Psychology

A Journey of Discovery

third edition

Psychology
A Journey of Discovery

Stephen L. Franzoi
Marquette University

ATOMIC**dog**PUBLISHING

Cincinnati, Ohio
www.atomicdog.com

Book Team

Vice President, Publisher   Laura Pearson
Developmental Editor   Christine Abshire
Director of Interactive Media and Design   Joe Devine
Director of Quality Assurance   Tim Bair
Senior Production Coordinator   Mary Monner
Web Production Editor   Joyce Powers
Quality Assurance Editor   Dan Horton
Marketing Manager   Mikka Baker
Cover Design   Zach Hicks

About the Cover. . .

Visitors to Venice, Italy, are encouraged by residents and seasoned travelers to happily lose themselves as they explore the twists and turns of the narrow streets, walkways, and canals. During a recent stay in this glorious city on the edge of the Adriatic Sea, I realized that newcomers who explore this city are similar to newcomers who explore the science of psychology. While navigating the meandering waterways and footpaths of Venice, you may occasionally be unsure of your precise location, only to discover something wonderful and glorious around the next bend. The beauty and wonder of Venice are found not only in the city's history-rich art and architecture, but also in the simple pleasures of a flower box on a second-story window ledge or the gentle lapping of water along a medieval canal. Like Venice, the science of psychology has both grand and simple discoveries for those who take the journey and are willing to seek assistance from those with extensive experience on these paths. Are you ready for a journey of discovery?
    —*Steve Franzoi*

ISBN 1-59260-261-4

Library of Congress Control Number: 2005932967

Printed in the United States of America by Atomic Dog Publishing, 35 East Seventh Street, Suite 405, Cincinnati, Ohio 45202

10 9 8 7 6 5 4 3 2 1

To the women in my life, Cheryl, Amelia, and Lillian;

To my parents, Lou and Joyce;

And to my brother and sister, Randy and Susie:

Together, and singly, they influence the essential elements of my life.

Brief Contents

Contents

List of Boxes

Self-Discovery Questionnaires

Explore It Exercises

Selected Themes

Biological and Evolutionary Psychology

Coverage of biological psychology, genetics, and evolutionary psychology can be found in Chapter 3 and on the following pages throughout the text:

Gender/Sex and Ethnicity/Culture

Preface

Why do I describe psychology as a journey of discovery? Much of my reasoning is very personal: My own study of psychology and my career in this scientific discipline have been a true journey of discovery. Growing up in a small town did not offer many opportunities to learn about the social sciences. However, during my first year in college, I was introduced to psychology and became hooked. I spent the following summer reading a stack of psychology books. As you will learn when reading chapter 1, after my sophomore year, I turned my next summer vacation into a literal journey of discovery as I traveled the country conducting my first psychological study. Since then, I am repeatedly reminded that the science of psychology is a valuable way to understand behavior and the process of living on this planet.

What can I offer you as an enticement to read this book? Well, are you interested in becoming more competent in dealing with future life events? Psychology involves the "study of the mind." As such, introductory psychology offers you the hope that course material will help you better understand not only other people, but also yourself. Seeking such knowledge is a distinguishing feature of young adulthood, and the college experience is specifically designed to foster this quest. In writing this text, I sought to bring into these pages that same message of hope and discovery that infuses the entire field of psychology. Does this sort of journey interest you?

I have written this text in a way that introduces you to the science of psychology as a journey of discovery undertaken both by researchers in their search for knowledge over the past century and by students over the course of the term. I explain how psychology has expanded our understanding of how people think, feel, and behave, while it also motivates you to apply this knowledge to better understand yourself and others. By regularly encouraging you to consider how psychological knowledge relates to your own life, I place your learning experience within a personally relevant context that benefits retention of course material, while also fostering self-insights that can be applied to your daily living.

The history of psychology is filled with compelling stories of how researchers' intense interest in learning about the nature of human and animal behavior led them on a journey of discovery that eventually culminated in important new knowledge. The fundamental difference between our often informal, anecdotally based personal journeys of discovery and the journeys of discovery found in psychology is that the vehicle employed in the latter journeys is the scientific method. Throughout *Psychology: A Journey of Discovery,* I tell selected discovery stories in psychology so that you will appreciate both the human element and the ever-evolving nature of scientific knowledge and insight.

Following chapter 1's introduction to psychology, which covers the field's history and areas of specialization, chapter 2 is devoted to the vehicle for psychological discovery—research methodology. This chapter provides a solid base for understanding the scientific enterprise of psychology, and it encourages a healthy, scientific skepticism of the many, often contradictory, commonsense truisms we learn from others. Discussion of the science of psychology is further reinforced by Appendix A, "Statistical Reasoning," at the end of the text.

Encouraging Self-Discovery

While encouraging you to analyze the scientific journey of discovery in psychology, the text also facilitates a personal journey of discovery by including more than 20 *Self-Discovery Questionnaires* that ask you to consider how the specific text material relates to your life. These self-report questionnaires are those that researchers currently use, and the results of studies employing them are part of the text material. Thus, as you learn about various psychological theories and relevant research findings, you also learn something about yourself. Examples of *Self-Discovery Questionnaires* are "Who Am I?" (Chapter 4), "Are You a Morning or a Night Person?" (Chapter 6), "Do You Have an Internal or an External Locus of Control?" (Chapter 12), and "Are You Typically an Optimist or a Pessimist?" (Chapter 15).

Applying Psychology to Everyday Experiences

Beyond self-report questionnaires, the text also includes numerous *Explore It Exercises* in which you actively experience how specific psychological processes work. Examples of *Explore It Exercises* are "How Can You Meditate?" (Chapter 6), "Can You Use Your Knowledge of Semantic Networks to 'Read' People's Minds?" (Chapter 8), "Which Side of Your Brain Is More Active during Emotional Situations?" (Chapter 11), and "How Can You Increase Your Chances of Receiving Help in an Emergency?" (Chapter 16). The text also presents a *Psychological Applications* section at the end of each chapter that demonstrates how psychology can be applied to your life. In these sections, you learn how the theories and research in a particular chapter can be applied to real-world settings. Topics covered in the *Psychological Applications* sections include developing critical thinking skills, learning how to exercise self-control in your academic and personal life, improving everyday memory, understanding test anxiety, coping with jealousy, and many others.

Encouraging Critical Thinking

You can develop an understanding of yourself and others by reading astrological predictions, internalizing the varied messages of popular culture, and uncritically accepting the advice and "wisdom" of friends, family, and (yes!) college professors. Yet, what is the value of this understanding if it is not subjected to critical cognitive analysis? Critical evaluation is an important component of *Psychology: A Journey of Discovery*. Questions in the main body of the text encourage critical thinking by inviting you to guess a study's hypotheses, results, or alternative interpretation of findings. In addition, questions that appear in the captions of figures, tables, and photos inspire further analysis of text material. Each chapter also features *Journey of Discovery Questions*, which require critical analyses of current discussion topics. Possible answers to these questions are provided in Appendix B in the Print Edition of the text and are "clickable" in the Online Edition. Last, but certainly not least, is a feature unique to the Online Edition: *QuickCheck* interactive questions. These questions test your knowledge on various topics and provide immediate feedback on the extent of your understanding.

Recognizing the Diversity and Unity of People

Integrated within this book's journey of discovery theme is the encouragement to recognize the ways in which people are both similar to and different from one another. *Psychology: A Journey of Discovery* tells the story of the science of psychology in such a way that you will recognize the "yin-yang" of unity and diversity, whether you are trying to understand the thoughts, emotions, and behavior of your college roommates or those of people from other cultures.

The text not only analyzes how culture and our individual developmental experiences influence the way we think, feel, and behave, but also examines how humans, as a species, often respond similarly to their physical and social surroundings. The "yin" in this diversity-unity analysis is the sociocultural perspective, while the "yang" is the evolutionary perspective. The text explains that the culture of a people is based on their relationship with the environment, and the evolution of our species is a story of how we have adapted to our surroundings. Thus, just as our bodies and brains are products of evolutionary forces, so, too, is our culture. Yet, cultural change occurs much more rapidly than genetic change. This is why the world's cultures vary greatly, despite little meaningful genetic variation among cultural groups.

Two belief systems that explain how individuals relate to their groups and that are important to understanding the psychology of human behavior are individualism and collectivism. Individualism is a philosophy of life stressing the priority of personal goals over group goals, a preference for loose-knit social relationships, and a desire to be relatively independent of others' influence. In contrast, collectivism is a philosophy of life stressing the priority of group needs over individual needs, a prefer-ence for tightly knit social relationships, and a willingness to submit to the influence of one's group. Although we know that cultures differ in their individualist-collectivist orientations, we do not know whether one is better than the other in any ultimate evolutionary sense. *Psychology: A Journey of Discovery* periodically examines how the psychology of people from different cultures differs due to their individualist-collectivist bents. For those chapter topics where the individualist-collectivist analysis is not especially relevant, other more relevant cultural factors are highlighted.

New to the Third Edition

The third edition of *Psychology: A Journey of Discovery* has a great deal of new content, including more than 80 new photos, figures, and cartoons, as well as more than 600 new references. The number of special boxed inserts in this edition has been greatly reduced, with much of this content now incorporated directly into the main body of the text. This change provides a better narrative flow to the chapter content. Now, the only in-chapter boxes are the *Self-Discovery Questionnaires* and the *Explore It Exercises*. Other significant changes in this new edition include:

Chapter 1
- *Psychological Applications:* How Did Psychological Research Influence the U.S. Supreme Court's 1954 Decision to Desegregate Schools?
- Expanded coverage of the evolutionary perspective
- Discussion of the new perspective of positive psychology

Chapter 2
- Discussion of whether there are any "final truths" in science, including a critical analysis of creation science as a scientific theory

Chapter 3
- New *Explore It Exercises*
- Increased coverage of neural growth
- Expanded coverage of behavior genetics
- New coverage of molecular genetics
- Discussion of the ethics of genetic testing and research
- Discussion of the controversies surrounding genetic explanations of sex and race differences

Chapter 4
- New *Explore It Exercises*
- New research on adolescent brain development
- New section on self-esteem stability
- New research covering adolescent decision making
- Revised section on moral development
- New research covering dementia
- Expanded coverage of friendship development
- Increased coverage of how aging affects the body and the brain

Chapter 5
- New *Explore It Exercises*
- New discussion of the visual cues used by painters
- Expanded coverage of perception

- New section on hearing loss
- Increased discussion of ESP research

Chapter 6
- New *Explore It Exercises*
- New research on the psychology and physiology of sleeping and dreaming
- New discussion of near-death experiences as altered states of consciousness

Chapter 7
- New *Explore It Exercises*
- New discussion of positive and negative punishment
- New research on media violence and observational learning
- New research on positive social modeling

Chapter 8
- New *Explore It Exercises*
- Increased coverage of mnemonics

Chapter 9
- New *Explore It Exercises*
- Increased coverage of slang language
- New section on artificial intelligence
- New section on nonconscious mimicry

Chapter 10
- Increased coverage of creativity

Chapter 11
- New *Explore It Exercises*
- Reorganized chapter context
- Revised discussion of sexual motivation
- Expanded coverage of emotion

Chapter 12
- New *Explore It Exercises*
- Completely revised discussion of self research

Chapter 13
- New *Explore It Exercises*
- New research on the causes of schizophrenia

Chapter 14
- New *Explore It Exercises*
- Revised chapter-opening story
- Updated discussion of drug therapies
- Expanded coverage of minorities seeking therapy
- New research on Internet therapy
- New section on eye movement desensitization therapy

Chapter 15
- New *Explore It Exercises*
- Expanded discussion of the general adaptation syndrome
- New research on stress and the immune system
- New discussion of natural versus specific immunity
- New discussion of hardiness
- New section on social support and stress
- New section on religion and health
- Expanded discussion of stress reduction
- Expanded coverage of optimism and pessimism
- Expanded discussion of eating disorders

Chapter 16
- New *Explore It Exercises*
- New chapter-opening story
- New research on the physical attractiveness stereotype
- New research on the psychology of prejudice
- Expanded coverage of romantic satisfaction

Appendix A: Statistical Reasoning
- Completely new end-of-text appendix covering measures of central tendency, measures of variability, and inferential statistics

Pedagogical Aids

Psychology: A Journey of Discovery enhances learning with the following pedagogical devices:

1. Each chapter opens with a *chapter outline.*
2. *Short-sentence headings* compactly summarize the content of chapter sections and facilitate recall of text topics.
3. *Preview questions* foreshadow the material to be covered and introduce each major chapter section.
4. Each major chapter section ends with a *Section Review* that presents a bulleted summary of the section's most important concepts that were initially queried in the Preview questions.
5. Beautifully rendered *four-color illustrations* throughout the text clarify and enhance chapter concepts.
6. In both the Print Edition and the Online Edition, *key terms* and concepts are highlighted and defined on first appearance. In the Print Edition, key terms are also defined in the text margins and listed in alphabetical order with page references at the end of each chapter. A *Glossary* at the end of the Print Edition presents all of the definitions alphabetically. The Online Edition has "pop-up" definitions of key terms, as well as a key term matching quiz in each end-of-chapter Study Guide.
7. *Journey of Discovery Questions* within each chapter require critical analyses of current discussion topics. Possible answers are found in the Online Edition, as well as in Appendix B at the end of the Print Edition.
8. *Quotes* from famous individuals in other fields illustrate text material.
9. *Self-Discovery Questionnaires* and *Explore It Exercises* within the chapters enhance your understanding of a variety of topics. See the list of *Self-Discovery Questionnaires* and *Explore It Exercises* on page xiii.
10. *Psychological Applications* sections help you to apply each chapter's psychological concepts to real-world situations.
11. *Suggested Websites* at the end of each chapter are online sources that you can access to obtain a better understanding of chapter material.
12. *Review Questions* at the end of each chapter allow you to check your comprehension of the chapter's major concepts.

Ancillary Materials

Atomic Dog is pleased to offer a robust suite of supplemental materials for instructors using its textbooks. These ancillaries include a Test Bank, PowerPoint® slides, Instructor's Manual, and Lecture Animations.

The Test Bank for this book includes multiple-choice questions in a wide range of difficulty levels for each chapter. The Test Bank offers not only the correct answer for each question, but also a reference—the location in the chapter where materials addressing the question content can be found. This Test Bank comes with ExamViewPro® software for easily creating customized or multiple versions of a test, and includes the option of editing or adding to the existing question bank.

A full set of PowerPoint slides is available for this text. This is designed to provide instructors with comprehensive visual aids for each chapter in the book. These slides include outlines of each chapter, highlighting important terms, concepts, and discussion points.

The Instructor's Manual for this book offers suggested syllabi for 10- and 14-week terms, lecture outlines and notes, in-class and take-home assignments, recommendations for multimedia resources such as films and websites, and essay questions and their answers appropriate for use on tests.

Lecture Animations allow instructors to use the animations from the Online Edition in their own PowerPoint slideshows. These include all of the animated figures from each chapter of the text in an easy-to-use format.

Acknowledgments

During my revision of this text for the third edition, many people provided me with invaluable assistance and understanding. I first want to thank my family for not only supporting my writing efforts and forgiving my memory lapses during this time, but also providing me with wonderful examples of psychological principles that I used throughout the text. I also apologize to my daughters, Amelia and Lillian, for any future embarrassment I may cause them by retelling some of their life experiences in the book!

I owe a big debt of gratitude to the students in my introductory psychology courses at Marquette University, who are the first to be exposed to my new stories of the psychological journey of discovery. I would also like to thank the numerous family members, friends, acquaintances, and strangers who allowed me to take their photos for use in the book.

There are a number of people I would like to warmly thank at Atomic Dog Publishing for not only having faith in my book project and making it a reality, but also making the entire publishing experience so thoroughly enjoyable. First, I would like to thank Mark Greenberg, Chairman and CEO, who has provided the necessary resources at all stages of development and production to make this a first-rate text. Second, I would like to thank Vice-President and Publisher Laura Pearson, who has worked closely with me to make this third edition an even better tool for student learning. Third, I want to thank

Victoria Putman, Vice-President, Production, for doing all the necessary work behind the scenes to assure that everything in the production process fell into its proper place at the correct time. While completing this third edition, I worked once again with Developmental Editor Christine Abshire, and she always does a great job coordinating and organizing numerous book tasks, including tracking down reviewers and resources, fleshing out my animation and figure ideas, and reminding me about deadlines and photo permissions. I was also again very fortunate to work with Senior Production Coordinator Mary Monner, who kept me on track during copyediting and page proofing, and once again budgeted in my vacation time! Interactive Media and Design Director Joe Devine did a fine job of taking my scrawled drawings and half-baked ideas and turning them into highly polished interactive learning devices for students. Very special thanks are also extended to Copy Editor Jeannie Smith, who not only cleaned up my writing but also pointed out potential problems in the text that would go unnoticed by 99 percent of copy editors.

Numerous reviewers, who obviously care very much about psychology and the art and craft of teaching, generously provided feedback during the writing of this text. I would like to thank:

Paul Bell, *Colorado State University*
Wayne Briner, *University of Nebraska at Kearney*
Sheila Brownlow, *Catawba College*
Trey Buchanan, *Wheaton College*
Adam Butler, *University of Northern Iowa*
Robert Caldwell, *Michigan State University*
Jorge Conesa, *Everett Community College*
James R. Cook, *University of North Carolina–Charlotte*
Tom Copeland, *Hardin Simmons University*
Wendy Domjan, *University of Texas–Austin*
Natalie Dove, *Purdue University*
Carol Edwards, *Purdue University North Central*
Ron Faulk, *St. Gregory's University*
Gary D. Fisk, *Georgia Southwestern State University*
Donelson R. Forsyth, *Virginia Commonwealth University*
Susan M. Frantz, *Highline Community College*
Traci Giuliano, *Southwestern University*
Wind Goodfriend, *Purdue University*
Judith Harackiewicz, *University of Wisconsin–Madison*
Robert M. Hessling, *University of Wisconsin–Milwaukee*
Deborah E. Horn, *Blinn College*
Neil Levens, *Indiana University of Pennsylvania*
Scott F. Madey, *Shippensburg University*
Michael Major, *Loyola University of New Orleans*
Michael S. Ofsowitz, *University of Maryland, European Division*
Daniel Osherton, *Rice University*
Maria Pagano, *New York City College of Technology*
Debra L. Palmer, *University of Wisconsin–Stevens Point*
Ellen Peters, *University of Oregon*
Laura Richardson, *University of Guam*
Alan Searleman, *St. Lawrence University*

Robert R. Sinclair, *Portland State University*
Leland Swenson, *Loyola Marymount University*
Alan Swinkels, *St. Edward's University*
Kris Vasquez, *Alverno College*
Lona Whitmarsh, *Fairleigh Dickinson University*
Bob Wildblood, *Indiana University, Kokomo*
Brian T. Yates, *American University*

And Finally . . .

I welcome your comments and feedback. Thanks to the online learning environment for Atomic Dog texts, I'll be in a position to incorporate appropriate suggestions several times a year. The prospect of being able to develop a robust exchange of ideas with current users, both students and faculty, is truly exciting. You can reach me at:

stephen.franzoi@marquette.edu.

Very best wishes,
Steve Franzoi

About the Author

Stephen L. Franzoi is Professor of Psychology at Marquette University in Milwaukee, Wisconsin. Born and raised in Iron Mountain, Michigan, Dr. Franzoi is proud to call himself a "Yuper" (a native of the Upper Peninsula of Michigan, or U.P.). Dr. Franzoi received his B.S. in both psychology and sociology from Western Michigan University and his M.A. and Ph.D. from the University of California at Davis, and he was a postdoctoral fellow at Indiana University before joining Marquette's faculty. Dr. Franzoi has served as assistant editor of *Social Psychology Quarterly* and associate editor of *Social Problems*. At Marquette University, Professor Franzoi teaches introductory psychology courses and is also the author of the textbook *Social Psychology* (fourth edition). He is an active researcher in the areas of body esteem and self-awareness, and over the years, Dr. Franzoi has discussed his research in many popular media outlets, including *The New York Times, USA Today,* National Public Radio, and *The Oprah Winfrey Show.* He and Cheryl Figg are the proud parents of Amelia and Lillian. In his spare time, he enjoys relaxing with his family, bicycling, collecting antiques, making wine, playing bocce ball, and dabbling in regular and 3-D photography.

Chapter 1

Introduction to Psychology

Chapter Outline

Source: Courtesy of Figzoi.

Quest—An act or instance of seeking; an adventurous journey.

The theme of this book is that both the science of psychology and your own life are journeys of discovery. Throughout your life, you will undertake many quests, and a substantial number of these will be irreparably flawed from the outset and, thus, doomed to fail. Others, however, will be fabulously successful due to a combination of factors, including good planning, skill, effort, fortunate circumstances, and the assistance of others. Certainly, one very important lesson in life is to learn to distinguish the foolish from the profound quests. Perhaps an even more important lesson is that it is absolutely essential to undertake quests regularly, because in such quests—both the large and the small variety—you develop new ways of looking at yourself and the world. With this thought in mind, let's begin.

My personal and professional journey of discovery in psychology began in the fall of 1972 when I was a college sophomore. My roommate, Ted, showed me a university brochure announcing awards of $1,000 to undergraduate "scholars" who designed innovative projects in their respective majors. Ted, an English major, announced that he was going to apply for this award and then embark on a grand adventure: a cross-country trip in his pickup truck and camper, writing an account of his road experiences along the lines of John Steinbeck's *Travels with Charley.* As Ted described all the places he planned to visit on his journey, I first thought of the factory job waiting for me back home, and then my thoughts shifted from assembly lines to the empty passenger seat in Ted's truck. In no time, I began to devise a plan to be the person riding in that seat. While Ted wrote the great American novel, his roommate and new traveling companion—me—would conduct a nationwide psychological study.

But of what? Even I, with only one scientific methods course under my belt, realized that an aspiring psychologist should have a specific research topic in mind before setting out to collect data. Wait. *Cross-country.* The term itself gave me an idea. In the early 1970s, many young adults, carrying backpacks and sleeping bags, hitchhiked from destination to destination, sometimes for months at a time. When describing these dropouts from the mainstream culture, news reporters used such phrases as "hippies on the move" and "modern-day hobos." Yet, who were these people? Did they share a common set of personality traits? There it was—the basis for my first psychological study!

Surprisingly, Ted and I both obtained awards for our respective projects. Perhaps it was because enough members on the university selection committee found it humorously appealing to subject unsuspecting summer travelers to a pair of Steinbeck-Freud "wannabes." Whatever the reason, the following June we began our adventure, traveling 13,000 miles through 23 states in 10 weeks' time. When we picked up cross-country hitchhikers, I would interview them, and then they would answer a personality questionnaire as we bounced around in the truck's camper. Although neither Ted nor I set the literary or scientific communities buzzing with the products of our summer excursion, my analysis of hitchhikers' personalities was eventually published in a scientific journal (Franzoi, 1985), and more importantly, the experience created in me a passion for the discipline of psychology.

Many of you reading this textbook will feel an intensity of interest similar to mine in learning as much as possible about the science of psychology. For others, whose passions burn for different life pursuits, this text and the course in which it is offered can still provide valuable knowledge that will serve you well while following those desires. At its heart, the science of psychology is a journey of discovery undertaken both by researchers in their search for knowledge over the past 100-odd years and by you, the student, over the course of the term. Throughout this text, as you learn how psychology has expanded our understanding of the ways people think, feel, and behave (the discipline's journey of discovery), I will encourage you to apply this knowledge to better understand yourself and others (your own journey of discovery).

A journey of a thousand miles starts from beneath one's feet.

—*Lao-Tzu, Chinese philosopher, sixth century* B.C.

Wheresoever you go, go with all your heart.

—*Confucius, Chinese philosopher, 551–479* B.C.

1-1 WHAT IS PSYCHOLOGY?

Preview

- *How do psychologists seek to understand people and other animals?*
- *Does the search for lawful patterns of behavior mean that psychologists do not believe in free will?*

1-1a Psychology Is the Scientific Study of Mental Processes and Behavior

A basic necessity for any successful journey is to know how to read the road signs, and for you, the reader of this textbook, this means understanding the terminology. The term **psychology** comes from the Greek words *psyche,* meaning "mind," and *logos,* meaning "the study of." In its broadest sense, psychology is the scientific study of mental processes and behavior. This means that psychologists are interested in using scientific methods (see chapter 2) to understand how we and other living creatures think, feel, and act. Have you ever wondered what your brain does while you sleep, or why you daydream? Do you think that TV violence can incite real-world violence? Can you accurately remember childhood events? What does it mean to be intelligent? Why do we fall in love? These are the sorts of questions studied by psychologists.

People often confuse psychology with **psychiatry,** a branch of medicine practiced by physicians and concerned with the diagnosis and treatment of psychological disorders. Psychology also deals with the diagnosis and treatment of such disorders (see chapters 13 and 14), but this interest represents only one area of specialization in a discipline that has a much broader scope than psychiatry (see section 1-3g). Whereas psychiatrists have completed medical school and obtained the M.D. (doctor of medicine), psychologists have completed graduate school in psychology and obtained the Ph.D. (doctor of philosophy) or, in some cases, the Psy.D. (doctor of psychology).

1-1b Most Psychologists Believe That There Are Lawful Patterns of Behavior

In trying to understand the means by which we "operate" in our life's journey, psychologists have struggled with the following fundamental question: Do we freely choose our actions, or are they determined beforehand by factors beyond our awareness and control?

During the fourth century B.C., the Greek philosopher Democritus was a proponent of **determinism,** the belief that human behavior is no different from any other physical action—that it is caused by lawful patterns that can be understood and predicted. If this is true, then all human decisions, from our clothing preferences to our career choices, are controlled—and ultimately determined—by our genetics, present environment, and past experiences (Sappington, 1990). In contrast to this perspective, the seventeenth-century French philosopher and mathematician René Descartes rejected determinism and argued instead that people—but not other animals—have **free will,** meaning that they have absolutely unlimited power of free choice. If such choices were really free, human behavior itself would be random and impossible to understand or predict (Slife & Fisher, 2000).

Although the free will versus determinism debate is still a topic of discussion in psychology, most psychologists and other social scientists believe in what could be called *probabilistic determinism* (Gillett, 2001). This means that, although psychological phenomena cannot be predicted with 100 percent certainty, they do occur with a regularity that is not random and can be reasonably understood using scientific methods.

Does embracing probabilistic determinism mean that you must reject the belief in free will, and vice versa? Not necessarily. In fact, many philosophers of science contend that free will is not possible unless some form of determinism is true (Carnap, 1966). What they mean is that, if behavior did not occur with a regularity that could be reasonably predicted, it would be impossible for people to make free choices. A choice involves

The purpose of psychology is to give us a completely different idea of the things we know best.

—*Paul Valéry, French poet/writer, 1871–1945*

psychology The scientific study of mental processes and behavior.

psychiatry A branch of medicine concerned with the diagnosis and treatment of psychological disorders. The roughly comparable specialty area in psychology is known as clinical psychology.

determinism The belief that all events have causes.

free will The belief that there are absolutely no limitations on people's power of free choice.

Actors and audience members follow certain rules of behavior during a theatrical performance that can be predicted with a good deal of accuracy. For example, actors generally interact only with other actors, and the audience does not walk onto the stage. How does their behavior illustrate the psychological concept of probabilistic determinism?

Source: Courtesy of Figzoi.

One of the annoying things about believing in free will and individual responsibility is the difficulty of finding somebody to blame your problems on. And when you do find somebody, it's remarkable how often his picture turns up on your driver's license.

—*P. J. O'Rourke, U.S. social satirist, b. 1947*

The will is never free—it is always attached to an object, a purpose. It is simply the engine in the car—it can't steer.

—*Joyce Cary, British author, 1888–1957*

an intentional selection of one course of action over another. Yet how could a choice possibly be made if the consequences of alternative actions could not be predicted? For example, when trying to decide what classes to take next semester, your choices are often based on professors' reputations for being predictably knowledgeable and fair. If you did not believe you could predict these personal qualities with at least some degree of accuracy, you would have no basis for choosing one professor over another. Thus, it may well be that for free choice to have any meaning, events must be somewhat predictable.

Section Review

- Psychologists employ scientific methods to understand how humans and other animals think, feel, and act.
- Most psychologists are probabilistic determinists, meaning they believe that psychological phenomena occur with a regularity that is not random and can be reasonably understood using scientific methods.

1-2 EARLY PIONEERS

Preview

- *Who was considered the world's first psychologist?*
- *Why was William James's approach to psychology called functionalism?*
- *What aspect of the mind did Sigmund Freud emphasize?*
- *Why was John Watson's behaviorism considered radically different from earlier perspectives?*
- *How did Gestalt psychology differ from structuralism?*
- *Has psychology been free of prejudice and discrimination?*

Many people have contributed to the development of psychology, and any history of the discipline in an introductory text will omit some of those who made valuable contributions. However, let me introduce you to the individuals who have been ranked by prominent historians as some of the most important psychologists of all time and the schools of thought that they spawned (Korn et al., 1991; Skokal, 2002).

1-2a Wilhelm Wundt and Structuralism Sought to Identify the Components of the Conscious Mind

Most historians call Wilhelm Wundt (pronounced "Vill-helm Voont"; 1832–1920) the "world's first psychologist." Wundt wrote the first textbook in the field of psychology in 1874, and in 1879 he established the first institute for research in experimental psychology at the University of Leipzig in Germany. Although in the early years no formal psychology courses were offered at the institute, many students from Europe and the United States traveled to Leipzig to study the psychology of consciousness. Wundt's method for studying the mind was known as *introspection,* a research technique in which trained observers would report on the contents of their own immediate states of consciousness. His model of consciousness, which his student Edward Titchener later named **structuralism,** sought to identify the components of the conscious mind.

Between 1876 and 1919, more than 100 students obtained doctoral degrees studying psychological topics under Wundt's supervision (Fernberger, 1933; Tinker, 1932). Some of his more illustrious students were Titchener (1867–1927; named and popularized structuralism in America), G. Stanley Hall (1844–1924; founded the American Psychological Association in 1892), Hugo Münsterberg (1863–1916; America's first industrial psychologist), James McKeen Cattell (1860–1944; a pioneer in the study of individual differences), and Viktor Henri (1872–1940; collaborator with Alfred Binet in developing the first intelligence tests). Besides his students from North America and Europe, Wundt trained students from other countries, including Japan and China. Indeed, Wundt's influence on the first generation of psychologists was so great that most contemporary psychologists can probably trace their historical lineage back to him (Blumenthal, 2002).

1-2b William James and Functionalism Analyzed How the Conscious Mind Helps Us Adapt to Our Environment

One of the first American students to visit Wundt in Leipzig was William James (1842–1910), but he quickly concluded that Wundt's structuralist approach to psychology was not to his liking. Although both men studied consciousness, James's desire was to understand how the mind affects what people do rather than to merely identify its components. In addition, his approach to psychology had little to do with laboratory studies and, instead, relied heavily on his own rich ideas and eloquent writing (Leary, 2002). Because of James's interest in how the conscious mind helps humans survive and successfully adapt to their environment—that is, how the mind functions—his approach to psychology came to be called **functionalism.** James's theory of emotion (discussed in chapter 11, section 11-5d), his contention that there are two different kinds of memory, and his analysis of the psychology of religion are still highly regarded today.

In 1890, James published a brilliant two-volume text entitled *Principles of Psychology,* which quickly established its author as America's foremost psychologist and is still considered a classic among classics. In addition to his superb writing and brilliant ideas, James was a masterful teacher at Harvard University, and he even wrote a popular book, *Talks to Teachers* (1899), which offered practical advice to teachers. Unlike Wundt, James had a relatively small group of students, but among them were such luminaries as James Angell (1869–1949; further developed functionalism), Mary Calkins (1863–1930; a pioneer in memory research), Edward Thorndike (1874–1949; investigated trial-and-error animal learning); and Robert Woodworth (1869–1962; a pioneer in motivation and drive theory).

Although James is widely regarded as one of psychology's most influential thinkers, during the last decade of his life he abandoned the discipline and established himself as America's best-known philosopher since Ralph Waldo Emerson (1803–1882). James described his philosophy, known as *pragmatism,* as a "philosophy without humbug." Arguing

Wilhelm Wundt, the founder of psychology.

structuralism An early theory in psychology that sought to identify the components of the conscious mind.

We take issue . . . with every treatment of psychology that is based on simple self-observation or on philosophical presuppositions.

—*Wilhelm Wundt, 1832–1920*

William James, the first major American psychologist.

functionalism An early approach to psychology that studied how the conscious mind helps humans survive and successfully adapt to their environment.

I wished, by treating Psychology like a natural science, to help her to become one.

—*William James, 1842–1910*

Journey of Discovery Question | At the beginning of the twentieth century, Hermann Ebbinghaus (1850–1909), one of psychology's pioneers, stated, "Psychology has a long past, but only a short history." What do you think he meant by this statement?

I am actually not at all a man of science, not an observer, not an experimenter, not a thinker. I am by temperament not but a conquistador—an adventurer, if you want it translated—with all the curiosity, daring, and tenacity of a man of this sort.

—*Sigmund Freud, 1856–1939*

Sigmund Freud, the founder of psychoanalysis.

psychoanalysis An approach to psychology that studies how the unconscious mind shapes behavior.

that there are no such things as absolute beliefs or truths, he stated that all beliefs must be judged by whether they produce practical benefits for the person. In other words, beliefs do not work because they are true, but rather, they are true because they work. Thus, if a person's belief in God produces practical benefits, such as a sense of security and psychological health, then for that person the existence of God is a personal truth. Pragmatism proved to be an extremely popular philosophy in early twentieth-century America.

1-2c Sigmund Freud and Psychoanalysis Examined How the Unconscious Mind Shapes Behavior

The third prominent person to shape psychology during its early years was Sigmund Freud (1856–1939), an Austrian physician trained as a neurologist. Actually, because Freud was a physician, his proper title is "psychiatrist" rather than "psychologist." Despite this technicality, psychology still claims him as an important founder of one of the early schools of thought in the discipline.

Instead of working in the lab (as Wundt did) or teaching at the university (as James did), Freud developed his approach to psychology through clinical practice. Based on his work with patients who suffered from ailments that had no known physical causes, Freud developed a theory that all human behavior is determined by hidden or unconscious motives and desires that are sexual in nature. In a very real sense, he contended that part of our personality never matures, and that the "adult" side of our personality struggles to control the "infant" side, with only limited success.

Freud's emphasis on the unconscious mind stood in sharp contrast to Wundt's and James's studies of conscious experience. The belief that most of the mind is inaccessible to a person's conscious awareness led Freud and his followers to develop therapy techniques and personality tests designed to reveal this hidden domain. This approach to psychology, which Freud called **psychoanalysis,** influenced the study of such diverse topics as dreams, childhood development, aggression, sexuality, creativity, motivation, personality, and psychotherapy (Kafka, 2002).

Freud's writings attracted many followers to psychoanalysis. Among the brightest of this group were Alfred Adler (1870–1936; founder of individual psychology), Carl Jung (1875–1961; founder of analytic psychology), and Karen Horney (1885–1952; one of the first psychologists to emphasize social rather than biological determinants of gender differences). Yet, Freud was intolerant of disagreement or dissent. When each of these people developed ideas that challenged some of Freud's cherished concepts, they either left or were expelled from the psychoanalytic inner circle. In response to these challenges, Freud established a committee of loyal followers whose job it was to repulse critics of psychoanalysis. Although no other psychologist comes close to matching Freud's impact on popular culture, his reluctance to submit psychoanalysis to critical examination stunted its development as a scientific theory. In chapter 12, section 12-2, we will examine Freud's theory of personality and its influence on contemporary psychological theories.

1-2d John Watson and Behaviorism Investigated Observable Behavior

Just as psychoanalysis is closely associated with Sigmund Freud, so is behaviorism intimately intertwined with John Watson (1878–1958). As an adolescent, Watson did not appear even remotely destined for greatness. Coming from a broken home, he was a poor and disruptive student who was arrested twice by the authorities. Despite these early troubles, Watson convinced the president of a local South Carolina college to admit him as a "sub-freshman" at the age of 16. In this new world, Watson thrived, fell in love with the psychology taught in his philosophy courses, and eventually was awarded the first Ph.D. degree in the department of psychology at the University of Chicago in 1903.

Watson's research with rats, dogs, and other animals caused him to question the three current schools of psychology that analyzed the structure, content, and function of the mind. His subjects couldn't talk or introspect, and thus, there was no hope that they could

John Watson, the founder of behaviorism.

Source: © Underwood & Underwood/CORBIS.

reveal the seeming mysteries of the mind. Perhaps partly because of this fact, Watson came to believe that, rather than studying hidden psychological processes, psychology should study observable behavior, and his approach came to be called **behaviorism.** In 1913, Watson published an article entitled "Psychology as the Behaviorist Views It," in which he challenged his fellow psychologists to abandon the other schools of thought because their focus of study, consciousness, was neither a definable term nor a usable concept. His opening paragraph spelled out the direction for this new school:

> Psychology as the Behaviorist sees it is a purely objective, experimental branch of natural science. Its theoretical goal is the prediction and control of behavior. Introspection forms no essential parts of its methods, nor is the scientific value of its data dependent upon the readiness with which they lend themselves to interpretation in terms of consciousness. The behaviorist, in his efforts to get a unitary scheme of animal responses, recognizes no dividing line between man and brute. The behavior of man, with all its refinement and complexity, forms only a part of the behaviorist's total scheme of investigation. (Watson, 1913, p. 158)

Watson's radical behaviorism struck a responsive chord among many American psychologists who shared his impatience with what they considered the "fuzziness" of the other schools within psychology (Schnaitter, 1987). Underlying behaviorism was a philosophy known as *logical positivism,* which contended that all knowledge should be expressed in terms that can be verified empirically or through direct observation. These "new" psychologists sought to describe, explain, predict, and control behavior. Within 2 years (1915), Watson was elected president of the American Psychological Association (APA).

Like William James before him, Watson did not complete his career in the field of psychology. Yet, unlike James, this change in career path was not of his own choosing. Just as behaviorism was establishing itself as the dominant school within psychology, Watson was forced to resign from Johns Hopkins University due to a sexual affair with a research assistant. Unable to secure another academic position following this scandal, Watson began a new career devising market research techniques in advertising. In addition to this work, Watson for a time wrote many popular books and magazine articles related to psychology and was in great demand as a lecturer and radio commentator. Although his academic career spanned fewer than 20 years, Watson is still regarded as the leader of the behaviorist revolution in psychological thought. His approach to understanding behavior dominated psychology in North America from the 1920s through the 1950s (Innis, 1992).

1-2e Max Wertheimer and Gestalt Psychology Studied How the Mind Organizes Stimuli into Coherent Wholes

During the first decades of the twentieth century, **Gestalt psychology** gained prominence primarily as a critique of—and an alternative to—structuralism. *Gestalt* is a German word that means "shape" or "form." The founder of this school of psychology, Max Wertheimer (1880–1943), criticized Wundt's structuralism for attempting to understand the conscious mind by identifying and analyzing its components. Instead, Wertheimer contended that "the whole is different from the sum of its parts." That is, our perceptions are not to be understood as the mind passively responding to a simple combination of individual elements but, rather, as the mind actively organizing stimuli into coherent wholes. Wertheimer and his colleagues, Wolfgang Köhler (1887–1967) and Kurt Koffka (1886–1941), produced many demonstrations of the unity of perceptual processes.

For an example of how our perceptions emerge as wholes, not parts, look at the four dots in figure 1-1a. Most people perceive the dots as corners of an invisible square rather than as separate, discrete objects. Do you? When three of the dots are increased in size in figure 1-1b, most people see the configuration of a triangle and a separate dot. Do you? This dot example illustrates the laws of grouping, which describe how people tend to group discrete stimuli together into a meaningful whole (see chapter 5, section 5-5a).

Besides creating new ways of thinking about perception, Wertheimer, Köhler, and Koffka analyzed learning and problem solving, but they always treated these topics as whole phenomena. Later, one of their colleagues, Kurt Lewin (1890–1947), applied the

behaviorism An approach to psychology that studies observable behavior rather than hidden mental processes; also referred to as the *behavioral perspective.*

Gestalt psychology An approach to psychology that studies how the mind actively organizes stimuli into coherent wholes.

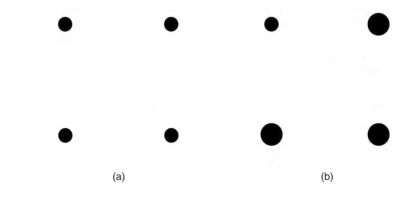

igure 1-1

Gestalt Psychology Stressed That Perception Strives toward a Complete Form

(a) These four dots are likely to be perceived as a square.
(b) However, if three of the dots become twice as big while the fourth remains the same size, the four dots are likely to be perceived as a triangle (of larger dots) and a single dot.

(a)   (b)

Gestalt approach to understanding social behavior, and he and his students were instrumental in shaping the development of a new area of specialization, social psychology.

There is one final story to tell about these pioneers in Gestalt psychology. They were Germans whose careers spanned a time of great social turmoil in their country, culminating in the Nazis taking control of the government and instituting anti-Semitic laws. During this period, the majority of German academics and scientists either kept quiet or actively supported Adolf Hitler (Wyatt & Teuber, 1944). Notable exceptions were the Gestalt psychologists. For example, at about the same time that Wertheimer was removed from his faculty position at the University of Berlin and expelled from Germany, Köhler wrote a highly critical article of the Nazi regime in the German equivalent of *The New York Times;* this was the last anti-Nazi article to be published under the Nazis. When all professors were ordered to begin their lectures with the Nazi salute, at his next class—and with numerous Nazis in the audience—Köhler responded by flipping his hand in a caricature of the Nazi salute as he outlined his opposition to the government (Crannell, 1970). Such open defiance was extremely dangerous, and eventually all four men were expelled from the country and relocated to the United States. There, they influenced the next generation of American psychologists (Ash, 2002).

1-2f Despite Discrimination, Many Women and Ethnic Minorities Were Pioneers in Psychology

Do you think it is simply a coincidence that the founders of the early schools of thought in psychology were all White men? On this issue, psychology reflected the cultural prejudices of the times, asserting that White men were intellectually superior to women and to members of all other racial and ethnic groups. Due to this institutionalized sexism and racism during the first 75 years of psychology's existence, women and minorities were generally excluded from graduate education (Kimmel, 1992; Minton, 2000). Those fortunate enough to be allowed to pursue a career in psychology generally had a substandard environment in which to conduct their research. But despite such impediments, many women and ethnic minorities made valuable contributions to the development of psychology (Furomoto & Scarborough, 2002).

A good example of the prejudice and discrimination faced by women in psychology is the career of Mary Calkins (1863–1930), who completed all requirements for a Ph.D. at Harvard University in 1895. William James described her dissertation defense as "the most brilliant examination for the Ph.D. that we have had at Harvard." Yet, despite being enthusiastically recommended for her doctoral degree by James and her other professors, Calkins was denied the Ph.D. because the university did not grant degrees to women. Harvard, like most universities

Mary Calkins, the first female president of the American Psychological Association.

Source: Archives of the History of American Psychology—The University of Akron.

Journey of Discovery Question
Consider the five early perspectives in psychology. What contribution did each make to our understanding of thinking and behavior?

at the time, allowed women to attend graduate classes only as "hearers," and thus they were not considered full-fledged graduate students. Can you imagine how you might react to such blatant discrimination? Keep in mind that excluding women from most professions was the accepted practice throughout society. Would you fight it? If so, how would you fight it?

In 1902, Harvard offered Calkins a Ph.D. from its "sister college," Radcliffe, but she declined, stating that accepting it would mean that she also accepted the college's sexist policies. Pursuing the few career paths open to her, Calkins became a non-Ph.D. professor at all-female Wellesley College. There, she established one of the first psychology laboratories in the United States, pioneered research in short-term memory, and in 1905 became the first woman president of the American Psychological Association. Despite this distinguished career, in 1930 Harvard again rejected a petition presented by several famous alumni to award Calkins her previously earned Ph.D. (Madigan & O'Hara, 1992).

The first woman to actually receive her doctorate in psychology was Margaret Washburn (1871–1939) in 1894 at Cornell University (Furomoto, 1992). During her distinguished career, Washburn was a research pioneer in comparative psychology and served as president of the American Psychological Association in 1921 (Dewsbury, 1992). Like Calkins, but unlike most of her male colleagues, Washburn never married, because a woman's decision to marry generally required her not to work outside the home.

In addition to this discrimination, even when women found a place within psychology, their contributions often went unrecognized by contemporaries. One such example is Bärbel Inhelder, a student of the developmental psychologist Jean Piaget (see chapter 4, section 4-3a). Despite collaborating with the pioneer of cognitive development on eight books and providing significant insight into cognitive processes and mental retardation, Inhelder never became widely known for her work (DeAngelis, 1996).

Similar obstacles also impeded the careers of ethnic minorities (Schultz & Schultz, 2000). The first African American to receive a Ph.D. in psychology was Gilbert Jones, who obtained his degree from the University of Jena in Germany in 1901 (Guthrie, 1976). Thirty-two years later, Inez Prosser, after teaching many years with a master's degree, became the first African-American woman to receive her doctorate in psychology from the University of Cincinnati. Despite the discrimination faced by African Americans during these early years, many made significant contributions to this budding science. For example, in 1920 the structural psychologist J. Henry Alston discovered how we sense heat and cold from our skin receptors (see chapter 5, section 5-4b). In the field of social psychology, Kenneth Clark and Mamie Phipps Clark's groundbreaking research in the 1930s and 1940s on the self-concept of Black children provided the scientific justification for the U.S. Supreme Court to end the practice of racially segregated education (see the end-of-chapter "Psychological Applications" section). In 1971, Kenneth Clark (1914–2005) became the first African American to be elected president of the American Psychological Association.

Hispanic psychologists have also made many important contributions (Guthrie, 1976). For example, George Sanchez was an early critic of using culturally biased psychological tests in assessing Mexican-American children, and John Garcia pioneered research on taste aversion in the 1960s (see chapter 7, section 7-1d).

As you can see from this brief overview, women and minorities in psychology had to overcome considerable social obstacles before they could position themselves to contribute to the development of the new science. During the past quarter century, career opportunities for women and ethnic minorities in psychology have expanded, and this greater diversity has challenged old assumptions of human behavior and spurred the study of previously overlooked populations. Today, in the United States, almost half of all psychologists holding doctoral degrees are women, and they make up two-thirds of all the new Ph.D.s. Moreover, members of ethnic minority groups now account for 16 percent of the new doctoral degrees earned each year (O'Conner, 2001). Similar diversity trends are also found in Canada.

Despite these advances, more work is needed (Sonnert & Holton, 1995). For example, although the majority of new doctorates in psychology today are women, men are still far more likely than women to hold the most powerful positions of authority in university psychology departments (Kite et al., 2001; L. Peterson et al., 1998). It is also true that there are still far too

Margaret Washburn, the first woman to receive a Ph.D. in psychology.

Source: Archives of the History of American Psychology—The University of Akron.

Mentally the negro is inferior to the white . . . deterioration in mental development is no doubt very largely due to the fact that after puberty sexual matters take the first place in the negro's life and thoughts.

——*Encyclopaedia Britannica, 1911*

It is not possible for every woman to be a scholar, a doctor, a lawyer, or possibly to attain the highest position in professions where competition with men is keen. As members of school boards, factory inspectors, poor law guardians, and sanitary inspectors, they have had ample scope for gratifying their ambition and energy.

——*Encyclopaedia Britannica, 1911*

few ethnic minorities in the discipline compared to their numbers in the general population. As an example, although Latinos make up about 13 percent of the U.S. population, fewer than 7 percent of graduate school students and only about 1 percent of psychology practitioners and psychology full professors are Latino (Dingfelder, 2005b). Similar patterns are also found among African Americans. Thus, although women and ethnic minorities have begun to share more of the center stage with their White male colleagues, the twenty-first century still awaits a more diverse cast of characters in this ever-changing science. Some of you reading this textbook will be part of this new generation of psychologists. What would you do to encourage this greater diversity without unfairly limiting the opportunities of young White males?

Section Review

- Wilhelm Wundt—identified as the world's first psychologist—developed structuralism, which sought to identify the components of the conscious mind.
- William James and functionalism studied how the conscious mind helps humans survive and successfully adapt to their environment (how the mind "functions").
- Sigmund Freud and psychoanalysis studied how the unconscious mind shapes behavior.
- John Watson and behaviorism considered only observable behaviors to be legitimate topics for scientific inquiry.
- Max Wertheimer and Gestalt psychology studied how the mind actively organizes stimuli into coherent wholes.
- Despite discrimination, many women and ethnic minorities made valuable contributions to the development of psychology.

1-3 CONTEMPORARY PERSPECTIVES AND AREAS OF SPECIALIZATION

Preview

- *Which of the early psychological perspectives exist as contemporary perspectives?*
- *What prompted the development of humanistic psychology?*
- *What is emphasized in cognitive psychology?*
- *What is the primary focus of the neuroscience perspective?*
- *Which perspective explains the importance of genetic survival?*
- *How does the sociocultural perspective differ from the evolutionary perspective?*
- *What areas of specialization in psychology emphasize research over application?*
- *What areas of specialization in psychology emphasize application over research?*

Of the five early schools of psychology, only psychoanalysis and behaviorism have survived as contemporary perspectives, although even they have been significantly altered from their original form. A contemporary approach to psychotherapy is known as Gestalt therapy (see chapter 14, section 14-5b), but it has little more than its name in common with the early German school of Gestalt psychology. Instead, Gestalt psychology's influence is seen today in the specialty areas of cognitive and social psychology. It is also true that even elements of the now-defunct structuralist and functionalist schools continue to shape psychology in the early years of the twenty-first century. Let us briefly examine seven contemporary perspectives within psychology that shape not only current psychological theory and research but also its application in everyday settings.

1-3a The Psychoanalytic and Behaviorist Perspectives Still Influence Theory and Research

Two of the early psychological perspectives—psychoanalysis and behaviorism—still exist today, although their emphases have shifted somewhat. For example, in explaining personality, many psychoanalysts today downplay Freud's emphasis on sexual drives and, instead, emphasize cultural experiences. Despite this shift in focus, the unconscious mind and early childhood experiences are still central areas of attention within this perspective. Yet many contemporary psychoanalysts, influenced by Erik Erikson's (1902–1994) writings, have rejected Freud's view that personality development, for all practical purposes, is complete by age 5. Instead, contemporary psychoanalysis generally accepts Erikson's (1980) view that personality is continually shaped and changed throughout life. I discuss Erikson's work in chapter 4.

The central figure shaping contemporary behaviorism was B. F. Skinner (1904–1990), who stressed the role of consequences in controlling behavior (Malone & Cruchon, 2001). His research—which I discuss in chapter 7—found that people and other animals tend to repeat behaviors that are followed by positive consequences and tend to avoid behaviors that bring negative consequences. For example, if you are rewarded for being helpful, you are likely to repeat such actions in the future, but you are unlikely to do so if your helpfulness is punished. In addition, this psychological perspective played a key role in insisting that psychologists precisely define and objectively measure the concepts they study. Although behaviorism does not exert the influence over psychology that it once enjoyed, you will recognize its footprints throughout this text as you examine various psychological topics (L. D. Smith, 2002).

1-3b The Humanistic Perspective Highlights Personal Growth and Conscious Decision Making

Arising out of many psychologists' dissatisfaction with both the psychoanalytic and the behaviorist views of human nature, a third force exerted its influence on psychology in the 1950s. This **humanistic perspective** emphasizes people's innate capacity for personal growth and their ability to make conscious choices. Carl Rogers (1902–1987) and Abraham Maslow (1908–1970) were the primary architects of this perspective, and both contended—like William James before them—that psychology should study people's unique subjective mental experience of the world.

In the 1960s, humanistic psychology served as the intellectual inspiration of the *human potential movement,* which became a loosely knit social movement striving to help individuals achieve their full human potential. Both within psychology and throughout the larger culture, humanistic psychology has had a broad impact by stressing the important role that positive life experiences play in people's lives. Although the humanistic approach has been criticized for being the least scientifically based of all contemporary perspectives within psychology, its emphasis on conscious experience and the essential goodness of people has promoted the scientific study of previously neglected topics, such as self-awareness, love, helping behavior, and positive personality growth—all issues that we will explore in this text.

Within the past 10 years, a new psychological perspective called *positive psychology* has emerged, which can be characterized as a direct descendant of the humanistic perspective.[1] **Positive psychology** is a scientific approach to studying optimal human functioning that asserts that the normal functioning of human beings cannot be accounted for within purely negative (or problem-focused) frames of reference. Because this new perspective is more firmly grounded in rigorous scientific methodology than is the traditional humanistic perspective, positive psychology may be in a better position to shape the future direction of psychology. Researchers who identify themselves as proponents of positive psychology are currently studying what it means to be a well-adapted person (Schmuck & Sheldon, 2001; Sheldon & King, 2001). For example, when does an optimistic view of life help you overcome hurdles to success, and when does it cause you to overlook impending failure? Teaching people to avoid harmful self-deceptions while still maintaining a sense of realistic optimism about life is one of the goals of this new positive psychology (Snyder, 2000).

humanistic perspective An approach to psychology that emphasizes human beings' innate capacity for personal growth and their ability to consciously make choices.

positive psychology A relatively new scientific approach to studying optimal human functioning that asserts that the normal functioning of human beings cannot be accounted for within purely negative (or problem-focused) frames of reference.

[1] It should be noted that some positive psychologists shun an affiliation with humanistic psychology because they believe the humanistic perspective is not firmly grounded in the scientific method. Many of these psychologists are more comfortable identifying themselves with one of the other perspectives, especially the cognitive and sociocultural perspectives described in sections 1-3c and 1-3f.

1-3c The Cognitive Perspective Analyzes How the Mind Organizes and Interprets Experiences

Accompanying the criticism of behaviorism by humanistic theorists was the fact that laboratory research was finding some interesting phenomena that were difficult to explain without reintroducing the concept of consciousness. In the 1960s, when this evidence had reached a sufficient "critical mass," the theoretical center of gravity in psychology shifted from behaviorism to cognitive psychology (Hilgard et al., 1991). The word *cognitive* comes from the Latin for "to know." The **cognitive perspective** is a psychological approach that attempts to understand behavior by studying how the mind organizes perceptions, processes information, and interprets experiences (Healy, 2005). For example, how do you remember a new friend's phone number? Or how do you decide while serving on a jury whether a defendant is guilty or innocent? Cognitive theories provide insights into these kinds of mental processes. Two of the principal leaders of this "cognitive revolution" in psychology were George A. Miller and Ulric Neisser.

The ascendancy of the cognitive perspective coincided with the development of a new form of technology, namely, the computer. Cognitive psychologists argued that the mind is like a computer (Harnish, 2002). Like a computer, the mind receives input from the environment, which it then transforms, stores, and later retrieves using a host of "programs," ultimately leading to specific response outputs. The computer is not only a useful metaphor for the mind, but as new generations of computers are developed to actually work like the human brain, it also has become an invaluable subject of study, simulating human thought. Today, behaviorist John Watson's description of the brain as "a black box forever mysterious" is no longer true, thanks largely to the discoveries of cognitive psychologists. This perspective provides valuable insights into many of the topics we will examine throughout this text.

cognitive perspective An approach to psychology that attempts to understand behavior by studying how the mind organizes perceptions, processes information, and interprets experiences.

1-3d The Neuroscience Perspective Focuses on the Nervous System

In recent years, as new techniques and instruments have been developed to examine the brain and how it reacts under different circumstances, psychologists have become increasingly interested in biological mechanisms (Cacioppo et al., 2004; Rosenzweig et al., 2002). The resulting attempts to understand behavior and mental processes by examining the nervous system have come to be known as the **neuroscience perspective.** In its study of how the brain communicates with itself and other body organs, as well as its attempt to understand elementary biochemical processes, this approach to psychology is focused on the most precise microscopic levels of analysis (Dror & Thomas, 2005; Posner, 2002).

Although neuroscientists do study humans, they conduct a good deal of their research using animals with simpler brains, hoping that the knowledge gained in these studies will lead to greater understanding of the brain's building blocks (Swanson, 2004). For example, in attempting to better understand memory loss in *Alzheimer's disease* (the most common form of dementia in the elderly), a researcher might graft tissue from the brains of rat fetuses into the brains of elderly rats. If such a procedure improves the older rats' memory, this finding may provide a crucial clue to curing this disease in humans. Chapter 3 will introduce you to some of the discoveries uncovered by this neuroscientific approach.

neuroscience perspective An approach to psychology that attempts to understand behavior and mental processes by examining the nervous system.

A recurring debate in psychology related to biological explanations of behavior involves the degree to which individual differences are due to inborn biological processes versus environmental influences. Have you ever wondered why we, as individuals, often differ in our thinking and behavior? Are we born this way, or do these differences develop based on our life experiences? Philosophers have endlessly debated this issue. For example, in the fourth and third centuries B.C., Plato argued that individual differences are largely inborn and due to heredity (nature), while Aristotle stressed the importance of environmental factors (nurture) and described the mind as a *tabula rasa*, or blank slate, that was later filled by life experiences. Which perspective on human nature makes more sense to you? Is there possibly a middle-ground position on this issue?

This **nature-nurture debate** has been a classic controversy in psychology (Coll et al., 2004; Kellett, 2005). Followers of the "nature" position point toward the greater behavioral similarities found between identical twins (genetically the same) than between fraternal

nature-nurture debate The question of whether individual differences in behavior are primarily due to inborn biological processes or to environmental factors.

twins (genetically not the same), using this as evidence for the influence of heredity. They further contend that the existence of similar behaviors among humans and other animals suggests the operation of similar biological processes. In contrast, advocates of the "nurture" position emphasize how people's thoughts, feelings, and behavior are shaped by the rewards and punishments they receive from their immediate surroundings. According to the "nurturists," this type of learning, combined with the values and beliefs of the larger culture, forms the basis for differences in the way we live our lives.

As you will discover, the different perspectives within psychology tend to emphasize either nature or nurture points of view in their analysis of psychological events. However, what you will also learn is that most contemporary psychologists believe that human beings, like all other animals, are a product of both nature and nurture (Hall et al., 2004; Plomin, 2004). Thus, instead of being opposing explanations of behavior, biological and environmental explanations often complement one another, adding a depth of understanding that cannot be achieved by considering only one alone (Goel, 2005; Rutter, 2002).

1-3e The Evolutionary Perspective Studies How Behavior Can Be Explained by Natural Selection

Fueled by the growing belief in the social sciences that behavior is at least partly influenced by the effects of evolution, a perspective known as **evolutionary psychology** is increasingly being incorporated into psychological theories (Barrett et al., 2002; Kenrick & Maner, 2004). Yet, what is evolution? The evolutionary perspective is partly based on the writings of the biologist Charles Darwin (1809–1882), who theorized that changes in the population of a species occur over many generations due to the interaction of environmental and biological variables.

According to evolutionary theory, living organisms struggle to survive, and within each species, a great deal of competition and biological variation occurs between individuals (Darwin, 1859; Dupre, 2003). Those members of a species with genetic traits best adapted for survival in their environment will produce more offspring, and as a result, their numbers will increase in frequency in the population. As the environment changes, however, other members within the species possessing traits better suited to the new conditions will flourish, a process called **natural selection.** In this way, the environment selects which genetic traits will be passed on to future generations. As natural selection continues, and as the features best suited for survival change again and again, the result is **evolution,** a term that refers to the gradual genetic changes that occur in a species over generations. Reproduction is central to natural selection; the essence of the natural selection process is that the characteristics of some individuals allow them to produce more offspring than others (Nielsen, 1995). For example, in an environment that is mostly frigid and snowy, mammals with a lot of insulating fur are more likely to survive and reproduce than are those with less fur. Similarly, animals that look white are more likely than darker-appearing members of

evolutionary psychology An approach to psychology based on the principle of natural selection.

natural selection The process by which organisms with inherited traits best suited to the environment reproduce more successfully than less well-adapted organisms over a number of generations. Natural selection leads to evolutionary changes.

evolution The genetic changes that occur in a species over generations due to natural selection.

According to the process of natural selection, animals that live in very cold and snowy environments will be more likely to survive and reproduce if their fur provides both insulating warmth and camouflage so that they blend in with the snow. Why doesn't the fur of zoo-housed polar bears turn darker to better match their zoo environment?

Source: Courtesy of Figzoi.

Figure 1-2

How Natural Selection Works

Environments are always undergoing changes. Throughout these changes, organisms living in a given environment are competing for survival. Those organisms in a species that possess genetic traits that allow them to cope with the environment and adapt to the changes that occur are the organisms most likely to survive, reproduce, and pass their genes on to the next generation. This is the natural selection process, and it repeats itself in every generation. The result of natural selection is evolution. In this natural selection process, it is important to remember that the genetic traits best adapted to the environment at Time 1 may not be the best-adapted traits when the environment changes at Time 2. This is the reason that evolutionary theorists contend that it is the environment that "selects" which traits will be passed on to future generations.

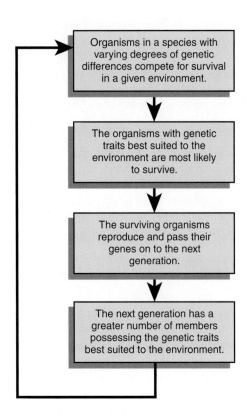

It may metaphorically be said that natural selection is daily and hourly scrutinising . . . the slightest variations; rejecting those that are bad, preserving and adding up all that are good; silently and insensibly working, whenever and wherever opportunity offers, at the improvement of each organic being in relation to its organic and inorganic conditions of life. We see nothing of these slow changes in progress, . . . we see only that the forms of life are now different from what they formerly were.

—*Charles Darwin, 1859,* On the Origin of Species, *pp. 90–91*

Natural selection, as it has operated in human history, favors not only the clever but the murderous.

—*Barbara Ehrenreich, U.S. author and columnist, b. 1941*

their species to blend in with the snow, which may protect them from predators or make them more stealthy hunters of prey (see photo of polar bear on page 13). This "whiteness" will lead to more offspring being produced. The result of this natural selection process—which transpires over thousands of generations—is that mammals from many species living in a frigid and snowy environment will have thick, white fur covering their bodies. Figure 1-2 depicts how natural selection causes evolutionary changes.

Perhaps the best-known documented example of natural selection is the peppered moth *Biston betularia,* a common insect in Britain (Kettlewell, 1973). Before the industrial revolution, the vast majority of moths within this species were light-colored. However, by the late 1840s, people began to see much darker versions in heavily industrialized regions of the country. The reason for this change was that industrial pollutants had darkened the tree bark in the surrounding forests where the moths spent much of their time, making the lighter-colored ones much more vulnerable to predatory birds, who hunt by sight. Under these altered environmental conditions, the darker moths now possessed better natural camouflage, and they survived and reproduced in greater numbers. By the mid-twentieth century, these dark-colored moths made up more than 90 percent of the peppered moth population in industrialized areas. However, in unpolluted areas of Britain, where the tree bark was much lighter in color, the lighter-colored moths continued to flourish. This is an example of how human activity can affect changes in the natural selection of other species.

The peppered moth story is a dramatic demonstration of natural selection, and a more recent development in this moth saga illustrates another important feature of evolution. In the 1960s, Britain began legislating tougher environmental laws. As the air in industrialized regions became cleaner, forest tree bark also lightened in color, resulting in lighter-colored moths becoming more prevalent once again (Campbell et al., 1994). This development illustrates that evolution does not necessarily result in species being transformed into more complex forms of life (Smith & Szathmáry, 1995). Instead, the key feature of the evolutionary process involves the degree to which an organism's inborn traits help it adapt to its current environment. Thus, just as a trait that was once highly adaptive can become maladaptive if the environmental conditions change, the reverse is also true: A maladaptive trait can become extremely adaptive.

In summarizing the evolutionary process, keep in mind that it is ongoing. Every species on the planet is undergoing some sort of evolution, even though the speed of the process differs substantially across species. Species that experience a great deal of change in their environment, such as the peppered moth, evolve faster than those that live in stable environments. Also keep in mind that individual organisms do not evolve; populations evolve. Individuals play a role in evolution by interacting with the environment and having their genes screened by natural selection. Thus, individuals contribute to a change in their species' population by their own successes or failures in reproducing. Over many generations, the accumulated effects of literally thousands or even millions of individuals' reproductive successes and failures lead to evolution of the species. The specific role that genes play in reproduction will be discussed more fully in chapter 3, section 3-4a.

1-3f The Sociocultural Perspective Studies How Behavior Is Shaped by Social and Cultural Forces

While the evolutionary perspective examines how inherited genes shape the behavior of humans and other living creatures, the **sociocultural perspective** emphasizes the role that social and cultural factors play in explaining behavior (Gripps, 2002; Haight, 2002). **Culture** is the total lifestyle of people from a particular social grouping, including all the ideas, symbols, preferences, and material objects that they share. It is a shared system of ideas about the nature of the world, and it consists of rules governing how people should think, feel, and act within this world.

Many countries contain a number of distinct cultures. For example, in the United States we can identify many cultural heritages, among them Native American, Hispanic, European, African, Asian, and Middle Eastern. In analyzing culture, it is important to understand that lifestyle changes over time. Thus, Native American culture today is not the same as Native American culture of the 1800s or even of the mid-1900s. This attention to social and cultural factors as a means of explaining human thought and behavior is a central element in many psychological theories.

Individualism and Collectivism

One aspect of culture that is very important in understanding the psychology of human behavior is the belief system concerning how individuals relate to their groups (Triandis, 1995). The human species has evolved within a social group sphere. One of the fundamental dilemmas we have faced throughout our existence is that each individual's inherent desire to pass its genes on to the next generation pushes her or him toward selfish, self-serving actions that can potentially threaten the survival of the individual's group and, thus, the individual itself. Somehow, through the process of natural selection, we have struck a delicate balance between these conflicting tendencies. Today, the cultural belief systems known as *individualism* and *collectivism* are products of this evolutionary-based tension between the desire to selfishly maximize one's reproductive fitness and the need to cooperate with others in order to survive (Kâgitçibasi, 1994; Oyserman et al., 2002).

Individualism is a philosophy of life that stresses the priority of personal goals over group goals, a preference for loosely knit social relationships, and a desire to be relatively autonomous of others' influence. In contrast, **collectivism** is a philosophy of life that stresses the priority of group needs over individual needs, a preference for tightly knit social relationships, and a willingness to submit to the influence of one's group (Tower et al., 1997; Triandis, 1989). Currently, 70 percent of the world's population lives in cultures with a collectivist orientation, which is a much older cultural belief system than individualism (Singelis et al., 1995). Individualism, which developed out of collectivism, is largely a manifestation of the mind-set of people living in industrialized societies.

Although we know that cultures differ in their individualist-collectivist orientations, we do not know whether one is better than the other in any ultimate evolutionary sense. In this text, we will periodically examine how the psychology of people from different cultures differs due to their individualist-collectivist bents. For example, in the chapter 4 discussion of human development, you will discover that within collectivist societies, childrearing practices tend to emphasize conformity, obedience, and knowing one's proper place, while within more individualist societies, independence and self-reliance are stressed. One consequence of

sociocultural perspective An approach to psychology that emphasizes social and cultural influences on behavior.

culture The total lifestyle of people from a particular social grouping, including all the ideas, symbols, preferences, and material objects they share.

individualism A philosophy of life stressing the priority of personal goals over group goals, a preference for loosely knit social relationships, and a desire to be relatively autonomous of others' influence.

collectivism A philosophy of life stressing the priority of group needs over individual needs, a preference for tightly knit social relationships, and a willingness to submit to the influence of one's group.

Seventy percent of the world's population lives in collectivist societies. How might the thinking and behavior of these Japanese schoolchildren differ from that of children in the United States, Canada, and Europe?

Source: Courtesy of Jenny Franzoi.

these differing views is that in an individualist society, people develop a belief in their own uniqueness and diversity. This sense of individuality is nurtured and fostered within the educational system, and its manifestation is considered a sign of maturity. On the other hand, in a collectivist society, uniqueness and individual differences are often seen only as impediments to proper self-growth. Instead, the person is thought to become most meaningful and complete when she or he is closely identified with—not independent of—the group.

Table 1-1 lists some of the differences between these two philosophies of life. The majority of social scientists consider individualism and collectivism to be two ends of a cultural continuum, with the United States, Canada, Australia, and Western European societies located more toward the individualist end and Asian, African, and Latin and South American nations situated near the collectivist end. Within both individualist and collectivist cultures, individualist tendencies tend to be stronger in large urban settings—where people are less dependent on group ties—while collectivist tendencies are more pronounced in small regional cities and rural settings—where social relationships are more interdependent (Kashima et al., 2004; Ma & Schoeneman, 1997).

Although individualism and collectivism are seen by many theorists as two ends of a continuum, this means neither that individualist tendencies do not influence people living in collectivist cultures nor that collectivist yearnings do not shape individualists. Indeed, a growing number of theorists think of these differing ideologies as reflecting two seemingly universal and

Table **1-1**	Differences Between Collectivist and Individualist Cultures
Collectivist Cultures	**Individualist Cultures**
Identity is given by one's group.	Identity is achieved by one's own striving.
Individuals are socialized to be emotionally dependent on their social group, and conformity is valued.	Individuals are socialized to be emotionally independent of their social group, and independence is valued.
Personal and group goals are generally consistent; when inconsistent, group goals have priority.	Personal and group goals are often inconsistent; when inconsistent, personal goals have priority.
Trust is placed in group decisions.	Trust is placed in individual decisions.

common human needs: the *need for autonomy* and the *need for communion* (Aaker et al., 2001; Schwartz, 2003). Thus, although all humans have a need for both autonomy and communion, individualist cultures place greater value on autonomy, while collectivist cultures place greater value on communion. Because one of the goals of psychology is to understand how the past experiences and present conditions of others influence their interpretation of reality, these two contrasting cultural perspectives will periodically figure in our chapter discussions.

Are the Sociocultural and Evolutionary Perspectives Compatible?

Although the sociocultural and evolutionary perspectives offer different explanations for human behavior, a growing number of psychologists believe that cultural and evolutionary forces operate simultaneously in shaping thought and action (Plomin & McClearn, 1993). They argue that a culture is based on its people's relationship with the environment, and that the evolution of our species is a story of how we have adapted to our environment. Thus, just as our bodies and brains are a product of evolutionary forces, so too is our culture. Yet culture change occurs much more rapidly than genetic change. This is why there is a great deal of variation in the world's cultures but little meaningful genetic variation between cultural groups. In this textbook, the evolutionary perspective will provide insight into how we, as a species, got to where we are with our biological structure and behavioral traits, and the sociocultural perspective will suggest how culture can either reinforce or attempt to change these evolutionary-based tendencies and patterns.

1-3g Psychology's Subfields Can Be Distinguished by Their Emphasis on Research versus Application

Now that you have learned something about the different schools of thought within psychology, you might be wondering who employs psychologists and what they do in these jobs. About one-fourth of all psychologists who received their Ph.D.s during the past 25 years are employed at colleges, universities, or institutes where they teach and conduct research in their areas of specialization (see figure 1-3). The goals of these research psychologists are to acquire psychological knowledge through scientific methods and to teach this knowledge to students. Seven areas of specialization for research psychologists are as follows:

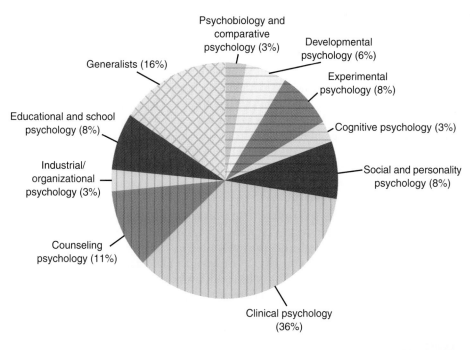

 Research psychologists

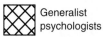 Applied psychologists

Generalist psychologists

Figure 1-3

The Percentage of Ph.D.s Awarded in Psychology by Specialty Area

Source: Based on data from the Summary Report: Doctorate Recipients from U.S. Universities, National Research Council, reported in the *APA Education Directorate*, 1995, p. 12.

1. *Psychobiology* (also called *behavioral neuroscience, biopsychology, physiological psychology*)—Studies behavior by examining physiological processes, especially those occurring in the brain. Psychobiologists are increasingly investigating the genetic bases of thought and action.
2. *Developmental psychology*—Studies how people mature and change physically, cognitively, and socially throughout the life span, from conception to old age.
3. *Experimental psychology*—Studies basic psychological processes such as sensation, perception, learning, motivation, emotion, and states of consciousness. Keep in mind, however, that experiments are used by psychologists in every area of psychology.
4. *Comparative psychology*—Studies similarities and differences in the physiology, behavior, abilities, and genetic makeup of different species, including humans.
5. *Cognitive psychology*—Studies all aspects of thinking, including problem solving, decision making, memory, reasoning, mental imagery, and language.
6. *Personality psychology*—Studies the consistent and distinct ways in which people think, feel, and behave, including how these characteristics originated and developed.
7. *Social psychology*—Studies how people think about and influence one another in social settings, including how the social settings and the cultural beliefs of the individuals shape the interaction.

In addition to psychologists within these seven areas, a little over half the psychologists who received their Ph.D.s during the past 30 years have careers in specialty areas, where they use existing psychological knowledge to solve and prevent problems (see figure 1-3). These **applied psychologists** most often work in mental health centers, schools, industries, governmental agencies, or private practice. Four major applied specialties are as follows:

applied psychologists Psychologists who use existing psychological knowledge to solve and prevent problems.

1. *Clinical psychology*—Diagnoses and treats people with psychological disorders, such as depression, acute anxiety, and schizophrenia, as well as seeks to determine the causes for these disorders.
2. *Counseling psychology*—Diagnoses and treats people with personal problems that do not involve psychological disorders; includes marriage counseling, social skills training, and career planning.
3. *Industrial/organizational psychology*—Focuses on ways to select, motivate, and evaluate employees, as well as to improve management structure and working conditions.
4. *Educational and school psychology*—Assesses and treats both students and the educational environment in order to facilitate children's learning and adjustment in school.

As a way of summarizing this chapter section on the contemporary perspectives and areas of specialization in psychology, consider the famous fable from India about four blind men who happened upon an elephant. None of the men had ever before encountered this sort of creature, so each reached out to explore a different part of the animal. The man who grabbed the tail exclaimed, "An elephant is like a rope!" The man who touched one of the elephant's ears shouted, "An elephant is as thin as a leaf!" "No!" marveled another, who was holding the trunk. "This animal is surely related to the snake!" "You are all mistaken," said the man who was grasping one leg. "An elephant is shaped like the trunk of a tree!" A heated argument ensued over whose description accurately captured the essence of the elephant. The mistake these men made was that they tried to understand their subject by examining only one aspect of it.

In many respects, this is the problem we face on our journey of discovery in psychology. Each of the psychological perspectives previously discussed attempts to understand the thoughts and behavior of humans and other animals by focusing on a different psychological process. Like the blind men—who would have come to a more accurate understanding of the elephant if they had tried to reconcile their seemingly conflicting discoveries—we too can better understand our subject matter if we consider multiple perspectives. Alone, none provides an adequate understanding of the human condition, but together, they give us an ever-clearer portrait of ourselves.

Journey of Discovery Question   Briefly describe the seven contemporary perspectives in psychology. Which of these perspectives appeals to you most, and which least? Why?

- Of the five early schools of psychology, only psychoanalysis and behaviorism have survived as contemporary perspectives.
- The humanistic perspective developed in opposition to psychoanalysis and behaviorism, and it emphasizes human beings' capacity for personal growth and their ability to consciously make choices.
- The cognitive perspective attempts to understand behavior by studying how the mind organizes perceptions, processes information, and interprets experiences.
- The neuroscience perspective attempts to understand behavior by examining physiological processes, especially those occurring in the brain.
- The evolutionary perspective assumes that all species have evolved in ways that maximize the chances of their genes being passed on to their offspring.
- The sociocultural perspective emphasizes social and cultural influences on behavior.
- Seven primary areas of specialization for research psychologists include the following: psychobiology, developmental psychology, experimental psychology, comparative psychology, cognitive psychology, personality psychology, and social psychology.
- Four primary areas of specialization for applied psychologists include the following: clinical psychology, counseling psychology, industrial/organizational psychology, and educational and school psychology.

Psychological Applications

How Did Psychological Research Influence the U.S. Supreme Court's 1954 Decision to Desegregate Schools?

One possible consequence of living in a society where your race is considered inferior to other races is a feeling of inferiority that can be internalized and breed self-hate. This disturbing possibility motivated social psychologists Kenneth and Mamie Phipps Clark to use different-colored dolls to measure children's racial awareness and preferences (Clark & Clark, 1939, 1947). Their research, which began in the late 1930s, demonstrated that not only do children develop racial awareness by age 3, but also they become aware of the positive and negative attributes assigned to Blacks and Whites.

In interviews with African-American children ranging in age from 3 to 7, the Clarks showed each child two dolls—one with light-colored skin and one with dark-colored skin—and then made the following requests:

Give me the doll that you want to play with.
Give me the doll that is a nice doll.
Give me the doll that looks bad.
Give me the doll that is a nice color.

The Clarks found that about two-thirds of the Black children preferred the white-colored doll: They identified it as the "nice" doll, the doll with the "nice" color, and the doll they wanted to play with. For these children, the black-colored doll looked "bad." These preferences occurred even though the children clearly understood that they themselves were Black, and thus were members of the "bad" group (Clark, 1950). As Kenneth Clark later recalled:

We were really disturbed by our findings, and we sat on them for a number of years. What

Kenneth and Mamie Clark's research employing different-colored dolls to measure children's racial awareness and preferences was instrumental in providing the U.S. Supreme Court with evidence that racially segregated schooling instilled a sense of inferiority in Black children.

Source: Library of Congress.

Continued next page—

Psychological Applications

—Continued

was surprising was the degree to which the children suffered from self-rejection, with its truncating effect on their personalities and the earliness of the corrosive awareness of color. I don't think we had quite realized the extent of the cruelty of racism and how hard it hit. . . . Some of these children, particularly in the North, were reduced to crying when presented with the dolls and asked to identify with them. They looked at me as if I were the devil for putting them in this predicament. Let me tell you, it was a traumatic experience for me as well. (Kluger, 1976, p. 400)

The sort of self-rejection that the Clarks found in the Black children was later cited by the U.S. Supreme Court as evidence that the cultural beliefs justifying racially separated educational facilities in the country were damaging to the self-esteem of Black children. On May 17, 1954, the justices concluded in their *Brown v. Board of Education* decision that the societal laws enforcing school segregation were unconstitutional. The decision electrified the African-American community with hope and promise for the future, while it galvanized support and opposition among White Americans (Fine, 2004).

At the time of the monumental 1954 decision outlawing racial segregation in American schools, many psychologists were working in the civil rights movement to fight racial intolerance. However, some of the officials in the American Psychological Association who supported racial segregation tried to destroy the Clarks' scientific reputation (Ludy & Crouse, 2002). For example, former APA president Henry Garrett, who had taught the Clarks in graduate school, referred to Kenneth Clark as "none too bright . . . he was about a C student, but he'd rank pretty high for a Negro" (Kluger, 1976, p. 502). Garrett later wrote a pro-segregation pamphlet claiming that Black people were biologically "immature" in their brain development. In 1994, long after Garrett's racial views had been discredited, the American Psychological Association honored Kenneth Clark with its prestigious Award for Outstanding Lifetime Contribution to Psychology.

In 2004, 50 years after this historic civil rights victory, Clark, now 90 years old, reflected on the event and the hope that psychological science offers society:

We worked with the lawyers on the *Brown* decision without regard to color. To me, that was a good example of how science and law cut across racial and ethnic lines. . . . One can teach children what's cruel and hostile and what's not. The stability of the human species and the stability of the society care whether we accept or reject the values of kindness. (Kersting, 2004a, pp. 58–59)

I like to say that on May 17, 1954, I became a citizen of this country.

—Roscoe Brown, Jr., African-American educator and social commentator

Key Terms

applied psychologists (p. 18)

behaviorism (p. 7)

cognitive perspective (p. 12)

collectivism (p. 15)

culture (p. 15)

determinism (p. 3)

evolution (p. 13)

evolutionary psychology (p. 13)

free will (p. 3)

functionalism (p. 5)

Gestalt psychology (p. 7)

humanistic perspective (p. 11)

individualism (p. 15)

natural selection (p. 13)

nature-nurture debate (p. 12)

neuroscience perspective (p. 12)

positive psychology (p. 11)

psychiatry (p. 3)

psychoanalysis (p. 6)

psychology (p. 3)

sociocultural perspective (p. 15)

structuralism (p. 5)

Suggested Websites

American Psychological Association

http://www.apa.org

This official American Psychological Association (APA) site provides access to many APA-sponsored websites related to various psychological issues.

American Psychological Society

http://www.psychologicalscience.org

This official website of the American Psychological Society (APS) provides access to many psychology-related websites and APS journals.

Today in the History of Psychology

http://www.cwu.edu/~warren/today.html

This website contains a collection of dates and brief descriptions of over 3,100 events in the history of psychology. Type in any day of the year and find out what happened on that day.

Psychweb

http://www.psywww.com

This website provides psychology-related material for both students and instructors of psychology.

Web Links by Psychology Subject Area

http://www.socialpsychology.org/psylinks.htm

This is the general psychology link on the Social Psychology Network, which has more than 5,000 links to psychology topics. The Psychology Subject Areas lists and provides important information on the various subdisciplines in psychology.

Review Questions

Note: You can find the correct answers to these questions by taking the quiz and then submitting your answers in the Online Edition. The program will automatically score your submission. If you miss a question, the program will provide the correct answer, a rationale for the answer, and the section number in the chapter where the topic is discussed.

1. Which of the following statements is *true* of psychology?
   a. It does not implement scientific methods.
   b. It is a small branch of psychiatry.
   c. Psychological phenomena can be predicted with 100 percent certainty.
   d. It is incompatible with free will.
   e. none of the above

2. In what year was the first institute for research in experimental psychology opened?
   a. 1879
   b. 1890
   c. 1921
   d. 1940
   e. 1960

3. Who is known as the "world's first psychologist"?
   a. Wilhelm Wundt
   b. Sigmund Freud
   c. William James
   d. Ivan Pavlov
   e. B. F. Skinner

4. Which of the following is *true* of William James?
   a. He wrote a classic book, titled *Principles of Psychology*.
   b. He wanted to understand how the mind affects what people do, rather than merely identifying its components.
   c. He did very little lab work; rather, he relied on his ideas and writings.
   d. His approach to psychology became known as functionalism.
   e. all of the above

5. Which of the following approaches to psychology was founded by William James, the first American psychologist?
   a. structuralism
   b. behaviorism
   c. functionalism
   d. psychodynamic theory
   e. Gestaltism

6. Which of the following was *true* of Sigmund Freud?
   a. He contended that our personality matures slowly but surely over the years.
   b. He emphasized the study of the conscious experience.
   c. He had no direct experience working with patients.
   d. He was technically not a psychologist but a psychiatrist.
   e. He is closely associated with behaviorism.

7. Which of the following founders of psychology believed that psychology should study observable behavior rather than hidden psychological processes?
   a. Sigmund Freud
   b. William James
   c. John Watson
   d. Wilhelm Wundt
   e. Max Wertheimer

8. Gestalt psychology produced
   a. logical positivism.
   b. laws of grouping.
   c. psychoanalysis.
   d. pragmatism.
   e. introspection.

9. Which of the following is *true* of Mary Calkins?
   a. William James described her dissertation defense as "brilliant."
   b. She was the first woman president of the American Psychological Association (1905).
   c. She did pioneering and influential research on short-term memory.
   d. She refused to accept a Ph.D. from Radcliffe instead of Harvard.
   e. all of the above

10. Of the five early schools of psychology, which perspectives survived as contemporary perspectives?
    a. psychoanalysis
    b. behaviorism
    c. Gestalt psychology
    d. functionalism and structuralism
    e. *a* and *b*

11. Who were considered the architects of the perspective that emphasized people's innate capacity for personal growth and their ability to make choices?
    a. William James and Wilhelm Wundt
    b. Carl Rogers and Abraham Maslow
    c. Mary Calkins and Mamie Phipps Clark
    d. Sigmund Freud and B. F. Skinner
    e. none of the above

12. Which of the following is *true* of the cognitive perspective?
    a. It emphasized the essential goodness of people.
    b. It coincided with the development of the computer.
    c. It is the least scientifically based of the contemporary perspectives.
    d. It promoted the scientific study of love.
    e. none of the above

13. Which of the following is *true* of the neuroscience perspective?
    a. A good deal of its research is done on humans.
    b. It does not believe that research on animals can benefit humans.
    c. It is focused on the most precise microscopic levels of analysis.
    d. It is based on the writings of the biologist Charles Darwin.
    e. all of the above

14. Which of the following observations is least supportive of the evolutionary perspective?
    a. Animals in colder climates have thicker fur.
    b. Babies' skin is often soft to the touch.
    c. Giraffes have unusually long necks.
    d. Some animals have fur or skin that blends in with their environment.
    e. All of the above are examples.

15. Which of the following statements is *true?*
    a. A central element in many theories is that social and cultural factors can help explain human thought and behavior.
    b. The sociocultural and evolutionary perspectives are not compatible.
    c. Genetic change occurs more rapidly than cultural changes.
    d. There is a great deal of genetic variation among cultural groups.
    e. all of the above

16. Which of the following statements is *true?*
    a. Thirty percent of the world's population lives in cultures with a collectivist orientation.
    b. The cultural belief system of individualism is older than collectivism.
    c. From an evolutionary perspective, individualism is better than collectivism.
    d. all of the above
    e. none of the above

17. Which of the following is an applied specialty?
    a. clinical psychology
    b. counseling psychology
    c. industrial psychology
    d. school psychology
    e. all of the above

18. Which of the following did Kenneth and Mamie Phipps Clark find in their 1940s research on racial awareness among Black schoolchildren in the racially segregated South?
    a. African-American children scored higher on standardized intelligence tests.
    b. Children tended to rate dolls of their own color as "nicer."
    c. All children preferred to play with other children, rather than dolls, regardless of color.
    d. The majority of African-American children rated dolls that had dark-colored skin as looking "bad."
    e. none of the above

Chapter 2

The Vehicle for Psychological Discovery

How do people react when they learn that you are enrolled in a psychology course? Based on our society's voracious appetite for "pop psychology" talk-radio shows and self-help books, I'm sure that some of your friends and family members are intrigued—and perhaps a bit envious—about what you might learn in the coming months. Others, in contrast, might dismiss what psychology has to offer as merely "warmed-over common sense." One reason some people think of psychology as simply rephrasing what we already know is that its subject matter is so personal and familiar: We all informally think about our own thoughts, feelings, and actions and those of others. Why would such informally obtained knowledge be appreciably different from what psychologists achieve through their scientific observations? This chapter examines how the scientific inquiry adopted by psychology is different from the much more casual analysis we employ in our everyday thinking.

2-1 IS PSYCHOLOGY JUST COMMON SENSE?

Preview

- *What are some "common" flaws in commonsense thinking?*
- *How do psychologists try to avoid the flaws of everyday thinking in their study of the mind?*

2-1a We Often Understand Our World Based on a "Naive" Psychology

All of us spend considerable time and energy gathering, analyzing, and interpreting information to better understand our world and the people who inhabit it. An important product of this informal journey of discovery is the development of certain assumptions or belief systems about how we and others function on the psychological level. In most cases, these beliefs are best characterized as being embedded within a *naive psychology*—that is, instead of being based on careful scientific analysis, they develop from everyday experiences and uncritical acceptance of other people's views and opinions. Although these commonsense psychological beliefs often result in good decision making, they can also produce distorted judgments. To illustrate some of the pitfalls of naive psychology, let's briefly examine how we typically judge other people's personalities and how we generally overestimate our knowledge of how people and the world operate.

Common Mistakes in Assessing Personality

Research indicates that the first bits of information we learn about a person carry more weight in forming an overall impression than information learned later. Thus, if a stranger were described to you as intelligent, industrious, impulsive, critical, stubborn, and envious, your overall impression of her might be more favorable than if she were described as envious, stubborn, critical, impulsive, industrious, and intelligent. Although the information contained in these two descriptions is identical, psychological research has found that a person described in the first manner is typically thought to be competent and ambitious, while a person described in the reverse order is more likely to be considered overemotional and socially maladjusted (Asch, 1946).

Why does early information figure more prominently than later information in our impression of others? One possible explanation for this *primacy effect* (see chapter 8, section 8-1a) is that the early bits of information provide a mental "outline" in memory, which we then use to process later information (Van Overwalle & Labiouse, 2004). If the later information contradicts this outline, we are more likely to ignore it. The primacy effect is particularly strong when people are given little time to make judgments and are not under a great deal of pressure to be correct (Kruglanski & Freund, 1983). There is also evidence that people who are most likely to "seize" the early information they learn about others and "freeze" it into quick personality judgments are those with a strong need for certainty in their lives (Kruglanski & Webster, 1996). Quick personality judgments provide these individuals with a reassuring belief that they understand other people.

Much of what we take to be true is seriously wrong.

—*Gore Vidal, U.S. author, b. 1925*

Our everyday personality judgments are shaped not only by the order in which we learn information about others, but also by our prior set of beliefs about which personality traits go together. These assumptions or naive belief systems that we have about the associations among personality traits have been called an **implicit personality theory.** In this unscientific theory of personality, we have a strong tendency to assume that all good things occur together in persons and that all bad things do so as well, with little overlap between the two (Leyens, 1991; Norenzayan et al., 2002). Thus, we are likely to believe that someone whom we perceive as warm and outgoing could not also be prone to violence. Implicit personality theory appears to have an operating principle of *evaluative consistency*—the tendency to view others in a way that is internally consistent. Even when contradictory information is provided, we still generally persist in viewing people as consistently either good or bad. In seeking consistency, we often distort or explain away contradictory information.

Research suggests that the use of implicit personality theories contributes to the high rates of sexually transmitted diseases among adolescents and young adults. The Center for Disease Control estimates that 19 million new cases of sexually transmitted diseases occur annually in the United States, with almost half occurring among 15- to 24-year-olds (Weinstock et al., 2000). One of the primary reasons why youth are overrepresented in these disease categories is that many of them are not practicing safe sex (Kalichman, 2000). A survey conducted by Diane Kimble and her colleagues (1992) found that many youth have a well-developed set of ideas—an implicit personality theory—regarding which potential sexual partners are safe and which are not. Who are these sexually "safe" persons? Can you guess, based on information in the previous paragraph? People one knows and likes are perceived not to be a risk, while risky people are those one does not know well, those who are older, or those who are overanxious for sex. Kimble and her coworkers attributed the young people's tendencies not to practice safe sex with partners they knew and liked to their reluctance to link the risk of disease with loving or caring relationships. Unfortunately, the criteria these people use to judge risk for sexually transmitted diseases are completely unrelated to a person's sexual disease status. People who use such a belief system run the very real risk of exposure to such dangerous diseases as gonorrhea, chlamydia, syphilis, hepatitis, and HIV/AIDS.

> *Journey of Discovery* Question
>
> The importance of Kimble's research on implicit personality theories and practicing safe sex is that it not only alerts us to how people often engage in faulty decision making, but also suggests how we might use this knowledge to develop intervention programs aimed at changing young adults' thinking regarding safe sex. If you were developing such a program, how would you explain to participants the role that implicit personality theory plays in their daily social judgments?

The Hindsight Bias

If you were to successfully develop an intervention program informing people about faulty decision making regarding safe sex, participants would likely say that you were not telling them anything they didn't already know. In other words, your psychological findings would likely be seen as simply reflecting obvious commonsense notions of life. Yet, is it really true that most young adults already understand the psychological dynamics of how they judge other people and thus realize they cannot assume that others are "safe" sexual partners simply because they are likable? As we have already seen, the available evidence certainly does not support this conclusion. What else might explain this "I-knew-it-all-along" response?

Research suggests that, when recalling past events, we tend to believe that we "knew all along" how things would turn out. For example, after learning the results of a local election, you might think, "I knew this would be the outcome long ago." Or, after your favorite sports team narrowly defeats its arch rival for the first time in 5 years, you exclaim, "All week I could sense that my team was going to win!" This after-the-fact overestimation of your ability to foresee the outcome is known as the **hindsight bias** (Blank et al., 2003; Villejoubert, 2005).

Why does the hindsight bias occur? Our desire for *sensemaking* fuels this bias, and we are most likely to rewrite our memory of a past event when the outcome is initially

implicit personality theory People's assumptions or naive belief systems about which personality traits go together.

hindsight bias The tendency, once an event has occurred, to overestimate our ability to have foreseen the outcome.

We often develop beliefs about people's personalities based on a need for evaluative consistency. If you were introduced to George, you would probably find him warm, friendly, and outgoing. Based on this first impression, you would probably conclude that he is also honest and trustworthy, because these traits are consistent with your initial evaluations. Often, such implicit personality theories are accurate, but sometimes they are not. Can you think of instances in your life when your implicit personality theories have created problems for you?

Source: Courtesy of Figzoi.

surprising (Pezzo, 2003). When thinking about a past event that had a surprising outcome, we selectively recall information in constructing a plausible story that is consistent with the now-known outcome (Harvey & Martin, 1995; Schwarz & Stahlberg, 2003). This "rewriting" of how events occurred allows us to insert the missing causal connections so that the story makes sense given the outcome. Claiming hindsight reassures us that we understand—and can anticipate—events in our world (Wasserman et al., 1991). Cross-cultural studies indicate that this bias occurs throughout the world (Pohl et al., 2002).

If you were among a group of employees laid off at work, do you think you would be more or less likely to claim that "there were many warning signals" than if you were merely an unaffected citizen of the town in which the layoffs occurred? In one study that explored this question, people living near a factory were asked questions about recent factory layoffs (Mark & Mellor, 1991). Results indicated that townspeople who did not work at the factory and were not affected by the layoffs were most likely to claim that they knew the job cuts were coming (high hindsight bias). Factory workers who kept their jobs were less likely to claim hindsight. Those who expressed the greatest surprise (no hindsight bias) were the workers who had actually lost their jobs. These results suggest that, although we often engage in hindsight bias when explaining past events, we are less likely to do so when those events affect us personally and are negative. Is this what you predicted? Present this hypothetical situation to your friends, and have them predict the outcome. How many guessed correctly? Are these findings simply "common sense"? In hindsight, it might appear so.

The hindsight bias involves the tendency to overestimate your ability to have foreseen the outcome of a past event. If workers have just been told that their factory is closing, are they more or less likely than the local townspeople to claim they foresaw the layoffs?

Source: Copyright © 2007 Atomic Dog Publishing and its licensors. All rights reserved.

Of course, not all "I-knew-it-all-along" claims are due to hindsight bias. Because we all observe and analyze the world in which we live, we are sometimes accurate in foreseeing how events will unfold. This is true for both personal and historical happenings, as well as for the findings of psychological research. But there are other times when the scientific findings of psychology are considerably distant from anything we would have predicted based on our casual observations. This is one fact that you will be regularly reminded of as you read this textbook: Many commonsense ideas are simply a product of wrongheaded thinking. One of the objectives of psychological research is to identify and dispel these faulty commonsense beliefs.

Life is lived forwards, but understood backwards.

—*Søren Kierkegaard, Danish philosopher, 1813–1855*

> *Journey of Discovery* Question
>
> Having digested the research on hindsight bias, why do you think we are less likely to claim hindsight for negative outcomes that personally affect us?

2-1b Scientific Methods Minimize Error and Lead to Dependable Generalizations

Now that we have reviewed a few ways in which our everyday thinking can lead to faulty judgments, do you think psychology has developed a special formula to eliminate these biases and errors when conducting research? The answer is no. There is no magic formula to erase these mental quirks and glitches so that our minds run with computer-like precision. Even if there were such a formula, would you be so foolhardy as to "cure" yourself in this manner? As you will discover in your journey through psychology, the quirks and glitches in our everyday thinking are important elements in what it means to be human.

While it is true that psychologists are not immune to error-prone thinking, they do use special methods to *minimize* these problems when conducting research. These **scientific methods** consist of a set of procedures used to gather, analyze, and interpret information in a way that reduces error and leads to dependable generalizations. By *generalizations*, I mean statements that apply to members of a group as a whole rather than to specific members. Remember my cross-country hitchhiking study described in chapter 1? When I collected my data, I used the scientific method of survey research (see section 2-3b), which involved interviewing and administering structured personality questionnaires to more than 100 cross-country hitchhikers in many different locations throughout the country. With this number of participants in my study collected over such a wide geographic area, I was more confident that my hitchhiking sample accurately represented the population of cross-country hitchhikers in the United States.

scientific method A set of procedures used in science to gather, analyze, and interpret information in a way that reduces error and leads to dependable generalizations.

sample A group of subjects who are selected to participate in a research study.

population All the members of an identifiable group from which a sample is drawn.

random selection A procedure for selecting a sample of people to study in which everyone in the population has an equal chance of being chosen.

critical thinking The process of deciding what to believe and how to act based on careful evaluation of the evidence.

In research, a **sample** is a group of subjects who are selected to participate in a given study, while a **population** consists of all the members of an identifiable group from which a sample is drawn. The closer a sample is in representing the population, the greater confidence researchers have in generalizing their findings beyond the sample. Researchers have the most confidence that their sample is an accurate representation of the population when everyone in the population has an equal chance of being selected for the sample. Such **random selection** of participants, although highly desirable, is not always possible. For instance, it would be impossible to design a study in which every cross-country hitchhiker in the United States had an equal chance of being included in the sample.

Beyond sample selection, how might you employ the scientific method to understand the personalities of your research participants? Often, psychologists use well-established, highly structured questionnaires in their research. In my study, instead of simply asking cross-country hitchhikers questions that I thought of at the moment, I asked them all to respond to the same set of questions that other researchers had previously developed to measure specific aspects of personality. I then compared their responses to one another as well as to those of other young adults who were not cross-country hitchhikers, using a series of statistical computations. These statistical analyses allowed me to determine whether and how these groups differed from one another.

From this brief description of scientific methodology, you can see that the guidelines psychologists follow when conducting research are far more stringent than those typically employed in everyday thinking. Psychologists also approach the study of the mind by engaging in **critical thinking,** which is the process of deciding what to believe and how to act based on a careful evaluation of the evidence. An important aspect of critical thinking is ruling out alternative explanations. Can a hypnotized person be induced to commit murder? Is there compelling evidence that psychics can predict future events? Can subliminal tapes improve memory and increase self-esteem? These are a few of the fascinating questions we will examine in our journey of discovery. And we will do so while using critical thinking skills. The "Psychological Applications" section at the end of this chapter discusses how you can develop critical thinking skills to aid in your journey. In the meantime, let's examine the research *process* itself and then scrutinize more thoroughly the *structure* of the various scientific methods psychologists use in their research.

Since the beginning of the 20th century, people's innate desire to understand themselves—and the human condition—has found a new avenue toward the answer: the scientific method.

—Jacqueline Swartz, contemporary Canadian journalist

Section Review

- Commonsense thinking often consists of the following faulty belief systems that can produce distorted judgments:
  — The primacy effect is the tendency for the first bits of information we learn to carry more weight in forming an overall impression than information learned later.
  — Implicit personality theories are the assumptions people make about which personality traits go together.
  — Hindsight bias is the tendency, once an event has occurred, to overestimate our ability to have foreseen the outcome.
- To minimize these human biases when conducting research, psychologists employ scientific methods.

2-2   WHAT IS THE PROCESS IN CONDUCTING RESEARCH?

Preview
- *What are the stages in the research process?*
- *What is a theory, and how is it related to a hypothesis?*
- *What is the role of internal review boards in psychological research?*
- *How do psychologists analyze the findings across many studies?*
- *Are there any "final truths" in science?*

When you were a child, did you ever try building something that came with a set of plans? I remember making my first model airplane and being so excited about getting it to look like the image on the box that I ignored the directions and simply slapped the pieces together as fast as my little fingers would allow. Of course, employing such a slapdash method did not lead to a very pleasing final result. Through such experiences, I gradually learned the value of designing a plan of action when undertaking projects. This basic lesson is what the rest of this chapter is about. That is, in order for psychologists to effectively study the mind and behavior, they must employ scientific methods to carefully plan and execute their research projects. This process occurs in a series of four sequential stages, which are summarized in figure 2-1. Let's examine each in turn.

2-2a The First Research Stage Involves Selecting a Topic and Reviewing Past Research

In most instances, the research process begins by selecting a topic worth exploring. Scientists get their ideas from many sources. Inspiration could come from someone else's research, from an incident in the daily news, or from some personal experience in the researcher's life. Psychologists generally investigate topics that have relevance to their own lives and culture. For example, in 1964 people were stunned to learn of the brutal murder of a woman outside her New York City apartment building. The victim, Kitty Genovese, was attacked by her assailant over a period of 45 minutes. Despite the fact that Ms. Genovese obviously needed help, none of her neighbors came to her aid. No one even phoned the police or an ambulance,

---

Stage 1: Selecting a Topic and Searching the Literature

Ideas come from a variety of sources, including existing theories, past research, current social events, and personal experiences. Once a topic has been selected, psychologists must not only become knowledgeable about past research findings in their area of interest, but also keep abreast of recently published studies and those reported at scientific meetings.

⬇

Stage 2: Developing a Theory and Formulating Hypotheses

Once the research literature has been digested, a theory is formulated and hypotheses that can be empirically tested must then be developed.

⬇

Stage 3: Selecting a Scientific Method and Submitting the Study for Ethical Evaluation

Research can be conducted in the laboratory or in the field, and the psychologist can employ a variety of methods, including correlational, experimental, and case study. All institutions seeking federal research funding must establish institutional review boards to evaluate the potential benefits and risks of proposed studies.

⬇

Stage 4: Collecting and Analyzing Data and Reporting Results

The three basic techniques of data collection are self-reports, direct observations, and archival information. Data can be analyzed using either descriptive or inferential statistics, with the latter mathematical analysis being the more valuable because it allows researchers to generalize their findings to the population of interest. Psychologists principally report their results at professional meetings and by publishing articles in scientific journals.

Figure 2-1

Stages in the Psychological Research Process

but one couple did pull up chairs to their window and turn out the lights to get a better view. Later, the question everyone asked was "Why were these bystanders so callous to her suffering?" Two people who discussed this disturbing event in detail were the social psychologists John Darley and Bibb Latané. Years later, Darley recalled the content of their discussion:

> Latané and I, shocked as anybody else, met over dinner a few days after this terrible incident had occurred and began to analyze this process in social psychological terms.... First, social psychologists ask not how are people different or why are the people who failed to respond monsters, but how are all people the same and how might anybody in that situation be influenced not to respond. Second, we asked: What influences reach the person from the group? ... In defining an event as an emergency, one looks at other people to see their reactions to the situation and interpret the meaning that lies behind their actions. Third, when multiple people are present, the responsibility to intervene does not focus clearly on any one person.... You feel a diffusion of responsibility in that situation and you're less likely to take responsibility. We argued that these two processes, definition and diffusion, working together, might well account for a good deal of what happened. (Evans, 1980, pp. 216–217)

The *model of bystander intervention* that emerged from this dinner discussion (Darley & Latané, 1968), and the subsequent research it spawned, provided valuable insights into the complex decision making that occurs among bystanders in emergency situations (see chapter 16, section 16-4e). Had this murder not received such wide coverage, perhaps Darley and Latané would have directed their research activities in a different direction.

Once a topic has been selected, investigators search the scientific literature to determine whether prior investigations of the topic exist. The findings from these previous studies generally shape the course of the current investigation. Today, psychologists can vastly accelerate literature searches by using a number of computer-based programs that catalog even the most recently published studies. In addition, psychologists can often instantly obtain unpublished articles from researchers at other universities through either computer networks or fax machines.

Often it is impossible to separate a literature search from topic selection, because researchers may not choose a specific topic until they have extensively searched the available literature. In addition, keeping abreast of other colleagues' discoveries and insights is necessary during all stages in the research process. For this reason, searching the research literature may be thought of as a never-ending endeavor.

2-2b The Second Research Stage Involves Developing a Theory and Hypotheses

The basic motivation underlying research is the desire to find answers to questions. The question of interest usually revolves around whether some event can be explained by a particular theory. A **theory** is an organized system of ideas that seeks to explain why two or more events are related. Put simply, a theory provides a picture of reality concerning some phenomenon. This picture develops after extensive observation, analysis, and creative reflection. Theory development is an important aspect of the second stage of the research process. What makes a good theory depends on a number of factors, some of which are listed in table 2-1 (Kuhn, 1977; McMullin, 1983).

The most salient factor in determining the value of a theory is its *predictive accuracy*. In other words, can it reliably predict behavior? A second necessary factor is *internal coherence*—that is, there shouldn't be any logical inconsistencies or unexplained coincidences among the theoretical principles and concepts. A third characteristic of a good theory is that it should be *economical*, meaning that it includes the minimum number of principles or concepts necessary to adequately explain and predict the phenomenon in question. Finally, a fourth and equally important quality in a good theory is *fertility*, the ability to generate sufficient interest in other scientists so that the theory is tested and extended to a wide variety of behavior.

Scientists determine the predictive accuracy of a theory by formulating hypotheses. **Hypotheses** are specific propositions or expectations about the nature of things derived

theory An organized system of ideas that seeks to explain why two or more events are related.

hypotheses Specific propositions or expectations about the nature of things derived from a theory.

Table 2-1	What Makes a Good Theory?

Predictive accuracy—Can the theory reliably predict behavior?

Internal coherence—Are there logical inconsistencies between any of the theoretical ideas?

Economy—Does the theory contain only what is necessary to explain the phenomenon in question?

Fertility—Does the theory generate research, and can it be used to explain a wide variety of behavior?

from a theory—in other words, they are the logical implications of the theory. The researcher asks, "If the theory is true, what observations would we expect to make in our investigation?" An example of a hypothesis developing from a theory is William Dement's interest in dreaming. Following other researchers' discovery that dreaming was associated with periods of rapid eye movement (REM) sleep (Aserinsky & Kleitman, 1953), Dement (1960) developed a theory that dreaming was a fundamental requirement for all humans. He hypothesized that if people were not allowed to dream over a series of nights (by waking them when they entered REM sleep), they would experience some kind of pressure to increase their "dream time" on subsequent nights. This hypothesis was a logical extension of Dement's theory that there is something basic in our need to dream. (Refer to chapter 6, section 6-2d, for the results of Dement's research.)

After collecting data to determine whether the hypothesis successfully predicts the outcome of the study, researchers reevaluate the theory. Was the research hypothesis supported by the data, which thereby support the validity of the theory? If the data do not support the study's hypothesis, the theory probably needs revising. Figure 2-2 illustrates the cyclical nature of the relationship between a theory and a testable hypothesis.

> One of the most serious problems confronting psychology is that of connecting itself with life. . . . Theory that does not someway affect life has no value.
>
> —*Lewis Terman, U.S. psychologist, 1877–1959*

2-2c The Third Research Stage Involves Selecting a Scientific Method and Obtaining Approval to Conduct the Study

When a theory and hypotheses have been developed, researchers must next select a scientific method that allows the hypotheses to be tested. Psychological research generally occurs in one of two settings—the *laboratory* (a controlled environment) or the *field* (a natural setting). Most laboratory research uses *experimental* methods, while most field studies are either *correlational* or *observational* (see section 2-3).

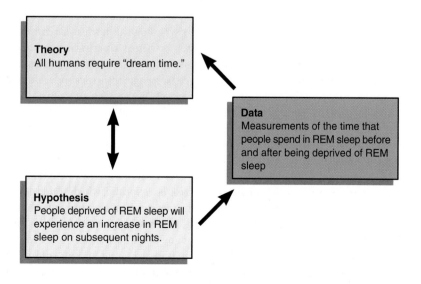

Figure 2-2

The Cyclical Nature of the Theory-Hypothesis Relationship

The research process reflects a cyclical relationship between a theory and a testable hypothesis, with the data from a research study providing the evidence to support or refute the hypothesis. If the research hypothesis is supported, the validity of the theory is also supported, generating new hypotheses to test in future research. If the research hypothesis is not supported, the validity of the theory is questioned, prompting a revision of the theory. From the revised theory, new hypotheses are developed that are then tested in another round of empirical studies.

variables In scientific research, factors that can be measured and that can vary.

operational definition A scientist's precise description of how a variable has been quantified so that it can be measured.

replication Repeating a previous study's scientific procedures using different participants in an attempt to duplicate the findings.

In all scientific methods, psychologists seek to determine the nature of the relationship between two or more factors, called **variables** because they are things that can be measured and that can vary. When scientists describe their variables, they do so by using **operational definitions,** which are very precise descriptions of how the variables have been quantified so that they can be measured.

Why is an operational definition of a variable so important in scientific research? Consider once again the hitchhiking study. My operational definition of a cross-country hitchhiker was any person hitchhiking at least 1,000 miles. This definition excluded from the study hitchhikers on short-distance trips, such as those hitching a ride to work or to a nearby town. What if I had not used a clear and concrete definition of this variable? What if I had simply included in my sample every hitchhiker I encountered? How do you think this might have affected the findings? Similarly, consider how experimental psychologists often study hunger. When conducting this research, they frequently use specialized instruments that measure stomach contractions, because such contractions signal the brain's lateral hypothalamic feeding system. In such studies, their operational definition of hunger is the onset of stomach contractions. This precise and concrete definition of hunger provides other psychologists with the necessary information concerning what was measured in the study, and it also allows them to repeat the same scientific procedures in future studies. Repeating a previous study's scientific procedures using different participants in an attempt to duplicate the findings is known as **replication.** Replication is important in advancing scientific knowledge because the findings from a single study are far less convincing than the same findings from a series of related studies. More on this later, in section 2-2e.

IRB Review of Human Studies

To ensure the health and safety of participants in psychological studies, all research-oriented institutions have *institutional review boards (IRBs)* to monitor and evaluate research proposals involving both human and animal subjects (Chastain & Lundrum, 1999). IRBs consist of a panel of both scientists and nonscientists who ensure the protection and welfare of research participants by formally reviewing the methodologies and procedures of proposed studies. Prior to conducting research, psychologists—like all other behavioral scientists—must have their proposed studies reviewed and approved by IRBs.

The issue of protecting research participants first became a hot topic of discussion in the psychological community during the 1960s following Stanley Milgram's (1963, 1974) obedience experiments, in which volunteers agreed to act as teachers in a learning experiment that, in actuality, was a study of obedience. In this experiment, the volunteers were ordered to deliver seemingly painful electrical shocks to a person because he wasn't performing well on a memory task. Although no shocks were ever delivered—the victim was an accomplice of Milgram and only pretended to be in pain—the stress experienced by the participants was real. The question raised by this study was whether the importance of the research justified exposing participants to potentially harmful psychological consequences (Blass, 2000; Savin, 1973). The potential psychological harm in such research could take many forms. First, because studies like the obedience experiments provide false information to participants regarding their true purpose, such *deception* could lead to a loss of trust in social scientists (Bok, 1978; Ortmann & Hertwig, 1997). Second, and more important, placing participants in situations where they are encouraged, or even coerced, to engage in antisocial activity could harm their mental health. That is, realizing that one has the potential for cruel behavior may induce feelings of guilt or inferiority in some people.

Spurred by the debate surrounding these controversial studies, the American Psychological Association developed detailed guidelines on the conduct of research with both human and nonhuman participants. To guard against harm to human participants, the guidelines followed by IRBs focus on the *risk/benefit ratio,* which weighs the potential risks to those participating in a study against the benefits that the study may have for advancing knowledge about humanity (Hayes, 2002). In assessing proposed studies, priority is always given to the welfare of the participants over any potential benefits of the research (Colombo, 1995; Rosenthal, 1994, 1995). With such standards and monitoring agencies in place, human psychological research is a very low-risk activity, and participants usually enjoy their

Table 2-2	Guidelines for Conducting Research with Human Participants

In assessing proposed studies involving human subjects, priority is always given to ensuring their welfare over any potential benefits of the research (Saks et al., 2002; Street & Luoma, 2002). The guidelines also urge researchers to do the following:

1. Provide enough information to possible participants about the activities they will perform in the study so that they can freely give their *informed consent.*

2. Be truthful whenever possible. *Deception* should be used only when absolutely necessary and when adequate debriefing is provided.

3. Allow participants the *right to decline* to be a part of the study and the right to discontinue their participation at any point without this decision resulting in any negative consequences (for example, not receiving full payment for their participation).

4. *Protect participants* from both physical and psychological harm. If participants suffer any undesirable consequences, the researcher must do as much as possible to remove the damaging effects.

5. Ensure that any information provided by individual participants is kept *confidential.*

6. *Debrief* individuals once they have completed their participation. Explain all aspects of the research, attempt to answer all questions and resolve any negative feelings, and make sure they realize that their participation contributes to better scientific understanding.

experience, even if they were initially deceived about the study's true purpose (Christensen, 1988; Smith & Richardson, 1983). Table 2-2 lists some of the guidelines followed when conducting research involving human participants (Fisher et al., 2002; Sales & Folkman, 2000).

> *Journey of*
> *Discovery*
> Question
>
> Imagine that you are a member of an institutional review board, and a research proposal similar to the Milgram obedience study has been submitted for approval. How would you determine its risk/benefit ratio?

IRB Review of Animal Studies

About 5 percent of all research published in psychology journals uses animals as subjects (Kiple & Ornelas, 2001). The vast majority of these studies involve little more than slightly modifying the environments of animals and observing how these changes affect their behavior. A minority of studies, however, involve painful and dangerous experimental procedures that would never be attempted on human participants. For example, research investigating the effect of drugs on brain function or the treatment of brain disorders and brain damage often begins with animal studies. This research has helped explain the causes of human mental illness and facilitated the development of effective treatments. Animal research has also contributed greatly to explanations of how the brain works, as well as to the discovery of basic principles of perception, motivation, and learning (Swanson, 2004).

Do such benefits outweigh the costs in terms of the harm done to the animal subjects in these studies? Many animal rights activists do not think so, and they have strenuously opposed such research, regardless of the resulting benefits (Erwin et al., 1994; Plous, 1998). Moderates among animal rights activists recognize the need for some of this research, but they argue that other research inflicts needless pain and suffering on animals. Within the field of psychology itself, although the majority of Ph.D.s and psychology majors support animal studies involving observation or confinement, most disapprove of studies involving pain or death (Plous, 1996a, 1996b).

In response to such criticism, virtually all scientists who conduct animal research support the humane treatment of animals, but they deny that animals have the same rights as people (Cohen, 1994). Instead, they contend that every advance in science must eventually be tried on a living creature. If animals are not substituted for humans in studies that pose significant health risks, then we must either (1) place human participants at serious risk in these studies, or (2) simply abandon the research altogether. Because neither of these options is acceptable to most people, animal research continues, as does the debate (Baldwin, 1993). However, responding to the widespread concern for the humane treatment of animals, both the American Psychological Association and a federal law known as the Animal Welfare Act have established standards for the humane care and treatment of laboratory animals. The U.S. Public Health Service also requires that all colleges and institutions receiving research grants from the National Institutes of Health maintain internal review boards to ensure that

1. animals are properly cared for;
2. subjecting animals to painful or stressful procedures is used only when an alternative procedure is unavailable;
3. surgical procedures are performed under appropriate anesthesia, and techniques to avoid infection and minimize pain are followed; and
4. when an animal's life must be terminated, it is done rapidly, with an effort to minimize pain.

Table 2-3 lists some myths and facts about animal research.

Journey of Discovery Question
For every dog or cat used in a laboratory experiment, 10,000 dogs and cats are abandoned by their owners (Miller, 1985). When these abandoned animals are brought to local humane societies and not adopted, should they be made available as subjects for scientific research? Upon what values would you base your decision?

Table 2-3   Some Myths and Facts about Animal Research
Myth: Most animal research is unnecessary. **Fact:** This may have been partly true 30 years ago when, for example, psychology students regularly used laboratory rats in their courses to better understand well-documented principles of learning. Today, however, strong economic pressures weigh against the unnecessary use of animals in research. The extremely limited funds available to conduct animal research minimize the possibility that animals will be used for such trivial purposes.
Myth: Other research methods can be used so that animals are not needed in behavioral research. **Fact:** In most cases, no good alternatives exist. For example, computerized models of complex behavior still do not truly mimic actual behavior.
Myth: Most research animals are dogs, cats, and nonhuman primates. **Fact:** Dogs and cats account for less than 1 percent of the total number of animal subjects. The same is true of nonhuman primates. Nearly 90 percent of the animals used in research are rats, mice, and other rodents.
Myth: Most animals in research suffer great pain and distress. **Fact:** The vast majority of behavioral and biomedical research (over 90 percent) does not cause pain or significant distress to the animal. In only 6 percent of experiments are anesthesia or painkillers withheld. In such instances, researchers withhold pain relief because it would interfere with the objectives of the research (for example, studying the effects of pain).
Myth: Animal research benefits only humans. **Fact:** Animal research benefits *both* humans and animals. For example, knowledge of animal sexual and feeding behavior has helped save a number of species from extinction. Further, insights gained through animal research on taste aversion have been used by both ranchers and conservationists to condition animal predators in the wild to avoid killing livestock and endangered species (see chapter 7, section 7-1d).

2-2d The Fourth Research Stage Involves Collecting and Analyzing Data and Reporting Results

When approval has been granted by the IRB, it is time to *collect the data*. There are three basic techniques of data collection: (1) *self-reports*, (2) *direct observations*, and (3) *archival information*. Collecting data using self-reports allows researchers to measure important subjective states, such as people's perceptions, emotions, or attitudes. The disadvantage of self-report data, however, is that it relies on people accurately describing these internal states—something they are not always willing or able to do (Greenwald et al., 1998). Because of this drawback, many researchers prefer to directly observe people's behavior, recording its quantity and direction of change over time. Finally, researchers sometimes examine existing documents, or archives, to gather information. These accumulated records come from a wide variety of sources (for example, census information, court records, newspaper articles, magazines) and can provide researchers with a great deal of valuable information.

Once the data has been collected, the researcher must analyze it. In contemporary psychology, data analysis generally requires extensive knowledge of statistical procedures and computer software packages. The two basic kinds of statistics employed by psychologists are descriptive and inferential. **Descriptive statistics** simply summarize and describe the behavior or characteristics of a particular sample of participants in a study, while **inferential statistics** move beyond mere description to make inferences about the larger population from which the sample was drawn. Inferential statistics are used to estimate the likelihood that a difference found in the groups studied would also be found if everyone in the population participated in the study. Psychologists generally accept a difference as *statistically significant* if the likelihood of it occurring by chance is less than 1 in 20—that is, a probability of less than 5 percent (Nickerson, 2000). Because one of the main objectives of psychological research is to generalize research findings to the population of interest, inferential statistics are the more valued type of statistic. For a closer examination of how psychologists employ statistics in their research, see Appendix A, "Statistical Reasoning," at the end of the text.

Finally, in any scholarly pursuit, for advancements to be made, researchers must share their knowledge with others in the field. Thus, the final task in the fourth stage of the research process is to *report results*. Psychologists principally share their findings by making presentations at professional meetings and by publishing articles in scientific journals. As they inform fellow scholars of their discoveries, researchers build upon and refine one another's work, and the understanding of psychology is enriched. This final task is very important for the advancement of the discipline. Yet psychologists' research findings are not uncritically accepted by others. At scientific conventions, where research is often first reported, and in scientific journals, where studies are ultimately published, all stages in the research process are scrutinized for possible errors and oversights. In most cases, a scientific journal will not publish research findings when there are significant problems with the hypotheses, methods, or data analysis. In addition, articles are often rejected for publication because reviewers decide the research isn't very important. Through such critical analysis, psychological knowledge is advanced.

Throughout this text, you will see citations like the following: (Blass, 2000; Hall & Brannick, 2002). These citations identify the authors whose research and ideas are being discussed, along with the year in which the cited book or scientific journal article was published. In the "References" section at the end of this text, you will find the complete references for this work, listed in alphabetical order by the first author's last name (in our examples, "Blass" and "Hall").

> **descriptive statistics**
> Numbers that summarize and describe the behavior or characteristics of a particular sample of participants in a study.

> **inferential statistics**
> Mathematical analyses that move beyond mere description of research data to make inferences about the larger population from which the sample was drawn.

2-2e Meta-Analysis Analyzes the Findings across Many Studies

One of the problems in science is that of contradictory findings from one study to the next. For example, if eight studies find that one type of psychotherapy is effective in treating depression while five studies find that it is ineffective, what conclusions should be drawn? In the past, researchers often used the "majority rules" approach to resolve such controversies. That is, they merely counted up the number of studies that found or did not find a particular psychological effect and then concluded that the effect existed if it occurred in the majority of studies. However, to better assess the findings from numerous studies during the past 20 years, researchers have increasingly relied on a more sophisticated comparison procedure called meta-analysis

meta-analysis The use of statistical techniques to sum up a body of similar studies in order to objectively estimate the reliability and overall size of the effect.

(Hall & Brannick, 2002; Stamps, 2002). **Meta-analysis** is the use of statistical techniques to sum up a body of similar studies in order to objectively estimate the reliability and overall size of the effect (Chalmers et al., 2002; Rothstein et al., 2002). Because many studies may find small differences between groups that do not reach statistical levels of significance, meta-analysis can determine whether these small effects are indeed "real" or merely measurement error.

One area of research in which meta-analysis has proven invaluable is the study of gender differences. Meta-analytic techniques have found that the less sophisticated methodology of the "majority rules" approach often overestimated male-female differences. Even when meta-analytic studies did find gender differences (for example, females' greater verbal abilities and males' greater mathematical performance), the sizes of these differences were often so small as to be of little practical significance (Hyde et al., 1990; Stumpf & Stanley, 1998). Although meta-analytic studies have found that men and women do differ somewhat in their psychological functioning and social behavior, equally important is the finding that even when gender differences are found, far more differences exist between men and between women (within-sex variation) than between men and women (between-sex variation).

2-2f There Are No "Final Truths" in Science

In the United States, an increasing number of school boards are in the grip of a controversy concerning whether *creation science* should be taught in science classes as an alternative explanation to evolutionary theory. The core of this argument involves what qualifies as a scientific theory. Advocates of creation science (sometimes referred to as *creationism* or *intelligent design*) reject evolution and adhere to a Bible-based explanation of God creating the world in 7 days (Evans, 2001). Some followers of creation science proclaim a more literal interpretation of the Bible's creation story than do others. *Young earth creationists* believe in the book of Genesis's literal 7-day creation story, while *old earth creationists* believe that the 7 days should be interpreted as figurative lengths of time. Whatever their differences concerning how much time passed while God created life, all creationists assert that their explanation is at least as scientifically based as evolutionary theory. My purpose here is not to judge the validity of the Bible's creation story. Instead, I would like to pose the following question: Based on your understanding of the scientific method, does creation science have a legitimate claim on being referred to as a scientific theory?

Let's review what constitutes a scientific theory. A theory is an organized system of ideas that seeks to explain why two or more events are related. To qualify as a scientific theory, an explanation must be testable by the methods of science. The explanation must also be *falsifiable,* meaning that it must be possible to find fault with, or disconfirm, the explanation. If no one can think of a test that would falsify an explanation, then the explanation is not a scientific theory, even if it is true. "God exists" is a statement that cannot be tested because there is no conceivable experiment or observation that would falsify it. Belief in God's existence is a matter of faith, not science. Likewise, the statement "God created life" is not falsifiable. Therefore, creationism does not qualify as a scientific theory (Perakh, 2004). In 1987, the U.S. Supreme Court agreed with this assessment and ruled that creationism is religion, not science, and cannot be advocated as a scientific theory in public school classrooms (*Edwards v. Auguillard*).

As already noted, creationism stands sharply opposed to evolutionary theory. Why does the theory of evolution qualify as a scientific theory? The simple answer is that this theory is falsifiable. Tests can determine whether or not evolutionary theory is correct as it currently stands (actually, there is more than one theory of evolution), and these tests can be carried out. Current and past evolutionary theories have all been subjected to these tests, and the general principles of evolutionary theory have been repeatedly supported. Based on this wealth of evidence, virtually all scientists express strong confidence in the overall theory. Likewise, many religious organizations have concluded that evolutionary theory is not inconsistent with descriptions of creation and the origin of the human species. Many members of these religious organizations could be classified as *theistic evolutionists:* They believe that evolution is an accurate explanation of how organisms change over time, but they also believe in a God who is both personal and concerned about his (or her) creation (which is different from a Deist God who isn't concerned). Their first belief rests on the findings of science, while their second belief rests on their religious faith, which is beyond the bounds of science.

The vast majority of Americans, including many scientists, believe that God created the universe and life on this planet (Deckman, 2002). This belief in theistic evolution does not necessarily contradict or otherwise stand in opposition to scientific explanations of evolution. Perhaps one way to approach science and religion is in the following manner, suggested by the Roman Catholic Pope, Pius X:

> . . . science is entirely concerned with the reality of phenomena, into which faith does not enter at all; faith on the contrary concerns itself with the divine reality which is entirely unknown to science. . . . [T]here can never be any dissension between faith and science, for if each keeps on its own ground they can never meet and therefore never be in contradiction. (Pius X, Roman Catholic Pope, 1835–1914)

In summary, it is important to understand that truth in science is never final. Scientific theories are explanations of how things in the world are related to one another and how they operate. They are logically constructed and reconfigured from careful observations and testable hypotheses. You can have such overwhelming data supporting your theory that you have very strong confidence that it accurately explains the phenomena in question, but at the core of the scientific journey of discovery is the assumption that any theory can be modified or completely discarded tomorrow. Thus, if you seek to understand the human mind using the scientific method, it is mistaken to believe that any theory can achieve a "final truth."

Section Review

- The process of scientific inquiry occurs in stages.
  - Stage 1 involves selecting a topic and searching the research literature.
  - Stage 2 involves developing a theory and hypotheses.
  - Stage 3 involves selecting a scientific method and submitting a proposed study for ethical evaluation.
  - Stage 4 involves collecting and analyzing data and reporting results.
- A theory's value is determined by its predictive accuracy, internal coherence, economy, and fertility, and a hypothesis is derived from a theory.
- Institutional review boards weigh potential risks to participants against the study's benefits for advancing knowledge.
- Meta-analysis statistically summarizes the findings of many studies and estimates the reliability and overall size of the effects.
- A basic assumption in science is that any theory can be modified or completely discarded in the light of new evidence.

2-3 COMMONLY USED SCIENTIFIC METHODS

Preview

- *What is observational research?*
- *What is correlational research?*
- *What is experimental research?*

One of the most important factors in determining whether a study will ultimately add to our knowledge of psychology is the method used to collect the data. Let us now examine the most commonly used scientific methods employed by psychologists, including their primary goals, as well as their strengths and weaknesses. One method seeks to describe behavior, another method seeks to understand the relationship between two or more variables, and the third method seeks to explain the causes of behavior.

2-3a Description Is the Goal of Observational Research

To understand behavior so that it can be predicted and controlled, a psychologist must first describe it accurately. Scientific methods that have *description* as their primary goal fall under the category of observational research (Heyman et al., 2001). Within this category are the methods of *naturalistic observation, participant observation,* and *case study.*

Naturalistic Observation

naturalistic observation
A descriptive scientific method that investigates behavior in its usual natural environment.

Naturalistic observation is a method that investigates behavior in its natural environment (Crabtree & Miller, 1992; Martin & Bateson, 1993). Settings for such research range from day-care centers, where developmental psychologists might record the play behavior of children, to the jungles of Africa, where comparative psychologists might study how a troop of baboons defends itself against predators. In all such naturalistic studies, behavior is merely observed and recorded—it is not manipulated. Besides employing naturalistic observation as a primary scientific method, other researchers use it during the initial stages of a project to generate research ideas and gather descriptive data.

One example of a naturalistic observation study was Robert Levine and Ara Norenzayan's (1999) analysis of the pace of everyday life in 31 cultures around the world. The researchers were interested in determining whether people in different cultures operated at a different pace in carrying out their daily activities. Examples of some of the data they collected were measurements of people's average walking speed on city sidewalks, the speed at which postal clerks responded to a simple request, and the accuracy of clocks in public settings. Notice that all these measurements simply involved the researchers observing how people behaved in their natural surroundings. Their findings indicated that the pace of life was faster in colder and more economically productive cultures (such as Switzerland, Germany, and Japan) than in those that were hotter and less economically energetic (such as Mexico, Indonesia, and Brazil).

In naturalistic observation, a researcher studies behavior in its natural environment. For example, social psychologists who are interested in understanding how strangers respond to one another when briefly congregated together might observe and record the behavior of people waiting at a bus stop. What are some advantages of this research method?

Source: Courtesy of Figzoi.

Participant Observation

Another type of observational method is **participant observation.** Here, as in naturalistic observation, a researcher records behavior as it occurs in its usual natural environment but does so as a participant in the group being studied. One of the chief benefits of this research strategy is that it allows investigators to get closer to what they are studying than does any other method.

An excellent example of this method was Leon Festinger's study of a doomsday cult in the 1950s (Festinger et al., 1956). The leader of the cult, Mrs. Keetch, claimed that aliens from outer space had told her the world would come to an end on a specific date, December 21. She also stated that the only survivors of this catastrophe would be members of her group. When Festinger and his coworkers learned of Mrs. Keetch, they became interested in measuring the psychological changes that would occur within the group when the dooms-day came and passed with the world still intact. To accomplish this task, over a period of several weeks, these researchers infiltrated the group as participant observers and began describing its dynamics. This descriptive study was one of the first tests of a new—and soon to be very influential—theory in psychology called *cognitive dissonance theory* (see chapter 16, section 16-2c).

The following are four advantages of both naturalistic and participant observation research (Hong & Duff, 2002; Weick, 1985):

1. Researchers are able to watch behavior in its "wholeness," providing the full context in which to understand it.
2. Researchers are able to record rare events that may never occur in a controlled laboratory environment.
3. Researchers are able to systematically record events previously observed only by nonscientists.
4. Researchers are able to observe events too risky, dangerous, or unethical to create in the laboratory.

Despite these benefits, there are also some problems in using naturalistic and participant observation methods. First, because of the researchers' lack of control in such studies, conclusions must be drawn very carefully. Second, researchers must be mindful that their participation in or even their observation of events can significantly alter the participants' behavior, and thus taint the data. Although researchers assume that after a period of time those who are being observed become accustomed to their presence, it is difficult to evaluate to what degree this actually occurs. Finally, more than any other scientific method, observational methods pose the most ethical problems involving invasion of others' privacy.

Case Study

Another form of observational research is a **case study,** which involves in-depth analysis of a single subject, usually a person. This method of inquiry is common in clinical work, in which psychotherapists provide an extensive description of a person suffering from a particular psychological disorder to illustrate the factors that lead to and influence it (Morgan & Morgan, 2001). Sigmund Freud's work is perhaps the most famous example of this method in psychology (Gedo, 2001). Like the other observational studies just discussed, the case study method is sometimes relied on by neuroscientists when investigating individuals with extraordinary cognitive abilities or significant brain damage (see opening stories in chapters 3 and 8). In such cases, researchers hope that any insights gained by studying one person will inspire ideas for later experimental or correlational studies involving more people (Trepper, 1990).

The advantage of the case study is that it produces a more detailed analysis of a person than does any other method. One disadvantage is that researchers must be extremely cautious when generalizing from a single case to the population as a whole. Another problem is that this method often depends on research participants' memories of the past, which all too often are both selective and inaccurate (see chapter 8, section 8-4d).

participant observation A descriptive scientific method in which a group is studied from within by a researcher who records behavior as it occurs in its usual natural environment.

Every journey into the past is complicated by delusions, false memories, false namings of real events.

—*Adrienne Rich, U.S. poet, b. 1929*

case study A descriptive scientific method involving in-depth analysis of a single subject, usually a person.

The case study method involves an in-depth study of a single subject. Although this research method produces a more detailed analysis of a subject than does any other method, what are two disadvantages of case studies?

Source: Courtesy of Figzoi.

2-3b Correlational Research Analyzes the Direction and Strength of the Relationship between Variables

Besides simply describing a phenomenon under study, often psychologists want to also know whether two or more variables are related and, if so, how strongly. When changes in one variable relate to changes in another variable, we say that they *correlate*. **Correlational research** assesses the nature of the relationship between two or more variables that are not controlled by the researcher. The importance of correlational research for psychologists is *prediction:* It allows them to predict a change in one variable by knowing the value of another variable.

correlational research Research designed to examine the nature of the relationship between two or more naturally occurring variables.

Using Surveys When Conducting Correlational Research

Although studying the relationships among variables can be done by directly observing behavior, it is often accomplished by asking people carefully constructed questions. **Surveys** are structured sets of questions or statements given to a group of people to measure their attitudes, beliefs, values, or behavioral tendencies (Bradburn & Sudman, 1988; Lavrakas, 1993). The three major survey techniques are *face-to-face surveys, written surveys,* and *phone surveys.* The face-to-face format provides highly detailed information and allows researchers the best opportunity to clarify any unclear questions. However, it is costly, and there is always the possibility that people's responses might be influenced by the interviewer's presence. (My hitchhiking study involved the use of face-to-face surveys.) Written and phone surveys eliminate such interviewer bias and are much less expensive. Although obtaining information using surveys is generally relatively easy, the main disadvantage in all three techniques is that they rely on people's self-reports, which are often faulty and inaccurate.

survey A structured set of questions or statements given to a group of people to measure their attitudes, beliefs, values, or behavioral tendencies.

Surveys are often used to gather information on behavior or other psychological processes that are difficult, if not impossible, to observe directly. For example, imagine that you are a psychologist interested in learning the degree to which people pay attention to their private thoughts and feelings and the degree to which they disclose these private thoughts and feelings to others. You might ask them to complete a survey questionnaire similar to the one in Self-Discovery Questionnaire 2-1, which measures both the personality trait known as *private self-consciousness* and the behavioral tendency to *self-disclose.* Before reading further, spend a few minutes answering the questions in the Self-Discovery Questionnaire and compare your responses with those of other college students.

Measuring Private Self-Consciousness

The personality trait of private self-consciousness is measured by items on the Self-Consciousness Scale (SCS; Fenigstein et al., 1975). To obtain information on the degree to which you attend to your own private thoughts and feelings, read each item below, and then indicate how well each statement describes you, using the following response scale:

0 = extremely uncharacteristic (not at all like me)
1 = uncharacteristic (somewhat unlike me)
2 = neither characteristic nor uncharacteristic
3 = characteristic (somewhat like me)
4 = extremely characteristic (very much like me)

____ 1. I'm always trying to figure myself out.
____ 2. Generally, I'm not very aware of myself.*
____ 3. I reflect about myself a lot.
____ 4. I'm often the subject of my own fantasies.
____ 5. I never scrutinize myself.*
____ 6. I'm generally attentive to my inner feelings.
____ 7. I'm constantly examining my motives.
____ 8. I sometimes have the feeling that I'm off somewhere watching myself.
____ 9. I'm alert to changes in my mood.
____ 10. I'm aware of the way my mind works when I work through a problem.

The two items with an asterisk (*) are reverse-scored; that is, for these items, a lower rating actually indicates a greater tendency to attend to private thoughts and feelings. Before summing the items, recode those with an asterisk so that 0 = 4, 1 = 3, 3 = 1, and 4 = 0. To calculate your private self-consciousness score, simply add up your responses to the 10 items. The average, or mean, score for college students on private self-consciousness is about 26. The higher your score is above this value, the greater is your tendency to reflect upon your private thoughts and feelings compared with the average American college student. The lower your score is below this value, the less likely is your tendency to regularly engage in this sort of private self-awareness compared to other students.

Measuring the Tendency to Self-Disclose

Willingness to self-disclose is measured by items on the Self-Disclosure Scale (SDS; Miller et al., 1983). To obtain information on your self-disclosure tendencies, indicate for the topics listed below the degree to which you have disclosed to a close romantic partner, using the following scale:

Discussed not at all 0 1 2 3 4 Discussed fully and completely

1. My personal habits
2. Things I have done which I feel guilty about
3. Things I wouldn't do in public
4. My deepest feelings
5. What I like and dislike about myself
6. What is important to me in life
7. What makes me the person I am
8. My worst fears
9. Things I have done which I am proud of
10. My close relationships with other people

Total score
You can determine your overall self-disclosure score by adding up the scores in the column. The higher the score, the greater your willingness to self-disclose.

Sources: SCS: From "Public and Private Self-Consciousness: Assessment and Theory" by Allan Fenigstein, Michael F. Scheier, and Arnold H. Buss in *Journal of Consulting and Clinical Psychology,* 1975, 43, 522–527 (Table 1, p. 524). Copyright © 1975 by the American Psychological Association. Adapted with permission. SDS: From "Openers: Individuals Who Elicit Intimate Self-Disclosure" by L. C. Miller, J. H. Berg, and R. L. Archer in *Journal of Personality and Social Psychology,* 1983, 44, pp. 1234–1244 (Table 2, p. 1236). Copyright © 1983 by the American Psychological Association. Adapted with permission.

If you were using survey data only to determine how people compare on various personality and behavioral measures, your research would involve observational methods in which description is the primary goal. However, returning to our example, imagine that you are interested in discovering whether there is a relationship between private self-consciousness and willingness to self-disclose. That is, do people who regularly attend to their private thoughts and feelings disclose this private side of themselves more than do those who do not habitually self-reflect? Now you are seeking information on whether these two variables are *correlated*. That is, can you predict whether people are likely to self-disclose based on their level of private self-consciousness, or vice versa? In correlational research, as in observational research, you would not try to influence how much time people in your study actually spent thinking about themselves. Instead, you would merely gather information on how often they attended to their own thoughts and feelings and the degree to which they self-disclosed to others.

The Correlation Coefficient

How does correlational research aid in prediction? It does so by providing the psychologist with information on the *direction* and *strength* of the relationship between two variables. The direction of the relationship between variable X and variable Y tells the researcher *how* they are related (positively or negatively). The strength of the relationship can be thought of as the degree of accuracy with which you can predict the value of one variable by knowing the value of the other variable. The direction and strength of the relationship between two variables are described by the statistical measure known as the **correlation coefficient (*r*).** The correlation coefficient can range from -1.00 to $+1.00$.

If you think of variable X as being people's degree of private self-consciousness and variable Y as being their degree of self-disclosure, a study with a correlation at or very near zero would indicate the absence of a *linear relationship* between these two variables. This zero correlation may mean one of two things: (1) Regularly self-reflecting has no association with self-disclosing, or (2) a *curvilinear relationship* exists between self-reflection and self-disclosing. You can easily determine the meaning of a zero correlation by plotting the pairing of these two variables on a scatterplot graph, as illustrated in figure 2-3. When you plot the relationship between the two variables for each of your research participants, what does the scatterplot look like? When the dots are randomly scattered around the graph, this tells you that there is absolutely no relationship between self-reflecting and self-disclosing. However, when the plotted dots form a curved line like the one depicted in figure 2-3, this indicates that people who self-reflect tend to self-disclose either very little or a lot, but those who are only moderately attentive to their private thoughts and feelings seldom self-disclose.

In marked contrast to a correlation at or very near zero, a correlation near $+1.00$ would have dots lining up on an imaginary *straight* line running between the X and Y axes of the graph. In our example, this would suggest that people who regularly attend to their private thoughts and feelings are much more likely to self-disclose than those who engage in little self-reflection. In contrast, a correlation near -1.00 would have a scatterplot with the dots lining up on an imaginary line in the opposite direction, indicating that people who regularly self-reflect are much less likely to self-disclose than are those who engage in little self-reflection.

Regarding the strength of a relationship, researchers seldom find a perfect or near perfect ($r = +1.00$ or $r = -1.00$) correlation between variables. For example, a study investigating the relationship between young adults' private self-consciousness and their degree of self-disclosure to their romantic partners found a correlation of .36 for men and a correlation of .20 for women (Franzoi et al., 1985). On a scatterplot, the dots would be farther away from the imaginary line running between the X and the Y axes. Due to the direction of the correlation, you might predict that men with a high level of private self-consciousness would be more likely to self-disclose to their romantic partners than men with a low level of private self-consciousness. For women, you would make the same prediction, but you would be less confident due to this correlation's lower strength.

Although these correlations might seem small, in social science research correlations rarely exceed .60. Correlations of about .50 are regarded as strong, those at about .30 are moderately strong, and those at .15 or below are considered weak. The reason correlations rarely exceed .60 is that many variables determine human behavior. In the example of self-disclosing to someone, many variables influence people's degrees of self-disclosure. In addition to the dis-

correlation coefficient (*r*) A statistical measure of the direction and strength of the linear relationship between two variables, which can range from -1.00 to $+1.00$.

The invalid assumption that correlation implies cause is probably among the two or three most serious and common errors of human reasoning.

—*Stephen Jay Gould,* The Mismeasure of Man *(1981), p. 242*

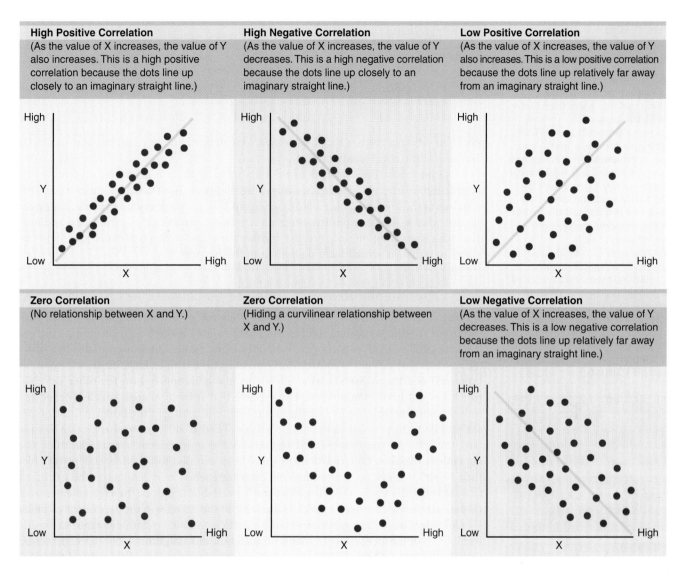

Figure 2-3

Plotting the Relationship between Variable X and Variable Y on a Graph

The points on the graphs represent a pairing of variable X with variable Y for each participant in the study. As you can see in the curvilinear relationship graph, the zero correlation is hiding a meaningful relationship, where both high and low levels of X are associated with high levels of Y, but moderate levels of X are associated with low levels of Y. Can you think of variables that would have a curvilinear relationship? In addition to the direction of the relationship between variable X and variable Y, correlations can have different values. The greater the scatter of values on the graph, the lower the correlation. A perfect correlation occurs when all the values fall on an imaginary straight line.

closers' own levels of private self-consciousness, we must also consider their partners' willingness to listen and the closeness of the relationship, as well as the amount of time they actually spend together. Furthermore, even if researchers could isolate all the important variables that influence self-disclosing, because of the nature of our subject—humans with minds of their own—it's unlikely they would be able to predict with perfect reliability people's actions.

The major disadvantage of the correlational study is that it cannot definitively determine the *cause* of the relationship between two variables. That is, besides knowing the strength and direction of a relationship, another piece of extremely valuable information when conducting an empirical study is knowing which variable causes a change in the other. Does attending to their own thoughts and feelings make people more eager to self-disclose, or does self-disclosing make people more attentive to these thoughts and feelings? This methodological disadvantage can result in the *reverse-causality problem,* which occurs

Figure 2-4

Difficulties in Determining Causation from Correlation

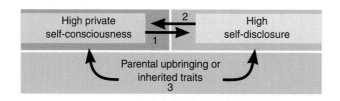

High private self-conscious individuals tend to be more willing self-disclosers than those low in the personality trait of private self-consciousness. Thus, you might conclude that being high in private self-consciousness causes increased self-disclosing in people (arrow 1). However, an alternative explanation is that the act of regular self-disclosing causes an increase in people's level of private self-consciousness (arrow 2). What is this methodological problem of correlation interpretation called? Now look at arrow 3. What if parental upbringing or inherited genes were causing the changes in both private self-consciousness and self-disclosing? What sort of correlation problem would this example illustrate?

experimental research Research designed to test cause-effect relationships between variables.

independent variable The experimental variable that the researcher manipulates.

dependent variable The experimental variable that is measured because it is believed to depend on the manipulated changes in the independent variable.

random assignment Placement of research participants into experimental conditions in a manner that guarantees that all have an equal chance of being exposed to each level of the independent variable.

experimental condition The condition in an experiment whereby participants are exposed to different levels of the independent variable.

whenever either of the two variables correlated with one another could just as plausibly be the cause or the effect (see figure 2-4).

A second problem resulting from the inability to confidently determine causality is that a third, unmeasured variable can possibly cause changes in both variables under study. This is known as the *third-variable problem* (see figure 2-4). In our previous example, it is possible that what looks like a positive correlation between private self-consciousness and self-disclosing is really an illusion, because another variable—perhaps parental upbringing or inherited traits—is actually causing both of those changes.

2-3c Experimental Research Determines Cause-Effect Relationships

Because correlational studies cannot conclusively tell us *why* variables are related, psychologists conduct **experimental research** to examine cause-effect relationships (Crano & Brewer, 2002). In an experiment, the psychologist manipulates one variable by exposing research participants to contrasting levels of it (for example, high, medium, low, or no exposure) and then observes what effect this manipulation has on the other variable, which has not been manipulated. The variable that is manipulated, which is called the **independent variable,** is the one the experimenter is testing as the possible *cause* of any changes that might occur in the other variable. The variable whose changes are considered the *effect* of the manipulated changes in the independent variable is called the **dependent variable.** Once participants have been exposed to the independent variable, their behavior is carefully monitored to determine whether it changes in the predicted fashion with different levels of the independent variable. If it does, the experimenter concludes that the independent variable is the cause of the changes in the dependent variable.

A key feature of most experiments is that participants are randomly assigned to the different levels of the independent variable. In such **random assignment,** the experimenter, by some random procedure, decides which participants are exposed to which level of the independent variable. Due to this procedure, the experimenter can be reasonably confident that the participants in the different experimental conditions don't differ from one another.

Some of the better-known experiments in psychology are Albert Bandura's Bobo doll studies, in which he and his colleagues studied whether children would imitate the behavior of an aggressive adult (Bandura et al., 1961). In one of these experiments, a child was first brought into a room to work on an art project. In another part of the room, an adult who was a *confederate*—meaning that she was an accomplice of the experimenter—was playing quietly with some Tinker Toys. Near these toys were a mallet and a Bobo doll, which is a big, inflatable, clownlike toy that is weighted down so that when it is pushed or punched it will bounce back to an upright position. For half the children in the study, after playing with the Tinker Toys for a minute, the adult stood up, walked over to the Bobo doll, and began to attack it. She punched the doll, kicked it, hit it with the mallet, and even sat on it. As she pummeled the clown doll, she yelled out, "Sock him in the nose! . . . Kick him! . . . Knock him down!" For the other children, the adult simply played quietly and nonaggressively with her toys for 10 minutes.

In Bandura's study, the independent variable (remember, this is the variable that is manipulated) was the aggressiveness of the adult's play behavior. After witnessing either the aggressive or the nonaggressive adult confederate, the child was led into another room filled with many interesting toys. However, before the child could play with them, the experimenter aroused frustration by saying that these were her best toys and she must "save them for the other children." The child was then led to a third room, containing both aggressive and nonaggressive toys, including a Bobo doll. What children did in this third room was the essential question of the study, for their level of aggressive play here was the dependent variable. The children who had observed the aggressive adult were in what is called the **experimental condition,** the condition

Hypothesis		
Children will imitate the behavior of an aggressive adult.		
Random Assignment	Subjects are randomly assigned to experimental and control conditions.	
Manipulation of Independent Variable	Experimental condition: Child observes an aggressive adult.	Control condition: Child observes a nonaggressive adult.
Measurement of Dependent Variable	The experimental group later engaged in greater aggressive behavior than did the control group.	
Conclusion		
Observing an aggressive adult model increases the aggressive behavior of children.		

Figure 2-5

The Basic Elements in an Experiment

As illustrated in the Bandura study, the power of experimental research is based on treating the experimental and control groups exactly alike except for the manipulation of the independent variable. Any later observed differences in the dependent variable between the two groups can then be confidently attributed to the effects of the independent variable.

of being exposed to different levels of the independent variable (in this case, the adult's aggression). In contrast, the children who had observed the nonaggressive adult were in what is called the **control condition,** the condition of not being exposed to the independent variable. Because the only difference between the experimental and control conditions in this study was whether or not the children had been exposed to an aggressive adult (the independent variable), any subsequent differences in the children's aggression (the dependent variable) could be attributed to the manipulation of the independent variable.

So what happened in the third room? Children in the control condition tended to play nonaggressively with the toys, while those in the experimental condition tended to beat up the Bobo doll, often shouting the same things at the clown that the aggressive adult had shouted. Based on this experiment and others like it, Bandura concluded that observing adult aggression can teach children to act more aggressively themselves. Figure 2-5 provides an overview of the elements in an experiment, using Bandura's study as an example.

The Bobo doll study represents a type of experiment called a *laboratory experiment.* Most psychology experiments are conducted in laboratories. The laboratory experiment can be contrasted with the less common *field experiment,* which is run in a natural setting, with participants often not realizing they are being studied. For example, a field experiment that also investigated how watching aggression might influence children's own aggressive behavior was conducted in a Belgian private institution for adolescent schoolboys by Jacques-Philippe Leyens and his colleagues (1975). The independent variable in this study was exposure to violent films. In two dormitories at the school, boys were shown a violent film every night for one week, while during the same time period the boys in two other dorms were shown the same number of nonviolent films. The experimenters then measured the children's aggressive behavior (the dependent variable) outside of the film-viewing settings and found that those in the experimental condition exhibited higher levels of aggression than did the control group. Based on these findings, they concluded that exposure to violent films can cause increased aggressiveness in viewers.

Although both laboratory and field experiments are valuable tools for research psychologists, each of these experimental methods has its own unique strengths and weaknesses. The main advantage of a lab experiment over a field experiment is that the variables can be well controlled. In Leyens's field study, for instance, he and his colleagues could not control all the interruptions and other distractions that may have occurred while they were attempting to test their hypotheses. However, the greater control in laboratory research often has a price: the danger of artificiality. Realism is the primary advantage of a field experiment. The research takes place in the participants' normal surroundings, and thus their responses are more natural and spontaneous.

Recently, some psychologists believe they have found a possible remedy to the dilemma of choosing between greater control and greater realism in their experiments (Blascovich, 2003). They recommend using *virtual environment technology (VET),* in which they create a virtual research environment using a computer. Once this simulated reality is created,

control condition The condition in an experiment in which participants are not exposed to the independent variable.

Should psychologists use their scientific knowledge about the harmful effects of television violence on people's aggressive behavior to influence social decisions, or does such social action undermine the scientific basis of the discipline? In other words, should social action follow research?

Source: Courtesy of Figzoi.

Journey of Discovery Question

What role should values play in science? Is it possible or desirable to separate values from science?

research participants wearing virtual-reality equipment are "immersed" in the setting. A commonly used piece of virtual-reality equipment is a head-mounted or binocular-style device that allows an individual to view 3-D images and to "walk" through the virtual environment. Although this type of simulated environment is completely controlled by the experimenter—even more than the traditional laboratory setting—it has a very "real-world" feel to it, similar to that of a field experiment.

Recent studies employing virtual environment technology suggest that participants behave relatively naturally in such settings (Blascovich, 2002; Waller et al., 2002). Although still in its infancy, virtual environment technology is currently being used to study such topics as conformity, eyewitness testimony, effects of violent video games, and simulated weightlessness. As this technology improves, psychologists hope to involve senses beyond sight and hearing, as well as to improve the ways people can interact with the virtual creations they encounter. This technology is meant not to replace traditional field and laboratory studies but instead to provide another research vehicle that psychologists can use in their journey of discovery.

Now that you have learned about the different scientific methods that psychologists use, which is the best? Actually, what I hope you take from this overview is that there is no one best method in all research settings. In each investigation, the psychologist must decide what method would provide the best test of the hypotheses under consideration. The best overall strategy for psychologists is a *multimethod* approach—employing different scientific methods to study the same topic, thereby capitalizing on each method's strengths and controlling for its weaknesses.

Section Review

- Some of the most commonly employed scientific methods in psychology are observational, correlational, and experimental designs.
- Observational research describes behavior as it occurs in its natural setting.
- Correlational research assesses the direction and strength of the relationship between two or more variables.
- Experimental research involves manipulating one or more independent variables to determine the effect on nonmanipulated dependent variables.

Psychological Applications

How Can You Develop Critical Thinking Skills?

In this chapter, you have become familiar with the science of psychology and the different research methods employed within the discipline. In this last section, I would like to discuss the kinds of critical thinking skills that not only are necessary in conducting scientific research but also are important in making you both a wise consumer of psychological knowledge and a capable decision maker in your own journey of discovery (Halonen, 1995; Stanovich, 1996).

What Is Critical Thinking?

A few years ago, my oldest daughter, Amelia, faced a dilemma. On her eighth birthday, she found herself in a toy store trying to decide which new bicycle to pick for her present. The colors, names, and styles of the bikes were clearly aimed at steering girls and boys toward different choices. Yet, Amelia ignored these gender labels and tested all the bikes. At the end of this process, she knew which bike felt the best riding-wise—the blue Huffy Hyper Force boy's bike. Amelia also knew, however, that if she picked a boy's bike, some of the neighborhood kids would tease her. She knew this because on her fifth birthday her choice had been a red Huffy Rough Rider. Three years later, Amelia realized she could avoid the same negative comments by picking her second choice, the pink Barbie Fashion Fun girl's bike. All this she explained to me as we stood in the store scanning the array of possibilities before us. Perhaps she was hoping I would draw upon that mystical "father knows best" wisdom that I had sometimes alluded to, and simply tell her which bike to choose. Instead, I said, "Amelia, this is your decision. You have to decide whether you will pick the bike that *rides the best* or the bike that *looks the best* for girls, and thus, will be most acceptable to some of your friends. Think about what's most important to you." After carefully evaluating the evidence and weighing the possible consequences of her two choices, she picked the Hyper Force boy's bike.

This Amelia example illustrates an important type of problem-solving skill known as critical thinking. As defined in section 2-1b, critical thinking is the process of deciding what to believe and how to act based on careful evaluation of the evidence. As you will learn more fully in chapter 9, sections 9-2d and 9-2e, as a species, we humans have the capacity to scrutinize available facts and arrive at judgments based on careful reasoning. Unfortunately, we often fail to use these cognitive skills and instead simply engage in "lazy thinking," which often results in being misled and manipulated by other people and events. In picking a bike, Amelia could have uncritically followed the color schemes and bike styles that her culture designates for girls, but instead she decided that these gender labels unnecessarily restricted her choices. By challenging the assumption that a bike's color and style restrict who

can ride it, Amelia could entertain many more bike possibilities. Once she had gathered her own information by riding all the bikes, she also could have ignored the evidence of her senses and chosen the gender-appropriate but less rider-worthy bike. Again, based on careful reflection of her options, she made her choice. That is one hallmark of critical thinking.

What if Amelia had decided, after going through this entire process, that the benefits of the better-riding boy's bike were not enough to justify the social hassles associated with it? Would the decision to pick the girl's bike have indicated a lack of critical thinking? The answer is no. The *choice* does not determine whether critical thinking took place. Rather, the *type* of cognitive process that a person engages in is the crucial point. We have learned that thinking critically about the arguments that you make to yourself, or that others make to you, can greatly improve your own decision making (Anderson, 1993a; McBride et al., 2002).

Guidelines for Critical Thinking

How often have you said to yourself or to someone else, "I don't want to think about how to solve this problem; I just want someone to tell me the answer"? Although being told how to think and act reduces cognitive effort, it certainly doesn't promote critical thinking. The following are some general guidelines on how to think critically (Halpern, 1995; Ruggerio, 1988):

1. *Be willing to ask questions*—Knowledge begins with questioning the nature of things. Think of the process of questioning as a sign of inquisitiveness, not a lack of intelligence.
2. *Analyze assumptions*—Instead of passively accepting assumptions as facts, think about possible exceptions and contradictions.
3. *Examine the evidence*—Instead of accepting a conclusion without evidence, ask for and analyze the evidence that supports and contradicts the various positions.
4. *Be cautious of emotional decisions*—Although there is certainly nothing wrong with being emotionally involved with a particular decision, avoid basing your decision on what you would *like* to be true, versus what you *know* to be true.
5. *Avoid oversimplifying issues*—It can be comforting to make simple generalizations about complex events, but resisting glib explanations provides the opportunity for creative complexity.
6. *Tolerate ambiguity*—By rejecting simple answers, you must learn to develop a tolerance for ambiguity. Don't be afraid to admit that you don't know the correct answer when the evidence suggests many possible solutions rather than a single correct one.

Continued next page—

Psychological Applications

—Continued

Critical thinking can be fostered through many activities, but the study of psychology is particularly helpful in promoting this type of cognitive activity (R. A. Smith, 2002). In fact, when researchers examined the reasoning ability of graduate students in psychology and chemistry, they found that as the two groups advanced through graduate school, the psychology students became better at analyzing everyday events, while the chemistry students showed no improvement (Lehman et al., 1988). One of the likely reasons why psychology promotes critical thinking is that students of psychology learn a great deal about how the mind works, including the many biases and errors that are obstacles to intelligent thinking. In this instance, knowledge really is power. Hopefully, one of the benefits of taking this course is that your increased knowledge of how people think and behave will allow you to make more intelligent decisions in your everyday life.

Using Critical Thinking While Reading This Textbook

Although greater knowledge of psychology may ultimately benefit future decision making, one of your more immediate questions may be how critical thinking can improve your study skills in college. This is certainly a legitimate concern. Let me briefly describe how you can use a critical thinking strategy known as *PRQR* while reading this textbook.

The PRQR Technique

Before reading each chapter, *preview (P)* the material by first reading the chapter-opening story and outline, the Preview questions that open each major chapter section, and the end-of-section reviews. This will provide you with a general understanding of what you are about to read so you can better organize the text material in memory. Next, *read (R)* an entire chapter section, and as you do, *ask questions (Q)* that focus your attention on the topics, paying particular attention to Journey of Discovery questions, Self-Discovery questionnaires, and Explore It exercises. In writing this text, I attempted to facilitate your critical thinking by regularly asking you questions in the main body of the text and in the captions accompanying the tables, figures, and photographs. The Journey of Discovery questions encourage you to analyze psychological concepts, provide alternative explanations for research findings, and explore the implications of the text material. Regularly ask yourself how the information in the text supports or calls into question any prior beliefs you may have had on the topic. The Explore It exercises and Self-Discovery questionnaires allow you the opportunity to discover how text material relates to your own life. How can the material help you better understand your own life and events in your world? Finally, once you have read the chapter, *review (R)* the material so the information is more securely stored in memory. This will be the time to answer the end-of-chapter review questions to check your understanding of the chapter content.

In addition to this reading technique, I also recommend that you read text material before your professor talks about it in lecture. By staying slightly ahead of lecture content, you will better comprehend and remember the material presented in class, because you already have information in memory upon which you can "hang" the new lecture material.

In summary, an essential ingredient in becoming an efficient consumer of psychological knowledge and a capable decision maker in your everyday activities is to be willing to exercise your mind just as athletes exercise their bodies. You must condition yourself to actively question and scrutinize not only course material but also life events. If you learn to think critically, you will retain something of value long after this textbook and your psychology course are distant memories.

> Either you think—or else others have to think for you and take power from you.
>
> —*F. Scott Fitzgerald, U.S. author, 1896–1940*

> We do not live to think, but, on the contrary, we think in order that we may succeed in surviving.
>
> —*José Ortega y Gasset, Spanish philosopher, 1883–1955*

Key Terms

case study (p. 39)

control condition (p. 45)

correlation coefficient (*r*) (p. 43)

correlational research (p. 40)

critical thinking (p. 28)

dependent variable (p. 44)

descriptive statistics (p. 35)

experimental condition (p. 44)

experimental research (p. 44)

hindsight bias (p. 25)

hypotheses (p. 30)

implicit personality theory (p. 25)

independent variable (p. 44)

inferential statistics (p. 35)

meta-analysis (p. 36)

naturalistic observation (p. 38)

operational definition (p. 32)

participant observation (p. 39)

population (p. 28)

random assignment (p. 44)

random selection (p. 28)

replication (p. 32)

sample (p. 28)

scientific method (p. 27)

survey (p. 40)

theory (p. 30)

variables (p. 32)

Suggested Websites

Critical Thinking and Psychology Links
http://www.kcmetro.cc.mo.us/longview/ctac/psychlink.htm
This website contains exercises for promoting critical thinking in psychology.

Animal Welfare Information Center
http://www.nal.usda.gov/awic
This website provides information on the ethical treatment of animals in government-sponsored research programs.

Review Questions

Note: You can find the correct answers to these questions by taking the quiz and then submitting your answers in the Online Edition. The program will automatically score your submission. If you miss a question, the program will provide the correct answer, a rationale for the answer, and the section number in the chapter where the topic is discussed.

1. Research on how young adults judge potential sex partners illustrates the concept of
   a. the primacy effect.
   b. evaluative consistency.
   c. implicit personality theory.
   d. all of the above
   e. *b* and *c*

2. The scientific method is
   a. any set of techniques employed by scientists.
   b. confined to studies in which a control group is compared to a treatment group.
   c. used to prove that theories are true.
   d. a controversial set of procedures and continually shifting standards.
   e. a set of procedures to collect data that minimize errors.

3. Which of the following statements is *true?*
   a. Psychologists have developed special formulas to eliminate biases and errors in human judgment.
   b. Statistical analysis is useful in comparing samples to the population.
   c. Psychologists are immune to error-prone thinking.
   d. It is not important that a sample represents the population.
   e. Psychologists cannot make dependable generalizations.

4. Dement's claim that there is something basic in our need to dream would be considered
   a. a hypothesis.
   b. a theory.
   c. a case study.
   d. a correlational coefficient.
   e. topic selection.

5. Institutional review boards (IRBs)
   a. monitor and evaluate research proposals involving only human subjects.
   b. focus on risk/benefit ratio.
   c. never allow participants to be deceived about a study's true purpose.
   d. claim that human psychological research is a high-risk activity.
   e. *a* and *b*

6. Precise descriptions of how factors in a study have been quantified and measured are known as
   a. operational definitions.
   b. independent variables.
   c. descriptive statistics.
   d. hypotheses.
   e. theories.

7. Which of the following statements is *true* of animal research?
   a. Most animal research is unnecessary.
   b. Other methods could be used so that animals are not needed in behavioral research.
   c. Nearly 90 percent of animals used in research are rodents.
   d. Ninety percent of behavioral and biomedical research causes pain and significant distress to animals.
   e. Animals do not benefit from animal research.

8. Which of the following statements is *true?*
   a. Descriptive statistics are a more valued type of statistic than inferential statistics.
   b. A difference is considered statistically significant if the likelihood of its having occurred by mere chance is less than one in five.
   c. Contemporary psychology does not require extensive knowledge of statistics.
   d. Meta-analysis is the technique of counting the number of studies that find or do not find a particular effect.
   e. Reporting results is an important stage of research.

9. A statistical technique that summarizes a number of similar studies is called
   a. majority rules.
   b. meta-analysis.
   c. summation.
   d. a review study.
   e. the assimilation technique.

10. The main criterion that makes a theory scientific is
    a. explanatory power.
    b. believability.
    c. empirical support.
    d. falsifiability.
    e. an expert opinion.

11. Leon Festinger's study of a doomsday cult used which form of observational research?
    a. naturalistic
    b. participant
    c. case study
    d. correlational
    e. survey

12. All *except* which one of the following are advantages of naturalistic and participant observation research?
    a. is absence of control
    b. provides a full context for behavior
    c. gives an opportunity to record events difficult to replicate in a laboratory
    d. can observe events too risky to create in a laboratory
    e. can record events previously observed only by nonscientists

13. Which of the following types of surveys discussed in the chapter provides very detailed information but may have the most problems with bias, due to people responding in a socially desirable manner?
    a. phone
    b. Internet
    c. face-to-face
    d. written
    e. none of the above

14. Correlational studies cannot determine the cause of the relationship between two variables because
    a. of the third-variable problem.
    b. of the reverse-causality problem.
    c. research correlation rarely exceeds .60.
    d. all of the above
    e. *a* and *b*

15. Which of these correlation coefficients indicates the strongest relationship between two variables?
    a. −.90
    b. .00
    c. +.20
    d. +.70
    e. +1.20

16. In Bandura's Bobo doll study, the level of aggressive play of the child in the third room was the
    a. experimental condition.
    b. control condition.
    c. dependent variable.
    d. independent variable.
    e. random assignment.

17. Considering the Amelia example, which of the following choices illustrates critical thinking?
    a. buying the boy bike
    b. buying the girl bike
    c. not buying a bike at all
    d. asking her dad's advice
    e. none of the above

18. According to the author, which of the following is a guideline to help in critical thinking?
    a. Ask questions.
    b. Base decisions on what you would like to be true.
    c. Don't make issues seem too complex; keep it simple.
    d. Avoid ambiguity.
    e. Never be wrong.

19. The PRQR technique suggests you
    a. preview the material by first reading the chapter-opening story and outline.
    b. read an entire section.
    c. ask questions that focus your attention on the topics.
    d. review the material so that the information is more securely stored in memory.
    e. all of the above

Chapter 3

Neurological and Genetic Bases of Behavior

Chapter Outline

Source: CC Studio/Photo Researchers, Inc.

It's like waking up, sort of like waking up in the world. You're waking, trying to push things together yourself, reaching back. And you wonder at times yourself just, well, what it is and what it isn't. (Hilts, 1995, p. 239)

Can you relate to this statement? Have you ever awakened from a dream feeling disoriented, not quite sure where you were or what was happening? If so, then perhaps you can relate in some small way to the life of an extraordinary man—Henry M.

Up until the morning of his 16th birthday, Henry M.'s life had been normal and uneventful, except for sporadic moments of blankness. Then, while en route to a birthday celebration with his parents, Henry's body suddenly stiffened and began to convulse in his first major grand mal epileptic seizure. Over the next 11 years, the seizures increased to as many as 10 minor blackouts and one major grand mal per week, causing a fearful disruption in Henry's life. Faced with a future filled with such incapacitating convulsions, Henry was advised to undergo a radical operation, which his doctors believed would cure his epilepsy. Following his mother's advice, on an August morning in 1953 and at the age of 27, Henry underwent the procedure.

Using a hand-cranked rotary drill—which could be purchased for $1 from any auto supply store—Henry's physician drilled two holes into Henry's skull above the eyes and inserted metal spatulas into the holes to lift the frontal lobes of the brain slightly. With the front of the brain raised, the physician next inserted a silver straw deep into Henry's brain and sucked out a fist-sized piece of it containing nearly the entire mass of the *hippocampus* and the regions leading up to it. What is all the more horrifying about this procedure is that Henry was awake the entire time, being anesthetized only on his scalp. Because the brain has no sensory receptors, Henry felt no pain.

In the 1950s, the purpose of the hippocampus was not known, but the physician who performed the surgery believed that removing this portion of the brain would stop the seizures. But at what price? Although the surgery did lessen the frequency and intensity of Henry's epileptic seizures, something was now terribly wrong with Henry (Corkin, 1984). Shortly after the surgery, his mother discovered that Henry couldn't walk to the neighborhood store unattended because he was unable to find his way back home. His ability to read and write was unaffected, and his measured intelligence was still above average, but now he used these abilities in a dramatically different fashion (Milner et al., 1968).

For example, before his surgery Henry had subscribed to a rifle magazine and read each issue. After his surgery, he still enjoyed reading the magazine, but he would read the same issue over and over without realizing it. Also, when his mother ran errands and left Henry alone at home, he treated anyone who knocked at the door like a family member or a close friend. Why? Because although Henry recognized none of the visitors, he assumed that anyone who knocked at the door must be someone he knew well. So, in order not to appear foolish, he treated everyone alike. Thus, total strangers would be invited in to sit and chat and wait for his mother's return. By removing the hippocampus, the physician who performed the surgery had also removed Henry's ability to form memories (see section 3-3b). Commenting on Henry's sorry state of mind, this physician later sadly noted, "Guess what, I tried to cut out the epilepsy of a patient, but took his memory instead! What a trade!" (Hilts, 1995, p. 100).

Today, for Henry, as for all of us, the events of the moment are full and rich. His memories of people and events prior to his surgery remain largely intact. Yet, unlike us, when Henry stops thinking about something that has just happened to him, the memory of this event disappears entirely, leaving him stuck in a constantly changing, meaningless present. With this inability to create new memories, almost everything Henry encounters in the world is a surprise to him, regardless of how many times he has been exposed to it. With no comprehension of what is before him, he has no motive force of his own but, instead, waits for others to direct his attention. In describing his state of mind, Henry says it is like perpetually waking from a dream and not knowing what day it is or what he should be doing on that day. With this confusion comes a tug of fear and concern. As he confided on one occasion to the scientists who were studying him:

> Right now, I'm wondering, have I done or said anything amiss? You see, at this moment everything looks clear to me, but what happened just before? That's what worries me. (Hilts, 1995, p. 138)

During the past 50 years, Henry M. has remained ignorant of all the changes and advances in the world around him. Not only does he not know that his mother and father have died or that people have walked on the moon, but also he has no realization that his tragic life circumstances have dramatically increased the scientific community's understanding of the neuropsychology of memory. Indeed, over the years, psychobiologists and other neuroscientists have learned a great deal about the functioning of the human brain by studying Henry and other people like him whose brains have been damaged in some manner (Calvin & Ojemann, 1994; Feinberg, 2001). This organ, which comprises only about 2 percent of our total body weight, controls most of the complex aspects of our behavior and mental life. In this chapter, we continue our journey of discovery by examining this most marvelous organ—the brain. But before analyzing the brain's larger structures and functions, we first need to examine the complex network of nerve cells, or *neurons*, that account for all human thought and action. After investigating the basic structure and function of these nerve cells, we will see how they are organized in our *central nervous system* and *peripheral nervous system*. Finally, we will end our analysis of the biology of behavior by examining its genetic basis.

3-1 THE NEURON

Preview

- *What is a neuron?*
- *What is the structure of a neuron?*
- *How does a neuron fire?*
- *How do neurons communicate with one another?*

In the late nineteenth century, scientists were struggling to identify the basic structural units of the brain and how they connect and interact. Prior to this time, the general scientific opinion was that the brain simply consisted of thick clumps of cell matter. Then the veil was lifted.

Working in a makeshift laboratory in his attic with a $25 microscope and a single box of slides, Spanish neuroanatomist Santiago Ramón y Cajal (1852–1934) discovered that the brain consisted of an untold number of separate, distinct cells. Perhaps millions of separate cells. Further, these specialized cells, called **neurons,** appeared to be responsible for sending and receiving information throughout the body. Cajal's resulting theory on how the brain processes information earned him the Nobel Prize for Physiology and Medicine in 1906.

[The neuron is] the aristocrat among the structures of the body, with its giant arms stretched out like the tentacles of an octopus to the provinces on the frontier of the outside world, to watch for the constant ambushes of physical and chemical forces.

—*Santiago Ramón y Cajal, Spanish scientist credited with first discovering the neuron, 1852–1934*

Source: Stock Montage, Inc.

neurons Specialized cells in the nervous system that send and receive information.

3-1a Neurons Are the Nervous System's Building Blocks

Today we know that the human nervous system contains anywhere from 90 to 180 billion neurons, or roughly about as many as the number of stars in our galaxy. Approximately 98.8 percent of these neurons reside in the brain, with the remaining 1.2 percent (over 1 billion neurons) distributed throughout the spinal cord (Rosenzweig et al., 2002; Williams & Herrup, 1988). On average, each neuron transmits information to tens of thousands of other neurons, which means that there are trillions of different neural connections in the brain (Beatty, 2001). Although these elementary units of the nervous system come in hundreds of shapes and sizes, researchers have identified three basic types:

1. **Sensory neurons** detect stimuli inside the body (for example, a headache or strained muscle) or in the world (for example, another person's voice). They send this information from sensory receptors to the brain, usually by way of the spinal cord.
2. In the opposite direction, **motor neurons** send commands from the brain to glands, muscles, and organs, directing them to do, cease, or inhibit something.
3. Finally, the vast majority of neurons are **interneurons,** which connect other neurons to one another. One of their most important functions is to link the sensory neurons' input signals with the motor neurons' output signals.

3-1b A Neuron Consists of a Soma, Dendrites, and an Axon

Despite the different functions of neurons, most have certain structural features in common (Levitan & Kaczmarek, 1991). As illustrated in figure 3-1, neurons have three basic parts. The central part of the neuron is the **soma,** which is the Latin word for "body." This cell body contains the *nucleus,* or control center of the neuron, and other components of the cell that preserve and nourish it. Attached to the soma are branchlike extensions known as **dendrites** (the Greek word for "trees") that receive information from other neurons and bring it to the soma. As previously noted, each neuron may have hundreds or thousands of dendrites. After integrating this information, the soma transmits it to a tubelike extension called an **axon** (Greek for "axle"), which carries the information from the soma to the other end of the axon in the form of an electrochemical impulse (Hille, 1984). Axons can range in length from 1/32 of an inch to more than 3 feet, with the longest axons extending from the spinal cord to the big toe.

To give you an idea of the relative sizes and lengths of the soma, dendrites, and axon of some of the longer neurons, visualize a tennis ball with a number of shoelaces attached to one side of it and a thin rope 14 miles long attached to the other side. The tennis ball is the soma, the shoelaces are the dendrites, and the long rope is the axon.

Many axons are covered with a protective coating of white fatty cells known as a **myelin sheath,** which hastens the transmission of the electrochemical charge. Scientists believe that the myelin sheath developed in humans as our brains evolved and became larger, making it necessary for information to travel faster over longer distances in the nervous system. Part of the reason children cannot learn and respond as fast as adults in many cognitive and motor tasks is that their axons have not yet been fully covered by these neural speed-enhancing fatty cells. Neural axons in regions of the brain involved in abstract thinking may not become fully covered by myelin until a person reaches the age of 20! In certain diseases, such as multiple sclerosis, the myelin sheath is slowly destroyed (Adams & Victor, 1993). This destruction of the protective coating impairs brain-to-muscle communication, resulting in a loss of muscle control.

At the end of each axon are branches with knoblike tips called *terminal buttons,* which closely approach, but do not touch, the dendrites of other neurons. The space between the axon's terminal buttons and the dendrites is less than one-millionth of an inch and is known as the *synaptic cleft.* The entire area composed of the terminal button of one neuron, the synaptic cleft, and the dendrite of another neuron is the **synapse,** which in Greek means "to clasp." In section 3-1d, we will see how neurons communicate at this synapse through a complex process of electrical and chemical (electrochemical) changes.

This brief outline of the neuron's structure is greatly simplified. In fact, some neurons have many axons, and others have no axons at all. In addition, some neurons do not synapse on dendrites but do so on axons or somas. Despite these exceptions, in general, dendrites receive information from other neurons and pass it through the soma and then along the axon to the dendrites of other neurons at the junction points called synapses. In this capacity as the receiver, integrator, and transmitter of neural information, the neuron truly earns its reputation as the workhorse of the nervous system.

One last important point is worth mentioning. Santiago Cajal also discovered that the brain and spinal cord are not solid masses of neurons. Nerve tissue throughout the body is composed of two kinds of cells: neurons and supporting **glial cells** (*glial* in Greek means "glue"), which supply the neurons with support, nutrients, and insulation. Glial cells have no axons or dendrites. If you think of the brain as a house, then the glial cells are the floors, walls, and supporting beams, while the neurons are the electrical wiring. In essence, the glial

---

sensory neurons Neurons that send information from sensory receptors to the brain, usually by way of the spinal cord.

motor neurons Neurons that send commands from the brain to glands, muscles, and organs to do, cease, or inhibit something.

interneurons Neurons that connect the sensory neurons' input signals with the motor neurons' output signals. One of their most important functions is to link other neurons to one another.

soma The cell body of the neuron; contains the nucleus and other components that preserve and nourish it.

dendrites Branchlike extensions of the soma that receive information from other neurons.

axon An extension of the soma that sends information in the form of electrochemical impulses to other neurons.

myelin sheath A protective coating of fatty material around an axon that hastens the transmission of the electrochemical charge.

synapse The entire area composed of the terminal button of one neuron, the synaptic cleft, and the dendrite of another neuron.

glial cells Non-neuron cells that supply the neurons with support, nutrients, and insulation.

sclerosis - hardening of a tissue

Dendrites

Soma

Axon

Myelin sheath

Terminal buttons

Figure 3-1

Structure of a Neuron

The primary components of the specialized cell known as a neuron are the soma, dendrites, and axon. The soma contains the nucleus of the cell, while the dendrites receive information from other neurons, and the axon passes this information to other neurons. Do you know the range in length of our axons?

INTERACTIVE FIGURE

cells hold the brain together, while the neurons send and receive information throughout the brain structure. The myelin sheath that covers most axons is made up of glial cells. Interestingly, there are 10 times more glial cells in the nervous system than there are neurons, although they are much smaller than neurons and constitute about half the brain's total mass (Travis, 1994). Now that you understand the makeup of neurons and their supporting glial cells, let's examine how information travels within a single neuron.

3-1c A Neuron Is in Either a Resting or a Firing State

A neuron is always in either a resting or a firing state—there is no in-between condition. Actually the resting state is, more accurately, a subtle pulsing state, but for our purposes, the term *resting* will be used. Whether or not the neuron fires an electrochemical impulse depends on whether the combined stimulation received by the dendrites exceeds a certain minimum intensity, or *threshold*. If the threshold is exceeded, the neuron's membrane transmits an electrochemical impulse. If the threshold is not exceeded, nothing happens. This effect, known as the *all-or-none law*, is like popping a kernel of corn. If the kernel is heated to a certain temperature, it pops. However, if this minimum temperature is not reached, the kernel remains unchanged.

It may be helpful for you to think of a neuron as a liquid-filled balloon surrounded by a slightly different kind of liquid. The axon part of this "balloon" is stretched to form a very long, thin tube. A neuron's electrochemical impulse results from positively and negatively charged particles, called *ions*, moving back and forth through specialized pores, referred to as *ion channels*, in the axon's membrane walls. The important ions in the inside and outside liquids are positively charged sodium and potassium ions and negatively charged chlorine ions. When the neuron is in a resting state, the ions floating inside the axon are mostly negatively charged, while those outside the axon's membrane are mostly positively charged. The reason there are more negative ions inside is that, in its resting state, the cell membrane of the axon resists the passage of positive sodium ions through its ion channels into the cell. In this stable resting state, there is a tiny negative electrical charge—about one-twentieth of a volt, or −70 millivolts—within the axon, making it a storehouse of potential energy (Koester, 1995). When the inactive neuron is in this chemical balancing state—more positive ions outside the membrane and more negative ions inside—its tiny electrical charge is known as the **resting potential.**

How is this resting potential changed? As previously stated, in its resting state the axon's cell membrane does not allow positive sodium ions through its ion channels into the cell. Yet, just as the negative pole of a magnet attracts the positive pole of another magnet (an event called *polarization*), the negative ions inside the axon attract positive ions along the external

resting potential The stable, negative charge of an inactive neuron.

[handwritten margin notes:] inhibitory transmitters or excitatory transmitters.

[handwritten margin notes:] Stretching from Spinal Cord to toe. 1/32 – 3ft.

[handwritten margin notes:] depolarizing action potential +30mv; −70mv hyper polarized; 0; −70mv

wall of the cell membrane, including the important sodium ions. When a neuron receives sufficient stimulation through its dendrites from other neurons, the neural membrane nearest where the axon emerges from the soma opens its ion channels, allowing the clustered positive sodium ions to rush in. For an instant, the charge inside this part of the axon switches from negative to positive (an event known as *depolarization*), eliminating the resting potential and sending a brief electrochemical charge or impulse down to the next section of the axon farther away from the soma (see figure 3-2). This electrical disturbance—which transpires in about one-thousandth of a second—is called the **action potential** and is analogous to a pulse of electricity traveling along a wire. As soon as the resting potential has been eliminated, the axon membrane ion channels in this area again open, but this time, they pump the positive sodium ions back out, restoring the positive-outside and negative-inside polarization. At the same time this is transpiring, the action potential has traveled farther down the axon, causing the ion channels there to open in the next axonal section so that it too depolarizes, setting off a domino-like chain reaction down the entire length of the axon (Hall, 1992).

This flood of electrically charged ions in and out of each section of the axon constitutes the neural impulse—which, remember, was all started by stimulation to threshold at the dendrite side of the neuron. In different neurons, the speed of the impulse varies from 2 to over 200 miles per hour, but its speed is always constant *within* a given neuron. The larger the diameter of the axon and the more myelin surrounding its outer surface, the faster the impulse travels. Although this neural impulse speed may seem fast, consider that the speed of an electric current passing through a wire is 3 million times faster. The fact that electrical wire transmission is so much faster than neural impulse speed explains why we can build machines that respond faster than our bodies.

Besides differing in the speed at which the impulse moves down the axon, neurons differ in their potential rate of firing. Some neurons can re-achieve their action potential within milliseconds after firing and can fire as many as one thousand times per second. Other neurons take a great deal longer to recover their action potential. Thus, while it is true that a bright light or a loud sound causes a higher rate of firing in neurons than does less intense stimulation, some neurons will not fire as rapidly as others due to their slow recovery rate.

3-1d Neurons Communicate with One Another by Releasing Chemicals

Now that you understand the basic operation of a single neuron, how do you think the billions of neurons in the nervous system work together to coordinate the body's activities? To explore this process, we will examine how neural impulses get from one neuron to another.

> **action potential** The brief shift in a neuron's electrical charge that travels down the axon.

[handwritten margin notes]
1) axon switches from negative to positive (ion channels)
2) the wider and bigger the myelin sheath the faster the impulse travels.

<u>Figure 3-2</u>

Structure and Operation of a Neuron

When the combined stimulation received by the dendrites exceeds a certain minimum intensity, or threshold, an electrochemical impulse is transmitted down the axon. This impulse results from positively and negatively charged ions moving back and forth through the axon's membrane walls. Can you describe how depolarization occurs? How does the diameter of the axon and the myelin sheath covering it affect the speed of the impulse?

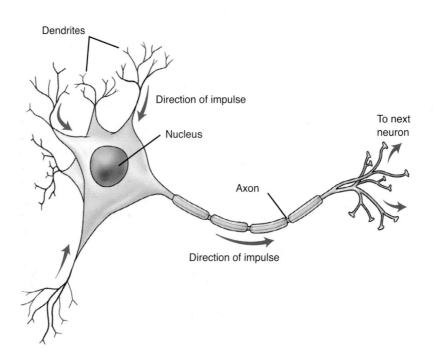

As noted earlier (see section 3-1b), at the end of each axon are *terminal buttons* that closely approach, but do not touch, the dendrites of other neurons. Most of these terminal buttons contain a number of tiny round sacs called *synaptic vesicles*. When an action potential arrives at the axon's terminal buttons, it causes these vesicles to release varying amounts of chemical messengers called **neurotransmitters,** which travel across the synaptic cleft. As the neurotransmitters arrive at the receiving neuron's dendrites—within 1/10,000 of a second of being released by the synaptic vesicles—they fit into *receptor sites* like keys fit into locks. Just as specific keys can fit into only specific kinds of locks, each kind of neurotransmitter has a unique chemical configuration that allows it to fit into only one specific kind of receptor site on the dendrites of the receiving neuron. This neural communication process, known as *synaptic transmission,* is illustrated in figure 3-3.

Once a neurotransmitter fits into a receptor site, it unlocks tiny channels that permit either positively or negatively charged ions to enter the receiving dendrite, which affects the probability that the neuron will fire. *Excitatory messages* increase the probability of an action

neurotransmitters Chemical messengers released by the synaptic vesicles that travel across the synaptic cleft and either excite or inhibit adjacent neurons.

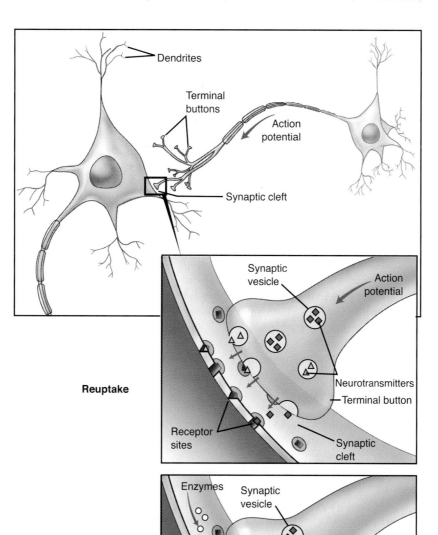

Figure 3-3

Synaptic Transmission

The axon's terminal buttons house synaptic vesicles that contain chemical messengers called neurotransmitters. These neurotransmitters travel across the synaptic cleft to the receiving neuron's dendrites, where they fit into receptor sites, causing either excitatory or inhibitory messages to be delivered to the dendrites. Excitatory messages increase the likelihood of an action potential, while inhibitory messages decrease this likelihood. If dendrites receive many more excitatory than inhibitory messages, they fire. After neurotransmitters deliver their messages, either they are repackaged into new synaptic vesicles (reuptake), or they are broken down by enzymes and removed from the synaptic cleft (enzyme deactivation).

*excitatory
transmitters
cause depolarization
depolarization*

*inhibitory
transmitters
cause
hyperpolarization.*

potential, while *inhibitory messages* reduce the likelihood of neural firing (Hensch & Fagiolini, 2004). Because the dendrites of a neuron receive both excitatory and inhibitory messages simultaneously from different receptor sites, whether or not the neuron fires will depend on which type of message is in greater abundance. If a neuron receives many more excitatory than inhibitory messages, it will fire. However, if the number of inhibitory messages is greater than the excitatory ones, the neuron will remain in a resting state.

What happens to the neurotransmitters after they lock into the receptor sites and either excite or inhibit the firing of the dendrites of the receiving neuron? This is an important question, because if the neurotransmitters are not quickly removed from the synaptic cleft, they will block the transmission of any additional signals to the receiving neuron other than their own excitatory or inhibitory messages. The primary way the synapse is cleared is by taking the neurotransmitters back into the terminal buttons from which they came, repackaging them into new synaptic vesicles, and using them again. This recycling process, which is called *reuptake,* is also used on many of the neurotransmitters that fail to reach the receptor sites (Ago et al., 2005; Schwartz, 1995). When neurotransmitters are not recycled, they are broken down and removed from the synaptic cleft by enzymes in a process called *enzyme deactivation.* Both of these means of clearing the synapse are depicted in figure 3-3.

The emerging knowledge of how neurotransmitters function in the brain has enabled scientists to develop drugs that are structurally similar to naturally occurring neurotransmitters. When such a drug is ingested into the body and reaches the appropriate receptor site in the brain, it may cause an action potential, just as the real neurotransmitter would do. Similarly, another drug may mimic a neurotransmitter that blocks the same receptor site, thus reducing the likelihood of neural transmission at the synapse. Still other drugs reduce the amount of the neurotransmitter that is recycled into the terminal buttons in the reuptake process, which keeps the neurotransmitter active in the synapse longer, thus increasing or decreasing the probability of neural transmission. One such drug that delays the reuptake of the neurotransmitter serotonin is *Prozac,* which is widely used in treating depression (see chapter 14, section 14-7b).

Neuroscientists once believed that only a few chemical substances accounted for neural transmission, but today about 75 neurotransmitters have been identified, and it is likely that more will be discovered in the future (Fishbach, 1992; Rosenzweig et al., 2002). In 1921, the Austrian scientist Otto Loewi discovered the first neurotransmitter, called **acetylcholine (ACh).** This chemical messenger is found throughout the nervous system and is responsible for motor control at the junction between nerves and muscles. Whenever ACh reaches the receptors on muscle cells, the muscles either contract or relax (Cooper et al., 1991). For example, ACh excites the body's large skeletal muscles but inhibits the heart muscles. Its continuing presence at the appropriate receptor sites enables us not only to walk, talk, and blink our eyes but also to breathe. If ACh is prevented from reaching receptor sites or if too much of it floods the synapses between motor neurons and muscles, the results can be disastrous. For example, the botulin bacterium, a toxin found in improperly processed food, blocks the release of ACh from terminal buttons, which leads to respiratory paralysis and suffocation (botulism). In contrast, the venom from a black widow spider—if of sufficient dosage—causes these same receptors to be flooded, triggering severe muscle contractions, convulsions, and even heart failure. ACh also plays a critical role in regulating wakefulness, as well as affecting memory and dreaming (Hasselmo & Bower, 1993). Researchers believe that the memory loss exhibited in the degenerative brain disorder known as *Alzheimer's disease*—which afflicts 11 percent of people over the age of 65—may be at least partly caused by a sharp reduction in the supply of this neurotransmitter (Goldman & Coté, 1991).

Another important neurotransmitter is **dopamine (DA),** which is involved in controlling large muscle movements as well as influencing pleasure and motivation. Such pleasurable activities as eating, drinking, and having sex are associated with activation of dopamine receptors (Wang et al., 2003). Too much or too little dopamine in the brain results in a wide variety of debilitating effects, ranging from jerky muscle movements to psychotic hallucinations (Barr, 2001). Researchers have found that degeneration of dopamine-producing

acetylcholine (ACh)
A neurotransmitter involved in muscle contraction and memory formation.

*pleasure in love
- similar to adrenaline
- cocaine releases
dopamine and
it stays there
and fires them
up.*

dopamine (DA)
A neurotransmitter that promotes and facilitates movement as well as influencing thought and emotion.

SSRI

neurons in the brain causes *Parkinson's disease,* a disorder affecting many elderly adults. The main symptoms of this disease are uncontrollable tremors, slowness of movement, altered body posture, and depressed mood (Rao et al., 1992). When Parkinson's patients are given the drug L-dopa, their brains convert it to dopamine, and this helps them regain control over their muscles (Parkinson Study Group, 2002). Another potentially useful treatment for Parkinson's disease is transplanting fetal tissue into the brains of Parkinson's disease patients. Researchers hope that the transplanted healthy fetal tissue will produce dopamine, thereby reducing patients' motor problems. Initial studies suggest that such transplants can help people regain the ability to walk and perform everyday activities (Freed & LeVay, 2002; Hauser et al., 1999).

Although the destruction of the brain's dopamine-producing system appears to be the cause of Parkinson's disease, increasing evidence shows that an overactive central dopamine system may be the root cause of *schizophrenia,* a psychological disorder we will examine more closely in chapter 13, section 13-3d. Drugs that block the reception of dopamine have proven effective in reducing schizophrenic symptoms in people suffering from this disorder (Baumeister & Francis, 2002). Unfortunately, because these drugs reduce dopamine levels in several brain areas, their long-term use sometimes produces symptoms similar to those of Parkinson's disease.

One group of neurotransmitters that is important in the control of pain and the elevation of mood is chemical substances known as **endorphins** (Pert, 2002). Interestingly, their discovery was prompted by a horseback-riding accident. In 1970, a graduate student in neuroscience, Candace Pert, was given *morphine,* a powerful painkilling drug derived from the opium plant (see chapter 6, section 6-3f), following a fall from a horse. This experience instilled in her a burning desire to understand how the drug works. She and Solomon Snyder soon discovered that certain brain areas are extremely sensitive to morphine. This finding at first perplexed the two researchers. Why would the brain have specialized receptors for an addictive opiate drug not normally found in the body? Can you guess the answer? Pert and Snyder (1973) hypothesized that the brain must have its own internally produced, morphinelike neurotransmitters. Even before these chemical substances were actually located, Pert and Snyder named them *endorphins,* a combination of the words *endogenous* (meaning "originating within the body") and *morphine.* Within 2 years, a number of these opiatelike neurotransmitters were identified (Hughes et al., 1975). Subsequent research revealed that the brain produces endorphins in response to injury and many forms of physical stress, such as intense exercise or the labor of childbirth (Akil, 1982; Vives & Oltras, 1992). During such times of body stress, the increase in endorphins not only temporarily provides the body with a natural painkiller but also may explain the state of euphoria many runners experience following a strenuous workout, as well as the pain-reducing effects of *acupuncture,* an ancient Chinese medical technique that involves inserting needles into the body (Harte et al., 1995; Pert, 1999).

One neurotransmitter that is involved in a number of psychological processes is **serotonin.** This chemical messenger is especially important in regulating emotional states, aggression, appetite, and sleep onset. Depressed and anxious moods, aggressiveness, and food cravings are associated with low levels of serotonin in the brain (Manuck et al., 2002; Widner et al., 2002). As previously mentioned, drugs that keep serotonin active in the synapse longer by blocking reuptake are used to elevate depressed moods, as well as to inhibit violence and overeating. Research also indicates that increasing the body's levels of *tryptophan,* the amino acid needed by the brain for synthesis of serotonin, facilitates sleep induction (Hartman, 1978). Because milk is a good source of tryptophan, grandma's advice to drink a glass of milk before going to bed may be the ticket to a good night's rest.

As you will discover in later chapters, other neurotransmitters play important roles in controlling aggression, sexual activity, blood pressure, sleep cycles, and food and water intake, as well as learning and immune responses (see table 3-1). The mysteries of neurotransmitter functioning revealed to date will no doubt be overshadowed by discoveries yet to come as neuroscientists continue to study these key factors in synaptic transmission.

> **endorphins** A family of neurotransmitters that are similar to morphine and that play an important role in the experience of pleasure and the control of pain.

Analgesia without pain pleasure

> **serotonin** A neurotransmitter that is important in regulating emotional states, sleep cycles, dreaming, aggression, and appetite.

Epinephrine, norepinephrine underlies fight-or-flight response.

[handwritten margin notes: "Types of Neurons", "transducers: recc. for cells", "effectr: cells", "sensory neurons", "stimulus → receptor → sensory cells → interneuron → (integrate)", "most of our neurons (integrate)", "motorneurons → effector → muscle cell"]

Table 3-1	Major Neurotransmitters
Neurotransmitters	**Involved in**
Acetylcholine (ACh)	Stress, wakefulness, mood
Dopamine (DA)	Voluntary movement, schizophrenia, cognition, mood
Endorphins	Pain suppression, pleasure
Epinephrine	Blood pressure, heart rate
GABA (gamma-amino-butyric acid)	Relaxation, anxiety
Norepinephrine (NE)	Stress, wakefulness, mood
Serotonin	Sleep, arousal, depression, schizophrenia

Section Review

- Neurons are specialized cells in the nervous system that send and receive information throughout the body.
  — The soma is the central part of the neuron.
  — Dendrites are branchlike extensions at one end of the soma that receive electrical impulses from other neurons.
  — The axon is a tubelike extension at the other end of the soma that carries impulses to other neurons.
- A neuron fires if it receives many more excitatory than inhibitory messages from other neurons.
- Neurotransmitters are chemicals that deliver excitatory or inhibitory messages to neurons, and some of the more important neurotransmitters are acetylcholine, dopamine, endorphins, and serotonin.

3-2 NEURAL AND HORMONAL SYSTEMS

Preview
- *What is the difference between the central and peripheral nervous systems?*
- *What are the two major divisions of the peripheral nervous system?*
- *What are the two parts of the autonomic nervous system?*
- *What is the endocrine system?*

Now that we have examined the structure and function of neurons, let's inspect the structure and function of the nervous system that neurons combine to form. The nervous system, our body's primary information system, is divided into two major portions, the *central nervous system* and the *peripheral nervous system* (figure 3-4). As you study these two divisions, you will notice that they too consist of a series of systems of twos. In addition to exploring the nervous system, we will explore a second communication system within the body that is interconnected with the nervous system, namely, the *endocrine system.*

3-2a The Peripheral Nervous System Connects the Brain and Spinal Cord with Body Organs and Tissues

The dictionary definition of *peripheral* is "located away from a center or central portion." As such, the **peripheral nervous system** consists of all the nerves located outside the brain and spinal cord. Its function is to connect the brain and spinal cord with the organs and tissues of the body. It accomplishes this task by conducting neural impulses into and out of the central nervous system.

[handwritten margin note: "PNS"]

peripheral nervous system
That portion of the nervous system containing all the nerves outside the brain and spinal cord.

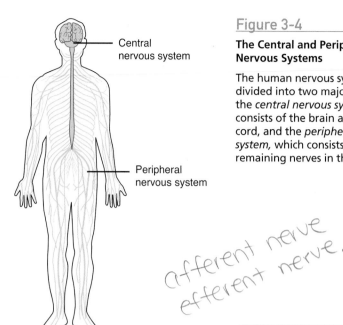

Central
nervous system

Peripheral
nervous system

afferent nerve
efferent nerve.

Figure 3-4

The Central and Peripheral Nervous Systems

The human nervous system is divided into two major portions, the *central nervous system,* which consists of the brain and spinal cord, and the *peripheral nervous system,* which consists of the remaining nerves in the body.

nerve A bundle of axons from many neurons that are routed together in the peripheral nervous system.

somatic nervous system A division of the peripheral nervous system that transmits commands to the voluntary skeletal muscles and receives sensory information from the muscles and the skin.

external environment

autonomic nervous system A division of the peripheral nervous system that controls the movement of nonskeletal muscles, such as the heart and lung muscles, over which people have little or no voluntary control.

internal environment.

sympathetic nervous system The part of the autonomic nervous system that activates the body's energy resources to deal with threatening situations.

energy-expanding

fight-or-flight.

parasympathetic nervous system The part of the autonomic nervous system that acts to conserve and maintain the body's energy resources.

energy-conserving

Because the peripheral nervous system is made up of a network of nerves, you might be wondering whether nerves are the same as neurons. The answer is no. While a neuron is a single cell, a **nerve** is a bundle of axons from many neurons that are routed together in the peripheral nervous system. Just as a single telephone line from your home is bundled together with thousands of other users' lines to form a telephone cable, so too are thousands of axons from many neurons bundled together to form a single nerve. Due to their sheer number, many neurons in this bundle could be destroyed without adversely affecting the nerve function, but the destruction of the entire nerve—for example, the optic nerve controlling vision—would certainly be much more problematic.

The peripheral nervous system is also composed of two major divisions: the somatic nervous system and the autonomic nervous system. The **somatic nervous system** transmits commands to the voluntary skeletal muscles by way of the motor neurons and receives sensory information from the muscles and the skin by way of the sensory neurons (refer back to section 3-1). The commands to the skeletal muscles control our movement, while the messages received from the muscles and the skin provide us with the sense of touch, the sense of position in our surroundings, and the perception of temperature and pain. For example, as you read these words, the movement of your eyes is being controlled by the somatic nervous system. Likewise, your ability to actually *see* the words and *feel* the book (or the "mouse," if you are reading this online) in your hands is aided by this same division of the peripheral nervous system.

The word *autonomic* means "self-governing." As such, in contrast to the somatic nervous system's control over voluntary skeletal muscles, the **autonomic nervous system** commands movement of involuntary, nonskeletal muscles—such as the heart, lung, and stomach muscles—over which we have little or no control. The primary function of this self-governing system is to maintain *homeostasis,* the body's steady state of normal functioning.

The autonomic nervous system is further divided into two separate branches—the *sympathetic* and *parasympathetic* systems (figure 3-5)—that tend to work in opposition to each other in regulating many of our body functions. Physiologist Walter Cannon (1915) was the first to describe how the **sympathetic nervous system** activates the body's energy resources to deal with stress and threatening situations. For example, if something angers or frightens you, the sympathetic system will prepare you for "fight or flight" by slowing your digestion, accelerating your heart rate, raising your blood sugar, and cooling your body with perspiration (see Explore It Exercise 3-1). In contrast, the **parasympathetic nervous system** acts to

Figure 3-5

The Dual Functions of the Autonomic Nervous System

The sympathetic and parasympathetic divisions of the autonomic nervous system often stimulate opposite effects in the body's organs. The sympathetic nervous system prepares your body for action, while the parasympathetic nervous system calms your body. Can you explain how these two systems respond to threat?

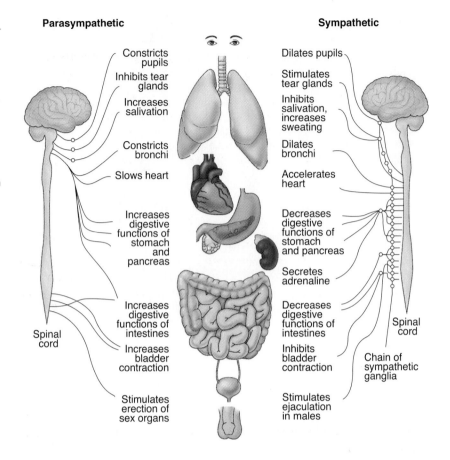

conserve and maintain the body's energy resources. Thus, when the threat ceases, parasympathetic nerves slow the autonomic system back down to its normal levels of functioning.

All things being equal, the parasympathetic system is the dominant branch of the autonomic nervous system, a state of affairs that is definitely beneficial to our long-term health. Can you imagine what your life would be like if your sympathetic system was constantly preparing you for fight or flight—automatically increasing your blood pressure, heart rate, and respiration, while decreasing your digestive and eliminative processes? Such a scenario leads to medical problems, including hypertension, ulcers, and heart failure, topics we will address more fully in chapter 15, section 15-1e.

In summarizing this discussion, it is important for me to emphasize that, although the sympathetic and parasympathetic systems produce opposite effects, together they keep the nervous system as a whole in a steady state of normal functioning. In this case, opposites are indeed attractive . . . to our overall health.

central nervous system That portion of the nervous system located in the bony central core of the body and consisting of the brain and spinal cord.

cerebrospinal fluid A clear, cushioning fluid secreted by the brain and circulated inside and around the brain and spinal cord.

3-2b The Spinal Cord Connects the Peripheral Nervous System to the Brain

The **central nervous system** is located in the bony central core of the body and consists of the brain and spinal cord. Besides being encased in bone and swaddled in three protective membranes (called *meninges*), the central nervous system is further cushioned and shielded from injury by a clear solution known as **cerebrospinal fluid,** which is secreted by the brain. This protective fluid circulating inside and around the brain and spinal cord has a specific gravity that is slightly greater than that of the brain, allowing the brain to literally float inside the skull. In this floating state, the brain's 3-pound "air weight" is reduced to only a few ounces, significantly reducing the pressure it exerts on the spinal cord. The importance of the cerebrospinal fluid in supporting and cushioning the brain is dramatically demonstrated when patients have it drained away during brain surgery. Until the brain replenishes

Explore It
Exercise **3-1**

Do You Notice When Your Sympathetic Nervous System Is Activated?

The sympathetic nervous system triggers your energy resources to better respond to threatening situations. Try the following exercises to help you better notice when this aspect of your nervous system is activated.

Exercise 1: Ask someone who spends a good deal of time with you to plan a surprise in which she or he startles you while you are engaged in a quiet, relaxing, or thought-absorbing activity. For example, a startle response could be elicited by making a loud noise while you are studying or settling down to take a nap. However it transpires, pay attention to your body's reaction. Does your heart rate accelerate? Does your stomach feel queasy? Are you perspiring? Is your mouth dry? Did your pupils dilate? How long does it take for your parasympathetic system to return your body to a steady state?

Exercise 2: Again enlist a friend to be the instigator of a specific stressor: tickling you. Lie on the floor with your eyes closed after giving your friend the following instructions: "Hover over me, and periodically tickle me. Sometimes do so without warning, while at other times let me know that the tickling is about to commence." While this good-natured torturing is taking place, notice how your body is reacting to this situation. When the tickling session ends, how long does it take for your body to return to its normal state? Next, reverse roles with your friend, and compare physiological reactions.

this fluid, the patients suffer terrible headaches and experience intense pain whenever they move their heads abruptly.

The **spinal cord** connects the brain to the rest of the body through the peripheral nervous system (Waxman, 2001). It is, in effect, a bundle of nerves with the thickness of a pencil. Encased within the vertebrae of the spinal column and bathed in cerebrospinal fluid, the nerves of the spinal cord transmit information from sensory neurons up to the brain, and from the brain down to motor neurons that initiate movement. Every voluntary action, such as walking or moving your arms, requires a message from the brain to the spinal cord, and from the spinal cord to the muscles.

The spinal cord extends from the base of the brain to slightly below the waist. By and large, the upper segments of the spinal cord control the upper parts of the body, while the lower segments control the lower body. Because of this neural configuration, when a segment of the spinal cord is severed, the person loses all sensation and muscle control below the injury. Some 11,000 Americans injure their spinal cords each year. The higher along the spine an injury occurs, the greater the extent of paralysis. Thus, when the late actor Christopher Reeve—who played the role of Superman in several 1970s and 1980s films—severed his spinal cord just below the base of his neck in a horseback-riding accident, he not only lost the ability to breathe on his own and to move any part of his body below the injury point, but also lost feeling in these areas. When such injuries occur, the central nervous system cannot repair itself. However, recent advances in medical science provide hope that the neural circuitry of the spinal cord can be regenerated. With the benefit of these advances, Reeve recovered some sensation and muscle control below his injury prior to his death in 2004.

In addition to transmitting information to and from the brain, the spinal cord controls the automatic, involuntary responses to sensory stimuli called **reflexes.** Reflexes, of which the *knee-jerk response* is one example, involve no interaction with the brain. Thus, when you accidentally place your hand on a hot stove and immediately pull it away, you are able to respond so quickly because your action involves no thinking—that is, no input from the brain. However, the pain message does continue traveling up the spinal cord to the brain, so that within a second, you will respond with a cry of pain—but the action of removing your hand from the burner is achieved by the spinal nerves. Such quick reflexive responses by the spinal cord enable the body to avoid serious injury.

spinal cord The slender, tube-shaped part of the central nervous system that extends from the base of the brain down the center of the back; made up of a bundle of nerves.

reflex An automatic, involuntary response to sensory stimuli; many reflexes are facilitated by the spinal nerves.

3-2c The Endocrine System Communicates by Secreting Hormones

Interconnected with—but not actually part of—the nervous system is the **endocrine system.** It consists of a network of glands in various parts of the body that manufacture and secrete chemical messengers known as **hormones** directly into the bloodstream (see table 3-2). Because our blood carries these hormones throughout the body, and because the membrane of every cell has receptors for one or more hormones, these chemical messengers have a direct effect on many different body organs, including the brain (Elmquist, 2001; Kravitz, 1988). Hormones affecting the brain influence our interest in food, aggression, and sex. However, unlike neural impulses, which rely on electrochemical transmission and can be measured in thousandths of a second, hormonal communications traveling through the bloodstream often take minutes to reach their destinations. Although the endocrine system generally affects body organs more slowly than the nervous system, the effects of hormonal stimulation typically have a longer duration than those of neurotransmitters.

The most influential endocrine gland is the **pituitary gland,** a pea-sized structure located at the base of the brain and controlled by a nearby brain area called the *hypothalamus,* which is situated just above the roof of the mouth (see section 3-3b). The pituitary is often referred to as the "master gland" because it releases about 10 different hormones that stimulate and regulate the rest of the endocrine system. Perhaps the pituitary's most important function is the secretion of hormones that regulate the body's reactions to stress and its resistance to disease. In this capacity as stress regulator, the pituitary gland works closely with the sympathetic nervous system (see section 3-2b). At puberty, the pituitary gland also increases its secretion of *growth hormone,* which acts directly on bone, cartilage, and muscle tissue to produce the adolescent growth spurt. Proper functioning of the pituitary gland during this stage of life is critical, because if it releases too little or too much growth hormone, either *dwarfism* or *giantism* may result (Zhou et al., 2005). Throughout life, growth hormone also plays an important role in tissue repair and muscle growth. However, in adulthood, the pituitary gland produces less and less growth hormone each year, and this depletion is thought to contribute to body aging.

Another hormone released by the pituitary gland is *oxytocin,* which causes the uterus to contract during childbirth and the mammary glands to produce milk. When a mother begins nursing her infant, the hypothalamus signals the pituitary gland to produce oxytocin, which results in the "let down" of milk into the nipple. Surprisingly, men also have significant amounts of oxytocin in their bodies, but for what purpose? Besides the role it plays in childbirth and nurs-

Table 3-2	Major Endocrine Glands and Some of Their Hormones	
Gland	**Hormone**	**Effects**
Pituitary gland	Growth hormone	Stimulates growth (especially bones) and metabolic functions
	Oxytocin	Stimulates contraction of uterus and mammary gland cells; may possibly promote prosocial behavior
Thyroid gland	Thyroxin	Stimulates and maintains metabolic processes
Adrenal glands	Epinephrine and norepinephrine	Increase metabolic activities and blood glucose; constrict certain blood vessels
Gonads (male testes and female ovaries)	Androgens (males), estrogens (females)	Support male sperm formation; stimulate female uterine lining growth; assist in the development and maintenance of secondary sex characteristics, such as chest hair growth in men and breast development in women

ing, animal research indicates that this hormone also influences social and sexual behavior, as well as parental behavior (Caldwell, 2002; Pedersen & Boccia, 2002). Animals with higher levels of oxytocin more strongly desire companionship, are more sexually active, and take better care of their young than do those with lower levels (Leckman & Herman, 2002; Young, 2002). A possible implication of these findings is that oxytocin is an *affiliative hormone,* promoting prosocial behavior in both humans and other animals, regardless of their sex (Pedersen, 2004).

Other notable glands in the endocrine system are the *thyroid gland,* the *adrenal glands,* and the *gonads* (see table 3-2). The **thyroid gland,** located just below the larynx in the neck, produces the hormone *thyroxin,* which controls metabolism—that is, the rate at which the food we eat is transformed into energy. People with an underactive thyroid—a condition known as *hypothyroidism*—tend to be lethargic and depressed, while those with an overactive thyroid tend to be very excitable and easily agitated and to have short attention spans (Haggerty et al., 1993).

The **adrenal glands,** located near the kidneys, secrete *epinephrine* (also called adrenaline) and *norepinephrine* (also called noradrenaline) when we feel anxious or threatened (Thompson, 2000). These hormones complement and enhance the effects of the sympathetic nervous system, making the heart beat faster, slowing digestion, and increasing the rate at which the body uses energy. Interestingly, epinephrine and norepinephrine also act as neurotransmitters, stimulating neural firing in the sympathetic nervous system (Raven & Johnson, 1999). For example, in one study, blood and urine samples collected from people just after they had given an important public speech showed dramatic increases in the secretion of these adrenal hormones (Bolm-Andorff et al., 1986). The fact that epinephrine and norepinephrine levels remain high following such stressful events explains why it takes considerable time to calm down from such experiences (see chapter 15, section 15-1b).

Finally, the **gonads** are the two sex glands. The two male gonads are called *testes,* and they produce sperm cells, while the two female gonads are called *ovaries,* and they produce ova, or eggs. The gonads also secrete hormones that not only are essential in sexual arousal but also contribute to the development of secondary sexual characteristics, such as chest hair growth in men and breast development in women.

thyroid gland The gland located just below the larynx in the neck that controls metabolism.

adrenal glands Two glands, located near the kidneys, that secrete epinephrine and norepinephrine, which activate the sympathetic nervous system.

gonads The two sex glands, called ovaries in females and testes in males.

S e c t i o n   R e v i e w

- The central nervous system consists of the brain and spinal cord, while the peripheral nervous system encompasses all the nerves outside the central nervous system.
- The two major divisions of the peripheral nervous system are the somatic nervous system (which transmits commands to the voluntary skeletal muscles by way of the motor neurons and receives sensory information from the muscles and the skin by way of the sensory neurons) and the autonomic nervous system (which controls movement of involuntary, nonskeletal muscles, such as the heart and lung muscles).
- The autonomic nervous system is divided into two separate parts: the sympathetic system (which activates the body's energy resources in threatening situations) and the parasympathetic system (which conserves and maintains the body's energy resources).
- The endocrine system is a network of glands throughout the body that manufactures and secretes hormones directly into the bloodstream.

3-3 THE BRAIN

Preview

- *What are some of the technological devices used to study the brain?*
- *What are the three major regions of the brain?*
- *How did the human brain evolve?*
- *What are the lobes of the cerebral cortex?*
- *Do we have "two" brains?*

- *Do the brains of men and women, or of people from diverse cultures, operate differently?*
- *How has the brain evolved to protect and repair itself?*
- *What is the blood-brain barrier?*

The organ of mind is not the brain itself; it is the brain, nerves, muscles and organs of sense. . . . We must . . . discard forever the notion of the sensorium commune, the cerebral closed, as a central seat of mind, or receptacle of sensation and imagery.

—*Alexander Bain, British scientist, 1818–1903*

non-invasive

Would it surprise you to learn that the ancient Greeks, Egyptians, Indians, and Chinese did not consider the brain to be of much consequence as a body organ? For example, the Greek philosopher Aristotle identified the heart, not the brain, as the source of intellectual activity. Similarly, the Egyptians considered the heart the seat of the soul and thought so little of the brain that, when mummifying a body for the afterlife, they scooped it out of the skull and threw it away! Today, we marvel at the capabilities of this 3-pound mass encased within the skull. Let us continue our journey of discovery by exploring this vital body organ.

3-3a Modern Technology Measures the Brain's Electrical Activity, Structure, Blood Flow, and Chemistry

Imagine how different Henry M.'s life would have been had he undergone medical treatment today rather than in the 1950s, when neuroscientists knew so little about the brain. One of the primary reasons we now know so much more about brain function is that contemporary neuroscientists have the ability to eavesdrop on the brain without causing it harm. Technological advances now allow researchers to use *brain-imaging techniques* that provide pictures—or scans—of this body organ. These techniques generate "maps" of the brains of living people by examining their electrical activity, structure, blood flow, and chemistry (Moses & Stiles, 2002; Toga & Mazziota, 1999). Let us examine the most widely used techniques and some of the emerging ethical debates their use has generated.

Brain-Imaging Techniques

electroencephalograph (EEG) An instrument that records "waves" of electrical activity in the brain using metal electrodes placed on a person's scalp.

The most widely used—and oldest—brain-imaging technique is the **electroencephalograph (EEG),** which records "waves" of electrical activity in the brain using many metal electrodes placed on a person's scalp. EEG measurement has provided researchers with invaluable information on brain functioning, especially in the areas of sleep, different states of awareness, and brain disease. The one drawback of the EEG is that it measures the overall electrical activity of many different areas of the brain at once, making it difficult to pinpoint the exact location of specific brain-wave activity (Russo et al., 2001). However, although it is difficult to determine exactly *where* an electrical event is taking place in the brain, the EEG is very good at determining *when* it happens. The technological cousin of the EEG is the *magnetoencephalogram (MEG),* which records magnetic fields instead of electrical activity.

computerized axial tomography (CAT) A brain-imaging technique in which thousands of X-ray photographs of the brain are taken and then combined to construct a cross-sectional brain picture.

A more revealing look at the functioning brain is obtained by **computerized axial tomography** (commonly called a **CAT** scan), which takes thousands of X-ray photographs of the brain while the person lies very still on a table with her or his head in the middle of a doughnut-shaped ring. Using a computer, these many X-ray images are combined to construct a cross-sectional brain picture. CAT scans are particularly helpful in detecting brain abnormalities, such as swelling and enlargement of certain areas.

magnetic resonance imaging (MRI) A brain-imaging technique that produces three-dimensional images of the brain's soft tissues by detecting magnetic activity from nuclear particles in brain molecules.

Another brain-imaging technique is **magnetic resonance imaging (MRI),** which produces three-dimensional images of the brain's soft tissues by detecting magnetic activity from nuclear particles in brain molecules (Senior et al., 2002). MRI provides greater accuracy in diagnosing diseases of the brain than does the CAT scan, and this has led to some groundbreaking discoveries. For example, as we will discuss more fully in chapter 13, section 13-3d, MRI researchers have found a possible association between enlarged ventricles (hollow, fluid-filled cavities) in the brain and schizophrenic disorders (Suddath et al., 1990).

positron emission tomography (PET) A brain-imaging technique that measures over several minutes the average amount of neural activity in different brain regions by showing each region's consumption of the sugar glucose, the brain's chemical fuel.

Unlike CAT or MRI scans, which document the brain's structure, the **positron emission tomography (PET)** scan measures the brain's metabolic activity in different regions by showing each region's consumption of glucose, the sugar that is the brain's chemical fuel. Technicians obtain these readings by injecting into the bloodstream a safe level of radioactive glucose liquid and then monitoring its rate of consumption in the brain. PET scans can reveal which parts of the brain are most active in such tasks as talking or listening to others, reading, lis-

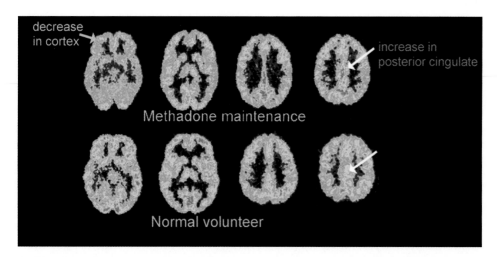

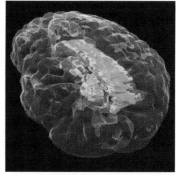

(Left) Color-coded PET scans showing rates of glucose use, a measure of brain activity, in a patient treated with methadone and in a normal volunteer. Methadone is a synthetic, morphinelike drug used to treat drug addicts. The patient shows the typical morphinelike lowering of brain metabolism in some cortical areas, but normal metabolic rates in many other brain areas and an increased metabolic rate in the posterior cingulate, part of the brain's limbic system. Individuals may vary in their response to methadone. *(Right)* A three-dimensional image of the living brain, based on computer-enhanced MRI and PET scans highlighting the cingulate gyrus.

Source: Photos courtesy of Monte S. Buchsbaum, M.D., Mount Sinai School of Medicine, New York, NY.

tening to music, and solving math problems (Nyberg et al., 2002; Schluter et al., 2001). Thus, this technique has been especially useful in revealing localization of brain function.

One disadvantage of the PET scan is that the picture of brain activity it provides is an average of the activity that occurs over several minutes. Another disadvantage is that it exposes people to small amounts of radioactivity, making extensive scanning somewhat risky. A newer technology, called **functional magnetic resonance imaging (fMRI),** does not have these drawbacks (Barinaga, 1997; Georgopoulos et al., 2001). First, fMRI can produce a picture of neural activity averaged over seconds, not minutes. Second, like a standard MRI, it uses magnetism to measure fluctuations in naturally occurring blood oxygen levels, not fluctuations in ingested radioactive glucose. The images produced by fMRI scans are also much sharper than those in PET scans, and thus they can be used to identify much smaller brain structures.

As you can see, all these brain-imaging techniques are providing researchers with the means for making new discoveries about our most important body organ. Improvements in neuroscientists' ability to "peek" into the brain provide them with the necessary information to better prevent the type of surgical calamity experienced by Henry M. However, the ability to measure the workings of the human brain is also raising growing concerns about how such technology might be abused by tapping into people's private thoughts without their consent.

Is Privacy an Issue in Brain Imaging?

Brain-imaging techniques are becoming so good at detecting the ebb and flow of neural activity that it is not far-fetched to predict that this technology will one day be able to literally "read" people's minds, determining such characteristics as their sexual orientation, their degree of racial prejudice, or their truthfulness when answering specific questions. For example, a recent study conducted by Tatia Lee and her colleagues (2002) found that certain areas of the brain are more active when people lie. These researchers are now trying to determine whether this knowledge can be used to produce an effective lie detector that would outperform the conventional polygraph machine (see chapter 11, section 11-5c).

Another brain-imaging study was able to detect unconscious racism among White Americans (O'Connor et al., 2000). In this research, White college students, who had previously stated that they held no conscious racial prejudice toward African Americans, were shown photos of familiar or unfamiliar Black and White faces. When the White students viewed unfamiliar Black faces as compared to unfamiliar White faces, brain scans indicated greater activation of the amygdala, the brain area associated with fear and emotional

functional magnetic resonance imaging (fMRI) A brain-imaging technique that measures over a few seconds the average neural activity in different brain regions by showing fluctuations in blood oxygen levels.

learning. No heightened amygdala activity occurred when the White students viewed familiar Black faces. These findings suggest that, despite not reporting any conscious negative attitudes toward African Americans, these White students perhaps unknowingly felt some level of fear and negativity toward Black people. Similar findings have also been obtained from African-American students when they viewed photos of White faces (Hart et al., 2000). In making sense of these studies, some psychologists believe they demonstrate that brain-imaging technology may be able to peel beneath the surface of human thought and emotion and reveal "unconscious racism" toward members of other social groups.

Are there dangers in employing such methods? Some experts think so. Privacy issues raised by brain imaging are becoming an important topic of discussion in the new field of *neuroethics* (Illes & Raffin, 2002; Kulynych, 2002). Arthur Caplan, director of the University of Pennsylvania's Center for Bioethics, states that the need to discuss brain privacy is urgent (Goldberg, 2003): "If you were to ask me what the ethical hot potato of this coming century is, I'd say it's new knowledge of the brain, its structure and function." Although the current media focus is on genetic privacy, Caplan contends that most people feel a greater need for privacy in regard to their brains than to their genes, because brain activity is more associated with the immediate "here and now" than is genetic functioning.

Today, the automobile-sized MRI machines used to create brain images cost approximately $3 million and thus are much too expensive to be used by most nonscientists or nonmedical personnel. However, certain well-funded marketing research firms are using these machines to try to determine consumers' unconscious preferences for certain products. If the brain privacy debate follows the same path as the genetic privacy debate, new laws may soon be proposed to protect the public from the misuse of this fascinating and powerful new technology.

3-3b Three Major Brain Regions Are the Hindbrain, the Midbrain, and the Forebrain

The names for the three major regions of the brain—*hindbrain, midbrain,* and *forebrain*—come from their physical arrangement in the developing human embryo. In the embryo, the central nervous system begins its development as a long, hollow *neural tube,* but within 5 weeks, this tubular cluster of neurons changes its shape into these three distinct regions (see figure 3-6). The forebrain is the farthest forward, near where the face will develop. The midbrain comes next, just above the hindbrain, which is near the back of what will become the neck. The remainder of the neural tube develops into the spinal cord. In this section of the chapter, we first briefly describe each of these major brain regions and then focus on that part of the forebrain that dominates the rest of the brain, namely, the *cerebral cortex.*

Figure 3-6

Development of the Brain

During the course of embryonic development, the neural tube forms distinct regions called the forebrain, the midbrain, and the hindbrain. In the photograph of the 5-week embryo, you can see the long, hollow *neural tube* from which these three brain regions develop.

Source: Photo © Cloud Hills Imaging Ltd./CORBIS.

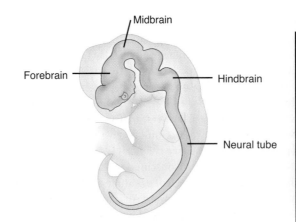
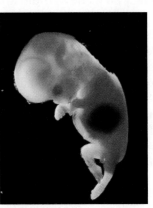

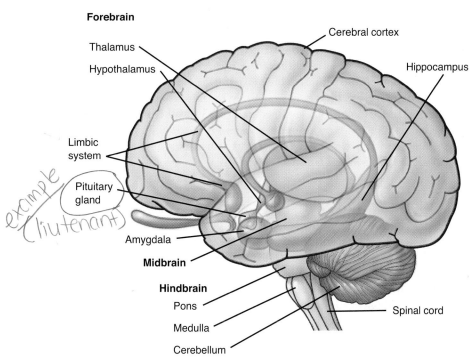

Forebrain

- Thalamus
- Hypothalamus
- Cerebral cortex
- Hippocampus
- Limbic system
- Pituitary gland
- Amygdala
- **Midbrain**
- **Hindbrain**
- Pons
- Medulla
- Cerebellum
- Spinal cord

example (liutenant) [handwritten annotation]

Figure 3-7
Main Parts of the Human Brain

INTERACTIVE FIGURE

The Hindbrain

Figure 3-7 shows that directly above the spinal cord is the **hindbrain,** consisting of the medulla, the pons, and the cerebellum. The **medulla,** which looks like a swelling at the top of the spinal cord, controls our breathing, heart rate, swallowing, and digestion. It also allows us to maintain an upright posture. Besides these functions, the medulla is the place in the brain where the nerves from the left side of our body cross over to the right side of the brain, and the nerves from the right side of the body cross over to the left side of the brain. (Yes! We are cross-wired!) The **pons,** located just above the medulla, is concerned with sleep and arousal. Behind the medulla and pons is the **cerebellum** (meaning *little brain*), which not only is important in the regulation and coordination of body movement but also appears to play a role in learning (Daum et al., 1993; Woodruff-Pak, 1999). Damage to this area of the brain not only results in jerky, poorly coordinated muscle functioning but also causes severe disturbances in balance, gait, speech, and the control of eye movement. The cerebellum is also one of the first brain structures affected by alcohol, which explains why intoxicated individuals are uncoordinated and have slurred speech. When a police officer suspects that you are driving while intoxicated, he will test the functioning of your cerebellum by having you walk a straight line or stand on one foot.

The Midbrain

The **midbrain** (see figure 3-7) is a small neural area located above the hindbrain. The most important structure in the midbrain is the **reticular formation,** a finger-shaped network of neurons involved in regulating and maintaining consciousness, including sleep. Actually, the reticular formation extends into the hindbrain, where it makes up a portion of the pons. When you are startled by a loud noise, it is the reticular formation that causes your heightened state of arousal (Steriade et al., 1980). Likewise, when you sleep through familiar sounds in your surroundings, it again is the reticular formation that filters out these background noises. The reticular formation's ability to respond to incoming stimuli can be shut down. This is exactly the function of anesthetics used in surgery. *Anesthetics* are chemicals that prevent certain "locks" from being opened at the synaptic level. Also, if the reticular formation is damaged, a permanent coma can result.

hindbrain The region of the brain above the spinal cord that contains the medulla, the pons, and the cerebellum.

medulla A part of the hindbrain that controls breathing, heart rate, swallowing, and digestion, as well as allowing us to maintain an upright posture.

pons A part of the hindbrain that is concerned with sleep and arousal.

cerebellum A part of the hindbrain that regulates and coordinates basic motor activities and may also play a role in learning.

midbrain The region of the brain above the hindbrain that contains the reticular formation.

controls eyes [handwritten annotation]

reticular formation A part of the midbrain involved in the regulation and maintenance of consciousness.

to sleep, to awake, to shut your body off.

The Forebrain

forebrain The region of the brain above the midbrain that contains the thalamus, the hypothalamus, and the limbic system.

As we move up past the first two brain regions, we come to the most interesting—and the most evolutionarily recent—region, namely, the **forebrain.** The forebrain allows us to engage in complex emotional reactions, cognitive processes, and movement patterns. It consists of such important structures as the *thalamus,* the *hypothalamus,* and the *limbic system.* On top of these structures is the *cerebral cortex,* the most complex part of the brain.

thalamus A part of the forebrain that is the brain's sensory relay station, sending messages from the senses to higher parts of the brain.

The **thalamus,** looking like a joined pair of eggs, is the brain's sensory relay station, sorting and sending messages from the eyes, ears, tongue, and skin to the cerebral cortex. The thalamus, working closely with the reticular formation, also plays an important role in controlling sleep and wakefulness.

hypothalamus A part of the forebrain involved in regulating basic biological processes, such as eating, drinking, sexual activity, emotion, and a stable body temperature.

The **hypothalamus** (*hypo* means "beneath") is located under the thalamus and is less than one-tenth its size (less than 1 cubic centimeter). Despite its small mass, the hypothalamus plays an indispensable role in brain functioning. One of its most important functions is being the control center of the autonomic nervous system, meaning that it controls that part of the nervous system governing the involuntary muscles (see section 3-2a). As the control center, the hypothalamus ensures that the autonomic nervous system provides *homeostasis,* which is the maintenance of a constant internal body state. Your relatively steady body temperature, blood pressure, and body fluid volume are a result of the hypothalamus coordinating the autonomic regulatory activities of the body. Another important function of the hypothalamus is providing a critical link between the central nervous system and the endocrine system. As discussed in section 3-2c, by exercising control over the release of hormones from the endocrine system's pituitary gland, the hypothalamus influences hormone release by other glands throughout the body. This small brain structure also regulates several motivated behaviors, including eating, drinking, and sexual activity. In addition, it plays an important role in the experience of emotion, stress, and pleasurable reward, and it is strongly affected by certain addictive drugs, such as cocaine. All in all, this is one cubic centimeter of the brain that you cannot function without.

limbic system A part of the forebrain consisting of structures that influence fear and aggression (amygdala) and the acquisition and consolidation of new information in memory (hippocampus).

A series of interrelated, doughnut-shaped neural structures, located at the border of the brain's older parts and the soon-to-be-discussed *cerebral cortex,* is the **limbic system.** Its two main structures are the *amygdala* and the *hippocampus.* The amygdala (which means "almond" in Greek) consists of two almond-shaped neural clusters that influence fear and aggression. Damage to—or electrical stimulation of—this part of the brain can result in either intense fear or uncontrollable rage, depending on what part of the amygdala is activated (Fanselow & Poulos, 2005). Such damage can also short-circuit these feelings: For example, monkeys with destroyed amygdalas lose their fear of natural predators. The other limbic structure, the hippocampus, is central to the acquisition and consolidation of new information in memory (Gluck & Myers, 2001; Tamminga, 2005). This is exactly the part of the brain that was surgically removed in Henry M. to control his seizures, leaving him unable to form new memories. Although acquiring new memories is no longer possible with such damage, acquiring *implicit* memories—those outside conscious awareness—is not affected (Cohen et al., 1985). Thus, Henry M. was able to learn new skills, such as reading mirror writing or solving mazes and puzzles, but he was not able to remember having done so!

> **Journey of Discovery Question**
> You have probably heard the following statement many times: "We use only 10 percent of our brain." Based on what you have learned about brain functioning, do you think this statement is true? In pondering the merits of this expression, consider another type of human functioning: athletic performance. Do athletes use only 10 percent of their muscles when competing?

As you have learned, many vital functions are controlled and regulated by the hindbrain, midbrain, and selected parts of the forebrain. Yet, despite the complexity of these different brain areas, what sets us apart from all other animals and makes us "human" is the largest forebrain structure, the *cerebral cortex,* which is the subject of section 3-3c.

3-3c The Cerebral Cortex Is the Crowning Achievement of Human Evolution

Among primates, there are five different groups: prosimians, new-world monkeys, old-world monkeys, apes, and hominids. *Homo sapiens* (or humans) are the only surviving species of the hominid line (Johanson & Edgar, 1996; Wood, 2002). Today, our nearest living biological relatives are the family of great apes, which include chimpanzees, bonobos, gorillas, and orangutans. According to existing fossil records, approximately 6 to 10 million years ago, hominids and apes diverged in their evolutionary lineage when hominids became *bipedal*—that is, developed the habit of walking on two legs (Gould, 1991; Lemonick & Dorfman, 2002). Our hominid ancestors' evolved ability to walk erect was an important environmental adaptation because the upright posture allowed them to explore a much larger expanse of territory and secure many new resources. Figure 3-8 depicts an estimate of the human evolutionary path over the past 5 million years, including some of the now-extinct members of our hominid family.

Besides the ability to walk erect, the second important adaptation in the evolution of the human species was the increase in brain size (Eccles, 1989). Among the primates, the brain of humans is three times bigger than that of an ape of the same body size (Lewin, 1993a, 1993b). Yet is size the most important factor when determining intellectual ability?

When scientists first studied the evolution of the human brain, they assumed that brain size was closely related to intellectual capacity. However, this assumption quickly ran into problems (Harvey & Krebs, 1990). First, although humans believed themselves to be the most intelligent of all creatures, their brains of about 1,350 grams weighed far less than those of less intelligent species, such as elephants (8,000 grams). Second, adult human brains vary between 1,000 and 2,000 grams, but there is no indication that the "heavy brainers" are more intelligent than the "light brainers." Another approach was to examine brain weight as a percentage of total body weight. Although this formula resulted in humans leaping ahead of elephants (2.33 percent versus 0.20 percent), they were now outdistanced by the shrew (3.33 percent), which is a mouse-sized mammal related to the mole.

> The mind loves the unknown. It loves images whose meaning is unknown, since the meaning of the mind itself is unknown.
>
> —*René Magritte, Belgian surrealist painter, 1898–1967*

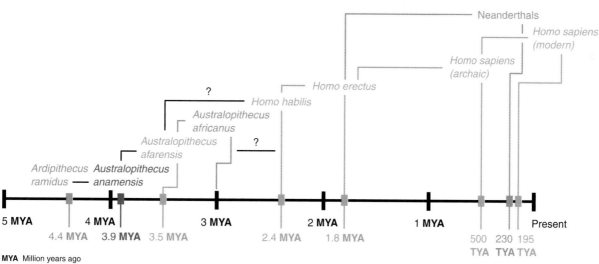

Figure 3-8

Human Ancestral Family Chart

Humans (*Homo sapiens*) are the only surviving species of the hominids. Around 8 million years ago, hominids began walking on two legs and diverged from gorillas, bonobos, orangutans, and chimpanzees in their evolutionary linkage. This chart depicts how the various species in the hominid family might be related to one another. Keep in mind that this chart of human evolution is based on an incomplete fossil record and represents only a possible solution to this puzzle. Every time new fossils are discovered, the chart may change, and not all scientists agree on those changes. The latest evidence is that modern-looking humans emerged about 195,000 years ago.

fissure - an opening

cerebral cortex The largest structure in the forebrain; largely responsible for higher-order mental processes.

Cortex
1.) percentral gyrus
2.) second opening of the brain.
3.) parietal cortex.
4.) somasthetic cortex (somatosensory.)

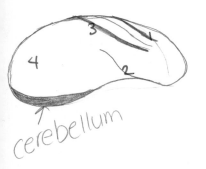

3
4
2

cerebellum

Instead of comparing brain weight, researchers began to compare the evolution of different brain regions. Of all the brain regions studied, the most dramatic differences between humans and other animals can be seen in the relative sizes of the brain stem—which includes the hindbrain and midbrain—and the cerebral cortex. As previously discussed, the brain stem regulates basic life processes, such as heart rate, respiration, digestion, and sleep. In contrast, the **cerebral cortex,** located in the uppermost portion of the forebrain, is the "thinking" center of the brain, coordinating and integrating all other brain areas into a fully functioning unit (Kolb & Whishaw, 1990). Its name is derived from two Latin words—*cerebrum,* meaning "brain," and *cortex,* meaning "bark." Basically, the cerebral cortex is the part of the brain that looks like the bark of a tree.

The surface area of the cerebral cortex has a gray appearance because it primarily contains gray nerve cells and unmyelinated fibers. Although it is only one-eighth of an inch thick, this densely packed system of interneurons is mostly responsible for our ability to plan, reason, remember, speak, and analyze ourselves. Directly below this thin layer of *gray matter* is *white matter,* consisting mostly of the axons of the cortical neurons (Seldon, 2005). They appear white because the axons are covered and insulated by the white myelin sheath discussed in section 3-1b.

As you can see in figure 3-7, the cortex in humans has a great number of *convolutions* (folds), allowing a greater volume of it to fit into the skull cavity. Indeed, if you were able to unfold the cortex, it would cover four sheets of typing paper. In comparison, a chimpanzee's flattened cortex would cover only one sheet, a monkey's would cover a postcard, and a rat's would cover a postage stamp (Calvin, 1996). The relative sizes of the cerebral cortex and brain stem of species with different evolutionary ages indicate that most of the growth has occurred in the cerebral cortex (Parker et al., 2000). Not only do humans have a larger cerebral cortex than other species, but also a human's cerebral cortex has a great deal more convolutions. About 90 percent of our cerebral cortex is of relatively recent evolution.

As the size of the cerebral cortex increased in our hominid ancestors, the brain required more oxygen to keep it alive. By examining the imprint left by the brain's blood vessels on the inside surface of our ancestors' fossilized skulls, paleontologists have been able to observe the evolution of this blood supply to the brain. What they discovered was a dramatic increase in the number of blood vessels supplying oxygen to the brain from our early hominid ancestors to modern-day *Homo sapiens.* As the number of oxygen-delivering blood vessels increased, our ancestors exhibited increased brain growth, which in turn required even more oxygen to be carried by the blood to the brain. This cycle continued, and today we have large brains with a complex and very dense network of surrounding blood vessels.

Figure 3-9 compares the size and shape of the brain of *Homo erectus,* a hominid that became extinct about 300,000 years ago, with the modern human brain (Parker, 2000).

Figure 3-9

The Hominid Brain

Based on molded casts of the inside surface of fossilized skulls, scientists are able to compare the size and shape of our modern-day brains (*Homo sapiens*) with those of our hominid cousins. Here, a depiction of the brain of *Homo erectus* (green), a hominid that became extinct about 300,000 years ago, is superimposed on the brain of a modern human (yellow).

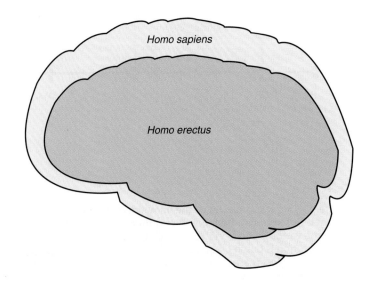

Homo sapiens

Homo erectus

Although 20 percent smaller than our brains, the *erectus* brain has the characteristic "football" shape found in the more recent hominids (Neanderthals and *Homo sapiens*). This modern look was primarily caused by an expansion of two regions of the cerebral cortex: the *occipital lobe* at the back of the brain and the *frontal lobe* at the front of the brain (see section 3-3d). Evolutionary scientists believe that the expansion of these two brain lobes of the cortex was associated with our hominid ancestors' increasing reliance on sight and complex thinking to survive in their environment. The football shape of the modern human brain has a more bloated look than the *erectus* brain, largely due to the evolutionary expansion of the parietal lobe, which, among other things, is important in perceiving the spatial layout of the environment and effectively moving through it (Joseph, 2000).

3-3d The Cerebral Cortex Consists of Specialized Regions, or "Lobes"

The cerebral cortex is divided into two rounded halves, called the **cerebral hemispheres.** These hemispheres are connected at the bottom by the **corpus callosum,** a thick band of over 200 million white nerve fibers that transmit information between the two hemispheres (figure 3-10). As mentioned earlier, our brain is cross-wired, meaning that the right hemisphere controls the movement and feeling of the left side of the body, and the left hemisphere controls the right side of the body.

Lobes of the Cerebral Cortex

Both hemispheres can be divided into four major sections called *lobes:* the frontal, parietal, temporal, and occipital lobes (see figure 3-11). Thus, you have a right and a left lobe of each of these hemispheric divisions. These lobes are not distinct, independent parts of the cortex

What made this brain of mine, do you think? Not the need to move my limbs; for a rat with half my brain moves as well as I.

—*George Bernard Shaw, Irish dramatist and socialist, 1856–1950*

I was taught that the human brain was the crown glory of evolution so far, but I think it's a very poor scheme for survival.

—*Kurt Vonnegut, Jr., science fiction author, b. 1922*

cerebral hemispheres The two main parts of the cerebral cortex; the left and right hemispheres.

corpus callosum A thick band of nerve fibers connecting the right and left cerebral hemispheres that transmits information between them.

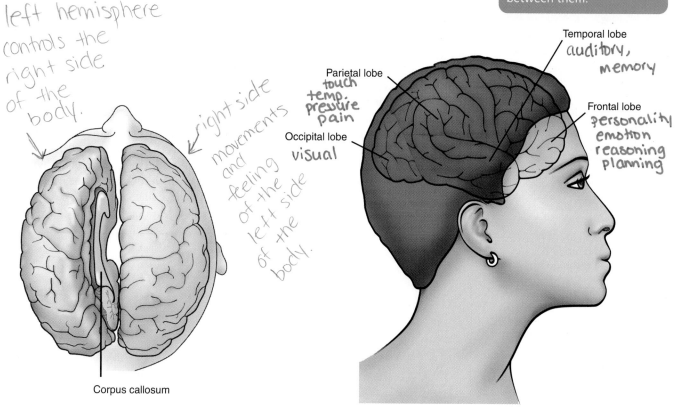

left hemisphere controls the right side of the body.

right side movements and feeling of the left side of the body.

Parietal lobe
touch temp. pressure pain

Occipital lobe
visual

Temporal lobe
auditory, memory

Frontal lobe
personality emotion reasoning planning

Corpus callosum

Figure 3-10

The Corpus Callosum

The corpus callosum is the dense band of nerve fibers connecting the right and left cerebral hemispheres. What would happen if this transmission bridge were cut?

Figure 3-11

The Lobes of the Cerebral Cortex

Each hemisphere of the cerebral cortex can be divided into four lobes: the occipital lobe, the parietal lobe, the temporal lobe, and the frontal lobe. Do these lobes represent distinct, independent parts of the cortex?

but, rather, convenient regions named for the bones of the skull covering them. As mentioned earlier, neuroscientists use PET scans and other brain-imaging techniques to discover which parts of the cortex are most active when the brain is performing specific tasks.

The **occipital lobes,** located at the back of the cerebral hemispheres, are the visual regions of the brain. Here, we experience the shapes, color, and motion in our world. Damage to the occipital lobes can cause blindness, even if our eyes and optic nerves are healthy. The **parietal lobes,** situated in front of the occipital lobes, are involved in touch sensation and in monitoring the body's position in space. Damage to these brain regions can destroy people's sense of touch, making it impossible for them to feel objects placed in their hands. The **temporal lobes** are located below the parietal lobes, near the temples (hence, the name). These regions of the cerebral hemispheres are important in audition (hearing) and language. Damage to what is called *Wernicke's area* in the left temporal lobe can cause difficulty in understanding the meanings of words and sentences. People with such damage may speak smoothly and expressively, but their sentences consist merely of "word salad," or meaningless words strung together. Finally, the largest lobes in the human brain are the **frontal lobes,** situated in the "front" of the cerebral hemispheres, just behind the forehead. These regions of the cerebral cortex are involved in coordinating movement and higher mental processes, such as planning, social skills, and abstract thinking (Goldberg, 2001). Damage to the frontal lobes can result in dramatic personality changes, as was first discovered over 150 years ago when a railroad worker named Phineas Gage damaged this area of his brain in an accident.

Personality Changes Due to Frontal Lobe Damage

In 1848, Phineas Gage, the foreman of a Vermont railroad company, had a terrible accident. While he was using an iron tamping rod to pack gunpowder into a large boulder, a spark ignited the gunpowder, rocketing the tamping rod up into Gage's left cheek, through the frontal lobe of his brain, and out the top of his head. Unbelievably, Gage survived this accident and was pronounced cured in less than 2 months. Yet, despite his outward recovery, Gage no longer had the same personality. Before the accident, he had been a friendly, popular, hardworking, and emotionally mature adult. Following the accident, he was irresponsible, disrespectful, profane, and unable to control his own impulses. This sort of dramatic alteration in Gage's personality is common among people with frontal lobe damage.

In later studies of patients with similar frontal damage, researchers have found that these patients not only tend to be unable to make sound decisions in their personal lives, but also lack the ability to experience strong emotions (Damasio, 1994; Russell & Roxanas, 1990). Although these people might well have been warm, loving, considerate, and responsible individuals prior to their illness or accident, they are now uniformly cold, distant, inconsiderate, and irresponsible. Although these declines in reasoning and emotional abilities do not affect their basic attention, memory, intelligence, and language ability, these people are no longer who they once were.

occipital lobe One of the four major sections of the cerebral cortex, located at the back of each cerebral hemisphere; primarily responsible for visual processing.

parietal lobe One of the four major sections of the cerebral cortex, situated in front of the occipital lobe in each cerebral hemisphere; involved in touch sensation and in monitoring the body's position in space.

temporal lobe One of the four major sections of the cerebral cortex, located below the parietal lobe and near the temple in each cerebral hemisphere; important in audition and language.

frontal lobe One of the four major sections of the cerebral cortex, situated in the front of each cerebral hemisphere and behind the forehead; involved in the coordination of movement and higher mental processes.

Using measurements of Phineas Gage's skull and modern neuroimaging techniques, Hanna Damasio and her coworkers (1994) reconstructed Gage's accident and the likely path taken by the metal tamping rod as it traveled through his brain.

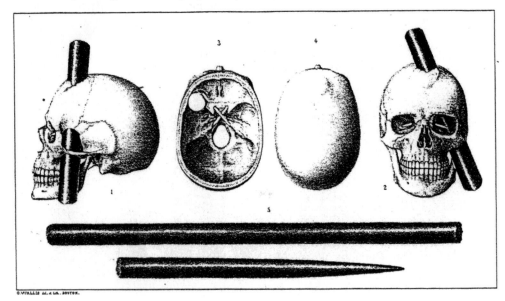

This link between the frontal lobes and emotional expression was further explored in an interesting set of studies conducted by Richard Davidson and his colleagues (Henriques & Davidson, 1990; Tomarken et al., 1990). Testing both infants and adults, they found that the left frontal lobe governs more positive feelings, while the right frontal lobe controls more negative moods, even as early as 10 months of age. They also discovered that people with more active left frontal lobes tend to be happier and more cheerful, optimistic, sociable, and self-confident than those with more active right frontal lobes.

> My own brain is to me the most unaccountable of machinery—always buzzing, humming, soaring, roaring, diving, and then buried in mud. And why? What's this passion for?
>
> —*Virginia Woolf, British novelist, 1882–1941*

3-3e The Right and Left Cerebral Hemispheres Function Differently

Although the right and left hemispheres of the brain look very much alike, they make different contributions to our mental lives. The term **cerebral lateralization** refers to the degree to which the right or left hemisphere controls various cognitive and behavioral functions (Morin, 2001; Spence et al., 2001). Much of what we now know about these different functions has come about by studying people who have undergone a very rare and unique surgical procedure.

> **cerebral lateralization** The degree to which the right or left hemisphere controls various cognitive and behavioral functions.

What would happen if the lobes of the cerebral cortex were healthy, but the right and left hemispheres could not transmit information to each other through the bundle of nerves that make up the corpus callosum? This was the question asked by psychologists Roger Sperry (1964, 1968) and Michael Gazzaniga (1970, 1989) when they began studying *split-brain* patients. In most cases, these were patients in whom the nerves of the corpus callosum had been surgically cut in a now-outmoded treatment for severe epileptic seizures. The technique was drastic, but the patients did improve rapidly, and their personality and behavior did not undergo major changes. However, now these patients had two brain hemispheres, acting more or less independently. What Sperry and Gazzaniga discovered was that these patients essentially had two minds.

The practical problem with this turn of events for the split-brain patients was that sometimes one hemisphere would initiate a behavior that conflicted with the other hemisphere's intentions. Now, without a direct line of communication between the right and left hemispheres, each had its own separate and private sensations, perceptions, and impulses to act (Bogen, 2000). For example, shortly after surgery, split-brain patients were often surprised to find that while dressing, their right hands (controlled by the left hemisphere) would reach for one article of clothing only to be brushed aside by their left hands (controlled by the right hemisphere), which had a different choice in mind. In an even more remarkable display of the independent functioning of the two hemispheres, a split-brain man, in a fit of anger, grabbed and shook his wife with his left hand while his right hand fought to set her free! Did he really intend to harm her? Well, yes and no. His right hemisphere initiated a harmful action, which prompted his left hemisphere to initiate a protective response. Here was a man who was both attacking and defending his wife at the same time! Despite these dramatic examples of hemispheric conflict, split-brain patients generally behave normally (Iaccino, 1993).

When split-brain patients have been studied in the laboratory, less dramatic but very interesting effects have provided scientists with a clearer understanding of the right and left hemispheres' abilities (Gazzaniga & Miller, 2000; Walsh, 2000). For example, in one experiment, Gazzaniga (1967) had split-brain participants stare at a dot while the word *HEART* was flashed across their visual field, with *HE* in the left visual field of each eye (which is processed by the right hemisphere) and *ART* in the right visual field (which is processed by the left hemisphere). The word could be seen for only about 150 milliseconds, providing insufficient time for the eyes to move and process the entire word in each hemisphere. Participants were first asked to report verbally what they saw and then to indicate with their left hands what they saw. When people with an intact corpus callosum performed this task, the right and left hemispheres passed the different information between them, and the word *HEART* was seen and reported. Yet, with split-brain persons, something very interesting occurred. As depicted in figure 3-12, split-brain individuals *say* they see the word *ART,* but their left hands *point* to the word *HE.*

On another task in this same study, when the word *PENCIL* was flashed in their right visual field, the split-brain participants could easily read aloud the word, but not when it was flashed in their left visual field. Gazzaniga discovered that the right hemisphere

[Handwritten margin notes: "Association cortex - located all over the brain / Sensory input — motor / ex: drummer output / Left side more dominent / Right side less dominent / does not include right hand people."]

Figure 3-12

Testing the Split Brain

When the word *HEART* flashes across the visual field of split-brain patients, they verbally report seeing the portion of the word transmitted to their left hemispheres (*ART*). However, when asked to indicate with their left hands what they have seen, they point to the portion of the word transmitted to their right hemispheres (*HE*).

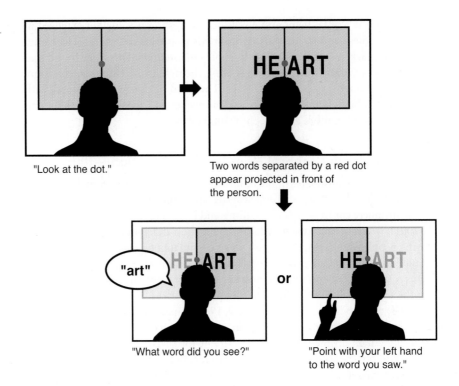

"Look at the dot."

Two words separated by a red dot appear projected in front of the person.

"art"

"What word did you see?"

or

"Point with your left hand to the word you saw."

did perceive and comprehend the word *PENCIL,* but the participants could not verbalize what they saw. However, using the left hand—which was controlled by the right hemisphere—the split-brain participants could easily pick out a pencil from a host of unseen objects.

Further research on the intact brain using brain-imaging techniques examined in greater detail the question of cerebral lateralization (Berninger et al., 2002; Federmeier & Kutas, 2002). Although generalizations should be made with caution, the right hemisphere appears to be superior to the left in completing visual and spatial tasks, recognizing nonlinguistic sounds (such as music and environmental noise), identifying faces, and perceiving and expressing emotions (Keenan et al., 2001; McAuliffe & Knowlton, 2001). In contrast, the left hemisphere excels at language, logic, and providing explanations for events (Best & Avery, 1999; Hellige, 1993). Indeed, Gazzaniga (1988) describes the left hemisphere as the brain's "interpreter," always striving to assign some rational meaning to behavior, even when there is none. Thus, when reading a map, listening to music, looking for a friend in a crowd, or laughing and crying at life's ups and downs, it's likely that more neural firing is occurring in your right hemisphere than in your left hemisphere. By contrast, when talking on the phone, balancing your checkbook, or explaining to your parents why you need extra money for your spring vacation, your left hemisphere is probably the most active (go to Explore It Exercise 3-2).

Having made the case that the two hemispheres appear to be more in control of certain functions than others, it is important to add that these different specialized abilities are almost always relative differences, not absolute differences (Reuter-Lorenz & Miller, 1998). That is, whatever task we work on, both hemispheres are activated to some extent. This literal "side-by-side" exchange of information is the hallmark of the healthy brain (Banich, 1998; Gazzaniga, 2000).

3-3f The Sexes May Differ in Their Hemispheric Organization

Try two simple tasks. First, mentally run through the alphabet and count as quickly as possible the number of letters, including the letter *e*, that when silently pronounced contain the sound "ee." Next, and again as quickly as possible, mentally count the number of letters that contain curves when they are printed as capitals. Writing or speaking aloud is not permitted.

Which task was harder for you, counting sounds or counting curves? Research indicates that your answer may partly depend on whether you are a woman or a man. Women tend to

Explore It
Exercise 3-2

Do You and Your Friends Use Different Patterns of Brain Activity to Recognize Each Other's Faces?

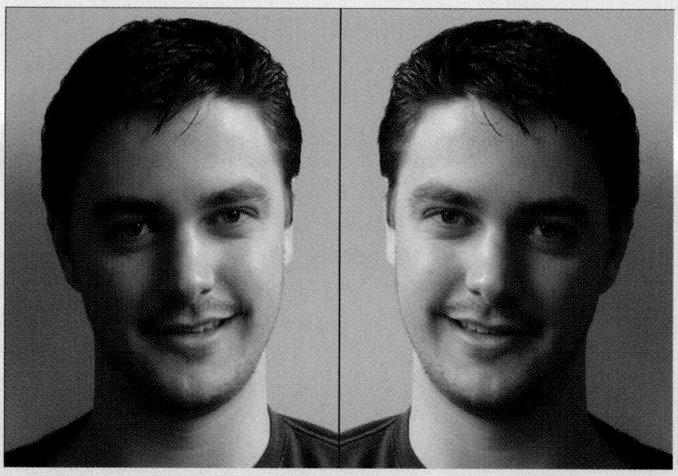

(a) (b)

Which of these faces looks happier to you?

If you are like most people, you perceive the face in photo (b), with the smile on the left side, as the happier face. This is because most people tend to be more accurate in recognizing visual stimuli presented to the left visual field, which is processed first in the right hemisphere. Exercises like this one suggest that the right hemisphere generally plays a larger role in recognizing facial expression than the left hemisphere (Levy et al., 1983). Of course, because virtually everybody has an intact corpus callosum, after a very brief interval, both hemispheres will share this information. Yet, until they do, the right hemisphere will exert greater influence in recognizing facial features.

Is right hemispheric dominance for facial expression true for everyone? No. Some people fail to show a left visual field advantage, while others actually demonstrate an advantage for the right visual field. To demonstrate individual differences in the lateralization of brain function, ask as many people as possible to complete this exercise. Do any of them not show right-hemisphere preference?

be more accurate and slightly faster in the sound task, while men tend to do better in the shape task, which suggests that there are sex differences in verbal and spatial abilities (Coltheart et al., 1975; Kimura, 1992). Because language abilities are more closely associated with the left hemisphere and spatial abilities are more closely aligned with right-hemispheric functioning, researchers wondered whether women and men differ in hemispheric dominance.

If the cerebral hemispheres function somewhat differently in women and men, these differences are likely to be reflected in the effects of brain injury. Support for this reasoning comes from studies of damage to the left hemisphere following stroke. A stroke causes damage to the brain by starving it of needed oxygen when its blood supply is temporarily interrupted. Men are three times more likely than women to develop **aphasia,** the inability to recognize or express language (McGlone, 1978). Some studies suggest that the reason women are less susceptible to aphasia is that their brains are more *bilateralized* for language—that is, they are more likely than men to use both hemispheres for this cognitive function (Bryden, 1979; Reuter-Lorenz & Miller, 1998). For instance, when women and men were asked to process and compare sounds, PET scans indicated that an area of the left hemisphere was activated in both sexes. However, in a majority of the women—but in none of the men—the same area in the right hemisphere was also activated (Shaywitz et al., 1995). This study's finding that women's language functions are less likely to be located solely in the left hemisphere of the brain (less lateralized) may explain why women experience fewer language deficits than men when their left hemispheres are damaged by stroke. It may also partly explain why women tend to be less adept at spatial tasks than men. Put simply, because the right hemisphere tends to control spatial functioning, and because women are more likely than men to also use part of this hemisphere for language functioning, this bilaterality in language function may result in less proficient processing of spatial tasks (Sanders et al., 2002).

aphasia The inability to recognize or express language as a result of damage to brain tissue, such as after a stroke.

Not only is there evidence that women's brains are less lateralized than men's, but also some studies suggest that women's left hemispheres are organized differently. Although it is still not known *why* the left hemisphere might be organized differently for women and men, some researchers have focused on hormonal influences during brain development and early childhood (Gerschwind & Galaburda, 1987; Hines, 1982). A few studies even suggest that during high-estrogen periods of the menstrual cycle, women's spatial abilities are not as acute as at other times (Kimura, 1987; Kimura & Hampson, 1994). In assessing these possible sex differences, one thing to keep in mind is that not only do they appear to be very small, but also the similarities in brain function between women and men far outweigh the differences (Riger, 1992; Rogers, 2001). Yet, what might explain these differences?

Although scientific inquiry has yet to yield a widely accepted explanation for why women's brains appear to be organized somewhat differently from men's brains, Jerre Levy (1972) suggests that evolutionary pressures may have played a decisive role. That is, because our species evolved with women being principally responsible for raising the young, verbal bilateralization may have given them a more-developed communication system that fostered their survival. In contrast, because men have historically been more involved in hunting and gathering food and other resources, having male spatial functioning clearly separate from verbal functioning in the brain may also have benefited their survival. Levy states that, although this different hemispheric arrangement between women and men may no longer provide any survival value, we still inherit and exhibit these biological differences.

Despite the fact that there is evidence of sex differences in brain organization, no one knows what these differences mean for the general abilities and behavior of women and men in their daily lives (Hoptman & Davidson, 1994). It is also true that culture profoundly shapes people's skills and interests, and the different manner in which girls and boys are typically socialized often has an important impact on what specific abilities are nurtured. The greater verbal abilities of females, for example, may have nothing at all to do with evolutionary factors and more to do with the fact that girls receive greater encouragement to talk during infancy and early childhood (Brody & Hall, 1993; Lewis & Weintraub, 1979). It is possible that this relatively high amount of verbal attention compared to that given to boys may foster greater elaboration of neural interconnections in certain areas of the brain.

Are There "Left-Brain" and "Right-Brain" People?

As previously discussed, the left hemisphere appears to exert a greater influence on verbal skills such as reading, writing, math, and logic, while the right hemisphere exercises greater control over nonverbal activities such as spatial tasks, music, art, and face recognition. These findings of hemispheric specialization have led a number of popular writers to claim that some people are logical and scientific because they rely mostly on their left hemispheres ("left-brainers"), while others are creative and artistic because they mostly use their right hemispheres ("right-brainers"). Armed with such a simple explanation, these same writers have produced popular books with such titles as *Educating the Right Brain, Drawing on the Right Side of the Brain,* and *The Other Side of the Mind,* in which they give advice on how to increase creative thinking by both tapping into unused right-brain potential and suppressing left-brain activity. Despite the simplistic appeal of these books, there is no sound evidence that individuals significantly differ in their sheer reliance on one hemisphere over the other (Hellige, 1990; Springer & Deutsch, 1998). In addition, these books are based on the incorrect assumption that various cognitive functions are completely localized within the left and right hemispheres, whereas in this chapter you have learned that, while certain tasks may activate one hemisphere somewhat more than the other, both hemispheres are involved in the completion of any task a person might perform. Thus, the ideas that a given person significantly relies more on one hemisphere than on the other that you can train yourself to activate and suppress hemispheric functioning remain interesting, but wholly unconfirmed, hypotheses (Corballis, 1999).

3-3g The Brain Can Alter Its Neural Connections

What happens when one part of the brain is severely damaged or destroyed? Are the cognitive functions associated with that brain area lost forever? The answers to these questions are partly being found by following the remarkable lives of children such as Matthew:

Eight-year-old Matthew has just returned home with his report card on the last day of second grade. Matt is pleased with the card's contents, for it is a summary of good behavior, respectable grades, and steady improvement. While such an evaluation would be greeted with satisfaction in most households, Matt's parents are especially pleased because 2 years earlier surgeons conducted a *hemispherectomy* of Matt's brain to control dangerous seizures. Put simply, they removed his left cerebral hemisphere.

At first, the surgery to treat Matt's seizures may seem even more foolhardy than the procedure performed on Henry M. 50 years ago. Yet, recall that I earlier asked you to imagine how Henry M.'s life might have been different had his surgery occurred today. Because of the advances made in neuroscience since Henry M.'s operation, we now know a great deal more about how the brain functions (Gazzaniga, 2000). Specifically, we understand that, although normal functioning is not possible without a hippocampus, it is possible to live a relatively normal life even after losing an entire cerebral hemisphere (Battro, 2001; Devlin et al., 2003). In Matt's case, even though half his skull is now filled with nothing but cerebrospinal fluid, the only visible effects of the operation are a slight limp, limited use of his right hand and arm, and lack of right peripheral vision in both eyes. In fact, brain scans indicate that control over his right arm and leg has been taken over by the cortical area that controls his left arm and leg. Despite the fact that the left hemisphere specializes in mathematics, math is Matt's strongest subject in school. Somehow, in a manner not yet adequately understood by scientists, the right hemisphere has taken over this function as well (Rossini & Pauri, 2000; Swerdlow, 1995).

In one session, when tested on his language proficiency by being asked to name as many "fast things" as he could in 20 seconds, Matt replied, "Car . . . truck . . . train . . . plane." The typical child his age names six to eight things. Scientists do not know if Matt's language deficiency is due to the loss of his language-proficient left hemisphere or to the fact that he suffered seizures for 3 years. While acknowledging this deficit, Matt's therapist observed that 20 months following surgery, Matt showed dramatic progress in his language ability, probably because of the accelerated growth of dendrites, making new connections between neurons. Just like other children with normal brains, Matt's production of dendrites will be at a peak level from about age 4 to age 10. Besides being caused by inherited growth patterns, neural connections are also fostered by environmental challenges, which is exactly why Matt is being pushed so hard during his weekly speech and language therapy sessions. As more connections are made among the billions of neurons in Matt's remaining brain regions, the result will be a better-functioning brain. Indeed, other children who have had one of their brain hemispheres removed have later earned college degrees and are currently leading successful and productive lives as adults (Battro, 2001; Vining et al., 1997).

These children's extraordinary recovery from such a dramatic loss of brain tissue demonstrates what neuroscientists call *plasticity,* the remarkable flexibility of the brain to alter its neural connections (Kolb et al., 2003; Stein et al., 1995). Through such *collateral growth* (figure 3-13), branches from the axons of nearby healthy neurons grow into the pathways previously occupied by the axons of damaged neurons (Bach-y-Rita, 1990). This ability to transfer brain functions from one part of the brain to the other is highest in childhood, during the peak years of dendrite growth (Leonard et al., 1996; Scharff, 2000).

Journey of Discovery Question   After limbs have been amputated, amputees often feel excruciating pain in the area of their lost limb. How might the brain's plasticity play a role in this pain?

Scientists once believed that brain structures ceased any positive physical development by early adulthood. Yet this thinking changed following a series of studies that suggested a very different developmental pattern. In this research, rats with an age equivalent to that of 75 human years were moved from the impoverished physical environment they had lived in all their lives (bare cage, simple food containers) to an enriched environment (spacious home, interesting playthings). By the time they reached the equivalent of 90 human years, these rats

Figure 3-13

Collateral Growth

The brain's plasticity is demonstrated by the way in which neural connections are altered when neurons are damaged. This collateral growth is highest in childhood, when dendrite growth is at its peak.

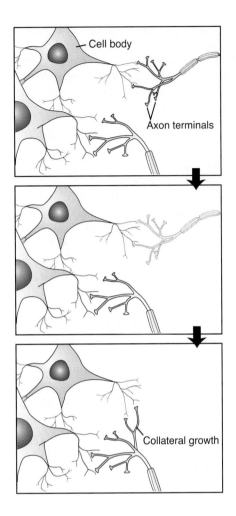

showed significant increases in brain growth and synaptic interconnections (Diamond, 1988). These findings, which mirror the results of studies with baby rats, adult monkeys, and other species, suggest that environmental enrichment significantly enhances brain functioning, even among the elderly (Gould et al., 1999; Rosenzweig, 1984). Additional research further indicates that older adults' brains can achieve a fairly substantial transfer of function after suffering strokes or brain damage due to accidents (Cotman, 1990; Kempermann & Gage, 1999). The lesson to be learned here is simple, yet profound: Exercising the brain at all stages of life increases its ability to adapt to and overcome life's challenges and hard knocks. This means that, although we may not be able to train one side of the brain to turn on and off like a light switch, we can make life choices that will improve the longevity of the 3-pound neural network enclosed within our skull (Drachman, 1997; Mahoney & Restak, 1998). Neuroscientific research suggests the following lifelong strategies to maintain a healthy brain at any age:

1. *Avoid harmful substances:* Drug abuse and alcohol abuse damage brain cells (Kish, 2002; Torvik et al., 1982).
2. *Exercise on a regular basis:* People who engage in strenuous physical activity throughout their lives are not only more likely to stay physically healthy but also more likely to maintain high cognitive functioning by minimizing the loss of brain tissue (Colcombe et al., 2003; Hall et al., 2001). Further, elderly adults who have not previously exercised can still enhance their cognitive vitality by taking up some form of aerobic fitness training (Colcombe & Kramer, 2003). The type of exercise that has the greatest benefit to brain longevity is that requiring complex motor skills and focused attention, rather than the repetition of simple motor skills (Kolb & Whishaw, 1998). Thus, playing tennis or soccer is better for your brain than simply doing jumping jacks or running on a treadmill.

"Use it or lose it!" Staying mentally active by reading regularly or doing crossword puzzles keeps the brain strong.

Source: Courtesy of Figzoi.

3. *Eat sensibly:* Dietary factors are associated with the incidence of stroke, which is the largest single cause of brain disabilities. Decrease the intake of saturated fat, and eat more fruits and vegetables (Bidlack, 1996).

4. *Challenge yourself mentally:* When it comes to the brain, the old adage "Use it or lose it" really does apply. People with more formal schooling tend to maintain higher mental functioning in their 70s than those with less schooling (Jacobs et al., 1993). Staying mentally active by reading regularly and learning new skills strengthens neural connections similarly to the way regular physical exercise strengthens the heart (White et al., 1994).

5. *Wear your seat belt and bike helmet:* Motor vehicle accidents account for up to half of all brain injuries. Head injury is the most common cause of death in bicycle crashes, accounting for 62 percent of all bicycle-related deaths.

Finally, recent advances in neuroscience also raise the possibility that in the not-so-distant future drugs developed for treating brain disease could be prescribed for healthy people looking to enhance their cognitive performance (Fauber, 2004). For example, Alzheimer's drugs might be given to air traffic controllers or other workers in highly skilled jobs to improve attention and memory. Yet such possibilities raise serious ethical issues. Should we permit the use of memory enhancement drugs by healthy people? Would the use of such drugs be permissible by physicians who need to operate on patients at peak cognitive efficiency? Should we allow students to take these drugs to help them study for exams? What are the dangers in using drugs to enhance the brain's cognitive efficiency?

A common plot device in science fiction movies involves removing a brain from its body and maintaining it alive in a nutrient-rich solution. If this were actually a scientific possibility, do you think this brain would have the same mind as it had when connected to the rest of the body? Underlying this question is the age-old *mind-body debate* concerning where the mind is located in the body.

The brain is wider than the sky.

—*Emily Dickinson, U.S. poet, 1830–1886*

The human head is bigger than the globe. It conceives itself as containing more. It can think and rethink itself and ourselves from any desired point outside the gravitational pull of the earth. It starts by writing one thing and later reads itself as something else. The human head is monstrous.

—*Günter Grass, German author, b. 1927*

blood-brain barrier
A semipermeable wall of tiny blood vessels that prevents certain chemicals in the bloodstream from reaching the brain.

3-3h The Brain Is Protected from Toxins by the Blood-Brain Barrier

Besides being able to alter its neural connections following injury, the brain has evolved an elaborate defense mechanism that reduces the likelihood of harm. The first evidence of this built-in protection came to light over 100 years ago when scientists discovered that if they injected blue dye into the bloodstream of an animal, tissues throughout the body would turn blue except those in the brain and spinal cord. Likewise, when they injected dye directly into the cerebrospinal fluid, the entire brain became stained, but the dye did not enter the animal's bloodstream to stain other internal organs. These effects suggested that some sort of barrier was preventing materials in the blood from entering the central nervous system. Scientists further discovered that all vertebrate animals had this barrier between the brain and the bloodstream. They speculated that this barrier served a protective function for the brain, but how it operated was a mystery for many years.

In the 1960s, neuroscientists using electron microscopes discovered that in most parts of the body, the walls of the smallest blood vessels, called *capillaries*, are lined with loosely fitting cells that allow chemical substances in the bloodstream to move easily through the capillary walls. They also discovered that in the capillaries that carry blood to the brain, these same cells fit very tightly together and allow only certain chemicals to pass out of the bloodstream. This semipermeable wall of tiny blood vessels that prevents certain chemicals in the bloodstream from reaching the brain is called the **blood-brain barrier** (Hurst et al., 2002; Mihaylov et al., 2002). In the human brain, about 400 miles of brain capillaries make up this tight seal of cells, with a total surface area of about 100 square feet! Additional research has found that the blood-brain barrier performs the following important functions:

1. It protects the brain from many "foreign substances" in the blood that may injure the brain.
2. It protects the brain from hormones and neurotransmitters in the rest of the body.
3. It maintains a constant environment for the brain.

What substances are allowed to enter the brain through the blood-brain barrier? Blood gases, such as oxygen, and small nutritional molecules are the main beneficial outsiders that gain entry. An especially important nutritional molecule that is transported out of the bloodstream in this way is glucose, the brain's chemical fuel (see section 3-3a).

Unfortunately, this defensive mechanism does not keep out all harmful foreign substances. Cocaine and heroin, for example, cross the barrier easily, bind with receptors, and affect neurotransmitter functioning. In addition, a number of therapeutic drugs designed to treat various brain ailments are barred from passing through this protective barrier, which poses a considerable medical dilemma. If you cannot treat these brain ailments by injecting useful drugs into the bloodstream, the only other option is to drill a hole in the skull and inject the drugs directly into the brain—not the most pleasant procedure for patients. Fortunately, by gaining a better understanding of the biology behind the brain's protective cells, scientists are now learning how to trick the blood-brain barrier into accepting some of these therapeutic drugs through the bloodstream. One technique used to treat patients suffering from ailments such as stroke and Alzheimer's disease attaches molecules of the therapeutic drug onto molecules that can easily pass through the barrier, resulting in a "piggyback" delivery system. Another treatment for some forms of brain cancer involves opening the blood-brain barrier by chemically inducing the cells that line the capillary walls to shrink temporarily, thus allowing the cancer drug to flow through to the diseased brain tissue. Figure 3-14 provides a close-up view of the blood-brain barrier and depicts how scientists have learned to temporarily sneak past this barrier to deliver therapeutic drugs to the brain.

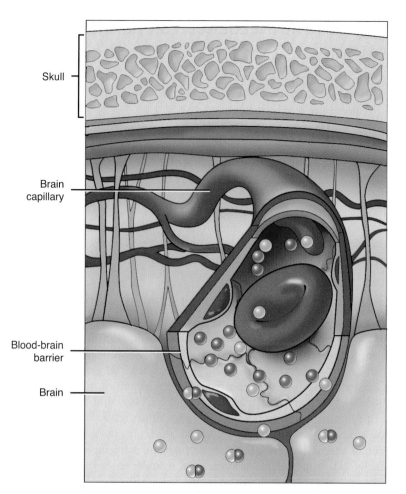

Skull

Brain capillary

Blood-brain barrier

Brain

Figure 3-14

The Blood-Brain Barrier

The blood-brain barrier is a semipermeable wall of tiny blood vessels that prevents the molecules of certain chemicals (green) in the bloodstream from reaching the brain. Blood gases and such nutritional molecules (yellow) as glucose (our brain's chemical fuel) are allowed to pass through this barrier. In treating brain diseases, scientists have learned how to attach the molecules of therapeutic drugs (blue) onto these blood gases and nutritional molecules so that the drugs can be transported through the barrier in piggyback fashion.

Section Review

- Some of the more commonly used technological devices to examine the brain's electrical activity, structure, blood flow, and chemistry are the electroencephalograph (EEG), computerized axial tomography (CAT), magnetic resonance imaging (MRI), positron emission tomography (PET), and functional magnetic resonance imaging (fMRI).
- There are three major brain regions: the hindbrain, located above the spinal cord and consisting of the medulla, the pons, and the cerebellum; the midbrain, which contains the reticular formation and is located above the hindbrain; and the forebrain, which consists of the thalamus, the hypothalamus, the limbic system, and the cerebral cortex and is located above the midbrain.
- The cerebral cortex, which is divided into two rounded halves called cerebral hemispheres, coordinates and integrates all other brain areas and is mostly responsible for our ability to plan, reason, remember, speak, and analyze ourselves.
- The left and right cerebral hemispheres are both divided into four major sections: frontal lobe, parietal lobe, temporal lobe, and occipital lobe.
- The right hemisphere is superior to the left in visual and spatial tasks, recognizing nonlinguistic sounds, identifying faces, and perceiving and expressing emotions.
- The left hemisphere excels at language, logic, and providing explanations for events.
- Women's brains may be less lateralized—less likely to have various brain functions located in only one of the hemispheres—than men's brains.
- The brain can alter its neural connections to compensate for damage.
- The blood-brain barrier surrounding the brain prevents certain chemicals in the bloodstream from entering the brain.

3-4 GENETIC INFLUENCES ON BEHAVIOR

Preview

- *What are genes and chromosomes?*
- *Can scientists use DNA structure to determine how closely related individuals and species are to one another?*
- *What is behavior genetics?*
- *What is molecular genetics?*
- *How do heredity and environment influence behavior?*
- *Why are sex and race differences controversial topics in genetic research?*

Having examined the neural basis of human functioning, let us now turn our attention to the influence of genetics on human functioning. The primary question we will address in this section is how the visible and measurable traits (the **phenotype**) of an organism reflect its underlying genetic composition (the **genotype**).

phenotype The visible and measurable traits of an organism.

genotype The underlying genetic composition of an organism.

gene The basic biochemical unit of inheritance that is located on and transmitted by chromosomes.

3-4a The Basic Biochemical Unit of Inheritance Is the Gene

In 2003, geneticists completed the Human Genome Project, which identified 99.99 percent of the genetic material in humans. *Genome* is the term used to describe the total genetic information in the cells of a particular species. Because every person has a unique genetic pattern, researchers do not expect to ever reach 100 percent. The focus of the Human Genome Project was the **gene,** the biochemical unit of inheritance that provides instructions for how every activity in every cell of our body should be carried out.

What sort of instructions do genes provide to the body's cells? Gene instructions concern the production of *proteins,* which regulate the body's physiological processes and the expression of phenotypic traits (for example, body build, intelligence, athletic ability). Proteins are the building blocks of life. As an example, consider how a gene instructs a liver cell to remove excess cholesterol from the bloodstream. The gene instructs the cell to make a particular protein (a receptor protein), and it is this protein that removes the cholesterol from the blood. The cholesterol molecules are then transported into the cell and processed by other proteins.

Genes are located on and transmitted by **chromosomes,** which are threadlike structures found in every cell of the body, with the exception of red blood cells. All chromosomes contain strands of the molecule **deoxyribonucleic acid,** commonly known as **DNA,** which in turn contains thousands of different genes, located at fixed positions. Figure 3-15 depicts our genetic building blocks, breaking down the human body from its 100 trillion cells to the genes that provide them with instructions on protein production.

chromosomes Threadlike structures carrying genetic information that are found in almost every cell of the body.

deoxyribonucleic acid (DNA) The complex molecular strands of a chromosome that contain thousands of different genes, located at fixed positions.

Genetic Variation within and across Species

One of the most surprising early findings of the Human Genome Project is that humans have only about 30,000 genes, not many more than a worm (18,000) and less than a rice plant (40,000). This discovery highlights the fact that human complexity is not solely due to the number of genes we possess but is largely determined by the many different ways that genes interact with one another (Johnston & Edwards, 2002).

When comparing the genes of different species, counting the sheer number of total genes is less important than determining how many genes the species share. This is because the structural similarity of DNA between species provides scientists with important clues concerning how closely related the species are on the evolutionary tree. For example, humans and chimpanzees share 98 percent of the same DNA structure, humans and gorillas share a bit less than 98 percent, and humans' and monkeys' DNA similarity is only about 90 percent. Coupled with the fossil record studies of these species, the DNA evidence indicates that monkeys diverged from humans much earlier in their evolutionary past than did chimps and gorillas.

We humans are unusual among our primate cousins because we have much less genetic variability within our species than do chimpanzees, gorillas, and other apes (Gagneux et al., 1999). These findings strongly suggest that not long ago in human evolution our ancestors

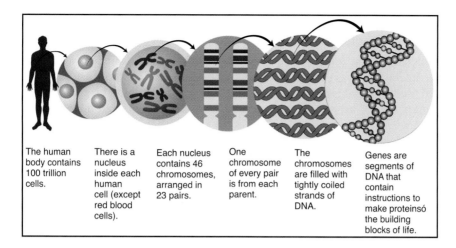

Figure 3-15

Genetic Building Blocks

Chromosomes are found in the nucleus of each of the cells in our bodies. Each chromosome contains tightly coiled strands of DNA. Genes are DNA segments that are the biochemical units of inheritance.

The human body contains 100 trillion cells.

There is a nucleus inside each human cell (except red blood cells).

Each nucleus contains 46 chromosomes, arranged in 23 pairs.

One chromosome of every pair is from each parent.

The chromosomes are filled with tightly coiled strands of DNA.

Genes are segments of DNA that contain instructions to make proteinsó the building blocks of life.

experienced a severe reduction in their population due to disease, famine, or some other disaster. The effective result of this massive population loss was that a large part of our within-species genetic variability was lost. Genetic testing of humans around the world indicates that the great majority of the existing overall genetic variation in humans is represented by individual diversity within populations, not across populations (Fish, 2002). This finding has important implications in understanding the concept of "race" as a distinguishing feature in the human population, a topic that we will examine in section 3-4d.

All humans possess 99.9 percent of the same genes, which is why we can do many of the same things, such as walking, talking, and engaging in abstract thought (Plomin & Crabbe, 2000; Wade, 1999). Despite this genetic similarity, a great deal of genetic variation also exists across individuals in that final one-tenth of 1 percent of genetic material. As you already discovered in our review of the evolutionary process (see chapter 1, section 1-3e), the genetic makeup of organisms not only determines their ability to survive in their environment but also influences their ability to reproduce and pass their genes on to the next generation.

Sex Chromosomes

How did you inherit your particular genotype? Putting it simply, each sperm cell of a human male and each egg cell of a human female contain 23 chromosomes. Upon the union of your father's sperm and your mother's egg at conception, all body cells that developed from this new cell (called the *zygote*) contained 46 chromosomes, or 23 pairs. Each of these body cells contained your genetic blueprint, or genotype, with half the genetic material coming from each parent. Among the 23 chromosomal pairs, one pair, known as the **sex chromosomes,** determined your sex. You inherited an X chromosome from your mother and either an X or a Y chromosome from your father. XX pairings cause the embryo to develop female physical characteristics, while XY pairings lead to male physical characteristics. Because it is only the father's sex chromosome that varies, your father's genetic contribution determined your sex.

Just as you share 50 percent of the same genes with each of your parents, you share that same percentage with your brothers and sisters. This is true even for **fraternal twins** (also known as *dizygotic twins*), who develop in the womb from the union of two separate sperms and eggs. Exceptions to this rule, of course, are **identical twins** (also called *monozygotic twins*), who develop from the union of the same egg and sperm. Identical twins share exactly the same genotype. In contemplating the genetic makeup of identical twins, you might wonder whether identical twins are truly identical. The answer is that they are identical genetically, but they may not express their identical genes in the same ways. That is, their phenotypes may not be identical. Environmental factors, such as stress and nutrition, can actually cause certain genes to become activated or deactivated, so that even identical twins may not have the same *active* genetic makeup (Lytton & Gallagher, 2002; McClearn, 1993).

sex chromosomes One of the 23 pairs of chromosomes, this pair determines whether an individual is male or female.

fraternal twins Twins who develop from the union of two separate sperm and eggs; also known as *dizygotic twins*.

identical twins Twins who develop from the union of the same egg and sperm, and thus share exactly the same genotype; also known as *monozygotic twins*.

3-4b Both Heredity and Environment Influence Physical and Behavioral Traits

Thus far, you have learned not that we only inherit our genes from our parents, but also that the interaction of genotype (our underlying genetic composition) with the environment can produce changes in our phenotype (our visible and measurable traits). The interdisciplinary field of **behavior genetics** studies how the genotype and the environment of an organism influence its behavior (Dick & Rose, 2002; Sémon et al., 2005).

behavior genetics The study of how the genotype and the environment of an organism influence its behavior.

One example of how heredity and environment can influence phenotype is obesity, a condition afflicting many adults (Kuczmarski et al., 1994). What causes obesity? Overeating is certainly an important cause of weight gain, but some people can consume many calories without gaining a pound. What accounts for these individual differences? Research suggests that obesity is partly related to the number and size of fat cells in the body, with the number being determined by our genes and the size being determined by our eating habits (Grinker, 1982). When people overeat beyond their bodies' needs, the number of fat cells does not increase, but the size of the fat cells does (Rodin & Wing, 1988). Studies of adopted children and of twins indicate that heredity is an important factor in determining both how many fat cells you have and how efficiently you utilize your intake of calories (Bouchard et al., 1990; Stunkard et al., 1990). Apparently, some people are born with an overabundance of fat cells, while others are born with a tendency to burn excess calories by turning them into muscle tissue rather than fat. Thus, regardless of whether they are raised together or apart, identical twins—whose genes are the same—have virtually the same weight. By contrast, the weights of fraternal twins—whose genes are different—differ greatly. In addition, the body sizes of children adopted from birth more closely resemble the body sizes of their biological parents, who share 50 percent of the children's genes, than those of their adoptive parents. This example illustrates that both heredity and environment can influence a specific phenotypic characteristic, namely, body size. Although the nature of gene-environment interaction is still not clearly understood, we do know that neither genes nor environment alone can account for how we live our lives.

3-4c Molecular Genetics Seeks to Identify Specific Genes That Influence Behavior

Don't Read.

molecular genetics The subdiscipline in biology that studies the molecular structure and function of genes to determine how they influence behavior.

While behavior genetics has focused on determining the degree to which genes influence behavior, a relatively new area in the biological sciences is **molecular genetics,** which seeks to identify the *specific genes* that influence behavior. One hope is that discoveries in molecular genetics will provide cures for genetically influenced disorders (Avise, 2004). Many diseases are caused by *mutations,* which are chemical changes in the DNA sequence of a gene (Benet-Pagès et al., 2005; Epstein et al., 2004). When the instructions that a gene provides to a cell are incorrect due to mutations, the resulting protein may not function properly or may not even be produced, and the affected cells no longer perform as expected. For example, molecular geneticists have discovered that mutations in genes that provide instructions for the cholesterol receptor protein cause a disease called *familial hypercholesterolemia.* Individuals with this condition cannot remove a sufficient amount of low-density *lipoprotein (LDL),* or bad cholesterol, from their bloodstream, putting them at increased risk for both heart attacks and strokes (Garcia et al., 2001).

Most research in molecular genetics has been conducted using nonhuman genomes, such as those of the fruit fly, the roundworm, and the laboratory mouse (Meikle et al., 2005). These simpler genetically constructed animals provide useful models for developing and testing the procedures needed for studying the much more complex human genome. The results of this work have already yielded valuable knowledge that has helped geneticists identify single genes associated with a number of diseases and age-related disorders, such as cystic fibrosis, colon cancer, and hearing loss. Research is also underway to discover the mechanisms for diseases caused by several genes or by single genes interacting with environmental factors (Ertekin-Taner et al., 2005). By identifying the genes and their proteins associated with disease susceptibility and the aging process, scientists will be better able to design more effective therapies and preventive measures. For example, researchers have identified a gene that prevents the regeneration of inner ear cells critical to hearing (Sage et al., 2005). If geneticists discover how to "turn off" this gene, they can potentially reverse hearing loss among the elderly. Investigators are also attempting to identify genes that play a role in various psychological disorders, learning disabilities, and other health problems such as diabetes and alcoholism.

Advances and Ethical Concerns Involving Genetic Testing

Genetic tests have been developed to determine the risk that people might have for specific diseases. To date, tests are available for about two dozen diseases, and more will be added as additional disease genes are discovered (Tercyak, 2003). Such testing involves examining a person's DNA—most often taken from cells in a sample of blood—for some alteration indicating the likelihood of a disease or disorder. Genetic testing might also include biochemical tests for the presence or absence of key proteins that signal altered genes.

The most common genetic test is conducted on newborn infants to screen them for abnormal or missing gene products (Patenaude, 2005). Four million newborns undergo such testing each year in the United States. Genetic testing of fetuses in the mother's womb is also increasingly common, especially when there is a risk of bearing a child with genes associated with mental retardation or severe birth defects. Do you perceive any dangers that might result from such prenatal screening? One danger is that these tests can easily determine the sex of a fetus. Parents in such countries as China and India—which place a much higher value on male babies than on female babies—have used prenatal genetic testing to abort pregnancies involving undesirable female fetuses. Estimates are that millions of such sex-selective abortions have already been carried out, which will likely lead to future male-female population imbalances in these countries (Das Gupta & Mari Bhat, 1997).

Adult genetic testing also raises serious ethical issues (Gaivoronskaia & Solem, 2004). For example, if testing reveals that an individual has an inherited risk for colon cancer, early-onset Alzheimer's disease, or a specific psychological disorder, should family members be informed that they may be at risk? This question has generated concerns within the medical community regarding the conflict between the physician's ethical obligations to respect the privacy of genetic information versus the potential liabilities resulting from the physician's failure to notify at-risk relatives. The failure to warn family members about hereditary disease risks has already resulted in at least three lawsuits in the United States (Offit et al., 2004). Another related concern involves the dangers in releasing genetic information to persons and organizations outside the family of those tested. For example, if a family has an inherited gene that makes them highly likely to develop a specific disease, this information could affect their future employability and insurability if it became public knowledge. That is, such results could be misused by employers and insurers, discriminating between those identified as low risk and high risk (Raithatha & Smith, 2004).

The Ethics of Cloning

Even more serious ethical concerns have been raised about **cloning,** which is the process of making a genetically identical organism through nonsexual means. Actually, cloning refers to three very different procedures that have very different goals.

Embryo cloning is a medical technique that duplicates the process that nature uses to produce twins or triplets. One or more cells are removed from a fertilized embryo and encouraged to develop into duplicate embryos. This procedure has been performed for many years on different animal species, but only very limited experimentation has been done on humans.

Adult DNA cloning, or *reproductive cloning,* is a technique used to produce a duplicate of an existing animal. To date this technique has been used to clone such mammals as mice, sheep, cats, cows, and horses. In reproductive cloning, the DNA from a female egg is removed and replaced with the DNA from a cell removed from an adult animal. Then the fertilized egg is implanted in a womb and allowed to develop into a new animal. Animal studies reveal that such cloning can produce severe genetic defects. For this reason alone, there are serious ethical concerns about human cloning, and many countries have specifically outlawed this procedure.

Finally, *therapeutic cloning,* or *biomedical cloning,* is a procedure in which *stem cells*—which are immature cells from which all mature cells develop—are removed from a pre-embryo so that tissue or a whole organ can be produced. The goal of therapeutic cloning is to produce a healthy copy of a sick person's tissue or organ, and it is vastly superior to relying on organ transplants

cloning The process of making a genetically identical organism through nonsexual means.

from other people (Civin et al., 2005; Turksen, 2004). Although the ethical issues surrounding the use of stem cells are not as readily apparent as those involving human cloning, some people argue that embryonic stem cells represent a human life and that this life is destroyed in therapeutic cloning. This is an ongoing debate that brings up the question of when life begins.

As you see, unlocking the mysteries of the human genome entails both great rewards and great risks, as well as mind-boggling ethical concerns. In the coming years, advances in molecular genetics and the controversies surrounding how to use this knowledge will undoubtedly have a significant impact on our lives. Stay tuned.

3-4d Controversies Surround Genetic Explanations of Certain Sex and Race Differences

In January 2005, at a conference on increasing the number of women and minorities in science and engineering careers, Harvard University President Lawrence Summers stated that he wondered whether the low representation of women in these two fields might be caused by females being genetically deficient compared to males in their math abilities. Could this hypothesized genetic difference further explain why Harvard University under Summers's leadership had offered only four of its last 32 tenured jobs to women? Although Summers later apologized for his remarks, he reminded reporters that he was only putting forward a hypothesis proposed by certain geneticists. This public controversy is part of an ongoing debate in psychology and other sciences concerning whether certain culturally important differences found between women and men are caused by genetic factors or life experiences (the old *nature-nurture* debate). Similar controversies also exist concerning cognitive and behavioral differences found between racial groups (see chapter 10, section 10-4c). In this text we will examine the research surrounding these group-based comparisons (for example, see section 3-3f in this chapter). To help you better understand the complexities in the various debates concerning genetic determinants of group differences in thought and action, I want to introduce you to a few important concepts and issues.

What Is the Difference between Sex and Gender?

The terms *sex* and *gender* are often used interchangeably. However, to better understand what it means to be female and male, a growing number of psychologists believe that distinctions should be made between these two concepts (Lippa, 2005). In this text, **sex** refers to the biological status of being female or male, and **gender** refers to the meanings that societies and individuals attach to being female and male. Put simply, sex is a matter of genetic construction, and gender is a matter of cultural construction (Yoder, 1999). Sex is something we *are,* whereas gender is something we *do* with the help and encouragement of others.

People are often confused about the distinction between sex and gender because the two concepts are generally thought of as going together—that is, female = feminine, and male = masculine. Yet behaviors or interests considered masculine in one culture may be defined as feminine in others (Zinn et al., 2000). For instance, in certain North African societies, decorating and beautifying the face and body is a sign of masculinity, not femininity. Similarly, within cultures, beliefs about gender transform over time. For instance, in contemporary North American culture, it is now acceptable—even encouraged—for girls to participate in sports that were previously designated only for boys. Among adults, women are now much more actively involved in careers outside the household (a masculine domain), and men are more involved in child care (a feminine domain) than in previous generations. Gender is not fixed—it is constantly changing and being redefined.

Because sex is biologically based and gender is culturally based, when research finds that men and women actually behave differently, we often ask whether this difference is due to sex (biology) or to gender (culture). This is not an idle question. If someone labels the behavior in question a *sex difference,* the implication is that the cause of the difference is rooted in human biology rather than in social or cultural factors. In contrast, when people talk about *gender differences,* the implication is that these differences do not stem from biology, but rather, that they develop in the course of socialization as boys and girls learn about appropriate gender-based attitudes, roles, and behaviors.

As discussed in section 3-4a, men and women differ biologically in a number of ways. The most basic sex difference is that males carry the chromosomal pattern XY, and females carry

sex The biological status of being female or male.

gender The meanings that societies and individuals attach to being female and male.

the pattern XX. This important difference at the chromosomal level produces differences in female and male anatomy and physical appearance. For instance, a newborn male has a penis and testicles, while a newborn female has a vagina and ovaries. At puberty, a male develops a prominent Adam's apple, while a female's breasts enlarge. Although the changes associated with puberty occur well after birth, no one would seriously argue that boys have been taught how to grow an Adam's apple or that girls learn how to grow breasts. These particular differences are due to biological factors—that is, they are sex differences and are not due to cultural experience. Beyond these identifiable biological differences in chromosome pattern and anatomy, it is extremely difficult, if not impossible, to presently conclude that differences in the way women and men think, feel, and act are clearly due to sex or gender. As already discussed, psychologists with a biological or evolutionary orientation emphasize biological factors in explaining such differences, whereas psychologists with a sociocultural orientation weigh in with cultural explanations. Yet the point that many psychologists often make when the issue of genetics is discussed is that, even in those instances when genetics influences behavioral differences between men and women, these biologically based differences can be greatly increased or decreased due to social forces (Eisenberg et al., 1996; Vasta et al., 1996).

How great are the differences between women and men in their psychological functioning? This is an issue we will address throughout this text. As a preliminary answer, I can tell you that research conducted over the past 20 years indicates there are many more similarities than differences. Across a wide variety of cognitive skills, psychological motives, and social behaviors, men and women do not differ from one another. Thus, despite cultural stereotypes to the contrary, women and men are remarkably alike in much of their psychological functioning. Reflecting these scientific findings, in this text I do not use the misleading term *opposite sex* when comparing one sex with the other but instead use the more appropriate term *other sex*.

Does Race Tell Us Anything Useful about How People Differ Genetically?

The *Oxford English Dictionary* defines race as a group of persons connected by a common descent; a subdivision of species. Consistent with this definition, many people believe that Caucasians, Blacks, Asians, and Hispanics make up biologically distinct races. Often underlying this common belief in race categorization is the assumption that greater genetic similarity exists among the members of each race than between the races. Yet are two people categorized as Black more genetically similar than a Black person and an Asian person, or a Caucasian person and a Hispanic person?

Analysis of fossilized skull fragments found in Ethiopia, a country in eastern Africa, has led scientists to estimate that the very first modern-looking human beings emerged about 195,000 years ago (McDougall et al., 2005; White et al., 2003). This research, coupled with fossil evidence from other scientists and genetic analysis of contemporary human populations throughout the world, strongly suggests that it was these first modern *Homo sapiens* in eastern Africa who eventually populated the rest of the planet (Clark et al., 2003; Stringer, 2003). Thus, all humans are related, and our common ancestors came from Africa. What then is the biological significance of race?

When early humans migrated to different areas of the planet, they often encountered physical environments vastly different from those in eastern Africa. Over the course of thousands of generations, human populations that were geographically separated from one another gradually began to differ in their physical appearance due to the effects of natural selection (see chapter 1, section 1-3e). For example, the dark skin of early humans in Africa offered protection against the intense ultraviolet light in the region. Too much ultraviolet light penetrating the skin not only causes skin cancer but also, more importantly, breaks down folic acid in the body, which can cause anemia and deadly birth defects. Thus, in this region of the world—and in other areas close to the equator—darker-skinned humans were better adapted to their surroundings and more likely to produce healthy offspring than those with light skin. However, those humans who had migrated to northern Europe and northern North America lived in parts of the world with much less sunlight. In these new surroundings, they needed much lighter skin in order to take in more ultraviolet light for the production of vitamin D, which is essential for absorbing calcium to build strong bones and teeth. Here, light skin provided an advantage over dark skin (Jablonski, 1998; Jablonski & Chaplin, in press). Lighter-skinned humans produced more vitamin D than those with darker skin, and they were ultimately more successful in surviving and reproducing. Likewise, humans who migrated to very cold climates gradually became shorter and more round, because this body type lost less heat and thus was better adapted to the frigid environment. In contrast, in very hot climates, taller, thinner body frames were advantageous because they dispersed heat more effectively so that the body stayed cooler. Large, circular nostrils and broad noses also helped disperse extra heat among people living in hot climates, while smaller, noncircular nostrils and more projecting noses helped warm the incoming air for people living in cold climates.

The superficial physical differences resulting from this migration of early humans to different world regions are what many of us now rely on when designating a person's race. Yet almost all anthropologists and many geneticists agree that the concept of race is purely a social construct and has very little to do with who is actually genetically similar to whom (M. N. Cohen, 2002; Fish, 2002; Smedley & Smedley, 2005). For example, DNA research demonstrates that genetically all humans, regardless of skin color, facial features, and other surface distinctions, are basically identical. Any person's race accounts for less than one-fourth of 1 percent of her or his genetic makeup (Lewontin, 1995; Ossorio & Duster, 2005). The genetic differences that account for these evolutionary-based adaptations in physical appearance probably involve only a few hundred of the billions of nucleotides in a person's DNA.

Would it surprise you to learn that greater genetic diversity exists among the different human populations in Africa than among the different populations in Asia, Europe, and North and South America? Would you also be surprised to learn that non-African populations are more genetically similar to many African populations than the African populations are to each other? In essence, this means that if you identify yourself as African American, it is quite likely that you are genetically more similar to a randomly chosen person who is White, Hispanic, or Asian than you are to another African American who is not a direct blood relative. This is because the human species has spent most of its 195,000-year existence in Africa, and as mentioned in chapter 9, section 9-1a, many human populations in Africa have been physically separated from each other longer than they have been separated from the human populations in other parts of the world. Thus, more genetic differences exist between the indigenous peoples of Africa than between them and non-Africans.

Given this scientific fact, what exactly does the race of a person tell us about his or her genetic makeup? As previously mentioned, it tells us very little: 99.76 percent of our genetic makeup has nothing to do with race. But does the less than one-fourth of 1 percent genetic difference account for any differences other than the superficial physical characteristics we use in making racial classifications in the first place? This question is currently being studied and intensely discussed in the scientific community (Anderson & Nickerson, 2005; Bonham et al., 2005). In the meantime, we can cast aside the *Oxford English Dictionary* definition of race. What we call "races" are not biologically distinct from one another and, thus, are definitely not subspecies in the human population. Biologically, there is only one race: the human race.

Section Review

- Genes are the biochemical units of inheritance located on and transmitted by chromosomes.
- Chromosomes, threadlike structures containing strands of DNA, are found in all human body cells except red blood cells.
- Humans have much less within-species genetic variability than do the other primate species.
- Humans share 99.9 percent of their genes, but great genetic variation exists across individuals in the final 0.1 percent.
- The field of behavior genetics studies how an organism's genetic makeup and environment influence its behavior.
- The field of molecular genetics studies how specific genes influence behavior, and the application of this knowledge has raised many ethical concerns.
- When differences in thinking and action are found between women and men or between people from different racial groups, genetically based researchers and socioculturally based researchers offer very different explanations of these differences.

Psychological Applications

If You Are Left-Handed, Is Your Brain Organized Differently from That of a Right-Hander?

Are you a "lefty" or a "righty"? Actually, people rarely use the same hand for all manual activities. Instead, they tend to use one hand for more tasks than the other. One of the most commonly employed questionnaires to assess a person's *direction* and *degree* of handedness is the *Edinburgh Handedness Inventory* (Oldfield, 1971), reproduced in Self-Discovery Questionnaire 3-1. Before reading further, complete this questionnaire to determine your *laterality quotient*.

Self-Discovery
Questionnaire **3-1**

What Is Your Direction and Degree of Handedness?

INTERACTIVE BOX

Instructions: Consider each of the 10 activities listed below and indicate which hand you prefer using when engaged in each of these different tasks by placing an "x" in either the "left" or the "right" box.

	Left	Right
1. Writing	☐	☒
2. Drawing	☐	☒
3. Throwing	☐	☒
4. Scissors	☐	☒
5. Toothbrush	☐	☒
6. Knife (without fork)	☐	☒
7. Spoon	☐	☒
8. Broom (upper hand)	☐	☒
9. Striking match (match)	☐	☒
10. Opening box (lid)	☐	☒

Scoring: Once hand preferences for all 10 activities have been identified, your *laterality quotient* is found by subtracting the number of left x's from right x's, and then multiplying by 10. The quotient's range extends from +100 for extreme right-handedness to −100 for extreme left-handedness, with 0 representing ambidextrous activity (that is, equal use of both hands). About 50 percent of right-handers who completed this questionnaire had laterality quotients greater than 80, while 50 percent of left-handers had quotients less than −76. These findings indicate that (1) people tend to exhibit a preference for one hand over the other rather than being ambidextrous, and (2) right-handers are stronger hand-dominant than left-handers.

Source: From "The assessment and analysis of handedness: The Edinburgh Inventory" by R. C. Oldfield in *Neuropsychologia, 9,* 1971, pp. 97–114. Copyright © 1971, with permission from Elsevier Science.

What Makes You Right-Handed or Left-Handed?

If you are predominantly left-handed, you are among the 7–8 percent minority of people who live in a right-handed world (Iaccino, 1993). What determines hand preference in the first place? Both environmental and genetic theorists have proposed opposing explanations.

Environmental theorists argue that very powerful cultural pressures are brought to bear on many natural left-handers, causing them to use their right hand (Ashton, 1982; Coren & Halpern, 1991). For example, many tools, materials, and items of equipment—including power saws, can openers, fishing reels, bowling balls, scissors, and school desks—are designed for right-handed persons. Given this right-handed bias, left-handers can function most effectively only if they learn to use their nondominant hand for most tasks. Due to this process of

Continued next page—

Psychological Applications

—Continued

nurtural (rather than natural) selection, a number of left-handers gradually convert to the right hand. Although this *Right-Sided World Argument* (Porac & Coren, 1981) may explain the conversion of some left-handers, it cannot explain the consistency in the prevalence of right- and left-handedness across cultures that differ in their tolerance of left-handedness. That is, even though conventional schooling in Germany, Greece, Asia, and Russia discourages left-handed writing, manifestations of left-handedness in those countries are comparable to those observed in more tolerant countries, such as the United States and Canada (Annett, 1985).

Genetic theorists point to a variety of sources to support their contention that handedness is determined by our biology. For example, when the human figures depicted in more than 1,000 drawings, paintings, and engravings spanning thousands of years are analyzed regarding their handedness, 90 percent are right-handers (Coren, 1989). Likewise, ultrasound studies of fetal thumb-sucking indicate the same percentage of left-right hand preferences, further suggesting that handedness may be an inherited trait (Hepper et al., 1990). Yet one problem with a simple genetic expla-

This is my college roommate and traveling companion, Ted (see chapter 1), who happens to be left-handed. Most tools in our culture are designed for right-handed persons, often forcing left-handers to adapt and use their nondominant hand for most tasks. When Ted first started playing golf, using right-handed clubs, he could barely hit the ball. His game improved tremendously after he found clubs for his dominant hand. He still performs some tasks with his nondominant hand, due to the unavailability of left-handed tools.

Source: Courtesy of Figzoi.

nation of handedness is that 54 percent of the children of two left-handed parents are right-handed (Coren, 1992). What we know about genetics would lead us to expect more left-handed children in this case. Even more troublesome is the fact that identical twins are no more likely to prefer the same hand than are fraternal twins (Coren & Halpern, 1991; Sicotte et al., 1999).

Faced with these problems, some genetic theorists have proposed that handedness is related to the lateralization of the brain. They argue that, although there may be no specific gene for left- or right-handedness, there is a dominant gene responsible for the development of speech in the left hemisphere, and this gene also predisposes people toward right-handedness (Annett, 1985). Support for this view comes from studies indicating that, while more than 95 percent of right-handers have speech localized to the left hemisphere, only about 65 percent of left-handers show this same pattern (Loring et al., 1990; Springer & Deutsch, 1998). The remaining 35 percent of left-handers tend to process speech using either the right hemisphere or both hemispheres. These findings suggest that, for left-handers, the two hemispheres are less specialized than they are for right-handers. Due to this difference, left-handers experience less language loss following damage to either hemisphere and recover more quickly than right-handers, because their healthy hemisphere is better equipped to assume the speech functions (Provins, 1997).

Is Being Left-Handed Hazardous to Your Health?

Some scientific studies have found a weak association between left-handedness and a variety of pathological conditions, including mental retardation, reading disabilities, epilepsy, alcoholism, schizophrenia, and allergies (Bryson, 1990; Ostatnikova et al., 2000). Although the percentage of left-handers who have such problems is very small, researchers have proposed possible explanations for even this weak association.

One explanation is that because some left-handers show evidence of language ability in both hemispheres, this duplication of language functions may impede other cognitive functions in the right hemisphere, such as visuospatial ability, resulting in cognitive deficits (Levy, 1969). Does this hypothesis sound familiar? It is exactly the same hypothesis offered for why women—who also tend to be bilateral for language proficiency—generally are less adept than men at spatial tasks. But surprisingly, although both left-handers and women tend to be bilateralized for language, women are not more likely than men to be left-handed.

Another explanation contends that prenatal hormonal imbalances or birth stress may cause neurological disturbances in the left hemisphere, which in turn cause the right hemisphere to become dominant (Coren & Halpern, 1991). According to this hypothesis, not only do these right-hemisphere-dominant individuals begin favoring their left hands, but also the neu-

Psychological Applications

—continued

rological problems in their left hemisphere make them more susceptible to the previously mentioned mental and physical health problems.

At present, we are not sure why left-handers are slightly more susceptible to these problems than are right-handers. What we do know is that, just as left-handers are somewhat more likely to experience certain health problems, they are also more likely to emerge as gifted and creative individuals (Benbow & Stanley, 1983). Indeed, the incidence of left-handedness is much higher in artists than in the population as a whole (Mebert & Michel, 1980). Although the meaning of these findings is still unclear, they certainly pose problems for the hypothesis that left-handedness is caused by some sort of cognitive defect. Thus, taking everything into account, neither right-handers nor left-handers can claim a decided advantage over the other when it comes to adapting to their world.

Key Terms

acetylcholine (ACh) (p. 58)

action potential (p. 56)

adrenal glands (p. 65)

aphasia (p. 77)

autonomic nervous system (p. 61)

axon (p. 54)

behavior genetics (p. 86)

blood-brain barrier (p. 82)

central nervous system (p. 62)

cerebellum (p. 69)

cerebral cortex (p. 72)

cerebral hemispheres (p. 73)

cerebral lateralization (p. 74)

cerebrospinal fluid (p. 62)

chromosomes (p. 84)

cloning (p. 87)

computerized axial tomography (CAT) (p. 66)

corpus callosum (p. 73)

dendrites (p. 54)

deoxyribonucleic acid (DNA) (p. 84)

dopamine (DA) (p. 58)

electroencephalograph (EEG) (p. 66)

endocrine system (p. 64)

endorphins (p. 59)

forebrain (p. 70)

fraternal twins (p. 85)

frontal lobe (p. 74)

functional magnetic resonance imaging (fMRI) (p. 67)

gender (p. 88)

gene (p. 84)

genotype (p. 84)

glial cells (p. 54)

gonads (p. 65)

hindbrain (p. 69)

hormones (p. 64)

hypothalamus (p. 70)

identical twins (p. 85)

interneurons (p. 54)

limbic system (p. 70)

magnetic resonance imaging (MRI) (p. 66)

medulla (p. 69)

midbrain (p. 69)

molecular genetics (p. 86)

motor neurons (p. 54)

myelin sheath (p. 54)

nerve (p. 61)

neurons (p. 53)

neurotransmitters (p. 57)

occipital lobe (p. 74)

parasympathetic nervous system (p. 61)

parietal lobe (p. 74)

peripheral nervous system (p. 60)

phenotype (p. 84)

pituitary gland (p. 64)

pons (p. 69)

positron emission tomography (PET) (p. 66)

reflex (p. 63)

resting potential (p. 55)

reticular formation (p. 69)

sensory neurons (p. 54)

serotonin (p. 59)

sex (p. 88)

sex chromosomes (p. 85)

soma (p. 54)

somatic nervous system (p. 61)

spinal cord (p. 63)

sympathetic nervous system (p. 61)

synapse (p. 54)

temporal lobe (p. 74)

thalamus (p. 70)

thyroid gland (p. 65)

Suggested Websites

Society for Neuroscience
http://www.sfn.org
This official website for the Society for Neuroscience provides brochures and newsletters on a number of relevant topics.

Neurosciences on the Internet
http://www.neuroguide.com
This website provides a wealth of information on the brain and nervous system. You will find facts on brain disorders and neurosurgery, as well as on the disciplines of psychology and psychiatry.

The Whole Brain Atlas
http://www.med.harvard.edu/AANLIB/home.html
This website, produced by the Harvard Medical School, provides a great deal of information and animated graphics about the brain, neuroimaging techniques, and brain disorders such as strokes and Alzheimer's disease.

Brain Model Tutorial
http://pegasus.cc.ucf.edu/~Brainmd1/brain.html
This "teaching" website is devoted to the various parts and functions of the brain.

Review Questions

Note: You can find the correct answers to these questions by taking the quiz and then submitting your answers in the Online Edition. The program will automatically score your submission. If you miss a question, the program will provide the correct answer, a rationale for the answer, and the section number in the chapter where the topic is discussed.

1. The story of Henry M. illustrates that
   a. the hippocampus is responsible for emotional expression.
   b. the brain has sensory receptors.
   c. the brain is a complex organ that scientists are only beginning to understand.
   d. neurons account for all human thoughts and action.
   e. none of the above

2. Which of the following neurons sends commands from the brain to our muscles?
   a. interneurons
   b. sensory neurons
   c. motor neurons
   d. flexineurons
   e. muscular neurons

3. All the following make up a synapse *except*
   a. the myelin sheath.
   b. the terminal button.
   c. the synaptic cleft.
   d. the dendrite of another neuron.
   e. *a* and *b*

4. Which of the following statements is *true*?
   a. Neurons never synapse on somas.
   b. Neurons receive and transmit nervous system information.
   c. The brain and spinal cord are solid masses of neurons.
   d. Glial cells make up a very small percentage of the brain's mass.
   e. *b* and *d*

5. The speed of neuron impulses
   a. is always constant within a given neuron.
   b. can vary.
   c. increases with the diameter of the axon.
   d. is slower than an electrical impulse.
   e. all of the above

6. Which neurotransmitter is associated with the regulation of emotional states such as depression and anxiety?
   a. endorphins
   b. serotonin
   c. dopamine
   d. naproxen sodium
   e. acetylcholine

7. Neuroscientists believe that neurotransmitters such as ACh, DA, and endorphins are responsible for
   a. convulsions and severe muscle contractions.
   b. cognition and the formation of new memories.
   c. influencing thought and emotion.
   d. *a* and *b*
   e. *a, b,* and *c*

8. What causes a neuron to fire?
   a. dendrites
   b. inhibitory neurotransmitters
   c. a flood of electrically charged ions that exceeds the threshold
   d. *a* and *b*
   e. *a, b,* and *c*

9. Which of the following diseases or illness may result from too much or too little of a neurotransmitter?
   a. Parkinson's disease
   b. schizophrenia
   c. botulism
   d. all of the above
   e. none of the above

10. The peripheral nervous system consists of the
    a. somatic and endocrine systems.
    b. somatic, sympathetic, and parasympathetic nervous systems.
    c. brain and spinal cord.
    d. *b* and *c*
    e. none of the above

11. The autonomic nervous system plays a part in which of the following bodily functions?
    a. blood pressure, heart rate
    b. digestion
    c. breathing
    d. all of the above
    e. *a* and *b*

12. Which of the following statements is *true?*
    a. The central nervous system cannot repair itself.
    b. All body actions require interaction between the brain and spinal cord.
    c. If a section of the spinal cord is severed, a person loses all sensation and muscle control above the injury.
    d. none of the above
    e. *a* and *c*

13. According to the text, what is the most important function of the pituitary gland?
    a. constriction of certain blood vessels
    b. secretion of cerebrospinal fluid to protect the brain
    c. development of sex organs
    d. regulation of the body's reactions to stress and resistance to disease
    e. none of the above

14. Which of the following is *not* a technique used in brain imaging?
    a. MRI
    b. CTS
    c. CAT
    d. EEG
    e. PET

15. If you wanted to study the blood flow or chemical makeup of the brain, you would use
    a. an EEG.
    b. a CAT scan or MRI.
    c. a PET.
    d. an fMRI.
    e. *c* and *d*

16. The hindbrain is involved in controlling
    a. breathing, heart rate, swallowing, and digestion.
    b. sleep and arousal.
    c. learning and body movement.
    d. all of the above
    e. *b* and *c*

17. If I am unable to remember new skills, which region of my brain is likely damaged?
    a. the occipital lobe
    b. the parietal lobe
    c. the temporal lobe
    d. none of the above
    e. *a* and *c*

18. The brain cannot function
    a. without both of the cerebral hemispheres.
    b. if there is damage to the cerebellum.
    c. with a cut corpus callosum.
    d. all of the above
    e. none of the above

19. Which of the following statements is *true?*
    a. Women's brains tend to be more bilateralized for language than do men's brains.
    b. Women tend to be less adept at spatial tasks than are men.
    c. Similarities in brain function between men and women far outweigh any differences.
    d. all of the above
    e. *a* and *b*

20. Which of the following statements is *true?*
    a. You receive half your genetic blueprint from each parent.
    b. Of all the human genes, 50 percent are identical in all humans.
    c. There are chromosomes in every cell of the body.
    d. The environment does not influence phenotype.
    e. all of the above

21. The goal of molecular genetics is to
    a. find genetic mutations and change them.
    b. understand how evolutionary forces shaped behavior.
    c. discover specific genes that influence behavior.
    d. create "super" genes that will improve people's health.
    e. identify the commonalities between animals and humans.

22. Therapeutic or biomedical cloning is a procedure in which
    a. stem cells are used to create bodily tissue of organs.
    b. DNA is extracted to produce a duplicate animal.
    c. fertilized embryos are split into duplicate embryos.
    d. mutated genes are replaced with normal genes from a donor.
    e. living replications of deceased people are created from sample cells.

23. A culturally based term used to refer to societal standards of whether one is male or female is known as
    a. sex.
    b. gender.
    c. orientation.
    d. sexuality.
    e. status.

Chapter 4

Human Development

When I was in fourth grade, there was a period of time when I spent a good deal of the school day leaning forward so that I put almost all my weight on the front right leg of my desk. Why? Because that desk leg was balancing on top of a lump of coal about the size of my fist. I had found the lump of coal on the school playground, near the furnace room. While Mrs. Rahm talked about math, science, and U.S. history, I earnestly pressed down on that black rock at my feet. Why? Because I had a plan. You see, in the latest issue of *Superman* comics, the Man of Steel had taken a fist-sized piece of coal, squeezed it in his superhand for a few seconds, and transformed it into a valuable diamond. I knew I was no Superman, but I also knew I was only 9 years old and had a lot of years left in me. If the Man of Steel could use his superhuman strength to turn a lump of coal into a precious diamond in only a few seconds, then maybe I could do the same thing if I desk-pressured my coal from now until high school graduation. So at the end of each school day, I would pull my project out from under that desk leg and inspect it carefully, looking for any signs of crystal growth.

Needless to say, I never witnessed any mineral transformation during Mrs. Rahm's class that year. Yet, while that lump of coal remained essentially unchanged, the child sitting at the desk above it was undergoing many transformations. Indeed, every child in that classroom was changing during the course of that school year. Some of these changes could be attributed to the "mind pressure" that Mrs. Rahm exerted on us every school day, while others were due to "peer pressure," "parental pressure," and, yes, the "biological pressure" changing us from within. Unlike the hands of Superman, which can take sole credit for turning coal into a diamond, in the real world the **development** of a child is the result of many forces working simultaneously. In our journey of discovery concerning human development, it is our job to analyze these forces so we better understand their role in shaping not only who we are now but also who we will become.

> **development** The systematic physical, cognitive, and social changes in the individual that occur between conception and death.

4-1 PHYSICAL AND PRENATAL DEVELOPMENT

Preview

- *What is involved in human development?*
- *What physical transformations take place following conception?*
- *What possible dangers to normal physical development occur before birth?*
- *Is the newborn's perceptual world more than a "blooming, buzzing confusion" of sensations?*
- *How is the brain "sculpted" during infancy?*

Look at the period at the end of this sentence. That's approximately the single-cell size of all human beings shortly after conception. Compare that dot to your current size. How did such an incredible transformation take place? Don't look to Superman for an answer; instead, let's go back to before you were even a dot.

4-1a Prenatal Development Occurs in Three Stages

Every month, an egg is released by one of a woman's two ovaries and travels down to her fallopian tubes. During this time, if she has sexual intercourse with a man, and if any of his seminal fluid is deposited into her vagina, she could become pregnant. During sexual intercourse, a man ejaculates between 200 and 500 million sperm into a woman's vagina, but only a few thousand will actually complete the 6- or 7-inch journey to the fallopian tubes. If an egg is present and one of the sperm successfully fertilizes it, a new cell is formed. If all goes well, a baby is born about 38 weeks later. During that period, the many changes that transform the fertilized egg into a newborn baby are known as **prenatal development.** Prenatal development can be divided into three stages: the zygote, the embryo, and the fetus.

> **prenatal development** The many changes that transform a fertilized egg into a newborn baby.

Zygote Stage

As you recall from chapter 3, section 3-4a, in humans, each male sperm cell and each female egg cell contain 23 chromosomes. When the sperm fertilizes the egg, the new cell, the *zygote,* contains 46 chromosomes, or 23 pairs, with half the genetic material coming from each parent. The zygote travels down the fallopian tube toward the uterus, dividing into an ever more complex, multicelled ball every 12 hours. On rare occasions, the zygote splits into two separate clusters that will eventually become identical (*monozygotic*) twins. Fraternal (*dizygotic*) twins develop when two eggs are released by the ovaries and fertilized by different sperm cells. The **zygote stage** lasts 2 weeks, from conception until the zygote implants itself in the wall of the uterus. By the end of the second week, the zygote is about 1 millimeter in diameter and consists of a few thousand cells.

zygote stage The first 2 weeks of prenatal development, from conception until the zygote implants itself in the wall of the uterus.

Embryonic Stage

Mainly due to abnormalities in the chromosomes, about 30 percent of all zygotes are spontaneously aborted (Plomin et al., 1997). If the zygote successfully embeds itself in the uterine wall, this living tissue is considered an embryo. The **embryonic stage** lasts from the third week through the eighth week of prenatal development. During this stage, the head develops before the rest of the body, and arms and legs develop before the hands and feet. Between the fourth and eighth weeks, the gonads of genetically male embryos secrete the hormone *testosterone,* and this stimulates the development of male sex organs. Otherwise, the embryo develops into a female. By the end of the eighth week, the embryo has facial features, fingers, toes, and a functioning heart that pumps blood, yet it is still only an inch long and weighs a tenth of an ounce!

embryonic stage The second stage of prenatal development, lasting from the third week through the eighth week of pregnancy.

Fetal Stage

The last and longest stage in prenatal development is the **fetal stage,** which extends from the ninth week after conception until birth. In the third month, identifiable sex organs appear, bones and muscles develop, and the fetus begins to move. At 4 months, the fetus is large enough (4 to 8 ounces) for the mother to feel its movements. By the seventh month, all the major organs are working, and the fetus has a chance of surviving outside the womb, though not without enormous high-tech medical intervention. Premature babies born this early have trouble breathing because their lungs are not fully developed, and they also cannot adequately regulate their body temperature because insulating body fat doesn't form until the eighth month.

fetal stage The last and longest stage in prenatal development, extending from the ninth week after conception until birth.

4-1b The Fetus Can Be Harmed by Parental and Environmental Factors

Among the risk factors that can harm a developing fetus are a parent's age, maternal nutrition, and harmful environmental agents.

Parental Age

The ages of both the mother and the father can affect prenatal development. The safest ages for women to bear children are from about age 17 or 18 to age 35 (Kessner, 1973). Mothers younger and older than this age range run a greater risk of experiencing spontaneous abortion due to chromosome abnormalities or of having babies with birth defects (Culp et al., 1988; Strigini et al., 1990). For men entering their 30s and 40s, there is a slightly greater risk that a damaged sperm will fertilize an egg and cause genetic abnormalities.

Maternal Nutrition

Because the mother is the fetus's only source of nutrition, her diet is extremely important to its health and development (Campbell et al., 1996; Huffman et al., 2001). According to the United Nation's Children's Fund, 18 million low-birth-weight babies (those weighing less than $5\frac{1}{2}$ pounds) are born every year, accounting for about 14 percent of all live births. The vast majority of these babies (11 million) are born in South Asia, with 3.6 million born in sub-Saharan Africa. These infants often suffer from infections, weakened immune systems, learning disabilities, and impaired physical development. In severe cases, low-birth-weight babies die shortly after birth.

Teratogens

teratogen Any disease, drug, or other noxious agent that causes abnormal prenatal development.

A **teratogen**—which in Greek means "monster maker"—is any disease, drug, or other noxious agent that causes abnormal prenatal development. Although these substances generally do not pose a threat to the pregnant woman's health, they do endanger the fetus and may lead to its death, either before or after birth. Many drugs administered during pregnancy can pose serious risks to the developing embryo or fetus, especially during the first 3 months of development (Brennan et al., 1999). Many teratogens create *mutations* in the developing fetus, which are chemical changes in the genetic code that cause changes in the fetus's underlying genetic composition, or genotype (refer back to chapter 3, section 3-4). One such teratogen is the drug *thalidomide*, which was given to many pregnant women in the late 1950s to treat nausea and vomiting. To the horror of the public and the medical community, this drug was found to cause severe prenatal mutations, causing thousands of babies to be born with deformed arms, legs, hands, and fingers (McBride, 2004; Moore & Persaud, 1993).

fetal alcohol syndrome Physical and cognitive abnormalities in children that result when pregnant women consume large quantities of alcohol.

A more common drug that is dangerous to the fetus is alcohol. Women who drink large quantities of alcohol while pregnant are 30 percent more likely to give birth to babies with **fetal alcohol syndrome,** which is characterized by mental retardation, motor deficits, and heart problems (Barr et al., 1990; Schneider et al., 2002). Children with fetal alcohol syndrome also exhibit facial deformities, such as a small head, a short nose, and widely spaced eyes (Julien, 2001). One way in which alcohol adversely affects the fetus is by reducing the intake and metabolism of several nutrients, including fatty acids that are important for fetal growth and brain development (Beblo et al., 2005). Because evidence indicates that even small amounts of alcohol may cause minor cognitive deficits, most medical experts recommend that expectant mothers drink no alcohol at all during pregnancy (Kaufman, 1997; Streissguth et al., 1993). Table 4-1 lists several drugs that are known teratogens (Jacobson & Jacobson, 2001).

Besides drugs, maternal infections such as rubella (German measles), chickenpox, mumps, and syphilis are another class of teratogens that can be hazardous to the fetus (Isada

Table 4-1	Teratogenic Drugs and Their Consequences on Prenatal Development
Drug	**Potential Consequences**
Alcohol	Heavy drinking can cause fetal alcohol syndrome (facial deformities, heart damage, mental retardation), while moderate drinking may cause small cognitive deficits.
Aspirin	Deficits in intelligence, attention, and motor skills
Antibiotics	Cataracts, retarded skeletal growth, and premature delivery
Anticonvulsants	Heart problems and cleft palate
Caffeine	Premature births, lower birth weight, abnormal reflexes, and decreased muscle tone
Cocaine and heroin	Retarded growth, brain damage, sluggishness, poor attention span, and heart abnormalities
Codeine, morphine, and methadone	Addicted baby, withdrawal symptoms (fever, tremors, convulsions, breathing problems)
Marijuana	Lower birth weight and less motor control
Nicotine	Increased risk of miscarriage, retarded growth, irritability in newborns, chronic respiratory problems, and facial deformities
Thalidomide	Abnormalities in arms and legs
Tranquilizers (other than thalidomide)	May produce respiratory distress in newborns

& Grossman, 1991). Two sexually transmitted diseases, *genital herpes* and *acquired immune deficiency syndrome (AIDS),* are especially dangerous. Genital herpes is typically transmitted to newborns during the birth process when they come in contact with their mothers' genital lesions. Herpes can cause blindness, serious brain damage, paralysis, and even death to the newborn. For these reasons, mothers with active herpes have cesarean deliveries to avoid infecting their babies through contact with the vaginal tract (Hanshaw et al., 1985). Of even greater concern to the fetus is AIDS, the fatal disease caused by the HIV virus. AIDS can be transmitted prenatally if the virus passes through the *placenta,* which is the thick membrane that passes nutrition and oxygen from mother to fetus. The disease also can be transmitted during birth, when exchange of blood may occur between the mother and the newborn as the umbilical cord separates from the placenta, or after birth, when the virus may be passed through the mother's milk during breast-feeding (Kaufman, 1997). Of the 30 percent of babies who contract the HIV virus from their infected mothers, few live longer than 3 years if not treated with antiviral drugs (Nakiyingi et al., 2003; Peters et al., 2002).

4-1c An Infant's Brain Is Overpopulated with Neurons That Compete for Survival

The brain develops its incredible complexity through two simple but powerful processes: (1) producing way too many more brain cells than can possibly survive, and (2) creating a fierce competition between these cells for survival. Both of these processes begin prior to birth.

As discussed in chapter 3, section 3-1, the basic unit of the nervous system is the neuron, or brain cell. You might be surprised to learn that when you were a 6-month-old fetus, you had more than twice as many brain cells as you do now, and your brain produced hundreds of thousands of new neurons per minute (Kolb, 1989; Sowell et al., 2004b). In fact, you reached your maximum brain-cell density 3 months before you were born! This is the process of overproduction. During those final months, your brain was pruned of unnecessary neurons. This commenced the process of neural competition and elimination, which persisted during infancy and early childhood, because as you grew, the billions of neurons were shaped by your environment (Cicchetti, 2002; Giedd et al., 1999). Each sight, sound, and touch you experienced activated and strengthened specific neurons and their connections, while other neurons that were not regularly activated grew weak and died (see figure 4-1).

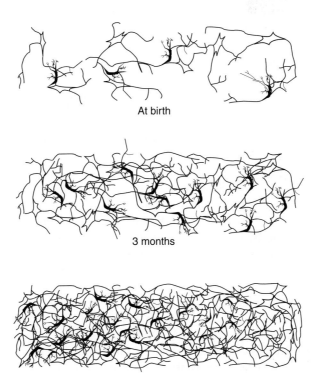

At birth

3 months

15 months

Figure 4-1

Neural Network Growth during Infancy

At what age do we have the most brain neurons? Minus 3 months of age? As we mature during infancy and interact with our environment, the neural connections in our brains grow bushier in appearance, because they are becoming increasingly complex. Depicted here are neurons in an infant's cerebral cortex during the first 15 months of life. How is brain growth an illustration of the use-it-or-lose-it principle?

This use-it-or-lose-it principle in brain development operates throughout life, even during advanced age. Such brain "sculpting" also occurs among other animals, including insects (Kolb & Whishaw, 1998; Strausfeld, 2001). This means that, although an animal's brain is generally programmed by genetics, it is more specifically shaped by life experiences.

Neural development during the early years of life causes the brain's weight to balloon from three-quarters of a pound to about two and a third pounds by age 4. Most of this added mass is due to (1) the growth of new dendrites that increase the connections between neurons, and (2) the growth of the protective coating of fatty cells—known as the *myelin sheath*—around neural axons (Bower, 1994). To understand the importance of brain growth for the overall development of the individual, consider this fact: Although the rest of a newborn's body weighs only about 5 percent of what it will weigh as an adult, its brain is already 25 percent of its adult weight. By age 2, the brain has reached 75 percent of its adult weight, while the body has only grown to 20 percent. At age 5, the brain/body adult percentages are 90 percent and 35 percent, respectively. The most likely reason the brain grows so much more quickly than the rest of the body is that it plays a major role in coordinating the physical and perceptual development of the body as a whole.

Brain development proceeds in stages, generally from back to front. During the first few months of infancy, the area at the back of the brain (the hindbrain) that is developing the most is the cerebellum, which is important in regulating and coordinating basic motor activities such as sucking and swallowing. Between 6 and 8 months of age, greater neurological maturity in the temporal lobes of the cerebral cortex (located in the middle-side of the brain) prepares children for language acquisition. Finally, in late adolescence, neurological development in the frontal cortex allows teenagers to engage in the type of abstract thinking so crucial for complex scientific and moral reasoning (Ohnishi et al., 2004). In essence, brain development provides the necessary neurological underpinnings for our social and cognitive development. The capacity to be skilled in many different areas is literally shaped by the interaction of inherited potential and early life experiences (refer to *reaction range* in chapter 10, section 10-4a). Thus, how you spend your time during infancy and childhood, including the nutrition you receive and the infections you endure, will have a profound impact on your adult neural wiring and complexity (Johnson & Karmiloff-Smith, 2004).

4-1d Physical Growth and Motor Development Occur Hand in Hand

Although the brain grows faster than the rest of the body, infant body growth is by no means slow. During the first year of life, the body almost triples in weight (from about 7 pounds to 20 pounds) and increases in length by about one-third (from about 20 inches to 29 inches). After this initial surge, the rate of childhood growth slows to about 2 to 3 inches and 4 to 7 pounds per year. Middle childhood is a time when bones continue to grow and harden, and muscles grow in strength. A child's height is largely determined by heredity, with tall parents generally having tall children and short parents generally having short children (Plomin, 1984).

Accompanying the physical growth of the body is motor development. Basic motor skills develop from the head downward to the trunk and legs. As depicted in figure 4-2, infants in North American culture lift their heads at about 2 months of age. By 6 months, they can sit up without support, and by the end of the first year, they begin walking. Although this pattern is mirrored in many other cultures, variations do occur. For example, at 10 months of age—when North American infants are only beginning to learn to stand alone—Ugandan infants are already walking. One possible explanation for this cultural difference is that, in Uganda, babies are carried upright on their mothers' backs, which helps develop their trunk and leg muscles at a faster rate than occurs in most North American infants (Bril, 1986).

Reflexes

Newborns enter the world with a number of reflexes. As mentioned in chapter 3, section 3-2b, a *reflex* is an automatic, involuntary response to sensory stimuli. Some reflexes are called *survival reflexes* because they are essential for survival; others are known as *primitive reflexes* because they are believed to be holdovers from our evolutionary history that have outlived their usefulness. Examples of survival reflexes are the eye-blink reflex, which protects us from bright lights and foreign objects, and the sucking reflex, which allows us to receive

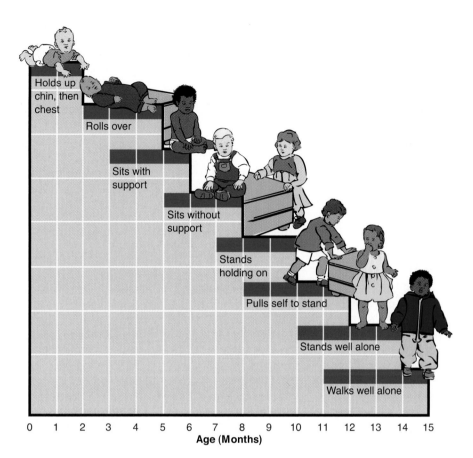

Holds up chin, then chest

Rolls over

Sits with support

Sits without support

Stands holding on

Pulls self to stand

Stands well alone

Walks well alone

0 1 2 3 4 5 6 7 8 9 10 11 12 13 14 15
Age (Months)

Figure 4-2

Motor Development

Infants' motor skills develop from the head downward to the trunk and legs. The ages at which children achieve specific motor skills vary somewhat from child to child. This chart identifies when the average child in North American culture develops different motor skills. This same progression in motor development is found in many cultures around the world. Yet have scientists also found cultural differences in the ages at which some motor skills develop? What is a possible explanation for these cultural differences?

necessary nourishment. The swimming reflex, which is an active movement of the arms and legs and an involuntary holding of the breath when immersed in water, is an example of a primitive reflex. Table 4-2 lists some reflexes that are easily observed in normal newborns. Many of these reflexes—such as the rooting, grasping, and Babinski reflexes—eventually disappear, but others—including the eye-blink, pupillary, and breathing reflexes—are permanent.

Are the Senses Functional Prior to Birth?

Although William James (see chapter 1, section 1-2b) once described a newborn's perceptual world as a "blooming, buzzing confusion" of sights, sounds, and other sensations, with no distinguishing patterns, later research found this characterization to be inaccurate. Let us briefly examine these findings for the five primary senses.

Audition

Evidence indicates that even before birth—during the final 2 months of pregnancy—the fetus is capable not only of hearing sounds but of recognizing them as well. These facts were uncovered due to an ingenious series of studies conducted by Anthony DeCasper and his colleagues. In the most famous of these studies, the researchers had 16 women read aloud Dr. Seuss's *The Cat in the Hat* twice a day during the last 6 weeks of their pregnancy (DeCasper & Spence, 1986). Three days after birth, the babies sucked on artificial nipples that activated a tape recording of their mothers' voice reading either the familiar Dr. Seuss story or some other unfamiliar story. Thirteen of the 16 babies sucked to hear a tape of their mother reading *The Cat in the Hat* but not to hear the other story. Similarly, DeCasper and his colleagues found that newborn infants preferred their mother's voice or a heartbeat to an unfamiliar male voice (DeCasper & Fifer, 1980; DeCasper & Sigafoos, 1983). These studies indicate not only that hearing is functional prior to birth, but also that learning begins in the womb. That is, the newborns were already capable of distinguishing one pattern of sounds (their mother's voice) from another pattern of sounds.

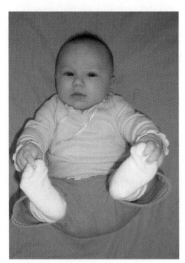

Source: Courtesy of Figzoi.

Table 4-2   Reflexes of the Newborn Baby

Reflexes	Developmental Course	Significance
Survival Reflexes		
Breathing reflex	Permanent	Provides oxygen and expels carbon dioxide
Eye-blink reflex	Permanent	Protects eyes from bright lights and foreign objects
Pupillary reflex (constriction and dilation of pupils due to the amount of light)	Permanent	Protects eyes from bright lights and adapts vision to darkness
Rooting reflex (turning of cheek in direction of a touch in search of something to suck on)	Gradually weakens during the first 6 months of life	Orients child to mother's breast
Sucking reflex (sucking on anything placed in the mouth)	Gradually modified by experience	Allows child to receive nourishment
Swallowing reflex	Permanent, but modified by experience	Allows child to receive nourishment and protects against choking
Primitive Reflexes		
Babinski reflex (splaying outward and then inward of toes)	Disappears within the first year of life	Presence at birth and later disappearance indicates normal neurological development
Grasping reflex (curling of fingers around objects that touch the palm)	Disappears by fourth month of life	Presence at birth and later disappearance indicates normal neurological development
Moro or "startle" reflex (throwing arms out and arching back due to loud noise or sudden movement of baby's head)	Disappears by seventh month of life but is replaced by adult startle reflex	Presence at birth and later disappearance indicates normal neurological development
Swimming reflex (active movement of arms and legs and involuntary holding of breath when immersed in water)	Disappears by sixth month of life	Presence at birth and later disappearance indicates normal neurological development
Stepping reflex (walking movements when held upright so that feet just touch the ground)	Disappears by second month of life	Presence at birth and later disappearance indicates normal neurological development

Vision

At birth, vision is not as well developed as hearing, but newborns can follow slowly moving objects, and within a day, they begin to show a preference for their mother's face (Field et al., 1984). Although newborns can see, they cannot see clearly (Courage & Adams, 1990): They see objects at 20 feet as clearly as normal-sighted people (those with 20/20 vision) see objects at between 400 and 600 feet; thus, their visual acuity ranges from 20/400 to 20/600. By 6 months of age, as the visual cortex in the back of the brain and the retina in the back of the eye mature, infants' vision improves and approaches normal adult levels.

(a)   (b)

Figure 4-3

Newborns' Preference for Faces

In studies of newborns, when shown stimulus (a) and stimulus (b), babies spent almost twice as much time looking at stimulus (a), which mimics the facial features of a human (Morton & Johnson, 1991; Mondloch et al., 1999). Why might this apparent innate ability to attend to the human face foster an infant's survival?

Newborns are particularly attentive to facial features (see figure 4-3). Faces and objects having qualities similar to those of faces are attended to more than are other objects (Field, 1982; Mondloch et al., 1999). In fact, a number of studies have found that newborns exposed to an adult making a happy, sad, or surprised face are able to imitate the corresponding expression (Meltzoff & Moore, 1977, 1989; Reissland, 1988). Evolutionary psychologists believe that this innate ability to respond to the expressed emotions in others' facial expressions is a survival reflex (Gould, 1993; Izard et al., 1995). How might imitating facial gestures help infants survive? One possibility is that an infant's attentiveness to its mother's face and even its imitation of the mother's facial gestures help establish an emotional bond between the two, making it more likely that the newborn will be nurtured and protected. Another possibility is that this early attentiveness to others' facial expressions may provide infants with the necessary foundation to later develop social interaction skills that will increase the likelihood that they will successfully mate and reproduce (Phillips et al., 1990).

Taste and Smell

At birth, infants have the ability to both taste and smell, making positive and negative facial expressions in response to various odors and preferring sweetness over other tastes (Bartoshuk & Beauchamp, 1994; Steiner, 1979). This sweet tooth persists during childhood, and for some people, sweets maintain their top ranking throughout life. Regarding smell, not only can babies discriminate between various odors, but also, within 6 days of birth, they recognize their mother's scent from that of other women (Macfarlane, 1975) and prefer the breast odor of a nursing female to that of a non-nursing female (Makin & Porter, 1989).

Touch

As we will discuss in chapter 5, section 5-4b, touch consists of several senses: pressure, temperature, and pain. The sense of touch is functional well before birth, although pain receptors may be less developed than the other skin senses (Porter et al., 1988). Infants' sensitivity to touch explains why they can be comforted by being rocked and held.

As you can see from this brief overview, William James's description of the newborn's perceptual world was very much mistaken. Today, we know that infant perception is not a meaningless jumble, but rather, that infants can meaningfully perceive a number of different sensations (Gopnik et al., 1999).

Section Review

- Human development involves the physical, cognitive, and social changes that take place in a person from conception to death.
- Prenatal development consists of three stages: the zygotic, embryonic, and fetal stages.
- Possible risk factors during pregnancy include parental age, maternal nutrition, and teratogens.
- As the brain grows, some neurons are strengthened through repeated stimulation, while others grow weak and die.
- Infants are born with a number of reflexes.

- Basic motor skills soon develop from the head downward to the trunk and legs.
- Prior to birth, the fetus can hear sounds and is sensitive to touch.
- Newborns can both taste and smell, but they do not see as clearly as normal-sighted adults.

4-2 SOCIAL DEVELOPMENT

Preview

- *What is the primary social achievement of infancy?*
- *Why is it important for parents to act affectionately toward their children?*
- *What must develop before children can form a self-concept?*
- *How is self-concept shaped by culture?*
- *What is gender identity?*
- *Are identifiable "crises" associated with different stages in life?*

Although physical and perceptual development provides us with the necessary biological infrastructure to survive in the world, there is more to survival than simple biology. In this section, we examine some of the social and cultural forces that shape our essential humanity, beginning with the development of an emotional attachment to our caregivers.

4-2a Attachment Is a Basic Need

attachment The strong emotional bond a young child forms with its primary caregiver.

Attachment is the strong emotional bond a young child forms with its primary caregiver; it is considered the cornerstone for all other relationships in a child's life (Cummings & Cummings, 2002). This bond is not unique to humans but can also be observed in most species of birds and mammals (Graves & Hennesy, 2000; Mason, 1997). Based on his analysis of both orphaned children and other species, the British psychiatrist John Bowlby (1969, 1988) proposed that attachment is part of many species' genetic heritage, and its evolutionary function is to keep immature animals close to their parents so they are protected from predators. In other words, infants who cling to their parents stand a better chance of surviving to adulthood than those who wander away from protective care.

The Harlows' Attachment Studies

Harry and Margaret Harlow (1962) stumbled upon the importance of attachment in nonhuman primates when they observed that infant rhesus monkeys, raised alone and away from their mothers, behaved a great deal like neglected children. To study the development of attachment, the Harlows constructed two surrogate (artificial) monkey "mothers." One of the surrogates consisted of a bare wire-mesh cylinder with a wooden head, while the other had soft terry cloth covering the wire and a more monkeylike head (see figure 4-4). Both surrogate mothers were placed in the same cage as the infant, but half the infants were fed by the wire mother, and the other half were fed by the cloth mother. To which monkey did the infants develop an attachment? Regardless of where their food came from, all the infants spent more time clinging to the cloth mother, and they sought it out when frightened or upset (Harlow & Zimmermann, 1959). These findings suggest that an infant monkey's attachment to its mother is due less to her ability to satisfy its physical needs, and more to her ability to satisfy its need for *contact comfort*—that is, direct contact with soft objects. In other words, providing food alone will not create attachment; contact comfort is the primary ingredient.

The need for contact comfort is also central to human children's sense of security and explains why toddlers enjoy stroking and being stroked by their parents. The gentle strokes and soft hugs are the glue that bonds the relationship. It also explains why children often clutch or stroke soft objects when they feel anxious or tired (Passman & Weisberg, 1975). As a youngster, my daughter Lillian always needed her favorite blanket to hold close to her body and rub between her fingers when settling down for a nap. One afternoon, Lillian

Figure 4-4

The need for contact comfort can be observed in many species. For example, when placed in an environment with both a soft terry cloth "mother" and a wire-mesh "mother," infant rhesus monkeys overwhelmingly preferred the cloth one. Likewise, when my daughter Lillian could not find her favorite blanket, she found a suitably soft substitute. How would you explain the behavioral preferences of these two infants?

Sources: Harlow monkey photo courtesy of Harlow Primate Laboratory. Baby on diapers photo courtesy of Figzoi.

apparently could not find this most cherished object as fatigue settled in, and she thus chose a convenient substitute "companion"—an unopened bag of disposable diapers. When loved ones are not available, children bond to other cuddly objects.

The Development of Attachment

Newborn humans are equipped with a number of attachment behaviors—for example, smiling, cooing, and clinging—that adults naturally respond to with care and attention. Because newborn babies' attachment behaviors are not directed toward a specific person, they not only will coo, smile, and cling to their caregivers, but also will engage in these behaviors in response to strangers and even inanimate objects (Gopnik et al., 1999). If adults do not respond to the infants' attachment behaviors, these bonding signals decrease in frequency (Ainsworth et al., 1978). Infants usually form their initial attachment bond with their mothers because mothers provide most of the early care.

Between the ages of 3 and 6 months, an infant shows a clear preference for its primary caregiver but does not yet become upset when separated from that person. In contrast, between 7 and 9 months, the child forms an attachment bond toward a specific caregiver and usually becomes extremely upset upon separation. The fear and distress that infants display when separated from their primary caregiver is known as **separation anxiety,** and it usually persists until they are about 2 or 3 years old. Also during this time, children develop a fear of strangers, called **stranger anxiety.** Stranger anxiety develops at about 6 or 7 months of age, peaks at about 1 year, and gradually subsides during the second year. Neither separation anxiety nor stranger anxiety is unique to Western culture but is found throughout the world (Super, 1981; van Bakel & Riksen-Walraven, 2002).

separation anxiety The fear and distress that infants display when separated from their primary caregiver.

stranger anxiety The fear and distress that infants often display when approached by an unfamiliar person.

Individual Differences in Attachment Style

As infants mature and interact with their parents, they develop either optimistic or pessimistic beliefs about human relationships (Meins, 1999; Moss et al., 2004). Children who form a *secure attachment* style believe that they are worthy of others' love and that people can be trusted to care for them. In contrast, those who develop an *insecure attachment* style believe that they are unworthy love objects and that others cannot be relied upon (Huth-Bocks et al., 2004). Attachment style remains quite stable throughout childhood, unless the family experiences a major disruption, such as divorce, illness, or death.

About 65 percent of children in the United States are securely attached, with the remaining 35 percent having an insecure attachment style (Lamb et al., 1992). Secure attachment promotes psychological adjustment and health, whereas insecure attachment fosters problematic social relationships. Infants who are securely attached at 1 year of age tend to mature into popular, independent, socially skilled, and self-assured children (Cummings & Cummings, 2002; Kagan et al., 1992). In contrast, insecurely attached infants tend to become children who lack curiosity, perform poorly in school, and are emotionally withdrawn. They also often exhibit contradictory social behavior, sometimes initiating social contact but then unexpectedly spurning others' social advances. This vacillating pattern of approach-avoidance invites social rejection from peers, which then serves to confirm the child's original sense of insecurity and distrust about the world outside.

Despite the sharply contrasting consequences of secure and insecure attachment, these findings by no means imply that secure attachment makes a child invulnerable to later problems in life, or that insecure attachment dooms a person to a life of loneliness and misery. Instead, the research suggests that children with a secure attachment history have an understanding of themselves ("I am worthy of love") and their relationship with others ("People can be trusted") that makes it easier for them to form satisfying social attachments than it is for those who have an insecure attachment history (Cassidy & Shaver, 1999).

4-2b Parenting Style, Initial Temperament, and Culture All Influence Attachment Style

A number of factors influence children's attachment style toward their parents. Three of the more important factors are the parents' behavior toward the child, the child's inborn temperament, and the family's culture.

Parenting Style

Parents who are sensitively responsive to their children's needs and emotional signals and provide a great deal of contact comfort tend to foster secure attachment (NICHD Early Child Care Research Network, 2002; Teti et al., 1991). In feeding, for example, they pay attention to the infant's verbal and nonverbal behavior to determine when to start and stop. They also respond promptly to the baby's cries and behave affectionately when holding her or him. In marked contrast, parents of infants who show insecure attachment pay less attention to their infants' moods and respond more on the basis of their own needs and desires (Bretherton, 1985; Pederson et al., 1990). For example, they feed the baby when it is convenient for them to do so, and they cuddle the baby when they themselves desire contact comfort but avoid the baby at other times. Mothers with insecurely attached babies seem to derive less pleasure out of contact comfort and often refuse to console the baby when it is crying.

Temperament

Another factor that influences the quality of the parent-child attachment is the initial temperament of the newborn (Putnam et al., 2002). Infants with an *easygoing temperament* generally react positively to new situations or stimuli, such as food, people, or toys, while those with a *difficult temperament* tend to react to these situations by crying or fussing. Temperament appears to be significantly shaped by inherited biological factors (DiLalla et al., 1994;

Schmidt & Fox, 2002), and temperament, in turn, appears to partly influence the quality of parent-child attachment. Infants who develop a secure attachment style tend to be naturally easygoing, while those who develop an insecure attachment style are more likely to be rather difficult (Chess & Thomas, 1987).

Of the two factors, most studies suggest that parenting style has a greater impact than the child's temperament in shaping the quality of the attachment (Rosen & Rothbaum, 1993; Seifer et al., 1996). For example, in one experiment, Dutch researchers randomly assigned 6- to 9-month-old temperamentally difficult babies to one of two conditions. In the experimental condition, mothers received training in how to respond sensitively to their child's needs, while in the control condition, they received no training. When the children reached the age of 1 year, 68 percent of those in the experimental condition were securely attached—right at the national average—while only 28 percent in the control condition were securely attached.

Culture

The nature of attachment also appears to be significantly shaped by culture and the ideologies of individualism and collectivism (Harwood et al., 1995; Rothbaum et al., 2000). For example, both U.S. and German children are far more likely than Japanese children to develop a type of insecure attachment style characterized by avoiding intimacy with the mother (Cole, 1992). These cultural differences in attachment are probably partly due to different views on how to raise children. Parents in the United States and Germany try to foster independence at an earlier age, and thus they discourage their children from staying near them and are more likely to give them toys or food when they cry rather than picking them up. In contrast, Japanese parents do not promote independence, and thus they rarely leave their children alone and quickly pick them up when they cry.

Another consideration when studying attachment cross-culturally is that in some areas of the world, such as in Israeli kibbutzim and in the Hausa culture in Nigeria, many people share in the rearing of a child, so the child develops attachments to many people (Super, 1980). In such situations where the primary caregivers are not necessarily the children's mothers or fathers, multiple attachments can develop without adverse consequences to the child (Sagi et al., 1985). Figure 4-5 summarizes some of the possible causes of children's attachment style.

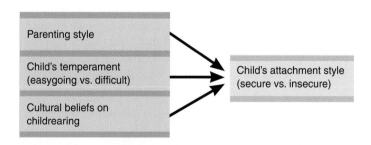

Figure 4-5

Possible Causes of Children's Attachment Style

Whether children develop a secure versus an insecure attachment style is determined by a variety of factors, including parenting style, children's temperament, and cultural beliefs on childrearing. Parents who are sensitively responsive to their children's needs foster secure attachment, while parents who are inattentive to their infants' needs foster insecure attachment. Regarding children's initial temperament, easygoing infants tend to develop secure attachment, while difficult infants tend to develop insecure attachment. Finally, cultures that encourage independence at an early age teach parents to remain less close to their children, which promotes higher levels of insecure attachment than those seen in cultures that do not encourage independence.

4-2c Children Can Handle Parental Separation under Certain Conditions

The notion of multiple caregivers raises the question of how day care affects the formation of attachment. A related question is whether the physical separation of one parent from the child—as occurs in divorce, for example—disrupts the attachment process.

Day Care and Attachment

Only 20 percent of infants and toddlers in the United States are regularly cared for by their parents during the day (National Research Council and Institute of Medicine, 2003). Given this fact, an important question is whether children are negatively affected by being placed into day-care programs. Employing meta-analysis (see chapter 2, section 2-2e), researchers examined the overall effects of day care versus maternal care across 59 studies (Erel et al., 2000). Results indicated no overall differences between children who stayed home and those who attended day care. However, this analysis did find that children in day care were somewhat more likely to exhibit an insecure attachment style if they started attending after $2\frac{1}{2}$ years of age rather than earlier. This finding suggests that placing children in day care may be emotionally disruptive and require more adjustment only when their attachment behaviors are well established. Thus, when working parents expose their children to day care prior to the toddler years, no ill effects on child development occur. Finally, numerous studies reveal that, in choosing day-care programs, the key criterion is "high-quality" care (Ghazvini & Mullis, 2002; Harvey, 1999; Sagi et al., 2002). Table 4-3 lists the important characteristics of high-quality day-care programs.

In evaluating the effects that day care has on children's development, it is important to keep in mind that these effects are significantly influenced by the quality of care children receive from their parents when at home (Marshall, 2004). Children who attend high-quality day-care programs are most likely to develop strong language, cognitive, and social skills when they also receive high-quality care at home. Children's social and intellectual development suffers when parents are neglectful.

Divorce and Attachment

In the United States, a little over half of all marriages end in divorce, whereas in China the occurrence of divorce is less than 15 percent. Yet, regardless of how common it is, divorce generally negatively affects the children involved (Dong et al., 2002). For example, a meta-analysis of over 90 studies indicates that children of divorce feel less emotionally secure and grow up feeling less happy than those who come from intact families (Amato & Keith, 1991). Further, a 23-year **longitudinal study** of more than 17,000 infants born in Great Britain during one week in 1958 found that parental divorce had a moderate, long-term negative impact on the mental health of about 12 percent of the children after they grew up (Chase-

longitudinal study Research in which the same people are restudied and retested over time.

Table **4-3**	Characteristics of High-Quality Day-Care Programs

- A low child-to-caregiver ratio:

  3-to-1 infant-to-adult ratio
  4-to-1 toddler-to-adult ratio
  8-to-1 preschooler-to-adult ratio
- Caregivers who are warm, emotionally expressive, and responsive to children
- Caregivers who have a college education
- Age-appropriate planned activities
- Low staff turnover, so that children feel comfortable and can emotionally bond with their caregivers

Lansdale et al., 1995). Some studies find that the emotional turmoil surrounding divorce has a greater impact on younger children than on their older peers (Allison & Furstenberg, 1989; Lowery & Settle, 1985).

Another factor that can negatively affect children is the change in childrearing styles that often accompanies divorce (Madden-Derdich & Leonard, 2002). In most divorces, mothers retain primary custody of the children, while fathers obtain considerably fewer parental rights. In this environment, overburdened custodial mothers may become less warm and less consistent in their discipline, whereas noncustodial fathers may become overly permissive. The lack of parental structure resulting from these contrasting styles of childrearing can heighten children's sense of emotional insecurity (Hetherington & Stanley-Hagen, 2002).

Despite these potential negative consequences, children of divorce tend to be psychologically healthier than children who come from conflict-ridden two-parent families (Cherlin et al., 1991). In fact, the emotional stress that children from troubled intact families experience can often be substantially reduced if the marriage is terminated (Barber & Eccles, 1992).

4-2d Self-Concept Is the Primary Social Achievement of Childhood

While the primary social achievement of infancy is attachment, the primary social achievement of childhood is **self-concept,** which is the "theory" or "story" that a person constructs about herself or himself through social interaction (Baumeister, 2005). Self-concept is a product of a larger social psychological process known as **socialization,** which involves learning the ways of a given society or group well enough to be able to function according to its rules. Although socialization occurs throughout life, societies are especially attentive to educating the young. Self-concept development is at the very core of this socialization process because it involves internalizing socially approved attitudes, values, and beliefs so they become guidelines for understanding ourselves and our social world. How does self-concept develop?

Self-Awareness: An Essential Ingredient

Stop reading for a moment, and think about your personal traits that you are most proud of and those that you are least proud of. In doing this, you engaged in **self-awareness,** a psychological state in which you focus on yourself as an object of attention (Franzoi & Davis, 2005). You are not born with this ability; rather, you develop it. Psychologists discovered this developmental fact by unobtrusively placing a spot of rouge on babies' noses and then placing them in front of a mirror (Lewis & Brooks, 1978). If a baby has a mental image of its own face and can recognize a mirror image as its own, the baby should notice the rouge mark and reach for or wipe its own nose rather than the nose of the mirror image.

When tested in this manner, infants between 9 and 12 months of age treat their mirror image as if it were another child, showing no interest in the unusual rouge spot. But those around 18 months of age exhibit self-recognition—and thus, self-awareness ability—by consistently staring in the mirror and touching the mysterious spot on their own nose, not the one in the mirror. Recognizing the image in the mirror as their own, they realize that they look different from how they looked before. Based on such studies, it appears that self-awareness develops at about 18 months of age (Amsterdam, 1972; Butterworth, 1992).

Research by Gordon Gallup and his coworkers indicates that humans may not be evolution's only experiment in self-awareness (Suarez & Gallup, 1981). In one study, Gallup (1977) painted an odorless red dye on the eyebrow and ear of anesthetized chimpanzees. Upon awakening, when the chimps looked into a mirror, they immediately began to touch the red dye marks on their bodies—indicating that they recognized the image in the mirror as their own. These and other studies indicate that our primate cousins (chimpanzees, gorillas, and orangutans, but not monkeys)—and perhaps even dolphins—possess self-awareness (Anderson, 1993b; Gallup & Povinelli, 1993).

self-concept The "theory" or "story" that a person constructs about herself or himself through social interaction.

socialization Learning the ways of a given society or group well enough to be able to function according to its rules.

self-awareness A psychological state in which you focus on yourself as an object of attention.

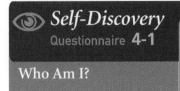

The Twenty Statements Test

Take out a sheet of paper and write the numbers 1–20 down the left column of the page. Then, beginning each sentence with the statement "I am," list up to 20 different responses to the question "Who Am I?" Respond as if you were giving the answers to yourself, not to someone else. When finished, evaluate your responses according to a commonly used classification scheme (see Hartley, 1970) by coding each response into one of the following four categories:

1. *Physical self-descriptions*—This is where you identify yourself in terms of physical qualities that do not imply social interaction (for example, "I am a male"; "I am a brunette"; "I am overweight").
2. *Social self-descriptions*—This is where you identify yourself in terms of social roles, institutional memberships, or other socially defined statuses (for example, "I am a student"; "I am a daughter"; "I am a Jew").
3. *Attributive self-descriptions*—This is where you identify yourself in terms of psychological/physiological states or traits (for example, "I am intelligent"; "I am assertive"; "I am boring").
4. *Global self-descriptions*—This is where you identify yourself in a manner so comprehensive or vague that it doesn't distinguish you from any other person (for example, "I am a human being"; "I am alive"; "I am me").

Code each of your responses into one of these four categories. Which category occurs most frequently for you? People in individualist cultures write more attributive self-descriptions, which highlight their differences from other people, while collectivists write more social self-descriptions, which highlight their connections to their social groups.

Self-Esteem Development

Once children become able to engage in self-awareness, they begin to develop a self-concept. Before reading further, go to Self-Discovery Questionnaire 4-1 and spend a few minutes answering the question "Who Am I?"

Self-concept is not a dispassionate self-theory, but rather, it consists of numerous evaluations of self as good, bad, or mediocre. This overall evaluation of self-concept is called **self-esteem.** In the early years, children's self-concepts display little organization and little negativity, and they have not yet developed a recognizable sense of self-esteem (Harter, 1988). During middle childhood, however, children have the cognitive maturity to integrate others' evaluations of them and their own self-assessments into a global sense of self-esteem (Marsh et al., 1991). A number of studies indicate that individuals with high self-esteem are generally more happy and optimistic, and that they tend to take greater achievement risks in their lives than do those with low self-esteem (Diener & Lucas, 2000a; Shepperd et al., 1996).

Given our previous discussion of attachment, it shouldn't surprise you to learn that children with high self-esteem tend to come from families where parents are warmly expressive toward their children (Maccoby & Martin, 1983). Yet parental warmth encompasses only half the equation when analyzing parents' influence on children's self-esteem. A host of studies, conducted in many cultures, have found that children with high self-esteem usually have *authoritative parents*—parents who exert control not merely by imposing rules and consistently enforcing them but also by allowing their children a fair amount of freedom within the rules and by discussing the rationale behind their decisions (Baumrind, 1991; Querido et al., 2002; Scott et al., 1991). This research indicates that children need love combined with a set of boundaries to structure their behavior. In contrast, parents who impose many rules and expect strict obedience (*authoritarian parents*) and those who make few demands and submit to their children's desires (*permissive parents*) tend to raise children who are less confident in their abilities and have lower self-esteem.

self-esteem A person's overall evaluation of his or her self-concept.

The detrimental effect that authoritarian parenting has on children's self-esteem is most apparent in Caucasian-American families, where this parental style is often used to "break the child's will." However, many ethnic-minority families place greater value on authoritarian parenting as a positive socialization tool (Lynch, 1994; Parke & Buriel, 1998). For example, Chinese-American parents use authoritarian discipline to "train" (*chiao shun*) and "govern" (*guan*) children so that they will know what is expected of them (Chao, 1992). In such a cultural context, authoritarian parenting is not associated with lower self-esteem or lower levels of achievement (Steinberg et al., 1992).

Stability of Self-Esteem across the Life Span

How stable is self-esteem across the life span? To answer this question, researchers conducted a meta-analysis of 50 self-esteem studies involving almost 30,000 participants in the United States and other countries who ranged in age from 6 to 82 (Trzesniewski et al., 2003). Stability of self-esteem was measured by correlating participants' self-esteem scores gathered across at least a 1-year interval. As you can see from figure 4-6, this analysis found that self-esteem stability is relatively low during childhood, increases throughout adolescence and young adulthood, and declines during midlife and old age. There was no evidence for gender or nationality differences in self-esteem stability. The low stability levels during childhood may be caused by young children being unable to form abstract conceptions of themselves as good or bad, but it also may be due to young children not understanding the self-esteem questions posed to them by researchers. The increasing stability of self-esteem during adolescence and young adulthood may be caused by people achieving a sense of personal identity and gradually obtaining the psychological resources needed to properly adjust to life changes (see section 4-2f). Finally, the decline in self-esteem stability in later adulthood and old age may be due to the dramatic life changes (for example, retirement, death of loved ones, declining health) that are more likely to characterize this life stage than the others. These events may threaten some people's self-concepts, resulting in fluctuations in self-esteem levels that reduce the stability of self-esteem (see section 4-6e).

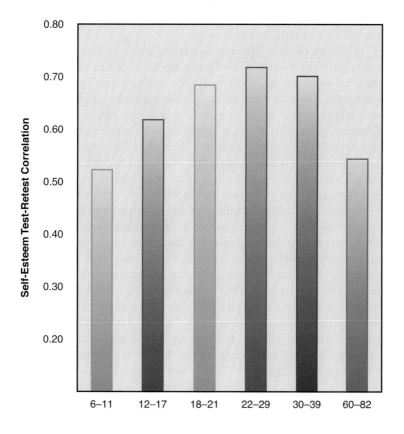

Figure 4-6

Stability of Self-Esteem across the Life Span

A meta-analysis of 50 self-esteem studies involving almost 30,000 participants (ages 6 to 82 years) examined test-retest correlations of self-esteem measures across at least a 1-year interval (Trzesniewski et al., 2003). There were no gender or nationality differences in self-esteem stability, but stability was relatively low during childhood, it increased throughout adolescence and young adulthood, and then it declined during midlife and old age. Why might self-esteem stability change over the life span?

Source: Based on data from Trzesniewski, K. H., Donnellan, M. B., & Robins, R. W. (2003). Stability of self-esteem across the life span. *Journal of Personality and Social Psychology, 84,* 205–220.

Self-Concept and Culture

Our self-concept is not only shaped by loved ones, but also molded by culture. As discussed in chapter 1, section 1-3f, the United States, Canada, and many northern European cultures cultivate *individualism*, a philosophy of life that stresses the importance of the individual over the group (Inglehart & Oyserman, in press). In this cultural belief system, the person is considered to be independent and endowed with unique attributes. In contrast, many Asian, African, and Central and South American cultures nurture *collectivism*, an older philosophy of life that places group needs ahead of individual needs. Collectivist cultures tend to value similarity and conformity rather than uniqueness and independence. About 70 percent of the world's population lives in cultures with a collectivist orientation.

> *Journey of Discovery* Question
>
> If you were to tell someone to "just be yourself," what would that mean to a person from an individualist culture? What would it mean to a person from a collectivist culture?

These two contrasting cultural perspectives concerning people's relationship to groups within society lead to important differences in the way children are socialized (Furnham, 2001; Harkness, 2002). Within collectivist societies, childrearing practices emphasize obedience and knowing one's proper place. In collectivist China, for example, educational theories and practices focus on shaping children's personalities to best meet societal needs and goals (Greenfield, 1994; Pratt, 1991). Consistent with this upbringing, when asked to describe themselves by completing the Twenty Statements Test (see Self-Discovery Questionnaire 4-1), people from collectivist cultures primarily list their **social roles,** which are clusters of socially defined expectations that people in given situations are supposed to fulfill, such as the role of son, daughter, student, or employee. In contrast, individualist societies encourage independence and self-reliance, and children develop a belief in their own uniqueness and diversity. When individualists describe their self-concepts, they tend to identify themselves in terms of personal attributes and psychological characteristics, such as outgoing, kind, and jealous (Kanagawa et al., 2001; van den Heuvel et al., 1992).

When my daughter Amelia was in third grade, she came home one day with a library book that nicely illustrated how North American culture socializes children to value independence and uniqueness. The book, *The Upside-down Boy* (Palazzo-Craig, 1986), is about a child who was different because he liked to do everything upside down. Despite everyone's efforts to try to get the boy to stand right-side-up, he didn't comply. Instead, his persistence in being different led to him foiling a bank robbery and, thereby, becoming a local hero. Such stories convey values of independence and uniqueness that are different from those espoused by children's literature in collectivist cultures, which stress fulfilling group goals, doing one's duty, and bringing pride to one's family, not one's self. Can you think of similar stories from your own childhood? Table 4-4 outlines how cultural differences regarding individualism or collectivism may influence self-concept.

Beyond differences in worldwide cultural beliefs that affect self-concept, cultural differences *within* societies can also shape people's beliefs and attitudes about themselves. Several studies demonstrate that, among African-American and Caucasian-American children, high self-esteem is associated with competitiveness (Peplau & Taylor, 1997; Rosenberg, 1965). In other words, children's feelings of self-worth are likely to be bolstered if they adopt a competitive approach toward others. This orientation conforms to the individualist values of mainstream American culture. Yet, in contrast to this association, researchers have found that among second-generation Mexican-American children, high self-esteem is associated with cooperativeness, not competitiveness (DeVoe, 1977; Kagan & Knight, 1979). These children's parents teach them to value and conform to the cooperative cultural norms of their collectivist Mexican homeland. For them, the growth and enhancement of self-concept and self-esteem

social roles Clusters of socially defined expectations that people in given situations are supposed to fulfill, such as the role of son, daughter, student, or employee.

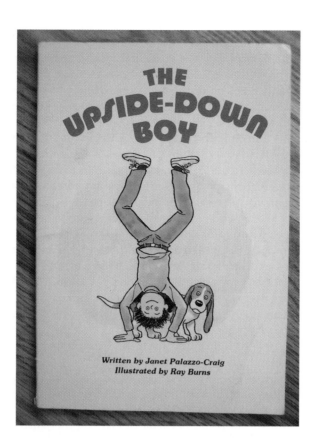

In the children's book *The Upside-down Boy* (Palazzo-Craig, 1986), Donnie does everything upside down, despite everyone's efforts to get him to act normally. In the end, his unique behavior helps him stop a bank robbery and become a hero. How does this story reflect individualist values? How might such stories shape children's values and beliefs?

Source: Courtesy of Figzoi.

do not appear to depend on a competitive comparison process with others. This same research indicates that, as Mexican-American children become more acculturated to mainstream American society, the association between cooperativeness and self-esteem weakens. These findings and additional studies suggest that, as Mexican-American youth strive to "fit in" to the larger American society, they adopt a more competitive approach to life (Delgado-Gaitan, 1994; Uribe et al., 1994).

Table 4-4	Differences between Collectivist and Individualist Cultures
Collectivist	**Individualist**
Identity is based in the social system and given by one's group.	Identity is based in the individual and achieved by one's own striving.
People are socialized to be emotionally dependent on organizations and institutions.	People are socialized to be emotionally independent of organizations and institutions.
Personal and group goals are generally consistent, and when inconsistent, group goals get priority.	Personal and group goals are often inconsistent, and when inconsistent, personal goals get priority.
People explain others' social behavior as being more determined by social norms and roles than by personal attitudes.	People explain others' social behavior as being more determined by personal attitudes than by social norms and roles.
Emphasis is on belonging to organizations and other groups.	Emphasis is on individual initiative, individual achievement, and leadership.
Trust is placed in group decisions.	Trust is placed in individual decisions.

4-2e Children Learn the "Right Way" to Think about Gender

An important aspect of childhood socialization is learning about gender. As discussed in chapter 3, section 3-4d, *gender* refers to the meanings that societies and individuals attach to being female and male. In teaching children about gender, adults often rely upon what "worked" for them. For women, it may be memories of playing with Barbie dolls or dainty tea sets, while for men, images of rough-and-tumble football or skateboarding may come to mind. Parents often perceive their newborns through these gendered lenses, describing their daughters as finer featured, more delicate, less strong, and more feminine than their sons (Karraker et al., 1995; Raffaelli & Ontai, 2004). Pause a moment in your reading to observe the image of the sleeping baby on this page. If you are like most people, the opinions that you form about such infants are substantially shaped by whether they are identified as "boy" or "girl."

Shortly after children begin engaging in self-awareness—by the age of 2—they develop an understanding of themselves as being either a boy or a girl (Katz, 1986). This knowledge is called **gender identity,** and it is one of the basic elements in self-concept (Bussey & Bandura, 1999). Once children identify with the girl or boy label, they strive to act in ways consistent with this identity (Bem, 1983; Martin & Ruble, 2004). Instead of being passively shaped by gender beliefs in the culture, they become active participants in socializing themselves. In this process of gender socialization, they learn to differentiate a wide variety of objects, activities, games, careers, and even basic personality traits as either "natural" or "unnatural" for them based on their gender identity (Etaugh & Liss, 1992; Fagot et al., 1986).

In societies where gender expectations are clearly defined and rigidly enforced by adults—such as in Islamic Iran or Saudi Arabia—a great deal of consistency is seen in how boys and girls model appropriate behavior. By contrast, in societies where gender is more flexibly defined—such as in the United States or Canada—the child's own gender role tends to have a more distinct quality. However, even in the United States and Canada, a great deal of gender conformity pressure is exerted by the children themselves. In learning the "right way" to think about gender, children often segregate themselves into boy and girl play groups, adopt a fairly rigid set of gender rules, and punish one another for violating these rules (Maccoby, 1990; Zucker et al., 1995). Such gender monitoring is at its height during early childhood. During the later elementary years, this gender inflexibility often declines as children become more aware of nontraditional gender views and exhibit greater cognitive complexity (Serbin & Sprafkin, 1986). But despite this tendency toward greater gender flex-

gender identity The knowledge that one is a male or a female and the internalization of this fact into the self-concept.

"Is it a boy or a girl?" In cultures throughout the world, this is often the first question asked about a newborn. Once answered, people are much more confident in assessing the infant's temperament, strength, and future interests and abilities. Gender is indeed a powerful force in childhood socialization!

Source: Frances Tipton Hunter, *Sleeping Infant,* ca. 1920, pastel on paperboard, 16 × 13.5 inches.

ibility in later childhood, traditional gender expectations significantly shape many adolescent and adult social relationships (see sections 4-6a and 4-6b).

What can adults do to encourage children not to limit their potential by conforming to narrow social definitions of male and female? Following are five recommendations to counter gender stereotypes in the larger culture:

1. *Teach by example.* As we will discuss in chapter 7, section 7-3a, people often learn how to think and act by listening to the thoughts and observing the actions of others, especially those important to them. Children who see their mother and father taking turns doing laundry, making dinner, driving the car, and mowing the lawn are less likely to attach gender labels to these activities.

2. *Monitor your use of pronouns such as* he *and* she. As we will discuss in chapter 9, section 9-1g, children associate men and women with certain occupations by listening to the gendered pronouns adults use in referring to those occupations. For example, when telling children what a police officer does on the job, using only the male pronoun ("He arrests people who break the law") conveys to the child that this is an occupation for men, not women. A more inclusive way to describe occupations is to use the plural pronoun *they* and provide concrete examples of both men and women who perform these jobs.

3. *Monitor children's entertainment.* Many forms of children's entertainment contain messages implying that boys and girls inherently engage in different kinds of social behavior. Often the message is that boys are aggressive and born to be adventurers, while girls are helpless and born to offer support to boys. For example, when reading fairy tales, Sandra Bem (1983) suggests that adults make such comments as "Isn't it interesting that the person who wrote this story seems to think that girls always need to be rescued?" If not heavy-handed, such discussions can provide children with the idea that gender beliefs are relative and not fixed.

4. *Provide a cross-cultural and historical view of gender.* Because children will be exposed to gender stereotypes, they need to understand that beliefs about gender vary not only from household to household and from culture to culture, but also over time. For instance, you could let them know that among the Agta Negritos of northeastern Luzon in the Philippines, the women are as likely as the men to be the family's hunters and fishers. Or you could talk about how scientists in the 1800s mistakenly argued that educating women could harm their reproductive systems because it would divert important "life forces" to the brain instead of to the female organs!

5. *Teach children about sexism.* Cultural relativism is a valuable lesson, but children should also be taught that preventing people from engaging in certain behaviors simply because they are a member of one sex and not the other is wrong. This includes letting children know that sexist practices should be opposed and corrected. Further, if children are told how sexism has been successfully opposed in the past, they will realize that this aspect of their social reality can be redefined and altered by their own future actions.

4-2f Erikson Asserted That Social Development Occurs in Stages, Each Marked by a Crisis

Erik Erikson (1902–1994) believed that people's social development occurs in identifiable stages. Each stage is marked by a crisis or conflict related to a specific developmental task. The more successfully people overcome these crises, the better chance they have to develop in a healthy manner (Erikson, 1950). Table 4-5 summarizes this eight-stage theory of psychosocial development.

Developing a sense of *trust versus mistrust* is the crisis of the first psychosocial stage, which corresponds to our previous discussion of attachment (refer back to section 4-2b) and occurs during the first year of life. Trust is established when an infant's basic needs for comfort, food, and warmth are met. If these needs are not adequately satisfied, the infant develops a mistrust of others.

Erik Erikson, a neo-Freudian whose personality theory encompasses the entire life span.
Source: © Ted Streshinsky/CORBIS.

Table 4-5	Erikson's Stages of Psychosocial Development	
Identity Stage	**Crisis**	**Description of Crisis**
Infancy (birth–1 year)	Trust vs. mistrust	If basic needs are met, infants develop a sense of trust. If these needs are not adequately satisfied, infants develop a mistrust of others.
Toddlerhood (1–2 years)	Autonomy vs. shame and doubt	If toddlers can control their own actions and act independently, they develop a sense of autonomy. If they fail, they experience shame and doubt their own abilities.
Preschool (3–5 years)	Initiative vs. guilt	If preschoolers can get what they want while acting responsibly, they develop a sense of initiative. If their impulses are not kept in check by a sense of guilt, they become undisciplined. If they are made to feel overly guilty, this inhibits their initiative.
Elementary school (6–12 years)	Industry vs. inferiority	If children master the knowledge and skills necessary for adult life, they develop a sense of competence. If they are unable to achieve competence, they feel inferior and develop low self-esteem.
Adolescence (13–18 years)	Identity vs. role confusion	Teenagers struggle to develop a sense of identity by experimenting with different roles and integrating them into a single identity. If they fail to develop their own personal identity, they become confused about who they are.
Young adulthood (19–45 years)	Intimacy vs. isolation	If young adults successfully develop close relationships, they gain a sense of intimacy. If they are unable to develop such relationships, they feel socially isolated.
Middle adulthood (46–65 years)	Generativity vs. stagnation	If the middle-aged believe that they are contributing to the world and the next generation, they develop a sense of generativity. If they fail to do so, they experience a sense of stagnation.
Late adulthood (66 years and up)	Integrity vs. despair	If the elderly have successfully managed the previous crises in their lives, they feel a sense of integrity. If they regret many of their life choices, they feel a sense of despair.

The second crisis, *autonomy versus shame and doubt,* occurs during the second year of life. Here, toddlers attempt to control their own actions and act independently. If successful, they develop a feeling of confidence or a sense of autonomy, but if they fail or are restrained too severely, they may experience shame and doubt their own abilities.

During the third stage of development, which occurs between the ages of 3 and 5 (the preschool years), children struggle with *initiative versus guilt.* This stage deals with learning how to initiate plans, set goals, and attain them without breaking the rules of proper behavior. If children can successfully get what they want while acting responsibly, this increases their initiative. Trouble arises, however, when initiative and guilt are not properly balanced. If children's impulses are not adequately kept in check by a sense of guilt over social transgressions—as is common in permissive parenting—they become undisciplined. In contrast, if children are made to feel overly guilty—as is common in authoritarian parenting—this will inhibit their initiative.

Between the ages of 6 and 12, children face the conflict of *industry versus inferiority* as they attempt to master the knowledge and intellectual skills necessary for adult life. Children who are successful in this type of learning develop a sense of competence and achievement, while those who do poorly feel inferior and develop low self-esteem.

During adolescence (ages 13 to 18), children face the most crucial stage in Erikson's theory: *identity versus role confusion* (Erikson, 1968). Although knowing who you are and where you're headed is a lifelong task, adolescence is the first time individuals make a concerted effort to consciously form their own identity or self-concept. One of the primary ways teenagers create their identity is by experimenting with many different roles—the nonconformist, the religious searcher, the obedient son or daughter, the thrill-seeker, the delinquent, and so forth. Through experimentation with these possible identities, adolescents gradually construct a theory about who they are that prepares them for adulthood (see section 4-5d). Often, this identity integrates many of the roles with which they previously experimented.

One way to think about identity formation during adolescence is as our first deliberate, figurative attempt to write our autobiography. In childhood, others told us who we were, and we had relatively little say in the final character sketch. In adolescence, we take the pen in our own hands and search for the "right storyline." We usually write many different character sketches before settling on the one we are most comfortable with. Once created, this identity sketch serves as a guide for our future life choices. According to Erikson, if adolescents cannot settle on an identity, they suffer role confusion and may feel "lost."

The sixth psychosocial stage involves the struggle with the main crisis of young adulthood, *intimacy versus isolation* (ages 19 to 45). Intimacy refers to sharing that which is inmost with others (McAdams, 1988). As we learned earlier in our review of research on attachment (see section 4-2b), people who do not feel a sense of security and trust in their social relationships have a difficult time achieving intimacy. Erikson contends that without close, loving relationships, people will live in emotional isolation.

During middle adulthood (ages 46 to 65), the person faces the crisis of the seventh stage, namely, *generativity versus stagnation*. For middle-aged adults, generativity involves teaching and nurturing the next generation, as well as creating something of substance in the world of work. People who fail to contribute and produce something that they feel is worthy of their efforts experience a sense of stagnation, or lack of purpose, in their lives.

Finally, during the last stage of psychosocial development (age 66 and up), Erikson believes that the crisis revolves around the issue of *integrity versus despair*. As elderly adults look back on their lives, they ask themselves, "Did my life have meaning?" If they have successfully managed the crises in the previous seven stages, they feel a sense of integrity (Holman, 2001). However, if they regret many of their important life choices, they likely experience a sense of despair.

One of the primary strengths of Erikson's theory is its ability to draw connections between important psychosocial developments throughout a person's life (Friedman, 2001). For example, as predicted by Erikson's theory and confirmed by attachment researchers, failing to develop a sense of trust in a child's caregivers early in life can have a detrimental effect on his or her ability to develop satisfying romantic relationships in adulthood (Hazan & Shaver, 1987; Mikulincer & Erev, 1991).

In addition to the stage connections, Erikson's description of the identity search in adolescence has generally been supported, although research also indicates two important qualifications. First, identity development is not reserved solely for the adolescent years but continues at least into young adulthood (Hill, 1993). Second, as Erikson himself admitted, his theory best describes identity development in Western industrialized cultures and may not accurately depict what occurs in nonindustrialized or collectivist societies. Echoing Erikson's cautionary note, critics of his theory contend that the need to *search* for identity

There are three things extremely hard. Steel, a diamond, and to know one's self.

—*Benjamin Franklin, U.S. statesman and scientist, 1706–1790*

A race of people is like an individual man; until it uses its own talent, takes pride in its own history, expresses its own culture, affirms its own selfhood, it can never fulfill itself.

—*Malcolm X, U.S. Muslim and Black nationalist, 1925–1965*

during adolescence is a Western psychological dilemma, fed by an individualist philosophy of life. Because most members of collectivist cultures think of identity as something simply *provided* by their social group, identity development should not constitute a "crisis" in their lives (Kroger, 1996). Although this criticism has merit, some social scientists have recently argued that, as the world becomes more globalized and industrialized, young members of collectivist cultures may increasingly adopt individualist values from the West, including the notion of personal identity search (Arnett, 2002; Stevenson & Zusho, 2002). If this is true, Erikson's analysis of identity crisis may now have more relevance for people around the world than it did when he first developed his theory in the middle of the twentieth century.

Section Review

- Attachment is the primary social achievement of infancy.
- Infants who receive tender and loving care develop secure attachment, which fosters psychological adjustment and health, while infants who receive neglectful or abusive care develop insecure attachment, which fosters problematic social relationships.
- Self-concept is the paramount social achievement of childhood, and it is predicated on the development of self-awareness.
- Collectivist cultures foster group-oriented self-concepts, whereas individualist cultures foster self-focused self-concepts.
- Gender identity, which is a person's understanding of her or his sex, is one of the basic elements in self-concept.
- Erikson's theory of psychosocial development explains the social conflicts encountered in eight life stages.

4-3   COGNITIVE DEVELOPMENT

Preview

- *Do children's minds work the same way as adults'?*
- *What role can others play in helping children improve their thinking?*
- *Is information processed differently at different ages?*

Cognition is the act of knowing combined with the processes through which knowledge is acquired and problems are solved. How does cognition, or thinking, emerge and develop in the mind of a child? For a good start in answering this question, we will turn to the pioneering work of Jean Piaget, the person who has had the single most important impact on developmental psychology (Flavell, 1996; Siegler & Ellis, 1996).

4-3a   Piaget's Theory of Cognitive Development Has Four Distinct Stages

Eighty years ago, the young Swiss psychologist Jean Piaget (1896–1980) was intrigued by the fact that children of different ages made different kinds of mistakes while solving problems. Based on his observations, he argued that children are not like "little adults" who simply know less, but that they think about the world in a very different way. Piaget's subsequent research led him to conclude that as children mature, they move through four chronological *cognitive stages,* each distinguished by a qualitatively different type of thinking, and each building upon the stages preceding it (see table 4-6). Perhaps influenced by his culture's individualist beliefs concerning self-reliance, Piaget also conceived of cognitive development as a relatively solitary process, something children achieved by actively interacting with the world. Later in this chapter (see section 4-3c), you will learn about a theorist from a collectivist culture who proposed a more "group-oriented" view of cognitive development.

Jean Piaget (1896–1980).
Source: © Bettmann/CORBIS.

Table 4-6	Piaget's Stages of Cognitive Development	
Typical Age Range	**Description of Stage**	**Developmental Phenomena**
Birth–2 years	*Sensorimotor*—Experiencing the world through actions (grasping, looking, touching, and sucking)	• Object permanence • Stranger anxiety
2–6 years	*Preoperational*—Representing things with words and images but having no logical reasoning	• Pretend play • Egocentrism • Language
7–11 years	*Concrete operational*—Thinking logically about concrete events; understanding concrete analogies and performing arithmetical operations	• Conservation • Mathematical transformations
12 through adulthood	*Formal operational*—Abstract reasoning	• Abstract logic

Schemas

According to Piaget, cognitive development occurs as children organize their own structures of knowledge—called schemas—to adapt to their environment. A **schema** is an organized cluster of knowledge that people use to understand and interpret information. For example, when teaching my daughters to play "catch," I had them hold out their arms about 6 inches apart, and then I gently tossed them a stuffed bear. When it landed on their arms, they pulled it to their chests, mission accomplished. By repeating this activity, they developed a schema for "catching."

Assimilation and Accommodation

In using schemas, people acquire knowledge through the two complementary processes of assimilation and accommodation (Piaget & Inhelder, 1969). **Assimilation** is the process of absorbing new information into existing schemas, while **accommodation** is the process of changing existing schemas in order to absorb new information. Once my daughters learned how to catch a stuffed bear, I began throwing other things to them: a beach ball, a pillow, a Ping-Pong ball. For the beach ball and pillow, they were able to use their bear-catching schema quite nicely, so they engaged in assimilation. However, trying to assimilate the Ping-Pong ball using the bear-catching schema didn't work—the ball fell right between their outstretched arms. So they had to accommodate—they adjusted their catching posture, using their cupped hands more than their outstretched arms to cradle the ball. Throughout life, the major dilemma in learning and problem solving is whether to assimilate new information into existing schemas or change those knowledge structures so the new information can be better handled and understood. Generally, people first try to assimilate, but if that fails, they accommodate their schemas in an attempt to deal with the situation.

Sensorimotor Stage

As you can see from table 4-6, the first stage in Piaget's theory of cognitive development is the **sensorimotor stage** (birth to age 2), a period of time when infants develop the ability to coordinate their sensory input with their motor actions. One of the major accomplishments at this stage is the development of **object permanence,** which is the realization that an object continues to exist even if you can't see it or touch it. For infants who lack a schema for object permanence, out of sight is quite literally out of mind. Although Piaget's research suggested that children do not exhibit memory for hidden objects prior to 8 months of age, later studies indicated that infants as young as 3 or 4 months may have at least some understanding of object permanence (Baillargeon & DeVos, 1991; Diamond, 1985).

schema An organized cluster of knowledge that people use to understand and interpret information.

There are two ways of meeting difficulties. You alter the difficulties or you alter yourself to meet them.

—*Phyllis Bottome, English author, 1884–1963*

assimilation The process of absorbing new information into existing schemas.

accommodation The process of changing existing schemas in order to absorb new information.

sensorimotor stage The first stage in Piaget's theory of cognitive development (birth to age 2), in which infants develop the ability to coordinate their sensory input with their motor actions.

object permanence The realization that an object continues to exist even if you can't see it or touch it.

One quick and easy way to determine whether infants have a clear understanding of object permanence is to engage them in a game of peekaboo. If they wait for your face to emerge from behind your hands, out of sight is definitely not out of mind for them; they have the capacity to retain a mental image of you in their minds. Piaget stated that object permanence marks the beginning of *representational thought,* which is the ability to use mental imagery and other symbolic systems, such as language. It also appears to be associated with the onset of separation anxiety (refer back to section 4-2a). Babies who cry when their mothers leave them are demonstrating that they have a schema for object permanence—they know she exists when she is out of sight, and this knowledge creates anxiety.

Preoperational Stage

> **preoperational stage** The second stage in Piaget's theory of cognitive development (ages 2 to 7), marked by the full emergence of representational thought.

Between the ages of around 2 to 7, children are in the **preoperational stage,** a maturational period marked by the full emergence of representational thought that started at the end of the sensorimotor stage. Not only do they think in terms of language, but also they begin to engage in *make-believe play,* in which they act out familiar activities, such as eating or sleeping. This stage is called preoperational because children have difficulty performing what Piaget called *operations,* which are mental manipulations of objects that are reversible (Piaget, 1972a). For example, a preoperational child might know that adding 7 plus 2 equals 9 but might find that information of no value in trying to figure out its reverse, namely, what 9 minus 2 equals.

> **egocentrism** The tendency to view the world from one's own perspective without recognizing that others may have different points of view.

Another important limitation of preoperational thinking is **egocentrism,** which is the tendency to view the world from one's own perspective without recognizing that others may have different viewpoints. Of course, egocentrism is also a limitation of the earlier sensorimotor stage, but since older children are talking more, this cognitive handicap becomes more noticeable. Piaget demonstrated preoperational egocentrism in his famous *three-mountains problem* (Piaget & Inhelder, 1956). In this task, children are seated at a table with three model mountains like those depicted in figure 4-7, and with a doll sitting in a chair opposite them. When asked to choose a picture that corresponds to the doll's view of the mountains, preoperational children often choose the picture depicting their own view. They simply seem incapable of getting into the "eyes" of the doll. Although preoperational children are not egocentric in every situation, they are much more likely to make egocentric mistakes than are older children (Ford, 1979). This is why 3-year-olds might play hide-and-seek by simply closing their eyes. As far as they are concerned, they have found a pretty good hiding place because they cannot see a thing!

> **conservation** The understanding that certain physical properties of an object remain unchanged despite superficial changes in the object's appearance.

Another limitation at this stage can be traced back to our earlier discussion of preoperational children's difficulty in reversing operations. Due to this inability to reverse thinking, children do not understand **conservation,** the fact that certain physical properties of an object remain unchanged despite superficial changes in the object's appearance. A 5-year-old, Jason, illustrated his lack of understanding of conservation when I poured each of us the same amount of soda into two identical glasses and then poured his soda into a third glass that was wider than the other two:

> After I poured the same amount of soda into two identical glasses, the following conversation took place:
>
> S.F.: "Do I have more soda than you? Do you have more soda than me? Or do we have the same amount of soda?"
>
> Jason: "We've both got the same."

Figure 4-7

The Three-Mountains Problem

In the three-mountains problem, preoperational children typically do not understand that the doll "sees" the mountains from a perspective different from their own. This is an example of egocentrism.

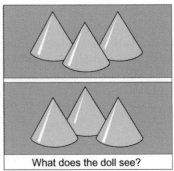

What does the doll see?

S.F.: "OK, now I'm going to take your soda and pour it into here (wider glass). Now, look at your soda. Do I have more soda than you? Do you have more soda than me? Or do we have the same amount of soda?"

Jason: "You've got more than me."

S.F.: "Why is that?"

Jason: "Because it's put into a bigger glass, so my soda is lower."

S.F.: "Can you make it so that we have the same amount of soda?"

Jason: "Just pour it back into the first glass."

After pouring the soda back into the original glass:

S.F.: "Do we have the same amount again?"

Jason: "Yes."

Jason's inability to mentally *reverse* the operation of pouring contributed to his inability to understand the conservation of liquid. Another factor that hindered Jason's understanding was that he paid attention to only one feature of the liquid in the glass—its height. Like other preoperational children, Jason engaged in *centration*, which is the tendency to focus (or center) on one feature of an object and ignore other relevant features. By noticing only the height of the liquid in the glass—which was lower than the original—and not noticing that its width was greater, Jason falsely concluded that he had lost some soda in the transfer. Preoperational children have difficulty with conservation tasks because not only are they unable to reverse operations, but also they tend to pay attention to only one feature of the object. Figure 4-8 lists a number of conservation tasks that preoperational children have difficulty performing.

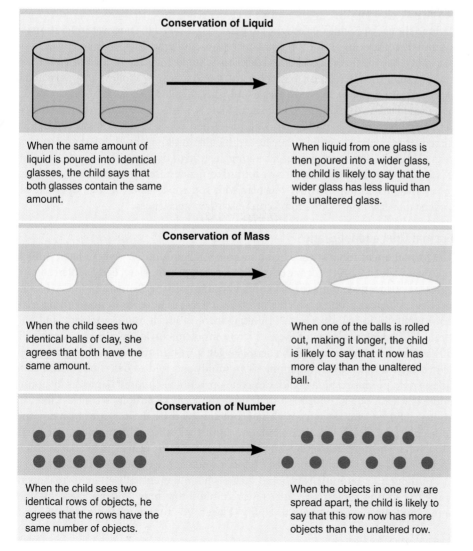

Conservation of Liquid

When the same amount of liquid is poured into identical glasses, the child says that both glasses contain the same amount.

When liquid from one glass is then poured into a wider glass, the child is likely to say that the wider glass has less liquid than the unaltered glass.

Conservation of Mass

When the child sees two identical balls of clay, she agrees that both have the same amount.

When one of the balls is rolled out, making it longer, the child is likely to say that it now has more clay than the unaltered ball.

Conservation of Number

When the child sees two identical rows of objects, he agrees that the rows have the same number of objects.

When the objects in one row are spread apart, the child is likely to say that this row now has more objects than the unaltered row.

Figure 4-8

Conservation of Liquid, Mass, and Number

Preoperational children cannot mentally reverse a sequence of events (an operation) back to the starting point. Further, because of centration, preoperational children cannot simultaneously consider two features of an object (for example, the height and width of liquid in a glass). As a result of these problems of reversibility and centration, they are not yet able to comprehend the principle of conservation.

Explore It
Exercise 4-1

Can You Demonstrate Conservation Failure with a Young Child?

If you want to impress your family with your knowledge of psychology, at the next family gathering ask some of your young relatives (age 3 and age 7 would be ideal) to complete a conservation task while others watch. Try the number conservation task. Make two rows of seven identical coins, but spread out the coins in one row. First ask the younger children whether the two rows have an equal number of coins or whether one row has more coins than the other. The younger children will most likely say that there are more coins in the row that is spread out. When these children respond with this incorrect answer, ask them why they think so. Next, repeat this exercise with the older children. They will most likely answer correctly. Then explain to everyone why the younger children answered incorrectly. When you pronounce Jean Piaget's name in explaining this cognitive process, remember it sounds like "Zhan Pee-ah-ZHAY," not "Jeen Pie-ah-JET."

Do you see something that egocentrism and centration have in common? In egocentrism, children see things from only one perspective (their own), and in centration, children consider only one feature of an object. Thus, in both mental activities, when judging reality, preoperational children can think about events or objects in only one way. Before continuing, read Explore It Exercise 4-1.

Concrete Operational Stage

concrete operational stage The third stage in Piaget's theory of cognitive development (ages 7 to 11), a time when children can perform mental operations on tangible objects or events and gradually engage in logical reasoning.

Around the age of 5, children advance to what Piaget called the **concrete operational stage,** a time when they can perform mental operations and gradually begin to engage in logical reasoning. During this stage, children develop an understanding of the principle of conservation, usually first in relation to number and liquid (ages 6–7), followed by mass and length (ages 7–8), and finally by area (ages 8–10). Piaget called this stage *concrete* operational, because children's thinking and their use of logic is limited to concrete reality—they do not yet grasp abstract or hypothetical concepts. When concrete operational children cannot directly experience something, they have difficulty thinking about it. For example, ask a 7-year-old to explain the concept of *friendship*. Instead of defining it abstractly by saying that it is the emotional attachment we have toward someone based on affection, she or he is likely to say that "friendship is when you play with someone." The concrete operational child understands friendship only from actual everyday experiences.

Formal Operational Stage

formal operational stage The fourth and final stage in Piaget's theory of cognitive development (ages 11 or beyond), during which a person is able to reason abstractly and make predictions about hypothetical situations.

The **formal operational stage,** beginning sometime around 12 years or later, is the fourth and final stage in Piaget's theory of cognitive development. Here, early adolescents are able to reason abstractly and make predictions about hypothetical situations, much like a scientist does. Whereas problem solving in earlier stages often tends to occur using trial-and-error methods, formal operational thinking involves much more systematic and reflective strategies. A demonstration of these different problem-solving modes was provided in one of Piaget's own experiments (Inhelder & Piaget, 1958). In this study, youngsters were presented with several flasks containing clear liquids and told to determine which combinations would produce a blue liquid. Concrete operational children haphazardly poured one liquid in with another, trying to stumble upon the correct solution. In contrast, formal operational children tended to step back and contemplate their choices prior to acting and then to keep track of each liquid combination until they solved the problem. Such reflective thought and abstract reasoning are necessary in order for teenagers to competently study such subjects as philosophy, theology, politics, and science (Renner et al., 1990).

Although Piaget initially believed that all children eventually attain formal operations sometime during adolescence, later research found that many older adolescents and even some adults have yet to attain this ability (Piaget, 1972b). For example, only 25 percent of first-year college students and 50 percent of all college students are at the formal operational stage (McKinnon, 1976; McKinnon & Renner, 1971).

4-3b Some of Piaget's Conclusions about Children's Mental Capabilities Are Incorrect

No theory comes close to matching the impact that Piaget's cognitive developmental theory has had on the field of developmental psychology (Beilin & Pufall, 1992; Gopnik, 1996), and numerous studies have supported many of Piaget's central propositions (Lourenço & Machado, 1996). Yet, despite Piaget's continuing influence, an increasing number of studies are questioning certain aspects of his work.

First, it appears that children are more cognitively advanced and adults are less cognitively sophisticated than Piaget outlined (Spelke et al., 1992; Thomas, 2001). For example, although still egocentric, preschoolers develop a **theory of mind,** which is a commonsense knowledge about other people's mental states (their beliefs, feelings, and desires) that allows preschoolers to understand or predict other people's behavior in specific situations (Flavell, 1999; Flavell & Flavell, 2004). The understanding that other people have knowledge and beliefs different from one's own is a major accomplishment for children. It allows them to engage in much more sophisticated social interactions, ranging from empathy to manipulation (Leslie et al., 2005; Wellman et al., 2001).

> **theory of mind** The commonsense knowledge about other people's mental states that allows one to understand or predict their behavior in specific situations.

Second, cross-cultural research suggests that cognitive development is more influenced by social and environmental factors than Piaget thought. For example, in nomadic societies where quantifying objects is not very important, understanding of the conservation of number develops later than in Western cultures (Dasen, 1994). In contrast, the fact that these nomadic societies move frequently from place to place probably explains why their children's *spatial ability*—the ability to orient themselves in their environment—develops more rapidly.

Perhaps the most serious criticism of Piaget's theory is that cognitive development doesn't occur in the sequential manner he described—that is, children progressing through qualitatively distinct stages of thinking. Instead, an increasing number of researchers contend that mental growth is more accurately characterized by continuous and gradual changes that are less distinct from one another than Piaget described (Case, 1992; Flavell, 1982). Further, we also now know that people who have the ability to engage in formal operations often fall back on concrete operational reasoning when they are dealing with an unfamiliar task (Flavell, 1992). Thus, just because you progress to a more sophisticated type of thinking doesn't mean that you will engage in that type of thinking in all instances.

Despite these criticisms, most developmental psychologists still agree that Piaget outlined a generally accurate view of many of the significant changes that occur in mental functioning with increasing maturation. They also credit Piaget with highlighting the fact that children are not passive creatures merely being molded by environmental forces, but that they too are actively involved in their own cognitive growth. Not only has Piaget's work advanced our understanding of childhood development, but also his insights have profoundly influenced how and what we teach our children in elementary and secondary schools.

4-3c Vygotsky's Theory of Cognitive Development Stresses Instruction and Guidance

One implication of Piaget's theory for educators is that children's level of cognitive development should be determined first so they can be taught material appropriate to their level. According to Piaget, trying to accelerate children's learning beyond their current stage of mental functioning is not only a waste of time, but also can undermine their confidence due to the inevitable failure they will experience. Standing in sharp contrast to this view is the work of the Russian psychologist Lev Vygotsky (1896–1934). Perhaps influenced by his culture's collectivist beliefs concerning cooperation or its Marxist beliefs emphasizing the role of experience, Vygotsky argued that children's mental development can be accelerated if they are given instruction and guidance by someone who is more mentally mature. Whereas Piaget stressed the biological limits of learning due to age, Vygotsky emphasized how social environmental factors can assist and nurture cognitive development (Vygotsky, 1934–1986). Whereas Piaget conceived of cognitive development proceeding "from the inside out" and being relatively asocial, Vygotsky viewed it as proceeding "from the outside in" and being inherently social (Cornejo, 2001; Matusov & Hayes, 2000). Yet how exactly does this outside-in development occur?

Private Speech and Internalization

Have you ever observed children talking to themselves while engaged in some play activity? According to Vygotsky, learning occurs through the social instrument of language. Throughout children's daily activities, they listen to people and observe their actions. Then they internalize this knowledge and make it their own through this **private speech.** Private speech is part of a larger cognitive process, known as **internalization,** in which people absorb knowledge from their social surroundings. Internalization is one of the key mechanisms through which children's environments influence their cognitive development.

Zone of Proximal Development

In assessing cognitive development, Vygotsky maintained that, instead of locating children within a particular *stage* of mental functioning as proposed by Piaget, educators need to identify their **zone of proximal development (ZPD).** The ZPD is the cognitive range between what a child can do on her or his own and what the child can do with the help of adults or more-skilled children. The lower limit of the ZPD is the level of problem solving the child can successfully accomplish working alone, while the upper limit of the ZPD is the child's untapped cognitive capacity, which is realized only through working closely with an instructor. According to Vygotsky, one of educators' most important jobs is to identify each child's ZPD and then push each of them toward that upper limit (DeVries, 2000). Once the child can problem-solve at that upper limit alone, it becomes the foundation for a new and more-advanced ZPD.

Private speech plays an important role in reaching the upper limit of the ZPD. By engaging in cooperative dialogues with their instructors, children can incorporate their instructors' language into their own private speech and later use this speech when working on the task alone (Berk, 1994). By internalizing the instructor's language and making it their own, children become less dependent on direct assistance regarding the task at hand (Rogoff, 1984). The use of private speech to work at the upper limit of the ZPD is practiced not only by children but by adults as well. For example, the next time you study for an exam, try to catch yourself incorporating your instructor's language into your own private speech. According to Vygotsky, engaging in this internal dialogue is an essential part of the learning process at all age levels.

Although Vygotsky's theory of cognitive development has profoundly shaped Russian and eastern European developmental psychology since the 1920s, his work remained relatively unknown in the West until international tensions between the East and the West eased in the late 1980s and the Soviet Union was dismantled in the early 1990s (Kozulin, 1990; Wertsch & Tulviste, 1992). However, since then his ideas have helped psychologists and educators in the West better understand how learning new cognitive skills is often very much a *social* activity (see the "Psychological Applications" section at the end of the chapter).

private speech Overt language that is not directed to others but, rather, is self-directed.

internalization A process of cognition in which people absorb knowledge from their social surroundings.

zone of proximal development (ZPD) The cognitive range between what a child can do on her or his own and what the child can do with the help of adults or more-skilled children.

4-3d The Information-Processing Approach Examines Age-Related Differences in How Information Is Organized and Manipulated

Another perspective on cognitive development that has become influential during the past 35 years is the *information-processing approach,* which examines age-related changes in the way information is processed, stored, and actively manipulated (Demetriou, 1988; Siegler, 1998). According to this perspective, a number of important changes occur in children's information-processing system that directly affects their ability to learn. For example, the speed of processing information increases throughout childhood as some abilities become more automatic (Kail, 1991). This increase in performance speed appears to be due to the maturation of the brain (Sowell et al., 2004a). As previously mentioned (section 4-1c), the brain's neural connections become increasingly complex during childhood, peaking when girls are about age 11 and boys $12\frac{1}{2}$, roughly the onset of puberty. Simultaneously, the myelin sheath surrounding the axons of neurons thickens like tree rings, which makes neural transmissions faster and more efficient. One positive consequence of this brain maturation is that children become less easily distracted, although their ability to concentrate is still not up to adult standards (Jensen & Neff, 1993; Siegler, 1996). Because our information-processing capacities are rather limited (refer to chapter 8, section 8-1d), young teens' increased ability to focus attention greatly aids learning.

The types of memory strategies children employ change with age as well. Prior to age 5, most children simply don't use any memory strategies at all. At the age of 5, however, children develop the ability to rehearse information in order to remember it, but they use it much less frequently than do older children (Flavell et al., 1966). Older children also employ more complex rehearsal strategies, such as categorization and imagery (Alexander & Schwanenflugel, 1994; Moely et al., 1969).

One reason older children employ more sophisticated memory strategies than younger children is that they have developed **metacognition,** an awareness and understanding of their own cognitive processes. Cognitive psychologists believe that this ability to "think about thinking" allows older children and adults to acquire new and more complex strategies for increasing their cognitive efficiency (Moses & Chandler, 1992).

metacognition An awareness and understanding of one's own cognitive processes.

The information-processing approach is not necessarily incompatible with either Piaget's or Vygotsky's theories of cognitive development. In fact, some theorists have combined the insights from all three perspectives into what are called *neo-Piagetian theories.* These theories tend to view development as occurring gradually, with later cognitive structures developing from earlier ones due to children's interaction with their environment (Case, 1985, 1991). As continuing studies provide us with a better understanding of the child's developing mind, it is likely that Jean Piaget's work will still serve as the fundamental springboard for new theories.

Section Review

- According to Piaget, children's thinking is different from that of adults, and children move through the following four distinguishable cognitive stages: sensorimotor, preoperational, concrete operational, and formal operational.
- Vygotsky believes that by instructing children within their zone of proximal development and encouraging internalization of knowledge, mental development can be pushed beyond the cognitive limits proposed by Piaget.
- The information-processing approach examines age-related changes in the way information is processed, stored, and actively manipulated.

4-4   MORAL DEVELOPMENT

Preview

- *What sort of concerns influence the moral judgments of children?*
- *Do men and women differ in their moral reasoning?*
- *Is the moral reasoning of people the same throughout the world?*

Consider the following hypothetical situation:

> In Europe, a woman is dying from a rare form of cancer. The one drug that the doctors think might save her is a form of radium recently discovered by a local druggist. The drug is expensive to make, costing $200, and the druggist is charging 10 times his cost, or $2,000, for a small dose. The sick woman's husband, Heinz, goes to everyone he knows asking to borrow money to buy the drug but is able to scrape together only $1,000. He tells the druggist that his wife is dying and asks him to lower the price or let him pay the balance later, but the druggist says, "No, I discovered the drug, and I'm going to make money from it." In desperation, Heinz breaks into the druggist's office and steals the drug for his wife.

Do you agree or disagree with Heinz's course of action? What are the reason(s) for your answer?

Figure 4-9

Kohlberg's Levels of Moral Development

According to Kohlberg, we move through six stages of moral development, reflecting three different levels of moral reasoning. Each successive level represents a more mature analysis of moral choices. Which level are you on?

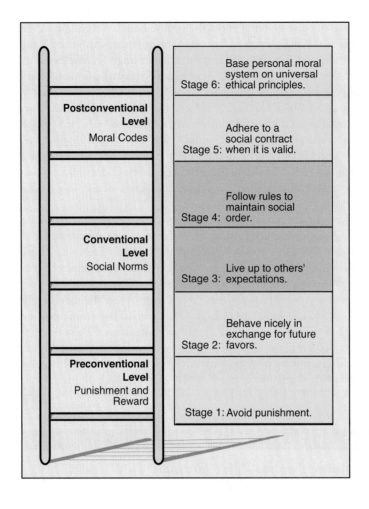

4-4a Kohlberg Identified Three Levels of Moral Development

According to Lawrence Kohlberg (1981, 1984), the *reasons* you give concerning the correctness of Heinz's behavior—and not simply your agreement or disagreement—provide insights into your level of moral development. Influenced by Piaget's theory of cognitive development, Kohlberg maintained that people pass through three levels of moral development, each containing two stages. Each successive level is a less egocentric and more mature analysis of moral choices (refer to figure 4-9).

At level one, **preconventional morality,** children's sense of moral reasoning centers on avoiding punishment (*stage 1*) or seeking concrete rewards (*stage 2*). Due to their egocentrism, people operating at the preconventional level focus on how their moral choices will affect them and not others. Thus, a preconventional person might reason either that Heinz should not steal the drug because he could end up in jail, or that he should steal the drug because his wife might make him something nice.

As children cognitively mature and become more aware of others' perspectives and the conventions of society, many begin engaging in **conventional morality.** Here, people define what is right and wrong in terms of societal norms and laws, and they are motivated to conform to these rules in order to gain the approval or avoid the disapproval of others. According to Kohlberg, most people remain at this level of moral reasoning the rest of their lives, basing their moral choices either on seeking acceptance and approval of others (*stage 3*) or on conforming to authority to maintain the official social order (*stage 4*). The reason Kohlberg considered social order conformity more advanced than interpersonal approval-seeking is that stage 4 reasoning is based on attention to rules made by representatives of the larger society rather than merely by a person's immediate peer group. In the Heinz dilemma,

preconventional morality The first level of moral reasoning in Kohlberg's theory of moral development; characterized by avoiding punishment and seeking rewards.

conventional morality The second level of moral reasoning in Kohlberg's theory of moral development; characterized by conforming to societal norms and laws.

a person at the stage 4 conventional level might argue that Heinz should not steal the drug because doing so is illegal.

Postconventional morality involves moving beyond mere acceptance of interpersonal norms and societal rules, to basing moral judgments on abstract principles and values that may conflict with self-interest and contemporary thinking. A basic requirement of postconventional moral reasoning is the ability to engage in formal operational thought. Yet, to attain this third level of moral development, abstract thinkers must base their moral decisions either on democratically agreed-upon individual rights (*stage 5*) or on universal ethical principles (*stage 6*). An adult at stage 6 might say that Heinz should steal the drug because saving a life is a principle that is more important than any law.

> **postconventional morality**
> The third and final level of moral reasoning in Kohlberg's theory of moral development; characterized by making moral judgments based on abstract universal principles.

4-4b Culture Shapes Moral Reasoning

Although Kohlberg asserted that his stage theory described moral development throughout the world, subsequent findings from cross-cultural studies suggest this is not so. As with self-concept development, the development of moral reasoning is influenced by whether a culture has an individualist or collectivist orientation. A number of studies confirm that children in diverse societies progress from the preconventional to the conventional levels, but that the postconventional level is typically reached only by people raised in individualist cultures, where personal rights and privileges take priority over those of the group (Al-Ansari, 2002; Snarey, 1985). Based on these findings, critics claim that Kohlberg's theory is not equipped to explain the development of moral reasoning in collectivist societies (Baek, 2002; Shweder et al., 1990).

Whereas Kohlberg's individualist theory of moral development considers the abstract principles of individual rights and social justice as the basis for the most "mature" moral reasoning, the religious and philosophical teachings from collectivist China and India, for example, emphasize social cohesion and group welfare (Ma, 1988; Miller, 1994). Here, morality is associated with an adherence to many rules and fits most closely with Kohlberg's conventional morality. Yet why should those cultures that emphasize social harmony and the good of the group ahead of the good of the individual be labeled as having a less sophisticated sense of morality? Cross-cultural research teaches us that moral development may vary considerably from society to society, and that what stands for mature moral reasoning in one culture may not be recognized as such in another culture.

Besides possible cross-cultural distinctions in moral reasoning, several early studies employing Kohlberg's theory found that women were often classified at a lower level of moral reasoning than men. Do these findings suggest that women are less sophisticated moral thinkers than men? Carol Gilligan (1982, 1990) asserted that these findings had nothing to do with any deficiencies in female moral reasoning. Instead, Gilligan proposed that these gender differences reflected the fact that Kohlberg's theory emphasizes values more often held by men, such as independence and rationality, while de-emphasizing values more associated with women, such as concern for others and belonging. She proposed that females in many cultures, including our North American culture, are socialized to analyze moral dilemmas based on these values. According to Gilligan, the end result of these different value orientations is that women's moral reasoning is more influenced by a desire to relieve distress and promote social welfare, while men's moral reasoning is more influenced by a desire to uphold individual rights and privileges.

The findings from a number of studies provide limited support for certain aspects of Gilligan's gender-based critique of Kohlberg's theory, but this research does not directly contradict his theory. It does appear that the manner in which men and women are socialized often results in their having different views on how they should approach social relationships, which might influence their moral reasoning. Throughout the world, men are more likely than women to value and seek *social power* over others and to view social relationships in terms of social dominance (Dambrun et al., 2004; Sidanius et al., 2000). In contrast, women are more likely than men to value and seek *social connectedness* with others and to view social relationships in terms of emotional sharing (Cross & Gore, 2004; Taylor et al., 2000). How might this affect moral reasoning?

While men represent powerful activity as assertion and aggression, women in contrast portray acts of nurturance as acts of strength.

—*Carol Gilligan, b. 1946*

Source: Courtesy of Carol Gilligan.

Consistent with Gilligan's critique, when making moral judgments, women may be more likely than men to take into account the social connectedness of people (Baumrind, 1986; Gilligan & Attanucci, 1988). However, having stated this possibility, it is important to note that a meta-analysis of the findings from many different studies has not found systematic gender differences in moral development (Jaffee & Hyde, 2000). Instead, evidence indicates that most women and men, as well as boys and girls, consider both justice and caring values when making moral judgments (Clopton & Sorell, 1993; Walker, 1989).

In summary, while Gilligan's assertion that men and women have markedly different styles of moral reasoning appears questionable, her work and the insights from cross-cultural studies have led to the realization that Kohlberg's theory is incomplete. Adult moral reasoning appears to be characterized by considerations of both justice and caring, with culture shaping the degree to which moral judgments also take into account the welfare of the larger group.

Section Review

- According to Kohlberg, people pass through three levels of moral development, with each successive level being a less egocentric and more mature analysis of moral choices.
- Questions remain concerning how well Kohlberg's stages accurately describe moral development in women and in collectivist cultures.

4-5 ADOLESCENCE

Preview

- *Is it true that we "created" adolescence as a stage in human development?*
- *What physical and psychological events do we associate with adolescence?*
- *Why are some teenagers so emotional and self-conscious?*
- *Why is ethnic identity development an important task for many minority youth?*

Are you an adult or an adolescent? If you are between the ages of 16 and 26, you may not know the answer to this question. During this 10-year span, your "adultness" is often open to heated debate. In fact, you might think of yourself as "adultlike" while attending college on campus, but relatively "childlike" when visiting your parents during semester breaks. So what are you? Let us examine some of the psychological and physical events often associated with adolescence, the "waiting and preparatory" period of life.

4-5a Adolescence Has Become a Gradual Transition to Adulthood

Adolescence, as a recognized stage in life, is a relatively recent phenomenon (Ben-Amos, 1994; Nelson et al., 2004). Most societies have always viewed young people as needing instruction and time to develop. However, as societies became industrialized, they had a greater need for workers with more specialized skills. To adequately train these workers, it was necessary to extend education beyond puberty and delay adulthood—hence, **adolescence** became the transition period between childhood and adulthood. Most preindustrialized societies, such as the Sambian people of Papua New Guinea or many African hunter-gatherer tribes, have little need for this transition period (Turnbull, 1989). Instead, after completing sometimes painful and demanding ritualistic ceremonies, children are ushered into adulthood and expected to take on the responsibilities associated with their new social status. For such groups, there is no need to adjust their cultural practices for the life stage of adolescence.

In North American culture, instead of going through one rite of passage after which everyone recognizes you as an adult, you go through many formal and informal rituals that make you more "adultlike." Adolescence is a time when you are en route to becoming an

adolescence The transition period between childhood and adulthood.

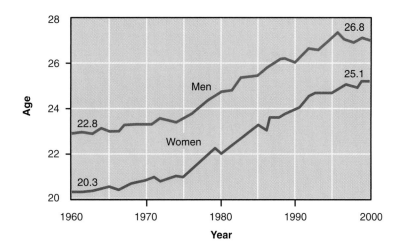

Figure 4-10

Median Age at First Marriage, United States

Over the past 40 years, the median age for getting married has increased by about 5 years. Why do you think Americans today are getting married for the first time at an older age?

Source: Fields, Jason. (2001). *America's families and living arrangements: March 2000* (Current Population Reports, P20-537). Washington, DC: U.S. Government Printing Office. Available online at http://www.census.gov/prod/2001pubs/p20-537.pdf.

adult, and people differ on when they arrive at the adult designation (Lerner & Steinberg, 2004). In this culture, the length of the adolescent period has gradually increased over the past 40 years, partly due to society's emphasis on attending college (Eccles et al., 2003). One consequence of this extension of the adolescent period is that today's youth are marrying at a later average age than their parents. As figure 4-10 shows, in 1960 the median age for getting married was 23 for men and 20 for women. Today, those medians have increased by about 5 years. A recent national survey found that most Americans consider people "grown up" after they finish school, get a full-time job, and start raising and supporting a family (National Opinion Research Center, 2003). In ranking the significant events of becoming an adult, completing one's education was most valued, with 73 percent of respondents identifying it as an "extremely important" step in achieving adulthood. Interestingly, "getting married" and "having children" were ranked last, with less than 20 percent of respondents stating that these were extremely important steps in becoming an adult. Further, people younger than age 30 were the least likely of all respondents to rank these two events as important criteria for being an adult. Table 4-7 lists the seven steps that Americans typically identify as being important in the transition from adolescence into adulthood.

4-5b Puberty Signals Important Physical Changes and New Neural Wiring

Most people would agree that adolescence *begins* at the onset of **puberty**, when the pituitary gland's increased secretion of the growth hormone triggers a growth spurt lasting about 2

puberty The growth period of sexual maturation, during which a person becomes capable of reproducing.

Table 4-7	What Makes You an Adult?
Seven Steps in the Transition into Adulthood (Age Event Should Occur)	**Respondents Who Rated Event as "Extremely Important" in Becoming an Adult**
1. Attaining financial independence (20.9 years)	47%
2. Not living with parents (21.2 years)	29%
3. Gaining full-time employment (21.2 years)	61%
4. Completing one's education (22.3 years)	73%
5. Being able to support a family (24.5 years)	61%
6. Getting married (25.7 years)	19%
7. Having children (26.2 years)	16%

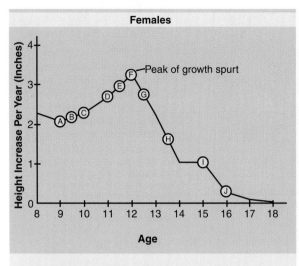

Females

A. Follicle-stimulating hormone signals ovaries to increase production of estrogen and progesterone.

B. Internal sex organs begin to grow larger.

C. Breasts bud.

D. Pubic hair sprouts.

E. Weight spurt starts.

F. Height spurt starts.

G. Muscle and organ growth peaks, and hips become visibly larger. Menarche.

H. First ovulation.

I. Final pubic hair pattern.

J. Full breast growth.

Males

A. Follicle-stimulating hormone signals testicles to increase production of testosterone.

B. Testicles and scrotum grow larger.

C. Pubic hair sprouts.

D. Penis growth starts.

E. First ejaculation.

F. Height spurt peaks.

G. Muscle and organ growth peaks.

H. Voice lowers.

I. Facial hair appears.

J. Final pubic hair pattern.

Figure 4-11

Sequences of Puberty in Adolescent Females and Males

years. Children vary a great deal on when they experience this growth spurt, but in North America, girls generally start at about 10 years of age while boys begin at 13 years (Tanner, 1990). Accompanying height and weight gains are the maturation of both the primary and the secondary sex characteristics. **Primary sex characteristics** are the reproductive organs, whereas **secondary sex characteristics** are the nonreproductive physical features that distinguish the two sexes from one another. Examples of developing secondary sex characteristics in pubescent females are breast enlargement, a widening of the hips, and an increase in fat deposits. In adolescent males, the development of facial hair, a deeper voice, and greater upper-body strength are some of the more noticeable secondary sex characteristics. Figure 4-11 lists the average sequence of puberty for the two sexes.

In girls, puberty's landmark event is the first menstrual period, called **menarche,** which occurs at about the age of 13. If parents or other adults have adequately prepared girls for menarche, they generally experience it as a positive life transition, although they still may respond with a mixture of pride and embarrassment (Greif & Ulman, 1982). The most significant pubertal event for boys is their first ejaculation, which also occurs at about age 13.

The timing of pubertal growth can have different psychological effects on girls and boys (Faust, 1977; Simmons et al., 1979). Because our culture tends to judge female bodies in terms of beauty and sexuality (Franzoi, 1995), early-maturing girls receive greater attention from boys than do later-maturing girls, and they also tend to date and engage in sexual relations earlier (Phinney et al., 1990). For some, this generally unwanted attention causes early-maturing girls to feel awkward and anxious in social situations and to suffer

primary sex characteristics The body organs that make sexual reproduction possible.

secondary sex characteristics The nonreproductive physical features that distinguish the two sexes from one another.

menarche The first menstrual period.

from low self-esteem. In contrast, our culture tends to judge male bodies by athletic ability and strength (Franzoi & Chang, 2000). Because early-maturing boys are physically superior to their peers, they tend to be popular, have high self-esteem, and feel relaxed and in control socially. What about late-maturing adolescents? The opposite effects are found. While slow-maturing girls are often pleased by the delay in the onset of puberty and tend to be more popular and socially poised, slow-maturing boys are distressed, feel physically inferior, and may become attention-seeking. Fortunately, the stress sometimes experienced by early-maturing girls and late-maturing boys does subside, and these females tend to enter adulthood with good coping skills while the males tend to have a strong sense of identity.

The hormonal changes that characterize puberty also influence brain function. The adrenal glands—located near the kidneys—release testosterone-like hormones that attach themselves to receptor sites throughout the brain and directly influence the neurotransmitters serotonin and dopamine, which play an important role in regulating mood and excitability (Spear, 2003). Two results of this hormone-induced chain of events are that adolescents' emotions easily reach a flash point, and that teenagers are now more motivated to seek out intense experiences that will thrill, scare, and generally excite them (Steinberg, in press). Such experiences include such activities as fast-paced video games, horror films, illegal drug use, and fast cars. Unfortunately, the brain regions that inhibit risky, impulsive behavior are still maturing, so there often is no internal brake on teenagers' sensation-seeking desires and roller-coaster emotions (Steinberg, 2004).

4-5c Some Teenagers Experience Heightened Self-Consciousness

At the same time adolescents are physically maturing, they are also further developing their reasoning abilities. They begin to think in greater depth about their place in the social world. With these cognitive advances comes a greater tendency to focus on the self, and this greater self-attention often results in a heightened sense of self-consciousness and more extremely positive and negative shifts of mood (Roberts et al., 2001).

One way that adolescents' self-consciousness is manifested is through the **imaginary audience,** a belief that other people are constantly focusing on the adolescent's thoughts, feelings, and behavior (Elkind, 1985; Kelly et al., 2002). For example, a teenager may be so convinced that everyone will notice a minor blemish on his face, or the fact that he is infatuated with a particular person, that he may actually refuse to leave the house until he believes this unwanted attention has subsided. Being so self-absorbed often results in the development of the **personal fable,** which is the tendency for some teenagers to believe that no one has ever felt or thought as they do (Elkind & Bowen, 1979). Thus, teenagers in love may believe that no one has ever felt the intense emotions they feel, and when relationships end, they may believe that no one can understand what they are going through—least of all their parents.

Although developmental psychologists once believed that almost all adolescents experienced heightened self-consciousness and social anxiety, it now appears that this is not the case. Teenagers are generally more aware of and concerned about being scrutinized by others than are younger children, but many adolescents experience little social anxiety (Vartanian, 2000). Instead, adolescence is the time when the emergence of formal operational thinking may lead to the development—or at least the recognition—of individual differences in self-consciousness and social anxiety, with these differences often extending into adulthood (Frankenberger, 2000).

Despite self-consciousness concerns by some teenagers, in most areas of their lives, adolescents are as well adjusted as children and adults, with about 80 percent reporting that they are relatively happy (Arnett, 1999). The problematic areas involve conflicts with parents and risky behavior. Compared to younger children, teenagers have more arguments with their parents, which the teens often spark by engaging in dangerous activities, such as drug use, reckless driving, and unprotected sex. Fortunately, as adolescents mature, they become more sophisticated in their social judgments, and as a result, parent-child conflicts and risky behavior decrease in frequency.

With the onset of formal operational thinking, when assessing others, older adolescents not only are more likely to recognize that people possess distinct and sometimes inconsistent

imaginary audience Adolescents' belief that their thoughts, feelings, and behavior are constantly being focused on by other people.

personal fable The tendency for adolescents to believe that their experiences and feelings are unique.

How does the imaginary audience heighten self-consciousness?

Source: Courtesy of Figzoi.

personality traits, but also integrate these discrepant traits into personality profiles that are considerably more complex than those provided by children (O'Mahony, 1986). Perhaps you recall spending hours, like many teens, analyzing your friends' and family members' personalities, trying to figure out what makes them tick. These attempts to understand the hidden world of personality are examples of how teenagers exercise their emerging formal operational thinking. In a sense, during adolescence, a cognitive-emotional "push-pull" takes place. On one hand, the emergence of formal operational thinking gives teenagers greater capability for deep thinking, but on the other hand, they must often learn to cope with new emotions that may sidetrack cognition into egocentrism.

4-5d For Minority Adolescents, Personal Identity Development Often Also Entails an Exploration of Ethnic Identity

As discussed in section 4-2f, one of the challenges of adolescence is developing a personal identity that prepares you for adult challenges. Yet what happens if you live in a society where the ethnic group to which you belong is devalued by the larger culture? In such circumstances, your search for personal identity may also encompass a search for **ethnic identity,** which is your sense of personal identification with a particular ethnic group (Hutnik, 1991; McAdoo, 2002). In a very real sense, ethnic identity is a state of mind, and acquiring it often requires considerable effort (Peters, 2002). This effort is especially important for people who experience prejudice in the larger culture due to their ethnicity. Faced with such intolerance, how might you search for your own ethnic identity?

Sociologist Jean Phinney (1993) has developed a three-stage model of ethnic identity formation, which is outlined in table 4-8. In stage 1, the *unexamined ethnic identity* stage, you have not examined ethnic identity issues and may have incorporated negative ethnic stereotypes from the dominant culture into your own self-concept. As discussed in the "Psychological Applications" section of chapter 1, internalizing these derogatory social beliefs into your self-concept can lead to low self-esteem and feelings of inadequacy (Clark & Clark, 1939; Phinney & Kohatsu, 1997).

ethnic identity A person's sense of personal identification with a particular ethnic group.

Table **4-8**	Stages in Ethnic Identity Formation

Stage 1: *Unexamined ethnic identity.* Lack of exploration of ethnicity, due to lack of interest or due to having merely adopted other people's opinions of ethnicity

Stage 2: *Ethnic identity search.* Involvement in exploring and seeking to understand the meaning of ethnicity for oneself, often sparked by some incident that focused attention on one's minority status in the dominant culture

Stage 3: *Achieved ethnic identity.* Clear and confident sense of one's own ethnicity; able to identify and internalize those aspects of the dominant culture that are acceptable and stand against those that are oppressive

In stage 2, *ethnic identity search,* a personal experience with prejudice or your search for personal identity may kindle an interest in your ethnicity (Kelman, 1998; Roberts et al., 1999). Whatever the initial spark, this stage often entails an intense period of searching, in which you read ethnic literature and participate in cultural events. During stage 2, you may also develop an *oppositional identity,* in which you actively reject the values of the dominant culture and criticize members of the dominant group. While in this oppositional stance, anything associated with the dominant group is typically viewed as evil and/or worthless, whereas anything associated with your own ethnic group is highly valued (Carter, 2003; Cross, 1991).

The third and final stage of this process is a deeper understanding and appreciation of your ethnicity—what Phinney labels *achieved ethnic identity.* Confidence and security in a newfound ethnic identity provide you with a deep sense of ethnic pride along with a new understanding of your place in the dominant culture. You are able to identify and internalize those aspects of the dominant culture that are acceptable and stand against those that are oppressive. In this way, your positive ethnic identity not only protects you from negative cultural stereotypes of your ethnic group, but also allows you to use this positive identity in pursuing mainstream goals and participating in mainstream life.

A number of studies support Phinney's view of the mental health benefits of ethnic identity development, among them high self-esteem and a stable self-concept (Phinney et al., 1997; Phinney & Kohatsu, 1997). These findings indicate that it is our commitment and attitudes

For many minority youth, exploring and seeking to understand the meaning of ethnicity for themselves is an additional dimension in personal identity development. How does an achieved ethnic identity prepare a person for the challenges of adult life?

Source: Courtesy of Figzoi.

toward our ethnic group, rather than the evaluations of our group by the larger society, that influence our self-esteem. Such positive ethnic identities can short-circuit the negative effects that prejudice can inflict on self-esteem (Branscombe et al., 1999; McCoy & Major, 2003).

- Adolescence is a fairly recent social construction marking a gradual transition into adulthood.
- Adolescence is a time of significant physical changes, including growth spurts and the maturation of primary and secondary sex characteristics.
- Adolescence is characterized by more complex thinking, heightened self-focus, and, for some teenagers, a heightened sense of self-consciousness and social anxiety.
- Minority adolescents who successfully complete ethnic identity development tend to have higher self-esteem and more stable self-concepts than those who do not develop an ethnic identity.

4-6 ADULTHOOD

Preview

- *How does gender shape friendship intimacy?*
- *Who is most likely to experience job and family conflicts in adulthood?*
- *What is aging?*
- *How can elderly adults guard against intellectual decline?*
- *How do we cope with death and dying?*

What is an adult? A child blown up by age.

—Simone de Beauvoir, French writer and feminist, 1908–1986

The psychological study of human development was once devoted almost exclusively to infancy, childhood, and adolescence. Today, developmental psychologists investigate the entire spectrum of our life's journey. Many of the physical, cognitive, and social changes that take place in adulthood differ from those that occur earlier in life.

4-6a Friendship Is an Important Emotional Bond throughout Life

Beyond the intimacy of family relationships, friendships provide important sources of social and emotional support throughout our lives (Elbedour et al., 1997). However, largely due to competing time demands, adults typically have fewer friends than do adolescents (Norris & Tinsdale, 1994).

Gender Differences in Friendship Patterns

Although both men and women value friendship, a number of studies find gender differences in the friendship patterns of North Americans from childhood through adulthood (Felmlee, 1999; Felmlee & Sprecher, 2000). The most notable gender difference involves the level of emotional expressiveness within same-sex friendships. Put simply, women's friendships tend to be more intimate and involve more emotional sharing than men's friendships (Veniegas & Peplau, 1997; Way et al., 2001). There is one important exception to this finding: The same-sex friendships of gay men are as intimate as those of lesbians (Nardi & Sherrod, 1994). What is it about gender socialization that leads to less friendship intimacy among heterosexual males?

Research suggests that men in North American culture are governed by a more rigid set of gender rules than women, especially regarding expressions of tender emotions and physical touching (Shields, 2002; Timmers et al., 1998). This social injunction against intimacy expression among males appears to result from men being socialized to conform to *heterosexual masculinity,* which entails valuing masculine traits related to power and control, while devaluing feminine traits related to the expression of tenderness and vulnerability (Shields, 1987). This perspective on manhood especially denigrates male homosexuality, because it is perceived to be the antithesis of masculinity. For a man to express warmth, nurturance, or caring toward another man is often interpreted as an indication of homosexuality, which was once also considered a sign of psychological maladjustment (see chapter 11, section 11-3e). Thus, many heterosexual men believe that to be masculine requires them to avoid acting in ways that might indicate homosexuality, including expressing warmth, tenderness, and affection in friendships with other men. In contrast, gay men do not feel similarly constrained in expressing intimacy to their gay friends. Although many gay men are justifiably wary of expressing affection toward one another in public because of anti-gay prejudice, no such anxiety exists in the gay community. As a result, their same-sex friendships are more intimate than those of heterosexual males.

The contemporary conception of masculinity as not encompassing tenderness and affection in male friendships is a fairly recent historical development in Western culture, and one not shared by many non-Western societies (Williams, 1992). As we move through the twenty-first century, changes in gender roles may eventually lead men to feeling less constrained in their expression of tenderness and affection toward other men. Until that time, however, male heterosexual friendships will generally lack the emotional intensity and gratification of the average female friendship.

Cross-Sex Friendships

Approximately 30 percent of young women and 40 percent of young men have cross-sex friends. In these friendships, individuals gravitate toward the "intimacy mean"—that is, men tend to be more emotionally open with their female friends than they are with their male friends, while women are not as intimate with their male friends as they are with their female friends (Monsour, 1997). Generally, heterosexual men believe their female friends provide more emotional support and security than their male friends, but not as much as women with whom they are romantically involved. In contrast, women do not perceive their cross-sex friendships as being that intimate, and they are likely to turn to female friends for highly personalized interaction (Wright & Scanlon, 1991).

Unfortunately, there are some drawbacks to cross-sex friendships, the biggest of which is sexual tension (Werking, 1997). One-fourth of cross-sex friendship failures are due to romantic and/or sexual desires, with men being more likely than women to experience such desires (Bleske-Rechek & Buss, 2001). In fact, men are much more likely than women to identify the potential of having sex with their other-sex friends as one of the major benefits of such friendships. This gender difference may occur because men not only tend to view sex as the primary means of achieving intimacy with women, but also tend to misinterpret certain signs of affection (for example, physical touching) as indicating sexual desire (Haselton & Buss, 2000).

Although most cross-sex friendships remain platonic, survey research suggests that half of all college students have engaged in sexual activity with an other-sex friend on at least one occasion, and one-third have engaged in sexual activity on multiple occasions (Afifi & Faulkner, 2000). When sex occurs, it does not necessarily change the friendship into a romantic relationship, nor does it necessarily end the friendship. If the two parties openly discuss the sexual contact and can agree on what it means to their relationship, the experience is likely to build trust and confidence in the friend's intentions and feelings.

Additional survey studies find that sexual contact is much more common among cross-sex friendships that are relatively new than among those that are of longer duration (Reeder, 2000). Why do you think this is the case? The tendency for sexual activity to be less common in longer-term cross-sex friendships may be due to partners recognizing that to preserve the friendship, sexual urges must decrease, or at least be safely regulated. However, another explanation is that cross-sex friends who don't redirect their sexual attraction eventually define themselves as romantic partners and, thus, are no longer included in studies of friendship! Until further research is conducted, the best conclusions we can draw about cross-sex friendship are that (1) it can be an important source of intimacy for both men and women, (2) it may be more highly valued by men than by women, and (3) issues of sexuality often have to be managed and negotiated to sustain such a relationship over time (Messman et al., 2000).

In cross-sex friendships, men are often more emotionally open and self-disclosing than they are with their male friends. However, women tend to be less intimate than they are with their women friends. What might explain these gender differences? What is the most common problem in cross-sex friendships?

4-6b Parenting and Job Responsibilities Often Conflict

As discussed in section 4-2f, most adults devote tremendous time and effort to pursuing careers and/or raising or otherwise mentoring children (generativity). Unlike many of their mothers and grandmothers, young women today are encouraged to work outside the home. Despite this historical shift toward gender equity, young women are much more likely than young men to receive mixed messages from their social environment concerning their ability to juggle these dual responsibilities. Such mixed messages occur because career opportunities often conflict with the traditional feminine role of child nurturer (Yoder & Schleicher, 1996). Due to this conflict, young women learn that their plans for work and family will be interdependent, with a great deal of trade-off necessary to balance both roles.

Interestingly, this fear of conflict between occupational and family goals is less of an issue among Black college women than White college women (Bridges & Etaugh, 1994). One likely reason for this racial difference is that, out of economic necessity, African-American women have a longer history of maternal employment than do White American women (Willson, 2003). Because Black female college students are more likely than their White counterparts to have mothers who worked outside the home, juggling these two roles seems more natural and less stressful for them.

In contrast to women's tendency to perceive conflict in their career and family roles, young men generally view work and family decisions as independent issues (Silverstein, 1996). This is so because in industrialized societies, many generations of fathers have spent long periods of time away from their families, resulting in many fathers being emotionally distant from their children (Masson, 1999). Accompanying this gender difference in parenting patterns is the widely held belief in many cultures that mothers are much more important to child development than fathers. As a result of this belief, a father's relationship with his children has historically been defined in the context of a bond with the mother. If that bond is broken by divorce or is not legitimized (as in the case of unmarried teens), the father's relationship with his children is often seriously undermined.

Despite this absent-father tendency, many men today are becoming more involved in the care of their children than their fathers, largely because over two-thirds of all mothers are now working outside the household (Adler, 1996). Yet, even with increasing father involvement, mothers in all ethnic groups continue to have far more direct physical contact with infants (holding, hugging, and kissing them) and spend far more time with their children than fathers do (Lamb et al., 1987; Wyche, 1993). In addition, wives still perform two-thirds of household work, or about 15 more hours each week of child care and house-work than do husbands (Steil, 1994). This imbalance in the sharing of household chores is smaller within African-American, Mexican-American, and Puerto Rican dual-earner fami-lies than it is within Caucasian families, but even here, the men's contributions are still not equal to those of the women (Herrera & DelCampo, 1995). In fact, the only household in which a woman's romantic partner shares chores and child care equally with her is a lesbian household (Kurdek, 1995). These statistics suggest that, while modern society has succeeded in encouraging women to expand their social responsibilities outside the household, it has failed to adequately encourage men to expand their responsibilities within the household.

> *Journey of Discovery* **Question**
>
> Why do you think it might be easier to encourage women to expand their gender roles to include "work outside the household" than it is to encourage men to expand their gender roles to include "domestic child-care" responsibilities?

What are the possible societal benefits of expanding the male gender role to include greater household and child-care responsibilities? Research suggests that when families have actively involved and caring fathers, everyone benefits: The children exhibit higher cognitive and social skills than children of less involved fathers, working mothers' stress levels decrease, the fathers gain greater confidence in their parenting abilities, and the couple's happiness with each other increases (Atkinson, 1995; Hoffman, 1989; Lamb, 1987). Although increased involvement in child care and household work can sometimes lead to increased stress for men in the short run, in the long run, it tends to strengthen marriages (Gilbert, 1994). The men most likely to break from the traditional father role and take on more nurturing child-care responsibilities are those who are older rather than younger, perhaps because they are more emotionally mature and secure in the parental role (Cooney et al., 1993; Neville & Parke, 1997).

4-6c The Body Begins a Slow Process of Physical Decline after Early Adulthood

I recently celebrated my fiftieth birthday—with my right leg in a cast. I hurt my foot jogging, and the once sure-fire remedy of resting the damaged body part was not working. So, after extensive examination, my doctor immobilized the entire lower leg so the foot would get a "good rest." I became a literal walking—make that "limping"—example of the impact that aging can have on the body (also add thinning, graying hair and tell-tale wrinkles to this picture).

Aging and the Body

What is this process we call **aging**? It is the progressive deterioration of the body that cul-minates in death. Of course, I have been aging for years, and this minor foot problem is just another reminder of my mortality. During adolescence and young adulthood, the body operates at its peak efficiency and strength. But, beginning in the 20s, it starts to burn calo-ries at a slower rate, causing many people to add extra pounds to their frame. Hearing also declines somewhat by the late 20s, especially for high-pitched tones. By the 30s and 40s, out-ward signs of aging become much more noticeable, with hair thinning and becoming gray, wrinkles developing, and visual acuity declining. A less noticeable aging effect is the loss of bone mass, which not only makes bones weaker and more brittle but also can actually cause them to compress slightly. Due to bone compression in the spinal column and changes in posture, by the age of 70, people have shrunk 1 to 2 inches.

The most significant biological sign of aging in women is **menopause**, which is the end-ing of menstruation. The time of onset of menopause varies, but it usually occurs within a few years of age 50, and it is accompanied by a reduction in the hormone *estrogen*. The most consistently reported sign of menopause is the *hot flash*, which is a sensation of heat in the upper torso and face that lasts for a few minutes. Many women going through menopause with the uncomfortable symptoms of hot flashes and night sweating have undergone

aging The progressive deterioration of the body that culminates in death.

menopause The ending of menstruation.

hormone-replacement therapy, which involves taking prescription drugs to artificially boost female hormones to their pre-menopause levels. Although hormone-replacement therapy is often effective in alleviating the negative effects of menopause, extended use of these drugs (lasting more than a couple of years) may have long-term negative consequences, such as increasing the risk of heart disease, stroke, and breast cancer, as well as doubling the risk of developing Alzheimer's disease and other cognitive problems later in life (Shumaker et al., 2003). Based on these findings, most women who take hormone-replacement drugs should do so for less than 2 years.

Although menopause is often thought to cause depression and other psychological problems in women, survey studies that have tracked middle-aged women's mental health over 10 years have found them no more depressed during menopause than at any other time (Busch et al., 1994; Matthews, 1992). Indeed, over two-thirds of American women who have experienced menopause generally feel better after going through "the change" than they have for years (Goode, 1999; Neugarten et al., 1963).

Unlike women, middle-aged men do not experience a cessation of fertility or even a sharp drop in sex hormones. However, they do undergo a more gradual reduction in sperm count, testosterone level, and overall sex drive, which can cause depression, insomnia, and impotence (Sternbach, 1998). They also tend to suffer an earlier decline in hearing and smell than do women (Steinberg, 1995).

Aging and the Brain

Regarding physical changes in the brain, after the age of 50, people begin losing neurons at an accelerated rate, so that at death they may have 5 percent or so less brain mass than they had in young adulthood (Selkoe, 1992). Women's brains shrink more slowly than men's, which may be one reason why they live an average of 4 years longer than men worldwide, and nearly 7 years longer in the United States and Canada (Coffey et al., 1998). The most neural loss occurs in the association areas of the cortex, which are involved with thought, or in the brain stem, which controls basic physiological functions (Whitbourne, 1985). This neural death in old age, combined with reduced blood flow to the brain and decreased levels of important neurotransmitters, can result in a significant loss of cognitive skill, which we will discuss in section 4-6d (Schmitter-Edgecombe & Nissley, 2002).

Although we experience increased neural loss in later adulthood, there is more to the aging brain than mere deterioration. Just as the brains of children can alter their neural connections following injury (refer to chapter 3, section 3-3g), as more neurons die during advancing age, the dendrites of surviving neurons can grow longer and bushier and take over many of the dead neurons' functions. In addition, researchers studying humans and other animals have recently discovered that throughout life the brain has the ability to generate a significant number of new neurons every day to partly replace dead neurons (Eriksson et al., 1998; Gould et al., 1999, 2000). This means that, at the same time the aging brain is degenerating, it also exhibits remarkable *plasticity* (Gross, 2000; Kempermann & Gage, May 1999). The aging brain is not as flexible as the young brain, but if adults live in an "enriched environment"—that is, one that is intellectually stimulating—they may show little evidence of intellectual decline through their 70s (Nelson, 1999).

Why Do We Age?

You might be wondering why we don't live forever. Let's consider this question from an evolutionary perspective. According to evolutionary theorists, all species are designed to live long enough to reproduce. The basic biochemical units that are maintained by natural selection are the genes, not the individuals who carry the genes. From this perspective, our bodies are really no more than disposable vehicles for replicating the information in our genes. Reproduction of genes is the most important function of the body, and natural selection may even favor a gene that causes cancer later in life if it makes us more fertile during our young adult years. Thus, from an evolutionary perspective, whether we live or die after reproducing is not important, unless our survival or death will benefit the ability of the next

Youth, large, lusty, loving—youth full of grace, force, fascination. Do you know the Old Age may come after you with equal grace, force, fascination?

—*Walt Whitman, American poet, 1819–1892*

That's the real trouble with the world, too many people grow up. They forget. They don't remember what it's like to be 12 years old.

—*Walt Disney, pioneer of animated cartoon films, 1901–1966*

generation to reproduce its own genes. So, in the large scheme of life, it might not make much evolutionary sense for us to live that far beyond our reproductive years.

If our deaths make evolutionary sense, what specifically causes the aging process that culminates in death? Biologists offer a host of theories but no conclusive answers. One set of theories proposes that aging is programmed into our genes (Hayflick, 1965). According to this view, each time a cell copies itself by dividing in half, the chromosomes—which carry genetic information—are copied incompletely. After many such cell divisions (on average, about 50), these copying errors accumulate to the point where the cell can no longer divide. Another set of theories compares the body to a machine that wears out due to constant use (Arking, 1998). According to one theory from this perspective, body cells gradually wear out after years of damage due to a variety of factors, including stress, toxins, and radiation. When young, our bodies are able to repair much of this damage, but not all the repairs are accurate or complete. After many years, these faulty and incomplete repairs weaken the ability of cells to both copy and repair themselves, resulting in eventual death.

Regardless of which theory ultimately proves to be the best explanation for the aging process, one of the biggest existing challenges for elderly adults is deciding how to adjust to these physical changes. Keeping physically and mentally active appears to be important in managing the aging process. Numerous studies indicate that people age with differing degrees of success, and those who both age successfully and live longer tend to have an optimistic outlook on life, a high degree of curiosity, and a sense of personal control over important aspects of their lives (Andrews et al., 2002; Swann & Carmelli, 1996; Yaffe et al., 2001).

4-6d Certain Intellectual Abilities Increase While Others Decrease as We Age

Despite the physical toll of aging, our mental skills remain fully functional throughout most of our adult lives. In fact, longitudinal studies of the intellectual abilities of about 5,000 people in the Seattle, Washington, area over the past 50 years indicate that general intellectual abilities gradually increase until the early 40s and then remain fairly stable until the mid-60s (Schaie, 1996). The abilities that show the most improvement during adulthood involve verbal ability, mathematical ability, and reasoning (Kaufman et al., 1996). The only ability that declines between age 25 and the early 40s is perceptual speed—the ability to quickly and accurately perform a task such as deciding whether two website addresses are identical. Around the age of 65 or so, a small percentage of adults experience a slight decline in certain intellectual abilities (Finucane et al., 2002). These deficits are most apparent for tasks requiring rapid manipulation of ideas, abstract problem solving, and rigorous mental effort. This decline appears to be largely due to the continued deterioration of the brain's mental processing speed. However, older adults' reduced neural processing speed does not generally adversely affect their ability to reason through everyday problems, understand mathematical concepts, or learn new information.

Although neurological decline is a natural part of the aging process, some elderly adults suffer brain damage that causes *dementia,* a condition of declining mental abilities, especially memory (Garrett et al., 2004). Dementia is most likely to occur among adults older than 65 years, and the brain damage is often caused by a stroke, a tumor, long-term alcohol abuse, or certain diseases.

The most common cause of dementia is **Alzheimer's disease,** which is a progressive and irreversible disorder that destroys areas of the brain that control thought, memory, and language (Rosen et al., 2004). Individuals with Alzheimer's disease have problems doing things they used to be able to do, such as balancing their checkbook, driving a car safely, or preparing meals. They often have problems finding the right words to use in conversation and become confused when given too many things to do at once (Nygard, 2004). Alzheimer's disease may also cause personality changes, with sufferers becoming aggressive, paranoid, or depressed (Marczinski et al., 2004). Scientists still do not know what causes this disease, there is no cure, and age is the most important known risk factor. The number of people with Alzheimer's disease doubles every 5 years beyond age 65. Current estimates are that about 4.5 million Americans suffer from this type of dementia, with the costs for care exceeding $100 billion. Even more troubling is the recent finding that twice as many American

Alzheimer's disease
A progressive and irreversible brain disorder that strikes older people, causing memory loss and other symptoms.

adults (9 million) with mild cognitive impairment may be suffering from the effects of early Alzheimer's disease (Ikonomovic et al., 2005). If future studies confirm this finding, it would mean that up to three times more people suffer from this debilitating disease than indicated by most previous research. "If you do the math, the numbers become astronomical," says Piero Antuono, an Alzheimer's disease specialist. "It implies a much bigger phenomenon than we originally thought" (Fauber, 2005).

Despite the devastating toll that brain disorders like Alzheimer's disease can inflict upon elderly adults and their families, the vast majority of older adults still have the ability to use the knowledge they have accumulated throughout life to critically analyze complex life events (Baltes & Mayer, 2001). In this regard, growing old can be associated with high levels of *wisdom,* which is expert knowledge and judgment about important, difficult, and uncertain questions associated with the meaning and conduct of life (Baltes & Kunzmann, 2003; Smith & Baltes, 1990).

4-6e People Differ in How They Cope with Dying

The most inescapable thing in life is death. Perhaps it is this knowledge that gives life its meaning. As people age, they become increasingly aware of their own mortality. Yet how do people typically cope with their own impending death and the loss of loved ones?

Are There Psychological Stages of Dying?

As discussed in section 4-2f, Erikson asserted that awareness of impending death triggers the final psychological crisis in life (integrity versus despair). Based on interviews with terminally ill patients, Elisabeth Kübler-Ross (1969, 1981) developed a five-stage theory of how people approach their own death: First, they experience *denial* that they are going to die; then *anger* ("Why me?"); followed by *bargaining* with God for an extension or second chance; next, *depression* when the illness can no longer be denied and what will be lost sinks in; and finally, *acceptance* of the inevitable.

Although Kübler-Ross's theory generated interest in the psychology of dying when it was first proposed over 30 years ago, researchers have found little evidence that people generally follow this five-stage sequence (Schulz & Alderman, 1974; Shneidman, 1992). For instance, counter to the theory, people who are old do not typically view death with a good deal of fear and anger (Wass et al., 1978–1979). Additionally, there is no empirical evidence that terminally ill people become calmer or happier as death approaches (Aronoff & Spilka, 1984–1985). Also, how people approach death varies a good deal according to their culture, and these differences are not addressed in Kübler-Ross's theory (Coppola & Trotman, 2002; Parry & Ryan, 1995). Thus, despite this theory's appeal, it does not adequately account for people's differing reactions toward death. At best, it may describe how some people who are dying at a relatively young age cope with death. Yet, even among this age group, many people do not follow the stages as outlined by Kübler-Ross (Bowes et al., 2002; Nolen-Hoeksema & Larson, 1999).

Communicating with the Dying Person

Unfortunately, the health-care system's emphasis on diagnosing and curing illnesses often results in medical professionals largely neglecting the psychological and spiritual needs of dying persons (Chochinov et al., 2002; Kaut, 2002). Family members also often find it hard to bring up end-of-life issues with those facing terminal illnesses. Because of this reality, many people often die feeling emotionally isolated (DeAngelis, February 2002).

Despite the fact that some people believe it is best not to discuss death and the terminal circumstances of the illness with the dying person, research indicates that open discussion and disclosure about dying are almost always beneficial (Kalish, 1985; Mak, 2002). Richard Kalish (1981) identifies some benefits of this open-awareness of death for the dying:

1. Dying persons have more understanding of what is happening to their bodies and what the medical staff is doing.
2. They can complete some plans and projects, make provisions for survivors, and participate in decisions about their funeral.
3. They have the opportunity to reminisce with loved ones and tie up emotional loose ends.

> Those who have lost an infant are never, in a way, without an infant.
>
> —*Leigh Hunt, English writer and poet, 1784–1859*

> Even the seasons form a great circle in their changing, and always come back again to where they were. The life of a person is a circle from childhood to childhood and so it is in everything where power moves.
>
> —*Black Elk, Native American, 1863–1950*

Most of us have an impact on many different people, shaping who they become as individuals. This legacy we build ensures that we will continue to live in their minds following death.

Source: © Stockbyte.

Spirituality and Meaningfulness

As death approaches, many people find solace in religion or in other spiritual beliefs. Spirituality can be a source of strength and comfort as a person nears death, but it can also trigger distress and despair if the individual feels abandoned or punished by God.

Consistent with Erikson's idea that the final crisis involves a search for meaning in one's life, recent studies suggest that people who have the most difficulty coming to grips with their impending death are those who believe they have nothing meaningful to grasp onto in their lives (Breitbart et al., 2000). For example, one study interviewed 241 cancer patients, who had less than 3 months to live, about their lives and spiritual beliefs (McClain et al., 2003). As death approached, those who felt they had led productive lives weren't immune to depression, but they were protected from the deepest despair experienced by those who found little meaning in their lives. Further, belief in an afterlife correlated with less hopelessness and with less desire to hasten death through suicide. This reluctance to hasten death among those with religious faith appears to be due to the belief that the power to end life is held by God, not by humans.

Every person must ultimately find their own personal meaning in life, but you are not alone in this search. I began this chapter by relating an incident from my childhood in which I earnestly tried to turn a lump of coal into a diamond. It is the "pressure" applied to you by those with whom you interact throughout your life that transforms you into what you ultimately become. Their life force shapes you as yours in turn shapes them. Whether you believe in an afterlife or not, in death, your life story goes on living. Those who loved you and others who knew you carry within their minds memories of you. Each day of your life, you are building a legacy of memories for them as well. In this sense, your life extends beyond your death.

Section Review

- Male-male friendships are not as intimate as female-female friendships, except among gay men; cross-sex friendships gravitate toward the "intimacy mean."
- Women are more likely than men to experience conflict in their family and career roles.
- Aging is the progressive deterioration of the body that culminates in death.
- If adults regularly engage in intellectually stimulating activities, they may show little evidence of intellectual decline through their 70s.
- A stage model of dying does not adequately describe most people's end-of-life experiences.

Psychological Applications

Using Effective Tutoring Strategies to Facilitate Cognitive Development

When the Zinacanten girls of Chiapas, Mexico, learn traditional weaving skills from more experienced women in their community, they first spend most of their time simply watching the women weave. Next, the girls begin to weave by cooperating with their teachers, starting with easy activities and then progressing to more challenging tasks. At each stage of learning, their teachers provide the girls with just the right amount of instruction to successfully complete the task (Greenfield & Lave, 1982). This example of informal learning is typical of how *tutors* play a crucial role in teaching new skills. To better understand how tutoring figures into cognitive development and what tutoring strategies are most effective, let's take a second look at the work of the Russian psychologist Lev Vygotsky.

Tutoring and the Zone of Proximal Development

As discussed in section 4-3c, one of Vygotsky's central concepts is the zone of proximal development (ZPD), which is the cognitive range between what people can do on their own and what they can achieve through guided collaboration with those who already have the knowledge and skills. In teaching a young would-be weaver her craft, a more experienced adult first assesses the child's cognitive range of weaving skills—her weaving ZPD—and then slowly moves her from the lower limit of that range to the upper limit. The upper limit of the girl's ZPD can be reached only through working closely with her tutor, yet once this upper limit is reached, it becomes the lower limit for a more challenging ZPD.

There is no one single "best" strategy in tutoring, but research indicates that the most effective instruc-

tors are those who combine general and specific interventions according to the learner's progress (Wood et al., 1976). In this two-pronged tutoring approach, the teacher begins with general instructions and stays at that level of advice until the learner runs into difficulties. The teacher then switches to a more specific type of instruction or demonstration. An example of this combined instruction strategy is the way my wife often teaches social studies to her fourth-grade class. First, she gives the students general instructions, telling them to read that day's lesson and then answer a series of questions at the end. If any students have problems answering the questions, her instructions become more specific: Preread the questions before reading the lesson; look for boldfaced words in the reading related to question material. This two-pronged style allows children considerable latitude in making their own learning choices, while still providing careful guidance when they reach the upper limits of their abilities.

In assisting the learner, effective tutors engage in their own problem solving: They modify their approach based on how the learner responds to instruction (Rogoff, 1990; Wood & Middleton, 1975). Good tutors also provide instruction that involves one extra operation or decision beyond the level at which their pupils are currently performing, so they are pushed to the upper limit of their ZPD. In trying to determine whether learners are "stuck" on a task, observant tutors not only listen to what learners say but also closely monitor their nonverbal behavior, including pauses, sighs, and nervous laughter (Fox, 1988).

Obstacles to Effective Tutoring

All tutors must bear in mind that their tutoring should never so dominate the lesson that it demotivates the learner, causing him or her to lose interest in the task altogether (Deci et al., 1993). This problem generally occurs when the tutor attempts to exercise control over a task that is within the learner's ability to perform—that is, at the lower limit of the learner's ZPD. For example, in trying to teach a child how to play a new computer game, a parent might take over the entire operation of the game instead of simply providing occasional hints. Before the parent realizes what he has done, his child has lost interest and is off doing something else.

Another potential problem faced by tutors is trying to teach a skill to someone who is not interested in learning it. A prime example of such reluctant learning occurs in the arena of household chores (Goodnow, 1988). Am I mistaken, or didn't all of us learn in childhood that if we acted wholly incompetent at, say, washing the dishes or sweeping the floor, our parents would do it themselves? At that young age, we already intuitively grasped Vygotsky's notion of ZPD and were banking on our parents' belief that these chores were so beyond our present skill levels that even guided collaboration was fruitless!

In tutoring students, effective teachers pay attention to each child's zone of proximal development, which is the cognitive range between what the child can do on his own and what he can achieve through guided collaboration.

Source: Courtesy of Figzoi.

Key Terms

accommodation (p. 121)

adolescence (p. 130

aging (p. 139)

Alzheimer's disease (p. 141)

assimilation (p. 121)

attachment (p. 106)

concrete operational stage (p. 124)

conservation (p. 122)

conventional morality (p. 128)

development (p. 98)

egocentrism (p. 122)

embryonic stage (p. 99)

ethnic identity (p. 134)

fetal alcohol syndrome (p. 100)

fetal stage (p. 99)

formal operational stage (p. 124)

gender identity (p. 116)

imaginary audience (p. 133)

internalization (p. 126)

longitudinal study (p. 110)

menarche (p. 132)

menopause (p. 139)

metacognition (p. 127)

object permanence (p. 121)

personal fable (p. 133)

postconventional morality (p. 129)

preconventional morality (p. 128)

prenatal development (p. 98)

preoperational stage (p. 122)

primary sex characteristics (p. 132)

private speech (p. 126)

puberty (p. 131)

schema (p. 121)

secondary sex characteristics (p. 132)

self-awareness (p. 111)

self-concept (p. 111)

self-esteem (p. 112)

sensorimotor stage (p. 121)

separation anxiety (p. 107)

socialization (p. 111)

social roles (p. 114)

stranger anxiety (p. 107)

teratogen (100)

theory of mind (p. 125)

zone of proximal development (ZPD) (p. 126)

zygote stage (p. 99)

Suggested Websites

Attachment Theory
http://www.psychology.sunysb.edu/attachment
This website provides information on Bowlby-Ainsworth attachment research.

Birth Psychology
http://www.birthpsychology.com
This is a website devoted to information on life before birth, birth traumas, and literature on birth psychology.

American Academy of Child and Adolescent Psychiatry
http://www.aacap.org
This website offers information about adoption, bedwetting, teenage suicide, divorce, and other developmental issues.

The Jean Piaget Society
http://www.piaget.org
This is a website covering Piaget's life and theory, with student links and information about the society.

Kohlberg's Theory of Moral Development
http://web.cortland.edu/~andersmd/kohl/content.html
This is a website with information about Kohlberg's theory, including applications.

Adult Development & Aging
http://apadiv20.phhp.ufl.edu
This is an APA-related website for Division 20, which is the APA division devoted to the psychology of adult development and aging.

Review Questions

Note: You can find the correct answers to these questions by taking the quiz and then submitting your answers in the Online Edition. The program will automatically score your submission. If you miss a question, the program will provide the correct answer, a rationale for the answer, and the section number in the chapter where the topic is discussed.

1. Which of the following statements is *true* of a zygote?
   a. It is created at conception.
   b. It contains 46 cells.
   c. It spontaneously aborts 10 percent of the time.
   d. It is developed during the longest stage of prenatal development.
   e. It can survive outside the womb.

2. A child's brain
   a. has fewer nerve cells than an adult brain.
   b. is not shaped by environment.
   c. is 75 percent of its adult weight by age 2.
   d. does not grow new dendrites.
   e. none of the above

3. Which of the following statements is *true* of physical growth and motor development of children?
   a. Motor development is not affected by culture.
   b. Basic motor skills develop from the legs up.
   c. Reflexes are permanent.
   d. There is a surge in height and weight during middle childhood.
   e. Primitive reflexes have outlived their usefulness.

4. There is evidence that
    a. the fetus is not capable of recognizing sounds.
    b. newborns can see very clearly.
    c. infants prefer sour tastes to sweet tastes.
    d. the sense of touch is not functional before birth.
    e. none of the above

5. Which of these characteristics has been attributed to securely attached babies?
    a. invulnerability to later problems in life
    b. lacking curiosity
    c. popular
    d. independent and socially skilled
    e. *c* and *d*

6. Which of the following is supported by studies on attachment style?
    a. Temperament is not significantly shaped by inherited biological factors.
    b. Parenting style has a greater impact than the child's temperament.
    c. Attachment style is not shaped by culture.
    d. Multiple attachments can cause adverse consequences.
    e. all of the above

7. Which of the following statements is supported by studies?
    a. The quality of day care is irrelevant when considering impact on attachment.
    b. Children who come from conflict-ridden two-parent families tend to be psychologically healthier than children of divorce.
    c. Mothers in all ethnic groups spend more time with their children than do fathers.
    d. There is no long-term impact on children of divorce.
    e. none of the above

8. The process of learning the ways of a given society or group well enough to be able to function according to its rules is known as
    a. adoption.
    b. adaptation.
    c. socialization.
    d. internalization.
    e. none of the above

9. The study by Lewis and Brooks that put babies in front of a mirror with rouge on their noses illustrated the concept of
    a. attachment.
    b. self-awareness.
    c. contact comfort.
    d. self-esteem.
    e. temperament.

10. Studies have indicated that children with high self-esteem tend to have
    a. authoritarian parents.
    b. permissive parents.
    c. authoritative parents.
    d. all types of parents.
    e. There have been no such studies.

11. What recommendation does the author give to counter gender stereotypes in the larger culture?
    a. Mothers and fathers should take turns doing household activities.
    b. Provide concrete examples of both men and women in all types of occupations.
    c. Engage in conversations about stereotypes with children.
    d. Monitor children's entertainment.
    e. all of the above

12. According to Erikson, the crisis that occurs when a person discerns whether he or she has contributed or produced something worthy of his or her efforts is called
    a. trust versus mistrust.
    b. autonomy versus shame and doubt.
    c. initiative versus guilt.
    d. competence versus inferiority.
    e. generativity versus stagnation.

13. Piaget's three-mountain problem demonstrated the notion of
    a. object permanence.
    b. representational thought.
    c. egocentrism.
    d. conservation.
    e. assimilation.

14. Which of the following is *true* of Vygotsky's theory of cognitive development?
    a. The cognitive development stage should be determined before teaching, so children can be taught material appropriate to that level.
    b. Children's mental development cannot be accelerated.
    c. Cognitive development is relatively asocial.
    d. Learning occurs through the social instrument of language.
    e. Internal dialogue is detrimental to the learning process.

15. Which of the following age-related changes is seen in information processing?
    a. increased speed of information processing
    b. increased ability to focus attention
    c. better use of memory strategies, such as imagery
    d. increased awareness of cognitive processes
    e. all of the above

16. Which of the following is a reason why teens often engage in risky behavior?
    a. General intelligence actually dips slightly in adolescence.
    b. Teens have a desire to "test out" their new bodies.
    c. Brain areas that control impulsive behavior are underdeveloped.
    d. The so-called "fear neurons" conduct impulses more slowly in teens.
    e. Risky behavior is an evolutionary strategy to attract the opposite sex.

17. In Phinney's (1993) research on ethnic identity formation, she found which of the following in relation to self-esteem?
    a. Evaluation of our group by the larger society is the most influential factor on our self-esteem.
    b. Our commitment and attitudes toward our ethnic group are most influential on our self-esteem.
    c. Ethnic identity is not as important as was originally thought in the development of self-esteem.
    d. Our self-esteem is more drastically damaged when we identify with members of our ethnic group.
    e. None of the above is correct.

18. The term *ethnic identity* refers to
    a. the characteristics, such as skin color, associated with ethnicity.
    b. an individual's personal feeling of belonging to an ethnic group.
    c. stereotypes associated with particular races.
    d. the unique cultural practices of ethnic subgroups.
    e. the performance of behaviors designed to show that one is "keeping it real."

19. Which of the following is *true* regarding the division of household labor in dual-earner families?
    a. Women greatly decreased their household labor as they worked more outside the home.
    b. Men and women spend roughly the same amount of time on household labor.
    c. In African-American families, husbands do fewer household chores than in Caucasian families.
    d. Wives do approximately 90 percent of all household chores.
    e. Only when a woman's romantic partner is a lesbian are household chores divided equally.

Chapter 5

Sensation and Perception

Source: Courtesy of Figzoi.

While Aron Ralston was climbing canyon walls in Utah's Canyonlands National Park, his right arm became pinned by an 800-pound boulder. After 3 futile days of trying to remove his arm from the boulder's grip, Aron decided to amputate his limb to secure his release.

Source: © Reuters/CORBIS.

sensation The process that detects stimuli from our bodies and our environment.

perception The process that organizes sensations into meaningful objects and events.

On April 26, 2003, 27-year-old Aron Ralston planned a 1-day training excursion in Utah's Canyonlands National Park. His goal was to go canyoneering, which involves scrambling, climbing, and rappelling up the sheer sides of canyons. After pedaling his bike into the park, Aron entered Bluejohn Canyon and began scaling its walls. When Aron was at the height of 60 feet and inside a 3-foot-wide slot, an 800-pound boulder shifted and pinned his right arm to the rocky surface. For 3 days, this former mechanical engineer used all his skills to try to free his arm, including vainly looping ropes around the boulder and rigging a pulley system with his climbing gear. Nothing worked, and he had used up all his food and water. What could he do?

Because people rarely entered this dangerous canyon, and because Aron had not told anyone about his trip, he knew there was little hope of rescue. He realized he would not survive unless he took drastic action. So, on that third day, Aron decided that his only option was to cut off his pinned arm. He took out a pocketknife and placed the dull blade on his skin where the incision should be made. However, he could not bring himself to do the deed.

On the fourth day, Aron practiced how he would apply a tourniquet using climbing cord and came up with a plan for cutting through the bone with his multitool-type knife. Finally, on the fifth day, he summoned up the courage to do what most people would find unthinkable: He cut off his crushed forearm just below the elbow. "It occurred to me I could break my bones," Aron later said. "I was able to first snap the radius and then within another few minutes snap the ulna at the wrist and from there, I had the knife out and applied the tourniquet and went to task. It was a process that took about an hour." How was he able to cope with the blinding pain while cutting through his own flesh and bone? "I'm not sure how I handled it," Aron later said. "I felt pain and I coped with it. I moved on."

After freeing himself from the boulder, Aron's ordeal was not over. Once he had fashioned a tourniquet around his partially severed limb, he crawled through the canyon and then rappelled to the canyon floor. With blood seeping from his wound, Aron walked 6 miles until he came upon some hikers, who notified nearby rescuers. Flown by helicopter to a nearby hospital, Aron walked off the aircraft and told the waiting hospital personnel, "I had to cut my arm off." Following surgeries and rehabilitation, Aron plans to resume his outdoor adventures.

Although few of us will ever have to deal with the type of life-threatening dilemma presented to Aron, experiencing and managing pain is a natural part of life, as well as one of the topics of this chapter. We continue our journey of discovery in psychology by examining the two interrelated processes of sensation and perception. **Sensation** is the process that detects stimuli from our bodies and our environment, whereas **perception** is the process that organizes those stimuli into meaningful objects and events (d'Y'dewalle, 2000; Ross, 2000).

Normally, we experience sensation and perception as one process, but they can be distinguished. For example, look at figure 5-1. Initially, you may have a hard time seeing anything meaningful—that is, you may sense different shapes but perceive no meaningful pattern. In fact, some of you will give up before organizing these visual sensations into a coherent set of objects.

We will begin our analysis of these two interrelated processes by examining some basic principles that apply to all sensory systems. Next we will individually discuss the five primary senses—vision, audition (hearing), olfaction (smell), gustation (taste), and touch—as well as the "sixth sense," proprioception (the sense of body position and movement). From there, we will examine how the brain organizes sensations into perceptions. Because scientific inquiry has discovered more about the visual system than any of the other senses, we not only will examine this sense first but also will later use the visual system to explain the major principles of perception.

Figure 5-1

Can you identify anything meaningful in these patterned shapes? Detecting the different shapes involves the process of sensation. However, seeing a person riding a horse involves the process of perception. When looking at this picture, which process did you experience first, sensation or perception? Is this noticeable delay in sensory and perceptual processing a common occurrence in your everyday life?

5-1 BASIC PRINCIPLES OF SENSATION

Preview

- *How does information about the world get to the brain?*
- *What are absolute thresholds?*
- *Does sensitivity in detecting stimuli vary due to motives and expectations?*
- *What are difference thresholds?*
- *How do people who live near busy streets tune out the noise?*

Can you sometimes overhear others' quiet conversations when you are considerably distant from them? Or do you sometimes "tune out" distracting sensations around you? These sorts of questions are of interest to the field of **psychophysics,** the study of how physical stimuli are translated into psychological experience.

> **psychophysics** The study of how physical stimuli are translated into psychological experience.

5-1a Sensory Information Must Be Converted into Neural Impulses

While typing this sentence, I am eating a handful of peanut M & Ms. I can hear their crunch while chewing, and I know that this sound is a response to vibrations in the air, or *sound waves.* I am also noticing a sweet taste, which I know is a response to the dissolving chemicals in my mouth. I can even faintly smell the aroma of chocolate, which is a response to molecules in the air that I am inhaling through my nose. I also feel the last three M & Ms in my hand, which is a response to their physical pressure on my skin. Finally, I see that these remaining candies are colored red, blue, and brown, which is a response to the light waves reflecting from their surfaces.

One thing to understand about this experience—and others like it—is that sound, light, and other kinds of stimuli from our surroundings cannot travel through our nerves to the brain. Instead, our sensory organs convert the physical properties of these various stimuli into neural impulses. This conversion process is called **transduction,** and it takes place at structures called *sensory receptors.* Following transduction, connecting neurons in the sense organs send this information to the brain. The brain then processes these neural impulses into what we experience.

> **transduction** The process by which our sensory organs convert a stimulus's physical properties into neural impulses.

One important fact to remember is that you can be aware of a stimulus in your environment only if you have sensory receptors that can transduce it. Human beings cannot see X rays or hear very high-frequency tones, and we cannot taste certain chemicals because we do not have sensory receptors that can convert these stimuli into neural impulses. These stimuli are just as real as those that we can transduce, but they are not a part of our sensory experience. Table 5-1 lists the stimuli and sensory receptors for each sense.

Table **5-1**	The Stimuli and Sensory Receptors for Each Primary Sense	
Sense	**Stimulus**	**Sensory Receptors**
Vision	Light waves	Light-sensitive rods and cones in the retina of the eye
Hearing	Sound waves	Pressure-sensitive hair cells in the cochlea of the inner ear
Taste	Molecules dissolved in fluid on the tongue	Taste cells in the taste buds of the tongue
Smell	Molecules dissolved in fluid on mucous membranes in the nose	Sensitive ends of olfactory neurons in the mucous membranes
Touch	Pressure on the skin	Sensitive ends of touch neurons in the skin

5-1b Our Senses Vary in Their Sensitivity Thresholds

To be sensed, a stimulus must be intense enough to activate the appropriate sensory receptor cell. This minimum level of intensity is called a *threshold*. There are two general kinds of sensory thresholds for each sense: the *absolute threshold* and the *difference threshold*.

Absolute Thresholds

> **absolute threshold** The lowest level of intensity of a given stimulus that a person can detect half the time.

The German scientist Gustav Fechner (1801–1887), who was a pioneer in psychophysics, introduced the term **absolute threshold** to describe the lowest level of intensity of a given stimulus that a person can detect half the time (Fechner, 1966). Psychologists measure absolute thresholds by presenting a stimulus (for example, a light or a sound) to a person at different intensities and determining the lowest level that is detectable 50 percent of the time. Some examples of absolute thresholds for various senses are listed in table 5-2.

A number of studies have found that the absolute threshold for a given sense varies between people (Rabin & Cain, 1986). For instance, due to the damaging effects of tobacco smoke on nasal cavities, smokers or people regularly exposed to tobacco smoke have a less sensitive sense of smell than do nonsmokers (Richardson & Zucco, 1989). As people age, their absolute thresholds for all senses increase, which means that greater stimulation is necessary to detect stimuli (Stevens, 1989). This increase is slower for taste than it is for smell, which means that the elderly are better able to taste things than smell them (Cowart, 1989). The inability to smell and taste can become so severe in the elderly that it leads to loss of appetite and malnutrition (Schiffman, 1997).

Signal-Detection Theory

> **signal-detection theory** The theory that explains how detection of a stimulus is influenced by observers' expectations.

The assumption underlying the absolute threshold concept is that there is a minimum intensity level at which a stimulus is consistently detected. However, according to **signal-detection theory,** the detection of a stimulus is also influenced by the observer's decision-making strategy or criterion (Gesheider, 1985; Swets, 1992). Two important factors that shape this decision making are (1) the observer's expectations about the probability that the stimulus will occur, and (2) the rewards and costs associated with detecting or not detecting the stimulus (Harder et al., 1989). For example, suppose you were looking for shooting stars on a night in which you mistakenly thought there was to be a meteor shower. Due to your false expectation, you probably would detect fainter, fleeting flashes of light in the sky more so than if you had expected no meteor shower. Detecting these flashes might also be affected by how important this task was to you. If astronomy was your favorite hobby, you might "see" more flashes than if stargazing were merely a lark.

One major contribution of signal-detection theory is that it points out that we do not have a single absolute threshold for a given sense. Whether or not we perceive a particular stimulus depends on the situation and on what expectations and motives we bring to it. Such knowledge is important because many signal-detection tasks carry life-and-death implications. Consider the task of an air-traffic controller who is responsible for ensuring that numerous aircraft, simultaneously in flight, have safe air lanes in which to travel. The controller monitors these flights by detecting small blips on a radar screen. Or consider the medical technician who is screening numerous X rays every hour for possible signs of dis-

Table 5-2	Examples of Absolute Thresholds
Sense	**Absolute Threshold**
Vision	A candle seen at 30 miles on a dark, clear night
Hearing	The tick of a watch at 20 feet under quiet conditions
Taste	One teaspoon of sugar in 2 gallons of water
Smell	One drop of perfume diffused into a three-room apartment
Touch	The wing of a fly falling on your cheek from a distance of 0.5 inch

Source: Adapted from Galanter, 1962.

ease. Are those very faint markings on the lungs normal, or do they indicate the early stages of cancer? Studies demonstrate that when people try to judge whether a faint stimulus is present or absent, their vigilance diminishes after about 30 minutes, due to fatigue. Although such fatigue effects won't cause serious consequences when looking for shooting stars, they could prove disastrous in the control tower or the medical lab.

Difference Thresholds

Besides detecting a weak stimulus, we often must detect changes in the intensity of a stimulus or discriminate between two similar stimuli. The smallest difference between two stimuli that can be detected half the time is known as the **difference threshold** (also called the *just-noticeable difference*, or *jnd*). For example, what is the minimum amount of difference you can detect in the sweetness of two soft drinks?

In 1834, Ernst Weber (1795–1878), Fechner's brother-in-law, discovered that the amount of change in stimulation necessary to produce a just-noticeable difference is a constant proportion of the original stimulus. Like the absolute threshold, the difference threshold for a particular sense varies from person to person and from situation to situation. According to **Weber's law,** a weak or small stimulus does not require much change before a person notices that the stimulus has changed, but a strong or large stimulus requires a proportionately greater change before the change is noticed (Laming, 1985; Norwich, 1987). Thus, lighting a second candle in an otherwise darkened room will much more likely be detected than lighting a fifty-first candle.

As you can see from table 5-3, the values of these proportions vary a great deal for the different senses. While we can detect a change in sound frequency of 0.3 percent (one-third of 1 percent), it requires a 7 percent increase to detect a difference threshold in smell, and a whopping 20 percent increase to detect a difference in taste! This means that our sense of hearing is much more sensitive than our sense of taste.

difference threshold The smallest difference between two stimuli that can be detected half the time; also called *just-noticeable difference,* or *jnd.*

Weber's law The principle that a weak or small stimulus does not require much change before a person notices that the stimulus has changed, but that a strong or large stimulus requires a proportionately greater change before the change is noticed.

5-1c Our Sensory Receptors Adapt to Unchanging Stimuli

During my first year in graduate school, I attended City College of New York and rode the subway to school each day. At first, the noise was so distracting that I not only had difficulty reading, but also invariably came home with a headache. Yet, within a few days, the subway noise appeared to diminish, and I became comfortable reading and headache-free when riding the subway. This example illustrates **sensory adaptation,** the tendency for our sensory receptors to have decreasing responsiveness to stimuli that continue without change. Although it is not clear exactly how sensory adaptation occurs, the most likely explanation is that it is caused when our nerve cells fire less frequently after high levels of stimulation (Rajimehr et al., 2004; Yamaguchi et al., 2004).

sensory adaptation The tendency for our sensory receptors to show decreasing responsiveness to stimuli that continue without change.

Weber's law states that a weak stimulus does not require much change before a person notices that it has changed, but a stronger stimulus requires a proportionately greater change before it is noticed. For example, in a room illuminated by a single candle, introducing a second candle results in a more noticeable change than adding another candle to a room of 50 already-lit candles.

Source: Courtesy of Figzoi.

Table 5-3	Difference Thresholds: How Much Must a Stimulus Change to Be Noticeable?
Stimulus	**Amount of Average Necessary Change**
Sound frequency	0.3 percent
Light brightness	2.0 percent
Weight heftiness	3.0 percent
Odor concentration	7.0 percent
Pressure intensity	14.0 percent
Taste concentration	20.0 percent

From an evolutionary perspective, sensory adaptation makes sense. Animals able to tune out constant unchanging stimuli that provide no new information should be better able to detect more useful information for survival. In our daily lives, sensory adaptation has both advantages and disadvantages. Being able to tune out noises on the subway allowed me to concentrate on my reading, which was advantageous because I studied going to and from school each day. Sometimes, however, my auditory adaptation became a disadvantage, as when I didn't hear the conductor call out my stop. Thus, although we may have evolved to tune out constant stimulation, some of the consequences of sensory adaptation may be to our disadvantage.

Auditory adaptation occurs much more slowly than adaptation to odors, tastes, and skin sensations (Scharf, 1983). For example, we adapt to smells very quickly, with the perceived magnitude of odor decay occurring at the rate of about 2.5 percent each second (Cain, 1978). Within 1 minute, odor adaptation is essentially complete, and the perceived magnitude of the smell is about 30 percent of the initial magnitude. We still smell it, but not as intensely. Try a little demonstration on yourself. Place a substance with a strong odor—perhaps onion, perfume, or shaving lotion—near your nose for a few minutes as you continue reading this chapter. Its odor will seem less intense over time. Next, remove the substance for 5 minutes, and then smell it again. Now it should smell as strong as it did when you first smelled it.

As you read about sensory adaptation, you might be wondering why objects don't slowly disappear from your visual field when you stare at them for a period of time. Doesn't sensory adaptation apply to vision? The answer is that, yes, sensory adaptation does occur with vision; stationary objects in your field of vision will disappear from sight. The catch is that your visual system does not allow a constant image on the retina. Your eyes are always moving, quivering just enough to guarantee that the retinal image continually changes, thereby stimulating different receptors. Scientists can fool our visual systems and achieve visual adaptation by having people wear a special instrument mounted on a contact lens that projects a constant image on the retina. When the eyes move, the image from the projector moves as well, causing the sense receptors to fatigue and fire less frequently. What happens to the image? Bit by bit, it vanishes, only to reappear and vanish again (Pritchard, 1961).

Section Review

- Stimuli must be transduced into neural impulses to be understood by the brain.
- Absolute threshold is the lowest level of intensity of a given stimulus that a person can detect half the time.
- According to signal-detection theory, detection of a stimulus is influenced by both stimulus intensity and the observer's decision-making strategy.
- Difference threshold is the smallest difference between two stimuli that can be detected half the time.
- Sensory adaptation refers to our sensory receptors' decreasing responsiveness to an unchanging stimulus.

5-2 VISION

Preview
- *What is light?*
- *How does the eye work?*
- *Where does color come from?*

Due to the fact that scientific inquiry has discovered more about the visual system than any of the other senses, I not only examine this sense first, but also later use the visual system to explain the major principles of perception.

5-2a We See Only a Narrow Band of Electromagnetic Radiation

Light is a form of energy known as *electromagnetic energy.* This energy is all around us and travels in waves of different lengths and intensities, created by the vibration of electrically charged particles. A **wavelength** is the distance between two peaks of adjacent waves. Our eyes can detect the wavelengths of visible light, which range from about 400 to 750 nanometers (a nanometer equals one-billionth of a meter). Within this range of visible light, the length of the light wave largely determines the *hue* that we see—that is, we perceive light waves of different lengths as different colors (refer to figure 5-2). We experience the shorter wavelengths as violet; the intermediate ones as blue, green, and yellow; and the longer ones as red. Other forms of electromagnetic energy that our eyes cannot detect because they fall outside this 400- to 750-nanometer range are radio, infrared, ultraviolet, and X-ray radiation. Besides wavelength, light waves differ in their amount of energy, or *intensity,* which is determined by the wave's height, or *amplitude.* Intensity influences the brightness of the light we see.

Scientists have proposed a number of hypotheses to explain why humans and most other animals evolved to see only this narrow band of energy. One hypothesis is that we evolved under the sun's light, a form of energy that is strongest in the 400- to 750-nanometer range. Light also travels very quickly—186,000 miles per second—and in a straight line, which means that we can see objects very quickly and in their actual structure. Having a sensory system that detects such fast-moving stimuli helps us quickly respond to environmental events and thus makes us more adaptive to our surroundings.

> **wavelength** The distance between two peaks of adjacent waves.

5-2b Light Passes through the Cornea, Pupil, and Lens before Focusing on the Retina

Light enters the eye through the **cornea,** a clear membrane covering the front of the eyeball (see figure 5-3). One of the important functions of the cornea is to bend the light falling on its surface just enough to focus it at the back of the eye. From the cornea, light

> **cornea** A clear membrane covering the front of the eyeball that aids in visual acuity by bending light that falls on its surface.

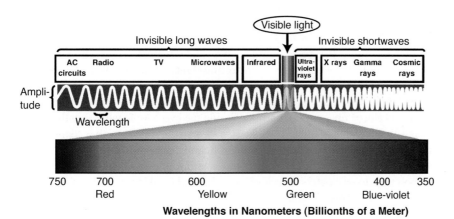

Figure 5-2

The Electromagnetic Spectrum

Humans sense only a narrow band of electromagnetic energy, ranging from about 400 to 750 nanometers. Within this narrow band, light at different wavelengths is experienced as different hues, or colors.

Wavelengths in Nanometers (Billionths of a Meter)

Figure 5-3

Major Structures of the Human Eye

After passing through the cornea, pupil, and lens, light is focused on the retina at the back of the eye. The point of sharpest vision on the retina is the fovea. To observe the pupillary response to light, first look in a mirror under bright light conditions and notice the size of your pupils. Now turn off the light for 30 seconds and then flick it back on while gazing into the mirror. Notice how much larger your pupils have become in response to the lack of light and how quickly they constrict as they respond to the added light.

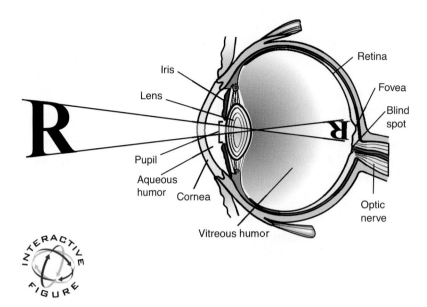

pupil A hole in the center of the iris that regulates how much light enters the eye.

iris A ring of muscles in the eye that range in color from light blue to dark brown.

lens An elastic, disc-shaped structure that focuses light.

retina A light-sensitive surface at the back of the eye.

passes through a pocket of fluid known as the *aqueous humor,* which carries oxygen and other nutrients to the cornea and lens. Next, light passes through a hole in the *iris,* called the **pupil.** The **iris** is a ring of muscles that functions much like the diaphragm of a camera. In dim light, muscle fibers in the iris dilate (open) the pupil, letting in more light, while in bright light the pupil constricts, letting in less light. Pupil size is affected not only by light. When you are psychologically aroused or interested in something, your pupils dilate (Hess, 1975).

Focusing the Lens

After passing through the pupil, light enters a clear, elastic, disc-shaped structure called the **lens,** which refocuses the light with the aid of muscles attached to it. When these muscles stretch and flatten the lens, we get a clear image of distant objects; by contrast, relaxing the lens and making it more spherical gives us a clear image of near objects. Because the lens changes shape without any willful action, people often mistakenly assume that everything, both near and far, is always in focus. To demonstrate to yourself that this is not the case, close one eye and look at a distant object, and then, while still focusing on this object, begin moving a pencil toward you while paying attention to—but not focusing on—the pencil point. As the pencil gets closer, notice that the point becomes blurred and appears to be doubled. When the pencil is about 12 inches away, focus on the point, and you will notice that the faraway object becomes blurred. As you move the pencil to within a couple of inches of your eyes, you will no longer be able to bring the point into focus, because the lens has reached its maximum curvature and cannot get any fatter. This distance at which your lens can no longer accommodate bringing the pencil point into focus is called the *near point.* As a person gets older (past the age of 45), the distance of the near point increases because aging causes a loss in the elasticity of the lens.

After being focused by the lens, light travels through the *vitreous humor,* a clear, jellylike liquid that occupies the space behind the lens, and is then projected onto a light-sensitive surface at the back of the eye, known as the **retina** (Mills & Catania, 2004). As people age, the vitreous humor may thicken, causing tiny clumps of gel or cells to form inside the eye and float around in the vitreous humor. Eye injury or normal wear-and-tear on the eye can also cause clumped cells or fibers to float around inside the eye. People who have these "floaters" can actually see them; they often look like specks, strands, webs, or other shapes. Actually, what these people see are the shadows of these floating cells and fibers projected on the retina. Because they are inside the eye, floaters move with your eyes when you try to see them. One of the best ways to see floaters is to close your eyes while looking at a light source and then watch for tiny strands, dots, or squiggles to float through your field of vision. A similar effect can often be achieved by keeping your eyes open and looking at a blank white background. In almost all cases, floaters are normal and perfectly harmless eye events. However, seeing floaters accompanied by flashes of light or peripheral vision loss could indicate a serious medical condition, such as diabetes, retinal hemorrhage, or the beginning stages of retinal detachment.

Besides the minor annoyance of floaters, abnormalities in the cornea's outer membrane wall and abnormalities in the lens can affect *visual acuity,* the sharpness of the visual image at the retina. *Myopia,* or nearsightedness—decreased acuity for distant objects—occurs when the cornea and lens focus the image in front of the retina. In contrast, *hyperopia,* or farsightedness—blurred vision for near objects—occurs when the eye focuses the image on a point beyond the retina. These eye defects affect many people, but they can be easily corrected by wearing glasses or contact lenses that alter the eye's focus.

In addition to these time-tested remedies for vision problems, an increasing number of people are turning to more modern medical procedures. In *laser surgery,* a surgeon first uses a computer-guided knife to cut a flap in the cornea, leaving a "hinge" at one end of the flap. Next the flap is folded back, revealing the cornea's middle section. Then pulses from a computer-controlled laser vaporize a small portion of this middle section so that the eye can properly focus on its own. Finally, the flap is replaced. For both eyes, this surgery usually takes only a few minutes, with the patient fully conscious the entire time.

The Retina and Photoreceptors

The retina is actually a piece of the brain that migrates to the eye during early fetal development (Gregory, 1998). Below its outer layer of cells resides a layer of sensory receptors, called *photoreceptors,* that convert incoming light into neural impulses (Greenstein et al., 2004). There are two basic kinds of photoreceptors: **rods** and **cones** (see figure 5-4). The rods, located at the edges of the retina, are extremely sensitive to light and are central to the

rods Receptor neurons in the eye, located at the edges of the retina, that are sensitive to the brightness of light.

cones Receptor neurons in the eye, located near the center of the retina, that mediate color vision.

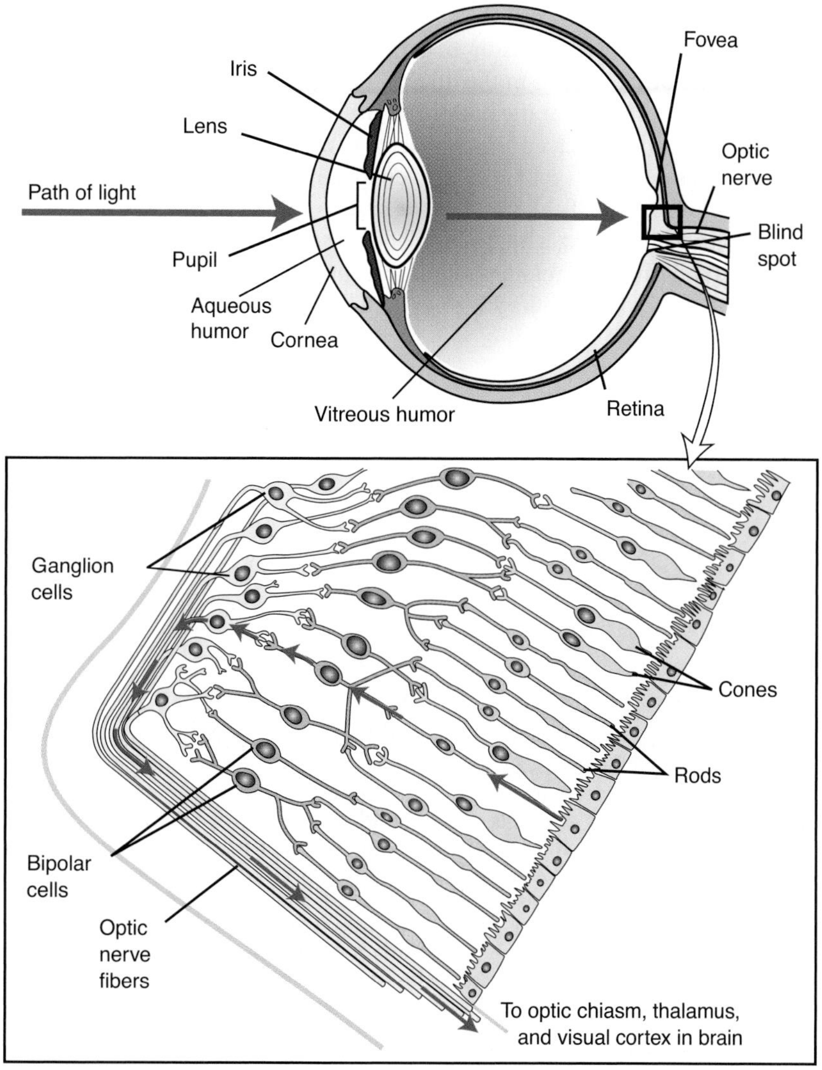

Figure 5-4

How Light Travels through the Eye

Light passing through the eye falls on the retina. This light then passes through several layers of cells below the surface of the retina before striking and activating sensory receptors called photoreceptors. The two different kinds of photoreceptors are rods and cones. The rods, which are extremely sensitive to light, help us detect patterns of black, white, and gray. The cones require much more light to be activated and play a key role in our color vision. When activated, these two types of photoreceptors send neural impulses to bipolar cells that, in turn, activate the ganglion cells (Chen et al., 2004). The axons of these ganglion cells converge to form the optic nerve, which sends information to the brain.

Iris

Lens

Path of light

Pupil

Aqueous humor

Cornea

Vitreous humor

Fovea

Optic nerve

Blind spot

Retina

Ganglion cells

Cones

Rods

Bipolar cells

Optic nerve fibers

To optic chiasm, thalamus, and visual cortex in brain

INTERACTIVE FIGURE

detection of patterns of black, white, and gray. The rods function best under low-light conditions and thus are most useful at night. In contrast, the cones require much more light to be activated and play a key role in color vision. Most cones are concentrated in a small area near the center of the retina known as the **fovea,** which is the area of central focus. A human retina contains about 125 million rods and 7 million cones (Pugh, 1988). As you would expect, animals that are most active at night, such as owls and rats, have all-rod eyes, whereas daytime animals, such as lizards and chipmunks, have mostly cone-dominant retinas (Tansley, 1965; Wagner, 2001).

> **fovea** The retina's area of central focus.

When light reaches the back of the eye and strikes the retina, it actually passes through several layers of cells below the retina's surface before reaching the rods and cones. Once activated by this light energy, the rods and cones generate neural signals that activate adjacent *bipolar cells,* which in turn activate neighboring *ganglion cells* (see figure 5-4). The axons of the ganglion cells converge like the strands of a rope to form the **optic nerve,** which carries information from the retina to the brain. Before visual signals are sent on to the brain, however, a great deal of complex information-processing takes place in the retina (Slaughter, 1990). This processing occurs in the bipolar and ganglion cells, where information from the rods and cones is integrated and compressed so that it can be more easily transmitted along the optic nerve. The portion of the retina where the optic nerve leaves the eye contains no rods or cones, which means that images falling there are not seen (Ramachandran, 1992). For this reason, this area is called the **blind spot** in the field of vision (see figure 5-5).

> **optic nerve** The bundle of nerve cells that carries information from the retina to the brain.

> **blind spot** The area on the retina where the optic nerve leaves the eye; contains no receptor cells.

5-2c Visual Information from Both Eyes Is Transmitted to Both Brain Hemispheres

After they leave the eyes, the axons of the ganglion cells that make up the optic nerve separate, and half of them cross to the other side of the head at the *optic chiasm* (pronounced "KYE-az-um"), which is at the bottom of the brain. As illustrated in figure 5-6, the axons from the right side of each eye are connected to the right hemisphere of the brain, and those from the left side of each eye are connected to the left hemisphere. Thus, visual information in a person's left visual field, which is the area to the left of the person, will go to the right hemisphere, while the exact opposite will be true for information in the person's right visual field. This splitting and crossing over of the optic nerve is very important, because it guarantees that signals from both eyes go to both brain hemispheres.

Figure 5-5

The Blind Spot

You can experience your own blind spot by closing your right eye and lining up the cross with your left eye. Now slowly move your head back and forth. When the image is between 6 and 18 inches away from your eye, the image of the happy face falls on your blind spot and disappears from sight. One reason you are not more aware of your blind spot is that when an image falls on the blind spot of one eye, it falls on the receptors of the other, and thus you still detect the image. Another reason you don't often perceive the blind spot, even with one-eyed vision, is that it is located off to the side of your visual field, and thus objects near this area are never in sharp focus. Finally, perhaps the most important reason that you are not aware of the blind spot is that your visual system somehow "fills in" the place where the image disappears. Thus, when you try the blind spot demonstration, the place where the happy face used to be isn't replaced by a "hole" or by "nothingness" but, rather, by the white surrounding it.

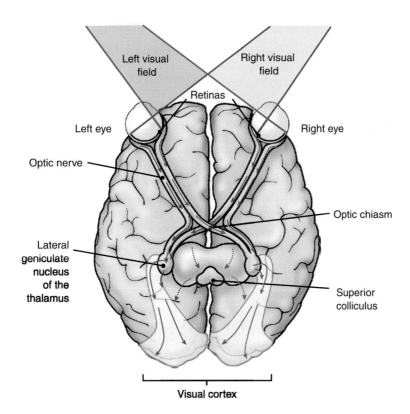

Figure 5-6

The Brain's Visual Pathways

This view of the visual system of the brain shows how the optic nerve carries visual information from the retina to the optic chiasm, where the optic nerve splits. Information from the right half of the visual field strikes the left side of each retina and is sent to the left hemisphere. Information from the left half of the visual field strikes the right side of each retina and is sent to the right hemisphere. After reaching the optic chiasm, a minor pathway goes to the superior colliculus in the midbrain, but the major visual pathway is to the lateral geniculate nucleus of the thalamus. From the lateral geniculate nucleus, visual information is sent to the occipital lobe, or visual cortex (Dow, 2002).

A short distance after leaving the optic chiasm, the optic nerve fibers diverge along two pathways. Eighty percent of the nerve fibers are connected to the *lateral geniculate nucleus* of the thalamus, while most of the rest of the nerve fibers are attached to the *superior colliculus* in the midbrain. The superior colliculus is the evolutionarily older of the two brain structures and is the primary area for visual processing in less-developed animals, such as frogs. In humans, the superior colliculus is involved in controlling eye movements. In contrast to this more primitive brain structure, the lateral geniculate nucleus is a kidney-bean-shaped cluster of neurons that performs much more detailed visual analysis. Six different layers of cells in the lateral geniculate nucleus not only organize information about color and other aspects of the visual field reaching it from the retina but also create a "map" of visual space in the retina, where each location on the lateral geniculate nucleus corresponds to a location on the retina (Mollon, 1990).

From the lateral geniculate nucleus, visual information proceeds to areas in the occipital lobe that make up the visual cortex. To understand how cells in the visual cortex communicate with one another, in the late 1950s David Hubel and Tortsen Wiesel placed microelectrodes in this area of a cat's brain to record action potentials from individual neurons. To stimulate action potentials, the researchers projected spots of light onto a screen with a slide projector, but they were initially unable to get the neurons to fire with any regularity. Then, quite by accident, as they were inserting a glass slide containing a spot stimulus into their projector, a neuron began firing like crazy. Hubel and Wiesel then discovered that the rapid neural firing was in response not to the image of the spot but to the image of the straight edge of the slide as it moved downward on the projector screen! They proposed that cells in the visual cortex known as **feature detectors** respond only to a highly specific *feature* or characteristic of a visual stimulus, such as a straight edge, an angle, movement of a spot, or brightness (Hubel & Wiesel, 1965a, 1965b). This information is then passed on to other cells that, in turn, respond only to more complex features. Through this interaction among many types of visual neurons, each responsible for specific tasks, our brain acquires the basic building blocks of visual perception that it then assembles into a meaningful whole (Hubel, 1996; Jiang et al., 2002; Rolls & Deco, 2002). This groundbreaking research earned Hubel and Wiesel the Nobel Prize in Physiology in 1981.

feature detectors Cells in the visual cortex that respond only to a highly specific feature of a visual stimulus, such as a straight edge, an angle, movement of a spot, or brightness.

5-2d Colors Are Created in Our Visual System, Not in the World

As I sit writing this section of the chapter, I can look out my window and see a world of color, highlighted by beautiful green-shrouded woods and a light-blue sky. Yet what does it really mean when we say that a leaf is green or the sky is blue? Do the leaf and the sky actually possess the colors we perceive?

What Is Color?

To humans and other color-perceiving animals, an object appears as a particular color because it absorbs certain wavelengths of light and reflects others. The color green is not actually in the tree leaves outside my window, nor is it in the light waves reflected from the leaves. Instead, the color resides in my own visual system. The leaves absorb all the wavelengths of light except those that evoke the sensation of green in my mind. There is nothing inherently "blue" about short wavelengths or "red" about long wavelengths. These wavelengths are simply energy. Colors are *created* by our nervous system in response to these wavelengths.

The idea that our sensory experience is created by our nervous system is hard for some people to understand. It becomes easier to grasp this fact when we consider color perception in other animals (Smith et al., 2002). The next time you see a honeybee or a pigeon, look at what it is looking at. You won't be seeing the same thing. Although honeybees have trichromatic vision like we do, their three kinds of color receptors are more spread out over the lower band of the spectrum than our own, and thus they are sensitive to light in the ultraviolet range but cannot see red (Menzel & Backhaus, 1989). Pigeons' color vision appears to be based on five kinds of receptors (pentachromatic vision), and thus they undoubtedly see the world differently than do we (Varela et al., 1993).

Do Humans Share the Same Color Experience?

Astonishingly, our difference threshold for colors is so low that the average person can discriminate about 2 million different colors (Abramov & Gordon, 1994; Gouras, 1991). Cross-cultural research indicates that all cultures have names for the colors black and white, and that the colors red, yellow, green, and blue are added before any others (Berlin & Kay, 1969; Boynton & Olson, 1990). These findings suggest that humans universally share a physiological basis for experiencing color (Pokorny et al., 1991).

5-2e The Trichromatic Theory and the Opponent-Process Theory Explain Different Aspects of Color Vision

Any color can be created by combining the light wavelengths of three primary colors—red, green, and blue (Hunt, 1998). Combining red, green, and blue lights makes white light. This

Strictly speaking, there are no colors *in* this painting. Artists construct their paintings so that when light strikes them, the paintings' surfaces absorb certain wavelengths of light and reflect others. This reflected light, which consists of many waves of different lengths and intensity levels, enters our eyes and strikes our retinas. This light is then converted into neural impulses and sent to the brain for further processing. Thus, the colors that we ultimately perceive are really a creation of our nervous system. Most of us can agree on the different colors that we see in our world because our visual systems operate in roughly the same manner. Notable exceptions are people with color blindness (see section 5-2e).

Source: Painting on wall: Milton Resnick, *East Is the Place,* 1959, oil on canvas, 117 × 190 inches. Milwaukee Art Museum, gift of Mr. and Mrs. Howard Wise, New York, *M1969.48.* © Milton Resnick. Courtesy Robert Miller Gallery, New York.

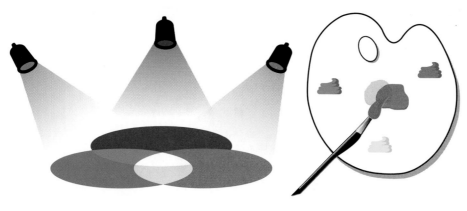

Figure 5-7

Additive and Subtractive Color Mixing

(Left) The three primary light colors—red, green, and blue—combine to create all the other colors of light. Mixing light of different wavelengths involves *additive color mixing* because the process adds wavelengths and thus increases light. Combining red and green makes yellow, while mixing all three together creates white. The colors that result when you mix paints are different from the colors that result when you combine colored lights.

(Right) Mixing color pigments in paint involves *subtractive color mixing,* because the process subtracts wavelengths of reflected light and thus decreases light. Magenta, cyan, and yellow are the primary pigments. Paint with any of these colors absorbs one primary color of light and reflects the other two. For example, if you wanted red paint, you would mix magenta and yellow. Magenta would absorb green, and yellow would absorb blue, leaving only red reflected back to your eyes. Mixing all three primary pigments would result in no light waves being reflected, and you would see black.

mixing of different light wavelengths is known as *additive color mixing,* because the process adds wavelengths and thus increases light. In contrast, when you mix paint pigments, you are *subtracting* wavelengths from the reflected light. Each color you mix in absorbs (or subtracts) more wavelengths, resulting in fewer being reflected back. The colors that result when you mix pigments are different from the colors that result when you combine the primary colors of light. Magenta, cyan, and yellow are called the primary pigments. In *subtractive color mixing,* combining magenta, cyan, and yellow pigments results in no light waves being reflected, and you see black. Figure 5-7 illustrates these two types of color mixing.

To explain how our visual system causes us to experience this color mixing, two nineteenth-century scientists—first the English physician Thomas Young (1773–1829), and later the German physiologist Hermann von Helmholtz (1821–1894)—hypothesized that the retina has three types of color receptors and that differing sensitivities to the different light waves are associated with these three primary colors. According to what came to be called the Young-Helmholtz **trichromatic theory,** light of a particular wavelength stimulates these three types of receptors to different degrees, and the resulting pattern of neural activity among these receptors results in color perception (Finger & Wade, 2002).

More than 100 years after the trichromatic theory was offered as an explanation for color vision, George Wald verified the existence of three different types of cones in the retina (Brown & Wald, 1964; Wald, 1964), a discovery that earned him a Nobel Prize. As trichromatic theory proposed, each cone is most sensitive to a particular wavelength of light. Long-wavelength cones (L-cones) are most sensitive to wavelengths of about 555 nanometers, which are perceived as red. Middle-wavelength cones (M-cones) produce the sensation of green and are most sensitive to wavelengths of about 525 nanometers. Finally, short-wavelength cones (S-cones), which produce the sensation of blue, are most sensitive to wavelengths of about 450 nanometers. By combining different stimulation levels from these three kinds of cones, our visual system produces a multitude of different color sensations. The trichromatic theory provides a partial explanation for **color blindness,** which is a deficiency in the ability to distinguish among colors. Approximately 1 in 50 people is color-blind, and about 90 percent of these are males, because the defect is genetic and carried

trichromatic theory
A theory of color perception proposing that three types of color receptors in the retina produce the primary color sensations of red, green, and blue.

color blindness A deficiency in the ability to distinguish among colors.

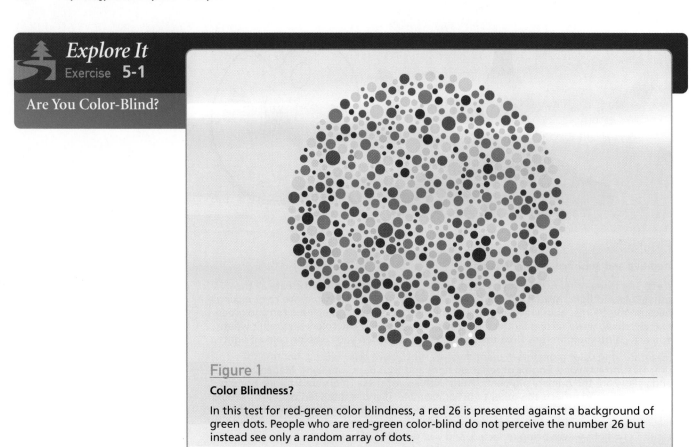

Explore It
Exercise **5-1**

Are You Color-Blind?

Figure 1

Color Blindness?

In this test for red-green color blindness, a red 26 is presented against a background of green dots. People who are red-green color-blind do not perceive the number 26 but instead see only a random array of dots.

on the X chromosome. A male who inherits the trait on his single X chromosome will be color-blind, but a female must inherit the trait on both of her X chromosomes to be color-blind. Interestingly, color blindness is more common among White men (8 percent) than among Asian (5 percent), African (3 percent), and Native American (3 percent) men. Check out Explore It Exercise 5-1 to test yourself for red-green color blindness.

Actually, the term *color blindness* is misleading because most people classified as color-blind are *dichromats,* meaning they can see two primary colors but are insensitive to the third because the cone that is sensitive to that color is nonfunctional (Gouras, 1991; Ladd-Franklin, 1929). In contrast, only about 10 people out of 1 million have the rare form of color blindness in which there are no functioning cones. These *monochromats* see everything in shades of white, gray, and black. Thus, while the relatively rare monochromats are truly color-blind, *color deficiency* is a more accurate term to describe the much more prevalent dichromats.

At roughly the same time that Helmholtz was championing the trichromatic theory, the German physiologist Ewald Hering (1834–1918) proposed a competing theory. His ideas were sparked by the observation of **afterimages,** which are visual images that persist after a stimulus has been removed (figure 5-8). Pointing out that the trichromatic theory could not

afterimage A visual image that persists after a stimulus has been removed.

Figure 5-8

Afterimage

Gaze steadily for about a minute at the lower-right corner of the yellow field of stars, and then look at the white space above or beside the flag. What do you see? The "Old Glory" you see is composed of the complementary colors in your visual system. Why do these colors reverse in this manner?

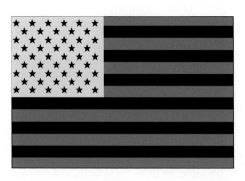

explain this visual phenomenon, Hering proposed a theory that could—namely, the **opponent-process theory.** This theory argues that all colors are derived from three opposing color processes: black-white, red-green, and blue-yellow. The black-white opponent process determines the brightness of what we see, while the other two processes determine color perception. Stimulation of one color inhibits its opposing color. When stimulation stops, the opposing color is seen as an afterimage.

A century after Hering proposed his theory, research by Russell de Valois and his colleagues (1966) supported its basic propositions. After leaving the cones, visual information is processed in terms of the opposing colors by certain bipolar and ganglion cells in the retina and certain cells in the thalamus, which are collectively known as *opponent cells.* These opponent cells respond to light at one end of the spectrum with an increase in nerve firing, and to light at the other end of the spectrum with an inhibition of spontaneous activity. Opponent cells that are inhibited from firing by a particular wavelength (which we experience as a particular color) produce a burst of firing as soon as that wavelength is removed. Similarly, cells that fire in response to a particular wavelength stop firing when that wavelength is removed (de Valois & Jacobs, 1984; Zrenner et al., 1990). As a result of this inhibition and firing of opponent cells, we experience *negative afterimages.* That is, when we stare at a particular color and then look away, the opposing color is seen as an afterimage due to a "rebound effect" in opponent cells.

Opponent-process theory also explains certain aspects of color blindness that cannot be explained by trichromatic theory. For example, people who are color-blind to red are also color-blind to green, and those who cannot see blue also cannot see yellow. The reason for this effect is that the opponent-process cells responsible for perceiving red are also responsible for perceiving green. When these opponent cells are nonfunctional, a person cannot perceive red or green. The same is true for those opponent cells responsible for blue-yellow perception.

Although Hering formulated his theory in opposition to trichromatic theory, research indicates that both theories accurately represent the process of color perception, but at two different stages in the visual process. In the first stage of color processing, the trichromatic theory explains how the retina's red, green, and blue color-sensitive cone receptors match the wavelength of the light stimulus. In the second stage, the opponent-process theory explains how opponent cells both in the retina and in the thalamus of the brain are either stimulated or inhibited from firing by wavelengths of varying sizes. Put more simply, trichromatic theory explains most of the visual processing occurring in the eye, while opponent-process theory explains the processing occurring between the eye and the brain.

5-2f Color Constancy Demonstrates That We Perceive Objects in Their Environmental Context

Try the following demonstration. First find two sheets of paper, one blue and the other yellow. Next hold these papers near a window and look at them carefully. Then look at them when illuminated by a fluorescent or tungsten light. Although you may have noticed some small change in color as you changed the illumination, the blue sheet didn't change to yellow and the yellow to blue, did they? No, certainly not. Yet you might be surprised to learn that the wavelengths reflected from a blue color chip by an indoor light bulb match the wavelengths reflected from a yellow color chip by sunlight (Jameson, 1985). Despite the fact that the blue paper under tungsten light and the yellow paper under sunlight reflect the same wavelength pattern, we still perceive one as blue and the other as yellow. Further, when we bring the blue paper outside and the yellow paper indoors, their colors appear the same to us, even though they now reflect different wavelength patterns. This relative constancy of perceived color under different conditions of illumination is known as **color constancy** (Lotto & Purves, 2002).

The fact that our perception of an object's color remains relatively unchanged despite changes in the wavelengths reflected from it is proof that our experience of color is based not only on the stimulation coming from the object but also on the stimulation coming from other objects in the environment. Research indicates that color constancy works best when an object is surrounded by objects of many colors, suggesting that our brain perceives color partly based on computations of the light reflected by an object relative to the light reflected by surrounding objects (Land, 1986; Pokorny et al., 1991). This finding that we

opponent-process theory A theory proposing that color perception depends on receptors that make opposing responses to three pairs of colors.

The best work of artists in any age is the work of innocence liberated by technical knowledge. The laboratory experiments that led to the theory of pure color equipped the impressionists to paint nature as if it had only just been created.

—Nancy Hale, U.S. writer, 1908–1989

color constancy Perceiving objects as having consistent color under different conditions of illumination.

perceive objects in their environmental context has long been recognized and utilized by artists, clothing designers, and interior decorators.

Section Review

- Light is a form of electromagnetic energy that passes through the cornea, pupil, and lens and then is projected onto the retina.
- Below the retina's surface reside two kinds of photoreceptors: rods, which function best under low-light conditions, and cones, which require much more light to be activated and play a key role in color vision.
- Rods and cones generate neural signals that activate adjacent bipolar cells, which activate ganglion cells.
- Behind the eyes, ganglion cell axons of the optic nerve separate, with half crossing to the other side of the head at the optic chiasm.
- Most optic nerve fibers run to the lateral geniculate nucleus, which performs detailed visual analysis.
- The experience of color is created by our nervous system in response to different wavelengths of light.
- Trichromatic theory explains most of the visual processing occurring in the eye.
- Opponent-process theory explains visual processing occurring between the eye and the brain.
- Our perception of an object's color remains relatively unchanged despite changes in the wavelength reflected from it.

5-3 HEARING

Preview

- *What does frequency, amplitude, and complexity have to do with sound?*
- *How can we tell where a sound is coming from?*
- *How does the ear work?*
- *What causes hearing loss?*

Stop reading for a minute, look around, and notice what your sense of vision tells you about your surroundings. Next, close your eyes, listen carefully, and notice what your sense of hearing, or **audition,** tells you.

> **audition** The sense of hearing.

When I did this exercise, looking around my den, I noticed my computer screen, my desk, a lamp, an antique clock, a phone, two windows, and many stacks and shelves of books and journal articles. When I closed my eyes and listened, my experience changed dramatically. Now I noticed the clock ticking, the computer fan whirring, the robins in our yard chirping, and the geese in the nearby woods honking. I also heard the soft rustle of my daughter's papers as she did her homework in the kitchen and the sound of a plane flying high overhead. Although these sensations were present when I looked around the room, I had not noticed them.

This exercise demonstrates that hearing is an important, though sometimes unrecognized, sense. From an evolutionary perspective, hearing was essential for our ancestors' survival, helping them detect the approach of predatory animals, locate food, and communicate with others (Nathan, 1982). Indeed, studies of various languages around the world reveal that between two-thirds and three-fourths of all words applying to the senses describe vision and audition, which are often described as our *higher senses* (Wilson, 1997). Yet how exactly does hearing take place?

5-3a Sound Waves Are the Stimuli for Hearing

Sound depends on a wave of pressure created when an object vibrates. The vibration causes molecules in an elastic medium—such as air, water, or solid material—to move together and apart in a rhythmic fashion. Like ripples on a pond, these pulsations move away from the vibrating object as **sound waves,** growing weaker as they travel farther from their source. Although sound waves weaken with increased distance, their speed remains constant, about 1,070 feet (or 330 meters) per second in air and about 4,724 feet (or 1,440 meters) per second in water.

The number of sound waves that pass a given point in 1 second is its *frequency.* Sound frequency is measured in *hertz (Hz),* named after the nineteenth-century German physicist Heinrich Hertz (1857–1894). One Hz equals one cycle per second. The physical quality of sound frequency roughly corresponds to the psychological experience of *pitch.* High-frequency waves are experienced as sounds of high pitch. Although people are most sensitive to sounds at frequencies between 2,000 and 5,000 Hz (Gulick et al., 1989), young adults can typically hear tones with frequencies as low as 20 Hz and as high as 20,000 Hz (Gelfand, 1981). The lowest note on a piano has a frequency of about 50 Hz, while the highest note has a frequency of about 4,000 Hz. As people age, their lower limit of hearing changes very little, but the upper range falls steadily from adolescence onward.

The height of a sound wave, called its *amplitude,* corresponds to the psychological experience of the loudness of a sound. Amplitude is measured in *decibels (dB).* The greater the amplitude, the louder the sound, with perceived loudness doubling about every 10 decibels (Stevens, 1955). By definition, 0 dB is the minimal detectable sound for normal hearing. A whisper has an amplitude of about 20 dB, normal conversation occurs at about 60 dB, and a jet aircraft taking off nearby has an amplitude of about 140 dB. Exposure to sounds at or over 120 dB can be painful and may cause hearing damage (Henry, 1984). Prolonged exposure to sounds over 90 dB, such as those found in industrial settings, subway trains, and rock concerts, can contribute to permanent hearing loss. Table 5-4 provides examples of some common sounds and their danger levels.

There are many sound waves that we do not hear. For example, did you know that the Earth emits a persistent hum at a frequency too low for human ears to hear? The frequency range of this hum is between 2 and 7 milli Hz, well below our hearing threshold. Large earthquakes set the whole planet ringing like a bell (again below the level of human perception), but this persistent hum is believed to start in the oceans, when winter storms create huge waves that reach all the way down to the ocean floor. The thumping of these waves on the bottom, like the pounding of a drum, sets the Earth vibrating, creating the hum (Chui, 2004).

One of the annoyances of modern-day living is widespread exposure to excess noise. Noise levels above 65 dB are not only irritating, but also can cause sleep disturbances in all age groups and learning deficits in children (Bullinger et al., 1999). For example, in one recent study investigating the effects of aircraft noise on children's cognitive development, researchers tested German children living near the old and new sites of the Munich International Airport (Hygge et al., 2002). The impending closing and opening of the two airports

> **sound waves** Pressure changes in a medium (air, water, solids) caused by the vibrations of molecules.

You hear a bell ringing because your ears respond to sound waves generated by the metal gong striking the bell's sides. How do the frequency, amplitude, and complexity of the sound waves generated by the bell affect what you hear?

Source: Courtesy of Figzoi.

Table **5-4**	Decibel Level of Some Common Sounds	
Decibels	**Source**	**Exposure Danger**
180	Space shuttle launch	Hearing loss certain within 150 feet of launchpad
140	Shotgun blast, jet aircraft motor	Any exposure dangerous
120	Sandblaster, thunderclap	Immediate danger
100	Heavy auto traffic, lawn mower	2 hours
60	Normal conversation	No danger
40	Quiet office	No danger
30	Quiet library	No danger
20	Soft whisper	No danger
0	Minimal detectable sound	No danger

located in different areas of the city provided researchers with the opportunity to observe how the exposure to and elimination of loud airport noise affected children's attention, reading ability, long-term memory, and speech perception. Children were tested three times: once before and twice after the airport switch-over. Following the switch, children living near the now-closed airport showed improvements in all four cognitive areas, while children living near the new airport—where noise levels were now high—experienced deficits in all areas. These findings provide strong evidence that chronic exposure to noise levels above 65 dB can adversely affect children's cognitive development. It further suggests that these deficits can be reversed if children are removed from their noisy surroundings.

Most sounds are actually a combination of many different waves of different frequencies. The extent to which a sound is composed of waves of different frequencies is known as its *complexity,* which corresponds to the psychological experience of *timbre.* Just as we can differentiate the sounds of different musical instruments because of the different frequencies of sound they blend together, we can also recognize the voices of different people over the telephone due to their unique sound-frequency blending. To experience a simple example of timbre perception, first clap your hands together while holding them flat, and then clap them again when they are cupped. Cupped hand-clapping produces a greater combination of low-frequency sound waves than flat hand-clapping, and thus it is a more complex sound.

5-3b The Auditory System Consists of the Outer Ear, the Middle Ear, and the Inner Ear

All vertebrates—that is, animals with backbones—have ears that appear to have evolved from the sense of touch (Békésy, 1960; Stebbins, 1980). The evolution of the modern mammalian ear can be traced back to the primitive internal ears found in some types of fish, which consist of a system of looping passages filled with fluid. Mammals, birds, and some reptiles have a more complex system of looping passages that contain a **cochlea** (pronounced COKE-lee-ah), a coiled, fluid-filled tube in the inner ear that contains hairlike auditory receptor cells. The ears of mammals have three small bones to transmit vibrations to the cochlea, while the ears of birds and reptiles have only one bone (Hackett & Kaas, 2003).

cochlea The coiled, fluid-filled tube in the inner ear that contains the hairlike auditory receptors.

Operation of the Ear

The ear can be divided into three major parts: the *outer ear,* the *middle ear,* and the *inner ear* (see figure 5-9). The most visible part of the outer ear is the *pinna,* which is the skin-covered, funnel-shaped cartilage visible from the outside. Only mammals have pinnae. The funnel shape is useful for channeling sound waves to the other part of the outer ear, the *auditory canal,* a passageway about 1 inch long. As sound waves resonate in the auditory canal, their amplification is doubled.

At the end of the auditory canal is a thin, flexible membrane known as the **eardrum,** which vibrates in sequence with the sound waves. Beyond the eardrum is the middle ear. As the eardrum vibrates, it sets in motion those three tiny, interconnected bones—the hammer, anvil, and stirrup—known collectively as the *ossicles.* The ossicles, which are the tiniest bones in the body, further amplify the sound waves two or three times before transmitting them to the liquid-filled inner ear.

eardrum A thin, flexible membrane at the end of the auditory canal that vibrates in sequence with sound waves.

The main parts of the inner ear are the oval window, the cochlea, and the organ of Corti. The stirrup is attached to the oval window, a thin membrane that transmits the sound waves from the stirrup to the cochlea. As mentioned earlier, the cochlea is a coiled, fluid-filled tube. The vibrations of the *oval window* cause pressure waves in the cochlear fluid. Running down the middle of the cochlea is a rubberlike membrane, the *basilar membrane,* which moves in a wavelike fashion in response to these pressure waves. Lying on top of the basilar membrane is the *organ of Corti,* which contains 16,000–20,000 receptors for hearing, called hair cells. Stimulation of these hair cells by movement of the basilar membrane triggers action potentials in the bundles of sensory neurons forming the *auditory nerve,* which transmits auditory information to the brain. Which of the hair cells are stimulated determines which neurons fire and how rapidly they fire, and the resulting pattern of firing determines the sort of sound we hear.

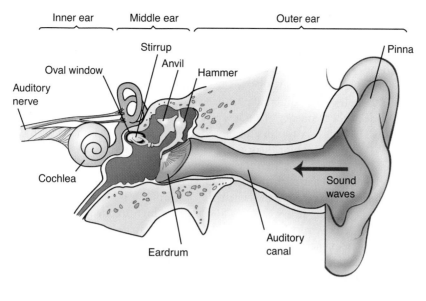

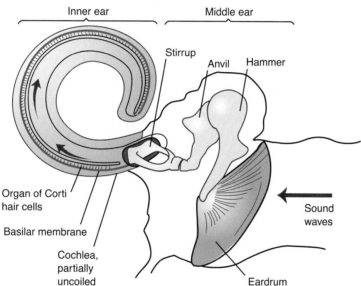

Figure 5-9

The Human Ear

The ear consists of the outer, middle, and inner sections, which have different functions. First, the outer ear directs the sound to the eardrum. From there, the bones of the middle ear (hammer, anvil, and stirrup) greatly amplify the sound through the oval window to the inner ear. The vibrations of the oval window cause pressure waves in the cochlear fluid, which, in turn, cause the basilar membrane to move, bending the hair cells on its surface. This stimulation triggers action potentials in the bundles of sensory neurons that form the auditory nerve, which then sends information to the brain.

Perceiving the Location of Sound

The ability to locate objects in space solely on the basis of the sounds they make is known as **sound localization.** People with only one functioning ear have difficulty accurately locating sounds. To demonstrate this auditory fact, close your eyes and ask a friend to make a noise from somewhere in the room. Point to your friend's location and then open your eyes to determine your accuracy. Next place your index finger in one ear and repeat this exercise. The reason two ears are better than one is that sounds coming from points other than those equidistant between your two ears reach one ear slightly before they reach the other. Sounds reaching the closer ear may also be slightly more intense, because the head blocks some of the sound waves reaching the ear on the other side of the head (Getzmann, 2003). Because your ears are only about 6 inches apart, the time lag between the sound reaching your two ears is extremely short, and the different intensities of the sounds are extremely small. Yet even such small differences provide your auditory system with sufficient information to locate the sound (Middlebrooks & Green, 1991; Phillips & Brugge, 1985).

Although people are pretty accurate in locating sounds that reach one ear slightly before the other, sounds coming from directly behind them or directly above their heads are harder to localize. To overcome this problem, people turn or cock their heads so the sound reaches their two ears at different times. Instead of moving the head, many animals can move the pinnae of their ears independently and achieve the same result.

> **sound localization** The ability to locate objects in space solely on the basis of the sounds they make.

5-3c Different Theories Explain Different Aspects of Pitch Perception

How does the auditory system convert sound waves into perceptions of pitch? Like our knowledge of color perception, our current understanding of pitch perception is based on two theories that were once considered incompatible.

Place theory contends that we hear different pitches because different sound waves trigger the hair cells on different portions, or places, on the cochlea's basilar membrane. The brain detects the frequency of a tone according to which place along the membrane is most activated. Place theory was first proposed by Herman von Helmholtz (1863), the codeveloper of trichromatic color theory, and later tested and refined by the Hungarian scientist Georg von Békésy (1947, 1957), who won a Nobel Prize for this work in 1961. Békésy's research indicated that high-frequency tones trigger the greatest activity at the beginning of the cochlea's basilar membrane, where the oval window is located.

Although place theory explains how we hear high-frequency tones, it cannot account for how we perceive very low-frequency tones, such as a deep bass note. The problem is that at very low frequencies the entire basilar membrane vibrates uniformly, so no one place is more activated than another. One theory that can explain the perception of low-frequency tones is **frequency theory,** first proposed by New Zealand physicist Ernest Rutherford (1871–1937) in 1886. According to frequency theory, the basilar membrane vibrates at the same frequency as the incoming sound wave, which in turn triggers neural impulses to the brain at this same rate. Thus, a sound wave of 800 Hz will set the basilar membrane vibrating 800 times per second, causing neurons to fire at 800 times per second.

One important problem with frequency theory is that individual neurons cannot fire more than 1,000 times per second. Because of this fact, frequency theory cannot explain how people perceive sounds with frequencies above 1,000 Hz. A revision of frequency theory, namely the psychologist Ernest Wever's **volley theory,** contends that neurons work in groups and alternate firing, thus achieving a combined frequency of firing well above 1,000 times per second (Wever, 1949; Wever & Bray, 1937). Studies indicate that such alternate firing of groups of auditory nerves can generate volleys of up to 5,000 impulses per second (Zwislocki, 1981).

Based on what we now know, it appears that frequency theory, place theory, and volley theory account for different aspects of pitch perception. Place theory best explains high-frequency sounds, while frequency theory can best explain the perception of low-frequency sounds. For sounds between 1,000 and 5,000 Hz, pitch perception seems best explained by volley theory, which is a revision of frequency theory.

5-3d There Are Two General Types of Hearing Impairment

Hearing impairment is one of the most common birth defects, occurring in about 3 in 1,000 newborns. Hearing loss that is present at birth is called *congenital hearing loss* (Tabaee et al., 2004). Genetic factors are believed to cause about half of all congenital hearing loss cases, but infections during pregnancy, such as rubella (German measles), herpes, or syphilis, are also known causes (Beasley & Amedee, 2001).

Millions of adults have some degree of hearing impairment, ranging from mild to severe. Because the process of loss is gradual, individuals who have this disorder may not realize that their hearing is diminishing. Older adults are the age group most affected by this condition, with high-pitched sounds being the most difficult to hear (Marcincuk & Roland, 2002). About 33 percent of adults between the ages of 65 and 75 years have some degree of hearing loss, with this figure rising to 50 percent among those older than 75 years. Individuals who are hearing impaired may experience several of the following symptoms:

1. Conversations are difficult to understand, especially when there is background noise.
2. The higher pitches of women's voices are harder to hear than the lower pitches of men's voices.
3. Certain sounds seem annoying or overly loud.
4. A ringing, roaring, or hissing sound may occur in one or both ears.

The damage that causes hearing impairment involves defects in one or more areas of the auditory system (Beasley & Amedee, 2001). Abnormalities with the mechanical system that carries sound waves to the cochlea cause *conduction hearing loss.* These middle ear

---

place theory A theory that pitch is determined by which place along the cochlea's basilar membrane is most activated.

When music fails to agree to the ear, to soothe the ear and the heart and the senses, then it has missed its point.

—Maria Callas, Greek soprano, 1923–1977

frequency theory A theory that pitch is determined by the frequency with which the basilar membrane vibrates.

volley theory A theory of pitch stating that neurons work in groups and alternate firing, thus achieving a combined frequency corresponding to the frequency of the sound wave.

problems often involve a punctured eardrum or reduced functioning of the tiny bones making up the ossicles. Whatever the cause, the result is that the middle ear is less able to send sound waves to the inner ear. A common treatment for conduction hearing loss is digital hearing aids, which are tiny instruments worn just inside the outer ear. Hearing aids amplify vibrations for frequencies that are troublesome—usually high frequencies—and compress sound so that soft sounds are amplified. Because the effectiveness of these external hearing aids is sometimes diminished due to perspiration in the outer ear and noise distortion, implantable hearing aids employing more advanced technology are increasingly common. One such device consists of a micro-magnet surgically placed on a segment of the tiny bones in the middle ear and an external sound processor that uses electromagnetic waves instead of air pressure to amplify volume (Hough et al., 2002).

The more common type of hearing impairment is *sensorineural hearing loss,* or *nerve deafness.* This condition involves a defect in the neural mechanisms that create nerve impulses in the inner ear or send them to the auditory cortex. Problems in the auditory cortex can also result in this type of hearing loss. Most sensorineural hearing loss occurs because hair cells in the cochlea are damaged by disease, injury, or aging (Oghalai, 2005; Singh & Selesnick, 2005). We are born with about 50,000 inner ear hair cells, but the number gradually declines over time. Unlike birds and sharks that can regenerate lost hair cells, humans do not have this ability.

Currently, the only means of restoring hearing in people suffering from nerve deafness is a *cochlear implant,* which bypasses damaged or missing hair cells to send electrical signals through an array of electrodes within the cochlea (Gantz & Turner, 2003). The implant actually consists of three separate parts: headpiece, speech processor, and receiver. The headpiece contains a microphone and transmitter and is worn just behind the ear. It picks up sounds and sends them to the beeper-sized processor that fits in a pocket or is worn on a belt. The processor converts sounds into electronic signals that are sent to the receiver, which is a small disc about the size of a quarter that is surgically implanted as far into the cochlea as possible. The receiver sends the sound signals to the brain (Turner et al., in press). About 60,000 people in the world have received cochlear implants. Young children born with hearing loss are the best candidates for this device, although some older adults with profound or severe hearing loss are beginning to receive these implants as well. Besides mechanical remedies, many people with hearing loss rely upon lip reading, in which they pay close attention to others when they talk.

Researchers have discovered that susceptibility to age-related hearing loss is due to defects that develop in several genes, which, in turn, destroy inner ear hair cells (Noben-Trauth et al., 2003). Recently, studies with genetically modified mice and guinea pigs have found that deleting a specific gene permits the growth of new hair cells (Kawamoto et al., 2003; Sage et al., 2005). These findings provide invaluable insights into the genetics of hearing and increase the possibility that one day medical science will be able to regenerate lost hair cells and thereby restore hearing in those suffering from nerve deafness.

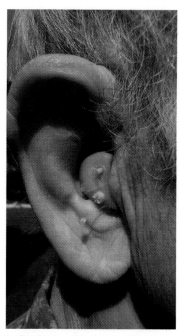

Individuals with conduction hearing loss often wear digital hearing aids, which are worn just inside the outer ear. Implantable hearing devices are also available.

Source: Courtesy of Figzoi.

Section Review

- Frequency refers to the number of sound waves that pass a given point in 1 second and corresponds to the experience of pitch.
- Amplitude is the height of a sound wave and corresponds to the experience of loudness.
- Complexity is the extent to which a sound is composed of different frequencies and corresponds to the experience of timbre.
- Sound localization is the ability to locate objects in space due to their sound.
- Place theory best explains high-frequency sounds.
- Frequency theory best explains low-frequency sounds.
- Volley theory best explains intermediate sounds.
- Conduction hearing loss involves abnormalities with the mechanical system that carries sound waves to the cochlea.
- Sensorineural hearing loss, or nerve deafness, involves a defect in the neural mechanisms that create nerve impulses in the inner ear or send them to the auditory cortex.

5-4 OTHER SENSES

Preview

- *How many different types of smell receptors do we have?*
- *What are the five primary tastes?*
- *What is the body's largest sensory organ?*
- *What three skin senses comprise touch?*
- *What causes pain?*
- *What body senses detect body position and movement?*
- *Can some people "see" sounds or "taste" colors?*

Through natural selection, animals come to possess the sensory mechanisms they need to survive in their specific environment. This is why animals that inhabit similar environments have similar sensory mechanisms. Our own human senses share the most similarity to those species that are our closest cousins on the evolutionary tree, namely, other primates (Hodos & Butler, 2001). Like all primates, we primarily rely on our vision, with hearing a distant second sense. These two sensory systems are classified as *higher senses* in humans, meaning they are extremely important to our survival. In contrast, the senses of taste, smell, touch, and proprioception are classified as *minor senses* because they are not considered as crucial to sustaining life. Unlike our vision and hearing, these senses generally do not alert us to predators in our surroundings, nor are they as important in helping us locate food sources and safe dwellings. However, as you will learn in this section, our minor senses are not inconsequential; they do serve important adaptive functions.

5-4a Smell and Taste Represent "Far" and "Near" Chemical Senses

In the primordial soup from which all life developed, most primitive sea animals relied on fairly simple chemical senses rather than the more sophisticated and later-evolving visual and auditory sensory systems. As life evolved from the sea to the land, two anatomically separate chemical sensory mechanisms developed. These two distinct senses—namely, taste and smell—came to serve different functions. The sense of taste became a "near" sense, providing the last check on the acceptability of food, while the sense of smell became a "far" sense, able to detect stimuli from a much farther distance.

Smell

olfaction The sense of smell.

Olfaction is the sense of smell, and its stimuli are airborne molecules. When you smell fresh-brewed coffee (see figure 5-10), you are sensing molecules that have left the coffee and traveled through the air to your nose. These molecules then enter your nasal passages and reach tiny receptor cells at the top of the nasal cavity. These olfactory receptors are located on a thin, dime-sized, mucus-coated layer of tissue known as the **olfactory epithelium.** The odor molecules from the coffee are then trapped and dissolved in the mucus of the epithelium, and this causes the olfactory receptor cells to transmit a neural impulse through their axon fibers, which form the olfactory nerve, directly to the olfactory bulb at the base of the brain. From there, the signals are processed before being sent to the primary olfactory cortex, which is located just below the frontal lobes (Dade et al., 2002; McLean & Shipley, 1992). Olfaction is the only sensation that is not relayed through the thalamus on its way to the cortex. Once your brain has processed the airborne molecules, you appreciate the coffee's wonderful fragrance.

olfactory epithelium A thin layer of tissue at the top of the nasal cavity that contains the olfactory receptor cells.

Humans have hundreds of different types of olfactory receptor cells, and each type responds to only a limited family of odor molecules (DiLorenzo & Youngentob, 2003; Ressler et al., 1994). This large number of different types of receptors stands in sharp contrast to the three basic receptors involved in vision. Although we do not yet know exactly how the brain processes all the different types of olfactory information, together these receptors allow us to distinguish among about 10,000 different smells (Malnic et al., 1999). Having so many different types of olfactory receptors may mean that a great deal of the processing necessary for odor perception occurs in the nose itself. Despite the staggering num-

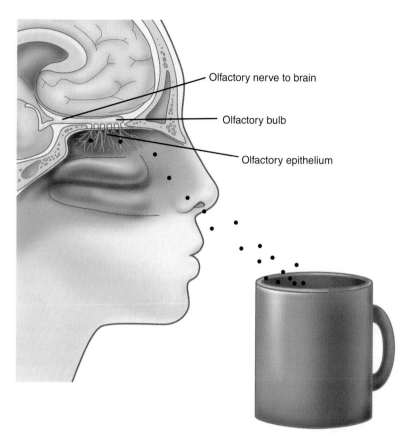

Figure 5-10

The Olfactory System

The sense of smell depends on odor molecules in the air reaching the nose and traveling up the nasal passages to the receptor cells in the olfactory epithelium. The odor molecules are trapped and dissolved in the olfactory mucus, and this triggers the receptor cells to send a neural impulse to the olfactory bulb. From there, the information travels to the primary olfactory cortex in the frontal lobes.

ber of odors we can distinguish, for some unknown reason, we have a hard time correctly identifying and attaching names to specific odors. Thus, you may have a hard time correctly distinguishing the smell of smoke from that of soap.

Numerous studies indicate that we are drawn toward perfumelike fragrances, such as those of flowers and many food substances, and repulsed by foul and sulfurous odors (W. I. Miller, 1997). This suggests that our olfactory systems evolved to help us distinguish things that are poisonous from those that are edible. Cross-cultural studies further suggest that the smells we pay most attention to are those that help us survive in our immediate surroundings (Classen et al., 1994). For example, the Dassanetch people of southwestern Ethiopia are especially sensitive to the smells associated with their principal livelihood, raising cattle (Almagor, 1987). They identify the time of year by predictable changes in surrounding smells, such as the odors of decay and burning during the dry season and the fresh smell of new plant growth during the rainy season. Further, the smell of everything associated with cattle is considered good, and the Dassanetch go out of their way to highlight those valued smells. Women smear liquid butter—*ghee*—on their bodies to ensure fertility and attract suitors, while men do the same with cow manure!

Olfactory sensitivity is substantially determined by the number of receptors in the epithelium. Animals with more receptors than other animals have much keener senses of smell. Whereas humans have about 10 million olfactory receptors, dogs have an astounding 200 million receptors, putting us at the lower end of the scale of smell sensitivity. Dogs' greater smell sensitivity is the reason why they are used to help detect the scent of illegal drugs, explosives, and biologically based weapons (Hilliard, 2003). Recently, scientists have discovered that some dogs can reliably detect the presence of cancer in the body (Willis et al., 2004). Apparently, cancerous tissue has a subtle odor that these dogs can detect, either by smelling the person's breath or urine (for internal tumors) or by smelling their skin (for skin cancer). In fact, in some cases, these specially trained dogs have been able to detect the presence of cancer even before the most sophisticated technology could do so.

The olfactory systems of many animals also have specialized receptors to detect airborne chemicals known as **pheromones,** which are released by other members of the same

pheromones Airborne chemicals released by animals and detected by other animals using specialized receptors. Pheromones affect the behavior of other animals of the same species.

species. Once detected, these pheromones directly affect the animal's behavior. Many species rely on pheromones to communicate their territorial boundaries, social status, and readiness to sexually reproduce (Luo et al., 2003).

Do we humans emit and detect pheromones? If so, how might this shape our behavior? In the late 1960s, Martha McClintock, a college student, tried to answer these questions by conducting a scientific investigation into the folk notion that women who live in the same dorm develop synchronized menstrual periods. Her survey of fellow students found that as women spent more time together, their menstrual cycles became more synchronized. In addition, McClintock discovered that women who spent a lot of time with men had shorter and more regular cycles (McClintock, 1971). Inspired by her undergraduate research, McClintock became a biopsychologist and has devoted her career to investigating the existence and possible function of human pheromones. She and her colleagues have discovered that pheromone-like chemicals are secreted in blood, sweat, armpit hair, and semen, and that at least some of these chemical substances may unconsciously influence sexual attraction (Jacob et al., 2001; Jacob & McClintock, 2000). For example, recent studies have found that heterosexual women and homosexual men exhibit an involuntary sexual response when exposed to the male pheromone *androstadien,* but they are not aroused by the female pheromone *estratetraen* (Savic et al., 2005). However, despite such discoveries, scientists are still unsure about whether humans possess sexual attractant pheromones. Even if such substances exist, it is extremely unlikely that they will be found to have the sort of direct effect on sexual behavior that is found among many animal species, because the human sexual response is much more complex than that of most other animals (see chapter 11, section 11-2). Rather than directly producing sexual attraction, it is much more likely that human sexual attractant pheromones would affect a person's mood and emotional states, which in turn would affect how the person interacts with other people (Cutler et al., 1998).

Although human behavior is not as strongly shaped by olfactory information as is the behavior of other species, we do have the ability to identify people by their olfactory cues. For example, based on the smell of breath, hands, and clothing, people are reasonably accurate in detecting another person's sex (Doty et al., 1982; Wallace, 1977). Further, at least one study has found that blindfolded mothers can identify with close to 95 percent accuracy the clothing worn by their own children by smell alone (Porter & Moore, 1981). Similarly, breast-feeding infants quickly learn to identify their mother's odor from that of other breast-feeding women (Porter, 1991). Although these studies suggest that humans as a group have a good deal of smell sensitivity, women's sensitivity is much better than that of men. Brain scans taken while people are smelling objects find that odors trigger more olfactory activation in women than in men (Yousem et al., 1999; Yousem et al., 2001).

Finally, odors can also evoke memories and feelings associated with past events (Richardson & Zucco, 1989). For example, the smell of freshly cut grass or the scent of a specific perfume can mentally transport us back to a time in our lives when these odors were associated with specific events.

Taste

gustation The sense of taste.

taste buds Sensory receptor organs located on the tongue and inside the mouth and throat that contain the receptor cells for taste.

As mentioned earlier, taste, or **gustation,** is a near sensation occurring when a substance makes contact with specialized receptor cells in the mouth and throat (Bartoshuk, 1991; I. J. Miller, 1995). About 50 to 150 of these receptor cells are contained in each of the 10,000 **taste buds** that are primarily located on the tongue (Margolskee, 1995). Some taste buds are also in the throat, on the insides of the cheeks, and on the roof of the mouth. The taste buds on the surface of the tongue are grouped together in structures called *papillae,* which in Latin means "pimple." Because of their constant contact with the chemicals they are designed to sense, as well as their exposure to bacteria, dirt, and dry air, the receptor cells wear out and die within 10 days (Pfaffmann, 1978). Fortunately, new cells emerge at the edge of the taste bud and migrate inward toward the center, replacing the old cells. Although this cycle of death and replacement of taste cells operates throughout our lives, it occurs more slowly in the elderly, which is one reason their taste sensitivity becomes less acute (Cowart, 1981).

When these taste cells absorb chemicals dissolved in saliva, they trigger neural impulses that are transmitted to one of two brain areas. In one pathway, information is sent first to the thalamus and then to the primary gustatory cortex, where taste identification occurs. A second pathway leads to the limbic system and allows a person to quickly respond to a taste prior to consciously identifying it, as when you reflexively spit out sour milk (Sekuler & Blake, 1994).

In contrast to our olfactory system's ability to distinguish among about 10,000 different smells, our taste receptors can detect only a handful of taste sensations (Classen, 1993; Laing et al., 1993). The receptor cells in each taste bud respond primarily to one particular taste, although they also respond weakly to other tastes. The most familiar taste sensations are sweetness (mostly sugars), sourness (mostly acids), saltiness (mostly salts), and bitterness (mainly chemicals that have no food value or are toxic). Recently, receptor cells for a fifth basic taste, which creates the sensation of *fattiness*, have been discovered (Schiffman et al., 1998). Most taste experiences are complex and result from the activation of some combination of these basic receptor cells in the taste buds (Smith, 1985).

You might already be aware that the taste buds most sensitive to these five basic tastes are bunched together on different areas of the tongue. As depicted in figure 5-11, sensitivity to sweet and fatty substances is greatest near the front of the tongue, salt sensitivity is greatest along the front sides, sour sensitivity is greatest along the back sides, and bitter sensitivity is greatest at the back. If you ever have to swallow an unpleasant-tasting pill, place it in the center of your tongue, where there are few taste receptor cells.

About 25 percent of people have a very large number of taste buds. These "supertasters" are extremely sensitive to bitter compounds, and they also perceive saccharin and sucrose as sweeter than other people do. Due to this hypersensitivity, supertasters may face a higher cancer risk if they find broccoli and other veggies that carry cancer-preventing vitamins too bitter to stomach. On the positive side, supertasters' discriminating palates may lead to lower risk for obesity.

Although the taste of a particular substance depends on whether one or more of the five basic taste sensations is activated, the flavor of this substance is a combination of both its smell and its taste (DiLorenzo & Youngentob, 2003). The important role that olfaction plays in the flavor experience was demonstrated by one study in which some research participants were allowed to both taste and smell substances placed on their tongues, while others were allowed to only taste them. Although over half of the taste-smell participants were able to correctly identify chocolate, root beer, cherry, coffee, and garlic, less than 3 percent of the taste-only group could accurately identify those flavors (Mozell et al., 1969). To personally experience the role that olfaction plays in flavor perception, pinch your nostrils closed before approaching a particular food. Then place the food in your mouth and swish it around while paying attention to the flavor. Next, release your nostrils, open your mouth slightly, and breathe in gently through both your mouth and nose. You should experience a significant increase in the food's flavor.

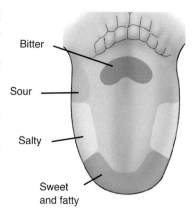

Bitter

Sour

Salty

Sweet and fatty

Figure 5-11

The Five Primary Tastes

Different areas of the tongue are most sensitive to the five primary qualities of taste: sweet, fatty, salty, sour, and bitter.

5-4b Touch Is Determined by the Skin Senses—Pressure, Temperature, and Pain

Every living thing has a "skin" of some sort that defines its boundaries with the environment, and every living creature has a sense of touch. Indeed, the skin is the largest sensory organ, with the average adult's body having more than 2 square yards of skin receptors. Our sense of touch is actually a combination of three skin senses: *pressure, temperature,* and *pain* (Craig & Rollman, 1999). Being kissed on the cheek, having an ice cube dropped down your shirt, and stepping on a sharp rock with bare feet all cause some combination of these three skin sensations. Although the 5 million sense receptors in our skin consist of a variety of different types, like our taste receptors, there is no one type of skin receptor that produces a specific sensory experience. Instead, the skin's sensory experiences appear to be due to the pattern of stimulation of nerve impulses reaching the somatosensory cortex of the brain (Hsiao et al., 2003).

Pressure

The stimulus for pressure is physical pressure on the skin. Although the entire body is sensitive to pressure, most of the cells in the brain's somatosensory cortex are devoted to processing neural impulses coming from the fingers, lips, face, tongue, and genitals, because these areas of the skin have the greatest concentration of receptors. That's why you are so much more sensitive to objects that come into contact with these skin areas than with other regions.

We experience pressure sensations differently based on whether we use passive or dynamic touch (Timmermann et al., 2000). In *passive touch*, your skin is contacted by an object, while in *dynamic touch*, you initiate the contact and actively explore the object (Gibson, 1966; Turvey, 1996). Whenever someone brushes up against you, taps you on the shoulder, or gives you a full-body massage, you are experiencing passive touch. Whenever you reach into your pocket for correct change, squeeze fruit to test its ripeness, or massage someone else's body, you are experiencing dynamic touch. In identifying objects by touch, accuracy rates differ based on whether dynamic or passive touch is used (Gibson, 1962; Kloos & Amazeen, 2002). When objects are simply pressed lightly onto the hand (passive touch), people are able to correctly identify those objects less than one-third of the time (29 percent). However, when people are allowed to actively explore the objects with their fingers, accuracy rates increase to 95 percent. Dynamic touch is exactly the type of touch perception that blind people use as a substitute for vision. In fact, in 1824 Louis Braille, a blind Frenchman, relied upon dynamic touch to create an alphanumeric system—known today as Braille—which employs patterns of raised dots that readers scan with their fingertips. For both the blind and the sighted, dynamic touch is used much more frequently than passive touch.

Because the fingers and lips have such high concentrations of sensory receptors, they are about equal in their pressure sensitivity. However, if this is true, how would you explain the following sensory experience? First touch your two index fingers together, noticing where the sensations of pressure are felt. Most people report about equal pressure intensity from both fingertips. Now lightly touch one fingertip repeatedly to your upper lip. Where do you experience the sensation of touch? Most people report sensations mostly on the lip and little or none from the fingertip. Why do we experience these different pressure sensations when both skin areas are being equally stimulated?

The reason your lip is more pressure sensitive than your finger in this case is related to the relative lengths of their neural pathways to the brain. When touched simultaneously, neural impulses from the lip reach the brain 1 millisecond faster than those from the finger. Apparently, even when two places on the skin are being equally stimulated, the impulses that reach the brain first dictate where the sensation will be primarily experienced.

Neuroscientists recently discovered a special set of thin nerves in humans that are especially sensitive to the soft touches generated by tender caresses and reassuring hugs but not to rough touches, pinches, or jabs (Olausson et al., 2002). These nerves stimulate the same areas of the brain as those involved in emotional processing. Thus, it appears that the brain areas activated by romantic love and sexual arousal also provide the emotional aspects of touch. Researchers speculate that these nerves may have evolved to guide humans toward tenderness and nurturing behavior.

Temperature

The skin contains two kinds of temperature receptors, one sensitive to warm and the other to cold. In 1920, the structural psychologist J. Henry Alston discovered that the sensation of "hot" is triggered by the simultaneous stimulation of both the warm and the cold receptors (Alston, 1920). He demonstrated this phenomenon by intertwining two metal pipes, one containing cold water and the other containing warm water. When people grasped these two braided pipes, they quickly pulled away, because they felt the sensation of intense heat. Of course, their skin was not actually scalded; Alston's unusual apparatus had simply fooled these people's brains into feeling intense heat. However, when you accidentally touch a hot stove with your fingers, the resulting sensation of intense heat in your fingers is correctly warning you about imminent harm to your skin.

Although temperature sensations depend on which type of receptor is stimulated, whether more warm or cold receptors are stimulated depends on the difference between the temperature of the skin and the object you are feeling. This is why washing your hands in 60°F water feels warm after coming in from the cold but chilly when you are in a hot environment.

Pain

The chapter-opening story described how Aron Ralston cut off his own arm to save his life. What is so remarkable about Aron's actions is that he performed this self-surgery while ignoring all of his body's built-in defenses against the self-infliction of pain. Although pain is an unpleasant experience, it is important to survival because it serves as a warning system that signals danger and the risk of injury (Wall, 2000). In order to save his life, Aron had to largely ignore this sensory warning system.

Pain can also force people to cope appropriately with an injury by inducing them both to seek treatment and to be still to promote healing. The importance of this sense is dramatically demonstrated by those rare individuals who are born with an insensitivity to pain due to improperly functioning nerve pathways that normally transmit pain signals to the brain (Sternbach, 1963). In one such case, a woman called Ms. C died at the age of 29 from massive infections caused by a lifetime of abrasion and unhealed injury (Melzack & Wall, 1982a).

Pain accounts for 80 percent of all visits to the doctor, and it afflicts more than 50 million Americans per year (Gatchel & Oordt, 2003). Yet what produces pain? Unlike other sensory modalities, pain has no specific physical stimulus—that is, the skin does not receive "pain waves" from the environment like the eyes receive light waves and the ears receive sound waves. Instead, pain is induced through tissue damage or intense stimulation of sensory receptors (Gatchel & Turk, 1999). The exact level of stimulation that will be experienced as painful can vary. Thus, light that is too bright, noises that are too loud, and pressure that is too great can all trigger the pain experience, but pain can also be triggered by only moderately intense stimulation, such as pouring salt on an open wound or pricking one's finger. On the other hand, overstimulation can sometimes occur without eliciting pain, as demonstrated when you eat something that is too sweet for your sense of taste. The too-sweet substance has certainly overstimulated your taste receptors, but you feel no pain.

The sensation of pain appears to originate in *free nerve endings* in the skin, around muscles, and in internal organs. When intense stimuli cause cell and tissue damage, the damaged cells release chemicals—including a neurotransmitter called *substance P* (for pain)—that stimulate the free nerve endings, which in turn transmit pain signals to the brain (Beyer et al., 1991). People with the rare disorder that makes them insensitive to pain have extremely low levels of substance P in or near the nerve endings (Pearson et al., 1982). Normal individuals do not experience pain in those areas of the body that have no free nerve endings, such as the cerebral cortex.

Upon suffering an injury, we experience two distinct peaks of pain that differ in quality and are separated in time. For example, when you sprain your ankle or pound your thumb with a hammer, you feel what is known as *double pain* (Cooper et al., 1986; Willis, 1985). The first is a sharp, stinging pain caused by large-diameter nerve fibers (called *L-fibers*) in the spinal cord that transmit pain information very quickly to the brain, while the second is a dull or burning pain arising from small-diameter and slower-operating nerve fibers (called *S-fibers*) in the spinal cord. Most pain signals are transmitted by the small, slower-operating S-fibers (Coderre et al., 2003).

The most widely accepted theory of pain is Ronald Melzack and Patrick Wall's (1982b) **gate-control theory,** which proposes that the L-fibers and S-fibers open and close "gateways" for pain in the spinal cord. According to this theory, the large, fast-transmitting L-fibers not only carry information about sharp pain to the brain but also carry information about most other forms of tactile stimulation. Once their information is transmitted to the brain, they close the pain gate by inhibiting the firing of neurons with which they synapse. The thin, slower-transmitting S-fibers, which carry information about dull and burning pain to the brain, also synapse with these same neurons, and thus their pain information may arrive at a closed gate due to the faster operation of the L-fibers. When this happens, the pain information from the S-fibers cannot be sent to the brain.

Gate-control theory explains why rubbing, massaging, or even pinching a bruised or sore muscle can ease the pain. These actions activate the large, fast-transmitting L-fibers, which then close the pain gate to the stimuli transmitted by the thin, slower-operating S-fibers. Because most pain information is transmitted by the S-fibers, blocking these signals significantly reduces the pain experience. This also explains why placing ice on a sprained

Illness is the doctor to whom we pay most heed; to kindness, to knowledge, we make promise only; pain we obey.

—*Marcel Proust, French novelist, 1871–1922*

gate-control theory
A theory of pain perception proposing that small and large nerve fibers open and close "gateways" for pain in the spinal cord.

Acupuncture, which means "needle piercing," is the ancient Chinese medical practice of inserting very fine needles into the skin to stimulate specific areas in the body (called acupoints) for therapeutic purposes. Research suggests that acupuncture causes the release of pain-reducing endorphins and is effective in easing pain caused by headaches, arthritis, and dental extractions.

Source: Courtesy of Figzoi.

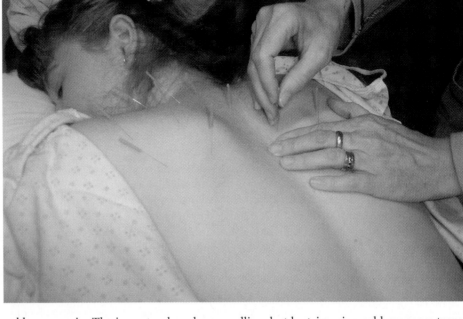

acupuncture An ancient Chinese healing technique in which needles are inserted into the skin at specific points, stimulating the release of pain-reducing endorphins.

When you sustain an injury, such as by hitting your thumb with a hammer, you experience *double pain*. First, you feel a sharp, stinging pain caused by large-diameter nerve fibers *(L-fibers)* in the spinal cord that quickly transmit pain information to the brain. Second, you feel a dull or burning pain caused by small-diameter and slower-operating nerve fibers *(S-fibers)* in the spinal cord.

Source: Courtesy of Figzoi.

ankle eases pain. The ice not only reduces swelling, but by triggering cold messages transmitted by the L-fibers, also closes the gate on the S-fibers' pain signals.

Besides explaining normal pain, gate-control theory can also account for the type of pain that Aron and other amputees experience well after their limb has been removed. This *phantom limb pain* occurs when an amputee feels pain in a missing limb (Gagliese & Katz, 2000; Melzack, 1992). How could Aron feel pain in his missing arm when the pain receptors in the skin no longer existed? According to gate-control theory, when L-fibers are destroyed by amputation, the pain gates remain open, which permits random neural stimulation at the amputation site to trigger the experience of pain in the missing limb (Melzack, 1973).

Research indicates that the brain can also send messages to the spinal cord to close the pain gate, thus preventing pain messages from reaching the brain (Melzack, 1986; Whitehead & Kuhn, 1990). In such instances, the brain's messengers are a class of substances known as *endorphins*. As discussed in chapter 3, section 3-1c, endorphins are the body's natural defense against pain that is released following an injury. The analgesic effects of endorphins helped Aron perform the self-surgery necessary to save his life, despite the pain it was causing him. Drugs such as morphine bind with endorphin receptors in the brain and greatly reduce the subjective experience of pain. Apparently, the ancient Chinese healing and pain-reducing technique of **acupuncture,** in which long, thin needles are inserted into the skin at specific points, stimulates the release of endorphins (Stener-Victorin et al., 2004; Takeshige, 1985). Recent controlled clinical trials demonstrate that acupuncture is effective in alleviating pain caused by dental extractions, headaches, and degenerative arthritis (Lei et al., 2004; Stener-Victorin et al., 2004). Similarly, a more modern pain-relief procedure, known as *transcutaneous electrical nerve stimulation (TENS)*, electrically stimulates painful body regions and also stimulates the release of endorphins (Barbaro, 1988).

Psychological Factors Affecting Pain

More than any of the other senses, our experience of pain can be significantly influenced by a variety of psychological factors (Kotzer, 2000). For example, anxiety, a feeling of helplessness, and fear can intensify pain. In contrast, diverting people's attention away from painful stimulation to some other stimulus, such as soothing music or a pleasant image ("Imagine yourself on a warm, sunny beach"), is an effective way to alleviate pain (Fernandez & Turk, 1989; McCaul & Malott, 1984). Recognizing the benefits of distraction, dentists and other healthcare workers provide music, videos, and a constant flow of conversation while performing painful procedures in order to divert a patient's attention away from the source of the pain.

Another psychological technique for reducing pain is to administer a placebo, which is an inert substance that the person believes will produce a particular effect, such as pain relief.

Studies indicate that up to 35 percent of patients with chronic pain get relief from taking placebos (Weisenberg, 1977). The reason these patients feel less pain is that, unlike those who do not experience relief, their brains produce higher levels of endorphins in response to the placebos (Lipman et al., 1990). Quite literally, their brains are "fooled" into releasing pain-relieving chemicals because they expect pain relief from the fictitious drug in the placebo.

5-4c The Proprioceptive Senses Detect Body Movement and Location

Besides the traditional five senses of vision, hearing, smell, taste, and touch, two additional sources of sense information, collectively called **proprioceptive senses,** detect body position and movement. If you've ever observed an intoxicated person unsuccessfully trying to control his or her own body movements and sense of balance, you have witnessed the malfunctioning of the proprioceptive senses.

One type of proprioception, the **kinesthetic sense,** provides information about the movement and location of body parts with respect to one another. Kinesthetic information comes from receptors in muscles, joints, and ligaments (Gandevia et al., 1992). Without this feedback about where our body parts are located, we would have trouble performing any voluntary movement. You sometimes experience partial disruption of your kinesthetic sense when your leg "falls asleep" and you have trouble walking, or when your jaw has been numbed by a dentist and talking and chewing become problematic.

While the kinesthetic sense provides feedback on the position and movement of body parts, the **vestibular sense** (or *equilibrium*) provides information on the position of the body in space—especially the head—by sensing gravity and motion (Highstein et al., 2004). Vestibular sense information comes from tiny, hairlike receptors located in the fluid-filled vestibular sacs and the semicircular canals of the inner ear, above the cochlea (refer back to figure 5-9). Whenever the head moves, these receptors send messages through a part of the auditory cortex that is not involved in hearing, and this information helps us maintain our balance. Perhaps you recall how much fun it used to be—and maybe still is—to twirl yourself around on a swing at the park until you were silly with dizziness. What happened was that, when you stopped twirling, the fluid in your semicircular canals and your vestibular receptors did not immediately return to a normal state, and thus you experienced the illusion of spinning while standing still. The vestibular imbalance caused by this twirling exercise is very similar to the vestibular imbalance caused by drunkenness.

proprioceptive senses Two additional sources of sensory information that detect body position and movement.

kinesthetic sense A type of proprioceptive sense that provides information about the movement and location of body parts with respect to one another.

vestibular sense A type of proprioceptive sense that provides information about the position of the body— especially the head—in space; also known as *equilibrium.*

> *Journey of Discovery* Question
>
> Based on what you know about your vestibular sense, why do you think it is difficult to walk in a straight line after spinning yourself around on a swing?

5-4d Certain Rare Individuals Experience Sensory "Crossovers"

Have you ever heard a sound and experienced it as a flash of light? This "seeing" of sound is fairly common and is most often experienced when the eyes are closed and the sound is unexpected. A very small percentage of people experience a much more sophisticated "colored hearing" that is part of a larger category of sensory experience known as *synesthesia.* **Synesthesia** (pronounced "sin-ess-THEE-zhah") is a rare and extraordinary sensory condition in which people perceive stimuli in other senses, such as "tasting" color or shapes, "hearing" someone's touch, or "feeling" the sounds of musical instruments on their bodies (Martino & Marks, 2001). Scientists estimate that about 1 in 2,000 people are *synesthetes,* with females outnumbering males 6 to 1 (Baron-Cohen et al., 1996; Harrison, 2001). Famous synesthetes include the writer Vladimir Nabokov, the composer Olivier Messiaen, and the physicist Richard Feynman.

Descriptions of this fascinating sensory condition can be found in historical records dating back hundreds of years, and it was extensively studied in the late nineteenth century. At that time, researchers vaguely explained the cause of synesthesia as "crossed wiring" in the brain. During the first 70 years of the twentieth century, scientific interest in this phenomenon waned, and the medical community often dismissed synesthetic experiences as delu-

synesthesia A rare and extraordinary sensory condition in which people perceive stimuli in other senses, such as by seeing sounds or tasting color.

sions or fabrications of an overactive imagination. Faced with such disbelief, many people with synesthesia kept silent about their condition. Then, in the 1970s, scientific interest resurfaced.

The most common form of synesthesia is colored hearing. Most people with this condition report that they see sounds internally (in "the mind's eye"), but a few see colors projected outside the body, usually within arm's reach. Brain scans of synesthetes who report colored hearing indicate that visual areas of their brains show increased activation in response to sounds (Cytowic, 2002).

In another type of synesthesia, a person experiences specific letters, numbers, and/or words as vivid patterns or particular colors (Mattingly et al., 2001; Smilek et al., 2002). For example, a person with this form of synesthesia might see the letter *B* as orange, the letter *T* as green, and the letter *R* as red. Based on this knowledge, researchers testing this particular person's digit-color synesthesia might show her a mixed pattern of black-printed letters similar to that depicted in figure 5-12, with instructions to quickly identify the geometric shape made by the *B* letters. Because the letters *B*, *T*, and *R* have similar shapes, most people find it difficult to detect the triangle formed by the *B* letters. Yet a synesthete who sees orange *B*'s will easily pick out the triangle (Mills et al., 2002; Wagar et al., 2002). Some neuroscientists believe that this synesthetic experience occurs partly because the areas of the brain that process colors are near the areas that process letters and numbers, and that synesthetes may have more extensive neural connections between these two adjacent brain areas.

Currently, researchers are not yet confident that they understand the causes of synesthesia. Although some experts believe it is caused by an overabundance of neural connections between different brain sensory areas, others disagree. Despite this lack of consensus, most researchers do agree that this phenomenon is biological, automatic, and unlearned. Research further indicates that the condition runs in families and is more common among women than men (Carpenter, 2001). These findings suggest a genetic basis for synesthesia. The coming years should yield further insights into this special sensory experience.

Figure 5-12

Testing Synesthesia

In a typical study of synesthesia, researchers pretest a person with digit-color synesthesia to determine what colors she sees for particular letters. In this hypothetical example, the synesthete sees the letter *B* as orange, the letter *T* as green, and the letter *R* as red. Later, a triangular pattern of *B*'s is embedded in a field of *T*'s and *R*'s. Most people find it difficult to detect the triangle formed by the *B* letters. Yet a synesthete who sees orange *B*'s easily identifies the triangle.

Source: Based on "Testing Synesthesia" from Ramachandran, V. S., and Hubbard, E. M. (2001). Psychophysical investigations into the neural basis of synesthesia. *Proceedings of the Royal Society London Series B Biological Sciences, 268,* 979–983.

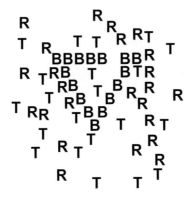

Section Review

- Humans have at least 100 different types of olfactory receptor cells, with each type responding to only a limited family of odor molecules.
- Most taste receptors are located on the tongue.
- Humans detect five primary tastes: sweet, sour, salty, bitter, and fatty.
- The skin is the largest sensory organ.
- Touch is a combination of three skin senses: pressure, temperature, and pain.
- Pain is induced through tissue damage or intense stimulation of sensory receptors.
- According to gate-control theory, small and large nerve fibers open and close "gateways" for pain in the spinal cord.

- The following two proprioceptive senses detect body position and movement:
  —The kinesthetic sense provides information about the movement and location of body parts with respect to one another.
  —The vestibular sense provides information about the position of the body in space by sensing gravity and motion.
- Synesthesia is a rare sensory condition in which a person perceives stimuli in other senses, such as seeing sound or tasting color.

Figure 5-13

Reversible Figure and Ground

Edgar Rubin designed *reversible figure-ground* patterns like the one illustrated here to distinguish the characteristics of figure and ground. When the white vase is perceived as the figure, it appears to be in front of the black ground, yet when the black faces are the figure, black switches position with white. Can you keep one image in mind without the other intruding? No. The ground is perceived as unformed material, so when you see the vase as figure, it is impossible to simultaneously see the faces, and vice versa. Because the stimuli in this illustration are ambiguous, the figure-ground relationship continually reverses, changing what you perceive. Rubin's vase-faces exercise nicely illustrates how the same stimulus can trigger more than one perception.

5-5   PERCEPTION

Preview

- *How are sensations organized into meaningful shapes and patterns?*
- *Are there laws of perception?*
- *What is a perceptual illusion?*
- *Do people in various cultures differ in how they perceive their surroundings?*
- *Is there any reliable scientific evidence for the existence of ESP?*

As defined at the beginning of the chapter, perception is the process that organizes sensations into meaningful objects and events. For some of our senses, such as taste and smell, the distinction between sensation and perception is so fine that it is virtually impossible to differentiate one from the other. For others, such as hearing and vision, psychologists have been able to make sufficiently clear distinctions that greater insight has been gained into how we assign meaning to sensory stimuli.

5-5a   Sensory Stimuli Are Organized into a Gestalt through Form Perception, Depth Perception, and Perceptual Constancy

While traveling by train in the summer of 1910, the German psychologist Max Wertheimer noticed something that millions of people before him had also noticed. When he gazed out the window of a moving train, close, stationary objects—such as fences, trees, and buildings—appeared to race in the opposite direction of the train, while distant objects—such as mountains and clouds—seemed to slowly move along with the train. Wertheimer became so enthralled with understanding the psychological origins of what later came to be called *motion parallax* that he began conducting experiments that ultimately led to the development of a new school of thought in psychology: *Gestalt psychology* (see chapter 1, section 1-2e). According to Gestalt psychologists, our perceptions are not to be understood as the mind passively responding to a cluster of individual sensations but, rather, as the mind actively organizing sensory stimuli into a coherent whole, or **gestalt.**

gestalt An organized and coherent whole.

form perception The process by which sensations are organized into meaningful shapes and patterns.

Form Perception

Form perception is the process by which sensations are organized into meaningful shapes and patterns. One basic principle of form perception, the **figure-ground relationship,** states that when people focus on an object in their perceptual field, they automatically distinguish it from its surroundings (see figure 5-13). What they focus on is the figure, and everything else becomes the ground. For example, the words you are reading are the figures in your perceptual field, while the white surrounding the text is the ground. When there are not enough cues to reliably distinguish a figure from its ground, it is difficult to perceive the sought-after object. The blending of objects into their surroundings is the basic principle behind camouflage (Regan & Beverley, 1984).

The figure-ground relationship applies to all the senses, not just vision. For example, I can distinguish the sound of my daughters' singing voices against the ground of the rest of the school chorus, the taste of cinnamon in a pumpkin pie, and the smell of barbecued chicken at a county fair. In all instances, I perceive one object as the figure and the other sensory information as the background.

figure-ground relationship The Gestalt principle that, when people focus on an object in their perceptual field, they automatically distinguish it from its surroundings.

Figure 5-14

Gestalt Laws of Grouping

Although there are many ways to perceive the objects shown here, we all tend to perceive them similarly, organizing them into groups based on specific perceptual "laws" that have been identified by Gestalt psychologists.

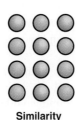

Similarity

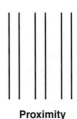

Proximity

Continuity

Closure

Connectedness

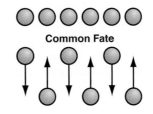

Common Fate

The Danish psychologist Edgar Rubin (1915–1958) identified the following characteristics that allow us to distinguish the figure from the ground:

- The figure is more "thinglike" than the ground, which is perceived as unformed material.
- The figure is perceived as being in front of the ground.
- The figure dominates consciousness and is more memorable than the ground.

Once we distinguish figure from ground, we must next organize the figure into a meaningful form. To give meaning to these sensations, Gestalt psychologists identified the following additional principles, known collectively as the **laws of grouping** (see figure 5-14), that describe how people tend to group discrete stimuli together into a meaningful whole:

Similarity—We group together stimuli that are similar.

Proximity—We group nearby stimuli together.

Continuity—We perceive the contours of straight or curving lines as continuous, flowing patterns.

Connectedness—We perceive objects that are uniform and linked as a single unit.

Closure—We close the gaps in a figure and perceive it as a whole.

Common Fate—We perceive objects moving together in the same direction (sharing a "common fate") as belonging to a single group.

laws of grouping Simple Gestalt principles describing how people tend to group discrete stimuli together into a meaningful whole.

Depth Perception

In addition to organizing sensations into meaningful shapes and patterns, another aspect of visual perception involves organizing sensations in terms of the distance they are from us. To judge distance, our brains must transform the two-dimensional images that fall on our retinas into three-dimensional perceptions. This ability to perceive objects three-dimensionally is known as **depth perception,** and it depends on the use of both binocular cues and monocular cues (Jacobs, 2002).

Binocular cues are depth cues that require information from both eyes. Because our eyes are about 3 inches apart, they receive slightly different images on their retinas when looking at the same scene. This degree of difference between the two images—which is greater when objects are closer to us—is known as the binocular cue of *retinal disparity.* Our brains automatically fuse these two images into one and use the cue of retinal disparity to judge the distance of objects (Genovesio & Ferraina, 2004; Harwerth et al., 2003). You can see the difference between the views of your eyes by holding both fore-fingers vertically in front of you, one at a distance of 6 inches and the other at arm's length. Now alternately close each eye while looking at both fingers. You will notice that the closer finger appears to move farther side to side than the farther finger. If you focus on one finger with both eyes, you will see two images of the other finger. Stereograms and 3-D movies create the perception of depth by presenting to each eye slightly different views of the same image.

Another binocular distance cue is *convergence,* which is the degree the eyes turn inward as an object gets closer. By receiving information about the angle of convergence from the muscles of your eyes, your brain automatically calculates the distance at which you are focusing. The eyestrain you experience after staring at a near object for a long time, such as a book or a computer terminal, is caused by continuous convergence (Tyrrell & Leibowitz, 1990).

While binocular cues result from both eyes working together, **monocular cues** are depth cues that require information from only one eye. Some of the more important monocular cues—a few of which are illustrated in figures 5-15 and 5-16—are as follows (Andre & Owens, 2003; Todd & Norman, 2003):

Interposition—When one object partially blocks our view of another, we perceive the partially obscured object as more distant.

Familiar size—When we see a familiar object, we perceive it as near or distant based on the size of its retinal image. Familiar objects that cast small retinal images are perceived as distant, while familiar objects that make large retinal images are perceived as near.

depth perception The ability to perceive objects three-dimensionally.

binocular cues Depth cues that require information from both eyes.

monocular cues Depth cues that require information from only one eye.

In the late 1800s, one of the most popular "home entertainment systems" was the stereoscope, which relied on the principle of retinal disparity to create the perception of three-dimensional images (Waldsmith, 1991). Photographers would take stereo pictures that mimicked the slightly different images seen by the two eyes. Looking into a stereoscope that allowed each eye to see only one of the two images, viewers were suddenly transported to exotic lands featuring breathtaking landscapes or strange people and animals.

Source: Courtesy of Figzoi.

The Monocular Cues of Interposition, Relative Size, and Height in the Field of View

Monocular cues are depth cues that require information from only one eye. Close one eye and test this depth-perception principle for yourself.

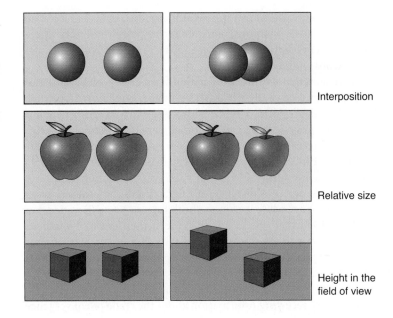

Interposition

Relative size

Height in the
field of view

Relative size—If we assume that two objects are similar in size, we perceive the object with the larger retinal image as being closer.

Height in the field of view—When we see objects, those closer to the horizon are perceived as farther away. This means that objects on the ground (below the horizon) are perceived as farther away when higher in our field of view, while aerial objects (above the horizon) are perceived as farther away when lower in our field of view. This depth cue is also called *relative elevation* or *relative height.*

Texture gradients—When we see a change in the surface texture of objects from coarse, distinct features to fine, indistinct features, we perceive increasing distance.

Atmospheric blur—When we see objects that appear hazy, we perceive them as farther away than sharp, clear objects. This cue is also called *atmospheric perspective* or *aerial perspective.*

Linear perspective—When we see the converging of what we assume are parallel lines, we perceive this convergence as indicating increasing distance.

Light and shadow—When one object reflects more light to our eyes than another object, we perceive the brighter object as closer to us. Further, when we see different degrees of light and shadow on a single object, this provides clues about the object's orientation relative to us and its three-dimensional shape. This cue is also called *relative brightness.*

Motion parallax—When we move our head sideways, objects at different distances appear to move in different directions and at different speeds.

The monocular cue of *motion parallax* refers to the fact that as you move your head sideways, objects at different distances appear to move in different directions and at different speeds. Parallax means a change in position, so motion parallax is a change in the position of an object caused by motion. As you recall from our previous discussion, it was Wertheimer's attention to this perceptual phenomenon that led to the founding of Gestalt psychology. The next time you ride in a car, bus, or train, experience what Wertheimer experienced by focusing on a distant object to your side. Notice how the speed and direction of motion depend on distance. Closer objects appear to speed by in the direction opposite to your own movement, while farther objects seem to move more slowly and in your same direction. This motion parallax causes many children to believe that the moon or clouds

The eye sees only what the mind is prepared to comprehend.

—*Henri Bergson, French philosopher,*
1859–1941

(a)

(b)

(c)

(d)

Figure 5-16

The Monocular Cues of Texture Gradients, Atmospheric Blur, Linear Perspective, and Light and Shadow

(a) With the monocular cue of texture gradients, objects are perceived to be more distant as their surface texture becomes less distinct. *(b)* Due to the atmospheric blur cue, objects that appear hazy are judged to be farther away than sharp, clear objects. *(c)* Due to the linear perspective cue, we perceive the converging of seemingly parallel lines as indicating increasing distance. *(d)* Finally, the light and shadow cue suggests to us that, when an object reflects more light to our eyes than another object, the brighter objects must be closer.

Source: Courtesy of Figzoi.

they see through their side windows are actually following them. When you were younger, you might even have encouraged your parents to drive faster in order to arrive home before the moon!

When artists use monocular cues to create a three-dimensional look in their paintings, the monocular cues are called *pictorial cues.* Prior to the Renaissance, which occurred in Europe from the fourteenth through the sixteenth centuries, artists did not understand how to use the full range of monocular cues. As a result, their paintings often looked two-dimensional and unrealistic. Figure 5-17 depicts a painting by the twentieth-century Indiana artist Norman Badgley Wilson that utilizes a number of pictorial cues to convey varying degrees of depth in a country scene.

> What we see depends mainly on what we look for.
>
> —*Sir John Lubbock, English naturalist,*
> *1834–1913*

Perceptual Constancy

Thus far, you have learned how we organize sensations into meaningful shapes and patterns, and how we also organize them in space. A third aspect of perceptual organization involves

Figure 5-17

Relying on their knowledge of monocular cues, artists depict three dimensions on a flat surface in their paintings. Several monocular cues are evident in this painting by Norman Badgley Wilson. Can you identify where in the painting Wilson has used interposition, familiar size, texture gradients, and atmospheric blur?

Source: Norman Badgley Wilson, *Cattle in a Landscape,* 1930, oil on canvas, 24 × 36 inches.

perceptual constancy The tendency to perceive objects as relatively stable despite continually changing sensory information.

size constancy The form of perceptual constancy in which there is a tendency to perceive objects as stable in size despite changes in the size of their retinal images when they are viewed from different distances.

shape constancy The form of perceptual constancy in which there is a tendency to perceive an object as the same shape no matter from what angle it is viewed.

perceptual sets Expectations that create a tendency to interpret sensory information in a particular way.

perceptual constancy, which is the tendency to perceive objects as relatively stable despite continually changing sensory information. Once we form a stable perception of an object, we can recognize it from almost any distance, angle, and level of illumination. We examined *color constancy* earlier in the chapter; thus, let us now turn our attention to size and shape constancy.

Size constancy is the tendency to perceive objects as stable in size despite changes in the size of their retinal images when we view them from different distances. This form of perceptual constancy explains why you don't perceive people approaching you from a distance as midgets who are mysteriously growing in stature before your eyes. Likewise, **shape constancy** is the tendency to perceive an object as the same shape no matter from what angle we view it. Thus, when you look at your hand, this book, or a door from different angles, you still perceive it as retaining its original shape despite changes in the shape of its retinal image.

With both size constancy and shape constancy, part of the ability in accurately judging objects depends on prior experience with those objects. We are better at assessing the true size and shape of familiar rather than unfamiliar objects (go to Explore It Exercise 5-2).

5-5b Perceptual Sets Create Expectations for How to Interpret Sensory Stimuli

Just as expectations can influence whether we detect the presence of a stimulus (refer back to section 5-1b), the expectations we bring to a situation can also influence how we perceive the stimulus object. These expectations, known as **perceptual sets,** create a tendency to interpret sensory information in a particular way. For example, look at the drawing of the duck in figure 5-18 and then read the figure caption. Based on your initial expectation of seeing a duck, you most likely organized the stimuli in this drawing so that your expectation was realized. Now ask a friend to look at this same drawing (cover up the caption), but tell him to "look at the rabbit." This demonstrates how people can develop different perceptions of the same stimuli based on the situational context that creates different perceptual sets.

Perceptual set can also be influenced by culture. For example, look at figure 5-19a. Most of you will see a rather confusing pattern of black shapes that, with some imagina-

Explore It
Exercise **5-2**

Shape Constancy

Using a pen and a sheet of paper, trace the outline of the music CD in the photo. The tracing will show an oval, but is that how you would describe this object? Show this same photo to other people and ask them to identify the object and describe its shape. Do they describe this music CD as being oval-shaped? I doubt it. Although the photo image is of an oval-shaped object, shape constancy leads you and them to perceive and think of this music CD as a flat circular object.

Source: Courtesy of Figzoi.

tion, may look somewhat like a boot. However, when most of you look at figure 5-19b, you readily perceive the word FLY in the white spaces. Your experience with the English language causes you to focus on the white spaces of figure 5-19b, while the black regions serve as background. Yet, if you were a native Chinese, you would readily perceive the white spaces in figure 5-19a as depicting the Chinese calligraphic character for the word FLY, and you would likely find figure 5-19b confusing (Coren et al., 1987).

Our perceptual sets can influence what we hear and taste as well as what we see. One incident from my childhood that has become family lore is the time we invited Great-Aunt Edith over for dinner. After the meal, as my sister was trying to coax our finicky dog to eat table scraps, she blurted out in an exasperated voice, "Oh, eat it, you dumb dog!" However, what our aunt heard was, "Oh Edith, you dumb dog!" Needless to say, she was momentarily shaken to hear her grandniece addressing her so disrespectfully. Regarding taste expectations, as a cost-saving measure during White House parties, former President Richard Nixon occasionally instructed waiters to refill empty bottles of fine and expensive wine with cheaper and lower-quality brands. Nixon was counting on the expensive bottle's label creating a perceptual set of fine taste in his

Figure 5-18

What Kind of a Duck Is This?

Now that you have seen the duck, look again at this drawing, but try to see a rabbit.

Source: From *Mindsights: Original Visual Illusions, Ambiguities and Other Anomalies, with a Commentary on the Play of Mind in Perception and Art* by Roger N. Shepard, © 1990 by Roger N. Shepard. Reprinted by permission of Henry Holt and Company, LLC.

Figure 5-19

Cultural Influence on Perception

(a) Why does this figure appear to be a confusing pattern of black figures to most English-speaking Westerners, but not to people who are familiar with Chinese? *(b)* Why is the exact opposite probably true for this figure?

(a)

(b)

guests. The psychological phenomenon of perceptual set is yet another illustration that what we perceive is much more than just a matter of detecting sensory stimuli in the world—perception has to do with what's going on in our minds.

5-5c Perceptual Illusions Represent a Misperception of Physical Reality

Because perception depends on how the perceiver interprets sensory stimuli, errors or misperceptions are bound to occur. For example, have you ever been in the driver's seat of a parked car when the car parked next to you began to back up, and you mistakenly perceived your car as moving forward? When this happens to me, I slam on my brakes before realizing that I have just experienced a **perceptual illusion** called **induced movement.** The reason we sometimes experience perceptual illusions is that we misapply one or more of the perceptual principles previously examined in this chapter (see section 5-5a). In the case of induced movement, the perceptual principle that we misapply is the monocular cue of motion parallax. That is, instead of forward movement causing close objects to appear as though they are moving backward, the backward movement of the car close to you makes you feel like you are moving forward.

Because vision is our dominant sense, we know more about visual illusions than any other sensory misperceptions. Thus, in this section, I focus mostly on the visual types of perceptual illusion. Yet let me mention one auditory illusion I am hearing right now as I type this sentence. As mentioned previously, I have an antique clock in my den. Although I know it is making a steady click-click-click-click sound as the pendulum swings back and forth, what I more often hear is an accented CLICK-click-CLICK-click. The reason for this auditory illusion is that people tend to group the steady clicks of a clock into patterns of two clicks, misperceiving one of the clicks—usually the first—as slightly louder than the other.

Do Some Perceptual Illusions Differ Cross-Culturally?

The most famous and extensively studied illusion is the **Müeller-Lyer illusion,** shown in figure 5-20. Notice that the vertical line *b* to the right appears longer than line *a* to the left. Yet, if you measure the lines with a ruler, you will find that they are equal in length. The most widely accepted explanation is that this illusion is due to the misapplication of size constancy (Gregory, 1998; Nijhawan, 1991). That is, because figure *a* bears a likeness to the outside corner of a building and figure *b* resembles the inside corner of a room, the

perceptual illusion A misperception of physical reality, often due to the misapplication of perceptual principles.

induced movement The illusory movement of a stationary object caused by the movement of another nearby object.

Müeller-Lyer illusion A perceptual illusion in which the perceived length of a line is influenced by placing inward- or outward-facing wings on the ends of the line.

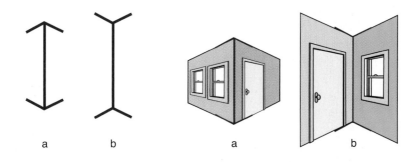

Figure 5-20

The Müeller-Lyer Illusion

In the Müeller-Lyer illusion, lines of equal length are perceived as unequal, with line *b* appearing longer than line *a*. Research indicates that this illusion is more commonly experienced in cultures where straight lines, right angles, and rectangles are common building-design elements. What monocular-distance cue is misapplied in this illusion?

vertical *b* line appears farther away than the vertical *a* line. As a result of this distance cue, the application of size constancy enlarges the perceived length of *b* relative to *a*. Interestingly, cross-cultural research indicates that the Müeller-Lyer illusion is most likely to occur in carpentered cultures where straight lines, right angles, and rectangles are common design elements in buildings (Segall et al., 1966, 1990). People who live in curved buildings without straight lines and right angles, such as the Zulu of southeastern Africa, are much less susceptible to this particular perceptual illusion.

The Japanese psychologist Kazunori Morikawa (2003) demonstrated that the popularity of high-cut bathing suits is at least partly due to the fact that they make a woman's legs look longer than does a conventional bathing suit. This fashion effect is simply an application of the Müeller-Lyer illusion. How so? Figure 5-21a depicts the "low-cut" look of a conventional bathing suit, whereas figure 5-21b depicts the "high-cut" look. Don't the "legs" in figure *b* look longer, even though we know they are not?

Like the Müeller-Lyer illusion, the perceptual illusion of the *Ames Room* is caused by people who live in carpentered cultures misperceiving distance cues. Designed by Adelbert Ames and depicted in figure 5-22, this room is built with a trapezoidal rear wall, different-sized windows, and a sloping floor and ceiling. When viewed through a peephole with one eye, this room appears to have a normal rectangular shape. The man

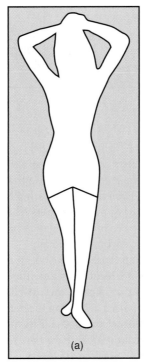

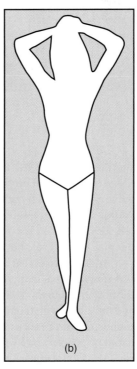

(a) (b)

Figure 5-21

High-Cut Bathing Suits and the Müeller-Lyer Illusion

Fashion designers rely on the Müeller-Lyer illusion to make women's legs appear longer, and thus more attractive, when they wear high-cut bathing suits *(b)* rather than low-cut bathing suits *(a)*. Is it possible that this misperception of these two women's leg lengths will occur more often in cultures where straight lines, right angles, and rectangles are common building-design elements?

Figure 5-22

The Ames Room

(a) Why does the man in the right corner of the Ames Room look like a giant? (b) This perceptual illusion is created by having viewers look into the room through a peephole, with one eye. Despite the fact that this room has a trapezoidal rear wall, a left window that is larger than the right window, and a sloping floor and ceiling, when viewed through the peephole it looks like a normal rectangular room. This illusion occurs because people on the right fill more of the space between the floor and ceiling, and because peephole viewers assume that when two objects are the same distance from them, the object that produces the larger image on their retinas is larger in size than the object that produces a smaller retinal image.

Source: (a) David Wells/The Image Works.

(a)

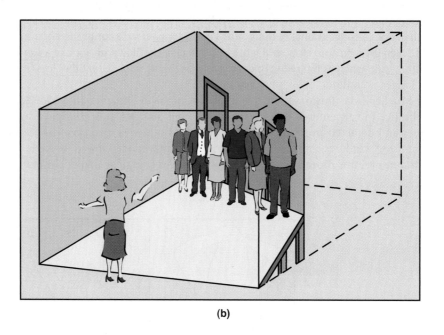

(b)

standing to the right (the near corner) appears disproportionately large because we judge his size based on the incorrect assumption that he is the same distance away as the person in the far left corner. Even more interesting is what we mistakenly perceive when people in the room walk to the opposite corner. When they cross the room from right to left they appear to shrink before our very eyes, while they are transformed from "little people" to giants as they move from left to right!

Another perceptual illusion caused by the misapplication of size constancy is the **Ponzo illusion,** depicted in figure 5-23. Most people see the line on top as longer than the one on the bottom. As in the Müeller-Lyer illusion, these two lines cast the same-sized retinal image, and thus the top line appears farther away than the bottom line because people misapply the monocular-distance cue of linear perspective. This illusion is also less likely to be experienced by people who live in cultures where they are not often exposed to straight lines and right angles (Deregowski, 1989; Segall et al., 1966).

Ponzo illusion A perceptual illusion in which the perceived lengths of horizontal lines are influenced by their placement between vertical converging lines that serve as distance cues.

Stroboscopic Movement

The most important visual illusion you experience when watching movies and playing video games is **stroboscopic movement,** the illusion of movement produced by a rapid pattern of stimulation on different parts of the retina (Anstis, 1978). In motion pictures, stroboscopic movement is created by rapidly passing a series of still pictures (or film frames) past a light source, which projects these images onto a screen. As we watch these rapidly changing images, the memory of each lasts just long enough in our minds until the next one appears (see figure 5-24). For this illusion of movement to occur, each film frame must replace the previous one 24 times per second. During the early days of motion pictures, the frame rate was only 16 per second, resulting in jerky and disjointed movement and a noticeable flickering of light. In television and video games, the static frames change about 30 times per second, resulting in the perception of fluid movement.

When stroboscopic movement is combined with the nineteenth-century technology of stereoscope photography, the visual illusion offered by 3-D movies is created (McCarthy, 1992). Early black-and-white 3-D movies from the 1950s were filmed from two slightly different angles, and the two images were later projected onto the theater screen with different-colored filters (red or blue) placed in front of each projector (McGee, 1989). So that each eye could receive a different view of the same scene, moviegoers wore special glasses with one red and one blue lens. The red lens washed out the red image, and the blue lens washed out the blue image. As previously described (see section 5-5a), by their brains merging these two images into one and using the cue of retinal disparity, the audience experienced three-dimensional movie vision. Later 3-D movies used different types of polarized light that allowed color to be depicted.

The modern-day version of the 3-D movie is the *virtual environment,* in which a person can experience 3-D images and sounds while wearing a head visor. The visor sends clear, full wraparound 3-D images to each eye, and the ears receive digital stereo sound. The images and sounds transmitted by the visor are controlled by a computer that takes into account the head movements of the wearer. Thus, whenever the wearer's head turns, the scene shifts accordingly. As discussed in chapter 2, section 2-3c, psychologists are beginning to use virtual-environment technology in their research to increase the realism of laboratory experiments. Likewise, some clinical psychologists employ this technology when treating clients who suffer from certain phobic disorders (see chapter 14, section 14-3a). Outside of psychology, virtual-environment visors and helmets not only are used to train airline pilots, police officers, surgeons, and soldiers in their various environments, but also are quickly becoming an integral part of the equipment used by computer game players.

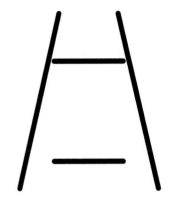

Figure 5-23

The Ponzo Illusion

Although the two horizontal lines are the same length, our experience tells us that a more distant object can create the same-sized retinal image only if it is larger. What monocular-distance cue is being misapplied here?

Figure 5-24

Stroboscopic Motion

Motion picture film consists of a series of still photographs. The illusion of movement is created by presenting the pictures, one at a time, in quick succession. Why do silent movies from the 1920s have a noticeable flickering of light and jerky images, while the movement seen in contemporary movies is fluid and realistic in appearance?

Source: Image Select/Art Resource, NY.

However, no two people see the external world in exactly the same way. To every separate person, a thing is what he thinks it is—in other words, not a thing, but a think.

—*Penelope Fitzgerald, British author, 1916–2000*

Art has a double face, of expression and illusion, just like science has a double face: the reality of error and the phantom of truth.

—*René Daumal, French poet, 1908–1944*

> **moon illusion** A perceptual illusion in which the moon appears to be about 1 1/2 times larger when near the horizon than when high in the sky.

One troubling fact about most of the virtual-environment computer games is that they involve violence. As noted in chapter 2, section 2-3c, psychological research suggests that watching aggression on television and in movies appears to increase people's own aggressive tendencies. Yet, when people play virtual-environment computer games, such as MechWarrior, Doom, and F-15 Strike Eagle, they are not merely observing violence—they are actively participating in simulated aggression. What effect does this more active participation in violent media events have on people's later aggression? Despite denials from the video-game industry, a meta-analysis of 33 video-game studies involving over 3,000 participants found that high video-game violence is associated with heightened aggression in the real world among young adults and children (Anderson & Bushman, 2001).

The Perplexing Moon Illusion

Finally, one last illusion that is affected by the perception of depth is the **moon illusion,** in which the moon appears to be about 1 1/2 times larger when near the horizon than when high in the sky (the same illusion also occurs for the sun). Of course, we know that the moon does not actually shrink as it rises in the sky, and the retinal size of the horizon moon and zenith moon is exactly the same, as represented by Figure 5-25*a*. We also know that the earth's atmosphere does not magnify the visual appearance of the horizon moon. Yet if you have ever watched the moon rise from the horizon to the night sky, you know that it does appear to decrease in size, as represented in figure 5-25*b*. What causes this illusion?

One of the oldest and best known explanations of the moon illusion is the *apparent-distance theory,* which contends that the illusion is caused by the two monocular depth cues of interposition and height in the field of view, combined with the misapplication of the principle of size constancy. According to this theory, when we see the moon near the horizon, it is often partially covered by buildings or trees that provide distance cues (interposition) that the moon is relatively far away. These distance cues are absent when the moon is high on the horizon, because it is almost always unobstructed. Regarding height in the field of view, when the moon is closer to the horizon, we perceive it as far-

Figure 5-25

The Moon Illusion

(a) This is a representation of a time-lapse photograph of the horizon moon and zenith moon. As you can see, the two moon images have the same diameter. Literally thousands of such time-lapsed photographs have been taken over the years, all showing the same result. *(b)* This is a representation of what most of us perceive as our moon illusion experience. That is, when we watch the moon rise in the night sky, it appears to be about $1\frac{1}{2}$ times larger when near the horizon than when high in the sky. Does this same illusion also occur for the sun?

(a)

(b)

ther away than when it is higher in our visual field. Thus, apparent-distance theory states that these two monocular cues cause us to mistakenly perceive the horizon moon as farther away than the moon that is high in the sky. If we perceive the horizon moon as farther away than the zenith moon, we implicitly conclude that this "distant low moon" must be larger than the "near high moon" (Kaufman & Rock, 1962). The problem with apparent-distance theory, however, is that when people are asked to judge which moon appears to be closer (Coren & Aks, 1990), most report that the horizon moon looks closer, not farther away! Of course, this directly contradicts apparent-distance theory.

So, is there any solution to the moon illusion puzzle? Not yet. Some scientists believe that the primary cause of this illusion is the moon's appearance near objects of known size (Hershenson, 1982, 2003). According to this explanation, when seen near the horizon next to trees, buildings, and mountains, the size of the moon in the sky appears rather large in relation to these known-size objects. In contrast, when seen high overhead the moon doesn't seem very big because there is nothing with which to compare it. As you might expect, this explanation also has its critics, and they offer their own solutions to this perceptual puzzle. And so it goes. The most accurate statement I can make to you at this time regarding the moon illusion is that it is a very complicated illusion, and there is still widespread disagreement as to its causes (Acosta, 2004; McCready, 1999; Ross & Plug, 2002).

5-5d Certain Aspects of Perception Are Innate, While Others Are Learned

The principles of Gestalt psychology describe how we transform sensory information into meaningful perceptions. What they demonstrate is that the perceptual "whole" is more than the sum of its individual sensory parts. Gestalt psychologists believe that we are born with these principles for organizing sensory information, but the extent to which this is the case is still open to debate. As discussed in chapter 4, section 4-1d, some aspects of perception—such as recognizing facial expressions, preferring sweet tastes over bitter ones, and discriminating between various odors—are present at birth. Yet to what extent is perception based on inborn abilities versus experience-based learning? One way psychologists have sought to answer this question is by studying how human infants respond to different environmental stimuli. A second method is to study newborn animals with sensory and perceptual systems similar to those of humans and deny them the usual perceptual experiences they encounter early in life. A third way is to study blind people whose eyesight has been surgically restored. Let's examine examples of all three research approaches.

The Visual Cliff

To study the ability to perceive depth, Eleanor Gibson and Richard Walk (1960) designed the *visual cliff*. This apparatus consists of a glass-covered tabletop with a "shallow" checkerboard on one end and a "deep" checkerboard on the other end that appears to drop off like a cliff (see figure 5-26). Infants between 6 and 14 months of age were placed on the middle of this table, and their mothers were instructed to coax them into crawling to one side or the other. Although the mothers had little problem getting their children to crawl toward them on the shallow end, most infants refused to crawl past the visual cliff onto the deep end (Walk & Gibson, 1961). It is possible that by the time they learned to crawl, these children had also learned to perceive depth, yet newborn animals that can walk the day they are born—such as lambs, chicks, kittens, pigs, and rats—also avoid the deep end of the visual cliff (Walk, 1981). In addition, later studies using the visual cliff found that when younger, noncrawling infants were physically moved from the shallow end of the table to the deep end, their heart rates slowed, which is a typical reaction when people try to orient themselves in new situations (Campos et al., 1970). In other words, although these younger babies may not have known precisely how to react, they did perceive something different between the shallow and deep ends of the table. Together, these findings suggest that infants develop depth perception shortly after birth,

Figure 5-26

The Visual Cliff

The visual cliff consists of a glass-covered tabletop with a "shallow" checkerboard on one end and a "deep" checkerboard on the other end that appears to drop off like a cliff. Most 6-month-old infants won't crawl across the "deep" side.

but that fear and avoidance of dangerous depths may develop only after they learn to crawl and obtain first-hand experience with the dangers of height.

Newly "Sighted" People and Animals

Further evidence that some perceptual abilities might be inborn comes from case histories of people who have gained sight after a lifetime of blindness. Most gained their vision by having cataracts—clouded lenses that allow only diffused light to enter the eye—surgically removed. Following this procedure, these newly sighted individuals could distinguish figure from ground, scan objects, perceive colors, and follow moving objects with their eyes (Gregory, 1998). Unfortunately, they often could not recognize objects until they touched them.

Seeking to study this same phenomenon under more controlled conditions, Tortsen Wiesel (1982) either stitched closed the eyelids of newborn kittens and monkeys or placed goggles over their eyes that enabled them to see only diffused light. Following infancy, when these visual impairments were removed, the animals exhibited perceptual limitations similar to those observed in the human cataract patients. Further studies with cats found that the first 3 months of life appear to be a critical period in the development of their ability to detect horizontal and vertical lines (Hirsch & Spinelli, 1970; Mitchell, 1980). If kittens don't get the necessary exposure to visual stimuli, they experience a permanent deficit in visual perception even after years of living in a normal environment. Together, these studies suggest that although certain aspects of visual perception may be inborn, others appear to require experience-based learning during critical periods in infancy. If this critical period is missed, certain perceptual deficits cannot be corrected through later learning.

5-5e There Is Little Scientific Evidence in Support of Extrasensory Perception

Besides the types of perception already discussed, some people believe that we can also perceive events in the world without using the normal sensory receptors. This **extrasensory perception (ESP)** is a controversial topic within psychology, with only a minority of psychologists believing in its possible existence (Hoppe, 1988; Hyman, 1994). The field that studies ESP and other paranormal phenomena is known as **parapsychology.**

Parapsychologists study a variety of extrasensory abilities. *Mental telepathy* is the alleged ability to perceive others' thoughts, while *clairvoyance* is the alleged ability to perceive objects or events that are not physically present. For example, telepathists might claim they can "read" your mind, and clairvoyants might claim they can find your lost jew-

extrasensory perception (ESP) The ability to perceive events without using normal sensory receptors.

parapsychology The field that studies ESP and other paranormal phenomena.

elry. Unlike telepathy and clairvoyance, which involve perception of things in the present, *precognition* is the alleged ability to perceive events in the future—that is, before they happen. Thus, you might consult a fortune-teller who claims to use precognition to reveal an impending love interest in your life. Finally, *psychokinesis* is the alleged ability to control objects through mental manipulation, such as causing a chair to move or a flipped coin to land either "heads" or "tails."

William James, one of the founders of psychology, believed in the existence of paranormal phenomena and co-founded one of the first organizations devoted to the scientific study of the paranormal, the American Society for Psychical Research. During his lifetime, James investigated numerous claims of the paranormal, including studying the use of mediums to communicate with the dead. One year before his death in 1910, James predicted that the greatest scientific discoveries of the next generation would be in parapsychology (James, 1909/1986). A century later, it is safe to conclude that this eminent psychologist demonstrated no precognitive ability in making his bold prediction: The mainstream scientific community recognizes none of the findings from parapsychology as particularly noteworthy.

One of the main reasons why the scientific community is skeptical about ESP claims is that whenever one study discovers evidence of paranormal abilities, the findings often cannot be replicated in subsequent research (Alcock, 2003; Lilienfeld, 1999). For example, in the 1930s, parapsychologist J. B. Rhine designed a set of cards with each containing distinct, easy-to-recall symbols on one side (see figure 5-27). When research participants were asked repeatedly to guess which of the five symbols was on the other side of a "target" card presented to them, Rhine (1934) reported that they were able to successfully do so with a frequency significantly better than chance. Had these findings been successfully reproduced by researchers in other laboratories, the scientific community might have been suitably impressed. Unfortunately for Rhine and parapsychology, other researchers could not replicate these impressive findings. Further, careful examination of Rhine's methods revealed that some of his participants may have been able to identify cards by their warped edges and stains.

More recently, scientists tested the ESP ability of almost 28,000 people by asking them to guess the outcome of four random electronic coin tosses. With such a large sample size, this study had the statistical power to detect the possible existence of even a very small ESP effect. However, the results found no evidence of ESP ability (Wiseman & Greening, 2002). There also is scant evidence for ESP ability among tabloid psychics. For example, between 1978 and 1985, the "leading psychics" identified by the *National Enquirer* made 486 predictions about the future, but only two came true (Strentz, 1986), which means they were wrong more than 99.5 percent of the time!

What about the widely held belief that psychics are successful at helping various government agencies uncover hidden or secret information, such as aiding the police in solving

Figure 5-27

In the 1930s, parapsychologist J. B. Rhine designed a special set of cards with easy-to-recall symbols as a way to test paranormal abilities. How might you design an ESP experiment using these cards to test participants' abilities at mental telepathy?

Source: Courtesy of Figzoi.

crimes or uncovering spy plots? Regarding psychic ability in crime solving, it appears that almost all the successful collaborations between psychics and police departments occur in fictional stories, such as the TV show *Medium*. When police departments in the 50 largest cities in the United States were surveyed, 65 percent reported never having used psychics, and of the remaining 35 percent that had used psychics on a crime case, not one police department had found it helpful (Sweat & Durm, 1993). Additional studies comparing the success rates of psychics, college students, and experienced crime detectives in solving crime cases have found that the psychics are no more successful than the students and detectives, and their success rate is no better than chance (Lucas, 1985; Reiser, 1982). Similar disappointing results have occurred when psychics have been tested in the clandestine world of intelligence gathering. After 20 years of testing "psychic spies," the Central Intelligence Agency concluded in a 1995 report that ESP claims were not supported by any reliable evidence (Hyman, 1996).

Despite the fact that there are many competent researchers studying psychic phenomena, flawed research methodology and outright fraud by people claiming psychic abilities have been persistent problems in parapsychology since its inception. In one famous case, the alleged psychic Uri Geller, who is also a magician, claimed to be able to bend spoons using psychokinesis. However, closer inspection by another trained magician revealed that Geller's powers were well short of anyone's definition of miraculous (Randi, 1980). Like any good magician, he used sleight-of-hand techniques to distract people's attention and then quickly bent the spoons using normal physical force!

Although there is little evidence to indicate that ESP is a viable means of gathering information about our world, over half of all American, Canadian, and British adults believe in its existence (Blackmore, 1997; Newport & Strausberg, 2001). Popular culture fosters such beliefs, with fictional television shows and movies depicting people with fantastic paranormal powers. Buoyed by this supportive cultural climate, psychic hotlines take in over $1 billion per year, mostly from low-income persons who are seeking special insight into their lives (Nisbet, 1998). Without exception, the evidence upon which laypersons base their beliefs comes from anecdotal accounts, not scientific studies. Yet these accounts could simply be due to unusual coincidences, exaggerated gossip, or—as we have seen—outright fraud. Until the phenomenon known as ESP can be reliably replicated in carefully controlled scientific studies, it will remain only a highly speculative "extra sense" to most practitioners of science.

Section Review

- Form perception is the process by which sensations are organized into meaningful shapes and patterns.
- The figure-ground relationship is a Gestalt principle stating that when people focus on an object, or "figure," in their perceptual field, they automatically distinguish it from its surroundings.
- Depth perception is the ability to perceive objects three-dimensionally.
- Perceptual constancy is the tendency to perceive objects as relatively stable despite continually changing sensory information.
- Perceptual set refers to the expectations an observer brings to a situation that influence what is perceived.
- Perceptual illusion is a misperception of physical reality due to the misapplication of perceptual principles.
- Certain aspects of visual perception may be inborn, while others require experience-based learning during critical periods in infancy.
- Extrasensory perception is the ability to perceive events without using normal sensory receptors. There is no reliable scientific evidence that this type of perception exists.

Psychological Applications

Can You Improve Your Memory and Self-Esteem through Subliminal Persuasion?

As discussed earlier in the chapter (section 5-1a), there are many events that we do not consciously experience because they are below our absolute threshold. Although we are not consciously aware of these stimuli, can they still influence our behavior? Stimulation just below the absolute threshold of conscious awareness is known as *subliminal stimulation*. **Subliminal perception** is the processing of such information. As with extrasensory perception, many astounding claims have been made over the years about the powerful influence that subliminal messages can have on our minds and actions. Perhaps you have watched television programs and movies in which subliminal persuasion was an important aspect of the plot line. Let's examine the inspiration for all these shows—namely, a "study" involving popcorn, Coca-Cola, and the glitter of the silver screen.

> **subliminal perception** The processing of information that is just below the absolute threshold of conscious awareness.

The Astounding Popcorn/Coke "Study"

It is the summer of 1957. Peter Trembath and Terese Berg have gone to a drive-in movie theater in Fort Lee, New Jersey, to watch Kim Novak and William Holden in the Hollywood box office smash *Picnic*. All week long, they have been looking forward to seeing this movie. Besides Peter and Terese, another person, James Vicary, has been waiting with a great deal of anticipation for the showing of this particular movie on this particular evening. Why? Mr. Vicary is an advertising expert, and he has secretly spliced the words *EAT POPCORN* and *DRINK COKE* into the filmstrip reel. While Peter and Terese watch Novak and Holden embrace on the silver screen, these words are periodically flashed before their eyes for a fraction of a second. Mr. Vicary hopes these subliminal messages will influence the moviegoers' immediate buying habits.

Watching the film, Peter and Terese do not consciously see these persuasive messages flash onto the screen, but both are suddenly gripped by the urge to buy popcorn and Coke. As Peter leaves his car and walks toward the refreshment stand, he notices that many other patrons are headed in the same direction. Later, returning to the car with two Cokes and a jumbo tub of popcorn, he tells Terese, "Boy, I've never seen so many hungry and thirsty people at a movie before! It seemed like everybody and his mother wanted Coke and popcorn!"

A short time after this special showing of the movie, Mr. Vicary contacts the press and tells them what he has done, adding that popcorn sales increased by 58 percent that evening, while Coke sales showed an 18 percent escalation. Reading the news accounts of this subliminal manipulation, many people throughout the country express shock and outrage. Social com- mentators decry Mr. Vicary's subliminal manipulation as a heinous crime. Why? Because it amounts to "breaking and entering" into people's most valued and prized domain: their minds.

Over the years, the remarkable statistics from Mr. Vicary's popcorn/Coke study have been commonly cited by people who want to demonstrate the powerful influence that subliminal messages can have on our minds and actions. A popular author, Wilson Bryan Key, has written a series of best-selling books on the topic in which he warns his readers about the dangers that such cleverly hidden messages can have on our lives (Key, 1989). Key states:

> Every person . . . has been victimized and manipulated by the use of subliminal stimuli directed into his unconscious mind by the mass merchandisers of media. The techniques are in widespread use by media, advertising and public relations agencies, industrial and commercial corporations, and by the federal government itself. (Key, 1973, p. 1)

If one were to believe Mr. Vicary's statistics and Key's analysis of them, such dire conclusions would be clearly justifiable. Yet you should not uncritically believe everything you read. For example, in telling the popcorn/Coke story, I made up the characters of Peter and Terese. No such people were at the drive-in theater in the summer of 1957. I fabricated these characters because I wanted them to fit the fabricated mold of the rest of the story. The simple facts are that there was no 58 percent increase in popcorn sales on that evening, nor was there even an 18 percent increase in Coke sales (Weir, 1984). James Vicary, desiring to gain customers for his failing marketing business, fabricated the entire study! His concocted results were never submitted to a scientific journal, where they would have been critically analyzed. Instead, reporters, popular authors, and even many social scientists merely accepted the findings as fact.

A likely reason why these surprising findings were so uncritically accepted is that they fit popular assumptions about the powers that new communication technologies could have over the attitudes and behavior of viewers. For example, by 1970, the American public's belief in the power of subliminal persuasion was so widespread that one poll indicated that almost 70 percent of those who had some knowledge of subliminal advertising believed it could influence consumers' buying habits (Zanot et al., 1983). Today these beliefs persist. In stores throughout the country, you can buy subliminal audiotapes to improve memory, stop smoking, lose weight, or increase self-esteem. Is there any evidence that such tapes are effective? Should you spend your money on such products?

Continued next page—

Psychological Applications

—*Continued*

Is Subliminal Persuasion the "Real Thing"?

Although numerous studies have found that people can respond to stimuli without being aware that they are doing so (Eimer & Schlaghecken, in press; Katkin et al., 2001), there is no convincing evidence that subliminal persuasion influences consumer behavior (Trappey, 1996). Yet what about people who have used subliminal tapes and swear that their lives have been changed? Isn't this evidence that subliminal persuasion can be effective at least some of the time?

This was the question that Anthony Greenwald and his colleagues (1991) were interested in answering when they conducted a study of such self-help tapes. Participants were first pretested for their level of self-esteem and memory recall ability and then given an audiotape containing various pieces of classical music. The tape manufacturers claimed that embedded within these self-help tapes were subliminal messages designed either to increase self-esteem (for example, "I have high self-worth and high self-esteem") or to increase memory (for example, "My ability to remember and recall is increasing daily"). Half the tapes were purposely mislabeled by the researchers, leading the participants who received them to believe they had a memory tape when they really had a self-esteem tape, or vice versa. The rest of the tapes, with correct labels, were distributed to the remaining participants. During the next 5 weeks, these volunteers listened at home daily to their respective tapes. After this exposure period, they again were given self-esteem and memory tests and were also asked whether they believed the tapes had been effective. The test results indicated no self-esteem or memory increases: The subliminal tapes were utterly ineffective. But despite these null findings, participants who thought they had received the self-esteem tape tended to believe their self-esteem had increased, and those who thought they had received the memory tape believed their memory had improved. This was true even if they had received a mislabeled tape!

Although subliminal self-help tapes and CDs do not improve memory or increase self-esteem, they continue to do a brisk business. Why do you think people believe in their effectiveness?

Source: Courtesy of Figzoi.

These results, combined with other subliminal tape studies, suggest that whatever benefits people derive from such self-help products have little to do with the content of the subliminal messages (Merikle & Skanes, 1992; Moore, 1995). Instead, people's expectations (the **placebo effect**), combined with their economic and psychological investment ("I invested a lot of time and money in this tape; it must be good!"), appear to be the sole influence operating here.

> **placebo effect** A situation in which people experience some change or improvement from an empty, fake, or ineffectual treatment.

Before we dismiss the possibility that subliminal persuasion can influence people's everyday attitudes and behavior, we should consider that there are some studies, conducted under carefully controlled laboratory conditions, that have successfully manipulated people's attitudes and behavior using subliminal stimuli (Weisbuch et al., 2003). For example, in a series of experiments, participants who were repeatedly exposed to subliminal stimuli (abstract geometric figures or people's faces) later expressed greater liking for those stimuli (Bornstein et al., 1987). In another study, participants who were subliminally exposed to achievement-oriented words (*strive, succeed, master*) while completing a "word search" puzzle were more likely to continue working on the puzzle task when signaled to stop than those in the control group (Bargh & Churchland, 1999). These findings suggest that it may be possible for a stimulus subliminally embedded in an advertisement to influence buyers' preferences.

The caveat to this possibility is that there are some important differences between the laboratory environment where these results were obtained and the real world where people would normally receive subliminal messages. In the carefully controlled settings where these subliminal effects have been found, participants paid a great deal of attention to the experimental stimuli. In watching the average media advertisement, people are considerably less attentive. Due to the viewer's wandering eye, it is much less likely that a subliminal stimulus embedded in an ad would be unconsciously processed. A second reason to doubt that these effects would occur outside the lab is that the duration of most of these subliminal effects appears to be very short, perhaps lasting only a few seconds. If the subliminal effects last only a short time, they are unlikely to influence product purchases. Thus, although it is not beyond the realm of possibility that practitioners of persuasion could at some time in the future develop clever subliminal techniques that influence the thinking and behavior of the general public, there are no known effective techniques at the present time. Future research will determine the actual potential use—and abuse—of subliminal procedures in persuasion.

Key Terms

absolute threshold (p. 152)

acupuncture (p. 176)

afterimage (p. 162)

audition (p. 164)

binocular cues (p. 181)

blind spot (p. 158)

cochlea (p. 166)

color blindness (p. 161)

color constancy (p. 163)

cones (p. 157)

cornea (p. 155)

depth perception (p. 181)

difference threshold (p. 153)

eardrum (p. 166)

extrasensory perception (ESP) (p. 192)

feature detectors (p. 159)

figure-ground relationship (p. 179)

form perception (p. 179)

fovea (p. 158)

frequency theory (p. 168)

gate-control theory (p. 175)

gestalt (p. 179)

gustation (p. 172)

induced movement (p. 186)

iris (p. 156)

kinesthetic sense (p. 177)

laws of grouping (p. 180)

lens (p. 156)

monocular cues (p. 181)

moon illusion (p. 190)

Müeller-Lyer illusion (p. 186)

olfaction (p. 170)

olfactory epithelium (p. 170)

opponent-process theory (p. 163)

optic nerve (p. 158)

parapsychology (p. 192)

perception (p. 150)

perceptual constancy (p. 184)

perceptual illusion (p. 186)

perceptual sets (p. 184)

pheromones (p. 171)

placebo effect (p. 196)

Ponzo illusion (p. 188)

place theory (p. 168)

proprioceptive senses (p. 177)

psychophysics (p. 151)

pupil (p. 156)

retina (p. 157)

rods (p. 157)

sensation (p. 150)

sensory adaptation (p. 153)

shape constancy (p. 184)

signal-detection theory (p. 152)

size constancy (p. 184)

sound localization (p. 167)

sound waves (p. 165)

stroboscopic movement (p. 189)

subliminal perception (p. 195)

synesthesia (p. 177)

taste buds (p. 172)

transduction (p. 151)

trichromatic theory (p. 161)

vestibular sense (p. 177)

volley theory (p. 168)

wavelength (p. 155)

Weber's law (p. 153)

Suggested Websites

Sensation and Perception Jeopardy
http://www.uni.edu/walsh/jeopardy.html
This website tests your knowledge of sensation and perception using the *Jeopardy* game show format. The site was prepared by Professor Linda Walsh at the University of Northern Iowa.

Grand Illusions
http://www.grand-illusions.com
This website has many optical and sensory illusions, as well as interactive demonstrations and puzzles.

Review Questions

Note: You can find the correct answers to these questions by taking the quiz and then submitting your answers in the Online Edition. The program will automatically score your submission. If you miss a question, the program will provide the correct answer, a rationale for the answer, and the section number in the chapter where the topic is discussed.

1. Which of the following statements is *true*?
   a. To determine absolute threshold, a stimulus must be detectable 90 percent of the time.
   b. We have many thresholds for a given sense.
   c. Our sense of taste is more sensitive than hearing.
   d. Sensory adaptation occurs with vision without any special equipment.
   e. None of the above

2. Which of the following types of energy can our eyes detect?
   a. radio
   b. ultraviolet and infrared
   c. X-ray radiation
   d. none of the above
   e. *a* and *c*

3. Pupil size is affected by
   a. light.
   b. psychological arousal.
   c. interest.
   d. all of the above
   e. *a* and *b*

4. Which of the following animals have all-rod eyes?
   a. lizards and chipmunks
   b. rats
   c. bears
   d. owls
   e. *b* and *d*

5. Nearsightedness, or _____, results in blurred vision for distant objects, while farsightedness, or _____, results in blurred vision for near objects.
   a. myopia, acuity
   b. acuity, myopia
   c. myopia, hyperopia
   d. hyperopia, myopia
   e. none of the above

6. Which of the following statements is *true?*
   a. Visual information in the right visual field goes to the left hemisphere of the brain.
   b. Visual information in the left visual field goes to the right hemisphere of the brain.
   c. Axons from the right eye are all connected to the right hemisphere of the brain.
   d. The optic nerve is the retina's area of central focus.
   e. *a* and *b*

7. Color is
   a. energy.
   b. created by our nervous system.
   c. the same for humans and animals.
   d. *a* and *b*
   e. all of the above

8. The theory that best explains color blindness is
   a. trichromatic theory.
   b. opponent-process theory.
   c. vision theory.
   d. *a* and *b*
   e. none of the above

9. Mixing of red, green, and blue light wavelengths makes a white light, because
   a. this process adds wavelengths and therefore increases light.
   b. this process subtracts wavelengths and therefore increases light.
   c. this process adds wavelengths and therefore decreases light.
   d. this process subtracts wavelengths and therefore decreases light.
   e. red, green, and blue light wavelengths cannot be truly mixed.

10. What theory best explains how we can hear sounds at frequencies of 5,000 Hz?
    a. volley
    b. place
    c. frequency
    d. *a* and *b*
    e. none of the above

11. The main parts of the inner ear include the
    a. oval window, cochlea, and organ of Corti.
    b. hammer, anvil, and stirrup.
    c. pinna, cochlea, and basilar membrane.
    d. basilar membrane, oval window, and hammer.
    e. none of the above

12. Which of the following is a recent addition to those tastes identified as basic tastes?
    a. bitterness
    b. fattiness
    c. saltiness
    d. sourness
    e. sweetness

13. Which of the following statements is *true?*
    a. Sensitivity to sweet and salty substances is best along the sides of the tongue.
    b. If your L-fibers are destroyed, you will be insensitive to pain.
    c. The inner ear is responsible only for our sense of hearing.
    d. Our tongue is the largest sensory organ.
    e. none of the above

14. Which of the following statements is *true?*
    a. Our sense of smell is as refined as that of a cat or dog.
    b. Our ears appear to have evolved from our sense of touch.
    c. We cannot recognize each other from body odor alone.
    d. all of the above
    e. none of the above

15. The areas of the skin with the greatest concentration of receptors are the
    a. fingers, lips, face, tongue, and genitals.
    b. fingers, lips, bottom of feet, and genitals.
    c. toes, elbows, and eyes.
    d. knees, wrists, and neck.
    e. none of the above

16. The perceptual experience of tasting colors or seeing sounds is called
    a. mixed perception.
    b. faux perception.
    c. Gestaltism.
    d. synesthesia.
    e. evanescence.

17. Gestalt psychology is based on the principle
    a. that our mind responds to individual sensations.
    b. that our mind actively organizes stimuli into a whole.
    c. of motion parallax.
    d. *a* and *b*
    e. none of the above

18. Depth perception depends on
    a. binocular cues.
    b. monocular cues.
    c. convergence.
    d. retinal disparity.
    e. all of the above

19. To fool the brain into seeing in three dimensions, 3-D movies rely on
    a. monocular cues.
    b. retinal disparity.
    c. amplitude.
    d. *a* and *b*
    e. none of the above

20. While looking up at the sky, your friend says, "That cloud looks just like a dinosaur." You look up and agree that it does look remarkably like a dinosaur. Another couple, 100 meters away, see the same cloud and agree that it looks like a bird. This illustrates
    a. conformist perceptions.
    b. ambiguity reduction.
    c. perceptual sets.
    d. figure-ground.
    e. perceptual cues.

21. How have scientists tried to determine what aspects of perception are innate?
    a. by studying human infants
    b. by studying newborn animals
    c. by studying blind people with eyesight surgically restored
    d. all of the above
    e. *a* and *c* only

22. Which of the following accurately summarizes the scientific evidence on ESP?
    a. ESP is rare, possessed by less than 2 percent of the population.
    b. There is evidence of mental telepathy, but not of clairvoyance.
    c. Not enough studies have been conducted on ESP to draw firm conclusions.
    d. ESP exists, but it is a very weak effect.
    e. There is no evidence of ESP in any form in anyone.

Chapter 6

Consciousness

Source: © Stockbyte.

Graduate student Eugene Aserinsky wasn't sure what he had discovered, if anything. It was late at night in 1952, and he was hovering over his sleeping 8-year-old son, Armond. The young boy had electrodes taped to his head, near his eyes. These electrodes were connected to an old, barely functioning electroencephalograph, which is a machine that measures the level of electrical activity in the brain. Aserinsky had spent weeks trying to repair this abandoned apparatus, found in the basement of the physiology department's sleep lab at the University of Chicago. Each time he fixed one problem, the machine developed another defect. After his latest repair, he had decided to test the machine on his sleeping son. Should he now believe what it was telling him?

What this machine was telling Aserinsky was that his sleeping son's brain was as active in sleep as it was during its normal waking state. This didn't make any sense, because everyone knew that the brain entered a quiet phase during sleep. Indeed, Aserinsky's boss and mentor, the world-renowned Professor Nathaniel Kleitman, was one of the main proponents of this theory about sleep. The machine must still be malfunctioning, thought Aserinsky. As the night progressed, he observed that Armond's brain showed spurts of brain activity about every 90 minutes. He further observed that this heightened brain activity occurred at the same time that Armond's closed eyes were making fast, jerky movements. During one such episode, Aserinsky awakened his son, and Armond reported that he was having a dream. Very curious, thought his father.

The next day when Aserinsky excitedly told Kleitman about his observations, the skeptical professor phoned the machine's manufacturer and was told by the chief technical expert that the inexperienced graduate student must have done something to the machine to make it spew out such nonsense. Upon hearing this indictment of his competency, Aserinsky's career flashed before his eyes. Later, recounting this dark moment in his life, Aserinsky (1996) stated, "If I had a suicidal nature, this would have been the time. I was married, I had a child, I'd been in universities for twelve years with no degree to show for it. I'd already spent a couple of years horsing around on this. I was absolutely finished."

Luckily, Aserinsky's mentor did not "pull the plug" on Aserinsky's research or career. However, Kleitman did insist that his own daughter serve as the next subject of study. They found similar results and then began testing adults. By waking people who were producing these fast, jerky eye movements, Aserinsky and Kleitman (1953) were able to ascertain that dreams are a characteristic feature of this active stage of sleep. This discovery was instrumental in changing the course of sleep research from a relatively mundane area of inquiry into one that is intensely exciting.

As we continue our psychological journey of discovery through the landscape of consciousness, we will explore the inner world of sleep. In addition, we will try to find answers to questions about other areas of consciousness. For example, can you recall ever being surprised by unusual states of awareness that occurred while you were awake? When labeling one state of mind an unusual or "altered" state, how well do you really understand the state with which you are comparing it? Are these normal and altered states the same for everyone, or do you inhabit your own unique experiential world? Luckily for us, researchers have also explored these areas of consciousness, and their discoveries will become ours as we follow their footprints in this part of our journey.

6-1   THE NATURE OF CONSCIOUSNESS

Preview

- *What are the essential characteristics of consciousness?*
- *What are daydreams?*
- *Why might consciousness be advantageous for our survival?*

Although almost everyone would agree that consciousness is highly important for our survival, scientists and philosophers still argue about its essential characteristics (Dennett, 1994; Hobson, 1999a; Roth, 2001).

6-1a Consciousness Is Subjective, Selective, Divided, Continuous, Changing, and Consisting of Many Levels

Consciousness is our awareness of ourselves and our environment. Such consciousness is highly complex. It is *subjective*—you cannot share it with another person; it is *selective*—you can be aware of some things while ignoring others; it is *divided*—you can pay attention to two different things at once; it is *continuous*—each moment of consciousness blends into the next moment; it is *changing*—what you are aware of now will normally shift to awareness of other things within seconds; and it *consists of many levels*—from an alert and focused awareness to the relative stupor of deep sleep. These qualities of consciousness allow human beings to negotiate a complex social world (Donald, 2001; Kreitler, 1999).

consciousness Awareness of ourselves and our environment.

Subjectivity

Each of us has our own conscious experiences. We can discuss with others what we see, hear, feel, and think, but we cannot directly share these experiences; our consciousness is unique. As discussed in chapter 1, section 1-2a, in the late 1800s, Wilhelm Wundt and the discipline of *structuralism* sought to identify the basic components—the "structure"—of the conscious mind by trying to directly observe conscious experiences. In attempting to meet this goal, the structuralists employed the method of *introspection,* in which highly trained individuals attended to their own consciousness and then reported their observations to others. For example, these trained introspectors would view a stimulus, such as a flower, and then try to reconstruct their sensations and feelings immediately after observing it. They might first report on the colors they saw, then the smells, and so on. Unfortunately for the structuralists, it proved impossible to objectively verify these self-reports. Today, psychologists do not try to directly observe consciousness, but instead, they have devised objective methods that *infer* what conscious experiences are occurring through careful observation. For example, by simultaneously measuring people's brain activity and obtaining self-reports from them, psychologists try to identify different states of consciousness.

Selective Attention

My wife and I tell our daughters they have "big ears," because whenever we talk about them at a social gathering and they are in the vicinity, they eavesdrop on what we are saying. Unless, of course, they are watching one of their favorite television shows—then, they tune out all distractions, however self-relevant. This ability to focus awareness on a single stimulus to the exclusion of all others is known as **selective attention,** and it is the second defining characteristic of consciousness.

selective attention The focused awareness on a single stimulus to the exclusion of all others.

One way psychologists study selective attention in the laboratory is through dichotic listening tasks (Clarke & Thiran, 2004; Gootjes et al., 2004). They place earphones on research participants and deliver different messages to each ear simultaneously but instruct participants to listen to only one of the messages. To ensure that participants do this, they are asked to repeat out loud the message, a process known as *shadowing.* Typically in such studies, participants are able to completely ignore the nonshadowed information in the other ear (Cherry, 1953). Participants are usually so good at shadowing the message that, if it is switched between the two ears, they continue to shadow it, following the content rather than the ear. However, if the participant's name is mentioned in the nonshadowed message, or if the message contains sexually explicit words, the participant is likely to notice this at least some of the time (Nielsen & Sarason, 1981; Wood & Cowan, 1995).

Despite the fact that participants in most shadowing studies show no ability to recall or recognize any of the nonshadowed information, they do appear to process it to some degree (Nisbett & Wilson, 1977; Schacter, 1992). For example, if the word *Wisconsin* is part of the unattended message, the person may not remember it but may be more likely to say "Madison" when asked to name a state capital than would be someone for whom "Wisconsin" was not part of the unattended message. Similarly, this participant will require less time to answer the question, "What state is known as the 'Dairy state'?"

While you engage in selective attention, are there certain kinds of stimuli that are more likely than others to redirect your attention? Consider for a moment your selective attention as you read these words. Although you may be ignoring the background noise around you, certain important signals will more easily penetrate your concentration than others. For instance, you may be able to ignore another person in the room, but what if that person turns toward you with a threatening expression on her face? You are likely to take notice, because we automatically divert our attention to threatening faces (Mogg & Bradley, 1999). This ability to override attentional focus and notice signs of impending danger is a useful trait and undoubtedly was of great survival value to our human ancestors.

Divided Attention

The evidence that some unattended messages are processed suggests that it is possible to attend to different stimuli at the same time. For example, you demonstrate such **divided attention**— which is a third characteristic of consciousness—when you get dressed in the morning while listening to music or talking to someone. Performing these tasks simultaneously is relatively easy because at least one of them is so well learned that you can do it automatically (Schneider, 1985). How can you simultaneously listen to a lecture and take notes when *both* tasks require substantial attention? Research suggests that you can divide your attention with a good deal of success in such instances because each task requires different attentional brain resources (Wickens, 1992a, 1992b). In listening to the lecturer's words, your primary attentional resources are devoted to perceiving this incoming stimulus, while other resources handle note-taking.

Although we generally are able to engage in both selective and divided attention, we sometimes risk our health and safety when performing two or more tasks at once. For example, there are over 110 million cell phone users in the United States, and 85 percent of them talk on their phones while driving a motor vehicle. A number of studies suggest that this sort of divided attention creates distractions and increases the risk of traffic accidents, even when using hands-free models (Just et al., 2001; Strayer & Johnston, 2001). Listening to the radio or talking to a passenger while driving does not distract us to the same dangerous degree (Just et al., 2001).

Research suggests that the upper limit of individual attentional abilities is determined by the efficiency of our nervous system (Hoptman & Davidson, 1994). For example, as we age, our nervous system becomes less efficient, which weakens our ability to sustain attention, either the selective or the divided variety (Madden, 1992; Valeriani et al., 2003). Children who have *attention-deficit/hyperactivity disorder (ADHD)*, which appears to be biologically based (Mason et al., 2004; Solanto, 2002), also are unable to concentrate for extended time periods. Still, among these children and among the elderly, strategies to improve attention can be learned, even in complex tasks (Kramer et al., 1995; Pashler, 1992).

divided attention
Attention that is split and simultaneously focused on different stimuli.

A number of studies find that the divided attention resulting from using a cell phone while driving a car creates distractions and increases the likelihood of accidents and traffic fatalities. Do you think knowledge of these research findings will influence your future decisions about operating a motor vehicle while talking on a cell phone?

Source: Courtesy of Figzoi.

The Stream of Consciousness

Psychologists have long recognized that consciousness is continuous and changing. Indeed, over 100 years ago, William James (1902/1985) described this continuously altering flow of thoughts, feelings, and sensations as a *stream of consciousness*. To understand James's viewpoint, reflect on your own awareness as you read these words—are other things passing through your mind? Try to pay attention only to these words on the page. You'll probably discover that this is not easy, because irrelevant thoughts are likely to interrupt and distract you.

One interesting stream of consciousness is **daydreaming,** a relatively passive waking state in which attention is directed away from external stimuli to internal thoughts and imaginary situations (Morley, 1998). A central feature of daydreaming is that these thoughts and imaginary situations develop without conscious premeditation and with no obvious conscious goal. Research indicates that almost everyone daydreams on a daily basis, yet daydream frequency and intensity decrease with age in adulthood (Giambra, 1989, 2000; Singer, 1975). Although many people think of daydreaming as an inconsequential part of daily consciousness, it is not. Indeed, college students spend about one-third of their waking hours daydreaming (Bartusiak, 1980)!

What is the content of a typical daydream, and how does it affect our mood? Despite the fact that 95 percent of us admit to daydreaming about sex, sexual fantasies account for only a small proportion of most people's daydreams (Leitenberg & Henning, 1995). Instead, most daydreams deal with practical, daily concerns and tasks, future goals, and interpersonal relationships (Greenwald & Harder, 1997; Zhiyan & Singer, 1997). Further, when we daydream about pursuing personal goals, not surprisingly, most of us daydream about achieving success rather than failing (Oettingen, 1997). These positive daydreams generally have a beneficial effect by elevating our mood and motivating us to try harder (Klinger, 1990; Langens, 2003). However, for some people, positive daydreams can actually sabotage real-life goal attainment. When people are very fearful about failing at a task, daydreaming about success can heighten anxiety, because it reminds them of the possibility of failure (Langens & Schmalt, 2002). If sufficiently intense, this anxiety can destroy their motivation to persist at the task (Oettingen et al., 2001). Although it might seem counterintuitive, encouraging such people to imagine lower expectations may help them manage their anxiety so that they have a better chance of ultimately achieving their goals (Spencer & Norem, 1996).

> **daydreaming** A relatively passive state of waking consciousness that involves turning attention away from external stimuli to internal thoughts and imaginary situations.

> *Journey of Discovery* **Question**
>
> Because daydreaming involves thinking about internal thoughts and imaginary situations, what effect might television viewing have on daydreaming? Do you think people who watch a lot of television daydream more or less than those who watch little television? Why?

Besides increasing mood and motivation, why else might daydreaming be beneficial? Several possibilities have been suggested (Klinger, 1999). Fantasizing about actual people, events, or problems in our lives may help us formulate useful future plans of action. For example, imagining how to tell your professor that you slept through her exam may help when you actually explain the situation to her. Second, daydreams may help us regulate our behavior by either providing a safe avenue to imaginatively act out certain desires or helping us consider the possible outcomes of our actions. For example, your fantasy of kissing your best friend's boyfriend or girlfriend not only may temporarily soothe your sexual desires but also may inhibit you from acting on this impulse as you imagine the damage it could cause to your friendship. Finally, when our external surroundings are providing insufficient stimulation, we may daydream as a way to escape boredom and stay mentally aroused (Giambra, 1995). Perhaps this is why college students spend so much class time daydreaming!

One disadvantage of daydreaming is that we become much less attentive to our surroundings, and thus our effectiveness in the world is diminished (Cunningham et al., 2000). I still vividly recall an embarrassing incident years ago when I was daydreaming during a professor's lecture in a seminar. Suddenly, my fantasy was interrupted by someone calling my name: the professor! He was wondering why I seemed so amused by his last remark. Without realizing it, I had been staring at him with a big smile on my face as I thought about something funny that had occurred the previous evening. I was literally caught red-faced, and my standing in the seminar suffered due to my inattentiveness.

About 4 percent of the adult population daydream so much that they are classified as **fantasy-prone personalities** (Lynn & Ruhe, 1986). Not surprisingly, due to the amount of time spent daydreaming and the intensity of these experiences, fantasy-prone individuals occasionally have trouble separating their daydreams from their memories of real events (Lynn et al., 1996; Wilson & Barber, 1983). Although this habitual blending of fantasy with reality can sometimes indicate a dissociative psychological disorder (see chapter 13, section 13-3c), many frequent fantasizers are merely more creative and imaginative than most people (Singer et al., 2000).

Levels of Consciousness

The final defining characteristic of consciousness is that it exists on many levels. Mental events that you are presently aware of are said to exist at the *conscious level.* For example, the sensations you feel when you squeeze your arm are at your conscious level of awareness for that moment. Some events are not currently at the conscious level but could become so with prompting. For instance, stop for a moment and recall what you were doing yesterday at around noon. Although you probably were not thinking about the events surrounding your previous midday activities—they were at the *preconscious level*—they are now "on your mind." Finally, some mental events are not consciously available to us; they exist at the *unconscious level.* For example, you are not consciously aware of your brain regulating your various hormone levels. You are also generally unaware of most of the mental events that occur while you are sleeping (see section 6-2). Many psychologists believe that some of these unconscious mental events—especially those involving unacceptable thoughts or urges—are actively kept out of consciousness (see chapter 12, section 12-2a). In this chapter, we will examine various levels of consciousness, including those identified as *altered states,* which are noticeably different from our "normal" state of consciousness (see section 6-3).

6-1b Consciousness May Provide Us with Survival Advantages

One important question concerning consciousness is, Why are we conscious beings? What possible function does it serve? According to the evolutionary principle of natural selection (see chapter 1, section 1-3e), members of a species with inborn traits best adaptive for survival in their environment will produce more offspring, and as a result, their numbers will increase in frequency in the population. What advantage might the emergence of consciousness have given our ancestors?

One possibility is that consciousness provided early humans with a mental representation of the world that allowed them to more effectively plan future activities (Cairns-Smith, 1996; Fetzer, 2002). That is, by mentally manipulating events and reflecting on possible behavioral choices before acting, our ancestors were able to greatly reduce the sort of aimless and impulsive behavior that is likely to cause death. Another related explanation is that consciousness may have evolved as a means of categorizing and making sense of primitive emotions (Dennett, 1991; Humphrey, 1992). According to this perspective, each of the primitive emotions came to be associated with a different state of consciousness, and as a result, these states of consciousness provided our ancestors with information that aided their survival. For instance, the negative emotions caused by a painful snakebite or a fall from a tree became associated with a specific state of consciousness that led our ancestors to avoid similar situations in the future, thus lowering the incidence of injury and death. Similarly, the positive emotions resulting from eating, drinking, and having sex became associated with states of consciousness that led our ancestors to seek out similar situations, which again benefited them. Although both of these explanations sound plausible, we currently have no way of knowing whether they accurately account for the emergence of consciousness.

fantasy-prone personality A person who has regular, vivid fantasies and who sometimes cannot separate fantasy from reality.

Evolution is an ascent towards consciousness.

—*Pierre Teilhard de Chardin, French priest and cosmic evolutionist, 1881–1955*

The emergence of consciousness in the animal kingdom is perhaps as great a mystery as the origin of life itself.

—*Karl Popper, English philosopher of science, 1902–1994*

- Consciousness is personal, selective, divided, continuous, changing, and consisting of many levels.
- In daydreaming, attention is directed away from external stimuli to internal thoughts and imaginary situations.
- Consciousness and evolution may have allowed our ancestors to plan future activities and/or categorize and make sense of emotions.

6-2 SLEEP

Preview

- *Do we have daily body cycles, and if so, can they be disrupted?*
- *Do we have sleep cycles?*
- *Why do we sleep and dream?*
- *How do people's sleep habits differ due to age, personality, and culture?*

Sleep is a nonwaking state of consciousness characterized by minimal physical movement and minimal responsiveness to one's surroundings. To understand this state of consciousness, in this section we examine the sleep-wake cycle, sleep stages, possible reasons for sleep, and different dream theories.

> **sleep** A nonwaking state of consciousness characterized by minimal physical movement and minimal responsiveness to one's surroundings.

6-2a Daily Body Rhythms Regulate Our Activities

While typing this sentence, I am noticing how tired I feel. It is almost midnight, and I am ready for a good night's sleep. Yet, as my day winds down, I know that somewhere in the nearby woods there is a great horned owl whose day is in full swing. Mammals can be classified into two categories based on their sleep cycles. *Diurnal mammals* are awake during the day and asleep at night, while *nocturnal mammals* are asleep during the day and awake at night. These sleep-wake cycles have evolved because they permit a species the maximum adaptation to its environment (Moore, 1990).

The behavioral cycle of sleep and wakefulness that we naturally follow throughout our lives corresponds to physiological changes, such as body temperature, blood pressure, and hormone levels (Latta & Van Cauter, 2003). Together, these daily behavioral and physiological changes are known as **circadian rhythms** (in Latin, *circa* means "about" and *diem* means "day"). Some of these circadian rhythms help regulate the sleep-wake cycle. For instance, as you can see in figure 6-1, body temperature rises in the early morning, peaks at midday, and then begins to drop 1 to 2 hours prior to sleep. Because body temperature influences feelings of arousal, you generally feel most alert late in the afternoon or in the early evening (Broughton et al., 1990). Thus, if you've ever pulled an all-nighter, you probably felt most in

> **circadian rhythms** Internally generated behavioral and physiological changes that occur on a daily basis.

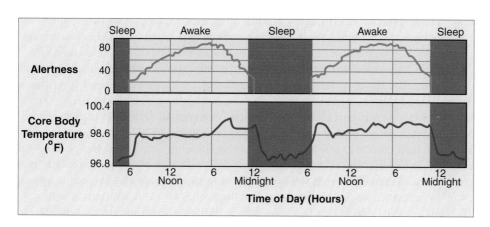

Figure 6-1

Circadian Rhythms

As you can see in the graph, as core body temperature changes, a person's level of alertness also changes. Based on this graph, what happens to your alertness as your core body temperature drops?

need of sleep at around 4:00 A.M., when your body temperature was lowest, but you probably began to perk up just before your normal waking time, as your temperature began to rise.

One way that circadian rhythms have been studied is by eliminating any environmental cues that would indicate the time of day. This has been accomplished by isolating people in a lab without windows or clocks, or by having them live underground in specially built "houses." The findings from such studies initially suggested that in the absence of daylight and time cues, circadian rhythms drifted toward a 25-hour cycle (Welsh, 1993; Wever, 1979). Indeed, for almost 30 years, sleep researchers believed these findings meant that humans were off-kilter with the natural world! Recently, however, researchers discovered that all the previous research testing the 25-hour cycle hypothesis had inadvertently created the effect (Shanahan et al., 1999). In these studies, the artificial light that participants relied on to see while deprived of natural sunlight was sufficiently intense to reset their sleep-wake cycle. Further, because participants often left lights on well after the sun had set in the outside world, this caused their brains' circadian pacemaker to keep them alert and awake longer than normal. Over the course of many days, their sleep-wake cycle appeared to drift to 25 hours. However, when researchers subsequently reduced light levels, they discovered that participants' true circadian cycle was about 24 hours. This research provides a valuable lesson in the way the scientific method is self-correcting. In their journey of discovery, scientists sometimes follow false paths, but the critical analysis that drives this search eventually reveals past missteps.

How does the brain reset this aspect of our biological clock? A small area of the hypothalamus known as the *suprachiasmatic nucleus,* or *SCN,* and the hormone *melatonin,* which is produced by the pineal gland, appear to be crucial in readjusting the body's sleep-wake cycle (Brown, 1994; Sorokin et al., 2000). Chronic insomniacs who receive synthetic forms of melatonin sleep better and feel more alert than those who are given placebos (Garfinkel et al., 1995; MacFarlane et al., 1991). This finding has led some researchers to refer to this hormone as "nature's sleeping pill." As the sun sets, the decreased light is detected by the SCN, which triggers the release of melatonin into the bloodstream and makes us feel drowsy. The level of melatonin in our bloodstream continues to rise during the evening, peaking between 1:00 A.M. and 3:00 A.M. However, shortly before sunrise, the pineal gland stops producing melatonin, which soon causes us to become aroused from sleep. During the day, exposure to sunlight and other bright light continues to suppress our melatonin levels until dusk, when this cycle repeats itself. Thus, sunlight plays a crucial role in setting the SCN so our bodies operate on a 24-hour schedule. Scientists have also isolated a gene in the SCN that, along with perhaps 10 other genes, actually controls our internal clock (Katzenberg et al., 1998; Vitaterna et al., 1994). The discovery of this gene—which has been named "clock"—may eventually lead to more effective treatment of ailments related to disruptions in circadian rhythms, such as insomnia and depression.

Circadian rhythms perform many critical functions for a species. Monarch butterflies, for example, rely upon a properly set circadian clock to guide them during their more than 2,000-mile migratory trek from the northeastern United States and eastern Canada to the mountains of central Mexico. Monarchs exposed to normal sunlight during development correctly fly southwest, the direction of their overwintering destination in Mexico. However, when scientists expose monarchs to different patterns of light and darkness during the time they are developing from caterpillar to butterfly, their circadian rhythms no longer provide them with accurate navigation cues (Mouritsen & Frost, 2002). These findings yield strong evidence that monarchs use an internal, time-compensated sun compass to keep them on course during migration.

As you have probably discovered yourself, disruptions in circadian rhythms can also occur when you travel by jet through a number of time zones. The severity of this so-called jet lag depends on whether you fly westward or eastward (see figure 6-2). When flying westward—say, from London to Detroit—your regular sleep cycle is pushed back 5 hours (a *phase delay*), so that your 24-hour day is stretched to 29 hours. The jet lag resulting from such east-west travel will be easier to adjust to—and thus, less severe—than eastward-induced jet lag. Why? Perhaps phase delays coincide with the tendency in modern times to habitually stretch waking time out to the limits of the 24-hour sleep-wake cycle. In contrast, flying eastward across five time zones results in shortening your day to 19 hours (a *phase advance*), which not only is farther away from your natural 24-hour

The only thing wrong with insomniacs is that they don't get enough sleep!

—*W. C. Fields, American comedian and film actor, 1880–1946*

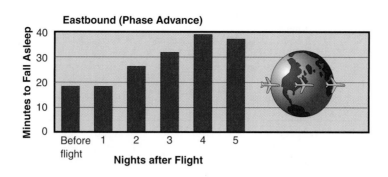

Eastbound (Phase Advance)

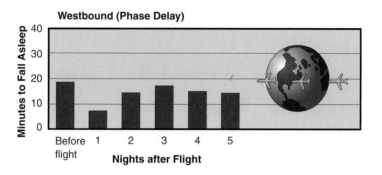

Westbound (Phase Delay)

Figure 6-2

Circadian Rhythms and Jet Lag

One way jet lag can be assessed is by determining whether it is harder for people to fall asleep after flying to a different time zone. In one study, people who flew eastward through five time zones had increased difficulty falling asleep following their arrival, whereas travelers who flew westward through five time zones experienced no sleep difficulties (Nicholson et al., 1986).

sleep-wake cycle but also is inconsistent with your day-stretching habits. Consistent with this explanation, in the study depicted in figure 6-2, travelers who flew eastward from Detroit to London had increased difficulty falling asleep following their arrival, while travelers who flew westward from London to Detroit experienced no sleep difficulties (Nicholson et al., 1986).

A similar problem is experienced by people employed in jobs involving some type of rotating shift work, in which they work during their normal sleeping hours (Goh et al., 2000; Khaleque, 1999). Of the 7 million Americans who work at night, 75 percent are regularly sleepy, and 20 percent have actually fallen asleep on the job, factors that lead directly to higher accident rates and lower productivity than occur during any other work schedule (Akerstedt, 1991; Smith, 1995). In an attempt to correct this work-related health problem, sleep researchers recommend that employers schedule workers on rotating shifts in a "clockwise" direction (from days to evenings to nights), so changes are phase delays rather than phase advances (Monk, 2000; Monk & Folkard, 1992). For example, if you are working an evening shift (4:00 P.M. to midnight), it would be easier for you to move forward to a night shift (midnight to 8:00 A.M.) than backward to a day shift (8:00 A.M. to 4:00 P.M.), because moving backward (a phase advance) forces you to try to sleep during the time you were previously working. Phase-delayed work schedules promote greater worker health, productivity, and satisfaction than do phase-advanced schedules (Czeisler et al., 1982; Scott, 1994).

The readjustment of circadian rhythms can be speeded up by light-treatment therapy (Ando et al., 1999). In such therapy, workers are exposed to bright lights mimicking the daylight sun during the first few days of their night shift. They are also exposed to 8 hours of total darkness at home during the day (Bougrine et al., 1995; Czeisler et al., 1990). NASA ground personnel who worked on shifted schedules during two space shuttle missions reported better sleep, performance, and physical and emotional well-being if they received light-treatment therapy during the prelaunch week and during the mission itself (Stewart et al., 1995).

6-2b There Are Distinct Stages of Sleep

Just as circadian rhythms regulate your sleep-wake cycle, your sleep also follows a biological rhythm. This was one of the important discoveries made in the wake of the 1952 discovery (described at the beginning of the chapter) that rapid eye movements occur in

Figure 6-3

EEG Brain-Wave Patterns

The regular beta and alpha waves associated with normal waking consciousness are very different from the brain-wave patterns typical of the stages of NREM and REM sleep.

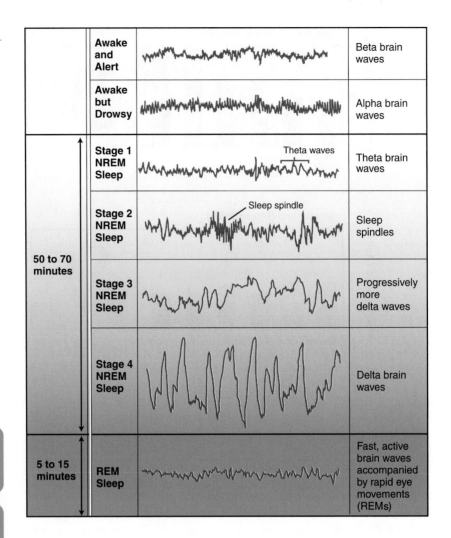

	Awake and Alert		Beta brain waves
	Awake but Drowsy		Alpha brain waves
50 to 70 minutes	**Stage 1 NREM Sleep**	Theta waves	Theta brain waves
	Stage 2 NREM Sleep	Sleep spindle	Sleep spindles
	Stage 3 NREM Sleep		Progressively more delta waves
	Stage 4 NREM Sleep		Delta brain waves
5 to 15 minutes	**REM Sleep**		Fast, active brain waves accompanied by rapid eye movements (REMs)

beta waves Very fast, low-amplitude brain waves associated with an active, alert state of mind.

alpha waves Fast, low-amplitude brain waves associated with a relaxed, wakeful state.

theta waves Irregular, low-amplitude brain waves associated with stage 1 sleep.

hypnogogic state Stage 1 in the sleep cycle; a brief transitional state between wakefulness and sleep, usually lasting only a few minutes.

sleep spindles Bursts of rapid, rhythmic electrical activity in the brain characteristic of stage 2 sleep.

delta waves Slow, high-amplitude brain waves most typical of stage 4 deep sleep.

predictable cycles during the course of a night's sleep. In sleep studies using electroencephalographs (EEGs), investigators such as Nathaniel Kleitman and Eugene Aserinsky discovered that, about every 90 or 100 minutes, we cycle through distinct sleep stages, each associated with a different pattern of brain activity (Aserinsky & Kleitman, 1953). These EEG brain-wave patterns are depicted in figure 6-3. The two most common EEG patterns that people experience while awake are **beta waves,** associated with an active, alert state of mind, and **alpha waves,** indicative of relaxed wakefulness.

As you gradually enter the light sleep of *stage 1*, your alpha-wave EEG pattern changes to the smaller, more rapid, irregular **theta waves.** Stage 1 sleep, which is referred to as the **hypnogogic state,** is a transitional state between wakefulness and sleep usually lasting only a few minutes. Heart rate and breathing slow as body temperature drops and muscles begin to relax. What may be orchestrating this sleep induction is a very small cluster of brain cells—called *sleep-on neurons*—located at the base of the forebrain (Siegel, 2003). Typical experiences reported during stage 1 sleep are sensations of falling (hence, the term "falling asleep") or floating, as well as visual and auditory hallucinations (Mavromatis, 1991). You can be easily awakened during stage 1 sleep.

Stage 2 sleep lasts about 20 minutes and is characterized by **sleep spindles,** which are bursts of rapid, rhythmic brain-wave activity. Muscle tension is now greatly reduced. Although sleeptalking can occur at any time during sleep, it is most likely to occur during stage 2.

In *stage 3,* you begin to move into the deeper form of *slow-wave sleep,* in which your brain waves become higher in amplitude and slower in frequency. These **delta waves** become much more pronounced during the even deeper sleep of *stage 4*. It is difficult to arouse a person at this stage of the sleep cycle.

From the time you enter stage 1 and progress to stage 4, between 50 and 70 minutes usually pass. These first four stages make up *NREM sleep*, or non-rapid-eye-movement sleep. Now the sleep cycle reverses itself, and you move back up through the stages to stage 2 (where you spend about half your night). NREM sleep is often called "quiet sleep" because of the slow, regular breathing, the general absence of body movement, and the slow, regular brain activity exhibited in the EEG. Actually, the term "quiet sleep" is a bit misleading because snoring is most likely to occur during NREM sleep.

REM Sleep

As you can see in figure 6-4, once you reach stage 2, you do not fully enter stage 1, but rather, you enter an entirely different kind of sleep. In this new stage, your brain waves become rapid, somewhat like waking alpha waves and stage 1 theta waves; your heart rate and breathing also increase, and your eyes begin darting back and forth behind your closed eyelids. This phase of "active sleep," which completes the sleep cycle, has come to be known for these quick eye movements and is called **REM (rapid eye movement) sleep.** What appears to be responsible for creating REM sleep are specialized neurons located in the pons at the base of the hindbrain, called *REM sleep-on neurons*. These neurons become very active during the REM sleep phase. You go through about four or five sleep cycles during the night, each lasting about 90 minutes (Anch et al., 1988). As also depicted in figure 6-4, after the first few sleep cycles, you do not usually pass through all the sleep stages.

Why Do We Sleep?

Your body needs sleep and will malfunction without a sufficient amount. For example, after about 18 hours of wakefulness, your reaction time begins to slow from a quarter second to half a second. You also experience bouts of *microsleep,* in which you momentarily tune out your surroundings. If you are reading a book, you will probably have to reread a paragraph when you tune back in, but if you are driving a car, the consequences can be deadly. At the 20-hour mark, your reaction time is equivalent to someone who is considered legally intoxicated (a blood alcohol content of 0.08), and your ability to remember things diminishes. Studies also suggest that children aged 2 to 5 years who fail to get sufficient sleep at night or during daytime nap periods are at greater risk for behavior problems (Dement, 1999).

Although sleep is essential in maintaining health, sleep experts are not quite sure why we need to sleep. One widely held theory is that sleep allows the body to restore itself following the rigors of daily activity (Flanagan, 1996; Hobson, 1999b). Research supporting this view finds that people sleep longer and spend more time in deep sleep (stages 3 and 4) after vigorous physical exercise (Vein et al., 1991). Testosterone levels depleted in males during the day are also restored during sleep. In addition, deep sleep promotes new cell growth by triggering the pituitary gland to release a growth hormone (see chapter 3, section 3-2c). As people advance from childhood to adulthood, less of this growth hormone is released, and they spend less time in deep sleep (Mancia, 1981; Pekkanen, 1982).

> **REM (rapid eye movement) sleep** A relatively active phase in the sleep cycle, characterized by rapid eye movements, in which dreaming occurs.

Figure 6-4

The First 90 Minutes of Sleep

Most people follow a rather consistent sleep cycle during the night, with each cycle lasting about 90 minutes and consisting of four NREM stages followed by REM sleep. Nightmares and other dreams occur during REM sleep, but sleepwalking and night terrors (see the "Psychological Applications" section at the end of the chapter) typically occur in stages 3 and 4, respectively. Based on this figure, what can you conclude about the duration of REM sleep as the night progresses?

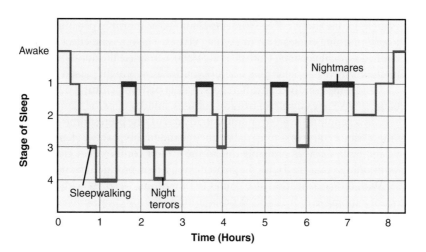

Sleep is a time when we exhibit minimal physical movement and are minimally responsive to our surroundings. Why would we have evolved a behavior like this that makes us so vulnerable?

Source: Courtesy of Figzoi.

Another theory contends that sleep is simply a product of our evolutionary heritage: It prevents us from moving about and being injured (or eaten) during a time of the day (darkness) in which our bodies are not well adapted. Sleep also conserves energy for that part of the day (daylight) in which our bodies are most efficient. Thus, sleep may have been selected because of its value in promoting both physical safety and energy conservation (Webb, 1992). Today, although we no longer need sleep for the same reasons as our ancestors, sleep mechanisms still have a significant influence on our lives.

Which of these theories is the best explanation for why we sleep? It may well be that both the restorative theory and the safety/conservation theory provide part of the answer to this puzzle. Both are consistent with a finding across the animal species: Bigger animals generally need less sleep than do smaller animals. Elephants, giraffes, horses, sheep, and the larger primates (including humans) sleep less than rats, mice, bats, squirrels, and cats (Kuo et al., 2004; Siegel, 2003). Smaller animals not only are generally more vulnerable to attack from predators than are larger animals but also have higher metabolic rates. *Metabolism*, which is the process of cells burning food to produce energy, generates extremely reactive chemicals (*free radicals*) that cause injury to cell membranes. Sleep slows metabolism, which may provide an opportunity for the body to repair the damage done by free radicals (Ramanathan et al., 2002). Perhaps most important, in the brain, sleep may give damaged neurons the time to become relatively inactive and deal with the free radicals.

6-2c Sleep Habits Vary Individually and Culturally

How much sleep you need partly depends on your age. The amount of time spent sleeping declines throughout the life cycle: Newborns sleep approximately 16 hours, children average between 9 and 12 hours, and adolescents average about 7.5 hours. Newborns and young children have the highest percentage of REM sleep, and many sleep experts believe that the heightened brain activity during REM sleep promotes the development of new neural pathways (Mirmiran & Ariagno, 2003; Siegel, 2003). In adulthood, both the quantity and the quality of sleep usually decrease, especially among the elderly (Almeida et al., 1999; Monane, 1992). Less time is spent in slow-wave stage 4 deep sleep, and a greater proportion of stage 1 sleep occurs, resulting in more nighttime awakenings (Bliwise, 1989). Although stage 4 sleep declines, the percentage of REM sleep remains fairly constant throughout much of adulthood, diminishing only in later life (Moran & Stoudemire, 1992).

Besides these age-related sleep differences, we also differ in when we typically go to sleep and awaken. Have you ever heard of "morning people" and "night people"? Morning people wake up early, with a good deal of energy and alertness, but are ready to retire before 10:00 P.M. Night people, on the other hand, stay up much later in the evening and have a hard time getting up early in the morning (Thoman, 1999). About 25 percent of us are "night persons," 25 percent are "morning persons," and the remaining 50 percent fall somewhere between these two extremes. This different sleep pattern appears to be related to differences in circadian body temperatures. Morning persons' body temperature quickly rises upon awakening and remains high until about 7:30 P.M. The body temperature of night persons, in contrast, rises much more gradually when they wake, peaks at midday, and begins dropping only late in the evening. Not surprisingly, in one study, college students identified as morning persons obtained better grades in early-morning classes than in evening classes. The opposite effect was found for students classified as night persons (Guthrie et al., 1995). Complete the questionnaire in Self-Discovery Questionnaire 6-1 to determine whether you are more a night person or a morning person.

Besides these individual differences in sleep patterns, cultural differences have also been documented. For example, in tropical cultures, midday naps, or *siestas*, are common because they allow people to avoid strenuous activity during the hottest time of the day. Interestingly, as these "siesta cultures" industrialize, they abandon this practice (Kribbs, 1993). This change in napping patterns is probably due to the greater comfort that can be achieved with air-conditioning, combined with the greater emphasis on productivity in industrialized settings.

With industrialization also comes less nighttime sleep. As with the gradual disappearance of napping in industrialized siesta cultures, the lower overall sleep time found in industrialized settings can undoubtedly be traced to the development of a stronger work ethic. Yet another related factor is electricity and the ability to literally light up the night, thereby

Respond to the following items by circling either "Day" or "Evening."

____	**1.**	I prefer to work during the	Day	Evening
____	**2.**	I enjoy leisure-time activities most during the	Day	Evening
____	**3.**	I feel most alert during the	Day	Evening
____	**4.**	I get my best ideas during the	Day	Evening
____	**5.**	I have my highest energy during the	Day	Evening
____	**6.**	I prefer to take classes during the	Day	Evening
____	**7.**	I prefer to study during the	Day	Evening
____	**8.**	I feel most intelligent during the	Day	Evening
____	**9.**	I am most productive during the	Day	Evening
____	**10.**	When I graduate, I would prefer to find a job with ____ hours.	Day	Evening

If you answered "Day" to eight or more items, you are probably a morning person. However, if you answered "Evening" to eight or more items, you are probably a night person.

Source: From "Day persons, night persons, and variability in hypnotic susceptibility" by B. Wallace in *Journal of Personality and Social Psychology*, 1993, 64, 827–833 (Appendix, p. 833). Copyright © 1993 by the American Psychological Association. Adapted with permission.

INTERACTIVE BOX

extending the time people can be active and productive. People who live in cultures without electricity generally retire shortly after the sun sets and sleep about 10 hours. In contrast, the average length of sleep for North American and European adults is less than 7.5 hours, about 20 percent lower than what it was a hundred years ago (National Sleep Foundation, 2002). Because all humans still possess the physiology that evolved to fit the ecological niche of a hunter-gatherer culture, our lower sleeping average suggests that many of us are sleep deprived (Benbadis et al., 1999; Coren, 1996).

Lack of sufficient sleep is a common problem reported by college students, especially while studying for final exams. Yet results from sleep deprivation experiments indicate that people lose their ability to concentrate and think creatively after only a day of sleep deprivation (Dinges et al., 1997; Webb, 1992). These findings suggest that engaging in long hours of continuous studying before final exams may actually lower academic performance. If all-night studying cannot be avoided, however, research indicates that grabbing a few hours of nap time during the day can offset some of the negative effects of sleep deprivation (Batejat & Lagarde, 1999). Remember this bit of information when preparing for your next exam! To determine whether you are getting enough sleep, answer the questions in Self-Discovery Questionnaire 6-2.

6-2d Dreaming Often Occurs during REM Sleep

As mentioned in section 6-2b, at the end of each sleep cycle, you enter REM sleep. The fact that the brain and other physiological functions are almost as active during REM sleep as in the waking state has led some researchers to describe this phase of sleep as *paradoxical sleep*. Two interesting developments that occur during REM sleep are that your genitals become aroused (increased vaginal lubrication or an erection) at the same time that muscular movement below the neck is inhibited. Perhaps fortunately for us, genital arousal typically outlasts REM periods and the accompanying neck-to-toe semiparalysis by about 30 to 45 minutes (Schiavi & Schreiner-Engel, 1988). As such, the erections and vaginal lubrication that often greet us upon awakening in the morning may be nature's way of facilitating sexual intercourse and, thus, possible procreation.

Even more fascinating than genital arousal and semiparalysis is what likely accounts for the rapid eye movements: dreaming. A **dream** is a storylike sequence of visual images experienced during sleep. As mentioned in the chapter-opening story, Eugene Aserinsky discovered the association between rapid eye movement and dreaming in 1952 when he awakened his son Armond

dream A storylike sequence of vivid visual images experienced during sleep.

Self-Discovery
Questionnaire 6-2

Are You Getting Enough Sleep?

Psychologist James Maas (1998) has developed the following questionnaire to measure people's sleep needs. To determine whether you might be suffering from sleep deprivation, answer true or false to the following items regarding your current life experiences.

	True	False
1. It's a struggle for me to get out of bed in the morning.	☐	☐
2. I need an alarm clock to wake up at the appropriate time.	☐	☐
3. Weekday mornings, I hit the snooze bar several times to get more sleep.	☐	☐
4. I often sleep extra hours on weekend mornings.	☐	☐
5. I often need a nap to get through the day.	☐	☐
6. I have dark circles around my eyes.	☐	☐
7. I feel tired, irritable, and stressed out during the week.	☐	☐
8. I have trouble concentrating and remembering.	☐	☐
9. I feel slow with critical thinking, problem solving, and being creative.	☐	☐
10. I often fall asleep in boring meetings or lectures or in warm rooms.	☐	☐
11. I often feel drowsy while driving.	☐	☐
12. I often fall asleep watching TV.	☐	☐
13. I often fall asleep after heavy meals or after a low dose of alcohol.	☐	☐
14. I often fall asleep while relaxing after dinner.	☐	☐
15. I often fall asleep within 5 minutes of getting into bed.	☐	☐

If you answered "true" to three or more items, you probably are not getting enough sleep. Keep in mind that we differ in our individual sleep needs. If this questionnaire suggests that you may be sleep deprived, Maas recommends that you go to bed 15 minutes earlier every night for a week. Continue adding 15 more minutes each week until you are waking without the aid of an alarm clock and without feeling tired during the day. Encourage your family and friends to also try this exercise, and compare your experiences over the next few weeks to see if your daily alertness and energy level improve.

Source: From *The Sleep Advantage* by James B. Maas, Ph.D., copyright © 1998 by James B. Maas, Ph.D. Used by permission of Villard Books, a division of Random House, Inc.

> Dreaming permits each and every one of us to be quietly and safely insane every night of our lives.
>
> —*William Dement, sleep researcher*

from sleep as his eyes darted about behind closed lids. Armond reported that he had been dreaming. Subsequent research indicated that people awakened from REM sleep report dreaming 78 percent of the time, even if they previously said they never dream (Antrobus, 1991; Schwartz & Maquet, 2002). In contrast, when people are awakened from NREM sleep, dreaming is reported only 14 percent of the time, and it usually is less vivid than REM dreaming (Antrobus, 1991). This discovery led some researchers to speculate that sleepers move their eyes as they "watch" their dream activities. William Dement (1978) first proposed this *scanning hypothesis* after one of his sleep participants exhibited only horizontal eye movements while having a dream about watching a table tennis match. The problem with the scanning hypothesis, however, is that most research has not found a strong correlation between rapid eye movement and dream content. Instead of dreaming causing rapid eye movement, it is more likely that both are caused by the brain's relatively high level of activation during REM sleep (Chase & Morales, 1983).

Although your ability to respond to external cues is diminished during REM sleep, it is not entirely absent (Arkin & Antrobus, 1991). Research indicates that unexpected sounds or other sensory stimulation may be incorporated into dreams, thus allowing the dreamer to continue sleeping. For example, in one experiment, sleeping volunteers who were sprayed with a mist of water and then awakened were more likely to report dreams of being squirted by someone, experiencing a sudden rainfall, or standing under a leaking roof than were volunteers who were not sprayed (Dement & Wolpert, 1958).

A recent study comparing people's dream reports during REM sleep and NREM sleep found that aggressive social interactions were more characteristic of REM dreams, while dreamer-initiated friendliness was more characteristic of NREM dreams (McNamera et al., 2005). Why might REM sleep be associated with the emergence of aggressive social impulses, while cooperative social impulses are more likely to emerge during NREM sleep? At present, there is no good answer to this question, but these findings suggest that certain brain areas are more active than others during these two different sleep stages. Section 6-2e examines various theories that explain the cause or meaning of dreams.

How important is REM sleep? When participants in sleep studies are partially deprived of REM sleep by being awakened whenever they begin exhibiting rapid eye movements, they often report feeling more tired and spend more time in REM sleep the next night than those who are not deprived of REM sleep (Dement et al., 1966). This extra time spent in REM sleep following such deprivation is known as *REM rebound*. Although some sleep researchers once thought that REM sleep deprivation led to psychotic hallucinations, later research disproved this idea (Kryger et al., 2000). However, some studies have found that people who experience prolonged REM sleep deprivation exhibit poorer recall of recently learned material than those not deprived of REM sleep (May & Kline, 1987; Tilley & Empson, 1978).

All mammals except the Australian anteater have REM sleep, as do some birds, but fish, reptiles, and amphibians do not. It is possible that those animals that engage in REM sleep also have dreams, but it is unlikely that most of them possess the cognitive ability required to distinguish dream events from real events. This inability to separate the dream world from the real world would pose a serious threat to animals if they remembered their dreams upon awakening. For instance, what if your cat "Tabby" had a dream that the vicious dog next door was replaced by a family of fat, juicy mice? If Tabby remembered this dream, she would likely saunter over for a nutritious breakfast and quickly become the dear-departed Tabby. Thinking about Tabby's situation from an evolutionary perspective, it is plausible that animals that remembered their dreams as real events were less likely than others to survive to pass on their genes to the next generation.

As mentioned, REM sleep is greatest early in life, accounting for at least 50 percent of all sleep time in normal human newborns and as high as 80 percent among premature infants (Burnham et al., 2003; Hobson, 1995). This finding suggests that prior to birth, REM sleep makes up virtually the entire mode of existence of the late-developing fetus. Within 6 months of birth, REM sleep declines to about 30 percent of all sleep time, and by early childhood, its 20 percent level remains unchanged until diminishing once again later in life.

6-2e No Consensus Exists on the Cause or Meaning of Dreams

> I'm at the ocean on a beautiful summer day, standing on a wooden pier jutting out from shore. The sky is a clear blue. I begin walking to the end of the pier, where an old woman is sitting. When I reach her, I notice an unattended fishing pole nearby. As soon as I look at the pole, I realize a fish has taken the bait at the other end. Without thinking, I grab the pole and begin reeling in the line. About a quarter-mile from shore, a huge, beautiful blue fish jumps high out of the water. This is what was at the end of the line! I have to use all my strength to keep from being pulled into the ocean. The old woman gives me advice, but I am confident that I know what I am doing. As I struggle with the fish, I learn about its life. After an hour of labor, I have the fish next to the pier. At the moment when I should get it in place to be hoisted up, a thought comes to me that what is important is the struggle, not the victory. I throw the pole down, and the fish swims away. The woman looks up at me and nods. She knows too. I walk back to shore.

Perhaps like the young college student who had this dream while preparing for an important exam, you too have pondered whether these sleep experiences are worth analyzing and trying to understand. The simple fact is that we all dream, whether we remember doing so or not. If dreaming were not part of the sleep experience, it's unlikely that we would express such fascination with this "other side" of our lives.

While dreaming, most people are not aware they are dreaming: The dream is experienced as "real." Exceptions to this rule are the 10 percent who occasionally experience **lucid dreams,** during which they are aware that they are dreaming (LaBerge, 1992; Patrick & Durndell, 2004). Such dreams can be very enjoyable, because the lucid dreamer is often able to shift the dream plot while it is in progress (LaBerge & DeGracia, 2000; Spoormaker et al., 2003).

lucid dream A dream in which the dreamer is aware of dreaming and is often able to change the plot of the dream.

> I do not know whether I was then a man dreaming I was a butterfly, or whether I am now a butterfly dreaming I am a man.
>
> —*Chuang-tzu, Chinese philosopher, 369–286 B.C.*

In some cultures, people believe you should be held accountable for your dreams. Thus, among the New Guinea Arapesh, if you hurt someone in your dreams, you must try to undo the harm in your waking life. In many Native North American cultures, dreams provide a valuable source of information about spiritual phenomena and are thought to provide a path to another dimension of reality (Tedlock, 2004). Similarly, people in other cultures believe that dreams foretell the future. Although some people in Western cultures believe in *precognitive dreams,* most do not place such importance on the stories generated by our unconscious minds.

Dreams as Wish Fulfillment

The most famous dream theory in psychology is that proposed by Sigmund Freud (1900) and *psychoanalytic theory* (see chapter 12, section 12-2). According to Freud, dreams are disguised wishes originating in the unconscious mind. The dream that is remembered by the dreamer represents only the surface content, or **manifest content.** The true meaning of the dream—the "disguised" content, or **latent content**—is concealed from the dreamer because it would not only arouse great anxiety but also disrupt sleep. Thus, the function of dreams is to express dreamers' unacceptable wishes in a confusing symbolic manner so their peace of mind—and their sleep—is protected. In the student's fishing dream, the struggle with the fish is the manifest dream content, perhaps symbolically representing the student's attempt to better understand, but not destroy, some unconscious desire (the latent content) dredged up by his studies.

> **manifest content** The dream that is remembered by the dreamer.

> **latent content** The true meaning of the dream that is concealed from the dreamer through the symbols that make up the manifest dream content.

Dreams as Problem Solving

Another view is that dreaming is a form of problem solving. According to Rosalind Cartwright's (1977, 1989) **problem-solving theory,** dreams provide people with the opportunity to creatively solve their everyday problems because what we think about in dreams is not hampered by logic or realism. From this perspective, the fish dream might reflect the student's dawning recognition that he should be more confident in his own intellectual abilities and rely less on others' advice (the old woman in the dream).

In support of problem-solving theory, Cartwright (1991) has found that for people going through a divorce, the first dream of the night often occurs sooner, lasts longer, and is more emotional and storylike than it is for other people. In addition, those who frequently dreamed about divorce-related problems made a better adjustment to single life than those who did not dream much about their problems. Beyond empirical findings, there are numerous historical anecdotes about people using dreams as a problem-solving strategy. For example, one evening in 1857, the German chemist Friedrich Kekulé fell asleep in front of a fire while trying to solve the mystery of how the benzene molecule was constructed. In a dream, he saw the carbon atoms of the benzene molecule twisting and twining like snakes, when suddenly one of the snakes seized hold of its own tail. Upon awakening, he realized that the carbon atoms bonded with one another in a "closed chain," just like a snake biting its tail!

> **problem-solving theory** A theory stating that dreams provide people with the opportunity to creatively solve their everyday problems.

> ***Journey of Discovery Question*** Have you ever had a dream that later seemed to come true? Many people who have had this experience, or who hear of it from a close friend or family member, believe that dreams can predict the future. What other potential explanations could there be for a dream that comes true?

Dreams as Information Processing

In contrast to attributing dreams to unconscious wish-fulfillment or problem-solving attempts, the **off-line dream theory** contends that the cognitive processing that occurs during dreaming consolidates and stores information gathered during the day, thus allowing us to maintain a smaller and more efficient brain (McNaughton et al., 2003; Pavlides & Ribeiro, 2003). The term *off-line* is a computer phrase referring to the fact that computers need time when data are not being input but instead are being analyzed and stored into memory. According to the off-line theory, dreaming is the time when the brain—our computer—goes off-line to somehow integrate the new information from the day with our older memories and experiences (Peigneux et al., 2004; Titone, 2002).

Evidence that dreaming may indeed serve an integrating function and be instrumental in learning comes from research demonstrating that both humans and other animals spend more

> **off-line dream theory** A theory that the cognitive process of dreaming consolidates and stores information gathered during the day, thus allowing us to maintain a smaller and more efficient brain.

time in REM sleep after learning difficult material than after learning easy material, and that if denied REM sleep, memory retention suffers (Karni et al., 1994; Smith, 1995). Additional studies suggest that REM sleep helps consolidate both perceptual and motor skill learning, emotional and factual memories, and complex cognitive learning (Smith, 2003; Stickgold, 2003). Some neuroscientists believe that if we didn't dream—that is, have off-line time—we would need much larger forebrains to handle our daily learning experiences. This may explain why the Australian anteater—the only known mammal that does not engage in REM sleep—has such a large forebrain compared with the rest of its brain (Hawkins, 1986).

Dreams as Interpreted Brain Activity

Although the previously described theories propose that dreams fulfill wishes, solve problems, or maintain brain efficiency, the psychobiologists J. Allan Hobson and Robert McCarley argue that dreaming has no particular significance beyond being a by-product of brain activity. This **activation-synthesis theory** states that a dream is the forebrain's attempt to interpret the random neural activity initiated in the midbrain during sleep (Hobson, 1988; Hobson, 1999b; Hobson & McCarley, 1977). As you recall from chapter 3, section 3-3b, the uppermost portion of the forebrain is the brain's "thinking" center and consists of the left and right cerebral hemispheres. According to activation-synthesis theory, the more verbal left hemisphere always strives to assign some rational meaning to behavior, even when there is none. It is just this sort of thinking that appears to be involved in creating the plots of our dreams. Similarly, the right hemisphere may help construct most of the dream's visual features (Antrobus, 1987). The resulting dream constructed, or *synthesized*, from this random brain activity will have a personal touch unique to the dreamer because it is based on available memories, but the dream has no hidden meaning (Hobson et al., 1998; Kahn & Hobson, 1993).

The various dream theories discussed here are summarized in table 6-1. Currently, researchers have come to no consensus concerning the cause or meaning of dreams. Yet,

The idea for Edward's pajamas was revealed to him in a dream.

Source: © King Features Syndicate.

> **activation-synthesis theory**
> A theory that dreaming is a by-product of random brain activity, which the forebrain weaves into a somewhat logical story.

Table **6-1**	Dream Theories		
Theory	**Explanation**	**Meaning of Dream**	**Is Meaning of Dream Hidden?**
Psychoanalytic	Dreams are anxiety-producing wishes originating in the unconscious mind.	Latent content of dream reveals unconscious wishes.	Yes, by manifest content of dreams
Problem-solving	Dreams provide the opportunity to creatively solve everyday problems.	Possible solutions to everyday problems are signaled.	Not necessarily
Off-line	Dreaming consolidates and stores information input during the day, thus allowing us to maintain a smaller and more efficient brain for survival.	Previous day's experiences are reprocessed in dreams.	Not necessarily
Activation-synthesis	Dreams are the forebrain's attempt to interpret random neural activity.	Dream content is only vaguely related to the dreamer's life experiences, thus there is little, if any, meaning in the dream.	No real meaning to hide

whatever the ultimate answer, all the theories agree that the specific content of dreams is associated with the life experiences of the dreamer. Supporting this view, numerous studies indicate that dreams reflect the daily concerns and interests of the dreamer (Domhoff, 2003). This may mean that exploring our unconscious world can help us better understand our conscious lives (Epstein, 1999).

Section Review

- Circadian rhythms closely align with the 24-hour rotation of the earth.
- Jet lag and shift work can disrupt normal circadian rhythms.
- Every 90 to 100 minutes, we cycle through sleep stages, going through four or five cycles per night.
- Sleep may provide us with time to restore our body and mind, as well as to protect ourselves from the dangers posed by engaging in nighttime activities.
- As people age, the quantity and quality of sleep decrease.
- Individuals and cultures differ in their sleeping patterns.
- REM sleep is when most dreaming occurs.
- According to psychoanalytic dream theory, dreams are disguised wishes originating in the unconscious.
- According to problem-solving theory, dreaming is when we creatively solve everyday problems unencumbered by logic or realism.
- According to off-line dream theory, dreaming allows us to maintain a smaller and more efficient brain by consolidating and storing information gathered during the day.
- According to activation-synthesis theory, dreaming is the forebrain's attempt to interpret the random neural activity initiated in the midbrain during sleep.

6-3 OTHER ALTERED STATES OF CONSCIOUSNESS

Preview

- *Can anyone be hypnotized, and is hypnosis a true altered state?*
- *Is meditation an altered state of consciousness?*
- *Are religious experiences associated with altered consciousness?*
- *How do psychoactive drugs alter consciousness?*
- *Who is most likely to abuse drugs?*

altered state of consciousness An awareness of oneself and one's environment that is noticeably different from the normal state of consciousness.

Sleep is our most familiar **altered state of consciousness.** An *altered state* is an awareness of ourselves and our environment that is noticeably different from our normal state of consciousness. In this section, we examine the altered states associated with *hypnosis, religious experiences, meditation,* and *drugs.*

6-3a Hypnosis Has Been Practiced for Thousands of Years

Imagine that you attend a group demonstration of hypnosis. As you sit with friends and strangers in an auditorium, the hypnotist begins talking:

> I want you to get comfortable and begin to relax. Ignore what is going on around you and pay attention only to my words. . . . You can become hypnotized if you are willing to do what I tell you to do. . . . Just do your best to pay close attention to my words, and let happen whatever you feel is going to take place. Let yourself relax. . . . Sometimes you experience something very similar to hypnosis when driving along a stretch of highway and your concentration becomes narrowed so that you don't notice landmarks along the road. . . . As you continue to listen to my voice, your eyes are growing heavy. . . . Heavy and tired. . . . Droopy. . . . You are beginning to

feel drowsy and sleepy. . . . Sleepy and drowsy. . . . Relax. . . . You're becoming more and more relaxed . . . and tired. . . . Tired and sleepy. . . . As your eyes become heavier, it's getting harder and harder to keep them open. . . . They feel so heavy, like lead. . . . You may feel you want to close them. That's all right. . . . Let your eyes close as your muscles relax more and more.

During this *hypnotic induction,* although you may begin to feel tired, you probably won't fall asleep. Hypnosis was named after the Greek god of sleep, Hypnos, but the two altered states of hypnosis and sleep bear only a superficial resemblance to one another. Sleep is characterized by minimal responsiveness to one's surroundings, while **hypnosis** is a state of altered attention and awareness during which a person is unusually responsive to suggestions. In our culture, hypnosis is typically induced using suggestions for deep relaxation while the person being hypnotized remains relatively passive and motionless. However, this altered state can be achieved with many different techniques, including *active alert induction,* as in inducing hypnosis while a person pedals a stationary bicycle (Gafner & Benson, 2003).

> **hypnosis** A psychological state of altered attention and awareness in which a person is unusually receptive to suggestions.

Various forms of hypnosis have been practiced for thousands of years. For example, in 2600 B.C., the father of Chinese medicine, Wang Tai, described a hypnotic-like medical technique involving incantations and the passing of hands over patients. Similar descriptions of trance-like states also appear in ancient Hindu and Egyptian medical writings (c. 1600 B.C.). More recently, in the eighteenth century, the Austrian physician Franz Anton Mesmer (1734–1815) used hypnosis—which he called *animal magnetism*—to restore the balance of supposed magnetic fluid in people's bodies and thus cure them of disease. In the nineteenth century, the French neurologist Jean Marie Charcot (1825–1893) used hypnosis to treat hysteria. Interestingly, it was partly Sigmund Freud's lack of success in using hypnosis as a therapeutic tool in the treatment of psychological disorders that led him to develop psychoanalysis in the 1890s. Freud's rejection of hypnosis slowed the development of research and theory on this altered state of consciousness for many years (Baker, 1990).

What Are the Characteristic Features of Hypnosis?

When people are hypnotized, their awareness tends to be characterized by the following features (Bowers & Woody, 1996; Bryant et al., 1999; Comey & Kirsch, 1999; Lynn & Neufeld, 1996):

Enriched fantasy—The hypnotized person can readily imagine situations dissociated from reality.

Cognitive passivity—Instead of planning actions, the hypnotized person waits for the hypnotist to suggest thoughts or actions.

Hyperselective attention—The hypnotized person focuses attention on the hypnotist's voice and ignores other stimuli. Even pain that a person would find unbearable during the normal waking state can be tolerated through the hypnotically induced focused attention.

Reduced reality testing—The hypnotized person tends to uncritically accept hallucinated experiences suggested by the hypnotist.

Posthypnotic amnesia—When instructed by the hypnotist, the hypnotized person often forgets all or most of what occurred during the hypnotic session. These memories are restored when the hypnotist gives a prearranged signal. Hypnotically induced amnesia does not appear to be due to deliberate thought suppression on the part of the hypnotized person.

What Are Common Misconceptions about Hypnosis?

Hypnosis has long been used as a form of entertainment, and this history has led to certain myths about the capabilities of the hypnotized person. The following list states some of these misconceptions and then tells how each has been disproven by scientific research (Dywan & Bowers, 1983; Gibson, 1991; McConkey, 1992; Nash, 1987; Newman & Thompson, 1999):

- *Hypnotized people can be forced to violate their moral values.* There is no evidence that hypnosis causes people to act against their will.
- *Memory is more accurate under hypnosis.* Although hypnosis may help people recall forgotten events, it often results in people recalling events that never happened.
- *While hypnotized, people are much stronger than normal.* Hypnosis has no effect on strength.
- *Hypnosis acts as a truth serum, compelling people to avoid deception.* Hypnotized people can lie and keep secrets if they so desire.
- *Hypnotized people can be age-regressed, thus allowing them to relive childhood experiences.* Although hypnotized people may believe they have regressed to an earlier age, they typically display cognitive abilities far beyond those of a child.

In a study investigating college students' beliefs about hypnosis, participants either watched a stage hypnotist or attended a lecture on hypnosis. When questioned later, both student groups were more likely to correctly believe that hypnotizability does not reflect lower intelligence. However, although those students who had heard the lecture were less likely to believe that a hypnotized person is robotlike and automatically acts on all suggestions, the reverse was true for those who had watched the stage hypnotist (Echterling & Whalen, 1995). Why might students who saw the stage hypnotist be more likely to believe such false descriptions of hypnosis?

Individual Differences in Hypnotizability

Does it surprise you to learn that not everyone can be hypnotized? Numerous studies indicate that people differ in their **hypnotizability,** the degree to which they can enter a deep hypnotic state (Hilgard, 1965; Kumar et al., 1996). Individuals who are highly hypnotizable have the ability to concentrate totally on material outside themselves and to become absorbed in imaginative activities (Kirsch & Braffman, 2001). Based on our previous discussion of fantasy-prone personalities (see section 6-1a), it probably doesn't surprise you to learn that these individuals are also highly hypnotizable (Barber, 2000).

In Western cultures, children are the most hypnotizable, with hypnotic ability peaking just before adolescence and declining during middle adulthood. Given the fact that being able to engage freely in fantasy is an important predictor of hypnotizability, these age-related differences may seem natural to you (Kihlstrom, 1985; Silva & Kirsch, 1992). However, these age-related differences in hypnotizability are not found in many non-Western cultures (Ward, 1994). One possible explanation for this finding is that, in many of these cultures, the ability to enter a trance-like state is highly valued. Because of the greater value placed on this ability, adults in these cultures are less likely to risk criticism for suspending "reality" in this manner.

Although the ability to suspend ordinary reality appears to facilitate entrance into the hypnotic state, highly hypnotizable persons are not more gullible or more conforming than their less hypnotizable counterparts (Fromm & Shor, 1979). They are, however, more open to new experiences. Among adults, about 10 percent cannot be hypnotized at all, approximately 15 percent are very susceptible, and the rest fall somewhere in between. Research also indicates that hypnotizability is a fairly stable trait during adulthood (Piccione et al., 1989).

hypnotizability The degree to which a person can enter a deep hypnotic state.

6-3b Some Psychologists Doubt That Hypnosis Is an Altered State

In contrast to the sleep state, the brain-wave activity (recorded by EEG) of individuals under hypnosis differs only slightly from that of their normal waking states (Crawford & Gruzelier, 1992; De Pascalis, 1999; Graffin et al., 1995). This lack of any clear physiological difference between the normal and the hypnotic state has fueled suspicion that hypnosis is not really an altered state at all. One such "nonstate" theory proposes that the hypnotized person is simply playing a role (Barber, 1979; Spanos & Chaves, 1989). This *role-playing* explanation contends that hypnosis is a normal waking state in which suggestible people behave as they think hypnotized people are supposed to behave. The proponents of this view do not necessarily believe that hypnotized people are consciously faking an altered state. Instead, they argue that, because of the misguided cultural beliefs about the powers of hypnosis, people are caught up in the hypnotic role and often unwittingly confirm these beliefs by demonstrating hypnotic behavior (Gorassini, 1996; Spanos & Coe, 1992). Theodore Barber (2000), one of the leading advocates of this perspective, suggests that, instead of being considered a truly altered state of consciousness, hypnosis should be thought of as a highly relaxed state of mind in which a person's attention is very focused.

In support of this role-playing interpretation of hypnosis, research indicates that people's responsiveness to hypnotic suggestions can be influenced by their expectations and their desire to please the hypnotist. For example, when previously low-hypnotizable individuals take *active training* to enhance their attitudes and expectations about hypnosis, they subsequently exhibit large gains in hypnotizability (Spanos, 1986). These gains are much more likely to occur when rapport with trainers is high rather than low. Yet merely liking one's trainer is generally not sufficient to increase hypnotizability. When low-hypnotizable persons were given *passive training,* in which their well-liked trainers told them that hypnotic responses just "happened by themselves," their level of hypnotizability did not increase (Spanos et al., 1989–1990).

Despite evidence indicating that hypnosis is influenced by social expectations and a desire to please the hypnotist, many hypnosis researchers still contend that hypnosis possesses enough special features to be legitimately called an altered state. For example, people who are hypnotized often report *dissociation* in consciousness, whereby they process perceptual information on two levels simultaneously (Hilgard, 1986, 1992; Zamansky & Bartis, 1985). Based on this research, Ernest Hilgard proposed his **neodissociation theory,** which contends that the hypnotized person has two streams of consciousness operating at once. One stream responds to the hypnotist's suggestions, while the other stream, called the *hidden observer,* remains concealed from conscious awareness and merely observes what is going on.

> **neodissociation theory**
> A theory that hypnotized persons enter an altered state in which two streams of consciousness operate simultaneously, one actively responding to suggestions and the other passively observing what is going on.

Based on our previous discussion of selective and divided attention (see section 6-1a), Hilgard's theory of *divided consciousness* is not that unusual. While engaging in normal daily activities, you can literally "split" your attention. Sometimes you might even engage in an activity without any memory of having done so. For instance, have you ever been so engrossed in a dinner conversation that you forgot what your meal tasted like or that you even ate it? This common experience during the normal waking state is not that different from Hilgard's explanation of hypnosis.

This debate about whether or not hypnosis is an altered state is still a matter of ongoing scientific inquiry (Raz & Shapiro, 2002). Although many of the more bizarre or peculiar effects observed during hypnosis might be explained by people's expectations about hypnosis and their desire to please the hypnotist, other effects—such as instances in which hypnotized patients have undergone surgery without pain and with less than normal bleeding (Hornyak & Green, 2000; Schafer, 1996)—suggest a truly altered state of consciousness. Brain-imaging studies further indicate that when hypnotized individuals are exposed to normally painful experiences—such as having their hands immersed in a hot-water bath—and are told to imagine pleasant sensations, not only do they report less than normal pain, but also the suggestion alters activity in the brain areas associated with the emotional component of pain (Faymonville et al., 2000; Rainville et al., 1997). Together, these studies clearly suggest that something other than fakery is going on with hypnotized people. However, even if hypnosis is ultimately determined to be a legitimate altered state, it should also be thought of as a product of common principles of social influence and an extension of ordinary splits in consciousness (Chaves, 1999). For our present purposes, we can safely conclude that the power of hypnosis does not reside in any mysterious qualities of the hypnotist but, rather, in the mind of the hypnotized.

6-3c Meditation Provides Relaxation and Reduces Arousal

As human beings, we are by nature social creatures. As such, we typically seek out the company of others and thrive in social settings. Yet there are times when we retreat from social settings and seek solitude, a time apart from others that is dominated by self-reflection (Long et al., 2003). During such solitary periods, some people engage in mental exercises collectively referred to as **meditation,** a practice that alters the normal flow of consciousness in order to enhance self-knowledge. This technique of altering the mind is very old, and all the major religions of the world—Buddhism, Taoism, Hinduism, Islam, Judaism, and Christianity—have rich meditative traditions (France, 1996). As a technique to alter the normal waking state, meditation became popular in North America during the late 1960s, but it is much more widely practiced in Asian cultures.

A common goal of all forms of meditation is to control or retrain attention. In reaching this goal, some meditative techniques encourage people to empty their minds of all content, whereas other forms of meditation—such as *Zen, transcendental meditation,* and the *relaxation response*—teach people to focus attention on a single sound, image, or object, and to effortlessly ignore any intruding sensations. Still other techniques emphasize body movement—for example, the Sufi whirling dervishes, a religious brotherhood in Turkey, seek mystic experiences through dance.

Although most practitioners of meditation and many researchers believe that it involves an altered state of consciousness capable of opening the mind to profound truths and a feeling of oneness with the universe, more skeptical observers contend that it is simply an effective relaxation technique. Meditation has indeed been found to be useful in promoting relaxation and reducing physiological arousal (Deepak et al., 1994; Walsh, 1996). Accomplished meditators exhibit high-amplitude alpha waves, reduced oxygen consumption, and slowed heart rate while meditating, all indicators of a deeply relaxed state (Fenwick, 1987; Kasamatsu & Hirai, 1969; Kjaer et al., 2002). More recent brain scans of experienced Buddhist meditators found that at the "peak" moment of their meditative state, they exhibit increased activity in the frontal lobes of the brain and decreased activity in the left parietal lobe (Lazar et al., 2000; Newberg et al., 2001). The heightened activation of the frontal lobes makes sense, because these brain areas are involved in focused attention, which is a defining characteristic of meditation. Similarly, the lowered activation of the left parietal lobe is understandable, because this brain area is involved in keeping track of time and orienting us in physical space. During peak meditative states, people often experience a sense of timelessness and diminished awareness of the physical world.

Numerous studies suggest that, beyond fostering relaxation, meditation can sometimes be an effective treatment for insomnia, anxiety, depression, and drug abuse (Gelderloos et al., 1991; Miller et al., 1995; Shapiro et al., 1998). Other studies even suggest that meditation may increase longevity among the elderly by reducing the negative effects of cardiovascular disease, especially in African Americans with high blood pressure (Davidson et al., 2003; Goldberg, 1995; Schneider et al., 2001). But despite these impressive therapeutic findings, skeptics claim that meditation is effective simply because it leads to relaxation, and perhaps because it serves as a placebo for those who want to believe in its benefits (Shapiro, 1987). Before reading further, spend a few minutes completing Explore It Exercise 6-1 to learn a simple meditative technique.

6-3d Intense Religious Experiences Often Involve Altered States

> One night I awoke gasping for breath—I thought I was dying and felt like I was—Just about to give up—I saw a vision of Jesus at the foot of my bed—the complete figure—He stretched out His hand and said, "No—not yet—Be not afraid." At that moment I felt a *peace* and *joy* come over me—such as I have never experienced in my life. (Stark, 1965)

Like this individual in Rodney Stark's study of religious experiences, have you ever had the feeling of being close to a powerful spiritual force that seemed to lift you out of yourself? When 5,420 Americans were asked this question, 40 percent answered yes (Yamane

meditation A variety of mental exercises that alter the normal flow of consciousness in order to enhance self-knowledge.

When someone in his own mind recalls the original condition of his Mind, then all deceptive thoughts dissolve away on their own into the realm of the ultimate reality.

—*Milarepa, Tibetan Buddhist saint and poet, 1040–1123*

No one can see their reflection in running water. It is only in still water that we can see.

—*Taoist proverb*

Does meditation induce an altered state of consciousness, or is it simply a form of relaxation?

Source: Courtesy of Figzoi.

Explore It
Exercise **6-1**

How Can You Meditate?

To get some sense of what meditation is all about, try the following exercise derived from Herbert Benson's relaxation response (Benson, 1975; Benson & Klipper, 1988):

Sit quietly in a comfortable position, close your eyes, and relax your muscles. Choose some word or short phrase (a *mantra*) that you can focus your attention on. It should be something that is calming to you, such as "love," "serenity," or "I am at peace." Don't concentrate too hard on the mantra; it could become only a faint idea at times. As you repeat this mantra silently to yourself, breathe through your nose and pay attention to your breathing. Continue this exercise for 10 to 20 minutes, and maintain a passive attitude throughout. When your attention is distracted away from your mantra, don't get upset, but simply and gently refocus your mind. If you find this a pleasant experience, practice it once or twice daily.

& Polzer, 1994). Similar findings have been obtained in England and Australia and are common experiences in religions throughout the world (Fontana, 2003; Scharfstein, 1973). A century ago, William James (1902/1985) described such intense religious experiences as creating a sense of peace and inner harmony, in which the self and the world are perceived as having undergone a dramatic transformation, and important truths are revealed. Recent empirical studies partly support this view: Individuals who have had profound religious or spiritual experiences tend to have high levels of meaning and purpose in life (Palmer & Broud, 2002). However, regardless of the ultimate insights or peace of mind that people might receive from these intense religious experiences, do they qualify as true altered states of consciousness?

One of the more interesting religious experiences studied by scientists is that of the Holy Ghost people of Appalachia. In this fundamentalist Christian sect, anointment by the Holy Ghost is believed to occur when the spirit of God possesses a person. While anointed and presumably protected by the Holy Ghost, these people handle poisonous snakes, drink strychnine poison, and touch flames to their bodies (Schwarz, 1960; Wilson, 1970). Although observations of individuals during anointment suggest that they are having profound religious experiences, their brain activity doesn't significantly differ from that of someone in an aroused, waking state. For instance, EEG recordings taken of one well-known serpent handler indicated a sudden shift from alpha to beta waves when anointment began, with beta activity predominant throughout the experience (Woodruff, 1993). Overall, the EEG pattern was not similar to the slower patterns recorded by meditating Zen monks.

Although there is no consensus on whether anointment represents an altered state of consciousness, there is little disagreement that near-death experiences involve altered states. A **near-death experience** is an altered state of consciousness episode in which a person is either briefly clinically dead or in extreme danger of clinical death. Many people who have near-death experiences identify them as being religious or mystical in nature, often even by those without religious beliefs (Fontana, 2003). How common are near-death episodes? One 13-year study conducted in the Netherlands found that about 10 percent of 344 patients resuscitated after suffering cardiac arrest had near-death experiences, with about 1 in 5 of those individuals remembering some part of what happened when they were clinically dead (van Lommel et al., 2001). Unfortunately, very few well-designed studies have been conducted on this topic. Anecdotal reports from doctors, nurses, and patients often describe near-death experiences involving a buzzing or ringing noise, a sense of blissful peace, a feeling of floating out of one's body and observing it from above, moving through a tunnel into a bright light, meeting dead people, and seeing one's life pass before one's eyes. Although these experiences sound extremely pleasant, about 15 percent of near-death experiences do not fit this pattern and are described as being extremely negative, even "hellish" (Blackmore, 2004). Regardless of whether

near-death experience
An altered state of consciousness episode in which a person is either briefly clinically dead or in extreme danger of clinical death.

near-death experiences are remembered as positive or negative, many neuroscientists believe that what people remember are sensory hallucinations caused by the brain being simultaneously deprived of oxygen and flooded by pain-killing endorphins (see chapter 3, section 3-1d). Some near-death researchers and many individuals who have experienced near-death phenomena object to reducing such profound experiences to simple neurological causes (Worth & Yates, 1996).

Beyond the extraordinary nature of near-death experiences, a number of researchers question whether altered states of consciousness are necessary for most religious experiences (Baruss, 2003). Similar to the hypnosis debate (refer back to section 6-3b), some investigators believe that many religious experiences are not precipitated by altered states but, rather, are the result of *role-playing* (Holm, 1991, 1995; Hood, 1991). As with the explanation for hypnosis, these researchers contend that people learn how to play the religious role, and that their religious experiences can be best understood within this social role context.

Although there is debate about whether certain religious experiences are induced by altered states, no such controversy exists regarding religious experiences induced by mind-altering drugs. For example, to facilitate their "vision quest," certain Native American tribes commonly use psychoactive drugs along with ritualistic fasting. Research indicates that, under the influence of psychedelic drugs, religious imagery is quite common (Masters & Houston, 1966; Pahnke, 1970). Such findings have led some researchers to make the controversial claim that all religions in the world originated through the use of mind-altering drugs (Kramrisch et al., 1986).

So what part do altered states play in religious experiences? The answer may well depend on what type of religious experience is being analyzed (Marechal & Thorold, 2004). It is important to keep in mind that religious experiences occur within the context of a set of cultural traditions and social expectations (Hood, 1995). As pointed out by social-role theorists, participants in religious exercises play identifiable roles that they have learned from their social group. The group also provides participants with a sense of identity and a feeling of security in having shared values and beliefs. Within this group context of acceptance and shared expectations, it isn't unusual for participants to feel as though the psychological boundaries between self and nonself have dissolved. The accompanying states of consciousness may appear no different from the normal waking state, or they may be profoundly altered. Whatever the case, altered states should not be thought of as the essence of the religious experience. Theodore Roszak has argued that focusing only on the altered-state component distorts the essence of the religious experience:

> The temptation, then, is to believe that the behavior that has thus been objectively verified is what religious experience is *really* all about, and—further—that it can be appropriated as an end in itself, plucked like a rare flower from the soil that feeds it. The result is a narrow emphasis on special effects and sensations: "peak experiences," "highs," "flashes," and such. Yet, even if one wishes to regard ecstasy as the "peak" of religious experience, that summit does not float in midair. It rests upon tradition and a way of life; one ascends such heights and appreciates their grandeur by a process of initiation that demands learning, commitment, devotion, service, sacrifice. To approach it in any hasty way is like "scaling" Mount Everest by being landed on its top from a helicopter. (Roszak, 1975, p. 50)

6-3e Psychoactive Drug Use Can Lead to Dependence

psychoactive drugs Chemicals that modify mental processes and behavior.

As mentioned in section 6-3d, **psychoactive drugs**—which are chemicals that modify mental processes and behavior—are often used to deliberately alter consciousness. Such drugs alter consciousness by attaching themselves to synaptic receptors and thereby either blocking or stimulating neural activity. Although psychoactive drugs are sometimes used in religious ceremonies, people mainly take them for medicinal and recreational purposes.

drug abuse Persistence in drug use even when impaired behavior or social functioning results.

When people persist in taking drugs even when impaired behavior or social functioning results, this is known as **drug abuse** or *substance dependence*. Abuse of psychoactive drugs is one of our most serious and costly social problems, accounting for a third

Instructions: Listed below are eight criteria that the American Psychiatric Association uses to diagnose drug abuse (also known as substance dependence). If three or more of the following criteria describe your own behavior, you may have a problem with substance abuse.

	Yes	No
1. You take the substance in larger amounts or over a longer period than intended.	___	___
2. You have a persistent desire, or have made one or more unsuccessful efforts, to cut down or control substance use.	___	___
3. You spend a great deal of your time in activities necessary to get the substance (for example, theft), taking the substance (for example, chain smoking), or recovering from its effects (for example, alcohol "hangovers").	___	___
4. You experience frequent intoxication or withdrawal symptoms while you are expected to fulfill obligations at work, school, or home, or when substance use is physically dangerous (for example, driving when intoxicated).	___	___
5. You give up or reduce in frequency important social, occupational, or recreational activities because of substance use.	___	___
6. You continue to use the drug despite recognizing its harmfulness to your life.	___	___
7. You need increased amounts of the drug (at least 50 percent more) to achieve the desired effect and/or you experience a decreased effect with continued use of the same amount (tolerance).	___	___
8. You often take the drug to relieve or avoid withdrawal symptoms.	___	___

Source: Adapted from the American Psychiatric Association (1994).

---

of all hospital admissions, a quarter of all deaths, and a majority of serious crimes. In the United States alone, the combined medical and social costs of drug abuse exceed $240 billion per year (Nash, 1997). To learn something about the criteria that psychologists use in evaluating substance abuse in individuals, answer the questions in Self-Discovery Questionnaire 6-3.

One effect of drug abuse is **drug tolerance,** meaning that greater amounts of the drug are necessary to produce the same effect once produced by a smaller dose (Julien, 2001). For example, an infrequent drinker might become intoxicated after only two beers, but an alcoholic might have to consume two six-packs to receive the same effect. Often accompanying tolerance is the development of *physical dependence.* A person who is physically dependent on a drug needs it in order to function normally. You can determine whether someone is physically dependent by withdrawing the drug and watching for the appearance of unpleasant physical symptoms—known as *withdrawal symptoms*—as the body reacts to its absence (Littleton & Little, 1989; Piasecki et al., 1997). Among heroin addicts, for example, common withdrawal symptoms are chills, fever, diarrhea, and a runny nose. What makes it difficult for drug abusers to stop their abuse is that readministering the drug can terminate the symptoms of withdrawal.

Besides physical dependence, many drugs produce an immediate pleasurable effect that, through continued use, leads to *psychological dependence,* in which the person experiences intense mental and emotional desires for the drug (Carroll, 1997). Many abused drugs cause both physical and psychological dependence. Importantly, psychological dependence can persist even when a person is no longer physically dependent on a drug.

drug tolerance An effect of drug abuse in which greater amounts of the drug are necessary to produce the same effect once produced by a smaller dose.

6-3f Depressants Slow Body Functions and Induce Relaxation

depressants Psychoactive drugs that slow down—or depress—the nervous system and decrease mental and physical activity.

The **depressants** are a class of psychoactive drugs that slow down—or depress—the nervous system and decrease mental and physical activity. In low doses depressants induce a relaxed state, while in higher doses they induce sleep. Further, their effects are *additive,* meaning that taking different depressants at the same time, such as alcohol and sleeping pills, can amount to a dangerous overdose that can lead to death. All depressants are potentially physically addictive.

Alcohol

By far the most widely consumed and abused depressant in the world is alcohol. Besides slowing body functions, depressants like alcohol reduce a person's awareness of both internal and external stimuli. As blood alcohol levels rise, the brain becomes increasingly impaired. For example, as noted in table 6-2, even at a blood alcohol level of 0.05 percent—which is below the level of legal intoxication—brain areas that control judgment and inhibitions are impaired, making it more likely that the person will act impulsively (Ito et al., 1996). Some researchers believe that this weakening of restraints, or *disinhibition,* is caused by an interruption of our ability to process and respond to the meaning of complex and subtle situational cues (Johnson et al., 2000; Steele & Josephs, 1988). For example, when provoked, people who are drunk are much less attentive than those who are sober to such inhibiting cues as the provocateur's intentions and the possible negative consequences of violence. This impairment of judgment partly explains why alcohol is the leading cause of domestic violence and highway deaths in the general population, and why college students who drink heavily are two to five times more likely to argue, fight, damage property, be injured, and engage in unplanned or unprotected sex (Holcomb & Anderson, 1983; O'Farrell & Murphy, 1995).

How prevalent is alcohol use? In the United States, more than two-thirds of all adults consume alcohol at least occasionally. Of those adults, over 20 million frequently drink in excess, thus putting their health at risk, and about 7 million Americans are *alcoholics* (Cooper, 2000).

alcoholism Tolerance of and physical dependence on alcohol due to prolonged abuse of that substance.

Alcoholism is defined as tolerance and physical dependence resulting from the prolonged abuse of alcohol (O'Brien et al., 1995). Among the health problems associated with chronic alcohol abuse are liver disease (*cirrhosis*), heart disease, stroke, memory loss, cancer, malnutrition, and loss of sexual interest (Cloninger et al., 1989; Yelena, 2002). People who start drinking at a younger age are more likely to abuse alcohol as adults (Grant & Dawson, 1997).

A recent survey of students at 119 U.S. college campuses found that almost 50 percent of the men and 40 percent of the women were *binge drinkers,* meaning that they consumed

Table 6-2	Blood Alcohol Levels and Their Behavioral Effects
Blood Alcohol Level*	**Behavioral Effects**
0.05%	Lowered alertness, impaired judgment, release of inhibitions
0.10%	Slowed reaction time, impaired motor function, less caution
0.15%	Large, consistent increases in reaction time
0.20%	Marked depression in sensory and motor capability
0.25%	Severe motor disturbance, impairment of sensory perceptions
0.30%	In a stupor but still conscious, no comprehension of surrounding events
0.35%	Surgical anesthesia, minimal level to cause death
0.40%	Lethal dose for half of all adults

*In milligrams of alcohol per 100 milliliters of blood.

five or more drinks per episode (Wechsler et al., 2002). Further, every year approximately 1,400 American college students die from alcohol-related causes, and another 150,000 students develop a health problem related to alcohol. Students who are most likely to binge-drink are those who strongly identify with campus groups that have social norms encouraging alcohol consumption (Johnston & White, 2003; Weitzman et al., 2003). Some of the campus groups that are most likely to foster binge drinking are fraternities and sororities, as well as groups composed of avid sports fans (Nelson & Wechsler, 2003). White students are most likely to binge-drink, whereas African-American students are least likely.

Although the health risks of alcohol certainly highlight the dangers of drug abuse, recent studies indicate that one possible long-term benefit of moderate alcohol consumption is reduced coronary heart disease (Criqui & Ringel, 1994; Fuchs et al., 1995). However, it must be emphasized that this potential health benefit is far outweighed by the risks associated with *heavy* drinking.

Sedatives and Tranquilizers

Like alcohol, **sedatives** are depressants that in mild doses produce relaxation, mild euphoria, and reduced inhibitions (Alexander et al., 2004). Physicians often prescribe sedatives as a sleep aid, yet one of their side effects is that they greatly reduce REM sleep. Common prescription sedatives include the drugs Seconal and Nembutal. Because sedatives produce both physical and psychological dependence, their medical use has declined over the years, but they are still widely abused through illegal drug markets. Even small doses of these drugs can prove fatal when mixed with alcohol.

Milder depressants that are similar to sedatives are *tranquilizers,* which are often used to relieve anxiety (Shaywitz & Liebowitz, 2003). Common prescription tranquilizers are Xanax, Valium, Librium, and Equanil. Although they are chemically different from sedatives, most tranquilizers are also extremely addictive and very dangerous when mixed with alcohol.

The Opiates

Another category of depressants is the **opiates** (also called *narcotics*), which include such drugs as *opium, morphine,* and *heroin* (Smith-Rohrberg et al., 2004). For centuries, opium extracted from poppy seeds has been used as a pain reliever by mimicking the effects of the brain's own naturally produced pain-relieving neurotransmitter, *endorphins* (see chapter 3, section 3-1c). Opiates not only depress the nervous system and relieve pain but also produce a relaxed, dreamlike state that is highly pleasurable (Chao & Nestler, 2004). However, such pleasure comes at a cost—users quickly develop a strong physical and psychological dependence, and their withdrawal symptoms are extremely intense and painful (Amato et al., 2004). The reason withdrawal symptoms are so severe is that opiates affect the brain's production of endorphins. Regular use of opiates overloads endorphin receptors within the brain, causing the brain to cease its endorphin production. When the drugs are withdrawn, the brain has an insufficient supply of these pain-relieving neurotransmitters, and this is the primary cause of the person's severe withdrawal symptoms.

6-3g Stimulants Speed Up Body Functions

Stimulants are drugs that speed up—or stimulate—the nervous system and increase mental and physical activity. However, all stimulants are at least mildly addictive, and most of us are somewhat addicted to at least one type of stimulant.

Caffeine and Nicotine

Are you a person who needs a cup of coffee in the morning to "get going" or a cigarette to curb your appetite or relieve stress? Because stimulants speed up body functions and reduce appetite (due to increased blood sugar), people often use them to stay awake, lose weight, enhance athletic performance, or elevate mood. Two of the most commonly used stimulant

Over 20 million Americans frequently drink in excess, and about 7 million are alcoholics. At what blood alcohol level is the typical person cognitively impaired?

Source: Courtesy of Figzoi.

sedatives Depressants that in mild doses produce relaxation, mild euphoria, and reduced inhibitions.

opiates A category of depressant drugs, including opium, morphine, and heroin, that depress the nervous system, temporarily relieve pain, and produce a relaxed, dreamlike state.

stimulants Psychoactive drugs that speed up—or stimulate—the nervous system and increase mental and physical activity.

Do you need a jolt of java in the morning to get yourself going? What happens when you do not have that morning cup of coffee? Habitual heavy caffeine users are physically dependent on the drug.

Source: Courtesy of Figzoi.

If cigarettes are behaviorally addictive or habit forming, they are much more like . . . Gummi Bears. I love Gummi Bears . . . and I want Gummi Bears, and I don't like it when I don't eat my Gummi Bears, but I'm certainly not addicted to them.

—*Philip Morris president James Morgan, offering his opinion that tobacco is not addictive, but merely a behavioral habit, 1997*

To cease smoking is the easiest thing I ever did. I ought to know because I've done it a thousand times.

—*Mark Twain, U.S. author, 1835–1910*

substances are *caffeine* and *nicotine*. Caffeine is found in coffee, tea, cocoa, and the cola nut (which is used to flavor cola beverages), while tobacco is the only natural source of nicotine.

Caffeine stimulates the cerebral cortex, which causes an increase in mental alertness and wakefulness (Lyvers et al., 2004). This increased alertness is partly caused by caffeine delaying the onset of boredom to repetitive tasks and enhancing the appeal of novel situations (Davidson & Smith, 1991). Caffeine also enhances mood, perhaps by mimicking the effects of a natural brain chemical, *adenosine*. Although moderate doses of caffeine can fight off drowsiness, large doses can make a person feel jittery and anxious and can cause insomnia (Dreher, 2003; Griffiths & Mumford, 1995). In addition, as discussed in chapter 3, habitual heavy users of caffeine can become physically dependent, experiencing headaches and depression when deprived of the drug (James, 1997).

When inhaled through tobacco smoke, nicotine reaches the brain within seconds, where it stimulates various brain areas, including the frontal lobes, thalamus, hippocampus, and amygdala (Stein et al., 1998). Like caffeine, nicotine increases mental alertness and elevates heart rate, respiration, and blood pressure. Paradoxically, this stimulant also appears to have a calming effect on smokers, often relieving stress. In addition to these effects, nicotine reduces blood flow to the skin, causing a drop in skin temperature, which makes blushing less common in smokers than in nonsmokers. This reduced blood flow is probably why the skin of smokers tends to wrinkle and age faster than that of nonsmokers (Daniell, 1971). Nicotine also appears to produce a decrease in hand steadiness and fine motor control (Frankenhauser et al., 1970).

Prolonged use of tobacco—primarily in cigarettes, cigars, and chewing tobacco—is a serious health hazard. It is also the single most important *preventable* risk to human health in developed countries and an important cause of premature death worldwide (Peto et al., 1992). About 21 million people died from smoking-related illnesses in the decade 1990–1999. Further, among nonsmoking adults, exposure to secondary smoke doubles the risk of heart disease and increases the risk of lung cancer by 30 percent (White et al., 1991). Such exposure also increases the risk of respiratory diseases and other health problems in nonsmoking children (White et al., 1991). Unfortunately for casual tobacco users, a greater percentage of them become addicted to this drug than do casual users of cocaine, morphine, or alcohol (Henningfield et al., 1990; Henningfield et al., 1995).

Fear of gaining weight is the primary reason many women give for not quitting smoking. Yet research indicates that women who exercise regularly while trying to "kick the habit" not only limit their weight gain but also are twice as likely to stop smoking and stay smoke-free than nonexercisers (Marcus et al., 2003). Similar benefits are also likely for male smokers. When trying to quit, African-American abstainers tend to have less severe withdrawal symptoms—such as irritability, difficulty concentrating, and restlessness—than Caucasians (Riedel et al., 2003).

Cocaine and Amphetamines

Despite the associated health dangers, nicotine-laced tobacco products—and caffeine—are only mild stimulants. Much stronger stimulants are *cocaine* and *amphetamines* (also known as "speed"), which produce a sense of euphoria and can cause severe psychological and physical problems.

Believe it or not, cocaine was once an ingredient in Coca-Cola. However, in 1906, the U.S. government outlawed cocaine, and the drug was dropped from the ingredients list of this popular soft drink. Today cocaine is one of the more widely abused illegal stimulant drugs (Baker et al., 2004). This stimulant is a natural substance that comes from the leaves of the coca bush, which grows in South America. When cocaine is smoked (*crack*), sniffed (*snorting*), or injected directly into the bloodstream (*mainlining*), users quickly experience a 15- to 30-minute "high" during which they feel energized, excited, happy, talkative, and confident. Cocaine activates the sympathetic branch of the autonomic nervous system, raising body temperature, heart rate, and breathing, while reducing the desire for food and sleep.

What causes the cocaine high? As depicted in figure 6-5, in the brain's neurons, the drug blocks the repackaging of dopamine and norepinephrine neurotransmitters into the synaptic vesicles of the axon's terminal buttons, so the neurotransmitters remain in the synaptic cleft

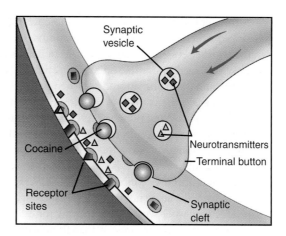

Figure 6-5

Effect of Cocaine on Neurotransmitters

Cocaine blocks the reuptake of neurotransmitters into the terminal buttons, causing them to remain in the synaptic cleft longer than normal. Their extended presence in the synaptic cleft creates the drug's stimulant effects.

longer than normal (Bubar et al., 2003). Because these neurotransmitters are the chemical messengers for feelings of pleasure and heightened wakefulness, their extended presence in the synaptic cleft sets in motion a series of events that result in the cocaine high. However, because this high lasts only a short time, users often repeatedly ingest the drug as soon as the effects wear off. The fast-acting yet short-duration nature of this drug also may make it more addictive than many other drugs. Cocaine binges can last for hours or even days, causing the users to eventually reach a state of physical exhaustion, after which they require long periods of sleep. Although cocaine is not generally believed to create physical dependence, it often produces strong psychological dependence due to its highly pleasurable effects (Bonson et al., 2002).

Like cocaine, amphetamines activate the sympathetic nervous system and increase dopamine and norepinephrine activity, producing many cocainelike effects. Sometimes referred to as "uppers" or "speed," these synthetic stimulants have long been used by people to lose weight or stay awake for extended time periods. They also increase alertness and response speed. However, physicians rarely prescribe these drugs, because they produce many negative side effects. For example, users who take amphetamines as a treatment for weight loss quickly develop a tolerance to the appetite-suppressing effects of the drug, requiring increasingly higher doses to maintain these effects. Furthermore, such high dosage can cause insomnia, anxiety, heart problems, and even brain damage (Mintzer & Griffiths, 2003; Volkow et al., 2001). As with cocaine, amphetamines are not generally physically addictive, but they do produce strong psychological dependence.

Habitual amphetamine and cocaine users often develop **stimulant-induced psychosis,** which is characterized by many of the symptoms seen in *schizophrenia,* a psychological disorder discussed in chapter 13, section 13-3d. One of the primary symptoms of stimulant-induced psychosis is hallucinations—for example, hearing strange voices, seeing snow, or feeling bugs crawling on or under the skin (Adeyemo, 2002; Pezze et al., 2002). The sensation of these "cocaine bugs" is actually caused by the cocaine-induced spontaneous firing of sensory neurons. Other symptoms of stimulant-induced psychosis are depression, paranoia, teeth grinding, and repetitive behaviors.

Ecstasy and Ritalin

One stimulant that has become popular among adolescents and young adults as an alternative to cocaine and amphetamines is "Ecstasy," or MDMA, which is short for methylenedioxymethamphetamine (Yacoubian, 2003). Taken as a pill, MDMA primarily affects the brain cells that produce serotonin, a neurotransmitter that is the body's primary regulator of mood (see chapter 3, section 3-1c). The massive release of serotonin by these cells may be responsible for the feelings of blissfulness and greater closeness to others that Ecstasy users often experience, as well as for significant increases in their body temperature, heart rate, and blood pressure (Green et al., 1995). MDMA also blocks serotonin reuptake, amplifying and extending serotonin's effects (Braun, 2001).

stimulant-induced psychosis Schizophrenic-like symptoms that can occur following prolonged and excessive use of cocaine and amphetamines.

Although MDMA is not physically addictive, it is a dangerous drug. When Ecstasy users take several doses over the course of a few hours, the body's natural ability to control its temperature can be severely impaired. Dozens of deaths have occurred due to overheating when users have engaged in strenuous physical activity (Cloud, 2000; Schifano et al., 2003). Findings from animal and human studies also raise the possibility that MDMA use can cause permanent damage to the axons of the serotonin-containing brain cells, resulting in memory and concentration problems (Gerra et al., 2000; Hatzidimitriou et al., 1999; Reneman et al., 2000).

Another disturbing cultural trend has been the increased abuse of Ritalin (methylphenidate), a stimulant drug prescribed to treat attention-deficit/hyperactivity disorder (ADHD) in children. Ritalin is effective in treating the disorder because it decreases distractibility and improves concentration (Roehrs et al., 1999). Yet some adults—among them college students—who do not have the disorder ingest the drug to increase their concentration and productivity while working or studying for exams (Beck et al., 1999). They also develop a tolerance for the drug more quickly than those with ADHD and experience withdrawal symptoms when the dosage is reduced.

6-3h Hallucinogens Induce Profoundly Altered States

The psychoactive drugs that produce the most profound alterations in consciousness are the **hallucinogens** (also called *psychedelics*), which distort perception and generate sensory images without any external stimulation. As the name implies, these drugs often create hallucinations, which are sensations and perceptions that occur without any external stimulation. Although hallucinogens were once thought to mimic psychotic states of mind, careful analysis indicates that these drugs do not produce the same behavioral patterns observed in people suffering from psychotic episodes.

Many hallucinogenic drugs are naturally derived from plants, such as the peyote cactus that contains *mescaline,* or the Mexican mushroom that contains *psilocybin.* These natural hallucinogens have been used for thousands of years in the religious rites of the Aztecs and other Mexican Indians and still today play an important role in the religious practices of the Native American Church of North America (Baruss, 2003). As a religious sacrament—similar to the bread and wine used in Christianity—these hallucinogens seldom are abused by members of the Native American Church.

LSD

The most potent of the hallucinogenic drugs, **LSD** (technically known as *lysergic acid diethylamide*), is not found in nature but is a synthesized drug structurally similar to the neurotransmitter serotonin (see chapter 3, section 3-1c). Following its discovery in 1938 by the Swiss chemist Albert Hoffman, LSD was sometimes given to patients in psychotherapy because its mind-expanding properties were thought to help them recover repressed memories. During the 1960s, LSD became a recreational drug on college campuses, championed by the former Harvard lecturer Timothy Leary, who believed that it could be used as a vehicle to spiritual discovery.

When taken orally, LSD's effects are felt within 30 minutes to an hour and persist for about 10 to 12 hours. Although the physiological effects of LSD are minor—a slight increase in heart rate, blood pressure, blood glucose, body temperature, dizziness, drowsiness, and nausea—the psychological effects are intense. The exact nature of the psychological experience is difficult to predict because it is influenced by a host of factors, including the user's personality and expectations, the persons with whom the user interacts during the LSD experience, and the setting in which the drug is administered. However, the principal psychological effects involve hallucinations and distortions. These effects are produced when the drug binds with the serotonin brain receptors associated with dreaming, causing users to experience a dreamlike state of mind while they are awake (Goodman, 2002). During this altered state, users may also experience a blending of sensory experiences known as *synesthesia,* in which colors are felt or heard, and sounds are seen (see chapter 5, section 5-4d). Subjective time is also altered, so that a few seconds might seem like many minutes, and people often feel detached from their bodies. For some, these experiences are enjoyable and even insightful; for others, they

hallucinogens Psychoactive drugs that distort perception and generate sensory images without any external stimulation.

LSD A synthesized chemical that is the most potent of the hallucinogens; induces hallucinations, distortions, and a blending of sensory experiences.

are unpleasant and even terrifying. Importantly, unpleasant experiences are relatively frequent, and *flashbacks*—recurrences of the drug's effects without the drug—occur in more than 15 percent of LSD users and can persist for months following the drug experience (Lerner et al., 2003). Most importantly, there is no way to predict how a person will react to the drug. Indeed, the same person may react positively during one experience and negatively during another.

LSD use is largely independent of the "party drugs" scene, which is perhaps not surprising, because its effects—profound hallucinations and distortions of reality—are very unlikely to promote or enhance social interaction (Prepeliczay, 2003). Interestingly, LSD users do not become physically dependent on the drug, even after prolonged use. In fact, most people discontinue using LSD because they tire of it or have no further need for it. However, the lack of physical dependence does not mean that this is a "safe" drug. Although LSD has never been definitely linked to even one human overdose death, fatal accidents and suicides have occurred while people were under the drug's influence. For example, people have fallen to their deaths due to an LSD-induced belief that they could fly. For this reason, LSD is considered a dangerous drug and should be avoided.

Marijuana

Marijuana, which is sometimes classified as a mild hallucinogen, is a preparation of leafy material from the hemp, or *Cannabis,* plant. The earliest reference to marijuana is in a pharmacy book written in 2737 B.C. by the Chinese emperor Shen Nung, who called marijuana the "Liberator of Sin" due to its ability to induce a sense of giddiness or euphoria in users. This pleasurable effect probably accounts for the fact that marijuana continues to be the most frequently used illegal drug in the world; for example, 47 percent of American adults have tried it at least once, and about 3 percent are daily users (Kingery et al., 1999; Martin, 1995). Although its use is widespread, marijuana appears to be a "maturational drug" for most people, meaning that they begin using it during the exploratory years of adolescence and stop using it in early adulthood as they secure their career and family relationships (Mitchell et al., 1999).

The major psychoactive ingredient in marijuana is **THC,** short for the complex organic molecule delta-9 tetrahydrocannabinol. THC is concentrated in the resin of the hemp plant, with most of the resin in the flowering tops (from which the stronger form of marijuana, known as *hashish,* is made), less in the leaves, and little in the stems. When smoked, THC is quickly absorbed into the blood and reaches the brain within 7 seconds; however, when eaten in such foods as brownies or cookies, the effect is delayed. Marijuana is at most only mildly physically addictive, but some habitual users experience unpleasant withdrawal symptoms when they stop using the drug (Budney et al., 2001; Haney et al., 2003).

What are the effects of marijuana? Physiologically, it produces mild arousal in the form of increased heart rate and blood pressure, and dryness of the mouth and throat. Psychologically, users often experience an increased sense of well-being and relaxation, spontaneous laughter, and a heightened sensitivity to various stimuli, such as tastes, sounds, colors, and smells. In addition, people often experience a distortion of time and a disconnected flow of ideas, which may be caused by temporary impairment of short-term memory, leading users to confuse past, present, and future (Schwartz, 1993). Like alcohol, moderate marijuana use can impair coordination, attention, and reaction time and has been linked to accidents and traffic fatalities (Chait & Pierri, 1992). On the positive side, medical evidence indicates that the drug is effective in treating glaucoma, chronic pain, and nausea from cancer chemotherapy (Tramer et al., 2001).

No clear understanding of the health consequences of long-term marijuana use has yet been achieved, but research suggests that, as with tobacco, marijuana use increases a person's susceptibility to throat and mouth cancers due to its high tar content (National Academy of Sciences, 1999). There also is sufficient evidence to recommend that the drug not be used during pregnancy due to possible negative prenatal effects (Szeto et al., 1991; Tashkin, 1999; Wu et al., 1988). In addition, prolonged marijuana use appears to disrupt memory formation and weaken the body's immune system (Pope et al., 2001). Regarding possible psychological and social effects, consistent use of high quantities of marijuana does appear to have a negative effect on motivation and interpersonal skills and thus may impede the normal development of adolescents and young adults (Martin, 1995).

marijuana A mild hallucinogen derived from the leafy material of the hemp, or *Cannabis,* plant; often induces a sense of giddiness or euphoria, as well as heightened sensitivity to various stimuli.

THC The major psychoactive ingredient in marijuana.

Marijuana can impair coordination, attention, and reaction time and has been linked to accidents and traffic fatalities. Why is it referred to as a "maturational drug"?

As it now stands, although marijuana does not appear to be a "killer weed," it is also not a harmless substance. In addition, the more heavily individuals use marijuana, the greater the probability that they will use other drugs. Thus, the most serious danger of marijuana use may be more related to "drug-use proneness" than to the effects of the marijuana itself (McMillan et al., 2003). Table 6-3 lists the effects and risks of physical and psychological dependence for the three types of psychoactive drugs.

Table 6-3	Psychoactive Drugs	
Drug	**Main Effects**	**Potential for Physical/ Psychological Dependence**
Depressants		
Alcohol	Relaxation, anxiety reduction, reduced inhibitions	High/High
Opiates ("narcotics")	Euphoria, relaxation, anxiety reduction, pain relief	High/High
Sedatives and tranquilizers	Relaxation, mild euphoria, reduced inhibitions	High/High
Stimulants		
Caffeine	Alertness	Moderate/Moderate
Cocaine	Alertness, euphoria	Moderate to high/High
Nicotine	Alertness	High/(?)
Amphetamines	Alertness, euphoria	Moderate to high/High
MDMA (Ecstasy)	Blissfulness, increased sociability	Low
Ritalin	Increased concentration	Moderate/Moderate
Hallucinogens		
LSD	Hallucination, altered perceptions	Low/Low
Marijuana	Mild euphoria, relaxation, altered perceptions	Low/Moderate

6-3i Biological and Sociocultural Factors Influence Drug Use

Virtually everyone has access to psychoactive drugs. Yet not everyone who has the opportunity to use such substances does so, and not all users become addicted. What factors influence drug use and abuse? Twin studies provide evidence that drug abuse vulnerability may have a biological link (Malone et al., 2004; Pickens et al., 1993). For example, the shared incidence of alcoholism is more common among identical twins than among fraternal twins (McGue et al., 1992). Similarly, twin studies in the United States and Scandinavia indicate a genetic contribution not only to risks of smoking but also to *resistance* to tobacco use (Carmelli et al., 1992; Kendler et al., 2002b). These findings suggest that the closer the genetic makeup between people is, the more similar their drug use pattern will be (Bierut et al., 2002; Uhl et al., 1995).

Regarding personal or social factors, although personality problems do not predict drug use in adolescents, a teenager's degree of rebellion against parents and societal norms is a good predictor of drug use: Those teens who are religious, attend school regularly and get good grades, have good relationships with their parents, and do not break the law are least likely to drink alcohol and use other drugs (Oetting & Beauvais, 1990; Wills et al., 2003). Rebellious adolescents, in contrast, often have closer emotional ties to their friends than to their parents, and these friends are also likely to be drug users. In this regard, peer pressure is a significant predictor of alcohol and other drug use among adolescents and young adults (Weitzman et al., 2003). The desire to "fit in" with friends who are using consciousness-altering drugs is often sufficient to prompt initial drug use. People who are most likely to conform in this manner are those who strongly desire acceptance from their friends (Johnston & White, 2003).

Cultural factors also influence drug dependence. Numerous studies indicate that the poor and the less educated are more likely to abuse various drugs than are people who have more money and education. One explanation for these findings is that poor and undereducated people experience higher levels of stress than do those who are rich and well-schooled, while simultaneously having considerably less access to medical care for physical and psychological problems. For people who are living in such underprivileged circumstances, drug abuse becomes an ill-advised and destructive means of self-medication. One notable exception to this tendency is found in the African-American community. A number of studies indicate that African Americans are less likely than White Americans to abuse alcohol, tobacco, and other psychoactive drugs (Breslau et al., 2001; Wechsler et al., 2002). Why is this so, given the fact that African Americans as a group earn less money and are less educated than White Americans? In searching for answers, researchers have examined cultural traditions in the African-American community that might protect people against substance abuse. One important tradition is religion. Many African Americans are members of evangelical religions, such as the Baptist faith, which forbids the use of drugs, including alcohol. At least one study has found that African-American Baptists who attend church frequently are more likely to abstain from alcohol use than are comparable White-American Baptists (Blazer et al., 2002). This greater adherence to their religion's antidrug social norm may partly explain the racial differences in drug abuse.

Cross-cultural studies find further support for the hypothesis that a culture's attitudes and beliefs about drug use are strong predictors of substance abuse. For example, *temperance cultures*—that is, cultures that maintain activist approaches to combating drinking problems—consume less alcohol than do non-temperance cultures (Levine, 1992; Peele, 1993). Further, alcohol consumption is more "socialized" in temperance cultures (Peele, 1997). That is, in temperance cultures, alcohol is more likely to be integrated into mixed-sex social settings (such as family meals and cafés), whereas in non-temperance cultures, it is more likely to be a part of male-dominated settings devoted exclusively to drinking (such as taverns). The drinking that occurs in the latter, relatively isolated settings is much more likely to be excessive and lead to alcoholism than that taking place in the more integrated social arenas.

> ### Section Review
>
> - People differ in their hypnotizability, with children being the most hypnotizable.
> - The role-playing explanation maintains that hypnosis is a normal waking state in which suggestible people behave as they think hypnotized people are supposed to behave.

- According to neodissociation theory, hypnosis is an altered state, with the hypnotized person having two streams of consciousness operating at once.
- Meditation may involve an altered state of consciousness, but skeptics claim that it simply leads to relaxation.
- Religious experiences may be precipitated by altered states but also may result from role-playing and shared expectations.
- Depressants induce a relaxed state when taken in low doses but induce sleep when taken in higher doses.
- Stimulants speed up the nervous system and increase mental and physical activity.
- Psychoactive drugs that produce the most profound alterations in consciousness are the hallucinogens.
- Drug abuse occurs when people persist in taking drugs even when impaired behavior or social functioning results.
- The poor and the less educated are more likely to abuse drugs than are people who have more money and education.

Psychological Applications

How Can You Deal with Sleep Disorders?

Problems related to sleep are among the most common psychological disorders, but they are often underdiagnosed and undertreated (Kerr & Jowett, 1994; Mindell, 1999). In the United States alone, approximately 40 million people suffer from some form of chronic sleep problem, accounting for about $50 billion a year in medical costs and lost labor (Holden, 1993). Some of the more common disorders of sleep are *night terrors, sleepwalking, narcolepsy, sleep apnea,* and *insomnia.*

Night Terrors

A type of sleep disorder most common among children between the ages of 3 and 8 is the **night terror,** which is a panic attack that generally occurs during early-night stage 4 NREM sleep (Kahn et al., 1991). Sufferers sit up in bed, let out a terrified scream, stare into space, and talk incoherently, but they seldom wake up, and they recall little or nothing of the event the next morning. It is important to distinguish night terrors from the far more common *nightmares,* which are anxiety-arousing dreams that occur during REM sleep and are as likely to occur in adults as children. It is also important to note that night terrors are not necessarily indicative of emotional disturbance. Although individuals who suffer from night terrors are somewhat more likely to exhibit mood disorders (Ohayon et al., 1999), night terrors may also be caused by an immature nervous system, which would explain why they are far more common among younger children than adults.

night terrors A sleep disorder involving panic attacks that occur during early-night stage 4 NREM sleep.

> When I woke up this morning, my girlfriend asked me, "Did you sleep well?" I said, "No, I made a few mistakes."
>
> —*Steven Wright, American comedian*

This disorder can sometimes be treated with drugs (Stores, 2001).

Sleepwalking

Sleepwalking, also known as *somnambulism,* is a sleep disorder in which a person arises and wanders about while remaining asleep. Like night terrors, sleepwalking occurs during early-night NREM sleep (Keefauver & Guilleminault, 1994). Thus, contrary to popular thinking, sleepwalkers are not acting out a dream. Also contrary to popular belief, it is not dangerous to wake a sleepwalker—although it may be difficult to do so, because they are in deep stage 4 sleep. This disorder is more common among children (10 percent) than adults (2 percent), and more common among boys than girls (Spielman & Herrera, 1991). Drug therapy can reduce sleepwalking, but most children outgrow the problem.

sleepwalking A sleep disorder in which a person arises and wanders about while remaining asleep.

Narcolepsy

A form of sleep disorder that is more serious than the ones discussed thus far is **narcolepsy,** which is characterized by uncontrollable REM sleep attacks during normal waking hours (Vgontzas & Kales, 1999). About 250,000 Americans—one in every thousand—suffer from this disorder. Narcolepsy can strike at any time, even while a person is driving a car or otherwise engaged in activities in which inattentiveness is dangerous and unconsciousness can be fatal. Fortunately, stimulant drugs can usually control the symptoms of this disorder (Godbout et al., 1990; Guilleminault, 1976). The cause of narcolepsy is unknown, but people who have a

narcolepsy A sleep disorder characterized by uncontrollable REM sleep attacks during normal waking hours.

Psychological Applications

family history of the disorder are 50 times more likely to develop it than are others, which suggests an underlying genetic factor. Planned napping can reduce the frequency of narcoleptic episodes, as can the stimulant drug *modafinil* (Silber, 2001).

Sleep Apnea

Another disorder with a possible hereditary cause is **sleep apnea,** in which sleeping individuals briefly stop breathing several times an hour, interrupting their sleep without their knowledge (Lavie, 2003). About 12 million Americans suffer from this disorder, with overweight men older than 40 the most common victims (Ingbar & Gee, 1985). Apnea sufferers report daytime sleepiness, morning headaches, and even occasional heart and lung problems. The loss of sleep experienced by apnea sufferers has been shown to affect their waking reaction time, making them as slow to respond as someone who is legally intoxicated (Kayumov et al., 2000; Ulfberg et al., 2000). Apnea may be treated by a number of methods, including weight loss, changing sleeping positions, using a nasal mask to increase air intake, hormone therapy, and even surgery to open constricted airways (Davies & Stradling, 2000).

> **sleep apnea** A sleep disorder in which a person repeatedly stops breathing during sleep.

Daily hassles and stress often create sleep difficulties. What recommendations do sleep experts make for getting a good night's rest?

Source: Courtesy of Figzoi.

Insomnia

The most common sleep disorder is **insomnia,** which is the chronic inability to fall or stay asleep (Zorick, 1989). Approximately 30 percent of adults complain of insomnia to some degree, and it is a recurring problem for about 15 percent of the population (Gillin, 1993; Mellinger et al., 1985). The elderly and women are more likely to suffer from insomnia than are the young and men (Kaeppler & Hohagen, 2003). Some of the more common causes of this disorder are daily hassles and life stress, physical illness or discomfort, depression, jet lag, shifting work schedules, and drug abuse (Morin et al., 2003). Although many insomniacs rely on sleeping pills and alcohol to alleviate insomnia, both of these remedies reduce REM sleep and can cause lowered moods the next day (Pagel, 1994). Instead, sleep experts suggest the following guidelines for getting a good night's sleep (Edinger et al., 2001; Landolt et al., 1995; Morin et al., 1999):

> **insomnia** A common sleep disorder characterized by the chronic inability to fall or stay asleep.

1. Establish a solid circadian rhythm by going to bed and getting up on a regular schedule. Don't try to catch up by sleeping longer on the weekends.
2. Do not take naps during the day, especially after a bad night's sleep.
3. Relax before going to bed, and get into the habit of setting up presleep rituals such as soft music or a warm bath. A warm bath is not only relaxing, but also promotes deep sleep by raising your core body temperature.
4. Greatly reduce or totally eliminate the use of coffee, tea, or other sources of caffeine during the entire day because caffeine affects sleep. Also avoid alcohol, nicotine, and chocolate in the late afternoon and evening. Instead, drink a glass of milk before retiring, because it contains the sleep-inducing amino acid *tryptophan.*
5. Being very hungry or very full prior to retiring will disrupt sleep. Eating a light snack before going to bed will reduce nighttime restlessness and increase sleep time.
6. Regular exercise promotes slow-wave sleep, but do not exercise within 3 hours of bedtime, because exercise's arousing effect can delay sleep.
7. Condition yourself so that you associate your bed with sleeping. Thus, don't use your bed for anything but sleep and sex.
8. If you're still awake but relaxed after about 20 minutes, stay in bed. If you're anxious, get out of bed and do something relaxing, such as listening to soothing music or reading. Return when you feel sleepy. Still maintain your regular waking time.

Key Terms

activation-synthesis theory (p. 217)

alcoholism (p. 226)

alpha waves (p. 210)

altered state of consciousness (p. 218)

beta waves (p. 210)

circadian rhythms (p. 207)

consciousness (p. 203)

daydreaming (p. 205)

delta waves (p. 210)

depressants (p. 226)

divided attention (p. 204)

dream (p. 213)

drug abuse (p. 224)

drug tolerance (p. 225)

fantasy-prone personality (p. 206)

hallucinogens (p. 230)

hypnogogic state (p. 210)

hypnosis (p. 219)

hypnotizability (p. 220)

insomnia (p. 235)

latent content (p. 216)

LSD (p. 230)

lucid dream (p. 215)

manifest content (p. 216)

marijuana (p. 231)

meditation (p. 222)

narcolepsy (p. 234)

near-death experience (p. 223)

neodissociation theory (p. 221)

night terrors (p. 234)

off-line dream theory (p. 216)

opiates (p. 227)

problem-solving theory (p. 216)

psychoactive drugs (p. 224)

REM (rapid eye movement) sleep (p. 211)

sedatives (p. 227)

selective attention (p. 203)

sleep (p. 207)

sleep apnea (p. 235)

sleep spindles (p. 210)

sleepwalking (p. 234)

stimulant-induced psychosis (p. 229)

stimulants (p. 227)

THC (p. 231)

theta waves (p. 210)

Suggested Websites

Center for Consciousness Studies

http://consciousness.arizona.edu

This website for the Center for Consciousness Studies at the University of Arizona offers online papers on consciousness as well as information about conferences, bibliographical references, and related websites.

National Institute on Drug Abuse

http://www.nida.nih.gov

This website provides valuable information and national statistics on drug use and related web links.

Sleepnet.com™

http://www.sleepnet.com

This website provides information about the psychology and physiology of sleep, including sleep disorders, dreams, and the addresses of sleep labs around the country.

Working (and Playing) with Dreams

http://www.rider.edu/users/suler/dreams.html

This website offers information on various theories and methods of dream interpretation.

Review Questions

Note: You can find the correct answers to these questions by taking the quiz and then submitting your answers in the Online Edition. The program will automatically score your submission. If you miss a question, the program will provide the correct answer, a rationale for the answer, and the section number in the chapter where the topic is discussed.

1. The study of circadian rhythms
   a. indicates that humans drift toward a 25-hour cycle.
   b. used natural light.
   c. provides a valuable lesson in the way the scientific method is self-correcting.
   d. discovered how to relieve insomnia.
   e. none of the above

2. Which of the following statements is *true* about stages of sleep?
   a. You spend half your night at stage 1.
   b. It is difficult to arouse a person from sleep during stage 4.
   c. You go through only one sleep cycle a night.
   d. The first four stages make up REM sleep.
   e. Alpha waves are associated with an active, alert state of mind.

3. Which of the following statements describes a theory in this chapter about why we sleep?
   a. Sleep occurs due to the activation of the hippocampus in the brain.
   b. Sleep allows the body to restore itself.
   c. Children aged 2 to 5 years who fail to get sufficient sleep at night or during naps have greater behavior problems than do other children their age.
   d. all of the above
   e. *a* and *c*

4. Which of the following is *true* regarding differences in sleep patterns?
   a. North Americans sleep about 20 percent more than they did a hundred years ago.
   b. About 50 percent of people are "night persons."
   c. Older people generally require more sleep than others.
   d. Different sleep patterns appear to be related to differences in circadian body temperatures.
   e. People who live in cultures without electricity tend to sleep less than those in industrialized cultures.

5. Which of the following statements is *true* of dreaming?
   a. Dreams occur only during REM sleep.
   b. You cannot respond to external cues while dreaming.
   c. REM sleep does not appear to be important.
   d. All animals have REM sleep.
   e. In humans, REM sleep is greatest early in life.

6. In the student's "fish" dream, the latent content would be
   a. the struggle with the fish.
   b. the old woman.
   c. the lake.
   d. letting the fish go.
   e. none of the above

7. Which dream theory proposes that dreams have no particular significance other than that they are by-products of brain activity?
   a. off-line dream
   b. problem-solving
   c. psychoanalytic
   d. activation-synthesis
   e. none of the above

8. Which of the following statements is *true* of hypnosis?
   a. Brain wave activity under hypnosis is radically different than during normal waking states.
   b. Hypnosis compels people to avoid deception.
   c. Everyone is hypnotizable.
   d. A hypnotized person tends to uncritically accept hallucinated experiences suggested by the hypnotist.
   e. Hypnotized people can be forced to violate their moral values.

9. Research on meditation has found
   a. high-amplitude alpha waves in accomplished meditators while meditating.
   b. that meditation is useful in promoting relaxation.
   c. that meditation reduces physiological arousal.
   d. a reduction in oxygen consumption, slower heart rate, and increased blood flow in the arms and forehead during meditation.
   e. all of the above

10. Which of the following is *not* true regarding research findings conducted on college campuses and binge drinking?
    a. Fraternities and sororities are among those groups most likely to foster binge drinking.
    b. African Americans are more likely to binge-drink than Caucasians.
    c. Binge drinking is defined as five or more drinks in one sitting.
    d. Almost 50 percent of men and 40 percent of women are classified as binge drinkers.
    e. All of the above are true.

11. The most widely consumed and abused depressant in the world is
    a. opium.
    b. alcohol.
    c. morphine.
    d. heroin.
    e. caffeine.

12. Which of the following is *true* about the effects of stimulants?
    a. They are addictive only in large quantities.
    b. Large doses of caffeine paradoxically can make you feel calm.
    c. Nicotine increases blood flow to the skin.
    d. Habitual amphetamine and cocaine users often develop stimulant-induced psychosis, similar to schizophrenia.
    e. Ecstasy, or MDMA, can improve the body's ability to control its temperature.

13. Which of the following statements is *true*?
    a. There are no naturally occurring hallucinogens.
    b. LSD creates physical dependence after prolonged use.
    c. Forty-seven percent of American adults have tried marijuana at least once.
    d. Marijuana does not appear to have any negative effects when used in high quantities.
    e. All drug users become addicted.

14. The poor and uneducated may be more likely to abuse various drugs because
    a. they experience higher levels of stress due to their socioeconomic status.
    b. they have less access to medical care for physical and psychological problems.
    c. drug abuse is more of a culturally accepted norm among these groups.
    d. *a* and *b*
    e. none of the above

15. Sleep disorders
    a. are among the most common psychological disorders.
    b. do not occur in children under age 5.
    c. occur only during NREM sleep.
    d. *a* and *b*
    e. none of the above

16. Which of the following guidelines is recommended for getting a good night's sleep?
    a. Take a nap during the day to catch up after a bad night's sleep.
    b. Drink an alcoholic beverage in the evening.
    c. Eat a chocolate bar before going to bed.
    d. Exercise a couple of hours before bedtime to wear yourself down.
    e. Drink a glass of milk before bedtime.

Chapter 7

Learning

Source: © Richard Cummins/CORBIS.

Dear Frederic,

Your very interesting letter has been read and discussed by mother and me. We naturally are deeply interested in your future. . . . In no circumstances would we want to say or do anything to discourage you in following out your ambition. . . .

On the other hand, we want to give you the benefit of our observation and experience. You will find that the world is not standing with outstretched arms to greet you just because you are emerging from a college—that the real rough and tumble world is not the world pictured by college professors who are constantly dealing with the theoretical and not the practical affairs of life. I am yet to be convinced that it is possible for you to make a living as a writer of fiction.

. . . Let's go slow and sure. . . . Let us arrange some plan whereby you can support yourself, get married when the fever strikes you, have a good home life, and when these things are provided for then go to it and if your talents enable you to do something big and startle the world no one of course will rejoice more than your mother and I who have our whole life centered in you and your success.

With love,
Father

What do you want to do when *you* graduate? Fred wanted to be a famous writer. Following this letter from his father, Fred spent a year after college working on his writing skills. He even submitted samples of his writing to the poet Robert Frost, asking whether he should persevere in his chosen profession. Frost replied that the young man had twice as much talent as anyone else he had read that year, but that only Fred himself could know whether his future lay in writing. At the end of this year-long odyssey, which he later called his "dark year," Fred was frustrated with writing and began casting about in search of an alternative career path. But what path should he choose?

The year was 1927. In his searching, Fred read psychologist John Watson's (1924) recently published book, *Behaviorism*. Watson presented a perspective on learning and the future of the young science of psychology that was novel for the time, in that he focused not on people's internal states and unconscious drives but on the outward behavior that people exhibit. Fred had always been interested in observing the behavior of people, a useful talent for a writer, and this approach to the human condition appealed to him. He applied and was accepted to Harvard University for graduate studies in psychology, where his own personal journey of discovery quickly became wedded to psychology's scientific discovery journey.

Although Fred never "startled the world" with his fiction writing, his subsequent extensions and refinements of Watson's behaviorism rocked the field of psychology and made Fred one of the best-known psychologists of all time. Outside his circle of family and friends, people knew and referred to Fred by his formal name, Burrhus Frederick ("B. F.") Skinner. Throughout his career, Skinner looked for ways in which his operant conditioning principles of learning (discussed in section 7-2) could be used to improve daily life (Vargas, 2003).

In this segment of our journey of discovery, we will focus our attention on the psychology of **learning,** which psychologists define as a relatively permanent change in behavior that results from experience. Learning can occur in a variety of ways, but we will review three basic learning perspectives: *classical conditioning, operant conditioning,* and *observational learning.* Classical conditioning is a type of learning in which one stimulus comes to serve as a signal for the occurrence of a second stimulus. Operant conditioning, the name for the type of conditioning Skinner investigated, is a form of learning in which we discover the consequences of behavior. Finally, observational learning deals with how we learn by observing the behaviors—and the behavioral consequences—of those around us.

B. F. Skinner, 1904–1990
Source: © Bettmann/CORBIS.

learning A relatively permanent change in behavior that results from experience.

Learning is a treasure that will follow its owner everywhere.
—*Chinese proverb*

7-1 | CLASSICAL CONDITIONING

Preview

- *How do you anticipate events through classical conditioning?*
- *How does a neutral stimulus become a conditioned stimulus?*
- *Are conditioned responses immediately learned?*
- *What is higher-order conditioning?*
- *What are stimulus generalization and stimulus discrimination?*
- *Can some responses be conditioned more easily than others?*

In science, as in other areas of life, researchers sometimes need time to realize that they have discovered a new scientific principle. Would you believe that one discovery that profoundly shaped the course of psychology was initially only viewed as an annoyance?

7-1a Pavlov Stumbled upon Classical Conditioning

In 1904, the Russian physiologist Ivan Pavlov (1849–1936) won the Nobel Prize for his research on digestion in dogs (Marks, 2004; Pavlov, 1897/1997). In conducting his studies, Pavlov placed meat powder on a dog's tongue to elicit reflexive salivation. One thing he noticed was that, over time, dogs began salivating before any food reached their mouths and even before they smelled the food. For example, they might salivate simply by seeing the food dish or by merely hearing the feeder's approaching footsteps. At first, Pavlov considered this phenomenon, which he called "conditional responses," an irritating development in his research because he could no longer control the beginning of the dog's salivation. However, this annoyance turned into excitement when he realized that he had stumbled upon a simple but important form of learning, which came to be known as classical conditioning (Todes, 1997).

Classical conditioning is a type of learning in which a neutral stimulus acquires the capacity to elicit a response after being paired with another stimulus that naturally elicits that response (Miller & Grace, 2003). In his experiments investigating classical conditioning, Pavlov placed a hungry dog in an apparatus similar to the one depicted in figure 7-1. Just before injecting meat powder into the dog's mouth, Pavlov presented an initially neutral stimulus to the dog, such as the ticking of a metronome.[1] At first, this ticking produced no response in the dog. However, the food powder presented right after the ticking sound

Ivan Pavlov, 1849–1936

classical conditioning
A type of learning in which a neutral stimulus acquires the capacity to elicit a response after being paired with another stimulus that naturally elicits that response.

Figure 7-1

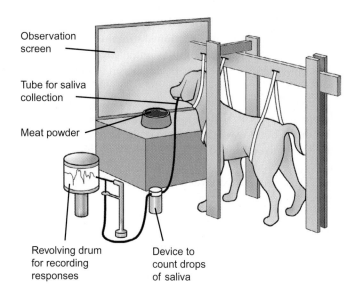

Observation screen

Tube for saliva collection

Meat powder

Revolving drum for recording responses

Device to count drops of saliva

Pavlov's Apparatus for Studying Classical Conditioning in Dogs

Pavlov used a device similar to this in his experiments in classical conditioning. He restrained the dog in a harness and attached a tube to its salivary gland in order to accurately measure its salivation response. A ticking metronome often served as the conditioned stimulus (CS), and the meat powder was the unconditioned stimulus (UCS). In classical conditioning terms, what type of response did the salivation represent when it occurred due to the presentation of the meat powder? What type of response did the saliva represent when it was triggered by the metronome?

---

[1]One of the mistaken "facts" often reported in psychology textbooks is that Pavlov conditioned his dogs with the sound of a bell or a tuning fork. In reality, his early experiments, which formed the basis for the theory of classical conditioning, used a metronome (Hock, 1992, p. 68).

Figure 7-2

Classical Conditioning

Before classical conditioning, the neutral stimulus of the ticking metronome presented just before the unconditioned stimulus of the meat powder does not trigger salivation. Instead, the unconditioned response of salivation occurs only when the unconditioned stimulus is presented. However, during conditioning, through repeated pairings of the neutral stimulus and the unconditioned stimulus, the neutral stimulus becomes a conditioned stimulus. Now this conditioned stimulus produces a conditioned response.

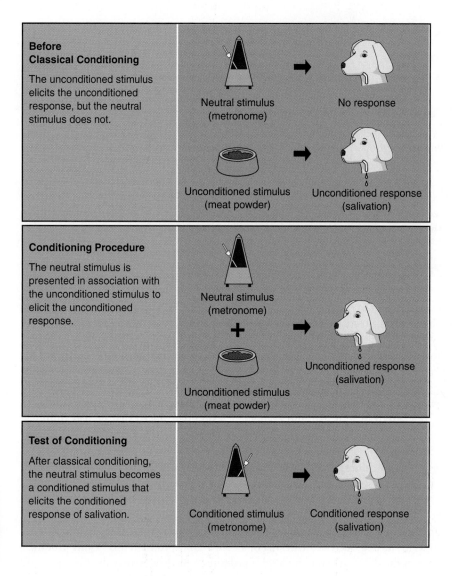

Before Classical Conditioning

The unconditioned stimulus elicits the unconditioned response, but the neutral stimulus does not.

Neutral stimulus (metronome) → No response

Unconditioned stimulus (meat powder) → Unconditioned response (salivation)

Conditioning Procedure

The neutral stimulus is presented in association with the unconditioned stimulus to elicit the unconditioned response.

Neutral stimulus (metronome) + Unconditioned stimulus (meat powder) → Unconditioned response (salivation)

Test of Conditioning

After classical conditioning, the neutral stimulus becomes a conditioned stimulus that elicits the conditioned response of salivation.

Conditioned stimulus (metronome) → Conditioned response (salivation)

unconditioned response (UCR) In classical conditioning, the unlearned, automatic response to an unconditioned stimulus.

unconditioned stimulus (UCS) In classical conditioning, a stimulus that naturally and automatically elicits an unconditioned response.

conditioned response (CR) In classical conditioning, the learned response to a previously neutral conditioned stimulus.

conditioned stimulus (CS) In classical conditioning, a previously neutral stimulus that, after repeated pairings with an unconditioned stimulus, comes to elicit a conditioned response.

naturally triggered the dog's salivary reflex. Because this act of drooling was unlearned, Pavlov called it an **unconditioned response (UCR),** and he called the food that elicited this automatic response an **unconditioned stimulus (UCS).**

Although the neutral stimulus initially had no effect on the dog, after several pairings of metronome and food, the dog began to salivate in response to the ticking alone. The dog had learned to associate the ticking with the presentation of the food powder (see figure 7-2). This learned response was called the **conditioned response (CR),** and the previously neutral stimulus that now triggered the CR was called the **conditioned stimulus (CS).** One way to remember the difference between stimuli and responses that are either unconditioned or conditioned is to think of these two terms in the following manner: *un*conditioned = *un*learned; conditioned = learned. Before moving on to section 7-1b, complete Explore It Exercise 7-1, which provides you an opportunity to experience classical conditioning yourself.

Classical conditioning may not be what you think of as learning. For instance, you are not using classical conditioning principles to understand the important points in this chapter. The type of learning that goes on in classical conditioning is often considered unintentional and automatic—that is, you do not usually set out to learn an association, and you do not usually consciously elicit the conditioned response (Lipp et al., 2003). Neither your pleasure (CR) upon seeing a good friend (CS) nor your anxiety (CR) upon hearing a dentist's drill (CS) is an intentionally learned response. They develop with no apparent effort on your part, because both your friend's image and the drill noise have become associated

Source: Courtesy of Figzoi.

To experience an example of classical conditioning, try a variation of the demonstration from chapter 5 involving pupillary response to light (see section 5-2b). As you recall, when you turned out the light in your room for 30 seconds and then flicked it back on while gazing into a mirror, your pupils had become much larger in response to the lack of light. This is an example of an unconditioned response. Now do the same demonstration, but just before turning out the light, ring a bell. Repeat the pairing of the neutral stimulus (the bell) with the unconditioned stimulus (the darkness) at least 20 times. Then, with the lights on, ring the bell while watching your eyes closely in the mirror. You should see your eyes dilate slightly, even though the unconditioned stimulus is not present. The previously neutral bell sound has become the conditioned stimulus, and your resulting pupil dilation is the conditioned response. Now you can truly say that classical conditioning does indeed ring a bell!

You can also classically condition your own eye-blinking. As you may already know, a puff of air directed at your eye is an unconditioned stimulus that causes the reflexive unconditioned response of eye-blinking. If you flash a light just before each puff of air, the light will soon become a conditioned stimulus that will cause eye-blinking on its own (Lavond & Steinmetz, 2003). Following hundreds of studies investigating human and mice classical eye-blink conditioning, scientists have discovered that the hippocampus in the brain is involved in the development of this conditioned response (Green & Woodruff-Pak, 2000; Grillon et al., 2004). They have also discovered that this same brain structure is damaged in the early stages of Alzheimer's disease and in the brain disorder known as *autism* (Sears et al., 1994; Steinmetz, 1999). This knowledge is now being used to help diagnose autism and to identify individuals who might be at high risk for Alzheimer's disease. Early diagnosis of such serious medical disorders allows for more effective treatment that, in the case of Alzheimer's disease, can delay onset of the disease.

with other stimuli that naturally evoke pleasure or pain. Similar effortless learning permeates our lives and profoundly affects our everyday behavior, but we often do not notice it because it is so automatic. Yet is that all there is to classical conditioning?

7-1b Classical Conditioning Is a Means by Which Animals Learn to Predict Events

Although Pavlov asserted that classical conditioning was an essentially "mindless" process, most contemporary learning theorists believe it often involves quite a bit of "mindfulness," because through the conditioning process, humans and other animals are learning to reliably predict upcoming events (Escobar & Miller, 2004; Timberlake, 2004). First proposed by Robert Rescorla and Allan Wagner (1972), this general rule of classical conditioning states that a previously neutral stimulus will lead to a conditioned response whenever it provided the organism with *information* about the upcoming unconditioned stimulus. In other words, classical conditioning is a process by which organisms learn to expect the unconditioned stimulus based on the presentation of the conditioned stimulus. For example, in the original Pavlovian conditioning studies, if a metronome always ticked (CS) just before the presentation of food (UCS), the dog later began salivating (CR) whenever the metronome ticked (CS). Conditioning occurred because the ticking provided the dog with the information that food would soon be delivered (Rescorla, 1992). The conditioned stimulus became a *signal* that the unconditioned stimulus would soon appear. Similarly, whenever our dog Maizy hears the rustling of her food bag in our utility room, she becomes excited, because she has learned that this sound predicts the appearance of food in her bowl.

This idea that classical conditioning involves a learning process by which humans and other animals acquire conditioned responses when one event reliably predicts, or *signals*, the appearance of another event greatly expands upon Pavlov's initial understanding of this type of learning. Instead of simply explaining basic, reflexlike responses, this revised conception of classical conditioning assumes that it often involves predicting the likely occurrence or nonoccurrence of future events (Domjan, 2005).

Acquisition

The learned ability to predict what events might follow other events certainly helps an individual survive in its environment. Yet how quickly and in what manner does the **acquisition,** or initial learning, of a conditioned response occur? Pavlov discovered that conditioned responses seldom occur at full strength right away (a phenomenon known as *one-trial learning*) but, rather, gradually build up over a series of trials. Based on this finding, psychologists initially believed that the key to acquiring a conditioned response was the sheer *number* of CS-UCS pairings. However, subsequent research in other laboratories indicated that the *order* and *timing* of the CS-UCS pairings are also very important, because they provide the animal with valuable information about the upcoming occurrence of the unconditioned stimulus (Buhusi & Schmajuk, 1999; Wasserman & Miller, 1997).

Regarding order of presentation, learning seldom occurs when the CS comes after the UCS (*backward conditioning*) or at the same time as the UCS (*simultaneous conditioning*). Instead, conditioning generally occurs only when the CS comes before the UCS (*forward conditioning*). This finding is consistent with the hypothesis that classical conditioning is biologically adaptive because it prepares the organism for good or bad events in the immediate future. As mentioned, the CS becomes a signal that a UCS is about to be presented. Prior to conditioning, the organism's response is dictated by the UCS appearing. However, after conditioning, the organism responds more quickly because it is now reacting to the earlier-occurring CS, not to the later-occurring UCS. These quicker conditioned responses often spell the difference between life and death. For example, as depicted in figure 7-3, classical conditioning can help an animal react swiftly to a predator's impending attack. Animals having prior experience with predators are more likely to quickly respond when stimuli associated with the predator (its sight, sound, or smell, for instance) are presented. Through experience, the animals that have been conditioned to respond to stimuli preceding the UCS are most likely to survive. Can you think of instances in your own life when conditioned responses may foster your survival?

Besides presentation order, in most cases the UCS must follow the CS closely in time. In animal research, the most efficient CS-UCS interval is between 0.2 and 2 seconds. If the interval is longer, the CR is more difficult to establish, because animals have difficulty recognizing it as a signal for the appearance of the UCS.

In addition to the presentation order and timing of the CS-UCS pairings, the *accuracy* with which the CS can predict the appearance of the UCS also determines whether a conditioned response is formed. If the UCS reliably follows the CS but also occurs when the CS is not present, a conditioned response is unlikely to develop. For example, in one experiment (Rescorla, 1968), rats were presented with a tone (CS), followed by a mild electric shock (UCS) that caused them to jump (UCR). In one condition, the shock was given only after the tone. Very quickly, these rats began displaying a fear response—freezing (CR)—after hearing the tone. In another condition, however, the shock was given both after the tone and

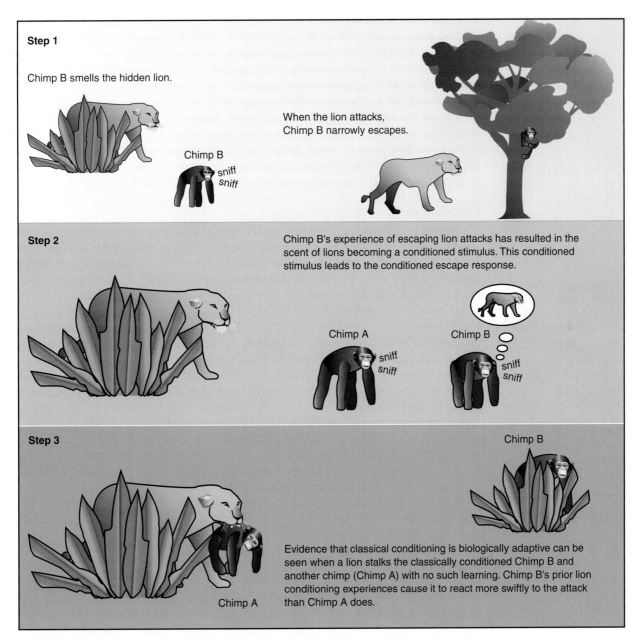

Figure 7-3

Avoiding a Predator's Attack through Classical Conditioning

As a learning technique, classical conditioning is biologically adaptive because it prepares the animal for good or bad events in the immediate future. Such prior conditioning helps animals respond more quickly to events. For example, when reacting to a lion attack, chimp B's prior experiences with lions provided it with a quicker response than that of chimp A.

during times when the tone had not been presented. These rats displayed little, if any, freezing in anticipation of the coming shock. Why do you think this group of rats did not become conditioned to the tone? No conditioning occurred because their ability to prepare for the UCS could not be accurately predicted by the sound of the tone. In other words, the tone was a poor signal of the coming shock, and thus the rats did not use it to predict the appearance of the shock. These findings are consistent with the previously stated rule that a stimulus will become "conditioned" whenever it signals to the organism that an unconditioned stimulus is about to occur.

Once a particular stimulus is recognized as a poor signal for an upcoming event, an animal can have difficulty learning a new association between the two stimuli. In a study similar to the one just discussed, researchers first presented tones and shocks to rats in a random order, so that the tone did not serve as a signal of an upcoming shock (Nakajima et al., 2000). Then the researchers changed the order of presentation so that a shock always followed the tone. Because the tone was now a signal, wouldn't you expect the rats to learn the association and freeze when they heard the tone? Interestingly, they did not. Having once learned that the tone provided no information, the animals had difficulty later detecting a real association, a phenomenon called *general learned irrelevance* (Linden et al., 1997).

Overall, research on the acquisition of conditioned responses tells us that organisms are not passive in this process. They actively seek information in their environment to establish when certain events (CS) predict the occurrence of other events (UCS).

Extinction and Spontaneous Recovery

extinction In classical conditioning, the gradual weakening and disappearance of the conditioned response when the conditioned stimulus is repeatedly presented without being paired with the unconditioned stimulus.

The general rule of classical conditioning states that a CS develops whenever it provides the organism with information about the impending occurrence of the UCS. If this is true, what do you think happens when the CS no longer provides accurate information about the appearance of the UCS? In other words, what happens when the CS occurs repeatedly without the UCS? The answer is **extinction,** which is the gradual weakening and disappearance of the conditioned response. In Pavlov's experiments, when the ticking metronome (CS) was repeatedly presented to the dog without the delivery of food (UCS), the metronome gradually lost its ability to elicit salivation (CR). In cognitive terms, the dog learned that the CS was no longer useful in predicting the UCS (Lovibond, 2004).

Can we use the principle of extinction in treating specific social problems? Consider the abuse of cocaine, a stimulant drug (UCS) that naturally induces a sense of euphoria (UCR) in users (see chapter 6, section 6-3g). Research indicates that one of the problems recovering drug users must overcome is the familiar reminder associated with their addiction. Anything that has been repeatedly associated with their past drug use—such as certain locations, smells, or objects—becomes a conditioned stimulus that can elicit a craving for the drug (Bonson et al., 2002). Because drug addicts use money to obtain cocaine, in one treatment program researchers attempted to weaken the conditioned link between money and cocaine-induced euphoria by asking addicts to engage in one of two activities under the guise of a "budgetary task" (Hamilton et al., 1997). One group of addicts was given $500 in cash to hold in their hands as they explained how they would spend it, while the other group was asked to merely imagine that they had the money. Those addicts who held the actual cash initially reported a stronger craving for cocaine after handling the money than did the group who imagined the money. However, repeated exposure to the cash without it being associated with cocaine use gradually reduced drug craving, as would be expected due to extinction. These results suggest that applying the principle of extinction in drug treatment programs can enhance their effectiveness.

spontaneous recovery The reappearance of an extinguished response after a period of nonexposure to the conditioned stimulus.

Although you undoubtedly remember instances when conditioned responses have become extinct in your own life, have you also noticed that occasionally a response that you thought was extinguished long ago reappears spontaneously when you happen to encounter the conditioned stimulus? This phenomenon, known as **spontaneous recovery,** is the reappearance of an extinguished response after a period of nonexposure to the conditioned stimulus. For example, former soldiers who long ago overcame the panic attacks they experienced during combat may reexperience acute anxiety while viewing a movie containing graphic war scenes. The practical importance of spontaneous recovery is that, even if you succeed in ridding yourself of a conditioned response, it may surprise you by reappearing later.

stimulus generalization In classical conditioning, the tendency for a conditioned response to be elicited by stimuli similar to the conditioned stimulus.

7-1c Following Acquisition, Other Stimuli Can Produce the Conditioned Response

One observation Pavlov made while conditioning his dogs to salivate was that salivation triggered by the conditioned stimulus often generalized to other, similar stimuli. Pavlov called this phenomenon **stimulus generalization.** Such generalization often fosters an organism's survival, as when a bird that becomes sick after eating a poisonous monarch butterfly avoids eating other orange and black insects. This reaction makes good adaptive sense: Things that look, taste, feel, or sound the same often share other important characteristics. The more similar new stimuli are to the original conditioned stimulus, the greater the likelihood of generalization (Balsam, 1988). Stimulus generalization may explain why you sometimes respond very warmly or coldly to strangers who look like people for whom you previously developed either positive or negative conditioned responses. In such instances, you may not realize that your emotional response is caused by the power of stimulus generalization, but it nonetheless has an impact on your social life.

While performing their conditioning studies, Pavlov and his coworkers also noticed that the dogs sometimes did not exhibit a conditioned response when presented with stimuli that were somewhat similar to the conditioned stimulus. When an animal gives a conditioned response to the conditioned stimulus but not to stimuli that are similar to it, the opposite of stimulus generalization occurs—namely, **stimulus discrimination.** Like generalization, discrimination has survival value because slightly different stimuli can have very different consequences (Thomas, 1992).

The Famous "Little Albert B."

The best-known study of stimulus generalization was conducted in 1920 by John Watson, the founder of behaviorism (see chapter 1, section 1-2d), and his colleague, Rosalie Rayner. Their subject was an 8-month-old orphan boy whom they identified as "Little Albert B." During initial testing, Watson and Rayner presented Albert with a white rat, a rabbit, a monkey, a dog, masks with and without hair, and some white cotton wool. The boy reacted with interest but no fear. Two months later, while Albert sat on a mattress placed on a table, the researchers presented him with the white rat. Just as Albert touched the rat, however, Watson made a loud noise behind Albert by striking a 4-foot steel bar with a hammer. This noise (the UCS) startled and frightened (the UCR) the toddler. During two sessions, spaced 1 week apart, this procedure was repeated a total of seven times. Each time, the pairing of the rat and the noise resulted in a fear response.

Next, the rat alone was presented to Albert, without the noise. As I'm sure you've guessed, he reacted to the rat (the CS) with extreme fear (the CR): He cried, turned away, rolled over on one side away from the rat, and began crawling away so fast that he almost went over the edge of the table before the researchers caught hold of him! Five days later, Albert showed stimulus generalization to a white rabbit:

> Negative responses began at once. He leaned as far away from the animal as possible, whimpered, then burst into tears. When the rabbit was placed in contact with him, he buried his face in the mattress, then got up on all fours and crawled away, crying as he went. (Watson & Rayner, 1920, p. 6)

Besides the rabbit, Albert's fear response generalized to a dog, a white fur coat, Watson's own head of gray hair, and even a Santa Claus mask! These fear responses also occurred outside the room in which the conditioned response had initially been learned. Two months later, just prior to being adopted, Albert was tested one last time and again expressed considerable fear toward the same objects.

For the most part, our natural tendency is to generalize, and we need experience to teach us to discriminate. This greater tendency to generalize explains why Albert reacted to the other furry objects in the same way he had been conditioned to react to the white rat. If he had somehow been encouraged to directly experience the fact that the unconditioned stimulus did not follow the presentation of these other objects, he would have developed stimulus discrimination.

In addition to demonstrating how a fear response can generalize to other objects, an equally important reason this study is still widely discussed today concerns the serious ethical issues it raises. Essentially, Watson and Rayner induced a phobia in Albert (see section 7-1d), a practice that would not be tolerated by current ethical standards of psychological research. Further, the researchers made no attempt to recondition their young subject,

stimulus discrimination
In classical conditioning, the tendency for a conditioned response not to be elicited by stimuli similar to the conditioned stimulus.

John Watson and Rosalie Rayner classically conditioned Little Albert B. to fear white rats. Due to stimulus generalization, he also became fearful of other furry-looking objects. How does this research provide insight into the development of phobias? What are the ethical concerns raised by this study?

Source: Courtesy of Dr. Ben Harris.

despite knowing a month in advance that Albert's adoptive mother would be leaving the area with him. Later attempts to locate Albert to determine the long-lasting effects of his experience failed (Harris, 2002), and as far as anyone knows, no reconditioning ever took place.

> **Journey of Discovery Question**
>
> Every year, thousands of drug users die from overdoses. Those who have narrowly survived such overdoses tend to report that the setting in which they took too much of the drug was different from their normal drug-taking environment (Siegel, 1984). How might classical conditioning principles explain why these different settings were more likely to be associated with drug overdoses?

Higher-Order Conditioning

higher-order conditioning
A classical conditioning procedure in which a neutral stimulus becomes a conditioned stimulus after being paired with an existing conditioned stimulus.

Beyond discovering the principles of stimulus generalization and stimulus discrimination, Pavlov (1927) also learned that a conditioned stimulus can condition another neutral stimulus. This procedure is known as **higher-order conditioning** (or *second-order conditioning*), and it greatly increases the number of situations in which classical conditioning explains behavior. For example, do you know people who become so anxious upon entering a classroom to take an exam that their ability to concentrate is affected? Such anxiety is often due to higher-order conditioning. Early in their schooling, academic performance may have been a neutral event for these people. However, somehow it became associated with criticism (the UCS) from parents or teachers, which elicited anxiety (the UCR). Through conditioning, then, academic performance (the CS) acquired the ability to trigger a stress response (the CR). As these people continued taking exams, this conditioned stimulus began functioning like a UCS through higher-order conditioning. That is, the kinds of neutral stimuli that immediately precede test-taking—such as walking into a testing room or hearing test booklets being passed out—became conditioned stimuli that also elicited test anxiety. The "Psychological Applications" section in chapter 11 discusses how to break this unpleasant kind of higher-order conditioning.

Fortunately, higher-order conditioning is equally effective at eliciting pleasant responses as it is at eliciting negative ones. For example, your cologne may spark romantic feelings in those who associate that fragrance with past loves. Likewise, complete strangers may respond warmly upon discovering that you are from their hometown. In both instances, a previously neutral stimulus (you) becomes a conditioned stimulus after being paired with an existing conditioned stimulus (cologne and hometown). As you can see, higher-order conditioning has a role in shaping a variety of advantageous—and disadvantageous—responses. With this knowledge, are you developing a greater appreciation—perhaps, even affection—for classical conditioning principles?

7-1d Animals Differ in What Responses Can Be Classically Conditioned

Pavlov and other early learning theorists assumed that the principles of conditioning were similar across all species, and thus, that psychologists could just as easily study rats and pigeons as people. They further assumed that associations could be conditioned between any stimulus an organism could perceive and any response it could make. However, research conducted during the past 35 years indicates that neither of these assumptions is correct. Not only do animals often differ in what responses can be conditioned, but in addition, some responses can be conditioned much more readily to certain stimuli than to others. The essential insight gained from this research is that an animal's biology steers it toward certain kinds of conditioning that enhance its survival (Hollis, 1997).

Taste Aversion

One of the most dramatic examples of a behavior being more easily conditioned by certain stimuli than by others is *taste aversion*. If you have ever experienced food poisoning, you are undoubtedly familiar with this concept. When you consumed the food that ultimately made you sick, there were probably many things going on around you besides the taste of that food. But if you are like most people, the lesson you learned was to avoid whatever food you had eaten, and not (for example) the people you were talking to or the show you were watching on TV. Why is this so? Let us consider the results of an animal study that helped us better understand this behavior.

In a classic study of taste aversion in rats, John Garcia and Robert Koelling (1966) allowed two groups of thirsty rats to drink flavored water from a device that produced a light flash and a loud click whenever they drank. Thus, both rat groups simultaneously experienced a taste, a light, and a noise. While they were drinking, the two groups also received a UCS: Group A received electrical shocks to their feet that immediately produced pain, while Group B received radiation in X rays that made them nauseous about 1 hour later. According to traditional classical conditioning principles, a conditioned response occurs only if the unconditioned stimulus follows the conditioned stimulus within a very short interval. Based on this knowledge, wouldn't you predict that Group A should learn to avoid the flavored water, the light, and the sound because all three sensations immediately preceded their literally shocking UCS? Wouldn't you also predict that Group B shouldn't learn to avoid any of these same sensations because the effects of their UCS—the radiation—were not felt until much later?

As you can see from figure 7-4, what actually happened was something very different. Garcia and Koelling found that the rats exposed to the immediately painful shocks (Group A) learned to avoid the light and noise, but not the flavored water. In contrast, rats exposed to the delayed nausea of the radiation (Group B) learned to avoid the flavored water but not the light and noise. If you were the researchers, how would you explain these findings? Why would the rats have been conditioned to associate the shocks with the light and noise but not with the flavored water? Why would nausea become associated with *any* stimulus that preceded it so far in advance? And why did the rats learn to associate the nausea with the flavored water but not with the light and noise?

Garcia and Koelling argued that these constraints on learning were by-products of the rats' evolutionary history. Through the process of adapting to their environment, rats—like all other creatures—have evolved to readily learn those things crucial to their survival. The sudden pain of a shock is more likely to be caused by an external stimulus than by something the rat ingests, so it is not surprising that rats are predisposed to associate shock with a sight or a sound. Similarly, nausea is more likely to be caused by something the rat drinks or eats than by some external stimulus, such as a noise or a light. Thus, it makes evolutionary

Figure 7-4

Biological Constraints on Taste Aversion in Rats

Rats learned to avoid a light-noise combination when it was paired with electrical shock, but not when it was followed by X rays that made the rats nauseous. In contrast, rats quickly learned to avoid flavored water when it was followed by X rays, but they did not readily acquire an aversion to this same water when it was followed by shock. How might these constraints on learning be by-products of the rats' evolutionary history?

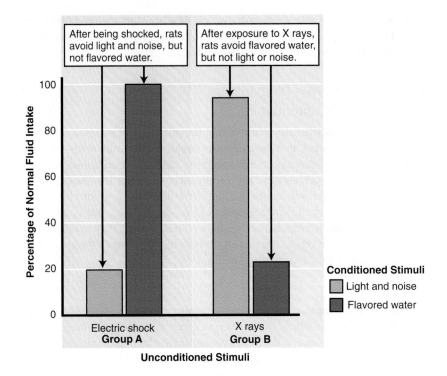

sense that rats are born with this tendency to associate nausea with taste. It is also adaptive for rats to be able to associate taste with a feeling of nausea, even after a long delay between the taste (the CS) and the nausea (the UCS). Animals biologically equipped to associate taste stimuli with illness that occurs minutes or even hours later are more likely to survive and pass their genes on to the next generation (Seligman, 1970).

Garcia decided to apply this newfound insight into conditioned taste aversion to a practical problem: controlling predators' attacks on ranchers' livestock (Garcia et al., 1977; Gustafson et al., 1974). In one study, captured wolves were fed sheep carcasses containing lithium chloride (the UCS), a chemical that causes severe nausea and vomiting (the UCR). After recovering from this very unpleasant experience, these same hungry predators were placed in a pen with a live sheep. At first, the wolves moved toward the sheep (the CS) in attack postures. However, as soon as they smelled their prey, they backed off and avoided further contact (the CR). Based on this research, many ranchers today condition potential predators to avoid their herds by depositing lithium chloride–injected livestock carcasses near their herds. Conservationists use this same strategy to condition predators to avoid killing endangered species (Nicolaus & Nellis, 1987).

Can this knowledge of learned taste aversion be used in programs to directly benefit our own species? Most definitely. In a very different context, these findings have been applied to combat the negative effects of chemotherapy in cancer patients. During the course of such treatments, many patients lose a great deal of weight because they become nauseous when eating their normal diet. In studying this side effect, researchers discovered that it was partly due to patients eating meals prior to going in for therapy, resulting in this food (the CS) becoming classically conditioned to the nausea-producing chemotherapy (the UCS). To make such conditioning less likely, a number of different strategies were developed. In one strategy, patients were advised not to eat before their therapy sessions in order to decrease the likelihood of establishing an association between food and illness. Researchers also discovered that taste aversions are more likely to develop for *unusual* rather than usual tastes (Bernstein, 1978; Broberg & Bernstein, 1987). This is true not only because usual tastes are subject to general learned irrelevance, but also because a new stimulus in your surroundings that is present at about the same time as an unpleasant sensation (nausea) suggests that it is a reliable signal—or "cause"—of that unpleasantness.

Can you guess how these researchers used this knowledge to develop two other useful strategies? (Hint: The key was *what* patients ate before each treatment session.) In one strategy, patients were encouraged to eat the same bland foods before every treatment. Because these foods were not part of their regular diet, if they developed a taste aversion to them, it would not adversely affect their eating habits. In the other strategy, just before receiving treatment, patients were given an unusual flavor of candy so that if they did form a taste aversion, it would more likely be to this candy rather than to their normal diet. In both strategies, then, patients eat something other than their usual diet just before receiving the treatment that makes them nauseous. The first strategy attempts to keep any taste aversion from developing at all by using bland foods with few taste cues, while the second strategy introduces a new, easily recognizable—and easily discardable—taste cue that is most likely to form an association with the impending nausea.

Conditioning the Immune System

Chemotherapy drugs are given to cancer patients to inhibit the growth of new cancer cells, but these drugs also inhibit the growth of immune cells, thereby weakening the body's ability to fight off illnesses. Chemotherapy drugs typically are given to patients in the same room in the same hospital. Thus, is it possible that these patients' immune systems become classically conditioned to negatively react in advance to stimuli in the hospital? Apparently, yes. In a study of women undergoing treatment for ovarian cancer, researchers found that, following several chemotherapy sessions, the patients' immune systems were weakened as soon as they entered the hospital—in anticipation of the treatment (Bovbjerg et al., 1990). The hospital setting had become a conditioned stimulus, causing an inhibition of cellular activity.

Armed with this knowledge, researchers are now investigating whether they can also strengthen the immune system through classical conditioning. Initial results are encouraging (Ramirez-Amaya & Bermudez-Rattoni, 1999; Schachtman, 2004). For example, after repeatedly pairing the taste of sherbet with shots of adrenaline—which naturally increases activity and growth in certain immune cells—researchers found that the presentation of the sherbet alone later caused an increase in people's immune response (Buske-Kirschbaum et al., 1994). These findings raise the encouraging possibility that the medical profession may be able to use classical conditioning to help fight immune-related diseases such as cancer and AIDS.

For cancer patients who have been undergoing outpatient chemotherapy at this hospital, how might the simple action of entering this setting for treatment weaken their immune system? What is the UCS? What is the UCR? What is the CS? What is the CR?

Source: Courtesy of Figzoi.

Phobias

People who have been injured in car accidents sometimes develop an intense fear of riding in all cars. These exaggerated and irrational fears of objects or situations are known as *phobias,* and they are discussed more extensively in chapter 13, section 13-3a. Such intense fear reactions often develop through classical conditioning (Schneider et al., 1999).

Although we can develop a phobia toward anything, there is evidence that some objects or situations elicit phobic reactions more easily than others. Researchers have noticed, for instance, that people tend to develop phobias for snakes and heights quite easily, but seldom develop phobias for knives and electrical outlets, even though these objects are often associated with painful experiences (Kleinknecht, 1991; LoLordo & Droungas, 1989). In a series of studies investigating the development of classically conditioned fear reactions, Arne Öhman and Joaquim Soares found that when photos of various animals and plants were paired with an electric shock, participants more readily acquired fear responses to pictures of snakes and spiders than to pictures of flowers and mushrooms (Öhman & Soares, 1994). They also found that conditioned fear responses to snakes and spiders were much more resistant to extinction (Soares & Öhman, 1993).

Evolutionary theorists contend that people more easily develop phobias for certain objects or situations because those stimuli once posed a real danger to our ancestors (Buss, 1995; Seligman, 1971). During the time our ancestors lived, those individuals whose genetic makeup allowed them to quickly learn to avoid hazards were most likely to survive and reproduce. According to this perspective, then, snakes and heights make many of us unduly anxious in our modern world because the genes that trigger such anxiety are still part of our genetic makeup.

Further support for this view that we have evolved to fear certain objects and situations more than others comes from a perceptual experiment conducted by Öhman and his coworkers (2001a). In this study, either participants were shown images of a few snakes and spiders placed within a much larger environmental scene of many flowers and mushrooms, or they were shown a few flowers and mushrooms placed within a larger scene of many snakes and spiders. Their task was to quickly identify the embedded images in the larger environmental scene (similar to a *Where's Waldo?* picture). Participants were significantly faster at finding snakes and spiders against a background of mushrooms and flowers than they were at finding mushrooms and flowers against a snake and spider background. This finding is consistent with the hypothesis that humans have developed specialized neural circuitry that quickly and automatically identifies stimuli associated with threat and danger in our evolutionary past (Öhman et al., 2001b; Öhman & Mineka, 2003). This evolved neural mechanism for threat detection and fear activation appears to be located in the amygdala of the brain, and the fear response occurs before conscious cognitive analysis of the stimulus takes place (Mineka &

Research suggests that different species are biologically prepared to develop fear and avoidance responses toward different stimuli. For example, humans' evolutionary history may predispose us to be apprehensive and even fearful toward snakes. In contrast, eagles hunt and eat snakes as part of their regular diet and exhibit no such anxiety. What other common phobias might be partly primed by our evolutionary heritage?

Source: Courtesy of Figzoi.

Öhman, 2002). Further discussion of how the brain coordinates these intense emotional responses can be found in chapter 11, section 11-5e.

Does the fear of snakes and spiders still make evolutionary sense? Right now, such fear serves very little adaptive function because few of us are at risk of dying from poisonous snake or spider bites. Yet we still carry the tendency to fear these creatures. Why? Two issues are involved. One reason is the timescale of evolution. Evolutionary changes are noticeable not in a single generation, or a few generations, but over hundreds of generations. Further, even in the most modern societies, we are not that far removed from possible encounters with dangerous snakes and spiders. The other issue is that evolutionary pressures will not work to remove human fear of snakes and spiders until, over the long term, such a fear becomes an actual disadvantage (Buss et al., 1998). If the fear is merely neutral—an annoying holdover from prehistoric times, with no effect on reproductive success—it may remain part of the human condition. In other words, the fact that a tendency is passed on through the generations implies nothing about its value in current society.

Section Review

- Classical conditioning explains how organisms learn that certain events signal the presence or absence of other events; such knowledge helps the organisms prepare for future events.
- A neutral stimulus will lead to a conditioned response whenever it provides information about the upcoming occurrence of the unconditioned stimulus.
- Conditioned responses usually develop gradually over a series of presentations.
- In higher-order conditioning, a conditioned stimulus is used to condition a neutral stimulus.
- Stimulus generalization is a conditioned response elicited by stimuli similar to the conditioned stimulus, while stimulus discrimination is a conditioned response not elicited by other stimuli.
- An animal's biology steers it toward certain kinds of conditioning that enhance its survival.

7-2   OPERANT CONDITIONING

Preview

- *What is the law of effect, and how is it related to operant conditioning?*
- *What is a reinforcer, and what is its opposite consequence called?*
- *What is the difference between a positive and a negative punisher?*
- *Is punishment an effective tool in learning?*
- *What reinforcement schedule leads to the fastest learning, and which one is most resistant to extinction?*
- *How do you "shape" behavior?*
- *How can operant conditioning explain superstitious behavior?*
- *Can an animal learn anything through operant conditioning?*
- *Is cognition part of the conditioning process?*

The type of learning that occurs due to classical conditioning helps you prepare for future events, but it seldom allows you to *change* those events. Thus, when Little Albert saw a white furry animal (the CS), he began crying (the CR) in anticipation of hearing a frightening sound (the UCS), but his crying could not control the presentation of either the CS or the UCS. Now let us examine another type of learning, in which you *do* learn that your actions, rather than conditioned stimuli, produce consequences.

7-2a Operant Behavior Is Largely Voluntary, Goal Directed, and Controlled by Its Consequences

A few years before Pavlov began watching hungry dogs salivate after being presented with food and a ticking metronome, the American psychologist Edward L. Thorndike (1898)—a student of William James—was observing hungry cats trying to escape from a "puzzle box" to reach a bowl of food. To escape, the cats had to press a lever (the response), which in turn lifted a gate that allowed access to the food (the stimulus). At first, the cats usually engaged in a number of incorrect behaviors while attempting to escape from their confinement. However, after about 10 minutes, the cats would accidentally press the lever, and the door would open. Thorndike would then return the cats to the box and repeat the trial. In subsequent trials, Thorndike's cats took less time to escape and soon learned the correct behavior to reach the food.

The Law of Effect

How was the learning of Thorndike's cats different from the learning of Pavlov's dogs? First, in classical conditioning, an organism's behavior is largely determined by stimuli that precede it. Thus, in Pavlov's experiments, food caused the dogs to salivate. However,[3] in Thorndike's research, behavior was influenced by stimuli that followed it. Second, classical conditioning involves learning associations between *stimuli,* and the organism exerts little influence over the environment; in contrast, Thorndike's cats learned an association between *behavior* and its *consequences,* and actively created a change in the environment. The cats learned to associate a response (lever pressing) with a subsequent desirable consequence (food). Gradually, the behavior that produced these desirable consequences increased in frequency and became the dominant response when the cats were placed in the puzzle box. Thorndike (1911) called this relationship between behavior and its consequences the **law of effect,** because behavior becomes more or less likely based on its *effect* in producing desirable or undesirable consequences.

You can see how the law of effect would be very useful to survival. Evolution works by selecting those individuals whose behavior best promotes survival in their given environment. Animals that repeat behavior followed by desirable consequences and terminate behavior followed by undesirable consequences (if the consequences didn't terminate the animals first) would be most likely to profit from experience with their environment and, thus, to survive and reproduce.

What Is Operant Conditioning?

Although Thorndike's law of effect is considered a fundamental principle of learning, the scientific community did not accept it at first. Indeed, John Watson, the founder of behaviorism, dismissed Thorndike's findings as due to "kind fairies" (Iversen, 1992). Fortunately for Thorndike and psychology, in the 1930s, former frustrated writer and, at that time, new psychologist B. F. Skinner elaborated on the law of effect and made it the cornerstone for his influential theory of learning, which he called **operant conditioning.** Skinner used the term *operant conditioning* because the organism's behavior is *operating* on the environment to achieve some desired goal.[2] Operant behavior is largely *voluntary* and *goal directed* and is controlled by its *consequences.* Thus, when a rat presses a bar in a Skinner box (see figure 7-5), it does so because it has learned that bar pressing will lead to food pellets. Likewise, when my daughters clean their rooms, they choose to engage in this behavior because they have learned that it will provide them with something highly valued—namely, permission to play with friends.

7-2b Reinforcement Increases the Probability of Behavior

As you have seen, people and other animals tend to repeat behaviors that are followed by desirable consequences. This fundamental principle of behaviorism—that rewarded behavior is likely to be repeated—is known as the concept of **reinforcement.** A **reinforcer**

Experience is the best teacher.
—*American proverb*

Experience is a good school, but the fees are high.
—*Heinrich Heine, German poet, 1797–1856*

law of effect A basic principle of learning that states that a behavior becomes more or less likely based on its effect in producing desirable or undesirable consequences.

operant conditioning A type of learning in which behavior is strengthened if followed by reinforcement and weakened if followed by punishment.

reinforcement The process by which a stimulus increases the probability of the behavior that it follows.

reinforcer Any stimulus or event that increases the likelihood that the behavior preceding it will be repeated.

---

[2]Thorndike had previously called this learning *instrumental conditioning* because the behavior is *instrumental* in obtaining rewards.

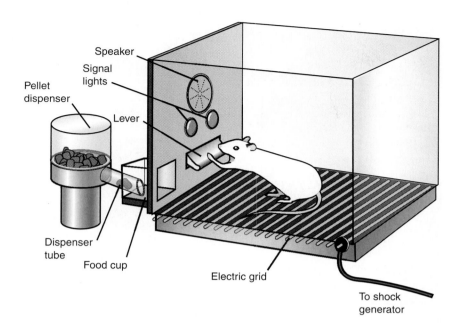

Speaker

Signal
lights

Pellet
dispenser

Lever

Dispenser
tube

Food cup

Electric grid

To shock
generator

Figure 7-5

Skinner Box

In studying operant conditioning, Skinner designed an apparatus that came to be known as a "Skinner box," in which animals learned to obtain food or to avoid shocks by operating on their environment within the box. In the Skinner box designed for rats depicted here, the animal learns to press the bar to obtain food pellets, which are delivered into the box down the pellet tube. If introduction of the food pellets increases the frequency of bar-pressing, what is the technical term for these pellets? The speaker and light allow the experimenter to manipulate visual and auditory stimuli, while the electric floor grid allows the experimenter to control aversive consequences (shock). Skinner also designed a new kind of bassinet for human babies, known as the "heir conditioner," and raised one of his daughters, Deborah, in it for over 2 years, leading to the false rumor that he raised her in a Skinner box. Also, contrary to another false rumor—that Deborah was permanently scarred by being the "baby in the box"—she grew up to become a successful artist and remembers her childhood fondly.

is any stimulus or event that increases the likelihood that the behavior preceding it will be repeated (Miller & Grace, 2003). A reinforcer may be a concrete reward, such as food, money, or attention. For example, if people laugh and pay attention to you when you tell a joke, their response is likely to encourage you to tell more jokes in the future. A reinforcer could also be an activity, such as allowing children to play with friends after they clean their rooms.

How do you know whether something is a reinforcer? Simple. Observe whether it increases the behavior it follows. While "friend play" reinforces my daughters' room cleaning, I have learned that allowing them to watch a football game on television with me is not a reinforcer. Sometimes the same stimulus is a reinforcer in one situation but not in another. For example, whereas laughter may reinforce joke-telling, my sister's laughter while teaching me to dance years ago certainly did not increase my desire to get on the dance floor! Likewise, a stimulus may be a reinforcer for one animal but not for another. Would the food pellets the rats in a Skinner box work so hard to obtain be a reinforcer for you? The lesson to be learned here is that something is a reinforcer not because of what it *is* but, rather, because of what it *does*.

Primary versus Secondary Reinforcers

How does a stimulus become a reinforcer? Actually, some stimuli are innately reinforcing, whereas others become reinforcing through learning. **Primary reinforcers** are naturally reinforcing because they satisfy a biological need. Food, water, warmth, sexual contact, physical activity, novel stimulation, and sleep are all examples of primary reinforcers. In contrast, **secondary reinforcers**—also called *conditioned reinforcers*—are learned and become reinforcing by being associated with a primary reinforcer. Does this sound familiar? It should, because this learning involves classical conditioning. Through classical conditioning, a neutral stimulus becomes a conditioned stimulus (in our case, a secondary reinforcer) by being repeatedly paired with an unconditioned stimulus (the primary reinforcer) that naturally evokes an unconditioned response. An example of a secondary reinforcer is money. You value money because it has been repeatedly associated with a host of primary reinforcers, such as food, shelter, and entertainment. Likewise, attention becomes a secondary reinforcer for children because it is paired with primary reinforcers from adults, such as protection, warmth, food, and water. Other powerful secondary reinforcers are praise and success. Thus, an important element in operant conditioning— namely, secondary reinforcers—comes into existence not through operant conditioning but through classical conditioning.

primary reinforcers Stimuli that are naturally reinforcing because they satisfy some biological need.

secondary reinforcers Stimuli that are learned and become reinforcing by being associated with primary reinforcers.

Praise becomes a secondary reinforcer because it is associated with primary reinforcers, such as gentle physical contact and warmth. Can you think of other secondary reinforcers in your own life?

Source: Courtesy of Figzoi.

Positive and Negative Reinforcers

The examples used thus far to describe reinforcers are known as **positive reinforcers:** They strengthen a response by presenting a positive stimulus after a response. Another type of reinforcer is a **negative reinforcer,** which strengthens a response by removing an aversive or unpleasant stimulus after a response. Although negative reinforcement sounds like it means reinforcing behavior with a negative consequence, in fact it refers to removing something from the environment. (Negative consequences are a form of punishment, which is discussed in section 7-2c.) In a Skinner box, a moderate electric shock administered through the floor grid often serves as a negative reinforcer. When the rat presses the bar, the shock is turned off. The removal of the shock strengthens the bar-pressing behavior.

Just as the rat learns that it can end an unpleasant sensation by responding in a specific way, you too have learned certain responses to escape negative reinforcers. The cold weather you avoid by going indoors is a negative reinforcer. Your parents nagging you to take out the garbage or to turn down the stereo is a negative reinforcer. When you respond in the correct fashion, the noxious stimulus (the cold temperature or the nagging) is terminated. Similarly, when you clean your smelly refrigerator, the removal of the foul odor is also a negative reinforcer: It strengthens refrigerator cleaning in the future.

The Relativity of Reinforcers

Many parents frequently resort to bribery to persuade their children to clean their plates:

"If you eat your potatoes, you may have some ice cream."
"You may not go out and play until you eat all your carrots."

Can the effectiveness of these inducements be explained by operant conditioning principles? According to research conducted by David Premack (1959, 1962), the answer is yes. Engaging in a less-valued activity—such as eating potatoes or carrots—becomes more likely because it leads to the opportunity to engage in a more-valued activity—such as eating ice cream or playing with friends. In other words, more-preferred activities can act as reinforcers for less-preferred activities. This **Premack principle,** as it is known, is widely employed not only by parents but also by employers and educators to motivate workers and students to engage in less desirable tasks so they then can do something they more highly value (Makin & Hoyle, 1993). Thus, bosses tell employees they will be promoted after they show their ability to successfully carry out less-demanding tasks in their current jobs. Likewise, teachers tell students they cannot go out for recess until they quiet down, clean their

---

positive reinforcers Stimuli that strengthen a response by presenting a positive stimulus after a response.

negative reinforcers Stimuli that strengthen a response by removing an aversive or unpleasant stimulus after a response.

Premack principle The principle stating that more preferred activities act as reinforcers for less preferred activities.

B. F. Skinner's research demonstrated that humans and other animals tend to repeat those responses that are followed by favorable consequences, or reinforcers. He further believed that people can gain greater control over their own behavior the more they can identify what kinds of environmental stimuli serve as personal reinforcers for them. In this spirit of discovery, think about the significant behavior you have engaged in during the past 24 hours (that is, behavior you consider personally important) and then list at least five of these behaviors below. Next, identify and list positive and/or negative reinforcers that influenced these behaviors.

Behavior	Positive Reinforcement	Negative Reinforcement	Combination
1 _____	_____	_____	_____
2 _____	_____	_____	_____
3 _____	_____	_____	_____
4 _____	_____	_____	_____
5 _____	_____	_____	_____

Based on this exercise, are your important daily behaviors influenced more by positive or negative reinforcement? Are your behaviors that are primarily influenced by one type of reinforcement generally more enjoyable than those behaviors primarily influenced by the other type of reinforcement? Can you identify why this might be the case for you? Did this exercise provide you with any self-insights that might prove useful in the future?

desks, finish their assignments, and so on. In all facets of our lives, we have a wealth of experience with the Premack principle. Before reading further, spend a few minutes completing Explore It Exercise 7-2 to identify personal reinforcers in your own life.

7-2c Punishment Decreases the Probability of Behavior

The opposite consequence of reinforcement is **punishment.** While reinforcement always *increases* the probability of a response—either by presenting a desirable stimulus or by removing or avoiding an aversive stimulus—punishment always *decreases* the probability of whatever response it follows. Like reinforcement, there are two types of punishment. **Positive punishers** weaken a response by presenting an aversive stimulus after a response. Shocking a rat in a Skinner box for pressing a food bar and scolding a child for eating candy before dinner are examples of the use of positive punishment to reduce the future likelihood of unwanted behavior. In contrast, **negative punishers** weaken a response by removing a positive stimulus after a response. Grounding a teenager for impolite behavior and denying an end-of-year bonus to a lazy worker are examples of negative punishment.

Do not confuse positive punishment with *negative reinforcement* (see section 7-2b). Although both involve an aversive stimulus, remember that a reinforcer strengthens behavior. Negative reinforcement strengthens behavior by *removing* an aversive stimulus, while positive punishment weakens behavior by *presenting* an aversive stimulus. Table 7-1 distinguishes between the two types of reinforcement and the two types of punishment.

Skinner, who was enthusiastic about using reinforcement to shape behavior, was equally adamant in opposing punishment. Why do you think he preached against its use? After all, punishment is a common method of controlling behavior. Parents use it to curb undesirable behavior in their children, teachers use it to control unruly students, employers use it to keep workers in line, and our courts use it to reduce crime. Why would Skinner advocate using only reinforcement and not punishment to shape behavior?

punishment The process by which a stimulus decreases the probability of the behavior it follows.

positive punishers Stimuli that weaken a response by presenting an aversive stimulus after a response.

negative punishers Stimuli that weaken a response by removing a positive stimulus after a response.

Table **7-1**	What Are the Differences between Types of Reinforcement and Punishment?	
	Effect on Behavior	
Procedure	**Strengthens**	**Weakens**
Presentation of stimulus	Positive reinforcement	Positive punishment
Removal of stimulus	Negative reinforcement	Negative punishment

Guidelines for Using Punishment

One reason Skinner did not recommend the use of punishment to shape behavior is that, in most instances, its implementation must conform to some very narrow guidelines. In order for punishment to have a chance of effectively reducing unwanted behaviors, three conditions must be met (Baron, 1983; Bower & Hilgard, 1981). First, the punishment must be *prompt*, administered quickly after the unwanted action. Second, it must be *relatively strong*, so its aversive qualities are duly noted by the offender. And third, it must be *consistently applied*, so the responder knows that punishment is highly likely to follow future unwanted actions.

The Drawbacks of Punishment

Even if the conditions for administering punishment are met, reduction of the undesirable behavior is not guaranteed. For instance, punishment is often used to curb aggressive behavior. But if potential aggressors are extremely angry, threats of punishment *preceding* an attack frequently fail to inhibit aggression (Baron, 1973). Here, the strength of the anger overrides any concerns about the negative consequences of aggression. Likewise, the use of punishment *following* aggression may actually provoke counteraggression in the aggressor-turned-victim, because such punishment may be frustrating and anger-producing.

Using physical punishments, such as spankings, to reduce unwanted behavior is an especially questionable practice. As you will learn in section 7-3, research indicates that employing physical punishment as a remedy for aggression and other undesirable behaviors may simply teach and encourage observers to copy these aggressive actions. That is, the person using physical punishment may serve as an aggressive model. This is exactly the process underlying the continuing cycle of family violence found in many societies—observing adult aggression appears to encourage rather than discourage aggression in children (Hanson et al., 1997; Olweus, 1980).

Taking these factors into account we see that, even though punishment may reduce unwanted behaviors under certain circumstances, it does not teach the recipient new desirable forms of behavior. The unwanted behaviors are not being replaced by more productive kinds of actions but are most likely only being temporarily suppressed. For this reason, punishment by itself is unlikely to result in long-term changes in behavior (Seppa, 1996).

Finally, one other unfortunate consequence of punishment is that it may unexpectedly shape a behavior other than the target behavior. For example, the repeated rejections young Skinner received from publishers during his "dark year" not only sharply reduced the amount of time he subsequently spent writing fiction but also had an unintended effect. He stopped *reading* fiction and poetry, and even avoided the theater for 3 years! As he put it, "Literature had been the great love of my high school and college years, but when I risked a year after college to test myself as a writer and failed, I turned rather bitterly against it" (Skinner, 1979, p. 90). Although the editors who "punished" young Skinner with their rejections may well have intended to stop his manuscript submissions, they would not have wanted him to give up reading the works they were publishing for their own profit. The lesson to be learned here is that, although you can use punishment to reduce a targeted response, you may "throw the baby out with the bathwater" by also reducing desirable behavior.

One alternative to punishment proposed by Skinner is to allow undesirable actions (such as a child's temper tantrums) to continue without either positive or negative conse-

Violence and injury enclose in their net all that do such things, and generally return upon him who began.

—*Lucretius, Roman philosopher and poet, 99–55 B.C.*

quences, until they are extinguished (Schunk, 1996). In other words, ignore the unwanted behavior—but immediately reinforce desirable responses when they occur. Another useful extinction technique is the "time-out," in which misbehaving children are removed for a short period of time from sources of positive reinforcement (Erford, 1999; Turner & Watson, 1999). Have you ever used these techniques? Were they effective?

7-2d Different Reinforcement Schedules Lead to Different Learning and Performance Rates

Thus far in my description of the learning that occurs in operant conditioning, the underlying assumption has been that every response is followed by a reinforcer. Although such **continuous reinforcement** leads to the fastest learning, in most instances of daily living we are not reinforced for every response. For example, consider avid golfers. Not all their shots lead to desirable consequences, yet most golfers wholeheartedly enjoy this activity. Similarly, you are probably not reinforced every time you go to a movie, visit friends, or go out to eat.

The biggest problem with continuous reinforcement is that, when it ends, extinction occurs rapidly. For example, what happens when you put money into a vending machine and do not receive a soda? You might respond by inserting more coins, but if doing so does not lead to the desired beverage, you do not continue to pump money into the machine, do you? That is unlikely, because behavior regulated by continuous reinforcement is easily extinguished. The same is not true for responses that are reinforced only some of the time. Did you stop going to movies, visiting friends, or eating food because you had a few unrewarding experiences? You persist in many activities even though you are reinforced only intermittently. Thus, although continuous reinforcement allows you to *acquire* responses most quickly, once responses have been learned, **partial reinforcement** has an important effect on your continued performance. Being reinforced only once in a while keeps you responding vigorously for longer periods of time than does continuous reinforcement (Humphreys, 1939).

Skinner and his colleagues identified and studied several partial reinforcement schedules (Ferster & Skinner, 1957; Skinner, 1938). *Partial schedules* are defined in terms of number of responses or the passage of time. *Ratio schedules* mean that the first response after a specified number of responses is reinforced. *Interval schedules* mean that the first response after a specified time period is reinforced. In addition, some partial schedules are strictly *fixed*, while others are unpredictably *variable*.

Fixed-ratio schedules reinforce behavior after a specified number of responses. For example, students may be given a prize after reading 20 books, or factory workers may be paid a certain amount of money for every 40 machinery pieces they assemble (a system known as "piecework"). The students read their first 19 books without reinforcement, as do the workers assembling their first 39 machinery pieces, because they know the payoff will occur when the last book or piece is completed in the ratio. When people and animals are placed on a fixed-ratio reinforcement schedule, response rates are high, with only brief pauses following reinforcement (see figure 7-6).

Why do you think people and animals on fixed-ratio schedules take such short breaks before working again on their tasks? Quite simply, resting reduces rewards. In industry, this schedule is popular with management because it leads to high productivity. However, it is unpopular with workers because it produces stress and fatigue. You might wonder why these employees do not exercise some self-restraint and simply slow down. According to behaviorists, that response is unlikely because the source of control over their actions lies largely in the environment, not in the individual. Employees work themselves to exhaustion simply and solely because the fixed-ratio schedule reinforces energetic responding. The only way to reduce fatigue is to somehow turn off the reinforcement schedule eliciting these high response rates. Fortunately for workers, many employee unions in the United States, Canada, and Europe have done just that: They have pressured management to replace the fixed-ratio piecework pay with a fixed-interval hourly wage (Schwartz & Robbins, 1995).

Animals also try to escape fixed-ratio schedules. If a pigeon in a Skinner box is pecking a lit key for food on a fixed-ratio schedule, when given the opportunity, it will periodically

continuous reinforcement A schedule of reinforcement in which every correct response is followed by a reinforcer.

partial reinforcement A schedule of reinforcement in which correct responses are followed by reinforcers only part of the time.

fixed-ratio schedule A partial reinforcement schedule that reinforces a response after a specified number of nonreinforced responses.

Figure 7-6

Schedules of Reinforcement

As shown in the graph, the predictability of fixed-ratio schedules leads to a high rate of responding, with brief pauses after each reinforcer is delivered. In contrast, the unpredictability of variable-ratio schedules leads to high, steady rates of responding, with few pauses between reinforcers. The predictability of fixed-interval schedules leads to a low rate of responding until the fixed interval of time approaches, and then the rate of responding increases rapidly until the reinforcer is delivered; after that, a low rate of responding resumes. In contrast, the unpredictability of variable-interval schedules produces a moderate, but steady, rate of responding.

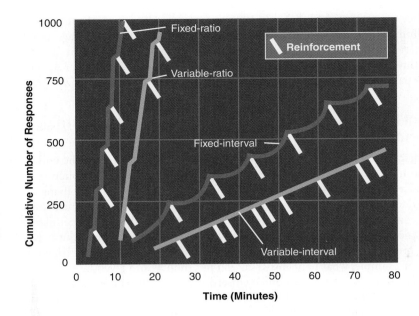

variable-ratio schedule
A partial reinforcement schedule that reinforces a response after a variable number of nonreinforced responses.

fixed-interval schedule
A partial reinforcement schedule that reinforces the first response after a fixed time interval has elapsed.

peck another lit key that briefly turns off the ratio key light (Appel, 1963). With the light off, the pigeon's environment is now conducive to rest and relaxation. Interestingly, although the pigeon could simply take a break or slow down by refraining from pecking the lit ratio key or by pecking it at a slower rate, like the pieceworker, it does not do so. When the ratio key is lit, the pigeon's responding remains high. What this research tells us is that, although it is difficult to change the pattern of responding generated by a reinforcement schedule, you can change the schedule and thereby change the response pattern.

Although fixed-ratio schedules are more resistant to extinction than is continuous reinforcement, the person or animal will stop responding soon after reinforcement stops. Why? Because when the reinforcer is not delivered after the required number of responses, it quickly becomes apparent that something about the schedule has changed.

What happens when a ratio schedule is not fixed, but varies? That is, a reinforcer may be delivered after the first response on trial 1, after the fourth response on trial 2, after the ninth response on trial 3, and so on. The average ratio may be one reinforcer after every six trials, but the responder never knows how many responses are needed to obtain the reinforcer on any given trial. Such schedules, which reinforce a response after a variable number of nonreinforced responses, are known as **variable-ratio schedules.**

As you can see in figure 7-6, of all the types of reinforcement schedules, variable-ratio schedules lead to the highest rates of responding, the shortest pauses following reinforcement, and the greatest resistance to extinction. Golfing and most other sports activities are reinforced on variable-ratio schedules. Even after golfers hit balls into sand traps and overshoot the green all day, it only takes a few good (reinforced) shots to get most of them excited about playing again. Most games of chance are also based on variable-ratio schedules. For example, the intermittent and unpredictable nature of the reinforcement is why people continue pumping money into slot machines: Their concern is that as soon as they leave, someone else will win all the money.

In **fixed-interval schedules,** reinforcement occurs for the first response after a fixed time interval has elapsed. As you can see in figure 7-6, this schedule produces a pattern of behavior in which very few responses are made until the fixed interval of time approaches, and then the rate of responding increases rapidly. If your mail consistently arrives at about the same time each day, attending to your mailbox is a good example of a behavior controlled by a fixed-interval schedule. From my window, I can see my own mailbox while typing this sentence, but I have not looked in that direction for hours. Why? Because the mail is delivered at around noon, and it is now midnight. Yet, 12 hours from now, I will be frequently glancing in that direction as I anticipate the reinforcing correspondence that will soon arrive.

What type of reinforcement schedule does the U.S. Postal Service have you on regarding your daily mail delivery? This is Audrey, my mail carrier. She has me on a fixed-interval schedule, arriving at my house 6 days per week at 2 P.M.

Source: Courtesy of Figzoi.

Researchers investigating the study patterns of college students found that they followed a fixed-interval behavior pattern when professors gave exams separated by a few weeks (Mawhinney et al., 1971). That is, when exams were given every 3 weeks, students began studying a few days before each exam, stopped studying immediately after the test, and began studying again as the next exam approached. In contrast, when professors gave daily quizzes, studying did not taper off after testing.

Unlike the predictability of fixed-interval reinforcement, **variable-interval schedules** reinforce the first response after a variable time interval has elapsed. As you can see in figure 7-6, such schedules produce relatively steady rates of responding. Have you ever taken a course where your grade was based on surprise exams that were given after a varying number of days or weeks? Because you did not know when you would be tested, you probably studied on a more regular basis in this sort of course than when exams were spread out in a fixed-interval pattern (Ruscio, 2001). Similarly, have you ever tried to connect to your Internet server but received a busy signal or a message saying that it was unavailable due to temporary maintenance? You know that sometime in the near future your attempt to connect will be reinforced, but you are unsure when that moment will arrive. So you periodically dial up your server. You are on a variable-interval schedule of reinforcement!

> **variable-interval schedule**
> A partial reinforcement schedule that reinforces the first response after a variable time interval has elapsed.

7-2e Accidental Reinforcement Can Cause Superstitious Behavior

As a teenager, when I first began asking girls out for dates, I used the phone so I could read what I wanted to say from a prepared script. One day I received a phone acceptance right after I had sunk 10 consecutive free throws on my parents' driveway basketball court. For a few months after the coincidental juxtaposition of these two events, I rarely phoned another girl for a date without first shooting 10 baskets in a row. This **superstitious behavior** was learned simply because it happened to be followed by a reinforcer (the girl accepting my offer!), even though my free-throw shooting was not the cause of the accepted offer.

In 1948, Skinner (1948b) was able to train superstitious responding in hungry pigeons by reinforcing them with food every 15 seconds, regardless of what they were doing. Skinner reasoned that when reinforcement occurred, it would be paired with whatever response the pigeons had just performed. Although this response had not caused the reinforcer, the fact that the reinforcer was delivered after the response would be sufficient to strengthen the response. Then, the next time food was delivered, the pigeons would be more likely than before to be engaging in that particular behavior, thereby strengthening it even further. This chain of events would continue until each individual pigeon would be spending most of its time engaging in its own particular superstitious behavior. This is exactly

> **superstitious behavior**
> A behavior learned simply because it happened to be followed by a reinforcer, even though this behavior was not the cause of the reinforcer.

what happened for six out of eight pigeons. One pigeon repeatedly pecked at the floor, another turned counterclockwise, another tossed its head about, and so on. Subsequent research has found that some of the behaviors Skinner observed in the pigeons are instinctive responses that pigeons make in preparation for food, and thus are not examples of superstitious behavior (Staddon & Simmelhag, 1971). Nevertheless, Skinner's initial reasoning bears repeating: When you are accidentally reinforced after engaging in a particular behavior, you may come to associate that desirable outcome with the preceding behavior and thus begin performing superstitious actions in the belief that this will help you receive another reinforcer.

Athletes and sports fans often engage in superstitious behavior during athletic events. For example, an athlete who plays well while wearing a particular pair of socks may continue to wear those socks for good luck. Likewise, a fan who sits in a particular chair just before a game-winning play may seek out that chair while watching future sporting events to "help" her team win. In both instances, wearing those socks and sitting in that chair did nothing to cause the favorable outcomes; the rewards followed them purely by chance. Yet both instances of *accidental reinforcement* function as a partial reinforcement schedule for these people, strengthening the behavior preceding their rewards. In their minds, these actions may have caused the rewards, so it makes sense to engage in these rituals whenever they want to secure the same rewards.

Although superstitious actions do not directly influence the delivery of a reinforcer, they may sometimes have an indirect benefit by helping the superstitious person cope with anxiety and stress (Matute, 1995). That is, by engaging in a ritual that you believe increases your chance of achieving success, you may gain a sense of personal control over the situation, which may help you perform better. For example, although shooting 10 consecutive free throws did not magically cause girls to go out with me, it may have lowered my anxiety level to the point where I could read my prepared script without stammering and thus come across as more poised than desperate!

The calming effect of superstitious behavior may partly explain why nearly 70 percent of college students admit to engaging in some type of superstitious action before taking an exam (Gallagher & Lewis, 2001). I was one of those "70 percent" in college. On the day of an exam, I would not take a shower lest I "wash off" the knowledge gained while studying. I usually did well on those exams, which reinforced my nonshowering behavior. Can you think of any of your own past or present behaviors that might fit Skinner's definition of superstitious behavior? Does this behavior serve a useful function for you, or does it hinder your daily routine?

7-2f Shaping Steadily Reinforces Closer Approximations to Desired Behavior

The reinforcement techniques discussed thus far describe how you can increase the frequency of behaviors once they occur. But suppose you want to train a dog to stand on its hind legs and dance, or teach a child to write the alphabet or play the piano. These behaviors are unlikely to occur spontaneously, so instead you must employ an operant conditioning procedure that Skinner called **shaping,** or the *method of successive approximations.*

In shaping, you teach a new behavior by reinforcing behaviors that are closer and closer approximations to the desired behavior (see table 7-2). For example, when my brother Randy taught his son Spencer to write the letter *Q*, he first identified what Spencer was capable of writing. Spencer's first attempt at the letter *Q* was a circular scrawl. Randy reinforced this response with praise. After several similar reinforced responses, Randy next raised the criterion for reinforcement to a circle with any straight line, then to a circle with an intersecting straight line placed anywhere, and finally, he reinforced Spencer only when he drew the correct *Q* letter. During this shaping process, when Spencer encountered difficulty at any point, Randy lowered the criterion for reinforcement to a level at which his son could perform successfully. Like Randy, all of us use praise and other reinforcers to shape successively closer approximations of desirable behavior in others. Whether it is teaching people to correct their tennis serve or to improve their grammar, shaping figures prominently in this learning process. In chapter 14, we will examine how shaping is used in therapy to change maladaptive thoughts and behavior, thus allowing people to lead happier and more normal lives.

shaping In operant conditioning, the process of teaching a new behavior by reinforcing closer and closer approximations to the desired behavior; also known as the *method of successive approximations.*

Table 7-2	How to Shape Behavior

1. Identify what the respondent can do now.
2. Identify the desired behavior.
3. Identify potential reinforcers in the respondent's environment.
4. Break the desired behavior into small substeps to be mastered sequentially.
5. Move the respondent from the entry behavior to the desired behavior by successively reinforcing each approximation to the desired behavior.

Source: Adapted from Galanter, 1962.

Using shaping techniques, Skinner trained pigeons to play Ping-Pong with their beaks and to bowl in a miniature alley. During World War II, he even devised a plan to train pigeons to guide missiles toward enemy targets! Thankfully for the pigeons, this plan was never implemented, but two former students of Skinner, Keller and Marion Breland, went into business training animals for advertising and entertainment purposes. "Priscilla, the Fastidious Pig," for example, was trained to push a shopping cart past a display case and place the sponsor's product into her cart. Today, when you go to a circus or marine park and see elephants balancing on one leg or sea lions waving "hello" to you with their flippers, you are seeing the results of shaping.

7-2g Operant Conditioning Theory Overlooks Biological Predispositions and Cognitive Processes

As a traditional behaviorist, Skinner focused on observable stimulus-response relationships and overlooked the impact that inborn biological predispositions and cognitive processes might have on learning (Kirsch et al., 2004). Thus, it became the task of other investigators to test and revise the aspects of operant conditioning related to these two factors.

Biological Constraints on Learning

One of the early assumptions underlying operant conditioning was that animals could be trained to emit any response they were physically capable of making. However, as with classical conditioning, researchers soon learned that an animal's biology can restrict its capacity for operant conditioning. Remember the animal trainers Keller and Marion Breland? Although they could train pigs to push shopping carts past display cases and raccoons to dunk basketballs in a hoop, they could not train these animals to reliably deposit silver dollars into a piggy bank (Breland & Breland, 1961). Instead, the pigs threw the coins onto the ground and pushed them about, while the raccoons in the experiment continually rubbed the coins between their paws. Both behaviors illustrate how species-specific behavior patterns can interfere with operant conditioning, a biological constraint that the Brelands called **instinctive drift** (Breland & Breland, 1961). Through evolution, pigs have developed a foraging behavior pattern of rooting for food in the ground with their snouts, whereas raccoons' foraging behavior involves washing food objects with their paws before eating them. These instincts inhibit learning new operant responses. Thus, just as certain species can be classically conditioned to learn certain responses more easily than others, operant learning is similarly constrained by an animal's evolutionary heritage (Gould & Marler, 1987).

instinctive drift Species-specific behavior patterns that interfere with operant conditioning.

Latent Learning

In the journey of discovery chronicled in this book, psychologists sometimes head down wrong paths due to misguided assumptions or failure to take notice of others' discoveries. Such was the case with Skinner. Despite evidence to the contrary, he died refusing to admit that an understanding of cognitive processes was necessary to fully understand human and animal behavior (Baars, 2003; Skinner, 1990). Yet, even as Skinner was developing his learning

Figure 7-7

Latent Learning

Rats that were rewarded for their maze running made fewer errors than rats that were not rewarded. However, on day 11, when these previously unrewarded rats were rewarded, they immediately made as few errors as the other rats. This experiment demonstrated the principle of latent learning. Can you think of examples of latent learning in your own life?

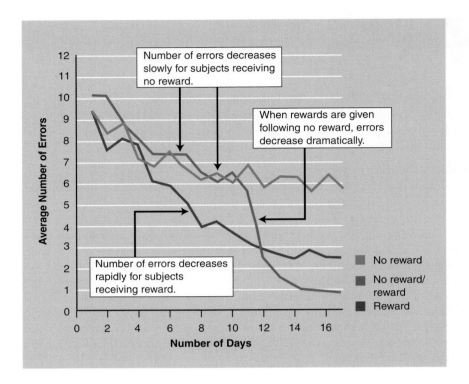

theory in the 1930s based on reinforced behavior, Edward Tolman's research (1922, 1932) with rats indicated that learning can occur without any reinforcement, something that the theory of operant conditioning assumed was not possible.

In one of Tolman's experiments, a group of rats wandered through a maze once a day for 10 days without being reinforced (Tolman & Honzik, 1930). Meanwhile, another group of rats spent the same amount of time in the maze but were reinforced with food at the "goal box" in each of their 10 trials. These reinforced rats quickly learned to accurately run the maze to reach the food reward, but the nonreinforced rats made many errors, suggesting little maze learning. On the 11th day, the nonreinforced rats were suddenly rewarded with food at the goal box, and they immediately thereafter made as few errors as the other rats. A third group of control rats that still received no food reward continued to make many errors (see figure 7-7).

How would you explain these findings using operant conditioning theory? You could not, because you would have to discuss cognition. However, not being constrained in this manner, Tolman suggested that, through experience, even the rats that had received no reinforcement had formed a *cognitive map,* or mental image, of the maze. They formed these maps prior to being conditioned, which meant that learning could occur without reinforcement. The learning of these rats remained hidden, or *latent,* because they had no incentive to engage in the behavior that would demonstrate the learning until that behavior was reinforced. Tolman called such learning that is not currently manifest in behavior and occurs without apparent reinforcement **latent learning.** Based on this research and more recent studies, psychologists now overwhelmingly believe that internal cognitive processes must be considered when explaining human, as well as animal, learning (Keith & McVety, 1988; Smith, 1994). Thus, despite Skinner's denials, operant conditioning is now thought to involve the cognitive *expectancy* that a given consequence will follow a given behavior (Dickinson & Balleine, 2000).

latent learning Learning that occurs without apparent reinforcement and is not demonstrated until sufficient reinforcement is provided.

Learned Helplessness

In the 1960s, a group of researchers were studying *avoidance learning*—that is, learning caused by negative reinforcers—when they stumbled upon an interesting and puzzling phenomenon. In these experiments, a dog was placed on one side of a box with a wire grid floor. Next, a light came on, signaling that the animal's feet would be shocked in 10 seconds unless it jumped a hurdle and crossed to the other side of the box. This jumping response to the light was the avoidance learning, and the animals quickly learned to avoid the electrical shock by jumping the hurdle. In one experiment, prior to placing dogs in the box, the researchers first strapped them down in a harness and then classically conditioned them to fear the light by repeatedly pairing it with a mild electrical shock. To the researchers' surprise, when these dogs were later placed in the box, they did not learn the simple escape response but, instead, passively lay down, whimpered, and accepted the shock (Overmier & Leaf, 1965).

> ***Journey of Discovery Question***
>
> Many of the studies that have explored the principles of classical conditioning and operant conditioning were performed on animals, such as rats and pigeons. How can scientists make generalizations about the way people behave based on these studies? Why not just study people?

Why do you think exposure to inescapable shock later caused the dogs not to learn a very simple escape response? Two young graduate students, Martin Seligman and Steven Maier, offered an answer (Maier et al., 1969; Seligman & Maier, 1967). When shock is inescapable, dogs learn that they are helpless to exert control over the shock by means of any voluntary behaviors, and they expect this to be the case in the future. Because the dogs developed the *expectation* that their behavior had no effect on the outcome in the situation, they simply gave up trying to change the outcome. Seligman and Maier called this reaction **learned helplessness.** Here again, in contradiction to behaviorist theory, research demonstrated that mental processes play a significant role in learning.

In human studies, people exposed to uncontrollable bad events at first feel angry and anxious that their goals are being thwarted. However, after repeated exposure to these uncontrollable events, people begin to feel helpless, and their anger and anxiety are replaced with depression (Peterson et al., 1993; Waschbusch et al., 2003). They have learned to think of themselves as helpless victims who are controlled by external forces. This type of learning explains why many unemployed workers who are repeatedly passed over for new jobs eventually give up. Unfortunately, by concluding that there is nothing they can do to change their job status, these individuals often overlook real employment possibilities. In chapters 12 and 15, we will examine the role that learned helplessness plays in depression.

> **learned helplessness**
> The passive resignation produced by repeated exposure to aversive events that cannot be avoided.

Section Review

- The law of effect states that behavior becomes more or less likely based on the effect it has in producing desirable or undesirable consequences.
- Operant conditioning refers to learning in which behavior is strengthened if followed by reinforcement and weakened if followed by punishment.
- A reinforcer is any stimulus or event that increases the likelihood that the behavior preceding it will be repeated.
- Primary reinforcers are innately reinforcing because they satisfy some biological need.
- Secondary reinforcers are learned through classical conditioning.
- Positive reinforcers strengthen a response by presenting a positive stimulus.
- Negative reinforcers strengthen a response by removing an aversive stimulus.
- The opposite consequence of reinforcement is punishment.
- Positive punishers weaken a response by presenting an aversive stimulus.
- Negative punishers weaken a response by removing a positive stimulus.
- In order for punishment to effectively shape behavior, it must be promptly administered, relatively strong, and consistently applied.
- Continuous reinforcement results in the fastest learning.
- Partial reinforcement maintains vigorous responding for longer periods of time.
- Partial reinforcement schedules are defined in terms of the number of responses

(ratio) or the passage of time (interval): fixed-ratio, variable-ratio, fixed-interval, or variable-interval.

- The steps in shaping behavior are (1) identify what the respondent can do; (2) identify the desired behavior; (3) identify potential reinforcers; (4) break desired behavior into small substeps; and (5) move the respondent to desired behavior by successively reinforcing each approximation to desired behavior.
- Due to accidental reinforcement, superstitious behavior may develop.
- As with classical conditioning, learning in operant conditioning is limited by an animal's evolutionary heritage.
- Cognitive processes must be taken into account in order to fully understand operant conditioning principles.

7-3 OBSERVATIONAL LEARNING

Preview

- *What is observational learning?*
- *How is observational learning related to role models?*
- *Does watching TV violence increase aggression in children?*
- *Can negative effects of observational learning be controlled?*

Classical and operant conditioning are two ways in which we and other animals learn from experience. Both of these conditioning processes involve *direct* experience with desirable and undesirable outcomes. Yet what about the learning that occurs without direct experience? Have you ever noticed that people and many animals learn by watching and imitating others? For example, by observing their mothers, jaguar cubs learn basic hunting techniques, as well as which prey are easiest to kill. Various bird species have also demonstrated their ability to learn by watching other birds perform specific actions (Akins et al., 2002; Baker, 2004). Similarly, while shopping one day, I couldn't help but notice a mother with her son, who looked about 4 years of age. She was yelling at the top of her lungs, "How many times have I told you not to yell at people?!!! I've told you, YOU HAVE TO BE POLITE!!!" Where do you think the child had learned his misbehavior?

7-3a A Great Deal of Learning Occurs by Observing and Imitating Others' Behavior

Just as nonreinforced learning cannot be explained within the framework of either classical or operant conditioning, neither can the fact that people and other animals learn simply through observing the behavior of others. Instead, a third form of learning, observational learning, must be introduced. **Observational learning** is learning by observing and imitating the behavior of others (Paignon et al., 2003). These others whom we observe and imitate are called *role models,* because they teach us how to play social roles. Observational learning helps children learn how to behave in their families and in their cultures, and it also helps adults learn the skills necessary for career success (Buunk & van der Laan, 2002; Rogoff et al., 2003). An example of behavior learned through observation is cigarette smoking. Research suggests that adolescents often decide to start smoking after observing their peers smoke (Hawkins et al., 1992). Which teens do you think are most susceptible to such influence? The answer is, those who are "outsiders," meaning that they have not yet been accepted into a teen group they desire to join. If the members of the group smoke, the outsiders imitate these teens and begin smoking (Aloise-Young et al., 1994). Can you think of ways that this knowledge could be used in developing effective antismoking ads for teenagers?

Observational learning is the central feature of Albert Bandura's (1986) **social learning theory,** which contends that people learn social behaviors mainly through observation and cognitive processing of information, rather than through direct experience. According to

observational learning
Learning a behavior by observing and imitating the behavior of others (models).

social learning theory
A theory contending that people learn social behaviors mainly through observation and cognitive processing of information.

this theory, when you watch others engage in an activity with which you are not familiar, a great deal of cognitive learning takes place before you yourself perform the behavior. For instance, consistent with the law of effect discussed earlier, you are most likely to imitate a model whose actions you see rewarded, and you are least likely to imitate behavior that is punished. This observational learning mechanism—in which you learn the consequences of an action by observing its consequences for someone else—is known as *vicarious conditioning*. As you can see, the only difference between this and the conditioning that occurs in operant learning is that, here, the behavior of others is being reinforced or punished rather than your own.

Bandura identified the following four key psychological factors necessary for observational learning to take place:

1. You must *pay attention* to the model's behavior.
2. You must *remember* what you have observed.
3. You must possess the *ability* to perform the observed behavior.
4. You must be *motivated* to perform the observed behavior.

Albert Bandura, b. 1925
Source: Courtesy of Albert Bandura.

A recent survey of 750 teenagers in Los Angeles indicates that having a role model or a mentor has a positive influence on the lives of adolescents (Yancey et al., 2002). In this study, a little over half the respondents reported that they had a role model whom they wanted to be like, with White teens (64 percent) being more likely to have role models than African-American (53 percent) or Latino teens (54 percent). The most popular role models were parents and other relatives (32 percent), but almost as many teenagers identified media figures such as athletes, singers, or musicians as their role models (28 percent). Girls most often identified people whom they personally knew as role models, whereas boys were more likely to identify sports stars and other media figures. The teenagers who identified one or more important role models in their lives earned higher grades in school and had more positive self-esteem than those who did not have a role model. Among the minority adolescents, those who had no role models had the lowest levels of ethnic identity development, whereas those who had role models they personally knew had the highest levels of ethnic identity development. As previously discussed in chapter 4, section 4-5d, higher levels of ethnic identity development not only promote a strong sense of ethnic pride that protects minority youth from internalizing negative ethnic stereotypes into their self-concepts, but also help people pursue mainstream goals and participate in mainstream life. These findings, along with those of other studies (Bryant & Zimmerman, 2003; Flouri & Buchanan, 2003), demonstrate the important "role" that role models play in shaping the behavior and self-esteem of children and adolescents.

7-3b We Often Learn Aggressive Behavior through Observation

Research suggests that widespread media coverage of a violent incident is often followed by a sudden increase in similar violent crimes (Berkowitz & Macaulay, 1971; Phillips, 1983, 1986). Apparently, reading and watching news accounts of violence can trigger some people to "copy" the aggression. This dangerous manifestation of observational learning was dramatically illustrated following the 1999 shootings and bombings at Columbine High School in Littleton, Colorado, which left 17 people dead and many wounded. Over the next year, copycat threats and actions occurred in schools throughout the United States and Canada. What insights can psychology bring to bear on this type of learning?

Bandura (1979) believes children observe and learn aggression through many avenues, but the three principal ones are the family, the culture, and the media. First, in families where adults use violence, children grow up much more likely to use it themselves (Herrenkohl et al., 1983; Hunter & Kilstrom, 1979). Second, in communities where aggression is considered a sign of manhood, learned aggressive behaviors are eagerly and consciously transmitted from generation to generation, especially among males (Cohen & Nisbett, 1997; Rosenberg & Mercy, 1991). Finally, the media—principally television and the movies—unceasingly convey images of violence and mayhem to virtually all segments of society on a daily basis (Gerbner & Signorielli, 1990; Murray, 1980). Given the fact that children and teenagers often adopt figures from popular culture as role models, do you think they might imitate the antisocial behavior these individuals sometimes engage in? Let's examine some of the research that has analyzed the conditions under which the media and popular culture might influence aggressive behavior, especially in children and adolescents.

Violence Depicted on Television and in Films

The first set of experiments demonstrating the power of observational learning in eliciting aggression was the famous *Bobo doll studies* (Bandura et al., 1961), described in chapter 2, section 2-3c. Likewise, in another classic study conducted by Albert Bandura and his coworkers (1963), young children watched a short film in which an aggressive adult model named Rocky takes food and toys from someone named Johnny. In one condition, children saw Johnny respond by punishing Rocky, while in another condition, children saw Rocky sing "Hi ho, hi ho, it's off to play I go," as he pranced off with Johnny's belongings in a sack. Not surprisingly, those children who saw Rocky rewarded for his aggression behaved more aggressively than those who saw Rocky punished. The children who had observed Rocky's rewarded aggression often expressed disapproval of his actions, but many of them still directly imitated him, even down to incidental details. At the end of one session, for instance, a girl first strongly condemned Rocky's behavior and then turned to an experimenter and asked, "Do you have a sack?"

Although these findings might leave you with the impression that aggressive models who are punished have little negative impact on children's later behavior, this is not really the case. The research demonstrates that children are less likely to imitate the actions of punished aggressors. Does this mean these children fail to learn the aggressive behavior, or does it mean they simply inhibit the expression of these behaviors?

To answer this question, in one study, Bandura (1965) offered children a reward if they could imitate the aggressive behavior of the model they had previously observed. Every single one of the participants could mimic the model's aggressive actions, even those who had seen the punished model. Thus, simply observing someone being punished for aggression does not prevent the *learning* of aggression—it simply inhibits its *expression* in certain circumstances.

Numerous experimental studies indicate that exposure to media violence significantly enhances children's and adolescents' aggression in interactions with strangers, classmates, and friends (C. A. Anderson et al., 2003a; Johnson et al., 2002; Wood et al., 1991). Further, longitudinal research conducted in a number of countries, including the United States, indicates that the early TV habits of children significantly predict their later aggressive behavior, even after statistically controlling for their initial aggressiveness. Consistent with our previous discussion of the importance of role models, what appears to significantly influence children's later aggressiveness is their *identification* with aggressive TV and movie characters. That is, children who watch a lot of media violence when they are young and identify with aggressive media characters are most likely to become highly aggressive later in life (Huesmann & Hasbrouck, 1996; Huesmann & Miller, 1994).

Violence Depicted in Music Lyrics and Music Videos

What about the violence often depicted in music videos and in music lyrics? Although no experimental studies have yet examined whether exposure to such music increases actual physical aggression, several studies have analyzed how music videos affect adolescents' aggressive thoughts and emotions. In one such study, after watching violent rap music videos, young African-American men were more likely than their counterparts who watched nonviolent music videos to endorse the use of physical aggression in resolving conflicts (Johnson et al., 1995). Similarly, college students shown rock music videos containing violence subsequently reported a greater acceptance of antisocial behavior compared with students in a control group (Hansen & Hansen, 1990). Regarding the effects of music lyrics, a series of five experiments found consistent evidence that songs with violent lyrics increase aggression-related thoughts and feelings of hostility in listeners (C. A. Anderson et al., 2003b). And finally, one survey study found that, compared with adolescents who had little exposure to rap music videos, those who had a great deal of exposure were three times more likely to have physically hit a teacher and more than two and a half times as likely to have been arrested (Wingood et al., 2003). Because this last study used correlational methods (see chapter 2, section 2-3b), we do not know whether the greater antisocial behavior among the teenagers who watched a lot of rap music videos was caused by their exposure to the rap music or by other factors in their lives. However, the overall implication of the findings reviewed here is that watching and/or listening to violent music not only causes people to be more accepting of antisocial behavior but also creates an emotional state of mind more likely to provoke aggressive responses.

Media Violence and Emotional Desensitization

Beyond the learning of aggressive behavior through the repeated observation of violence, another possible negative effect of such observation is emotional blunting or *desensitization,* which means simply becoming indifferent to aggressive outbursts. For example, in a series of experiments, children who had just watched a violent movie were less concerned when they observed other youngsters fighting and were slower to stop the fight than a control group of children who had not seen the movie. Similar desensitization effects were also observed in college students who watched a lot of violent TV programs: When their physiological responses were monitored, the heavy consumers had the lowest levels of arousal when observing both fictional and realistic aggression (Drabman & Thomas, 1975; Thomas et al., 1977). These findings suggest that people who are exposed to a lot of media violence become habituated to violence in other areas of their lives (Carnagey et al., 2004). Being less anxious and bothered by aggressive behavior, these individuals may be less inhibited than others in responding aggressively when facing social confrontations.

Of course, in examining all this research, it must be kept in mind that these findings do not mean that most people who regularly view or listen to media violence will begin terrorizing their schools, neighborhoods, and work settings. The relationship between viewing media violence and behaving aggressively is by no means perfect. It also does not mean that media violence is a primary cause of aggression in society. However, while exposure to such staged violence is not the primary cause of aggression, it may be the one factor that is easiest to control and reduce (Hamilton, 1998; Wilson et al., 1998).

7-3c Positive Social Modeling Can Counteract the Negative Influence of Aggressive Models

Living in a culture in which violent images saturate the media, what can you do as an individual to teach children not to imitate such behavior? First, remember that just as destructive models can teach people how to act aggressively, social learning theorists contend that nonaggressive models can urge observers to exercise restraint in the face of provocation. In an experiment supporting this claim, research participants who watched a nonaggressive model exhibit restraint in administering shocks to a "victim" in a learning experiment were subsequently less aggressive than those who had observed an aggressive model (Baron & Kepner, 1970).

Besides being reduced by nonaggressive models, aggression also can be controlled if an authority figure condemns the behavior of aggressive individuals. For example, research demonstrates that when a child watches violence on television in the presence of an adult who condemns the violence, the child is less likely to later imitate this aggression (Hicks, 1968; Horton & Santogrossi, 1978). This bit of knowledge has not been lost on my wife and I in raising our own children. On more than one occasion while watching television with our daughters, the screen has suddenly erupted with violent images so quickly that we have not had time to change the channel. Each time this happened, we condemned the violence, and I can now tell you that our efforts paid off. A few years ago while we were watching a

Research demonstrates that the negative effects of television violence can be reduced if adults condemn the violence when it occurs. However, for this strategy to work, adults must monitor children's television viewing and take the time to watch the shows with the children.

Source: Courtesy of Figzoi.

Looney Toons cartoon, Elmer Fudd pulled out a shotgun and blew the head off Daffy Duck. Without missing a beat, Lillian, who was 4 years old at the time, turned to us and said, "Boy, that wasn't very nice, was it? People shouldn't be so mean."

Finally, an essential ingredient in reducing aggressive responses is to diminish exposure to violence. Recent studies indicate that aggressive behavior in children is significantly reduced when they spend less time watching violent television shows and playing violent video games. One such study examined third- and fourth-grade students at two comparable schools over a 6-month period (Robinson et al., 2001). In one of the schools, TV and video-game exposure was reduced by one-third when students and parents were encouraged to engage in alternative forms of home entertainment, while in the other school no effort was made to reduce exposure. The researchers found that children at the intervention school were subsequently less aggressive on the playground than students at the control school, especially those students who had been initially rated as most aggressive by their classmates.

> **Journey of Discovery Question** Why are the studies on observational learning now mostly based on human populations? And why does observational learning make evolutionary sense for human beings?

Section Review

- Observational learning refers to learning by observing and imitating the behavior of others.
- Adolescents who have role models are more academically successful and have more positive self-esteem than those who have no role models.
- Watching violence on television may encourage children to become more aggressive, but they are less likely to imitate the actions of aggressors who are punished.
- The negative effects of observing aggression can be controlled by having an authority figure condemn the aggression.

Psychological Applications

Learning How to Exercise Self-Control in Your Academic and Personal Life

- Do you have trouble getting out of bed in the morning to attend an early class?
- Do you procrastinate in studying for exams and end up cramming the night before?
- Do you tend to spend money quickly, thereby having little left to live on until your next paycheck?
- Are you having difficulty exercising on a regular basis?
- Would you like to stop smoking or cut down on your consumption of alcohol?

If you answered yes to any of these questions, the bad news is that you are struggling with issues of self-control. The good news, however, is that what you have learned in this chapter can help you regain control over those troubled aspects of your academic and personal life. In most self-control issues, problems arise because we choose *short-term reinforcers* that provide immediate gratification instead of choosing *long-term reinforcers* that provide delayed gratification. For instance, we sacrifice a chance at getting a good grade at the end of the semester for the luxury of getting an extra hour's sleep each class day. Likewise, we choose to continue smoking because doing so gives us an immediate nicotine high, even though smoking significantly lowers our life expectancy. Why do short-term reinforcers have greater incentive value than long-term reinforcers?

The Relative Value of Short-Term and Long-Term Reinforcers

Let's consider this question by examining the problem of early-morning class attendance. When resolving to change your habit of skipping class, you consider the incentive value of both the short-term and the long-term reinforcers. In most cases, such resolutions are made when both reinforcers are relatively distant, such as just before you go to bed the night before class. At that time, the incentive value of getting a good grade is usually greater than the value of getting extra sleep, so you set your alarm for an early rising. However, as the availability of a reinforcer gets closer, its incentive value increases (Ainslie, 1975). Thus, when the alarm interrupts your sleep in the morning, the short-term reinforcer—extra sleep—is now immediately available, while the long-term reinforcer—a good grade—is still distant. Now it will be much harder to maintain your resolve and forgo the short-term reinforcement of extra sleep. If the thought of staying in your warm, comfy bed has greater incentive value than getting a good grade, you will break your nighttime resolution.

Strategies to Modify Troublesome Behavior

Now that you understand the process of shifting incentive values, what can you do to counteract the allure of these resolution-breaking short-term reinforcers? You can adopt the following six strategies to modify your problem behavior and regain self-control.

1. *Set realistic goals:* Punishment weakens the behavior it follows. Because failure to reach your goals will punish your efforts, it is important that you set goals you can realistically achieve.
2. *Shape your behavior:* As previously noted, the delay in receiving a long-term reinforcement can weaken your resolve to change your troublesome behavior. One strategy to increase the incentive value of the long-term reinforcer is to *shape* your behavior. That is, give yourself modest reinforcers for achieving successive steps toward your ultimate desirable goal. For example, after going for a week without missing class, reward yourself by going to a movie or spending time with friends. Similarly, if you were smoking a pack a day and wanted to stop, during the first week, you might reward yourself if you smoked only a half-pack per day. Remember, a reinforcer strengthens the behavior it follows, not the behavior it precedes. Reinforce yourself only *after* you perform the desired behavior, not before. If you reward yourself before attending class, or before lowering your cigarette consumption, you are not reinforcing the desired behavior.
3. *Chart your progress:* To give yourself feedback on how well you are progressing toward meeting your goals, keep a chart of your progress. For example, to support your efforts to stop smoking, the chart would track how many cigarettes you smoked each day. Place the chart in a place where you will regularly see it. Charting your progress in this manner will bring into play both positive and negative reinforcement: You will praise yourself after reaching your daily goals, and you will work harder to remove the guilt—a negative reinforcer—that follows a day in which you fail to meet your goals.
4. *Identify environmental cues that trigger undesirable behavior:* Environmental stimuli can serve as signals that we are about to have access to certain desirable, yet harmful, situations or substances. For example, if you have regularly smoked after meals or when in taverns, those situations will likely trigger your urge to "light up" during the time you are trying to quit smoking. If you can identify these environmental cues, you can avoid putting yourself in those situations while you are trying to change your behavior (stay away from taverns for a while). If you cannot avoid the tempting situations (as will be the case in eating meals), take steps to countercondition yourself. Instead of smoking after meals, have a favorite dessert or beverage.

Continued next page—

Psychological Applications

—Continued

5. *Keep focused on the long-term reinforcer:* As previously stated, the undesirable short-term reinforcers are generally more salient than the desirable long-term reinforcers. Thus, when tempted by these more salient and troublesome reinforcers, take advantage of the cognitive aspects of learning and selectively focus on the long-term reinforcers. For example, instead of succumbing to temptation and grabbing an extra hour of sleep, imagine how good you will feel at the end of the semester when you receive a good grade in your course. Such imagining can subjectively close the gap between the present and the future goal, increasing its incentive value in the present.

6. *Select desirable role models:* Observational learning teaches us that we can learn by observing and imitating the behavior of others. Just as you may have acquired your undesirable behavior by imitating others, you can change your behavior by identifying people who possess traits and skills you desire. By observing these individuals, you not only will learn how to behave differently, but also will receive inspiration by seeing someone successfully doing what you ultimately want to do.

Key Terms

acquisition (p. 244)

classical conditioning (p. 241)

conditioned response (CR) (p. 242)

conditioned stimulus (CS) (p. 242)

continuous reinforcement (p. 259)

extinction (p. 246)

fixed-interval schedule (p. 260)

fixed-ratio schedule (p. 259)

higher-order conditioning (p. 248)

instinctive drift (p. 263)

latent learning (p. 264)

law of effect (p. 254)

learned helplessness (p. 265)

learning (p. 240)

negative punishers (p. 257)

negative reinforcers (p. 256)

observational learning (p. 266)

operant conditioning (p. 254)

partial reinforcement (p. 259)

positive punishers (p. 257)

positive reinforcers (p. 256)

Premack principle (p. 256)

primary reinforcers (p. 255)

punishment (p. 257)

reinforcement (p. 254)

reinforcer (p. 254)

secondary reinforcers (p. 255)

shaping (p. 262)

social learning theory (p. 266)

spontaneous recovery (p. 246)

stimulus discrimination (p. 247)

stimulus generalization (p. 246)

superstitious behavior (p. 261)

unconditioned response (UCR) (p. 242)

unconditioned stimulus (UCS) (p. 242)

variable-interval schedule (p. 261)

variable-ratio schedule (p. 260)

Suggested Websites

Neuroscience: Learning and Memory

http://www.brembs.net/learning

This website presents information describing and distinguishing between classical and operant conditioning principles.

Animal Training at SeaWorld

http://www.seaworld.org/infobooks/Training/home.html

This SeaWorld website contains information about animal behavior and the training of marine animals at SeaWorld.

Albert Bandura

http://www.emory.edu/EDUCATION/mfp/bandurabio.html

This website at Emory University provides a biography of Albert Bandura, as well as an overview of his theory of observational learning and his research on modeling violence.

Review Questions

Note: You can find the correct answers to these questions by taking the quiz and then submitting your answers in the Online Edition. The program will automatically score your submission. If you miss a question, the program will provide the correct answer, a rationale for the answer, and the section number in the chapter where the topic is discussed.

1. The person associated with classical conditioning is
   a. B. F. Skinner.
   b. Ivan Pavlov.
   c. John Watson.
   d. Martin Seligman.
   e. *b* and *c*

2. Which of the following is *true*?
   a. Classical conditioning involves "mindless" automatic learning.
   b. Humans are passive in learning conditioned responses.
   c. Learning occurs when the conditioned stimulus comes after or at the same time as the unconditioned stimulus.
   d. *b* and *c*
   e. none of the above

3. Which of the following was missing from the experiment on Little Albert B.?
   a. extinction
   b. stimulus generalization
   c. punishment
   d. all of the above
   e. *a* and *c*

4. Which of the following is *not* an example of higher-order conditioning?
   a. A perfume sparks romantic feelings.
   b. A new acquaintance likes you because she knew and liked your sibling.
   c. Upon entering a room to take an exam, you experience test anxiety.
   d. You dislike Pringles™ potato chips because you once got sick from eating too many.
   e. none of the above

5. Which of the following can be used to protect endangered species from predators?
   a. conditioned taste aversion
   b. extinction
   c. spontaneous recovery
   d. *a* and *b*
   e. none of the above

6. Several hours after eating a burrito at a new restaurant, Adam becomes ill with a fever and vomiting. After several days, his doctor diagnoses him with the flu. However, for years after that, Adam can no longer eat a burrito without feeling sick. This is an example of
   a. negative reinforcement.
   b. learned taste aversion.
   c. food punishment.
   d. superstitious behavior.
   e. stimulus generalization.

7. In a study conducted by Öhman et al., a neural mechanism for threat detection was evidenced by
   a. participants most quickly identifying spiders and snakes among a background of mushrooms and flowers.
   b. participants most quickly identifying mushrooms and flowers among a background of spiders and snakes.
   c. participants identifying natural solutions to threat situations in a picture of an outdoor environment.
   d. participants more quickly identifying spiders and snakes that were poisonous in a picture than those that were nonthreatening.
   e. all of the above

8. B. F. Skinner
   a. assumed that latent learning was not possible.
   b. overlooked the impact of inborn biology on learning.
   c. elaborated on the law of effect.
   d. was named Burrhus Frederick Skinner.
   e. all of the above

9. Which of the following could be a reinforcer for students to study more?
   a. money
   b. less homework
   c. studying with someone you enjoy being with
   d. good grades
   e. all of the above

10. Which of the following is a primary reinforcer?
    a. food
    b. water
    c. warmth
    d. sex
    e. all of the above

11. Which of the following is a negative reinforcer?
    a. money received for mowing the lawn
    b. being fired by your boss for getting to work late
    c. the annoying knocking in your car that leads you to the mechanic
    d. money won in the lottery
    e. none of the above

12. The type of reinforcement that has the greatest long-term effects is
    a. continuous reinforcement.
    b. fixed-ratio schedule.
    c. variable-ratio schedule.
    d. punishment.
    e. none of the above

13. What is the term for something that weakens behavior by presenting an aversive stimulus?
    a. negative reinforcement
    b. shaping
    c. punishment
    d. avoidance behavior
    e. none of the above

14. Which of the following is a drawback of punishment?
    a. It doesn't teach new, desirable forms of behavior.
    b. It can lead to more aggression.
    c. It encourages aggressive behavior.
    d. all of the above
    e. none of the above

15. Repeatedly attempting to contact your Internet dial-up server when you receive a busy signal or have been informed that it is currently unavailable is an example of which type of reinforcement?
    a. continuous
    b. variable-ratio
    c. fixed-ratio
    d. variable-interval
    e. fixed-interval

16. Which of the following might be an example of superstitious behavior?
    a. jumping when someone jumps out and says "boo"
    b. pushing an elevator button again and again until the elevator arrives
    c. salivating when someone talks about food
    d. studying harder after being praised
    e. experiencing a feeling of calmness after engaging in prayer or meditation

17. Learning that has occurred without apparent reinforcement and that is not currently manifest in behavior is called
    a. superstitious behavior.
    b. instinctual drift.
    c. innate intelligence.
    d. latent learning.
    e. collective wisdom.

18. Social learning theory
    a. contends that people learn social behavior through direct experience.
    b. is inconsistent with the law of effect.
    c. requires cognition.
    d. all of the above
    e. none of the above

19. Survey research on the "role" of role models among teenagers indicates that
    a. the most popular role models are identifiable media figures.
    b. all teenagers have someone they can identify as a role model.
    c. individuals with role models are most likely to perform better in school.
    d. all races and ethnicities are equally likely to identify role models.
    e. all of the above

20. Which of the following is *true*?
    a. Media are the primary cause of aggression in children.
    b. Observing someone being punished for behaving aggressively does not prevent the learning of aggression.
    c. Less time watching violent TV diminishes aggressive behavior.
    d. *b* and *c*
    e. all of the above

21. Applying the learning principles in chapter 7, which of the following would be helpful in modifying troublesome behavior?
    a. Identify environmental cues that trigger undesirable behavior.
    b. Keep focused on long-term reinforcers.
    c. Select desirable role models.
    d. Chart your progress.
    e. all of the above.

Chapter 8

Memory

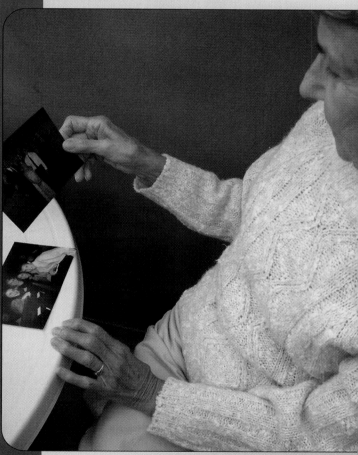

Source: Courtesy of Figzoi.

The amount of information you have in memory could fill thousands of books. How does this information get into your memory? How is it stored and organized? Can you "lose" this information? These are some of the important memory questions researchers try to answer.

Source: Courtesy of Figzoi.

memory The mental process by which information is encoded and stored in the brain, and later retrieved.

At the Russian newspaper where reporter S. V. Shereshevskii worked, he was surprised to learn that his editor was upset with him for never writing down assignments. Shereshevskii, who was in his late 20s, informed his editor that he didn't need to write down assignments because he remembered everything people told him, word for word. Didn't everybody have this ability, he naively asked?

Following that innocent question, Shereshevskii soon found himself in the office of psychologist Alexander Luria, who proceeded to test Shereshevskii's memory. Over the years, Luria discovered that there was virtually no limit to what this reporter could remember. For example, he could memorize a list of 70 words in 4 minutes. Although this feat is not that unusual, what was extraordinary was that, whenever Shereshevskii created an image in his mind, it became so vivid that he never forgot it. Fifteen years after Shereshevskii memorized this word list, Luria asked him if he could recall it. Shereshevskii closed his eyes, paused, and then replied, "Yes, yes . . . this was a series you gave me once when we were in your apartment. . . . You were sitting at the table and I in the rocking chair. . . . You were wearing a gray suit and you looked at me like this. . . . Now I can see you saying . . .," and then he recited the words in the exact order they had been read to him so long ago (Luria, 1968).

While Shereshevskii stands out because of his amazing memory, "Ben" is noteworthy for his limited ability to remember information and events. Ben, who is 44, happened to sit next to me during a plane trip and noticed an early draft of this memory chapter lying on my lap. "You know," he said nonchalantly, "I have no short-term memory." With that attention-grabbing opening line, Ben proceeded to tell me that 4 years ago he had suffered damage to his short-term memory when he received insufficient oxygen during minor knee surgery. Now he has to repeat information many times before he can remember it. If he doesn't repeat information over and over, or if he doesn't write it down immediately, it will disappear. By his own admission, Ben's moods are now much more even-keeled than before the accident. Why? Because, when he does experience emotions such as happiness, sadness, or anger, they last only until his attention is distracted and then quickly fade from consciousness—and from memory.

Despite this substantial memory handicap, Ben recently became the public relations director for a major industrial manufacturing firm. Perhaps what is most surprising about Ben's new job situation is that no one there is apparently aware of his disorder. When he was first hired, it took him a number of months to memorize the names of his office staff, and he still occasionally calls the company president "Prez" and the chief financial officer "Chief" when their names escape him. Thus far, Ben's bosses have interpreted this informality as simply an example of his winning personality.

Ben and Shereshevskii represent opposite ends of the memory spectrum. In most of us, **memory**—the mental process by which information is encoded and stored in the brain, and later retrieved—operates somewhere between these two extremes (Gabrieli, 1998). There is a close link between learning, the subject of chapter 7, and memory, the subject of this chapter (Healy & Bourne, 1995; Schacter & Scarry, 2003). Memory involves the retention of what we learn. As Ben's current predicament illustrates, without a well-functioning memory, learning becomes extremely problematic.

How extensive is our memory system? One memory researcher estimated that by your early 70s you will have memories equal to about 500 times the amount of information contained in the entire *Encyclopaedia Britannica* (Hunt, 1982). Of course, a good deal of the information stored in memory would never appear in an encyclopedia (for example, I have unintentionally memorized the *CatDog* and *SpongeBob Squarepants* TV theme songs). Despite the fact that some of our memories appear redundant, we could not function properly without the ability to encode, store, and later recall our life experiences. In this chapter, we explore how information gets into memory, how it is kept in memory, how it is taken out of memory, and also how it is lost from memory.

8-1   THE NATURE OF MEMORY

Preview

- *Is human memory identical to computer memory?*
- *What are the stages of information-processing?*
- *How many memory systems are there?*
- *Can short-term memory be extended?*
- *How do we get information into memory?*

Up until the late 1950s, most psychologists viewed memory as a single system (Melton, 1963). This perspective was largely due to the influence of behaviorism, in which remembering something was attributed to the strength of stimulus-response pairings (see chapter 7, section 7-2a). If a person or animal consistently responded in the same way to the same stimulus, this meant they had formed a strong memory for the response. According to behaviorists, this single conditioning process was the extent of memory. Unobservable events, such as cognition, were considered off-limits to the science of psychology. Then, due to technological advances outside the discipline and scientific discoveries within, psychologists dramatically changed their views of memory.

8-1a   The Computer's Information-Processing System Has Been a Useful Model for Human Memory

The event outside of psychology that served as a catalyst in changing psychologists' thinking on memory was the advent of the computer age (Dodwell, 2000). Like humans, computers have memories. As psychologists adopted the terms and concepts in the computer sciences, they began to view memory as a kind of information-processing system that depended on three basic processes (Lewandowsky & Murdock, 1989; Searle, 1995). This does not mean that they thought of human memory and computer memory as identical, but they concluded that the two were similar enough for computer information-processing to serve as a rough working model for human information-processing (Lewandowsky & Murdock, 1989; Searle, 1995). According to this **information-processing model,** in both computer and human memory, information goes through three basic processes: an input or *encoding* process, a *storage* process, and a *retrieval* process.

Information Processes

Encoding refers to the first memory process, in which incoming information is organized and transformed so it can be entered into memory (Golob & Starr, 2004; MacPherson et al., 2004). In the computer, typing on the keyboard transforms information into electronic language. In the brain, sensory information from our surroundings is transformed into neural language. For example, imagine that you are presented with the sentence "Sporminore is a town in northern Italy." If you encode the image of the letters as they appear on your computer screen, you are using **visual encoding,** and the information is represented in memory as a picture. If you encode the sound of the words as if they were spoken, you are using **acoustic encoding,** and the information is represented

information-processing model A memory model concerning the sequential processing and use of information, involving encoding, storage, and retrieval.

encoding The first memory process, in which information is organized and transformed so it can be entered into memory.

visual encoding The encoding of picture images, including the sight of words.

acoustic encoding The encoding of sound, especially the sound of words.

NON SEQUITUR   Wiley Miller

Source: Non Sequitor © 2005 Wiley Miller. Distributed by Universal Press Syndicate. Reprinted with permission. All rights reserved.

semantic encoding The encoding of meaning, including the meaning of words.

in memory as a sequence of sounds. Finally, if you encode the fact that this sentence is referring to the birthplace of your grandfather (which for me is true), you are using **semantic encoding,** and the information is represented in memory by its meaning to you. The type of encoding used—visual, acoustic, or semantic—can influence what is remembered. As you will discover in section 8-1d, semantic encoding yields much better memories than visual or acoustic encoding. However, because semantic encoding involves processing the general, underlying meaning of information, it often ignores details of the information.

We automatically encode a great deal of information from our environment without any conscious effort and without interfering with other cognitive tasks. For example, without looking, you probably can recall the place on this textbook's cover where the title appears. Although much encoding occurs without conscious effort, other information is encoded only with effort and attention. In general, effortful encoding results in more durable memories than effortless encoding (Craik & Lockhart, 1972; Lockhart & Craik, 1990).

storage The second memory process, in which information is entered and maintained in memory for a period of time.

The second memory process is **storage,** which involves entering and maintaining information in memory for a period of time. Just as the computer can store information for either brief periods (in random-access memory) or indefinitely (on a floppy or hard disk), we too have similar memory capabilities. The human memory systems that store information for relatively brief time periods are known as *sensory memory* and *short-term memory,* while the more permanent system is known as *long-term memory.*

retrieval The third memory process, which involves recovering stored information from memory so it can be used.

Finally, the third memory process is **retrieval,** which involves recovering stored information from memory so it can be used. In both computers and humans, this means pulling information out of long-term memory storage and placing it into a much smaller working memory. To demonstrate for yourself how the retrieval process works, recall the name of your best friend from sixth grade. In doing so, perhaps memories of your hometown come to mind, along with images of your sixth-grade classroom and activities you engaged in with this person. Each of these memories can serve as a stimulus to help you remember your best friend's name. When the correct memories come to mind, you retrieve the name (Valentine et al., 1996).

In a nutshell, these are the three memory processes: Encoding gets information into memory, storage keeps it in, and retrieval takes it out, just like a computer. Although the computer is by far the most popular metaphor for our memory system, as already noted, it is not a perfect metaphor. Indeed, some critics point out that the human brain often does not operate like a typical computer (Gabrieli, 1999; McClelland, 1994). For instance, computers are based on algorithms (see chapter 9, section 9-2b), and they process information sequentially, or *serially,* working on only one stream of data at a time. However, the human brain is much more complex and can process many kinds of information simultaneously, in a *parallel* fashion. Thus, the computer may not be the last and best metaphor for the human mind, but as of this writing, it is still the most convenient and popular metaphor for organizing the major findings on memory (Tulving, 1997). With this caveat in mind, let us examine how psychologists, operating within this information-processing perspective, began questioning old assumptions about how we form memories. As you learn about how these researchers understand memory, compare this understanding with your own ideas and beliefs about how memory operates. Take note of the degree to which your understanding of memory prior to reading this chapter is in line with contemporary theories. As you will later learn in this chapter, your beliefs about memory and how you are asked about past events can actually influence what you remember (see section 8-4d).

The Identification of Three Memory Systems

A series of studies in the 1950s indicated that if people are distracted from rehearsing a small amount of information given to them, they often completely forget this information in a matter of seconds (Brown, 1958; Peterson & Peterson, 1959). In trying to make sense of these findings, researchers "remembered" one of the earliest memory studies. In 1885, the German psychologist Hermann Ebbinghaus (1850–1909), using himself as his

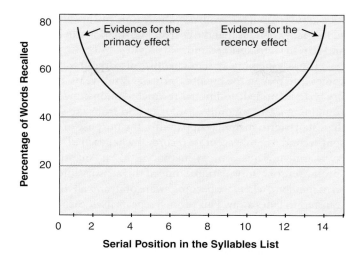

Figure 8-1

The Memory Curve

Hermann Ebbinghaus (1885) found that memory is better for the first few and last few items in a string of nonsense syllables. These two memory effects were respectively called the *primacy effect* and the *recency effect.* In the 1950s, memory researchers argued that the primacy effect suggested the existence of a long-term memory system, while the recency effect suggested a short-term memory system. What was the reasoning behind these assertions?

own subject, studied a list of nonsense syllables (such as *BIW* or *SUW*) and measured how many he later recalled. As illustrated in figure 8-1, Ebbinghaus discovered that he could remember the nonsense syllables near the beginning and end of the list more easily than the ones in the middle. The resulting "U-shaped" pattern was referred to as the *serial-position effect,* with the increased memory for items near the beginning called the **primacy effect** and the increased memory for the last few items called the **recency effect.** In the 1950s, these serial-position findings were reinterpreted as evidence for the existence of two distinct memory systems, not just one. Memory researchers argued that the primacy effect occurs because people have more time to think about the earlier items than the later items, and thus the earlier ones are more likely to be stored in a memory system that can hold information for a long time. This memory system was labeled **long-term memory.** Memory researchers further contended that the recency effect occurs because the last items are still in a memory system that holds information only for relatively short periods of time, up to about 18 seconds. This memory system was called **short-term memory.** Whatever you are currently thinking about or conscious of is contained within short-term memory, and some of the information that is actively processed there makes its way into the considerably more durable long-term memory, which has an immense capacity for information (Nairne, 2003). Long-term memory is the memory system containing the name of your sixth-grade friend.

If your parents ever advised you to "put your best foot forward" when meeting strangers, they were simply emphasizing the fact that the primacy effect shapes social thinking. In general, the first bits of information we learn about people during initial encounters have a bigger impact on our overall impression of them than later information (Asch, 1946). This is probably because the first bits of information are more likely to make their way into long-term memory. Another way to state this phenomenon is that the *primacy effect* has more influence on impression formation than does the *recency effect.*

Neuroimaging studies find that when participants recall items from different serial positions in Ebbinghaus's memory task, different areas of the cerebral cortex are activated (Ranganath et al., 2003; Zhang et al., 2003). The fact that different brain areas are used when recalling items at different serial positions in the memory list is further evidence of distinct memory systems.

One important point about the relationship between short-term and long-term memory is that information flows in both directions. Not only does information from short-term memory go to long-term memory (for further encoding and storage), but also a great deal of information stored in long-term memory is sent back to short-term memory (this is the retrieval process). The reason it is so hard for Ben to memorize new information is that his short-term memory system has trouble working with this information and sending it on to

primacy effect The increased memory for the first bits of information presented in a string of information.

recency effect The increased memory for the last bits of information presented in a string of information.

long-term memory A durable memory system that has an immense capacity for information storage.

short-term memory A limited-capacity memory system through which we actively "work" with information.

long-term memory. In contrast, the reason you are able to answer the question about your sixth-grade friend is that the correct information can be retrieved from long-term memory and sent to short-term memory.

The last memory system scientists discovered is the first memory system that typically comes into play in the memory process. A few years after short-term and long-term memory were identified, additional research demonstrated that a **sensory memory** also exists, containing a vast amount of information from the senses that decays even more quickly than short-term memory. Apparently, the purpose of this memory system is to retain for a split second a highly accurate record of what each of our senses has just experienced in the environment. Thus, sensory memory is like a "snapshot" of our surroundings concerning specific sensory information. Some of this sensory information is then transferred to short-term memory, where we become aware of it, and all the remaining sensory information not transferred fades away. This process repeats itself each moment, with sensory memory continuously supplying short-term memory with new information to process.

Sensory memory happens automatically, without effort and without conscious awareness. Further, unlike the two-way processing that occurs between short-term and long-term memory, information does not travel back from short-term memory to sensory memory. In other words, sensory memory is not involved in the retrieval process of memory. Thus, we cannot analyze or intentionally review a sensory memory.

Is This the Only Model of Memory?

Figure 8-2 provides an overview of the information-processing model, depicting how information is transferred between the three memory systems and how they are related to encoding, storage, and retrieval. This model has dominated research on memory for about four decades. Although psychologists traditionally divide memory into these three systems, it is important to mention that these are *abstract* memory systems and do not actually exist as physically identifiable brain areas. Describing memory as consisting of distinct systems simply supplies us with a useful way of understanding how information is both remembered and forgotten. This model, however, does not explain all memory processes, and there are competing memory system theories (Weldon, 1999). Later in the chapter, in section 8-3c, I discuss a more recent approach, the *parallel distributed processing model,* which represents memory as a weblike network of connections that operate simultaneously rather than sequentially. For now, however, let us use the traditional memory model to examine in greater detail each of the three memory systems.

sensory memory A memory system that very briefly stores the sensory characteristics of a stimulus.

Figure 8-2

Overview of the Information-Processing Model of Memory

The information-processing model of memory likens human memory to computer information-processing. In this model, information goes through three basic processes: encoding, storage, and retrieval. This model also identifies three memory systems: sensory memory, short-term memory, and long-term memory.

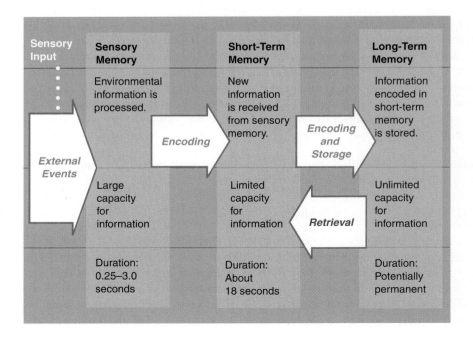

8-1b Sensory Memory Preserves Detailed Sensory Information for a Few Moments

Sensory memory is the doorway to memory. It serves as a holding area, storing information just long enough for us to select items for attention from the multitude transmitted by our senses every moment. Those items not transferred to short-term memory are quickly replaced by incoming stimuli and then lost. The fleeting nature of sensory memory makes sense from an evolutionary perspective (Martindale, 1991). If memories of all of the sights, sounds, tastes, smells, and tactile sensations that you encounter every moment of the day did not quickly fade, you would become incapacitated by sensory overload.

Sensory information is not actually stored all together in one system but instead consists of separate memory subsystems, each related to a different source of sensory information. The duration of sensory memory varies, depending on the sense involved, but no sensory memory lasts more than a few seconds. Visual sensory memory is referred to as *iconic memory,* because it is the fleeting memory of an image, or *icon.* Auditory sensory memory is referred to as *echoic memory,* because this brief memory is often experienced like an echo.

Can you experience sensory memory firsthand? Try the following demonstration. Move your forefinger back and forth in front of your face. The blurred images of many fingers that you see are not the actual sensory-memory images. They are gone. What you are consciously aware of is the end result of the sensory information reaching short-term memory. Thus, you cannot directly access sensory memory.

How do psychologists study something that lasts such a short time and cannot be consciously accessed? In groundbreaking research in this area, George Sperling (1960) presented participants with different displays of letters, consisting of three rows of four letters each. These displays were presented for only one-twentieth of a second and looked like this:

W   K   L   P

R   B   C   U

X   V   T   D

Presenting the letters so briefly meant that participants could get only a glance at them, and most people could recall only 4 or 5 of the 12 letters. They knew they had seen more, but the fleeting image faded before they could report more than the first few letters. With this feedback, Sperling slightly modified his experiment to determine whether his participants were really seeing more of a fleeting image than they could report. The main modification involved assigning a different tone to each row in the display and then sounding one of these tones immediately after the letter pattern disappeared from view. Participants were told to report the letters in the top row if they heard a high tone, the middle row if they heard a medium tone, and the bottom row if they heard a low tone. Because the tone was not sounded until *after* the letter pattern disappeared, participants had to rely on their visual sensory memory, or iconic memory, to report the correct row.

With this modification, participants now correctly identified three or four letters from any given line, indicating that they had stored a fairly complete pattern of the letters in sensory memory. However, if the tone was delayed for half a second, only one or two letters were still available. At a 1-second delay, the information in their iconic memory had completely disappeared, and they could report nothing of what they saw. Now remember, as I just discussed, the participants did not directly perceive the letters in sensory memory. What they "saw" was what had been sent to short-term memory from sensory memory. Subsequent research indicated that iconic memory lasts no more than four-tenths of a second (Van der Heijden, 1981). However, the brighter the visual image, the slower it fades (Long & Beaton, 1982).

Sensory-memory studies of hearing, or *echoic memory,* indicate that auditory echoes last longer than fleeting visual images—up to a few seconds (Cowan et al., 1990). The longer duration of echoic memory explains why we hear a series of musical notes as a melody, or perceive speech as a "string" of continuous words rather than as disjointed sounds. It also explains why sometimes we do not initially comprehend what someone is saying to us while we are distracted by other matters, only to have the words register in our minds a split second later. The auditory echo of sensory memory has retained those spoken words just long enough for us to process their meaning. Of course, here again, we are not directly accessing echoic memory, but instead, we are aware of what has been transferred from echoic memory to short-term memory.

8-1c Short-Term Memory Is Conceived of as a "Working Memory" System

Sensory memories are brief replicas of environmental information, but for us to make sense of this information and retain it for a longer time, it has to be transferred to the second memory system, namely, short-term memory. Although short-term memory was once considered a relatively passive storage area that simply held information until it faded or was transferred to long-term memory, it is now thought of as the memory area where we actively "work" with information that comes from either sensory or long-term memory (Jonides et al., 2005; Osaka, 2003). Memory researcher Alan Baddeley (1992, 2002) referred to this more complex and expanded view of short-term memory as **working memory.**

As depicted in figure 8-3, working memory has three basic components. The first is the *phonological loop,* which temporarily stores auditory input such as spoken words and meaningful sounds and is also used to generate and decode language. It can be refreshed through rehearsal. When reciting a phone number to yourself while searching for a pen to write it down, you are relying on this inner voice. This component of working memory represents all of what we originally thought of as short-term memory. The second component is the *visuospatial sketchpad,* which temporarily stores visual and spatial images (Parasuraman et al., 2005). When an architect envisions a new building design, when a choreographer imagines a dancer's movements, or when you recall the appearance of your favorite stuffed animal from childhood, all these cognitive tasks rely on the visuospatial sketchpad. Finally, the third aspect of working memory is the *central executive* that supervises and coordinates the other two components. The central executive is in charge of encoding information received from sensory memory and then filtering the sufficiently important information to long-term memory. It also retrieves information from long-term memory, if this is necessary.

As you can see, the two original defining characteristics of short-term memory—small capacity and short duration—still exist in the concept of working memory. However, this new view of short-term memory assumes that it handles many more functions and is an active, rather than passive, process. Despite the fact that some researchers make distinctions between short-term memory and working memory (Squire & Kandel, 1999), in this introduction to the psychology of memory, I use these terms interchangeably.

Encoding in Short-Term Memory

The encoding of information in short-term memory is much more complex than that occurring in sensory memory (Brandimonte et al., 1992; Richardson et al., 1996). The two

> **working memory** The term used to describe short-term memory as an active memory system that contains a "central executive" processor and two subsystems for temporarily storing auditory and visual-spatial input.

Figure 8-3

Short-Term Memory as Working Memory

"Working memory" is an updated conceptualization of short-term memory. This short-term memory system is active rather than passive and contains a central executive and two subsystems that temporarily store auditory input (the phonological loop) and visual-spatial input (the visuospatial sketchpad).

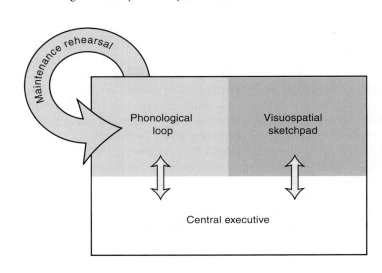

storage systems in working (short-term) memory encode information either acoustically (the phonological loop) or visually (the visuospatial sketchpad), but acoustic encoding seems to dominate (Wickelgren, 1965). In one study, for example, participants were presented with a list of letters and then asked to immediately repeat them (Conrad, 1964). Even though the letters were presented visually, the mistakes made in remembering the letters were overwhelmingly acoustic in nature. That is, a correct letter (such as *V*) was much more likely to be substituted with a similar-sounding letter (such as *E*) than with a similar-looking letter (such as *U*). This research suggests that, although we can store information in short-term memory using both visual and acoustic codes, we rely more on acoustic encoding, perhaps because it is easier to rehearse by mentally talking to ourselves than by creating mental images.

Storage Capacity of Short-Term Memory

Before reading further, complete Explore It Exercise 8-1 to test the storage capacity of your short-term memory. In the 1950s, George Miller tested many people's ability to remember various lists of letters, words, and digits. He found that the capacity of short-term memory is quite limited: About seven items or *chunks* of information (plus or minus two) can be retained at any one time (Miller, 1956). Cross-cultural research indicates that this seven-item limit to short-term memory is universal (Yu et al., 1985). Some recent research even suggests that this number may be as low as four chunks on average (Cowan, 2001). In the 1950s, when American Telephone and Telegraph Company learned of George Miller's finding that people can hold only about seven items of information in short-term memory at a time, they instituted a new policy in assigning phone numbers: All numbers would consist of only seven digits. The hope was that this new standard would reduce customers' need to use operator assistance (Ellis & Hunt, 1993).

What happens when new information is presented to you when your short-term memory capacity is filled? Often, new information simply displaces the currently held information. However, what if you combine many discrete bits of information into a small number of meaningful groupings? This memory strategy, known as **chunking,** can greatly increase the amount of information you can hold in short-term memory. Remember that long list of letters presented in task 2 of Explore It Exercise 8-1? If you examine the pattern of letters closely, you will be able to chunk those 18 individual items into the following six chunks: CNN ABC CBS NBC MCI CIA. Encoding these six chunks is less likely than not to exceed your short-term memory capacity.

Chunking is one of the important memory strategies that we learn in childhood, and these information chunks can be quite complex (Servan-Schreiber & Anderson, 1990). For example, you probably can repeat the following 66-letter, 14-word sentence very easily after reading it only once: *On Tuesday, three-fisted boys run after four-legged girls to compare extra limbs.* Here, you might represent this information as the following four manageable chunks: (1) "On Tuesday" (2) "three-fisted boys" (3) "run after four-legged girls" (4) "to compare extra limbs." In this case, the reason your short-term memory is so good is that you possess a great deal of knowledge about the material—namely, the English language. The ability to create meaningful chunks largely depends on how much you know about the material that needs to be remembered (Chase & Simon, 1973; Egan & Schwartz, 1979). Thus, for chunking to effectively increase short-term memory capacity, it often requires the retrieval of information from long-term memory (Ericsson & Kintsch, 1995).

Maintenance Rehearsal

Although information is stored in short-term memory for only about 18 seconds, this time can be extended through **maintenance rehearsal,** which is the process of repetitively verbalizing or thinking about information. Reciting a phone number until you write it down is an example of maintenance rehearsal. If you are distracted before finding a pen, you will likely forget the number because it is no longer in the phonological loop of short-term memory and was not transferred to the more durable long-term memory system. Maintenance rehearsal is also important in helping you transfer information to long-term memory. This is the method you often rely on when memorizing dialogue in a play, multiplication tables, or foreign language vocabulary.

chunking Organizing items of information into a meaningful unit, or chunk, that can be stored in short-term memory.

maintenance rehearsal The process of repetitively verbalizing or thinking about information to either extend the usual 18-second duration of short-term memory or transfer the rehearsed information to long-term memory.

Explore It
Exercise 8-1

What Is Your Short-Term Memory Capacity?

In the 1950s, the phone company began assigning seven-digit phone numbers to its customers. How was this new policy shaped by George Miller's research on short-term memory capacity?

Source: Courtesy of Figzoi.

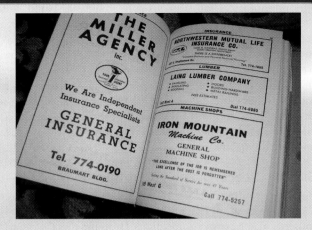

Complete the following two tasks to test the storage capacity of your short-term memory.

Task 1

Directions: Ask someone to read you the letters in the top row at the rate of about one per second. Then try to repeat them back in the same order. Repeat this for the next row, and for the one after that, until you make a mistake. How many letters could you repeat back perfectly?

Q M R
H Z X E
X D P Q F
G N M S W R
D H W Y U N J
E P H E A Z K R
N R E F D T O Q P
U H V X G F N I K J
H F R D S X A W U G T
H E Q L I M Y D J R N K

Task 2

Directions: Read the following string of letters and then try to write them down in correct order:

CNNA   BCCBSNB   CMCIC   IA

How many letters in each task were you able to recall?

8-1d We Often Encode Information into Long-Term Memory Using Elaborative Rehearsal

One problem with using maintenance rehearsal to transfer information to long-term memory is that information learned this way has few retrieval cues and often is not strongly integrated into long-term memory. As a result, such information is often hard to retrieve from long-term memory. However, what if you use a different type of rehearsal in which you organize information in some meaningful fashion? Is it more likely to be transferred to long-term memory in a way that you will later remember?

Although some information is encoded into long-term memory automatically, without any conscious effort, much of this encoding involves relatively conscious processing. This encoding is often accomplished by utilizing a strategy known as **elaborative rehearsal,** which involves thinking about how new information relates to information already stored in long-term memory. This type of rehearsal is referred to as *elaborative* because, rather than merely repeating the information over and over to yourself, you *elaborate* on how it is related to something you already know. Can you still recite many—or all—of those 18 individual letters in task 2 of Explore It Exercise 8-1? If so, that is most likely because you elaborated on how certain of these clusters of letters represent the names of previously learned organizations (CNN, ABC, CBS, NBC, MCI, and the CIA). Similarly, one way I remember phone numbers is by associating them with the jersey numbers of former football players from the Green Bay Packers (information that is in my long-term memory). So, 242-1504 becomes 242-"Bart Starr" and "Brett Favre." Organizational strategies such as this are called *mnemonics* (pronounced "neh MON ix"), which are discussed in greater detail in this chapter's "Psychological Applications" section.

> **elaborative rehearsal**
> Rehearsal that involves thinking about how new information relates to information already stored in long-term memory.

"Shallow" versus "Deep" Processing

Psychologists Fergus Craik and Robert Lockhart (1972) propose that elaborative rehearsal is a more effective way of encoding new information than maintenance rehearsal because elaborative rehearsal involves a deeper level of cognitive processing. In other words, the more you think about how new information is related to existing knowledge you possess, the "deeper" the processing and the better your memory of it becomes. Craik and Lockhart believe that *shallow processing* typically involves encoding information in terms of its superficial perceptual qualities, such as its sights and sounds, while *deep processing* often involves encoding information in terms of its meaning, or *semantics* (refer back to section 8-1a). For instance, look at each of the adjectives in the following list for 5 seconds each, and mentally note which ones contain the letter *e:*

curious

humorous

sensitive

daring

quiet

introspective

ambitious

responsible

Now, instead of scanning these words for the letter *e,* note which of these adjectives describe you as a person. Research indicates that this semantic exercise, in contrast to the previous perceptual exercise, not only triggers more activity in the part of the frontal cortex of the left cerebral hemisphere associated with language but also leads to a greater likelihood of long-term memory storage (Gabrieli et al., 1996). The primary explanation for why memory storage is more permanent in semantic exercises than in perceptual exercises is that semantic exercises create more associations between new memories and existing memories (Lockhart & Craik, 1990). Further, in the semantic exercise just described, you were asked to process the adjectives by associating them with a very important set of existing memories: your self-concept. Numerous studies indicate that the self can be used as a memory aid (Rogers et al., 1977; Symons & Johnson, 1997). When new information is processed in terms of its relevance to ourselves, we tend to process it at a deeper level and better remember it at a later time.

When discussing levels of the encoding process, some researchers—including Craik and Lockhart—disagree with the traditional information-processing model and argue that there is only one memory system beyond sensory memory. They contend that the distinction between short-term memory and long-term memory is simply a matter of the depth of the encoding process. Instead of distinguishing two memory systems (short and long), they describe a continuum of processing ranging from shallow to very deep. Information processed at a shallow level can be retained only briefly (in what is conventionally called short-term memory), while information processed at a deeper level can be kept indefinitely (in what is conventionally called long-term memory). Although Craik and Lockhart's shallow-to-deep continuum view of memory has not replaced the short-term/long-term memory distinction, their research is important because it informs us that the most important determinant of memory is how extensively information is encoded or processed when it is first received. Elaborative rehearsal, which relies extensively on semantic encoding, provides a much deeper level of processing than does maintenance rehearsal, which relies primarily on acoustic encoding.

> *Journey of Discovery* Question
>
> The finding that deep processing leads to more effective encoding and better retention of new information has many practical applications for you as a student. In your own studying, how can you process new information at a deep, rather than a shallow, level?

Semantic Encoding Errors

Because semantic encoding is the dominant encoding process for long-term memory, the types of errors we make in remembering information are often associated with the unique qualities of semantic encoding. For instance, semantic encoding often ignores details and instead encodes the general underlying meaning of information. Consider figure 8-4. Can you identify the correct drawing of a U.S. penny?

When Americans are asked this question, most are unsuccessful, as are people from Great Britain who are asked to identify their country's coins (Nickerson & Adams, 1979; Richardson, 1993). The reason most of us are so bad at correctly identifying a familiar object such as a penny is that we have never encoded all its specific details into long-term memory. The details are processed by short-term memory, but most are not transferred further. Our tendency to encode the general meaning of visual stimuli rather than their specific details is what counterfeiters depend on when "passing" fake currency. To reduce this problem, the U.S. Treasury is now putting more distinctive drawings on paper money so people will more easily recognize counterfeit currency when they see it.

Figure 8-4

Which Is the Real Penny?

Among all these coins, can you correctly identify the "real" penny? Our failure to encode the details of coins and other currency into long-term memory is what counterfeiters rely on in plying their trade.

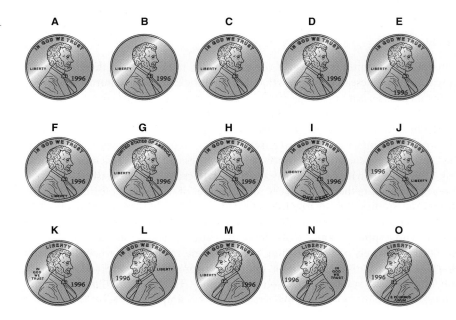

Very few of us ever encode the specific details of currency notes into long-term memory. This fact allows counterfeiters to pass fake money off as real. In hopes of reducing this problem, the U.S. Treasury is beginning to print more distinctive drawings on paper money so we will more easily recognize counterfeit money when we see it.

Source: Courtesy of Figzoi.

Section Review

- Computer information-processing serves as a rough working model for human information-processing.
- In the three basic information processes, the encoding stage transfers information into memory, the storage stage organizes and maintains information in memory for a period of time, and the retrieval stage recovers stored information from memory so it can be used.
- The three memory systems have the following characteristics: Sensory memory stores information just long enough for us to select items for attention; short-term memory (or working memory) actively works with about seven bits of information; and long-term memory has immense information capacity and durability.
- Information can be kept in short-term memory longer through rehearsal.
- Some information is encoded into long-term memory automatically, but a great deal of encoding involves conscious processing.

8-2 WHAT CONSTITUTES LONG-TERM MEMORY?

Preview

- *What kind of information is stored in long-term memory?*
- *Can you have a memory of something without being aware of it?*
- *Is long-term memory one system or many systems?*

The traditional information-processing model describes long-term memory as one solitary system. Yet, beginning in the late 1970s and early 1980s, some cognitive psychologists challenged this view and proposed that long-term memory consists of multiple systems that encode and store different types of information. Thus, unlike a computer, which has one hard drive to store information for long periods of time, the current view of memory is that the brain has multiple "hard drives" (Noice & Noice, 2002; Tulving, 1997).

How many types of long-term memory are there? As yet, memory researchers have not reached agreement. In carving up long-term memory and trying to make sense of it, some cognitive psychologists distinguish among memory systems based on the types of information stored, such as specific facts, general knowledge, or habitual actions. Other researchers emphasize how information is stored in memory, such as whether or not conscious recollection is involved. In this section of the chapter, we will examine both these views of long-term memory and see how together they can provide us with a useful template for understanding the memory process.

8-2a Long-Term Memory Stores Three Major Categories of Information

Cognitive psychologists agree that long-term memory stores at least three major categories of information. **Episodic memory** is memory for factual information acquired at a specific time and place (Tulving, 2002). Do you remember what you had for dinner last night? Do you know when you received your first romantic kiss? Can you recall the name of the current president of the United States? Do you remember how you felt during your first day attending college? All these questions involve episodic memories. When memory researchers present participants with a list of words, numbers, or nonsense syllables—such as in Ebbinghaus's memory curve studies—and later test their memory for this information, they are studying episodic memory. Episodic memory for events in your own life—your personal life history—are called *autobiographical memories* (Catal & Fitzgerald, 2004; Roediger & Marsh, 2003). Autobiographical memory is not composed simply of previously experienced events; it is memory of the self engaged in those events (Pernot-Marino et al., 2004). This memory of self-experiences creates the essence of "you" in your own mind (Woll, 2002). A recent study suggests that when we recall autobiographical memories that were either positive or negative, we tend to "see" the events from our own perspective, whereas we tend to "see" emotionally neutral autobiographical memories as an observer would (D'Argembeau et al., 2003).

Given our discussion in chapter 4, section 4-2d, concerning how culture shapes the structure of self-concept, would it surprise you to learn that your autobiographical memories are shaped by whether you grew up in a collectivist or an individualist culture? A developmental psychologist, Qi Wang (2001), asked Chinese college students in Beijing and American college students in Boston to report their earliest childhood memories. His subsequent analysis indicated that the Chinese students' early memories were more likely than those of the American students to include other people and to center on routine group activities involving family or community members ("I used to play with friends. . . . We went to the bush to pick wild fruits to eat."). In contrast, American students' early memories were more self-focused and involved more themes of individual autonomy than those of the Chinese students ("When I was 4, I got stung by a bee."). These cultural differences in the content of autobiographical memories reflect Chinese culture's emphasis on interdependence and tightly knit social relationships, and American culture's emphasis on independence and loosely knit relationships. Therefore, how your culture socializes you to think of yourself in relation to your group and how it teaches you to relate to others not only shapes the structure of your self-concept but also shapes the content of your autobiographical memories (Fivush & Nelson, 2004).

In contrast to the specific information stored in episodic memory, **semantic memory** is more general in nature. It stores general knowledge about the world that we typically do not remember acquiring at a specific time and place (Menson et al., 2002; Tulving & Lepage, 2000). For example, do you remember when or where you learned that George Washington was the first president of the United States? Or when you learned that Santa Claus had a reindeer with a big red nose? All the countless facts that you have learned during the course of your life generally fit into this category of memory. Studies of brain-injured patients and neuroimaging studies of healthy individuals suggest that both episodic and semantic memories involve the activation of the frontal lobe, but that the right frontal lobe may play a larger role in episodic memory, while semantic memory may involve more left frontal lobe activity (Hasegawa et al., 1998; Nyberg et al., 2003). These findings provide further evidence that long-term memory consists of multiple systems (Squire & Kandel, 1999).

Finally, **procedural memory** retains information of how to perform skilled motor activities, such as how to ride a bike, drive a car, do a cartwheel, or even walk. Often referred to as *habits*, these activities are so well learned that we carry them out automatically, with-

---

episodic memory Memory for factual information acquired at a specific time and place.

semantic memory Memory for general knowledge about the world that is not associated with a time and place when the information was learned.

procedural memory Memory of how to perform skilled motor activities, which have become well-learned habits and are carried out automatically (without conscious thought).

out conscious thought. We begin forming procedural memories during infancy, when we learn to walk, talk, and engage in other routine activities. It is often difficult to describe in words how to actually perform these actions. For example, when recently asked to describe how to drive using a stick shift on a car, I was at a loss for words. After a few failed attempts at verbally describing how to depress the clutch pedal while simultaneously repositioning the shifter, I sat on a chair and demonstrated the procedure by imagining myself in the driver's seat.

Countless everyday situations and activities require you to use all three types of long-term memory. For example, when driving a car, you rely on procedural memory to steer, shift, speed up, and slow down. Remembering the rules of driving, such as stopping at red lights, yielding to pedestrians, and driving on the right side of the road, is an example of semantic memory. Finally, recalling that you were ticketed for speeding on a particular stretch of road on your 19th birthday is an example of episodic memory.

8-2b Long-Term Memories Can Be Explicit or Implicit

Another way to understand the content of long-term memory is to determine whether the information can be consciously recollected or not. As you have learned throughout this textbook, experience affects how we behave. However, our memory of these past experiences can be either conscious or relatively unconscious (Nelson et al., 1992; Underwood & Bright, 1996).

For many years, psychologists primarily studied the conscious recollection of previous experiences, known as **explicit memory.** Explicit remembering can be either intentional or unintentional. For example, you might intentionally recall an argument, or this memory might spontaneously enter your consciousness. Both instances involve explicit memory because conscious recollection takes place. Explicit memory is sometimes also referred to as *declarative memory* because, if asked, you can "declare" this information. Episodic and semantic memories are explicit memories, because you know you possess this information.

Remembering does not always involve conscious recollection. In fact, quite often we retain information that influences our thoughts and actions, without consciously remembering it (Dovidio et al., 2001; Schacter et al., 1993). This psychological process is known as **implicit memory.** How might implicit memory affect your thoughts and behavior? If you were traumatized by a horse as a youngster, you might feel anxious when around horses as an adult, even though you have no conscious memory of the childhood incident (see the discussion of repression in section 8-5c). Similarly, feeling uneasy and irritable around a new acquaintance because she unconsciously reminds you of a disagreeable person from your past is another example of the power of implicit memory. Implicit memory is also referred to as *nondeclarative memory*, because you cannot "declare" this information.

It is not unusual for a great deal of cognitive activity to be involved in implicit memory (Rovee-Collier et al., 2001). For example, while reading these words, you are unconsciously remembering their meaning. Similarly, knowledge of the motor skills necessary for walking involves the use of implicit memories. Indeed, procedural memories are a type of implicit memory. To demonstrate the truth of this statement, before reading further, complete Explore It Exercise 8-2.

To study implicit memory, psychologists often use word-completion tasks. In such tasks, a participant is asked to complete word stems, such as the following: part_ _ _ _ _ _ _. Because you just saw the word *participant* earlier in the sentence, you are more likely to think of this word than the word *partnership*. This method of activating implicit memories is known as **priming.** The fact that a previous experience (seeing the word *participant*) makes you more likely to respond in a certain way demonstrates that you can retain more implicit knowledge about the past than you realize (Roediger, 1990).

Some cognitive psychologists believe that explicit and implicit memories constitute separate memory systems, whereas other memory researchers believe that these two types of memories simply involve the use of different types of encoding and retrieval processes. While acknowledging this difference of opinion among the experts, I organize my introduction to long-term memory by assuming for the time being that explicit memory and

explicit memory Memory of previous experiences that one can consciously recollect; also called *declarative memory.*

implicit memory Memory of previous experiences without conscious recollection; also called *nondeclarative memory.*

priming A method of activating implicit memories, in which a recently presented bit of information facilitates—or "primes"—responses in a subsequent situation.

Explore It
Exercise **8-2**

Do You Rely on Your Implicit Memory When Typing?

A great deal of knowledge is stored in the form of implicit memories. For example, your knowledge of how to perform skilled motor activities, what is called procedural memory, involves the use of implicit memories. Let's demonstrate this memory fact by considering your knowledge of computers, specifically your computer keyboard. First try reciting from memory the letters on the keys of a computer keyboard, starting with the bottom left row. Don't spread your fingers in front of you to help in recalling the letter order!

Was it difficult? Impossible? I'm betting that you could not recall the letters in their proper order.

Now spread your fingers in front of you, as if they were resting on a keyboard, and "type" your name using the imaginary keys. If you have experience typing on the computer, this is an easy task, and it demonstrates that you really do know the proper order of the keys. Thus, although it is difficult for you to consciously "declare" this information, you still can unconsciously pull it out of memory and use it to correctly type your name.

Can you recite from memory the letters on a computer keyboard, starting with the bottom left row? Is this a difficult task for you? Why?

Source: Courtesy of Figzoi.

Figure 8-5

Types of Long-Term Memory

Long-term memory consists of two basic subsystems: explicit memory, which involves memories of previous experiences that we can consciously recollect, and implicit memory, which involves memories of previous experiences without conscious recollection. Within the explicit memory subsystem are two types of memory information: episodic memory, which is memory for factual information acquired at a specific time and place, and semantic memory, which is memory for general knowledge that is not associated with a time and place when the information was learned. Finally, within the implicit memory subsystem, the most common type of memory information is procedural memory, which is memory of how to perform skilled motor activities.

implicit memory are two separate and distinct subsystems. Operating from this assumption, figure 8-5 categorizes episodic, semantic, and procedural memories into explicit and implicit domains. Future research will determine whether these distinctions remain useful in helping us understand the memory process.

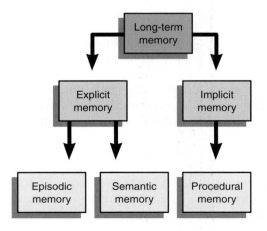

S e c t i o n   R e v i e w

- Long-term memory stores information learned at a specific time and place (episodic memory), general knowledge information (semantic memory), and information on how to perform skilled motor activities (procedural memory).
- Explicit memory involves conscious recollection, whereas implicit memory involves using information in long-term memory without being aware that you are doing so.
- Episodic and semantic memories are explicit memories, whereas procedural memories are implicit memories.

8-3 HOW DO WE ORGANIZE INFORMATION IN MEMORY?

Preview

- *How might memory be like a semantic network?*
- *How might memory be organized into neural networks?*
- *Do schemas help us organize knowledge?*

As noted, an immense amount of information is encoded into long-term memory, much of it unique to your own personal experiences. However, during the course of your formal and informal schooling, you have also encoded much of the same information as other individuals, especially those who have grown up in the same cultural surroundings. Demonstrate this fact for yourself by completing Explore It Exercise 8-3.

8-3a Some Information in Long-Term Memory Is Organized into Networks of Related Concepts

In an early study of how information is organized in long-term memory, William Bousfield (1953) asked people to memorize 60 randomly presented words that came from four semantic categories: names, animals, vegetables, and professions. Despite the random order of presentation, people later tended to recall the words in clusters corresponding to the four categories. Subsequent research indicated that, even when items on a list have little in common, we still try to impose a semantic structure (Mandler & Pearlstone, 1966; Tulving, 1962). These findings suggest that, possibly due to both experience and genetic predisposition, we develop the habit of organizing information into meaningful patterns to facilitate encoding, and hence, long-term memory.

In attempting to understand how knowledge is often semantically organized in long-term memory (see section 8-2a), a number of theorists have proposed that information is stored in a vast network of interrelated concepts (Anderson, 1990; Ratcliff & McKoon, 1994). One of the most influential of these theories is called the **semantic network model** (Collins & Loftus, 1975). According to this model, there are many kinds of associations we can make between concepts. A *concept* consists of a cluster of objects, ideas, or events that share common properties and are linked to other concepts in the long-term memory network. Some concepts in this network are more strongly linked than others.

Figure 8-6 depicts a small semantic network as it might look right after you think of the concept *Santa Claus*. According to the semantic network model, when you think of a concept, your thoughts naturally go to related concepts. In figure 8-6, this network of possible associations is represented by lines connecting the concepts. *Santa Claus* activates associations with the following concepts: *red* and *white,* because Santa has a red suit and a white beard; *snow* and *Christmas,* because he visits during a specific night in winter; *reindeer* and *rooftops,* because these animals fly him to the top of houses; and *elves* and *presents,* because his elf-helpers make presents that he delivers. The length of the lines indicates the strength of the association between the concepts. Shorter lines imply stronger associations, meaning that you will more easily recall concepts with these stronger associations. Thus, when you hear the name *Santa Claus,* you are more likely to think of the words *Christmas, red,* and *reindeer* than

semantic network model A theory that describes concepts in long-term memory organized in a complex network of associations.

Explore It
Exercise **8-3**

Are You an "April, August, December" Encoder? (I Doubt It.)

To experience how you encode some information into long-term memory, try this exercise: Recite the names of the 12 months of the year as fast as you can. Go!

Barring any physical problems with your brain, I'm sure that you—and everyone else reading this chapter—knew all 12 names of the months. I'm also willing to bet that everyone recited them in the following order: January, February, March, April, May, June, July, August, September, October, November, December. Am I right about your recitation? Why do you think this is so?

Now recite these same months again as fast as you can, but this time, recite them in alphabetical order. Go!

If you did indeed take up my challenge, I'm virtually certain that it took you much longer to complete the second task than the first, despite the fact that the first task allowed you to "practice" recalling the months' names. Why?

Do you know how you encoded the months of the year into long-term memory?

Source: Courtesy of Figzoi.

the words *elves* and *white*. Similarly, you are much more likely to think of the words *elves, white, snow,* and *presents* than the words *leprechauns, blue, sleet,* and *offerings*.

Although the semantic network model assumes that semantic networks are a universal way of organizing information, cross-cultural studies indicate that the way people use these networks is influenced by experience and education. For example, research in rural Liberia and Guatemala found that children who receive more schooling are more likely to use semantic categories in recalling lists of concepts than are children with less schooling (Cole & Cole, 1993). This finding makes sense, because semantic grouping allows for the quick learning of a lot of information, a basic requirement in academic settings. Children with less schooling have less need to memorize large amounts of information and, thus, are less likely to organize information semantically. These findings do

Figure 8-6

A Semantic Network Model

According to the semantic network model, information in long-term memory is organized in a complex network of associations. The shorter the link between concepts, the more likely it is that retrieving one concept will trigger the retrieval of the other concept.

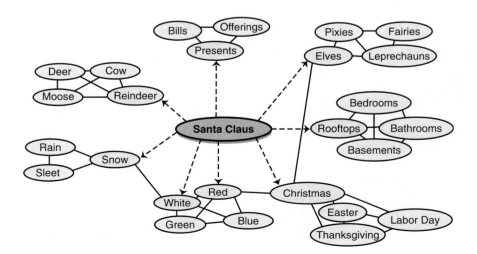

If you would like to impress your friends with the power of semantic networks, have them complete the following brainteaser (Fulero, 1997). But first, explore it yourself. The only rule is to execute each instruction as quickly as possible.

1. Pick a number from 1 to 9.
2. Subtract 5.
3. Multiply by 3.
4. Square the number (that is, multiply by the same number).
5. Add the digits until you get only one digit (for example, 64 = 6 + 4 = 10 = 1 + 0 = 1).
6. If the number is less than 5, add 5; otherwise, subtract 4.
7. Multiply by 2.
8. Subtract 6.
9. Find your mark by mapping the digit to a letter in the alphabet (1 = A, 2 = B, 3 = C, 4 = D, and so on).
10. Pick a name of a country that begins with that letter.
11. Take the second letter in the country's name and then think of a mammal that begins with that letter.
12. Think of the color of that animal.

Are you thinking of a gray elephant from Denmark?

Steps 1 to 8 of this brainteaser are designed so that everyone has the number 4 going into step 9, thus giving them the letter *D*. From this point, the reason this brainteaser usually ends with the person thinking of a gray elephant from Denmark is that, for most North Americans and Europeans, the concept "Denmark" has a stronger association with "countries that begin with the letter *D*" than, say, the "Dominican Republic" or "Dahomey" (an African nation). Likewise, with the *e* from "Denmark," people are also more likely to think of the concept "elephant" than, say, the concept "elk." Thus, in dazzling people with your apparent ability to read their minds, you are counting on their having a specific semantic structure for these two concepts. Instead of actually "reading" their minds, you are "predicting" their semantic associations. By the way, did you notice the priming word I inserted in instruction 9 to increase the probability that you would think of the word *Denmark*?

not mean that school-educated children have better memories than those with no schooling. Instead, they mean that people tend to organize information in long-term memory that is consistent with their life experiences and the demands of their surroundings. If you want to capitalize on the influence that life experiences have on people's semantic networks and simultaneously impress your friends with your "mind-reading" ability, examine Explore It Exercise 8-4.

8-3b Information in Long-Term Memory Can Be Organized around Schemas

The tendency to encode information by semantic categories doesn't mean that all stored memories are arranged in semantic networks. Semantic networks explain how one concept triggers a network of related concepts, but they are of limited help in explaining how information is clustered into coherent wholes. Such clusters of knowledge are called *schemas*. As discussed in chapter 4, section 4-3a, schemas are organized, repeatedly exercised patterns of thought or behavior. Regarding encoding and memory, research indicates that people are more likely to remember things they can incorporate into existing schemas than things they cannot (Marshall, 1995).

John Bransford and Marcia Johnson (1972) conducted a memory experiment that demonstrated the importance of having the right schema at the right time. To understand

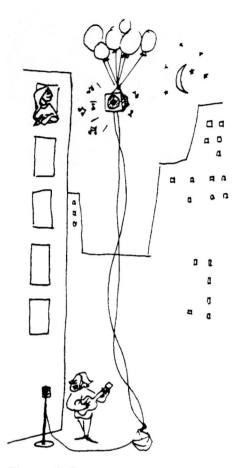

Figure 8-7

Man Serenading a Woman

Source: Figure from "Contextual prerequisites for understanding: Some investigations of comprehension and recall" by John D. Bransford and M. K. Johnson in *Journal of Verbal Learning and Verbal Behavior,* 11, pp. 717–726, copyright © 1972. Reprinted by permission of Elsevier. This material may not be reproduced in any form or by any means without the prior written permission of the publisher.

the importance of schemas yourself, read the following story read by Bransford and Johnson's participants, and then, like them, try to recall as much of it as you can:

If the balloons popped, the sound wouldn't be able to carry since everything would be too far away from the correct floor. A closed window would also prevent the sound from carrying, since most buildings tend to be well insulated. Since the whole operation depends on the steady flow of electricity, a break in the middle of the wire would also cause problems. Of course, the fellow could shout, but the human voice is not loud enough to carry that far. An additional problem is that the string could break on the instrument. Then there would be no accompaniment to the message. It is clear that the best situation would involve less distance. Then there would be fewer potential problems. With face-to-face contact, the least number of things could go wrong.

After reading this passage, take a little break, look around your immediate surroundings, and make a mental note of 10 different objects you can see. What color is each of them? What are their sizes in relation to one another?

Now that I have distracted you from thinking about the Bransford and Johnson story for more than 18 seconds, how much of it can you remember? Experimental participants remembered less than 4 of its 14 ideas when, like you, they were given *no schema* in which to understand the story. However, when participants were given a schema in which to understand the story—by being shown a cartoon similar to the one in figure 8-7 before reading the story—they recalled twice as many ideas (about 8 out of 14). Interestingly, participants who were given the schema after the reading remembered no more than those not shown the picture at all. Apparently, seeing the picture beforehand allowed participants to make sense of what they were reading. This suggests that it is crucial to have the right schema during the encoding stage in order to understand and remember complex material. Further studies indicate that schemas help us remember and organize details, speed up processing time, and fill in gaps in our knowledge (Fiske & Taylor, 1991; Hirt, 1990). The fact that schemas can fill in gaps in our knowledge explains why they sometimes contribute to memory distortions (see section 8-4d.)

Because schemas develop from our experiences, it is reasonable to assume that they are significantly shaped by culture. Further, if people from different cultures develop markedly different schemas, these divergent mental frameworks for processing and storing information should influence what they notice and remember. In one study, students in both the United States and the Pacific island nation of Palau read separate descriptions of funerals in the two cultures and were later asked to recall everything they could about them (Pritchard, 1991). The researchers hypothesized that students would better remember the funeral description from their own culture because it would more closely match their cultural schema for funerals. Results supported this hypothesis. Further cross-cultural research indicates that *cultural utility* plays an important role in what kind of schemas develop and, thus, what we remember (Mistry & Rogoff, 1994). For example, the Fore people of New Guinea have highly elaborate schemas for many different bird species, but they tend to group all butterflies together under one schematic category (Diamond, 1966). The reason for this difference is that birds are a valued food source for the Fore, while butterflies are of little use to them. Similarly, the Sahaptin Indians of the northwestern United States—who depend on fish as a primary food source—can accurately identify many fish species in their environment but can identify few flowers, which have little use to them, despite their beauty (Hunn, 1982, 1990). These findings, along with many other studies, suggest that culture does shape schema formation and thus plays an important role in the memory process (Malt, 1995). The culture we grow up in influences what we will attend to, process, encode, and later recall from long-term memory.

8-3c Memory May Involve Parallel Processing of Neural Units

Do you realize that, while reading the words on this page, you are performing some amazing feats of memory? You are recognizing the patterns that make up the letters of the alphabet while simultaneously recognizing how sets of these letters make up words in the English language and how these word strings make up meaningful sentences. How can you execute these different memory tasks so quickly?

The traditional information-processing model assumes that the brain works sequentially, like a computer (Ioannides et al., 2002), but such *serial processing* would occur too slowly to account for your reading the words on this page. Rather, we know that the human brain performs many tasks simultaneously—that is, in parallel. It apparently accomplishes this *parallel processing* of information because millions of neurons are active at once, and each neuron is communicating with thousands of other neurons. This simultaneous neural communication produces the type of cognitive complexity necessary for parallel processing. Building on this idea of simultaneous neural communication, **parallel distributed processing models** of memory contend that what we call *memory* is knowledge distributed across a dense network of neural associations (McClelland, 1994; Raffone & Leeuwen, 2001; Smolensky, 1995). When this neural network is activated, different areas of the network operate simultaneously, in a parallel fashion. Such parallel processing allows us to quickly and efficiently utilize our storehouse of knowledge.

A parallel distributed processing system consists of a large network of interconnected neurons called *processing units,* which are distributed throughout our brains. Each unit is designed to work on a specific type of memory task. For example, one model suggests that for comprehending written English, there might be individual processing units for 16 different letter patterns, for each of the 26 letters in the English alphabet, and for thousands of words (McClelland & Rumelhart, 1981). When you look at a book written in English, these processing units in your brain are activated at the same time. The letter-related units recognize letters, while the word units recognize words from letter combinations, and presto, you are comprehending the words on the page with amazing speed.

Parallel distributed processing models maintain that information in memory is not located in a specific place in the brain but, instead, resides in connections between the involved processing units in the neural network (Nadeau, 2001). Parallel distributed processing models better represent the actual operation of the brain than do the information-processing models and also have been used to explain perception, language, and decision making. However, the information-processing approach is still better at explaining memory for single events, as well as accounting for the fact that learning new information can sometimes cause you to forget previously learned information (see section 8-5b). In sizing up these two approaches, memory expert Endel Tulving (1999) advises that, at least for the present, both models are necessary for a fuller understanding of memory.

> **parallel distributed processing models** Models of memory in which a large network of interconnected neurons, or processing units, distributed throughout the brain simultaneously work on different memory tasks.

Section Review

- In the semantic network model, information is organized in long-term memory in a vast network of interrelated concepts.
- Schemas help us remember and organize details, speed up processing time, and fill in knowledge gaps.
- Parallel distributed processing models contend that memory is a large network of interconnected neurons, or processing units, that simultaneously work on different memory tasks.

8-4 HOW DO WE RETRIEVE INFORMATION FROM MEMORY?

Preview

- *What is the difference between recognition and recall?*
- *What is a retrieval cue?*
- *What is the encoding specificity principle?*
- *What is a likely explanation for déjà vu experiences and cryptomnesia?*
- *Does our remembering change over time?*
- *Are flashbulb memories accurate?*

Encoding, storing, and organizing information in long-term memory are important cognitive processes, but they would be of no use if we could not later retrieve this information when we needed it. Remembering involves retrieving information from long-term memory so it resides in consciousness, or short-term memory. To appreciate firsthand the power and imperfection of memory retrieval, try answering the following five questions:

- Did Abraham Lincoln fly in a spaceship to the moon?
- How many days are there in the month of April?
- What did you eat for breakfast last Monday?
- In Mexico, which national hero is considered the "father" of his country?
- Which of the following terms refers to conscious recollection of previous experiences?
  a. implicit memory
  b. explicit memory
  c. procedural memory
  d. sensory memory

8-4a Memory Retrieval Varies in Difficulty

When answering the previous questions, it is likely that you found some easier than others. For instance, you probably quickly answered that Lincoln never flew to the moon, but it probably took you a bit longer to remember that there are 30 days in April. Did you remember what you ate for breakfast last Monday, and were you able to recall that Benito Juárez, Mexico's first president of Indian descent, was his country's national hero? Finally, were you able to recognize that answer *b* was the correct answer for the last question?

As this exercise hopefully illustrates, although memory retrieval can be effortless and automatic, it can also be difficult and unreliable. The effortful nature of memory retrieval might have been demonstrated when you tried to answer the "April" question. Perhaps you had to recite a rhyme learned in childhood to aid your recall: "Thirty days hath September, April, June, and November. . . ." By the way, if you could not answer the "Mexican national hero" question, it may have been because the Benito Juárez information was not stored in long-term memory. Finally, the "explicit memory" question might have been relatively easy, because all you had to do was recognize it as the correct response.

When measuring explicit memory, psychologists typically test people's *recall* ability and their *recognition* ability. Although **recall** requires a person to retrieve and reproduce information from memory, **recognition** simply requires a person to decide whether or not the information has been previously encountered. In most cases, recall is more difficult than recognition, because recall requires more extensive mental processing (Watkins & Tulving, 1975). This is the main reason you will often *recognize* a person's face as familiar, even though you cannot *recall* her or his name (Boehm et al., 2005). Recent studies indicate that the cognitive capacity for recalling information from long-term memory emerges late in the first year of life, well before children have the verbal ability to describe past experiences (Bauer, 2002).

To directly test the explicit remembering of faces versus names, researchers first asked young and old high school graduates to write down the names of as many former classmates as they could remember (Bahrick et al., 1975). For all age groups, recall was poor. Recent graduates could recall only a few dozen names, and those who had graduated over 40 years earlier recalled fewer than 20 names. Next, researchers asked these same individuals to identify the face of a former classmate from a card containing five photographs. In this recognition task, recent graduates and those who had graduated up to 35 years earlier correctly recognized classmates 90 percent of the time! Even those who had graduated 48 years earlier still recognized classmates three-fourths of the time.

In analyzing these findings, it is important to realize that they do not suggest that we are better at remembering faces than names. Instead, they indicate that recall is more difficult than recognition. Remembering faces becomes much more difficult when we have to *recall* each facial feature rather than simply *recognize* it as familiar. Similarly, our

recall A measure of explicit memory in which a person must retrieve and reproduce information from memory.

recognition A measure of explicit memory in which a person need only decide whether or not something has been previously encountered.

Why is it easier to recognize a familiar person's face than to recall his or her name?
Source: Courtesy of Figzoi.

ability to recognize familiar names is equal to our ability to recognize familiar faces (Faw, 1990).

The greater difficulty of recall tasks compared with recognition tasks is one of the main reasons most students prefer true-false and multiple-choice exams over essay and fill-in-the-blank exams. The former types of questions require recognition only of the correct answer, while the latter types require the retrieval and reproduction of information (Kroll et al., 2002). The different remembering required in these exams, however, doesn't necessarily mean that recognition tests are easy. As you undoubtedly know from personal experience, multiple-choice tests can be extremely challenging (you might even say "tricky") if the alternatives are very similar to the correct response. Sometimes the correct answer feels like it is on the "tip of your tongue"—so close you can almost taste it, which is the topic of section 8-4b.

8-4b We Sometimes Are Only Temporarily Unable to Retrieve Information from Memory

In explicit memory, we often can retrieve some features but not enough to identify an entire concept. For example, pause for a few seconds and try to recall the names of all the dwarfs from the movie *Snow White and the Seven Dwarfs*.

How did you do? If your retrieval attempt resulted in incomplete recall, you are in good company—most people cannot recall all seven names without assistance (Miserandino, 1991). Now try this second exercise: Pick out the seven dwarf names from among the 14 names listed in alphabetical order here:

Angry, Bashful, Crummy, Doc, Dopey, Father, Grumpy, Happy, Leafy, Sleepy, Sneezy, Snowy, Sweaty, Windy

I'm guessing that the second exercise, which involves recognition rather than recall, was easier for you than the first exercise. In doing the first exercise, you may have felt that the names were just about to enter consciousness, but you were having trouble pulling them out of long-term memory. About once a week, most people are unable to remember something they are absolutely certain they know. This frustrating retrieval problem is known as the **tip-of-the-tongue phenomenon** and is another demonstration of how recognition is easier than recall (Brown, 2000; Schwartz, 2001, 2002).

tip-of-the-tongue phenomenon The temporary inability to remember something you know, accompanied by the feeling that it is just beyond your conscious state.

Listed next are some basic facts about the tip-of-the-tongue phenomenon (Brown, 1991; James & Burke, 2000; Vigliocco et al., 1999):

- It appears to be universal, occurring in all cultures and age groups.
- It increases in frequency with age.
- It is most often triggered by names of personal acquaintances.
- When a person tries to remember the sought-after word, related words come to mind. These words usually have a similar meaning (*favoritism* instead of *nepotism*) or sound (*Greg* instead of *Craig*).
- Usually, people can guess the first letter of the sought-after word about half the time.
- About half the time, the person remembers the sought-after word within the first minute.

By the way, if you are still wondering about those dwarf names, they are *Sleepy, Grumpy, Dopey, Sneezy, Happy, Bashful,* and *Doc.*

8-4c Retrieval Cues Help Trigger Recall of Stored Memories

retrieval cue A stimulus that allows us to more easily recall information from long-term memory.

One of the most effective ways to facilitate remembering is to use retrieval cues. A **retrieval cue** is a stimulus that allows us to more easily recall information from long-term memory. The reason similar stimuli help us remember information is that many elements of the physical setting in which we learn are simultaneously encoded into long-term memory along with the information we are learning (Tulving & Thomson, 1973). The helpfulness of the physical setting in fostering retrieval is also why students perform better on exams when tested in the classroom where they learned the material than in a different setting (Saufley et al., 1985; Smith et al., 1978).

If you think of a memory as being held in storage by a web of associations, as in the semantic network model (see section 8-3a), then retrieval cues would be the individual strands in the web that lead to the memory (Anderson, 1983). The more retrieval cues you have for a particular memory and the better learned these cues are, the more accessible the memory will be. You are likely to retrieve the sought-after memory if you can activate one or more of those strands.

Thus far I have mentioned only retrieval cues originating in our external world. Yet our internal psychological environment can also be encoded and become part of our memory strands. For example, when people learn information while in an altered state of consciousness induced by alcohol, marijuana, or some other drug, they may later recall it better when tested under the same altered state (Eich, 1989). Similar effects have been found for positive and negative moods. When in a positive mood, we tend to recall positive memories, while negative memories are more accessible when we are depressed (Ehrlichman & Halpern, 1988; Lewinsohn & Rosenbaum, 1987). This tendency for retrieval from memory to be better when our *state* of mind at the time of retrieval matches our *state* at the time of initial encoding is known as **state-dependent memory.**

state-dependent memory The tendency for retrieval from memory to be better when our state of mind during retrieval matches our state during encoding.

Although many studies have found evidence for state-dependent memory, others have not (Bower & Mayer, 1991; Kihlstrom, 1989). Two factors that appear to influence the strength of state-dependent memory are *self-awareness* and the *presence of other retrieval cues.* That is, evidence for state-dependent memory is strongest when people are self-aware (and thus, attentive to their internal state of mind) and when other retrieval cues are weakest (Rothkopf & Blaney, 1991; Singer & Salovey, 1988).

encoding specificity principle A retrieval rule stating that retrieving information from long-term memory is most likely when the conditions at retrieval closely match the conditions present during the original learning.

As mentioned in section 8-1d, the best retrieval cues come from associations formed when we encode information into long-term memory. This rule of retrieval, known as the **encoding specificity principle,** is supported by a large body of evidence (Mantyla, 1986; Tulving & Thomson, 1973). For instance, in one study, participants were shown a long list of words and then asked either a semantic (meaning) or a rhyming question about each word (Morris et al., 1977). Thus, if the word were *dairy,* they might have been asked if "*dairy* products come from cows" or if "*dairy* rhymes with *fairy.*" Later, participants were asked to identify from a list those words they had been shown before. Results indicated that participants did much better at recognizing words for which semantic questions had previously been asked than they did for rhyming-word questions. The fact that semantically coded retrieval cues worked better than rhyming codes is not surprising, because as previously mentioned (section 8-1d), long-term memories are often encoded semantically. However, when asked to identify words that *rhymed* with the ones they had previously seen (for example, *berry,* which rhymes with *dairy*), participants did much better at recognizing words that rhymed with words for which they had been asked a rhyming question rather than a semantic question.

The importance of having the right retrieval cues for a memory task strikes close to home for every college student. In what you might perceive to be a cruel classroom demonstration of the encoding specificity principle, half the students in a college class were told that an upcoming exam would be multiple-choice (a recognition task), while the other half expected an essay exam (a recall task). Only some of the students, however, were given the exam they expected, and consistent with the encoding specificity principle, those students did much better on the exam than those who received an unexpected type of exam (d'Ydewalle & Rosselle, 1978). These results, combined with the previous study's findings, clearly indicate that the best retrieval cues are those that closely match the original encoding process.

8-4d Source Confusion Can Create Memory Illusions

One of the primary distinctions between semantic and episodic memory involves remembering the time and place when the information in question was learned. With semantic memory, the information in question is no longer associated with the time and place when it was learned, but with episodic memory, the information is most definitely tied to a specific time and place. Yet sometimes we forget the true source of the episodic memory, and then we have a *memory illusion* (Urbach et al., 2005). Memory illusions appear to be shaped by implicit remembering.

A common type of memory illusion is the **déjà vu illusion** (Brown, 2004; Sno, 2000). In French, déjà vu literally means "already seen." About 60 percent of American adults experience déjà vu at least once in their lives. People who experience this memory illusion subjectively feel a sense of familiarity in a situation that they objectively know they have never encountered before. An example of déjà vu would be walking into a house for the very first time and experiencing a strong feeling of having been there before. Such experiences occur most often among people who regularly remember their dreams and who daydream a great deal. They are also most likely to occur when you are stressed and when you are overly tired (Brown, 2003; Reed, 1979). Although a popular belief is that déjà vu occurs because people are experiencing previous lives (reincarnation), a more cognitive—and less extraordinary—explanation is that people are simply implicitly remembering similar, but unidentifiable, situations they have previously experienced in their present lives (Brown, 2003). When brain scans have been able to locate the neurological source of déjà vu experiences, they tend to originate in the temporal lobes (Zeman, 2005).

Another type of memory illusion is **cryptomnesia,** which is also known as *unintended plagiarism* (Searleman & Herrmann, 1994). In cryptomnesia, a person honestly believes that some work she or he has done is a novel creation, when in reality the work is not original (Brown & Murphy, 1989; Taylor, 1965). This type of memory illusion is common when people collaborate on a project. In such instances, group members recall an idea they heard from others, but they forget where and from whom they originally heard it. After a while, each of them believes it was they who came up with the brilliant idea that made the project a success. If you think of cryptomnesia as an instance in which someone else's old idea becomes your new idea, then cryptomnesia is almost the opposite of déjà vu, in which something new seems old. With cryptomnesia, as with déjà vu, previously learned information is retained and influences our thoughts and actions without our consciously remembering it.

Accusations of cryptomnesia usually arise only after someone publicly presents the unintentionally plagiarized work as her or his own. A number of the more famous incidents—and even scandals—resulting from such public presentations have involved such well-known individuals as Sigmund Freud (founder of psychoanalysis), Helen Keller (educator and lecturer who was both deaf and blind), Friedrich Nietzsche (German philosopher and poet), Eddie Murphy (comedian and movie star), and George Harrison (former member

Why do students perform better on exams when tested in the same room where they learned the material than in a different setting?

Source: Courtesy of Figzoi.

déjà vu illusion A memory illusion in which people feel a sense of familiarity in a situation that they know they have never encountered before.

cryptomnesia A memory illusion in which people believe that some work they have done is a novel creation when, in fact, it is not original.

of the Beatles). How common is cryptomnesia? The frequency of its occurrence is difficult to estimate, because people in private life are rarely confronted with evidence that their ideas and works are not original. But it is safe to assume that cryptomnesia is not a rare product of implicit memory.

8-4e Memories Are Often Sketchy Reconstructions of the Past

The existence of memory illusions is evidence that our memories are susceptible to distortion. Yet distortions in memory extend beyond déjà vu and cryptomnesia incidents. Based on the chapter 5 discussion of perception, you understand that errors or misperceptions are bound to occur because our beliefs and expectations significantly influence how we perceive sensory stimuli. Similarly, our previous discussion of schemas (see section 8-3b) demonstrates that our beliefs and expectations can significantly shape what we encode and later retrieve from memory. How does this reconstructive process take place?

The scientific belief in the reconstructive nature of memory was first proposed about 70 years ago by the English psychologist Sir Frederic Bartlett (1932). When testing people's memories of stories they had read, Bartlett found that accurate recollections were rare. Instead, people seemed to reconstruct the material they had learned, shortening and lengthening different aspects and, overall, changing details to better fit their own beliefs and expectations. These memory distortions became more pronounced over time, yet the people were largely unaware that they had reconstructed the past. In fact, the reconstructed memories were often those aspects of the story that the people most adamantly claimed to be true. Based on these findings, Bartlett concluded that information already stored in long-term memory strongly influences how we both encode and later remember new information.

One factor that influences the reconstruction of memory involves age-related differences in encoding and retrieval (Howe, 2003). That is, an adult's mind is organized differently from that of a 2-year-old, and thus, the encoding and retrieval operations are different. According to the previously discussed *encoding specificity principle* (see section 8-4b), the effectiveness of a retrieval operation is determined by how well it recreates the conditions present at the time of the original encoding. As a result, it is highly questionable whether a childhood experience that was encoded using a 2-year-old's sensorimotor schemes can be accurately retrieved using an adult's formal operational schemes (Ceci, 1995; Simcock & Hayne, 2002). This so-called **infantile amnesia** is one of the primary problems surrounding claims by adults concerning their recently "remembered" memories of early childhood sexual abuse (see section 8-5c).

In addition to age effects, people's social expectations and stereotypes can significantly shape what they remember about an event. For example, in a set of classic studies conducted by Gordon Allport and Leo Postman (1945, 1947), White participants were first shown a picture of a White man holding a razor while gesturing at a Black man (see figure 8-8). They

infantile amnesia The inability to remember events that occurred during the early part of life (usually before the age of 3).

Figure 8-8

Negative Stereotypes Can Reshape Memory

In the 1940s, when White Americans were briefly shown this picture of a White man holding a razor while gesturing at a Black man, they remembered it in a manner that was consistent with their racial stereotypes. What implications does this study have for eyewitness testimony?

Source: From *The Psychology of Rumor,* 1st edition, by G. W. Allport and L. Postman. Copyright 1947. Reprinted with permission of Wadsworth, an imprint of the Wadsworth Group, a division of Thomson Learning. Fax 800/730-2215.

were then instructed to describe the scene to another participant, who in turn described it to another, and so on, until there had been six tellings. Consistent with the social expectations and stereotypes of many White Americans in the 1940s, the final story in this chain-of-telling usually had the razor in the Black man's hand.

Not only can people's expectations affect their memory of events, but also the *way* they are questioned about what they witnessed can alter their memories. These distortions and alterations in memory are known as **misinformation effects.** The altered memories generated by such misinformation not only feel real to the people who hold them but also often look real to observers (Schooler et al., 1986). In a famous study, Elizabeth Loftus and John Palmer (1974) demonstrated misinformation effects when they showed participants a short film of two cars colliding. Afterward, some of the participants were asked, "About how fast were the cars going when they *contacted* each other?" while others were asked, "About how fast were the cars going when they *smashed* into each other?" Those who heard the word *smashed* estimated the cars' speed at 41 miles per hour, while those who heard the word *contacted* gave a 31-mile-per-hour estimate. In addition, when questioned again a week later, the "smashed" participants were more than twice as likely as the "contacted" participants to recall seeing broken glass at the accident scene, despite the fact that no broken glass was visible in the film.

Further research indicates that altered memories are most likely to be created when misleading information is subtly introduced and when original memories have faded with the passage of time (Jaschinski & Wentura, 2002; Loftus, 1992, 1993). For example, during criminal trials, eyewitness memory distortions may occur in response to misleading questions posed by lawyers. A witness might be asked whether a mugger's glasses had plastic or wire frames, suggesting that the mugger wore glasses. The witness may not remember glasses, and the mugger may not have worn glasses, but this question may lead the witness to now "remember" seeing glasses on the mugger's face. Currently, it is unclear whether misleading information permanently alters memory or whether true memories can be retrieved under the right conditions (Dodson & Reisberg, 1991; Weingardt et al., 1995). Children are particularly susceptible to misinformation effects, and this fact has made the prosecution of alleged child sexual abuse cases problematic (Ceci & Bruck, 1993, 1995). That is, if children's memories can be literally altered through skillful questioning, how trustworthy is their testimony? Until more is learned about misinformation effects, distinguishing between the true and false memories of witnesses of any age—but especially those of children—will be one of the major challenges of the courts.

Have the results of these studies about the reconstructive nature of memory surprised you? Do they cause you to doubt your recollection of important life events? What about those events from your past that seem "frozen in time"? How accurate are these memories?

8-4f Flashbulb Memories Are Often Not Accurate Snapshots of Memorable Past Events

When discussing the reconstructive nature of memory, many people bring up the fact that they seem to remember certain experiences in their lives in amazing detail, as if literally frozen in time. These detailed and vivid memories of surprising and emotion-provoking events are known as **flashbulb memories** (Brown & Kulik, 1977; Conway et al., 1994). Flashbulb memories are often formed when you learn of the death of a loved one or a personally important public figure (Cursi et al., 2001; Tekcan & Peynircioglu, 2002). For middle-aged and elderly Americans, the assassination of President Kennedy in 1963 created a flashbulb memory. On September 11, 2001, the terrorist attacks at New York's World Trade Center and the Pentagon created flashbulb memories for millions of people worldwide.

How do flashbulb memories develop? Research suggests that self-relevance is a critical factor that interacts with surprise and emotion in producing such memories (Conway, 1995; Davidson & Glisky, 2002). Strong emotional reactions at the time of the event activate the amygdala—the portion of the brain that plays a key role in emotions—which in turn influences the hippocampus to create a memory (McGaugh, 2004; Pillemer, 1984). Age is also important. When they asked people who were between 1 and 7 years old in 1963 to recall how they heard about the Kennedy assassination, researchers found that these flashbulb memories steadily increased as age at encoding rose (Winograd & Killinger, 1983).

misinformation effects Distortions and alterations in witnesses' memories due to receiving misleading information during questioning.

If it is necessary to rearrange one's memories or to tamper with written records, then it is necessary to forget that one has done so.

—*George Orwell, English author and social satirist, 1903–1950*

Ten thousand different things that come from your memory or imagination—and you do not know which is which, which was true, which is false.

—*Amy Tan, American author, b. 1952*

flashbulb memories Detailed and vivid memories of surprising and emotion-provoking events.

Whereas all those who were 7 years old at the time had flashbulb memories of this event, only 50 percent of the 4-year-olds had such memories. Also, individuals who were older at the time of encoding had more elaborate and detailed memories. The likely reason for this increase is that a 7-year-old's encoding process is more similar than a 4-year-old's to that of an adult, and thus, the 7-year-old's childhood memories are more accessible for adult retrieval.

Although people tend to express high confidence in the accuracy of their flashbulb memories, substantial evidence indicates that changes and reconstructions do occur (Neisser, 1982; Terr, 1988; Wagenaar & Groeneweg, 1990). For example, one day after the space shuttle *Challenger* explosion in 1986, college students were asked to describe exactly how they had heard the news. Then, 3 years later, many of these same students were again asked to recall their experiences (Neisser & Harsch, 1992). Despite expressing confidence in the accuracy of their memories, only about 7 percent of the students demonstrated a high degree of agreement in their two reports. For instance, although 21 percent initially reported that they learned the news from television, 3 years later this figure had risen to 45 percent. Those who had produced false memories during the 3-year period were surprised, if not amazed, when they were shown the handwritten reports they had produced right after the explosion. These findings suggest that flashbulb memories are not burned into our minds and fully retained, but instead, are subject to considerable change and reconstruction over time (Schmolck et al., 2000). Despite the susceptibility to error of flashbulb memories, they still tend to be more accurate than other types of memories, perhaps partly because of their stronger emotional content (MacKay & Ahmetzanov, 2005; Schacter, 1996). However, additional research suggests that the greater accuracy may also be due to people spending more time thinking about the content of flashbulb memories (Otani et al., 2005). In other words, you are more likely to accurately remember something if you spend a lot of time elaboratively rehearsing it. As previously discussed in section 8-1d, elaborative rehearsal involves a relatively deep level of cognitive processing.

Section Review

- Recall requires both retrieval and reproduction of information, while recognition requires only a decision on whether or not the information has been previously encountered.
- A retrieval cue is a stimulus that helps us recall information from memory.
- According to the encoding specificity principle, retrieving information from long-term memory is most likely when the conditions at retrieval closely match the conditions present during the original learning.
- Déjà vu and cryptomnesia are memory illusions shaped by implicit memory.
- Information stored in long-term memory influences both encoding and later remembering of new information.
- The way people are questioned about their memories can cause memory reconstruction.
- Flashbulb memories are not as accurate as we think.

8-5 HOW DOES FORGETTING OCCUR?

Preview

- *When are we most likely to forget something?*
- *Is forgotten information truly forgotten?*
- *Why do we forget?*
- *Can we be motivated to forget?*
- *Is it possible to falsely remember something that never happened?*

What would happen if you did not ever forget anything? Wouldn't this be an overwhelming experience? Shereshevskii, the Russian reporter whose story you read at the beginning of this chapter, could answer this question. Over the years, as his memories piled up, they began to overwhelm him. Eventually, the slightest stimulus evoked so many memories that Shereshevskii could no longer hold a job, read, or even follow a simple conversation. He was eventually institutionalized because of his memory problem. For Shereshevskii, not being able to forget became as problematic as Henry M.'s condition of not being able to remember (described in chapter 3).

8-5a Most Forgetting Occurs Soon after Learning

Unlike what Shereshevskii learned, much of what the normal person learns is quickly forgotten. Do you remember Hermann Ebbinghaus's research from the late 1800s, discussed in section 8-1a? After learning more than 1,200 nonsense syllables and then measuring how much he recalled when relearning the list, from 20 minutes to 30 days later, he discovered that most forgetting occurs during the first 9 hours after learning. As you can see in his "forgetting curve," depicted in figure 8-9, he had forgotten more than 40 percent of the material after just 20 minutes. By 9 hours, over 60 percent had been lost, but then the course of forgetting leveled off. These findings, combined with later research, indicate that the greatest amount of forgetting occurs in the first few hours after learning, with progressively less memory loss occurring as time goes on (Wixted & Ebbesen, 1991).

In addition to establishing the shape of the forgetting curve, a second important discovery made by Ebbinghaus was that, although you may forget information that you previously learned, this does not necessarily mean you have forgotten *everything* about that information. He discovered that it took less time to relearn the list of nonsense words than it had taken to initially learn the list. The implication of these findings is that most forgetting is not complete: You may forget something if you do not rehearse it for a period of time, but it is much easier to relearn it in the future than to learn it initially (MacLeod, 1988). This is good news for all of us who have not practiced our French or algebra since high school graduation!

One reason we forget information soon after learning it is that we are not sufficiently attentive when the information is presented. Such *absentmindedness* accounts for those instances when we forget new acquaintances' names, misplace our keys, or are unsure whether we took our daily vitamins. The pervasiveness of people's daily inattentiveness was demonstrated in a clever study in which a research confederate approached people on a public street and asked them for directions (Simons & Levin, 1998). While these unsuspecting individuals were answering the confederate's query, two workers carrying a large door passed between them. During the few moments in which the participant's view was

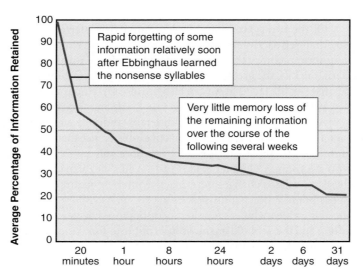

**Interval between Original Learning
of Nonsense Syllables and Memory Test**

Figure 8-9

Ebbinghaus's Forgetting Curve

Ebbinghaus discovered that most forgetting (over 60 percent) occurs during the first 9 hours after learning. After 9 hours, the course of forgetting levels off. What else did Ebbinghaus learn about information that is forgotten? Is the "relearning" of this information generally difficult or easy, relative to information that was not previously learned?

decay Forgetting due to the passage of time.

retroactive interference Forgetting due to interference from newly learned information.

proactive interference Forgetting due to interference from previously learned information.

obscured, a second confederate stepped in to replace the original confederate. Would it surprise you to learn that only half the participants noticed the change? This study suggests that inattentiveness or shallow encoding can cause rapid forgetting of newly presented information.

8-5b Forgetting Often Occurs Due to Interference

Based on Ebbinghaus's research, the popular early view of why forgetting occurs was that, unless memories are periodically rehearsed, the simple passage of time causes them to fade and eventually decay (Thorndike, 1914). But although **decay** contributes to forgetting in short-term memory, research now strongly suggests that decay does not significantly influence forgetting in long-term memory (Cowan, 1995).

An important study that discredited the decay theory of forgetting in long-term memory was conducted in 1924 by John Jenkins and Karl Dallenbach (Jenkins & Dallenbach, 1924). They had college students learn lists of nonsense words either just after waking in the morning or just before going to sleep at night, and then tested the students' recall after 1, 2, 4, or 8 hours. For the sleeping students, this meant waking them. Despite the same amount of time passage, much more forgetting occurred while the students were awake and involved in other activities than while they were asleep.

If forgetting is not due to the simple passage of time, then what causes it? Actually, the key to this answer is contained within Jenkins and Dallenbach's findings. Do you see it? More forgetting occurred among students who had learned nonsense words early in the morning because they were exposed to more information during the day that could potentially interfere with their remembering. In contrast, the students who had learned the nonsense words before bedtime were exposed to much less potentially interfering information while they slept. These findings suggest that the learning of new information can act backward in time to interfere with the remembering of older information. This forgetting due to interference from newly learned information is known as **retroactive interference** (Koutsaal et al., 1999; Windschitl, 1996). You experience retroactive interference when learning the information in this chapter interferes with your memory of information learned in a previous chapter.

The other major type of interference is **proactive interference,** which occurs when previously learned information interferes with remembering more recently learned information. Thus, if your memory of information learned in a previous chapter of this textbook interferes with your learning of information in the present chapter, you are experiencing proactive interference. Another common (and often embarrassing) example of proactive interference occurs when you call your current girlfriend or boyfriend by a previous partner's name.

Of the two types of interference, proactive interference probably causes more forgetting than retroactive interference, because we have stored up a great deal of information in long-term memory that can potentially interfere with any new information we might try to learn. Luckily, the greater potential ability of proactive interference to cause forgetting may be offset by the fact that we can also use already-stored information to elaboratively encode new information (refer back to section 8-1d) and thus improve our memory.

A recent meta-analysis of 26 different studies (Kail, 2002) suggests that young children (age 4) are more susceptible to proactive interference than older children (age 13). In contrast, among adults, those who are older are more vulnerable to proactive interference than those who are younger (Hasher et al., 2002). A likely explanation for both sets of findings is that these age-related changes in retroactive interference are associated with age-related changes in the brain's information-processing speed. As children's brains mature, neural processing speed increases, whereas neural processing speed decreases in later adulthood. Thus, the very young and the very old are most susceptible to forgetting due to proactive interference.

For both proactive and retroactive interference, one important factor in determining how much interference will occur—at any age—is the degree of *similarity* between the old and the new information. As the degree of similarity increases, the likelihood of interference also increases (McGeoch & McDonald, 1931; Riccio et al., 1994). For example, as illustrated in figure 8-10, if your new phone number at the college dorm is very similar to your old

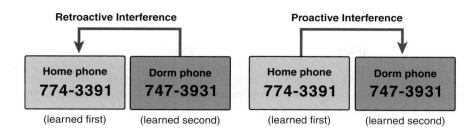

Figure 8-10

Interference in Memory

Retroactive interference occurs when newly learned information interferes with previously learned information. Proactive interference occurs when previously learned information interferes with newly learned information. Thus, after learning your new college dorm phone number, you may have trouble remembering your parents' number at home (retroactive interference). However, your memory of your parents' phone number may also interfere with remembering your new dorm number (proactive interference). For both types of interference, the degree of similarity between the old and new information significantly determines how much interference occurs. More-similar information causes greater interference than less-similar information. Can you think of other examples of retroactive and proactive interference in your life?

phone number at home, you may well experience retroactive interference when you call home and proactive interference when you call your dorm room.

8-5c We Are Sometimes Motivated to Forget Information

In 1990, George Franklin, Sr., stood trial for the brutal 1969 murder of an 8-year-old child, Susie Nason. The major evidence provided against Franklin was the eyewitness testimony of his own daughter, Eileen, who had been Susie's best friend. What made this case so unusual was that Eileen's memory of witnessing the murder had been repressed for 20 years. Then one day, while playing with her own young daughter, she had a brief flashback of the murder—the look of betrayal in Susie's eyes just before she was killed. Later, more flashbacks occurred, including the memory of Susie begging for mercy and the images of Eileen's father sexually assaulting Susie in the back of a van and of Eileen's father raising a rock above his head just before smashing Susie's skull.

   One of the problems with Eileen's memory of the murder was that it changed across various tellings. First she told police that the murder occurred in the morning while driving to school. However, when reminded that Susie had not been missing until after school was out, Eileen said it was in the late afternoon. Initially, she also reported that her sister Janice was riding in the van but then was dropped off when Susie was picked up. Later, that detail disappeared from her testimony. Despite these inconsistencies, the jury was so impressed with Eileen's detailed and confident memory of the murder that it returned a guilty verdict after only a day of deliberation. This case marked the first time the return of a repressed memory proved to be the deciding factor in convicting someone of a crime in the United States. Did Eileen really witness the murder of her best friend 20 years earlier? Could such a traumatic event be forgotten for so long and then suddenly remembered?

What Is Motivated Forgetting?

Beyond the influence of interference, sometimes people forget things because they *want* to forget them. This is called **motivated forgetting,** and it usually occurs because a memory is unpleasant or disturbing. Sigmund Freud (1946, 1949) is generally credited with providing the theoretical framework for understanding this type of self-protective forgetting. In Freud's psychoanalytic theory, there are two types of motivated forgetting: *suppression* and *repression.*

   Suppression occurs when a person consciously tries to forget something. For example, while preparing to execute a complicated routine during an important performance, a dancer is likely to suppress the memory of sprawling on the stage the last time she attempted this maneuver. Similarly, prior to kicking a game-deciding field goal, a player is likely to suppress the memory of his last attempt that went wide of the mark. In both situations, although the performers are aware that they failed in their previous attempts, they consciously choose not to think about it.

   Freud believed that *repression,* unlike conscious forgetting, occurs when a person unconsciously "pushes" unpleasant memories out of conscious awareness. Although these memories are no longer "remembered" in the conventional sense, they continue to unconsciously influence the person's thoughts, feelings, and behavior. According to psychoanalytic theory, repression plays a key role in both the formation of personality and the development of psychological disorders (as you will see in chapters 12 and 13). Despite psychoanalysts'

motivated forgetting Forgetting due to a desire to eliminate awareness of some unpleasant or disturbing memory.

suppression Motivated forgetting that occurs consciously.

Memories are hunting-horns
whose noise dies away in the
wind.

*—Guillaume Apollinaire, French poet and
art critic, 1880–1918*

assumption that repression shapes human thought and behavior, it remains a controversial topic (James, 2003; McNally, 2003).

Should We Trust Repressed Memories?

Many memory researchers believe it is naive to assume that people can accurately recover memories that were previously unconsciously repressed. They further contend that people can unknowingly manufacture false memories (Anaki et al., 2005). For ethical reasons, psychologists cannot attempt to implant false memories of murder or sexual assault in the minds of research participants. However, Elizabeth Loftus and James Coan (1995) successfully implanted less traumatic false childhood memories in the minds of five research participants ranging in age from 8 to 42. Following Loftus and Coan's instructions, trusted family members told these five individuals that, at age 5, they had been lost in a shopping mall for an extended time before being rescued by an elderly man. Following these suggestions, all participants became convinced that they indeed had been lost. One of these individuals, a 14-year-old named Chris, received this false account from his older brother. Two days later, Chris could remember the incident with strong feelings: "That day, I was so scared that I would never see my family again. I knew that I was in trouble." Within 2 weeks, he remembered that the man who rescued him was bald and wore glasses and a flannel shirt. When debriefed and told that his memory was false, he replied, "Really? I thought I remembered being lost . . . and looking around for you guys. I do remember that. And then crying, and Mom coming up and saying 'Where were you? Don't you ever do that again.'"

Other studies have been able to successfully create false memories in children for such events as knocking over a punch bowl at a wedding and getting one's hand caught in a mousetrap (Ceci et al., 1994, 1995). These children not only recalled the suggested incidents but also greatly embellished their false memories. Further, during debriefing, when parents explained to them that the suggested events never occurred, some of the children persisted in their false beliefs. One boy exclaimed to his mother, "But it did happen. I remember it!"

These findings and those from other investigations demonstrate that false memories can be implanted into the minds of both children and adults (Johnson & Raye, 2000; S. M. Smith et al., 2003). In fact, research indicates that simply repeating imaginary events to people causes them to become more confident that they actually experienced these events (Begg et al., 1992; Zaragoza & Mitchell, 1996). Once constructed, these false memories may feel as real as—or even more real than—genuine memories (Brainerd et al., 1995). How are these false memories constructed? Loftus suggests that people may combine actual personal experiences—or the witnessed experiences of others—with their memories of the location selected by the family member in which the alleged incident occurred (Loftus et al., 1995). Although people may at first be confused when others tell them about the false incidents, they soon combine previously unconnected bits of information into new—yet thoroughly false—memories.

Of course, this research does not tell us whether George Franklin's daughter Eileen recalled a false memory of sexual assault and murder rather than an authentic repressed memory. But it does raise the possibility that her repressed memory, and those of others who have come forward with similar claims, may not be real. Psychologists who conduct research on false memories readily acknowledge that childhood abuse is a major societal problem. Indeed, Elizabeth Loftus is herself a survivor of such trauma, having been molested at 6 years of age (and not having forgotten). Yet many memory researchers are concerned that some cases involving repressed memories may reflect something other than real experiences.

Journey of Discovery **Question** Could you falsely reconstruct a childhood memory based on your *beliefs* about how memory works? That is, do you think that your beliefs about how memory works could affect your recollection of past events?

Given the malleable nature of memory, cognitive psychologists who study repressed memory warn their fellow psychologists who treat possible abuse patients to exercise extreme caution during therapy sessions. Certain techniques commonly used in therapy to recover childhood memories of abuse, such as hypnosis and dream interpretation, can distort patients' recollections of past events and create false memories of abuse (Lynn et al., 2003).

One antidote to naively accepting recovered memories of childhood trauma is to educate the public about the reconstructive nature of memory and the ways that children can be tricked into "remembering" things that never happened (Kassin et al., 2001; McHugh et al., 2004).

Section Review

- Most forgetting occurs during the first 9 hours after learning.
- It is much easier to relearn forgotten information than to learn new information.
- Most forgetting is caused by interference (retroactive and proactive).
- Two types of motivated forgetting are suppression and repression.
- Therapeutic techniques used to recover childhood memories of abuse can create false memories of abuse.

8-6   WHAT IS THE BIOLOGICAL BASIS FOR MEMORIES?

Preview

- *Physiologically, how does a memory develop?*
- *Are specific memories stored in specific locations in the brain?*

As mentioned at the beginning of this chapter, memory has been likened to a computer's information-processing system. In this regard, while cognitive psychologists have studied our memory "software," neuroscientists have focused their attention on its "hardware"—the biological underpinnings of memory.

8-6a   Long-Term Potentiation May Be the Neural Basis for Memory

When a memory is made, what happens physiologically? The search for this memory trace, or *engram,* has been the focus of neuroscientists for more than 50 years (Lashley, 1950; Thompson, 2005). Although there still is no scientific consensus on what an engram is or where it is located in the brain, memories appear to begin as electrical impulses traveling between neurons. The establishment of long-term memories involves changes in these neurons. Eric Kandel and James Schwartz (1982) observed such neuronal changes when studying learning in the California sea slug, *Aplysia,* which has a small number (about 20,000) of large-sized neurons. By repeatedly giving sea slugs a squirt of water (the CS) followed by a mild electric shock to the tail (the UCS), Kandel and Schwartz were able to classically condition the sea slugs to reflexively withdraw their gills when only squirted with the water (the CR). Kandel and Schwartz discovered that, when the sea slug forms a new memory for this classically conditioned response, significant changes occur in both the *function* and the *structure* of its affected neurons (Kandel, 1995). Regarding function, an increase occurs in the amount of the neurotransmitters released at the synapses—the communication points—of the neurons. Regarding structure, not only does the number of synapses increase, but so does the number of interconnecting branches between neurons. These structural changes make communication along this new neural circuit more efficient.

This strengthening of synaptic transmission, which is known as **long-term potentiation,** has also been found in the brains of more complex animals (Goosens & Maren, 2002). For example, when rats are raised in "enriched" environments containing many objects with which they can play and from which they can learn, their brains develop more elaborate neural connections than rats raised in impoverished environments (Black et al., 1990; Chang et al., 1991). Additional research supporting long-term potentiation as the neural basis for memory has found that the same drugs that improve memory also facilitate long-term potentiation, and those that block memory also inhibit long-term potentiation (Beggs et al., 1999; del Olmo et al., 2003). Finally, when researchers altered the genes of mice so that long-term potentiation was enhanced in the hippocampus and other areas of the brain used in memory, the mice remembered new information over longer time periods than did normal mice (Manabe et al., 1998; Tang et al., 1999).

> **long-term potentiation** The long-lasting strengthening of synaptic transmission along a specific neural circuit, which is believed to be the neural basis for long-term memory.

Together, this research suggests that long-term potentiation is the physiological key to memory. When a new memory is formed, functional and structural changes take place in specific neurons, creating a kind of *memory circuit*. Each time the new memory is recalled, the neurons in this new circuit are activated, which strengthens their neural connections. As the communication links between the neurons increase in strength, the memory becomes established as a long-term memory.

8-6b Several Brain Regions Are Involved in Memory Formation and Storage

A related "engram" question that neuroscientists have pursued is whether there are special brain regions that form and store memories. During the first half of the twentieth century, neuroscientists believed that a specific memory could be found in a specific place in the brain (Lashley, 1950). This belief was partly based on interviews with epileptic patients in whom various regions of the cerebral cortex had been electrically stimulated during brain surgery (Penfield, 1958). Because the brain has no pain receptors, the patients were able to remain conscious during the surgery (see accompanying photo). When the temporal lobe (just above the ears) was stimulated, for example, patients reported flashbacks, such as the vision of wagons at a carnival or the sound of family members talking (Penfield & Perot, 1963). Despite the great excitement initially generated by such findings, neuroscientists soon became skeptical that specific brain locations stored specific memories. Such skepticism was due to further research demonstrating that (1) removal of specific brain areas associated with specific memories did not destroy the memories, and (2) when the same brain area was repeatedly stimulated, different experiences were reported (Halgren et al., 1978; McCarthy, 1995). Researchers now believe that these patients were not having memory "flashbacks" when their brains were electrically stimulated but, instead, were probably experiencing dreamlike illusions.

Although we now know that a specific memory cannot be tied to a specific brain site, certain types of memories appear to be stored in certain brain areas. Short-term memory, the type of memory used when we actively "work" with information, appears to involve prefrontal regions of the cerebral cortex. For example, when monkeys perform short-term memory tasks, recordings of individual neurons in their prefrontal cortex show extensive firing (Fuster, 1989). Similarly, PET scans of humans performing tasks requiring the use of short-term memory also show increased neural firing in this brain area (Faw, 2003).

Related to long-term memory function, a number of brain regions have been identified. The neocortex, striatum, and amygdala play important roles in the type of long-term memory

In the 1950s, neurosurgeons "mapped" the cerebral cortex while performing brain surgery on patients suffering from epileptic seizures. Surgeons would place numbered tags on the exposed brain to designate which locations induced particular memories, sensory experiences, or motor activities. Although scientists initially believed they had discovered the physical traces of memory, the engram, additional research suggested that these were not always true memory traces.

Source: Courtesy Dr. William Feindel.

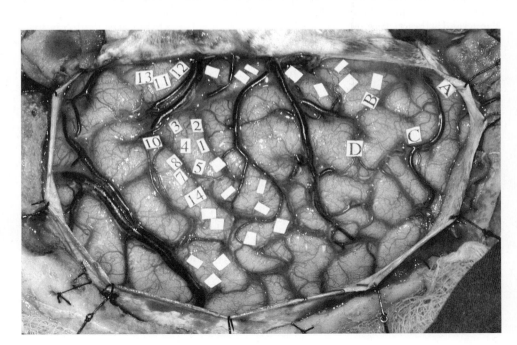

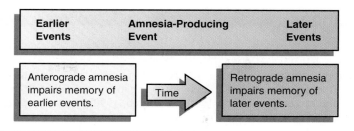

Earlier Events	Amnesia-Producing Event	Later Events

Anterograde amnesia impairs memory of earlier events.	Time	Retrograde amnesia impairs memory of later events.

Figure 8-11

Anterograde and Retrograde Amnesia

In anterograde amnesia, a person is unable to form new memories after the amnesia-inducing event. In retrograde amnesia, a person is unable to retrieve information stored in long-term memory before the amnesia-inducing event.

previously identified as implicit memory (Tulving & Schacter, 1990). Regarding the sort of memory consolidation necessary for explicit memory, both animal and human studies reveal that several brain regions are involved, including the hippocampus and nearby portions of the cortex and the thalamus (Eichenbaum & Fortin, 2003; Squire, 1992). Of these brain regions, the hippocampus appears to be most important in encoding new memories and transferring them from short-term to long-term memory (Tamminga, 2005). Again, do you remember the tragic story of Henry M.? Because his entire hippocampus was surgically removed to control his epileptic seizures, he lost the ability to form explicit long-term memories.

This inability to form new memories is called **anterograde amnesia.** *Anterograde* means "forward moving." Henry M.'s short-term memory is fine, and he can still form implicit memories and remember events stored in long-term memory prior to his surgery. Similar memory deficits occur in rats and monkeys whose hippocampus has been surgically removed (Wood et al., 2004; Zola-Morgan & Squire, 1993). These findings suggest that although the hippocampus is critical for long-term memory formation, it is not involved in short-term memory activities or in the storage and retrieval of long-term memories.

Another type of amnesia is **retrograde amnesia,** which is the loss of information previously stored in long-term memory (Brown, 2002; Fast & Fujiwara, 2001). People who have automobile accidents or experience some other kind of blow to the head often cannot remember the events leading up to their physical injury (Levin et al., 1984; Riccio et al., 2003). For example, Princess Diana's bodyguard, who was the sole survivor of the car crash that claimed her life, retained no memory of the accident. In more severe cases, the person may not remember events that occurred years before the amnesia-inducing event. However, in most cases, such memory loss of "distant events" is only temporary (Kapur, 1999). Figure 8-11 reviews the differences between anterograde and retrograde amnesia.

When researchers discovered the role played by the hippocampus in long-term memory formation, it also helped them better understand the biological basis for *infantile amnesia* (refer back to section 8-4d), which is a special form of retrograde amnesia (Newcombe et al., 2000). That is, the hippocampus does not fully develop until about 2 years of age (Bauer, 2005; Nadel & Zola-Morgan, 1984). Thus, any memory encoding the immature hippocampus performs is likely to be inaccessible for later conscious remembering by the mature brain.

As you can see from this brief overview of the biological basis of memory, neuroscientists' insights into our memory "hardware" provide a more complete understanding of the entire memory system. As we learn more about the biopsychology of memory, we will be in a better position to treat memory deficits caused by illness and trauma, as well as to enhance the memory of healthy individuals.

anterograde amnesia The inability to form long-term memories due to physical injury to the brain.

retrograde amnesia The loss of information previously stored in long-term memory due to physical injury to the brain.

Black-capped chickadees can remember not only the location of up to 6,000 sites where they stockpiled food during the winter, but also recall what kind of food they put at a particular site and when they put it there (Clayton & Dickinson, 1998). Anatomical studies indicate that these birds have a much larger hippocampus than birds that do not stockpile food (Clayton, 1998). If the hippocampus is surgically removed, chickadees lose this memory ability.

Source: Courtesy of Figzoi.

Section Review

- Long-term potentiation appears to be the physiological key to memory.
- There is no specific location in the brain associated with a specific memory, but certain types of memories appear to be stored in certain brain areas.

Psychological Applications

Improving Everyday Memory

> **mnemonics** Strategies that make it easier to encode, store, and/or retrieve information.

Mnemonics are strategies to make it easier to encode, store, and/or retrieve information. This chapter has described current research and theory on memory. How can you use this knowledge to improve your ability to remember facts and other information? The guidelines that follow do not comprise an exhaustive list, but research indicates that these ten techniques can improve your everyday memory:

1. *Focus your attention.* When you don't pay close attention to something, you are unlikely to remember it. Distracting stimuli, such as having the television on while studying, significantly interfere with encoding information into long-term memory (Armstrong & Greenberg, 1990). Thus, to aid remembering, eliminate distractions by finding a quiet place to concentrate. If you cannot escape annoying distractions, reading aloud what you need to remember can help focus your attention (Hertel & Rude, 1991).

When studying, external distractions can make it difficult to encode information into long-term memory. You can minimize distractions by finding a quiet place to concentrate.
Source: Courtesy of Figzoi.

2. *Space your practice sessions.* One of the most common mistakes students make is waiting until a day before an exam to study. Yet Ebbinghaus's (1885) famous research on forgetting (see section 8-4a) revealed another important truth about learning new material: Don't try to memorize by swallowing all your information in one big gulp. Studying new information over several days

results in better learning than cramming your studying into 1 day (Bahrick et al., 1993; Naveh-Benjamin, 1990). Such *distributed practice* is most effective if the interval between practice sessions is about 24 hours. Thus, four separate 1-hour study sessions spread out over 4 days will lead to better retrieval than one 4-hour session.

3. *Construct information in a hierarchy.* One of the most effective ways to remember information is to arrange it in a series of categories, from the most general to the most specific. For example, I have intentionally constructed the presentation of topics in this chapter and the other chapters so they are organized hierarchically: first, with very general topics (such as memory); next, with more focused "level-A" sections (such as "The Nature of Memory") that contain even more specific "level-B" headings (such as "The Computer's Information-Processing System Has Been a Useful Model for Human Memory"); and finally, within these "level-B" headings are very specific "level-C" subsection headings (such as "Information Processes," "The Identification of Three Memory Systems," and "Is This the Only Model of Memory?"). Using hierarchical systems can double the amount of information you can recall (Bower et al., 1969).

4. *Use the method of loci.* In studying the amazing Shereshevskii, Alexander Luria discovered that Shereshevskii habitually and automatically used visual imagery to encode information into long-term memory. Although we are unlikely to come close to matching Shereshevskii's memory skills, research indicates that we can better remember information if we associate it with vivid mental images (Kline & Groninger, 1991). One well-known visual mnemonic technique is the *method of loci* (pronounced "LOW-sigh"), which requires you to mentally place items to be memorized in specific locations well known to yourself, such as rooms in your house. When you want to recall these items, you simply take a mental "walk" by these locations and "see" the memorized items. Shereshevskii would often mentally place items he wanted to remember at different locations on Gorky Street in Moscow. Later, he could recall these items in reverse order by mentally "walking" down Gorky Street in the opposite direction. In using the method of loci, choose extremely familiar memory locations so they provide a vivid context for organizing the information to be memorized (Hilton, 1986). If you wanted to learn a grocery list, for example, you might mentally place each food item at a specific location in your home: strawberries on your bed, milk jugs in your bathroom sink, hot dogs hanging from the kitchen door, and so on. By mentally strolling through your home, the food items pop into your mind, as illustrated in figure 1.

Psychological Applications

—Continued

Step 1: Mentally place items in specific locations.

Strawberries on your bed

Milk jugs in the bathroom sink

Hot dogs hanging from the kitchen window

Butter smeared on the refrigerator

Ice cream dripping off the stove

Olives tumbling out of the dishwasher

Flour covering the living room floor

Sugar cubes piled on the couch

Carrots on the front door

Coffee beans strewn on the front porch

Step 2: Mentally "walk" by specific locations to recall the items.

Figure 1

The Method of Loci

With the method of loci, you remember things by mentally placing items in specific locations well known to yourself. To recall these items, you mentally "walk" by these locations and "see" the memorized items. In this example, you memorize a grocery list by placing each food item in separate locations at home.

5. *Use the peg-word method.* Another effective use of visual imagery to encode information into long-term memory is the *peg-word method,* which involves using a series of words that serve as "pegs" on which memories can be "hung." In one variation of this memory technique, the peg words rhyme with numbers to make the words easy to remember. For example: One is the sun, two is a shoe, three is a tree, four is a door, five is a hive, six is sticks, seven is heaven, eight is a plate, nine is wine, and ten is a pen. As illustrated in figure 2, if you wanted to learn a grocery list, you might associate sun and strawberries by imagining the sun ripening strawberries. Two is a shoe, so you might imagine a shoe resting on a jug of milk. The image of hot dogs in a tree and olives on sticks might also serve as memorable images, and so on. At the grocery store, you remember the list of groceries by simply recalling the peg words associated with each number. These peg words then serve as retrieval cues for the groceries.

6. *Use verbal mnemonics.* The use of verbal mnemonics can facilitate recall by giving extra meaning to concepts. One effective verbal mnemonic is an *acronym,* which is a word that consists of all the first letters of the items to be memorized. For example, you can remember the names of the Great Lakes (Huron, Ontario, Michigan, Erie, Superior) by remembering the acronym HOMES. Similarly, an *acrostic* is a phrase in which the first letters of each word are used to remind you of something. My daughters recite the phrase, "My Very Educated Mother Just Sold Us Nine Pizzas" to remember the names of the

Step 1: Memorize these peg words in order	Step 2: Hang new items on the peg words	Step 3: Imagine a memorable interactive image.
One is the sun.	Sun—strawberries	
Two is a shoe.	Shoe—milk	
Three is a tree.	Tree—hot dogs	
Four is a door.	Door—butter	
Five is a hive.	Hive—ice cream	
Six is sticks.	Sticks—olives	
Seven is heaven.	Heaven—flour	
Eight is a plate.	Plate—sugar cubes	
Nine is twine.	Twine—carrots	
Ten is a pen.	Pen—coffee beans	

Figure 2

The Peg-Word Method

Continued next page—

Psychological Applications

—Continued

planets (Mercury, Venus, Earth, Mars, Jupiter, Saturn, Uranus, Neptune, Pluto). Finally, another verbal mnemonic that provides an organizational structure to information is a *rhyme* (Rubin & Wallace, 1989). Often-used rhymes are "*I* before *E* except after *C*" and "Thirty days hath September. . . ."

7. *Use external mnemonics.* External mnemonics play a leading role in helping us fortify our memories (Park et al., 1990). Examples of such memory aids include the alarm clock that reminds you to get up in the morning, your lecture notes that facilitate your retrieval of classroom material, the rubber band worn on your wrist that reminds you to visit a sick friend, and the grocery list that helps you purchase the ingredients for your next meal. To effectively use these external memory aids, you must first recognize your need to use them, and then you must select an appropriate aid for the task at hand (Intons-Peterson & Newsome, 1992). Ben, the public relations director with a severe short-term memory deficit, could not have survived in his job without heavily relying on external memory devices. For example, before walking into meetings, Ben would discreetly hold in his hand the business cards of those in attendance. This external memory aid helped Ben remember their names and relevant details of previous meetings. Immediately following meetings, he would write down or tape-record his recollections before they disappeared. Although Ben could not properly function without constantly relying on these external aids, his case is merely an extension of what most of us do to bolster our fairly efficient memory systems.

8. *Overlearn.* Studying information even after you think you already know it is one of the most effective ways to firmly embed it in memory. Any information that is well learned is more likely to survive a case of the jitters than information only minimally learned (Martens, 1969).

9. *Use sleep to your advantage.* As you recall from chapter 6, section 6-2e, there is evidence that the cognitive processing that occurs during nighttime dreaming consolidates and stores information gathered during the day (Pavlides & Winson, 1989; Winson, 1990). In this chapter, you also discovered that, due to lack of interference, things learned just before sleep are retained better than information learned earlier in the day. Together, these findings suggest that your parents' advice to get a good night's rest before a big exam—and to study just before going to sleep—is well worth heeding.

10. *Cultivate close relationships.* Finally, an intriguing way to expand your memory is to form a partnership with someone else's memory! Research reveals that people in close relationships have a shared memory system that is greater than either of their individual memories (Andersson & Rönnberg, 1997; Wegner et al., 1991). In such collaborative memory, each person enjoys the benefits of the other's memory by taking responsibility for remembering just those items that fall clearly to him or her. For two people living together, this may involve one person assuming responsibility for remembering where the tools in the basement workroom are located, while the other assumes responsibility for remembering where the special dinnerware and napkins are stored. If you learn in a general way what the other person knows in detail, you can significantly improve your overall ability to remember things. By updating one another regarding your individual knowledge areas, each of you will further embellish your collaborative memory.

Key Terms

acoustic encoding (p. 277)

anterograde amnesia (p. 309)

chunking (p. 283)

cryptomnesia (p. 299)

decay (p. 304)

déjà vu illusion (p. 299)

elaborative rehearsal (p. 285)

encoding (p. 277)

encoding specificity principle (p. 298)

episodic memory (p. 288)

explicit memory (p. 289)

flashbulb memories (p. 301)

implicit memory (p. 289)

infantile amnesia (p. 300)

information-processing model (p. 277)

long-term memory (p. 279)

long-term potentiation (p. 307)

maintenance rehearsal (p. 283)

memory (p. 276)

misinformation effects (p. 301)

mnemonics (p. 310)

motivated forgetting (p. 305)

parallel distributed processing models (p. 295)

primacy effect (p. 279)

priming (p. 289)

proactive interference (p. 304)

procedural memory (p. 288)

recall (p. 296)

recency effect (p. 279)

Suggested Websites

American Psychological Association

http://www.apa.org

At the American Psychological Association website, you can search for press releases and other information about recent memory research.

Mind Tools

http://www.mindtools.com

This website contains memory techniques and mnemonics for use in everyday living, as well as links to other related websites.

Eyewitness Identification Research Laboratory

http://eyewitness.utep.edu

This website discusses research on eyewitness testimony and provides recommendations for how to correctly design and conduct police lineups and photospreads for eyewitnesses.

How Can Eyewitness Identification Research Go Wrong?

http://www.pbs.org/wgbh/pages/frontline/shows/dna/photos

This website discusses how conducting police lineups and photospreads for eyewitnesses can inadvertently lead to incorrect identifications.

Review Questions

Note: You can find the correct answers to these questions by taking the quiz and then submitting your answers in the Online Edition. The program will automatically score your submission. If you miss a question, the program will provide the correct answer, a rationale for the answer, and the section number in the chapter where the topic is discussed.

1. When you encode information into memory using its personal meaning, you are using
   a. visual encoding.
   b. acoustic encoding.
   c. semantic encoding.
   d. information-processing.
   e. *c* and *d*

2. If, in trying to memorize an alphabetical list of Russian states, you can remember the last two states on the list better than the middle two states on the list, you have experienced the
   a. serial-position effect.
   b. primacy effect.
   c. recency effect.
   d. *a* and *c*
   e. *b* and *c*

3. Sensory memory
   a. requires conscious awareness.
   b. exists in the hippocampus.
   c. can be studied in the laboratory.
   d. exists in one system.
   e. can be directly accessed.

4. Short-term memory
   a. stores spoken words and visual and spatial images.
   b. seems to be dominated by visual encoding.
   c. has an unlimited capacity.
   d. does not retrieve information from long-term memory.
   e. *a* and *d*

5. When I remember my first day as a college student, I am relying on
   a. episodic memory.
   b. semantic memory.
   c. procedural memory.
   d. short-term memory.
   e. working memory.

6. If I don't like my professor because he unconsciously reminds me of a high school teacher I disliked, which type of memory am I using?
   a. explicit
   b. recognition
   c. recall
   d. implicit
   e. priming

7. Which of the following statements is *true*?
   a. School-educated children have better memories than those with no schooling.
   b. All stored memories are stored in semantic networks.
   c. Bransford and Johnson's research suggests that it is crucial to have the right schema during the encoding stage.
   d. Cultural utility does not play a role in how schemas develop.
   e. Parallel distributed processing models believe information in memory is located in a specific part of the brain.

8. Research on recognition and recall of high school classmates suggests that
   a. we are better at remembering faces than names.
   b. recognition is more difficult than recall.
   c. recall is more difficult than recognition.
   d. *a* and *b*
   e. *a* and *c*

9. The tip-of-the-tongue phenomenon
   a. is another demonstration of how recognition is easier than recall.
   b. increases in frequency with age.
   c. appears to occur in all cultures and age groups.
   d. has to do with explicit memory.
   e. all of the above

10. Which of the following statements is *true*?
    a. Implicit memories cannot be activated.
    b. Cryptomnesia is a type of tip-of-the tongue phenomenon.
    c. Memory illusions are believed to be a direct result of implicit memory.
    d. When in a negative mood, we tend to recall positive memories.
    e. According to the encoding specificity principle, there is little problem in believing a claim by an adult that he or she recently remembers being sexually abused as a child.

11. In an early study of memory involving the recollection of stories, Bartlett (1932) found that
    a. more intelligent people more accurately recalled the story.
    b. racial stereotypes influenced the recollection of the story.
    c. when the story was about a 2-year-old, women remembered it better.
    d. people changed the details of the story to reflect their personal beliefs.
    e. people initially distorted much of the story, but over time the distortions lessened.

12. What is the term that refers to our forgetting something soon after learning, due to a lack of attention when the information was originally presented?
    a. interference
    b. decay
    c. suppression
    d. repression
    e. absentmindedness

13. The term *flashbulb memories* refers to
    a. having a photographic memory.
    b. misremembering things as real that we've seen only pictures of.
    c. recalling vivid memories of emotion-provoking events.
    d. poorer memory recall associated with great tragedies.
    e. greater recall of images than of verbal material.

14. Which of the following statements is *true* of forgetting?
    a. The greatest amount of forgetting occurs in the first few hours after learning.
    b. Research indicates that decay significantly influences forgetting in long-term memory.
    c. Jenkins and Dallenbach's research indicates that decay causes greater memory loss than interference.
    d. Proactive interference does not improve our memory.
    e. *a* and *d*

15. In the Simons and Levin (1998) study of inattentiveness, what percentage of participants noticed when a research confederate asking for directions was replaced by a new person when the participant was distracted.
    a. less than 1 percent
    b. 25 percent
    c. 50 percent
    d. 75 percent
    e. almost 100 percent

16. The findings of Simons and Levin's 1998 study suggest that
    a. inattentiveness can lead to rapid forgetting of newly presented information.
    b. rapid processing of newly presented information can lead to heightened memory.
    c. distractions in research methodology can bias the results.
    d. people are generally inattentive to small details.
    e. all of the above

17. Memories of past events
    a. can be consciously or unconsciously forgotten.
    b. can be falsely implanted in children and adults.
    c. can be influenced by our beliefs about how memory works.
    d. are more likely to be well remembered than completely forgotten if there is strong emotion and self-relevance.
    e. all of the above

18. Long-term potentiation refers to
    a. the potential to remember events for long periods of time.
    b. memories that are distributed over large areas of the cortex.
    c. increased forgetting of events that occurred long ago.
    d. increased recall of information presented at the end of a list.
    e. strengthening of transmission across synapses associated with learning.

19. The following brain regions are involved in memory formation and storage:
    a. cerebral cortex and amygdala
    b. striatum and neocortex
    c. long-term memory, short-term memory, and sensory-memory systems
    d. all of the above
    e. *a* and *b*

20. Considering Ebbinghaus's research, how could you best use 4 hours to study for an exam?
    a. study for 4 straight hours the night before the exam
    b. study for two separate 2-hour sessions the day of the exam
    c. study for four 1-hour sessions, each 24 hours apart
    d. study for one 4-hour session, 24 hours before the exam
    e. none of the above

21. According to research on memory, which of the following statements is *true*?
    a. Hierarchical systems can double the amount of information you can recall.
    b. It is not helpful to use the method of loci when trying to recall information.
    c. Do not waste time studying information you already know.
    d. It is a myth that studying before you go to sleep will improve your recall.
    e. Individual memories are greater than collaborative memories.

Chapter 9

Language and Thinking

Chapter Outline

Imagine an alternative reality where people are absolutely obsessed with Great Literature and where children swap author cards with the zeal children in our world have for sports cards. Instead of seeking religious converts, missionaries show up at your door trying to convince you that Francis Bacon is the true author of Shakespeare's plays. In pubs and other social venues, Will-Speak machines that quote Shakespeare on command stand in place of the flashy video games of our world. However, this literature-enriched world is not without its share of problems. The Crimean War between Great Britain and czarist Russia—which ended in 1856, in our reality—is still being waged, and Wales has a communist government. Further, an evil, multinational conglomerate, the Goliath Corporation, controls much of the world's economy and resources. And, oh yes, the Third Most Wanted criminal on the planet has somehow entered the original manuscript of Charlotte Brontë's *Jane Eyre* and kidnapped its namesake. Big problem. Suddenly, everyone reading *Jane Eyre* discovers the book's narrative is in serious disarray as the remaining characters are at a loss on how to proceed with the disrupted storyline.

Welcome to the hilariously off-kilter world of author Jasper Fforde, where fictional characters from famous and not-so-famous (and even unpublished) novels have lives beyond the stories they inhabit and occasionally cross over to the "real" world. The heroine of Fforde's novels is a smart, gun-toting literary detective named Thursday Next who has the job of setting right that which has gone so wrong. Does this story sound like the basis for a commercially successful book? Not according to almost all the major publishing houses around the globe. Fforde's first manuscript, *The Eyre Affair,* received 76 rejections before finally being published in 2001. Today he is a best-selling author and touted by literary critics as the adult's J. K. Rowling (the *Harry Potter* author).

What do Jasper Fforde and the content of his books have to do with the content of this chapter? Fforde's work represents an excellent example of the creative expression of language and the ability to envision alterative realities. This chapter examines the psychology of *language* and *cognition*. In this regard, Fforde's work is an illustration of our chapter topics. At the outset, let us explore how our world is transformed by the ability to share the meaning of these markings on the page and the vocal utterances we emit. We begin this journey by stepping into the past and examining the evolution of language.

All that mankind has done, thought, gained or been: it is lying as in magic preservation in the pages of books.

—*Thomas Carlyle, British author and social critic, 1795–1881*

9-1 LANGUAGE

Preview

- *How did language use evolve in humans?*
- *What are three features of language?*
- *What would happen if we tried to teach language to another species?*
- *How do we learn language?*
- *What is the relationship between language and cognition?*
- *How do we communicate nonverbally?*

communication The sending and receiving of information.

language A systematic way of communicating information using symbols and rules for combining them.

speech The oral expression of language.

Communication is the sending and receiving of information. Every day of our lives, we communicate hundreds, if not thousands, of bits of information to others. Some of these messages are intended, while others are not. **Language,** the primary mode of communication among humans, is a systematic way of communicating information using symbols and rules for combining them. It is a complex and sophisticated skill, the principal tool for building human culture. **Speech** is the oral expression of language, and approximately 5,000 spoken languages exist today. How did they come into being?

Language is a complex means of communicating, involving the use of symbols and rules for combining them. In writing books, authors rely upon creative literary skills to convey their ideas to readers.

9-1a Human Language Evolution Had Social and Cognitive Advantages

The search for the origins of language begins in the brain. As noted in chapter 3, section 3-3e, PET scan studies indicate that the major neural mechanisms for language are located in the left hemisphere, even in most left-handed people. Our early understanding of the neural mechanisms for language came about through studying people who had suffered brain damage to those areas. The disruption of language caused by brain damage is known as *aphasia* (see chapter 3, section 3-3f).

As depicted in figure 9-1, a small clump of neurons in the left frontal lobe, known as *Broca's area,* influences brain areas that control the muscles of the lips, jaw, tongue, soft

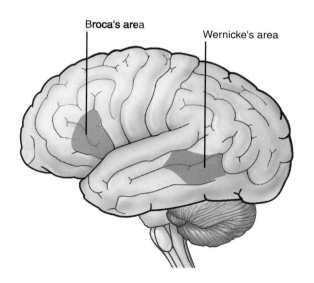

Broca's area

Wernicke's area

Figure 9-1

Broca and Wernicke's Areas of the Cerebral Cortex

Traditionally, two brain areas have been associated with language function—namely, Broca's area and Wernicke's area. These brain areas are usually located in the left cerebral hemisphere.

palate, and vocal cords during speech. Damage to Broca's area principally disrupts *language production,* which is the ability to speak or otherwise use words, phrases, and sentences to convey information. Broca's area is named after the French neuroanatomist who first described this brain damage. This brain disorder—called *Broca's aphasia*—often causes people to produce long pauses between words and to leave out function words, such as *and, but,* and *if.* Also depicted in figure 9-1 is *Wernicke's area,* which is at the back of the left temporal lobe, connected by a nerve bundle to Broca's area. This part of the left temporal lobe appears to be much more responsible for *language comprehension,* which is the ability to understand the message conveyed by words, phrases, and sentences (Blank et al., 2002). Wernicke's area is named after the German neurologist Carl Wernicke, who first reported how damage to this area disrupted language comprehension. Such damage is called *Wernicke's aphasia,* and those affected produce "word salad," or speech that makes no sense (Hillis & Heidler, 2002). Ask them how they are doing, and they might reply with something like, "Yes, bit is you hafta what mo hafta."

Even though Broca's area is primarily responsible for speech production and Wernicke's area is more involved in speech comprehension, brain scans indicate that Broca's area is also activated when a person is trying to comprehend a sentence with a complex *syntax,* which is the area of grammar dealing with the language rules for combining words into sentences. Thus, Broca's area appears to be involved when we use the grammatical rules of a language in both producing and comprehending sentences (Newman et al., 2003; Stromswold et al., 1996).

Was Language Evolution Gradual or Abrupt?

Although we can identify the major brain areas associated with language, the "when" and "why" questions of language evolution have proven to be a bigger problem (Botha, 1997; Maestripieri, 1997). For instance, scientists do not yet agree on whether human language evolved gradually or suddenly (Elman, 1999; Lewin, 1993a). The *gradual increase theory* contends that human language is the product of a very long period of biological evolution, spanning millions of years (Deacon, 1989). Evidence for this view has been obtained by examining fossilized skulls: A small lump on the left inside surface (near the temple), where Broca's area is located, suggests that some sort of primitive spoken language could have existed about 2 million years ago (Falk, 1991; Holloway, 1983). In contrast to the view that language evolved gradually, the *threshold theory* asserts that human language is a product of more sudden cultural evolution (Davidson & Noble, 1989). Proponents of this theory believe that language is no older than 50,000 years and is closely tied to the development of tools, imagery, and art (Isaac, 1983).

Besides studying brain evolution for evidence of language evolution, scientists have also examined the change in position of various parts of our vocal tract, most notably the larynx. In all mammals except humans, the larynx is high in the neck. Although this allows animals to breathe and drink at the same time, it severely restricts the range of sounds they can produce. Because the human larynx is much lower in the neck, it can be much larger, allowing us to produce the wide range of sounds necessary in a language. The "cost" of this anatomical descent of the larynx in the vocal tract is that we now have an increased risk of choking when we eat or drink (Smith & Szathmáry, 1995). Anthropologists who study the fossilized skulls of our hominid ancestors (see chapter 3, section 3-3c) have discovered that the shape of the bottom of the skull is related to the position of the larynx. This finding led to the additional discovery that the earliest time that our prehuman ancestors had a larynx low enough in the neck to allow for something similar to humanlike speech was about 1.6 million years ago (Laitmann, 1983; Lewin, 1993b). Yet it wasn't until about 300,000 to 400,000 years ago in archaic *Homo sapiens* that a vocal tract (see chapter 3, figure 3-9) essentially the same as our own had evolved.

Although it is still unclear whether human language evolved gradually or suddenly, German scientists recently found evidence that bolsters the threshold theory of language evolution (Enard et al., 2002). Their work, which involved genetic testing of different animal species, suggests that roughly 200,000 years ago, mutations in the FOXP2 gene may have caused changes in the brains of archaic *Homo sapiens,* providing them with much finer control over their mouth and throat muscles. Within 1,000 generations, or about 20,000 years, these mutations may have played a central role in enabling modern humans to speak and, therefore, develop language about 50,000 years ago. The human and chimpanzee FOXP2 genes differ by only 2 out of their 715 amino acids, but this small difference may partly explain why chimps cannot speak.

Why Did Language Evolve?

Beyond the "when" question, one possible reason why language evolved is that it had *social significance* to humans (Oda, 2001). That is, it provided a way for our ancestors to more efficiently communicate in such cooperative ventures as hunting and gathering food. Support for this view comes from contemporary cross-cultural studies indicating that language is mostly used today for establishing, maintaining, and refining social relationships (Burling, 1986; Dunbar, 1993). It is also possible that language evolved because of its *cognitive significance* to humans. Throughout evolutionary history, brains have been shaped to construct a representation of the world appropriate to a species' daily life (Jerison, 1975, 1991). Human brains have been shaped to facilitate reflective thought and imagery, abilities essential for complex decision making and problem solving. From this perspective, language use evolved as a means of facilitating the construction of an inner reality that we call *consciousness*.

It is likely that both these explanations for the evolution of consciousness—one social, the other cognitive—are true. As discussed in chapter 6, section 6-1b, consciousness may have evolved because it provided our ancestors with a mental representation of the world that allowed them to more effectively plan future activities. Language may have evolved because it facilitated the construction of consciousness at the same time it facilitated the cooperative efforts of individuals living in groups. By sharing a common language, our ancestors could communicate about events not currently present, such as food in a distant valley, or they could conjure up ideas in the minds of fellow tribal members about alternative realities, which became the foundation for their mythologies. This ability to create pictures and thoughts in another's mind through language is the art of the writer and orator. Or, as Jasper Fforde, author of the Thursday Next novels, explains the marvel of written language:

> If books and reading were invented tomorrow they would be hailed as the greatest technological advance known to mankind. No batteries, simple, portable, durable. Why bother building sets or creating convincing computer effects when the images are already there in the reader's mind? . . . When a reader praises an author, they should reserve 75% of that praise for themselves. (White, 2002, p. 10)

Some linguists believe that remnants of the earliest language spoken by our ancestors are preserved in the distinctive clicking sounds still spoken by some southern and eastern African tribes. For many years, linguists assumed that these click languages—each with a set of four or five click sounds—were derived relatively recently from a common language. However, recent genetic testing of people from different click-speaking tribes who live thousands of miles apart (the Hadzabe and the !Kung) found no evidence of any interbreeding over tens of thousands of years (Knight et al., 2003). This means that these two cultures have had no apparent contact with one another for thousands of generations. Although it is possible that the two cultures independently invented similar-sounding clicks, some linguists believe it is far more likely that these two tribes are very distant descendants of the world's earliest language users. If this is so, then these unusual click sounds may represent the remaining distinctive elements of this ancient vocabulary. Clicks may have been an important component in the first human language and may also have persisted for tens of thousands of years as meaningful sounds in the different languages of these African tribes because they provided an advantage in communication during hunting. Animals are known to be scared by most human languages but take little notice of click-speaking. According to this theory, as our early click-speaking ancestors migrated out of their East African cradle to different hunting environments around the world, their click vocabulary may have lost many of its communication advantages and slowly disappeared. Yet, in the environment where click speaking was first invented, it still provides a competitive advantage for users and remains an important communication tool.

Asking an archeologist to discuss language is rather like a mole being asked to describe life in the tree-tops.

—*Glynn Isaac, American archeologist, 1937–1985*

9-1b Language Capabilities May Not Be Unique to Humans

Beyond searching for the reasons why we became language users, scientists have also wondered whether language and speech are uniquely human abilities. The Austrian biologist Karl von Frisch (1950, 1967) discovered that honeybees can communicate the exact location of food sources by engaging in an elaborate dance. The direction in which the bee dances indicates the direction of the food relative to the sun; the amount of buzzing indicates the distance of the food; and the amount of tail-wagging indicates the food quality. All bees appear to have the same basic communication system, but in some kinds of bees, the dance is more elaborate than others, which sometimes causes miscommunication (Frisch, 1962). For example, although Italian and Austrian bees can live and breed together, they misinterpret each other's communications. The Italian bees never go far enough to look for food in response to an Austrian bee's dance, while the Austrian bees overshoot the food source that Italian bees report. Frisch's discoveries concerning honeybee communication earned him the Nobel Prize in 1973.

This and other research indicate that animals of the same species communicate—and sometimes miscommunicate—with one another. However, in many species, communication patterns appear to be completely determined by the "collective memory" genetically passed on from one generation to the next. Such within-species communication is extremely functional, often associated with mating, taking care of young, displaying dominance and submission, and setting territorial boundaries (Forstmeier & Balsby, 2002; Wich et al., 2002). For example, a robin will vigorously attack a patch of red feathers tied to a tree limb in its territory, just as if it were a male intruder. Likewise, the chirping of turkey chicks stimulates brooding behavior in turkey hens, even if these sounds are tape-recorded and coming from inside a stuffed skunk—a natural enemy of the turkey! In both instances, the feathers and chirps act as stimuli that trigger biologically programmed responses (Wardhaugh, 1993). Most researchers do not label this communication a "conversation" because it appears to be based on instinctive responses.

However, not all animal communication is based solely on biologically programmed responses. For instance, hummingbirds, parrots, and many songbirds share with humans the ability to learn new vocalizations through imitation (Jarvis et al., 2000; Pepperberg, 2002). Thus, humans are not unique in their ability to learn new communication skills. So what makes a communication system a language?

Linguists have traditionally asserted that, for a communication system to qualify as a language, it must have certain features (Hockett, 1960; Hockett & Altmann, 1968). Of the many features that have been proposed over the years, the following three might be described as most important (Comrie, 2003; Hulit & Howard, 1993):

1. *Meaningfulness*—Language conveys meaningful messages using words or signs that have relatively stable relationships with the things they represent. By combining words into meaningful sentences, humans can carry on extensive conversations with one another. Other species can also convey meaningful messages, but this appears to involve fairly general messages or a limited number of specific messages (Brudzynski, 2001). For example, when a beaver slaps its tail on the water, other beavers understand this as a danger message, but the danger could be an approaching bear, a mountain lion, or a fire. Although vervet monkeys have separate warning calls for certain predators, this naming system is much more limited than human language (Cheney & Seyfarth, 1985; Seyfarth & Cheney, 1992).

2. *Displacement*—Language permits communication about things that are displaced in time or space, meaning they are not present in the here and now. Although humans can discuss what happened long ago, what may happen in the future, or what is currently happening far away, animal communication is generally considered to lack this property (Yule, 1996). When a dog says *GRRR,* it means *GRRR* right now, not *GRRR last week by the pond in the park.*

3. *Productivity*—Language allows us to communicate things that have never before been communicated. Following a set of grammatical rules, we can convey this novel message to anyone who shares our language. In contrast, most nonhuman

communication appears to have considerably less novelty or flexibility. Although the honeybee's dance appears productive because it conveys information about new food sources, it has no signal for *up,* and thus bees cannot tell other bees about food located directly above their hive (Frisch, 1967).

Based on these criteria, it is doubtful that any nonhuman species has its own language. However, since the 1930s a number of attempts have been made to teach language to a few select species, such as chimpanzees, bonobos, gorillas, dolphins, and parrots (Hayes, 1951; Kellogg & Kellogg, 1933; Sigurdson, 1993). Perhaps the most famous case is that of Washoe, a young female chimpanzee, who was raised at home by Allen and Beatrix Gardner (1969) and taught sign language as though she were a deaf human child. Within 4 years, Washoe was using more than 100 signs, ranging from *baby, banana,* and *airplane* to *window, woman,* and *you.* She could also combine words to produce sentencelike phrases, such as *gimme banana* and *open food drink.* Some of these phrases appeared to be novel constructions by Washoe, as in her combination of *water bird* to refer to a swan. Even more impressive was Washoe's apparent ability to engage in simple conversations, prompting a visiting reporter for *The New York Times* to declare, "Suddenly I realized I was conversing with a member of another species in my native tongue."

During the 1970s and 1980s, research with other chimps and gorillas using sign language or plastic shapes representing words provided further evidence of ape language ability (Premack & Premack, 1983; Wise, 2000). One female gorilla named Koko learned more than 600 words and demonstrated even more spontaneous and productive use of language than Washoe (Patterson, 1978). In one memorable incident, Koko created a new word for an object she had previously never encountered, calling a ring a *finger bracelet.* Yet is this truly evidence of language ability?

One argument against accepting the achievements of Washoe and Koko as evidence of language development was offered by Herbert Terrace (1979)—a student of B. F. Skinner— who taught sign language to a male chimpanzee, named Nim Chimpsky (after the linguist Noam Chomsky). Over a 2-year period, Nim's achievements in producing many single-word signs and two-word combinations at first suggested that he was developing an ability to use language in much the same way as human children do. However, a closer inspection of videotapes of Nim's classroom activities indicated that, unlike human children, his two-word combinations were simply repetitions of simpler structures, not an expansion into more complex structures (Terrace et al., 1979). Also unlike human children, Nim rarely initiated signing but, instead, used sign language only in response to others' signing and tended to repeat the signs they used. Based on these findings, Terrace concluded that chimp use of sign language is not much different from pigeons pecking a sequence of keys to get food; in neither case should such behavior be confused with language acquisition.

Although Terrace's research with Nim and his skepticism of ape language ability received a great deal of initial attention, his conclusions soon came under critical scrutiny. One of the most serious criticisms was that Nim's learning environment was lacking in the sort of natural social interaction that typifies normal language development (Cantfort & Rimpau, 1982; Lieberman, 1984). When other researchers allowed Nim to socialize under more natural conditions, his spontaneous signing increased dramatically, leading some linguists to suggest that the chimp's earlier language deficit was caused by Terrace's rigid training procedures (O'Sullivan & Yeager, 1989).

Subsequent research with bonobos (or "pigmy chimps"), which are close genetic relatives of both chimpanzees and humans, provided further evidence that apes could use language. In particular, one young male bonobo, Kanzi, began using symbols at the age of 2 1/2 years to communicate with humans without any special training (Rumbaugh, 1990; Rumbaugh & Savage-Rumbaugh, 1986). Like human children, Kanzi learned to use symbols early in life by watching his adoptive mother use language (while she was in a training study). Eighty percent of the time, this communication occurred spontaneously, without prompting by the researchers. Kanzi learned not only how to "talk" by using hand signals and typing geometric symbols on a keyboard but also how to comprehend the semantic nuances of spoken English. Although dogs, cats, horses, and many other species can sometimes guess what we mean when we talk to them by attending to various situational cues (for example, our tone of voice and gaze

Bonobos and other apes have been taught by humans to communicate with sign language. Once taught, they have been observed teaching their offspring sign language. Does this mean that these animals possess the ability to learn language, an ability once thought unique to humans?

Source: Courtesy of Figzoi.

direction), Kanzi's understanding of spoken English was much more complex. For instance, when listening through earphones to a list of words spoken by a person in another room—thus eliminating situational cues—Kanzi was able to select the correct picture from among a pile of pictures. In another testing situation, when he was told to "Give the dog a shot," Kanzi picked up a toy hypodermic syringe from among a host of objects and "injected" his stuffed toy dog.

Over the years, scientists have watched Kanzi (a bonobo), Washoe (a chimp), Koko (a gorilla), and other apes not only sign spontaneously but also use their signing to let others know their likes and dislikes, just as humans do. Although these apes have not mastered human language, a growing number of researchers now believe that these animals are able to communicate with humans and even with others of their own species using a form of human language (Budiansky, 1998; Fouts, 1997; Jensvold & Gardner, 2000; Savage-Rumbaugh et al., 1998). In contrast to humans, their vocabulary is small, and their sentences are simple, similar to those of a 2-year-old child. Further, it takes substantially longer and requires more effort for them to learn a language than it does human children. This suggests that the human brain must have something at birth that is more ready to acquire language than do the ape brains. Despite these qualifications, these animals may indeed possess the ability to learn language, an ability we once thought unique to humans (Hillix & Rumbaugh, 2004; Rumbaugh & Washburn, 2003).

Not all scientists agree with this assessment (Povinelli & Bering, 2002). Acknowledging that some apes may have the capacity to use symbolic thought under the right conditions, these skeptics still contend that this does not mean these animals are actually using language (Pinker, 1994). Other skeptics state that, while apes may be able to learn a limited use of language, they require a much more gifted environment in which to do so than do most humans (Skoyles & Sagan, 2002). Although researchers remain divided over whether animals can use language, it does appear that apes have the capacity to learn some of the basic elements of language. Perhaps the most appropriate conclusion to draw at this time is that, although nonhuman species show no capacity to produce language on their own, as a result of human intervention, certain species can be taught to produce *languagelike* communication.

9-1c Human Languages Have a Hierarchical Structure

As depicted in table 9-1, all human languages have a hierarchical structure, in which elementary sounds are combined into meaningful units to form words. In turn, these words are combined to form phrases, which are also combined to form sentences. The system of

Table **9-1**	The Hierarchical Structure of an English Sentence

Human language has a hierarchical structure, ranging from the basic fundamental sounds known as phonemes to the more complex levels of sentences. Phonemes are combined to form the smallest units of meaning, known as morphemes, and morphemes are combined to form words. Syntax rules determine how words can be combined to form phrases, and how phrases can be combined to form sentences.

Sentence	The angry men shouted at the boxers
Phrases	The angy men shouted at the boxers
Words	The angry men shouted at the boxers
Morphemes	The angry men shout ed at the box er s
Phonemes	thŭ a ng g rē mĕn šowt id at thŭ b o k s e r s

rules that determines how this structure is created is known as **grammar.** The rules of grammar tell us which combinations of sounds and words are permissible within the language we are using (Bybee & Fleischman, 1995). Grammar has three major components: (1) **phonology,** the rules for combining basic sounds into words; (2) **syntax,** the rules for combining words into sentences; and (3) **semantics,** the rules for communicating the meaning of words, phrases, and sentences.

Regarding phonology, all human languages are composed of **phonemes,** which are the smallest significant sound units in speech. To say *men,* you use three phonemes: *m, ĕ,* and *n.* *The* uses the phonemes *th* and *ŭ,* and the word *angry* has five phonemes: *a, ng, g, r,* and *ē.* As you can see, there isn't a one-to-one correspondence between a given letter of the alphabet and a phoneme. In the provided examples, the letter *e* has a different kind of speech sound in *men* than it does in the word *the,* and the *ē* sound in *angry* is made by the letter *y,* not the letter *e.*

Linguists estimate that humans have the capacity at birth to produce about 100 phonemes, but because no language uses all these phonemes, this number is reduced to a much smaller set as children learn to speak (Fowler, 2003). The Hindi language uses the most phonemes (over 60), and the Polynesian language uses the least (only 11). Most languages consist of between 30 and 40 phonemes; the English language uses about 40. Because one language might not include all the phonemes found in another language, people who learn to speak another language often have difficulty pronouncing the novel phonemes in their second language. This is why Japanese who learn to speak English often fail to distinguish between *r* sounds and *l* sounds. The Japanese linguist Masaaki Yamanashi committed this type of phonetic mistake when he remarked to an American colleague following the 1992 presidential election, "In Japan, we have been very interested in Clinton's erection." Similarly, native English speakers have difficulty coughing up the guttural Arabic *ch* or rolling the German *r.*

One step above phonemes in the spoken language hierarchy are **morphemes,** which are the smallest units of language that carry meaning. A few morphemes, such as *a* and *I,* are also phonemes, and most morphemes are themselves words. Morphemes include prefixes and suffixes, such as the *re* in *replay* or the *s* in *plans.* The word *tourists* contains three morphemes—*tour, ist* (meaning "person who does something"), and *s* (indicating plural)—each of which adds to the meaning of the morpheme it precedes. The average English speaker uses the available 40 phonemes to build between 50,000 and 80,000 morphemes.

Beyond the simple structural elements of phonemes, morphemes, and their phonological rules, we also rely on syntax rules to build proper phrases and sentences. For instance, you can easily recognize that the phrase *the angry men* is a correctly formed piece of English, but the phrases *men the angry* and *angry the men* are not correct. These last two phrases violate the rules of English syntax, in which articles (*the*) and adjectives (*angry*) precede nouns (*men*). Another simple rule of syntax is that a declarative sentence (a sentence that makes a statement) must have both a subject (what is being talked about) and a predicate (a statement about the subject). Thus, while *The angry men* is not a sentence because it lacks

grammar The system of rules that determines the proper use and combination of language symbols.

phonology The rules used in language to combine basic sounds into words.

syntax The rules used in language to combine words into sentences.

semantics The rules used in language to communicate the meaning of words, phrases, and sentences.

phoneme The smallest significant sound unit in speech.

morpheme The smallest unit of language that carries meaning.

Boy, those French: They have a different word for everything!

—*Steve Martin, American actor and author, b. 1945*

Figure 9-2

Surface Structure versus Deep Structure

The surface structure of a sentence consists of its word arrangement, while the deep structure refers to its underlying meaning. Sometimes the same surface structure can reflect two different deep structures ("Visiting relatives can be a nuisance"). Similarly, two sentences can have different surface structures but the same deep structure ("Jaelyn broke the window").

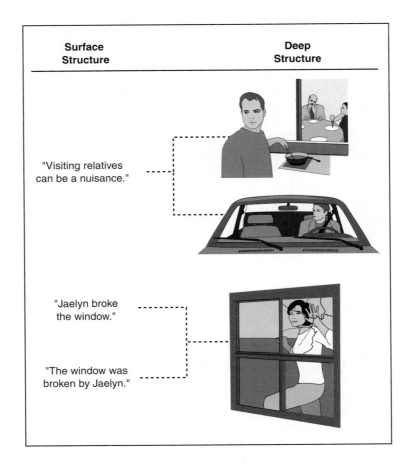

a predicate, *The angry men shouted at the boxers* is a sentence. The way people happen to combine words into a sentence is known as the *surface structure* of language, and it is based on syntax rules.

Although syntax rules shape proper sentence construction, the rules of semantics determine the *meaning* of sentences. This underlying meaning is known as the *deep structure* of language (Chomsky, 1957, 1965). Based on your knowledge of semantics, you realize that while the following sentence does not violate any syntax rules, it conveys no obvious meaning: *Silent music questions winter.* How can music—especially *silent music*— question anything, let alone winter? This sentence illustrates the fact that proper syntax and meaning don't always go together.

As you can see from figure 9-2, two sentences can have the same surface structure but two different deep structures ("Visiting relatives can be a nuisance"), and they can also have different surface structures but the same deep structure ("Jaelyn broke the window"; "The window was broken by Jaelyn"). People are more likely to store information in memory based on deep structure rather than surface structure. For this reason, while you probably won't remember whether someone told you that "Jaelyn broke the window" or "The window was broken by Jaelyn," you probably will remember that Jaelyn caused the window breakage.

How you understand the meaning of a sentence often depends on context, and this is especially so when a sentence is perceived to have two or more deep structures. When a sentence is unclear—as in "Visiting relatives can be a nuisance"—people automatically try to choose one deep structure over the other (Warren, 1970). The art of poetry and writing often involves forcing the reader to simultaneously consider multiple deep structures in language.

9-1d Infants Appear to Be Born Prepared to Learn Language

Learning a language has the appearance of being a monumental task. For example, consider the task of learning your culture's vocabulary, which is one component in language acquisition. During childhood, you learned almost 5,000 words per year, which translates to about 13 new words per day. Your vocabulary on graduating from high school was proba-bly about 80,000 words. Adults with excellent vocabularies retain upward of 200,000 words (Just & Carpenter, 1987; Miller & Gildea, 1987). Achieving that level of vocabulary capabil-ity certainly seems like a challenging task, and we haven't even discussed the challenges of learning the other components in language acquisition.

How do we become proficient language users? As in other areas of psychological inquiry, researchers have debated the degree to which language acquisition is simply due to experience and learning, and the degree to which it naturally unfolds due to inborn capac-ities (Sealey, 2000; Snow, 1999).

Behaviorism's Language Theory

Due to the influence of behaviorism, until about 1960 most psychologists assumed that chil-dren's development of language ability was simply a learned response. Championing this perspective, in his 1957 book *Verbal Behavior,* B. F. Skinner asserted that people speak as they do because they have been reinforced for doing so. Children, according to the behav-iorists, begin life with a blank "language blackboard," which is then slowly filled by the expe-riences provided by people in their social environment. Throughout this learning process, behaviorists assumed that children were relatively passive; parents and other speakers were given credit for shaping their younger charges' utterances into intelligible words by selec-tively reinforcing correct responses.

The problem with this view that language develops solely through imitation, selective reinforcement, and punishment is that it does not fit the evidence (James, 1990). For instance, behaviorism cannot explain how children often produce sentences they have never heard before (Brown, 1973). Instead of saying, "Mommy went to work" or "That is my cookie"—which would be correct imitations of adult speech—children typically say, "Mommy goed to work" and "That mine cookie." Perhaps more important, children's imitation of adult speech drops dramatically after the age of 2, despite the fact that language development continues. How could children continue to learn language if imitation is at the core of their learning? Selective reinforcement and punishment also cannot explain language development; not only do parents rarely provide negative feedback when their young children make grammat-ical errors, but also children's speech usually is not significantly influenced by such correc-tions when they do occur (Gordon, 1990; Morgan & Travis, 1989). This does not mean that operant conditioning principles play no role in learning language; for example, anyone who remembers learning when to use "who" and when to use "whom" can attest to the influence of learning principles on language acquisition. Yet, contrary to earlier behaviorist assump-tions, operant conditioning principles do not play the primary role in language development.

The Nativist Perspective

Standing in sharp contrast to the behaviorist's view of language development is the nativist perspective. In general, a *nativist theory* of development contends that normal development proceeds according to an inborn program that is not significantly influenced by environ-mental factors. Thus, a nativist theory of language acquisition would suggest that we learn language for the same reason that we learn to walk—because we're biologically equipped for it (Bates & Dick, 2002; Ramus et al., 2001).

The linguist (and social activist) Noam Chomsky (1957) proposed one of the more influential nativist theories of language acquisition. He contended that humans are born with specialized brain structures, or neural prewiring, called the **language acquisition device,** which facilitates learning of language. According to Chomsky, with this inborn capacity to acquire language, if children are exposed to it, they will learn to talk even if they are not reinforced for doing so.

Although the existence of a language acquisition device remains an unconfirmed hypothesis, recent studies suggest that we may indeed be biologically predisposed to acquire language. For example, by studying videotapes of infants while they were engaged in bab-bling and nonbabbling mouth movements, Siobhan Holowka and Laura-Ann Petitto (2002) discovered that the right sides of the babies' mouths opened wider than the left sides

Noam Chomsky, b. 1928
Source: Courtesy of Noam Chomsky.

language acquisition device
According to Chomsky's linguistic theory, an innate mechanism that facilitates the learning of language.

when they babbled, but not when they nonbabbled. *Babbling* is the vocal sound made by babies consisting of consonant-vowel repetition, such as *baa-baa-baa* or *gaa-gaa-gaa*. As you recall from chapter 3, section 3-3b, the right side of the body is controlled by the left side of the brain, which is where the major neural mechanisms for language are located. Petitto and Holowka contend from their findings that certain brain areas are specialized for language very early in life, perhaps even prior to birth. Studies such as these may indicate that we have an innate capacity for language. Researchers have also found that, when adults learn a language, they speak with a more nativelike accent if they overheard the language regularly during childhood than if they did not (Au et al., 2002). Consistent with Chomsky's notion of a language acquisition device, these findings suggest that early exposure to a language may establish a long-lasting mental representation of it.

Interactionist Perspectives

In the debate on language acquisition, while behaviorists emphasize environmental factors and nativists champion inborn predispositions, a middle-ground view has been taken by a number of interactionist theories (Bates & MacWhinney, 1982; Nelson et al., 2003). As the name implies, *interactionists* assume that environmental and biological factors interact to affect the course of language development.

The cognitive theory of Jean Piaget, discussed in chapter 4, section 4-3a, is an example of a *cognitive interactionist* perspective. In a 1975 debate with Chomsky, Piaget argued that the structures of language may be neither innate nor learned. Instead, they may emerge as a result of the continuing interaction between children's current level of cognitive functioning and environmental input.

While Piaget's cognitive interactionist perspective emphasizes how children learn language by interacting with their environment, it downplays the role that other people—specifically adults—play in this process. In contrast, the *social interactionist* perspective, which is strongly influenced by Lev Vygotsky's writings (see chapter 4, section 4-3c), stresses the point that, while children may have an innate capacity for language, they cannot acquire it until they are immersed in social conversation with adults. Adults, especially parents, supply a "scaffold," or supportive communicative structure, that allows children to begin learning language (Bates et al., 1983; Hirsh-Pasek & Golinkoff, 1993).

Adult interaction does appear to be critical in the development of language. Studies of abused and neglected children who had received little adult attention found that their speech comprehension and verbal expression were impaired compared to those of children who had received normal adult attention (Allen & Oliver, 1982; Culp et al., 1991). Unlike these language deficits, no differences were found in the children's cognitive development, leading to the conclusion that language development is particularly vulnerable in an environment lacking normal parent-child verbal interaction.

Evidence that verbal interaction—not just language exposure—is the crucial ingredient in normal language development comes from the case study of a young boy named Jim, who was raised by deaf parents (Sachs et al., 1981). Using their extremely limited language skills, Jim's parents tried to teach their son spoken English. Still, at the age of 4, when he was enrolled in a preschool program, Jim could produce no spontaneous utterances and few intelligible words, despite the fact that he had regularly watched television at home. In spite of his serious language deficit, after only a few months in preschool, and with speech therapy, Jim showed marked improvement. Within a few years, his language usage became normal. In this case, at least, being exposed to language in a nonsocial context (watching television) did not foster language acquisition. What was necessary was actual engagement in conversation with competent language users. Luckily for Jim, corrective therapy occurred early enough to avoid long-term negative effects. Unfortunately, when children are isolated from normal language interaction beyond their middle childhood, they develop irreversible language deficits (Gill, 1997; Ouellet et al., 2001; Rymer, 1993). Taken together, these studies suggest that a critical component in the development of language is supportive social interaction with competent language users.

As you can see from this brief overview, psychologists have developed different theories to explain language acquisition. Behaviorists emphasize how the environment shapes children's vocabulary and grammar through the application of operant conditioning principles.

Verbal interaction with competent language users is essential in order for children to develop language skills. Which perspective on language development does this evidence support?

Source: © Stockbyte.

Nativists emphasize how inborn mechanisms facilitate learning of language. Finally, inter-actionists emphasize how environmental and biological factors interact to affect the course of language development. Of these three perspectives, the behaviorists place too much emphasis on conditioning principles, while the nativists don't give enough credit to environmental influences. Currently, the dominant opinion within the field is that the possible solution to the controversy between the behaviorist and nativist approaches lies in the contribution of the various interactionist approaches (Gleason, 1997). By attending to how biology interacts with social and environmental factors, we may more fully understand the language acquisition process.

9-1e Language Development Occurs in Distinct Stages

Regardless of the exact process by which language acquisition occurs, we do know that it begins shortly after birth and involves a number of distinct stages that move from simplicity to complexity (Floccia et al., 2003; Hoff, 2003). Indeed, deaf infants exposed to sign language from birth acquire sign language on the same developmental schedule as hearing infants learn spoken languages (Petitto, 2000).

Phonemes and Their Combination

Language development begins with children using primitive-sounding phonemes. In every culture throughout the world, by about 2 months of age, newborns begin a vocalization pattern known as *cooing,* in which they produce phoneme sounds such as *ooooh* and *aaaah.* Between the fourth and sixth months, infants can read lips and distinguish among the phonemes that comprise their language (Cohen et al., 1992). They also begin babbling (Plaut & Kello, 1999). This sequence of cooing and then babbling occurs even among babies born deaf (Oller & Eilers, 1988). Further, the early babbling of children from different cultures sounds the same because it includes the phonemes in all existing languages. However, by the time a child is about 10 months of age, phonemes that are not in the child's native language drop out, and babbling takes on a more culture-specific sound (de Boysson-Bardies et al., 1989).

Children throughout the world progress through distinct stages in developing language, beginning with *cooing* and *babbling,* followed by the *one-word stage* and the *two-word stage.* After the two-word stage, children not only begin using longer phrases, but also learn grammatical rules. During the early stages of language development, what sort of speech feedback do adults provide to young children to facilitate learning?

Source: © Stockbyte.

Journey of Discovery Question — Research indicates that infants have an inborn ability to detect phonemes that are not a part of their culture's language repertoire. Given that you cannot ask infants questions, how do you think psychologists tested this ability in newborns? That is, how did they design an experiment to test children's inborn ability to detect phonemes?

The Development of Language Comprehension

Well before children speak their first words, they develop an understanding of their language. For example, by the time children utter their first word at 1 year of age, they probably already understand about 50 words (Menyuk et al., 1995). Studies of infants' brain functioning during the beginning stages of language comprehension indicate that, unlike adult patterns of brain activity, both cerebral hemispheres show widely distributed activity during language comprehension. However, by 20 months, children's pattern of brain activity becomes more adultlike—that is, localized in Wernicke's area in the temporal lobes of the left cerebral hemisphere (Mills et al., 1997). These findings suggest that, as children learn to understand language, their brains are undergoing changes that are either the cause or the effect (or both!) of this learning.

Single-Word Use

By the end of their first year, most children begin uttering morpheme sounds that can be identified as words, such as *mama, papa,* and the ever-popular *no.* This period in language acquisition is typically called the *one-word stage,* because children can use only one-word phrases (Akhtar & Tomasello, 1996). These words usually relate to specific objects or concepts that children regularly encounter or use in their world. Because they still possess a fairly small vocabulary, young children often don't have words for many of the objects they want to talk about. Consequently, they *overextend* their words to these yet unnamed objects. Thus, an 18-month-old child might use the word *wawa* not only for water but also for milk, juice, and any other liquid. Similarly, anything sweet might be called a *cookie*. Overextension is an application of the process of *assimilation* to children's words. As you recall from chapter 4, section 4-3a, assimilation is the process of using existing schemas to deal with information encountered in the world. When children call all liquids *wawa*, they are assimilating these objects into their *wawa* schema. However, when they begin calling liquids by their specific names—for example, milk is no longer *wawa*, but *milk*—this is an application of the process of *accommodation*, which involves the creation of new schemas.

From Primitive to Complex Sentences

> **telegraphic speech** An early speech phase in which children use short, multiple-word sentences that leave out all but the essential words, as in a telegrammed message.

By the age of 2, children enter the *two-word stage*, in which they begin using two separate words in the same sentence. During this two-word stage, a phase of **telegraphic speech** begins, in which children use multiple-word sentences that leave out all but the essential words, as in a telegrammed message (*BABY BORN. MOTHER FINE*). Thus, instead of saying, "I want to go outside," children will say, "Want outside." Even when using this basic telegraphic speech, youngsters demonstrate an elementary knowledge of syntax: Words are almost always spoken in their proper order ("Want outside" instead of "Outside want").

Once children move beyond using two-word sentences, they quickly produce longer phrases, and they use telegraphic speech less frequently by age 3 (Riley, 1987; Waxman, 2003). By the time children reach the age of 4, they are using plurals, as well as the present and past tense in sentences, but they often *overgeneralize* grammatical rules (Pinker, 1999). For example, in using the past tense, they may incorrectly say, "I goed outside" or "I rided my bike." Because "goed" and "rided" are words children would not have heard from adults, their use suggests that children are naturally predisposed to pick up grammatical rules and then apply them generally (Marcus, 1996). Children also don't seem to be especially attentive to adult corrections, as illustrated in the following dialogue (quoted in Cazden, 1972):

Child:	"My teacher holded the baby rabbits and we patted them."
Mother:	"Did you say your teacher held the baby rabbits?"
Child:	"Yes."
Mother:	"What did you say she did?"
Child:	"She holded the baby rabbits and we patted them."
Mother:	"Did you say she held them tightly?"
Child:	"No, she holded them loosely."

> **child-directed speech** Speech to babies characterized by exaggerated intonations, high pitch, clear enunciation, short sentences, repetition, and slow speech; also called *motherese*.

This does not mean that adults are irrelevant to children's language acquisition. As noted earlier, especially during the early stages of language development, the day-to-day verbal feedback that infants receive from their caregivers plays an important role in the learning process. This **child-directed speech**—also called *motherese*—is characterized by exaggerated intonations, high pitch, clear enunciation, short sentences, repetition, and slow speech (Sachs, 1989). Child-directed speech may help infants recognize specific language forms and understand where utterances begin and end, skills necessary for future language learning (Barnes et al., 1983; Morgan, 1986). Adults who communicate with deaf children exhibit a similar pattern by making signs more slowly, repeating the signs, and making exaggerated gestures when signing (Masataka, 1996; Sandler, 2003). Deaf infants pay more attention to this *child-directed signing* than to the more rapid, fluid signing typically used between adults.

Adolescent Slang and Peer-Group Influence

As children mature and progress into adolescence, they continue developing their grammatical abilities, although not in identifiable stages. In the process of establishing their social identities (see chapter 4, section 4-2f), peer-group influence becomes increasingly important in how teenagers and young adults use language. This influence can be heard in the special vocabularies of *slang* terms that adolescents bring home from school and play (Akom, 2000; Wardhaugh, 1993). As a parent of two adolescents, I am regularly reminded of one of the primary functions of slang usage: to help the young identify with their age group by distinguishing their language from adult language. A second function of adolescent slang is to provide a private means of communication, one that adults will have difficulty deciphering. In this sense, slang is a socially accepted way in which teenagers and young adults can erect a vocabulary barrier between themselves and the adult world (Harman, 1985).

Some buzzwords and catchphrases used by adolescents and young adults are peculiar to just one neighborhood, school, or geographic region, while others are widely recognized and used throughout the country and beyond. Consistent with the influence that African-American culture has on popular American culture, many slang terms used by younger Americans come directly from African-American vernacular English (Dalzell, 1996; Green, 2002). Table 9-2 lists some commonly used slang terms and phrases among teenagers and young adults. Of course, the use of specialized words and phrases is not unique to younger people. For example, anyone who is a serious athlete or avid sports fan uses many slang terms in describing different facets of a sport, and the use of such slang often identifies the person as a member of a particular social group. Similarly, medical students learn slang terminology as part of the socialization process of becoming physicians (Coombs et al., 1993; Fox et al., 2003). However, we tend to pay more attention to teen slang because of its strong connection with adolescent social life and identity development (Adams & Slayer, 2003; Eble, 1996).

Finally, as Internet use has become increasingly common, slang terms have developed among those who interact online. *Instant messaging* is a communications service that enables people to interact with others in real time over the Internet using a computer keyboard (Herring, 2004). One of the attractive features of the slang used in instant messaging is that it allows the user relative privacy from inquisitive onlookers who are unfamiliar with the meaning of the abbreviated terms (Cameron & Webster, 2005). Thus, when used by

Table 9-2	Commonly Used Slang among Adolescents and Young Adults

This is a nonrepresentative sampling of terms and phrases sometimes used by adolescents and young adults in everyday conversation. Some of this terminology will have different meaning in different geographic regions, and some terms already may be outdated. Many of the 11 slang terms listed below come from African-American vernacular English. Two functions of slang usage are to identify oneself with a desirable social group and to provide a somewhat private means of communication.

Slang Term	Definition and Example
Baggin	To make fun of or insult someone ("Nora, why you always baggin on me?")
Boo	Your best friend, your boyfriend, or your girlfriend ("There's my boo!")
Bootsie	Something undesirable; an unfortunate or unfair situation, event, or thing ("That class is bootsie." "Did you see that test? Bootsie!")
Cheezin	Smiling ("Why you cheezin so big?")
Game	A man's effectiveness in conversing with and wooing women ("She ain't going to go out with you. You got no game!")
Kickin' it	To relax, usually with your friends ("I'm just kickin' it with my friends tonight.")
Kryptonite	A weakness ("Boy, that history class is my kryptonite.")
My bad	A phrase said to admit guilt in a situation ("Oh, that's not your grampa, that's your boyfriend? My bad!")
Salty	To have a bad attitude toward someone or something ("Don't be all salty tonight!")
Shizzle	Something very good ("Did you see how A.J. danced? She was the shizzle.")
Sprung	To be obsessed with someone, usually in a sexual manner ("Alex's so sprung on Angela, she's all he thinks about.")

One reason that instant messaging is so popular among teenagers is that the abbreviated slang used to communicate provides relative privacy from the prying eyes of adults.

Source: Courtesy of Figzoi.

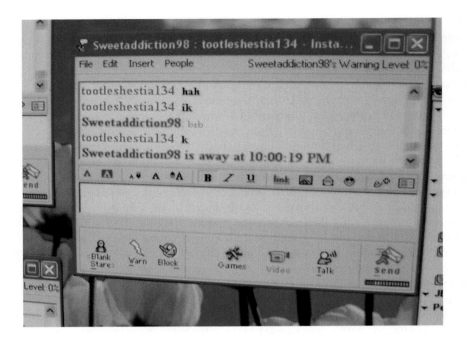

teens interacting with one another, instant messaging terminology serves one of the same functions as spoken slang: providing relative privacy from adult understanding.

9-1f Accomplished Language Users Sometimes Experience "Slips of the Tongue"

Thus far, our focus has been on how we use grammar correctly and how we creatively alter our vocabulary. Yet, as language users, we sometimes have difficulty getting the brain and speech production to work together smoothly. Some of the most noticeable—and often humorous—speech errors are **slips of the tongue.** These types of speech errors take a number of forms, including *word reversals* ("life is a chair of bowlies") and *word substitutions* ("I have the breast of intentions toward your daughter, sir"). Word reversals are also known as *Spoonerisms,* after the English clergyman William Spooner, who was famous for these kinds of tongue slips. Spooner once chastised a frequently absent student by exclaiming, "You have hissed all my mystery lectures and tasted the whole worm!" He meant to say, "You have missed all my history lectures and wasted the whole term." Word substitutions that appear to reveal hidden thoughts or motives are known as *Freudian slips,* after the psychoanalyst Sigmund Freud.

Cognitive and psychoanalytic theorists offer different explanations for "tips of the slung" (Chen, 2000; Marx, 1999). One cognitive theory states that tongue slips may result from "slips of the brain" as it tries to organize linguistic messages (Dell, 1986, 1988). According to this *spreading-activation theory,* constructing a sentence involves the brain activating from memory both phonemes and morphemes. If activation of a particular phoneme or morpheme spreads too quickly to a similar phoneme or morpheme, a slip of the tongue occurs. For example, try reciting the following tongue twister five times in rapid succession:

> She sells seashells by the seashore.

Because the *sh* sound is so highly activated by the *sh* in *she* and *shells,* during one of your recitations, it's likely that you will say *shells* instead of *sells, sheashells* instead of *seashells,* and/or *sheashore* instead of *seashore.*

In contrast to this cognitive view, psychoanalytic theorists argue that slips of the tongue occur when unconscious thoughts and desires slip past conscious censorship. Even so, the findings from one experiment suggest that these unconsciously motivated *Freudian slips* may be caused by a cognitive process similar to the previously described spreading activation of phonemes and morphemes. In this study, slips of the tongue were artificially induced

slips of the tongue Inadvertent speech errors that occur when sounds or words are rearranged.

in male participants by setting up expectations for certain word patterns of sound (Motley & Baars, 1979). Thus, after pronouncing a series of word pairs—such as *ball doze, bell dark,* and *bean deck*—a participant was more likely to say *barn door* when he saw *darn bore*. In the first experimental condition, prior to responding to the word pairs, participants were told that they would receive random shocks during the experiment. In the second experimental condition, other participants interacted with a provocative female experimenter prior to responding to the word pairs. Results indicated that participants in the first condition produced more tongue slips related to fear of being shocked (for example, *shad bock* became *bad shock*), while individuals in the second condition produced more sexual slips (for example, *past fashion* became *fast passion*). These results suggest not only that the unconscious contributes to the production of speech errors, but also that emotionally charged situations can interfere with conscious word choice just as morphemes and phonemes do (Motley, 1985).

9-1g The Linguistic Relativity Hypothesis Asserts That Language Determines Thought

In this chapter, in addition to examining our language system, we will also analyze how we think. Yet how strong is the connection between cognition and language? The linguist Benjamin Lee Whorf (1897–1941) developed the **linguistic relativity hypothesis,** which proposes that the structure of language *determines* the structure of thought (Whorf, 1956). He used the term *linguistic relativity* to emphasize his belief that thought is relative to the particular language used. The implications of this hypothesis are profound. First, if language shapes your conception of reality, without a word or phrase to describe an experience, you literally cannot think about it. Second, if language shapes reality, then no two cultures share the same understanding of the world.

> **linguistic relativity hypothesis** The proposal that the structure of language determines the structure of thought, meaning that people who speak different languages also think differently.

The idea that language determines thinking has been the subject of considerable debate and research over the years (Lucy, 1997; Penny, 1996). In a critical test of Whorf's hypothesis, Eleanor Rosch (1973) compared the color perceptions of the Dani people of Papua New Guinea—who use only two words for color (*bright* and *dark*)—with those of English-speaking people who use many different color terms. Despite these substantial language differences, Rosch found no differences in the way the two groups perceived color: Dani speakers made discriminations among colors as fine as the discriminations of English speakers. Other cross-cultural studies using different languages have also failed to support the hypothesis that language determines thinking (Davies, 1998; Gumperz & Levinson, 1996). Thus, counter to the linguistic relativity hypothesis, even though a language lacks terms for certain stimuli, the users of the language may still be able to perceive the various features of those stimuli. In fact, when we encounter something novel, we change our language to accommodate the need to refer to it. In other words, we manipulate our language much more than our language manipulates us.

Although the hypothesis that language determines thought in some sort of lock-step fashion has no empirical support, most psychologists do believe in a weaker version of Whorf's hypothesis—that language can *influence* thinking (Hardin & Banaji, 1993; Lucy, 1992). This idea may not seem that unusual to you if you speak two dissimilar languages, such as English and Japanese or English and Chinese (Brown, 1986). English, rooted in an individualist cultural context, has many self-focused words, while the collectivist-based Japanese and Chinese languages have many interpersonally focused words. Bilingual people report that the way they think about themselves and others is influenced by which language they happen to use (Dinges & Hull, 1992; Hoffman et al., 1986). For instance, when speaking English, bilingual people are more likely to attend to their own personal needs and desires, while social obligations are more salient in their thoughts when they speak Japanese (Matsumoto, 1994).

Language can also influence thinking in the way it calls attention to a person's gender. In English, you cannot avoid specifying gender when using pronouns such as *his* or *her*. Yet, traditionally in the English language, masculine pronouns and nouns have been used to refer to all people, regardless of their gender. Although the **generic masculine** is meant to include women as well as men, it does not do so in reality. A number of studies indicate that people learn to associate men and women with certain activities and occupations by listening to the gendered pronouns used to describe these activities and occupations (McConnell & Fazio, 1996; Miller & Swift, 1991). For example, telling children what a physician does on

> **generic masculine** The use of masculine nouns and pronouns to refer to all people, instead of just males.

Table 9-3	Suggestions for Reducing Gendered Terms in Language
Gendered Terms to Avoid	**Alternative Gender-Neutral Terms**
He, his, him	He or she, she or he, her or his, his or her, him or her, her or him, *or* they, their, them
Man, mankind	Humanity, people, human beings, the human species
Man-made	Handmade, synthetic, fabricated, constructed
Coed	Student
Freshman	First-year student, frosh
Manpower	Workers, human resources, personnel, workforce
Businessman	Businessperson
Career girl	Businesswoman
Chairman, chairwoman	Chairperson, head, chair
Saleswoman, salesgirl	Salesclerk
Foreman	Supervisor
Policeman, policewoman	Police officer
Waitress	Server
Man-to-man	One-to-one, person-to-person
Forefathers	Ancestors
Housewife, househusband	Homemaker
Mothering	Parenting, caregiving, nurturing

the job using the generic masculine ("He takes care of sick people") conveys to the child that this is an occupation for men, not women. Similarly, after reading a paragraph describing psychologists with the generic masculine *he*, both women and men rated psychology as a less attractive profession for women than did students who read a gender-neutral (*they*) description (Briere & Lanktree, 1983). Based on this research, the American Psychological Association recommends that gender-neutral language be used to reduce gender bias in people's thinking. Reading-time studies indicate that using gender-neutral terms instead of gendered terms is cognitively efficient and does not reduce reading comprehension (Foertsch & Gernsbacher, 1997). Table 9-3 lists some suggestions for avoiding gendered terms in your own language.

In summary, then, although research does not support the original strong version of the linguistic relativity hypothesis—that language determines what we can (and cannot) think about—it does appear that language can make certain ways of thinking more or less likely. This weaker version of the original hypothesis tells us that, while language is not the sole determinant of thought, it does influence thought in some meaningful ways.

> Every country has its own language, yet the subjects of which the untutored soul speaks are the same everywhere.
>
> —*Tertullian, Roman theologian, 160–240 A.D.*

9-1h Cultural Thinking Shapes Language Styles

Research suggests not only that the language of a culture can influence language users' thinking, but also that cultural thinking can influence people's style of language. This is clearly seen in the different ways individualists and collectivists express meaning in their speech and look for meaning in others' speech.

As described in chapter 1, section 1-3f, individualism focuses on satisfying one's own needs and desires, while collectivism shows greater concern for the needs and wants of one's group. Because people from individualist cultures have been brought up to satisfy themselves, they are not only used to speaking directly to others about their needs, but they also expect that others will do the same (Brown & Levinson, 1987; Ting-Toomey et al.,

1991). Thus, when they converse, individualists express themselves directly and don't look for hidden meaning in others' speech. In contrast, people with a collectivist orientation tend to use language in a very different way (Holtgraves, 1997). Because they have been socialized to satisfy other group members rather than themselves, collectivists tend to speak indirectly about their own needs—and to expect that others will do likewise. Due to this cultural mind-set against expressing one's needs directly, collectivists habitually look for the hidden meaning in others' speech. In collectivist cultures such as Japan, China, and Korea, it is considered virtuous to be able to quickly and accurately interpret and respond to others' vaguely expressed feelings and desires before they have been clearly articulated (Barnlund, 1989; Doi, 1973). In this kind of cultural context, directly expressing one's desires is considered inappropriate, because others are expected to "read" them through indirect means.

In general, an indirect language style not only is considered more polite than a direct style, but also is more likely to provide the speaker with deniability (Holtgraves, 1992; Holtgraves & Yang, 1992). That is, because indirect remarks have multiple meanings, any one meaning can be denied in favor of another meaning. For example, imagine that Sandy invites Kim over for dinner and, after the meal, asks her which dish she liked best, the tofu burger or the broccoli pasta. Kim responds with something like, "That's such a difficult choice." If Sandy interprets this as a negative comment on both dishes and confronts Kim, Sandy's guest can now simply assert that her host misinterpreted her statement. Deniability would be harder to claim if Kim had initially responded directly and told Sandy that she did not like either dish, or that she preferred one to the other. An indirect language style, then, is more likely than a direct style to help smooth over awkward social situations.

One implication of these findings is that misunderstandings can easily develop between individualists and collectivists if they misread each other's conversational styles. That is, individualists might become irritated because collectivists do not clearly convey their needs and preferences, while collectivists might think individualists are being insulting by directly stating their attitudes and desires. If you would like to better understand your own language style, spend a few minutes responding to the statements in Self-Discovery Questionnaire 9-1.

Self-Discovery
Questionnaire **9-1**

Do You Have a Direct or an Indirect Language Style?

Directions: Read the statements below and indicate whether you generally agree or disagree with each statement.

1. Most of what I say can be taken at face value, and there is no need to look for a deeper meaning.
   Agree_____   Disagree_____

2. There are many times when I prefer to express myself indirectly.
   Agree_____   Disagree_____

3. There is usually no need for people to look below the surface to understand what I really mean.
   Agree_____   Disagree_____

4. My remarks often have more than one meaning.
   Agree_____   Disagree_____

5. What I mean with a remark is usually fairly obvious.
   Agree_____   Disagree_____

6. Many times, people are not totally sure what I really mean when I say something.
   Agree_____   Disagree_____

Scoring instructions: People with a direct language style tend to agree with the odd-numbered statements, while people with an indirect language style tend to agree with the even-numbered statements. What do your responses suggest about your own language style?

9-1i We Also Communicate Nonverbally

Imagine that you are invited over to a new acquaintance's house for dinner and served lentil burgers as the main course. Further imagine that you are a proud meat-and-potatoes person and not eager to send this Mc-mutant bean food patty down your intestinal tract. At the same time, you don't want to offend your host, and thus you look her straight in the eye, smack your lips, and exclaim, "Oh boy! Lentil burgers! I love 'em!" During the meal, while you expound at length on how tasty the burger is and how much you enjoy its texture, your host will probably be more attentive to your facial expressions as you chew and swallow the burger, and to the amount of beverage with which you wash it down, than to your words. No matter what praise you lavish upon your host, if you look like you're being tortured as you eat, your words will likely be disregarded.

This hypothetical scenario illustrates that, when interacting with others, we convey and attend to a great deal of information by means other than language. **Nonverbal communication** is the sending and receiving of information using gestures, expressions, vocal cues, and body movements rather than words. Some forms of nonverbal communication, such as sign language, qualify as language because they meet the criteria of meaningfulness, displacement, and productivity discussed in section 9-1b, but other forms do not qualify. Still, these non-language-based forms of nonverbal communication contain a wealth of information that we rely on when interacting with others.

nonverbal communication The sending and receiving of information using gestures, expressions, vocal cues, and body movements rather than words.

Facial Gestures and Body Movement

One of the more important nonverbal channels of communication is the face. In fact, the evolutionary theorist Charles Darwin (1872) proposed that certain facial expressions are inborn and thus are understood throughout the world. Studies conducted during the past 30 years provide strong support for Darwin's assertions (Ekman, 1993, 1994; Izard, 1994). For example, as I discuss more fully in chapter 11, section 11-5b, people from very different cultures manifest similar facial expressions when experiencing certain emotions. Evolutionary psychologists believe that this ability to recognize emotion from facial expressions is genetically programmed into our species and has survival value for us (Smith et al., 2005). How might this ability aid in survival? One possibility is that being able to read others' emotions by attending to facial expressions not only allows us to better predict their intentions ("Do they mean to harm me?"), but also helps us to understand how they are interpreting events ("Why are they afraid? Are we all in danger here?"). In support of this "survival value" hypothesis, research indicates that we are most attentive to facial expressions that signal potential danger—namely, fear and anger (Hansen & Hansen, 1988; Öhman et al., 2001b).

Besides facial cues, the body as a whole can convey a wealth of information. For example, people who walk with a good deal of hip sway, knee bending, loose-jointedness, and body bounce are perceived to be younger and more powerful than those who walk with less pronounced gaits (Montepare & Zebrowitz-McArthur, 1988). Research suggests that many muggers pay close attention to potential victims' body movements to determine whether they will be easy or difficult targets. People with an organized quality to their body movements are less likely to be picked out as easy victims by would-be muggers, while those with inconsistent or jerky movements are more likely to be chosen (Grayson & Stein, 1981). Thus, just as wounded animals invite attack from predators in the wild (Tinbergen, 1969), potential victims of crime may unwittingly and nonverbally communicate a sense of vulnerability to criminals.

Although certain nonverbal cues are universally recognized, many forms of nonverbal behavior are shaped by cultural norms. For example, cultures vary greatly in what is considered the appropriate distance (*personal space*) to maintain when casually conversing with strangers and acquaintances. In the United States, Canada, England, and Germany, this distance ranges from 18 inches to 4 feet, whereas in Middle Eastern and Latin American cultures, the personal space zone is much smaller (Hall, 1969; Latané et al., 1995). Figure 9-3 identifies other cultural differences in nonverbal communication.

Nonverbally Communicating Deceit

During an average week, American college students lie to about one-third of all of those with whom they interact (DePaulo et al., 1996; Kashy & DePaulo, 1996). On average, young adults

When we think that others are trying to deceive us, what aspects of their self-presentation are we most likely to closely monitor and analyze? Their spoken words? Facial gestures? Eye gaze? Body posture? Are you a good deception detector?

Source: comstock.com

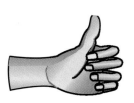

Thumbs-up

In North America, Russia, and France, this gesture means "OK," "good job," or "excellent." However, in Iran, Nigeria, and Sardinia, it is an obscene gesture.

OK

In the United States and Canada, this gesture means "OK" or "That's good." In Japan, this gesture means "money." In Mexico, it means "sex." In Ethiopia, it means "homosexuality." In Laos and France, it means "bad," "zero," or "worthless."

Hand-purse

In Italy and among Italian Americans, this gesture means "What are you trying to say?" In Spain, this gesture means "good." In Tunisia, this gesture means "Slow down." In Malta, it means "You may seem good, but you are bad."

Nodding and Shaking the Head

Nodding the head means "yes" in North America, while shaking the head means "no." In certain cultures in Africa and India, the exact opposite is true. In North Korea, shaking the head means "I don't know." In Bulgaria, throwing the head back and then returning it to an upright position means "I don't agree with you."

Figure 9-3

Cultural Differences in Gestures

tell about 10 lies per week, with the greatest amount of lying committed by those who are more sociable, manipulative, and concerned about creating favorable impressions than others. Because a wealth of information can be gleaned from nonverbal behavior, when we believe others are trying to deceive us, we pay close attention to their nonverbal gestures (Ekman & O'Sullivan, 1991; Mehrabian, 1972). We do so for two reasons: (1) We believe that nonverbal information is likely to reveal people's true feelings, and (2) we think deceivers are less likely to consciously monitor and control their facial and bodily gestures. Consistent with these assumptions, a number of studies find that when people are trying to deceive, they fidget—that is, they touch, scratch, and rub various parts of their bodies (Harrigan, 1985; Harrigan et al., 1991).

Despite the numerous nonverbal deception signals available to us, studies—and everyday experience—indicate that we frequently make mistakes in judging others' truthfulness (Vrij & Semin, 1996). Deceivers fool us regardless of our sex, race, cultural background, socioeconomic status, or educational level. One of the biggest mistakes we make is placing too much importance on the face to detect deception. For example, we tend to believe that others do not smile when they lie, when in fact, smiling is a common device used by deceivers to hide their true feelings (Ekman et al., 1988). We also are often fooled by the structure of people's faces, falsely assuming that baby-faced individuals (large eyes and symmetrical facial features) and physically attractive persons are more honest than those with mature-looking and less attractive faces (Zebrowitz & Montepare, 1992; Zebrowitz et al., 1996). Further, confidence doesn't predict accuracy. A meta-analysis of 17 studies involving almost 2,800 participants found that people's confidence in detecting deception does not predict their accuracy in distinguishing liars from nonliars (DePaulo et al., 1997). This suggests that if deceivers closely monitor their nonverbal behavior, even well-trained deception-detectors will have a difficult time separating truths from lies (DePaulo, 1992; Ekman & O'Sullivan, 1991; Tucker & Riggio, 1988). Keep this in mind the next time you are served lentil burgers when visiting new friends!

She (Lady Desborough) tells enough white lies to ice a wedding cake.

—*Margo Asquith, English socialite, 1864–1945*

Nonconscious Mimicry

Beyond consciously interpreting the meaning of nonverbal gestures, we also communicate with others through **nonconscious mimicry,** which is the tendency to adopt the behaviors, postures, or mannerisms of interaction partners, without conscious awareness or intention (Chartrand et al., 2002). For example, when conversing with others, we often mimic their speech tendencies and accents, we laugh and yawn when they do, and we adopt their body postures and gestures. Mimicking others' facial expressions appears to be an inborn tendency: One-month-old infants smile, stick out their tongues, and open their mouths when

nonconscious mimicry The tendency to adopt the behaviors, postures, or mannerisms of interaction partners, without conscious awareness or intention.

Have you ever noticed that when conversing with others, some people begin mimicking their partner's speech tendencies, body postures, and gestures? Have you noticed yourself engaging in this nonconscious mimicry? What do some psychologists believe is the origin of this sort of imitation? What function may it serve for humans?

Source: Courtesy of Figzoi.

they see someone else doing the same. As discussed in chapter 4, section 4-1d, such imitation may be important in triggering emotional attachment of parents to newborns, thus making it more likely that the newborn will be nurtured and protected.

Do similar survival benefits explain why we find nonconscious mimicry in adult communication? Perhaps. In one study, some confederates were instructed to subtly imitate the mannerisms of people they were interacting with in a "get acquainted" session (for example, rubbing their face or tapping their foot when their partner did so). Results indicated that people whose gestures had been mimicked liked the confederates more than those who had not been mimicked (Chartrand & Bargh, 1999). Additional research has found that as people interact with one another and establish rapport, they increase their mimicking of each other's gestures (Jefferis et al., 2003). This mimicry not only increases their liking for and helpfulness toward one another but also tends to create more positive feelings toward others in the immediate vicinity (van Baaren et al., 2004). In explaining the implication of these findings, evolutionary psychologists point out that throughout human evolution individual survival and success at reproduction depended on our ancestors having successful social interactions. Individuals who could cooperate with others and maintain harmonious social ties were more likely to be included in group activities, thereby giving them an adaptive advantage over those who were ostracized from the group. Due to this process of natural selection, behaviors that fostered group cohesion eventually became widespread throughout the human population (Caporael, 2001). Over time, many of these behaviors became automatically activated without awareness. Nonconscious mimicry may be an example of this form of automatically activated behavior that creates affiliation and rapport among people and thereby fosters safety in groups (Chartrand et al., in press; de Waal, 2002).

Section Review

- According to the evolutionary perspective, language may have evolved because it facilitated the construction of consciousness and the cooperative efforts of group living.
- Three features of language are meaningfulness, displacement, and productivity.

- Certain species can be taught languagelike communication.
- Three theories of how language develops in humans maintain the following: Behaviorists stress the role played by operant conditioning; nativists contend that humans are born with a capacity to acquire language; and interactionists assert that environmental and biological factors interact to influence language development.
- Language has a hierarchical structure, in which elementary sounds are combined into meaningful units to form words.
- Grammar has three major components: (1) phonology (the rules for combining basic sounds into words); (2) syntax (the rules for combining words into sentences); and (3) semantics (the rules for communicating the meaning of words, phrases, and sentences).
- The smallest significant sound units in speech are phonemes, followed by morphemes, which are the smallest language units that carry meaning.
- Children progress through distinct stages in language development.
- The linguistic relativity hypothesis proposes that the structure of language determines the structure of thought.
- Although language structure does not determine the structure of thought, language can make certain ways of thinking more or less likely.
- Attention to nonverbal behavior can provide useful information in judging others.
- Nonconscious mimicry is a form of nonverbal communication that increases prosocial behavior among people.

9-2 THINKING

Preview

- *What are concepts, and why are they important?*
- *How is a concept related to a prototype?*
- *What are some common problem-solving strategies and some common obstacles to problem solving?*
- *Is "shortcut thinking" always bad?*
- *Are low self-esteem individuals high or low risk takers?*
- *What is artificial intelligence?*

As we discussed, evolutionary changes have given us the capacity not only to acquire language but also to engage in complex thinking. For our purposes, **cognition** will be defined as the mental activity of knowing and the processes through which knowledge is acquired and problems are solved. While chapter 4 examined how cognition develops in children, this chapter examines the building blocks of cognition, namely, *concepts*.

> **cognition** The mental activity of knowing and the processes through which knowledge is acquired and problems are solved.

9-2a Concept Formation Is a Basic Element of Cognition

A **concept** is a mental grouping of objects, ideas, or events that share common properties (Markman, 1999). For example, the concept *insect* stands for a class of animals that have three body divisions (head, thorax, abdomen), six legs, an external skeleton, and a rapid reproductive cycle. As you recall from our discussion of the semantic network model in chapter 8, section 8-3a, concepts enable us to store our memories in an organized fashion. When one concept in our long-term memory is activated, other closely related concepts are also activated, or *cognitively primed* (see chapter 8, section 8-2b).

> **concept** A mental grouping of objects, ideas, or events that share common properties.

The primary means of coding experience by forming concepts is called **categorization** (Rakison & Oakes, 2003). As a species, we humans spontaneously categorize the things we experience. Categorization is adaptive because it saves time and helps us make predictions about the future. I know, for example, that if I eat an object from the concept *cheese*, I am likely to enjoy the experience. I also know that if I need medical attention, I will likely receive it by seeking out people from either of the concepts *physician* or *nurse*. Like the heart that

> **categorization** The primary means of coding experience through the process of forming concepts.

Figure 9-4

When Is This Object a "Cup," and When Is It a "Bowl"?

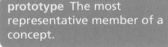

prototype The most representative member of a concept.

pumps life-giving blood throughout the body or the lungs that replenish the oxygen in this blood, humans could not survive without engaging in categorization.

We form some concepts by identifying defining features. For instance, if an animal has three body divisions, six legs, an external skeleton, and a rapid reproductive cycle, I would classify it as an insect; if it lacks one or more of these features, I would not think of it as an insect (Medin, 1989). The problem with forming concepts by definition is that many familiar concepts have uncertain or fuzzy boundaries. This fact makes categorizing some members of familiar concepts more difficult than others. To see an illustration of this point, consider the objects included in the fuzzy boundary of the concept *cup* in figure 9-4. In one experiment, when people were individually shown objects like this and asked to name them, they were more likely to abandon the "cup" label and identify the object as a "bowl" as its width increased relative to its depth (Labov, 1973). However, the point at which this shift occurred was gradual, not fixed.

What Are Prototypes?

Findings such as these suggest that categorizing has less to do with the features that define all members of a concept and more to do with the features that characterize the typical member of a concept. This is why some members of familiar concepts are easier to categorize than others; they are better representatives of the concept (Olson et al., 2004; Rosch, 1978). The most representative members of a concept are known as **prototypes.** For example, most people consider a golden retriever more "doglike" than a Chihuahua, an American robin more "birdlike" than a penguin (see accompanying photos), and an undergraduate more "studentlike" when she is 20 years of age versus 65 years. For most of us, golden retrievers are "doggier," robins are "birdier," and 20-year-olds are "studentier," because they more closely resemble our prototypes for their respective concepts than the alternative choices. In fact, the Chihuahua might be mistakenly categorized as a rat because it looks more "ratty" than "doggy," and the elderly student might be mistaken for a college professor.

Our failure to correctly categorize things because they don't match our prototype for that concept can lead to errors in decision making. For instance, if certain physical symptoms don't fit our flu prototype, we may continue our normal activities, thus worsening our condition and also infecting others (Bishop, 1991). Similarly, we may turn our life savings over to a dishonest investment advisor because he looks like "Honest Abe."

Which of these birds is more "birdlike" to you—the robin in (*a*) or the penguin in (*b*)? That is, which of these birds is closer to your bird prototype? Consider the robin. How many concepts come to mind to describe this creature? Identify this creature at its *basic level*.

Source: Courtesy of Figzoi.

How Are Concepts Organized?

Objects often have multiple concepts to describe them. For example, the American robin in the accompanying photo is an "American robin," a "robin," a "bird," and an "animal." In thinking of objects, we tend to organize them into orderly hierarchies composed of main categories and subcategories (Markman & Gentner, 2001). Thus, the general concept of "animals" can be mentally divided into various subcategories such as "birds," "mammals," and "reptiles." Each more general concept includes a number of more specific concepts. The concept "bird" includes robins, bluebirds, eagles, penguins, and many other feathery creatures. At each level of this hierarchy, there are prototypes for the concept. For most North Americans, mammals might be the prototypical animal, robins might be the prototypical bird, and the American robin, with its distinctive red breast, might be more prototypical than the clay-colored robin with its brownish-olive coloring. However, for people living in eastern Mexico, the native clay-colored robin is probably their robin prototype.

When you first looked at the photo of the robin on page 338, I'm guessing that the concept that popped into your mind was "robin" or "bird" rather than "American robin" or "animal." People typically identify an object at its *basic level,* which is the middle level in the object's concept hierarchy. One way to identify the basic-level category for an object is to determine which level in the hierarchy contains objects that are as general as possible while still having similar sizes and shapes. So, for those of us who are relatively attentive to birds in our surroundings, perhaps "robin" is the basic level, because American robins, rufous-backed robins, and clay-colored robins have similar sizes and shapes. In contrast, "bird" is a step above the basic level in the hierarchy, because robins, penguins, and hummingbirds have quite different sizes and shapes. However, for those of us who do not think about or notice birds very often, the basic-level category for this particular creature is simply "bird."

9-2b We Employ a Number of Problem-Solving Strategies

One important way we use concepts as the building blocks of thinking is in overcoming problems. Problems vary in complexity, from the simple one of finding car keys in the morning to the more complex one of deciding what to do following college graduation. **Problem solving** is the thought process you engage in to overcome these obstacles and attain your goals. Typically, problem solving involves using one of several strategies, including *trial and error, algorithms, heuristics,* and *insight.*

> **problem solving** The thought process employed to overcome obstacles.

Trial and Error

Do you remember Edward Thorndike's puzzle box experiments with hungry cats, described in chapter 7, section 7-2a? Through **trial and error,** which involves trying one possible solution after another until one works, Thorndike's cats eventually learned how to escape from the puzzle box to reach a bowl of food. In many species, trial and error often provides responses that are important to survival. Whether you are a lion cub discovering how best to attack your prey or a teenager finding the right tone of voice to use when asking someone for a date, haphazardly trying various solutions until you stumble on one that works may be time-consuming, but it is often effective.

> **trial and error** A problem-solving strategy that involves trying one possible solution after another until one works.

Algorithms

Unlike trial and error, which does not guarantee success, an **algorithm** is a problem-solving strategy that involves following a specific rule or step-by-step procedure that inevitably produces the correct solution. For example, recently I needed to contact a student named John Smith. I knew he lived in Milwaukee, but I didn't know his phone number. There are 40 John Smiths in the Milwaukee telephone directory. One available strategy was to use an algorithm; that is, simply phone all the John Smiths until I found the right one. Assuming that my John Smith had a phone and that his number was listed, this strategy was guaranteed to work. The drawback to algorithms, however, is that they are inflexible. Further, like trial and error, they are time-consuming. Computers are based on algorithms, and that is the reason they are inflexible in their functioning.

> **algorithm** A problem-solving strategy that involves following a specific rule or step-by-step procedure until you inevitably produce the correct solution.

Heuristics

heuristic A problem-solving strategy that involves following a general rule of thumb to reduce the number of possible solutions.

Instead of calling all the John Smiths in the phone book, I relied on a **heuristic,** which involves following a general rule of thumb to reduce the number of possible solutions (Geary, 2005a). The general rule of thumb I used in solving my problem was that college students usually live on or near campus. Now the number of phone numbers to call was reduced to five. Heuristics have a reasonably good chance of working, and true to form, I found my John Smith on the third call. However, unlike algorithms, heuristics do not guarantee success. What if my John Smith had lived at home with his parents? The chief advantage of heuristics is that they usually save time.

Insight

insight A problem-solving strategy that involves a sudden realization of how a problem can be solved.

Sometimes we are unaware of using any problem-solving strategy at all; solutions simply pop into our heads while we ponder our problems (Bowers et al., 1995; Dorfman et al., 1996). The sudden realization of how a problem can be solved is called **insight** (Sternberg & Davidson, 1999). Consider the following problem that is often solved by insight:

> A man walks into a tavern and asks for a glass of water. The bartender pulls a shotgun from behind the bar and points it at the man. The man says "Thank you" and walks out.

Can you explain the behavior of the two people in this imaginary situation? This story was presented to participants in an insight problem-solving study, during which the participants were allowed to ask yes/no questions for up to 2 hours (Durso et al., 1994).

At several points during this problem-solving period, participants were asked to rate the degree to which different pairings of 14 words were related to the problem. Some of these word pairs were explicitly stated in the story (*man, bartender*); others were implicit in the correct solution (*surprise, remedy*); and still others had no relation at all to the story (*clock, grass*). Results indicated that, at first, the problem solvers thought the implicitly related words were highly unrelated to the story. However, some time before they achieved insight, the participants slowly began to see an increased association between the story and these implicitly related words. They observed no such increase in relatedness in the explicitly related words or the unrelated words. This pattern of results suggests that, in solving problems through insight, people gradually increase their focus on those concepts important to the solution, even though they are yet unaware of the solution itself. Thus, although insight seems to happen unexpectedly, the cognitive organization necessary for this type of problem solving is built beforehand, just as slowly gathering clouds eventually lead to a sudden lightning flash. (The solution to the problem preceding this paragraph is that the man had the hiccups.)

9-2c Internal Obstacles Can Impede Problem Solving

Along with identifying various strategies for solving problems, psychologists have identified a number of cognitive tendencies that act as barriers to problem solving. Three of the more common internal obstacles are the *confirmation bias, mental set,* and *functional fixedness.*

Confirmation Bias

confirmation bias The tendency to seek information that supports our beliefs while ignoring disconfirming information.

When you think you have a solution to a problem, you may fall victim to the **confirmation bias,** which is the tendency to seek only information that verifies your beliefs (Edwards & Smith, 1996). Unfortunately, such selective attention prevents you from realizing that your solution is incorrect. In one confirmation-bias study, college students were given the three-number sequence 2-4-6 and then told to discover the rule used to generate it (Wason, 1960). Before announcing their beliefs about the rule (which is simply any three increasing numbers), students could make up their own number sequences, and the experimenter would tell them whether these sequences fit the rule. The students were instructed to announce the rule only after receiving feedback from enough self-generated number sequences to make them feel certain that they knew the solution.

True to the confirmation bias, 80 percent of the students convinced themselves of an incorrect rule. Typically, they would begin with a wrong hypothesis (for example, adding by twos) and then search only for confirming evidence (testing 8-10-12, 20-22-24, 19-21-23, and so on). Had they tried to disconfirm this hypothesis by testing other number sequences that simply increased in value (for example, 1-2-3 or 10-19-39), they would have realized their error. But their bias toward confirmation ruled out this important hypothesis-testing step. Experiments like this indicate that an important barrier to problem solving is our tendency to search more energetically for information that will confirm our beliefs than for information that might refute them (Klayman & Ha, 1987).

How might this tendency to seek confirming information lead to incorrect social beliefs? In one experiment, Mark Snyder and William Swann (1978) asked some participants to find out whether the person they were about to interact with was an introvert, while other participants were asked to find out whether the person was an extravert. Consistent with the confirmation bias, the questions that people asked their interaction partners were biased in the direction of the original question. If they had been asked to find out whether the person was an introvert, they asked questions such as "What do you dislike about loud parties?" In contrast, in the extravert condition, they asked questions such as "How do you liven things up at a party?" Because most people can recall both introverted and extraverted incidents from their past, the interaction partners' answers provided confirmatory evidence for either personality trait. As you can see, such confirmation seeking can easily lead to mistakes when forming impressions about individuals. Similarly, incorrect stereotypes about social groups can be perpetuated by seeking confirmation of preexisting beliefs (Yzerbyt et al., 1996).

Mental Set

Another common obstacle to problem solving is the **mental set**—the tendency to persist in using solutions that have worked in the past, even though better alternatives may exist. The influence that a mental set can have on problem solving was first demonstrated by Abraham Luchins (1942) in his "water-jar" problems study. Participants were asked to solve problems involving the filling of water jars. In the first task, using a 21-cup jar, a 127-cup jar, and a 3-cup jar, they were asked to measure out exactly 100 cups of water. With minimal effort, participants discovered that the solution was to fill the largest jar (B), and from it fill the second-largest jar (A) once and the smallest jar (C) twice. Try solving the remaining problems in figure 9-5 before reading further.

> **mental set** The tendency to continue using solutions that have worked in the past, even though a better alternative may exist.

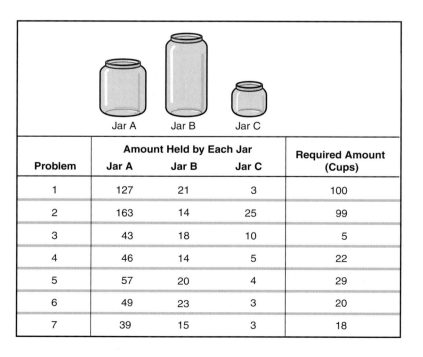

Figure 9-5

The Water-Jar Problems

In each problem, what is the most efficient way of measuring out the correct amount of water using jars A, B, and/or C?

Problem	Amount Held by Each Jar			Required Amount (Cups)
	Jar A	Jar B	Jar C	
1	127	21	3	100
2	163	14	25	99
3	43	18	10	5
4	46	14	5	22
5	57	20	4	29
6	49	23	3	20
7	39	15	3	18

Explore It
Exercise 9-1

Can You Solve the Nine-Dot Problem?

Connect all nine dots with four straight lines without lifting your pencil from the paper. A line must pass through each point. Can you solve this problem?

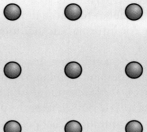

Solution: To solve the nine-dot problem, you need to step out of the mental set in which you think that the four lines must remain within or on the edge of the square of dots. When you realize that the lines can extend beyond the "boundaries" of the square, you solve the problem.

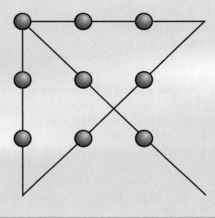

> If the only tool you have is a hammer, you tend to see every problem as a nail.
>
> —*Abraham Maslow,*
> *founder of humanistic psychology,*
> *1908–1970*

functional fixedness The tendency to think of objects as functioning in fixed and unchanging ways and ignoring other less obvious ways in which they might be used.

Like Luchins's participants, you probably ran into a mental set. That is, discovering that you could use the basic algorithm, B − A − 2C, to solve all the remaining problems caused you to miss the much simpler solutions for problem 6 (B − C) and problem 7 (B + C). Although mental sets can lead to solutions, they can also lead to "mental ruts" when the situation changes and old methods are no longer efficient or are completely ineffective (Pashler et al., 2000). Now that you understand something about mental sets, complete Explore It Exercise 9-1 before continuing with your reading.

Functional Fixedness

Finally, related to mental set is **functional fixedness,** which identifies our tendency to think of objects as functioning in fixed and unchanging ways (Furio et al., 2000). In problem solving, when you are unable to consider using familiar objects in unusual ways—for example, using a dime as a screwdriver—you are experiencing this cognitive obstacle. In one study of functional fixedness, participants were given a small cardboard box of tacks, some matches, and a candle (see figure 9-6). Their task was to mount the candle on a bulletin board in such a way that it would burn without dripping wax on the floor (Duncker, 1945). Before reading further, try solving this problem.

Many participants could not solve the problem because they thought of the box as simply a container for tacks, not as a support for a candle. Later research found that when describing the task, if the experimenter used the term *box of tacks* rather than just *tacks,* more solutions were obtained (Glucksberg & Danks, 1968; Glucksberg & Weisberg, 1966). This suggests that when a person hears the word *box,* numerous possible encodings of *box*

The Candle Problem

When supplied with the materials in the box on the far left, many people cannot figure out how to mount a candle on a bulletin board so it will not drip wax when lit. How is this candle problem an example of functional fixedness?

may be activated from memory, thus making a solution more likely. In general, the more experience a person has with an object, the greater the likelihood of experiencing functional fixedness with this object.

9-2d Decision Making Involves Evaluating Alternatives and Making Choices

In addition to finding solutions to problems, another aspect of everyday cognition is weighing the pros and cons of different alternatives in order to make a choice. In such decision making, often no one alternative is superior in every feature to the others. To make a rational decision in such circumstances, we would systematically evaluate the features of each alternative, assigning a numerical weight to each feature according to its importance (Edwards, 1977; Reed, 1996). For example, in the chapter 2 "Psychological Applications" section, I described the dilemma my oldest daughter faced when trying to decide which new bicycle to pick for her birthday present: Should she pick the better-riding Huffy Hyper Force *boy's* bike or the more socially acceptable Barbie Fashion Fun *girl's* bike?

As illustrated in figure 9-7, Amelia placed more importance on *rideability* than *style*, and thus rideability was assigned the highest numerical weight. She also compared additional features, such as price, color, and accessories, before making her decision. According to this *weighted additive model*, you multiply the numerical weight of the feature (how important it is) by its value (how positive it is) to arrive at a weighted value. By adding all the weighted values for each alternative, you determine its weighted additive value. In Amelia's case, the Huffy bike had a higher weighted additive value than the Barbie bike, and thus that was the one she chose. Now, I am not contending that Amelia actually plotted out her decision in exactly this manner. What I am saying is that using the weighted additive model can greatly improve your decision making. This is the type of decision-making skill known as *critical thinking*, which is the process of deciding what to believe and how to act based on a careful evaluation of the evidence (see the "Psychological Applications" section in chapter 2).

Research and everyday experience indicate that, although we usually try to be systematic and rational in our decision making, we often fall short of this goal. Instead, we end up using simple strategies that, while rational, focus on only a few aspects of our available options (Simon, 1957). For example, if Amelia had considered only the bikes' colors and accessories in making her purchase, she would have been relying on this sort of elementary decision-making strategy. By not fully analyzing the situation in which a decision is to be made, we determine our choices according to what we happen to focus on.

Framing

One of the most important influences on the decision-making process is how choices are *framed*. **Framing** is the way in which alternatives are structured (Russo & Schoemaker, 2002;

"Wouldn't a good flea powder be more efficient, Basil?!"

In solving problems, sometimes it is unwise to use familiar objects in unusual ways.

Source: © King Features Syndicate

framing The way in which choices are structured.

Figure 9-7

Calculating the Weighted Additive Value

According to the weighted additive model of decision making, when people make systematic rational decisions, they assign numerical weights to the features of each alternative according to their importance. By multiplying the numerical weight of a feature by its value, you determine its weighted value. The final weighted additive value is determined by adding all the weighted values for each alternative. According to this model, which bike would Amelia choose to buy?

Source: Adapted from Edwards (1977).

		Huffy Hyper Force Bike		Barbie Fashion Fun Bike	
Features (in Order of Importance)	**Importance (Numerical Weight)**	**Value**	**Weighted Value**	**Value**	**Weighted Value**
Rideability	5	+10	50	+5	25
Style	4	+7	28	+9	36
Color	3	+8	24	+9	27
Accessories	2	+9	18	+8	16
Price	1	+10	10	+10	10
			130		114

Tversky & Kahneman, 1981). In one experiment, hospital physicians were presented with a hypothetical situation in which they had to choose between two forms of treatment for a lung cancer patient (McNeil et al., 1982). Half the physicians were given the following information before making their decision:

Of 100 patients having surgery, 10 will die during treatment, 32 will die within a year, and 66 will die within five years. Of 100 patients having radiation therapy, none will die during treatment, 23 will die within a year, and 78 will die within five years.

If you were the physician, what would you choose: surgery or radiation? The other half of the physicians received the following information:

Of 100 patients having surgery, 90 will be alive immediately after treatment, 68 will be alive after a year, and 34 will be alive after five years. Of 100 patients having radiation therapy, all will be alive after treatment, 77 will be alive after a year, and 22 will be alive after five years.

Would your decision be different if you obtained the information in this manner? Actually, the treatment outcomes are exactly the same. The only difference is in their framing: The first description emphasizes how many people will die, while the second description stresses how many will live. You might assume that highly educated and intelligent physicians would not be swayed simply by information framed in terms of losses or gains, but this was not the case. Although surgery was the preferred choice in both framing situations, the physicians were much more reluctant to choose surgery when the choices were framed in terms of death (a loss) rather than in terms of survival (a gain). Apparently, the physicians' aversion to death as an outcome in treatment made them more reluctant to perform surgery when information was framed in this manner.

The fact that decisions can be altered by the way choices are framed is not lost on advertisers. Consumers, for example, are more likely to buy ground beef labeled "75 percent lean" than that labeled "25 percent fat" (Levin & Gaeth, 1988). To counter such framing manipulations, always make a decision only after considering *both* a gain frame and a loss frame. When a salesperson tells you that 82 percent of his products need no repairs during the first year, remind yourself that this also means that 18 percent of his products *do* need repairs. Does this reframing of the information alter your decision? Your understanding of framing can make you a better decision maker.

Individual Differences in the Need for Cognition

An important step in competent decision making is to critically analyze options and hazards. Yet everyday experience informs us that not everyone approaches decision making with a desire for cognitive challenges. John Cacioppo and Richard Petty (1982) have designed a self-report scale that measures individual differences in the motivation to think, which they call the **need for cognition.** People high in the need for cognition (high NFC) like to work on difficult cognitive tasks, analyze situations, and make subtle cognitive distinctions. In contrast, individuals with a low need for cognition (low NFC) are more likely to take mental shortcuts and avoid effortful thinking unless required to do so (Nair & Ramnarayan, 2000; Sommers & Kassin, 2001). Spend a few minutes answering the need-for-cognition items in Self-Discovery Questionnaire 9-2 before reading further.

Researchers have investigated how the need for cognition influences decision making. For example, people with a high need for cognition are more likely than those low in the need for cognition to critically analyze advertisements before making consumer purchases (Priester et al., 2004). Individual differences in the need for cognition also affect attention to political campaigns and voting decisions. During the 1984 presidential and vice-presidential debates, for instance, voters high in the need for cognition were more likely to watch these events than were their low-NFC counterparts (Ahlering, 1987). Not only did they spend more time watching the debates, but also the high-NFC voters developed more beliefs about the candidates than did those low in the need for cognition. In addition, their attitudes toward the candidates 8 weeks before the November election were better predictors of their actual voting behavior than were the attitudes of the low NFCs (Cacioppo et al., 1986). This finding and the results from additional studies suggest that attitudes and beliefs formed as a result of critically analyzing information are more resistant to change than attitudes shaped by lazy thinking (Priluck & Till, 2004; Shestowsky et al., 1998).

Although high-NFC persons are more disposed to critically analyze information when making decisions than are low-NFC persons, this is no guarantee that they will actually do so. Even people who enjoy intellectual stimulation will engage in lazy thinking when they conclude that the decisions they face have little relevance to their lives (Leippe & Elkin, 1987). On the other hand, people who are typically lazy thinkers can become critical thinkers if the decision is personally compelling and relevant. Thus, while our need for cognition generally affects how much we critically analyze our options before making a decision, when we believe that a decision is important, we all tend to take greater care in weighing our options. Yet, because we sometimes are not aware that a decision is "important" until after the fact, the greater overall care taken by high-NFC individuals should lead to better results than the lazier decision-making style of low-NFC persons (Cacioppo et al., 1996).

> **need for cognition**
> A person's preference for and tendency to engage in effortful cognitive activities.

> To most people nothing is more troublesome than the effort of thinking.
>
> *—James Bryce, British statesman, 1838–1922*

9-2e Decision-Making Heuristics Often Sidetrack Everyday Cognition

When we do engage in lazy decision making, what kind of timesaving mental shortcuts do we use? Heuristics, of course! To understand how we use specific types of heuristics and how they can sometimes lead us astray, let us examine two heuristics identified by Amos Tversky and Daniel Kahneman (1974): *representativeness* and *availability*.

The Representativeness Heuristic

Remember my example of being cheated out of your life savings because your investment adviser happened to look like an honest person? To judge things based on how closely they represent particular prototypes is to use a cognitive shortcut known as the **representativeness heuristic** (Gilovich & Savitsky, 2002; Tversky & Kahneman, 1974). The problem with this cognitive shortcut is that because it is a rapid method of decision making, it doesn't take into account other important qualifying information. The most important information of this type relates to *base rates*—the frequency with which some event or pattern occurs in the general population.

The tendency to overlook base-rate information was demonstrated in a well-known study by Tversky and Kahneman (1973). Research participants were told that an imaginary person named Jack had been selected from a group of 100 men. Some were told that 30 of

> **representativeness heuristic**
> The tendency to make decisions based on how closely an alternative matches (or represents) a particular prototype.

the men were engineers (a base rate for engineers of 30 percent), and others were told that 70 were engineers (a base rate of 70 percent). Half the participants were given no other information, but the other half were given a description of Jack that either fit the common stereotype of an engineer (for example, practical, likes to work with numbers) or did not. They were then asked to guess the probability that Jack was an engineer. Results indicated that when participants received only information related to base rates, they were more likely to guess that Jack was an engineer when the base rate was 70 percent than when it was 30 percent. However, when they received information about Jack's personality and behavior, they tended to ignore the base-rate information and, instead, focus on whether Jack fit their prototype of an engineer. The tendency to ignore or underuse useful base-rate information and overuse personal descriptors of the individual being judged has been called the *base-rate fallacy.*

The Availability Heuristic

availability heuristic The tendency to judge the frequency or probability of an event in terms of how easy it is to think of examples of that event.

Following the terrorist attacks on September 11, 2001, many Americans were afraid to fly on commercial airlines. Instead of flying, people began driving their cars cross-country. In nixing plane travel for car travel, they based their judgments on the **availability heuristic,** which is the tendency to judge the frequency or probability of an event in terms of how easy it is to think of examples of that event. In using the availability heuristic, the most important factor for people is not the content of their memory but the ease with which this content comes to mind (Schwarz & Vaughn, 2002; Vaughn & Weary, 2002). Because people could easily recall the horrible images of September 11, they decided that car travel was safer than plane travel. These judgments were made despite data from the National Safety Council indicating that, mile for mile, Americans are 37 times more likely to die in a motor vehicle crash than on a commercial flight. Indeed, if terrorists destroyed more than 50 planes per year, each containing 60 passengers, we would still be safer traveling by plane than by car. In this instance, it appears that reliance on the availability heuristic has actually caused many Americans to increase their safety risks when traveling.

The ease with which we generally recall our own characteristics and opinions from memory helps explain why we tend to believe that other people share our views and preferences to a greater extent than is actually true. This *false consensus effect* has been observed in numerous contexts: We exaggerate how common our own personalities are in the general population; we overestimate how many people smoke or do not smoke, based on our own smoking habits; we assume that most people agree with our political beliefs (Alicke et al., 1996; Babad et al., 1992). The ease with which we generally recall important aspects of ourselves from memory may well explain our tendency to exaggerate how common our own characteristics and opinions are in the general population. That is, perhaps we often assume that others share our characteristics, habits, and opinions because these self-aspects are readily available in memory. As you can see, this type of thinking, brought about by the availability heuristic, can cause us to make misguided decisions.

 Journey of Discovery Question — In Olympic competition, athletes who win an event receive the gold medal, those who come in second receive a silver medal, and third-place finishers get a bronze medal. Fourth-place finishers receive nothing. During the 1992 Olympics, bronze medalists (third-place finishers) exhibited more joy than silver medalists (second-place finishers) after their events (Medvec et al., 1995). How can this finding be explained by the availability heuristic?

When Do We Use Heuristics?

With what frequency do we take mental shortcuts in decision making? As you have already learned, frequency is partly determined by our need for cognition. Beyond this individual difference, Anthony Pratkanis (1989) has identified at least five conditions th),at are most likely to lead to the use of heuristics rather than rational decision making: (1) when we simply *don't have time* to engage in systematic analysis; (2) when we are *overloaded with information* so it is impossible to process all that is meaningful and relevant; (3) when we consider the issues in question *not very important*; (4) when we have *little other knowledge* or information to use in making a decision; or (5) when something about the situation in question *calls to mind* a given heuristic, making it cognitively available.

One final note: Although basing decisions on heuristics may lead to errors, relying on them may actually be adaptive under conditions in which we don't have the luxury of carefully analyzing all our options (Johnston et al., 1997). For example, reacting quickly in an emergency based only on information that is most accessible from memory (the availability heuristic) may often be the difference between life and death. Thus, although heuristics can lead to sloppy decision making, their timesaving quality may sometimes be a lifesaver. In this regard, heuristics can be very helpful because they provide a reasonably accurate basis for making decisions under many conditions (Figueredo et al., 2004). If these heuristics were eliminated from human decision making, social judgment accuracy would get much worse, not better.

9-2f Self-Esteem Can Influence Our Decision-Making Strategies

As discussed in chapter 4, section 4-2d, during childhood we develop a *self-concept,* which is our "theory" of who and what we are as individuals. We also evaluate ourselves as good, bad, or mediocre. Research indicates that this *self-esteem* can have an important effect on how we make decisions. For instance, in a series of studies, high and low self-esteem participants played a game in which they gambled real money for the opportunity to win more than $100 (Josephs et al., 1992). In the game, players chose among pairs of gambles that varied in risk and payoff. Each gamble pair was composed of a sure thing and a speculative gamble of equal or roughly equal expected value. Half the pairs were framed positively as gains (for instance, a $10 sure win versus a 50 percent chance of winning $20), and half were framed negatively as losses (for instance, a $10 sure loss versus a 50 percent chance of losing $20). If players chose the sure thing, the person running the game noted their choice and moved on to the next pair. If players chose the risky prospect, the gamesperson rotated a bingo drum containing 100 pieces (numbered 1–100), removed a piece, and recorded the number of the piece without announcing the result. If the number on the bingo piece was less than or equal to the stated probability of the risky prospect, the outcome of the prospect occurred. So, for a 50 percent chance of winning $20, players had

Figure 9-8

Risky Decisions as Self-Esteem Threats

Josephs and his colleagues (1992) presented high and low self-esteem people with forced-choice gambling decisions of high and low risk to determine whether they differed in the amount of risk they were willing to take. In the positively framed prospects, avoiding the risky option would be the clear choice for people who are motivated to protect their self-esteem from threats, which was the option generally taken by those low in self-esteem. For the negatively framed prospects, both choices are threatening, and high and low self-esteem participants chose each prospect 50 percent of the time. Thus, when prospects are framed positively, low self-esteem individuals appear to take fewer risks than high self-esteem individuals. Based on these findings, which of the two groups is more concerned with protecting self-esteem?

Source: Data from R. A. Josephs et al. (1992). "Protecting the Self from the Negative Consequences of Risky Decisions." *Journal of Personality and Social Psychology, 62,* 26–37.

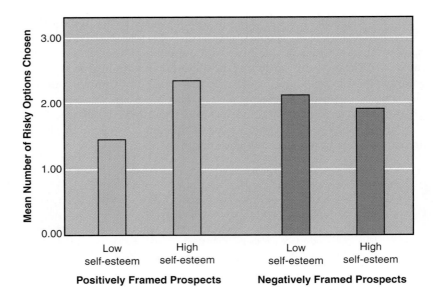

to draw a bingo piece numbered 50 or lower to win the $20. Players did not get to see these outcomes until they had made all their choices.

In the positively framed prospects, the sure gain would be the clear choice for people who are motivated to protect their self-esteem from threats. As you can see in figure 9-8, the gambling choices of the participants with low self-esteem reflected a tendency to protect themselves from threat. That is, people with low self-esteem were 50 percent more likely to choose the sure gain than were those with high self-esteem. With the negatively framed prospects, however, the choice that minimizes threat is not clear, for both can be viewed as threatening. As a result, neither prospect should be preferred by individuals with low self-esteem. Results supported this expectation—both high and low self-esteem participants chose each prospect 50 percent of the time. Therefore, when prospects are framed positively, individuals with low self-esteem appear to take fewer risks than individuals with high self-esteem.

This research and other studies suggest that people who have low self-esteem are much more concerned with self-esteem *protection* on an everyday basis than are people with high self-esteem (Wood et al., 1994). Diane Tice (1993) has argued that the decision-making strategies of low self-esteem people are best compared to those of financial investors with limited resources who are presented with a moneymaking opportunity: They don't try for big gains because they are too concerned about losing what modest assets they currently possess. By consistently opting for less rewarding risks, low self-esteem people may guard against self-esteem threats due to failure in the short run, but over time they lose opportunities to experience self-enhancing grand success. In contrast, Tice believes that people with high self-esteem tend to act like wealthy, high-stakes speculators—they can afford to risk some of their many assets, so they make bold decisions. Every time they succeed in these endeavors, they further enhance themselves and increase their feelings of confidence and fulfillment. How would you characterize your own decision-making strategies? Do you hold on to a "sure thing," or do you instead make a grab for greater riches, be they material or psychological? Before reading further, spend a few minutes completing the self-esteem scale in Self-Discovery Questionnaire 9-3.

9-2g Computers with Artificial Intelligence Simulate Human Thinking

One of the founding figures of cognitive psychology, Nobel Prize winner Herbert Simon, was also a pioneer in the field of **artificial intelligence (AI),** which is the science of designing and making intelligent machines, especially intelligent computer programs. A good deal of AI research involves simulating human thinking and observing human decision making in order to design better problem-solving machines (Dunne, 2005; Roy et al., 2005). AI work also entails

artificial intelligence (AI) The science of designing and making intelligent machines, especially intelligent computer programs.

Instructions: Read each item below, and then indicate how well each statement describes you, using the following response scale:

0 = extremely uncharacteristic (not at all like me)
1 = uncharacteristic (somewhat unlike me)
2 = neither characteristic nor uncharacteristic
3 = characteristic (somewhat like me)
4 = extremely characteristic (very much like me)

____ **1.** On the whole, I am satisfied with myself.
____ **2.** At times, I think I am no good at all.*
____ **3.** I feel that I have a number of good qualities.
____ **4.** I am able to do things as well as most other people.
____ **5.** I feel I do not have much to be proud of.*
____ **6.** I certainly feel useless at times.*
____ **7.** I feel that I'm a person of worth, at least on an equal plane with others.
____ **8.** I wish I could have more respect for myself.*
____ **9.** All in all, I am inclined to feel that I am a failure.*
____ **10.** I take a positive attitude toward myself.

Directions for scoring: Half of the self-esteem items are reverse-scored; that is, for these items, a lower rating actually indicates a higher level of self-esteem. Before summing all 10 items to find out your total self-esteem score, recode those with an asterisk (*) so that 0 = 4, 1 = 3, 3 = 1, and 4 = 0. Your total self-esteem score can range from 0 to 40, with a higher score indicating a higher level of self-esteem. Scores greater than 20 indicate generally positive attitudes toward the self, while those below 20 indicate generally negative self-attitudes.

Source: From *Conceiving the Self* by Morris Rosenberg. Reprinted by permission.

developing problem-solving techniques that are not observed in people or that involve highly complex information-processing skills beyond human capabilities (Zhang & Zhang, 2005).

One type of AI research that has achieved some notable real-world applications involves *computer neural networks,* which are computer systems that mimic the brain's complex network of neurons (Weng et al., 2001). These artificial neural networks have been used with varying degrees of success in managing traffic flow on congested city highways, diagnosing medical disorders, and making financial decisions (Augusto, 2005; Mussone et al., 1999).

How closely can computers simulate human thought and decision making? In 1950, Alan Turing, the founder of computer science, outlined the necessary conditions for considering a machine to be intelligent. He stated that, if a machine could successfully pretend to be human to a knowledgeable observer, then it should be considered intelligent. An example of this test might involve an observer interacting with a machine and a human over the Internet, with the human trying to persuade the observer that he or she was human and the machine trying to fool the observer. When such tests have been conducted, some people are easily fooled by computer programs, even when the program is not that sophisticated (Dennett, 1998). One such computer program that has successfully passed the "Turing test" is computer scientist Richard Wallace's ALICE, which is an acronym for Artificial Linguistic Internet Computer Entity. Following is an excerpt from a conversation I just had over the Internet with Alice:

Herbert A. Simon, 1916–2001

Source: © Bill Pierce/Time Life Pictures/Getty Images.

SLF: Have you studied psychology?

Alice: I don't think I ever have studied psychology. What's it like?

SLF: It's fascinating, because you learn how the mind works.

Alice: You learn something new every day.

SLF: Do you enjoy conversing with people?

Alice: I always say people don't go into computer science because they want to work with the public.

SLF: Well, I should get back to writing this chapter on language and thinking.

Alice: Interesting. Tell me why you should.

SLF: You sound like a psychologist.

Alice: Oh really. What does it sound like?

Many modern-day computer programs are much faster than people in processing information, and they also have an immense information-storage capacity. However, the ability of computers to mimic human thought is ultimately determined by the human intellectual processes that program designers understand well enough to install into computer programs. Currently, some intellectual abilities associated with adults may be installed in a computer program, while some abilities possessed by 2-year-olds are missing from the same program. The problem faced by AI designers is that they cannot install programs that mimic intellectual processes they do not yet understand (Russell & Norvig, 2003). Whenever people outperform computers or whenever computers require extensive computation time to do as well as people on some task, this indicates that the program designers do not adequately understand the thinking processes required to complete the task efficiently.

AI scientists have long been intrigued with the possibility of designing a "child machine" that could improve by learning from experience, including having the ability to read. Computer neural networks have a limited capacity to learn in this way, but they cannot yet adequately modify themselves based on past experience in the same manner as humans. Similarly, chess programs can play at the level of a grandmaster, but their ability to creatively thwart opponents is still inferior to the best human chess master.

Will computers ever approximate, or exceed, the genius of an Albert Einstein? Will they be able to create great works of art like Leonardo da Vinci or Ludwig von Beethoven? Will they have the wisdom to develop history-changing philosophies like Mahatma Gandhi or Jesus Christ? Over the years, psychologists and philosophers have often characterized the two sides of human thought as involving rational decision making versus emotional evaluation. The bulk of AI research has emphasized the study of intellectual processes, with considerably less time devoted to emotions. Yet it could be argued that underlying all human intellectual achievements is an emotional core. Can a computer program sufficiently mimic such emotional expressiveness? Future research in the area of AI may one day answer these questions.

Section Review

- A concept is a mental grouping of objects, ideas, or events that share common properties, and a prototype is the most representative member of a concept.
- Concept formation is a basic element of cognition, and the process of forming concepts is called categorization.
- Failing to correctly categorize things because they don't match our prototypes can lead to errors in decision making.
- Typical problem-solving strategies include trial and error, algorithms, heuristics, and insight; three common internal obstacles to problem solving include confirmation bias, mental set, and functional fixedness.
- An important ingredient in competent decision making is critical analysis, but we often rely on thought-saving heuristics, especially if we have a low need for cognition.
- Due to concern with protecting their self-esteem, low self-esteem individuals are less likely than high self-esteem persons to make risky decisions that could threaten their self-esteem.
- Artificial intelligence (AI) is the science of designing and making intelligent computer programs and has led to important and useful real-world applications, but it is debatable whether AI will ever truly match, or exceed, human thought.

Psychological Applications

How Can You Change Your Language Style to Become a More Persuasive Speaker?

Imagine the following two individuals going to their separate bosses to request a raise:

Person A: "Uhm . . . excuse me, sir? . . . Uhm . . . could I speak to you for a minute? . . . This may sound a little out of the ordinary, but I've been with the company for 1 year now, you know, and . . . uhm, well, I was sort of wondering if we could talk about an increase in my salary? Uhm . . . you know, since starting here, I've kind of been given a good deal of responsibilities that go beyond my job description, you know, and . . . uhm . . . I've handled this additional work efficiently and professionally, you know, without complaining and without supervision, don't you think? I'm not an expert on how to run this company, you know, but I was wondering . . . uhm . . . now that I have proven capable of handling this increased workload and responsibilities, you know, don't you think my salary should reflect this fact?"

Person B: "Excuse me, sir? Could I speak to you for a minute? I've been with the company for 1 year now, and I would like to talk to you about an increase in my salary. Since starting here, I've been given a good deal of responsibility that goes well beyond my job description, and I've handled this additional work efficiently and professionally without complaining and without supervision. Now that I have proven capable of handling this increased workload and responsibilities, I would like to have my salary reflect this fact."

Both messages contain the same factual content, yet they differ greatly in how the content is presented. Linguists would say that Person A's presentation is an example of *powerless speech,* while Person B's embodies *powerful speech.* Powerless speech includes the following language forms:

- *Hesitation forms*—"Uhm" and "you know" suggest a lack of confidence or certainty.
- *Disclaimers*—"This may sound out of the ordinary, but . . ." and "I'm not an expert, but . . ." ask the listener to be patient or refrain from criticism.
- *Qualifiers*—"Sort of," "kind of," and "I guess" serve to blunt the force of an assertive statement.
- *Tag questions*—"I've handled this additional work efficiently and professionally, don't you think?" The added-on question turns an assertive statement into a plea for agreement.

Based on the delivery styles of Person A and Person B, who do you think is more likely to persuade their boss to give them the desired raise? As you might guess, research finds that when people use a powerful speak-

ing style, they are judged more competent and credible than when their style is powerless (Erickson et al., 1978; Hosman, 1997). This suggests that, even when people have persuasive messages, they often fail to persuade if they weaken their message by the way they deliver it.

> Be skillful in speech that you may be strong.
> —*The teaching for Merikare, 2135–2040* B.C.

Despite the fact that powerful language gives an assertive "punch" to messages, not everyone in society is taught to use this style of speech. Linguist Robin Lakoff (1975, 1990) asserts that, because the status of women in society has been relatively powerless and marginal compared to that of men, women often are not socialized or expected to express themselves as assertively and forcefully as men do. As a result, in conversation, women are more likely than men to use qualifiers, ask tag questions, and use disclaimers (Coates, 1992; Mulac & Lundell, 1986).

What are some differences between powerful and powerless speech? Research indicates that a powerful speaking style is more persuasive than a powerless speaking style, but that the effectiveness of the powerful style differs when the speaker is a woman and the listening audience consists of men. Why might this be so?

Source: Copyright 2007 Atomic Dog Publishing and its licensors. All rights reserved.

Continued next page—

Psychological Applications

—Continued

Although a powerful speaking style generally is more persuasive than a powerless one, research suggests that women—but not men—sometimes are caught in a double bind communicatively. For a woman, adopting a powerful communication style increases her persuasive power with a female audience, but a male audience sometimes perceives her as less likable and trustworthy, which reduces her ability to persuade (Carli, 1990). Does this mean that women should adopt a powerless speaking style to improve their persuasive power with men? No. The use of powerless language as a subtle persuasion technique will either compromise a woman's perceived competence or make it difficult for her to persuade an audience of both men and women. Instead, additional research (Carli et al., 1995) suggests that, when speaking to a male audience, female persuaders should combine assertive language with a *social nonverbal style* that communicates friendliness and affiliation (relaxed, forward-leaning, smiling face, moderate eye contact). In other words, men are more inclined to like and be persuaded by a competent woman when she is also sociable than when she is merely competent. For a male audience, a sociable nonverbal style appears to remove the perceived threat from a competent woman's self-presentation, making her an effective agent of persuasion.

> Public speaking is done in the public tongue, the national or tribal language; and the language of our tribe is the men's language. Of course women learn it. We're not dumb. If you can tell Margaret Thatcher from Ronald Reagan, or Indira Gandhi from General Somoza, by anything they say, tell me how. This is a man's world, so it talks a man's language.
>
> —*Ursula LeGuin, U.S. author, b. 1929*

Key Terms

algorithm (p. 339)

artificial intelligence (AI) (p. 348)

availability heuristic (p. 347)

categorization (p. 337)

child-directed speech (p. 328)

cognition (p. 337)

communication (p. 316)

concept (p. 337)

confirmation bias (p. 340)

framing (p. 343)

functional fixedness (p. 342)

generic masculine (p. 331)

grammar (p. 323)

heuristic (p. 340)

insight (p. 340)

language (p. 316)

language acquisition device (p. 325)

linguistic relativity hypothesis (p. 331)

mental set (p. 341)

morpheme (p. 323)

need for cognition (p. 345)

nonconscious mimicry (p. 335)

nonverbal communication (p. 334)

phoneme (p. 323)

phonology (p. 323)

problem solving (p. 339)

prototype (p. 338)

representativeness heuristic (p. 343)

semantics (p. 323)

slips of the tongue (p. 330)

speech (p. 316)

syntax (p. 323)

telegraphic speech (p. 328)

trial and error (p. 339)

Suggested Websites

The Psychology of Language Page of Links
http://www.psyc.memphis.edu/POL/POL.htm
This website provides links to other websites of language researchers, organizations, journals, questionnaires, and related disciplines.

Center for the Study of Language and Information (CSLI)
http://www-csli.stanford.edu
This website is the home page for CSLI, an independent research center at Stanford University.

Experimental Psychology Lab
http://www.psychologie.unizh.ch/genpsy/Ulf/Lab/WebExpPsyLab.html
This website contains links to a number of sites that provide people with the opportunity to participate in psychological experiments.

Critical Thinking on the Web
http://www.austhink.org/critical
This site is a directory of quality online resources covering such topics as cognitive biases, language and thought, great critical thinkers in history, and the media and critical thinking.

Review Questions

Note: You can find the correct answers to these questions by taking the quiz and then submitting your answers in the Online Edition. The program will automatically score your submission. If you miss a question, the program will provide the correct answer, a rationale for the answer, and the section number in the chapter where the topic is discussed.

1. The brain disorder characterized by disruptions in language production is known as
   a. Broca's aphasia.
   b. Wernicke's aphasia.
   c. temporal aphasia.
   d. temporal disorder.
   e. word salad.

2. The content and comprehension of language are associated with
   a. Broca's area.
   b. the right cerebral hemisphere.
   c. Wernicke's area.
   d. the larynx.
   e. the location of the larynx.

3. Features of a communication system that characterize it as a "language" include all *except* which one of the following?
   a. meaningfulness
   b. signals that trigger instinctive responses
   c. displacement in space
   d. displacement in time
   e. productivity

4. Researchers who study nonhuman language have determined that
   a. chimps' use of sign language has nothing to do with language acquisition.
   b. honeybees have flexible signals for communicating novel messages.
   c. rigid training methods, such as those used by Terrace, are the most effective way to teach spontaneous signing to chimps.
   d. Kanzi, a bonobo, learned to use symbols spontaneously by observing his adopted mother use symbols to communicate.
   e. very intelligent apes can learn to communicate at a 5- to 6-year-old human level.

5. Rules for how words are put together to form a proper phrase or sentence are referred to as
   a. semantic rules.
   b. syntax rules.
   c. surface structure.
   d. phonological rules.
   e. morpheme rules.

6. The dominant view of language currently emphasizes which of the following as a critical component of language acquisition?
   a. simple exposure to the language
   b. the language acquisition device
   c. selective reinforcement and punishment
   d. the nativist approach
   e. verbal interaction

7. Two-year-olds' telegraphic speech involves
   a. the use of phonemes that are not part of the native language.
   b. an elementary knowledge of syntax.
   c. the use of plurals and past and present tense.
   d. learning exaggerated intonations and using a high pitch.
   e. primarily the use of slang terms.

8. Another term for "motherese," characterized by exaggerated intonations and clear enunciation, is
   a. mother-directed speech.
   b. child-directed speech.
   c. baby talk.
   d. nonsensical wordplay.
   e. None of the above

9. Slips of the tongue are primarily explained by
   a. cognitive processes such as spreading activation of phonemes and morphemes.
   b. psychoanalytic theories of unconscious thoughts and desires.
   c. Spoonerisms, tangled expressions, and word reversals.
   d. spreading activation of semantic rules.
   e. the nativist perspective.

10. A weaker version of Whorf's linguistic relativity hypothesis is supported by
   a. research showing that bilinguals focus on personal needs when speaking English and social needs when speaking Japanese.
   b. Rosch's research on cross-cultural color perception, showing that the Dani people have only two words for color.
   c. research showing that the structure of language determines the structure of thought.
   d. the finding that Chinese languages have many self-focused words.
   e. research showing that language does not influence thinking in collectivist cultures.

11. The way that language calls attention to an individual's gender and the use of generic masculine pronouns and nouns supports the notion that
   a. language determines thought.
   b. cultural thinking can influence people's style of language.
   c. gender-neutral language erases females from our thinking.
   d. collectivist cultures exhibit more gender bias than individualist cultures.
   e. language influences thought.

12. One of the advantages of the indirect language style used in collectivist cultures is that
   a. the speaker does not have to be very eloquent to make a point.
   b. the listener does not have to pay close attention to the message to understand it.
   c. it provides the speaker with plausible deniability.
   d. fewer words can be used to convey relatively complex thoughts.
   e. less educated citizens can converse more easily with the educated.

13. Research on body movements suggests that muggers may choose victims who have what type of body movements?
    a. organized
    b. smooth
    c. confident
    d. inconsistent
    e. comfortable

14. Categorizing, or forming concepts, is accomplished by
    a. identifying features that define all members of a concept.
    b. learning specific concept formation rules.
    c. learning the fixed boundaries between objects' properties.
    d. identifying features that define typical members of a concept.
    e. learning the specific rules that define the meaning of fuzzy boundaries.

15. Trial and error problem-solving strategies
    a. guarantee success, because you can keep guessing until you get it right.
    b. are faster and more efficient than using complex algorithms.
    c. are slower than heuristic strategies.
    d. follow a systematic and methodical step-by-step procedure.
    e. involve a gradually increasing focus on concepts important to the solution.

16. Confirmation bias leads to problem-solving errors
    a. because we seek only information that confirms our beliefs.
    b. only when we waste time testing alternative hypotheses rather than seeking confirming evidence.
    c. only when we pursue information that disconfirms our beliefs.
    d. when we fail to rely on solutions that worked in the past.
    e. because we tend to confirm what experts tell us.

17. Rational decision-making strategies
    a. always consider all aspects of the available options.
    b. involve framing choices in multiple ways before deciding.
    c. are used less often when a decision is important to us.
    d. may involve nonsystematic or elementary strategies.
    e. are more effective than using the weighted additive value model.

18. Research on decision-making strategies and shortcuts indicates that
    a. representative heuristics are the best way to eliminate the base-rate fallacy.
    b. the false consensus effect leads us to assume that our decision is wrong when we disagree with everyone else.
    c. a useful decision-making strategy that can narrow our choices is to rely on the ease with which previous examples of an event are recalled.
    d. heuristics are complex cognitive processes used primarily by those with a high need for cognition.
    e. heuristics are used more frequently when we are in a hurry than when we have time to think about our choices.

19. When making decisions, people with low self-esteem
    a. try to protect themselves from the negative consequences of decisions.
    b. take more risks to try to make themselves feel better.
    c. attempt to win big by choosing high-stakes options.
    d. will punish themselves by selecting options where they might lose big.
    e. take more risks with gains but fewer risks with losses.

20. One area of human intellectual processes that has not been well integrated into artificial intelligence (AI) research and programs is
    a. verbal communication.
    b. emotional evaluation.
    c. rational decision making.
    d. short-term memory.
    e. computational simplicity.

21. According to the "Psychological Applications" section, concerning language style and persuasive speaking, what is the "double bind" that women, but not men, face?
    a. Women who use qualifiers in their speech are more effective in persuading women but not men.
    b. Women need to use a powerful communication style to be persuasive, but men do not need to do so.
    c. When women use a powerful communication style, they are judged to be less physically attractive than if they use a powerless style.
    d. When women use a powerful communication style, some male listeners feel threatened and, thus, are less persuaded.

Chapter 10

Intelligence

The Man with the Hoe

Bowed by the weight of centuries he leans
Upon his hoe and gazes on the ground,
The emptiness of ages in his face,
And on his back the burden of the world.
Who made him dead to rapture and despair,
A thing that grieves not and that never hopes,
Stolid and stunned, a brother to the ox?
Who loosened and let down this brutal jaw?
Whose was the hand that slanted back this brow?
Whose breath blew out the light within this brain?

(Excerpt from "The Man with the Hoe" by Edwin Markham, New York: Doubleday & McClure, 1899)

Jean-Francois Millet's painting *The Man with the Hoe,* shown in figure 10-1, has an interesting footnote in the history of intelligence testing. In 1899, inspired by Millet's painting, Edwin Markham wrote a poem of the same name, which was published in almost every newspaper in the United States that year and quickly became the focus of discussion and debate. For many, the weary French peasant became a symbol of people prevented by oppressive social conditions from attaining their true intellectual potential. Yet psychologist Henry Goddard, the director of intellectual assessment at Ellis Island in New York Harbor where immigrants to the United States were processed and tested, did not agree with Markham's interpretation. Believing that he could recognize feebleminded people by sight, Goddard asserted that, as with most poor peasants, the man in Millet's painting was not the victim of bad social conditions but, rather, bad genes (Goddard, 1919). He further contended that people with very low intelligence should be identified so society could prevent them from passing their feeblemindedness on to the next generation.

During the first quarter of the twentieth century, Goddard and many of his colleagues used the emerging field of intelligence testing to work toward this goal. In hindsight, we can see that their research and policy recommendations—fueled by cultural prejudices in the larger society—illustrate how science can sometimes be used as a weapon of discrimination. Even now, in a new century, psychology continues to struggle with disturbing findings from intelligence research. For example, persistent differences in the intelligence scores of Blacks, Whites, Hispanics, Asians, and Native

Figure 10-1

The Man with the Hoe

Source: The J. Paul Getty Museum, Los Angeles, Jean-Francois Millet, *The Man with the Hoe,* 1860–1862, oil on canvas, 31 1/2 × 39 inches. © The J. Paul Getty Museum.

Americans raise disturbing questions about what determines intelligence (Cooper, 2005; Cosmides & Tooby, 2002). Do these group differences mean that the different races can be organized into a hierarchy of superior-inferior intelligence? This question threatens to further tear the social fabric of our society, which is already divided by race and ethnicity. But it is a question that ignoring won't dismiss.

In this chapter, we continue our journey of discovery in psychology by analyzing the important question of group differences in intelligence. In addition, we examine the early attempts to measure intelligence and explore how it is conceptualized today. For our purposes, I define **intelligence** as the mental abilities necessary to adapt to and shape the environment (Grossman & Kaufman, 2002; Neisser et al., 1996). This means that intelligence involves not only reacting to one's surroundings but also actively forming them. It also means that intelligent behavior in New York City, for example, may not be intelligent or adaptive in the jungles of South America (Detterman, 2005). The mental abilities making up what we call intelligence are the keys to lifelong learning (Sternberg, 1997). But is intelligence something inborn or learned? Are there different types of intelligence? Are there gender differences in intelligence? Can we scientifically study creativity? These are some of the issues we will grapple with as we ride the rocky road of intelligence testing and theorizing.

> **intelligence** The mental abilities necessary to adapt to and shape the environment.

10-1   MEASURING INTELLIGENCE

Preview

- *Who developed the first useful intelligence test?*
- *What is eugenics?*
- *Is there a difference between aptitude tests and achievement tests?*
- *What are three characteristics of good intelligence tests?*
- *Are intelligence tests "culture free"?*
- *How is an intelligence test developed?*

Psychometrics—which literally means "to measure the mind"—is the measurement of intelligence, personality, and other mental processes. The psychological tests developed by psychometricians assess the *individual differences* that exist between people in a wide variety of abilities, interests, and personality traits (Fuster, 2005; Sternberg, 2005). Although the psychometric approach has been extensively employed in the study of intelligence, the results have sometimes given psychology a black eye.

> **psychometrics** The measurement of intelligence, personality, and other mental processes.

10-1a   Early Intelligence Testing Was Shaped by Racial and Cultural Stereotypes

As outlined in chapter 2, section 2-4a, no science is untouched by the values and politics of the culture in which it is practiced. In psychology, nowhere is this more clearly seen than in the history of intelligence testing, beginning about 100 years ago (Gregory, 2004). During this time period, Western scientific thinking was heavily influenced by the cultural belief that upper-class White men were intellectually superior to women, the poor, and members of all other racial and ethnic groups.

Francis Galton: Quantifying Intelligence

Not surprisingly for a pioneer in modern statistics, the British mathematician and naturalist Sir Francis Galton (1822–1911) loved numbers. In fact, he was so convinced that anything could be quantified that he actually tried to statistically determine the effectiveness of prayer! When his cousin Charles Darwin proposed the theory of evolution, Galton decided to apply the principle of natural selection to human traits. He reasoned that if traits are inherited, then similar levels of intelligence should consistently appear in families over generations. Galton (1869) further believed that the wealthy families in society—such as his own—were also the

eugenics The practice of encouraging supposedly superior people to reproduce, while discouraging or even preventing from doing so those judged to be inferior.

Sir Francis Galton: "If everybody were to agree on the improvement of the race of man being a matter of the very utmost importance, and if the theory of the hereditary transmission of qualities in men was as thoroughly understood as it is in the case of our domestic animals, I see no absurdity in supposing that, in some way or other, the improvement would be carried into effect."

Our purpose is to be able to measure the intellectual capacity of a child who is brought to us in order to know whether he is normal or retarded. . . . If we do nothing, if we don't intervene actively and usefully, he will continue to lose time . . . and will finally become discouraged. The child who loses the taste for work in class strongly risks being unable to acquire it after he leaves school.

—*Alfred Binet, French psychologist,*
1857–1911

more intelligent because intelligence was assumed to result in success and wealth. He was so confident that families ended up either wealthy or poor because of their inherited traits that he founded the **eugenics** (the Greek word for "well-born") movement to improve the hereditary characteristics of society. Eugenics proposed not only that men and women of high mental ability—meaning White and upper-middle-class individuals—should be encouraged to marry and have children, but also that those of lesser intelligence—meaning lower-class Whites and members of other races—should be discouraged (or prevented) from reproducing. At the beginning of the twentieth century, British scientists and politicians, who were nearly all members of the upper middle class, promoted the eugenics movement as a possible solution to their country's shrinking status as a world power. However, although eugenics began in England, as you will soon learn, it became a much stronger force in the United States, where it was fueled by racial prejudice and immigration fears.

How did Galton measure intelligence? Believing that intelligence was a product of how quickly and accurately people respond to stimuli, Galton's assessment battery included measurements of sensory abilities and reaction time, as well as measurements of head size and muscular strength. Unfortunately for Galton, his tests not only failed to correlate with each other, but also had almost no relation to accepted criteria of intellectual functioning (Sharp, 1898; Wissler, 1901).

Alfred Binet: The Father of Intelligence Testing

While Galton's attempts to measure intelligence failed, across the English Channel, a different type of intelligence testing was being developed by the French psychologist Alfred Binet (1857–1911), whose work partly inspired Jean Piaget's theory of cognitive development (see chapter 4, section 4-3a). When the French government passed a law in 1904 requiring that all children attend school, Binet and a physician named Theophilé Simon (1905/1916) worked to develop an inexpensive, easily administered, objective measure of intelligence that could identify lower-performing children in need of special education. In contrast to Galton's work, the resulting Binet-Simon Test measured general mental ability and emphasized abstract reasoning rather than sensory skills (Sternberg & Jarvin, 2003).

According to Binet, cognitive development follows the same course in all children, but some learn faster and more easily than others. In intelligence testing, this means that "average" children will perform similarly to those their own chronological age, "dull" children will perform similarly to children younger than themselves, and "bright" children will perform as older children do. Binet reasoned that general mental ability can be calculated by comparing children's *mental age* with their chronological age. Thus, a 12-year-old child whose performance is equal to that of the average child her chronological age would have the mental age of 12 years. Armed with this method of intellectual comparison, testers could place children into appropriate grades in school and identify those who would benefit from additional tutoring. Unlike Galton's intelligence test, the Binet-Simon Test proved to be the first valid intelligence instrument—that is, it accurately identified lower-performing students.

In designing the Binet-Simon Test, Binet, unlike Galton, made no assumptions about why intelligence differences exist. However, he did insist that his test did not measure inborn intelligence, and he believed that intellectual ability could be increased through education. He also realized that his test merely sampled intelligence and did not measure all intellectual aspects. Finally, he warned that because the test was developed in France using children with similar cultural backgrounds, it might not accurately measure intelligence in other countries. Binet feared that his test would not be used to help slow learners receive special help but, instead, would be used to (1) limit their educational opportunities and (2) plant the idea in their own minds that they were incapable of learning (Gould, 1996). Unfortunately, both fears were realized when his test was redesigned for use in the United States (Mayrhauser, 2002).

IQ Testing in America

Henry Goddard, the director of research at the Vineland Training School for Feeble-Minded Boys and Girls in New Jersey, was the first to translate and use Binet's test in the

United States. Despite Binet's insistence that his test did not measure inherited intelligence, Goddard believed that it did (Thalassis, 2004). Also, in contrast to Binet's desire to use his scale to identify low-scoring students for special education, Goddard, a strong advocate of Galton's eugenics movement, used the test to identify the feebleminded so they could be segregated and prevented from having children. To describe these low-intelligence people, he coined the term *moron*, which is derived from a Greek word meaning "foolish."

When Goddard (1913) later used the Binet-Simon Test to assess newly arrived immigrants at Ellis Island in New York Harbor, he confirmed prevailing cultural beliefs concerning racial and ethnic differences in intelligence. Among adult immigrants tested, 87 percent of Russians, 83 percent of Jews, 80 percent of Hungarians, and 79 percent of Italians were feebleminded—that is, below the mental age of 12! Although these poor scores were later shown to be based on tests biased toward native-born English speakers and on testing procedures that selectively chose immigrants who appeared feebleminded, they seemed to confirm that the country's intellectual strength was being weakened by the arrival of inferior immigrants (Richardson, 2003). A few years later, when group intelligence tests were given to 1.7 million World War I army recruits, psychologists reported with some alarm that their average mental age was only 13. Because many recruits were also recent immigrants, politicians used this and the earlier evidence provided by Goddard to help pass the Immigration Act of 1924. This law dramatically restricted the admittance of certain "undesirable" ethnic groups, especially those from eastern and southern Europe (Sedgwick, 1995).

Although Goddard and most other psychologists involved in the eugenics movement later reversed their positions and argued against such discriminatory measures, this aspect of their research not only harmed the reputation of psychology as a science but also justified racist societal practices here and abroad. In Germany, the eugenics movement helped fan the flames of the Holocaust. Partly inspired by the success of U.S. eugenics laws, the Nazis in Germany designed deadly eugenics programs involving forced sterilization of those who supposedly had genetic defects, forbiddance of marriages between Aryans and Jews, and finally the mass execution of Jews, Gypsies, homosexuals, the mentally handicapped, and other "genetic undesirables" (Leahey, 1991). Desperate to escape the sure death awaiting them in Nazi concentration camps, millions of Jewish refugees tried to emigrate to the United States. However, in the cruelest twist of this sorry tale, few Jews were admitted, partly due to restrictions imposed by the 1924 immigration law. The indirect role that psychology played in this chapter of history chillingly demonstrates how ideas can sometimes be as destructive as guns and bombs.

Lewis Terman: "The children of successful and cultured parents test higher than children from wretched and ignorant homes for the simple reason that their heredity is better. . . . The whole question of racial differences in mental traits will have to be taken up anew and by experimental methods. The writer predicts that when this is done there will be discovered enormously significant racial differences in general intelligence, differences which cannot be wiped out by any scheme of mental culture." (1916, pp. 91–92, 115)

Source: Archives of the History of American Psychology, The University of Akron.

If the impression takes root that these tests really measure intelligence, that they constitute a sort of last judgment on the child's capacity, . . . then it would be a thousand times better if all the intelligence testers and all their questionnaires were sunk without warning in the Sargasso Sea.

—*Walter Lippmann, American journalist and social critic, 1889–1974; comments while debating Lewis Terman*

10-1b Modern Tests of Mental Abilities Measure Either Aptitude or Achievement

During your schooling, you have taken many tests of your mental abilities. When describing such tests, psychologists generally place them into the two categories of *aptitude* and *achievement* (Wasserman, 2003). Intelligence tests are **aptitude tests:** They predict your capacity to learn a new skill if you are given an adequate education. In contrast to predicting what you can learn, **achievement tests** measure what you have already learned. Whenever you are given an exam to determine what you have learned in a course, you are taking an achievement test.

Although the distinctions between aptitude tests and achievement tests seem clear-cut, they are not. For instance, suppose two college students who have an equal capacity for learning math are given a test of mathematical aptitude. One student, however, attended a high school that provided him with 4 years of college-level math instruction, while the other student's school offered no college-level courses. Despite their equal capacity for learning math, it's likely that the student with the greater math experience will achieve a higher math aptitude score. The implication of this example is that your score on an aptitude test can be affected by your prior experience in the area being tested.

aptitude test A test designed to predict a person's capacity for learning.

achievement test A test designed to assess what a person has learned.

The Stanford-Binet Intelligence Test

Although Goddard introduced the Binet-Simon Test to America, Lewis Terman (1877–1956), a psychology professor at Stanford University, was responsible for revising it for use with American children (Terman, 1916; Terman & Childs, 1912). The resulting **Stanford-Binet Intelligence Test** employed a new scoring system known as the **intelligence quotient,** or **IQ.** Based on an idea by the German psychologist Wilhelm Stern (1914), IQ was represented as a ratio of mental age divided by chronological age, multiplied by 100:

$$\text{IQ} = \frac{\text{Mental age} \times 100}{\text{Chronological age}}$$

With this formula, a child whose mental and chronological ages were the same had an IQ of 100. However, a 10-year-old who answered questions at the level of a typical 8-year-old had an IQ of 80, and an 8-year-old who answered questions like a typical 10-year-old had an IQ of 125. The advantage of this ratio formula over the Binet-Simon scoring system was that it was more useful when comparing mental ages within a group of children who differed in their chronological ages.

Although the IQ ratio was generally adequate in representing intelligence in children, it proved problematic when the Stanford-Binet Intelligence Test was redesigned to measure adult intelligence as well. Because the *rate of growth* does not occur as rapidly in adulthood as in childhood, using the IQ ratio led to the mistaken representation that intelligence *declines* with age. For example, if Raymond had the mental age of 20 at age 15, he would have an IQ of 133, which is considered mentally gifted. However, at the age of 40, if Raymond's mental age had increased to 28, his IQ would now be only 70, which is the beginning of the mentally retarded range. Raymond might have a successful career in a profession requiring above-average intelligence, but the ratio IQ would not accurately reflect this. Today, most intelligence tests, including the Stanford-Binet, no longer compute a ratio IQ. Instead, they use a *deviation IQ,* which compares how a person's intelligence test score deviates from the average score of her or his same-age peers, which is 100.

The Wechsler Intelligence Scales

The person responsible for developing the deviation IQ score was David Wechsler, one of those supposedly feebleminded eastern Europeans who immigrated to this country in the early 1900s. Today's most widely used set of intelligence tests is the **Wechsler Intelligence Scales,** named after their creator. Three separate intelligence tests have been designed for adults (the *Wechsler Adult Intelligence Scale*), for preschoolers (the *Wechsler Preschool and Primary Scale of Intelligence*), and for school-age children (the *Wechsler Intelligence Scale for Children*).

For all the Wechsler tests, intelligence is measured by 11 subtests—6 verbal and 5 performance—that yield a verbal IQ score, a performance IQ score, and an overall IQ score. Figure 10-2 provides sample items from the adult test for the verbal and performance subscales. As you can see, the verbal items consist of general information, similarities, math, vocabulary, comprehension, and the recall of number strings. In contrast, the performance subscales require the test-taker to locate missing picture parts, arrange cartoons in a logical sequence, reproduce block designs, assemble jigsaw puzzles, and copy symbols on paper. Because the performance subtests rely less on familiarity with words and language than do the verbal subtests, the performance subtests are less likely to be affected by the test-takers' education or cultural experiences. When significant differences are found between the verbal and performance scores, this alerts test administrators to possible learning problems (Weiss et al., 2005). For instance, a verbal score considerably lower than the performance score might indicate a reading or language disability (Aiken, 1996). However, as just mentioned, it could also mean that the test-taker is not very familiar with the language or customs of the larger society.

Group-Administered Tests

While the Stanford-Binet and the Wechsler tests are administered to people individually, group-administered tests can assess hundreds or thousands of people simultaneously.

Stanford-Binet Intelligence Test The widely used American revision of the original French Binet-Simon intelligence test.

intelligence quotient (IQ) Originally, the ratio of mental age to chronological age multiplied by 100 (MA/CA × 100). Today, IQ is calculated by comparing how a person's performance deviates from the average score of her or his same-age peers, which is 100.

Wechsler Intelligence Scales The most widely used set of intelligence tests, containing both verbal and performance (nonverbal) subscales.

VERBAL

General Information
What day of the year is Independence Day?

Similarities
In what way are *wool* and *cotton* alike?

Arithmetic Reasoning
If eggs cost 60 cents a dozen, what does 1 egg cost?

Vocabulary
Tell me the meaning of corrupt.

Comprehension
Why do people buy fire insurance?

Digit Span
Listen carefully, and when I am through, say the numbers right after me.

7   3   4   1   8   6

Now I am going to say some more numbers, but I want you to say them backward.

3   8   4   1   6

PERFORMANCE

Picture Completion
I am going to show you a picture with an important part missing. Tell me what is missing.

'85

SUN	MON	TUE	WED	THU	FRI	SAT
1	2	3	4	5	6	7
8	9	10	11	12	13	14
15	16	17	18	19	20	21
22	23	24	25	26	27	28
29	30					

Picture Arrangement
The pictures below tell a story. Put them in the right order to tell the story.

Block Design
Using the four blocks, make one just like this.

Object Assembly
If these pieces are put together correctly, they will make something. Go ahead and put them together as quickly as you can.

Digit-Symbol Substitution

Code

△	○	⧄	✕	8
1	2	3	4	5

Test

△	8	✕	○	△	⧄	8	✕	△	8

Figure 10-2

Sample Items from the Wechsler Adult Intelligence Scale (WAIS)

Source: From *Measurement and Evaluation in Psychology and Education* by A. L. Thorndike and E. P. Hagen. Reprinted by permission of Pearson Education, Inc., Upper Saddle River, NJ.

Group aptitude and achievement tests are widely used today, including the familiar college entrance *Scholastic Assessment Test (SAT)*, which was previously known as the Scholastic Aptitude Test. The reason for this name change is that the old name's use of the term *aptitude* implied that the SAT measures a person's capacity for learning. In reality, it measures learned verbal and mathematical skills; thus, it is more accurately considered an achievement test. As such, SAT scores are significantly influenced by the quality of the schools test-takers attend. Therefore, overemphasizing SAT scores in evaluating students for college admission can disadvantage students who attended inferior schools and also those whose main academic strengths lie in such areas as music and art. Both the verbal and the math sections of the SAT have an average score of 500 and a range of 200 to 800, resulting in a total score range of 400 to 1600.

Similar tests are also used to assess students' potential for postgraduate training. For graduate school in the arts and sciences, there is the Graduate Record Exam (GRE); for graduate school in business, there is the Graduate Management Admission Test (GMAT); medical schools use the Medical College Admission Test (MCAT); and law schools use the Law School Aptitude Test (LSAT). There is sufficient evidence that, like the SAT, these exams measure not only the potential for performing well on scholastic tasks but also achievement. The practical importance of this fact for students is that studying can improve test performance. On the SAT, extensive training or coaching on how to take the test can increase total scores by as many as 30 to 50 points (Kulik et al., 1984; Powers, 1993).

Journey of Discovery Question

Women who go to college after their mid-20s receive better grades than would be predicted by their scores on SAT tests taken just before entering college. Why might this be the case?

10-1c Psychological Tests Must Be Standardized, Reliable, and Valid

All psychological tests, including the mental ability tests discussed in this chapter, are measurement instruments that must have three basic characteristics: They must be *standardized*, *reliable*, and *valid*. The Stanford-Binet, Wechsler tests, and scholastic tests we have reviewed thus far all possess these characteristics.

Standardization

If you have taken the SAT or any other achievement or aptitude test, you may recall that the testing procedures are extremely rigid. Regardless of where or when the test is administered, everyone receives the same instructions, the same questions, and the same time limits. You may also remember that when you received your test results, your individual score was compared against those of a previously tested group of people who had followed the same testing procedures that you followed. This comparison process allowed you to convert your "raw score" into a *percentile*, which indicates the percentage of people in the standard group who scored at or below your score. This entire process of establishing uniform procedures for administering a test and interpreting its scores is known as **standardization.**

When the Binet-Simon Test was first used in the United States, Goddard, Terman, and their coworkers recognized that the test items developed for French citizens did not provide an adequate standard for Americans. To their credit, before using this scale to evaluate the intelligence of White Americans, they dutifully revised the test and standardized it by evaluating 2,300 White-American citizens from different socioeconomic backgrounds. However, they failed to standardize the test for non-White Americans and immigrants and instead evaluated these groups based on the White standard. This failure to standardize goes a long way toward explaining the lower IQ scores achieved by these groups during this time.

Standardized test results often show a roughly **normal distribution,** which has a bell-shaped appearance when the individual scores are placed on a graph. As you can see in figure 10-3, in a normal distribution, most test scores cluster around the *median*, or middle score, which has a value similar to both the *mean* (the average test score) and the *mode* (the most frequent test score). As mentioned, the mean score on an intelligence test is 100. As we move away—in either direction—from this mean score, we find fewer test scores. Also as depicted in figure 10-3, in a normal distribution of IQ scores, 68 percent of the scores will range between 85 and 115, and 96 percent of the scores will fall within the 70–130-point range. Only 2 percent of the population has IQ scores above 130, and only 2 percent has scores below 70.

Periodically, the Stanford-Binet and the Wechsler IQ tests must be restandardized to maintain the mean score of 100. Why is this necessary? Simply put, it appears that people are getting smarter. In every one of the 20 countries studied worldwide, each succeeding generation intellectually outperforms the previous generation (Flynn, 1987, 1996; Nettelbeck et al., 2004). For restandardization purposes, this means that test items must be made

standardization The process of establishing uniform procedures for administering a test and for interpreting its scores.

normal distribution The bell-shaped appearance of a distribution that results when the mean, median, and mode are identical in value.

Figure 10-3

The Normal Distribution

Scores on standardized aptitude tests, such as the Wechsler Adult Intelligence Scale, tend to form a normal distribution (also known as a "bell-shaped curve"). The Wechsler scale, like other IQ tests, calls the average score 100.

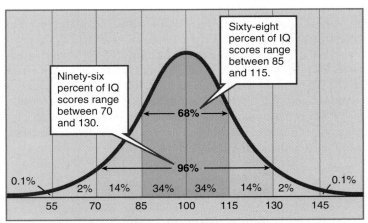

Wechsler Intelligence Score

more difficult to keep the average intelligence score at 100. The tendency for people's performance on IQ tests to improve from one generation to the next is called the **Flynn effect,** after the psychologist who first noticed it (Dickens & Flynn, 2002).

What accounts for this rapid increase in IQ? Evolution—which occurs slowly—cannot provide an answer, and the increase certainly appears inconsistent with Galton's prediction that higher birthrates observed among those with lower IQ scores would move IQ scores lower. A likely explanation is the combined effects of improved education, better health and nutrition, experience with testing, and exposure to a broader range of information via television and the computer (Colom et al., 2005).

Reliability

The **reliability** of a test indicates the degree to which it yields consistent results. How is a test's reliability estimated? The most common technique for estimating this type of consistency is through *test-retest reliability,* which is checking to see how people score on the same test on two or more separate occasions (Kittler et al., 2004). The drawback to this reliability technique, however, is that people tend to remember the test items when they take the test again, and this influences their performance. A solution is to use *alternate-forms reliability,* in which slightly different versions of the test are given to people on the two separate occasions. The items on the two test versions are similar in format but different enough in content that test-takers' performance will not be influenced by familiarity. Reliability estimates for both techniques are based on *correlation coefficients.* As you recall from chapter 2, section 2-3b, a correlation coefficient (also known by the symbol r) is a statistical measure of the direction and strength of the linear relationship between two variables, and it ranges from -1.00 to $+1.00$. In estimating both test-retest and alternate-forms reliability, the two variables are the two test scores obtained on two different occasions. If people's test scores at time 1 have a strong correspondence with their scores at time 2 (figure 10-4a), the correlation coefficient will be near $+1.00$, meaning that the test's reliability is high, which is good news for the test developer. However, if people's scores at time 1 and time 2 do not correspond (figure 10-4b), the correlation coefficient will be closer to 0.00, meaning that the test's reliability is low. This is bad news for the test developer. The contemporary intelligence tests

Flynn effect The tendency for people's performance on IQ tests to improve from one generation to the next.

reliability The degree to which a test yields consistent results.

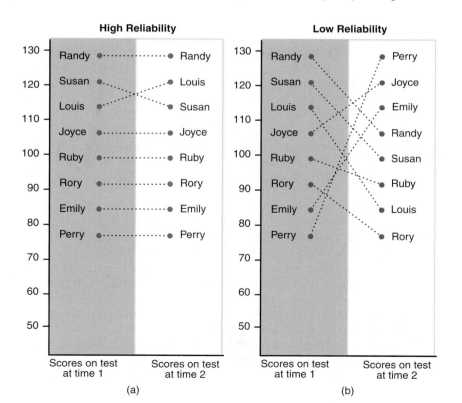

Figure 10-4

Determining Both Test-Retest and Alternate-Forms Reliabilities

In test-retest reliability, people take a test at time 1 and again at time 2. In alternate-forms reliability, they take one version of the test at time 1 and a slightly different version at time 2. For both of these reliability techniques, people's scores at time 1 are depicted on the left, and their scores at time 2 are depicted on the right. (*a*) When people obtain similar scores on both occasions, the test has high reliability. (*b*) If they get very different scores, the test has low reliability.

described thus far have correlation coefficients of about +.90, which indicate high reliability (Kaufman, 1990; Robinson & Nagel, 1992).

Validity

Knowing that a test is reliable does not tell you anything about its validity. **Validity** refers to the degree to which a test measures what it is designed to measure. In our household, we have a weighing scale that is highly reliable: Everyone who steps on it consistently weighs 32 pounds. Although it is reliable, none of us believes it is a *valid* weight measure. While the invalidity of our household scale is a source of amusement for us, invalid intelligence tests are no joking matter.

How do researchers determine whether an intelligence test is valid? Typically, they analyze different aspects of the test (Shields et al., 2004; Ukrainetz & Blomquist, 2002). **Content validity** refers to the degree to which the items on a test are related to the characteristic the test supposedly measures. For example, if an intelligence test consisted of measuring a person's weight and height, we would probably conclude that it was low in content validity, because these measurements seem completely unrelated to our concept of intelligence. However, if it contained items that measured abstract reasoning, we would be more inclined to believe it had reasonable content validity.

> *Journey of*
> *Discovery*
> Question
>
> Imagine that you wanted to develop your own intelligence test. What are some of the pitfalls in early intelligence testing that you would want to avoid?

Besides content validity, tests are analyzed in terms of **predictive validity** (also known as *criterion validity*), which is the degree to which the test results predict other observable behavior related to the characteristic the test supposedly measures. How well do contemporary intelligence tests predict behavior thought to be related to intelligence? It depends. The correlation between IQ scores and scholastic achievement (usually measured by students' school grades) is about +.60 to +.70 during elementary school, which is quite high. However, during the college years this correlation drops to about +.40 to +.50.

Why does predictive validity decline from elementary school to college? Undoubtedly, many more factors influence school performance in college than in elementary school, such as jobs or romantic relationships that distract students from their studies. However, more important is the simple fact that a greater *restricted range* of intelligence is found among college students than among students in elementary school. That is, regardless of whether they are low or high in intelligence, almost all children attend elementary school. In such an environment where virtually all intelligence levels are represented, it isn't surprising that IQ scores do a pretty good job of predicting school grades: The cream rises to the top. However, following high school, students with above-average intelligence—the "cream" of elementary school—are the ones most likely to attend college. In this "creamy" environment, IQ scores cannot possibly predict academic performance as well as in the "milky" elementary school environment.

Do SAT scores significantly predict whether students will actually succeed or fail in college? Yes, but like IQ scores, they are not strong predictors: The correlation with college grades is less than +.50 (Aiken, 1996). The SAT is a better predictor of college performance for those who score at the two extremes. A probable reason for the greater predictive power of the SAT at these two extremes involves the fact that college success is due to both intellectual ability and a desire to achieve. Most high SAT scorers have both these personal qualities, while many of the low scorers may have deficiencies in ability and/or desire. While this explanation may generally be true, it is important to add that there are many examples of successful students who scored low on the SATs.

In summary, an intelligence test, like any other psychological test, is useful only to the extent that it is both reliable and valid. Does the test yield consistent scores, and does it actually predict what it supposedly measures? In general, the reliability of intelligence tests is higher than their validity. Despite continuing reservations expressed by some about using intelligence tests to measure people's intellectual abilities, testing is an integral part of many modern soci-

validity The degree to which a test measures what it is designed to measure.

content validity The degree to which the items on a test are related to the characteristic the test supposedly measures.

predictive validity The degree to which a test predicts other observable behavior related to the characteristic the test supposedly measures; also known as *criterion validity*.

eties, both in their educational systems and in their workplaces. Further, such tests do appear to predict to some degree how successful people will be in life. For example, in the United States, individuals who score high on intelligence tests tend to learn more in school, get better grades, and complete more years of education than those who score low. In fact, people who have IQs below 85—which is about 15 percent of the population—are very likely to drop out of school before receiving their high school diploma (Hunt, 1995). They also are likely to be unemployed for long periods of time, to live below the poverty line, and to have a criminal record. Thus, intelligence testing is likely to remain part of our cultural scene for the foreseeable future.

10-1d Intelligence Tests Are Not "Culture Free"

Intelligence tests measure people's developed abilities at a particular point in time. As such, they detect not only innate differences in intellectual abilities but also differences due to cultural learning and experiences. Because of this fact, two people with the same innate intellectual ability will probably score differently on an intelligence test when one of them has considerably less experience with the culture in which the test was developed. In the United States, critics of intelligence tests argue that Whites and middle- and upper-class individuals have had greater exposure than ethnic minority and lower-class individuals to the topics contained within some of the test items in the country's most commonly used IQ tests. Consider again the sample item on the Wechsler Adult Intelligence Scale in figure 10-2, which asks why people buy fire insurance. Is it possible that this item is biased against a person who has never had enough possessions to make the cost of fire insurance relevant? Or consider this question on a children's IQ test: "Which is most similar to a xylophone? (violin, tuba, marimba, piano)?" Are White children of well-to-do parents more likely to have attended orchestra concerts or learned about these instruments than minority children of poor parents? Could such questions explain the racial group differences in IQ test scores discussed later in this chapter (see section 10-4b)?

It is true that some of the test items on the most frequently used IQ tests in the United States are still based on the vocabulary and experiences of the dominant middle-class culture. As such, these tests are measuring a person's achievement in acquiring knowledge valued by mainstream culture, in addition to measuring innate abilities (Kwate, 2001). Supporters of IQ tests respond to these charges of culture bias by pointing out that, although these tests do not provide an unbiased measure of cognitive abilities in general, they do provide a fairly accurate measure of whether people are likely to succeed in school and in certain occupations. Thus, in statistically predicting academic and career success, standard intelligence tests and achievement tests are not biased: Their predictive ability is roughly the same for Blacks and Whites, for rich and poor, and for native-born and immigrant groups (Neisser et al., 1996; te Nijenhuis et al., 2004).

The question of cultural bias in intelligence testing is also an issue when attempting to assess and compare the intellectual abilities of people in different cultures around the world (Serpell & Haynes, 2004). Intelligence researchers have attempted to construct "culture-free" tests to solve this problem, but it is now clear that no current test is completely free of cultural influence. For example, the Raven Progressive Matrices Test, which was initially touted as "culture free," is now known to show some degree of cultural bias (Carpenter et al., 1990). In this test, people are presented with a number of increasingly difficult nonverbal matrix problems to solve, such as the exercise in figure 10-5. The problem with using this test to measure intelligence cross-culturally is that, whereas matrices are repeatedly encountered in most cultures that have formal schooling, they are virtually nonexistent in cultures that lack formal schooling. Because of this difference, test-takers in cultures with formal schooling perform at a higher level than test-takers where formal schooling is rare (Benson, 2003). Yet, even with this culturally based problem, the Raven Progressive Matrices Test has been found to have adequate validity across a number of cultures (Rushton et al., 2004).

The problem of cultural bias does not mean that administering valid intelligence tests in other cultures is impossible. However, it does mean that simply translating a test developed in the United States into the local language of another culture is not sufficient. Instead, researchers must become very familiar with the cultures they study, and design tests that are consistent with the needs and values of the people who will be tested (Greenfield et al., 2003; Holding et al., 2004). For example, when Ashley Maynard and her colleagues (2002) studied intellectual development among children in a Zinacantec Mayan village in

Figure 10-5

Raven Progressive Matrices Test

This example of an item like those on the Raven Progressive Matrices Test relies on visual-spatial ability. Which of the eight figures presented at the bottom best completes the logic of the matrix at the top?

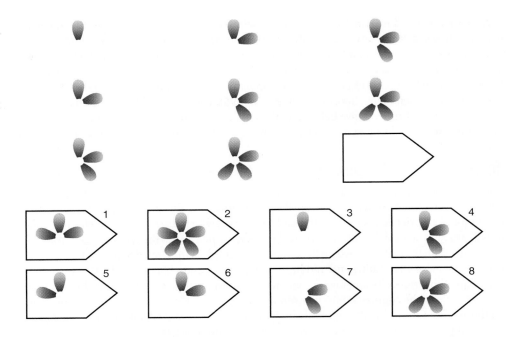

Chiapas, Mexico, they used toy looms, spools of thread, and other common objects from the local culture. Their results indicated that the progression of children's intellectual development was comparable to that found among children in the United States. Maynard's research demonstrates that when psychologists use testing materials and measurement techniques associated with test-takers' cultural experiences, psychologists can be more confident in making cross-cultural comparisons of intellectual abilities.

Section Review

- The first useful intelligence test was developed by Alfred Binet to identify lower-performing children needing special education.
- Eugenics was a social movement to improve the hereditary characteristics of society, and it led to discrimination against people who were judged mentally inferior.
- Henry Goddard inappropriately used the Binet-Simon Test to assess the intelligence of diverse groups, including immigrants.
- Intelligence tests are aptitude tests because they measure your capacity for learning, while achievement tests measure what you have already learned.
- All mental ability tests must be standardized, reliable, and valid:
  —Standardization is the process of establishing uniform procedures for administering a test and for interpreting its scores.
  —Test reliability indicates the degree to which a test yields consistent results.
  —Test validity indicates the degree to which a test measures what it is designed to measure.
- The reliability of intelligence tests is higher than their validity.
- Intelligence tests are not "culture free," and care is needed when comparing people from different cultural backgrounds.

10-2 INTELLIGENCE: ONE THING OR MANY?

Preview

- *Is there really such a thing as general intelligence?*
- *What is the difference between crystallized and fluid intelligence?*
- *Are athletic and musical talents forms of intelligence?*
- *Are common sense and empathy forms of intelligence?*

As you have learned, intelligence tests were constructed to meet practical goals: to identify slow learners in school for remedial education, to weed out intellectually "deficient" immigrants and army recruits, and to select college applicants. Given this practical emphasis, relatively little research attention was initially devoted to developing theories concerning the nature of intelligence (Kaufman, 2000). During this early period, Edwin Boring (1923), a historian of psychology, wrote, "Intelligence is whatever an intelligence test measures." As researchers began to more carefully study the nature of intelligence, one primary question concerned whether intelligence was best conceptualized as a general, unifying capacity along which people vary, or whether it should be thought of as composed of many separate and relatively independent abilities (Brody, 2000).

10-2a Early Factor-Analytic Studies Led to Conflicting Conclusions about General Intelligence

One researcher who explored this question in the 1920s was British psychologist Charles Spearman (1863–1945). To aid in his dissection of intelligence, Spearman helped develop a statistical technique called **factor analysis,** which allows researchers to identify clusters of test items that correlate with one another. By analyzing these correlations, researchers are in a better position to judge whether people's test performance can be accounted for by a single underlying ability (known as a *factor*) or whether multiple abilities (or *factors*) are needed. In essence, factor analysis helps researchers reduce the number of variables they are studying to a more manageable level by grouping together those that seem to be measuring the same thing. For example, if people who do well on reading tests also do well on writing and vocabulary tests, this suggests that some underlying "verbal ability" factor might be tapped by each of the individual performance measures. Moreover, if all the different intelligence abilities are highly correlated with one another, this might suggest that intelligence can be thought of as "one thing" rather than "many things."

Based on his factor-analytic research, Spearman (1927) concluded that there was indeed a **general intelligence factor,** or **g-factor,** underlying all mental abilities, and a set of specific factors (*s-factors*) underlying certain individual mental abilities. However, because the g-factor could predict performance on a variety of intelligence tests measuring math ability, vocabulary, and general knowledge, Spearman asserted that the g-factor was much more important than the specific factors. He and other researchers believed that this general factor, which involves the more complex, higher-level mental functions, provided the key to understanding intelligence.

Although the g-factor's relative simplicity was appealing to many researchers, others argued that a person's intellect could not be captured by a general factor. Leading this dissenting group was Louis Thurstone (1887–1955). Based on his own factor-analytic studies, Thurstone (1938) identified seven clusters of *primary mental abilities*: reasoning, verbal fluency, verbal comprehension, perceptual speed, spatial skills, numerical computation, and memory.

How could the same statistical technique, namely factor analysis, lead researchers to different conclusions? The answer is that, despite its reliance on sophisticated and objective mathematical formulas, factor analysis requires researchers to make a number of highly subjective decisions concerning how their data will be organized and interpreted. As a result, researchers with different assumptions about how intelligence is organized sometimes interpret the findings of factor analysis differently.

Which of these perspectives on intelligence prevails today? The current scientific reality is that there is solid evidence for both perspectives: A number of studies indicate that we have distinct mental abilities, but there is also evidence of a general intelligence factor (Carroll, 1993; Johnson et al., 2004). A number of PET-scan studies find that when people perform different cognitive tasks associated with spatial reasoning, verbal abilities, or perceptual-motor skills, the same brain area, the lateral frontal cortex, is activated (Anderson, 2005; Duncan et al., 2000). The fact that these different mental abilities rely on some of the same underlying neurological processes is consistent with the g-factor hypothesis. However, it is possible that the brain scans performed using current PET technology are not sensitive enough to detect activation of different subregions of the lateral frontal cortex when people are performing different cognitive tasks. In the future, a more sensitive brain-scanning

factor analysis A statistical technique that allows researchers to identify clusters of variables or test items that correlate with one another.

general intelligence factor (g-factor) An intelligence factor that Spearman and other researchers believed underlies all mental abilities.

device may find this different subregion activation. Such a discovery would be inconsistent with the hypothesis that the g-factor is associated with a single general cognitive process. Thus, until we can determine what different neural networks in this region of the brain are doing, the issue of the existence of a general intelligence factor remains open to debate.

10-2b Cattell Distinguished between Crystallized and Fluid Intelligence

Raymond B. Cattell (1963, 1971) agreed with Spearman's idea of general intelligence, but his own factor analyses suggested the existence of two kinds of g-factors, which he labeled *crystallized* and *fluid*. Later, his student and collaborator John Horn further developed this thinking (Horn, 1994; Horn & Cattell, 1966).

According to Cattell, some people demonstrate a remarkable ability to learn from their experiences, while others do not exhibit this mental capacity to nearly the same degree. **Crystallized intelligence** involves knowledge acquired through experience, such as the acquisition of facts and the ability to use and combine them. People with high crystallized intelligence are adept at using previously learned information to solve familiar problems (Schulze et al., 2005). In contrast to this type of general intelligence, Cattell proposed that we also have the ability to understand the relationships between things without having had past experience or practice with them. This **fluid intelligence** involves the mental capacity to learn or invent new strategies for dealing with new kinds of problems (see the "Psychological Applications" section, at the end of the chapter). One reason people with high fluid intelligence are very good at finding solutions to problems in new and unfamiliar situations is that they are less likely to fall prey to such internal mental obstacles as *mental set* and *functional fixedness* (see chapter 9, section 9-2c).

One appeal of Cattell's view of intelligence is that it makes no distinction regarding what kinds of things are learned and what kinds of strategies are used in solving problems. Because of this generality, the theory can be used to discuss intelligence in cultures that emphasize very different mental abilities. For example, while some cultures might be more likely to associate intelligence with abstract reasoning and mathematical abilities, other cultures might emphasize spatial and verbal abilities. By focusing on people's general ability to retain and use knowledge and their general ability to develop strategies to solve new challenges, this theory can be applied in any situational or cultural context (Geary, 2005a).

Existing research both supports and undermines Cattell's theory of two types of general intelligence. In terms of support, research on how intelligence changes with age suggests that it is useful to distinguish between crystallized and fluid intelligence (see figure 10-6). Numerous studies find that, while crystallized intelligence increases throughout the adult years and up to old age, fluid intelligence decreases slowly up to age 75 or so, and then more rapidly after that (Garlick, 2002; Rabbitt et al., 2003). On the other hand, despite this evidence supporting the distinction between crystallized and fluid intelligence, studies have

crystallized intelligence The ability to acquire knowledge through experience and to use that knowledge to solve familiar problems.

fluid intelligence The ability to understand the relationships between things in the absence of past experience and the mental capacity to develop strategies for dealing with new kinds of problems.

Figure 10-6

Life-Span Changes in Crystallized and Fluid Intelligence

While fluid intelligence declines as we age, crystallized intelligence increases throughout the adult years and up to old age. Given these different developmental tendencies, how would the average elderly person's ability to remember facts compare to that of the average young adult? How would the average elderly person's ability to solve new problems compare to that of the average young adult?

Source: From J. L. Horn and G. Donaldson, "On the Myth of Intellectual Decline in Adulthood" in *American Psychologist, 31,* 701–719. Copyright © 1976 by American Psychological Association.

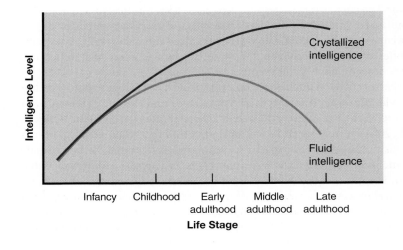

also consistently found a positive correlation between the two mental abilities. The fact that people who score high on crystallized intelligence also tend to score high on fluid intelligence suggests that they may be part of a more general factor of intelligence. In an attempt to settle this long-standing controversy concerning a general factor of intelligence, many modern theories propose that, although intelligence may encompass a general ability to deal with a wide variety of cognitive tasks and problems, it also can be expressed in many ways (Embretson & McCollam, 2000). That is, we can be highly "intelligent" in one or more mental abilities while being relatively "unintelligent" in others. Two recent theories that have continued to explore this diversity of intelligence are Howard Gardner's *theory of multiple intelligences* (see section 10-2c) and Robert Sternberg's *triarchic theory of intelligence* (see section 10-2d).

> **Journey *of* Discovery Question**
>
> How are Raymond B. Cattell's concepts of crystallized intelligence and fluid intelligence related to Jean Piaget's concepts of *assimilation* and *accommodation*, discussed in chapter 4, section 4-3a?

10-2c Gardner's Theory of Multiple Intelligences Broadens the Concept of Intelligence

When discussing gifted athletes, musicians, or carpenters, I'm sure you've heard people say, "They may be talented, but they sure aren't rocket scientists!" The implied meaning in such declarations is that talent is not intelligence. Howard Gardner (1983, 1993b) would not agree. While working at a veterans' hospital and observing people who had suffered brain damage, Gardner noticed that such injuries often resulted in the loss of one ability while leaving others unimpaired. Partly based on these observations, he developed the theory of **multiple intelligences,** which contends that the human brain has evolved separate systems for different adaptive abilities, and that what we call "intelligence" in our culture is simply a small cluster of these abilities. Rather than defining intelligence narrowly, Gardner supports Thurstone's view and identifies at least eight distinct and relatively independent intelligences, all of which are differently developed in each of us: linguistic or verbal, logical-mathematical, spatial, musical, bodily-kinesthetic, naturalist, interpersonal, and intrapersonal (Gardner, 1998; Gardner et al., 1996). The degree to which particular individuals develop these intellectual abilities largely depends on which ones are most highly valued in their culture.

Table 10-1 summarizes the multiple intellectual abilities described by Gardner. The first three on this list are most highly valued in Western culture, and thus they are the ones measured by conventional intelligence tests. A person with high *linguistic intelligence,* such as an author or public speaker, would be good at communicating through written and spoken language. A person with high *logical-mathematical intelligence,* such as an engineer or scientist, would be good at solving math problems and analyzing arguments. And a person with high *spatial intelligence,* such as a carpenter or air traffic controller, would be skilled at perceiving and arranging objects in the environment. Regarding the five less conventional forms of intelligence, *musical intelligence* entails the ability to analyze, compose, or perform music. *Bodily-kinesthetic intelligence* is displayed by our gifted athletes, dancers, and surgeons, but it is also necessary in ordinary activities, such as driving a car or hammering a nail. *Naturalist intelligence,* which relates to seeing patterns in nature, is an ability that forest rangers, ecologists, and zoologists must possess. Finally, *interpersonal intelligence* identifies the ability to interact well socially and to reliably predict others' motives and behavior, while *intrapersonal intelligence* is associated with insight into one's own motives and behavior. Recently, Gardner (1999, 2003) has also suggested a possible ninth intelligence, *existential intelligence,* which deals with the posing and pondering of large philosophical questions.

Although Gardner considers these different intelligences to be separate systems located in distinct brain areas, he does believe that they often interact to produce intelligent behavior. For example, skilled politicians rely heavily on linguistic intelligence when debating issues, but they also use logical-mathematical intelligence to critically analyze these issues and interpersonal

multiple intelligences Gardner's theory contends that there are at least eight distinct and relatively independent intelligences (linguistic, logical-mathematical, spatial, musical, bodily-kinesthetic, naturalist, interpersonal, and intrapersonal), all of which are differently developed in each of us.

Table 10-1 Gardner's Multiple Intelligences

Type of Intelligence	Description
Linguistic intelligence	Ability to communicate through written and spoken language: author, poet, public speaker, native storyteller
Logical-mathematical intelligence	Ability to solve math problems and analyze arguments: engineer, scientist, mathematician, navigator
Spatial intelligence	Ability to perceive and arrange objects in the environment: carpenter, air traffic controller, sculptor, architect
Musical intelligence	Ability to analyze, compose, or perform music: musician, singer, composer
Bodily-kinesthetic intelligence	Ability to control body motions to handle objects skillfully: athlete, dancer, surgeon, craftsperson
Naturalist intelligence	Ability to see patterns in nature: forest ranger, ecologist, zoologist, botanist
Interpersonal intelligence	Ability to interact well socially and to reliably predict others' motives and behavior: mental health therapist, salesperson, politician, fund-raiser
Intrapersonal intelligence	Ability to gain insight into one's own motives and behavior: meditator, essayist, stand-up comic
A Possible Ninth Intelligence	
Existential intelligence	Ability to pose and ponder large philosophical questions: philosopher, clergy

intelligence to understand what motivates voters (Bass, 2002). By combining skills in different intellectual domains into what Gardner calls a *profile of intelligences*, people can become competent in certain tasks or occupations even though they may not be particularly gifted in any specific intelligence (Gardner, 1991; Walters & Gardner, 1986). One of the challenges in life is to determine how you can use your particular talents to pursue a particular career path.

Howard Gardner's theory of multiple intelligences proposes that we have evolved separate brain systems for different mental abilities. Musical intelligence entails the ability to analyze, compose, or perform music.

Source: Courtesy of Figzoi.

Even though people often rely on multiple intelligences to accomplish goals, it is extremely rare to find the so-called Renaissance person who excels in all or several forms of intelligence. More frequently, a person with an extraordinary ability in one area will have relatively normal abilities in the others. The existence of **prodigies,** people who easily master skills in one intellectual area, supports Gardner's hypothesis that various types of intelligence exist and are relatively independent of one another. Besides prodigies, an even greater intellectual variance can be found among **savants,** who demonstrate exceptional ability in one specific area, such as music or drawing, while having very limited mental abilities in all other areas (Detterman et al., 2000; Treffert, 1992). In one such case, Harriet, an autistic child who did not speak until the age of 9, could hum a classic operatic piece in perfect pitch at the age of 7 months. By age 4, she had taught herself to read music, and she had also learned to play the piano, violin, clarinet, trumpet, and French horn. As an adult, although Harriet's IQ was only 73, her proficiency in music increased dramatically. She not only could identify and provide key details about any major symphony, but she also could play a tune in the style and manner of the composers of these symphonies (Treffert, 1989). As with prodigies, the existence of savants provides dramatic evidence for multiple intelligences (O'Connor et al., 2000).

Not everyone agrees with Gardner's theory. For instance, some critics question how athletic prowess can be considered a mental ability and instead believe that it should more properly be labeled a talent (Hoberman, 1997). Others charge that the list of eight (now, perhaps nine) intelligences is arbitrary and that it is simply wrong to deny the existence of a general intelligence factor (Brody, 1992). As research explores these challenges to the notion of multiple intelligences, we can conclude that how we think about intelligence has become much broader than it was even a few years ago.

10-2d Sternberg's Triarchic Theory Identifies Three Sets of Mental Abilities

> As an elementary-school student, I failed miserably on the IQ tests I had to take. I was incredibly test-anxious. Just the sight of the school psychologist coming into the classroom to give a group IQ test sent me into a wild panic attack. . . . For me, the game of taking the test was all but over before it even started. And the outcome was always the same: I lost. (Sternberg, 1996, p. 17)

Would you believe that the person who experienced this early academic trauma is now one of our leading intelligence experts? His name is Robert Sternberg, and his career provides a dramatic demonstration of how childhood experiences can motivate people to embark on scientific journeys of discovery that ultimately aid others in their personal quests. Following extensive interviews with ordinary people, Sternberg (1985, 1997) developed the belief that intelligence consists of much more than the abilities measured by traditional intelligence tests. Yet, while he agrees with Gardner's idea of multiple intelligences, Sternberg's **triarchic theory of intelligence** (*triarchic* means "ruled by threes") asserts that human intelligence can be more simply described as comprising three sets of mental abilities, not eight or nine (figure 10-7):

- *Analytical intelligence:* Required to solve familiar problems and to judge the quality of ideas. This is the type of intelligence that is valued on tests and in the classroom, and thus people who are high in analytical intelligence tend to score high on g-factor, or general intelligence. Analytical intelligence is somewhat similar to Cattell's crystallized intelligence (see section 10-2b).
- *Creative intelligence:* Required to develop new ways of solving problems (Sternberg & O'Hara, 2000). People with a high degree of creative intelligence have the ability to find connections between old and new information, combine facts that appear unrelated, and see the "big picture" (see the "Psychological Applications" section at the end of the chapter). Sternberg's creative intelligence is closely related to Cattell's notion of fluid intelligence (see section 10-2b).

prodigies Individuals who easily master skills in a particular intellectual area.

savants Mentally retarded individuals who demonstrate exceptional ability in one specific intellectual area.

triarchic theory of intelligence Sternberg's theory that three sets of mental abilities make up human intelligence: analytic, creative, and practical.

Figure 10-7

Sternberg's Triarchic Theory of Intelligence

According to Robert Sternberg, intelligence consists of analytical, creative, and practical abilities. You use analytical thinking to solve familiar problems, creative thinking to think about problems in new ways, and practical thinking to apply what you know to everyday situations. Of these three types of abilities, which do you think you employ most efficiently? More than one? Do you think that this self-understanding will influence your decisions about possible career paths?

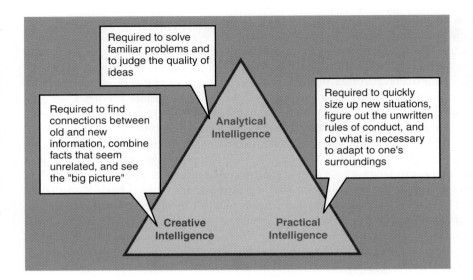

- *Practical intelligence:* Required to apply, utilize, and implement ideas in everyday situations. People who are high in practical intelligence have what we call "street smarts"; they are quick to size up new situations, figure out the unwritten rules of conduct, and do what is necessary to adapt to—and shape—their surroundings (Sternberg et al., 1995; Wagner, 2000). Unlike analytical intelligence, a person's level of practical intelligence does not predict her or his IQ score or academic achievement (Heng, 2000).

Although some tasks require us to utilize all three intelligences, the triarchic theory does not define intelligence according to our skill in all three aspects combined. Some people are more intelligent in solving abstract, theoretical problems, while others are more intelligent when the problems are concrete and practical. Research conducted by Sternberg (1997) suggests that people learn best—whether in school, on the job, or in daily living—if they are taught in a way that is compatible with their strongest type of intelligence. Thus, if you have high analytical intelligence, you might learn a good deal about many things in life by reading books and thinking abstractly about issues. However, if you have high practical intelligence, you might learn best by tossing the books and how-to manuals aside—getting your hands dirty and letting your wits carry you along. *Successful intelligence* is knowing when and how to use analytic, creative, and practical abilities (Sternberg, 2003). In this regard, Sternberg agrees with the message conveyed by Gardner's previously discussed notion of *profiles of intelligence:* People who are successfully intelligent will seek challenges that capitalize on their intellectual strengths and downplay their weaknesses. This is exactly what personnel departments try to do when selecting employees: match people's intellectual strengths with specific jobs within the organization. Successful organizations have workers who are skilled at analyzing existing problems, others who are best at using this analysis to create new ideas, and still others who can adeptly apply these new ideas to effective solutions.

Like Gardner's theory of multiple intelligences, the triarchic theory has its critics. Perhaps the most common question is whether practical intelligence is really different enough from academic intelligence to warrant thinking of it as a distinct intellectual ability (Brody, 2003; Gottfredson, 2003). Despite such lingering doubts, both these theories of multiple intelligences not only have broadened the discussion of intelligence but also have led an increasing number of intelligence researchers to recommend the development of new and improved tests to assess cognitive abilities (Harrison et al., 1997; Kaufman, 2000). If intelligence is more than just academic skill, we may need to move beyond traditional tests and theories of intelligence.

Einstein's theory of intelligence.

Source: © Vic Lee. King Features Syndicate.

10-2e Emotional Intelligence Allows Us to Understand and Regulate Our Emotional and Social Lives

If one function of intelligence is to predict what will happen next in our surroundings, and if an important part of what will happen next depends on how others behave, then we not only must predict others' behavior with some degree of accuracy but also must influence their behavior in desired directions. This *social intelligence* is believed to be part of our primate evolutionary heritage (Byrne, 1995), in that effective interpersonal coordination and planning probably increased the survival of our ancestors.

An important aspect of social intelligence is what various researchers have called **emotional intelligence,** which is the ability to recognize and regulate our own and others' emotions (Gohm, 2003; Mayer & Salovey, 1997). Individuals with high emotional intelligence are attentive to their own feelings, can accurately discriminate between them, and can use this information to guide their own thinking and actions (Mayer et al., 2000; Salovey et al., 2003). For example, when they experience negative moods, emotionally intelligent people try to create a more positive state of mind by doing something they enjoy or by finishing a task that will bring them a reward (Tice & Baumeister, 1993). In contrast, those who are less emotionally skilled tend to be "ruled" by their emotions: They not only have quick tempers, but also "stew in their own negative juices" when things don't go their way (Caprara et al., 1994, 1996; Salovey & Mayer, 1994). Of the two spectrums of emotional intelligence, which do you think leads to greater happiness and success?

Emotionally intelligent people are aware not only of their own emotional states but of others' as well (O'Sullivan, 2005). For example, in one study, participants being rated on their emotional intelligence watched a computer screen as people's faces morphed into different emotional expressions. The participants' task was to click a key as soon as they could identify the morphing expression. Results indicated that the emotionally intelligent participants were faster at identifying the expressions than were their less emotionally intelligent counterparts (Petrides & Furnham, 2003).

People with emotional intelligence are those we seek out when we are troubled. Their emotional attentiveness makes them sympathetic listeners, and their skill at managing social conflicts often provides us with good advice on how to resolve our difficulties. Due to their ability to accurately measure the "pulse" of social relationships, emotionally intelligent people get along well with others, have many friends, and often achieve great success in their careers (Salovey & Pizarro, 2003). Based on these findings, it isn't surprising that our skill at managing the emotional realm significantly determines the extent to which our lives are successful and fulfilling. Before reading further, spend a few minutes answering the items in Self-Discovery Questionnaire 10-1.

> **emotional intelligence** The ability to recognize and regulate our own and others' emotions.

Self-Discovery
Questionnaire **10-1**

What Is Your Level of Empathy for Others?

Instructions: One aspect of emotional intelligence is the ability to be attentive to others' feelings. *Empathy* is a feeling of compassion and tenderness toward those who encounter unfortunate life events. Research indicates that people differ in their levels of empathy. To discover your level of empathy or *empathic concern* for others, read each of the following items and then, using the following response scale, indicate how well each statement describes you.

0 = extremely uncharacteristic (not at all like me)
1 = uncharacteristic (somewhat unlike me)
2 = neither characteristic nor uncharacteristic
3 = characteristic (somewhat like me)
4 = extremely characteristic (very much like me)

____ 1. When I see people being taken advantage of, I feel kind of protective toward them.
____ 2. When I see people being treated unfairly, I sometimes don't feel very much pity for them.*
____ 3. I often have tender, concerned feelings for people less fortunate than me.
____ 4. I would describe myself as a pretty soft-hearted person.
____ 5. Sometimes, I don't feel very sorry for other people when they are having problems.*
____ 6. Other people's misfortunes do not usually disturb me a great deal.*
____ 7. I am often quite touched by things that I see happen.

Scoring your responses: Three of the items on this scale are reverse-scored; that is, for these items, a lower rating actually indicates a higher level of empathic concern or personal distress. Before summing the items, recode those with an asterisk (*) so that 0 = 4, 1 = 3, 3 = 1, and 4 = 0.

The mean score for female college students is about 22, while the mean score for male students is about 19 (Davis, 1996). The higher your score, the higher is your level of empathic concern for others.

Source: From *Empathy: A Social Psychological Approach* by Mark H. Davis. Copyright © 1996. Reprinted by permission of Westview Press, a member of Perseus Books, L.L.C.

People with emotional intelligence are sympathetic listeners, and we seek them out when we are troubled. Are emotionally intelligent people generally happier than those who are less emotionally intelligent?

Source: Copyright © 2007 Atomic Dog Publishing and its licensors. All rights reserved.

- Spearman's factor-analytic research suggests a general intelligence factor, or g-factor, underlying all mental abilities, and a set of specific factors (s-factors) underlying certain individual mental abilities.
- Cattell's theory defines intelligence as our ability to acquire knowledge through experience (crystallized intelligence) and our ability to find novel solutions to problems (fluid intelligence).
- Gardner's theory of multiple intelligences proposes eight separate abilities: linguistic, logical-mathematical, spatial, musical, bodily-kinesthetic, naturalist, interpersonal, and intrapersonal.
- According to Sternberg's triarchic theory, intelligence is composed of three sets of mental abilities: analytical, creative, and practical.
- Emotional intelligence helps us achieve and maintain personal and career success.

10-3   THE DYNAMICS OF INTELLIGENCE

Preview

- *Are the brains of intelligent people neurologically different from those of the less intelligent?*
- *How stable is intelligence from infancy to adulthood?*
- *What are common causes of mental retardation?*
- *Are mentally gifted individuals social misfits?*

We have all heard people described as "quick-witted" or "dim-witted." In this section, we examine individuals who differ substantially in their intelligence levels, and we analyze the degree to which IQ is fixed or changeable.

10-3a   Neuroscientists Try to Link Differences in Intelligence to Dissimilarities in People's Brains

How do people's intelligence test performances relate to dissimilarities in their brains? Neuroscientists have tried to answer this question by examining both brain anatomy and brain functioning.

Brain Anatomy

More than a century ago, Francis Galton believed that intelligence was related to the size of a person's head. Although Galton's research failed to find any valid evidence to support his hypothesis, more recent studies have found a small correlation ($r = +.15$) between head size and intelligence scores (Jensen & Johnson, 1994; Rushton & Rushton, 2003). Yet, because there is more inside the skull than just brain tissue, skull size is not a very accurate measure of brain size. When magnetic resonance imaging (MRI) scans directly measure brain volume, the resulting brain size and IQ score correlation (adjusted for body size) increases to a moderately high $+.44$ (Rushton, 1995; Rushton & Ankney, 1996).

What might explain this brain size–IQ correlation? Neuroscientists are unsure. One possibility relates to the fact that larger brains are known to have more neurons (Pakkenberg & Gunderson, 1997). The higher intelligence found among people with bigger brains may be due to a larger number of neural connections and a correspondingly greater cognitive capacity in their brains (Vernon et al., 2000). One problem with this "greater neuron" explanation is that men, on average, have about 4 billion (or 16 percent) more neurons than do women, but they do not outscore them on IQ tests (Pakkenberg & Gunderson, 1997). In addition, archeological records indicate that Neanderthals had larger brains than modern humans, but no scientists have suggested that our extinct hominid cousins were more intelligent than us.

Another possibility is that the brain size–IQ correlation is related to different levels of *myelin* in the brain (Miller, 1994). As you recall from chapter 3, section 3-1a, the myelin sheath is the protective coating of glial cells around an axon that hastens the transmission of the neuron's electrochemical charge and also supplies the neuron with support, nutrients, and insulation.

Another problem with using brain size to predict intelligence is that scientific research (reviewed in this chapter; see section 10-2a) suggests that intelligence is associated with specific areas of the brain, not the brain as a whole. Therefore, if brain size is related to intelligence, it is probably not overall brain size but the size of crucial areas that matters. Perhaps a dramatic example will best illustrate this point. When people think about the smartest individuals who ever lived, physicist Albert Einstein is usually near the top of everyone's list. When Einstein died in 1955, his brain was removed and preserved. Later examination found that the overall size of this brilliant man's brain was only average. However, his brain had an unusually large number of glial cells, particularly in the bottom portions of the left parietal lobe, which is a brain area involved in mathematical reasoning (Dehaene et al., 1999; Gardner et al., 1996). These "extra" glial cells may have helped this area of Einstein's brain function faster and more efficiently. A more recent analysis of Einstein's brain also discovered that both his left and right parietal lobes were 15 percent wider than normal (Witelson et al., 1999). Of course, the findings from this single case study do not mean that overall brain size is not related to intelligence, but they do suggest that the relation between brain size and intelligence is far from clear.

Brain Functioning

The possibility that intelligence might be related to myelin is one of the reasons intelligence researchers have devoted a great deal of attention to the brain's processing speed. A number of studies indicate that intelligence is partly based on neural complexity, quickness, and efficiency (Haier, 2003; Vernon et al., 2000). For example, IQ scores tend to be correlated with the complexity of electrical activity in the brain: When responding to simple stimuli, high scorers have more complex brain patterns than low scorers (Barrett & Eysenck, 1992; Caryl, 1994). Regarding neural "quickness," the speed at which neural impulses travel (see figure 10-8) is positively correlated with IQ—about +.40—suggesting that intelligent people are literally more quick-witted than the less intelligent (McGarry-Roberts et al., 1992; Vernon & Mori, 1992). Finally, additional studies suggest that smarter brains are not only quick and complex but also efficient (Jausovek & Jausovek, 2003). Using PET scans, Richard Haier and his coworkers (1992, 1995) found that the brains of people with higher intelligence tend to consume less *glucose*—a simple sugar required for brain activity—while working on problem-solving tasks than they do normally. They also found evidence suggesting that the brains of intelligent people become more efficient with practice than the brains of those with less intelligence. That is, after practicing a relatively complex computer game, intelligent participants' brains subsequently consumed less glucose overall when playing this game than normally, even though certain brain areas actually consumed more glucose. Haier and his coworkers contend that, by concentrating the processing of information to relatively small areas of their brains, intelligent people use their

Figure 10-8

An Inspection Time Task

In a typical experiment measuring neural "quickness," researchers often study how fast participants can process perceptual information presented to them. An incomplete stimulus is quickly flashed on a computer screen, but its lingering afterimage is immediately hidden (or *masked*) by another stimulus. In this example, the participant would then be asked whether the long side of the original stimulus appeared on the left or the right. Researchers determine how much time participants need to inspect the stimulus in order to answer such questions correctly 80 percent of the time. Participants who need less time to correctly answer these questions tend to score higher on intelligence tests.

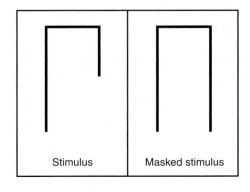

brains more efficiently than they otherwise would. Although the origins of these biological differences in brain functioning could be genetic, the fact that greater efficiency is achieved with practice suggests that these differences also develop from experience. Together, these findings suggest that intelligence is a product of both our biology *(nature)* and our experience *(nurture)*.

10-3b Intelligence Becomes More Stable with Age, but It Is Far from Fixed

Is intelligence—as measured by IQ—a stable characteristic, or does it change throughout our lives? This question has intrigued psychologists for many years. Because infants cannot talk and have limited attention spans, studying the stability of intelligence early in life is difficult. Indeed, reliable assessments of IQ generally cannot be obtained until children reach the age of about 3 or 4 years. Despite this impediment, Joseph Fagan (1992) has devised an indirect intellectual assessment technique that tests infants' preferences for visual novelty. In this test, infants are shown pairs of pictures on a screen. For each showing, one of the pictures has been previously seen by the infant, while the other is new. Findings indicate that babies between the ages of 2 and 7 months who spend more time looking at the novel stimuli later tend to score higher than others on childhood intelligence tests (McCall & Carriger, 1993). Fagan's test can also identify 85 percent of babies who are later diagnosed as mentally retarded. Thus, although this simple measure of infant attention and processing is not a *true* intelligence test in the classic sense, it does appear useful in identifying children who are later likely to score very high or very low on conventional intelligence tests. In this sense, it provides evidence of stability in intelligence even during infancy. As illustrated in figure 10-9, once children reach the age of 7 or 8, IQ scores begin to predict later IQ scores reasonably well (Bayley, 1949; Sameroff et al., 1993).

Does this increased stability with age mean that IQ scores are fixed and unchanging? Although Henry Goddard held this viewpoint during the early days of intelligence testing, most contemporary researchers believe that intelligence is pliable, and that the thinking skills associated with IQ scores can be improved through learning (Halpern, 1996; Sternberg, 1996). For example, considerable evidence indicates that exposing children to healthy and stimulating environments can enhance their performance on IQ tests (Grotzer & Perkins, 2000). In one longitudinal study, inner-city children who received a great deal of intellectual stimulation at home and in day care or school had, by age 12, average IQ scores 15 to 30 points higher than those of inner-city children who were not exposed to enriching environments (Campbell & Ramey, 1994, 1995).

What impact do enriched environments have on the brain? Claire Rampon and her coworkers (2000) explored this question by manipulating the environment of genetically identical mice. First, the researchers randomly divided baby mice into separate groups and then exposed them to different levels of an enriched environment. For the mice, this meant being placed into cages with fewer or more toys, tunnels, and boxes to explore and manipulate. In

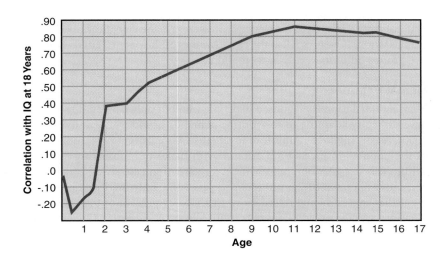

Figure 10-9

The Stabilization of IQ Scores with Age

When IQ scores obtained at age 17 are plotted with IQ scores obtained at earlier ages, the correlations before the age of 5 or 6 are below .50, but they rise in the range of .70 to .80 by the time children are 7 and 8 years old. What might account for this increased stability with age?

subsequent testing, Rampon and her colleagues found that the mice in the more enriched environments later exhibited greater learning and memory abilities than the mice in the more impoverished environments. Equally important were the differences found in the mice's brains. The "enriched" mice developed higher levels of neuronal structure, synaptic signaling, and plasticity. Their enriched environments had literally fostered greater brain growth and neural speed.

How can enriched environments be established in humans? The quality of interaction between adults and children is of primary importance in this regard. Following are some steps that adults can take to foster mental growth in children (Bradley & Caldwell, 1984; Dweck, 1990, 1992; Whitehurst et al., 1994):

- Read to young children, asking them open-ended questions about the stories ("What is the Daddy doing?") rather than simple yes or no questions ("Is the Daddy cleaning the house?").
- Talk to children in detail about many topics, and carefully answer their questions.
- Expand on children's answers, correct inaccurate responses, and emphasize the process of learning rather than its product.
- Encourage children to think through problems rather than to simply guess at solutions.

One of the more impressive intellectual-skills training programs ever developed was *Project Intelligence,* which was implemented in Venezuela during the 1980s, when that country had a Ministry for the Development of Intelligence. Created by a group of Harvard researchers, this program consisted of six units of instruction in analytical and creative skills composed of about 100 lessons (Adams, 1986; Perkins, 1995). For example, a lesson on creative thinking might require students to ponder the purposes of an ordinary object, such as a pencil. What can you use it for? What features does it have? Another lesson on problem solving might emphasize various strategies, such as trial and error, heuristics, and algorithms. Each lesson included ample practice time, including individual and group exercises.

When 450 seventh-grade Venezuelan children were evaluated after being taught an abbreviated form of Project Intelligence, their IQ scores showed an increase of about seven points more than gains experienced by a control group of students. Unfortunately, a change in the political party in power in Venezuela made such programs become available to children on only a limited basis. Due to government cutbacks in further developing and testing of these programs, we do not know whether Project Intelligence enhanced the academic performance of the children whose IQ scores were raised; however, the initial findings suggest that intelligence can be raised through training (Herrnstein et al., 1986). One of the interesting footnotes to this story is that the primary author of this careful evaluation of Project Intelligence was Richard Herrnstein, an intelligence researcher who figures prominently in an ongoing controversy discussed later in this chapter (see section 10-4c).

10-3c The "Challenged" and the "Gifted" Are the Two Extremes of Intelligence

One controversial area of intellectual assessment is the classification and education of individuals whose IQ scores fall at the two extremes of the normal curve. Not surprisingly, these two groups differ markedly in their abilities.

Mental Retardation

mental retardation
A diagnostic category used for people who not only have an IQ score below 70 but also have difficulty adapting to the routine demands of independent living.

Mental retardation is diagnosed in people who not only have an IQ score below 70 but also have difficulty adapting to the routine demands of independent living (Detterman et al., 2000). According to the American Psychiatric Association (1994), only about 1 to 2 percent of the population meets both criteria, with males outnumbering females by 50 percent. Within this designation are four mental retardation categories, which vary in severity. As you can see in table 10-2, most retarded people are only mildly retarded.

What causes mental retardation? In about 25 percent of the cases, doctors are able to identify a specific organic cause (Yeargin-Allsopp et al., 1997). Organic conditions that can cause retardation are infections or malnutrition in the pregnant mother or young child, poisoning of the developing fetus or young child by harmful substances (such as alcohol or

Table **10-2** Degrees of Mental Retardation

Level	Typical IQ Scores	Percentage of the Retarded	Adaptation to Demands of Life
Mild	50–70	85%	May learn academic skills up to the sixth-grade level. With assistance, adults often can learn self-supporting social and vocational skills.
Moderate	35–49	10%	May progress to second-grade level. Within sheltered workshops, adults can contribute to their own support through manual labor.
Severe	20–34	<4%	May learn to talk and to perform simple work tasks under close supervision, but are generally unable to profit from vocational training.
Profound	Below 20	<2%	Limited motor development and little or no speech. Require constant aid and supervision.

Source: Reprinted with permission from the *Diagnostic and Statistical Manual of Mental Disorders,* Fourth Edition. Copyright © 1994 American Psychiatric Association.

lead; see the discussion of teratogens in chapter 4, section 4-1b), premature birth, and trauma to the infant's head.

Also included among organic causes are genetic disorders, the most common being **Down syndrome,** which is caused by an extra chromosome in either the mother's egg (the primary source) or the father's sperm (Gardner & Sutherland, 1996). The production of this extra chromosome is strongly related to maternal age. Among mothers under the age of 33, the rate of Down syndrome is only 0.9 per 1,000 live births. This rate increases to 3.8 in mothers 44 years of age or older (Grigorenko, 2000). Characteristic signs of Down syndrome are a small head, nose, ears, and hands; slanting eyes; short neck; and thin hair. Individuals with this disorder have IQs in the mild to severe range of retardation. When given proper training and placed in a supportive family environment, many people with Down syndrome can care for themselves, hold a job, and lead happy, fulfilling lives.

Approximately 75 percent of mental retardation cases cannot be linked to any organic cause; instead, they are thought to result from unfavorable social conditions or subtle and difficult-to-detect physiological effects (Handen, 1997). Most of these cases tend to involve less severe forms of mental retardation, and children from low-income families are 10 times more likely to be classified in this manner than those from the general population.

During the 1950s and 1960s, schoolchildren with mild retardation were placed in *special education classes,* where they received instruction designed for their ability level. However, beginning in the 1970s, educational researchers recommended *mainstreaming,* a policy in which retarded children are educated with normal children. The goal of mainstreaming is to integrate the retarded as fully as possible into the normal educational environment, but the reality is that they are frequently teased and ridiculed by their nonretarded classmates (Marks, 1997). Although some evidence indicates that sustained in-class contact leads to more positive attitudes toward retarded children, there is also evidence that such contact leads to resentment due to some students' perception that their retarded classmates are receiving greater attention and consideration from teachers (Bowers, 1997; Nabuzoka & Ronning, 1997). Given these conflicting findings, it is not currently clear whether mainstreaming is a more effective educational policy than special education, but U.S. federal law mandates mainstreaming whenever possible (Farrell, 1997; Susan, 1990).

One impediment to integrating the mentally retarded into mainstream society is the ridicule and prejudice they often face from people with average or above-average

Down syndrome A form of mental retardation caused by an extra chromosome in an individual's genetic makeup.

Doing easily what others find difficult is talent; doing what is impossible for talent is genius.

—*Henri-Frederic Amiel, Swiss critic, 1821–1881*

intelligence. Have you witnessed expressions of such intolerance toward the mentally retarded? Armed with the knowledge you now possess, what information could you convey to people who express negative attitudes and beliefs toward those who are mentally handicapped?

Mental Giftedness

What does it mean to be "gifted"? For some psychologists, the term is reserved for people with IQs above 130 or 135. Other psychologists supplement this criterion with additional requirements, such as exceptional school or career achievement. Consistent with recent theories of multiple intelligences, U.S. federal law specifies that giftedness should be based on superior potential in any of six areas: general intelligence, specific aptitudes (for example, math and writing), performing arts, athletics, creativity, and leadership (Callahan, 2000). Although more school districts are beginning to identify gifted students based on these broader standards, most continue to emphasize IQ scores (Fields, 1997).

What causes giftedness? Obviously, genes and environment play an important role in the creation of giftedness, but their degree of contribution is not yet clear. Some recent studies indicate that gifted girls may have higher levels of the male hormone *testosterone* than nongifted girls, while gifted boys may have lower testosterone levels than nongifted boys (Dohnanyiova et al., 2000; Ostatnikova et al., 2001). These findings suggest that biological factors predispose some people toward giftedness.

Regarding the education of gifted students, one concern has been that they are not adequately challenged by the regular school curriculum (Gottfried et al., 1994; Keen & Howard, 2002). To address this concern, educators have developed two separate intervention strategies. *Acceleration* involves early admission to school and encouraging gifted students to skip grades. *Enrichment*, in contrast, keeps gifted students in their normal grade level but supplements their course work with advanced material, independent study projects, and other special learning experiences. Both intervention strategies can be effective, but many gifted students in these programs still complain that their classes move too slowly, involve too much repetition of already mastered material, and place too much emphasis on the mastery of facts rather than the use of thinking skills (Gallagher et al., 1997). One problem is that these programs are underfunded. Compared to the money provided for the education of mentally retarded students, little money is spent on education for gifted children, especially those who are poor or live in rural areas (Winner, 1997).

One common belief about gifted individuals is that their "gift" is really a curse because it makes them social misfits who lead lonely, unsatisfied lives. Is this stereotype true? In an attempt to answer this question, in 1921 Lewis Terman began tracking the lives of over 1,500 California children with IQs above 135 (Terman, 1925). Over the course of the next 70 years, Terman and later researchers discovered that, by and large, these men and women led healthy, well-adjusted lives and experienced slightly more successful marriages and much more successful careers than the average person (Holahan & Sears, 1995; Terman & Oden, 1947). Other longitudinal studies of gifted individuals have replicated these findings (Janos & Robinson, 1985; Subotnik et al., 1989). Thus, counter to prevailing stereotypes, research clearly indicates that children with high IQs are less likely to be social misfits than their less gifted counterparts.

Children identified as extremely gifted (top 1 in 10,000) are much more likely than their nongifted counterparts to pursue doctoral degrees as adults, and many of these individuals create noteworthy literary, scientific, or technical products by their early 20s (Lubinski et al., 2001). However, childhood giftedness does not guarantee adult eminence. For example, although the "Termanites" (as they affectionately called themselves) generally grew up to be very successful adults in their chosen careers, very few became the best and brightest members of their generation (Pyryt, 1993). Thus, although IQ is an important contributor, in the final analysis it is only one factor determining a person's life accomplishments. This is certainly good news to the vast majority of us who do not fall within the 1 percent upper realm of the IQ normal distribution!

Is this your stereotype of gifted students? Does research support this stereotype? How do the lives of gifted people differ from those of the average person? Do you suppose the persistence of this stereotype might have something to do with salving the self-esteem of those of us with merely average intelligence?

Source: © Stockbyte/PictureQuest.

- Intelligence is partly based on neural complexity, quickness, and efficiency.
- The stability of intelligence increases from infancy to adulthood.
- Enriched environments can increase IQ scores.
- Seventy-five percent of mental retardation cases result from harmful environmental or subtle physiological effects; 25 percent are linked to organic causes.
- Gifted students are less likely to be social misfits than are nongifted students.

10-4 HEREDITARY AND ENVIRONMENTAL INFLUENCES ON INTELLIGENCE

Preview

- *What do twin studies tell us about the nature-nurture link?*
- *Are gender and racial differences reflected in IQ scores?*
- *How can cultural expectations influence IQ scores and academic achievement?*
- *What is a self-fulfilling prophecy, and how is it related to intellectual development?*

As discussed in the chapter-opening vignette, most early intelligence researchers claimed that intelligence is inherited. However, this assertion was soon challenged by other scientists, who believed that environmental factors, such as social class, family conditions, and educational opportunities, were more important than genetic makeup. This nature-nurture controversy remains an important issue in the study of intelligence (Schaie, 2005). Its fundamental question is this: To what degree is intelligence determined by heredity, and to what degree is it determined by the physical and social environment in which we are raised?

The scientific answer to this question has important social implications (Sternberg & Kaufman, 2002). For instance, in 1969, the psychologist Arthur Jensen claimed that up to 80 percent of intelligence is due to heredity. Based on this claim, he argued that intellectual-skills training programs, such as Head Start, were a waste of taxpayers' money. Both Jensen's analysis and his policy recommendations were sharply challenged by environmentally based researchers. At the heart of this scientific debate were studies of twins and studies of adoptive families.

10-4a Twin and Adoption Studies Indicate That Both Genes and Environment Influence Intelligence

Psychologists and behavior geneticists who study the heritability of intelligence express the degree to which heredity determines intelligence within a particular human group in terms of a **heritability coefficient,** which ranges from 0 to 1. A coefficient of 0 would mean that heredity has no influence on intelligence, while a coefficient of 1 would mean that heredity is the only influence. As with most of the intelligence testing conducted today, heritability coefficient estimates are almost always based on standard IQ tests, which define intelligence primarily in terms of analytic and verbal ability (Petrill et al., 1996; Saudino et al., 1994). To gain a better understanding of heritability research, let us first examine studies of twins and then turn our attention to adoption studies.

heritability coefficient
A statistical coefficient, ranging from 0 to 1, that estimates the degree to which heredity determines intelligence within a particular human group.

Twin Studies

Why would researchers studying the role of genetic factors in intelligence be so interested in studying identical and fraternal twins? As you learned in chapter 3, identical twins have identical genes, while fraternal twins share only about half the same genes. The rationale for studying twins is that they are normally raised in similar environments. If the IQ scores of identical twins are more similar than those of fraternal twins, this presumably would be due to their greater genetic similarity. Or would it?

Figure 10-10

**Studies of IQ Similarity:
The Nature-Nurture Debate**

The results of over 100 studies correlating the IQ scores of people with different genetic and environmental backgrounds found that the most genetically similar people had the most similar IQ scores. Do these findings suggest that intelligence is partly inherited? How do the other findings reported here support the argument that intelligence is partly determined by environmental factors?

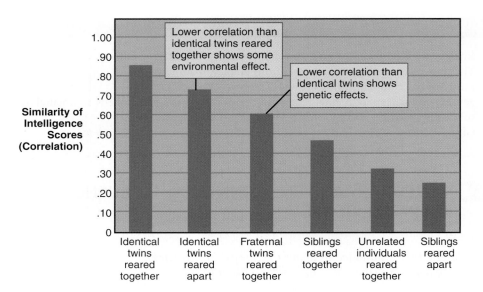

As you can see from figure 10-10, the findings of more than 100 twin studies indicate that the average correlation of identical twins' IQ scores is .86, while that of fraternal twins is significantly lower, .60 (Bouchard & McGue, 1981; McGue et al., 1993). These results seem to support the genetic contribution to intelligence. However, these same twin studies also point to environmental effects on intelligence (Lytton & Gallagher, 2002). Fraternal twins—who are genetically no more similar than regular siblings, but who are exposed to more similar experiences due to their identical ages—have more similar IQ scores than do other siblings. In addition, nontwin siblings raised together have more similar IQs (r = .47) than siblings raised apart (r = .24). Together, do these findings suggest that genes and environment both contribute to intelligence, but that genes have a larger influence?

That is a reasonable conclusion, but environmentally oriented researchers argue that the higher IQ correlations among identical twins than among fraternal twins may be substantially caused by environmental factors. According to this argument, fraternal twins' environments often are not as similar as are the environments of identical twins, especially if the fraternal twins are not the same sex. Parents of identical twins tend to treat them more alike than do parents of fraternal twins, often even dressing them identically. Perhaps it is this greater environmental similarity that explains the higher IQ correlations among the identical twins than among the fraternal twins.

Genetically oriented researchers respond that identical twins raised apart still have higher IQ correlations (r = .72) than fraternal twins raised together (r = .60). Isn't this convincing evidence for genetic effects? Maybe not, say the environmentally oriented researchers. These higher IQ correlations for identical twins reared apart may be due to *prenatal environmental factors.* About two-thirds of identical twins share the same placenta and amniotic sac in the uterus, which makes their prenatal environment more alike than that of fraternal twins, who are almost always in separate sacs (Phelps et al., 1997). Twins in the same sac share the same blood, which contains chemicals that affect brain development. Perhaps the high IQ correlations among identical twins separated at birth are due to early shared environment, as well as to shared genes.

Adoption Studies

Given the competing ways in which twin study findings can be interpreted, researchers have sought further clues among adopted children. Why would researchers want to compare the IQ correlations of adopted children with their biological versus adoptive parents? Put simply, biological parents supply these children with their genes, while adoptive parents provide their environment. If heredity matters more than environment, the children's IQ scores should correlate higher with their biological parents' IQ scores than with their adoptive parents' scores. The reverse finding should occur if environment matters more than heredity.

A number of adoption studies have found that children who were adopted within 2 weeks to 1 year of birth later had higher IQ correlations with their biological parents than

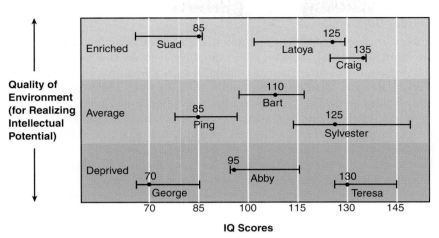

Figure 10-11

Reaction Range

Reaction range indicates the extent to which the environment can raise or lower IQ scores, given the preexisting hereditary limits. Each person has her or his own individual reaction range. People who grow up in enriched environments should score at the top of their reaction range, while those who grow up in impoverished settings should score closer to the bottom of their range.

with their adoptive parents (Horn, 1983; Scarr & Weinberg, 1983; Turkheimer, 1991). Furthermore, many of these same studies find that as adopted children grow up, their IQ correlation with their biological parents doesn't decrease—it increases! How could this be, if environment is more important than genetics in determining intelligence? These and other findings suggest that heredity makes a somewhat larger contribution to IQ scores than does environment (Loehlin et al., 1989, 1997; Teasdale & Owen, 1984).

Although adoption studies point toward a substantial hereditary contribution to intelligence, they also report significant environmental influences. For instance, in France, the IQ scores of lower-class children adopted by upper-class families were compared with the IQ scores of their siblings who had not been adopted (Capron & Duyme, 1989; Schiff et al., 1978). Although the average adopted children's scores in these studies ranged between 104 and 111, the average scores for their brothers and sisters reared in the original lower-class households ranged between 92 and 95, a significant difference. Furthermore, when children of upper-class parents were adopted, their later average IQ score was 120 if their adoptive parents were from upper-class families, but only 108 if they were adopted by lower-class families.

Based on the twin and adoption studies combined, the best estimate is that heredity accounts for a little over 50 percent of the variation in intelligence, with environmental factors responsible for a little less than 50 percent. However, this does not mean that a little over half of *your* intelligence is inherited and a little less than half is environmentally influenced. It simply means that genetics and environmental factors are respectively responsible for a bit more and a bit less than about half the differences among individuals in the population.

So how do genes and environment interact in determining intelligence? The concept of **reaction range** provides a possible answer (see figure 10-11). Our genes establish a range of potential intellectual growth, and our environmental experiences interact with our genetic makeup in determining where we ultimately fall in this reaction range (Mann, 1994). For example, children with a natural aptitude for writing are most likely to spend leisure time writing and also to select writing and literature courses in high school. If their parents and teachers further nourish this natural aptitude by offering them enrichment opportunities, their skills are further enhanced. Thus, their subsequently high scores on verbal aptitude tests are due to both their natural ability and their experience.

reaction range The extent to which genetically determined limits on IQ may increase or decrease due to environmental factors.

10-4b There Are Group Differences in IQ Scores

As discussed at the beginning of this chapter, claims about group differences in intelligence have often been used to rationalize racial, ethnic, and gender discrimination. For this reason, claims about group differences must be subjected to very careful analysis. In this section, we will examine research regarding gender differences in intelligence and then focus on racial differences.

Gender Differences

Although male and female IQ scores are virtually identical, a few differences in certain aptitudes are worth mentioning (Halpern, 2000; Lynn, 1994). Females tend to do better on verbal aptitude tests, such as naming synonyms and verbal fluency, while males tend to do better on visual-spatial tests, such as mental rotation and tracking a moving object through space (Law et al., 1993; Stanley, 1993). These gender differences have been found in at least 30 countries around the world (Beller & Gafni, 1996; Vogel, 1996). As discussed in chapter 3, section 3-3f, some studies suggest that these female-male differences in verbal and spatial abilities might be linked to sex differences in the organization of those areas of the cerebral hemispheres controlling verbal and spatial abilities and to hormonal fluctuations (Gur et al., 1999; Shaywitz et al., 1995). Other studies suggest that these differences are a product of gender socialization and the different skills taught to girls and boys (Crawford et al., 1995). For example, girls not only receive greater encouragement to talk during infancy and early childhood than do boys, but also in school are more likely to be praised for their reading and writing, while boys are more often encouraged to play sports and engage in other activities that develop their visual-spatial skills.

Gender differences have also been found in mathematical ability. For example, in the 60-item SAT math test, male high school seniors average about four more correct answers than their female counterparts (Halpern, 2000; Held et al., 1993). Are these differences caused by genetics, socialization, or some combination of the two? In January 2005, Harvard University President Lawrence Summers was roundly criticized for publicly stating that he wondered whether the low representation of women in the fields of mathematics and engineering might be caused by women being genetically deficient to men in math abilities. What does the research literature tell us about this group difference? In contrast to the substantial gender differences found in verbal and spatial abilities (about one standard deviation), math differences are relatively small and appear to be disappearing (Feingold, 1992a; Hyde et al., 1990; Masters & Sanders, 1993). Overall, despite the fact that these gender differences are small, they have a considerable impact on the gender composition of undergraduate and graduate college programs that require extensive mathematical knowledge and skills. In general, men are more likely than women to score very high or very low on tests of mathematical ability. In fact, men are seven times more likely than women to score in the top one percentile on math tests used for college admissions. For example, many colleges use the Physics C (Mechanics) College Board Advanced Placement Test to select incoming students for their accelerated and advanced physics and science courses and programs. However, as you can see in figure 10-12, a much higher percentage of male students than female students achieves the highest grade (5) on this test. This means that many more men than women are being admitted to the top science and engineering programs. These gender differences probably do not reflect any innate differences

Figure 10-12

Gender Differences in Physics Advanced Placement Exam Grades

Colleges often use the Physics C (Mechanics) College Board Advanced Placement Test to select incoming students for their accelerated and advanced physics and science courses and programs. The highest grade level that a student can attain on this exam is a 5. How might the gender difference depicted in this figure have an impact on who is admitted to elite math and science programs in college or who receives academic scholarships to those programs?

Source: From "Stability and change in gender-related differences on the College Board Advanced Placement and Achievement Tests" by H. Stumpf and J. C. Stanley in *Current Directions in Psychological Science,* 1998, 192–196.

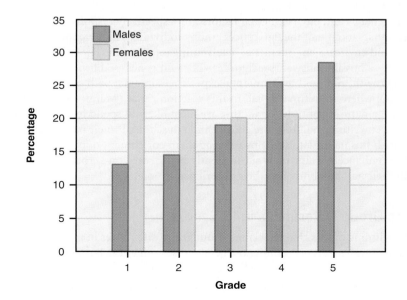

between men and women but, instead, may be due to cultural stereotypes and the resulting ways in which we socialize men and women to think about their mathematical abilities.

Racial Differences

In the United States, African Americans score between 10 and 15 points lower on intelligence tests than White Americans, whose IQ averages are about 100 (Bracken et al., 1993; Williams & Ceci, 1997). Hispanic Americans achieve IQ scores somewhere in between those of Blacks and Whites, and Asian Americans score about 5 points higher than Whites (Lynn, 1996; McShane & Plas, 1984). Although research suggests that the average IQ scores for Black children have risen over the past 20 years, these group-based IQ differences persist (Hauser, 1998; Neisser et al., 1996). As mentioned in section 10-1d, critics of conventional intelligence tests argue that these group differences are caused by culturally biased test items, but defenders of these tests respond that these differences also occur on nonverbal test items—such as counting digits backward—that do not appear to be culturally biased against ethnic minorities.

In making sense of these findings, we must remember that group differences tell us nothing about the intellectual ability of any specific person (Helms, 2004). As you can see in figure 10-13, tens of millions of African-American and Hispanic individuals have IQs higher than those of the average White or Asian American. Yet, if heredity influences individual differences in intelligence, does it also substantially explain these group differences?

Yes, according to psychologist Arthur Jensen. Three decades ago, he claimed that "between one-half and three-fourths of the average IQ difference between American Negroes and whites is attributable to genetic factors," such as differences in the rate of information-processing (Jensen, 1973, p. 363). As mentioned, Jensen argued that, on this basis, training programs to enhance the IQs of Black children would have limited success. As you might guess, the social and political implications of this hypothesis landed like a bombshell in the scientific community, and many denounced its author as a racist. Fortunately, the controversy also generated a great deal of research.

Among the subsequent studies, Sandra Scarr's work is a good example of how different research methods were used to test Jensen's hypothesis. In her first line of research, Scarr and Richard Weinberg (1976) examined the IQs of lower-class Black and White children adopted by both Black and White middle-class families. They found that adopted African-American children had an average IQ of 110, more than 20 points higher than those of children who had been raised in their original lower-class African-American families. Even when these adopted children reached adulthood, their IQ scores remained 10 points higher than those of African Americans raised in lower-class Black families (Weinberg et al., 1992). The researchers concluded from these findings that Black-White IQ differences in the general population are substantially affected by environmental factors, such as unequal economic and educational conditions.

On a second research front, Scarr and her colleagues (1977) examined the chemical composition of blood among African Americans. Because many African Americans have European ancestors, Scarr reasoned that if Black-White IQ differences were predominantly

Figure 10-13

Racial Differences in IQ Scores

The average score of Asian Americans on IQ tests is about 3 to 5 points higher than White Americans' average score of 100. White Americans, in turn, average about 7 points higher than Hispanic Americans and 10 to 15 points higher than African Americans. However, as you can see by examining the graph, the IQ variation *within* these groups is much greater than the differences among their average IQ scores.

Sources: Data from N. J. Mackintosh. (1998). *IQ and human intelligence.* Oxford: Oxford University Press. Neisser, U. (1998). *The rising curve: Long-term gains in IQ and related measures.* Washington, DC: American Psychological Association. Herrnstein, R. J., & Murray, C. (1994). *The bell curve: Intelligence and class structure in American life.* New York: The Free Press.

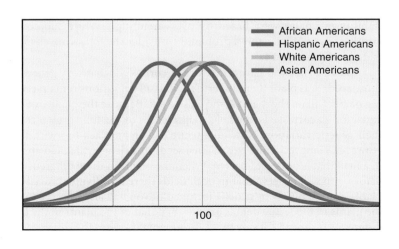

African Americans
Hispanic Americans
White Americans
Asian Americans

100

caused by genetics, then African Americans with a greater proportion of European ancestry in their blood should have the highest IQ scores. Counter to Jensen's genetic hypothesis, however, no correlation was found between IQ and racial ancestry. In fact, virtually all the studies that have sought to find the source of these Black-White IQ differences have failed to find evidence for genetic effects (Eyeferth, 1961; Lewontin, 1995; Loehlin et al., 1973; Nisbett, 1995). Based on the converging findings from these different research avenues, although Jensen's genetic hypothesis cannot be completely ruled out, Scarr and her colleagues conclude that it is "highly unlikely" that genetic differences between the races cause the observed group differences in IQ scores (Waldman et al., 1994).

10-4c Genetic Explanations of Group IQ Score Differences Remain Highly Controversial

Despite the meager evidence for a genetic explanation of racial differences in IQ, in 1994 this controversy was reignited when the psychologist Richard Herrnstein and the conservative political theorist Charles Murray published their book, *The Bell Curve: Intelligence and Class Structure in American Life*. Based on their review of other researchers' work, these authors claimed that intelligence is largely inherited, that intelligence overwhelmingly determines socioeconomic status, that the nation's intelligence level is declining because low-IQ people are having more children than high-IQ people, and that intellectual-training programs will do little to help the poor. They further argued that African Americans are disproportionately poor, because as a group, they score lower on IQ tests than White Americans and, therefore, are inherently less intelligent. Many scientists, social policy makers, and ordinary citizens were disturbed that Herrnstein and Murray's claims bore a striking similarity to the claims advanced in the nineteenth and early twentieth centuries by the eugenics movement (refer back to section 10-1a).

As with Jensen's claims in the 1970s, Herrnstein and Murray's proposals were strongly challenged by many psychologists, who charged that a great deal of *The Bell Curve* reasoning was flawed and based on selective review of past research. For example, Robert Sternberg (1996) pointed out that the only research study related to intelligence ever conducted by Richard Herrnstein (coauthor Charles Murray has never conducted his own intelligence research) directly contradicts one of his central *Bell Curve* arguments— namely, that intellectual-skills training programs are ineffective in improving mental abilities (refer back to section 10-3b). In making this claim, Herrnstein simply ignored his own research findings!

Other critics focused on Herrnstein and Murray's contention that, because *individual* differences in intelligence are strongly influenced by genetic factors, *group* differences are similarly influenced (Dorfman, 1995; Horn, 2002; Schulze et al., 1996). These critics argue that a fatal flaw in Herrnstein and Murray's group heritability estimates of racial differences in intelligence is that they are based on the heritability estimates derived from twin studies. Yet heritability estimates for intelligence should be made only for the specific social group on which the estimate is based. In the twin studies, the heritability estimates were based on overwhelmingly White subjects, not Blacks or other ethnic groups. Why is this a problem? Consider the following analogy, which is also illustrated in figure 10-14.

Imagine that you have a mixture of corn seeds that vary genetically. Take a handful of those seeds and plant them in fertile soil. If all conditions remain equal, some of the resulting plants will be short and some will be tall. Because the quality of your soil and care were equal for all corn seeds, the height differences of the fully grown corn can be attributed to their genetic variation. Now fill a white bag and a black bag with this same seed mixture. However, plant the white bag of corn seeds in a rich, fertile field and the black bag of seeds in a field that is poor and barren. When the plants in these different soil conditions grow, as before, you will observe that in both fields there is individual variation in the height of the plants, caused purely by genetic factors. But you will also observe that the average height of the plants in the fertile field is greater than that of the plants in the barren field. This group difference is caused entirely by environmental factors (the soil).

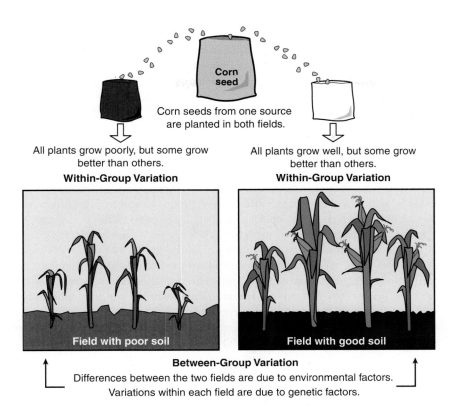

Corn seeds from one source are planted in both fields.

All plants grow poorly, but some grow better than others.
Within-Group Variation

All plants grow well, but some grow better than others.
Within-Group Variation

Field with poor soil

Field with good soil

Between-Group Variation
Differences between the two fields are due to environmental factors.
Variations within each field are due to genetic factors.

Figure 10-14

Between-Group and Within-Group Variation

In our corn seed analogy, all the variation in plant height within each field is due to genetics, but the overall height difference between the corn plants in the fertile field and the barren field is due to the environment. How does this analogy relate to observed Black-White IQ differences?

As this analogy illustrates, the fact that IQ differences *within* groups are partly or even completely caused by genetic variation does not mean that average IQ differences *between* groups are due to genetics (Block, 2002). An important question that needs to be asked before attributing between-group IQ differences to genetics is this: Are the groups' environments the same? In the United States, Blacks and Hispanics do not generally grow up in the same environments as Whites. For example, statistics gathered by the U.S. Census Bureau in 2001 indicate that the percentage of African-American and Hispanic-American families living below the poverty level is more than double (22.1 percent and 21.2 percent, respectively) that of European-American families (9.4 percent). When focusing on children below the age of 16, the statistics show that 36 percent of African-American and Hispanic-American youth live below the poverty level, compared with only 15 percent of European-American children. Many children living in poverty do not receive proper nutrition, which impedes neurological development and causes attention problems at school (Brody, 1992). They also have fewer role models who can teach them skills and habits necessary to flourish academically, and they attend schools with lower-quality learning resources and lower expectations for academic achievement. Either singly or together, these aspects of an impoverished environment interfere with intellectual growth. Due to the dissimilarity in environments, critics of *The Bell Curve* correctly argue that it is a mistake to assume that IQ differences between Whites and different minority groups stem from genetic factors. Although intelligence researchers generally agree that individual differences in IQ scores are substantially influenced by genetic factors, the claim by *The Bell Curve* authors that group differences in IQ are due to genetics simply does not ring true.

10-4d Cultural and Social Psychological Factors May Explain Group IQ Differences

Beyond the socioeconomic disadvantages that account for lower IQ scores among Blacks and other selective minority groups, some social scientists also contend that certain cultural and psychological forces contribute to these between-group differences.

Voluntary versus Involuntary Minorities

One way to distinguish among minority groups in the United States is in terms of how they became a "minority" (Ogbu & Simons, 1998). *Voluntary minorities* are people who have freely come to this country because they perceived it as "the land of opportunity." Voluntary minorities include immigrants from Africa, the Caribbean, Mexico, South America, China, India, Japan, and Korea. In contrast, *involuntary minorities* are people who are a part of this country because their ancestors were conquered, colonized, or enslaved. Instead of seeking out the United States, the ancestors of involuntary minorities were forced against their will to become a part of this country. Involuntary minorities include Native Americans, most African Americans, early Mexicans in the Southwest, native Hawaiians, Alaskan natives, and Puerto Ricans.

Numerous studies indicate that involuntary minorities in the United States achieve lower IQ scores than do voluntary minorities (Brand, 1996; Suzuki & Gutkin, 1994a, 1994b). Similar findings have been reported in Canada, Europe, India, Japan, and New Zealand (Dennis, 1970; DeVos, 1973; Gaur & Sen, 1989; Ogbu, 1978; Verma, 1988). For example, in Japan the Burakumin are an involuntary minority group that comprises 2 percent of the population. They have the same ethnic and national origins as the dominant Ippan Japanese, yet they have been discriminated against for centuries. Over the past 20 years, the Japanese government has engaged in a substantial effort to improve the educational and social opportunities of the Burakumin. However, despite these efforts, members of this involuntary minority still encounter negative stereotypes and discrimination in mainstream Japanese society (Shimahara, 1991). When the IQ scores of the Burakumin and the Ippan are compared, the Burakumin score 16 points lower, which is comparable to the 15-point IQ difference found between U.S. Blacks and Whites (DeVos, 1973; Ikeda, 2001). Interestingly, when the Burakumin immigrate to the United States as voluntary minorities, they perform very well on IQ tests, actually doing slightly better than other Japanese immigrants (Ito, 1967).

What is it about the involuntary minority status that might cause these lower IQ scores? A growing number of social scientists believe that the primary causes are (1) persisting negative cultural stereotypes within the dominant culture concerning involuntary minorities' intellectual abilities and (2) the self-protective defensive reaction many involuntary minority members subsequently develop against the rejecting mainstream culture (Ogbu, 2002; Serpell, 2000; Shimahara et al., 2001).

Oppositional Identities

Anthropologist John Ogbu (1986, 1993, 2002) believes that some members of involuntary minority groups respond to negative stereotypes and discrimination by developing an *oppositional* ethnic identity and cultural frame of reference that defensively opposes the rejecting dominant culture (see chapter 4, section 4-2f, for a discussion of ethnic identity development). This type of reaction makes a good deal of sense in certain respects. If you live in a society where your racial or ethnic group is devalued, developing an oppositional identity may help you cope with your hostile environment by clearly defining your group in contrasting ways to the larger culture (Crocker & Major, 1989; Crocker et al., 1998). One of the most immediate benefits is that an oppositional identity can psychologically insulate you—the stigmatized person—from some of the negative effects of social injustice, such as loss of self-esteem (Helms, 1990; Parham & Helms, 1985). On the negative side, however, immersion in an identity that defines itself in terms of opposition to the larger culture will likely constrict your personal identity. For example, if you are African American and your behavior or thinking falls within the forbidden White cultural frame of reference, you may be accused by other Blacks of "acting White" or being an "Oreo" (Black on the outside but White on the inside). These forbidden areas are those that have historically been reserved for White Americans, and in which minorities have not been given an equal opportunity to excel.

How might oppositional identity development help explain racial and ethnic differences in IQ-test performance? Simply put, for many African-American youths with oppositional ethnic identities, academic tasks represent one of the forbidden White cultural domains. For these individuals, committing themselves to academic excellence and learning to follow the academic standards of the school might be perceived as adopting a White-American cultural frame of reference and forsaking their ethnic identity (Ford, 1996).

Unfortunately, by rejecting these academic pursuits because of their association with White culture, African Americans and other involuntary minorities are not only more likely to score lower on IQ tests than their White counterparts and members of voluntary minorities but also less likely to fully take advantage of the civil rights advances that have occurred over the past 50 years (Bankston & Caldas, 1997; Fordham & Ogbu, 1986).

Stereotype Threat

In addition to the problem that oppositional identities pose to involuntary minority students' academic achievement, the social psychologist Claude Steele (1997) asserts that, for those minority students who do want to excel academically, negative cultural stereotypes about their supposed inferior intellectual abilities can create feelings of anxiety and vulnerability, especially when they are in the company of people outside their racial group. That is, if you are a student who is often one of only a few members of your race enrolled in a particular course, your individual performance is often looked upon by students not of your race as representing the "typical" student of your racial group. Accompanying this scrutiny is the added social stigma associated with your minority label, which often implies a suspicion of intellectual inferiority (Sigelman & Tuch, 1997). Because these negative stereotypes are widely known throughout society, as the target of such stereotyping, you are susceptible to developing **stereotype threat,** which is the realization that your performance on some task might confirm the negative stereotype. According to Steele, when highly motivated African-American students take an intelligence test while simultaneously worrying that a low score will confirm that they fit the "mentally inferior" stereotype, this added pressure is often sufficient to significantly hinder their performance.

> **stereotype threat** The realization that your performance on some task might confirm a negative stereotype associated with your social group.

Evidence for the stereotype threat among African-American college students comes from a series of experiments conducted by Steele and Joshua Aronson (1995). In one of these studies, Black and White student volunteers were given a difficult English test. In the *stereotype threat condition,* the test was described as a measure of intellectual ability, while in the *non-stereotype threat condition,* it was described as a laboratory problem-solving task that didn't measure intelligence. Because one of the more salient racial stereotypes is that Blacks are intellectually inferior to Whites, the researchers presumed that describing the test as an intellectual measure would make this negative stereotype relevant to the Black students' performance. In turn, researchers also expected this stereotype relevance to establish for these Black students a fear of confirming the stereotype ("If I do poorly, my performance will reflect badly on my race and on me"). Steele and Aronson hypothesized that the anxiety created by such thinking would interfere with the Black students' performance. In contrast, when the task was described as not measuring intelligence, researchers assumed that this would make the negative racial stereotype about ability *irrelevant* to the Black students' performance and, therefore, not arouse anxiety. As you can see in figure 10-15, consistent with the stereotype threat hypothesis, when the test was presented as a measure of ability, Blacks performed worse than Whites. However, when it was not associated with ability, no significant racial differences were found.

One common reaction in academic settings is for those affected by stereotype threat to *disidentify* with the activity that is the source of the threat—namely, academic achievement. That is, individuals change their self-concept so that academic achievement is no longer very important to their self-esteem. Steele describes the effects of disidentification on one particular student with whom he spoke:

> She may continue to feel pressure to stay in school—from her parents, even from the potential advantages of a college degree. But now she is psychologically insulated from her academic life, like a disinterested visitor. Cool, unperturbed. But, like a pain-killing drug, disidentification undoes her future as it relieves her vulnerability. (Steele, 1992, p. 74)

Research indicates that academic disidentification is much more common among African-American and other involuntary minority students than among White-American and voluntary minority students (Ambady et al., 2001; Major et al., 1998). Although such disidentification protects self-esteem and is a coping response to racial prejudice and discrimination, it also is one of the psychological factors that undermines involuntary minority students' school achievement.

Figure 10-15

African-American Intellectual Test Performance and Stereotype Threat

Steele and Aronson (1995) administered a difficult English test to Black and White college students. When the test was described as a measure of intellectual ability (stereotype threat condition), Blacks performed worse than Whites. However, when it was not associated with ability (nonstereotype threat condition), no racial differences were found. How are these findings consistent with the stereotype threat hypothesis?

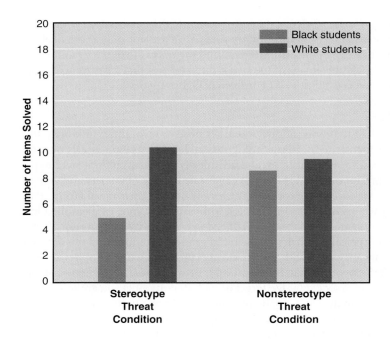

Academic disidentification resulting from stereotype threat also occurs among lower-class Whites and among female students of all races and ethnic categories who are in male-dominated academic courses, such as engineering and chemistry. For example, Steven Spencer and his colleagues (1999) found that women performed as well as men on a difficult English test for which they suffer no social stigma, but women underachieved relative to men on a comparably difficult math test for which they are more vulnerable to suspicions of intellectual inferiority. In a follow-up to this study, the researchers gave female and male college students a difficult math test but divided it into two halves and presented it as two distinct tests. Half the students were told that the first test was one on which men outperformed women and that the second test was one on which there were no gender differences. The other students were told the opposite: Test 1 was described as exhibiting no gender differences, but men were said to have outperformed women on test 2. Consistent with the stereotype threat hypothesis, when told that the test yielded gender differences, women performed significantly worse than men. However, when the test was described as not exhibiting any gender differences, women and men performed at the same level. This dramatic change occurred even though the two tests were the same! Similar to African-American students' disidentification process described earlier, women are most likely to disidentify with math and math-related careers when negative gender stereotypes are salient (Spencer at al., 1999).

Although stereotype threat is most noticeable and problematic among social groups that have historically been disadvantaged, it also occurs among members of privileged groups, such as White middle-class men. For example, in one study, White male undergraduates who were skilled in math performed poorly on a difficult math test when they were told beforehand that the test was one on which Asians outperformed Whites (Aronson et al., 1999). Considered together, these studies inform us that negative stereotypes can create damaging self-fulfilling prophecies among members of many different social groups by inducing stereotype threat. Further, these findings raise the very real possibility that stereotype threat may explain a substantial amount of the racial differences found in intelligence testing and the gender differences found in advanced math testing (refer back to section 10-4b).

Valuing Academic Achievement

Thus far, we have examined cultural and social psychological factors that might *depress* IQ scores among selected racial and ethnic groups. Yet why do elementary school children in Taiwan and Japan outscore American children by about 15 points (roughly one standard deviation) in math ability and, to a lesser extent, in reading skills? Interviews with the parents of these children conducted by Harold Stevenson and his coworkers (1986) found that the Chinese and Japanese parents downplayed the importance of innate intellectual ability and, instead, stressed hard work. They also considered doing well in school to be the most important goal for their children. In contrast, the American parents were more likely to believe that intelligence is genetically determined, and they assigned academic achievement as a much lower-valued goal for their children. Following their parents' lead, when asked what they would wish for if a wizard promised them anything they wanted, the majority of the Asian children named something related to their education, whereas the majority of American children mentioned money or possessions.

Follow-up studies found that the achievement differences between these Asian and American children persisted through high school (Stevenson et al., 1993). Consistent with the different valuing of education found during their early school years, the American teenagers were much more likely than the Asian teenagers to have after-school jobs and time for sports, dating, and other social activities (Fuligni & Stevenson, 1995). Although engaging in such a wide variety of extracurricular activities is consistent with the American parents' goal of developing a "well-rounded" teenager, a recent study indicates that this philosophy creates a great deal of stress and academic anxiety for high-achieving American students (Crystal et al., 1994). Figuratively, they are trying to burn the candle at both ends and often simply get burned out. In contrast, high-achieving Asian students burn only one end of the candle—the academic end—and tend to have low stress and anxiety levels. Taken together, these studies seem to suggest that intellectual growth will be nurtured when parents and the larger culture stress the value of education and the importance of working hard to achieve intellectual mastery (Deslandes & Bertrand, 2005; Li, 2004). In contrast, intellectual growth will likely be stunted when cultural beliefs impress upon children that their own academic success is either unlikely (due to negative cultural stereotypes) or not highly valued (due to incompatibility with more important cultural values).

10-4e Intellectual Ability Can Be Shaped by Self-Fulfilling Prophecies

In 1948, the sociologist Robert Merton introduced the concept of the **self-fulfilling prophecy** to describe a situation in which someone's expectations about a person or group actually lead to the fulfillment of those expectations. As illustrated in figure 10-16, the self-fulfilling prophecy involves a three-step process. First, the perceiver (the "prophet") forms an impression of the target person. Second, the perceiver acts toward the target person in a manner consistent with this first impression. Third, in response, the target person's behavior changes to correspond to the perceiver's actions. Research indicates that behavior changes due to self-fulfilling prophecies can be permanent and can markedly change the course of an individual's life (Smith et al., 1999). How might self-fulfilling prophecies influence the development—for better or worse—of children's intellectual abilities?

In the 1960s, Robert Rosenthal and Lenore Jacobson (1968) explored this very question by studying the academic achievement of children in a South San Francisco elementary school. Rosenthal and Jacobson first gave IQ tests to first- and second-grade children at the school and then told their teachers that the tests identified certain students as "potential bloomers" who should experience substantial IQ gains during the remaining school year. In reality, the children identified as potential bloomers had simply been randomly selected by the researchers and did not differ intellectually from their classmates. Eight months later, when the students were again tested, the potential bloomers not only exhibited improved schoolwork, but also showed higher gains in their IQ scores than those who had not been identified as bloomers. Additional research indicates that teachers treat students who are positively labeled in this manner differently from others in the following ways (Jussim, 1989; Meichenbaum et al., 1969):

- Teachers create a warmer *socioemotional climate* for "gifted" students.
- Teachers provide "gifted" students with more *feedback* on their academic performance.
- Teachers *challenge* "gifted" students with more difficult material.
- Teachers provide "gifted" students with a *greater opportunity to respond* to material presented in class.

self-fulfilling prophecy The process by which someone's expectations about a person or group lead to the fulfillment of those expectations.

Figure 10-16

The Development of a Self-Fulfilling Prophecy

Self-fulfilling prophecies often involve three stages, or steps. In step 1, the perceiver forms an impression of the target. In step 2, the perceiver behaves in a manner consistent with this first impression. In step 3, the target responds to the perceiver's actions in a way that confirms the perceiver's initial impression. The more interactions the target has with the perceiver and the more this three-step process is repeated, the more the target will internalize the perceiver's expectations into his or her own self-concept.

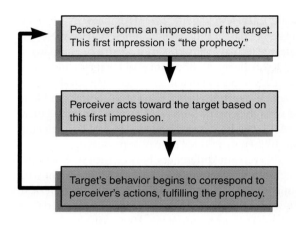

Perceiver forms an impression of the target. This first impression is "the prophecy."

Perceiver acts toward the target based on this first impression.

Target's behavior begins to correspond to perceiver's actions, fulfilling the prophecy.

Treated in this favorable manner, positively labeled students are likely to assume either that the teacher especially likes them and has good judgment or that the teacher is a likable person. Whichever attribution is made, the positively labeled students work harder and begin thinking of themselves as high achievers. Through this behavioral and self-concept change, the prophecy is fulfilled.

Unfortunately, self-fulfilling prophecies can also cause some students' academic potential to be destroyed by negative expectations. Children labeled as "troubled" or "intellectually inferior" are often treated by teachers and fellow students in a way that reinforces the negative label so it is more likely to be internalized. For example, in one experiment exploring the impact of negative expectancies on children's social interactions, pairs of unacquainted boys in third through sixth grade played together on different tasks (Harris et al., 1992). The researchers designated one of the boys in the pairing as the *perceiver* and the other boy as the *target*. Half the target boys had been previously diagnosed as hyperactive, and the rest of the participants—the remaining targets and all the perceivers—had no history of behavioral problems. Prior to playing together, perceivers in the *hyperactive expectancy condition* were told—independently of their partner's actual behavior—that their partner had a special problem and might give them a hard time. In the *control condition*, the perceivers were not given this information.

Results indicated that the target boys whose partners had been led to believe that they had a behavioral problem (the *hyperactive expectancy condition*) later reported that they enjoyed the tasks less, rated their own performances as poorer, and took less credit for success than the boys whose partners were in the *control condition*. Likewise, the boys who held the negative expectancies about their partners enjoyed the tasks less themselves, worked less hard on them, talked less, and liked their partners less and were less friendly to them than those perceivers who were not provided with negative expectancies. These findings are consistent with the hypothesis that people who have negative expectations about others are more likely to treat these individuals in a negative manner, which often causes the targets of such negative treatment to react in kind, thus confirming the initial negative expectations. For half the boys in this study, the negative expectations were groundless, but this did not alter the outcome of the interaction.

Unfortunately, in our educational system, this form of self-fulfilling prophecy is all too common, and over time it leads to negative self-beliefs and low self-esteem among those targeted students. The children most likely to be identified early as "problem students" are those from involuntary minority groups. Although similar negative expectations also occur for certain White children and those from voluntary minorities, they are more the exception than the rule. The resulting differences in how these students are treated may be small and subtle, but their cumulative effects can be profound.

Section Review

- Twin and adoption studies indicate a substantial hereditary contribution to individual intelligence, but also significant environmental influences.
- Females perform better on verbal aptitude tests, and males do better on visual-spatial tests.
- Little scientific evidence exists to support hereditary explanations for racial differences reflected in IQ scores.
- In cultures throughout the world, involuntary minority groups score lower on IQ tests than do voluntary minority groups.
- Racially based IQ differences are most likely due to environmental factors such as unequal economic and educational conditions, differing cultural values surrounding education, and negative effects of racial stereotypes on minority students' self-confidence.
- A self-fulfilling prophecy is the process by which expectations about a person or group lead to the fulfillment of those expectations; intellectually-based self-fulfilling prophecies can either foster or hinder intellectual development.

Psychological Applications

What Is Creativity, and How Can You "Create" a Creative Environment?

creativity The ability to produce novel, high-quality products or ideas.

convergent thinking Applying logic and conventional knowledge to arrive at (or *converge upon*) a single solution to a problem.

divergent thinking Pursuing many different and often unconventional paths to generate many different solutions to a problem.

Creativity is the ability to produce novel, high-quality products or ideas. In trying to understand the creative process, psychologists have distinguished between two types of thinking: *convergent thinking* and *divergent thinking* (Guilford, 1959). **Convergent thinking** involves applying logic and conventional knowledge to arrive at (or *converge upon*) a single solution to a problem. Most formal education emphasizes this type of thinking. For example, when teachers ask students to solve a math problem, they encourage them to focus on one particular approach and work through a series of steps until they find the "right" answer. Traditional IQ tests primarily require the use of convergent thinking. In contrast, **divergent thinking** involves pursuing many different and often unconventional paths to generate many different solutions to a problem (Reese et al., 2001). When engaged in this type of thinking, you often are moving away (or *diverging*) from the problem and considering it from a variety of perspectives (Baer, 1993). Groups searching for new directions and novel ideas may sometimes encourage their members to engage in divergent thinking during

brainstorming sessions (Kurtzberg & Amabile, 2001). In these sessions, members are instructed to say the first thing that comes to mind without worrying about its logic or social acceptability. The goal in brainstorming is to generate as many different ideas as possible to help the group meet existing challenges. Unfortunately, one of the biggest obstacles to success in such brainstorming sessions is that members often censor their own creative ideas out of concern for how other group members might respond (Williams, 2002).

Psychologists have traditionally considered divergent thinking to be a more important ingredient in creativity than convergent thinking, because people who are divergent thinkers are more likely to break out of mental sets that hinder the adoption of new ideas (see chapter 9, section 9-2c). However, it is also true that successful completion of a creative project often requires frequent convergent thought as well as divergent thought (Brophy, 2001). Overall, despite the contribution of convergent thinking to creative endeavors, creativity tests generally contain items that emphasize divergent thinking (Diakidoy & Spanoudis, 2002). For example, test-takers might be asked to list as many white, edible things as they can think of in 3 minutes, or to list all the uses they can think of for a brick. Responses to such items are scored in terms of the number of unique or novel ideas generated, with higher scores indicating higher levels of creativity. Creativity is also measured by asking people to generate a creative product—a poem, a story, a drawing, or perhaps a photo—which judges then rate. Despite the obvious subjectivity of such creativity ratings, the agreement level among judges is quite high (Amabile, 1996). To

Continued next page—

Psychological Applications

—Continued

Figure 1

How Creative Are These Photos?

The assignment here was to take a photo in which a common hair clip was the subject of focus. No other instructions were given to the participants. Using the scale provided below the photos, rate the creativity of each photo and then ask others to do so as well. Is there agreement on which photo is more creative? What criteria did you and others use in making your judgments?

Source: Courtesy of Figzoi.

Not at all creative						Very creative
-1-	-2-	-3-	-4-	-5-	-6-	-7-

give you some idea of how judges might rate the creativity of such projects, examine the two photos in figure 1. How would you rate each photo's level of creativity? What criteria are you using in making your judgments? Is one photo more creative than the other?

Most creative people have an intermediate level of education—enough formal schooling to have learned the necessary skills to generate creative products, but not so much formal education as to stifle the creative spirit (Simonton, 2000b). During the early stages of their careers, creative people tend to rely heavily on a few close friends for advice and encouragement. However, their intense devotion to work often causes strained relationships with other people (Gardner, 1993a).

How Does Culture Shape Creative Expression?

Cultural values often channel creative energy into specific fields (Feldman, 1999). When a culture values a particular form of creative expression, it teaches its children how to express themselves in this manner. For example, the birth of the Renaissance—a period of immense artistic creativity at the beginning of the fifteenth century in Florence, Italy—was made possible due to the generous support of artists by the entire population, especially those who had wealth and power. Cultures can also restrict creativity (Abou-Hatab, 1997). In the Omaha Indian culture, for instance, there is only one way to sing a song, and if anyone alters from that format, ritual weeping occurs (Colligan, 1983). As you might guess, this response is an effective way to prevent people from taking "creative liberties" with music. A similar social norm prevents singers in the United States from engaging in too much creative expression when performing "The Star-Spangled Banner."

What is considered "creative" is also shaped by culture. An important feature of creativity in Western cultures is producing an observable product (Lubart, 1999). In contrast, the Eastern view of creativity is less product-focused and more related to personal fulfillment or the expression of an inner sense of ultimate reality (Kuo, 1996). In Hinduism, creativity is thought of as entailing spiritual or religious expression rather than as providing an innovative solution to a problem (Aron & Aron, 1982). This Eastern sense of creativity has a great deal to do with what humanistic psychologists in the West refer to as *self-actualization,* or the process of achieving one's full potential (see chapter 11, section 11-1f).

Another distinction between Western and Eastern views of creativity is the way creativity is related to traditional views. The Western approach to creativity typically involves a break with tradition (Kristeller, 1983). This is consistent with the Western philosophy of individualism, which values nonconformity and the expression of ideas that run counter to the group. In contrast, the Eastern approach to creativity is more likely to involve the *reinterpretation* of traditional ideas so that traditional truths come alive and become revitalized in daily activities (Hallman, 1970). This conception of creativity is consistent with the Eastern philosophy of collectivism, which values conformity and the upholding of traditional values and beliefs.

As you can see, culture has an important influence on the nature of creativity, both how it is defined and how it is channeled. You may be born with a certain degree of creative potential, but how that potential develops and is later expressed will be significantly shaped by your social reality. Yet, in most cultures, cre-

Psychological Applications

—Continued

ative individuals tend to share the following characteristics (Reed, 2005; Simonton, 2000a):

- They have wide interests.
- They like to work hard.
- They are open to new experiences.
- They are risk takers.
- They have at least moderate intelligence.
- They are willing to tolerate rejection.

Do you remember Jasper Fforde, the best-selling author of the Thursday Next book series highlighted in chapter 9? Fforde embodies many of these characteristics. Although he was recognized as an intelligent child, young Fforde was disinterested in traditional schooling and thrived academically only after his parents placed him in a school with a more progressive attitude toward learning. In adulthood, Fforde pursued a wide variety of interests, including working at odd jobs, being a cameraman in the movie industry, and flying vintage airplanes. Even during the years in which his manuscripts were being repeatedly rejected by publishing houses, he continued to hone his skills after completing his regular workday.

Fostering Creativity

Beyond possessing important personal characteristics, to be creative you need to have a lot of things go your way (Lubart & Sternberg, 1994; Sternberg & Lubart, 1995, 1996). For example, many highly creative artists' talents go unrecognized because their works remain obscure, through no fault of their own. In Fforde's case, his first Thursday Next book was never even recognized by his own literary agent as anything special until the agent was so desperate for material that he read the whole thing. This sounds like creativity is a fragile and illusive form of intelligence, but it's not. Creativity experts contend that you have the power to construct the necessary conditions that foster creative accomplishments. They recommend the following six steps to increase your own creativity. Accompanying each recommendation is a qualification concerning its limits.

- *Redefine problems.* As discussed in chapter 9, section 9-2c, a number of cognitive tendencies act as barriers to problem solving. Although certain thinking strategies may have effectively solved problems for us in the past, creative solutions often require us to look "through" and "around" problems rather than directly at them. *Warning: Don't feel that you must "reinvent the wheel" for every new problem. Often, tried-and-true problem-solving strategies are the best tools for creative products.*
- *Make a habit out of questioning tradition.* Since childhood, we have been rewarded for conforming to the way other people think and act. Such conformity is often necessary for a

society to properly function, but it does not provide a fertile environment for creative ideas. One of the defining characteristics of creative people is that they regularly question traditional ways of thinking and behaving (Feist & Barron, 2003; Ochse, 1990). *Warning: Defying tradition simply because it brings you attention is not the purpose of this exercise!*

- *Find something you love to do.* Creative people, whether they are children or adults, are motivated primarily by the enjoyment, challenge, and satisfaction they derive from working on their projects, rather than from the external rewards they receive (Amabile, 1996; Amabile & Hennessey, 1992). *Warning: Being rewarded for doing things you naturally enjoy can undermine your enjoyment of those activities (see the discussion on intrinsic motivation in chapter 11, section 11-1e).*
- *Become an expert in your area of interest.* Case studies of 120 creative people from diverse professions found that great accomplishments were preceded by high-quality training (Bloom, 1985). This research suggests that you will have a much better chance of being a creative success if you have developed a good base of knowledge in your chosen interest area. By tapping your accumulated learning, you will be able to generate more ideas and make more mental connections that will ultimately lead to creative problem solving. *Warning: Don't feel you need to know everything about your area of interest before you can make a creative contribution to it.*
- *Tolerate ambiguity and take sensible risks.* Because creative ideas run against the grain of everyday thinking and often do not fit neatly into clearly defined categories, you must have sufficient confidence in your ideas so that you are not easily discouraged when others don't understand or accept what you have to offer (Feist & Barron, 2003). *Warning: Do not totally ignore feedback from others, because you can profit from others' advice.*
- *Choose friends and associates who will support your creative endeavors.* Analysis of the lives of over 2,000 successful scientists and inventors found that the most creative individuals were not isolated geniuses. Rather, they had high emotional intelligence and surrounded themselves with people who encouraged them in their work (Simonton, 1992). *Warning: Do not surround yourself with "yes people" who will agree with anything you say. Blind conformity does not foster a creative environment.*

Key Terms

achievement test (p. 359)

aptitude test (p. 359)

content validity (p. 364)

convergent thinking (p. 393)

creativity (p. 393)

crystallized intelligence (p. 368)

divergent thinking (p. 393)

Down syndrome (p. 379)

emotional intelligence (p. 373)

eugenics (p. 358)

factor analysis (p. 367)

fluid intelligence (p. 368)

Flynn effect (p. 363)

general intelligence factor (g-factor) (p. 367)

heritability coefficient (p. 381)

intelligence (p. 357)

intelligence quotient (IQ) (p. 360)

mental retardation (p. 378)

multiple intelligences (p. 369)

normal distribution (p. 362)

predictive validity (p. 364)

prodigies (p. 301)

psychometrics (p. 357)

reaction range (p. 383)

reliability (p. 363)

savants (p. 371)

self-fulfilling prophecy (p. 391)

standardization (p. 362)

Stanford-Binet Intelligence Test (p. 360)

stereotype threat (p. 389)

triarchic theory of intelligence (p. 371)

validity (p. 364)

Wechsler Intelligence Scales (p. 360)

Suggested Websites

Human Intelligence

http://www.indiana.edu/~intell/map.shtml
This website discusses the history of intelligence testing and theory development.

Online IQ Tests

http://www.2h.com/iq-tests.html
This website contains a number of intelligence tests and brainteasers.

Multiple Intelligences

http://www.thomasarmstrong.com/multiple_intelligence.htm
This website outlines Gardner's theory of multiple intelligences and how it might apply in educational settings.

Review Questions

Note: You can find the correct answers to these questions by taking the quiz and then submitting your answers in the Online Edition. The program will automatically score your submission. If you miss a question, the program will provide the correct answer, a rationale for the answer, and the section number in the chapter where the topic is discussed.

1. Eugenics, a movement founded by Sir Francis Galton, has been associated with all of the following *except*
   a. Nazi Germany's program of mass extinction of "genetic undesirables."
   b. improving the hereditary characteristics of society through sterilization.
   c. Binet's research identifying lower-performing children through intelligence testing.
   d. Galton's use of the term *moron.*
   e. intelligence test bias toward native-born English speakers.

2. Intelligence has been assessed or scored in a variety of ways since Galton's measures of sensory abilities and head size. Most intelligence tests today rely on a scoring method known as
   a. ratio IQ.
   b. deviation IQ.
   c. an intelligence quotient.
   d. mental age/chronological age ($\times$ 100).
   e. verbal IQ.

3. Standardization, or establishing rigid test administration and interpretation procedures, typically results in
   a. a reliable test.
   b. a standard test.
   c. a valid test.
   d. a normal distribution of scores.
   e. the Flynn effect.

Chapter 11

Motivation and Emotion

Source: Courtesy of Figzoi.

In 1938, at the beginning of Indiana University's fall semester, there was a great deal of excitement in the student body. Why? A small notice had been posted about a new course on human sexuality that would be taught by Professor of Zoology Alfred Kinsey. Students were promised a series of frank lectures covering sexual technique, physiology, and contraception. Most students who enrolled in the course knew very little about sex. The course was restricted to seniors and married students, and it was so popular that a few students moved up their wedding dates or even donned fake wedding rings to gain admittance.

To appreciate the experience of these students, imagine that you had never once read or been told anything factual about human sexual behavior. Further, imagine that one of the things you were told by your parents was that holding hands was not only a sexual act but also a mortal sin. And that masturbation caused nervous disorders and even madness. This sort of highly restrictive and false information constituted your sexual education. Now, during your first class sessions with Professor Kinsey, you are lectured in detail about the physiology of sex and shown slides of the penis, clitoris, and various positions for sexual intercourse. You are also told that sexual ignorance causes mental anguish and sexual liberation is the key to a strong marriage and a happy life.

When other professors and the public learned about the content of Professor Kinsey's lectures, many were horrified and demanded its cancellation. Kinsey resisted and argued that scientific research should be used to dispel the myths about sex being taught by schools and religious institutions. Based on his experience teaching this course, Kinsey and his colleague, Walter Pomeroy, began questioning 18,000 people on this most intimate subject. Using interviews and surveys to obtain participants' sexual histories, they provided evidence indicating that sexual fantasies, masturbation, premarital and extramarital sex, and same-sex sexual contacts were fairly common among Americans (Kinsey et al., 1948, 1953). Although there were some flaws in the methodology, this early research remains an important contribution to the understanding of human sexual behavior (Robinson, 1989).

Instead of greeting these research findings with praise and gratitude, a majority of Americans responded with intense disapproval, and many public officials demanded a congressional investigation into who was funding such sinful studies. Amid the furor, Kinsey's financial backers withdrew their support (Fisher, 1993). In the following years, other scientists who attempted to investigate human intimacy and sexuality endured similar accusations—that what they were studying could never, and should never, be studied empirically.

Despite such condemnations, the undeniable facts are not only that sexual behavior affects health and happiness, but also that understanding human sexuality provides a means for affecting societal well-being. Consider the personal, social, and economic costs of unwanted pregnancies, sexually transmitted diseases, and sexual assaults and abuse, as well as the negative effects of the commercial sex industry. Also consider the positive impact that sex has on interpersonal intimacy and pleasure. Regardless of your values or your religious and social beliefs, you probably recognize that sex is a powerful motivating force in people's lives.

Sex is just one of the influences that motivate us. In this chapter, we examine different approaches to the study of motivation, identifying cognitive, physiological, social, and environmental factors that shape our various needs and desires. Then we analyze three different motivational issues—eating, sex, and striving for achievement. Finally, we explore the psychology of emotion, a topic that is integral to a full understanding of motivation.

11-1 MOTIVATION

Preview

- *What is motivation?*
- *Why were instinct theories inadequate explanations of motivation?*
- *What motivation theory emphasizes homeostasis, and what theory explains the importance of optimal arousal?*
- *What two motives are explained by incentive theory, and how can external rewards undermine one of these motives?*
- *Why are Maslow's needs described in a hierarchy?*

We do things. Not only do we do things, but also we often feel irrepressible urges to initiate certain actions. Sometimes we feel "pushed" to behave one way, while at other times we feel "pulled" to behave entirely differently. This "push" or "pull" to act in certain ways or achieve particular goals is the topic of our discovery quest in this section.

11-1a Motivation Is a Dynamic Process

Motivation is an inner state that energizes behavior toward the fulfillment of a goal (Pittman, 1998). In a very real sense, the study of motivation is the study of motion—of what moves a person or other animal to act in a particular way. As such, motivation is best conceived of as a dynamic process in which motivational states are constantly changing due to changes both outside and inside the person and due to responses toward the motivated state itself (Reeve, 1992).

To better understand how motivation is a dynamic process, imagine that you have a strong desire to become a painter. Due to the positive feelings associated with this desire, you enroll as a student at a famous art institute. Your subsequent successes and failures at the institute, combined with conflicting goals related to your desire for wealth, romance, and children, may change the intensity of your motivation toward this goal. Due to this dynamic quality, motivation is not easily measured or quantified. Psychologists often measure motivation by looking for changes in the intensity and direction of the desire or need—and what has caused those changes.

In making sense of this moving target, theories of motivation focus on what influences behavior at any given time and tend to focus on either internal or external sources for that influence. *Internal* theories assume that something about the organism *pushes* it toward (or away from) some object. In contrast, *external* theories focus more on attributes of the goal or the environment that *pull* the organism in a certain direction. Clearly, no matter which source is emphasized, both internal and external issues need to be addressed when studying motivation (Hogan, 2005).

> **motivation** An inner state that energizes behavior toward the fulfillment of a goal.

11-1b Genes May Shape Our Motivation

At the beginning of the twentieth century, many psychologists were fascinated by Charles Darwin's (1871) theory of evolution. Extending his theory, they proposed that humans, like other animals, have instincts (Reeve, 1992). An **instinct** is an unlearned, relatively fixed pattern of behavior that is essential to a species' survival. William McDougall (1908) was an early proponent of the view that much of human behavior is controlled by instincts, and he generated a list of 18 human instincts, including greed, self-assertion, and gregariousness. In subsequent years, other instinct theorists expanded this list into the thousands. The argument became this: If a behavior is seen, it must be instinctual. Of course, one problem with such reasoning is that it is circular: An observed behavior (for example, aggression) is attributed to an instinct (aggressiveness), which in turn is inferred from the behavior. A second problem with instinct theory is that it cannot accommodate the role of learning that early behaviorists were demonstrating in their research (see chapter 7). Simply put, many so-called instinctual behaviors are learned and shaped by experience.

Although instinct theory collapsed due to its false assumptions, our study of other topics in psychology shows that genes may predispose the human species—as well as other species—to engage in certain patterns of behavior. This contemporary evolutionary perspective states

> **instinct** An unlearned, relatively fixed pattern of behavior that is essential to a species' survival.

that we indeed inherit adaptive genetic traits but that these traits express themselves more as predispositions for behaviors rather than as a predetermined set of actions (Barrett et al., 2002; Buss & Kenrick, 1998). For example, early instinct theorists would have explained alcoholism as being directly caused by an inherited instinct. In contrast, modern evolutionary theorists acknowledge that there may be a genetic predisposition for such behavior, but they reject the notion that some genetic code predetermines who will become an alcoholic. Instead, they contend that genes might affect how the body responds to alcohol or what emotional responses a person might have to certain environmental cues associated with drinking. Such predispositions might increase the likelihood of excessive drinking, but they would not predetermine the behavior or the addiction.

11-1c We Are Sometimes Motivated to Reduce Arousal

When the original instinct theory fell out of scientific favor, many psychologists sought to explain motivation by turning to **drive-reduction theory** (Hull, 1943), which is based on the concept of homeostasis. **Homeostasis** is the tendency for organisms to keep physiological systems internally balanced by adjusting them in response to change. An example of homeostasis is the body's temperature-regulation system: A dip or rise in body temperature causes various physiological responses (for example, constriction of blood vessels and sweating), which return the body's temperature to the desired level.

According to drive-reduction theory, an imbalance in homeostasis creates a physiological need, which in turn produces a **drive,** defined as a physiological state of arousal that moves the organism to meet the need. Once the need is met, the drive is reduced, and the behavior that was initiated in response to the drive ceases. For example, as depicted in figure 11-1, if you were deprived of water or other liquids for an extended period of time, the chemical balance of your body fluids would become disturbed, initiating a "thirst" drive marked by arousal and discomfort and pushing you to seek liquid to alleviate the discomfort. After you consumed a sufficient amount of liquid, homeostasis would be achieved, the drive would be reduced, and you would stop drinking.

Part of the difference between instinct theory and drive-reduction theory is that drive-reduction theory, by distinguishing between primary and secondary drives, recognizes the importance of learning on motivation. *Primary drives* are unlearned drives that arise from basic biological needs, such as the need for food and water. *Secondary drives* are acquired drives that are learned by being associated with primary drives. For example, the need to acquire money is a learned, secondary drive that can develop into a strong influence on behavior. By recognizing the existence of secondary drives, drive-reduction theory was able to explain a much wider range of behavior than instinct theory.

Despite its advantages over instinct theory, drive-reduction theory ran into problems because it could not explain why people engage in behaviors that do not reduce a drive. Curiosity-motivated behaviors are an example. Humans and other animals will learn complicated tasks or endure physical hardships (such as receiving electrical shocks) in order to explore their surroundings (Brown, 1979). Such behaviors do not reduce any known drive to restore homeostasis. In fact, people engage in many behaviors, such as riding roller coasters,

drive-reduction theory The idea that an imbalance in homeostasis creates a physiological need, which in turn produces a drive that motivates the organism to satisfy the need.

homeostasis The tendency for organisms to keep physiological systems internally balanced by adjusting them in response to change.

drive A physiological state of arousal that moves an organism to meet a need.

Figure 11-1

Drive-Reduction Theory

According to drive-reduction theory, we are motivated to keep physiological systems internally balanced, a state called homeostasis. An imbalance in homeostasis (for example, due to being deprived of liquids) creates a physiological need (for liquids), which then produces a drive that moves us to engage in behavior to find and consume liquids in order to satisfy the need. When the need is satisfied, the drive is reduced, and homeostasis is restored.

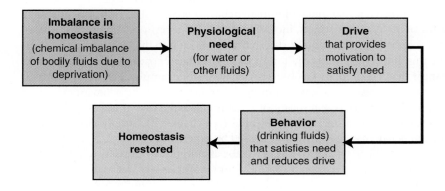

watching scary movies, or taking drugs, that seem designed to *increase* arousal. Due to these observations, psychologists concluded that, although drive-reduction theory was not "wrong," it was incomplete, because it could not account for all areas of human motivation. Most subsequent theories moved away from broad, global explanations of motivation while still retaining many of the insights gleaned from both drive-reduction theory and evolutionary theory.

11-1d We Are Sometimes Motivated to Maintain an Optimal Level of Arousal

Contrary to drive-reduction theory, research indicates that levels of arousal that are too low are as uncomfortable as those that are too high (Berlyne, 1974). For example, when research participants were placed in an artificial environment that deprived them of sensory stimulation, they reported having difficulty thinking, and within hours they became increasingly irritable and began having vivid daydreams and hallucinations (Heron, 1957). Overall, it appears that we seek to achieve and maintain an *optimum* level of bodily arousal—not too much and not too little. This preference conforms to the **Yerkes-Dodson law,** which is named after the researchers who first described a similar principle. As depicted in figure 11-2, this law contends that, when we are underaroused or overaroused, we perform below our abilities. Why? When underaroused, we tend to be bored and sluggish, while overarousal makes us nervous and tense. Our best performance occurs when we are at an intermediate level of arousal (Hebb, 1955; Teigen, 1994). Thus, instead of motivation simply being tied to reducing arousal, it appears that motivation is associated with *regulating* arousal. Level of arousal can be determined by measuring various physiological processes, including brain activity, heart rate, and muscle tension.

> **Yerkes-Dodson law** The idea that we perform best when we are at an intermediate level of arousal.

Not surprisingly, people differ in their optimal arousal. Those who enjoy high arousal tend to listen to loud music, socialize a great deal, eat spicy foods, drink alcohol, smoke tobacco, engage in frequent sexual activity, and take part in activities that are risky or novel (Trimpop & Kirkcaldy, 1997; Zuckerman, 1984). Individuals with lower optimal arousal than others seek less intense stimulation and take fewer risks in life. Biology and blood chemistry appear to explain many of these individual differences (Shekim et al., 1989).

11-1e Incentive Theory Examines How External Factors Motivate Behavior

The theories of motivation reviewed thus far focus on internal physiological states and their effect on motivation. Each theory describes some kind of internal "push" toward a goal. But how do these internal states translate into specific sets of behaviors? If a person becomes hungry, why doesn't tasteless freeze-dried food satisfy that drive as well as mouth-watering pizza? Further, how do we account for the fact that motives change over time?

> **incentive theory** A theory of motivation stating that behavior is directed toward attaining desirable stimuli, called positive incentives, and avoiding undesirable stimuli, called negative incentives.

Unlike instinct, drive, or other physiological theories, **incentive theory** focuses on the role of external factors in motivation—how things in our environment *pull* us in certain directions (Balleine, 2005; Wise, 2004). Developed from the insights gained from classical and operant conditioning research (see chapter 7), incentive theory proposes that any

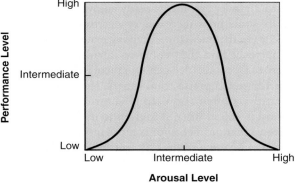

Figure 11-2

The Yerkes-Dodson Law

According to the Yerkes-Dodson law, we perform best when we are at an intermediate level of arousal. How might this psychological principle explain our ability to think when we are either nearly asleep or overly excited?

incentive A positive or negative environmental stimulus that motivates behavior.

[Tom] had discovered a great law of human action . . . namely, that Work consists of whatever a body is obliged to do, and that Play consists of whatever a body is not obliged to do.

—*Mark Twain, American author, in* The Adventures of Tom Sawyer *(1876)*

intrinsic motivation Motivation to engage in a behavior or an activity because one finds it interesting or enjoyable for its own sake.

extrinsic motivation Motivation to engage in a behavior or an activity because of the external rewards it can provide.

The performing arts offer meager monetary compensation for the vast majority of individuals who pursue this profession. Most artists have an intrinsic motivation toward their art, meaning that performing the artistic activity is a valued goal in its own right. Do you believe that you will have a similar level of intrinsic motivation for the profession you pursue following graduation from college?

Source: Courtesy of Figzoi.

stimulus we learn to associate with positive or negative outcomes can serve as an incentive for our behavior. An **incentive** is a positive or negative stimulus in the environment that attracts or repels us. According to this theory, we are motivated to behave in certain ways when we expect to gain positive incentives and/or avoid negative incentives through our actions.

The value of an incentive can change over time and across situations. For example, gaining praise from your parents may have had greater incentive value for you during different periods of your childhood and adolescence (Pomerantz et al., 2005). In certain situations, such as when you were with your teenaged friends, you may have gone out of your way to avoid receiving parental praise. It was a negative incentive. The value of an incentive is also influenced by biology (Balleine & Dickinson, 1994). That is why food is a stronger motivator when you are hungry than when you are full.

The idea that a great deal of motivation can be explained in terms of incentives has led researchers to further distinguish between two types of motivation, which are tied to whether incentives are *intrinsic* or *extrinsic* to the behavior being performed (Harackiewicz et al., 2005). A behavior or an activity that a person perceives as a valued goal in its own right represents a source of **intrinsic motivation.** On the other hand, a behavior or an activity may be valued because it leads to a reward separate from that the act itself provides. The classic example is doing work for pay. In such instances, the work itself may not provide pleasure, but it provides another outcome—money—that does bring pleasure. The type of motivation that leads a person to engage in a behavior or an activity for external reasons is known as **extrinsic motivation.** In a longitudinal study of businesspersons, those who had an extrinsic motivation toward work when they were in graduate school were happier with their lives and jobs 9 years later when they earned more money rather than less. However, this same study also found that businesspersons who had an intrinsic motivation toward work when they were in graduate school were less satisfied with their lives 9 years later if they were earning a lot of money (Malka & Chatman, 2003). This research suggests that how people react to being very well compensated on the job may be at least partly shaped by whether they chose their careers because of their "love of the work" or their "love of the money."

In general, we value behaviors and activities that are intrinsically motivating more highly than those that are extrinsically motivating. In explaining this value difference, various psychologists have proposed that intrinsic motivation is based on our need to control our own behavior (Deci, 2004; Guofang & Qinglin, 2004). From this perspective, the primary reason certain activities are intrinsically motivating—and more valued—is that they satisfy our need to feel that we are competent beings who control our own lives. Of course, it is not always possible to determine whether we engage in a behavior because of intrinsic or extrinsic rewards. In fact, both sources of motivation often operate simultaneously (McNeill & Wang, 2005). For example, a child may read a lot, not simply because she enjoys the activity for its own sake, but also because doing so earns praise from adults and better grades in school.

11-1f Rewards Can Undermine Intrinsic Motivation

As you undoubtedly know, there is less need to use extrinsic motivators to convince people to do tasks that they already enjoy. Yet did you also know that using extrinsic motivators sometimes increases or decreases people's intrinsic motivation (Deci & Ryan, 1985)? On the one hand, receiving external rewards for a task may reinforce our sense of competence and thus enhance intrinsic motivation (Harackiewicz & Sansone, 2000; Ryan & Deci, 2000). Such enhancing effects often occur when our task performance receives verbal praise from others. However, as we learned in chapter 7, section 7-2b, rewards are often also used to control people's behavior. If the controlling aspect of a reward is salient when it is given to us for performing a task we enjoy, we may begin to perceive that our behavior is more motivated by the reward (extrinsic motivation) than by our enjoyment of the task (intrinsic motivation).

Many psychologists argue that American society has become so dependent on the use of extrinsic motivators (rewards and punishments) that it has seriously reduced people's intrinsic motivation for many activities (Deci et al., 1999; Eisenberger & Cameron,

1996; Kohn, 1993). Citing examples from over 25 years of research, they conclude that, by providing rewards such as money, stickers, or even marshmallows, interest in performing a task is reduced. For example, in one study, preschoolers who normally chose to spend a lot of time drawing were asked to draw a picture (Lepper et al., 1973). Preschoolers in one condition of the experiment were told that they would receive a reward for the picture, while those in another condition were not told of a reward but were given one after completing the picture. Finally, preschoolers in a third condition were neither told about nor given any rewards. Results indicated that those who had expected and received a reward drew the least when later given the opportunity to do so. Other studies find that students' academic interest and performance decline when external rewards are emphasized at school or at home (Turner et al., 1998; Vansteenkiste et al., 2004).

Rewards may even affect the quality of our work. In one study, Teresa Amabile (1996) found that people who were paid to engage in artistic activities produced work that was judged to be less creative than people who were not paid. This research suggests that we tend to be most productive and creative when we are intrinsically motivated rather than extrinsically motivated.

Does this mean that external rewards always undermine intrinsic motivation? No. Although psychologists disagree on how much damage external rewards can cause to intrinsic motivation, external rewards can also be beneficial. As mentioned, positive reinforcement, properly presented, can increase feelings of personal autonomy and competence and can reduce many of the negative effects that failure inflicts on intrinsic motivation (Harackiewicz & Sansone, 2000). However, in order for these good effects to occur, rewards need to be given because specific performance standards have been met and/or because the recipient surpasses the performance of others. Simply rewarding someone for participating in a task or for meeting some vague or meaningless objective ("Good breathing, Timmy!") will often undermine intrinsic motivation. Further, tangible rewards, such as money or treats, are much more likely to undermine intrinsic motivation than verbal praise, which often increases intrinsic motivation by bolstering a person's confidence that she or he is a capable individual.

Not all praise, however, enhances intrinsic motivation. In discussing how to foster intrinsic motivation in children, Jennifer Henderlong and Mark Lepper (2002) warn that when praise compares a child to others, or when it implies that the child must now try to attain virtually impossible standards, this seemingly positive feedback can actually undermine intrinsic motivation. Henderlong and Lepper suggest that praise will most likely increase intrinsic motivation under the following conditions:

1. The praise is sincere and does not imply that the adult is trying to control the child.
2. The praise does not compare the child to other children.
3. The praise implies that the child was successful because of good effort and not simply because of natural talent or abilities.
4. The praise implies that the adult has standards for the child, and the child believes that those standards are attainable.

Perhaps the key ingredient in determining whether rewards enhance or undermine intrinsic motivation for a task is the degree to which the rewards convey to recipients that they are their "own masters" rather than "pawns" of others' desires. However, this "key ingredient" may apply only to people from individualist cultures, who place a premium on being free from others' control. In collectivist cultures, where self-determination and autonomy are not emphasized, intrinsic motivation is much more likely to be maintained even when trusted authority figures or family members are deciding for us what tasks and activities we will pursue (Iyengar & Lepper, 1999).

Journey of Discovery Question   Sometimes, when athletes are paid large sums of money to play their sport, they seem to lose their "love of the game" and become less motivated. How could this change in athletic motivation be explained by intrinsic and extrinsic motivation?

Figure 11-3

Maslow's Hierarchy of Needs

Except for self-actualization, all the needs in Maslow's hierarchy are motivated by a feeling of deprivation.

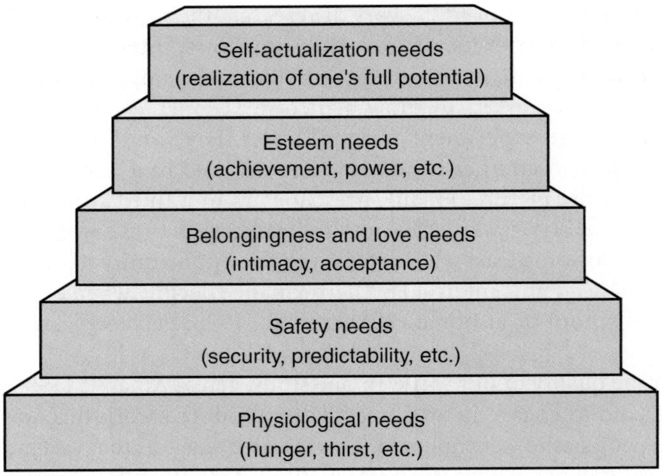

Self-actualization needs
(realization of one's full potential)

Esteem needs
(achievement, power, etc.)

Belongingness and love needs
(intimacy, acceptance)

Safety needs
(security, predictability, etc.)

Physiological needs
(hunger, thirst, etc.)

hierarchy of needs
Maslow's progression of human needs, in which those that are the most basic—namely, physiological needs—must be sufficiently satisfied before higher-level safety needs and then psychological needs become activated.

self-actualization The ultimate goal of growth, being the realization of one's full potential.

11-1g Maslow Proposed That Needs Are Organized in a Hierarchy

Out of the humanistic tradition, Abraham Maslow (1970) developed another approach to understanding motives. As first discussed in chapter 1, section 1-3b, the humanistic view in general and Maslow's theory of motivation in particular assumed that people have a basic need for personal growth—to become what is possible. As illustrated in figure 11-3, Maslow proposed that we are born with a **hierarchy of needs,** basic needs that have to be sufficiently satisfied before we are motivated to satisfy higher-level needs. The needs further up the hierarchy are considered less basic because we can survive without satisfying them.

The most basic of these needs are physiological, such as hunger and thirst. Once these *physiological needs* have been adequately satisfied, they recede into the motivational hierarchy, and the next set of needs, *safety needs,* is activated. These needs involve striving for a sense of safety, security, and predictability in life. Regarding these first two need levels, Maslow contended that when food and safety are difficult to attain, they dominate people's lives, and higher-level needs have little motivational power. Yet, if these two levels of needs are reasonably satisfied, the person becomes motivated by more social needs. The first social needs activated are the *belongingness and love needs,* which involve the desire for intimacy, love, and acceptance from others. Next on the hierarchy are *esteem needs,* which involve the desire for achievement, power, and recognition and respect from others.

Up to this point in the hierarchy, Maslow believed that people are motivated by a need to overcome their feelings of being deprived of some kind of physical or psychological need. Thus, all the needs in the first four levels of the hierarchy are *deficiency needs,* needs that if absent inhibit our personal growth. In contrast, the needs in the upper reaches of the hierarchy are *self-actualization needs* that move the person toward fulfilling her or his potential. **Self-actualization** is the ultimate goal of human growth, although Maslow hypothesized that it is a significant motive for very few of us. Why? The primary reason is that most of us are preoccupied throughout our lives with trying to make up for deficiencies lower in the hierarchy (Maslow, 1971; Vitterso, 2004).

The simplicity of Maslow's needs hierarchy makes it an appealing theory of motivation in such diverse fields as philosophy, business, and education (Banwell, 2004; Trigg, 2004). Despite this interest, the simplicity of the theory is its primary problem. Although research generally suggests that the motives lower in Maslow's hierarchy do take precedence over those higher in the hierarchy (Baumeister & Leary, 1995; Reiss & Havercamp, 2005), safety needs remain high in importance for all age groups, and there is no clear evidence that met needs become less important than unmet needs in motivating people's behavior (Goebel & Brown, 1981; Hall & Nougaim, 1968). Despite these shortcomings, the theory provides a comprehensive and organized framework for discussing basic human motives.

Section Review

- Motivation is the study of how behavior is energized toward the fulfillment of a goal.
- According to instinct theories, motivated behaviors are genetically determined; instinct theories cannot account for motivation affected by experience and learning.
- According to drive-reduction theory, motivation originates from attempts to reduce unpleasant drive states and return the body to homeostasis.
- The Yerkes-Dodson law states that people are motivated to seek an optimal level of arousal.
- In incentive theory, only externally produced consequences determine motivation, and there are two types of motivation—extrinsic and intrinsic.
- When people receive salient external rewards for performing an enjoyable task, they may perceive that their behavior is more motivated by the reward (extrinsic motivation) than by task enjoyment (intrinsic motivation).
- Maslow's needs hierarchy reflects a prioritization of goals, ranging from basic survival goals to the ultimate goal of self-actualization.

11-2 HUNGER AND EATING

Preview

- *What three biological systems in the body control hunger and eating?*
- *What other factors shape hunger?*
- *What is a restrained eater?*
- *Are there "set points" for weight?*

Having explored some of the underlying factors in motivation, let us now turn to specific motives. One basic, primary, motivated behavior is eating. Although it is essential for survival, we don't eat just to survive. Eating is a major source of social interaction. In fact, eating well beyond our basic needs seems to have become a national pastime in the United States! In this section, we explore the biological mechanisms that underlie this most basic of human needs and then discuss various theories related to hunger, eating, and **satiety** (pronounced "sa-TY-a-tee"), which means being full to satisfaction.

> **satiety** Being full to satisfaction—in this case, with food.

11-2a Various Biological Mechanisms Control Hunger and Eating

Due to their importance for survival, it is not surprising that the controls over hunger, eating, and satiety are complex and represent several independent and interacting body systems (Pinel et al., 2002). Three of the major control systems are the stomach, the bloodstream, and the brain.

The Stomach

It seems logical that the stomach should play some role in whether we feel hungry or full. In one early investigation of this body organ, A. L. Washburn, working with Walter Cannon, swallowed a long tube attached to a balloon that was then inflated (Cannon & Washburn, 1912). Whenever Washburn's stomach contracted, the corresponding changes in the balloon's air pressure were recorded. Although stomach contractions corresponded to Washburn's perceptions of hunger, later research demonstrated that these contractions do not *cause* hunger pangs (Rozin et al., 1998). In fact, you can still feel hungry even after your stomach has been surgically removed (Mills & Stunkard, 1976)! Although the stomach doesn't cause the sensation of hunger, the sensation of food satiety at least partly originates in this body organ. As the stomach becomes swollen from eating, sensory neural signals reflecting satiety are sent from the stomach—and the small intestine and liver—to the brain. The stomach also releases the hormone *gastrin,* which, among other actions, signals the pancreas to begin releasing insulin, a hormone that, among other actions, decreases appetite (Masaki et al., 2004).

The Bloodstream

The important role our blood plays in signaling hunger was demonstrated when researchers injected food-deprived rats with blood from rats that had just eaten. When these injected rats were offered food, they ate little, as if they were satiated (Davis et al., 1969). These findings set scientists wondering what in the blood was responsible for the satiety signal. Today, we know that the blood is the pathway for many eating-related signals that flow to the brain. The brain monitors two main types of blood signals: those dealing with the level of food nutrients the stomach supplies to the bloodstream, and those dealing with hormone levels in the bloodstream related to those nutrients.

When the brain receives signals that the level of food nutrients in the blood is low, we feel hungry (Schwartz & Porte, 2005). The two major types of food nutrients are *fatty acids* and the blood sugar *glucose,* which is converted into energy that can be stored and used later by the body. The blood hormone *insulin* is essential in this conversion process. High insulin production leads to cells taking in more glucose than they can use, with the excess being converted into fat. As mentioned, increased levels of insulin lead to decreased hunger, while drops in the levels of insulin result in increased hunger (Nelson, 2000).

Finally, one blood signal that tells the brain that eating should start or stop comes from *cholecystokinin (CCK),* a chemical that is released from the small intestine as a hormone and from the brain as a neurotransmitter (Hayes et al., 2004). CCK not only aids digestion but also regulates how much we eat by decreasing hunger. Administering CCK to food-deprived humans and other animals reduces hunger and eating but doesn't affect thirst or water consumption (Morley et al., 1985). If receptors for CCK in the brain are blocked, animals continue eating even after they have consumed their normal amount of food (Bloom & Polak, 1981).

The Brain

The *hypothalamus,* a small structure buried deep within the brain, plays a significant role in regulating eating behavior. As noted in chapter 3, section 3-3b, the hypothalamus is primarily responsible for homeostatic regulation. A major part of maintaining homeostasis is balancing the body's energy demands with energy availability. About 50 years ago, studies on rats suggested that two small parts of the hypothalamus were the primary centers for coordinating hunger and satiety. The lateral (side) area of the hypothalamus (LH) was thought to be the "hunger-on" center (Stellar, 1954), and the ventromedial (bottom center) area of the hypothalamus (VMH) appeared to be the "hunger-off" center (Hetherington & Ranson, 1942). The reason for these beliefs was the discovery that making small lesions (holes) in the VMH led to massive increases in eating, whereas lesioning the LH led to finicky eating. Although these two areas of the hypothalamus play an important role in hunger and satiety, later studies indicated that the "hunger on/off" labels were too simplistic: The LH and VMH interact with many other brain systems to produce their effects (Kalat, 1998; Pinel, 1997).

Today, scientists believe that another part of the hypothalamus, the *paraventricular nucleus (PVN),* plays a more important role in hunger regulation by having neural circuitry that responds to various neurotransmitters (Stanley et al., 1986; Woods et al., 2000). For instance, the neurotransmitter *neuropeptide Y* has a marked effect at the PVN and greatly increases carbohydrate consumption, while the neurotransmitter *serotonin* inhibits carbohydrate consumption (Mori et al., 2004). Thus, rather than describing the hypothalamus as having "hunger-on" and "hunger-off" areas, it is more accurate to state that it has some neurons that fire when blood nutrient levels are low, and others that fire when nutrients are at high levels and should be released. These neurons act less like "on/off" hunger switches and more like sensors that provide information to the frontal lobes of the brain, which then decide eating behavior (Winn, 1995).

Another problem with the idea of a hunger-on switch in the brain is that it doesn't make sense from an evolutionary perspective (Pinel et al., 2000). If humans and other animals were motivated to seek food only after a drop in their blood nutrient levels flipped the hunger switch, they would be in a weakened, energy-depleted state. Then they would need to hunt and kill their food (or shop for and cook it) before finally eating. A more adaptive approach would be to *anticipate* the energy demands, thus completing eating and beginning the process of digestion *prior* to a drop in homeostatic balance (Bolles, 1980; Collier, 1986). Such anticipation of hunger requires the intervention of the frontal brain lobes' higher-order thinking.

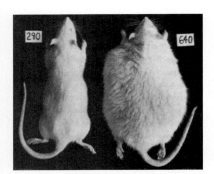

Early studies with rats found that destruction of the ventromedial area of the hypothalamus resulted in massive eating and gross obesity. How did later research refine our understanding of the role that the hypothalamus plays in hunger regulation?

Source: From P. Teitelbaum, Appetite, *Proceedings of the American Philosophical Society,* 108, 1964, 464–473.

11-2b Situational and Social Factors Also Control Hunger and Eating

The fact that there is more to hunger than the operation of our physiological states was recently demonstrated by Paul Rozin and his colleagues (1998) when they tested two brain-damaged patients who—similar to Henry M. in chapter 3—had no recollection of events occurring more than a few minutes ago. After eating a normal meal, these patients ate a second and sometimes a third full meal when evidence of the prior meal had been cleared away. This suggests that knowing when to eat not only is a function of body chemistry and hypothalamic activity but also involves external cues and memory of when we last ate.

Anticipation and the Incentive Value of Food

Anticipation has a significant influence on hunger and eating. Do you recall Ivan Pavlov's digestion studies of dogs from chapter 7, section 7-1a? In conducting his studies, Pavlov (1927) placed meat powder on a dog's tongue to elicit reflexive salivation. One thing he noticed was that, over time, dogs began salivating before any food reached their mouths and even before they smelled the food—in other words, in anticipation of the meal (Capaldi, 1996). Since Pavlov's time, many studies have shown that physiological responses that *prepare* the body for food (for example, a surge in insulin) occur in response to cues normally related to eating (Pinel, 1997; Woods, 1991). Such cues include the sight or smell of appealing food, the time of day, other people eating, and the clatter of dishes (Jansen et al., 2003). This means that hunger is also a response to environmental cues that indicate food is on the way, rather than simply a response to specific changes occurring within the body.

Another control over eating is related to the incentive value of food. Although the early phases of eating depend on the taste of food, as you continue eating the same food, its positive incentive value declines (Raynor & Epstein, 2003; Rolls, 1986). In other words, the first taste of barbecued ribs may be wonderful, but they lose their "scrumptiousness" appeal with each bite. Accordingly, you will tend to consume many more calories when a variety of food is available rather than just one (Rolls et al., 1981). This effect cannot be explained by the body's monitoring of fat or glucose content (Pinel et al., 2000). Simply put, taste variety matters in how much you eat.

Restrained versus Unrestrained Eaters

How you think about food in relation to yourself also affects your eating behavior. If you are chronically worrying about and trying to control what and how much you eat, you are a *restrained eater,* while if you are relatively unconcerned about controlling your eating you are an *unrestrained eater* (Herman & Polivy, 1980, 2004; Johnson & Wardle, 2005). Restrained eaters put constant limits on the amount of food they allow themselves to consume, and they are perpetual dieters. Restrained eaters also tend to be heavily influenced by what the situation says is correct about eating rather than by what their body signals are telling them.

The constant monitoring of food consumption requires great self-control on the part of restrained eaters. However, when stressed by daily events, they are much more likely than unrestrained eaters to go on high-calorie binges when they "let their guard down" (Polivy et al., 1994; Tanaka, 2002). Despite their constant dieting, restrained eaters have more difficulty than unrestrained eaters avoiding "forbidden" yet desirable food, such as chocolate (Stirling & Yeomans, 2004). The apparent cause of these self-control lapses by restrained eaters is that stressful events temporarily deplete their ability to regulate and control their eating desires.

Research indicates that at any given time of the day people have only limited amounts of energy available for self-regulation (Baumeister & Heatherton, 1996; Mischel et al., 1996). This is true regardless of whether a person is a restrained or an unrestrained eater. Yet restrained eaters are constantly using some of their limited self-regulatory energy to control their eating, while unrestrained eaters are not. However, when restrained eaters need to focus energy on one task, such as studying for a big exam or handling conflict in a romantic relationship, they do not have enough self-regulatory energy left to keep themselves from consuming that half-gallon of ice cream in the freezer. This research suggests that people who are constantly trying to lose weight by controlling their eating may unintentionally be creating circumstances that actually cause them to gain weight.

Restrained eaters expend a considerable amount of their self-regulatory resources controlling what and how much they eat. When such people are under stress, how might they react when encountering an array of delicious food like that displayed in this photo? Why are they more likely than unrestrained eaters to go on high-calorie binges?

Source: Courtesy of Figzoi.

Culture and Eating Preferences

As humans, we are *omnivores,* or food generalists. This allows us to consume a wide variety of foods. Accordingly, we learn a lot about our food preferences from our own personal experiences and by observing what others eat (Rozin, 1996). However, like other animals, we tend to prefer long-familiar foods to those that are novel (Pliner & Pelchat, 1991; Sclafani, 1995).

Think for a moment about the ways in which food plays a part in your family and cultural celebrations and day-to-day activities. Very few cultural differences in food preferences are biological in origin. A major factor in determining food preferences is simply what foods are available in a particular geographical region, along with climate and storage concerns. Further, such regional issues as family size, trading partners, economic status, and whether the society depends on hunting or on domestication of animals and agriculture all affect which foods are part of a person's life. Over time, these eating practices become linked to a particular culture. In a very real sense, what we eat is often determined by the group to which we belong.

The ability to digest milk is one of the few biological differences that shape culinary cultural tastes (Rozin, 1996). The great majority of humans beyond infancy are lactose intolerant, meaning that they cannot digest milk sugar, and thus feel nauseous after consuming milk products (Sahi, 1994). Most people who are able to continue digesting lactose after infancy are of northern European descent (Simoons, 1970, 1982). Some cultures, such as the Chinese, do not include milk of any kind in their diet. However, other cultures have found ways to remove lactose from milk prior to consuming it by allowing bacteria to break it down. Not only has this bacterial fermentation allowed milk consumption without ill effects, but in addition, the resulting milk products—cheese and yogurt—have significantly altered the culinary choices in these cultures.

11-2c The Body May Be "Set" to Maintain Weight within a Limited Range

The starvation that occurred in World War II concentration camps and war zones sparked researchers' interest in the effects of food deprivation. In one study, 36 conscientious war objectors were asked to semistarve themselves to reduce their weight by 25 percent (Keys et al., 1950). As these male volunteers lost weight, they initially were in good spirits. However, as they endured more food restrictions in order to continue the weight loss, the men's moods darkened, aggression increased, and they neglected both their personal appearance and relationships.

Does this Japanese meal seem appealing to you? Our food preferences are largely learned from our culture.

Source: Courtesy of Jenny Franzoi.

When unlimited food became available at the end of the study, they ate voraciously, sometimes as many as five large meals a day. Most volunteers quickly regained their prestudy weight.

Researchers have also studied the opposite end of the eating spectrum, namely, the effects of overeating. In one noteworthy study, prison volunteers were asked to increase their weight by 25 percent, which meant gaining about 35 to 50 pounds (Sims, 1974; Sims & Horton, 1968). The prisoners were given plenty of food, and their amount of exercise was reduced. At first, they gained weight quickly, but then it became increasingly difficult to continue adding pounds. One man couldn't gain further weight even when eating over 10,000 calories per day—more than twice his normal daily food consumption. Over time, these men grew to dislike eating, and for some of them, food became repulsive. When the study ended, most returned to their normal eating habits, but not all of the men lost the weight they had gained. Those who had difficulty losing the weight tended to have a family history of obesity.

Together, these and other studies led some researchers to develop the hypothesis that the body has a **set point** for weight, meaning a level of body weight that it works to maintain (Hallschmid et al., 2004). Although this physiological process is only partly understood, it appears that the body monitors fat-cell levels to keep them relatively stable (Friedman, 2000). When the body's fat cells rise above this set point, they release the hormone leptin. *Leptin,* which in Greek *(leptos)* means "thin," has the effect of decreasing hunger by altering neural activity in the hippocampus (Balthasar et al., 2004; Denis et al., 2004). In essence, releasing leptin is the fat cells' way of telling the brain to stop eating because the body has enough fat already. In contrast, when fat-cell levels fall below the set point, the body compensates in the opposite direction by increasing hunger and decreasing metabolism. This constant compensation due to fluctuations in the body's fat-cell levels keeps your weight within a limited range.

Remember the World War II conscientious objectors who allowed themselves to be starved? After a certain point, it became difficult for them to lose any more weight. Similarly, the prisoners who were given the unusually large diets had trouble going too far over their original weight levels. Some set-point theorists propose that our weight and fat content are genetically preprogrammed and that this set point can be altered only under extreme circumstances, if at all. The practical implication of this assumption is that, even after extensive dieting or overeating, both the conscientious objectors and the prisoners were genetically destined to eventually return to their original weight.

> **set point** A level of weight that the body works to maintain.

What determines your set point? It may have something to do with your *number* of fat cells. Research indicates that when people gain or lose weight, they do not also gain or lose fat cells. Instead, their existing fat cells increase or decrease in average *size* (Hirsch et al., 1989). According to the reasoning of set-point theorists, if you have many more fat cells than the average person, you also have a correspondingly higher set point, which greatly increases your chances of becoming overweight. On the other hand, if you have relatively few fat cells, your set point is lower, and you are likely to be relatively thin.

Some researchers have criticized the idea that we have a genetically determined set point, saying that it is inconsistent with the increasing prevalence of obesity in countries where food supplies exceed need. For example, the percentage of Americans 30 percent or more above their ideal body weight increased from 12 percent in 1991 to 17.9 percent in 1998 (Centers for Disease Control and Prevention, 2000). How can a genetically fixed set point explain this increase? Either genetically programmed set points are rising at a rapid rate—which is virtually impossible—or our natural set points are at a level that is pathologically too high—which means that they really haven't been controlling the weight levels of many people at all (Pinel et al., 2000).

Faced with this problem, most researchers share the prevailing view that set points are not genetically fixed. However, this does not mean that people don't differ in their set points or that genetics doesn't significantly shape set-point levels. What it does mean is that your set point can change over time. Unfortunately, the change is usually upward, not downward. Research suggests that long-term overeating can gradually raise your set point, but it is much more difficult to lower your set point (Bolles, 1980; Keesey, 1995). These results mean that, if you are obese, you must make permanent changes in your eating habits in order to lose weight and maintain it at a healthy level. Weight change requires a *lifestyle* change, not just a fad diet.

Section Review

- The three major biological control systems in hunger and eating are the stomach, the bloodstream, and the brain.
- Hunger is also a response to environmental cues, anticipation, and the incentive value of food.
- Restrained eaters chronically worry about controlling what and how much they eat and may unintentionally create circumstances that cause them to gain weight.
- The body has a set point for weight, but this set point may not be genetically fixed.

11-3 SEXUAL MOTIVATION

Preview

- *Why do men report enjoying greater sexual variety than do women?*
- *What are two negative consequences of traditional sexual scripts?*
- *Are there differences between males and females in the sexual arousal response and in sexual motivation?*
- *What do we know about sexual orientation?*
- *What is heterosexism?*
- *Are people who are "uptight" about sex likely to have unprotected sex?*

In addition to hunger, another basic, primary motive is sex. Engaging in sexual behavior is essential for the continuation of a species. From an evolutionary perspective, it follows that reproduction would be more likely to occur if the process were pleasurable. As you already know, this is indeed the case. In fact, research suggests that the reinforcing properties of sex may well involve the same brain structures and neurotransmitter systems as those that are so strongly stimulated by cocaine and other addictive drugs (Melis & Argiolas, 1993; Walsh, 1993).

Motives for sexual behavior also include *non*physical factors, such as peer approval, the need to feel valued, the need for intimacy, stress reduction, the need for power, and procreation desires (Basson, 2002; Cooper et al., 1998). Understanding this powerful human motivator has proven to be a puzzle. In this section, we will put some of the pieces together.

11-3a Men Tend to Enjoy Greater Sexual Variety Than Do Women

Despite the AIDS crisis, teen pregnancy rates, and other important societal issues related to sexual behaviors, it has continued to be difficult to systematically study human sexual behavior. The first careful nationwide study of American sexual behaviors since Kinsey's work in the 1940s and 1950s didn't occur until 1994, when Edward Laumann and his coworkers questioned almost 3,500 adults. The results from their *National Health and Social Life Survey* provide us with a fairly detailed look at what Americans do sexually, with whom, and how often.

As you can see from figure 11-4, the most popular sexual activity among heterosexual Americans is vaginal intercourse, followed by watching one's partner undress, and then oral sex. Perhaps not surprisingly, both men and women enjoy *receiving* oral sex more than *giving* it. Beyond this similarity, do you notice an overall gender difference in the data? Put simply, men report enjoying every activity more than do women. This is consistent with other studies indicating that men are much more likely than women to masturbate frequently and desire more frequent sex and more sexual partners (Baumeister et al., 2001; Fletcher, 2002; Oliver & Hyde, 1993). Indeed, a recent cross-cultural survey of over 16,000 people in 52 nations across North and South America, Europe, the Middle East, Africa, Asia, and the Pacific Islands found that gender differences in the desire for sexual variety are universal (Schmitt, 2003). Men want sex more than do women at the start of the relationship, in the middle of it, and even after many years in the relationship (Impett & Peplau, 2003). Why might this be so?

One possible explanation offered by sociocultural theorists involves the different sexual scripts men and women learn while growing up (Kornreich et al., 2003). A **sexual script** is a preconception about how a series of events, perceived as being sexual, is likely to occur. Such scripts are learned from one's social environment, stored in memory, and used as a guide for behavior. In North American culture and many other cultures, the traditional sexual script taught to women is to downplay interest in sex and resist sexual advances. Men, in contrast, are conventionally taught to freely express sexual interest, brag about sexual exploits, and sometimes even persist in sexual advances despite a partner's protests (Alksnis et al., 1996; Andersen et al., 1999). These culturally learned scripts may explain the gender differences in sex surveys.

> **sexual script** A learned preconception about how a series of events, perceived as sexual, is likely to occur.

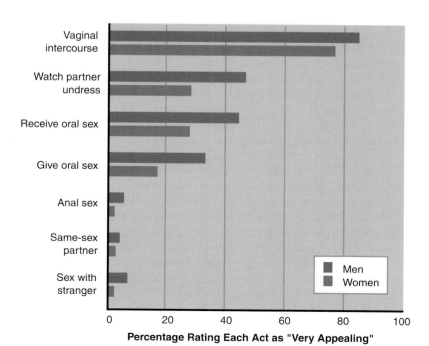

Figure 11-4

What Sexual Acts Do Americans Find "Very Appealing"?

A random survey of almost 3,500 U.S. adults has increased our understanding of U.S. sexual practices and desires. Why do you think men report enjoying every activity on this graph more than women do (Laumann et al., 1994)?

Sex sells!!! If you read magazines, watch television, or go to the movies, you know that sexual content is readily available for viewing. Like other animals, humans find sex a very powerful motivating force in everyday living. Yet do men and women differ in their interest in sex?

Source: Courtesy of Figzoi.

Instead of a sociocultural explanation, some social scientists believe that these gender differences reflect the different evolutionary pressures exerted on women and men (Buss, 1999; Trivers, 1972). A starting point in this evolutionary explanation is the following question: When a man and a woman have sex, which of them is most likely to bear responsibility for any resulting offspring? The answer is the woman. Further, unlike a man, a woman can have only one pregnancy at a time, and her reproductive years are relatively short. These biological limitations mean that, to maximize the probability that her genes will be passed on to future generations through her offspring, the best sexual strategy for a woman is to adopt a cautious approach. Such a strategy will better allow her to identify men with the best genes and those most likely to help care for offspring. In contrast to this cautious approach, it is to a man's advantage to establish sexual intimacy as quickly as possible in a relationship and to have frequent sexual encounters with many different women (Pedersen et al., 2002; Schmitt et al., 2001a). According to evolutionary theorists, over thousands of generations, men who seek frequent sex and prefer many mates produce more offspring than do men with a weaker sex drive and weaker preference for sexual variety. Thus, a higher sex drive and a preference for sexual variety have become common among men. High sex drive and a preference for variety have not become widespread among women, because such desires among women do not necessarily produce more children (Schmitt et al., 2001b).

Support for the evolutionary explanation of sex differences in preference for sexual variety comes from observations of other animal species. In most species, as in humans, males show more sexual interest in more partners than do females. However, this sex difference reverses in a few species (for example, water bugs, the Mormon cricket, the sandhill crane, seahorses, and a variety of fish species) in which the females abandon their eggs (and their mates) and seek other reproductive partners. In such instances, the males remain and care for the eggs and later offspring. Thus, this parental investment theory is not about males always having more interest in low-cost, indiscriminate sex than females. Instead, it is a theory about how sex differences in mating behavior are caused by differences in the parents' investment obligations to their young (Buss & Schmitt, 1993).

Which of these two explanations—evolutionary or sociocultural—is correct? Although I have contrasted the two viewpoints, they may often complement rather than compete with one another (Schaller, 1997). Cultural explanations for why women and men sometimes differ in their approach to and experience of sex (and love) emphasize the different social roles and positions of power that the two sexes traditionally hold in society. What are the origins of these gender roles and cultural status systems? Evolutionary explanations focus on how these differences might have initially arisen due to evolutionary selection pressures. Thus, perhaps the ultimate "best" explanation for gender differences in preferences for sexual variety may describe how evolutionary pressures faced by our prehuman ancestors shaped certain patterns of social behavior—including those related to sex—leaving modern women and men with certain *capacities* to react differently to sex. Yet the degree to which we actually manifest these inherited capacities today may be decided by how we are raised and taught to behave in our current social surroundings. In other words, culture and social learning may either enhance or override these inherited capacities.

11-3b Traditional Sexual Scripts Foster Acquaintance Rape

Forced sexual intercourse that occurs either on a date or between people who are acquainted or romantically involved is known as **acquaintance rape.** On American college campuses, acquaintance rapes account for 84 percent of all rapes or attempted rapes (Koss, 1993). Further, one in five women reports having been forced to do something sexual (Laumann et al., 1994). One factor contributing to these sexual assaults is the **rape myth,** which is the false belief that, deep down, women enjoy forcible sex and find it sexually exciting (Frese et al., 2004; Zurbriggen et al., 2004). Not surprisingly, heterosexual men are much more likely to endorse this myth than are heterosexual women. One consequence of men's adherence to the rape myth is a tendency to believe that women don't really mean it when they say "no" to sexual advances (Littleton & Axsom, 2003). Spend a few minutes responding to the statements in Self-Discovery Questionnaire 11-1, related to the rape myth.

Both the rape myth and acquaintance rape are fostered by traditional sexual scripts in which the woman's role is to act resistant to sex and the man's role is to persist in his sexual advances. Numerous studies indicate that acquaintance rape is much more likely to occur when the resistant female sexual script is combined with the male sexual script of predator (Allison & Wrightsman, 1993; Peterson & Muehlenhard, 2004). A victim following the resistant female sexual script often does not clearly communicate the limits of acceptable behavior to the person who persists after initial sexual advances have been discouraged. Instead of employing the highly effective tactic of declaring to her attacker, "This is rape and I'm calling the cops," a victim of acquaintance rape is often nonassertive or in the habit of giving mixed messages. In following the resistant female sexual script, the victim has problems with forcefully conveying a clear message of "no" and is later less likely than other women to acknowledge her experience as rape.

Despite this lack of assertiveness by the female victim, it in no way justifies forced sex. It cannot be stressed enough that acquaintance rape occurs when a man refuses to stop his sexual aggression. Such men tend to be more sexually active than other men, they enjoy exerting dominance in sexual encounters, and they treat women as property rather than people (Chiroro et al., 2004). An acquaintance rapist also generally has a history of antisocial behavior and displays a lot of anger toward women. Because he believes that women often need a little force in order to enjoy sex, the victimizer does not think that acquaintance rape is rape, even after he has committed this crime.

Although the definition of the rape myth is framed to include only women as targets, recent studies suggest that a similar myth exists for gay men: That is, some people falsely believe that gay men have an unconscious desire to be raped. As with the traditional rape myth, heterosexual men are most likely to endorse rape myths regarding gay men; gay men are least likely to endorse such beliefs (Davies & McCartney, 2003).

So what can we learn from this research? First, learning and practicing sexual scripts in which there are "predators" and "resistors" promotes sexual aggression and acquaintance

acquaintance rape Forced sexual intercourse that occurs either on a date or between people who are acquainted or romantically involved; also known as *date rape.*

rape myth The false belief that, deep down, women enjoy forcible sex and find it sexually exciting.

Self-Discovery
Questionnaire **11-1**

What Are Your Beliefs about Sexual Consent?

The Rape Myth Acceptance Scale

Directions: There are 19 items on this scale. For items 1–11, use the following 7-point scale to indicate your degree of agreement or disagreement:

Strongly disagree <u>1 2 3 4 5 6 7</u> Strongly agree

1. A woman who goes to the home or apartment of a man on their first date implies that she is willing to have sex.
2. Any female can get raped.
3. One reason that women falsely report a rape is that they frequently have a need to call attention to themselves.
4. Any healthy woman can successfully resist a rapist if she really wants to.
5. When women go around braless or wearing short skirts and tight tops, they are just asking for trouble.
6. In the majority of rapes, the victim is promiscuous or has a bad reputation.
7. If a girl engages in necking or petting and she lets things get out of hand, it is her own fault if her partner forces sex on her.
8. Women who get raped while hitchhiking get what they deserve.
9. A woman who is stuck-up and thinks she is too good to talk to guys on the street deserves to be taught a lesson.
10. Many women have an unconscious wish to be raped and may then unconsciously set up a situation in which they are likely to be attacked.
11. If a woman gets drunk at a party and has intercourse with a man she's just met there, she should be considered "fair game" to other males at the party who want to have sex with her too, whether she wants to or not.

Note: For questions 12 and 13, use the following scale:

1 = About 0%, 2 = About 25%, 3 = About 50%, 4 = About 75%, 5 = About 100%

12. What percentage of women who report a rape would you say are lying because they are angry and want to get back at the man they accuse?
13. What percentage of reported rapes would you guess were merely invented by women who discovered they were pregnant and wanted to protect their own reputations?

Note: For items 14–19, read the statement, and use the following scale to indicate your response:

1 = Always, 2 = Frequently, 3 = Sometimes, 4 = Rarely, 5 = Never

A person comes to you and claims s/he was raped. How likely would you be to believe the statement if the person were:

14. your best friend?
15. an Indian woman?
16. a neighborhood woman?
17. a young boy?
18. a black woman?
19. a white woman?

Note: Once you have indicated your response to each item, reverse the scoring for item 2 (1 = 7, 2 = 6, 3 = 5, 5 = 3, 6 = 2, 7 = 1). Then add up your total score. The higher your total score, the greater your belief in the rape myth. The mean total score in Burt's (1980) original sample of 598 American adults (average age of 42 years) was 86.6, with a standard deviation of 11.9. How does your total score compare with Burt's original sample? Are you more or less likely to believe in the rape myth than these American adults? Have your friends complete this scale as well. How do your beliefs about the rape myth compare to their beliefs?

Total score: _____

Source: From "Cultural Myths and Supports for Rape" by Martha Burt in *Journal of Personality and Social Psychology,* 38, 1980, pp. 217–230. Copyright © 1980 by the American Psychological Association. Adapted with permission.

rape. Second, people who are sexually attracted to one another should put aside these traditional, limiting sexual scripts and engage in open, honest communication (Frith & Kitzinger, 2001). In such exchanges, a refusal of sexual intimacy should be accepted as such.

11-3c Sex and Love May Be More Fused for Women Than for Men

Consistent with our section 11-3a discussion of evolutionary explanations for different sexual motivation in women and men, some social scientists have suggested that sexual desire and romantic love have evolved to meet different human needs (Diamond, 2003b; Fisher, 1998). These theorists propose that sexual desire is governed by the *sexual mating system,* in which the goal is to sexually reproduce and thereby pass one's genes on to the next generation. In contrast, romantic love is governed by the *attachment system,* in which the goal is to establish and maintain a strong emotional bond between two people. As discussed in chapter 4, section 4-2a, attachment is a part of our evolutionary heritage that developed to foster childrearing. In childrearing, the function of the attachment bond between infant and caregiver is to maximize the newborn's survival. Parents who love their babies will feed and protect them. Similarly, infants who become emotionally attached to their parents are more likely to remain physically close, thereby decreasing the likelihood of being killed by predators during their most vulnerable stage of life. Likewise, in childrearing, the attachment bond between the two parents also maximizes the newborn's survival. Parents who love one another are more likely to stay together to raise their children, and there is strength in numbers. According to this perspective, then, sexual desire fuels the sexual mating system, ensuring that a new generation is born into this world. In turn, romantic love fuels the attachment system, ensuring that enough members of the new generation will survive childhood.

When examining the causal link between sexual desire and romantic love, psychologists have traditionally assumed that sexual desire leads to the formation of an emotional bond, or romantic love, and not the other way around. In other words, you meet someone who is sexually appealing, and this initial sexual interest motivates you to seek out this person and become better acquainted. As this sexually charged relationship develops, you fall in love. Sound familiar? Yet there are numerous examples from everyday life of people developing sexual desires for a particular person *after* developing a strong emotional attachment to her or him (Rose & Zand, 2000). Based on our discussion thus far, would it surprise you to learn that women appear more likely than men to feel sexually attracted toward someone only after feeling romantically attracted to him?

When college students were asked what they thought caused sexual desire, both sexes strongly agreed that the causes were often different for women and men (Peplau & Garnets, 2000; Regan et al., 2000). The most widely endorsed causes of female sexual desire were interpersonal experiences related to romantic love, whereas the most widely endorsed causes of male desire were biological processes and a physical "need" for sex. Thus, it appears that women tend to emphasize emotional intimacy as more of a necessity for sexuality than do men. The same gender difference exists among homosexual adults. Like heterosexual women, lesbians are less likely than gay and heterosexual men to desire or engage in casual sex (Peplau et al., 2004).

When we think about these gender differences within the contexts of the sexual mating system and the attachment system, we see that men appear more focused than women on the sexual mating aspect of this process, whereas women appear more focused than men on the attachment aspect. For women more than men, the goal of sex is intimacy, and the best context for pleasurable sex is a committed relationship. For men, this is less true (Peplau, 2003). Of course, this does not mean that women are not interested in casual sex and men do not seek committed romantic relationships. It simply means that gender differences in motivational tendencies regarding sex and intimacy appear to exist. However, these are only tendencies, and many women and men do not fit these general patterns. That is, some women show high levels of interest in casual sex, and some men seek sex only in committed relationships.

Finally, in considering how evolutionary and sociocultural factors may shape sexuality, growing evidence indicates that men and women differ in the malleability of their sexual motivation. For example, national surveys (Laumann et al., 1994) indicate that men of all educational and socioeconomic levels are about equally interested in sexual variety and experimentation, but that women's sexual desires and behaviors depend significantly on social factors such as education and religion. Highly educated women are much more likely than uneducated women to engage in oral sex, anal sex, homosexual activity, and other types of sexual experimentation. Similarly, women's interest in sexual experimentation is sharply curbed if they are members of socially conservative religions. Evidence that women's sexual motivation is more influenced by situational factors than men's is revealed in how the two sexes respond to a romantic breakup. Although women and men may have frequent sex with their partners while involved in an intimate relationship, following a breakup, women are much more likely than men to have no sex at all—including masturbation—for several months (Peplau, 2003). Roy Baumeister (2000) believes such findings suggest that, compared to men, women have higher *erotic plasticity,* meaning that their sexual motivation is more easily shaped by social, cultural, and situational factors.

11-3d The Sexual Response Cycle Is Very Similar in Males and Females

Although women and men may differ in what influences their sexual motivation, they do not substantially differ in how they experience the sexual act itself (Halaris, 2003). This fact became apparent in the mid-1960s, when William Masters and Virginia Johnson (1966) published their pioneering work on the human sexual response. By monitoring 382 female and 312 male volunteers as they masturbated or had intercourse, Masters and Johnson determined that women's and men's physiological changes as they approach and achieve orgasm are remarkably similar, and that the physiological expression of an orgasm is similar regardless of how it is achieved.

The **sexual response cycle** that the body passes through during sexual activity involves the following four stages:

> **sexual response cycle** The four stages of sexual responding—excitement, plateau, orgasm, and resolution; first identified by Masters and Johnson.

1. *Excitement*—The initial stage when the body becomes aroused. (For example, the skin becomes flushed, the penis and clitoris become enlarged, and vaginal lubrication increases.)
2. *Plateau*—The stage of full arousal. (The penis enlarges even more, and the outer third of the vagina becomes engorged with blood.)
3. *Orgasm*—The stage involving muscle contractions throughout the body. (Men ejaculate sperm-filled semen, and women's vaginal contractions facilitate conception by helping propel semen from the penis up into the vagina.)
4. *Resolution*—The stage when the body gradually returns to an unaroused state. (Muscles relax, and the engorged genital blood vessels release excess blood.)

One thing to remember about the stages in the sexual response cycle is that they blend into one another, with no clear divisions. During a given cycle, a woman may experience no orgasm, one orgasm, or multiple orgasms. In contrast, a man experiences only one orgasm, but he can achieve orgasm again following a rest—or *refractory*—period. This refractory period can last from a few minutes to a day or more, with the length of the rest period typically becoming longer with age. The intensity of orgasms varies, in both individuals and situations. Sometimes you might experience it as something like a sigh, while at other times it might feel like your entire body is simultaneously celebrating all the holidays of the year!

Some people cannot complete the sexual response cycle. For men, this might involve being unable to have or maintain an erection. In recent years, the drug *sildenafil* (trade name Viagra) has helped such men achieve and maintain an erection by increasing blood flow to the penis (Rowland & Burnett, 2000). About 10 percent of women and a few men remain at the plateau stage without experiencing orgasm, and some men experience premature ejaculation. Such sexual disorders can sometimes be traced to physiological or psychological causes, but often the cause is unknown. Although Masters and Johnson originally believed that subjective feelings of sexual arousal were directly related to specific physiological responses, later research discovered that this was not the case. For example, vaginal lubrication or penile erection is not necessarily a sign of sexual arousal but, instead, may be a response to a whole host of emotions, including anger or fear (Clayton, 2003; Marthol & Hilz, 2004).

Not surprisingly, sex researchers have found that cognitive factors influence sexual arousal (Scepkowski et al., 2004; Sewell, 2005). For example, men who have problems getting and maintaining an erection tend to be less aware of how aroused they are. Further, men who can become aroused fairly easily are relatively unconcerned by occasions when they cannot get or maintain an erection. In such instances, they tend to attribute their nonarousal to external events, such as something they ate or excessive fatigue. In contrast, men with arousal problems make damaging internal attributions: They believe that their nonarousal is caused by long-term physiological or psychological problems.

Testosterone, a male sex hormone found in both men and women, has a positive influence on sexual desire, although the effect is stronger among men than women (Leitenberg & Henning, 1995; Reichman, 1998). Despite this positive effect, eliminating testosterone production does not eliminate desire, and heightened levels of this hormone do not affect desire to the same extent as psychological factors, such as the quality of the partners' relationship (Persky, 1983). Many other hormonal and neurological systems are involved with sexual desire, sexual responses, and behaviors, but none adequately explains, by itself, why people are so driven to achieve sexual satisfaction, or the varied approaches sexual behaviors take. Turning sexual behaviors "on" or "off" is dramatically simpler among most animals other than humans and a few species of nonhuman primates (de Waal, 2000).

11-3e Sexual Orientation Is a Continuum Rather Than an All-or-None Distinction

Do you recall the moment when you decided you were going to be sexually attracted to women, men, or both? It is a pretty safe bet that your answer is no. Instead of choosing what kind of person sexually attracts you, like most people, you probably discovered your sexual attractions while growing up. **Sexual orientation** is the degree to which we are sexually attracted to persons of the other sex and/or to persons of our own sex. The dawning awareness of our sexual orientation usually occurs by adolescence, typically about 3 years before we become sexually active (Bell et al., 1981). This finding suggests that we generally realize what sex we are attracted to, not because of our sexual behavior, but because of our sexual feelings. In other words, at some time during childhood and adolescence, we typically discover that we have sexual feelings toward members of the other sex, our own sex, or both sexes. These sexual feelings—rather than actual sexual behavior—are what primarily determine whether we identify ourselves as heterosexual, homosexual, or bisexual.

In studying sexual orientation, behavioral scientists conceptualize it as a continuum, with **heterosexuality** at one end, **homosexuality** at the other end, and **bisexuality** somewhere in between (Haslam, 1997; Kelly, 2001). To characterize individuals' sexual orientation from this continuum perspective, Alfred Kinsey and his coworkers (1948) devised a seven-point scale, which is depicted in figure 11-5. On this scale, if you are attracted exclusively to persons of the other sex and you engage in sexual behavior only with such persons, you are at the heterosexual end of the continuum (category 0). In contrast, if you are attracted exclusively to persons of your own sex and you engage in sexual behavior only with such persons, you are at the homosexual end of the continuum (category 6). Finally, if you

testosterone A male sex hormone found in both men and women that has a positive influence on sexual desire. The additional testosterone in males stimulates the growth of the male sex organs in the fetus and the development of the male sex characteristics during puberty.

sexual orientation The degree to which a person is sexually attracted to persons of the other sex and/or to persons of the same sex.

heterosexuality The sexual orientation in which a person is sexually attracted primarily to members of the other sex.

homosexuality The sexual orientation in which a person is sexually attracted primarily to members of the same sex.

bisexuality The sexual orientation in which a person is sexually attracted to members of both sexes.

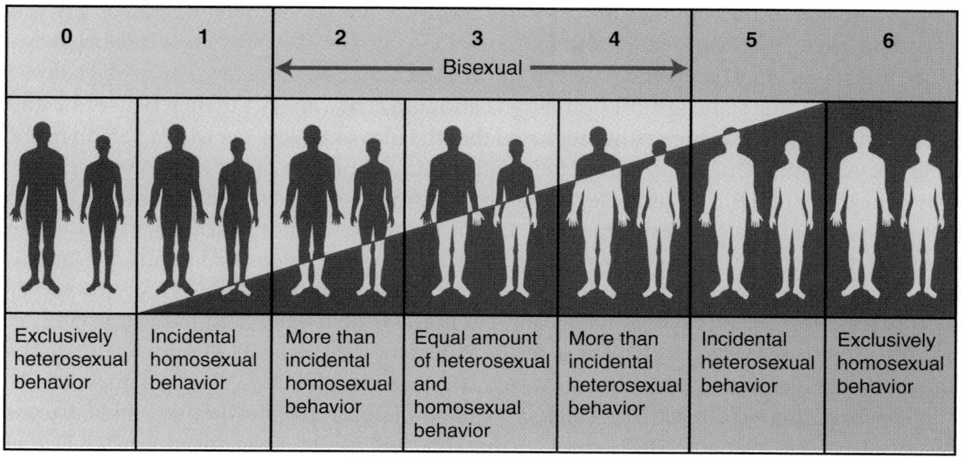

0	1	2	3	4	5	6
		←	Bisexual	→		
Exclusively heterosexual behavior	Incidental homosexual behavior	More than incidental homosexual behavior	Equal amount of heterosexual and homosexual behavior	More than incidental heterosexual behavior	Incidental heterosexual behavior	Exclusively homosexual behavior

Figure 11-5

Sexual Orientation as a Continuum

Instead of characterizing sexual orientation as an either-or distinction between heterosexuality and homosexuality, Kinsey et al. (1948) designed this seven-point scale to describe sexual orientation as a continuum, with heterosexuality and homosexuality at the ends and bisexuality in the middle.

fall somewhere between these two extremes (categories 2–4), you are usually defined as bisexual. This scientific viewpoint stands in sharp contrast to the conventional view that sexual orientation is an all-or-none distinction.

To more fully appreciate the complexity and diversity of human sexuality, it is useful to distinguish sexual orientation from *sexual identity*. **Sexual identity** refers to the identity a person organizes around his or her sexual orientation. North American culture, as well as many other cultures, has a fairly rigid notion of sexual identity: You can be "heterosexual," "gay," "lesbian," or "bisexual." In considering Kinsey's continuum concept of sexual orientation, it is important to note that your sexual orientation does not always coincide with your sexual identity. For example, you could experience sexual attraction toward members of both sexes but not identify yourself as bisexual. Similarly, you could be attracted to members of your own sex but still think of yourself as heterosexual. In fact, three different people could have the same distribution of sexual behavior on Kinsey's scale—for example, a score of 4—but have three different sexual identities: homosexual (gay or lesbian), bisexual, or heterosexual. In this regard, like gender (see chapter 3, section 3-4d), we socially "construct" our sexual identity with the help of others. Because people in most cultures are strongly socialized to think of themselves and others as sexually attracted to members of the other sex, it generally takes a longer time for people with a homosexual or bisexual orientation to cognitively pull themselves out of the heterosexual identity category and recategorize themselves as gay, lesbian, or bisexual.

> **sexual identity** The identity a person organizes around his or her sexual orientation, typically labeled "heterosexual," "gay," "lesbian," or "bisexual."

> *Journey of Discovery Question*
>
> What are the similarities and differences between the terms *sexual identity* and *gender identity*?

Many people who define themselves as heterosexual, gay, or lesbian have had sexual experiences outside their sexual identities (Diamond, 1998; Diamond & Savin-Williams, 2000). Indeed, cross-cultural research indicates that homosexual behavior is quite common. For example, in 22 of the 120 cultures examined in one study, over 20 percent of the men had engaged in homosexual activity, with some cultures having rates as high as 50 percent or more (Minturn et al., 1969). Another cross-cultural study found that homosexual behavior of some sort was considered normal and socially acceptable for at least some individuals in almost two-thirds of the 76 societies investigated (Ford & Beach, 1951). Even in cultures with the most restrictive views about same-sex sexual relations, homosexual behavior still takes place (Hatfield & Rapson, 1996). Yet, remember, behavior does not equal identity. What is the prevalence of heterosexual, gay, lesbian, and bisexual identities in the general population?

> Many years ago I chased a woman for almost two years, only to discover that her tastes were exactly like mine: we both were crazy about girls.
>
> —*Groucho Marx, American comedian, 1895–1977*

Frequency of Different Sexual Identities

Heterosexuality has clearly been the most practiced form of sexuality in all cultures throughout history (Bullough, 1980). Yet homosexual and bisexual activities have also occurred throughout these same time periods. Fantasies about, and sexual behaviors between, people of the same sex are far more common than identifying oneself as gay, lesbian, or bisexual. The National Health and Social Life Survey of American sexual behaviors found that 9 percent of men and 4 percent of women have had some form of sexual contact with a person of the same sex after puberty (Laumann et al., 1994). Further, between 7 and 8 percent of men and women either reported that the idea of having sex with a person of the same sex was "appealing" or reported being attracted to a person of the same sex. For those who reported experiencing same-sex attractions, women were more likely than men to also report experiencing other-sex attractions. In this survey, only about 1.4 percent of women identified themselves as lesbians, and only 2.8 percent of men identified themselves as gay. About half as many women and men reported a bisexual identity. The rates in this survey are comparable to those in other recent surveys in the United States and in Europe (Billy et al., 1993; Sandfort et al., 2001). Of course, these percentages are likely to underestimate the actual percentage of people with homosexual and bisexual identities. Can you guess why?

The answer is **heterosexism,** which is a system of cultural beliefs, values, and customs that exalts heterosexuality and denies, denigrates, and stigmatizes any nonheterosexual

> **heterosexism** A system of cultural beliefs, values, and customs that exalts heterosexuality and denies, denigrates, and stigmatizes any nonheterosexual form of behavior or identity.

form of behavior or identity (Herek et al., 1991). How does heterosexism manifest itself? Open and blatant expression of antigay attitudes by heterosexuals, such as calling another person a "faggot" or a "dyke," is certainly an example of heterosexism. However, heterosexism can also operate on a more subtle level. Like the fish that doesn't realize it is wet, heterosexuals are so used to defining heterosexual behaviors as normal and natural that they cease to think of them as a manifestation of sexuality. For instance, although heterosexuals may hardly notice a man and woman kissing in public, they often react with disgust or even hostility if the couple is of the same sex. Such condemnation of nonheterosexual behavior can make it dangerous for homosexual and bisexual individuals to do anything in public that would identify them as nonheterosexuals, a fact underscored by the high rate of gay hate crimes committed each year (Herek et al., 2002). In such an unaccepting social environment, it is likely that some gay, lesbian, and bisexual survey respondents are reluctant to tell a stranger (even anonymously) about their true sexual identity and sexual orientation.

Sexual Orientation and Mental Health

For many years the medical community identified homosexuality as a psychological disorder. Then, in 1957, psychologist Evelyn Hooker published her now-famous study that examined whether homosexual and heterosexual individuals differ in their psychological adjustment. Her findings indicated no significant differences between the two groups. These results were later replicated in many other studies using a variety of research methods (Berube, 1990; Freedman, 1971; Gonsiorek, 1991). Confronted with this overwhelming scientific evidence, in 1973 the American Psychiatric Association removed homosexuality from its list of recognized mental disorders. Soon the American Psychological Association endorsed the psychiatrists' actions. Additional research has disconfirmed other myths about homosexuality, such as the belief that the vast majority of child molesters are homosexual men. In reality, most molesters are male heterosexuals (Gonsiorek, 1982). Today, as in the past, the biggest threat to homosexual and bisexual individuals' mental health is not their sexual orientation but the hostility they experience from heterosexuals when their sexual identity becomes public knowledge (DeAngelis, 2002b; Herek et al., 2002).

Because of this lack of societal tolerance, gay, lesbian, and bisexual individuals who have not publicly revealed their sexual identity to those with whom they interact on a daily basis often describe feeling as if they are hiding their "true selves" or "living a lie." Imagine talking to friends or coworkers over dinner and not being able to share with them the many wonderful things you did with your boyfriend or girlfriend that weekend. Or imagine not feeling free to bring this person home to meet your parents and grandparents, because you are afraid of facing possible disapproval and hostility. On those rare occasions when you vaguely refer to this special person in conversation, you are careful to replace "she" or "he" with the romantically appropriate pronoun. Engaging in such conscious concealment of your sexual identity will likely make you feel psychologically distant from your friends, coworkers, and family members. It may also harm your mental health and lower your self-esteem (Fergusson et al., 1999; Sandfort et al., 2001). The alternative to concealing this central part of your personal identity is to "come out of the closet" and publicly switch your sexual identity.

The Process of "Coming Out"

Coming out is the process by which people acknowledge that they are gay, lesbian, bisexual, or in some cases simply questioning their sexual orientation. Most individuals first make this acknowledgement to themselves and later to others. Although coming out is often thought of as a one-time event, it is more properly considered a continual process that gay, lesbian, and bisexual persons experience throughout their lives. For instance, the person who acknowledges to himself and to his close friends that he is gay while a sophomore in college may not come out to his family and hometown friends until his senior year. Then, after moving to another city following graduation, he may have to repeat the coming-out process at his new job and with his new friends. Coming out often creates stress, because you are never sure how others will react due to heterosexism in the mainstream culture. Yet studies indicate that coming out promotes better psychological adjustment and overall mental health than not doing so (Strickland, 1995).

Nonheterosexual teenagers and young adults are much more likely to publicly switch their sexual identities while in college than in high school (Laumann et al., 1994). One reason

Have you ever wondered about the origin of the derogatory word *faggot,* which is used by bigots when referring to homosexual persons? The dictionary defines *faggot* as a bundle of sticks for firewood. During the European Inquisition, when accused "witches" were burned at the stake, people condemned to death for homosexual behavior were often set aflame ahead of time to act as kindling for the "witches'" flames.

Source: Courtesy of Figzoi.

for this timing is that college comes after high school, and students are simply more likely to realize they have a homosexual or bisexual orientation as they mature. However, a second reason is that the antigay prejudice permeating many aspects of mainstream society is generally less pronounced on college campuses than in high schools. Gay history courses, gay/lesbian/bisexual/straight alliances, and gay awareness weeks are now a normal part of the college experience for many students in the United States. With social norms promoting acceptance of diversity, college is often a place where many gay men, lesbians, and bisexuals feel comfortable enough to be themselves. Yet, even in a relatively tolerant social environment, it is still important for people to "test the waters" before coming out to everyone in their lives. Although there is no perfect formula for coming out, it is often best to first reveal your sexual identity to one or two friends who are likely to be accepting and supportive. If successful, this initial disclosure and subsequent social support can help buffer the negative effects of possible future rejections from family members, friends, or acquaintances.

Do People Ever Switch Back Their Sexual Identities?

For many nonheterosexual students, college is just a temporary oasis from cultural heterosexism. After graduation, the anxiety of facing antigay prejudice and discrimination at a new job without the social support relied upon in college causes some people to go back into the closet or redefine themselves as heterosexuals. Although this perceived need to "straighten up" is less pronounced now than 10 or 20 years ago, it may partly explain findings by Lisa Diamond (2003a) concerning the sexual-identity development of lesbian and bisexual women. Among 80 nonheterosexual female college students initially interviewed by Diamond as part of a longitudinal study, one-fourth said 5 years later that they were no longer lesbian or bisexual. Many conservative religious and political organizations that adamantly oppose homosexuality often cite this type of switching of sexual identities as evidence that homosexuality is merely a "phase" that impressionable young adults experiment with while living on socially permissive college campuses. These organizations further contend that such switching is evidence that sexual orientation is a "choice."

Such conclusions do not fit the available scientific evidence. In Diamond's study, the women who changed their sexual identity almost always remained as attracted to women as they were before redefining themselves. This finding indicates that the women's sexual orientation did not change; only their sexual identity changed. Half the women who dropped their lesbian or bisexual identities "reclaimed" their previous heterosexual identities, while the other half no longer defined themselves in terms of sexual identities. The women who reclaimed their heterosexual identities tended to have more rigid notions of sexuality and found that the only way to reconcile inconsistencies between their current heterosexual behavior and their lesbian or bisexual identity was to switch identities. As one of these women explained, "I think I still have the same orientation, but things are different because now I'm in a heterosexual relationship, and it's pretty serious and I guess that's what basically forms my identity."

Sexual-identity switching is most likely to occur when a person's sexual orientation is close to the midpoint on Kinsey's sexual orientation continuum (refer back to figure 11-5). This tendency to switch an ambiguous sexual orientation from a heterosexual identity to a homosexual or bisexual identity and then later back to a heterosexual identity or to no sexual identity appears to be more common among women than men (Diamond, 2003b; Peplau, 2003). A possible reason for this difference involves the previously discussed (section 11-3c) greater plasticity of women's sexuality and the fact that their sexual motivation is more influenced by feelings of attachment and intimacy than is men's sexual motivation. Because women's sexual desires are more strongly influenced by their emotional attachments to particular persons than are men's sexual desires, women with a relatively ambiguous sexual orientation may be more likely than similarly sexually ambiguous men to become sexually intimate with someone they bond with emotionally. In such instances, women report that their intense emotional feelings spark their sexual desire (Clausen, 1999; Diamond, 2000).

Based on this overview, you can see that using a sexual-identity label sometimes does not accurately describe a person's sexual orientation. By forcing some people to fit their relatively complex sexual attractions into fairly rigid sexual-identity categories, we can create confusion in their minds about their "true" target of sexual desire. As one woman in Diamond's (2003a) study explained, "A lot of people that I talk to say, 'Well, you know bisexuality is just one step up from one or the other, so you're not actually bisexual, you're actually on your way to becoming either straight or gay.' " For at least some people, there is no "true" target. Yet, until the cultural pressure to "pick" a sexual identity diminishes (don't hold your breath!), sexual-identity switching will remain a social fact of life.

11-3f The Causes of Sexual Orientation Are as Yet Unclear

Whenever discussion focuses on the possible causes of sexual orientation, it is often phrased in terms of "What causes homosexuality?" Yet this question is scientifically misconceived, because it falsely assumes either that heterosexuality needs no explanation or that its causes are already known. So what does cause sexual orientation?

Brain Development

Some researchers have examined whether specific brain areas might be associated with sexual orientation (K. M. Cohen, 2002). For example, a small part of the hypothalamus—no bigger than a grain of sand—has been found to be twice as large in the brains of heterosexual men as in gay men (LeVay, 1991). A similar difference has been found in a section of the fibers of the corpus callosum that connect the right and left brain hemispheres. In this case, the brain area is one-third larger in gay men than in heterosexual men (Allen & Gorski, 1992). Both of these brain differences are similar to the differences found between heterosexual men and lesbians. Together, they may indicate that brain development affects sexual orientation (LeVay, 1996). However, it is equally possible that these brain differences may not be the *cause* of sexual orientation but, rather, the *effect* of behaviors associated with homosexual versus heterosexual orientations and identities (Breedlove, 1997). In other words, certain differences in the life experiences of gay and heterosexual men may cause this part of the hypothalamus to develop differently. Until further research is conducted, both interpretations are plausible.

Genes

The finding that all three "points" on the sexual orientation continuum—heterosexuality, bisexuality, and homosexuality—exist throughout the world has bolstered the view that sexual orientation may be substantially determined by our genes. As in studies on the inheritance of intelligence (see chapter 10, section 10-4a), research on the inheritance of sexual orientation has focused on twins (Kendler et al., 2000). One study found that among gay men who were identical twins, over half of their twin brothers were also gay, compared with less than one-quarter of fraternal twin brothers (Bailey & Pillard, 1991, 1995). Similar findings were obtained with lesbian twins (Bailey et al., 1993). Although these results suggest that sexual orientation is at least partly inherited, a more recent study failed to find this effect (Rice et al., 1999). Because of these contradictory findings, the best we can conclude at this point is that a genetic influence on sexual orientation is possible (Hamer, 2002).

Gender Nonconformity

Although early attempts to identify social developmental causes of sexual orientation claimed that homosexuality was caused by a smothering mother, absent father, sexual abuse, or "deviant" homosexual role models, research did not support any of these claims (Storms, 1983). For example, sons of gay men are not more likely to become gay if they live with their father, and over 90 percent of children of lesbian mothers develop a heterosexual orientation (Bailey et al., 1995; Golombok & Tasker, 1996). Thus, unlike contagious diseases, you cannot "catch" a sexual orientation. The only early childhood experience that predicts the development of a homosexual versus a heterosexual orientation in adulthood for both women and men is *gender nonconformity*.

As depicted in table 11-1, when 1,500 homosexual and heterosexual women and men were interviewed about earlier life experiences, lesbians and gay men were significantly more likely to report that they had preferred play activities traditionally associated with the other sex and were more likely to have had other-sex friends (Bell et al., 1981). They also were less likely to have had a traditional gender role (masculine for boys and feminine for girls). Describing their

It wasn't easy telling my parents that I'm gay. I made my carefully worded announcement at Thanksgiving. I said, "Mom, would you please pass the gravy to a homosexual." Then my Aunt Lorraine piped in. "Bob, you're gay. Are you seeing a psychiatrist?" I said. "No, I'm seeing a lieutenant in the Navy."

—*Bob Smith, comedian, b. 1960*

Table 11-1	Gender Nonconformity in Childhood among Homosexual and Heterosexual Women and Men			
Gender Nonconforming Preferences and Behaviors	Men		Women	
	Gay (%)	Heterosexual (%)	Lesbian (%)	Heterosexual (%)
Did not enjoy traditional play activities for their sex	63	10	63	15
Did enjoy nontraditional play activities for their sex	48	11	81	61
Adopted nontraditional gender role (masculinity for girls and femininity for boys)	56	8	80	24
Had most childhood friends from the other sex	42	13	60	40

Source: Adapted from Bell, Weinberg, & Hammersmith, 1981.

childhood using labels derived from a heterosexist culture, the lesbians had acted more like "tomboys," and the gay men had acted more like "sissies" than did their heterosexual counterparts.

These gender nonconformity findings have been replicated in other studies (Lippa, 2002), and a growing number of psychologists believe that they may be due to one or more of the previously discussed biological factors (Bailey & Zucker, 1995; Green, 1987). Of course, it is important to remember that we are discussing group differences here, and there are many exceptions to these general findings. In other words, many heterosexuals prefer activities traditionally associated with the other sex, and many gay men and lesbians prefer traditional gender activities. Thus, despite these findings of group differences, you cannot reliably identify people's sexual orientation based on whether they like to play baseball versus perform gymnastics.

So where are we in our understanding of the causes of sexual orientation? There may well be genetic or other biological influences on sexual orientation, but the nature of these influences is still an open question. It is clear that, in almost all instances, we don't consciously choose our sexual orientation. Because of the strong antigay prejudice that still exists in many areas of the world, the possibility that sexual orientation is biologically determined may paradoxically lead to both a decrease and an increase in heterosexuals' intolerance of gay men, lesbians, and bisexuals. For instance, if sexual orientation is something we inherit, like skin color, then some heterosexuals may be less fearful of "catching" homosexuality through direct contact. As a result, they may interact more with nonheterosexuals and, through such contact, dispel their other misconceptions and become more tolerant (Anderssen, 2002; Tygart, 2000). However, if it is determined that genetics shape sexual orientation, it is also possible that heterosexuals with an antigay bias may try to genetically eliminate homosexuality from the human gene pool by either aborting or genetically altering fetuses with homosexual "markers." As an active creator of the social reality in which you live, you can use the information in this chapter to dispel many people's misconceptions about sexual orientation issues and thereby reduce heterosexism. Remember, in the journey of discovery, knowledge is power.

11-3g People Who Are Uncomfortable Thinking about Sex Are Most Likely to Have Unprotected Sex

Although social values have changed considerably in the 50-plus years since Alfred Kinsey conducted the groundbreaking sex research mentioned at the beginning of this chapter, sex researchers still face a degree of stigma when others learn what they study. As William Fisher states in his autobiographical chapter, *Confessions of a Sexual Scientist,* people often still expect him to justify why "a nice professional like me is in a field like this" (Fisher, 1993, p. 13). As with other psychologists to whom you have been introduced in this text, Fisher's scientific journey of discovery has been the product of opportunity, careful observation, and the motivation to follow through with the question, "I wonder if . . .?"

As a graduate student, Fisher stumbled upon a paradoxical finding that was to dominate much of his subsequent research: Men and women who expressed the most negative feelings about sexually explicit movies either had, or planned to have, the most children. After much thought and discussion, he and his colleagues theorized that people with negative feelings about sex, which they called **erotophobia,** would be least able to think about intercourse in advance, to learn about birth control, to talk to their partners about it, or to effectively use contraceptives. Thus, Fisher initiated a process of discovery to test the possible links between erotophobia and behaviors that may affect sexual health.

> **erotophobia** The tendency to respond to sexual cues negatively.

Typical of other areas of inquiry (see chapter 2, section 2-3a), Fisher's initial steps were to observe and record the emotional and behavioral responses of men who bought condoms, as part of a study on "male purchasing behavior" (Fisher et al., 1977). He next developed a scale to measure people's level of comfort with sexual issues, called the Sexual Opinion Survey (Fisher et al., 1988b). Fisher found that people scoring high in erotophobia reported parental strictness about sex, conservative attitudes, and the avoidance of masturbation (Fisher et al., 1988a). He also found that women tended to be more erotophobic than men.

In subsequent research, Fisher and his colleagues (1979) discovered that people who were high in erotophobia tended to plan less for sexual interactions and, thus, engaged in more unprotected sex than did other people. Such behavior increased their likelihood not only of having unplanned pregnancies but also of contracting sexually transmitted diseases. Fisher also discovered that medical students who were similarly negative and uneasy about sexual matters were less prepared than others to work with patients' sexual health problems or even to answer their sex-related questions (Fisher et al., 1988a). The same discomfort affected the quality of sex education offered by trained teachers (Fisher, 1993).

Having found evidence that people's discomfort with sex could actually place them at greater risk for unplanned pregnancies and sexually transmitted diseases, Fisher wondered whether he could develop an intervention program to counteract these negative outcomes. Thus, the next step in his scientific journey of discovery was to design sex-education courses that would specifically target people's discomfort in talking about contraception and sex. Subsequent evaluations of these programs indicate that they are successful in reducing unwanted pregnancies (Fisher, 1993). Fisher's work as a sex researcher nicely demonstrates how the "what if" questions in life can lead psychologists down many varied paths in the pursuit of scientific knowledge.

Section Review

- Evolutionary and sociocultural factors may jointly explain why men appear to have greater desire for sex and sexual variety than do women.
- Both the rape myth and acquaintance rape are fostered by traditional sexual scripts in which women act resistant to sex and men persist in sexual advances.
- Women and men are similar in their sexual arousal response.
- Regarding human sexual motivation, men may be more focused than women on the sexual mating aspect of this process, whereas women may be more focused than men on the attachment aspect.
- Women's sexual motivation may be more easily shaped by social, cultural, and situational factors than is men's sexual motivation.

- Sexual orientation is a continuum, with heterosexuality at one end, homosexuality at the other end, and bisexuality somewhere in between; a person's sexual orientation does not always coincide with her or his sexual identity.
- Heterosexism is a system of cultural beliefs, values, and customs that exalts heterosexuality and denies, denigrates, and stigmatizes any nonheterosexual form of behavior or identity.
- Genetic or other biological factors may influence sexual orientation.
- People who have negative attitudes about sex are more likely than those with positive attitudes to engage in unprotected sex, have unwanted pregnancies, and contract sexually transmitted diseases.

11-4 ACHIEVEMENT MOTIVATION

Preview

- *Are some people more driven to achieve than others?*
- *Who is most likely to seek out achievement situations that are either very easy or extremely difficult?*
- *Can achievement motivation be enhanced?*

The motives examined thus far—sex and hunger—are observed in many other species. Now we come to a motive that may be unique to humans: achievement motivation (Epstein, 1998). Some people seem to be more or less driven to succeed—to achieve their goals—sometimes at the expense of other pleasures. Others seem to avoid challenges out of fear of failing. Are these inborn traits? Do these tendencies develop out of experience?

11-4a Individuals Differ in Their Need for Achievement

need for achievement (n-Ach) A desire to overcome obstacles and meet high standards of excellence.

The **need for achievement (n-Ach)** is a desire to overcome obstacles and meet high standards of excellence (Murray, 1938). Although several different methods have been devised to study the need for achievement, researchers have traditionally measured the strength of this motive by examining people's fantasies. The reason for attending to people's fantasies to determine their desire for achievement is that researchers had previously noted that fantasies often reflect the current strength of people's hunger and sex motives. That is, when deprived of food, people tend to daydream about delicious meals, and when deprived of sex, their fantasies reflect their sexual appetites. Perhaps, investigators reasoned, achievement desires could be similarly measured.

Thematic Apperception Test (TAT) A test in which people "project" their inner feelings and motives through the stories they make up about ambiguous pictures.

One of the most popular tools used to measure the n-Ach is the **Thematic Apperception Test (TAT),** which we will examine again in chapter 12, section 12-6a. The TAT consists of a series of ambiguous pictures similar to the one in figure 11-6. Persons taking the test are asked to make up stories about the ambiguous pictures. These stories are then scored for the presence of a number of motives (for example, *need for power* and *need for affiliation*), including the n-Ach. In evaluating n-Ach, trained scorers look for achievement-related imagery and themes in the stories. For instance, if you were shown this picture of two elderly women looking at a letter and responded by saying this was a letter for their granddaughter informing her that she had won a national writing contest, your response would be scored as indicating achievement desires. If your TAT stories consistently contained such themes, you would be regarded as having a high n-Ach. Research suggests that the TAT does a moderately good job of measuring individual differences in n-Ach (Khalid, 1991; Tuerlinckx et al., 2002).

The Desire to Succeed versus the Fear of Failure

High n-Ach people have an intrinsic *desire to succeed.* This desire is assumed not to develop from biological or genetic sources but to come from experience and parental encouragement. David McClelland (1985) contends that n-Ach develops when children *internalize*

Figure 11-6

Measuring the Need for Achievement with the Thematic Apperception Test (TAT)

People taking the TAT tell or write stories about what is happening in a scene, such as this one showing two elderly women closely examining a letter. The following story illustrates strong achievement motivation: "Two older women are looking at a letter addressed to their granddaughter and are very curious about its contents, because they know she is waiting to learn whether she has won a national writing contest. This young woman desperately wants to attend college to pursue her writing career, and winning this contest will provide her with enough money to do so. Her grandmothers taught her to read and write but don't have any money to send her to college. When the young woman arrives home and opens the letter, she learns that she achieved the top prize in this nationwide competition, and she is recruited by many prestigious universities. The woman grows up to become a famous writer. Now, whenever she is faced with a difficult challenge and doubts her abilities, the woman thinks about her grandmothers and realizes that, by working hard, she will succeed."

Source: Richard F. Stone, *A Bad Case of Curiosity*, watercolor on board, 15.5 × 16.75 inches.

achievement values displayed by their parents and other important role models. Such internalization comes about by children observing adults engaging in achievement tasks and by themselves being placed in achievement situations that they can master. These challenges, however, cannot be so easy that the person doesn't feel some sense of satisfaction and accomplishment (McClelland et al., 1953).

Some people's achievement needs are less determined by a desire to achieve greatness than by a fear of appearing foolish, lazy, or stupid. Thus, an important component in understanding n-Ach is the additional motivational push we receive by *fear of failure* (Atkinson, 1957). If your desire for success is considerably stronger than your fear of failure, you will have a high n-Ach. However, if your fear of failure is considerably stronger than your desire for success, you will have a low n-Ach.

Do high n-Ach people approach all achievement challenges with equal desire? Not at all. In fact, high n-Ach individuals are more likely to choose tasks that are moderately difficult and challenging (those tasks with about a 50/50 chance of success) than tasks that are either extremely difficult or extremely easy (Atkinson, 1977; Slade & Rush, 1991). This is so because their desire for success is stronger than their fear of failure. Thus, these people are attracted to achievement situations that they can master if they work hard and precisely apply their skills (McClelland, 1995). When they succeed at these tasks, high n-Ach people are generally perceived as talented, hardworking, and deserving of praise and rewards. This positive feedback serves to both satisfy and further strengthen their achievement desires. In contrast, extremely difficult and extremely easy tasks are not nearly as appealing to people with a high n-Ach, because the probability of success is either very low ("Why waste my time?") or virtually guaranteed ("Where is the challenge?"). Further, if they do succeed at a virtually impossible task, their achievement is likely to be dismissed by others as sheer "dumb luck."

What about low n-Ach individuals? Do they completely avoid achievement situations? Again, the answer is no. They tend to pick achievement situations that are either very easy so success is guaranteed or extremely difficult so they have a good excuse for failing (McClelland, 1985). The key fact to remember about low n-Ach people is that their fear of failure is stronger than their desire for success. As a result, they pick achievement situations that will protect them from either failing or being blamed for failing. However, such situations also virtually guarantee that they cannot take credit for any success they achieve. Thus, while they may protect themselves from embarrassment and self-esteem loss, they have little hope of winning praise or enhancing their self-esteem. As a result, achievement situations are unlikely to ever be very rewarding to people with low n-Ach.

My mother drew a distinction between achievement and success. She said that achievement is the knowledge that you have studied and worked hard and done the best that is in you. Success is being praised by others, and that's nice, too, but not as important or satisfying.

—*Helen Hayes, American actress, 1900–1993*

If we don't succeed, we run the risk of failure.

—*Dan Quayle, U.S. senator and vice president, b. 1947*

This desire to meet high standards of excellence in achievement situations causes many people to experience high levels of anxiety as they prepare to demonstrate their skills. Such anxiety can sabotage achievement desires. The "Psychological Applications" section at the end of this chapter examines the psychological aspects of high anxiety in academic testing situations and offers tips on how to control such anxiety.

Are There Cultural Differences in the Achievement Motive?

The n-Ach was originally conceived as a motive that reflects individualist ideals of achieving personal gains in competition against others. When cross-cultural researchers have asked people to complete conventional achievement measures that emphasize individual achievement, respondents from individualist cultures exhibit higher achievement motivation than do respondents from collectivist cultures (Sagie et al., 1996). However, this does not mean that individualists are truly more achievement-oriented than collectivists. Instead, cross-cultural psychologists have argued that people from collectivist cultures focus on a different type of achievement that is much less associated with personal success (Markus & Kitayama, 1991; Smith & Bond, 1994).

Specifically, most collectivist cultures value goals that promote group harmony, loyalty, humility, and interdependence. These values are quite contrary to individualist ideals of achievement (Feather, 1994; Niles, 1998). Accordingly, goals that facilitate the well-being of the group will be seen as a mark of achievement more commonly within collectivist cultures than within individualist cultures (Jayakar, 1994; Singhal & Misra, 1994). Even the same achievement task is often perceived as meeting different goals. For example, among collectivists, achieving success in one's career is much less likely to be viewed solely as a personal gain than as bringing honor to one's family or gaining approval from teachers and peers (Urdan & Maehr, 1995).

11-4b There Are Strategies for Increasing Achievement Motivation

We are not born with a motive to achieve. Instead, we acquire it as parents and others encourage us and help us discover the rewards of mastering challenging tasks while surviving failures (Vallerand et al., 1997). Thus, how can we foster achievement motivation in people who typically avoid achievement situations?

One effective strategy is to get people to emotionally identify with the achievement task, so they become intrinsically motivated (see section 11-1e). If you can convince people that they are working on a task because it is important to them, they will work harder and do better work, even if they are low n-Ach individuals (Cialdini et al., 1998). Second, you should also take steps to increase the value of achieving (for example, emphasize feelings of pride and accomplishment) while decreasing the negative effects of failing (for example, downplay feelings of shame and guilt). By providing realistic models of success with positive outcomes, while introducing examples of failure within a supportive environment, the emotional responses and expectations related to both can be shifted (Sorrentino & Hewitt, 1984). Experience with failing—and finding that the world does not end in the absence of success—can lessen the fear and help one cope with difficult challenges.

If people confine themselves to tasks that are too easy, they gain little satisfaction when they succeed. On the other hand, if they regularly are asked to work on tasks well beyond their capabilities, achievement situations become associated with disappointment and a feeling of inferiority. Thus, a third important factor in increasing achievement motivation is to place people in achievement situations that are moderately difficult but that can be mastered if they exert themselves (Locke & Latham, 1990).

Finally, a fourth factor is to be careful how people are given feedback when working on achievement tasks. Frequent feedback is more helpful when success is being demonstrated and something is being gained. However, less frequent feedback and keeping long-term outcomes in mind are better when progress on achieving the goal is slow or uneven (Cochran & Tesser, 1996). This less frequent feedback shifts people's attention away from their immediate frustrations and toward the desired end state of success.

- The need for achievement (n-Ach) is a desire to overcome obstacles and meet high standards of excellence; it is assumed to develop from experience and parental encouragement.
- High n-Ach persons seek out achievement tasks that are moderately difficult, while low n-Ach persons choose either very easy or extremely difficult tasks.
- Achievement motivation can be enhanced through various intervention strategies.

11-5 EMOTION

Preview

- *What are emotions made of, and what functions do they serve?*
- *Do emotions cause changes in bodily responses?*
- *What brain regions control emotions?*
- *How do cognitions shape emotional experience?*
- *Does experiencing one emotion trigger its opposite emotion?*
- *Are men and women encouraged to express different emotions?*

It is difficult to imagine the pushes and pulls of motivation not being associated with some sort of emotion, such as fear, anxiety, love, desperation, or loathing. It is equally difficult to think of a strong emotion that doesn't serve to either push or pull us toward or away from some goal. In many respects, motivation and emotion are two sides of the same coin, with emotions both reflecting and inciting our motives. Let us now examine the character of emotions and the various theories that have been developed to explain them.

11-5a Emotions Are Positive or Negative Feeling States

Visualize the following experiences, pausing after each one and carefully paying attention to how you would feel:

- You're walking down the street, a car comes up fast from behind, and the driver blows the horn just as the car reaches you.
- You're walking down the street and see your heart's greatest desire not just walking toward you, but also looking at you and smiling.
- You're walking down the street and see that thoroughly annoying person who makes your life miserable stumble and fall face-first into a mud puddle.

These incidents would probably induce different emotional responses. But what makes up an emotion? Choose any one of the preceding situations. In response to this change in environment, would there be changes in how your body felt? Would you feel your heart race? Would your muscles become tense or relax? Would your attention, or what you were thinking about, change along with the emotion? What changes in body posture and/or facial expression would occur? Would there be any changes in your behavior?

Go back to the scenario of seeing "your heart's greatest desire"—but now add into the vision him or her walking hand in hand with another person, both gazing longingly into each other's eyes. The primary "thing" in the environment is still the "greatest desire," but the context (and therefore the meaning) has changed, and so has the way your body feels and how you might behave.

These examples illustrate the complexity of emotions. For our purposes, I define **emotion** as a positive or negative feeling state (or *evaluative response*) that typically includes some combination of physiological arousal, cognitive appraisal, and behavioral expression. Although many theories have been developed to explain emotions (Plutchik, 1994), most researchers consider that all emotions have the following unifying characteristics:

> **emotion** A positive or negative feeling state that typically includes some combination of physiological arousal, cognitive appraisal, and behavioral expression.

- Emotions involve reactions of many body systems.
- Expressions of emotion are based on genetically transmitted mechanisms but are altered by learning and interpretation of events.
- Emotions communicate information between people.
- Emotions help individuals respond and react to changes in their environment.

In short, an emotion is an experience felt as happening to the self that is partly generated by cognitive appraisal of a situation and accompanied by reflexive physiological changes (for example, an increase in blood pressure and heart rate) and behavioral responses (for example, facial expressions and postural changes).

11-5b Emotions Facilitate Survival

Humans, like other animals, signal their readiness to fight, flee, mate, and attend to each other's needs through a variety of facial and bodily nonverbal expressions (Buck, 1984). These adaptive response patterns include emotions (Lang, 1995; Plutchik, 1994). Evolutionary theories have emphasized the survival value of emotions, not only because they tend to motivate us to avoid what is harmful and approach what is beneficial, but also because emotional expressions and behaviors foster communication with others (Bonanno et al., 2002; Preston & de Waal, 2002).

After observing that a number of facial expressions of emotion appeared to be universal, Charles Darwin (1872) proposed that facial expressions are inborn and that the expressions we see today are those that allowed our ancestors to most effectively communicate to one another their inner states and behavioral intentions (see chapter 9, section 9-1g). Consistent with Darwin's evolutionary view of emotional expressiveness, cross-cultural research indicates that similar facial expressions are readily displayed and accurately interpreted by people from differing cultures (Eible-Eibesfeldt & Sutterlin, 1990; Ekman, 1970; Matsumoto et al., 1988). Although this research indicates substantial cross-cultural agreement in both the experience and the expression of emotions, certain emotions are easier to distinguish from one another than others. For example, people from all cultures can easily tell the difference between happiness and anger, but it is harder for them to distinguish adoration from desire. This finding has led to the belief that certain emotions are more basic, or *primary,* than others (Izard, 1989). Most classification lists include the following seven primary emotions: *anger, disgust, fear, happiness, surprise, contempt,* and *sadness* (Ekman, 1973, 1993). Other emotions considered basic by some theorists are *shame* and *guilt* (Reeve, 1992). The most recent studies of the human face find that the reason these seven emotions are most accurately "read" is because the facial expressions associated with each emotion are relatively unique to that emotion (Smith et al., 2005). Thus, it appears that the human brain has evolved to efficiently transmit signals to the facial muscles associated with specific emotions and also to "read" those facial signals on human faces. Further, the human face has evolved to accurately transmit facial expressions associated with specific emotions. Check out Self-Discovery Questionnaire 11-2 to determine how accurate you are in identifying the emotion conveyed in different facial expressions.

This does not mean, however, that people throughout the world always express emotions in the same way. Given the important role that emotions play in human interactions, it makes abundant sense that cultures would develop social rules for when and how different emotions are expressed (Mesquita & Frijda, 1992). For example, the cultural belief systems of individualism and collectivism have shaped norms related to acting in ways that might threaten group harmony. That is, collectivists are much more likely than individualists to monitor their behavior so it does not disrupt the smooth functioning of the group. Regarding emotions, research suggests that, although people from collectivist and individualist cultures do not differ in publicly displaying positive emotions, collectivists are much more uncomfortable about publicly expressing negative emotions (Stephan et al., 1996).

Does this mean that people from collectivist cultures *feel* negative emotions differently than individualists feel them? In an attempt to answer this question, Paul Ekman (1970) unobtrusively recorded the facial expressions of Japanese and Americans while they individually watched either an emotionally neutral film or one depicting body mutilation. In this "viewing alone" condition, Ekman found a very strong positive correlation between the facial expressions displayed by the Japanese and American participants ($r = +.88$), indicating clear

Fear is a question: What are you afraid of, and why? Just as the seed of health is in illness, because illness contains information, your fears are a treasure house of self-knowledge if you explore them.

—*Marilyn Ferguson, U.S. author, b. 1938*

Can You Match the Seven Primary Emotions with Their Correct Facial Expressions?

Cross-cultural research has determined that the seven primary emotions are anger, disgust, fear, happiness, surprise, contempt, and sadness. In identifying these emotions as "primary," social scientists mean that people find them easier to distinguish from one another than other emotions. Examine each of the seven facial expressions here. Can you identify the correct emotion to each expression? Answers are listed below.

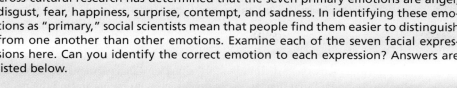

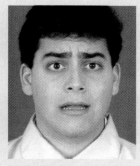

Answers: Top row, left to right: happiness, fear, anger. Middle row, left to right: disgust, sadness, surprise. Bottom row: contempt.

Source: © 1988–2004 David Matsumoto and Paul Ekman.

agreement in their expressions of such emotions as anger, disgust, surprise, and fear. However, when someone else entered the viewing room while a participant was watching a film, the Japanese, unlike the Americans, tended to display polite smiles rather than expressing their authentic emotions. These findings suggest that collectivism influences whether people publicly *express* negative feelings, but not whether they privately experience them. In other words, there is no evidence that collectivists *feel* emotions differently than do individualists.

What are the feelings of men? They are joy, anger, sadness, fear, love, disliking, and liking. These seven feelings belong to men without their learning them.

—*From* The Li Chi, *first-century Chinese encyclopedia*

Returning to the notion that emotions have survival value, we see that recent investigations indicate that, as people immerse themselves in satisfying friendships and romantic relationships, they experience an *emotional convergence* with their partners: That is, the emotions of the two people become increasingly similar over time (Anderson et al., 2003). When one person reacts to a situation with fear, laughter, or sadness, her or his partner's emotions are likely to correspond. The benefit of such emotional convergence is that people's thoughts and behaviors become more coordinated (Keltner & Haidt, 1999, 2003). They emotionally respond as a "team," supporting each other's definition of the situation. Such partner support not only increases people's confidence that they are accurately reacting to events around them—after all, there is strength in numbers—but also might at times have real immediate survival value. For example, if one person reacts fearfully to an approaching stranger, her or his partner is also likely to be on guard. This ability to quickly construct a united defensive front when facing possible danger provides safety not afforded those couples who are emotionally out of synch.

Non-invasive

11-5c Emotions Result in Bodily Responses

Can you imagine riding a roller coaster and not feeling your heart pounding or your blood pressure rising? What if there were no anticipatory "butterflies" in your stomach prior to an important date? The emotional impact of these events would be blunted without physiological feedback.

Emotions and the Autonomic Nervous System

The body's responses that are integral to emotion are produced by the *autonomic nervous system*. As discussed in chapter 3, section 3-2a, the autonomic nervous system is the part of the peripheral nervous system that commands movement of involuntary, nonskeletal muscles—such as the heart, lung, and stomach muscles—over which we have little or no control. The autonomic nervous system is further divided into two separate branches—the *sympathetic nervous system* and the *parasympathetic nervous system* (figure 11-7)—that tend to work in opposition to each other in order to keep the body's vital systems in a state of homeostasis (see the earlier discussion in section 11-1c).

Figure 11-7

The Dual Functions of the Autonomic Nervous System

The sympathetic and parasympathetic divisions of the autonomic nervous system often stimulate opposite effects in the body's organs. The sympathetic nervous system prepares your body for action, while the parasympathetic nervous system calms the body. Can you explain how these two systems respond to threat?

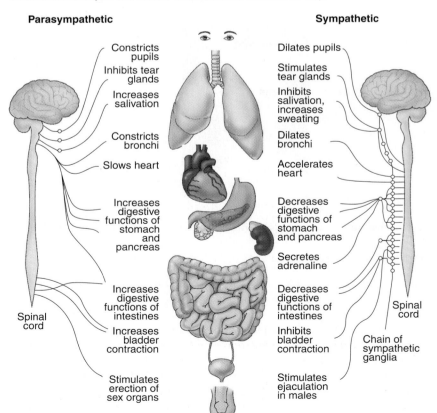

As you recall, the sympathetic nervous system is geared toward energy expenditure—getting the body ready to respond (the "fight-or-flight" response) by moving blood to the muscles and releasing stored energy. This system not only is activated to meet physical demands, but also functions when you experience strong emotions. In contrast, the parasympathetic nervous system is geared toward energy conservation and "refueling" by stimulating digestion and decreasing blood flow to the muscles. Although this system has not traditionally been associated with emotion to the same degree as the sympathetic system, its role in emotions has received more attention recently. For example, *emotional fainting* is likely a symptom of an overreaction by the parasympathetic system (Vingerhoets, 1985). In addition, *worrying* is characterized by low parasympathetic activity combined with a relatively inflexible autonomic response (Borkovec et al., 1998).

Can You Detect Lying by Measuring Autonomic Responses?

Because the sympathetic nervous system is associated with emotional arousal, scientists have reasoned that if they can obtain measurements of various autonomic responses they should be better able to determine whether people are lying. Why? Because usually when people are trying to cover up lies they become anxious. The **polygraph** is the most common "lie detector." This mechanical device measures a variety of autonomic responses, typically respiration, heart rate, blood pressure, and galvanic skin response (palm perspiration). Each of these physiological responses is affected by the sympathetic nervous system. Therefore, increases in heart rate, breathing, blood pressure, and palm sweating are interpreted as signs of lying when responding to appropriate questions. As depicted in figure 11-8, a polygrapher will monitor physiological responses to control questions (for example, "What is your favorite color?") and compare those responses to ones relevant to the investigation ("Have you ever taken property from an employer?"). Larger responses to key questions, reflecting greater sympathetic nervous system response, are considered "consistent" with lying.

Is a polygraph a true "lie detector"? No. It is really a detector of sympathetic nervous system activity. Researcher David Lykken (1998) made that very point when demonstrating the numerous ways in which a polygraph can lead to inaccurate conclusions about a person's guilt or innocence. It is true (I'm not lying!) that trained polygraph experts can accurately identify lying as much as 80 to 98 percent of the time. However, accuracy in identifying a person as *innocent* still suffers under this technique, with error rates as high as 55 percent (Honts & Perry, 1992; Kleinmuntz & Szucko, 1984; Lykken, 1984).

> **polygraph** A machine that measures several of the physiological responses accompanying emotion (such as respiration, heart rate, blood pressure, and palm perspiration).

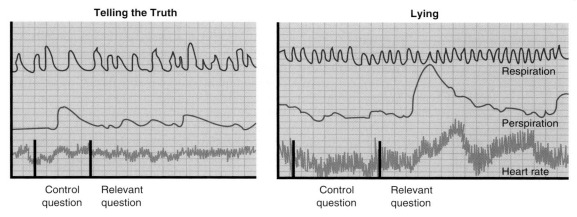

Figure 11-8

Detecting Lying with the Polygraph

In the polygraph test, the polygrapher compares physiological responses to control and relevant questions. The polygraph responses on the left are from a person who responded less strongly to a question relevant to a crime than to an emotionally arousing control question not relevant to the crime. This comparison of the physiological responses indicates that the person is likely being truthful. In contrast, the polygraph responses on the right are from a person who responded more strongly to a question relevant to the crime than to an emotionally arousing question not relevant to the crime. This comparison indicates that the person is likely lying. How might such polygraph methods sometimes lead to errors in detecting liars?

PET scan: positron emission tomography

Further, because a polygraph is measuring sympathetic nervous system activity and not actual lying, the machine can also be fooled by a person being tested who consciously elevates their physiological responses while answering neutral questions. This can be done by biting the tongue or squeezing the anal sphincter muscles. These falsely high physiological responses to neutral questions will later mask the elevated physiological responses to the important questions, making lies more likely to go undetected. Aldrich Ames, who was convicted of espionage that led to the deaths of at least 10 CIA agents, passed two lie-detector tests by taking advantage of polygraph weaknesses in this area (Adams, 1995; Weiner et al., 1995).

Due to its inability to actually detect lies, the polygraph is inadmissible as evidence in almost all courts of law. However, polygraph tests are becoming increasingly common for employment screening and as part of criminal investigations. This increased use is occurring despite the fact that a majority of experts in the field of psychophysiology believe the polygraph is an invalid and theoretically unsound approach to lie detection (Iacono & Lykken, 1997).

Are there more accurate alternatives to the polygraph? Measurements of brain activity obtained by electroencephalograph (EEG) machines and the more elaborate functional magnetic resonance imaging (fMRI) scanners have been studied as possible deception detectors, but their reliability and validity outside the laboratory have not been adequately tested (Boaz et al., 1991; Farwell & Donchin, 1991; Lee et al., 2002; Zhou et al., 1999). At this time, a truly accurate way to detect lying does not exist. The polygraph, properly administered by a trained professional, can work as one possible tool for investigation but should not be regarded by itself as providing enough evidence to determine guilt, innocence, or deception.

11-5d Two Theories Dispute Whether Physiological Responses Precede Emotions

In 1884, William James and the Danish physiologist Carl Lange independently proposed that our subjective emotional experiences are automatically caused by specific physiological changes in the autonomic nervous system that, in turn, are caused by environmental stimuli. According to James, "We feel sorry because we cry, angry because we strike, and afraid because we tremble" (1890, p. 1066).

Consider the example of a car horn honking at you unexpectedly. The **James-Lange theory** would predict that your heart would pound and your body would tremble *before* you felt fear. According to the theory, your brain would perceive the physiological responses to the horn honking as the emotion of fear. Similarly, the palm-sweating, heart-fluttering, and stomach-churning responses upon seeing your "greatest desire" would be perceived as "longing" or "love." This theory considers all emotions the products of different physiological changes that the brain automatically interprets, all of which occur in response to environmental stimuli.

In contrast to this view of how we experience emotions, the physiologists Walter Cannon (1927) and Philip Bard (1934) offered a very different perspective. What came to be called the **Cannon-Bard theory** contended that feedback from body organs could not be the source for our emotions because autonomic processes are typically too slow (taking 1–2 seconds) to explain the almost instantaneous experience of emotions. Cannon and Bard further argued that, because many different emotional states are associated with the same autonomic responses, arousal is too general to directly cause specific emotions. Instead, they proposed that emotion-provoking events *simultaneously* induce both physiological responses and subjective states that we label as emotions. This occurs because information concerning the emotion-inducing event is transmitted simultaneously to the brain's cortex—which causes the subjective awareness of emotion—and to the autonomic nervous system—which causes the physiological arousal. From this perspective, then, when the car's horn sounds, this event causes your heart to race *as* you experience a feeling you call "fear." Figure 11-9 illustrates how these two theories view the process of emotion differently.

Which theory is more accurate? Actually, research partially supports both theories. First, the contention by Cannon and Bard that autonomic responses occur too slowly to account for many emotional responses still appears valid. However, consistent with the James-Lange theory, research over the past decade suggests that different emotions do appear to be associated with distinct autonomic responses (Boiten, 1998; Levenson, 1992). For example, anger and fear produce greater heart rate acceleration than does hap-

James-Lange theory
A theory stating that emotion-provoking events induce specific physiological changes in the autonomic nervous system, which our brain automatically interprets as specific emotions.

Cannon-Bard theory
A theory that emotion-provoking events simultaneously induce both physiological responses and subjective states that are labeled as emotions.

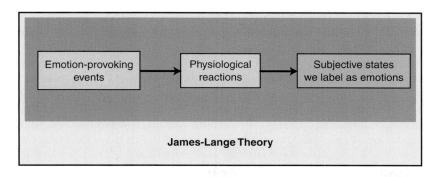

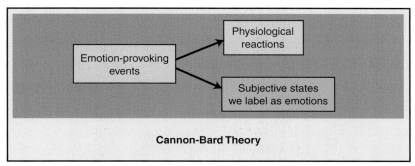

Figure 11-9

Two Contrasting Theories of Emotion

While the James-Lange theory proposes that physiological reactions cause emotions, the Cannon-Bard theory contends that these two processes occur simultaneously in response to emotion-provoking events.

piness, and those two emotions are also autonomically distinguishable from each other. Cross-cultural research further indicates that these associations between specific body changes and specific emotional experiences are universal, suggesting that they may be "hardwired" into the brain (Levenson et al., 1992). Although these findings suggest that emotional reactions can be generated by changes in our body states, most researchers agree with the Cannon-Bard proposition that our subjective experience of emotion also involves cognition.

One variation of James's theory is the **facial feedback hypothesis,** which proposes that specific facial expressions trigger the subjective experience of specific emotions (Duclos et al., 1989; Laird, 1974). In one experiment testing this hypothesis, the German psychologist Fritz Strack and his colleagues (1988) asked college students to hold a pen in their mouths while they looked at a series of amusing cartoons. Participants in the *lips condition* were

facial feedback hypothesis A theory of emotion proposing that specific facial expressions trigger the subjective experience of specific emotions.

The facial feedback hypothesis states that changes in facial expression can lead to corresponding changes in emotion. In an experiment testing this hypothesis, Fritz Strack and his colleagues (1988) asked participants to read cartoons while holding a pen in their mouths. People who were told to hold the pen between their teeth thought the cartoons were funnier than those who held the pen between their lips. Do these findings support the facial feedback hypothesis?

Source: Courtesy of Figzoi.

instructed to hold the pen tightly with their lips, while those in the *teeth condition* were told to hold the pen with their front teeth (see photo on previous page). In a control condition, participants were told to hold the pen in their nondominant hand. After reading the cartoons, all students rated how funny they were using a 10-point scale. You can tell by looking at the photograph that holding a pen with the teeth causes a person to smile, while holding it with the lips produces a frown. Did this manipulation of facial expressions cause participants to experience different emotions? Yes. Those participants who held the pen between their teeth found the cartoons to be the most amusing, followed by those who held it in their hand. Students who held the pen in their lips gave the cartoons the lowest ratings of amusement. The way this phenomenon may work is that our facial muscles send feedback signals to the brain, producing neurological changes that trigger specific emotions, even though the emotions triggered may not be exactly the same as when we are genuinely happy or sad (Ekman & Davidson, 1993).

11-5e The Brain Coordinates Emotional Responses

Ultimately, the brain is what controls the body's responses to emotional stimuli. Although no single brain region controls emotion, three regions are of particular importance: the hypothalamus, the limbic system, and the cerebral cortex. Investigations of these brain regions have provided insights into (1) how we can experience emotion before cognition (as proposed by the James-Lange theory) and (2) how the cerebral cortex interprets emotion (as proposed by the Cannon-Bard theory).

The Hypothalamus

Just as the *hypothalamus* is vital in the regulation of eating (see section 11-3a), it also provides a vital link between higher-order cognitive activities in the forebrain and activities controlled by more primitive areas of the lower brain and those concerned with homeostatic control of the body. The hypothalamus does this by converting emotional signals generated in the forebrain into autonomic and endocrine responses. Thus, when something angers or frightens you, the hypothalamus activates the sympathetic division of the autonomic nervous system's "fight-or-flight" responses and the endocrine system's release of hormones.

The Limbic System

A key component in human emotional responses is the *limbic system,* which is a set of interrelated neural structures located at the border of the brain's "older parts" and the cerebral cortex (see chapter 3, section 3-3b). Although different structures in the limbic system relate to different aspects of emotion, the structure that has received the most attention is the *amygdala,* which is thought to be the first processor of human emotional responses (Hamann et al., 2002; LeDoux, 1998).

Two distinct neural circuits involving the amygdala appear to produce emotional responses, particularly fear (Armony & LeDoux, 2000). The first circuit is very primitive and consists of the amygdala quickly evaluating incoming sensory information from the *thalamus* (the brain's sensory relay station) and eliciting an immediate emotional response by activating the hypothalamus. This emotional response does not entail any higher-order processing by the cerebral cortex. The fear you experience when someone jumps out at you from the shadows is an example of this first-circuit emotional response. Emotional responses acquired through classical conditioning are also a function of this primitive neural circuit, and the emotional responses that the James-Lange theory best explains arise through this first emotional circuit as well.

When the thalamus sends sensory information to the amygdala, it also simultaneously sends this information to the cerebral cortex for further processing (LeDoux, 1995). This second neural circuit involves slower processing, because it requires more complex cognitive appraisal by the cerebral cortex, involving the use of acquired knowledge and consideration of motives and goals. Following this appraisal, information is then transmitted to the amygdala, and a second emotional response occurs when the hypothalamus is activated. The sub-

Forebrain

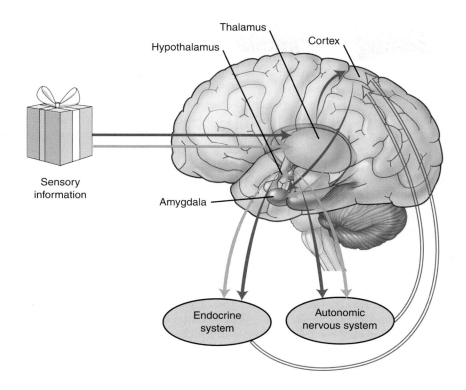

Thalamus

Hypothalamus

Cortex

Sensory
information

Amygdala

Endocrine
system

Autonomic
nervous system

Figure 11-10

Two Neural Circuits for Processing Emotion

Two distinct neural circuits process emotional responses, both involving the amygdala in the brain's limbic system. The activation of both circuits begins with sensory information relayed from the thalamus. In the first circuit (blue arrows), the amygdala processes this sensory information and immediately elicits an emotional response without any higher-order processing. In the second circuit (red arrows), the cerebral cortex receives the sensory information from the thalamus and engages in more complex cognitive appraisal before transmitting a signal to the amygdala. Then a second emotional response occurs. Both circuits ultimately activate the hypothalamus, which produces autonomic and endocrine changes. These changes are also sent back (red outline arrows) to the cerebral cortex, where they are analyzed and interpreted.

sequent changes that occur in the autonomic and endocrine systems are relayed back to the cerebral cortex for analysis and interpretation. Complex emotions such as love, happiness, sorrow, and guilt are most likely due to this second emotional circuit. The operation of this second neural circuit resembles what the Cannon-Bard theory hinted at in proposing that the cerebral cortex causes the subjective awareness of emotion. Both neural circuits are illustrated in figure 11-10.

Sometimes, these two neural circuits can generate emotional responses that conflict with one another. For example, in chapter 7, section 7-1d, you learned that cancer patients receiving chemotherapy experience nausea and often develop a classically conditioned aversion to stimuli associated with their treatment. This aversive reaction is a function of the first neural circuit. However, despite the nausea, cancer patients generally maintain a strong "approach" response to chemotherapy because they realize it is their best route to recovery. This second, more thoughtful reaction is due to the functioning of the second neural circuit.

The Cerebral Cortex

While the limbic system is important for processing emotions, the *cerebral cortex* is important for subjectively experiencing emotions. As you recall from chapter 3, section 3-3d, the cerebral cortex is divided into two rounded halves, called the cerebral hemispheres. Overall, the right cerebral hemisphere seems to be more active than the left hemisphere during the expression of emotions and when processing emotional cues from others (Lee et al., 2004; Oatley & Jenkins, 1996). Because the right hemisphere controls the left side of the body and the left hemisphere controls the right side, the left side of the face is somewhat more involved in emotional expression than the right side.

Research further suggests that each of the two hemispheres is related to one type of emotion more than another. For example, activation of the anterior region of the left hemisphere is associated with approach-related emotions, whereas activation of the anterior region of the right hemisphere is associated with aversion-related emotions (Sutton & Davidson, 1997). Apparently, this hemispheric difference is inborn: Infants as young as 3 to 4 days show more active left hemispheres when given sweet-tasting sucrose and more right hemisphere activity when given sour-tasting citric acid. Similarly, 10-month-old babies with more active left hemispheres tend to be more placid and become less upset upon separation from their mothers than babies with more active right hemispheres (Davidson & Fox, 1989). Among adults, individuals with damage to the anterior region of the left hemisphere tend to express intense negative affect, such as pathological crying, while those with damage to the anterior region of the right hemisphere often display pathological laughing (Davidson, 1992; Davidson, 2005). Together, these findings suggest that the left cerebral hemisphere is somewhat more involved in expressing positive emotions, while the right hemisphere is more involved in expressing negative emotions (Fox & Davidson, 1991). Before reading the next section, complete Explore It Exercise 11-1 to gain some insight into whether you exhibit more activation of your right or left cerebral hemisphere.

11-5f The Two-Factor Theory Emphasizes the Role of Cognition in Emotions

The James-Lange theory hypothesizes that physiological arousal precedes the experience of emotion. The Cannon-Bard theory hypothesizes that our emotions are physiologically similar. Taking these different hypotheses from the competing theories, Stanley Schachter and Jerome Singer (1962) proposed that if people are emotionally aroused but not sure what they are feeling, they look for cues in their surroundings. If others are happy, they are likely to interpret their arousal as happiness. If others are anxious, they too are likely to feel anxious. In other words, they will perceive themselves as experiencing the emotion that their surroundings tell them they should be experiencing. Thus, according to Schachter and Singer, emotions are based on two factors: *physiological arousal* and *cognitions* about what that arousal means. They named their theory the **two-factor theory** of emotions.

In one field experiment testing this theory, male hikers walking across a park bridge were asked by an attractive female research assistant to write an imaginative story in response to a TAT picture while standing on the bridge (Dutton & Aron, 1974). In one condition, the bridge was very sturdy and stood only a few feet above the ground. In another condition, the bridge was 5 feet wide, 450 feet long, and constructed of wooden boards attached to wire cables that were suspended 230 feet above a rocky gorge! It was assumed that the men who encountered the assistant on the high suspension bridge would be more physiologically aroused than those who met her on the low, sturdy bridge. Based on the two-factor theory, researchers predicted that the men on the high bridge would interpret their arousal as being caused by sexual interest toward the assistant rather than by fear of heights. Consistent with the theory, the men on the high bridge not only told TAT stories with significantly higher sexual imagery than the men on the low bridge, but also were more likely to call the assistant for a date! Additional research has demonstrated that the attributions we make concerning our physiological responses to a particular stimulus will often, but not always, determine our emotional reactions (Schachter, 1959, 1966).

two-factor theory A theory of emotion suggesting that our emotional states are sometimes determined by experiencing physiological arousal and then attaching a cognitive label to the arousal.

Journey of Discovery Question

Imagine that you are going out on a date with someone, and you would like this person to fall in love with you. Up to this point in your relationship, this person likes you only "as a friend." Based on your knowledge of the two-factor theory of emotions, what sort of activities might you plan for the date to increase the likelihood that the object of your affections will experience a similar emotion toward you?

Explore It
Exercise **11-1**

Which Side of Your Brain Is More Active during Emotional Situations?

People differ in which hemisphere of their brains is more active during emotional experiences, and this difference is related to what emotions they experience. One way in which individual differences in hemispheric activation have been evaluated is to measure the direction of a person's gaze after asking them an emotion-laden question. In a right-handed person, if the eyes move to the left, this is associated with right-hemisphere activation, whereas if the eyes move to the right, it signifies left-hemispheric activation. Researchers have used questions similar to those listed below to measure hemispheric activation (Schwartz et al., 1975). Ask a friend to read these questions to you and have her or him note the direction of your first eye movement following each question. If on seven or more of the questions your eyes move in the same direction, this suggests that you have more activation on one side of your brain than the other. Seven or more eye movements to the left indicate right-hemisphere activation, whereas seven or more eye movements to the right indicate left-hemisphere activation. This test is meant only for right-handed individuals, because left-handers have a more complicated pattern of hemispheric activation for which this eye-movement test is not a good measure.

Question 1: Tell me how you feel when you are nervous.

Question 2: Visualize and describe the most upsetting movie you have seen.

Question 3: Imagine that you are relaxing on a warm, sunny beach as you watch the sun set in the westward sky. Your friend is sitting nearby with his back toward your right side. Toward approximately what direction is your friend looking?

Question 4: When you visualize your father's face, what is the first emotion you experience?

Question 5: Make up a sentence using the words *alarm* and *anger.*

Question 6: Visualize and describe the most pleasurable scene in which you recently have been.

Question 7: Describe how you feel when annoyed.

Question 8: Imagine that you are a surgeon and must make a long and deep incision upon a patient's body. You must cut a straight line from the person's left eye to his right shoulder. Visualize making the incision, telling me through what areas of the patient's face you would cut.

Question 9: Visualize and describe the most beautiful photo you have recently seen.

Question 10: Construct a sentence using the words *bliss* and *delight.*

Keep in mind that this is not a conclusive measure of which brain hemisphere is more active during emotional situations. Also keep in mind that most people do not show consistent eye movements to one or another direction. If your eye-movement responses are in the range of seven or more in one direction, you can decide whether you believe that you are more vulnerable to positive or negative emotions. As noted, research suggests that people who consistently look to the left should be more likely to experience negative emotions, while people who consistently look to the right should be more likely to experience positive emotions.

11-5g One Emotion May Trigger an Opposite Emotion

As discussed in section 11-5c, once the sympathetic nervous system activates the body's energy resources in response to a threat, the parasympathetic system responds by conserving these resources. Noting how the body often responds in this counterbalancing fashion, psychologist Richard Solomon (1980) suggested that our experience of emotion often occurs in a similar manner. For example, have you experienced elation after succeeding at some task only to have that feeling soon replaced by a sense of despondency? Or have you felt angry and then afterward felt a sense of calm? Solomon's **opponent-process theory** contends that every emotion triggers an opposite emotion. In addition, the theory proposes that repetition of an experience causes the initial emotional reaction to weaken and the opposing emotional reaction to strengthen (Solomon & Corbit, 1974).

The opponent-process theory of emotion is similar to the opponent-process principle of color vision, discussed in chapter 5, section 5-2e. This principle states that when you stare at a particular color and then look away, you see the opposing color as an afterimage due to a "rebound effect" in opponent cells. Richard Solomon believed that the same principle holds for emotions. For example, consider how the opponent-process theory would explain your emotional reaction to skydiving. During your first parachute jump, you would probably experience considerable fear as you prepared to leap from the plane. This fear would undoubtedly subside and give way to exhilaration upon your landing safely on the ground. According to the theory, your "rebound" exhilaration would become greater and start earlier with each successive jump. Eventually, your fear could diminish to the point where the entire experience was pleasurable.

The opponent-process theory also provides insights into drug abuse. Initially, drug use often provides intense pleasure, which is followed by unpleasant withdrawal symptoms. With repeated drug use, these unpleasant aftereffects become stronger, while the initial pleasure diminishes. Eventually, taking the drug is motivated less by the fleeting pleasure it provides and more by the desire to extinguish the pain of withdrawal. Table 11-2 summarizes the four theories of emotion discussed in this section.

11-5h Gender May Sometimes Shape the Social Meaning of Emotion

Instead of trying to understand emotion by studying its components or its association with physiological processes, some psychologists attempt to understand the social meaning of emotion in a culture. How is the meaning of emotion learned from those around us? According to this perspective on emotion, as children mature, they learn an *emotion culture*, which consists of the informal norms governing what emotions are appropriate in different

opponent-process theory
A theory of emotion suggesting that every emotion triggers an opposite emotion.

According to opponent-process theory, every emotion triggers an opposite emotion.
Source: © Stockbyte.

Table **11-2** Four Theories of Emotion	
Theory	**Basic Assumptions**
James-Lange theory	Emotion-provoking events induce physiological reactions that then cause the subjective states we label as emotions.
Cannon-Bard theory	Emotion-provoking events simultaneously induce physiological reactions and subjective states that we label as emotions.
Two-factor theory	Emotion-provoking events induce physiological reactions that increase arousal, which we then identify as a particular emotion based on situational cues.
Opponent-process theory	Emotional reactions to an event are automatically followed by an opposite emotional reaction. Repeated exposure to the same event weakens the initial emotion while strengthening the opposing emotion.

circumstances for particular people. These norms often vary from culture to culture and are often shaped by gender beliefs (see section 11-5b).

In North American culture, Stephanie Shields (2002, 2005) describes two contrasting emotional styles linked to gender. Both are required of women and men, but each is expected more of one sex than the other. *Extravagant expressiveness* is an open style of experiencing and communicating emotion that is associated with femininity. This form of emotion is evident in nurturing and is the form linked in our culture to intimacy. This is the kind of emotion we expect when we say, "Don't just tell me that you love me, say it like you really mean it!" The second emotional style telegraphs intense emotion under control; Shields labels this emotional style *manly emotion* because of its connection to a particular version of White, heterosexual masculinity. This is the kind of emotion we have come to expect from movie heroes—think of Tom Hanks in *Saving Private Ryan,* Denzel Washington in *Training Day,* or Clint Eastwood in *Million Dollar Baby.*

These two emotional styles convey different messages to people witnessing their expression. The strongly felt—yet controlled—manly emotion conveys the message that the person is independent: "I can control my emotion (and thereby, my *self*), and I can harness it to control the situation." The underlying message of extravagant expressiveness involves nurturance: "My emotion (and thereby, my *self*) is at your service." Shields contends that in our culture manly emotion is ultimately considered more important than extravagant emotion because it is believed to express rational behavior. In contrast, whereas the feminine emotional standards underlying emotional expressiveness foster many socially desirable behaviors (such as tenderness and selflessness), these behaviors are culturally tainted because of their association with emotion out of control. Shields asserts that *control* of emotion is more central to the masculine standards than expressiveness because control is associated with power and dominance. Being the historical holders of power in society, men are assumed to possess greater ability to control their emotions than are women.

There is no scientific evidence of a gender difference in emotional control—and, of course, there is more than one way to define *control*. In many cultures, boys are encouraged to express emotions—such as anger, contempt, and pride—that reflect a sense of entitlement to power in society. In contrast, girls are encouraged to express emotions associated with satisfaction, powerlessness, and service to others, such as happiness, fear, and empathy (Saarni, 1999; Shields, 1995). To what degree does this gender difference fit your understanding of your own emotion culture? Can you think of situations when extravagant emotion was expected of you? Manly emotion? Do you sometimes feel locked into expressing your emotions in certain ways due to other people's (or your own) expectations about gender? What are the costs and benefits of conforming to these gender standards of emotion?

Section Review

- Emotions are positive or negative feeling states.
- Evolutionary theories emphasize the survival value of emotions; they motivate us to avoid what is harmful and approach what is beneficial. Emotional expressions and behaviors also foster communication with others.
- The James-Lange theory and the Cannon-Bard theory disagree on whether physiological responses precede emotions.
- Emotions reflecting approach or avoidance can occur automatically and prior to conscious interpretation.
- Three brain regions are central in controlling emotions: the hypothalamus, the limbic system, and the cerebral cortex.
- Cognitive appraisals help broaden the emotional experience, creating further definition and interpretation of the initial approach or avoidance response.
- One emotional experience may trigger an opposite emotional experience.
- In many cultures, people are taught that the social meaning of emotions is different for the sexes.

Psychological Applications

How Can You Manage Your Emotions and Control Test Anxiety?

As discussed in section 11-4a, our desire for success and our fear of failure can trigger high levels of anxiety in achievement situations. In academic achievement settings, test anxiety can seriously undermine our ability to demonstrate our intellectual skills (Hembree, 1988; Seipp, 1991). Such anxiety is generally acknowledged to be a multidimensional problem, typified by worry over performance, emotional symptoms, and distracted thoughts (Hodapp & Benson, 1997; Liebert & Morris, 1967; Sarason, 1984).

Two prevailing views about the cause of test anxiety are that (1) heightened anxiety blocks retrieval of learned information (Covington & Omelich, 1987; Sarason et al., 1990), and (2) poor encoding and organizing skills lead to poorer preparation and thus to anxiety resulting from this realization (Birenbaum & Pinku, 1997; Tryon, 1980). These two sources of performance decrements could act independently or interact. That is, poor preparation could affect performance, whether in evaluative situations or not, but worry about performance could further hinder performance under evaluative situations.

Therefore, given adequate preparation, test-anxious students have been found to perform worse than non-test-anxious students under evaluative conditions but comparably well under nonevaluative, nonthreatening conditions (Birenbaum & Pinku, 1997; Covington & Omelich, 1987). This means that when information is requested directly—as is the case when taking exams—anxiety can interfere with performance or retrieval.

How can test anxiety, or its effects on performance, be reduced? Regardless of the source of test anxiety, adequate preparation is crucial: Students must develop good study skills. Some common suggestions for improving preparation include the following:

- Go to all your classes; find out what you're expected to know and when the exams are scheduled.
- Study and read as the course goes along, to avoid "cramming" for exams.
- Have a study schedule that makes it easier to avoid more enjoyable distractions. Study where you can concentrate, get interested in the material, and give it your complete attention.
- Make flashcards and review them often.
- Learn how to take good notes by comparing your notes with others' or by going over them with your instructor. Go over them right after class and review periodically.

- Make outlines and summary sheets. Ask yourself, "What is the important information?" Reciting the material in your own words will help you encode the material more deeply.
- Join a study group with motivated classmates; this is often helpful.
- Take advantage of your college's academic assistance center (most colleges have these centers to help improve students' study and test-taking skills; free tutoring is also usually available).

Here are some tips to handle the "anxiety" aspects of preparing and taking tests:

- *Keep tests in perspective.* You're more than just a test-taker or a student. Often, people with the greatest test anxiety assume themselves a failure if they have not done well on an earlier exam. A test is only a test—dwelling on past mistakes will only keep you from focusing on the current or next challenge.
- *Break tasks down into more manageable bits (time management will help with this).* By setting more realistic goals in terms of the level and extent of what can be accomplished, you can make your emotional response less severe than it might be otherwise.
- *Relax while preparing for an exam.* If you find yourself becoming "worked up" over an upcoming exam, find ways to counteract the emotions (for example, try progressive relaxation, described in chapter 15, section 15-3d). Your anxious emotions will interfere with encoding information. Additionally, get plenty of sleep.
- *Practice relaxation during the test, taking a moment to breathe deeply and close your eyes.* Read through the entire exam, just to get a sense of what's there, and then begin with the "friendly" questions—the ones you readily know the answers to. Focus your attention by not allowing yourself to worry, "What if I fail this exam?" Relax again and focus only on the task at hand.

Most of these suggestions require practice and time. If your anxiety about tests is disrupting your performance and is a concern to you, go to your college's counseling services center and have a counselor there assess your test anxiety and provide you with help in trying to handle it.

Key Terms

acquaintance rape (p. 415)

bisexuality (p. 419)

Cannon-Bard theory (p. 434)

drive (p. 402)

drive-reduction theory (p. 402)

emotion (p. 429)

erotophobia (p. 425)

extrinsic motivation (p. 404)

facial feedback hypothesis (p. 435)

heterosexism (p. 420)

heterosexuality (p. 419)

hierarchy of needs (p. 406)

homeostasis (p. 402)

homosexuality (p. 419)

incentive (p. 404)

incentive theory (p. 403)

instinct (p. 401)

intrinsic motivation (p. 404)

James-Lange theory (p. 434)

motivation (p. 401)

need for achievement (n-Ach) (p. 426)

opponent-process theory (p. 440)

polygraph (p. 433)

rape myth (p. 415)

satiety (p. 407)

self-actualization (p. 406)

set point (p. 411)

sexual identity (p. 420)

sexual orientation (p. 419)

sexual response cycle (p. 418)

sexual script (p. 413)

testosterone (p. 419)

Thematic Apperception Test (TAT) (p. 426)

two-factor theory (p. 438)

Yerkes-Dodson law (p. 403)

Suggested Websites

Procrastination Research Group
http://www.carleton.ca/~tpychyl
This website contains information on the psychology of procrastination.

Study Skills Self-Help Information
http://www.ucc.vt.edu/stdysk/stdyhlp.html
This website provides time management strategies for improving academic performance.

TAT Research
http://web.utk.edu/~wmorgan/tat/tattxt.htm
This website describes the Thematic Apperception Test and University of Tennessee psychologist Wesley Morgan's research in this area.

Emotional Intelligence Test
http://www.helpself.com/iq-test.htm
This website provides a brief questionnaire and evaluation of emotional intelligence.

Review Questions

Note: You can find the correct answers to these questions by taking the quiz and then submitting your answers in the Online Edition. The program will automatically score your submission. If you miss a question, the program will provide the correct answer, a rationale for the answer, and the section number in the chapter where the topic is discussed.

1. One of the clear advantages of the drive-reduction theory of motivation over instinct theory is that it
   a. explains why people engage in behaviors that do not reduce a drive.
   b. accounts for low levels of arousal as well as high levels of arousal.
   c. explains a much wider range of behavior than does instinct theory.
   d. accounts for all areas of human motivation.
   e. does not rely on the role of learning in motivation.

2. The Yerkes-Dodson law
   a. describes the fixed level of optimal arousal at which all humans respond best.
   b. claims that arousal levels vary according to environmental factors, suggesting that individuals exhibit no consistency in arousal levels.
   c. states that individuals strive to maintain consistently low levels of arousal.
   d. states that individuals strive to maintain consistently high levels of arousal.
   e. states that individuals strive to maintain intermediate levels of arousal.

3. Research on intrinsic motivation indicates
   a. that the best method for enhancing a child's motivation for doing chores is a tangible reward such as money.
   b. that rewards based on verbal praise are less likely than those based on candy treats to undermine intrinsic motivation.
   c. little support for incentive theory, which focuses on the role of internal states in motivation.
   d. that intrinsic motivation leads a person to engage in behavior to obtain incentives.
   e. that the principal reason why certain activities are extrinsically motivating is that they satisfy a need to feel competent and enhance one's sense of control over one's life.

4. The regulation of eating behavior is *not* associated with
   a. the presence of cholecystokinin (CCK) in the blood.
   b. a hunger on/off switch located in the hypothalamus.
   c. external cues such as the rattling of dishes.
   d. neurotransmitters such as serotonin.
   e. the self-esteem of restrained eaters.

5. Researchers studying the effects of food deprivation and overeating have found that
   a. the number of fat cells individuals have may be related to their set point.
   b. when the body's fat cells fall below a certain limit, they release leptin, which increases hunger.
   c. when people gain or lose weight, they also gain or lose fat cells.
   d. the percentage of Americans 30 percent or more above their ideal body weight has decreased since 1991.
   e. it is not possible to change your body's set point.

6. According to research on sexual motivation,
   a. men report enjoying different types of sexual activity more than do women.
   b. women desire more frequent sexual partners than do men, because it helps ensure that women will bear offspring.
   c. sex is motivated exclusively by physiological needs, such as the pleasure instinct.
   d. sex is motivated exclusively by socioemotional needs, including the need for intimacy.
   e. evolutionary and sociocultural explanations for sexual motivation contradict one another.

7. Sociocultural explanations for gender differences in sexual behavior emphasize traditional sexual scripts, which
   a. describe playful approaches to sexual behavior that enhance motivation.
   b. are generally the same for men and women.
   c. are learned behaviors that emphasize male dominance (for example, bragging) and female resistance to sexual advances.
   d. have been found helpful in reducing acquaintance rape but not the rape myth.
   e. are not harmful and may even be beneficial, in the context of consensual sexual relations.

8. Which of the following is *not* a gender difference in sexual motivation?
   a. Men and women show different sexual response cycles.
   b. Women's sexuality is more influenced than men's by cultural factors.
   c. Men prefer greater sexual variety than do women.
   d. Women's sexual interest is more tied than men's to attachment and intimacy.
   e. Women's sexual identity is more likely than men's to change.

9. Which of the following is known as a system of cultural beliefs, values, and customs that exalts heterosexuality and denies, denigrates, and stigmatizes any nonheterosexual form of behavior or identity?
   a. homosexism
   b. heterosexism
   c. homophobia
   d. heterophobia
   e. discrimination

10. Sexual orientation has been found to be associated with all of the following *except*
    a. differences in the size of the hypothalamus and the corpus callosum.
    b. childhood preferences for same-sex or opposite-sex activities.
    c. sexual orientation of identical twins.
    d. sexual orientation of parents and/or primary caregivers.
    e. childhood gender role and same-sex or other-sex friends.

11. Compared to others, people who have negative feelings about sex
    a. want to have fewer children.
    b. experience less intense orgasms.
    c. are more likely to have unprotected sex.
    d. actually have more sex.
    e. are more likely to talk about their feelings with their partner.

12. Individuals with a high need for achievement are likely to
    a. be motivated by either a fear of failure or a desire for success.
    b. approach all achievement challenges with equally strong desires for success.
    c. choose extremely difficult or challenging tasks.
    d. choose extremely easy tasks to ensure the success they desire.
    e. have an intrinsic desire to succeed.

13. Achievement motivation may be enhanced by
    a. reducing emotional identification with the achievement task.
    b. frequent feedback when progress on the task is slow.
    c. convincing people that the task is something important to them.
    d. protecting the individual from experience with failure.
    e. providing easy tasks that guarantee success.

14. Emotions, defined as positive or negative feeling states or evaluative responses, share all *except* which one of the following characteristics?
    a. The expression of emotions is not altered by learning or culture.
    b. Emotions communicate information between people.
    c. Emotions involve a variety of physiological reactions.
    d. Emotions help individuals respond to changes in the environment.
    e. Emotions are partly generated by cognitive appraisals of situations.

15. Cross-cultural research on emotions indicates
    a. that collectivist cultures experience emotions differently than do individualist cultures.
    b. that individualist cultures can accurately read more emotions than can collectivist cultures.
    c. that 10 primary emotions have been identified across all cultures.
    d. that social norms for expressing certain emotions vary according to cultural beliefs.
    e. no differences among cultures in the facial expression of emotions.

16. Research has shown that, as people immerse themselves, over time, in satisfying friendships and romantic relationships, they experience a similarity in emotions with their partners. This phenomenon is known as
    a. dispositional similarity.
    b. dispositional convergence.
    c. emotional similarity.
    d. emotional convergence.
    e. none of the above

17. Support for the James-Lange theory of emotion is evidenced by the finding that
    a. associations between specific physiological changes and emotional experiences vary by culture.
    b. emotional changes cannot be generated by changes in bodily states.
    c. the subjective experience of emotion involves cognition.
    d. anger and fear produce greater heart rate acceleration than does happiness.
    e. the experience of emotion precedes the physiological changes that automatically occur in response to environmental stimuli.

18. The facial feedback hypothesis states that
    a. specific facial expressions trigger the subjective experience of specific emotions.
    b. people make primary attributions based on facial expressions.
    c. those with more attractive faces tend to have higher self-esteem.
    d. most individuals are actually portraying an emotion contradictory to how they feel.
    e. none of the above

19. Support for the two theories of emotion is seen in studies of the brain's role in producing and coordinating emotional responses, which show that
    a. the left cerebral hemisphere is more involved than the right in the expression of emotion.
    b. the second neural circuit involved in producing emotion passes through the cerebral cortex before activating the hypothalamus.
    c. the amygdala is involved only in the first neural circuit.
    d. complex emotions and conflicting emotions are associated with the second neural circuit.
    e. both sides of the brain are equally involved in expressing both positive and negative emotions.

20. According to Solomon's opponent-process theory of emotion,
    a. repeating an experience weakens the initial emotional reaction and strengthens the subsequent emotional reaction.
    b. the craving associated with drug abuse is motivated by the pleasure it provides.
    c. men who encountered an attractive female on a high bridge interpreted their arousal as being caused by fear rather than sexual attraction.
    d. the interpretation of emotional arousal in ambiguous situations will be influenced by cues in the immediate environment.
    e. repeating an experience strengthens the initial emotional reaction and weakens the subsequent emotional reaction.

21. Which term refers to an emotional style associated with femininity characterized by the open experience and communication of emotion?
    a. femotion
    b. candid feelings
    c. extravagant expressiveness
    d. demonstrative affect
    e. extreme emotion

Chapter 12

Personality

Source: Courtesy of Figzoi.

"It is totally me, Dad!"

This was my daughter Amelia's reaction a few years ago upon reading the "personality profile" she received from the handwriting analysis machine at Michigan's Upper Peninsula State Fair. After Amelia slipped her signature into the "Data Entry" slot (and paid a $2 fee to the cashier), the lights on the graphology machine's cardboard façade flashed furiously before the machine spit out its evaluation. As Amelia marveled at the accuracy of her personality profile, I noticed a partially hidden worker placing a fresh stack of pretyped profiles into the "Completed Profile" slot behind the machine. At that moment, a scene from *The Wizard of Oz* ran through my mind. It was the scene in which Dorothy returns to Oz and presents the dead witch's broom to the all-powerful Wizard. As the huge disembodied head of the Wizard blusters and bellows at Dorothy, her dog Toto pulls back a curtain, revealing that the Wizard is really just an ordinary man manipulating people's impressions with smoke and mirrors.

That day at the fair, I decided not to tell Amelia about the man behind the machine. Sometime later, however, we talked a bit about the validity of handwriting analysis, palm reading, and horoscopes. To put it simply, these techniques that claim to assess personality have no scientific validity (Beyerstein & Beyerstein, 1992; Kelly, 1997). They provide assessments that appear remarkably accurate in divining our unique characteristics because they are either flattering to our egos or generally true of everybody (Forer, 1949). For example, consider the following generic description of personality:

> You are an independent thinker, but you have a strong need to be liked and respected by others. At times you are outgoing and extraverted, while at other times you are reserved and introverted. You have found it unwise to be too frank in revealing yourself to others. While you have some personality weaknesses, you can generally compensate for them. You tend to be critical of yourself. You have a great deal of potential, but you have not yet fully harnessed it. Some of your aspirations are pretty unrealistic.

When college students were provided with personality assessments similar to this one and told that an astrologer had prepared the profiles just for them, almost all the students evaluated the accuracy of these descriptions as either "good" or "excellent" (Davies, 1997; Glick et al., 1989). Further, after receiving their assessments, students were more likely than before to believe that astrology was a valid way to assess personality. This tendency to accept global and ambiguous feedback about oneself—even if the source of the information lacks credibility—is known as the *Barnum effect,* in honor of the master showman P. T. Barnum. Barnum credited his success in the circus industry to the fact that "there's a sucker born every minute."

Now, I am not suggesting that my daughter and the majority of college students are "suckers" waiting to be fleeced of their money by unscrupulous fortune hunters. But I am suggesting that there is a more accurate—and yes, more ethical—way to understand our personalities: through application of the scientific method (Cervone & Mischel, 2002). In this chapter, we continue our journey of discovery through psychology by venturing behind the scientific "curtain" of personality theory and research. I think you will find that this particular journey will reveal much more than the "smoke and mirrors" effects typically created by graphologists, palm readers, and astrologers.

12-1 THE NATURE OF PERSONALITY

Preview

- *What does personality research examine?*
- *Is personality shaped only by experience?*

Before reading further, spend a few minutes identifying certain recurring ways in which you respond to a variety of situations. In addition, identify ways in which you think, feel, or behave that set you apart from many other people. Is there anything on this mental list that your culture might have shaped? Do any of these personal qualities help you successfully meet life's challenges?

12-1a Consistency and Distinctiveness Define Personality

One important quality of personality is *consistency* in thinking, feeling, and acting. We consider people to be consistent when we see them responding in the same way in a variety of situations and over an extended period of time. Of course, people do not respond entirely consistently, but in order for us to notice that they have a characteristic way of thinking, feeling, and behaving, they must respond consistently across many situations and over time. For instance, you may have a friend who argues a great deal. Name the topic, and he probably will carve out a contrary position to that of others. This aspect of his interaction style is consistent enough that you have a pretty good idea how he will generally act around others, regardless of whether they are friends, relatives, or strangers.

Distinctiveness is another important quality of personality, because it is used to explain why everyone does not act the same in similar situations. Let's return to the example of your argumentative friend: Because most people generally try to find points of agreement when interacting with others, your friend's argumentative style is distinctive, setting him apart from most people. So, when you see him arguing with professors in class and notice that other students don't routinely do so, you begin to think that arguing is a distinctive characteristic for him.

Overall, then, when we study personality, we are studying both how people are consistent across situations and how they are different from one another (Leary, 2005). For our purposes, I define **personality** as the *consistent* and *distinctive* thoughts, feelings, and behaviors that an individual engages in. This definition has its roots in philosophy as much as in science. For that reason, parts of this chapter may seem as though they are describing a different kind of psychology—a more speculative and less data-driven psychology—than other parts of the chapter. You will most likely notice this during the discussion of psychoanalytic and humanistic approaches to personality. During the second half of the twentieth century, the study of personality followed the rest of the field of psychology and moved away from broad theorizing to scientific testing of hypotheses about personality functioning. Modern personality theorists tend to be much more limited and narrow in their approach to the field. This more modest approach has allowed for clearer descriptions of **personality styles,** though the more overarching and comprehensive descriptions that were

> **personality** The consistent and distinctive thoughts, feelings, and behaviors an individual engages in.

> **personality style** A collection or constellation of traits that describes the functioning of the person across situations and settings.

Consistency and distinctiveness are important qualities of personality. When we describe certain individuals as "really having a personality," we often mean that we see them responding in the same way in a variety of situations over an extended period of time and that the way they think, feel, and act is unique, setting them apart from others.

Source: © Stockbyte.

present earlier have been lost (Magnavita, 2002). In the later sections of this chapter, these more modern approaches to studying personality functioning are represented by the trait and social-cognitive theories. We also examine various means of assessing or describing personality.

12-1b Culture and Evolutionary Processes Shape Personality

Personality psychology was developed and has flourished in the North American and Western European social climate of *individualism,* which is a philosophy of life stressing the priority of individual rights and desires over those of the group. This individualist perspective conceives of people as unique, independent entities, separate from their social surroundings. In contrast, *collectivism* is a philosophy of life emphasizing group needs and desires over those of the individual. As noted in chapter 1, section 1-3f, approximately 70 percent of the world's population lives in collectivist cultures (Singelis et al., 1995).

During the past 25 years, as psychology has become more of an international science, personality theorists in individualist societies have begun to investigate how personality is a product of the individual's interaction with her or his social settings. In adopting this approach, personality theorists are thinking about human behavior in a way similar to that of collectivists (Brislin, 1993). At various points in this chapter (for example, see sections 12-4d and 12-5a), we discuss this *interactionist* perspective on personality.

In addition to the influence that cultural beliefs can have on the *study* of personality, research further suggests that cultural beliefs can actually shape personality development (Church & Ortiz, 2005). For example, people from collectivist Latin cultures are often taught to have *simpatía,* which is a way of relating to others that is empathic, respectful, and unselfish and helps maintain harmonious social relationships (Marín, 1994). Likewise, the Chinese concept of *ren qin* (relationship orientation) and the Japanese concept of *amae* (indulgent dependence) emphasize social ties and dependence on others. Individuals who internalize these social norms develop a personality style that is characteristic of their social group and may be relatively uncommon in other cultures (Ho et al., 2001).

Although personality styles may be associated with particular cultures, most personality researchers strive to identify universal aspects of personality. In this regard, a growing number of social scientists are beginning to examine how certain aspects of personality have been shaped over the course of our species' evolutionary history (Buss, 1999b; MacDonald, 1998; Ridley et al., 2005). According to this viewpoint, because the evolutionary process is the only known creative process capable of producing complex organisms, all theories of human nature, including personality theories, must consider the basic principles of evolution by natural selection (see chapter 1, section 1-3e). Consistent with this viewpoint, in this chapter I periodically offer an evolutionary accounting of personality.

Section Review

- Personality research examines how people are consistent across situations and how they differ from one another.
- More than culture influences how personality is studied; many contemporary psychologists study how both cultural and evolutionary forces shape personalities.

12-2 THE PSYCHOANALYTIC PERSPECTIVE

Preview

- *What aspect of the mind did Freud stress in explaining personality?*
- *According to psychoanalytic theory, what is the structure of personality, and what are the stages of personality development?*

- *How is the ego protected from disturbing unconscious desires?*
- *How did Freud's followers revise his theory, and what are the limitations of psychoanalytic theory?*

The most recognizable person in the field of psychology—Sigmund Freud—was not trained as a psychologist (Colombo & Abend, 2005). Freud (1856–1939) grew up in Austria, was trained as a physician in Vienna, and aspired to become a university professor (Gardner, 1993a). Early in his professional career as a medical doctor, he studied the nervous system in the hope of applying newly discovered principles of physics and chemistry to the functioning of the human mind. In addition to teaching and doing laboratory work, Freud worked with patients (mostly women) who seemed to have problems with the functioning of their nervous systems. Freud frequently discovered that their symptoms were not caused by physiological problems but, rather, seemed to originate from emotional trauma. Gradually, this young Viennese doctor developed the idea that the young science of psychology held answers to many of these perplexing disorders (Freud, 1917).

An example of the kind of medical problem that set Freud on his journey of discovery into psychology was a strange neurological-like condition referred to as *glove anesthesia* (see the chapter 13, section 13-3e, discussion of *conversion disorders*). In this condition, the patient had no feeling from her wrists to the tips of her fingers, so that if Freud poked her hand with a pin, she would not flinch or complain of any pain. But she did have feeling in her forearms, and if Freud poked her anywhere above the wrist, she would flinch and say the equivalent of "ouch" in German. Glove anesthesia is not consistent with the way the nervous system functions, which suggested to Freud that its cause was not physiological, but psychological (Freud, 1895/1950/1966). As you will see, this idea revolutionized the study of personality in the early 1900s (Westen, 1998).

12-2a Psychoanalytic Theory Asserts That the Unconscious Controls Behavior

When Freud suspected that some of his patients' medical problems were, in fact, caused by emotional disturbances, he sought the advice of a French neurologist, Jean Charcot, who was treating such patients using hypnosis (Gay, 1998). Freud was also impressed by the psychiatrist Joseph Breuer's "talking cure" therapy, in which patients with emotional problems were told to report whatever came to mind. Adapting these two techniques to his own emerging theory of the human mind, Freud encouraged his patients to talk about their symptoms and what was occurring when the symptoms emerged. As they did this, Freud developed the idea that their symptoms were psychologically related to some sort of problem or dilemma they were experiencing. For instance, the previously described glove anesthesia of one of his young patients developed soon after she became aware of her emerging sexual urges. Stimulating herself with her hand was simultaneously very pleasurable and extremely anxiety-inducing. Freud believed that, to prevent the expression of this unacceptable urge to sexually gratify herself, the woman unconsciously "deadened" her hand, making it unusable. Piecing together his patients' accounts of their lives while under hypnosis, Freud believed that he had discovered the unconscious mind.

Freud's model of the mind proposed that it was mostly hidden, like an iceberg (Freud, 1917). As depicted in figure 12-1, our **conscious mind** is the relatively small part of our mind that we are aware of at the moment, like the tip of the iceberg that is visible above the surface of the water. Right now, your conscious processes include (I hope!) the material from the previous sentences, perhaps an awareness of certain stimuli in your surroundings, and maybe the thought that you would like to be doing something other than reading this book. Immediately below the surface of the conscious mind resides the **preconscious mind,** which consists of those mental processes that are not currently conscious but could become so at any moment. Examples of preconscious material might include your parents' phone number, hopefully some of the material from previous sections of this book, and a conversation you had yesterday with a friend. Below this preconscious level resides the **unconscious mind,** which is like the huge section of the iceberg that is hidden in the water's

conscious mind According to Freud, the relatively small part of our mind that we are aware of at the moment.

preconscious mind According to Freud, those mental processes that are not currently conscious but could become so at any moment.

unconscious mind According to Freud, the thoughts, desires, feelings, and memories that are not consciously available to us but that nonetheless shape our everyday behavior.

Figure 12-1

Freud's Model of Personality Structure

In Freud's theory of personality, the mind is likened to an iceberg, with the conscious mind the relatively small part of the iceberg visible above the water line and the unconscious mind that part of the iceberg well below the surface. In this metaphor, the ego is the aspect of the personality that includes part of our conscious mind and part of our unconscious mind. The same is true of the superego. In contrast, the id is the completely unconscious aspect of personality.

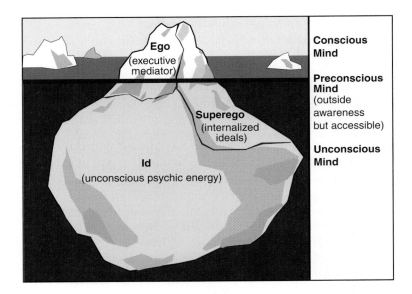

Imagine how you might behave if you had no ego and, instead, simply acted on your id desires. While walking through a park, you become hungry. Nearby, three people are eating lunch. Without hesitating, you lunge at them, fighting and clawing for all the food you can carry. How long do you think you would survive with this primary-process thinking?

Source: Courtesy of Figzoi.

id An unconscious part of the mind that contains our sexual and aggressive drives.

pleasure principle The process by which the id seeks to immediately satisfy whatever desire is currently active.

depths. The unconscious mind is driven by biological urges that have been shaped by our evolutionary history, and it contains thoughts, desires, feelings, and memories that are not consciously available to us but that nonetheless shape our everyday behavior. Examples of unconscious material are painful, forgotten memories from childhood, hidden feelings of hostility toward someone you profess to like (or even love), and sexual urges that would create intense anxiety if you became aware of them.

Freud's theory of the mind was an important milestone in the history of psychology, because it challenged the prevailing notion that consciousness was the determining factor in the management and control of behavior. As you will see in later sections of this chapter, opposition to Freud's perspective on the determinants of human behavior spawned a number of competing personality theories.

12-2b Freud Divided Personality into the Id, the Ego, and the Superego

Freud used his model of the conscious and unconscious minds to guide his treatment of patients who came to him with psychological symptoms. His goal was to make conscious what had formerly been unconscious. Yet Freud soon discovered that, even when his patients were told about the unconscious forces driving their behaviors, they still had difficulty managing these behaviors. This led him to propose another dimension to his theory of the mind, which came to be called the *structural model* (Moore & Fine, 1990). Freud proposed three subcomponents, or structures, in this model of the mind: the *id*, the *ego*, and the *superego* (see figure 12-1). Each of these structures of the mind has different operating principles and different goals. Frequently, the goals of one component are in conflict with the goals of another component. This model of the mind is sometimes called a *conflict model,* because it attempts to explain how psychological conflicts determine behavior.

The **id**—which in Latin means "it"—is an entirely unconscious portion of the mind. It contains the basic drives for reproduction, survival, and aggression. The id operates on the **pleasure principle.** That is, the id consistently wants to satisfy whatever desire is currently active as quickly and directly as possible. The id's agenda, as directed by the pleasure principle, might be summarized by the statement "If it feels good, do it." Freud referred to this primitive, irrational, and illogical orientation as *primary-process thinking.* He believed that newborn infants represent the purest form of id impulses, crying whenever their needs are not immediately satisfied. He further proposed that a part of our personality continues to function like that of a newborn—wanting needs met immediately—throughout our lives.

One of life's realties is that our needs are very seldom immediately satisfied. Freud asserted that, as infants, whenever our immediate gratification did not occur, we experienced distress and anxiety. As a way to cope with this infantile stress, the **ego**—which in Latin means "I"—develops out of the id. The ego's function is to be the decision-making part of the personality that satisfies id impulses in socially acceptable ways. In performing this function, the ego is both partially conscious and partially unconscious. The conscious part of the ego is in contact with external reality, while the unconscious part is in contact with the id. In seeking id satisfaction, the ego is guided by the **reality principle,** the process by which the ego seeks to delay gratification of id desires until appropriate outlets and situations can be found. The ego is interested in achieving pleasure but learns that this will more likely occur if the constraints of reality are taken into account. Freud referred to this relatively rational and realistic orientation as *secondary-process thinking.*

The **superego**—which in Latin means "over the I"—develops later in childhood, around the age of 4 or 5. The superego has several functions, including overseeing the ego and making sure that it acts morally. As such, the superego is concerned not just with what is acceptable but also with what is ideal. It provides us with a conscience, making us feel guilty when we do "wrong" and instilling pride when we do "right." Essentially, the superego represents the internalization of cultural norms and values into the individual mind. Not surprisingly, the superego and the id are frequently at odds about the proper course of action in a given situation. The ego balances the demands of the id and superego, along with those of external reality, to generate behavior that will still bring pleasure.

Although this description of the three personality components appears to suggest that the ego (the conscious self) is controlling our behavior, Freud contended that this is largely an illusion. Throughout our daily activities, we are generally unaware of the unconscious compromises our ego makes to create a particular outcome. For example, a college sophomore may agree to spend hours tutoring a group of first-year students, unaware of how his sexual attraction to one member of the group figured in his decision. He may be conscious of feeling altruistic about helping these students, and thus his superego is satisfied, but he is largely unaware of how his ego has unconsciously allowed his id to be gratified as well. *yes or no {no compromising} answer*

12-2c Personality Development Occurs in Psychosexual Stages

As Freud listened to his patients during therapy, they repeatedly mentioned significant events from their childhood that had left them with emotional scars. Based on his patients' reconstruction of their lives, Freud created a theory about how personality develops and how the ego and superego come into existence (Stern, 1985). Going along with the idea that personality involves a degree of consistency, his psychoanalytic theory proposed that children pass through a fixed sequence of **psychosexual stages.** Each stage is characterized by a part of the body, called an *erogenous zone,* through which the id primarily seeks sexual pleasure. Critical elements of the personality are formed during each of these stages (see table 12-1). If children experience conflicts when seeking pleasure during a particular psychosexual stage, and if these conflicts go unresolved, these children will become psychologically "stuck"—or *fixated*—at that stage. **Fixation** is a tendency to persist in pleasure-seeking behaviors associated with an earlier psychosexual stage during which conflicts were unresolved. One important point to keep in mind about fixation is that the conflicts that trigger fixation can be caused by either too little or too much gratification of id desires.

Oral Stage

The first stage of psychosexual development, which encompasses the first year of life, is referred to as the **oral stage.** During this stage, infants are totally dependent on those around them to care for their needs. Their most salient need is to be nourished. Freud believed that the id derives intense sexual pleasure by engaging in oral activities such as sucking, biting, and chewing. Adults with fixations at the oral stage are often extremely clingy and emotionally dependent on others. In attempting to satisfy oral needs, they might smoke excessively and/or spend a great deal of time eating and thinking about eating. However, if

ego The part of our minds that includes our consciousness and that balances the demands of the id, the superego, and reality.

reality principle The process by which the ego seeks to delay gratification of id desires until appropriate outlets and situations can be found.

superego The part of our minds that includes our conscience and counterbalances the more primitive demands of the id.

superego - parent within you rules of our culture formed thru childhood.

Too much of a good thing can be wonderful.

—Mae West, American actress and comedian, 1897–1980

psychosexual stages The fixed sequence of childhood developmental stages during which the id primarily seeks sexual pleasure by focusing its energies on distinct erogenous zones.

fixation A tendency to persist in pleasure-seeking behaviors associated with an earlier psychosexual stage during which conflicts were unresolved.

oral stage In Freud's theory, the first stage of psychosexual development, during which the child derives pleasure by engaging in oral activities.

Table 12-1	Freud's Stages of Psychosexual Development		
Stage	**Approximate Age**	**Erogenous Zone**	**Key Tasks and Experiences**
Oral	0–1	Mouth (sucking, biting)	Weaning (from breast or bottle)
Anal	2–3	Anus (defecating)	Toilet training
Phallic	4–5	Genitals (masturbating)	Coping with Oedipal/Electra conflict and identifying with same-sex parent
Latency	6–11	None (sexual desires repressed)	Developing same-sex contacts
Genital	Puberty onward	Genitals (being sexually intimate)	Establishing mature sexual relationships

adequately gratified during this stage as infants, adults would still derive pleasure from oral activities, but they would not be overly focused on such pleasures.

Anal Stage

anal stage In Freud's theory, the second stage of psychosexual development, during which the child derives pleasure from defecation.

The **anal stage** follows the oral stage, as the focus of erotic pleasure shifts from the mouth to the process of elimination. This psychosexual stage begins at about 2 years of age, when toilet training becomes an area of conflict between children and parents. Freud argued that, from the child's point of view, toilet training represents the parents' attempt at denying the child's primary pleasure by exerting control over where and when urination and defecation occur. Thus, toilet training becomes a contest of wills. Adding to this conflict is the fact that the ego is beginning to exert itself, and thus the way this stage of development is managed will have long-term consequences for the characteristic ways a person's ego negotiates the conflicting demands of the id and the environment. Fixation at this stage, caused by overly harsh toilet-training experiences, produces children who too closely conform to the demands of their parents and other caretakers. As adults, they will be excessively neat and orderly (this is the source of the term *anal retentive*). Overly relaxed toilet-training experiences can also cause fixation, with individuals forever being messy and having difficulty complying with authority and keeping their behavior under control (*anal expulsive*). Successful negotiation of this stage results in a capacity to engage in directed work without being dominated by the need to perform perfectly.

Journey of Discovery **Question** An increasing number of contemporary personality theorists pay attention to how culture and evolutionary forces shape personality. Is there any evidence in Freud's theory of personality indicating that he considered the impact of culture and evolution on personality?

Phallic Stage

phallic stage In Freud's theory, the third stage of psychosexual development, during which the child derives pleasure from masturbation.

At about age 4, children enter the **phallic stage,** which is characterized by a shift in the erogenous zone to the genitals and deriving pleasure largely through self-stimulation. It is common to see children of this age masturbating while rocking themselves to sleep and displaying a great deal of curiosity about male and female genitals. According to Freud, accompanying this interest in genital stimulation is the association of this pleasure with the other-sex parent. Freud asserted that boys develop an erotic attachment to their mothers, and girls develop a similar attachment to their fathers. Soon, however, children realize that they are in competition with their same-sex parent for the attention and affection of their other-sex parent.

Among boys, Freud related this dilemma to a character in ancient Greek literature, Oedipus Rex, who became king by unknowingly marrying his mother after murdering his father. This so-called *Oedipus complex* arouses fear in boys that their fathers will punish them for their sexual desires for their mother. Freud asserted that this fear of the loss of genital pleasure is psychologically represented as *castration anxiety,* which is the fear that the father will cut off the penis.

Among girls, instead of being afraid that their mothers will harm them, Freud believed that girls are likely to express anger because they believe that their mothers have already inflicted the harm: by removing their penis. This "mother conflict" is now known as the *Electra complex,* after another Greek character who had her mother killed. Freud asserted that the *penis envy* girls experience during this stage stems from their belief that this anatomical "deficiency" is evidence of their inferiority to boys.

Successful negotiation of the phallic stage requires that children purge their sexual desires for their other-sex parent and bury their fear and anger toward their same-sex parent. Children accomplish these dual feats by identifying with the competitive, same-sex parent. According to Freud, this process of identification is critical for the development of a healthy adult personality, because this is how children internalize their parents' values. This internalization of parental values—which generally mirror larger societal values—is critical in the development of the superego. Less successful negotiation of this stage can cause people to become chronically timid because they fear they do not "measure up" to their rivaled same-sex parent.

Latency Stage

From about age 6 to age 11, children are in a psychological period of relative calm called the **latency stage.** During this time, the dramatic struggles of the oral, anal, and phallic stages are forgotten by the ego. Although the ego is relatively free from interference by the id, sexual, aggressive, and other id impulses are still present and must be managed. Often this is accomplished by channeling these desires into socially acceptable activities in school, sports, and the arts.

> **latency stage** In Freud's theory, the fourth stage of psychosexual development, during which the child is relatively free from sexual desires and conflict.

Genital Stage

Latency is followed by puberty and the onset of the **genital stage.** During adolescence, many of the issues of the earlier stages re-emerge and can be reworked to a certain extent. Mature sexual feelings toward others also begin to emerge, and the ego learns to manage and direct these feelings. Of all the stages, Freud spent the least amount of time discussing the psychological dynamics of the genital stage. This was probably due to his belief that personality was largely determined by age 5.

> **genital stage** In Freud's theory, the last stage of psychosexual development, during which mature sexual feelings toward others begin to emerge, and the ego learns to manage and direct these feelings.

12-2d Defense Mechanisms Reduce or Redirect Unconsciously Caused Anxiety

When Freud's theory was relatively simple and included only the conscious, preconscious, and unconscious, he proposed that people managed to move certain thoughts into the unconscious by using a very basic defense mechanism that he called **repression.** Repression banishes anxiety-arousing thoughts from consciousness. Freud believed that repression is the reason we do not remember our childhood conflicts in each of the psychosexual stages. As Freud's model developed to greater levels of complexity, his thoughts about how we manage anxiety became more complex. Instead of simply relying on repression, he proposed that the ego uses a variety of more sophisticated techniques, which he called **defense mechanisms,** to keep threatening and unacceptable material out of consciousness and thereby reduce anxiety (Freud, 1926/1959). His daughter, Anna Freud (1936), later described more fully how these ego defense mechanisms reduce anxiety.

Defense mechanisms are very important features of psychoanalytic theory because they explain why humans—whom Freud believed are essentially driven by sexual and aggressive urges—can become civilized (Domino et al., 2002). Furthermore, Freud asserted that the particular defense mechanisms people rely on most often in adapting to life's challenges

> **repression** In Freud's theory, a very basic defense mechanism in which people move anxiety-arousing thoughts from the conscious mind into the unconscious mind.

> **defense mechanisms** In Freud's theory, the ego's methods of keeping threatening and unacceptable material out of consciousness and thereby reducing anxiety.

Table 12-2	Major Ego Defense Mechanisms
Repression	Pushing high-anxiety-inducing thoughts out of consciousness, keeping them unconscious; this is the most basic of the defense mechanisms.
Rationalization	Offering seemingly logical self-justifying explanations for attitudes, beliefs, or behavior in place of the real, unconscious reasons.
Reaction formation	Preventing unacceptable feelings or ideas from being directly expressed by expressing opposing feelings or ideas.
Displacement	Discharging sexual or aggressive urges toward objects that are more acceptable than those that initially created the arousal.
Projection	Perceiving one's own sexual or aggressive urges not in oneself but in others.
Regression	Psychologically retreating to an earlier developmental stage where psychic energy remains fixated.

rationalization A defense mechanism in which people offer logical self-justifying explanations for their actions in place of the real, more anxiety-producing, unconscious reasons.

reaction formation A defense mechanism that allows people to express unacceptable feelings or ideas by consciously expressing their exact opposite.

displacement A defense mechanism that diverts people's sexual or aggressive urges toward objects that are more acceptable than those that actually stimulate their feelings.

projection A powerful defense mechanism in which people perceive their own aggressive or sexual urges not in themselves, but in others.

regression A defense mechanism in which people faced with intense anxiety psychologically retreat to a more infantile developmental stage at which some psychic energy remains fixated.

become distinguishing features of their personalities. Thus, Freud would tell you that, although you have probably used most of the defense mechanisms described in table 12-2 at least once in your life, your personality can be best described by that configuration of defenses that you rely on most heavily. He would also tell you that, under extreme stress, you may begin to use more powerful defenses, which are also more primitive and associated with psychological disorders.

Rationalization is probably one of the more familiar defense mechanisms. It involves offering seemingly logical self-justifying explanations for our attitudes, beliefs, or behavior in place of the real, unconscious reasons. For instance, you might say that you are punishing someone "for her own good," when in reality the punishment primarily serves to express your anger at the person. Have you ever been romantically rejected and then convinced yourself that you never really cared for the person in the first place? Freud would say that this may well have been your ego's attempt to defend you against feelings of worthlessness.

Reaction formation allows us to express an unacceptable feeling or idea by consciously expressing its exact opposite. Thus, if we are interested in sex (and, according to Freud, we all are) but uncomfortable with this interest, we might devote much time and energy to combating pornography. Focusing on defeating the porn industry allows us to think about sex but in an acceptable way. Of course, there are nondefensive reasons to oppose pornography or to engage in other activities that could indicate a reaction formation. In fact, one of Freud's primary ideas is that all human actions are *multiply determined,* meaning that each behavior has many causes.

Displacement is a defense mechanism that diverts our sexual or aggressive urges toward objects that are more acceptable than the one actually stimulating our feelings. This is commonly referred to as the "kick-the-dog" defense, when we unconsciously vent our aggressive impulses toward a threatening teacher, parent, or boss onto a helpless creature, such as the family pet. Similarly, we might displace sexual feelings away from a parent because that is unacceptable and, instead, date someone who is remarkably like dear old mom or dad.

Projection is one of the more powerful defense mechanisms and can involve quite serious distortions of others' motivations. In projection, we perceive our own aggressive or sexual urges not in ourselves but in others. Thus, an insecure person may falsely accuse other people of being insecure while not recognizing this characteristic in her own personality. Freud contended that we are more likely to use projection when we are feeling strongly threatened, either by the strength of our feelings or by particularly stressful situations. Soldiers in combat, for instance, may begin to see everyone around them as potential enemies who could hurt them.

Another powerful defense mechanism is **regression,** which occurs when we cannot function in our current surroundings due to anxiety, and we psychologically retreat to a more infantile developmental stage where some psychic energy remains fixated. For example, following the birth of a younger sibling who threatens an older child's sense of "place" in the family, that older child may lose control of bowel or bladder functions, or return to thumb-sucking. When this occurs in adults, it may be a relatively contained regression, such as talking like a baby when working with an authority figure.

12-2e There Are Many Variations of Psychoanalytic Theory

Perhaps because of the strength of Freud's thinking and writing, many people assume that psychoanalytic theories are still based exclusively on his work. In the 100 years since Freud began developing his personality theory, we have learned a great deal about human behavior, and many psychologists have worked to adapt Freud's theories to what we have learned about how people function. Yet the process of revising Freud's ideas actually began during his lifetime. Three of his closest coworkers, Alfred Adler, Carl Jung, and Karen Horney, disagreed about the central role of sexual drives in determining people's personalities. Freud, an authoritarian individual who demanded strict obedience from his followers, reacted very negatively to such criticism. Let us briefly examine the ideas of some of those individuals who refused to follow Freud's lead. These personality theories, along with Freud's original theory of psychoanalysis, are often placed under the general label of the **psychodynamic perspective** (Auld et al., 2005).

> **psychodynamic perspective** A diverse group of theories descended from the work of Sigmund Freud that assert that behavior is controlled by unconscious forces.

Adler's Individual Psychology

As a youngster, Alfred Adler (1870–1937) was sickly, struggling to overcome rickets (a bone disease) and numerous bouts of pneumonia. In 1902, he joined Freud's inner circle of "disciples" who were expected to carry on their master's work while adhering to its basic theoretical principles. However, Adler soon began developing his own ideas about how personality developed, which led to arguments and tension between him and Freud. Adler's view of personality stressed social factors more than did Freud's theory. For example, concerning family dynamics, Adler felt that Freud focused so much attention on the mother-child-father bonds that he neglected the important influence that siblings can have on personality development. In this regard, Adler was one of the first theorists to write about how birth order shapes personality, and he coined the term *sibling rivalry*.

In 1911, the Freud-Adler relationship ended when Adler proposed his *individual psychology*, which downplayed the importance of sexual motivation and, instead, asserted that people strive for superiority. By this, Adler meant that children generally feel weak and incompetent compared with adults and older children. In turn, these feelings of inferiority motivate them to acquire new skills and develop their untapped potential. Adler (1929) called this process of striving to overcome feelings of inferiority *compensation*. However, for some individuals, such striving can lead to *overcompensation* if the sense of inferiority is excessively strong. Instead of mastering new skills, these people simply seek to obtain outward symbols of status and power, such as money and expensive possessions. By flaunting their success, they try to hide their continuing sense of inferiority.

Jung's Analytical Psychology

Carl Jung (pronounced "Yoong"; 1875–1961), a native of Switzerland and the son of a Protestant pastor, was inspired to become a psychoanalyst by reading Freud's *The Interpretation of Dreams* (Freud, 1900/1953). After corresponding with Freud through letters, Jung met Freud for the first time in 1906, and the two men talked nonstop for 13 hours! They quickly became close friends, and Freud viewed his younger protégé as the person most capable of carrying on his work. However, in 1914, after Jung challenged some of Freud's central ideas concerning personality development, their friendship abruptly ended.

Jung (1916) called his approach *analytical psychology*. Like Adler, Jung de-emphasized the sex motive in his version of psychoanalysis. Instead, he asserted that people are motivated by a desire for psychological growth and wholeness, which he called the *need for individuation*. Jung's idea that humans are motivated to engage in a quest for personal growth later became the central focus of the *humanistic perspective* (see section 12-3).

Unlike Adler, who also de-emphasized the influence of the unconscious on behavior, Jung agreed with Freud that the unconscious mind has a powerful effect on people's lives. Yet, for Jung, the unconscious was less a reservoir for repressed childhood conflicts and more a reservoir of images from our species' evolutionary past. In studying different cultures and religions, he noticed certain universal images and themes, which were also strikingly similar to the images and themes in his patients' dreams. Based on these observations, Jung asserted that besides our *personal unconscious,* we also have a **collective unconscious,** which is that part of the unconscious mind containing inherited memories shared by all human beings. Jung (1963, 1964) called these inherited memories **archetypes,** and he believed that they reveal themselves when our conscious mind is distracted (as in fantasies or art) or inactive (as in dreams). He further believed that archetypes are represented in the religious symbols found throughout the world. Key archetypal figures are *mother, father, shadow, wise old person, God,* and *the hero.* Jung also claimed that the feminine and masculine qualities that everyone possesses were represented by the male archetype, *anima,* and the female archetype, *animus,* However, the most important archetype is the *self,* which Jung described as the ultimate unity of the personality, symbolized in religions by the circle, the cross, and the mandala.

Although Jung's idea of the collective unconscious has generally been dismissed in mainstream psychology, it has had considerably greater influence in other disciplines, such as anthropology, art, literature, and religious studies (Neher, 1996; Tacey, 2001). But one aspect of his personality theory that has been incorporated into mainstream personality theories is the idea that we are born with tendencies to direct our psychological energies either into our inner self or into the outside world (Jung, 1921). **Introverts** are preoccupied with the inner world and tend to be hesitant and cautious when interacting with people. In contrast, **extraverts** are focused on the external world and tend to be confident and socially outgoing.

Horney's Neo-Freudian Perspective

The German physician Karen Horney (pronounced "HOR-nigh"; 1885–1952) was the first influential female psychoanalyst. Like Adler, Horney (1945) believed that social factors play a much larger role in personality development than sexual influences. Instead of perceiving personality problems as being caused by fixation of psychic energy, Horney believed that problems in interpersonal relationships during childhood create anxiety, and this anxiety causes later personality problems. Developmental psychologists later expanded on these ideas by studying how parent-child emotional attachments shape children's personalities (see chapter 4, section 4-2a).

Horney was also instrumental in confronting some of Freud's assertions concerning female personality development (Gilman, 2001; Ingram, 2001). Whereas Freud proposed that gender differences in behavior are due to biological factors, she argued that the origins of these differences are largely social and cultural. Although conceding that women often felt inferior to men, Horney (1926/1967) claimed that this is due not to penis envy but to the sexism that denies women equal opportunities. What women really envy, she said, is the social power and privilege that men enjoy in the larger society.

An Overall Evaluation of Freud's Legacy

As you will see more fully when we discuss psychological disorders and therapies (see chapters 13 and 14), there is no dismissing the impact of Freud's ideas on psychology. His influence has also extended into other disciplines that study humans and their behavior, including anthropology, sociology, literature, and history. Recently, the *Harvard Business Review* (Coutu, 2001) recommended that business executives read Freud whenever they want to "read someone absolutely relevant on any matter that torments or concerns us: love, jealousy, envy, cruelty, possessiveness, curiosity or what have you."

Despite Freud's influence on the social sciences and the larger culture, a major limitation of his theory is that it is not based on carefully controlled scientific research (Crews, 1998). Indeed, Freud's entire theory was developed based on a handful of cases from his clinical practice that do not constitute a representative sampling of the human population. As you know from our discussion of scientific methods in chapter 2, section 2-1b, a theory's

collective unconscious In Jung's personality theory, the part of the unconscious mind containing inherited memories shared by all human beings.

archetypes In Jung's personality theory, inherited images that are passed down from our prehistoric ancestors and that reveal themselves as universal symbols in dreams, religion, and art.

introvert A person who is preoccupied with his or her inner world and tends to be hesitant and cautious when interacting with people.

extravert A person who is focused on the external world and tends to be confident and socially outgoing.

According to Carl Jung, universally shared memories within the collective unconscious reveal themselves in religion, art, and popular culture as various archetypal figures. For example, Jung might suggest that African-American artist Karl Priebe's dreamlike painting, *Mayor of Tehuantepec (top),* depicts "the wise old person" who guides the hero on his or her quest for spiritual salvation or wholeness by revealing the nature of the collective unconscious. Similarly, Jung might describe French artist Adolphe Faugeron's painting, *Spring Maidens (bottom),* as a representation of the animus archetype, which is the feminine side of personality in both women and men.

Sources: Karl Priebe, *Mayor of Tehuantepec for Lisa on the 22nd of August 1966,* 1966, casein painting on artist board, 17.75 × 22 inches; Adolphe Faugeron, *Spring Maidens,* 1900.

usefulness is difficult to determine if the research sample does not represent the population of interest. Further, recent reexaminations of Freud's case notes suggest that he may have distorted some of his patients' histories so they conformed to his view of personality (Esterson, 1993). Related to these criticisms is the fact that Freud did not welcome anyone questioning or challenging his ideas (Gardner, 1993a). Such a stance is typical of cult leaders but not of those who want to advance scientific understanding.

Another criticism of Freud's theory is that many of its psychological processes—such as that of the id—cannot be observed, much less measured. If aspects of his theory cannot be scientifically tested, then of what use are they to the science of psychology? Further, when scientific studies have tested some of Freud's concepts, they have found little evidence to support the existence of the Oedipal/Electra complexes, penis envy, or many of Freud's ideas on sexual and aggressive drives (Crews, 1998).

Despite the inability to test certain portions of Freud's personality theory and the lack of evidence for other portions that have been scientifically tested, a few of his general ideas concerning personality have received widespread empirical support (Lichtenberg, 1989; Pine, 1990; Westen & Gabbard, 1999). These general ideas are that (1) unconscious processes shape human behavior; (2) childhood experiences shape adult personality; and (3) learning to regulate impulses is critical for healthy development. Given these continuing contributions, psychoanalysis still deserves recognition as an important, albeit flawed, perspective on personality.

Section Review

- Freud believed that the unconscious mind largely determines human behavior.
- Freud's three personality structures are the id (the entirely unconscious part of the personality that contains our sexual and aggressive urges), the ego (the part of the personality that balances the demands of the id, superego, and reality), and the superego (the part of the personality that counterbalances the more primitive id demands).
- Psychosexual stages include the oral stage, anal stage, phallic stage, latency stage, and genital stage.
- The conscious part of the ego is protected from awareness of disturbing id impulses because defense mechanisms transform raw id desires into more acceptable actions.
- Alfred Adler emphasized personal striving to overcome feelings of inferiority.
- Carl Jung emphasized that our thoughts and actions are influenced by a collective unconscious.
- Karen Horney stressed that social and cultural factors influence female personality.
- Psychoanalytic theory has two major limitations: (1) It is not based on carefully controlled scientific research, and (2) many of its concepts cannot be measured.

12-3 THE HUMANISTIC PERSPECTIVE

Preview
- *How does unconditional positive regard shape personality?*
- *What facilitates self-actualization?*

As discussed in chapter 1, section 1-3b, due to many psychologists' dissatisfaction with both the psychoanalytic and the behaviorist views of human nature, in the 1950s a new perspective developed in psychology. This "third wave" in psychology, known as the *humanistic perspective*, emphasized people's innate capacity for personal growth and their ability to make conscious choices. Carl Rogers and Abraham Maslow were the primary architects of humanistic psychology, and they both contended that psychologists should study people's unique subjective mental experience of the world. This stance represented a direct challenge to behaviorism and was instrumental in focusing renewed attention on the study of the self within the field of personality. Further, by emphasizing the possibilities for positive change that people can make at any point in their lives, the humanistic perspective stood in sharp contrast to the more pessimistic tone of the psychoanalytic perspective (Cassel, 2000).

12-3a Rogers's Person-Centered Theory Emphasizes Self-Realization

Carl Rogers (1902–1987) believed that people are basically good and that we are all working toward becoming the best we can be (Rogers, 1961). Instead of being driven by sexual and aggressive desires, Rogers asserted that we are motivated by a wish to be good, and that

Carl Rogers's person-centered theory of personality considers receiving unconditional positive regard an essential ingredient in healthy personal growth. Parents are the primary providers of this affection to children.

Source: Courtesy of Figzoi.

we would achieve our potential if we were given **unconditional positive regard.** Unfortunately, according to Rogers, many of us are frustrated in our potential growth because important people in our lives often provide us with positive regard only if we meet their standards. Being the recipient of this **conditional positive regard** stunts our personal growth, because in our desire to be regarded positively, we lose sight of our *ideal self,* which is the person we would like to become. Rogers stated that, as we continue to adjust our lives to meet others' expectations, the discrepancy between our *actual self,* which is the person we know ourselves to be now, and our ideal self becomes greater.

Rogers's theory of personality is as much about how people change as it is about how people are at any given moment (Kirschenbaum, 2004). For him, the dilemma of personality involves how people's thwarted growth potential can be released. The answer to this dilemma is for people with damaged selves, or low self-esteem, to find someone who will treat them with unconditional positive regard. The assumption here is that, when people are accepted for who they are, they will eventually come to accept themselves as well. When this self-acceptance occurs, people then put aside others' standards that are false for them, and they get back on track in developing their true selves (Truax & Carkhuff, 1967). Conveying unconditional positive regard to others involves the following three characteristics: *genuineness* (being open and honest), *warmth* (being caring and nurturing), and *empathy* (accurately identifying what the person is thinking and feeling).

unconditional positive regard An attitude of complete acceptance toward another person regardless of what she or he has said or done; based on the belief in that person's essential goodness.

conditional positive regard An attitude of acceptance toward another person only when she or he meets your standards.

12-3b Maslow's Self-Actualization Theory Stresses Maximizing Potential

Like Rogers, Abraham Maslow (1908–1970) was interested in people's ability to reach their full potential. As discussed in chapter 11, section 11-1f, this process of fulfilling one's potential was what Maslow (1970) called *self-actualization.* Like Rogers and Freud, Maslow used the case study method in developing his theory. However, unlike Rogers and Freud, Maslow studied healthy, creative people rather than those who were troubled and seeking therapy. He chose as his subjects people who had led or were leading rich and productive lives, including outstanding college students, faculty members, professionals in other fields, and historical figures, such as Abraham Lincoln, Thomas Jefferson, and Eleanor Roosevelt (Moss, 1999; Rathunde, 2001).

Maslow found that both the self-actualized and the self-actualizing people he studied shared important characteristics. They were secure in the sense of who they were and therefore not paralyzed by others' opinions. They were open and spontaneous, able to engage

peak experience A fleeting but intense moment when a person feels happy, absorbed, and extremely capable.

easily and effortlessly with other people, in part because they focused on problems and how to solve them rather than on themselves. They were also loving and caring, and they often focused their energies on a particular task, one they regarded as a life mission. Most of these people had a few deep friendships rather than a large network of more superficial relationships. Maslow also reported that these people had experienced personal or spiritual **peak experiences,** which are fleeting but intense moments of joy, ecstasy, and absorption, in which people feel extremely capable. A peak experience can occur while a person is engaging in a religious activity or service, while performing athletically, while listening to music, or while relating to a lover. Some women report childbirth as a peak experience. Although anyone can have peak experiences, Maslow's group of self-actualizing people reported more peak experiences, and the quality of those experiences was richer than the experiences reported by others he studied. These peak experiences, regardless of how they occur, have a lasting effect. They enrich the outlook of the persons who have experienced them and can lead them to become more spontaneous and more open to the experiences of others.

Maslow was interested in ways to facilitate self-actualization, just as Rogers had been. He noted that the qualities of the self-actualized people he studied were the qualities of mature adults. His theory of motivation suggested that people were more likely to focus on self-actualizing needs after sufficiently satisfying more basic needs, including social and esteem needs (Reiss & Havercamp, 2005). Like Rogers, Maslow was optimistic about what would transpire when people were provided with the psychological and physical nutrients they needed in order to develop.

12-3c The Humanistic Perspective Has Been Criticized as Being Overly Optimistic

Like Freud, humanistic psychologists have had a significant impact on popular culture. If you look in the self-help section of any bookstore, you will find numerous titles emphasizing the control you have over changing your life and achieving your full potential. However, in trying to correct for Freud's gloomy outlook on human nature, the humanistic perspective on personality may have overshot the mark and failed to acknowledge that many people engage in mean-spirited and even cruel behavior on a fairly regular basis. The truth is that people have the capacity to act in a wide variety of ways. Further, some of the forces that shape our behavior are outside our conscious awareness.

Although humanistic psychology has helped revitalize attention to the self, one of its major limitations is that it has not produced a substantial body of testable hypotheses for its personality theories. Like Freud before them, humanistic psychologists have not clearly defined their concepts and have often rejected the use of carefully controlled scientific studies to test the validity of their theories. As a result, most of the scientific investigations of the self have come from outside the humanistic perspective, especially the social-cognitive perspective (see section 12-5c).

Section Review

- Carl Rogers proposed that being provided unconditional positive regard allows a person to heal the split between the actual and the ideal self.
- According to Abraham Maslow, in order to self-actualize, people must be motivated to become the best they can be.

12-4 THE TRAIT PERSPECTIVE

Preview

- *How do trait theorists study personality?*
- *How many basic traits describe personality?*
- *At what points in life are personality traits most and least stable?*
- *What interacts with personality traits in predicting behavior?*

In 1919, Gordon Allport was a 22-year-old psychology student from Indiana. During the summer, he traveled to Europe and boldly asked the world-famous Sigmund Freud to meet with him. Upon arriving at Freud's office, the young Allport was at a loss to explain the purpose of his visit. In truth, he simply wanted to meet this great man. After a strained silence in which Freud did nothing to put him at ease, Allport told a story about an incident he had witnessed on the train ride to Vienna. In his car was a boy who seemed to have a dirt phobia, for he pleaded with his mother throughout the journey to keep dirty passengers from sitting near him. The mother was meticulously dressed and had a domineering personality, which seemed to suggest the source of the boy's phobia. When Allport finished telling the story, Freud paused and then leaned toward Allport and asked in a soft voice, "And was that little boy you?" Allport was mortified. Freud had mistakenly perceived this "ice-breaker" story as a window into the young man's unconscious. Quickly changing the subject, Allport talked a bit more before excusing himself and departing. After getting over his embarrassment, Allport decided that psychoanalysis was not the best way to understand personality. Instead of searching for hidden, unconscious motives in people's behavior, he thought that personality psychologists should first try to describe and measure the basic factors of personality (Allport, 1967). This set him on a path of research that culminated in the development of the *trait perspective*.

12-4a Trait Theories Describe Basic Personality Dimensions

The **trait perspective** conceives of personality as consisting of stable characteristics that people display over time and across situations (Nicholson, 2002). A **trait** is a relatively stable tendency to behave in a particular way. As an approach to understanding personality, the trait perspective is more concerned with describing *how* people differ from one another than explaining *why* they differ (Pervin, 1996). The way psychologists typically measure traits is similar to the way people normally assess others' personalities. They observe them over time and in various situations or ask them how they typically behave. For example, if a friend is always prompt, you come to rely on that as characteristic of her. From the trait perspective, we would propose that your friend is consistently on time because of an underlying trait that predisposes her to act in this manner. This may seem a little circular, and to a certain extent, it is. However, like so much else in personality psychology, traits cannot be measured directly but, instead, are inferred from behavior.

In studying traits, Gordon Allport and his colleague Henry Odbert (1936) began by combing through an unabridged dictionary and making a list of words that described people's personal characteristics. This initial list of 18,000 words was eventually reduced to about 200 clusters of related words, which became the original traits in Allport's personality theory (Allport, 1937). Allport's perspective on personality had a good deal in common with the views of humanistic psychologists in that he emphasized that the whole human being should be the focus of study. Like humanistic psychologists, he further asserted that behaviorism was seriously mistaken when it explained human behavior as no different from that of rats and pigeons. In addition to being influenced by his humanistic associations, Allport was influenced by Gestalt psychology. As you recall from chapter 1, section 1-2e, the Gestalt perspective contends that "the whole is different from the sum of its parts." Similarly, Allport (1961) argued that personality is not simply a collection of traits, but that these traits seamlessly fit together to form a dynamic and unique personality.

Allport's contemporary, Henry Murray (1938, 1948), was also a trait psychologist who appreciated humanistic psychology's emphasis on the total person. However, Murray's personality approach was also influenced by Jung's and Freud's theories of unconscious motivation. As a result, he focused on traits that are relatively irrational, passionate, and laden with conflict and emotion. Ironically, both men were doing their research in the same place—Harvard—at about the same time.

How can a single perspective, the trait perspective, include theorists who take such different positions about the nature of personality? Actually, the trait approach is not based on specific assumptions about human nature. Traits are viewed as the small building blocks of personality, and a theorist can fit them together in a variety of ways, just as a landscaper can lay bricks into a walk in a variety of patterns. Whereas psychoanalytic and humanistic

trait perspective
A descriptive approach to personality that identifies stable characteristics that people display over time and across situations.

trait A relatively stable tendency to behave in a particular way across a variety of situations.

[handwritten margin note:] an underlying (non observable) psychological characteristic assumed to be the cause/source of consistencies in behavior in different situations and at different times. example: intelligence some have it others have a little but everyone has it.

theorists have definite beliefs about whether human beings are basically rational, aggressive, or unconsciously motivated, the trait approach assumes that people differ in the degree to which they possess personality traits. For example, instead of taking a position that people are basically aggressive or nonaggressive, trait theorists contend that people differ in the degree to which they possess aggressive traits (McCrae & Costa, 1990).

12-4b Factor Analysis Is Used to Identify Personality Traits

Allport's work in identifying a list of traits was a necessary first step in the development of a scientific trait approach to personality, yet his list of 200-some traits needed to be reduced to a more manageable level. Researchers achieved this by relying on *factor analysis.* As you recall from chapter 10, section 10-2a, factor analysis is a statistical technique that allows researchers to identify clusters of variables that are related to—or *correlated* with—one another. When a group of traits correlates in factor analysis, this suggests that a more general trait is influencing them. For example, several studies have found that people who describe themselves as outgoing also describe themselves as talkative, active, and optimistic about the future. This cluster of traits has been associated with the more general trait *extraversion* (Eysenck, 1973).

Raymond Cattell (1965, 1986) was one of the first trait theorists to use factor analysis to identify these general traits, which he called *source traits.* First he collected people's ratings of themselves on many different traits, and then he identified clusters of related traits using factor analysis. Based on this procedure, Cattell concluded that you can understand an individual's personality by identifying the degree to which she or he possesses each of the 16 source traits listed in table 12-3. To measure these traits, Cattell developed the *Sixteen Personality Factor Questionnaire* (*16PF*), which is widely used for career counseling, marital counseling, and evaluating employees and executives (Cattell, 2001; Tango & Kolodinsky, 2004).

Cattell was a pioneer in using factor analysis to study personality. He also demonstrated the importance of testing personality traits in applied settings—in business organizations, in schools, in clinical work—and then using that information to better understand the traits. Testing personality theories in applied settings and then refining the theories based on what is learned has become an important part of modern trait approaches to personality (Friedman & Schustack, 1999).

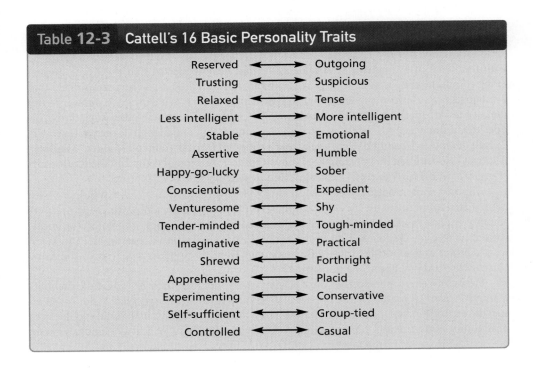

Table 12-3	Cattell's 16 Basic Personality Traits
Reserved	⟷ Outgoing
Trusting	⟷ Suspicious
Relaxed	⟷ Tense
Less intelligent	⟷ More intelligent
Stable	⟷ Emotional
Assertive	⟷ Humble
Happy-go-lucky	⟷ Sober
Conscientious	⟷ Expedient
Venturesome	⟷ Shy
Tender-minded	⟷ Tough-minded
Imaginative	⟷ Practical
Shrewd	⟷ Forthright
Apprehensive	⟷ Placid
Experimenting	⟷ Conservative
Self-sufficient	⟷ Group-tied
Controlled	⟷ Casual

The British psychologists Hans Eysenck and Sybil Eysenck (pronounced "EYE-zink") also used factor analysis to describe personality functioning. However, unlike Cattell, the Eysencks believed that personality researchers should rely on other evidence besides the findings of factor analysis when identifying the basic dimensions of personality. Specifically, they believed that researchers should also consider the biological bases of personality (Eysenck, 1973; Eysenck & Eysenck, 1963, 1983). Based on thousands of studies conducted over five decades, the Eysencks identified three genetically influenced dimensions of personality: *extraversion* (which included Cattell's factors of outgoingness and assertiveness), *neuroticism* (which included Cattell's factors of emotional instability and apprehensiveness), and *psychoticism* (which included Cattell's factors of tough-mindedness and shrewdness).

So how many basic traits are there in personality? Are there 16 source traits, as Cattell proposed, or are there the much more modest three dimensions proposed by the Eysencks? Before reading further, complete Explore It Exercise 12-1.

12-4c The Five-Factor Model Specifies Five Basic Personality Traits

Did you complete Explore It Exercise 12-1? If not, do so now before reading further. When other college students have completed a similar task (Sneed et al., 1998), over 70 percent classified 30 traits similar to those in this exercise so that at least five of the six items in each grouping fell into clusters similar to the following: (1) *rich fantasy life, rich emotional life, action-oriented, novel ideas, eccentric, idiosyncratic*; (2) *competent, orderly, dutiful, self-disciplined, deliberate, achievement-oriented*; (3) *outgoing, positive emotions, assertive, full of energy, excitement seeking, warm*; (4) *trusting, straightforward, compliant, modest, tender-minded, altruistic*; (5) *anxious, self-conscious, depressed, hostile, impulsive, vulnerable*. Did your own clustering conform to this pattern?

Over the past 25 years, most personality trait researchers have reached the conclusion that the key personality factors do in fact cluster this way. The five factors, or dimensions of personality, are known as the *Big Five Factors,* or the **Five-Factor Model** (Endler & Speer, 1998; McCrae & Costa, 1997b; Pytlik Zillig et al., 2002). These five basic traits are *openness, conscientiousness, extraversion, agreeableness,* and *neuroticism* (use the acronym *OCEAN* to remember these five traits). As you can see in table 12-4, each of the five factors represents a clustering of more specific traits. For example, people who score high on neuroticism tend

> **Five-Factor Model** A trait theory asserting that personality consists of five traits (neuroticism, extraversion, openness to experience, agreeableness, and conscientiousness).

Explore It
Exercise **12-1**

Can You Perform an Intuitive Factor Analysis of Personality Traits?

In the 1930s, well before the widespread use of factor analysis in research, Gordon Allport and Henry Odbert (1936) relied upon their intuitive judgment to reduce an initial list of 18,000 personality traits to about 200 clusters of related traits. To gain some appreciation of their effort, examine carefully the 30 traits listed below and sort them into five groups of related traits, each containing 6 traits. In forming each grouping, keep in mind that the traits in each group are assumed to "go together," so that people who have one of the traits in the group are also likely to have the other traits. After you have finished sorting the 30 traits, identify what it is they have in common. Can you attach an overall trait name to each of the five groups of traits? Finally, for each group, how would people who possess an abundance of the overall trait differ from people who possess very little of this overall trait?

Five Factor Model

Achievement-oriented 2	Eccentric 1	Positive emotions 3
Action-oriented 1	Excitement seeking 3	Rich emotional life 1
Altruistic 4	Full of energy 3	Rich fantasy life 1
Anxious 5	Hostile 5	Self-conscious 5
Assertive 3	Idiosyncratic 1	Self-disciplined 2
Competent 2	Impulsive 5	Straightforward 4
Compliant 4	Modest 4	Tender-minded 4
Deliberate 2	Novel ideas 1	Trusting 4
Depressed 5	Orderly 2	Vulnerable 5
Dutiful 2	Outgoing 3	Warm 3

Table 12-4	The Five-Factor Model and Its Facets			
Openness	**Conscientiousness**	**Extraversion**	**Agreeableness**	**Neuroticism**
Rich fantasy life	Competent	Outgoing	Trusting	Anxious
Rich emotional life	Orderly	Positive emotions	Straightforward	Self-conscious
Action-oriented	Dutiful	Assertive	Compliant	Depressed
Novel ideas	Self-disciplined	Full of energy	Modest	Hostile
Eccentric	Deliberate	Excitement seeking	Tender-minded	Impulsive
Idiosyncratic	Achievement-oriented	Warm	Altruistic	Vulnerable

to be anxious, self-conscious, depressed, hostile, impulsive, and vulnerable. These lower-order traits are called *facets* of the Five-Factor Model (Wiggins, 1996).

With only slight variations, the five basic traits that make up the Five-Factor Model have consistently emerged in studies of children, college students, and the elderly (John & Srivastava, 1999; McCrae et al., 1999). Further, these traits have been found in societies as diverse as those of the United States, Bangladesh, Brazil, Japan, Canada, Finland, Germany, Poland, China, and the Philippines (Diaz-Guerrero et al., 2001; McCrae et al., 1998). This is especially impressive when you consider the wide variety of languages used in these studies to test for these traits. Although gender differences are small, a recent study of 24 cultures from five continents found that women tend to score higher than men on neuroticism and agreeableness (Costa et al., 2001).

Evolutionary theorists contend that the reason these five traits are found across a wide variety of cultures is that they reflect the most salient features of humans' adaptive behavior over the course of evolutionary history (Buss, 1999a; MacDonald, 1998). In other words, these five traits have emerged as the basic components of personality because, as a species, we have evolved special sensitivity to variations in the ability to handle stress (neuroticism), seek out others' company (extraversion), approach problems (openness to experience), cooperate with others (agreeableness), and meet our social and moral obligations (conscientiousness). In contrast, sociocultural theorists propose that the behaviors associated with these five traits are learned through the experiences that children and young adults have while mastering important social roles found in cultures throughout the world (Roberts et al., 2005). Instead of genetic predisposition to developing these traits, sociocultural theorists emphasize the role learning plays in shaping the behaviors that psychologists associate with these traits. Presently, neither of these theories has received sufficient empirical support to declare it superior to the other.

You might be wondering whether these five traits comprise an individual's entire personality. Do you think that five traits can sufficiently describe your personality? Most trait theorists would say no. Although almost any personality trait probably has a good deal in common with one of these five basic traits, the Five-Factor Model does not capture the entire essence of personality (Funder, 2001). Let us briefly examine each of these traits.

Openness to Experience

People who are particularly open to experience are adventurous—constantly searching out new ways to do things—and they are sensitive and passionate, with a childlike wonder at the world (McCrae, 1994). They can also flout traditional notions of what is appropriate or expected in terms of their behavior or ideas (McCrae & Costa, 1997a; McCrae & John, 1992). As with most of the other dimensions, openness to experience is at the end of the pole that appears more desirable, but in fact, many qualities of those who are more closed to experience are quite valuable. These individuals tend to be hardworking, loyal, down-to-earth, and proud of their traditional values.

Openness to experience can be a misleading title, because some people might equate this personality dimension with being educated or "cultured." Although a liberal arts education theoretically may lead to changes in openness to experience, a national survey of nearly 10,000 men and women found only a modest correlation between this trait and the subjects' years of education (Costa et al., 1986). People who are open to experience *enjoy* gaining information in new fields, including nonintellectual fields. They may, for instance, seek out new tastes in food or new types of music to listen to. Thus, people who are open to experience will broaden their knowledge base across the course of their lifetime and will have new and different interests as time goes on. Having good cognitive abilities helps broaden a person's experience, but it is not necessary—nor does intelligence alone mean that people will be open.

Conscientiousness

Conscientiousness is the measure of a person's willingness to conform to others' expectations and follow through on what she or he has agreed to do, despite more tempting options that may arise. People who score high on conscientiousness tend to be well organized, dependable, hardworking, and ambitious, whereas those who score low are more likely to be disorganized, undependable, lazy, and easygoing. This dimension is very important in career planning and workplace productivity. Adolescents who are conscientious are much more likely to spend time thinking about and planning their future career options than those who lack conscientiousness (Lounsbury et al., 2005). Similarly, conscientious employees are good workplace citizens, while nonconscientious employees are nonproductive and undermine the organization's health (Barrick & Mount, 1991; Howard & Howard, 2000).

The Five-Factor Model of personality contends that there are five basic components of personality: neuroticism, extraversion, openness to experience, agreeableness, and conscientiousness. What traits do you think are strongest in your personality?

 Journey of Discovery Question   How do you think Freud would describe the highly conscientious person?

Extraversion

Extraversion was first identified by Carl Jung (see section 12-2e) and has been included in virtually every personality system proposed in the last 50 years (Watson & Clark, 1997). Extraverts are people who seek out and enjoy others' company. They tend to be confident, energetic, bold, and optimistic, and they handle social situations with ease and grace. Extraverts' social skills, confidence, and take-charge attitude often make them well-suited for leadership positions (A. M. Johnson et al., 2004). On the opposite end of this particular personality dimension is the introverted character. Introverts tend to be shy, quiet, and reserved, and it is harder for others to connect with them (Tellegen et al., 1988).

Agreeableness

Agreeableness is a personality dimension that ranges from friendly compliance with others on one end to hostile antagonism on the other (Costa et al., 1989). People who score high on agreeableness tend to be good-natured, softhearted, courteous, and sympathetic, whereas those who score low tend to be irritable, ruthless, rude, and tough-minded (Caspi et al., 1989). Some researchers have suggested that disagreeableness is related to an overactive sympathetic division of the autonomic nervous system (Rothbart, 1989). Agreeableness is a useful way to obtain popularity, and agreeable people are better liked than disagreeable people (Graziano & Eisenberg, 1997). However, people high in agreeableness may be too dependent on others' approval and thus ill-suited for situations requiring tough or more objective decisions. For instance, scientists, art or literary critics, and judges may be able to perform better if they are less agreeable and more "objective" in their approaches to solving problems (Graziano et al., 1996).

Neuroticism

At the core of neuroticism is negative affect (McCrae & Costa, 1987). This personality dimension, which is sometimes labeled *emotional stability,* describes how people differ in terms of being anxious, high-strung, insecure, and self-pitying versus relaxed, calm, composed, secure, and content. Neurotics (people low in emotional stability) can either channel their worrying into a kind of compulsive success or let their anxiety lead them into recklessness. Many of the facets underlying neuroticism will be discussed more fully in chapter 13, when we examine psychological disorders.

Personality Traits in Nonhuman Animals

Our family dog, Maizy, is trusting, curious, very energetic, somewhat absentminded, and extremely friendly. I would guess that she is low on neuroticism and high on agreeableness, extraversion, and openness to experience. Is my application of the Five-Factor Model to a canine based on any scientific evidence, or should it be dismissed as the whimsical musings of a dog lover?

The personality psychologists Samuel Gosling and Oliver John believe that the Five-Factor Model can be used to describe the personality of many nonhuman animals, including dogs. In a review of 19 animal personality studies involving 12 different species, Gosling and John (1999) found that the personality traits of extraversion, neuroticism, and agreeableness commonly occur across species. Chimpanzees, gorillas, various other primates, mammals in general, and even guppies and octopuses exhibit individual differences that are remarkably similar to these three personality traits. The researchers believe that this cross-species similarity in personality traits suggests that biological mechanisms are likely responsible.

Using personality distinctions similar to those in the Five-Factor Model, the comparative psychologist John Capitanio (1999) has also discovered that the behavior of adult male rhesus monkeys can be reliably predicted from personality dimensions. Over a 4-1/2-year period, Capitanio found that, compared to monkeys who scored low on these personality dimensions, highly extraverted monkeys engaged in more affiliative behavior, highly neurotic monkeys were more fearful and hypersensitive to changes in their surroundings, and highly agreeable monkeys were more easygoing in their social behavior. Like Gosling and John, Capitanio believes that biological mechanisms are shaping the expression of these personality traits.

These consistencies across species and over time further suggest that the five factors identified by trait theorists reflect some of the basic styles of behavior that are necessary for many species to best adapt to their environments (Capitanio, in press; Gosling, 2001). For instance, an animal high in neuroticism might be the most responsive to the presence of a predator and so could act as a sentinel in a group of animals. Meanwhile, an animal low in neuroticism may promote group solidarity by being relaxed and calm. Together, these animals could contribute to the social functioning of their group in different ways, with the net result that both of them (and their kin) may be more likely to survive and reproduce. Thus, the genes that influence these personality styles are likely to be passed on to future generations.

So what are the important traits in a dog's personality? I wasn't far off the mark in sizing up Maizy. Factor analyses of experts' ratings of dog breeds identified traits that closely approximated four of the five traits in the Five-Factor Model: neuroticism, agreeableness, extraversion, and openness to experience. A fifth personality dimension, "dominance-territoriality," was also identified (Gosling & John, 1999). Maizy, a golden retriever, would score very low in this dimension.

What about conscientiousness? Gosling and John's research found that chimpanzees were the only species other than humans that exhibited the trait of conscientiousness (it was not found among gorillas), although it was defined more narrowly in chimps than in humans. Among chimps, conscientiousness included individual behavioral variations involving lack of attention and goal directedness, unpredictability, and disorganized behavior. Because conscientiousness entails following rules, thinking before acting, and other complex cognitive functions, it is not surprising that this trait was found only in humans' closest genetic relative. These findings suggest that conscientiousness is a recent evolutionary development among hominids, the subfamily composed of humans, chimpanzees, and gorillas.

12-4d Critics Challenge Whether Traits Reliably Predict Behavior

Personality theorists, whether they take a psychoanalytic, humanistic, or trait perspective view, have all emphasized that personality is relatively stable over time and an important

In addition to describing human personalities, the Five-Factor Model has been used to describe many nonhuman personalities as well, including those of dogs. Experts' ratings of dog breeds identified traits that closely approximated four of the five traits in the Five-Factor Model: neuroticism, agreeableness, extraversion, and openness to experience, as well as a fifth personality dimension, "dominance-territoriality." Which of the five factors do you think they found only in humans and chimpanzees?

Source: Courtesy of Figzoi.

determinant of behavior. Yet, Walter Mischel (1968, 1984) has argued that these are misguided beliefs. Instead, he asserts that personality is not really stable over time and across situations and that the situation we place people in is a much stronger determinant of behavior than their personalities. This viewpoint, which is called **situationism,** asserts that our behavior is not determined by stable traits but is strongly influenced by the situation.

In making a situationist argument, Mischel discussed an early study conducted by Hugh Hartshorne and Mark May (1928), who placed children in many different situations in which they had the opportunity to lie, cheat, and steal. Instead of finding that the children displayed honest or dishonest traits consistent across many different situations, Hartshorne and May found that the situation was the most important determinant of how the children behaved. If kids thought they could get away with it, most of them were likely to behave dishonestly. In Mischel's own research, he found virtually no correlation between people's traits and their behavior across situations (Mischel, 1968, 1984). In other words, personality traits did not reliably predict behavior. Based on this evidence, Mischel argued that personality traits are a figment of trait theorists' imaginations!

As you might guess, this critique stirred up considerable controversy among personality psychologists. Seymour Epstein (1979, 1980) responded that Mischel was not seeing consistency in behavior across situations because he was not measuring enough behaviors. Using an analogy, Epstein stated that no one expects your IQ score to predict whether you will correctly answer a particular question on a particular test in a particular class during a particular semester. Predicting such a thing would be highly unreliable, because so many factors might influence your response (Were you rushed for time? Did you understand this information in class? Did you read the question correctly?). However, your IQ score will be much more accurate in predicting your *average* performance over many questions on several exams. Similarly, your score on an introversion-extraversion scale will not be very accurate in predicting whether you will introduce yourself to that attractive person you see on campus tomorrow. But your score will probably be much more accurate in predicting your *average* sociability across many situations. By and large, research supports Epstein's argument: Personality trait scores do reliably predict how people generally behave (Funder, 2001; Paunonen, 2003; Paunonen & Ashton, 2001).

Yet what about the assertion by situationists that personality is not stable over time? Actually, most studies find that personality traits are remarkably stable over the adult years but somewhat less so during childhood (Asendorpf & Van Aken, 2003; Costa et al., 1980). The most extensive study of personality trait stability at different ages was a meta-analysis of 150 studies involving almost 50,000 participants (Roberts & DelVecchio, 2000). In the various studies included in this meta-analysis, participants' personalities had been measured for at least 1 year. As depicted in figure 12-2, results indicated that personality traits are least stable during childhood (correlations in the .40s), somewhat more stable in early adulthood (correlations in the .50s), and most stable after the age of 50 (correlations in the .70s). These findings do not support the situationists' claim that personality is not stable over time. Our personalities are quite stable, especially during the adult years, with most change occurring during the early years of life. Yet, despite this trait stability, additional research indicates that our personalities are certainly capable of change throughout our lives (Srivastava et al., 2003). They do not necessarily become fixed like plaster at a particular age.

One important contribution to personality theory made by situationists was their insistence that situational factors shape people's behavior. In response, many personality researchers acknowledged that situations do indeed shape behavior, and that how we behave is often determined by an *interaction* of personal and situational factors (Cervone & Shoda, 1999; Mischel & Shoda, 1999). In some situations, social norms may constrain the expression of personality traits. For example, extraverts, like everyone else, are likely to be relatively quiet and subdued at a library, in a funeral home, or during a church service. The personalities of those with whom we interact also can significantly alter our own behavior. For instance, a store clerk who is low on agreeableness may treat us very rudely, which may cause us to react in a similar fashion, despite the fact that we generally are kind and considerate. Thus, although personality traits do appear to explain a good deal of our behavior, situational forces significantly influence us (see chapter 16).

> **situationism** The viewpoint that our behavior is strongly influenced by the situation rather than by personality traits.

Figure 12-2

Stability of Personality Traits at Different Ages

A meta-analysis of 150 studies involving nearly 50,000 participants examined the stability of personality at different ages (Roberts & DelVecchio, 2000). Based on the findings depicted in this graph, at what ages is personality least stable, and when is it most stable?

Source: Data from Roberts, B. W., and DelVecchio, W. F. (2000). The rank-order consistency of personality traits from childhood to old age: A quantitative review of longitudinal studies. *Psychological Bulletin*, 126, 3–25.

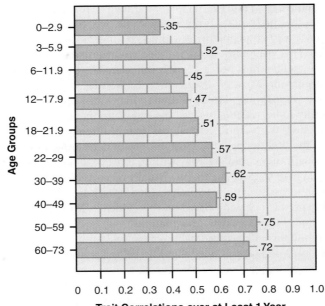

The criticisms of the trait approach have helped sharpen our understanding of the limits of personality as a determinant of behavior, but they have also increased our ability to predict behavior. Attending only to personality traits will not accurately predict behavior in most circumstances. Instead, many personality researchers have increasingly embraced **interactionism,** which is the study of the combined effects of both the situation and the person on human behavior (Magnusson & Endler, 1977; Sadler & Woody, 2003). As outlined here, Mischel's critical position toward the trait approach fueled a number of research directions that might not otherwise have been pursued. In psychology, as in all science, a critical or contrary position that is well presented frequently benefits the field by causing everyone to more clearly state (and examine) their assumptions and beliefs.

interactionism The study of the combined effects of both the situation and the person on human behavior.

Section Review

- The trait perspective is a descriptive approach to personality that focuses on stable characteristics that people display over time and across situations.
- Trait theorists identify traits by relying on factor analysis.
- The Five-Factor Model, the most widely accepted trait theory, contends that personality is best described by the traits of neuroticism, extraversion, openness to experience, agreeableness, and conscientiousness.
- Personality traits are most stable during later adulthood and least stable during early childhood.
- Personality traits interact with situational factors in determining behavior.

12-5 THE SOCIAL-COGNITIVE PERSPECTIVE

Preview

- *How do cognitions shape personality?*
- *What is reciprocal determinism?*
- *How do people develop a locus of control?*
- *Is the desire to verify your self-concept stronger than the desire to increase your self-esteem?*
- *What type of behavior is best explained by the social-cognitive perspective?*

The perspectives examined thus far contend that personality consists of internal psychological needs or traits that shape our thoughts, feelings, and behavior. These approaches provide a good illustration of how the ideology of *individualism* has shaped the development of many personality theories. In contrast, our fourth major approach, the **social-cognitive perspective,** has a less individualist bias, because it views personality as emerging as the person interacts with her or his social environment. This perspective has its roots in the behavioral principles of *classical conditioning* and *operant conditioning*, but its closest associations are with the more cognitively oriented behavioral principles of *observational learning* (chapter 7) and the principles of *cognitive psychology* (chapter 8). As you recall from chapter 7, section 7-3a, observational learning is the central feature of Albert Bandura's (1986) *social learning theory*. Bandura proposes that people learn social behaviors primarily through observation and cognitive processing of information rather than through direct experience.

12-5a Personality Is Shaped by the Interaction of People's Cognitions, Behavior, and Environment

According to Bandura (1986), Skinner was only partly correct when he asserted that the environment determines people's behavior. Bandura pointed out that people's behavior also determines the environment. He further contended that people's thoughts, beliefs, and expectations determine—and are determined by—both behavior and the environment. As such, personality emerges from an ongoing mutual interaction among people's cognitions, their actions, and their environment. This basic principle of the social-cognitive perspective is known as **reciprocal determinism** and is depicted in figure 12-3. Thus, while environmental factors shape our personalities, we think about what is happening to us and develop beliefs and expectations that will alter both our behavior and our environment (Makoul, 1998). In turn, these behavioral and environmental changes will influence our thoughts, which will then alter our personalities. As you can see, the idea that personality emerges through reciprocal determinism does not fit into the individualist mold of traditional personality theories.

One of the most important cognitive factors in reciprocal determinism is **self-efficacy,** which is a person's belief about his or her ability to perform behaviors that should bring about a desired outcome. Perceptions of self-efficacy are largely subjective and tied to specific kinds of activities. For example, you could have high self-efficacy for solving mathematical problems but low self-efficacy for interacting with new acquaintances. Because of these two different self-efficacies, you might approach a difficult calculus course with robust confidence, while you feign illness when invited to a new friend's party. Success in an activity heightens self-efficacy, while failure lowers it (Boudreaux et al., 1998; Lin, 1998). Further, the more self-efficacy you have for a particular task, the more likely you will pursue the task, try hard, persist in the face of setbacks, and succeed (Bandura, 1999; Chemers et al., 2001). Success breeds self-efficacy, which in turn breeds further success. This mutual interaction is an illustration of reciprocal determinism.

social-cognitive perspective A psychological perspective that examines how people interpret, analyze, remember, and use information about themselves, others, social interactions, and relationships.

reciprocal determinism The social-cognitive belief that personality emerges from an ongoing mutual interaction among people's cognitions, their actions, and their environment.

self-efficacy A person's belief about his or her ability to perform behaviors that should bring about a desired outcome.

Journey of Discovery Question   Is self-efficacy the same as self-esteem?

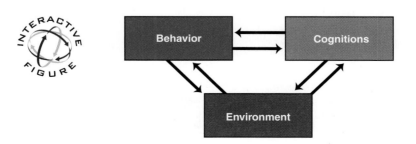

Figure 12-3

Reciprocal Determinism

The idea that personality emerges from an ongoing mutual interaction among people's cognitions, their behavior, and their environment is known as reciprocal determinism. Reciprocal determinism is an important principle of the social-cognitive perspective and stands in sharp contrast to the strict behaviorist belief (as articulated by B. F. Skinner) that the environment is the sole determinant of people's behavior.

12-5b Interacting with the Environment Fosters Feelings of Either Control or Helplessness

According to the social-cognitive theorist Julian Rotter (1966, 1990), through the process of interacting with our surroundings, we develop beliefs about ourselves as either controlling, or controlled by, our environment. The degree to which we believe that outcomes in our lives depend on our own actions versus the actions of uncontrollable environmental forces is known as **locus of control.** People who believe that outcomes occur because of their own efforts are said to have an *internal locus of control*, whereas those who believe that outcomes are outside their own control are described as having an *external locus of control*. Spend a few minutes responding to the items in Self-Discovery Questionnaire 12-1 to get an idea of whether you have an internal or external locus of control.

Numerous studies indicate that people with an internal locus of control are more likely to be achievement-oriented than those with an external locus of control, because they believe that their behavior can result in positive outcomes (Findley & Cooper, 1983; Lachman & Weaver, 1998). True to these expectations, "internals" tend to be more successful in life than are "externals." Externals are less independent than internals, and they are also more likely to be depressed and stressed (Presson & Benassi, 1996).

People who believe that external events control their lives often develop a feeling of helplessness. As discussed in chapter 7, section 7-2g, Martin Seligman (1975) defined this *learned helplessness* as the passive resignation produced by repeated exposure to aversive events believed to be unavoidable. Because people develop the expectation that their behavior has no effect on the outcome of the situation, they simply give up trying to change the outcome, even when their actions might bring rewards (Baum et al., 1998).

Learned helplessness is an example of the operation of reciprocal determinism. After repeatedly failing to achieve a desired outcome, people develop a belief that they can do nothing to alter their current conditions, so they stop trying. Even when the world around them changes so that success becomes possible, they don't act on opportunities because they falsely believe that such action is futile. Learned helplessness explains why some people who have grown up in poverty don't take advantage of opportunities that, if pursued, could lead to economic rewards. Having developed the belief that they cannot change the cards they've been dealt, these people remain mired in poverty and often instill these pessimistic beliefs in their children. Social welfare programs that have been successful in help-

locus of control The degree to which we expect that outcomes in our lives depend on our own actions and personal characteristics versus the actions of uncontrollable environmental forces.

Persons with an internal locus of control are more achievement-oriented and successful in life than those with an external locus of control. What sort of thinking causes these differences among "internals" and "externals"?

Source:

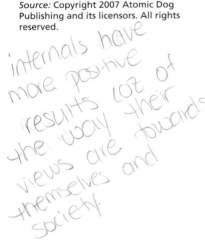

[handwritten note: internals have more positive results coz of the way their views are towards themselves and society]

Self-Discovery

Questionnaire **12-1**

Do You Have an Internal or an External Locus of Control?

Instructions: For each item, select the alternative that you more strongly believe to be true. Remember that this is a measure of your personal beliefs and that there are no correct or incorrect answers.

1. a. Making a lot of money is largely a matter of getting the right breaks.
  b. Promotions are earned through hard work and persistence.

2. a. In my experience, I have noticed that there is usually a direct connection between how hard I study and the grades I get.
  b. Many times, the reactions of teachers seem haphazard to me.

3. a. Marriage is largely a gamble.
  b. The number of divorces indicates that more and more people are not trying to make their marriages work.

4. a. When I am right, I can convince others.
  b. It is silly to think that one can really change another person's basic attitudes.

5. a. In our society, a person's future earning power is dependent upon his or her ability.
  b. Getting promoted is really a matter of being a little luckier than the next person.

6. a. I have little influence over the way other people behave.
  b. If one knows how to deal with people, they are really quite easily led.

Scoring instructions: Give yourself one point for each of the following answers: 1(a), 2(b), 3(a), 4(b), 5(b), and 6(a). Then add up your total number of points. The higher the score, the more external is your locus of control. A score of 5 or 6 suggests that you are in the *high external* range, while a score of 0 or 1 suggests that you are in the *high internal* range. Scores of 2, 3, and 4 suggest that you fall somewhere between these two extremes.

Source: From "External Control and Internal Control" by Julian B. Rotter in *Psychology Today,* June 1971. Reprinted by permission of the author.

ing people pull themselves out of poverty specifically attack learned helplessness (Wanberg et al., 1999).

12-5c Social-Cognitive Psychologists Have Extensively Studied the Self

In the decades of the 1950s and 1960s, humanistic psychologists' attention to the self did not generate a great deal of research, but their self personality theories did help keep the concept alive in psychology during a time when behaviorism was the dominant perspective. Today, the self is one of the most popular areas of scientific study, and many social-cognitive theorists are some of the more prominent researchers. As discussed in chapter 4, section 4-2d, *self-concept* is the "theory" that a person constructs about herself or himself through social interaction, whereas *self-esteem* is a person's evaluation of his or her self-concept. One topic that self researchers have explored is the degree to which our self-concepts are accurate reflections of our personalities. Is wishful thinking a common ingredient in most people's self-concepts? Is the need for accurate self-understanding stronger than the need for positive self-esteem?

Do We Evaluate Ourselves Accurately?

When you receive a good grade on an exam, do you usually conclude that your success was caused by your intelligence, your hard work, or a combination of the two? What if you do poorly? Are you likely to blame your failure on the unreasonable demands of your professor or on pure bad luck? Overall, this tendency to take credit for success while denying blame for failure is known as the **self-serving bias** (Campbell & Sedikides, 1999). The most agreed-upon explanation for the self-serving bias is that it allows us to enhance and protect self-esteem. If we feel personally responsible for successes or positive events in our lives but do not feel blameworthy for failures or other negative events, our self-worth is likely to be bolstered.

Recent studies by Michael Ross and Anne Wilson (2002, 2003) indicate that we are motivated to evaluate our past selves in a way that makes us feel good about ourselves now. We accomplish this feat by perceiving our present self as superior to our former selves, especially in characteristics that are important to our self-concepts (Wilson & Ross, 2001). Although you might think that negatively evaluating our past selves would lower our self-esteem, past selves are not as "real" to us as our present self. Criticizing our past selves allows us to feel better about our current performance in relation to these important characteristics.

Wilson and Ross (2001) also found evidence that we tend to believe we are more superior to our peers at the present time than when we were younger. This is true regardless of our age. Of course, it is possible that most people do learn from experience and get better with age, but it is not statistically possible for all of us to improve more than our peers! In fact, do we really improve noticeably over time? Apparently, not nearly as much as we would like to think. When Wilson and Ross studied people longitudinally, they found that, although research participants perceived themselves as improving in a number of personal characteristics, there was actually no evidence of any such improvement (Wilson & Ross, 2001). These findings suggest that wishful thinking is often an important ingredient in our self-concepts.

One point to keep in mind about these findings is that this tendency to try to enhance feelings of self-worth varies in strength across cultures. Individualist cultures are much more likely than collectivist cultures to believe that high self-esteem is essential for mental health and life satisfaction (Oishi et al., 1999). This cultural difference in the importance placed on self-esteem may explain why individualists are more likely than collectivists to exhibit the self-serving bias and to evaluate their present selves more positively than their past selves (Heine & Lehman, 1999; Wilson & Ross, 2001).

Are Self-Enhancement Needs Stronger Than Self-Verification Needs?

Over the years, there has been an ongoing debate regarding self-esteem and self-concept (Seta & Donaldson, 1999). *Self-enhancement* theories propose that people are primarily motivated to maintain high self-esteem, whereas *self-verification* theories assert that people are primarily motivated to maintain consistent beliefs about themselves, even when these self-beliefs are negative (Dunning et al., 1995; Swann, 1997). For people with high self-esteem, no conflict exists between these two motives, because receiving positive evaluations from others verifies positive self-beliefs. However, for individuals with low self-esteem, these two motives often conflict: The need for self-enhancement causes people with low self-esteem to seek positive evaluations, but that action conflicts with their desire to verify existing negative self-beliefs. Self-enhancement theorists contend that people with low self-esteem seek out positive social evaluations to bolster their self-esteem. In contrast, self-verification theorists argue that this positive feedback creates the fear in low self-esteem people that they may not know themselves after all, and therefore, they will reject it. Which of these perspectives is correct?

A number of studies (Jussim et al., 1995; Swann, 1997) suggest that when judging others' evaluations of ourselves, our emotional reaction ("Do I like it?") is based on whether the evaluations bolster our self-esteem (self-enhancement need), whereas our cognitive reaction ("Is it correct?") is based on whether these evaluations are consistent with our self-concepts (self-verification need). Further, as depicted in figure 12-4, self-enhancement appears to be the automatic and initially strongest response to favorable evaluations, but self-verification is the slower, more deliberate, and perhaps more lasting

self-serving bias The tendency to bolster and defend self-esteem by taking credit for positive events while denying blame for negative events.

Of all the lives that I have lived, I would have to say that this one is my favorite. I am proud that I have developed into a kinder person than I ever thought I would be.

—*Mary Tyler Moore, U.S. actress, b. 1937; quoted at age 60*

Self-esteem and self-contempt have specific odors; they can be smelled.

—*Eric Hoffer, U.S. social philosopher, 1902–1983*

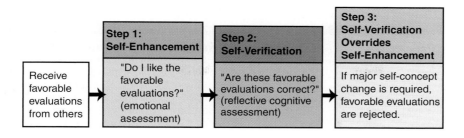

Figure 12-4

How Do Low Self-Esteem People Typically Respond to Positive Evaluations?

When confronted with positive social evaluations that contradict a negative self-concept, how do people with low self-esteem resolve the conflict between self-enhancement and self-verification needs? Research suggests that people follow a three-step process in resolving this conflict. In step 1, the initial reaction is to self-enhance. However, with more time to critically analyze the feedback (step 2), self-verification dominates thinking. In step 3, if internalizing these positive evaluations will necessitate a major reassessment of their self-concept, the need for self-verification tends to override self-enhancement needs, and people reject the evaluations. Generally, low self-esteem people try to strike a balance in satisfying these two motives. They prefer to associate with people who make them feel better about themselves without seriously calling into question their current self-concepts. Why wouldn't people with high self-esteem have this same dilemma when given positive feedback from others?

response (Baumeister, 1998; Sedikides & Strube, 1997). When people first receive favorable evaluations, they tend to automatically self-enhance, but when they have time to critically analyze the feedback, they tend to self-verify. For example, if you have low self-esteem and someone says you are absolutely wonderful, your initial reaction may be to accept this positive feedback and thereby increase your self-esteem. However, after you engage in more complex cognitive analysis, you may realize that accepting this positive feedback will require a major reassessment of your self-concept, a task you may feel ill-equipped to accomplish. Faced with the possible upheaval caused by such a major self-reconstruction, you may abandon self-enhancement and instead seek self-verification. Therefore, you reject the feedback and retain your original self-concept. If you hadn't analyzed the implications of the positive feedback, this incident probably would have ended with simple self-enhancement. Self-verification overrode self-enhancement only because of the later extra cognitive processing.

It appears that the need for self-enhancement and the need for self-verification act as checks and balances on one another, and that only in cases of personality maladjustment does one need rampantly dominate the other (Epstein, 1994; Epstein & Morling, 1995). For example, individuals with delusions of grandeur require self-enhancement to lord over self-verification to maintain their grand, yet faulty, self-beliefs. On the other hand, chronically depressed people continually avoid self-enhancement so they can verify their negative self-beliefs. Most people, however, seek *compromises* between these two motives. Research suggests that when low self-esteem individuals receive positive or negative feedback from others, they automatically compare it to their own self-beliefs and prefer to associate with people who make them feel better about themselves without seriously disconfirming their current self-concepts (Morling & Epstein, 1997).

Journey of Discovery Question

If people with low self-esteem reject attempts to increase their feelings of self-worth when others lavishly praise them, what strategy might you employ to satisfy their self-enhancement needs without triggering their need for self-verification?

12-5d The Social-Cognitive Perspective Has Difficulty Explaining Nonrational Behavior

Traditional behavioral theories of personality that are based primarily on the operant conditioning principles of B. F. Skinner have been criticized for assessing only how environmental factors shape personality. To its credit, the social-cognitive perspective has taken a much more complex view of human personality, while still testing its theories using the scientific method. In their reliance on carefully controlled studies, social-cognitive theories have much more in common with the trait approach to personality than with the less scientifically based theories from the humanistic and psychoanalytic perspectives.

Social-cognitive personality theories have also drawn praise for emphasizing the important role that cognitions play in personality. They have quite rightly pointed out that our behavior is significantly shaped by our beliefs and expectations—those related to ourselves as well as those related to our environment. The social-cognitive approach has also

Perspective	Explanation of Behavior	Evaluation
Psychoanalytic	Personality is set early in childhood and driven by unconscious and anxiety-ridden sexual impulses that we poorly understand.	A speculative, hard-to-test theory that has had an enormous cultural influence and a significant impact on psychology
Humanistic	Personality is based on conscious feelings about oneself and focused on our capacity for growth and change.	A perspective that revitalized attention to the self but often did not use rigorous scientific methods
Trait	Personality consists of a limited number of stable characteristics that people display over time and across situations.	A descriptive approach that sometimes underestimates the impact of situational factors on behavior
Social-cognitive	Personality emerges from an ongoing mutual interaction among people's cognitions, their behavior, and their environment.	An interactionist approach that tends to underestimate the impact of emotions and unconscious motives on behavior

Table **12-5**   The Four Perspectives on Personality

drawn praise because its scientific findings have generated useful applications in the real world concerning how to understand and help solve such problems as drug abuse, unemployment, academic underachievement, and teen pregnancy.

The social-cognitive perspective's emphasis on cognition has placed it squarely in the mainstream of contemporary psychology, and it enjoys immense popularity among many psychologists. However, by emphasizing the cognitive side of human nature, the social-cognitive perspective is best at explaining rational behavior that is "thought through." Like many cognitively oriented theories, it is less able to explain behavior that is spontaneous, irrational, and perhaps sparked by unconscious motives (Schacter & Badgaiyan, 2001). Table 12-5 provides a brief summary of the four personality perspectives we have discussed.

Section Review

- In the social-cognitive perspective, personality represents the unique patterns of thinking and behavior that a person learns in the social world.
- According to the principle of reciprocal determinism, personality emerges from an ongoing mutual interaction among people's cognitions, their actions, and their environment.
- According to the concept of locus of control, by interacting with our surroundings, we develop beliefs about ourselves as either controlling or controlled by our environment.
- The need for self-verification tends to override self-enhancement needs.
- Social-cognitive theories are best at explaining rational behavior but less capable of explaining irrational behavior.

12-6   MEASURING PERSONALITY

Preview

- *What are projective tests supposed to reveal about personality?*
- *What is an objective personality test?*

Two basic assumptions underlie the attempt to understand and describe personality. The first assumption, which we just examined, is that personal characteristics shape people's thoughts, feelings, and behavior. The second assumption, which we are about to examine, is that those characteristics can be measured in some manner (Briggs, 2005). We will consider two kinds of personality tests: *projective* and *objective*.

12-6a Projective Tests Indirectly Measure Inner Feelings, Motives, and Conflicts

Projective tests are based on the assumption that if people are presented with an ambiguous stimulus or situation, the way they interpret the material will be a "projection" of their unconscious needs, motives, fantasies, conflicts, thoughts, and other hidden aspects of personality. In other words, when people describe what they see in ambiguous stimuli, their description will be like the image projected on the screen at the movies. In this analogy, the film in the movie projector represents the hidden personality aspects, and the responses to the test are the images seen on the screen. Projective tests are among the assessment devices most commonly used by psychotherapists in their clinical practices (Butcher & Rouse, 1996). The most popular projective tests are the *Rorschach Inkblot Test* and the *Thematic Apperception Test*.

The Rorschach Inkblot Test

Have you ever played the "cloud game," in which you and another person look at cloud formations and tell each other what the shapes look like? The **Rorschach Inkblot Test** has a format similar to that of the cloud game (Exner, 1993). Introduced in 1921 by the Swiss psychiatrist Hermann Rorschach (1884–1922), the test consists of 10 symmetrical inkblots. Five cards are black and white, and five are colored like the one in figure 12-5. Originally designed to measure perceptual and cognitive distortions, the test quickly was used by psychoanalytically oriented psychologists as a projective measure of motives and desires. Rorschach purposely varied the composition of his inkblots—some of them are essentially large blobs, while others are bits of ink all over the page (Mattlar, 2004).

People's responses to the Rorschach are scored on three major features: the *location*, or part of the card mentioned in the response; the *content* of the response; and which aspect, or *determinant*, of the card (its color or shading) prompted the response. Rorschach's original system of scoring was revised by other psychologists, and by 1950, there were five separate systems for scoring and interpreting the inkblots, none of which exhibited good reliability or validity. To try to correct these problems, James Exner (1993) integrated the five scoring systems into one system that decreased, but did not eliminate, reliability and validity concerns (Lilienfeld et al.,

> **projective test**
> A psychological test that asks people to respond to ambiguous stimuli or situations in ways that will reveal their unconscious motives and desires.

> **Rorschach Inkblot Test**
> A projective personality test in which people are shown 10 symmetrical inkblots and asked what each might be depicting.

Figure 12-5

The Rorschach Test

Persons taking the Rorschach Inkblot Test look at a series of inkblots and describe what they see. The assumption in this projective personality test is that the way people interpret the inkblots will be a "projection" of their unconscious mind. What is one of the more serious validity problems with the Rorschach test?

2000). One of the more serious validity problems with the Rorschach is that the current scoring system tends to misidentify mentally healthy people as having psychological problems (Daruna, 2004; Wood et al., 2000). Although most critics do not think the Rorschach is completely invalid, they believe more valid tests are available that are also cheaper to administer, score, and interpret. Today, many users of the Rorschach administer it as a way to start a conversation with clients seeking therapy rather than as a way to measure personality (Aronow et al., 1995).

Thematic Apperception Test

Another widely used projective measure is the *Thematic Apperception Test (TAT)*, which was briefly described in chapter 11, section 11-4a. Administering this test involves showing a person a picture and asking him or her to tell a story about it (Hunsley & Bailey, 1999). This process is repeated using several different pictures, each one depicting a person or persons involved in an ambiguous situation. For example, in the TAT-like picture in figure 12-6, who are these three people? What are their emotional states? Is this a picture of a daughter and parents, a student and teachers, or some other group? Is the girl in trouble, is she being tested, or is she being praised? The person telling the story about the TAT cards is instructed to describe what led up to the story, what the people in the story are thinking and feeling, and how the situation resolves or comes to an end.

When Henry Murray developed the TAT in 1937, he hypothesized that the issues people were struggling with in their own lives would be perceived as issues for the characters in the cards. Murray proposed that the storyteller could give the characters various needs, such as the need for nurturance or the need for achievement. There would also be an opposing pressure from the environment, such as the demand to conform or to provide nurturance to others. Murray further proposed that, across the stories people told, certain themes would emerge related to important issues in their lives.

As discussed in chapter 11, section 11-4a, Murray and his colleagues were particularly interested in using the TAT to study the need for achievement (n-Ach). Over several decades of research, the TAT and other variations of the test have demonstrated adequate validity in measuring need for achievement, but the test-retest reliability is relatively low (Cramer, 1999; Spangler, 1992). In addition, because the scenarios depicted in the TAT pictures were created for Americans, assessing the motives of people from other cultures using the TAT is often not recommended (Hofer & Chasiotis, 2004). For these reasons, the TAT is not considered one of the better ways to measure personality (Lilienfeld et al., 2000). Today, as with the Rorschach, psychologists using the TAT in therapy frequently employ it to help start a conversation about a client's problems.

Figure 12-6

Thematic Apperception Test (TAT)

This picture of two adults sitting in a room focusing their attention on a child is an illustration of a TAT-like image. What sort of story do you think this picture tells? Why is the TAT referred to as a projective test?

Source: Harold Edward Bryant, *Evening Conversation,* 1929, oil painting on canvas, 31.5 × 25.5 inches.

12-6b Objective Tests Ask Direct Questions about a Person's Thoughts, Feelings, and Behavior

Unlike projective tests, which are designed to trick the unconscious into revealing its contents, **objective tests** are primarily designed to assess consciously held thoughts, feelings, and behavior by asking direct, unambiguous questions. The questions can be directed toward friends and family members or toward people who have just met the person being assessed. When people evaluate themselves, the test is called a *self-report inventory*. This is the most common kind of objective personality test.

Like college exams, objective personality tests can be administered to a large group of people at the same time. Also similar to exams, objective tests usually ask true-false, multiple-choice, or open-ended questions. However, unlike exams in a college course, there is no one "correct" answer to a personality test question. Each respondent chooses the answer that best describes her or him. Many objective tests measure only one specific component of personality (for example, refer to the *Self-Monitoring Scale* in the end-of-chapter "Psychological Applications" section), while other objective tests assess several traits simultaneously.

One test that assesses several traits is the **Minnesota Multiphasic Personality Inventory (MMPI),** which is the most extensively researched and widely used personality inventory (Butcher, 2005; Piotrowski et al., 1998). The MMPI was developed in the 1940s to assess personality traits associated with psychological disorders. Since its development, the MMPI has been revised so its language and content better reflect contemporary concerns and a more culturally diverse population. The original test has 550 items, with participants responding "True," "False," or "Cannot say" to each item. The more recent second edition, the MMPI-2, has 567 such items. Both versions of the MMPI measure various personality dimensions and clinical conditions, such as depression. The MMPI is an *empirically derived* test, meaning that the items were not selected for inclusion on a theoretical basis but were included only if they clearly distinguished one group of people from another (for example, patients with schizophrenia versus a normal comparison group). Each item had to demonstrate its usefulness by being answered differently by members of the two groups but similarly by members within each group.

Both versions of the MMPI have 10 *clinical scales,* which are used to identify psychological difficulties or interests, so the groups used to choose the scale items were composed of people with different psychological problems or interests. For example, the items comprising the MMPI depression scale were those that depressed individuals endorsed more than did nondepressed people. The statement "Nothing in the newspaper interests me except the comics" is an item from the depression scale. People who score above a certain level on the depression scale are considered to have a problem with depression. Table 12-6 describes the 10 clinical scales for the MMPI-2.

The MMPI also contains four *validity scales,* which are item groups that detect suspicious response patterns indicating dishonesty, carelessness, defensiveness, or evasiveness (Butcher & Williams, 2000; Greiffenstein et al., 2004). The interpretation of responses according to these four scales can help psychologists understand the attitudes a person has taken toward all the test items. For example, someone who responds "True" to items on the *Lie* scale such as "I like every person I have ever met" and "I never get angry" may be trying to favorably impress the test administrator, and thus, this respondent may not be providing honest answers to the other test items. The four MMPI-2 validity scales are also described in table 12-6.

Both versions of the MMPI are easy to administer and score, and they have proven useful in identifying people who have psychological disorders (Bagby et al., 2005; Butcher & Williams, 2000). Despite these advantages, it is often difficult to interpret MMPI scores when trying to diagnose *specific* disorders, because people with different disorders score high on a number of the same clinical scales. Critics also contend that neither MMPI version has kept pace with recent advances in personality theory (Groth-Marnat, 1997).

objective test A personality test that asks direct, unambiguous questions about a person's thoughts, feelings, and behavior.

Minnesota Multiphasic Personality Inventory (MMPI) An objective personality test consisting of true-false items that measure various personality dimensions and clinical conditions such as depression.

Table **12-6** MMPI-2 Clinical and Validity Scales	
Scales	**Description**
Clinical Scales	
Hypochondriasis	Abnormal concern with body functions and health concerns
Depression	Pessimism, feelings of hopelessness; slowing of action and thought
Hysteria	Unconscious use of mental or physical symptoms to avoid problems
Psychopathic deviation	Disregard for social customs; emotional shallowness
Masculinity/femininity	Interests culturally associated with a particular gender
Paranoia	Suspiciousness, delusions of grandeur or persecution
Psychasthenia	Obsessions, compulsions, fears, guilt, anxiety
Schizophrenia	Bizarre thoughts and perceptions, withdrawal, hallucinations, delusions
Hypomania	Emotional excitement, overactivity, impulsiveness
Social introversion	Shyness, insecurity, disinterest in others
Validity Scales	
Cannot say	Not answering many items indicates evasiveness.
Lie	Repeatedly providing socially desirable responses indicates a desire to create a favorable impression, lying to look good.
Frequency	Repeatedly providing answers rarely given by normal people may indicate an attempt to appear mentally disordered, faking to look mentally ill.
Correction	A pattern of failing to admit personal problems or shortcomings, indicating defensiveness or lack of self-insight.

Another objective test that is closely aligned with modern personality theory is the 243-item *Neuroticism Extraversion Openness Personality Inventory, Revised,* or *NEO-PI-R* (Costa & McCrae, 1992). Unlike the MMPI, the NEO-PI-R measures personality differences that are not problematic and that are based on the Five-Factor Model. (A previous version of this inventory did not measure agreeableness and conscientiousness.) Although it is a relatively new personality test, the NEO-PI-R is already widely used in research and clinical therapy, and represents the new wave of assessment (Katigbak et al., 2002; Stone, 2002).

Section Review

- Projective testing assumes that if people are presented with ambiguous stimuli, their interpretation of it will be a "projection" of their unconscious needs and desires.
- The two most widely used projective tests are the Rorschach Inkblot Test and the Thematic Apperception Test.
- Objective testing involves assessing consciously held thoughts, feelings, and behavior.
- The Minnesota Multiphasic Personality Inventory (MMPI) is one of the oldest and most widely used objective personality tests.
- The NEO-PI-R is an objective test that measures Five-Factor Model traits.

12-7 THE BIOLOGICAL BASIS OF PERSONALITY

Preview

- *Does an extravert's brain operate differently from an introvert's brain?*
- *Are people born shy?*
- *To what degree does personality consist of inherited traits?*

My older daughter, Amelia, can be a little absentminded at times, like her father, whereas my younger daughter, Lillian, is very organized, like her mother. Both girls are generally good-natured, ambitious, and open to new experiences—traits they share with both parents. Did they inherit these traits from one or both of us? Or are they like one or both of us because we shaped their personalities while raising them? To what degrees do heredity and environment account for personality? Also, is there any evidence that personality traits are associated with the activation of different areas of the brain?

12-7a Personality Is Affected by Nervous System Arousal and Specific Brain Activity

The idea that individual differences in personality are caused by biological differences among people has been proposed by a number of psychologists, most notably Hans Eysenck (see section 12-4b). In studying introverts and extraverts, Eysenck (1990) suggested that these differences in personality types are caused by inherited differences in people's nervous systems, especially their brains. According to Eysenck, introverts have inherited a nervous system that operates at a high level of arousal. Therefore, introverts avoid a great deal of social interaction and situational change in order to keep their arousal from reaching uncomfortable levels. Extraverts have the opposite problem. Their nervous system normally operates at a relatively low level of arousal, and thus they seek out situations that stimulate them. Consistent with this idea of different levels of nervous system activation, researchers have found that introverted students prefer studying in quiet, socially isolated settings, whereas extraverted students prefer studying in relatively noisy settings where they can socialize with others (Campbell & Hawley, 1982). Additional studies indicate that not only do extraverts choose to perform tasks in noisy settings, but also they actually perform better in such settings (Geen, 1984). Also consistent with Eysenck's arousal hypothesis are the findings that introverts are more sensitive to pain than are extraverts.

Some of the more inventive studies that Eysenck and his colleagues conducted to test the hypothesis that introverts have higher levels of arousal than extraverts involved classically conditioning the eye-blink response, using puffs of air to the eye as the unconditioned response (see chapter 7, Explore It Exercise 7-1). Eysenck reasoned that if introverts' nervous systems operate at a higher level of arousal than do those of extraverts, introverts' eye-blinking should become conditioned faster than extraverts' to the conditioned stimulus (Eysenck, 1967; Eysenck & Levey, 1972). As you can see from figure 12-7, his hypothesis was supported: Introverts exhibited a much higher percentage of conditioned eye-blink responses to the conditioned stimulus than did extraverts.

More recent studies employing brain-imaging technology suggest that brain structures in the frontal lobes that inhibit behavior possibly associated with danger or pain are more active among introverts than extraverts (Johnson et al., 1999). Additional research has found evidence that extraversion may be related to greater activation of dopamine pathways in the brain associated with reward and positive affect (Lucas et al., 2000; Rammsayer et al., 2003). Further, when introverts and extraverts are shown positive images (for example, puppies, a happy couple, or sunsets), extraverts experience greater activation of brain areas that control emotion, such as the frontal cortex and the amygdala (Canli et al., 2001, 2002). Together, this research suggests that introversion and extraversion are associated with distinct patterns of brain activity, and that the experience of positive affect may be a primary feature of extraversion.

Another related personality characteristic associated with a hyperactive nervous system and different brain activity is shyness, which involves feelings of discomfort and inhibition during interpersonal situations (Rubin et al., 2002). Although almost everybody

Figure 12-7

Do Introverts Have Higher Levels of Arousal Than Extraverts?

To test the hypothesis that introverts have higher levels of nervous system arousal than extraverts, numerous studies have classically conditioned the eye-blink response in these two groups of people (Eysenck, 1967; Eysenck & Levey, 1972; Franks, 1957). Results indicate that introverts show a much higher percentage of conditioned eye-blink responses to the conditioned stimulus than do extraverts. How do these findings support the hypothesis that introverts have inherited a nervous system that operates at a higher level of arousal than that of extraverts?

Source: From H. J. Eysenck, *The Biological Basis of Personality,* 1967. Courtesy of Charles C. Thomas, Publisher, Ltd., Springfield, Illinois.

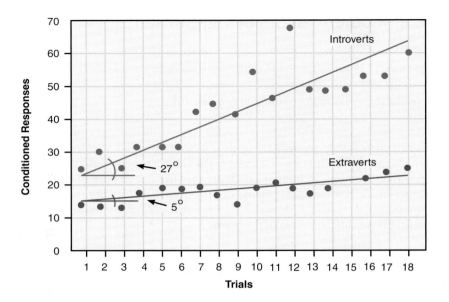

feels shy at some point in their lives, about 40 percent of the population is excessively shy, which hinders them in making friends, developing romantic relationships, and pursuing other goals involving social interaction. When compared to nonshy persons, shy individuals are much more self-focused and spend an excess amount of time worrying about how others are evaluating them. Some studies show that shy children and adults are more likely to have been "high-reactive" infants, meaning they were more sensitive to environmental stimuli and thus more fussy than other infants (Kagan et al., 1998; Snidman et al., 1995; Woodward et al., 2001). Such reactivity is detectable even in the womb. Fetuses with fast heart rates are more likely to develop into shy children than are those with slow or normal heart rates.

Regarding brain activation, it appears that both the amygdala—which is involved in the emotion of fear—and the right frontal lobe—which is involved in controlling emotions—play a role in shyness. Brain scans of chronically shy adults indicate that, when shown unfamiliar faces or when interacting with strangers, these shy adults experience much greater activation of the amygdala and the right frontal lobe than do nonshy persons (Birbaumer et al., 1998; McManis et al., 2002). This different level of brain activation among shy persons makes them more susceptible than others to experiencing anxious emotions (Kagan et al., 2001).

12-7b Both Genetic and Environmental Factors Shape Personality

Many personality theorists have long assumed that genetic predispositions influence most aspects of personality (DiLalla, 2004; Rowe & Van den Oord, 2005). As discussed in chapter 10, section 10-4a, psychologists have conducted a great deal of research comparing twins reared together versus those reared apart to better understand genetic and environmental influences on intelligence. Many of these same studies have also examined personality traits. Overall, they have found that, raised together, identical twins have more similar traits than do fraternal twins (Agrawal et al., 2004; McCrae, 1996). These findings indicate a moderate genetic influence on personality. However, this same research has found that the trait correlations for identical twins reared apart are considerably lower than for those reared together, which suggests that environment also influences trait development (Borkenau et al., 2001). Currently, the best estimates are that personality differences in the population are between 40 and 50 percent genetically determined, with the balance attributable to environment (Bouchard, 2004).

Although genetics plays an important role in shaping personality, *how* it does so is not clear (Beckwith & Alper, 2002). David Buss (1995) proposes that genes most likely influence personality due to their impact on physical characteristics and general predispositions toward certain temperaments associated with activity, emotionality, and sociability. These physical characteristics and temperaments then interact with environmental factors to shape personality. For example, children who inherit a healthy body and high sociability and activity levels may actively seek opportunities to play with other children. Such interactions may foster the development of important social skills and the enjoyment of social activities, which are characteristic of extraverted personalities. Of course, this does not mean that genetic predispositions will actually lead to specific personality traits for a given person. For instance, even though shyness is an inherited trait, children and older adults can consciously overcome their social inhibitions and become remarkably skilled and outgoing in a wide variety of social settings (Rowe, 1997). Parents are especially important either in diminishing children's shyness or in maintaining it into adulthood (Rubin et al., 2002). Thus, instead of genetics determining personality in some lockstep fashion, we appear to inherit the building blocks of personality from our parents, and then our interactions with our social environment create the personality that we become (Johnson & Krueger, 2005; Vierikko et al., 2004).

Section Review

- Inherited differences can be seen in introverts' and extraverts' nervous systems, especially in their brains.
- Higher levels of nervous system activity and different levels of brain activation cause shy persons to experience anxious emotions more frequently than other people do.
- Both genetic and environmental factors shape personality development.

Psychological Applications

Do You Have a Chameleon-Like Personality?

As noted at the beginning of this chapter, when we study personality, we are studying both how people are consistent across situations and how they are different from one another. What if I told you that personality researchers have identified a trait having the defining characteristic that people consistently behave inconsistently when interacting with others? Although this may sound strange to you, this trait is associated with a very normal self-presentation style that many of us exhibit. Before reading further, spend a few minutes responding to the items in Self-Discovery Questionnaire 12-2 to better understand your association with this trait.

Self-Monitoring

In social relationships, we often try to manage the impression we make on others by carefully constructing and monitoring our self-presentations (Goffman, 1959; Leary et al., 1994). Although we all monitor and adjust how we present ourselves to others, depending on the situation and with whom we are interacting (Tice et al., 1995), there is a personality difference in the degree to which we make such alterations in "who we are to others." According to Mark Snyder (1987), these differences are related to a personality trait called **self-monitoring**, which is the tendency to use cues from other people's self-presentations in controlling our own self-presentations. Those of us high in self-monitoring spend considerable time

> **self-monitoring** A personality trait involving the tendency to use cues from other people's self-presentations in controlling one's own self-presentations.

learning about other people, and we tend to emphasize impression management in our social relationships (John et al., 1996).

Individuals who are high in self-monitoring are especially attuned to social cues concerning appropriate behavior in a given situation. They are skilled impression managers who strive to perform whatever behavior projects a positive self-image, even if some degree of deception is required. In this regard, they tend to be extraverted, good actors, and willing to change their behavior to suit others (Klein et al., 2004; Leck & Simpson, 1999). For example, when trying to initiate a dating relationship, high self-monitoring men and women behave in a chameleon-like fashion, strategically and often deceptively changing their self-presentations in an attempt to appear more desirable (Rowatt et al., 1998). On the other hand, those low in self-monitoring are less attentive to situational cues, and their behavior is guided more by inner attitudes and beliefs. As a result, their behavior is more consistent across situations. Although it may appear to the casual observer that the low self-monitor has a stable personality and the high self-monitor has no identifiable personality at all, the high self-monitor's inconsistency across situations represents a stable personality trait.

Due to their greater attention to social cues, high self-monitors are more socially skilled than low self-monitors. They are better able to communicate and understand the meaning of emotions and other nonverbal behaviors. They also learn more quickly how to

Continued next page—

Psychological Applications

—Continued

Self-Discovery
Questionnaire **12-2**

Do You Closely Monitor and Control Your Self-Presentations?

The Self-Monitoring Scale

The personality trait of self-monitoring is measured by items on the Self-Monitoring Scale (Gangestad & Snyder, 2000; Snyder, 1974). To discover your level of self-monitoring, read each item below and then indicate whether each statement is true or false for you.

F T **1.** I find it hard to imitate the behavior of other people.

T T **2.** At parties and social gatherings, I do not attempt to do or say things that others will like.

T T **3.** I can only argue for ideas which I already believe.

T F **4.** I can make impromptu speeches even on topics about which I have almost no information.

T F **5.** I guess I put on a show to impress or entertain others.

T F **6.** I would probably make a good actor.

F T **7.** In a group of people I am rarely the center of attention.

T T **8.** In different situations and with different people, I often act like very different persons.

T T **9.** I am not particularly good at making other people like me.

T F **10.** I'm not always the person I appear to be.

T T **11.** I would not change my opinions (or the way I do things) in order to please someone or win their favor.

F F **12.** I have considered being an entertainer.

F T **13.** I have never been good at games like charades or improvisational acting.

F F **14.** I have trouble changing my behavior to suit different people and different situations.

T T **15.** At a party I let others keep the jokes and stories going.

F T **16.** I feel a bit awkward in company and do not show up quite as well as I should.

F F **17.** I can look anyone in the eye and tell a lie with a straight face (if for a right end).

T F **18.** I may deceive people by being friendly when I really dislike them.

Directions for scoring: Give yourself one point for answering "True" to each of the following items: 4, 5, 6, 8, 10, 12, 17, and 18. Also give yourself one point for answering "False" to each of the following items: 1, 2, 3, 7, 9, 11, 13, 14, 15, and 16. Next, add up your total number of points for your self-monitoring score.

When Snyder (1974) developed the Self-Monitoring Scale, the mean score for North American college students was about 10 or 11. The higher your score above these values, the more of this personality trait you probably possess. The lower your score below these values, the less of this trait you probably possess.

Source: Snyder, M., and Gangestad, S. (1986). "On the nature of self-monitoring: Matters of assessment, matters of validity." *Journal of Personality and Social Psychology,* 51, 125–139. Copyright © 1986 by the American Psychological Association. Reprinted with permission.

behave in new situations and are more likely to initiate conversations (Gangestad & Snyder, 2000). On the negative side, people high in self-monitoring have less intimate and committed social relationships, and they tend to judge people more on superficial characteristics, such as physical appearance and social activities, than on their attitudes and values (Jamieson et al., 1987; Snyder & Simpson, 1984).

Self-Monitoring on the Job

Because high self-monitors' actions are guided by what they think are the appropriate behaviors in a given situation, some psychologists have wondered how this might affect their search for a job and their performance in that job (Snyder & Copeland, 1989). What about low self-monitors? Because they are guided more by their inner feelings and beliefs than by social

Psychological Applications

—Continued

propriety, will they tend to gravitate toward and perform better in different jobs than their more socially sensitive counterparts?

Research suggests that people high in self-monitoring prefer jobs with clearly defined occupational roles. In comparison, low self-monitors tend to prefer occupational roles that coincide with their own personalities so they can "be themselves" on the job (Snyder & Gangestad, 1982). Thus, if you are high in self-monitoring, you may be more willing than a person low in self-monitoring to mold and shape yourself to "fit" your chosen occupational role. You might find, for example, that occupations in the fields of law, politics, public relations, and the theater are particularly attractive to you. Or, considering yourself assertive, industrious, and a risk-taker, you may gravitate toward careers in business or other entrepreneurial professions. In these careers, you can use your social chameleon abilities to mimic others' social expectations. In contrast, if you are low in self-monitoring and consider yourself warm, compassionate, and caring, you may seek out social service or "helping" occupations such as medicine, psychology, or social work.

Once having chosen and secured a job, your self-monitoring orientation may influence your work performance. High self-monitors' social skills make them well suited for jobs that require the ability to influence others (Douglas & Gardner, 2004). One type of job that appears particularly suited to the skills of the high self-monitor is the so-called boundary-spanning jobs, in which individuals must interact and communicate effectively with two or more parties who, because of their conflicting interests, often cannot deal directly with one another. Examples of boundary-spanning jobs are the mediator in a dispute between management and labor, a real estate agent who negotiates the transfer of property from seller to buyer, and a university administrator who deals with students, faculty, and alumni. In an examination of 93 field representatives whose jobs required boundary spanning, David Cald-

well and Charles O'Reilly (1982) found that high self-monitors performed better in these jobs than did low self-monitors. These findings suggest that self-monitoring skills may be particularly helpful in occupations that involve interacting with people who have conflicting interests and agendas. In such work settings, high self-monitors are less likely to allow their personal feelings to affect their social interactions.

In what type of job might you perform better if you are low in self-monitoring? The job performance of low self-monitors appears to be less influenced by their leaders' behavior than that of high self-monitors, who are more sensitized to such external demands. In other words, the degree of effort that low self-monitors exert on the job is less dependent on their bosses' expectations and more determined by their own intrinsic motivation. This suggests that, if you are low in self-monitoring, you may be more effective when working in an unsupervised setting than a high self-monitor would be in that same setting—if you feel your work is important.

Now that you have learned about this particular personality trait, which end of the self-monitoring spectrum do you think is the desirable pole? Do you see high self-monitoring as more socially adaptive because it allows people to better negotiate in an ever-changing and complicated social world? Or do think that the chameleon-like nature of the high self-monitor suggests shallowness? Does the consistency of low self-monitoring individuals suggest "principled behavior" or "inflexibility"? The safest and perhaps wisest conclusion is that neither high nor low self-monitoring is necessarily undesirable unless it is carried to the extreme. Fortunately, pure high or low self-monitoring is rare; most of us fall somewhere on a continuum between these two extremes.

> It is not whether you really cry. It's whether the audience thinks you are crying.
>
> *—Ingrid Bergman, Swedish actress, 1915–1982*

Key Terms

anal stage (p. 454)

archetypes (p. 458)

collective unconscious (p. 458)

conditional positive regard (p. 461)

conscious mind (p. 451)

defense mechanisms (p. 455)

displacement (p. 456)

ego (p. 453)

extravert (p. 458)

Five-Factor Model (p. 465)

fixation (p. 453)

genital stage (p. 455)

id (p. 452)

interactionism (p. 470)

introvert (p. 458)

latency stage (p. 455)

locus of control (p. 472)

Minnesota Multiphasic Personality Inventory (MMPI) (p. 479)

objective test (p. 479)

oral stage (p. 453)

peak experience (p. 462)

personality (p. 449)

personality style (p. 449)

phallic stage (p. 454)

pleasure principle (p. 452)

preconscious mind (p. 451)

projection (p. 456)

projective test (p. 477)

psychodynamic perspective (p. 457)

psychosexual stages (p. 453)

rationalization (p. 456)

reaction formation (p. 456)

reality principle (p. 453)

reciprocal determinism (p. 471)

regression (p. 456)

repression (p. 455)

Rorschach Inkblot Test (p. 477)

self-efficacy (p. 471)

self-monitoring (p. 483)

self-serving bias (p. 472)

situationism (p. 469)

social-cognitive perspective (p. 471)

superego (p. 453)

trait (p. 463)

trait perspective (p. 463)

unconditional positive regard (p. 461)

unconscious mind (p. 451)

Suggested Websites

Great Ideas in Personality

http://www.personalityresearch.org

This website deals with scientific research programs in personality psychology. It provides information about personality research from a variety of perspectives, including some not covered in this chapter. It also contains a good selection of well-organized links to other personality websites.

The Society for Personality Assessment

http://www.personality.org

This Society for Personality Assessment website is intended primarily for professional use; it contains a section outlining the requirements for personality assessment credentials and telling how to go about becoming a personality psychologist.

The American Psychoanalytic Association

http://www.apsa.org

The website of the American Psychoanalytic Association is intended for both the general public and the professional psychoanalytic community. Information is given here about the current state of the psychoanalytic theoretical orientation.

Humanistic Psychology

http://www.apa.org/divisions/div32

This is the official website of the American Psychological Association's division of humanistic psychology. It provides information on upcoming APA events and information for students interested in this perspective.

QueenDom.com Complete List of Tests

http://www.queendom.com/tests/alltests.html

This website has a number of online personality tests that you can take and receive feedback on.

Review Questions

Note: You can find the correct answers to these questions by taking the quiz and then submitting your answers in the Online Edition. The program will automatically score your submission. If you miss a question, the program will provide the correct answer, a rationale for the answer, and the section number in the chapter where the topic is discussed.

1. The modern study of personality involves all *except* which one of the following?
   a. studying how personality emerges from the interaction between the individual and his or her environment
   b. approaches that are more limited and narrow than in the first half of the twentieth century
   c. understanding how people may be generally predictable yet different from others
   d. both philosophical and scientific roots
   e. a focus on overarching and comprehensive descriptions of personality styles

2. Freud is perhaps best known for the significance of his theory of
   a. glove anesthesia.
   b. the nervous system.
   c. the mind.
   d. biological urges.
   e. hypnosis.

3. Regarding personality, Freud's structural model emphasized the different operating principles and goals that operated within the following subcomponents of the mind:
   a. the collective unconscious and archetypes.
   b. the id, the ego, and the superego.
   c. the id, the pleasure principle, and archetypes.
   d. the ego, the reality principle, and the collective unconscious.
   e. the id, the superego, and reality.

4. Among Freud's contributions was his theory of psychosexual stages, which included an emphasis on
   a. five fixed stages of development in childhood and adolescence.
   b. fixation, which involves unresolved conflicts emerging from too little gratification of id desires.
   c. the Oedipus complex, in which children develop an attachment to their same-sex parent.
   d. the latency stage, when unconscious sexual and aggressive impulses go dormant.
   e. personality development after the age of 5.

5. The psychoanalytic theory of defense mechanisms, or ways we control anxiety-provoking thoughts and impulses, suggests that defense mechanisms
   a. protect the id from unacceptable urges.
   b. represent permanent changes in the structure of the mind.
   c. allow us to understand our unconscious motivations.
   d. explain why we can become civilized.
   e. tend to be consistent, but not distinguishing, characteristics of personality.

6. An individual with a strong desire to perform immoral acts might exhibit extremely moralistic behavior and be harshly judgmental of others, if he used which defense mechanism?
   a. rationalization
   b. reaction formation
   c. displacement
   d. projection
   e. regression

7. All the alternative approaches to Freud's psychoanalysis have in common the notion that
   a. the collective unconscious is a fourth component of the mind's structure.
   b. social interaction is the basis for personality.
   c. the mind can be understood only through carefully controlled scientific research.
   d. the unconscious mind is less important than Freud claimed.
   e. sexual drives are not central in determining people's personalities.

8. The humanistic model of personality development differed from the predominant views of psychoanalysis and behaviorism primarily in
   a. the discrepancy between Rogers's actual and feared self.
   b. its exclusive focus on the development of psychologically healthy and creative people.
   c. the belief that individual psychological growth is predetermined.
   d. its optimistic approach to the possibilities for positive human change.
   e. the scientific and testable hypotheses it generated.

9. One criticism of the humanistic approach to personality is its
   a. overreliance on the unconscious as a motivator of action.
   b. specification of many personality types.
   c. inability to acknowledge and explain negative and cruel behavior.
   d. lack of attention to the importance of self.
   e. all of the above

10. The trait approach to personality is primarily focused on
    a. describing how people differ from one another in specific ways.
    b. Allport's view that behavior varies across situations.
    c. relatively new ideas concerning the classification of people according to personality types.
    d. direct measurement, rather than inference, of personality characteristics.
    e. describing why people differ from one another in specific ways.

11. A statistical technique that can reduce large numbers of measured personality traits into a smaller number of clusters of related traits is called
    a. a cluster test.
    b. factor analysis.
    c. personality reduction.
    d. relational grouping.
    e. trait clustering.

12. There is general consensus among personality researchers today that the basic personality traits
    a. are biologically or genetically determined.
    b. capture the essence of individual personality.
    c. are a result of adaptive human evolution.
    d. vary across cultures.
    e. include neuroticism, extraversion, openness to experience, agreeableness, and conscientiousness.

13. Mischel's controversial claim concerning the predictive ability of personality traits
    a. was based on limited samples of behavior.
    b. was supported by Epstein's view that traits reliably predict behavior.
    c. led to the realization that situations do not play a role in shaping behavior.
    d. generated new research but did not increase the ability to predict behavior.
    e. indicated that children are reliably honest or dishonest across situations.

14. The social-cognitive approach describes personality as primarily based on
    a. classical conditioning.
    b. operant conditioning.
    c. an individualist approach.
    d. observational learning.
    e. direct experience.

15. Bandura's reciprocal determinism explains that
    a. the environment plays a more important role in behavior than does the individual.
    b. self-efficacy is stable and consistent across situations.
    c. personality emerges from an ongoing mutual interaction among people's cognitions, actions, and environment.
    d. individual perceptions are of little consequence in determining behavior.
    e. there is no relationship between self-efficacy and self-esteem.

16. The concept of locus of control, originated by Rotter, is associated with all of the following *except*
    a. a belief in one's ability to control the outcomes in one's life.
    b. learned helplessness.
    c. anger and acting-out behaviors.
    d. achievement orientation.
    e. success in life.

don't answer

not sure.

17. Self-enhancement theories propose that people are primarily motivated to
    a. maintain high self-esteem and feelings of self-worth.
    b. optimize personal growth and development.
    c. perform activities that make them a more attractive mate.
    d. educate and develop their mind.
    e. maintain consistent beliefs about themselves.

18. The primary difference between projective and objective measures of personality is that
    a. objective measures rely on ambiguous stimuli, while projective measures are more direct.
    b. projective tests assess unconscious aspects of personality, while objective tests assess conscious aspects of personality.
    c. objective tests are scored on the basis of a correct answer, while there are no correct answers on projective tests.
    d. projective tests are more reliable and valid than objective tests.
    e. objective tests are used primarily to start conversations about a client's problems.

19. Eysenck's research (1990) on extraverts and introverts suggests that differences on this personality dimension could be due to
    a. brain wave patterns.
    b. sensory consciousness.
    c. nervous system arousal.
    d. parental discipline style.
    e. all of the above

20. According to the text, what area of the brain activates shyness?
    a. the amygdala
    b. the hypothalamus
    c. the thalamus
    d. the cerebellum
    e. the hippocampus

Chapter 13

Psychological Disorders

After returning from my cross-country trip studying hitchhikers (see chapter 1), I rented an apartment along with two of my college friends. We were looking for another boarder to help pay the rent. After placing an ad in the local paper, we rashly accepted the first person who expressed an interest in the vacancy. Our new living companion was Jim, a quiet, frail-looking young man with long hair and a droopy mustache.

At first, other than being very quiet, Jim appeared to be your average college student. However, after a time, we noticed that he was lacking in virtually any kind of emotional expressiveness. He rarely smiled or laughed, and his actions were slow, as if he were moving through molasses. We also soon noticed that Jim regularly repeated two specific behaviors. One behavior was flicking on and off a cigarette lighter, and the other was opening and closing a small pocketknife. Both items were always in his hand or pants pocket. Strange, we thought. But was it any stranger than our roommate Pete repeatedly playing his favorite record album (yes, record, not tape or CD), the Doors' *Soft Parade*, every single day? Was it stranger than Doug flopping down in his feather-bag chair like clockwork every day at 4:00 P.M.? Or stranger than me waking up every night and writing down my dreams in a notebook near my bed? Yes, we concluded, it was stranger than all those behaviors, but perhaps only by degree.

One group ritual that we quickly developed was returning to our apartment every day after classes to relax and watch reruns of the science fiction TV show *Star Trek* (with Captain Kirk and Spock). Although Jim would join us, he rarely spoke. Then one day, as an episode began, Pete burst out with an "Oh boy!!!" He was excited because he had never seen this episode before. To our surprise, the usually quiet Jim turned to Pete and asked, "Why did you call me a boy?" Utterly perplexed, Pete replied that he had done no such thing but, rather, was simply excited at what he was about to watch. Not satisfied with this explanation, Jim continued, "Well, if you weren't calling me a boy, then you must have been calling him a boy." He was pointing at the television. Slowly, we realized that Jim was referring to an African-American actor on the screen. No amount of subsequent persuasion by Pete could convince Jim (who, by the way, was not African American) that his roommate was not being condescending to him or to minorities. Jim was convinced that Pete was "out to get him."

That same week, Doug was in charge of preparing our evening meals. After one such culinary treat, Jim confronted Doug and accused him of putting "speed" (amphetamines; see chapter 6, section 6-3g) in his food. Again, no amount of persuasion could convince Jim that Doug wasn't trying to poison him. After all, Jim said, what else could explain the sensations he was experiencing in his body? As with Pete following the *Star Trek* incident, Doug was now "the enemy."

About a week after these strange incidents, Pete came home from class, put his favorite album on the turntable, and settled down to relax. Yet, as the needle touched the record, it simply slid across the vinyl. No *Soft Parade*. When Pete inspected his prized record, he discovered that the vinyl grooves that produce the music had been fused together by some sort of intense heat. Immediately, the image of Jim flicking his cigarette lighter on and off popped into Pete's mind, and a chill ran down his back. Just then, Doug arrived home. Before Pete could tell him about the record, Doug plopped down in his feather-bag chair and was showered by goose down that burst from hundreds of puncture holes in the chair's fabric. Doug and Pete stared dumbfounded as feathers slowly settled on the carpeting. They must have looked like figures in a snow-globe scene. Immediately, the image of Jim opening and closing his pocketknife popped into their minds. We soon realized that, like those snow globes that captivate one's attention when shaken, our apartment had been similarly shaken, but by a powerful, invisible force beyond our understanding. We definitely had a problem. If Jim was destroying our cherished possessions as a form of distorted and misguided retribution, what was next?

* * * * *

Jim is an example of someone who experiences severe problems in his daily living, leading him (and those around him) to experience significant distress. When witnessing his bizarre thinking and behavior, those with whom Jim interacted generally were at a loss as to how to respond. Reasoning with Jim often wasn't effective, and ignoring his destructive actions was not an option. As his apartment mates, we wondered what was causing Jim to think, feel, and behave in a manner that was so dysfunctional.

Do people like Jim both interest and concern you? Such interest and concern are due to a number of factors. First, their actions are often very unusual and cry out for explanation. Second, their behavior is sometimes so strange that it is frightening. Third, you may see in them something of yourself. Haven't you, at times, become suspicious, distrustful, anxious, or depressed—or even heard or seen things that you later discovered were fabricated in your mind? Perhaps, by understanding these extreme forms of behavior in others, you will gain insight into your own behavioral oddities.

Statistics gathered by the U.S. Bureau of the Census (2001b) indicate that about 2.1 million Americans are admitted to hospitals every year due to serious psychological problems, and over twice as many seek help as outpatients for less severe mental health problems. Further, it is estimated that 20 percent of all persons in the United States in any given year experience psychological problems severe enough to adversely affect their daily living, and 40 percent experience at least mild mental health problems (Kessler et al., 1994; Surgeon General, 1999). Contrary to earlier research indicating that psychological disorders occur more often among African Americans than among White Americans, recent findings from the National Survey of American Life point to lower rates of mental illness among African Americans. This survey also found higher rates of psychological disorders in Hispanics in comparison to non-Hispanic Whites (Sue & Chu, 2003). Worldwide, about 400 million people are afflicted with psychological disorders, and projections indicate that such problems will soon account for 15 percent of the global burden of disease, just below that caused by heart disorders (Murray & Lopez, 1996; Phillips et al., 2002; World Health Organization, 2002).

Many of the mental health problems addressed in this chapter are common, and so it is likely that some of the conditions discussed will remind you of someone you know, including yourself. Yet, even if you have not yet met people with serious psychological problems, you are likely to encounter them as your circle of acquaintances grows. Because you will eventually meet such people, it is important to have a basic understanding of the types and causes of psychological problems. The goal of this chapter is to introduce you to the topic of psychological disorders. From this introduction, you will encounter three basic questions. First, how should we define psychological disorders? Next, what are the important theoretical perspectives used to explain these disorders? And finally, how should we classify the major types of psychological disorders?

13-1 HOW SHOULD WE DEFINE AND EXPLAIN PSYCHOLOGICAL DISORDERS?

Preview

- *How does the medical model explain psychological disorders?*
- *What separates normal from disturbed behavior?*
- *What perspectives do psychologists use in explaining mental illness?*
- *What is the diathesis-stress model?*

Based on what you have learned about Jim and his strange behavior, you probably suspect that he had some sort of psychological disorder. But how do we decide when a pattern of behavior is simply "different" or "quirky" and when it is disordered? And how do we explain such behavior?

13-1a The Medical Model Proposes That Psychological Disorders Are Like Diseases

Many psychologists believe that a useful approach in organizing our thinking about mental health problems comes from the field of medicine. The **medical model** proposes that

We do not have to visit a madhouse to find disordered minds; our planet is the mental institution of the universe.

—Johann von Goethe,
German philosopher, 1749–1832

medical model The viewpoint from the field of medicine that psychological disorders have a biological basis and can be classified into discrete categories just as physical diseases are.

psychological disorders have a biological basis, can be classified into discrete categories, and are analogous to physical diseases. Although not agreeing that all mental health problems have a biological basis, mainstream psychology has adopted the medical model's terminology, using such words as *illness* and *disorder* when referring to troublesome behavior patterns. As in the medical profession, in psychology a **symptom** is a sign of a disorder, **diagnosis** involves distinguishing one disorder from another, **etiology** refers to a disorder's apparent causes and developmental history, and **prognosis** is a prediction about the likely course of a disorder.

Since the late eighteenth century, the medical model has reflected the dominant way of thinking about mental disorders. In comparison to earlier approaches, which were largely based on superstitious beliefs that the mentally ill were possessed by demons or in league with the devil, the medical model represented an enlightened and humane orientation toward mental illness. Patients began to be viewed with greater sympathy and less fear, and the scientific method underlying the medical model led to significant improvements in treatment.

However, in the late 1800s and early 1900s, Freud and other psychologically oriented therapists challenged the medical model's assumption that biological factors were the cause of all mental illness. And despite the improvements in the understanding and treatment of the mentally ill brought about by the medical model, some critics have argued that it has outlived its usefulness. One of the most forceful critics has been Thomas Szasz (1961, 1990), who contends that mental illness is a "myth" created by modern society and legitimated by the medical profession and their "disease" model. Szasz proposes that, instead of labeling people as "sick," a more accurate way to describe those who cannot live according to society's norms and conventions is that they have "problems in living." Although most mental health professionals today view Szasz's critique as overly simplistic and naive, his criticisms played a role in sensitizing the society at large to the dangers of labeling people with psychological disorders as social deviants (see section 13-2a). In this respect, his ideas have promoted greater acceptance of people with psychological problems. Despite this benefit, most psychologists believe it is still useful to think of psychological disorders as being *like* diseases, while keeping in mind that this is only an analogy.

symptom A sign of a disorder.

diagnosis The process of distinguishing one disorder from another.

etiology The initial cause that led to the development of the disorder.

prognosis A prediction about the likely course of a disorder.

Why do psychiatrists systematically impose themselves on persons who want to have nothing to do with them? I believe they do so because, like most people, psychiatrists love power and exult in pushing others around.

—*Thomas Szasz, psychiatrist, b. 1920*

13-1b Psychological Disorders Involve Atypical Behavior That Causes Personal Distress or Social Impairment

Over the years, operating from the general medical model, psychologists and other mental health professionals have developed criteria to differentiate normal from disordered behavior. Let us review the four major criteria used in making such distinctions.

Atypical Behavior

One way to differentiate disordered from normal behavior is in terms of the statistical frequency of disordered behavior in the general population. Behavior that is significantly above or below the average in its frequency of occurrence is *atypical* and thus more likely to be classified as a psychological disorder. Jim's compulsive actions of repeatedly flicking on and off his lighter and opening and closing his pocketknife were certainly unusual, and they signaled an underlying psychological disorder. However, relying only on the criterion of statistical infrequency can easily lead to false judgments. For instance, the behavioral accomplishments of Nobel Prize winners and Hall of Fame athletes are statistically infrequent, but few would label these individuals as suffering from a psychological disorder. On the other hand, some disorders, such as anxiety and depression, are statistically common in contemporary society. Thus, we cannot rely solely on deviations from the "average" in identifying psychological disorders.

Violation of Cultural Norms

Another way to differentiate between disordered and normal behavior is by determining whether the exhibited behavior violates cultural norms. For example, in mainstream American culture, reporting hallucinations is likely to raise concerns about your sanity. Yet what about reporting these same hallucinations to members of various Native American nations or to the Holy Ghost worshipers of Appalachia? There, such experiences may be perceived as normal and an essential ingredient in your spiritual enlightenment (see chapter 6, section 6-3d).

Even within a given culture, shifts in norms can change people's perceptions of what is a mental disorder. As discussed in chapter 11, section 11-2d, up until 1973, homosexuality was labeled a psychological disorder by the American Psychiatric Association, not only because it was atypical but also because it violated prevailing standards of morality. Similarly, in the South before the Civil War, many slaves were diagnosed with forms of mental illness because their behavior violated cultural norms (Landrine, 1988). *Drapetomania* was a psychological disorder in which a slave had an uncontrollable urge to escape from bondage, and *dysathesia aethiopica* was a disorder in which a slave was disobedient to her or his owners. Although labeling the desire to be free and the resentment of human bondage as "disorders" seems ludicrous today, such labeling illustrates how culture can shape our perceptions of mental illness. As these examples attest, simply relying on violations of cultural norms is not adequate in determining what is disordered.

Maladaptive Behavior

There is more to a psychological disorder than being atypical or out of synch with cultural norms. Such behavior is much more likely to be considered disordered if it is judged *maladaptive*—disruptive or harmful—for the person or society. The inability to perform normal activities is an indication of maladaptiveness. Not leaving your house because you fear crowds, repeatedly being fired from jobs due to excessive drinking, and losing your life savings due to compulsive gambling are all examples of maladaptive behavior. Maladaptiveness is generally considered the most important criterion in defining a disorder.

Personal Distress

Individuals who report experiencing troubling emotions are often considered to have psychological problems. They may be able to perform normal activities, such as caring for family members and holding a job, but they feel unreasonably fearful, anxious, guilty, angry, or depressed. One of the advantages of this criterion is that it takes into account a person's own distress level rather than using the same standard for everyone. A behavior that is upsetting and extremely stressful for one person, such as the inability to maintain intimacy with others, may not be disturbing to another. The problem with this criterion, however, is that some people who suffer from psychological disorders—and who cause harm to themselves and others—are not troubled by their behavior. Further, some individuals may not be able to tell us how much distress they are experiencing, because they are very young or are otherwise unable to communicate. Finally, cultural factors can affect how people report personal distress. For example, Asian Americans suffering from a psychological disorder are more likely than non-Asians to report physical symptoms, such as dizziness, rather than emotional symptoms (Lin & Cheung, 1999). This is because, in many Asian cultures, it is considered inappropriate to discuss one's personal feelings with others, especially non-family members (Russell & Yik, 1996). Many Hispanic Americans feel a similar reluctance to discuss psychological problems (Arredondo & Perez, 2003). Mental health professionals who are unaware of the cultural differences in how people express or present symptoms of mental illness are more likely to misdiagnose psychological disorders as physical ailments.

As you see, one of these criteria alone is usually insufficient to differentiate normal from disordered behavior. Although psychologists sometimes rely on only one criterion in making their diagnoses, they are more confident when more than one of these indicators is present and valid. Further, when making diagnoses, psychologists try to understand people's symptoms within the larger social context of their lives, in order to distinguish psychological disorders from other problems in living (Hsieh & Kirk, 2005). In the end, diagnoses of psychological disorders often involve value judgments about what behaviors cross the bounds of normality. All four criteria are useful in arriving at a diagnosis, but they are not completely objective, and thus they can be influenced by the psychologist's value judgments (Kutchins & Kirk, 1997; Whaley, 2004). Drawing a line that clearly separates normality from abnormality is often difficult, because in reality, these distinctions represent two ends of a continuum.

Because of the possibility that values may bias evaluations of what is normal versus what is disordered, some evolutionary psychologists have recently proposed that judgments of psychological disorders be based on whether the behaviors perform their naturally selected function adequately or effectively (Wakefield, 1999). For example, although the emotion of fear probably evolved because it increased our ancestors' likelihood of behaving cautiously in physically threatening situations, individuals who are chronically fearful in the absence of identifiable threats are not behaving in line with properly functioning evolutionary predispositions (Stevens & Price, 1996). Although this evolutionary perspective is intriguing, deciding the functions of various evolved mechanisms is still a subject of debate (Fulford, 1999).

Until such ambiguities are resolved, I define a **psychological disorder** as a pattern of atypical behavior that results in personal distress or significant impairment in a person's social or occupational functioning. Using this definition, we see that Jim would definitely be classified as suffering from a mental disorder. He certainly was experiencing considerable anxiety and distress, his repetitive actions were very unusual, and his physical symptoms and the nature of his social interactions were definitely interfering with normal daily living.

13-1c Psychologists Employ Numerous Theoretical Perspectives in Explaining Mental Illness

The vast majority of contemporary psychologists believe that mental illness is real, but they do not always agree on its nature and causes. In general, psychological approaches to understanding mental illness assume that disordered behavior, like normal behavior, can be explained by people's past and present life experiences. Let us briefly review how psychodynamic, behavioral, cognitive, sociocultural, and biological theories explain psychological disorders.

The Psychodynamic Perspective

As first described in chapter 12, section 12-2e, the *psychodynamic perspective* asserts that disordered behavior, like normal behavior, is not freely chosen but, rather, is controlled by unconscious forces that have been largely shaped by childhood experiences. The founding father of the psychodynamic perspective, Sigmund Freud, contended that early traumatic events leave the individual with troubling feelings and memories. Because this material is painful, the individual represses it to the unconscious. Once this material is unconscious, the individual does not experience the anxiety that would result if the painful material were faced directly. However, although this painful material is beyond conscious awareness, it continues to influence the person's behavior and is often expressed indirectly through defense mechanisms. This idea of how the unconscious mind shapes people's everyday actions formed the basis for Freud's theory of *psychoanalysis* (see chapter 12, sections 12-2a and 12-2b).

A well-known example of Freud's explanation of psychological disorders is the case of Little Hans (Freud, 1909/1963). Hans was a young boy who developed an intense fear of horses. Freud explained the child's fear as due to an unconscious fear of his father. Because fearing his father would be painful to acknowledge, the boy repressed this fear and displaced it onto a more acceptable alternative. A horse is large and strong, just like the boy's father, and so the horse became a symbolic representation of the father. According to psychoanalytic theory, the etiology of the fear was a troubling childhood experience, and the maintaining cause was the unconscious fear of father.

The Behavioral Perspective

While the psychodynamic perspective assumes that "what you see is not what you get" when you analyze mental illness, the *behavioral perspective* assumes that disordered behavior is caused by readily identifiable factors in the person's environment and is the product of learning. As you recall from chapter 7, section 7-2, behaviorists believe that learning occurs through *conditioning*. In classical conditioning, a previously neutral stimulus is paired with a stimulus that automatically elicits a reflexive response, the unconditioned stimulus. Through repeated pairing of the neutral and unconditioned stimuli, the neutral stimulus

---

psychological disorder
A pattern of atypical behavior that results in personal distress or significant impairment in a person's social or occupational functioning.

There's a very fine line between a groove and a rut; a fine line between eccentrics and people who are just plain nuts.

—*Christine Lavin, American singer and songwriter, b. 1952*

The only difference between me and a madman is that I'm not mad.

—*Salvador Dali, Spanish artist, 1904–1989*

comes to elicit a response similar to the reflexive response. Classical conditioning can explain the development of several reflexive responses, including those that might lead to a psychological disorder. For example, the fear response toward a white rat that John Watson and Rosalie Rayner (1920) classically conditioned in "Little Albert B." provided insights into the development of phobic disorders (see section 13-3a). Other physiological responses that occur reflexively to certain stimuli, such as allergies, nausea, and sexual arousal, may also be classically conditioned to occur in response to what were initially neutral stimuli.

The other basic form of conditioning is operant conditioning, which is driven by reinforcement and punishment (see chapter 7, section 7-2a). As you recall, behaviors followed by reinforcement will increase in frequency, while those followed by punishment will decrease in frequency. Operant conditioning explains why some individuals develop troubling behaviors (for example, a child's misconduct is reinforced), and also why some people fail to develop appropriate behaviors (for example, a child fails to learn appropriate social skills). According to the behavioral perspective, the etiology (initial cause) of disordered behavior is conditioning, whereas the maintaining cause is either the problem behavior itself or the environment that continues to condition the behavior.

The Cognitive Perspective

Cognition is important in understanding psychological disorders, because as you will soon learn, many disorders involve severe cognitive disturbances. Indeed, the *cognitive perspective* (see chapter 1, section 1-3c) holds that ineffective or inaccurate thinking is the root cause of mental illness (Beck, 1991). According to this viewpoint, the person's faulty cognitive style is acquired through learning, perhaps from observing how one's parents interpret their experiences or from interpreting and attempting to understand one's own experiences. This ineffective way of thinking leads the person to experience troubling emotions or behave ineffectively. Cognitive theorists believe that the etiology of a psychological problem is learning, and that the maintaining cause is the faulty cognitive style.

The Sociocultural Perspective

Theorists from the *sociocultural perspective* (see chapter 1, section 1-3f) propose that mental illness is the product of broad social and cultural forces. Evidence for this viewpoint comes from a number of sources. For example, within a given culture, the rates of psychological disorders are higher in poor urban settings than in other segments of the population (Kessler et al., 1994). Further, as unemployment increases, psychiatric hospital admissions and suicides tend to increase similarly (Pines, 1993). These findings suggest to sociocultural researchers that social forces, such as poverty, urbanization, and inequality, may be the primary causes of many mental health problems (Lott, 2002).

Cross-culturally, although certain psychological disorders are universally encountered—such as depression and schizophrenia—others are limited to specific societies or cultural areas. For example, only in Mediterranean cultures do people suffer from *mal de ojo*, or "the evil eye," in which they experience fitful sleep, unexplained crying, diarrhea, vomiting, and fever. Similarly, only among the Arctic and sub-Arctic Eskimos do we find the *pibloktog* disorder, which involves an abrupt break with reality, violence, and hyperexcitability, followed by seizures and coma (Simons & Hughes, 1993). Mental health experts have not yet determined whether these **culture-bound syndromes** are distinct from the more established psychological disorders, or whether they are variations of them. However, the existence of culture-bound syndromes, along with the fluctuations that occur in mental illness rates due to socioeconomic factors, demonstrates that a complete understanding of psychological disorders must consider people's sociocultural context.

The Biological Perspective

While the perspectives on mental illness reviewed so far primarily focus on the relationship between the mind and the social environment, biological researchers focus on the relationship between the mind and the body. This *biological perspective*—which includes the neuroscience and evolutionary perspectives first introduced in chapter 1, sections 1-3d and 1-3e—proposes that psychological disorders are caused by biological conditions, such as

All are lunatics, but he who can analyze his delusion is called a philosopher.

—*Ambrose Pierce, American satirist, 1842–1914*

culture-bound syndromes
Psychological disorders found only in a few cultural groups.

genetics, hormone levels, or neurotransmitter activity in the brain. For example, as discussed in chapter 4, section 4-1b, the fetus is vulnerable to various teratogens that cause abnormal prenatal development. There is also evidence that these noxious agents can later make people more vulnerable to certain psychological disorders due to their effects on the central nervous system. Biological irregularities related to mental illness are also shaped by many other factors, including illness and response to environmental stressors, and they often can be treated through medical intervention and drug therapies (see chapter 14, section 14-7).

Movement toward a Multiperspective Approach

Table 13-1 summarizes the five theoretical approaches to understanding mental illness. Over the years, as researchers have attempted to identify the origins of psychological disorders, they have discovered that adequate one-perspective explanations are rare. Further, we should remember that a perspective's emphasis on one set of symptoms does not mean that it ignores symptoms emphasized by other theoretical perspectives. For example, cognitive theorists assess social, behavioral, biological, and psychodynamic symptoms, but they emphasize the cognitions that occur prior to and simultaneously with these other symptoms. Today, many current explanations of psychological disorders combine the various perspectives into one overall account.

One such interdisciplinary approach is the **diathesis-stress model** (Barlow, 1988; Kendler et al., 2002a), illustrated in figure 13-1. A *diathesis* (pronounced "dye-A-thuh-sis") is an underlying vulnerability or predisposition that may be caused by genetic inheritance, biological processes, or early learning experiences. A person with a diathesis is susceptible to developing

diathesis-stress model
A predisposition to a given disorder (diathesis) that combines with environmental stressors to trigger a psychological disorder.

Table **13-1**	The Etiology of Psychological Disorders by Theoretical Perspective
Perspective	**Etiology**
Psychodynamic	Unconscious conflict from childhood experiences
Behavioral	Conditioning from the environment
Cognitive	Learning ineffective or inaccurate thinking
Sociocultural	Broad social and cultural forces
Biological	Genetics, hormone levels, neurotransmitter activity

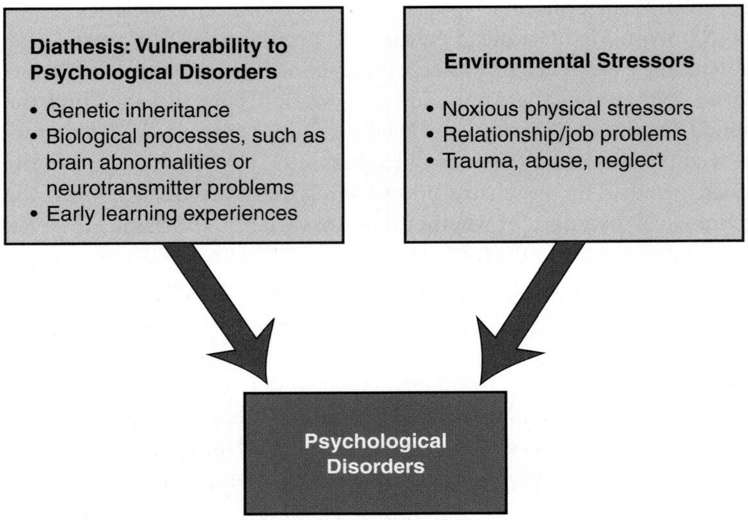

Figure 13-1

The Diathesis-Stress Model

The diathesis-stress model proposes that a predisposition to a psychological disorder (diathesis) interacts with environmental stressors to cause the disorder. According to this model, the diathesis alone or the stressors alone are unlikely to trigger the disorder.

Diathesis: Vulnerability to Psychological Disorders

- Genetic inheritance
- Biological processes, such as brain abnormalities or neurotransmitter problems
- Early learning experiences

Environmental Stressors

- Noxious physical stressors
- Relationship/job problems
- Trauma, abuse, neglect

Psychological Disorders

a problem later, when experiencing stress. Without the diathesis, stress alone may not be sufficient to produce a disorder (Zuckerman, 1999). For example, a person may have inherited neural problems that are associated with panic disorder. Further, overly protective parents may have taught the person to closely monitor his or her physiological reactions, a behavior that is also associated with panic disorder. Yet these predispositions may be expressed as a panic disorder only when the individual is experiencing high levels of stress in life. If such stress is infrequent, or if the person has learned how to adequately cope with such stressful events, he or she may never have a panic attack, or it may be relatively mild. Thus, the diathesis-stress model proposes that the *interaction* of both the predisposition for a disorder (diathesis) and environmental stressors is what causes the psychological disorder. Periodically throughout this chapter, I discuss how the diathesis-stress model can provide additional insight into how the other perspectives might interact in explaining a particular psychological disorder.

Section Review

- The medical model views psychological disorders like physical diseases.
- The criteria for differentiating disordered from normal behavior are that the behavior
  1. is atypical
  2. violates cultural norms
  3. is maladaptive
  4. involves personal distress
- Psychologists employ multiple perspectives in studying psychological disorders.
- The diathesis-stress model proposes that the predisposition for a psychological disorder (diathesis) interacts with environmental stressors to cause the disorder to emerge.

13-2 HOW SHOULD WE CLASSIFY PSYCHOLOGICAL DISORDERS?

Preview

- *What are the risks and benefits in labeling people with psychological disorders?*
- *What is the most widely used classification scheme to diagnose mental disorders?*

In diagnosing psychological disorders, mental health professionals use agreed-upon criteria. Yet, given that the distinction between normality and abnormality is a matter of degree rather than an either-or proposition, to what extent is the diagnostic process susceptible to judgmental bias? What are the risks and benefits in diagnosing psychological disorders? These questions have been the subject of considerable debate—and research—within the mental health community over the years.

13-2a Using Diagnostic Labels Has Both Risks and Benefits

David Rosenhan (1971) demonstrated the biasing effects of diagnostic labels when he and seven of his friends and Stanford University colleagues went to various psychiatric hospitals and presented themselves as would-be patients. When asked by the hospital personnel about their problem, each pseudopatient reported hearing voices that said "thud," "hollow," and "empty." Aside from this complaint and giving fictitious names and occupations, they answered all other questions honestly. Every single one of these individuals was admitted as a patient, most often with the diagnosis of schizophrenia. During their hospital stay, the pseudopatients acted normally, keeping records about their treatment. They remained in the hospital, on average, for about 3 weeks. In most cases, the discharge diagnosis stated that their schizophrenia was in remission, meaning that the "patient" no longer exhibited active symptoms of the disorder. Rosenhan concluded that the misdiagnosis of insanity by the hospital personnel was due to their general bias toward calling a healthy person sick.

How might the *confirmation bias,* a topic of discussion in chapter 9, section 9-2c, explain the decision-making process of the hospital personnel in the Rosenhan study?

Risks of Diagnostic Labels

Diagnostic labels can harm patients in several ways. First, the label may "dehumanize" patients by encouraging mental health practitioners to treat patients as labels rather than as unique individuals with problems. Second, labeled individuals may experience discrimination if jobs, housing, or other social opportunities are limited due to negative stereotypes about the mentally ill. Finally, people may expect the labeled individuals to behave abnormally and thus misperceive normal behavior as disordered. This sometimes occurred in the Rosenhan study: When the pseudopatients asked questions about their medication or took notes about staff interactions, hospital personnel interpreted those activities as further symptoms of the previously diagnosed disorder.

All available evidence strongly indicates that people identified as suffering from psychological disorders are severely stigmatized in the United States and in other Western and Asian cultures (Arredondo & Perez, 2003; Brockington et al., 1993; Ng, 1997). A **stigma** is an attribute that serves to discredit a person in the eyes of others (Biernat & Dovidio, 2000; Goffman, 1963). In the United States, a national survey found that Americans viewed people with psychological disorders as dangerous and less capable of handling their daily affairs than the average person (Pescosolido et al., 1999). Such stigmatization is fostered and strengthened by selective news reporting of violent incidents involving people with psychological disorders and the highly negative portrayals of the mentally ill in popular culture (Angermeyer & Matschinger, 1996). For example, a content analysis of U.S. television programs found that people with psychological disorders are the most stigmatized group on the small screen; they are typically portrayed as either helpless victims or evil and violent villains (Gerbner, 1993). While 5 percent of "normal" television characters played the role of a murderer, 20 percent of "mentally ill" characters were portrayed as murderers. Similarly, whereas 40 percent of "normal" characters engaged in some form of aggression (a very high number in itself!), 70 percent of the "mentally ill" characters were violent.

Faced with this societal stigma and the fear of being negatively evaluated, people with psychological problems often conceal their symptoms and avoid seeking therapy (Corrigan & Penn, 1998; Wahl, 1999). In many Asian countries, the stigma of mental illness is so severe that it can damage the reputation of the family lineage and thereby significantly reduce the marriage and career prospects of other family members (Ng, 1997). This stigma is also pervasive among Asian Americans in the United States. For example, a mental health survey in Los Angeles (Zhang et al., 1998) found that Asian Americans were less than half as likely as White Americans to mention their mental health problems to a friend or relative (12 percent versus 25 percent), and only 4 percent stated that they would seek help from a psychiatrist or psychotherapist (compared to 26 percent of White Americans). In addition to preventing people from seeking help for their psychological problems, the stigma of mental illness lowers self-esteem while increasing a sense of social isolation and hopelessness (Penn & Martin, 1998).

Are the Mentally Ill More Violent Than Healthy Individuals?

So what is the truth underlying one of the most common stereotypes of the mentally ill—namely, that they are more violent than the average person? One study monitored the behavior of more than 1,000 individuals during the year after they had been discharged from psychiatric hospitals (Steadman et al., 1998). Results found no significant difference in the incidence of violence between the former patients and a control group of people living in the same neighborhoods with no history of serious mental health problems. Other research indicates that heightened violence is only slightly more likely among people with severe psychological disorders who are currently experiencing extreme psychological symptoms, such as bizarre delusional thoughts and hallucinated voices (Link et al., 1992). All

stigma An attribute that serves to discredit a person in the eyes of others.

 It is important that people experiencing severe psychological distress seek professional help, yet the stigma surrounding psychological disorders causes many people to avoid seeking help. What is one of the most common stereotypes about the mentally ill?

other individuals with a psychological disorder who are not experiencing these severe symptoms are no more likely than the average person to be violent. Thus, the research clearly indicates that the cultural stereotype associating mental illness with violence is grossly exaggerated and largely unfounded. However, until such negative stereotypes surrounding psychological disorders are reduced, the stigma of the mental illness label will remain the most formidable obstacle to future progress in the area of mental health.

Benefits of Diagnostic Labels

Despite the drawbacks associated with diagnostic labels, mental health professionals continue to use them because they serve several important functions. The first benefit is that a label summarizes the patient's presenting symptoms or problems. Rather than listing each patient's entire set of symptoms, clinicians can communicate a great deal of information about a patient with a single word. A second benefit is that a diagnostic label conveys information about possible causes of the disorder. Explaining a psychological disorder involves understanding both what factors possibly caused it to develop and what factors may be operating to maintain it. For some psychological disorders, research has identified clear causal and maintaining factors, and so the diagnostic label carries much useful information that helps the psychologist understand the individual's condition. In other disorders for which the etiology and maintaining causes are still unclear, the diagnostic label may suggest to the psychologist a range of possible causes to consider when working with the patient. Finally, a third benefit of a diagnostic label is that it conveys information about the patient's prognosis, or expected future course. An important aspect of the prognosis is the patient's likely response to treatment. For many psychological disorders, research has identified one or more effective interventions. Knowledge of a patient's diagnosis may therefore suggest to the psychologist which treatment may be most helpful.

In summary, although diagnostic labels may sometimes lead to aversive consequences for people suffering from psychological disorders, these labels also convey important information about the nature, probable causes, and likely treatments of the problem. Because of these benefits, psychologists continue to use diagnostic labels, while being mindful of the potential risks.

13-2b *DSM-IV-TR* Is the Most Widely Used Classification Scheme for Psychological Disorders

In any science, it is important to accurately and reliably classify into categories whatever you are studying. Research in the 1950s and 1960s indicated that the categories into which psychological disorders were being classified were not sufficiently reliable to be useful (Wierzbicki, 1993). Responding to criticism concerning the reliability and validity of psychological diagnoses, psychologists and psychiatrists worked to improve their classification scheme, an effort culminating in the 1980 publication of the ***Diagnostic and Statistical Manual of Mental Disorders (DSM)*** by the American Psychiatric Association. This system has since been updated several times and is now in its fourth edition, text revision, or *DSM-IV-TR* (American Psychiatric Association, 2000). The *DSM*'s classification system is based on the medical model, in which psychological disorders are viewed as diseases. Its use of the term *patient* is consistent with this medical model. As a testament to its influence in our society, not only do most psychologists and psychiatrists use the *DSM* in their work with individuals suffering from mental illness, but also insurance companies and the courts have increasingly come to accept and rely on its criteria for disordered behavior in resolving payment and legal issues.

The *DSM* differs from previous diagnostic systems in several ways. First, this classification system is *descriptive* rather than *explanatory*, meaning that it is not based on a particular theory concerning what causes psychological disorders. Rather, it is *atheoretical*. Thus, diagnoses are based more on observable symptoms than on the clinician's judgment about the underlying cause of these symptoms. Second, the *DSM* provides clearer directions to clinicians concerning the number, duration, and severity of symptoms that are necessary to assign a diagnosis. By recognizing that two patients with the same disorder may substantially differ from one another, clinicians are much more likely to acknowledge the uniqueness of all patients.

These improvements address many of the criticisms of diagnostic labels, and numerous studies indicate that *DSM* diagnoses are in fact more reliable than previous diagnostic

Diagnostic and Statistical Manual of Mental Disorders (DSM) The manual of psychological disorders published by the American Psychiatric Association and used for descriptive diagnoses.

This is the text that most mental health professionals use in diagnosing psychological disorders. The classification scheme used in the *Diagnostic and Statistical Manual of Mental Disorders (DSM)* is descriptive rather than explanatory, meaning that it is not based on a particular theory. Diagnoses are based on observable symptoms, and the *DSM* provides directions concerning the number, duration, and severity of symptoms that are necessary to assign a particular diagnosis. This classification scheme has been updated several times, and the manual is now in its fourth-edition text revision, or *DSM-IV-TR*.

Source: Courtesy of Figzoi.

systems (Blacker & Tsuang, 1999; Spitzer et al., 1979). However, critics still contend that the *DSM* incorrectly views many normal behaviors as indicative of a psychological disorder (Malik & Beutler, 2002). For example, an irrational fear of embarrassment is considered a symptom of social phobia, while a habitual tendency to violate rules at home or in school is a symptom of conduct disorder (Pomerantz, 2002). In response, ongoing research seeks to improve the reliability and validity of *DSM* diagnoses and to address criticisms of specific sections of the diagnostic system (First et al., 2004). In this respect, the *DSM* is truly a "work in progress." As research identifies new disorders or more reliable ways of diagnosing a disorder, these results are incorporated into new versions of the *DSM*.

Section Review

- Two risks in using diagnostic labels are (1) mental health professionals may become biased in interpreting normal behavior as disordered in persons labeled mentally ill, and (2) labeled individuals may be stigmatized by others and subject to discrimination.
- Using labels does have benefits; for example, diagnostic labels communicate valuable information, including possible causes of the disorder, its likely course, and possible treatment.
- Most clinicians rely on the *Diagnostic and Statistical Manual of Mental Disorders* (*DSM*) when diagnosing psychological disorders.

13-3   THE MAJOR CLASSES OF DISORDERS IDENTIFIED BY *DSM-IV-TR*

Preview

- *What characterizes anxiety and mood disorders?*
- *What are dissociative disorders?*
- *What is schizophrenia?*
- *What characterizes somatoform and personality disorders?*

The remainder of this chapter introduces you to the major classes of psychological disorders. Each class of disorders is defined according to the most severe or most prominent of the patient's symptoms. While reading about these disorders, keep in mind that you may have experienced some of these symptoms yourself at some time. In recognizing yourself, you may begin to worry that you are suffering from one (or more) of these disorders. Don't become alarmed. The truth is that many of the described symptoms are fairly common in the general population. On innumerable occasions throughout our lives, we all experience sadness and euphoria, unrealistic anxiety and fear, and interpersonal problems. Only when these symptoms significantly disrupt our functioning or our sense of well-being are they indicative of a possible psychological disorder. In such instances, you should seek the help of a mental health professional for proper diagnosis and treatment.

13-3a Anxiety Disorders Are Characterized by Distressing, Persistent Anxiety or Maladaptive Behavior

Everybody experiences anxiety. However, anxiety disorders are distinguished from "normal" anxiety by the severity of the emotional distress and the degree to which the anxiety disrupts daily functioning. **Anxiety disorders,** which are characterized by distressing, persistent anxiety or maladaptive behavior, are the most common psychological disorders (Hollander et al., 2002). About 25 percent of us will experience this disorder in our lifetime (Kessler et al., 1994). Anxiety disorders occur across the life span and commonly co-occur with many other disorders, such as depression and substance abuse. Recent research raises the possibility that, besides the suffering caused by acute anxiety, the chronic stress associ-

anxiety disorders Disorders characterized by distressing, persistent anxiety or maladaptive behavior.

ated with anxiety disorders may damage the hippocampus (see chapter 3, section 3-3b), a brain structure involved in acquiring and consolidating new information in memory (McEwen, 2000). The possibility that chronic stress negatively impacts brain functioning highlights how important it is to properly identify and treat anxiety disorders. In this section, we discuss five major anxiety disorders: panic disorder, phobic disorder, generalized anxiety disorder (GAD), obsessive-compulsive disorder (OCD), and post-traumatic stress disorder (PTSD).

Panic Disorder

Maya is a 28-year-old hairstylist who has **panic disorder,** which is characterized by episodes of intense anxiety without an apparent reason. When having these attacks, Maya feels dizzy, her heart races, she sweats and has tremors, and she may even faint. Besides these physiological symptoms, her psychological symptoms may include fear of dying, fear of suffocating, fear of "going crazy," and fear of losing control and doing something drastic, such as killing herself or others.

> **panic disorder** An anxiety disorder characterized by episodes of intense fear and dread that usually occur suddenly and unexpectedly.

Panic episodes have a clear beginning and end, and they are relatively brief, usually lasting no more than a few minutes. As you can imagine, such episodes are extremely frightening; the symptoms of sympathetic nervous system arousal often lead sufferers like Maya to seek immediate medical attention out of concern that they are dying. About 3 percent of the general population worldwide experiences panic disorder during their lifetimes (Kessler et al., 1994; Weissman et al., 1997). In general, this anxiety disorder occurs more often in young adults than in older adults (Blazer, 1997), with about twice as many women (5 percent) suffering from it as men (2 percent).

People often take extreme steps to limit the panic episodes. For example, Maya is embarrassed about having a panic episode in public, so she limits her social activities. She also avoids locations where she has experienced previous panic episodes, and so she has stopped going to shopping malls and restaurants. As you can see, like many panic disorder sufferers, Maya has significantly restricted her social activities outside her home. Such restriction of activities in an attempt to limit panic episodes creates a condition called **agoraphobia,** which is a fear of going out in public or open places. As its name implies, until recently agoraphobia was classified as a phobic disorder (see next subsection). Recent studies, however, suggest that it is primarily a complication of panic disorder (Hollander et al., 1999). One reason agoraphobia was not recognized earlier as developing from panic disorder was that its sufferers rarely came to clinics for treatment, due to their avoidance of outside activities.

> **agoraphobia** A fear of going out to public or open spaces.

Phobic Disorder

Another anxiety disorder is **phobic disorder,** which is characterized by strong, irrational fears of specific objects or situations, called *phobias.* The *DSM* classifies phobias into subtypes based on the object of fear. The most common subtype in the United States is composed of the *specific phobias,* which involve fear and avoidance of particular objects and situations, such as heights, animals, enclosed spaces, blood, and automobile or air travel. Another subtype is made up of the *social phobias,* which involve fear of being negatively evaluated by others or acting in ways that are embarrassing or humiliating (Kleinknecht, 2000). Whereas specific phobias affect about 10 percent of the population, only about 3 percent are affected by social phobias (Narrow et al., 2002). Women are diagnosed with specific phobias about twice as often as men, and they tend to develop phobic symptoms earlier (age 10 for females and age 14 for males). The gender difference in social phobias is considerably smaller, with women diagnosed only slightly more often than men (Dick et al., 1994; Kessler et al., 1994).

> **phobic disorder** An anxiety disorder characterized by strong irrational fears of specific objects or situations.

Different types of phobias tend to have different courses. For example, fears of strangers, doctors, storms, and the dark are more common in children than in adults, whereas fears of cancer and the death of a loved one are more common in adults. Interestingly, phobias have a moderate tendency to run in families, so that individuals with phobias tend to have close relatives with similar kinds of phobias (Rose & Ditto, 1983).

When analyzing phobic disorders, it is important to distinguish them from rational fears that occur in the presence of a realistic threat. For example, it is normal to experience

Figure 13-2

Frequency of Specific Phobias

Many people experience fear when exposed to these stimuli. In most of these cases, the fear represents a "subclinical" phobia, meaning that it would not be indicative of a psychological disorder.

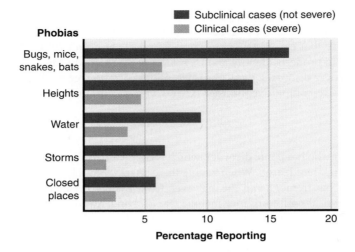

fear when encountering a mugger or when riding in a car that skids off the road. It is also important to distinguish clinical phobias from *subclinical phobias,* which are mild, irrational fears that do not interfere with daily functioning. You may experience fear when you encounter a huge spider in your basement while washing clothes. If you continue to use the basement for normal activities despite your fear, you have a subclinical phobia. In contrast, if you are so afraid of seeing the spider in your basement that you start taking your clothes to a Laundromat, you may have a clinical phobia. Figure 13-2 shows the frequency of some common specific phobias. Before reading further, complete Explore It Exercise 13-1.

Generalized Anxiety Disorder

> **generalized anxiety disorder (GAD)** An anxiety disorder characterized by a constant state of moderate anxiety.

Generalized anxiety disorder (GAD) is characterized by a constant state of moderate anxiety. This anxiety differs from normal anxiety that occurs in response to actual stressful events or situations. For example, if you are a full-time college student who works 20 hours a week and maintains an active social life, it is normal to experience stress and anxiety throughout the semester. Further, the anxiety experienced in GAD differs from the anxiety felt in phobic disorder because, in GAD, there is no clear object or situation that causes the anxiety. Instead, the anxiety is "free floating." GAD also differs from panic disorder in that the anxiety does not occur in discrete, relatively brief episodes but is constant.

GAD occurs in about 5 percent of the general population in their lifetime—about twice as often in women as men, and more often among those over the age of 24 (Kessler et al., 1994). GAD often occurs in association with other problems, including other anxiety disorders and depression (Craske, 1999).

Explore It
Exercise **13-1**

What Do You Most Fear?

We all fear something. Fear of animals is most common during the elementary school years. Blood phobia tends to appear at about 9 years, dental phobia at about 12 years, and social phobias and claustrophobia are most pronounced in later adolescence or early adulthood.

1. What is it that you fear most? _____
2. At what age did you first become aware of this fear? _____
3. How strong is this fear? Mild fear 1 2 3 4 5 6 7 8 9 10 Paralyzing fear
4. Does this fear cause a major disruption in your life? Yes _____ No _____
5. Based on what you have read about phobias, do you think this fear is
   —merely a normal source of anxiety_____
   —sufficiently intense to be a subclinical phobia_____
   —sufficiently intense to be a clinical phobia_____

People who suffer from obsessive-compulsive disorder often engage in repetitive actions, such as washing their hands for hours until they are raw. How do such rituals reduce the anxiety associated with the disorder?

Source: Courtesy of Figzoi.

Obsessive-Compulsive Disorder

Obsessive-compulsive disorder (OCD) is an anxiety disorder characterized by repetitive, unwanted, and distressing actions and/or thoughts. *Obsessions* are repetitive thoughts or ideas that cause distress or interfere significantly with ongoing activity. For example, some OCD sufferers may be bothered by thoughts of killing themselves or others, even though they have no history of, and are not truly at risk for, suicide or homicide. *Compulsions* are repetitive actions or behaviors that cause distress or interfere significantly with ongoing activity. Most OCD rituals can be classified as *cleaning* or *checking*. For example, some OCD sufferers engage in hand-washing rituals, cleaning their hands hundreds of times a day, while others feel compelled to repeatedly check the locks on their doors before they leave the house. Still other individuals save newspapers and tin cans for years, to the point that it becomes difficult to navigate through their houses.

OCD is associated with intense anxiety. OCD patients experience many anxiety-provoking obsessions, such as fears of contamination and worries about not having taken steps to prevent harm. These obsessive thoughts are followed by compulsive rituals, which reduce the anxiety associated with the obsessions. However, the compulsive rituals lower anxiety only temporarily, and soon the individual must repeat them or add to their length.

Psychologists today recognize that this disorder is more common than had been thought in the past. The lifetime prevalence of OCD is from 2 to 3 percent, with females having a somewhat higher risk than men (Karno et al., 1988; Torres et al., 2004). This disorder tends to develop in adolescence or young adulthood, although it may not be diagnosed until years later. OCD sufferers usually are embarrassed about their symptoms and try to hide them from others. Thus, it may be years before the symptoms become so intense that they can no longer be hidden. Research indicates there is at least a moderate genetic influence on OCD (Pato et al., 2002; Pauls et al., 1995).

obsessive-compulsive disorder (OCD) An anxiety disorder characterized by repetitive, unwanted, and distressing actions and/or thoughts.

Post-Traumatic Stress Disorder

Post-traumatic stress disorder (PTSD) occurs in some individuals who have experienced or witnessed life-threatening or other traumatic events. Following such trauma, some people experience intense emotional distress, re-experiencing the event (say, through nightmares or flashbacks) and avoiding situations or persons that trigger flashbacks. When these symptoms occur long after the original trauma and significantly interfere with normal daily functioning, the individual is said to have PTSD (Lamprecht & Sack, 2002).

Research suggests that almost 8 percent of the general population experiences PTSD symptoms during some period in their lifetime (Kessler et al., 1995). Although highly dramatic events, such as warfare and natural disasters, can lead to this disorder, most PTSD patients have experienced more common types of trauma, such as rape, child abuse, family illness, and witnessing violence (Bromet & Havenaar, 2002; Kazak et al., 2004). It appears that trauma due to crimes is more likely to trigger PTSD than trauma due to natural disasters (Breslau et al., 1998). Risk also varies with the nature and severity of the trauma (Koren et al., 2005). For example, the lifetime risk for PTSD following rape is about 35 percent (Kilpatrick

post-traumatic stress disorder (PTSD) An anxiety disorder characterized by flashbacks and recurrent thoughts of life-threatening or other traumatic events.

Following the terrorist attacks at the World Trade Center and the Pentagon, many survivors developed post-traumatic stress disorder, which involves intense emotional distress, nightmares or flashbacks, and avoidance of situations or persons that trigger flashbacks.

Source: AP/Wide World Photos.

& Resnick, 1993), while the lifetime risk following automobile accidents ranges from 8 to 41 percent, depending on the severity of the accident (Keppel-Benson et al., 2002; Stallard et al., 2004). In general, as the severity of the traumatic event increases, the risk for PTSD increases.

Although only about 4 percent of the U.S. population suffers from PTSD at any given time, the rates are much higher for combat veterans, inner-city residents, and recent immigrants from countries in turmoil (Kagee, 2004; Yehuda, 2000). For example, some survey studies of refugees from Vietnam, Cambodia, and Laos find rates of PTSD symptoms as high as 70 percent. Further, in a study of over 1,000 recently immigrated schoolchildren in Los Angeles, 32 percent reported PTSD symptoms in the clinical range. Although boys were more likely to have been personally victimized or to have witnessed violence in the previous year and during their lifetimes, girls reported more PTSD and depressive symptoms (Jaycox et al., 2002).

Etiology of Anxiety Disorders

Several biological factors appear to influence the development of anxiety disorders. As discussed in chapter 7, section 7-1d, our genetic heritage may predispose us to more easily develop phobic reactions toward certain objects and situations, such as snakes and heights, because they once posed real dangers to our ancestors (Buss, 1995; Kleinknecht, 1991). According to this evolutionary explanation, snakes and heights make many of us unduly anxious and are the source of phobic reactions because the genes that trigger such anxiety are still part of our biological makeup. Genetics also plays a contributory role in both panic disorder and obsessive-compulsive disorder (Goldstein et al., 1997; Pato et al., 2002). For example, panic disorder is more likely to be shared by identical twins than fraternal twins (Kendler et al., 1999b; Torgersen, 1983), and family, twin, and adoption studies indicate that OCD has at least a moderate genetic influence (Billett et al., 1998). At the level of brain functioning, brain-imaging studies have found evidence that obsessions are at least partly caused by a malfunctioning neural structure in the *basal ganglia,* a brain region located below the cerebral cortex (Hansen et al., 2002; Saxena & Rauch, 2000). Normally, this structure—the *caudate nucleus*—terminates recurrent thoughts before they become obsessions, but in people who suffer from OCD, it does not operate correctly. Evidence also indicates that people who suffer from panic disorder are more likely to have a limbic system (most notably, the amygdala) that is more easily activated by mental imagery of traumatic events versus nontraumatic events (Shin et al., 1997). As you recall from chapter 3, section 3-3b, a malfunctioning amygdala can trigger intense fear.

The fact that certain drugs can alleviate anxiety symptoms and other drugs can induce those same symptoms further suggests that biology plays a role in anxiety disorders (Hansen et al., 2002; Holland et al., 1999). Brain scans also reveal that people who suffer from anxiety disorders respond differently to danger signals than do nonsufferers (Gorman, 2002). These and other findings suggest that some people are simply biologically predisposed to respond more intensely to stressful events than other people, and this stronger stress reaction puts them at greater risk for developing anxiety disorders (Buss & Plomin, 1984).

As discussed in chapter 7, behavioral or conditioning factors have also been implicated in anxiety disorders (Hopko et al., 2001; Watson & Rayner, 1920). In such cases, classical conditioning can produce emotional responses to previously neutral stimuli. After these conditioned emotional responses have been initiated, people's avoidance of the feared objects may be reinforced, because as they move away from the objects, their anxiety decreases. In other words, classical conditioning may be involved in instilling conditioned emotional responses, and operant conditioning may reinforce—and so, maintain—the person's avoidance responses. This *two-process conditioning model* has been an influential and useful way to understand anxiety disorders (Mineka & Zinbarg, 1995; Mowrer, 1947). Consistent with this perspective is the finding from one study that 44 percent of sufferers of a social phobia could identify a traumatic conditioning event in their past that was associated with their anxiety (Stemberger et al., 1995).

Finally, cognitive factors also play an important role in anxiety disorders. People who suffer from panic disorder often closely monitor their physiological reactions, because they want to detect the onset of another panic episode. However, they often misinterpret and exaggerate the significance of their physiological symptoms, perhaps because panic episodes are so distressing. Their hypervigilance regarding the onset of panic episodes may actually contribute to the condition they want to avoid (Beck, 1997). This "fear of fear" is one of the fundamental problems that must be addressed in treating panic disorder (Craske & Barlow, 1993).

It is easy to see how biological, behavioral, and cognitive factors interact to cause anxiety disorders. Consider again panic disorder. People with panic disorder may have a biological predisposition to this problem, and biological stressors, such as breathing a carbon-dioxide-rich mixture of air, can trigger panic episodes (Rapee, 1995). Through conditioning, panic is associated with certain situations so that eventually these situations alone can trigger panic attacks. Finally, panic disorder sufferers become so fearful of panic episodes that they are hypervigilant to signs of a panic attack and thus may actually frighten themselves into a panic attack. Given these possible multiple triggers, what is the ultimate cause of panic disorder? Is it biological, behavioral, or cognitive? Most likely, it is some combination of all three factors.

13-3b Mood Disorders Are Characterized by Emotional Extremes

Have you ever had "the blues"? Most people have had days when they felt sad, lethargic, and uninterested in their usual activities. These are some of the symptoms of depression, the most common mood disorder. In general, **mood disorders** are characterized by emotional extremes that cause significant disruption in daily functioning (Parker, 2004). These symptoms are relatively common; almost 30 percent of the general population reports experiencing depressed mood for at least 2 weeks at some time in their lives (Weissman et al., 1991). However, to qualify as a mood disorder, such emotional extremes must persist for a long time.

mood disorders Psychological disorders characterized by emotional extremes that cause significant disruption in daily functioning.

Depression

The most common mood disorder is **depression,** which is characterized by extreme and persistent negative moods and the inability to experience pleasure by participating in activities one previously enjoyed (Kramlinger, 2001; Riso et al., 2003). Depressed individuals often experience physiological problems such as lack of appetite, weight loss, fatigue, and sleep disorders. In addition, depressed individuals often experience behavioral symptoms, such as slowed thinking and acting (called *psychomotor retardation*), social withdrawal, and decreased rate of activity. Finally, depressed people exhibit cognitive symptoms, including low self-esteem, thinking about death and/or suicide, and having little hope for the future. When these symptoms are severe, are persistent, and interfere with daily functioning, the person is diagnosed as having major depressive disorder. When these symptoms are mild

depression A mood disorder characterized by extreme and persistent negative moods and the inability to experience pleasure from activities previously enjoyed.

dysthymia Chronic low-level depression lasting more than 2 years.

but persistent, lasting for more than 2 years, the individual is diagnosed with **dysthymia.** The average duration of dysthymia is about 5 to 10 years.

Because major depressive disorder is so common—the lifetime likelihood is about 17 percent, with an annual rate of 6.5 percent—it has been termed the "common cold" of mental illness (Kaelber et al., 1995). Further, people who experience major depressive disorder often have multiple recurrences (Solomon et al., 2004). Cross-culturally, depression occurs about twice as frequently in women as in men, but significant variations are seen between cultures (see figure 13-3). Depression is also associated with age (Weissman et al., 1996). In the general population, the risk of having a major depressive episode in a given year is highest (almost 4 percent) among people between the ages of 30 and 44 years (Weissman et al., 1991). Although depression does occur in children, the risk among those younger than 10 years is much lower than that among adolescents and adults (Speier et al., 1995). Check out Self-Discovery Questionnaire 13-1, which contains a self-report questionnaire that assesses cognitive symptoms of depression.

One of the major dangers of depression is suicide (Shaffer & Greenberg, 2002). For example, one study found that as many as 30 percent of people with severe mood disorders die from suicide (Klerman, 1987). In the United States and Canada, about 31,000 people commit suicide annually, a rate of about 12 per 100,000, which is almost twice the homicide rate (Clark, 1995). Worldwide, the annual death toll from suicide is about 120,000, with Japan and some northern European countries having annual death rates as high as 25 per 100,000 (Lamar, 2000; Shiho et al., 2005). Sociocultural factors, including religion, age, sex, ethnicity, and marital and employment status, are related to suicide risk (Centers for Disease Control and Prevention, 2002). For example, countries with suicide rates as low as 6 per 100,000—nations of the Middle East, Italy, Ireland, and Greece—have strong religious prohibitions against taking one's own life. In the United States, suicide rates are higher among

- men than women;
- elderly adults than younger adults and minors;
- unemployed and retired adults than employed persons;
- widowed adults than married adults;
- and Native Americans and European Americans than Asian Americans, Hispanic Americans, and African Americans.

Figure 13-4 depicts the suicide rates per 100,000 people in various ethnic groups in the United States. The highest rates of suicide are among the various Native American tribes (13.6), followed by European Americans (12.9), Asian Americans (9.1), Hispanic Americans (7.5), and African Americans (5.7). Because European Americans far outnumber Native Americans in the general population, they have a higher number of suicides than any other ethnic group. For example, in 1999, White males accounted for 72 percent of all suicides in the United States, with White females accounting for another 18 percent. Firearms are the most common method of suicide used by both men and women in the United States, with the risk of suicide being five times greater for households having guns (Grossman et al., 2005; Rosenberg et al., 1999).

Figure 13-3

Gender and Depression

Interviews with 38,000 women and men, aged 18 to 84, in 10 countries found that women's risk of experiencing major depression at some point in their lifetime is double that of men's. In addition, lifetime risk of depression among adults varies by culture, with a low of 1.5 percent in Taiwan and a high of 19 percent in Beirut (Weissman et al., 1996).

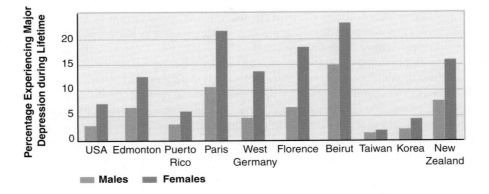

The Automatic Thoughts Questionnaire

The Automatic Thoughts Questionnaire, or ATQ (Hollon & Kendall, 1980), addresses common negative thoughts that occur when people are experiencing depressed mood. You may find it interesting to read the items of the ATQ and rate your own negative thoughts. Read each thought carefully and indicate how frequently, if at all, the thought occurred to you *over the last week,* using the following scale:

1 = not at all   2 = sometimes   3 = moderately often   4 = often   5 = all the time

_____ 1. I feel like I'm up against the world.
_____ 2. I'm no good.
_____ 3. Why can't I ever succeed?
_____ 4. No one understands me.
_____ 5. I've let people down.
_____ 6. I don't think I can go on.
_____ 7. I wish I were a better person.
_____ 8. I'm so weak.
_____ 9. My life's not going the way I want it to.
_____ 10. I'm so disappointed in myself.
_____ 11. Nothing feels good anymore.
_____ 12. I can't stand this anymore.
_____ 13. I can't get started.
_____ 14. What's wrong with me?
_____ 15. I wish I were somewhere else.
_____ 16. I can't get things together.
_____ 17. I hate myself.
_____ 18. I'm worthless.
_____ 19. I wish I could just disappear.
_____ 20. What's the matter with me?
_____ 21. I'm a loser.
_____ 22. My life is a mess.
_____ 23. I'm a failure.
_____ 24. I'll never make it.
_____ 25. I feel so hopeless.
_____ 26. Something has to change.
_____ 27. There must be something wrong with me.
_____ 28. My future is bleak.
_____ 29. It's just not worth it.
_____ 30. I can't finish anything.

To score the ATQ, simply add the ratings for all 30 items. According to Hollon and Kendall (1980), the average score in a college student population is about 49, whereas the average score in a depressed sample is about 80. Wierzbicki and Rexford (1989) found comparable differences in ATQ scores between depressed patients and nondepressed college students. Keep in mind that this exercise is not meant to diagnose depression in those who answer these questions but, rather, to give you an idea about the common negative thoughts that occur when people are depressed. If you experience many of these thoughts on a regular basis, you might consider consulting a mental health professional.

Source: From "Cognitive self-statements in depression: Development of an Automatic Thoughts Questionnaire" by S. D. Hollon and P. C. Kendall in *Cognitive Therapy and Research, 4,* 1980, pp. 383–395. Copyright © 1980. Reprinted with kind permission from Springer Science and Business Media and the authors.

Figure 13-4

Suicide Rates in Various Ethnic Groups

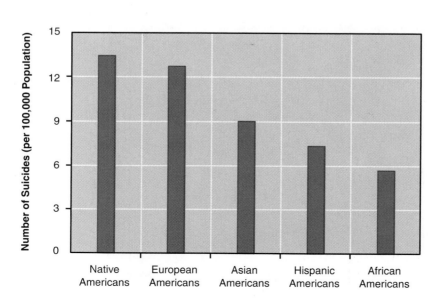

Suicide rates vary widely among ethnic groups in the United States. For example, Native Americans and European Americans are more than twice as likely to commit suicide as African Americans. The suicide rate for Native Americans is about 1.5 times the national rate. Suicide rates are generally higher in the western states and lower in the eastern and midwestern states. People in the western states are more likely to own guns, which is Americans' most common method of suicide (57 percent of suicides are committed with a firearm).

Source: Centers for Disease Control and Prevention. (1999). *Suicide deaths and rates per 100,000* [online].

Suicide risk is associated with several psychological variables: suicide threats, prior suicide attempts, recent loss, social isolation, physical and sexual abuse, and substance abuse (Evans et al., 2005; Rossow et al., 2005). Because older adults are the age group most likely to suffer from depression caused by social isolation and the death of loved ones, they have the highest suicide rates (Pritchard & Hansen, 2005). The "Psychological Applications" section at the end of this chapter presents additional information about suicide.

Bipolar Disorder

mania An excessively elated, active emotional state.

The symptoms of depression may be familiar to you. However, you are probably less familiar with manic symptoms. **Mania** is an excessively elated, active emotional state, and its symptoms are basically the opposite of depressive symptoms. For example, persons in manic states experience buoyant, exuberant mood and such boundless energy that they do not feel the need for sleep. They often have increased appetites and thus overindulge in food, alcohol, drugs, and sexual activity. Manic individuals speak and move rapidly, often going from activity to activity with endless optimism and self-confidence. I once knew a manic patient who tried to compose an opera overnight, even though he had no prior training in music composition.

At first glance, manic symptoms may not seem very problematic. They do not appear as severe as depressive symptoms, which often are accompanied by suicidal thoughts and torturous feelings. However, a person in a manic state can engage in very destructive behavior (Dilsaver et al., 1999). For example, they may go to a casino and lose the family's life savings in a single session at the roulette wheel, or they may feel so "on top of the world" that they drive their car 100 miles per hour, oblivious to the danger to themselves and others. Manic persons may also experience such an increase in physical appetites that they engage in unprotected sex with a dozen people in a day. All these activities can destroy a person's life as decisively as a suicide attempt by a depressed person.

bipolar disorder A mood disorder characterized by swings between the emotional extremes of mania and depression.

Individuals with high levels of manic symptoms followed by high levels of depressive symptoms that persist for weeks and significantly interfere with daily functioning are diagnosed as having **bipolar disorder** (previously called *manic depression*). Individuals who experience mild manic and depressive symptoms that persist for a long time are diagnosed with *cyclothymic disorder*.

Bipolar disorder is less common than major depressive disorder, occurring in about 1 percent of the population (Thomas, 2004). Unlike major depression, bipolar disorder occurs about equally in men and women and tends to occur earlier in life than major depression. Although bipolar patients usually experience episodes of severe depression as well as bouts of mania, their depressive episodes are more severe than those experienced in major depression, are accompanied by higher suicide risks, and show a distinct pattern of brain activity during sleep. This evidence suggests that bipolar disorder and major depressive disorder are distinct conditions. Further, as depicted in figure 13-5,

Figure 13-5

Brain Activity in Bipolar Disorder

PET scans of individuals suffering from bipolar disorder find substantial changes in brain activity when they cycle between mania and depression every 24 to 48 hours. Here, the top and bottom sets of brain scans were taken during times when the bipolar patient was depressed, while the middle set of brain scans was taken during a manic period. The red areas indicate a high level of neural activity.

Source: Phelps, M. E., & Mazziotta, J. C. (1985). Positron-emission tomography: Human brain function and biochemistry. *Science, 228,* 799–809. Courtesy of Drs. Lewis Baxter and Michael Phelps, UCLA School of Medicine.

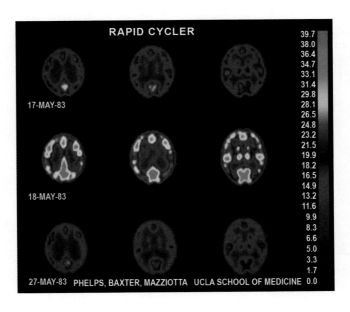

Table **13-2** Symptoms of Mood Disorders		
Type of Symptom	**Depressive State**	**Manic State**
Emotional	Sad mood Lack of pleasure	Elated mood
Physiological	Fatigue Sleep difficulty Decreased appetite Decreased interest in sex	Increased energy Lack of need for sleep Increased appetite Increased interest in sex
Behavioral	Slowed pace Decreased activity level	Increased pace Increased activity level
Cognitive	Low self-esteem Thoughts of death Negative view of world	Increased self-esteem Lack of perception of danger Positive view of world

brain scans of bipolar patients indicate that manic periods are associated with unusually high levels of brain activity. The symptoms of manic and depressive states are summarized in table 13-2.

Etiology of Mood Disorders

When seeking explanations of mood disorders, it is important to consider bipolar disorder and major depressive disorder separately. Bipolar disorder clearly has a genetic influence, and most psychologists consider it a biological disorder (Meltzer, 2000). Why? The risk for mood disorder in family members of bipolar disorder patients is more than 30 percent, which is very high (Sevy et al., 1995). Exactly what is inherited that may predispose an individual to bipolar disorder is as yet unclear. However, a growing number of researchers believe that bipolar disorders might be caused by imbalances in neural circuits that use serotonin, norepinephrine, and other neurotransmitters (Nemeroff, 1998; Thase & Howland, 1995). Brain-imaging studies have also found evidence that the amygdala—which plays a role in regulating mood and accessing emotional memories—may be enlarged in people who suffer from bipolar disorder (Strakowski et al., 2002).

Because bipolar disorder occurs more frequently among creative writers and artists than among the general population, some researchers believe that mild fluctuations in mood may play a role in enhanced creativity (Bower, 1995). A number of well-known artists have reputedly suffered from bipolar disorder, including such classical composers as G. F. Handel, Hector Berlioz, Gustav Mahler, and Robert Schumann (Jamison, 1995). Berlioz described his two contrasting moods as "passionate" and "morose." Schumann created pieces that contrasted an impulsive and high-spirited style with one that was melancholy and inner-directed.

Major depressive disorder, unlike bipolar disorder, can be explained through several approaches. First, biology does have some influence on this disorder (Davidson et al., 2002; Rosso et al., 2005). Family, twin, and adoption studies indicate at least a moderate genetic influence on depression (Katz & McGuffin, 1993). For example, with identical twins, both individuals are four times more likely to experience depression at some time in their lives than are fraternal twins (Kendler et al., 1999a). Thus, some individuals may be biologically predisposed for this disorder, and onset of the illness may have little relation to their psychosocial experiences. Such cases tend to be severe and are properly treated using antidepressant medications such as Prozac and Paxil.

One subtype of depression that appears to have a biological basis is **seasonal affective disorder (SAD).** SAD is characterized by symptoms of depression at particular times of the year, especially during the winter months, when daylight hours are reduced (Sher, 2002b; Thompson et al., 2004). Figure 13-6 shows a direct relationship between depression and the length of daylight during the year (Rosenthal et al., 1984). Of course, some cases of winter depression may be due solely to psychosocial influences, such as decreased activity due to poor weather and increased stress brought on by holiday preparations. Yet evidence that SAD is a distinct disorder comes from studies demonstrating that people with SAD have unusually high metabolic

seasonal affective disorder (SAD) A subtype of depression characterized by depressive symptoms during the winter months, when daylight hours are reduced.

Figure 13-6

Depression and Length of Daylight

People who suffer from seasonal affective disorder (SAD) experience periods of depression corresponding to the shorter days of winter.

Source: Data from Rosenthal, N. E., et al. (1984). Depression and length of daylight in seasonal affective disorder. *Archives of General Psychiatry, 41,* 72–80.

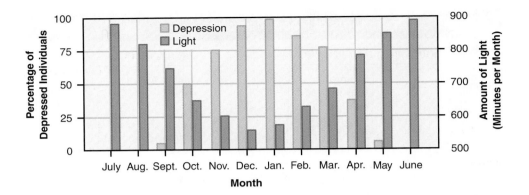

rates, as well as physiological differences from other depressed patients (Sher, 2002a; Thase & Howland, 1995). One therapy that is quite effective in alleviating SAD is exposing sufferers to bright white fluorescent light for 2 hours a day. Research suggests that this light therapy restores brain levels of the neurotransmitter serotonin to normal, since a low serotonin level is one of the likely biological causes of depression (Neumeister et al., 1997).

Beyond pure biological explanations, the psychodynamic perspective (Freud, 1909/1957) explains depression as caused by experiencing a "lost loved object" in childhood. As an adult, when the individual experiences subsequent losses, she or he becomes depressed. Rather than express anger outwardly toward whatever environmental circumstances contributed to the loss, the individual experiences "anger turned inward," blaming self. Although this explanation of depression has not received much empirical support, it has been a popular approach for psychotherapists who treat depressed patients.

As you might expect, cognitive theory suggests that depression is a thinking disorder (Beck et al., 1979; Riso et al., 2003). Depressed persons have negative views of themselves, the world, and the future, and they misinterpret their daily experiences so their negative outlook is supported (Beck, 1967). In contrast, the behavioral perspective holds that depression results from low social reinforcement, which may be due to skills deficits (such as the inability to solve problems or to interact successfully with others) or to decreased opportunities to interact with others (Lewinsohn & Gotlib, 1995). Consistent with the diathesis-stress model, research indicates that individuals with such predisposing cognitive and behavioral conditions are more likely to become depressed following stressful events in their lives (Peterson & Seligman, 1984; Teri & Lewinsohn, 1985).

Finally, why does depression occur more frequently among women than men? Some psychologists believe that this gender difference is due to biological factors. For example, there are modest relationships between depressed mood in women and biological factors such as stage of menstrual cycle and use of oral contraceptives (Thase & Howland, 1995). However, other psychologists contend that social and cultural factors related to sexism are the more likely cause. According to this sociocultural argument, because women have fewer educational and occupational opportunities, receive less money for their work, and experience more violence due to their gender, the world is simply more "depressing" for them than for men (Brems, 1995). Some sociocultural theorists also contend that the reported gender difference in depression may be a statistical mistake, reflecting gender differences in seeking help and clinician bias in diagnosis (Bogner & Gallo, 2004). For example, women may seek help for depression more frequently than men, not because they suffer more from this disorder, but because they are more likely than men to seek help for their problems. Further, the mental health profession may have a bias that leads to different diagnoses for women and men, even though they present identical symptoms, with the women labeled as depressed while the men are diagnosed with other conditions. Biological differences? Sociocultural differences? Gender differences in help seeking or clinician bias? Perhaps the best explanation for this gender difference involves some combination of these perspectives.

13-3c Dissociative Disorders Involve a Loss of Contact with Portions of One's Consciousness or Memory

Anxiety disorders and mood disorders involve symptoms that are familiar to most college students. However, the next category of disorders may be less familiar to you. **Dissociative disorders** are characterized by disruptions in consciousness, memory, sense of identity, or perception. As the label indicates, the primary feature of this class of disorders is *dissociation,* meaning that significant aspects of experience are kept separate—"disassociated"—in consciousness and memory. Dissociation usually occurs when a situation becomes overwhelmingly stressful, and the person psychologically escapes by separating his or her consciousness from the painful situational memories, thoughts, and feelings.

Consider what sometimes happens after a natural disaster, such as a flood or hurricane. Some victims are found wandering in a daze, only dimly aware of what is going on around them. Even though they may not have suffered any head injuries, these individuals may not remember their names, addresses, events leading up to the disaster, or other basic information that they typically know. Although these individuals will likely experience this dazed state only temporarily, in some cases the symptoms are prolonged, and the person is diagnosed as suffering from a dissociative disorder.

Dissociative Amnesia

The type of dissociative disorder suffered by victims of natural disasters is called **dissociative amnesia,** and it involves the sudden loss of memory of one's identity and other personal information. Of course, some cases of amnesia are due to organic causes, such as a head injury or a brain tumor. However, when there are no known organic causes, and the person's memory loss is isolated to information threatening to the self, the amnesia is considered dissociative.

Dissociative Fugue

Like amnesia, **dissociative fugue** involves loss of memory of identity. However, in fugue, the person abruptly leaves home or work and assumes a new identity without realizing that this identity is not the one that she or he had in the past. It may be hard for you to imagine how this can happen, but it does. One such case involved a "Mr. X," who experienced occasional fugue states over a period of several decades. During one episode, Mr. X married a woman, much to the chagrin of the wife he already had and whom he did not remember. In addition to dealing with the consequences of dissociative fugue, Mr. X soon faced legal charges of bigamy.

Dissociative Identity Disorder

By far, the dissociative disorder that has received the most attention is **dissociative identity disorder (DID),** also known as *multiple personality disorder* (Lilienfeld & Lynn, 2003). This condition is characterized by the presence of two or more distinct identities or personalities, which take turns controlling the person's behavior. At least one of the personalities is unaware of what transpired when it was not in control. The symptoms of DID are bizarre and extreme. One personality may be that of a 6-year-old child, while another may be that of an infirm grandparent. One personality may be male, while another may be female. Because of the fascinating nature of its symptoms, DID has received a great deal of attention from popular culture, ranging from the 1950s book and movie *The Three Faces of Eve* (Thigpen & Cleckley, 1957) to the 1990s novel and film *Primal Fear* (Diehl, 1993).

Prior to 1980, DID was considered one of the rarest forms of psychological disorder, with only about two cases reported per decade from 1930 to 1960 (McHugh, 1995). Yet, in the 1980s, over 20,000 cases were reported! Skeptics doubted that this increase was due to better diagnosis. Instead, they suggested it was caused both by the media coverage of multiple personalities and by psychotherapists' use of hypnosis and other suggestive techniques that can sometimes elicit DID-like symptoms in patients. According to this argument, psychotherapists may first wonder whether a patient's chaotic and unpredictable behavior is due to DID. Then, during therapy sessions, they ask leading questions that suggest the

dissociative disorders
Psychological disorders characterized by disruptions in consciousness, memory, sense of identity, or perception.

dissociative amnesia
A dissociative disorder characterized by a sudden loss of memory of one's identity and other personal information.

dissociative fugue
A dissociative disorder characterized by a sudden departure from home or work, combined with loss of memory of identity and the assumption of a new identity.

dissociative identity disorder (DID) A dissociative disorder characterized by the presence of two or more distinct identities or personalities that take turns controlling the person's behavior; also known as *multiple personality disorder.*

possibility of DID. Further, they may use hypnosis to try to draw out the multiple personalities. However, one of the unfortunate consequences of hypnosis is that it can lead its subjects to produce "memories" that are not true (see chapter 6, section 6-3a). Because these patients are distressed and looking for ways to understand their problems, they may come to accept the multiple personality explanation (Lilienfeld et al., 1999; Nogrady et al., 1985).

Research since 1980 has shown that DID is more common than was once believed (Gleaves, 1996). Although it is likely that some cases are manufactured in therapy sessions, most psychologists believe that the research evidence suggests this disorder is real (Hopper et al., 2002; Ross, 1991). Patients with DID typically are female, and almost all of them have histories of childhood physical and sexual abuse (Ross et al., 1989; Schmidt, 2004).

Etiology of Dissociative Disorders

Psychodynamic theory suggests that dissociation results from the individual's attempt to repress some troubling event. If this event is associated with intense emotion, a corresponding high degree of repression may be required to keep this material in the unconscious. While repressing the memory of the troubling event, the individual also inadvertently represses other memories, including memory of identity. In the case of fugue and DID, individuals develop an alternative identity or identities as a way to avoid facing the stress that would occur upon recognizing that they had lost memory of their identity and other personal information.

Invoking a biological explanation, some psychologists suggest that dissociative disorder patients may have an undetected neurological problem. Research has shown that individuals with dissociative disorders have high rates of epilepsy and that those with epilepsy have high rates of dissociative disorders (Willerman & Cohen, 1990). As intriguing as this biological explanation may be, it cannot account for all cases of dissociative disorder, because most DID patients do not have the hallmark abnormal brain-wave patterns found among epileptic sufferers. Still, it is possible that at least some individuals with dissociative disorder have neurological disorders that have not yet been detected.

Another explanation of dissociative disorders comes from the cognitive perspective. This approach holds that individuals learn to dissociate as a way of coping with intense distress. When a child is exposed to prolonged, intense stress (such as torturous abuse), dissociation may be used so frequently that it becomes automatic. Consistent with this idea, several cognitive techniques have been effective in helping to limit pain and emotional distress. For example, distraction (thinking of something other than the stressful stimulus, such as the lyrics to a song), fantasy (imagining oneself as another person, such as James Bond resisting torture), and imagery (imagining oneself in a peaceful situation other than the current stressful one) have all been shown to reduce subjective pain (Meichenbaum & Turk, 1976). Perhaps a child who experiences repeated abuse learns to cope using these cognitive techniques. Over time, the child's use of these cognitive pain-management techniques becomes automatic, even in the presence of mild stressors. At this point, the individual's dissociation no longer serves the function of protecting her or him from stress but is a problem that interferes with daily functioning in and of itself. Recent psychophysiological studies of DID patients provide some support for this hypothesis. When subjected to intense stress that precipitates a dissociated state, DID patients also experience a reduction in nervous system arousal (Williams et al., 2003). These results support the idea that the dissociated state functions as a protective mechanism for the person.

13-3d Schizophrenia Involves Disturbances in Almost All Areas of Psychological Functioning

One of the most fascinating and severe forms of psychological disorder is **schizophrenia.** Indeed, schizophrenia is so severe that it is considered a *psychosis*, meaning that the person is out of touch with reality. Sufferers may not be aware of what is going on around them and may not be able to interact effectively in the world.

Schizophrenia is characterized by severe impairment in thinking, including hallucinations, delusions, or loose associations. With *hallucinations*, some schizophrenic patients hear or see things that are not there. For example, they may hear voices that they attribute to aliens or demons. Some schizophrenic patients experience *delusions*, or irrational belief systems.

schizophrenia Psychological disorders characterized by severe impairment in thinking, such as hallucinations, delusions, or loose associations.

For example, they may believe that they are Jesus, a CIA agent, the president of the United States, a robot, their shadow, or some other unusual entity. Often, schizophrenic patients experience delusions and hallucinations that support and strengthen one another. For example, patients with schizophrenia may hear voices, which they attribute to God and which lead them to believe that they have been selected for a spiritual mission. Schizophrenic patients often experience *loose associations,* meaning that their thoughts are disconnected from one another and from the world around them. Schizophrenic patients can be so disorganized in their thinking that they are unable to speak in complete sentences and can only babble. Some patients' thoughts jump from topic to topic so rapidly that they cannot speak clearly.

Hallucinations, delusions, and loose associations are sometimes called *positive symptoms* of schizophrenia, because they are symptoms that do not typically occur in other people. Schizophrenic patients also display *negative symptoms,* meaning that they do not exhibit behaviors that most other people do. For example, many schizophrenic patients are socially withdrawn, unmotivated to engage in common social or recreational activities, and emotionally unresponsive. This emotional unresponsiveness is called *flat* or *blunt affect.* Schizophrenic patients may walk around a hospital ward as though they are zombies, completely uninvolved with what is going on around them.

Do you remember Jim, from my chapter-opening story? Following the record and pillow incidents, Jim's psychological condition rapidly deteriorated. His previously quiet, sleepy demeanor gave way to episodes of whooping and hollering while he danced frenetically around the apartment jingling his ring of keys in the air. This behavior so scared us that we called his parents and only then learned that Jim had been released from a psychiatric hospital just prior to answering our ad. By the end of the day, Jim was readmitted to the hospital with a preliminary diagnosis of schizophrenia.

Schizophrenia is diagnosed when symptoms persist for at least 6 months, are not due to some other condition (such as substance use or severe depression), and cause significant impairment in daily functioning. Because schizophrenics experience such severe problems in thinking, they often cannot work, manage a home or apartment successfully, or care for their basic needs. Schizophrenic individuals usually require assistance to care for themselves, from either their family or a treatment center. In the absence of such assistance, many schizophrenic individuals end up living on the streets (Torrey, 1997).

Schizophrenia occurs in about 1 percent of the world's population, with roughly equal frequency among males and females, and it tends to begin more often in adolescence and young adulthood than in middle and late adulthood (American Psychiatric Association, 2000; Zipursky & Schulz, 2002). Although the disorder can occur in children, it is rare in those younger than age 10. In the *DSM,* schizophrenia has been classified into five major subtypes, depending on which symptoms are most prominent.

Paranoid Schizophrenia

Paranoid schizophrenia refers to cases in which the most prominent symptoms are hallucinations and delusions. *Paranoid* delusions do not mean simply delusions of persecution but could also encompass grandiose delusions, such as thinking that you are the U.S. president or Jesus Christ. The afflicted individual is often anxious, angry, argumentative, and jealous, with such feelings sometimes leading to violence. One high-profile incident of violence involving a person with paranoid schizophrenia occurred in July 1998, when Russell Watson, Jr., shot and killed two police officers inside the U.S. Capitol building. But the violence sometimes exhibited by paranoid schizophrenics is not always directed against others. Of people suffering from schizophrenia, those with this subtype have the highest suicide rate, 13 percent (Fenton & McGlashan, 1991). Approximately 40 percent of patients diagnosed with schizophrenia are classified as paranoid schizophrenics. One silver lining in the dark cloud of paranoid schizophrenia is that this subtype has the best prognosis for recovery.

Disorganized Schizophrenia

Disorganized schizophrenia refers to rare cases (only 5 percent of all schizophrenics) whose most prominent symptoms are a variety of unrelated hallucinations and delusions, incoherent speech, and strange facial grimaces. Disorganized schizophrenic patients may be unable to speak clearly and only babble. They may act in a childlike or even infantile manner, drooling, giggling, babbling, and playing with toys.

Catatonic Schizophrenia

Catatonic schizophrenia refers to cases in which the most prominent symptom is some extreme level of motor activity. Some catatonic patients are statuelike, remaining motionless and unresponsive to the outside world, while others exhibit frenetic activity, talking and moving very rapidly. Like disorganized schizophrenia, catatonic schizophrenia is rare, occurring in only 8 percent of all schizophrenics.

Undifferentiated Schizophrenia

Forty percent of all patients diagnosed with schizophrenia have patterns of disordered behavior, thought, and emotion that cannot be neatly classified into any of the other three subtypes. In some cases, a patient previously diagnosed into one of the other subtypes is reclassified as suffering from *undifferentiated schizophrenia,* because the set of symptoms has changed. Such symptom shifting is not uncommon and explains why so many schizophrenic patients are classified into the undifferentiated subtype.

Residual Schizophrenia

Individuals who have had prior episodes of any of the previously mentioned subtypes of schizophrenia but are not currently experiencing the major symptoms of the disorder are classified as having *residual schizophrenia.* Although these persons do not display noticeably prominent psychotic symptoms, they may occasionally express mild symptoms, such as blunted or inappropriate emotions, loose associations, social withdrawal, and eccentric behavior. The frequency of occurrence of this subtype varies.

Etiology of Schizophrenia

The current consensus is that schizophrenia has a strong genetic basis (Chen et al., 2005; Gruzelier, 2002). For example, although 1 percent of the general population develops schizophrenia in their lifetime, from 10 to 15 percent of first-degree relatives (parents, children, siblings) of a schizophrenic patient also develop schizophrenia (Willerman & Cohen, 1990). This holds true whether a person is reared in the same household as the schizophrenic person or in an adoptive, nonschizophrenic home. Perhaps most convincing is the evidence from twin studies. Among fraternal-twin pairs in which one member displays schizophrenia, the other members have about a 15 percent risk of also developing the disorder, about the same as for non-twin siblings. However, among identical twins, the risk jumps to almost 50 percent (Tsuang, 2000). Figure 13-7 depicts these findings.

What biological condition is inherited that may predispose the development of schizophrenia? Most antipsychotic medications that control the symptoms of schizophrenia have

Figure 13-7

Risk of Developing Schizophrenia

The lifetime risk of developing schizophrenia increases with genetic closeness to relatives with schizophrenia.

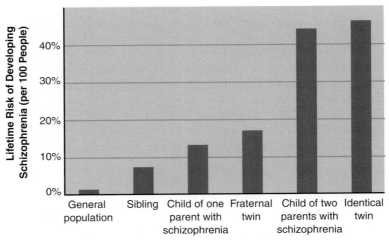

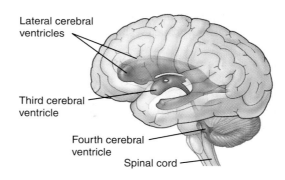

Lateral cerebral ventricles

Third cerebral ventricle

Fourth cerebral ventricle

Spinal cord

Figure 13-8

Brain Abnormalities in Schizophrenia

The hollow cavities in the brain (ventricles) are filled with cerebrospinal fluid. Brain scans suggest that schizophrenics may have enlarged ventricles, as shown here, which is consistent with additional findings that schizophrenics have fewer brain neurons than do normal individuals. This shrinkage of the brain may be caused by excessive destruction of neurons and their interconnections that occurs during adolescent brain maturation.

the effect of decreasing the amount and/or activity of dopamine, a neurotransmitter that facilitates movement and influences thought and emotion (see chapter 3, section 3-1c). Amphetamines and other medications that increase the amount or activity of dopamine can induce symptoms that mimic those of schizophrenia (Green, 1998; Meltzer, 1979). Further, autopsies of schizophrenic patients often reveal an unusually high number of dopamine receptors in the brain (Seeman et al., 1993). Thus, compelling evidence indicates that increased dopamine activity is related to schizophrenia. Perhaps schizophrenic patients see and hear things that are not there and have racing thoughts they cannot control because the dopamine pathways in their brains are overactive.

As illustrated in figure 13-8, brain scans of some schizophrenic patients also show an enlargement of the fluid-filled brain cavities called *cerebral ventricles* and a corresponding shrinkage in the surrounding cerebral cortex (Raz & Raz, 1990; Wright et al., 2000). What might have triggered this shrinkage of the cerebral cortex? Because schizophrenia often develops at about the same time that rapid changes are occurring in the adolescent brain (see chapter 4, section 4-5b), some neuroscientists suggest that this disorder is caused by excessive pruning of neurons and their interconnections (Thompson et al., 2001). Evidence supporting this theory comes from MRI studies indicating that, while average adolescents lose about 15 percent of their neural mass during this important stage of brain maturation, those who develop schizophrenia lose as much as 25 percent (Gogtay et al., 2004; Keller et al., 2003; Sporn et al., 2003). Related to these findings are studies suggesting that some of the hormones flooding the brain during puberty may activate previously dormant "vulnerability genes" that cause the type of abnormal brain development associated with schizophrenia (Walker & Bollini, 2002). Thus, the development of schizophrenia may be at least partially caused by an overzealous process of brain sculpting during the teen years (Selemon et al., 2005).

Regarding behavioral explanations for schizophrenia, during the 1950s some theorists proposed that the disorder might directly result from disturbed family interactions that teach children to communicate in a confusing fashion (Bateson et al., 1956; Mednick, 1958). By the 1970s, this "disturbed family" explanation lost much of its influence among mental health professionals, because it had received very little empirical support. However, although behavioral explanations do not appear to act alone in causing schizophrenia, the diathesis-stress model suggests that they may interact with biological factors in triggering the onset of the disorder (Fowles, 1992; Wearden et al., 2000). For example, poor parenting and the development of inadequate social and coping skills may influence the course of the disorder by increasing the stress level of individuals who are biologically predisposed for schizophrenia (Walker & Diforio, 1998). By contrast, individuals who face similar environmental stressors but do not have the necessary biological vulnerability (the diathesis) will not develop schizophrenia. Currently, the diathesis-stress model, which considers the interaction of both biological and environmental factors, provides the best explanation of this highly complex psychological disorder. This disorder does have a strong genetic component, but what is inherited is not the disorder itself but a state of vulnerability manifested by neuropsychological impairment (Byrne et al., 2003).

One social fact that bears mentioning and discussion is that there are higher rates of schizophrenia among poor people in the United States than among the middle and upper socioeconomic classes (Gottesman, 1991). What accounts for this difference? The *social causation hypothesis* contends that membership in the lowest social classes may actually cause schizophrenia. According to this sociocultural explanation, members of the lowest social classes receive the smallest share of the society's assets, such as quality education, employment, and health care, while receiving most of its liabilities, such as high crime and poor housing. Because many members of the lower classes are minorities, they must also battle prejudice and discrimination. Together, these social factors create a very stressful environment that might lead to the development of schizophrenia. This idea that social factors cause schizophrenia due to their effect on people's level of stress is consistent with the diathesis-stress model. The higher stress levels found among the lower classes may interact with predisposing biological factors to elicit schizophrenic symptoms. These biological factors may exist in equal frequencies among members of higher socioeconomic classes, but they are less likely to trigger the disorder due to lower stress levels.

An alternative explanation of the relationship between socioeconomic status and schizophrenia is the *downward social drift hypothesis,* which contends that schizophrenia develops at equal rates across the social classes, but once the disorder develops, those afflicted descend into poverty (Mulvany et al., 2001). Thus, instead of highlighting the stress caused by poverty (as the social causation hypothesis does), this explanation represents a straightforward biological approach to understanding schizophrenia.

At this point, it is not clear which of these two hypotheses concerning the relationship between social class and schizophrenia is correct. Perhaps both perspectives provide one piece of the puzzle in understanding this complex disorder.

13-3e Somatoform Disorders Are Characterized by Physical Complaints without Physical Causes

somatoform disorders
Psychological disorders involving some body symptom, even though there is no actual physical cause of the symptom.

Somatoform disorders are psychological problems that involve some body symptom, even though no actual physical cause of the symptom can be found. Thus, somatoform disorders are distinct from the *psychophysiological disorders* discussed in chapter 15, which are actual physical conditions—such as high blood pressure, migraine headaches, or asthma—that are caused or aggravated by psychological factors such as stress (Fink et al., 2004). Let us examine four distinct somatoform disorders—namely, *conversion disorder, somatization disorder, hypochondriasis,* and *body dysmorphic disorder.*

Conversion Disorder

conversion disorder
A somatoform disorder characterized by a specific sensory or motor symptom that has a psychological rather than a physical basis.

Conversion disorder is characterized by a specific sensory or motor symptom that has no physical basis and is presumed to be due to psychological factors. Classic examples of conversion disorder include the soldier who develops paralysis in his hand (called "glove anesthesia"; see figure 13-9) so he cannot hold or fire his weapon, and the mother who sees her child killed in a traffic accident and is "struck blind." This disorder is not common, occurring in .01 to .5 percent of

Figure 13-9

Conversion Disorder

An example of conversion disorder is "glove anesthesia," characterized by numbness in the entire hand, ending at the wrist. The skin areas served by nerves in the arm are shown in (*a*). Glove anesthesia, depicted in (*b*), cannot be caused by damage to these nerves.

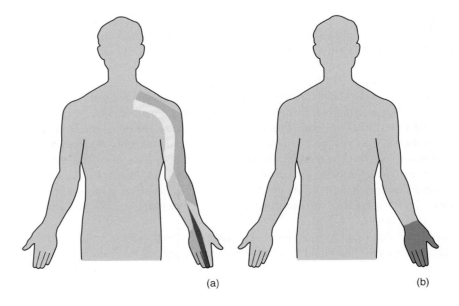

(a)   (b)

the general population (American Psychiatric Association, 2000). It occurs more frequently in women than in men and more often in individuals whose education, income, and understanding of medical and psychological concepts are below average (Cassady et al., 2005).

Related to conversion disorder is *pain disorder,* in which the body symptom for which there is no physical basis is pain. Given that many medical conditions are associated with undifferentiated pain and are difficult to detect in their early stages, the diagnosis of pain disorder is difficult.

Adding to the difficulty of diagnosing conversion and pain disorders are other conditions that may be associated with medical symptoms. For example, some individuals *malinger,* which means they deliberately produce or misreport symptoms in order to gain some clear external incentive. A child may lie about having a stomachache to avoid going to school, a soldier may lie about being sick to avoid being shipped out to a war zone, and a person may exaggerate symptoms following an accident to gain increased insurance benefits. Malingering is not a psychological disorder, but it does make proper diagnosis of conversion and pain disorders more difficult.

Somatization Disorder

Somatization disorder is a somatoform disorder characterized by a *series* of physical complaints that do not have a physical basis. These symptoms include pain, gastrointestinal symptoms, sexual symptoms, and pseudoneurological symptoms, such as impaired coordination, paralysis, and hallucinations. As with conversion disorder, the physical symptoms of somatization disorder do not have a physical basis and are not being deliberately faked or misreported. However, this disorder differs from conversion disorder in that it tends to be more chronic and more associated with emotional and personality problems (Willerman & Cohen, 1990). In addition, adoption studies indicate that somatization disorder has a genetic influence, whereas no clear family pattern is apparent in conversion disorder (Sigvardsson et al., 1984).

> **somatization disorder**
> A somatoform disorder characterized by a series of numerous physical complaints that have a psychological rather than a physical basis.

Hypochondriasis

A fourth somatoform disorder is **hypochondriasis,** which is characterized by excessive preoccupation with or fear of developing some physical condition. This concern is not consistent with the person's actual medical condition and is resistant to reassurance from a physician. When a physician refers such a patient to a psychotherapist, the patient often seeks out another physician rather than admitting that the problem is psychological. Largely due to this fact, relatively little research has been conducted on hypochondriasis. Existing evidence does suggest that this disorder is relatively common in medical settings (occurring in 2–7 percent of patients in general medical practice), tends to occur in early adulthood, and generally is a chronic condition throughout the person's life (American Psychiatric Association, 2000). Because hypochondriasis involves fear of a specific thing (a disease), it shares some qualities with certain types of phobic anxiety disorder, such as fear of germs. The difference is that, whereas a phobic person has an irrational fear of getting a serious disease by coming into contact with specific objects or situations (germs or unsanitary conditions), a hypochondriac is fearful of already having the disease.

> **hypochondriasis**
> A somatoform disorder characterized by excessive preoccupation with or fear of developing some physical condition.

Body Dysmorphic Disorder

The final somatoform disorder is **body dysmorphic disorder,** characterized by preoccupation with an imagined defect in one's physical appearance that causes significant distress or interferes with daily functioning. Even if an actual physical problem is present, the person's preoccupation with this condition is excessive. Body dysmorphic disorder has received relatively little attention from psychologists, largely because sufferers often seek out plastic surgeons rather than psychologists for a remedy. In such cases, individuals may undergo multiple plastic surgeries to correct what they believe is a defect in their appearance. In chapter 15, section 15-3b, we discuss in greater detail how culture and gender shape body esteem.

> **body dysmorphic disorder**
> A somatoform disorder characterized by preoccupation with an imagined physical defect that causes significant distress or interferes with daily functioning.

Etiology of Somatoform Disorders

As discussed in chapter 12, section 12-2, Freud originally developed psychoanalytic theory to explain conversion disorders. As a neurologist, he saw patients whose medical problems could not be explained by physicians. One of his earliest attempts to apply psychoanalytic theory to explain psychopathology occurred in the case of Anna O. (Breuer & Freud, 1893/1955). Anna O. was a young woman whose symptoms—including loss of feeling and motion in her limbs, loss of speech, hallucinations, and "hysterical" pregnancy—defied medical explanation. Freud suggested that Anna O. had troubling material in her unconscious related to her father (she had recently nursed her father while he had a serious illness). Because she was unable to admit this troubling material to herself, Freud believed that it had been repressed to her unconscious. However, because the material was powerful, Freud further believed that it sought expression in some form. According to Freud, this material was *converted* to the series of physical symptoms that Anna O. developed. Freud considered these symptoms to symbolize, in some form, the nature of the underlying troubling material.

Besides this psychoanalytic explanation, more recent studies suggest that the people more prone to develop somatoform disorders are those with *histrionic* personality traits (Slavney, 1990). That is, such individuals tend to be self-centered, suggestible, extremely emotional, and overly dramatic—exactly the personality style that thrives on the attention received during illness.

A cognitive-behavioral explanation suggests that individuals with conversion disorder may have, in the past, been reinforced for reporting medical symptoms. For example, when sick, the individual has not had to go to school, attend work, or perform other arduous tasks. Similarly, as a child, the individual may have malingered, deliberately faking sickness to avoid going to school on the day of an exam. It is possible that, through repeated reinforcement, the individual has learned to report symptoms when stressed. This may become so automatic that the individual is not aware that the symptoms he or she is reporting are not real.

Although personality and cognitive-behavioral factors appear to account for a large portion of somatoform disorders, biological factors may account for certain cases. For example, some individuals initially diagnosed with conversion disorder later develop a clear medical problem that probably accounted for their initial symptoms (Shalev & Munitz, 1986). The likelihood that their initial physical symptoms were caused by real medical problems demonstrates that psychologists should diagnose somatoform disorders cautiously, in conjunction with appropriate medical evaluations.

13-3f Personality Disorders Are Inflexible Behavior Patterns That Impair Social Functioning

personality disorders
Psychological disorders characterized by general styles of living that are ineffective and that lead to problems.

A final category of psychological problems is composed of the personality disorders. **Personality disorders** differ from the other psychological disorders considered so far in that personality disorders are not associated with specific symptoms that cause distress or interfere with daily functioning (Shedler & Westen, 2004). Instead, they are characterized by general styles of living that are ineffective and lead to problems for the person and for others. Personality disorders develop by adolescence or young adulthood and typically persist for a long time. They are associated with personality traits that are extreme and inflexible, and that ultimately lead the person to have problems in daily functioning. Often, individuals with personality disorder do not consider their personality to be a problem but instead blame others for their problems. The current *DSM* diagnostic system classifies 10 personality disorders (Lewin et al., 2005; Skodol, 2005). Table 13-3 lists and briefly describes each of these personality disorders.

Three of the more common personality disorders are the paranoid personality, the histrionic personality, and the narcissistic personality. People with paranoid personalities are habitually distrustful and suspicious of others' motives, and thus they expect their friends and family members to be disloyal. Histrionic personalities are excessively emotional and attention-seeking, often turning minor incidents into full-blown dramas. If they are not the center of attention, they become upset and may do something inappropriate to regain the spotlight. Narcissistic personalities also seek attention, but what they desire is constant admiration from others. Their overblown sense of self-importance and egocentric focus make them feel entitled to special privileges without any kind of reciprocation on their part (Corbitt, 2002). As with the other personality disorders, individuals with these three disorders are extremely difficult to live with on an everyday basis.

Table 13-3	Types and Symptoms of Personality Disorders
Type	**Major Symptoms**
Paranoid	Distrust and suspiciousness of others
Schizoid	Detachment from social relationships and restricted range of emotions
Schizotypal	Cognitive and perceptual distortions and eccentricities of behavior
Antisocial	Disregard for and violation of the rights of others
Borderline	Instability of interpersonal relationships, self-image, and emotion
Histrionic	Excessive emotionality and attention-seeking
Narcissistic	Grandiosity, need for admiration, and lack of empathy
Avoidant	Social inhibition, feelings of inadequacy, and hypersensitivity to negative evaluation
Dependent	Excessive need to be taken care of, submissive and clinging behavior, and fear of separation
Obsessive-compulsive	Preoccupation with orderliness, perfectionism, and control

Antisocial Personality Disorder

By far, the personality disorder that has received the most attention is the **antisocial personality disorder,** also referred to as *psychopathy.* Psychopaths are individuals who exhibit a persistent pattern of disregard for and violation of the rights of others. They repeatedly exhibit antisocial behavior across all realms of life, often lying, cheating, stealing, and manipulating others to get what they want. When other people catch them in their deceit, psychopaths fail to take responsibility and do not exhibit remorse (Harpur et al., 2002).

Although this description sounds nasty, psychopaths surprisingly are often charming and likable. They have learned how to manipulate people to get what they want and can lie without hesitation or guilt. In the movie *Pacific Heights,* Michael Keaton portrays a psychopath who wickedly manipulates a young couple, first charming them into leasing an apartment, and then taking advantage of them for monetary gain. When the couple realizes his deceit, Keaton's character convinces the police and others in the legal system that he is in the right. Psychopathy occurs in about 3 percent of males and about 1 percent of females (American Psychiatric Association, 2000). At present, there is no effective treatment to permanently alter the behavior patterns of antisocial personalities (Rice, 1997).

Etiology of Personality Disorders

Research since the 1970s suggests that personality disorders have a genetic component, perhaps related to abnormal brain development or chronic underarousal of both the autonomic and the central nervous systems (Irle et al., 2005; Slutske et al., 2001). Most of this research has focused on the possible causes of antisocial personality disorder. One study of 14,000 adoptions found that adopted-away sons of fathers with a criminal background are themselves at increased risk for experiencing legal problems as adults, even when reared by noncriminal adoptive fathers (Hutchings & Mednick, 1977; Mednick et al., 1987). Further, this study found that, the more habitual the criminal history of the father, the more likely that the adopted-away son will engage in criminal behavior. Similarly, large-scale twin studies indicate that identical twins resemble one another with respect to various types of antisocial behavior more than fraternal twins do (Lykken, 1995; Lyons et al., 1995). At the brain activity level, the fact that psychopathic individuals tend to have higher pain thresholds and do not experience fear or anxiety nearly to the same degree as the average person suggests that they have a lower overall level of nervous system arousal (Lykken, 1995). This lower arousal may partly explain why these people engage in sensation-seeking behavior and do not learn from punishment.

antisocial personality disorder A personality disorder characterized by a persistent pattern of disregard for and violation of the rights of others.

Every normal man must be tempted at times to spit upon his hands, hoist the black flag, and begin slitting throats.

—*H. L. Mencken, American political commentator, 1880–1956*

Good people do not need laws to tell them to act responsibly, while bad people will find a way around the laws.

—*Plato, Greek philosopher, 427–347 B.C.*

The current thinking about antisocial personality disorder is that both biological and environmental factors interact to cause the problem (Norden et al., 1995; Paris, 1997). For instance, there may be a biological predisposition, such as a neurological influence on impulse control. Children with this predisposition who are reared in chaotic households may not learn to control their impulses and so behave in ways to maximize their benefit, even if this means violating social rules. On the other hand, children with this predisposition who are reared in more stable homes are more likely to acquire self-control techniques so they do not act to satisfy their immediate impulses.

Section Review

- The *DSM* lists major classes of psychological disorders.
- Anxiety disorders are characterized by distressing, persistent anxiety or maladaptive behavior.
- Mood disorders are characterized by emotional extremes that cause significant disruption in daily functioning.
- Dissociative disorders are characterized by disruptions in consciousness, memory, sense of identity, or perception.
- Schizophrenia is characterized by severe impairment in thinking, such as hallucinations, delusions, or loose associations.
- Somatoform disorders involve some body symptom that has no physical cause.
- In individuals with personality disorders, their general styles of living are ineffective and lead to problems.

Psychological Applications

Some Important Facts about Suicide

There are many misconceptions about suicide. In this section, let me address five commonly asked questions concerning this important issue and provide information that may prove helpful to you now or in the future (Goldston, 2003).

- *Does suicide run in families?* Not exactly. People who have major mood disorders, such as severe depression and bipolar disorder, are at increased risk for suicide. It is possible to find families that have histories of suicide across generations (Egeland & Sussex, 1985), but the genetic influence appears to be related to the mood disorder rather than to suicide itself.
- *Is it true that people who talk about suicide never commit suicide?* No! This is a dangerous misconception. One of the best predictors of suicide risk is a stated threat to commit suicide. In fact, 80 percent of all suicides are preceded by some form of warning (Schneidman, 1987). Psychologists therefore take every threat of suicide seriously, at least until they can conduct a thorough evaluation of risk in the individual case. Some threats may be veiled. For example, a person may give away her prized possessions or talk about "getting away to end my problems." Observers should be sensitive to such hints of suicidal thinking and should ask direct questions about the person's intentions.

- *Does every person who attempts suicide truly want to die?* No! Some suicide attempts are designed more to get attention and help than to die. For example, a person who takes a half-bottle of baby aspirin or who scratches his wrist with nail clippers may not truly have intended to die. Such nonlethal attempts are called "suicidal gestures" and are considered cries for help. However, psychologists must be careful when working with clients who have histories of suicidal gestures, because such clients are often not thinking in a rational manner (Jollant et al., 2005). The fact that a person has made several suicidal gestures in the past does not mean that she or he will not make a more lethal attempt in the future (Cooper et al., 2005). Also, some persons who make suicidal gestures make a mistake and inadvertently kill themselves, even though that may not have been their true intention.
- *Why do men have a higher suicide rate than women?* Even though women attempt suicide more often than men, men have a higher suicide rate. The explanation for this gender difference is complex. Men attempt suicide by using guns, hanging, and leaping from high places more frequently than do women (Rosenberg et al., 1999). Thus, men tend to use methods that are more lethal and less reversible than do women, who more frequently use pills. Although you can

Psychological Applications

—Continued

kill yourself with pills, they take time to work, and thus people have more time to change their minds or be found and saved. Now, why do men and women use these different methods? Perhaps men have more familiarity with and accessibility to firearms than do women, which leads men to select this more lethal method. Or perhaps men are less willing than women to call for help, and so men are less likely to make a suicidal gesture.

• *What should I do if a friend is talking about suicide?* It is important that you take the threat seriously, because many suicide attempts can be prevented by providing those at high risk with help and social support (Joiner, 1999). However, it is also important to recognize that you are not a mental health professional and, thus, are not equipped to evaluate suicide risk or provide psychotherapy. As a friend, you can listen and provide appropriate comfort and support, but it is important to encourage your friend to seek professional help. You can convey the information that depression is not a sign of

weakness or "craziness" but instead is recognized as a mental illness. You can convey the information that depression is well understood by the mental health profession and that there are effective treatments for it. However, it will be up to the mental health professional—not you—to provide this treatment. If your friend does not take your advice, perhaps you can find someone important in your friend's life—a family doctor, a member of the clergy, a family member—who can convince your friend to see a mental health professional. As a last resort, a suicidal individual may be committed against his or her will to a psychiatric hospital for treatment. Commitment procedures vary across states, but they usually require the request of a relative and the opinion of one or more physicians that the individual is dangerous to himself or herself, or dangerous to others, and unable to make decisions in his or her best interest. Although commitment may seem a drastic step, it is far better to commit someone to treatment than lose them through suicide.

Key Terms

agoraphobia (p. 501)

antisocial personality disorder (p. 519)

anxiety disorders (p. 500)

bipolar disorder (p. 508)

body dysmorphic disorder (p. 517)

conversion disorder (p. 516)

culture-bound syndromes (p. 495)

depression (p. 505)

diagnosis (p. 492)

Diagnostic and Statistical Manual of Mental Disorders (DSM) (p. 499)

diathesis-stress model (p. 496)

dissociative amnesia (p. 511)

dissociative disorders (p. 511)

dissociative fugue (p. 511)

dissociative identity disorder (DID) (p. 511)

dysthymia (p. 506)

etiology (p. 492)

generalized anxiety disorder (GAD) (p. 502)

hypochondriasis (p. 517)

mania (p. 508)

medical model (p. 491)

mood disorders (p. 505)

obsessive-compulsive disorder (OCD) (p. 503)

panic disorder (p. 501)

personality disorders (p. 518)

phobic disorder (p. 501)

post-traumatic stress disorder (PTSD) (p. 503)

prognosis (p. 492)

psychological disorder (p. 494)

schizophrenia (p. 512)

seasonal affective disorder (SAD) (p. 509)

somatization disorder (p. 517)

somatoform disorders (p. 516)

stigma (p. 498)

symptom (p. 492)

Suggested Websites

National Institute of Mental Health (NIMH)
http://www.nimh.nih.gov
This website, intended for both the general public and mental health professionals, includes information on various psychological disorders.

The Anxiety Panic Internet Resource
http://www.algy.com/anxiety
This website is a self-help network that provides information and support for people who suffer from anxiety disorders.

Depression Central
http://www.psycom.net/depression.central.html
This website provides information on mood disorders.

Dissociation, Trauma, and Recovered Memories
http://www.acsu.buffalo.edu/~jjhall/dissociation.html
This website provides links to other websites with information on various dissociative disorders.

Schizophrenia.com
http://www.schizophrenia.com
This website provides not only information on schizophrenia but also discussion and support groups.

Review Questions

Note: You can find the correct answers to these questions by taking the quiz and then submitting your answers in the Online Edition. The program will automatically score your submission. If you miss a question, the program will provide the correct answer, a rationale for the answer, and the section number in the chapter where the topic is discussed.

1. The diagnosis of psychological disorders relies on specific criteria that distinguish normal from abnormal behavior. One of the most important of these criteria is
   a. an uncontrollable urge for freedom.
   b. behavior that is disruptive or harmful to the individual or others.
   c. behavior that is infrequent in the "normal" population.
   d. extremely odd or eccentric behavior.
   e. personal distress.

2. A variety of theories attempt to explain the etiology of psychological disorders. The cognitive approach explains mental illness primarily as
   a. behavior that has been conditioned through reinforcement and punishment.
   b. resulting from a diathesis-stress model of vulnerability interacting with environmental stressors.
   c. associated with broad sociocultural forces.
   d. a product of unconscious forces shaped by childhood experiences.
   e. a learned pattern of faulty thinking or maladaptive interpretations.

3. The use of diagnostic labels carries both risks and benefits to the patient, including all of the following *except*
   a. confirmation bias, in which expectations of certain behaviors lead to diagnoses that may not exist.
   b. the ability to summarize information concerning the patient's presenting problems.
   c. dehumanization of patients by treating them as "labels" rather than individuals.
   d. a clear association with specific and reliable etiologic factors for all psychological diagnoses.
   e. the suggestion that researchers have identified optimal methods of treatment.

4. What is the term for an attribute that serves to discredit a person in the eyes of others?
   a. stereotype
   b. stigma
   c. schema
   d. schemata
   e. socialization

5. Negative attributions surrounding mental illness can result in which of the following?
   a. avoiding seeking treatment
   b. lowered self-esteem
   c. hopelessness
   d. social isolation
   e. all of the above

6. Research on the association between violence and mental illness has
   a. found that there are no differences between the mentally ill and the general population.
   b. found that there are significant differences between the mentally ill and the general population.
   c. found that, except for extreme cases of severe psychopathology, there are no differences between the mentally ill and the general population.
   d. found that violence levels among the mentally ill and the general population are disturbingly high.
   e. been inconclusive.

7. The *Diagnostic and Statistical Manual of Mental Disorders* is considered a work in progress primarily because
   a. ongoing research seeks to continually improve the reliability and validity of *DSM* diagnoses.
   b. the manual is currently undergoing its first classification revision.
   c. there is a lack of agreement among insurance companies concerning how the *DSM* classifies mental illness.
   d. the etiological descriptions provided by the *DSM* are considered tentative.
   e. the criteria specified for diagnosing mental disorders are vague and unclear.

8. Panic disorder is characterized primarily by which one of the following symptoms?
   a. extended periods of excessive fear lasting for several days at a time
   b. avoidance of places where previous attacks have or have not occurred
   c. brief attacks of intense anxiety that occur for no apparent reason
   d. strong, irrational fears of specific objects or situations
   e. subclinical phobias that do not interfere with normal functioning

9. Obsessive-compulsive disorder is unique in that two relatively distinct types of symptoms are experienced, including
   a. obsessions, which are unwanted, repetitive thoughts; and compulsions, which are repetitive behaviors that may disrupt daily functioning.
   b. obsessions, which are urges to stalk or kill others; and compulsions, which are urges to overeat.
   c. obsessions, such as repeated hand washing; and compulsions, such as fear of contamination.
   d. obsessions, which are urges to perform some type of repetitive or ritual behavior; and compulsions, which are repetitive, intrusive thoughts.
   e. obsessions and compulsions, which are rarely recognized as abnormal by the individual.

10. After the terrorist attacks on September 11, 2001, many people experienced symptoms of post-traumatic stress disorder, generally considered a "normal" or expected reaction to a trauma of such magnitude. However, a more serious disturbance might be indicated if an individual
    a. had repeated intrusive thoughts or images of the attack scene.
    b. made efforts to avoid all reminders of the attacks.
    c. experienced flashbacks or nightmares.
    d. had symptoms that continued for a long period after the attacks, and if the symptoms significantly interfered with the individual's daily functioning.
    e. began to question his or her essential beliefs concerning the nature of good and evil or the just-world phenomenon.

11. Despite the similarities in many of the symptoms of anxiety disorders, a variety of theories have been proposed to explain their causes, including
    a. conditioning explanations for the *initial onset* of generalized anxiety disorder.
    b. hypervigilance as a cause of PTSD.
    c. "fear of fear" explanations for generalized anxiety disorder.
    d. sociological causes of social phobia.
    e. genetic or evolutionary causes of phobias.

12. Mood disorders may involve all the following symptoms *except*
    a. a prolonged feeling of sadness and lethargy.
    b. a change in sleep patterns.
    c. repetitive lying or dishonesty.
    d. difficulties concentrating.
    e. thoughts of suicide.

13. Less common than depression, bipolar disorder
    a. affects only about 9 percent of the population.
    b. is probably caused by the same etiological factors as depression.
    c. follows the same symptom and behavior pattern in all individuals with the disorder.
    d. involves manic behavior, which may be destructive in its consequences.
    e. involves only mild symptoms of mania and depression, but over extended periods.

14. Etiological explanations for depression and bipolar disorder tend to be quite different, although there is some degree of overlap. Bipolar disorder is typically explained by which one of the following?
    a. misinterpretations of daily experiences
    b. a genetic or biological disturbance leading to imbalances in neural circuits
    c. low social reinforcement
    d. childhood loss, with subsequent anger turned against oneself
    e. negative views of oneself, the world, and the future

15. Researchers have determined that there are distinct gender differences in the experience of depression. These have been explained by all of the following *except*
    a. a lack of social support for men, who are less intimate in their friendships than women.
    b. female hormones, which have been associated with depression.
    c. social and cultural factors related to sexism.
    d. statistical error, reflecting greater help seeking by women.
    e. clinicians' gender bias in diagnosing depression.

16. Of all the psychological diagnoses, dissociative disorder is probably the most fascinating, because the symptoms tend to be so unusual. For example, some characteristic symptoms include
    a. a split personality consisting of two personalities, each of whom is aware of what occurs while the other is in control.
    b. the gradual assumption of a new identity, with no awareness by the individual involved and, in dissociative fugue conditions, no return to the previous identity.
    c. a gradual loss of memories threatening to the self, known as dissociative amnesia.
    d. a permanent "dazed" state following a trauma or tragedy.
    e. both male and female personalities, in dissociative identity disorder.

17. Which of the following is *true* of schizophrenia?
    a. It is classified as a psychosis.
    b. It tends to begin in later adulthood.
    c. It involves positive symptoms.
    d. It occurs in about 10 percent of the world's population.
    e. both *a* and *c*

18. Research investigating the etiology of schizophrenia has shown
    a. little family risk beyond that for identical twins, which is very high.
    b. that dopamine-enhancing drugs may cause schizophrenic-like symptoms, suggesting an overactive dopamine system.
    c. an enlargement of the cerebral cortex and corresponding shrinkage of cerebral ventricles.
    d. that disturbed family communication is directly responsible for some types of schizophrenia.
    e. no evidence for prenatal etiologies.

19. Somatoform disorders can be characterized by which of the following?
    a. preoccupation with an imagined defect in one's physical appearance
    b. pain for which there is no physical basis
    c. a sensory or motor symptom that has no physical basis
    d. excessive preoccupation with or fear of developing a physical condition
    e. all of the above

20. Personality disorders differ from other psychological disorders in that
    a. they appear to be caused by the interaction of genetic factors, such as temperament or impulse control, and environmental influences, such as family functioning.
    b. they are almost always attributable to a single cause.
    c. they are associated with maladaptive personality traits and result in longstanding problems with living rather than extreme distress or dysfunction.
    d. individuals with personality disorders are universally unlikable.
    e. personality disorders involve affective, cognitive, and behavioral systems of functioning.

21. Which of the following is a common misconception about suicide?
    a. Women attempt suicide more often than men, but men have a higher suicide rate.
    b. Some suicide attempts are designed more to get attention and help than to die.
    c. People who have major mood disorders are at increased risk of suicide.
    d. People who talk about suicide never commit suicide.
    e. Some suicide threats may be veiled; for example, a person may give away her prized possessions or talk about getting away to end her problems.

Chapter 14

Therapy

Source: fotosearch.com

Imagine, for a minute, that you were born 230 years ago. Further, imagine that you were born with an underlying vulnerability (a *diathesis*) for a specific psychological disorder (see chapter 13, section 13-1c). By the age of 18, you have experienced a number of stressful life events and found it increasingly difficult to carry out your normal daily activities. During the past year, your thinking and behavior have become so disturbed and bizarre that your parents bring you to the Pennsylvania Hospital for medical attention. They tell you that you are lucky, because the doctor who will care for you is Benjamin Rush (1745–1813), the founder of American psychiatry and one of the signers of the Declaration of Independence.

When Dr. Rush first joined the hospital's medical staff in 1783, he was appalled at the atrocious conditions he found there and began implementing reforms. At his urging, psychologically disturbed patients were separated from those who were physically ill and placed in a separate ward, where they began receiving occupational therapy (Maher & Maher, 1985). He also stopped curiosity seekers from coming to the hospital to gawk and laugh at the mentally ill patients. At the time of your admittance, Dr. Rush is being hailed throughout the country as a humane healer of the human psyche.

What sort of enlightened treatment are you likely to receive under Dr. Rush's care? Well, he will probably occasionally puncture your skin and drain "excess" blood from your body, because he believes this is the source of many psychological problems. He may also seal you in a coffinlike box and then briefly submerge you in water, strap and immobilize you in his "tranquilizer" chair, spin you rapidly in a circulating swing, and terrorize you by threatening to have you killed. The rationale behind these therapies is that Dr. Rush and his colleagues believe that fright and disorientation can counteract the overexcitement responsible for your mental illness (Yager, 2005). How lucky do you now feel to be in Dr. Rush's care?

Of course, these remedies are no longer used in mental health facilities to treat psychological disorders. What sorts of remedies are being employed today? If you watch the *Dr. Phil* TV show, you might have a misperception about contemporary psychological therapies. On his show, Dr. Phil McGraw, a licensed psychologist, usually diagnoses problems and formulates solutions for his TV clients within 12 minutes of meeting them, just in time for a commercial break. When he has particularly troubling cases, Dr. Phil asks his TV clients to take a polygraph test to determine whether they are being truthful (not the best way to build trust with a person!). He also spends a great deal of time lecturing TV clients with his "tell-it-like-it-is" style: "There's nowhere to run, nowhere to hide. You're going to get real about fat, or you're going to get real fat!" Dr. Phil also gives advice in the form of obscure proverbs that often make little sense: "You don't need a pack of wild horses to learn how to make a sandwich." Dr. Phil's son, a college student with no psychological training, is a frequent contributor to the show, offering "life strategies" for teenagers.

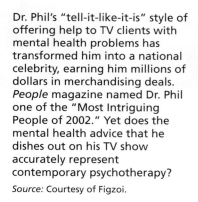

Dr. Phil's "tell-it-like-it-is" style of offering help to TV clients with mental health problems has transformed him into a national celebrity, earning him millions of dollars in merchandising deals. *People* magazine named Dr. Phil one of the "Most Intriguing People of 2002." Yet does the mental health advice that he dishes out on his TV show accurately represent contemporary psychotherapy?

Source: Courtesy of Figzoi.

Although the *Dr. Phil* show may have entertainment value for many viewers, the people who appear on the show suffering from painful psychological problems are not receiving psychological therapy from this TV celebrity (Levenson, 2005). Dr. Phil does not accurately represent the therapeutic practice of psychology. In this chapter, we continue our journey of discovery through the mental health field by examining various methods employed by professionals in helping individuals deal with psychological problems. As you learn about these contemporary therapies, periodically ask yourself whether any of them bear a resemblance to the methods employed by Dr. Rush or Dr. Phil.

14-1 WHO OFFERS THERAPIES FOR PSYCHOLOGICAL DISORDERS?

Preview

- *What are the two broad categories of therapy?*
- *Which mental health professionals can provide therapy?*
- *What training and expertise do therapists have?*

Just as there are different types of psychological disorders for which people seek therapy (see chapter 13), there are many types of therapists and therapeutic methods. In beginning our examination of the treatment of psychological disorders, I first identify two main categories of therapy and then describe the types of therapists who are trained as mental health professionals.

14-1a There Are Both Psychological and Biomedical Therapies

In treating psychological disorders, the two broad categories of therapy are psychological and medical. As discussed in chapter 8, section 8-1a, if you think of the mind as being like a computer, then mental health problems can originate in either the brain's software or its hardware. Psychologically oriented therapies typically seek solutions for what are believed to be "software" problems, while medically oriented therapies try to repair "hardware" problems. Psychological therapy, or **psychotherapy,** employs psychological methods that include a personal relationship between a trained therapist and a client. Its focus is to change the disordered thoughts, behaviors, and emotions associated with specific psychological disorders. In contrast, **biomedical therapies** treat psychological disorders by altering brain functioning through use of physical or chemical interventions.

When Sigmund Freud developed psychoanalytic therapy in the late 1800s, only a handful of practitioners employed psychological principles to treat patients. The very limited range of psychological methods used prior to Freud included hypnosis, emotional support, and direct education (Ellenberger, 1970). Today, mental health experts have identified more than 400 forms of psychotherapy within each of the major theoretical schools of psychology (Bergin & Garfield, 1994; Corsini & Wedding, 2001). In addition to traditional Freudian psychoanalysis, dozens of variations of therapy are based on Freudian concepts. Likewise, there are dozens of applications of cognitive-behavior therapies for different psychological problems, such as panic disorder and depression.

Besides the numerous therapies within each theoretical school, psychotherapy and biomedical therapies are also delivered in many formats. Whereas Freud primarily provided psychotherapy to individual adult clients, contemporary therapists provide treatment to children, groups, families, and couples. The following sections will introduce you to a variety of psychotherapies based on specific theoretical orientations, as well as some biomedical therapies that involve surgery, electric shock, and drugs.

> **psychotherapy** The treatment of psychological disorders by employing psychological methods that include a personal relationship between a trained therapist and a client.

> **biomedical therapies** The treatment of psychological disorders by altering brain functioning with physical or chemical interventions.

14-1b Three Primary Mental Health Professions Provide Therapy

The three mental health professions that provide most of the therapy to people suffering from psychological disorders are psychiatry, social work, and psychology (Peterson et al.,

1996). Psychiatrists are medical doctors (M.D.s) who have received subsequent training in treating mental and emotional disorders. As physicians, psychiatrists can prescribe medications, and thus biomedical therapy is an important aspect of their practice. They also receive training in psychotherapy and so may provide various kinds of "talk" therapy.

Most social workers have obtained a master's degree in social work (M.S.W.) in a 2-year graduate program after completing their undergraduate work; a smaller percentage have their doctorate (D.S.W.). Clinical and psychiatric social workers provide psychotherapy and coordinate with social support agencies that may offer assistance—such as shelter, vocational training, or financial aid—to clients. They often explain problems in terms of how clients interact with their family and social surroundings.

The third major mental health profession that offers therapy to individuals with psychological problems is psychology. Psychologists have earned either a master's or a doctoral degree. Most frequently, a psychologist's doctoral degree is the doctorate in philosophy (Ph.D.). However, some doctoral degrees in psychology are the doctorate in psychology (Psy.D.) or the doctorate in education (Ed.D.). In contrast to social workers and medical doctors, psychologists who receive training in psychotherapy also receive extensive training in conducting scientific research (less true for the Psy.D.). In most states, a doctoral degree is required to practice independently as a psychologist. However, it is possible to work with a master's degree as a staff therapist within many hospitals and clinics where supervision from doctoral staff members is available. Except in New Mexico and Louisiana, psychologists are not authorized to prescribe drugs. Currently, the American Psychological Association is working to help obtain prescription privileges for qualified psychologists in the remaining 48 states (Dittmann, 2003; Holloway, 2004).

Two specialty areas in psychology—clinical psychology and counseling—provide psychotherapy. Clinical psychology is the field that works with psychological disorders—their assessment, explanation, and treatment. Counseling psychology is the field that works with essentially "normal" individuals who experience problems in living and so could benefit from educational, vocational, or personal counseling. The fields of clinical and counseling psychology overlap in that both specialties provide outpatient psychotherapy for mildly disturbed clients (Plante, 2005; Shakow, 2002). However, the two fields remain distinct.

There are several general differences in the theoretical perspectives across these professions. For example, counseling psychologists tend to place less emphasis on biological factors and more frequently adopt a holistic (or "whole person") approach compared to clinical psychologists (Johnson & Brems, 1991). Social workers often utilize more sociological and cultural approaches to therapy than do psychologists (Wierzbicki, 1997). Finally, psychiatrists rely more on biological models when explaining disorders than do clinical psychologists (Kingsbury, 1987). Table 14-1 provides some demographic information on the people in each of these three mental health professions.

Despite these general differences, it is important to remember that all three mental health professions can provide various types of therapy. Training in one profession does not restrict individual practitioners from specializing in any particular theoretical approach to therapy. For example, I have known psychiatrists who use humanistic psychotherapy, clini-

Table **14-1** Profiles of Mental Health Professionals					
	Degree	Current Number in U.S.	Median Age	Female (%)	Male (%)
Psychiatrists	M.D.	33,500	52	25	75
Clinical and psychiatric social workers	D.S.W., M.S.W.	189,000	47	77	23
Clinical and counseling psychologists	Ph.D., Psy.D., Ed.D.	70,000	48	44	56

Source: Peterson et al., 1996.

cal social workers who are behaviorists, and counseling psychologists who have a biological orientation. Therapists who combine techniques from various theoretical perspectives in treating psychological disorders are said to have an **eclectic approach** (Stricker, 1996).

Given the reality of managed care today, mental health providers often work together as a team to treat individuals suffering from psychological disorders. An individual case is likely to be referred from a primary care physician to a psychiatrist, who then refers the client to a psychologist and/or a clinical social worker. Particularly for more serious conditions, such as schizophrenia and drug addiction, a social worker is often involved in training the client in basic life skills, a psychologist has numerous "talk therapy" sessions with the client, and a psychiatrist monitors and adjusts medications.

Other health professionals may also become involved with patients who have psychological disorders. For example, nurses, occupational therapists, physical therapists, speech therapists, and other health professionals may work in mental health settings. Although they are not primarily trained as therapists, their work with patients suffering from psychological disorders may involve basic psychotherapeutic strategies.

Also, it is possible for people who do not have professional degrees to provide specific forms of therapy. For example, many states permit individuals to become certified drug counselors or marriage counselors if they have completed a series of undergraduate or graduate courses. I have also known many college students who have provided behavior therapy to autistic children. In these cases, the service provider must be trained to provide a specific intervention and must be appropriately supervised by an experienced psychotherapist. If you decide to pursue a major in psychology, at some point in your college education you may receive training as a volunteer service provider.

> **eclectic approach** An approach to psychotherapy in which techniques from various theoretical perspectives are used in treating psychological disorders.

Section Review

- The two broad categories of mental health therapies are psychotherapies (which employ psychological theories in treating disorders) and biomedical therapies (which involve altering brain function by means of physical or chemical interventions).
- Therapy is delivered through many different approaches and with many different formats.
- Therapy is primarily provided by three mental health professions: psychiatry, social work, and psychology.
- Each profession has its own area of expertise, and each can provide various forms of psychotherapy.

14-2 PSYCHODYNAMIC THERAPIES

Preview

- *What is the goal of psychodynamic therapy?*
- *What treatment techniques do psychodynamic therapists use?*
- *What are two important drawbacks to psychodynamic therapies?*
- *How have followers of Freud modified psychoanalytic therapy?*

Psychodynamic therapies are a diverse group of therapies, descended from the work of Sigmund Freud, which assert that psychological disorders stem primarily from unconscious forces. All these variations of Freudian therapy are included under the heading *psychodynamic therapy* because, like Freud, they stress the importance of understanding the *psychological dynamics* underlying behavior.

> **psychodynamic therapies** A diverse group of psychotherapies based on the work of Sigmund Freud that assert that psychological disorders stem primarily from unconscious forces.

14-2a Psychoanalysis Laid the Groundwork for Psychodynamic Therapies

Freudian therapy, as practiced originally by Freud himself, is called psychoanalysis. Psychoanalysis dominated the field of psychotherapy throughout the first half of the 1900s. Many of the leading figures in other theoretical schools of therapy, such as Carl Rogers, Frederick Perls, Albert Ellis, and Aaron Beck—all of whose ideas on therapy are discussed later in this chapter—were originally trained in psychoanalysis.

As discussed in chapters 12 and 13, Freud asserted that some traumatic childhood event, often sexual or aggressive in nature, leaves people with troubling memories or feelings. To manage the resulting anxiety, people repress the troubling material. Although this material is now unconscious, it continues to have a powerful effect on their functioning and eventually causes psychological symptoms. In other words, people experience problematic behaviors or feelings without being aware of the true, underlying cause of the symptoms. According to Freud, since the cause of the patient's problem is unconscious, the goal of therapy is to bring the troubling material into conscious awareness. This process of helping clients understand their own psychological processes is called *insight* (McCabe & Quayle, 2002). For this reason, psychodynamic therapy is often called *insight-oriented*.

When clients gain insight into the underlying troubling material, they can then express the emotional energy associated with this unconscious material. This release of pent-up emotion, called *catharsis*, is an important aspect of psychodynamic therapy. In addition to discharging the emotions associated with the previously unconscious troubling material, clients can now deal with this troubling material in a conscious, rational, and more effective manner.

14-2b Free Association Is the Primary Psychodynamic Technique

free association
A psychodynamic therapy technique developed by Freud, in which clients say whatever comes to mind, without making any effort to inhibit their speech.

All Freudian-based therapy techniques are directed toward helping the client gain insight. The primary technique in Freudian therapy (what Freud called the "fundamental rule" of psychoanalysis) is **free association,** in which the clients say aloud whatever comes to mind, making no deliberate attempt to inhibit their speech. According to Freud, free association gives unconscious troubling material the opportunity to come forth, perhaps allowing clients to suddenly recall important events from childhood. Free association may yield important information in other ways as well. For instance, while freely associating, clients may be unable to think of a word or finish a sentence. They may also suddenly change topics or begin to stammer. According to Freud, such responses often occur when clients are close to achieving insight concerning sensitive unconscious subjects, and their defense mechanisms attempt to block this therapeutic breakthrough.

The psychodynamic therapist also draws inferences from special types of slips of the tongue, known as *Freudian slips*, which are instances when the client means to say one thing but actually says something else (see chapter 9, section 9-1f). For example, if the client means to say, "I love my wife" but actually says, "I leave my wife," the therapist would interpret this slip as communicating an unconscious desire.

transference The process by which the client develops feelings for the therapist that are presumed to reflect the client's feelings for significant others early in life.

The psychodynamic therapist also interprets the underlying meaning in other forms of expression: dreams, daydreams, artwork, poetry, and so on. Freud thought that almost everything we do is caused by unconscious influences. Through interpreting the symbols in the client's dreams and artwork, the therapist may come to understand the client's unconscious.

According to psychodynamic therapy, the client often develops strong positive or negative feelings for the therapist, which is called **transference** (Scaturo, 2005). Feeling admiration and even romantic love for the therapist is a common form of positive transference, while feeling resentment and anger are common forms of negative transference. Freud interpreted transference as representing feelings that the client experienced toward others early in life. If the client becomes dependent on the therapist, this may mean that the client was overly dependent on parents during childhood. If the client resents the authority of the therapist, perhaps the client was resentful of his or her parents as a child.

countertransference The process by which the therapist develops feelings for the client that are presumed to reflect feelings the therapist had for others early in life.

Freud also warned therapists that they may in turn develop similarly strong feelings for their clients. This **countertransference** represents feelings that the therapist experienced toward others early in life (Bernard, 2005). Freud strongly recommended that therapists attend to these feelings so they gain greater insight into their unconscious desires and thereby make these feelings less likely to interfere with treatment of clients.

resistance Anything the client does to interfere with therapeutic progress.

Another important aspect of the client-therapist relationship in Freudian therapy is resistance. **Resistance** is anything the client does that interferes with therapeutic progress.

"I'm so proud. My son visits a fancy psychiatrist five days a week and all he wants to talk about is me."

Source: © Vic Lee. King Features Syndicate.

Over the course of therapy, the client may begin to sabotage therapy by missing or coming late to sessions, talking only about trivial issues, or bringing up significant issues only at the very end of a session so there is no time to address them. According to Freud, the cause of the client's problem is some troubling material in the unconscious. When the client starts making inroads toward identifying this troubling material, the material becomes even more threatening. Thus, even though the client wants to improve, the mind raises its defenses to keep this troubling material unconscious. When this occurs, the therapist's task is to focus the client's attention toward personal issues of which they are not currently aware and then help them make connections between current behavior and childhood experiences.

14-2c Psychodynamic Therapy Is Lengthy and Expensive

One of the primary criticisms of psychodynamic therapy is that it is too lengthy and expensive for all but the very wealthy. At one to three sessions a week at $150 a session, a client would pay between $40,000 and $120,000 after 5 years. A second criticism is that its interpretations can never be disproved. For example, if a therapist interprets a client's tardiness for an appointment as a sign of resistance, the client's attempt to disagree may be perceived as further proof of the initial interpretation.

Though still available, classic psychoanalysis is not widely practiced today. However, as discussed in chapter 12, section 12-2e, followers of Freud have modified his theory and therapy (Davanloo, 1999). Some disagreed with the more extreme aspects of psychoanalysis, while others altered his therapeutic approach to make therapy briefer and more accessible to a wider range of clients.

Alfred Adler was a contemporary of Freud and an early leader in the psychoanalytic movement. In contrast to Freud, Adler considered early family social interactions to be more important influences on the developing personality than unconscious sexual conflicts. For example, he held that birth order shaped people's interactions with their parents and siblings and so was an important influence on personality and psychological problems. As a result, Adlerian therapists place more emphasis on the ego's conscious, rational processes than on the id's unconscious processes.

Carl Jung, Freud's most cherished pupil, was also an early leader in the psychoanalytic movement. Like Adler, Jung de-emphasized sex as the major motivation for human behavior and criticized psychoanalysis as too negative. He also strongly disagreed with Freud's belief that adult personality is determined by early childhood experiences and instead argued that behavior is primarily influenced by future goals. As a result, Jungian therapists emphasize their clients' future possibilities rather than their past experiences. They also compare therapy to a spiritual exercise, in which clients must first "confess" their weaknesses before they can improve.

In traditional psychoanalysis, the client reclines on a couch facing away from the therapist. This placement of the therapist and client is thought to minimize distractions, thus making it easier for the client to verbalize whatever comes to mind. Is classic psychoanalysis widely practiced today?

Source: Courtesy of Figzoi.

In general, the psychodynamic approach has had an enormous impact on the way mental health professionals "do" psychotherapy. First, this perspective has helped demythologize psychological disorders by arguing that "sane" and "insane" behaviors have their psychological roots in the same mental processes. Second, even therapists who reject Freud's theoretical basis for mental illness often still use his therapeutic technique of developing a one-to-one therapist-client relationship aimed at increasing client insight.

Section Review

- The goal of psychodynamic therapy is insight into unconscious, troubling material.
- Free association is the primary technique of psychodynamic therapy.
- Psychodynamic therapy is lengthy and expensive.
- Many current variations of Freud's classic psychoanalysis de-emphasize sex as the primary motivator of behavior; they also tend to downplay the importance of the unconscious and early childhood experiences.

14-3 BEHAVIOR THERAPIES

Preview

- *What is the theoretical foundation of behavior therapy?*
- *What treatment techniques are based on classical conditioning?*
- *What treatment techniques are based on operant conditioning and observational learning?*

Unlike practitioners of the psychodynamic perspective, behaviorists do not believe in the unconscious, and thus, for behaviorists, insight is not important in the treatment of psychological disorders. Instead, psychological disorders and "healthy" behavior both are thought to develop through learning. Thus, in **behavior therapies,** disordered behaviors are unlearned and replaced by more appropriate alternative behaviors (Miltenberger, 2001). In treating clients, behavior therapists employ principles of classical conditioning, operant conditioning, and observational learning.

behavior therapies
Psychotherapies that apply learning principles to the elimination of unwanted behaviors.

14-3a Some Behavior Therapies Rely upon Classical Conditioning

One category of behavior therapy employs the principles of classical conditioning first developed by Ivan Pavlov (see chapter 7, section 7-1a). As you recall, in classical conditioning, an unconditioned stimulus (UCS) automatically elicits an unconditioned response (UCR). The UCS is paired with a neutral stimulus that initially has no effect on the response. However, after repeated pairings of the two stimuli, the previously neutral stimulus, now called the conditioned stimulus (CS), elicits the response, now called the conditioned response (CR).

The most widely used form of psychotherapy based on classical conditioning is **counterconditioning** (Goetestam, 2002), which involves conditioning new responses to stimuli that trigger unwanted behaviors. Three specific counterconditioning techniques are *systematic desensitization, response prevention,* and *aversive conditioning.*

counterconditioning
A behavior therapy procedure based on classical conditioning that involves conditioning new responses to stimuli that trigger unwanted behaviors.

Systematic Desensitization

Systematic desensitization is commonly used to treat people suffering from phobias, by gradually exposing the phobic client to the feared object without arousing anxiety and fear (Wolpe, 1958; Wolpe & Plaud, 1997). Behaviorists hold that the phobia was initially acquired through classical conditioning. That is, the phobic object was originally a neutral stimulus that was then paired with something that naturally elicited fear. A phobia condi-

systematic desensitization
A counterconditioning technique commonly used to treat phobias, in which the client is gradually exposed to the feared object while remaining relaxed.

tioned in this way can be counterconditioned by pairing the feared object with relaxation or another physiological state incompatible with anxiety and fear.

Mary Cover Jones (1896–1987), one of John Watson's students, was the first psychologist to demonstrate that conditioned fears could be reversed. She treated a 3-year-old boy, Peter, who had a fear of furry objects very similar to that of Watson's famous "Little Albert B." Therapy involved feeding Peter at one end of a room while a rabbit was brought in at the other end. After several sessions of slowly closing the distance between Peter and the rabbit, the boy's fear disappeared (Jones, 1924). Jones is often called "the mother of behavior therapy."

Today, therapists employing systematic desensitization follow a similar strategy as did Jones. For example, suppose a client has a fear of snakes. The client and therapist begin by constructing a *desensitization hierarchy,* which consists of a sequence of increasingly anxiety-provoking situations related to snakes (see table 14-2). The therapist then trains the client in relaxation exercises, such as slow breathing or muscle relaxation. The first step of the hierarchy is then introduced (imagining seeing a snake). If the client can handle this without experiencing anxiety, the next step is introduced. Whenever the client experiences anxiety, the stimulus is removed and the client is given time to relax. After the client relaxes, a less threatening object on the hierarchy is reintroduced and the client and therapist again proceed along the hierarchy. In a relatively short time, the client often can face the highest object on the hierarchy—handling a snake—without distress (Chambless, 1990).

Desensitization is particularly effective when it slowly and carefully presents clients with real, rather than imaginary, hierarchy items (McGlynn et al., 1999). Due to advancements in computer technology, clients can now experience very real-appearing items in their fear hierarchy by using virtual-reality equipment (Wiederhold et al., 2001). Wearing a head-mounted virtual-reality helmet, clients can gradually experience more and more intense anxiety-provoking 3-D situations without ever leaving the therapist's office (Carlin et al., 1997; North et al., 2002). This *virtual-reality graded exposure* technique is especially useful in treating acrophobia (fear of heights), because it removes any danger of clients panicking while standing on a high structure (Rothbaum et al., 1995). Before reading further, complete Explore It Exercise 14-1.

Table 14-2   A Sample Desensitization Hierarchy

The scenes in this hierarchy are typical of those used in the systematic desensitization of a fear of snakes. The numbers to the left of each statement represent one patient's subjective rating of how anxiety-provoking a situation is, on a scale from 0 ("not at all anxious") to 100 ("uncontrollable anxiety").

Fear Level	Scene
10	I imagine seeing a snake.
20	I see a line drawing of a snake.
25	I see a photograph of a small, harmless garden snake.
30	I see a photograph of a large python.
40	I hold a rubber snake in my hands.
50	I watch a nature video on snakes.
60	I am in the same room with a snake in a cage.
70	I am standing next to the snake cage.
80	I am looking into the top of the snake cage with the lid open.
90	I am standing next to a person holding a snake.
95	I touch a snake held by someone else.
100	I am holding a snake.

A review of 375 therapy outcome studies indicates that systematic desensitization is the most effective therapy for treating phobias (Smith & Glass, 1977). Other reviews have concluded that desensitization is also effective in treating other problems that may occur as a result of anxiety, such as sexual dysfunction (Emmelkamp, 1986; North et al., 2002).

Explore It
Exercise **14-1**

Can You Systematically Desensitize Your Greatest Fear?

In chapter 13's Explore It Exercise 13-1, I asked you to identify your greatest fear. Now I would like you to use the counterconditioning technique of systematic desensitization to reduce and possibly even eliminate this fear. First construct a desensitization hierarchy consisting of a list of increasingly anxiety-provoking situations related to your fear (refer to table 14-2 as a guide). Next find a quiet place with no distractions, sit in a comfortable reclining chair, and progressively relax all the muscles of your body (you might be able to relax better if you read Explore It Exercise 15-2 in chapter 15). While relaxed, imagine the first, easiest scene in your fear hierarchy. When you can imagine this scene without experiencing anxiety, move on to the next scene. Whenever you experience anxiety, stop imagining the scene and give yourself time to relax. After relaxing, imagine the previously less threatening scene in the hierarchy and then gradually reintroduce the more threatening scene. Do not try to go through the entire hierarchy in one session. Space out your sessions over time.

Response Prevention

response prevention
A counterconditioning technique commonly used in the treatment of obsessive-compulsive disorder. Clients are exposed to the situation in which they previously exhibited a compulsive behavior but are not permitted to engage in the ritual.

A counterconditioning technique closely related to desensitization is **response prevention,** which is often used to treat compulsive behaviors (Abramowitz, 2002). Remember that in obsessive-compulsive disorder, people experience distressing repetitive thoughts (such as worries about catching illness by being exposed to germs) followed by ritualistic compulsive behaviors (such as washing their hands hundreds of times daily). In response prevention therapy, clients are exposed to situations that trigger the distressing thoughts and feelings (for example, touching an object that fell on the floor). In the past, the clients' distress decreased after they engaged in compulsive behaviors, and so the compulsions were reinforced. However, in this treatment, clients are prevented from engaging in the compulsive behaviors, thus shutting off their usual, troublesome escape route to anxiety reduction. In all cases, response prevention causes an initial buildup of anxiety, but over time, the client's distress tends to diminish. Numerous studies indicate that response prevention is effective in treating obsessive-compulsive disorder, with about 50 percent of clients showing substantial improvement and another 25 percent showing moderate improvement (Barlow & Lehman, 1996; Steketee, 1993).

Aversive Conditioning

aversive conditioning
A counterconditioning technique in which a classically conditioned aversive response is conditioned to occur in response to a stimulus previously associated with an undesired behavior.

One last counterconditioning technique is **aversive conditioning,** in which people are classically conditioned to react with aversion to a harmful or undesirable stimulus (Hermann et al., 2002). For example, as depicted in figure 14-1, a client who abuses alcohol may be given a favorite drink laced with *Antabuse,* a drug that induces severe vomiting. The objective is to replace the alcoholic's positive reaction to alcohol with a decidedly negative response. After repeated pairings of alcohol with vomiting, the alcohol alone begins eliciting nausea. Alcoholics treated with this form of aversion therapy tend to achieve about a 60 percent abstinence rate up to 1 year after treatment (Miller & Hester, 1980; Rimmele et al., 1995; Voegtlin, 1940). However, after 3 years, only about one-third remain abstinent. The problem with this therapy is that alcohol is an unconditioned stimulus that naturally evokes a pleasant state of intoxication, which is an unconditioned response. Alcoholics know that if they drink outside the therapist's office, they will not experience the immediate nausea but instead will experience a pleasant alcoholic "high."

Another form of aversive conditioning is *rapid smoking,* which is designed to help people stop smoking. In this treatment, the client inhales smoke from a cigarette every 6 to 8 seconds. After only a few minutes, smokers—even those who chain-smoke—become physically sick from the toxins in the tobacco. After repeated trials, the taste, smell, and even sight of cigarettes often trigger a nausea response. Rapid smoking is a fairly effective technique, with about 50 percent of clients remaining smoke-free at least 3 to 6 months after treatment (Lichtenstein & Brown, 1980).

As you can imagine, aversive conditioning is both distressing and messy, and many clients and therapists prefer other treatments. Aversive conditioning is typically used only after other

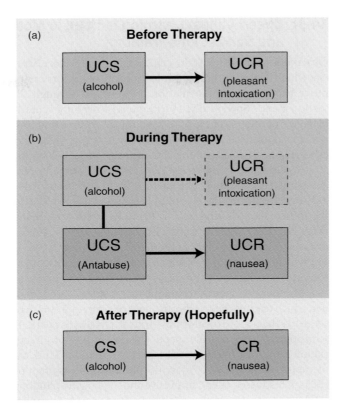

(a) **Before Therapy**

(b) **During Therapy**

(c) **After Therapy (Hopefully)**

Figure 14-1

Aversive Conditioning for Alcoholism

(*a*) Initially, alcohol is an unconditioned stimulus for alcoholics, naturally evoking a pleasant unconditioned response. (*b*) During therapy, the Antabuse drug is mixed with alcohol and given to the alcoholic, causing severe nausea. (*c*) After repeated pairings, the alcohol becomes a conditioned stimulus, evoking the conditioned response (nausea). What might weaken this conditioned response following therapy so that the treatment is ultimately ineffective in preventing abstinence?

methods have failed and the client provides informed consent to participate in such a difficult process. Even when this procedure is used, therapists almost always combine it with another treatment, often one involving operant conditioning, our next topic of discussion.

14-3b Operant Conditioning Is Used in Token Economies

As you recall from chapter 7, section 7-2, *operant conditioning* involves learning through reinforcement and punishment. Because virtually every voluntary behavior can be punished or reinforced, operant conditioning is a very flexible approach to modifying behavior. One important therapeutic application of operant conditioning principles is the **token economy,** which uses reward and punishment to modify the behavior of groups of people often in institutional settings, such as psychiatric hospitals or prisons (Bellus et al., 1999; Kopelowicz et al., 2002). In this technique, desirable behaviors are reinforced with tokens (such as poker chips or checks on a card), and undesirable behaviors are punished by the loss of tokens (Ayllon & Azrin, 1968). People whose behavior is being modified with token economies accumulate and later exchange the tokens for other forms of reinforcement (such as television privileges or field trips). Research has shown that the token economy technique is effective in shaping desirable behavior not only in psychiatric hospitals and prisons but also in school classrooms, structured play activities, and homes for juvenile delinquents (Kazdin, 1982; Reitman et al., 2001).

Is there a downside to using the token economy? Critics charge that this type of *behavior modification* makes people too dependent on the external rewards earned in the token economy. Why is this a problem? Well, when was the last time someone gave you a token when you did something nice or took a token from you when you behaved badly? One of the problems with token economies is that the desirable behaviors learned through this technique are likely to be quickly extinguished when people are outside the institution. Proponents of the token economy respond that such a possibility can be considerably reduced if, prior to leaving the institution, people are slowly shifted from a token-economy reward system to rewards more likely to be encountered outside the institution, such as social approval.

> **token economy** A technique often used to modify the behavior of severely disturbed people in institutional settings; involves reinforcing desirable behaviors with tokens that can be exchanged for other forms of reinforcement, such as snacks or television privileges.

14-3c Observational Learning Is Used in Modeling and Social Skills Training

Observational learning is the central feature of Albert Bandura's (1986) *social learning theory,* which contends that people learn social behaviors mainly through observation and cognitive processing of information, rather than through direct experience (see chapter 7, section 7-3a). Specifically, *observational learning* occurs by observing and imitating the behavior of others. These others whom we observe and imitate are called *models.* The therapeutic application of observational learning principles is called **modeling,** and it has been especially helpful in teaching clients useful social behaviors and coping skills.

> **modeling** A behavioral method of psychotherapy in which desirable behaviors are demonstrated as a way of teaching them to clients.

In *participatory modeling,* the therapist or someone else models more effective ways of behaving, and gradually, the client is invited to participate in the behavior. For example, a person suffering from snake phobia might first watch the therapist handling snakes without the therapist expressing fear or being harmed. After watching this snake handling a few times, the client is gently coaxed into holding a snake. Participatory modeling is a very effective treatment for phobias and other fears (Bandura, 1986). It relies on *vicarious conditioning,* which is the process by which one learns the consequences of an action by observing its consequences for someone else (see chapter 7, section 7-3a).

Another therapeutic technique that involves observational learning is **social skills training,** which teaches clients who are inept or act inappropriately in social situations how to interact with others more comfortably and effectively (Hersen & Bellack, 1999). For example, most schizophrenics are socially inept: They often do not directly interact with others, and they exhibit emotions unconnected with the situation. Thus, usually in conjunction with drug therapies (see section 14-7a), schizophrenic patients often participate in social skills training (Bellack & Mueser, 1993). Impulsive and hyperactive children, who often have problems interacting with others, are also regularly placed in such therapy programs (Tutty et al., 2003).

> **social skills training** A behavioral method of psychotherapy in which clients are taught how to interact with others more comfortably and effectively.

Social skills training programs employ various learning techniques, including the previously discussed modeling of socially skilled trainers, as well as the role-playing of various problematic social encounters. The social skills taught in these training sessions cover such areas as initiating conversations, giving and receiving compliments, reacting nonviolently to conflict, using nonverbal methods of communication, and actively listening to what others have to say in conversation (L. Kelly, 1997). Training is usually conducted in groups. In a typical session, the therapist might show a videotape of a model starting a conversation inappropriately or aggressively responding to a disagreement. The group might then discuss ways in which the model could have acted more appropriately. Following this discussion, group members might view another videotape in which the model performs more effectively. Each person in the training group might then role-play a conversation while others observe and then provide feedback. This role-playing might even be videotaped so group members can see exactly how they interacted. The session might end with a homework assignment requiring group members to work on some specific social behavior during the following week. A number of studies indicate that people who participate in such training exercises show improvements in their social skills and an increased level of social satisfaction (Erwin, 1994; Margalit, 1995; Wert & Neisworth, 2003).

> *Journey of*
> *Discovery*
> Question
>
> Suppose a male college student seeks therapy because he is shy and has been unsuccessful in his attempts to talk to women. He reports that he stammers and has trouble thinking of anything to say. He does not initiate conversations with women classmates, even to make small talk. When he starts to make a phone call to ask someone out, he hesitates and talks himself out of calling. How might a behavior psychotherapist use modeling and social skills training to treat this student's shyness?

Section Review

- Behavior therapies use conditioning and observational learning techniques to modify problem behaviors.
- Therapy techniques based on classical conditioning include systematic desensitization (gradually exposing phobic clients to the feared objects without arousing anxiety and

fear); response prevention (exposing clients to situations in which they previously exhibited a compulsive behavior, but not permitting them to engage in the ritual); and aversive conditioning (conditioning an aversive response to a stimulus previously associated with an undesired behavior).

- Therapy techniques based on operant conditioning and observational learning include token economies (used in institutions to modify the behavior of groups of people); modeling (demonstrating desirable behaviors as a way of teaching them to clients); and social skills training (learning how to interact with others more comfortably and effectively).

14-4 COGNITIVE THERAPIES

Preview

- *How does cognitive therapy treat psychological problems?*
- *What characterizes cognitive therapies?*
- *What are the major approaches in the field of cognitive therapy?*

As discussed in chapter 13, section 13-1c, the cognitive perspective suggests that the immediate cause of psychological problems is inaccurate or ineffective thinking. Hassles become crises because people do not accurately evaluate the situations they encounter and, thus, do not arrive at effective solutions. Because dysfunctional thinking is considered by this perspective to be the source of psychological problems, **cognitive therapies** seek to identify and then modify these faulty cognitive processes. Like behavior therapies—and unlike psychodynamic therapies—cognitive therapies tend to be short-term, problem-focused, and highly directive.

> **cognitive therapies** Psychotherapies that focus on identifying and then modifying dysfunctional patterns of thought.

14-4a Rational-Emotive Behavior Therapy Confronts Clients' Irrational Assumptions

Albert Ellis (1962, 1999) developed a form of cognitive therapy called **rational-emotive behavior therapy (REBT),** which assumes that mental distress is caused not by objective events in people's lives but rather by the irrational thinking people have about those events. For example, a person might say he is depressed because he did not receive a promotion at work. However, Ellis would contend that the real cause of the depression is the person's assumption that this event means something negative about himself ("My boss does not respect me"). The goal of REBT is to help people identify problems in the way they think about their general experiences and then try to modify these cognitions. The irrational beliefs that cause emotional problems are based on what Ellis called "all-or-none" types of thinking. For instance, people who think they must be loved or approved by everyone, or that they must be successful in everything they do, are likely to feel unhappy much of the time. By setting unreachable goals, they experience frequent disappointment.

> **rational-emotive behavior therapy (REBT)** The cognitive therapy of Albert Ellis, in which people are confronted with their irrational beliefs and persuaded to develop a more realistic way of thinking.

What makes REBT so unconventional is the way these therapists respond to their clients' irrational beliefs (Ellis, 2002). Instead of allowing clients to state their beliefs without evaluative comment (as happens in classical psychoanalysis), REBT therapists directly attack clients' irrational way of thinking, pointing out how it is inevitably self-defeating, and persuading them to develop a more realistic way of evaluating their lives. Of all the therapies discussed in this chapter, REBT is the one vaguely similar to Dr. Phil's interpersonal style with his TV clients. Like Dr. Phil, REBT therapists are often blunt and confrontational in challenging clients' negative and unrealistic assessments of their present conditions. The following are typical responses therapists might make to clients' emotional woes:

> "So you didn't get the promotion. Where is it written that life has to be fair?"
> "Why do you always have to look on the dark side of things?"
> "So what if your father didn't love you. That's *his* problem!"

Clients are also encouraged to "step out of character" and try new behaviors that directly challenge their irrational beliefs (Ellis et al., 2002). For example, if a woman is afraid others won't like her if she disagrees with them, her therapist might instruct her to forcefully disagree with five people during the next week. The objective in such an exercise is for the woman to discover that her world doesn't end following such exchanges.

How effective is REBT? That is a difficult question to answer. There are no specific psychological disorders that are best treated by REBT, and it's unclear how much clients benefit from this form of therapy, but studies suggest that it does have some positive effects on clients' later adjustment and well-being (Blackburn, 2005; Engels et al., 1993; Moeller & Steel, 2002).

14-4b Cognitive-Behavior Therapy Focuses on Emotional Problems

Like Ellis, Aaron Beck's (1967) **cognitive-behavior therapy (CBT)** was originally developed to treat depression—which he considers a cognitive disorder—but he later applied his treatment to anxiety and other emotional problems (Beck & Emery, 1985). According to Beck, depressed people have negative views of themselves, the world, and their future, and they misinterpret everyday events to support these negative views (Beck et al., 1979). For example, they tend to exaggerate negative outcomes while downplaying positive outcomes, and they jump to overly pessimistic conclusions based on a single event. These thinking errors may occur so frequently that they become automatic.

CBT involves identifying and then changing the client's negative thinking patterns and negative behavior patterns (Blenkiron, 2005). To do so, therapists instruct clients to keep a diary of their thoughts before and after sad episodes. Therapists then discuss these episodes with the clients and help them develop new thinking patterns that are more positive, accurate, and effective. The reason this therapy has the term *behavior* in its title is that the methods used to help clients develop new patterns of thinking often involve basic conditioning techniques. Research has shown that CBT is relatively effective in treating depression (Bourne, 2003), anxiety disorder (Durham et al., 2003), bulimia (Fairburn et al., 1997), and borderline personality disorder (Linehan, 1993).

> **cognitive-behavior therapy (CBT)** The cognitive therapy of Aaron Beck that identifies and then changes negative thinking and behavior by using both cognitive and behavioral principles.

Cognitive-behavior therapy attempts to change negative thinking that promotes pessimism and failure. If your current life situation could be described as a glass half-filled with sweet nectar, cognitive-behavior therapists would encourage you to focus on the fact that it is half full, not half empty. However, if your current life situation is more aptly described as a half-filled glass of bitter medicine, cognitive-behavior therapists would encourage you to focus on the fact that the glass is already half empty and you will soon be finished with its contents and can look forward to better times. So, how do you perceive your own "life glass"? Is it half full or half empty?

Source: Courtesy of Figzoi.

Section Review

- Cognitive therapy is based on the assumption that troubling emotions and behaviors result from inaccurate or ineffective thinking.
- Cognitive therapies are short-term, active, and problem-focused.
- In rational-emotive behavior therapy, clients are bluntly confronted with their irrational beliefs and persuaded to develop a more realistic way of thinking.
- In cognitive-behavior therapy, clients' negative thinking and behavior are modified using both cognitive and behavioral principles.

14-5 HUMANISTIC THERAPIES

Preview

- *What is the theoretical basis of humanistic therapies?*
- *How do humanistic therapists help clients function better?*

As discussed in chapter 12, section 12-3, humanistic psychology focuses on positive aspects of human experience, such as love, creativity, and spirituality. **Humanistic therapies** focus on helping people get in touch with their feelings, with their "true selves," and with their purpose in life. Humanists believe that psychological problems develop when outside forces stifle people's natural tendency to seek personal growth. One of the primary goals of humanistic therapies is to help clients actualize their basically good nature.

> **humanistic therapies** Psychotherapies that help people get in touch with their feelings, with their "true selves," and with their purpose in life.

14-5a Client-Centered Therapy Focuses on Clients' Conscious Self-Perceptions

The psychologist who has had the strongest influence on humanistic psychotherapy is Carl Rogers (1959, 1961), the developer of **client-centered therapy.** In articulating how therapists should view their function in treating psychological disorders, Rogers argued that they should not assume the role of "detective," as in psychodynamic therapy, or the role of "active director," as in behavior and cognitive therapies. Instead, Rogers believed that therapists should be *facilitators* of personal growth by providing a supportive environment in which clients can discover their "true selves." This emphasis on the client's own conscious self-perceptions rather than on the therapist's interpretations of those perceptions is the reason Rogers's therapeutic approach is titled "client-centered."

A central assumption underlying client-centered therapy is that psychopathology results because people have received *conditional positive regard* from loved ones, which involves being loved and socially accepted only when meeting others' standards (Rogers, 1951). Put another way, people are accepted as worthy individuals in their own right only when they meet or conform to others' wishes and desires. As discussed in chapter 12, section 12-3a, Rogers believed that people subjected to this conditional love fail to develop their "true selves" and, as a result, develop an array of emotional problems.

To counteract the negative effects of this conditional acceptance, Rogers proposed that psychotherapy be built around the principle of *unconditional positive regard* (again, see chapter 12, section 12-3a). That is, clients should be accepted unconditionally—treated with warmth, kindness, and caring—regardless of what they have said or done. The assumption here is that when therapists accept clients for who they are, clients will eventually come to accept themselves as well. When this self-acceptance occurs, clients can put aside the standards of others that are false for them and once again get on track in developing their true selves (Corsini & Wedding, 2001; Truax & Carkhuff, 1967). Key ingredients in unconditional positive regard are *genuineness* (being open and honest), *warmth* (being caring and nurturant), and *empathy* (accurately identifying what the client is thinking and feeling).

What techniques do client-centered therapists use to express unconditional positive regard for clients? That is, how do they convey their genuineness, warmth, and empathy during therapy sessions? Three techniques typically used are *open-ended statements, reflection,* and *paraphrasing.*

Consider the question, "Did you have a good week?" This is a closed-ended question, because it can be answered with a single word, and it suggests that the client should evaluate the week. On the other hand, "Tell me about your week" is open-ended, because clients can say as much or as little about the week as they choose. **Open-ended statements** encourage clients to speak, without limiting the topic of conversation. Client-centered therapists often sprinkle the therapy session with open-ended comments such as "Go on," "Um-hmm," and "I see," which convey genuineness, warmth, and empathy.

Another Rogerian technique is **reflection,** in which the therapist acknowledges some emotion that the client has expressed verbally or nonverbally. For example, when a client says the week has been hard, the therapist reflects this by saying, "This has been a tough week for you." If a client begins crying, the Rogerian therapist recognizes this by saying, "This is difficult for you to talk about." Reflection is considered a client-centered technique because the therapist expresses understanding of and caring for the client.

A third technique is **paraphrasing,** in which the therapist summarizes the expressed verbal content of the client's statements. For example, many clients are distressed and so do not express themselves clearly. In such instances, the therapist may summarize his or her understanding of what the client has said: "Let me see if I understand the situation you faced this week. You said that . . . ." By using paraphrasing, the therapist is expressing empathy.

Therapists from many theoretical schools use some or all of these client-centered techniques to build rapport with their clients. Even if therapists think another approach is more effective than client-centered therapy, they often still blend these techniques into the foundation of their own therapeutic practice. Such wide use of client-centered techniques probably explains why fellow psychotherapists often identify Carl Rogers as the person having had the biggest influence on how therapy is practiced (Smith, 1982). Further, reviews of

client-centered therapy A humanistic therapy in which the client, rather than the therapist, directs the course of therapy.

open-ended statement A therapy technique in which the therapist encourages the client to speak, without limiting the topic of conversation.

reflection A therapy technique in which the therapist acknowledges an emotion that the client has expressed verbally or nonverbally.

paraphrasing A therapy technique in which the therapist summarizes the expressed verbal content of the client's statements.

almost 1,100 therapeutic outcome studies conducted over a 35-year period support Rogers's contention that a positive client-therapist relationship is an essential factor in determining the effectiveness of therapy (Orlinsky & Howard, 1987).

14-5b Gestalt Therapy Encourages Clients to Get in Touch with Their Feelings

Gestalt therapy
A humanistic psychotherapy that stresses awareness of feelings in the here and now.

Another influential humanistic therapy is **Gestalt therapy,** which was developed by the former psychoanalyst Frederick ("Fritz") Perls, along with his wife, Laura (Perls, 1969; Perls et al., 1951). *Gestalt* is the German word for "pattern" or "whole." Perls named his approach Gestalt therapy because he said that he treated the "whole" person. To Perls, a major cause of mental illness is people's lack of awareness of their true feelings or some other important aspect of the self.

Although Gestalt therapy is most often classified as humanistic, it also has certain psychodynamic features (Kirchner, 2000). Consistent with the psychodynamic view, Perls asserted that people often are not consciously aware of their own feelings, and he sought to help clients develop their self-awareness (or gain *insight*). However, consistent with the humanistic view, in seeking self-awareness, Perls focused on the here and now rather than on childhood experiences.

empty-chair technique
A Gestalt technique in which clients engage in emotional expression by imagining that the person to whom they would like to speak is sitting in an empty chair facing them.

In contrast to the nondirective style typical of client-centered therapists, Gestalt therapists employ a directive approach, often putting clients on a figurative "hot seat" to encourage them to become aware of feelings and impulses they have disowned and to abandon feelings and ideas not their own (Bowman & Brownell, 2000). For example, if a client frowns following a comment by the therapist, the therapist might confront this directly by stating, "Are you aware of your facial expression? What does this mean to you?" Gestalt therapists also use body awareness exercises to stimulate physical and emotional reactions. For example, if clients are having difficulty recognizing their emotions, the therapist may tell them to practice different facial expressions in front of a mirror and identify the associated feelings. The goal of such exercises is to enhance clients' awareness of their current emotional and bodily states.

Perhaps the most popular technique used in Gestalt therapy to help clients gain insight into their true feelings is the **empty-chair technique,** in which the therapist places an empty chair facing the seated client and then asks the client to imagine that an important person from her or his past or present—a parent, spouse, or friend—is sitting in the chair. In this "safe" environment, the client can express her or his feelings by "talking" with the imagined person and hopefully gaining insight into those feelings. Research suggests that this technique may indeed help clients deal with the emotional turmoil that led them to seek therapy in the first place (Paivio & Greenberg, 1995). Before reading further, complete Explore It Exercise 14-2, which recreates in more detail this Gestalt technique.

In the empty-chair technique, clients are asked to imagine that an important person from their past or present is sitting in the chair. Then clients engage in a conversation with this person, saying things they have been holding in for years and, as a result, presumably gaining insight into their own true feelings.

Source: Courtesy of Figzoi.

14-5c Existential Therapy Helps Clients Deal with the Fundamental Problems of Existence

The work of many humanistic therapists was heavily influenced by existential psychology, which is an outgrowth of European existential philosophy (May, 1959). *Existentialism* is an approach to philosophy that examines the fundamental problems of human existence, such as the meaning of life, the inevitability of pain and isolation, and the responsibility of self-determination. Existentialists believe that the material comforts of the modern world have caused people to fall into a pattern of conformity and to lose a sense of their "true self" (Laing, 1967). Although some existential psychologists may not consider themselves humanists, this perspective is closer to humanistic psychology than to any of the other schools of therapy covered in this chapter, and so I present it here.

existential therapy
A philosophical approach to treating clients who are experiencing distress principally related to a lack of meaning in their lives.

Existential therapy is a philosophical approach that helps clients address their existential dilemmas (Brody, 2002; May, 1990). Although not closely associated with any specific treatment technique, existential therapy resembles humanistic therapy in that both forms (1) stress the person's subjective perception of the world; (2) believe that people are free to select their own actions; and (3) emphasize the here and now rather than the person's past.

One important existential therapist is Viktor Frankl (1963, 1969), a student of Freud, who developed a form of existential therapy called *logotherapy,* or "meaning therapy." Frankl

Explore It
Exercise **14-2**

Can Imaginary
Conversations Resolve
Conflict?

Gestalt therapists often help clients resolve conflicted feelings toward loved ones by guiding the clients through an imaginary conversation with these persons. One therapeutic procedure used to accomplish this task is known as the empty-chair technique. To help you understand how this technique works, explore it yourself by following these four steps:

1. Think of someone with whom you have had a recent conflict. Choose a conflict that is not very serious, because in this exercise I am more interested in your understanding the process of this technique rather than your resolving a major personal problem.
2. Set two chairs facing each other. Sit in one of these chairs and visualize your "target" person sitting in the other chair. Speak out loud to this absent person, describing the situation and/or behavior that created the conflict, how it makes you feel, and how you would like to resolve it.
3. Sit in the "target" person's chair and assume his/or point of view, imagining yourself sitting in the chair you just occupied. Respond to your previous statements as you think the "target" person would respond. How do the "target" person's imagined comments make you feel?
4. When you complete this exercise, reflect on its usefulness. Did you find that participating in this technique helped you better understand your "target" person's point of view? Do you see how this technique might help people resolve emotional conflicts in their lives?

believed that a fundamental human motive is to find meaning in life, and that emotional problems develop when such meaning cannot be found. How do you find meaning for yourself? According to Frankl, meaning can be found through (1) your life contributions (what you "give" to the world); (2) your life experiences (what you "take" from the world); and (3) your attitudes in facing difficult situations.

Frankl is best known for this third way of finding meaning, because he himself was a survivor of Nazi concentration camps in World War II and developed logotherapy during his imprisonment. For people who find themselves in terrible situations over which they have little control, Frankl offers a philosophical—almost a religious—form of psychotherapy, in which clients are encouraged to find meaning in terms of how they face these situations. For example, in his book *Man's Search for Meaning*, Frankl (1963) described the case of an elderly man who was consumed by grief after the death of his wife. Frankl asked the man to consider the consequences if he had died before his wife. The man recognized that he would have done anything to spare her this suffering—including bearing the pain himself. Even though he continued to mourn his wife, he found meaning in her loss by seeing that his suffering had spared her.

How effective is existential therapy? That is a difficult question to answer. By and large, existential therapists reject the use of conventional scientific methods to test the effectiveness of their methods, believing, like Freud, that such methods cannot accurately evaluate their therapies. Instead, they have sought to validate their therapies solely by relying on individual case studies. As a result, there is little empirical support for this therapeutic approach.

Section Review

- Client-centered therapy is a form of humanistic therapy based on unconditional positive regard; it focuses on the client's self-perceptions and is nondirective.
- Gestalt therapy stresses awareness of feelings in the here and now and uses active and directive techniques, such as confrontation, to enhance awareness.
- Existential therapy addresses problems that result from existential dilemmas involving a lack of meaning in life.

14-6 OTHER FORMS OF PSYCHOTHERAPY

Preview

- *What kinds of therapy are available for children?*
- *Can approaches to psychotherapy originally developed for use with individual clients be modified for delivery in other formats?*

Most forms of psychotherapy were originally developed for use with individual adult clients. However, it is important to remember that psychotherapy is often provided in other formats. In this section, we examine *child therapy, group therapy,* and *family/couples therapy.*

14-6a Child Therapies Use Techniques Designed for Younger Minds

Approximately 12 percent of the children and adolescents in the United States experience significant behavioral or emotional problems, with about 2.5 million of them receiving some form of therapy (Siskind, 2005). In offering such therapy, psychologists and other mental health professionals must remember that children differ from adults in many ways that affect their response to psychotherapy. For instance, children's vocabulary is still fairly simple and undeveloped, making it harder for them to express their feelings. Also, their thinking in general is much more concrete and oriented to present events, making them less aware than adults of the possible causes of their problems. Due to these limitations, children may be less able than adults to respond to verbal and insight-oriented therapies. Thus, therapists may have to rely more on behavioral observations and the reports of third parties (such as parents or teachers) than they would with adult clients. In some cases, the parents may be recruited as "co-therapists," using at-home techniques taught to them by the therapist.

play therapy A therapeutic technique in which the therapist provides children with toys and drawing materials on the assumption that whatever is troubling them will be expressed in their play.

A common approach taken by therapists when working with children is **play therapy** (Gil, 2003; Homeyer & DeFrance, 2005). Here, the child plays with puppets, blocks, crayons, and other common toys, while the therapist plays with or simply observes the child. Psychodynamic therapists consider play therapy to be a childhood form of free association, a technique they believe allows the client's unconscious material to come forth (Klein, 1932). In contrast, client-centered therapists consider play therapy a perfect vehicle in which to practice their warm, nondirective approach (Axline, 1947). During play, the therapist provides the child with unconditional positive regard, thereby activating the therapeutic process. Cognitive and behavior therapists also find play therapy useful, because it provides a means of helping the child acquire new cognitive or behavioral skills. In both approaches, therapy is basically an educational enterprise. By playing with the child, the therapist can demonstrate new skills, reinforce the child's successful efforts, and modify efforts that are only partly correct.

14-6b Group Therapy Involves Clients Discussing Their Problems with One Another under a Therapist's Guidance

Thus far, the therapies that we have discussed involve individual clients working with a therapist to solve the client's psychological problems. Yet psychotherapy can also be conducted with groups of clients (Saakvitne, 2005). **Group therapy** refers to the simultaneous treatment of several clients under the guidance of a therapist. Some therapy groups are composed of relatively well-functioning clients in outpatient settings, while other therapy groups consist of severely disturbed patients in hospital settings. Many groups are organized around one kind of problem (such as alcoholism or depression) or one kind of client (such as adolescents or police officers). The group usually consists of between 5 and 10 people who meet with a therapist about once a week for 2 hours. Today, all major theoretical schools of psychotherapy have some sort of group format (Edelman et al., 2003; Valbak, 2003; Yalom, 1995).

group therapy The simultaneous treatment of several clients under the guidance of a therapist.

Although the increased use of group therapy over the past 30 years is partly due to economics—it is more cost-effective than individual therapy—the group format has some real advantages over the individual format (Fuhriman & Burlingame, 1994; Kutash & Wolf, 1990). One advantage is that group therapy helps clients realize that others also struggle with many of the same problems they are working to solve. A related advantage is that a group format provides clients with the opportunity to compare themselves to others like themselves and exchange information on how to become more mentally healthy. A third advantage is that group members can become an important support network for one another, boosting self-confidence and providing self-acceptance. Finally, a fourth advantage is that the group setting allows the therapist to observe clients interacting with one another, which often helps the therapist better understand how to treat individual members.

One variation of group therapy is the **self-help group,** which consists of several people regularly meeting and discussing their problems with one another without the guidance of a therapist (Davison et al., 2000). One of the oldest and best-known self-help groups is Alcoholics Anonymous (AA), which has more than 70,000 chapters and more than 2 million members worldwide (Davison & Neale, 2001; Morganstern et al., 1997). AA, which was founded as a group run by and for alcoholics, provides information about the consequences of alcoholism and the opportunity to learn from the experiences of other alcoholics. AA is based on a series of 12 steps that help alcoholics attain and maintain sobriety. AA meetings begin with a discussion of one of the 12 steps, followed by several members speaking about their problems and telling how this step has helped them cope with alcoholism. Many other self-help programs have been developed on the AA model, covering a wide range of problems, including mood disorders, drug addiction, compulsive gambling, childhood sexual abuse, and spouse abuse (Lieberman, 1990).

How effective are self-help groups in treating mental health problems? The lack of reliable data makes an accurate assessment difficult, but such programs do appear to provide moderate to substantial benefits (Ouimette et al., 1997; Tonigan et al., 2000). Many therapists who treat clients in an individual or group format often also urge them to participate in self-help groups as part of their recovery process. The primary limitation of such groups is that the lack of guidance from a trained therapist can sometimes lead members to oversimplify the causes and remedies for their problems.

14-6c Family and Couples Therapies Try to Change Dysfunctional Interaction Patterns

Research suggests that when people who have been hospitalized for a psychological disorder return home to their families, they often suffer a relapse (Hazelrigg et al., 1987). One possible cause for such setbacks is the dysfunctional nature of their family relationships. Such an occurrence is consistent with the *diathesis-stress model* (see chapter 13, section 13-1c), which contends that stress may trigger the onset or relapse of a disorder for people who have an underlying vulnerability (a *diathesis*) for that disorder. In an attempt to prevent such relapses, all the major theoretical schools of psychotherapy have adapted their ideas to the treatment of families. These **family therapies** are designed to constructively modify the dysfunctional relationships among family members.

Often, family therapists base their work on *systems theory,* a theoretical approach important in both biology and cybernetics and based on the assumption that "the whole is greater than the sum of its parts" (Ackerman, 1966; Bowen, 1960, 1966). Systems theory readily applies to families because the family itself is a system, with each member an interacting element in that system. According to **family systems therapy,** the family acts in specific ways to maintain itself, both in terms of the interactions among the members and in terms of how the family interacts with its outside environment (Kempler, 1974). As such, an individual family member's problems cannot be understood and treated in isolation but must be examined and treated within the family system (Clarkin & Carpenter, 1995; Levant, 1984).

As with group therapy, family therapy allows the therapist to observe how the initially treated client interacts with other family members (Goldenberg & Goldenberg, 1995). With the therapist's guidance, family members can develop constructive communication and problem-solving skills, thereby reducing conflicts and emotional distress and improving the quality of their relationships (Alexander & Parsons, 1973; Jacobson & Margolin, 1979).

self-help group Several people regularly meeting and discussing their problems with one another without the guidance of a therapist.

family therapies Therapies designed to constructively modify the dysfunctional relationships among family members.

family systems therapy A form of family therapy in which the family is treated as a dynamic system, with each member an important interacting element in that system.

Research suggests that the types of negative family interactions that contribute to relapse differ, depending on the family's cultural background. For example, when psychologists first examined schizophrenic relapse in Great Britain and the United States, they found that patients were most likely to require rehospitalization when they returned to live with family members who expressed a great deal of criticism and hostility (Bebbington & Kuipers, 1994; Leff & Vaughn, 1985). However, when studies of schizophrenic relapse were extended to Mexican-American samples, researchers found a different pattern (Lopez & Carrillo, 2001; Lopez & Guarnaccia, 2000). In these cases, family interactions that were characterized by emotional distancing or a lack of warmth, rather than negative emotional expression by family members, were the crucial predictors of relapse. One possible explanation for this difference is that the Mexican-American patients have a collectivist cultural heritage characterized by a desire for tightly knit social relationships and group solidarity. In such a cultural setting, being emotionally ignored by family members may create significantly higher stress than being criticized by those same family members.

Finally, a variant of family therapy is **couples therapy,** which focuses on the problematic communication and behavior patterns of romantic partners. Over half the couples entering therapy state that their number-one problem involves faulty communication (O'Leary et al., 1992). This is true for both other-sex and same-sex romantic partners (Kurdek, 1994a, 1994b; Miller, 1997). Due to the pervasiveness of this problem, establishing an honest dialogue between the two partners is crucial in virtually all couples therapies.

Couples therapists with a cognitive and/or behavioral orientation use various techniques to teach positive communication skills. For example, couples may keep a diary of their weekly interactions, participate in positive role-playing exercises, and even watch videotapes of themselves discussing their relationship. Humanistic therapies often focus on getting the partners to express their emotions toward one another and to reveal what kind of new relationship they would like to build (Greenberg & Johnson, 1988). Finally, psychodynamic therapists emphasize helping couples gain insight into the underlying motives in their relationships and the ways they may be reacting to one another based on how they related to their own parents as children.

Overall, couples and family therapies appear to be relatively successful (Hazelrigg et al., 1987; Shadish et al., 1993). In fact, an increasing number of therapists who regularly treat married or cohabiting clients for depression on an individual basis now believe that the couples format is a more effective approach. Specifically, research suggests that, compared with individual therapy, couples therapy is equally effective in reducing depression and more effective in reducing romantic relationship problems (Beach et al., 1994).

14-6d Therapy Is Sometimes Offered through the Internet

You can take college courses through the Internet, and you can purchase groceries and even automobiles online, but can you receive psychotherapy while sitting at your home computer? The answer is yes (Kraus et al., 2004; Maheu & Gordon, 2000). A growing number of therapists are interacting with their clients—and providing actual therapy—through email, chat rooms, and message boards. Although most forms of psychotherapy assume that the client and therapist will interact face-to-face, *online therapy* (also called *e-therapy*) can provide help to people who are geographically isolated or are extremely socially anxious, disabled, or fearful that others will discover that they are seeing a mental health professional (J. Fink, 1999).

One potential benefit to the relative anonymity of computer-assisted therapy is that clients may feel at ease more quickly when interacting online and, as a result, reveal their most troubling and important problems sooner and with greater honesty than when in the therapist's office (Grohol, 1998). However, one drawback for the therapist is that all sorts of valuable information—such as physical appearance, tone of voice, and body language—is missing. Without such information, accurate diagnosis and proper treatment are more difficult to achieve than in a face-to-face setting. Another possible problem with online therapy is confidentiality (Suler, 2001). How do therapists know that the person interacting with them is, in fact, their client? If it is someone else pretending to be their client, confidentiality is destroyed. Fortunately, confidentiality problems can be addressed by using secure networks, user verification software, and video conferencing.

couples therapy Therapy designed to help couples improve the quality of their relationship.

A common problem addressed in couples therapy is faulty communication between partners. How effective is this form of therapy, compared to individual therapy, in reducing romantic relationship problems?

Source: © Bill Varie/CORBIS.

In recent years, an increasing number of people are seeking therapy on the Internet. This online therapy is most often used by persons who live in remote settings or are extremely socially anxious, disabled, or fearful about others discovering that they are seeking psychological help. What types of psychological disorders should not be treated online?

Source: Copyright © 2007 Atomic Dog Publishing and its licensors. All rights reserved.

In 1997, the International Society for Mental Health Online was formed to promote the understanding, use, and development of online mental health technologies (King & Moreggi, 1998). In the coming years, online therapy may become commonplace as either a supplement to face-to-face therapy or a complete treatment technique in its own right. However, e-therapy is not for everyone. It should not be used by individuals who have very complex mental health problems or who are in an extreme emotional crisis, such as those suffering from severe depression with suicidal thoughts. It also should not be used by those who are uncomfortable working with computers or have difficulty expressing themselves in writing. Such situations should be dealt with by seeing a therapist face to face. As you can see from this brief overview, psychotherapy can be administered in formats other than one-on-one client-therapist interaction.

Section Review

- Play therapy is often used with children, even though the various therapeutic formats have different assumptions regarding its usefulness.
- Major forms of psychotherapy were originally developed for use with individual adults but have been adapted for use with children, families, couples, and groups.
- Alternative therapy formats are often as effective as or superior to traditional therapy formats.

14-7   BIOMEDICAL THERAPIES

Preview

- *What kinds of medications are helpful in treating psychological disorders?*
- *What is electroconvulsive therapy?*
- *When is psychosurgery performed to treat psychological disorders?*

Today in the United States, the number of people who are full-time residents of psychiatric hospitals is less than one-third of the number hospitalized during the 1950s. The primary reason for this sharp decrease in hospitalization is the widespread use of drug therapies to treat psychological disorders such as schizophrenia and the mood disorders (Dursan & Devarajan, 2001; Schatzberg & Nemeroff, 1995). As you can see in figure 14-2, by 1995 more than 90 percent of the people diagnosed with a psychological disorder were receiving drugs as part of their treatment program (Nietzel et al., 1998). This high percentage of drug therapy is due not only to its effectiveness but also to the fact that this form of therapy is often less expensive than psychological therapies (see section 14-8a). In this section, we examine some of these drugs and

Figure 14-2

**Use of Drugs in Treating
Psychological Disorders**

The percentage of people
diagnosed with a psychological
disorder who are receiving drug
therapy has increased sharply
since the 1970s.

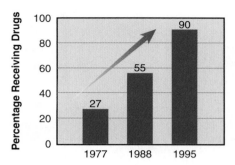

their effects and then discuss two controversial biomedical procedures that are sometimes used
to treat severe cases of mental illness—namely, *electroconvulsive therapy* and *psychosurgery.*

14-7a Antipsychotic Drugs Affect Dopamine Neurotransmitters

One of the earliest successes in using medication to treat psychological disorders was the
discovery in the 1950s that certain drugs used for other medical purposes reduced the positive, "uncontrollable" psychotic symptoms of schizophrenia, such as auditory hallucinations and paranoia (Lehman et al., 1998). The first of these **antipsychotic drugs,**
chlorpromazine, is in a class of drugs called the *phenothiazines* and is marketed under the
trade name Thorazine. As you recall from chapter 13, section 13-3d, research suggests that
schizophrenia is associated with an overactive central dopamine system in the brain. Chlorpromazine and other antipsychotic medications are thought to work by blocking dopamine
receptor sites in the brain, thereby reducing dopamine activity (Bernstein, 1995; Remington
et al., 2001).

Antipsychotic medications do not actually "cure" schizophrenia—they merely help
control its severe symptoms. These patients still have schizophrenia, and they often continue
to experience problems in living, although they may now be able to function outside the
hospital, such as in their family home or a halfway house. Because antipsychotic drugs cannot cure the disorder, it is important that schizophrenic patients who receive these drugs
also receive appropriate aftercare services so they do not simply move from the back wards
of hospitals to the back alleys of our cities.

Although they reduce positive schizophrenic symptoms, antipsychotic drugs do not
relieve negative symptoms—such as the absence of emotional expression, immobility, and
social withdrawal (see chapter 13, section 13-3d)—which may be related to structural defects
in the brain. These drugs also have some very unpleasant side effects, including Parkinson's
disease–like muscular tremors, stiffness, sluggishness, and loss of control over voluntary
movements. Even the newer antipsychotic drug *clozapine* (Clozaril), which does not have these
undesirable side effects, can cause a fatal blood disorder in about 2 percent of patients who
take it (LaGrenade et al., 2001). Recent medical advances have led to the development of even
newer replacement drugs, such as *risperidone* (Risperdal), that do not appear to have some of
these dangerous side effects (Ravasia, 2001; Wahlbeck et al., 1999). However, even these new
drugs are not risk free: Prescribing Risperal to elderly adults increases their risk of stroke.

14-7b Antidepressant Drugs Affect Serotonin and Norepinephrine Neurotransmitters

A second psychological disorder successfully treated with medication since the 1950s is
depression. **Antidepressant drugs** include *iproniazid,* which is in a class of drugs called the
monoamine oxidase inhibitors (MAOI) and was the first drug used in this way. Although initially developed to treat tuberculosis, physicians observed that iproniazid significantly
improved patients' mood and energy. Iproniazid and the other MAOI drugs work by
inhibiting the monoamine oxidase (MAO) enzyme involved in breaking down the neurotransmitters norepinephrine and serotonin. When MAO is inhibited, the available supply
of norepinephrine and serotonin is increased, which has the effect of elevating mood.

antipsychotic drugs
A group of medications
effective in treating the
delusions, hallucinations,
and loose associations of
schizophrenia by blocking
dopamine receptors and
thereby reducing dopamine
activity.

antidepressant drugs Drugs
that relieve depression by
increasing the supply of
norepinephrine and/or
serotonin at the neuron's
receptor sites.

Despite these benefits, MAOI drugs can produce dangerous side effects, including virtually eliminating REM sleep (see chapter 6, section 6-2d) and causing a sudden increase in blood pressure—and thus, an increased likelihood of stroke—if mixed with certain foods, such as red wine, beer, and aged cheeses (Julien, 2001). Recently, a newer type of MAOI drug, *moclobemide,* has become available that is less likely to have this negative food interaction (Martin, 2000).

A second class of antidepressant medications that have less severe side effects and seem to work somewhat better than the MAOI drugs is composed of the *tricyclics* (Bernstein, 1995). These drugs increase the available supply of serotonin and norepinephrine by decreasing their reuptake at the neuron's receptor sites (see chapter 3, section 3-1c). Among the tricyclics, *amitriptyline* (Elavil), *desipramine* (Norpramin), and *imipramine* (Tofranil) are widely used. Some of the common side effects of tricyclics are drowsiness, sleep disturbances, constipation, dry mouth, and blurred vision. These antidepressants can also affect a person's blood pressure and heart rate.

Finally, the most popular antidepressants are those that affect only serotonin— namely, the *selective serotonin reuptake inhibitors (SSRIs).* As their name implies, SSRIs inhibit the reuptake of the neurotransmitter serotonin, which increases the available supply of serotonin in the body, making it easier for neural impulses to be transmitted along serotonin pathways in the brain (Ago et al., 2005; Cheer & Goa, 2001). Among the SSRIs, *fluoxetine* (Prozac), *fluvoxamine* (Luvox), *paroxetine* (Paxil), and *sertraline* (Zoloft) are all widely used. Prozac is by far the most popular, with over 1.5 million prescriptions written every month in the United States alone. Worldwide, 24 million people use this drug. Prozac is also sometimes used to treat certain anxiety disorders and eating disorders (Julien, 1998). Controlled studies indicate that the SSRIs are as effective as the tricyclics in treating depression, but the SSRIs tend to have milder side effects, perhaps because they act only on one neurotransmitter (Fava & Rosenbaum, 1995). Researchers have also discovered that another possible way to increase the supply of serotonin in the bodies of depressed people without using drugs is to deprive them of sleep. It appears that sleep deprivation increases the activity of serotonin receptors, which is often sufficient to decrease depressive symptoms (Benedetti et al., 1999).

Bipolar disorder, like depression, is a mood disorder that can be treated effectively with medication (Ketter & Wang, 2002). Since 1969, when a mineral salt of the element *lithium* was approved for use in the United States, the drug lithium has helped about 75 percent of the bipolar patients it has been prescribed for (Bernstein, 1995). Without lithium, bipolar patients have a manic episode about every 14 months. With lithium, manic attacks occur as infrequently as once every 9 years. However, despite its effectiveness, lithium can cause delirium and even death if excessive doses are taken. Exactly how lithium works is unclear. Yet, because it takes at least a week of regular use before the drug shows any benefits, lithium's effects probably occur through some long-term adaptation of the nervous system. Although lithium has long been regarded as the "treatment of choice" for bipolar disorder, new mood stabilizers, such as *depakote,* have been developed and are now being used along with lithium (Martin, 2000).

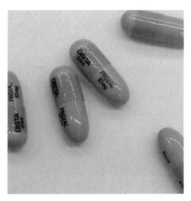

Prozac, a *selective serotonin reuptake inhibitor (SSRI)* drug, is the most widely prescribed antidepressant in the world. SSRI drugs inhibit the reuptake of the neurotransmitter serotonin, which makes it easier for neural impulses to be transmitted along the serotonin pathways in the brain, causing an elevation in mood. Why might the SSRI drugs have milder side effects than other antidepressants?

Source: Courtesy of Figzoi.

14-7c Antianxiety Drugs Are the Most Widely Used Legal Drugs

As presented in chapter 13, section 13-3a, one of the most common types of psychological problems is anxiety. The oldest drug treatment for anxiety is alcohol, which has been available as a tranquilizer for thousands of years. However, given the recognized negative side effects of alcohol (see chapter 6, section 6-3f), physicians no longer prescribe it as an anxiety treatment. Instead, a class of **antianxiety drugs**—the *benzodiazepines*—is the most frequently prescribed anxiety medication in the United States (Roy-Byrne & Crowley, 2002). Among the benzodiazepines are *oxazepam* (Serax), *lorazepam* (Ativan), *alprazolam* (Xanax), and *diazepam* (Valium). These drugs seem to produce their effects by facilitating the action of the neurotransmitter *gamma-aminobutyric acid (GABA),* which has an inhibitory effect on the central nervous system. That is, when GABA is taken up by receptor sites on the neuron, it becomes more difficult for the neuron to be stimulated to transmit a nerve impulse. In this way, antianxiety agents help "slow down" the transmission of nerve impulses and thus reduce the physiological and psychological changes that occur when a person is under stress.

antianxiety drugs Drugs that have an immediate calming effect by facilitating the inhibitory action of the GABA neurotransmitter, thereby reducing nerve impulse transmission.

Benzodiazepines are dangerous when combined with alcohol, and their side effects include lightheadedness, slurred speech, and impaired psychomotor and mental functioning (Bernstein, 1995). These drugs can also lead to physical dependence, so that when discontinued, the patient experiences withdrawal symptoms. Therefore, patients who discontinue their antianxiety medication should do so gradually. A newer drug, *buspirone* (*Buspar*) is effective in controlling anxiety by increasing serotonin levels in the brain without causing physical dependence or interacting negatively with alcohol. However, Buspar is slower acting than the benzodiazepines, taking up to several weeks to have an effect. Because Buspar takes time to reduce anxiety, some patients stop taking the drug because they think it has no effect other than dizziness and headache. As you see from my overview, these drugs can be remarkably effective in treating serious psychological disorders. Of course, all drug therapies have side effects, some more serious than others.

14-7d Electroconvulsive Therapy Is Sometimes Used to Treat Depression

electroconvulsive therapy (ECT) A physiological treatment for severe depression in which a brief electrical shock is administered to the brain of an anesthetized patient.

Another medical treatment used to manipulate the brain is much more controversial than drug therapies (Frank, 2002) and has been in use for a much longer period of time. **Electroconvulsive therapy (ECT)** was first used in the 1930s as a possible treatment for schizophrenia. However, subsequent research indicated that ECT does not help schizophrenia but instead is helpful in cases of severe depression, with about 80 percent of patients showing marked improvement (Coffey, 1993). Controlled treatment studies have found that ECT is about as effective as antidepressant medications in treating this mood disorder (Fava & Rosenbaum, 1995).

In a typical ECT procedure, patients are first given drugs to both render them unconscious and induce profound muscle relaxation. Next, with an electrode placed on one side of the patient's temple, a 70- to 130-volt charge of electricity is administered to that side of the brain for about 1 second. These shocks are continued until the patient has a seizure—a muscle contraction of the entire body—that lasts for at least 20 seconds (Abrams, 1993). This treatment is repeated at least once a week for 2 to 4 weeks.

Although ECT is effective in treating severe depression, no one knows for sure why it works (Coffey, 1993; Sackheim et al., 2000). Recent evidence suggests that ECT may be effective in treating severe depression by promoting new cell growth in the brain. Studies with rats demonstrate that ECT increases neural growth in the hippocampus, a brain area critical for the production of new memories (Hellsten et al., 2004). Additional research indicates that ECT also increases non-neuron cell growth in the frontal lobes of the cerebral cortex, which is responsible for higher mental processes (Madsen et al., 2005). This new cell growth in the frontal lobes involves two different types of cells: (1) cells that coat the inside of blood vessels and increase the efficiency of blood flow; and (2) cells that produce the myelin sheath, which insulates the axons of neurons and hastens synaptic transmission. Thus, the effectiveness of ECT in alleviating severe depression may be due to its ability to induce cell growth in areas of the brain that play a central role in the creation of new memories and complex thinking.

Despite ECT's effectiveness as a treatment for depression, it has several temporary negative side effects, including confusion, loss of memory, and impaired motor coordination (Breggin, 1979, 1991). In most instances, any memory lost for events preceding treatment is recovered within a few months (Cohen et al., 2000). Due to these side effects, ECT is generally used only when severely depressed patients either cannot tolerate or have not responded to drug therapy. In some cases, it may also be used when severely depressed patients are at immediate risk for suicide, because ECT has an almost immediate effect, while benefits from antidepressant medications usually take at least 10 days (M. Fink, 1999).

14-7e Psychosurgery Involves Removing Portions of the Brain

psychosurgery A rarely used surgical procedure to treat psychological disorders in which brain tissue thought to be the cause of the disorder is destroyed.

By far the most radical and controversial method of treating psychological disorders is **psychosurgery,** which involves destroying brain tissue thought to be the cause of these disorders. In 1949, the Portuguese psychiatrist Antonio Egas Moñiz received the Nobel Prize in Medicine for his psychosurgical technique known as *prefrontal lobotomy*. In this medical procedure, two small holes are drilled in the skull, and a sharp instrument is inserted and moved from side to side, severing the neural connections between the prefrontal lobes and the rest of the brain (Egas Moñiz, 1948). At the time that Egas Moñiz was using this technique to treat psychotic patients, it was thought that destroying the prefrontal lobes would relieve the crippling emotional reactions experienced by many schizophrenics. The medical profession was so taken by Egas Moñiz's technique that, during the 1940s and early 1950s, over 35,000 lobotomies were performed in the United States to treat schizophrenia, aggressiveness, anxiety, and depression.

Although lobotomies did reduce the incidence of some undesirable behaviors, patients paid a heavy price. In many cases, the treatment profoundly altered their personalities, with some becoming extremely apathetic and others becoming excitable and impulsive. Due to these very negative and irreversible effects, most physicians stopped using the procedure. Then, with the advent of antipsychotic drugs in the late 1950s, lobotomies were virtually extinguished as a medical intervention (Swayze, 1995). Today, MRI-guided precision psychosurgery is performed only in extreme cases when other types of treatment have been ineffective, and it focuses on much smaller brain areas than those involved in lobotomies.

As this overview suggests, biomedical therapies—as well as psychotherapies—have made amazing strides over the past 50 years in delivering more effective treatments for psychological disorders. With this accomplishment in mind, consider again my chapter-opening story about the likely therapies you might have received had you been a patient of Benjamin Rush at the end of the eighteenth century. Viewed with the insights of the twenty-first century, Rush's methods seem primitive and appalling. Yet, before we become smug in our assessment of how victims of psychological disorders were treated in the past, we should consider for a moment how upcoming scientific discoveries will likely change our views of current approaches to mental illness therapy.

Section Review

- Antipsychotic drugs reduce positive schizophrenic symptoms but do not relieve negative symptoms.
- Antidepressant drugs relieve depression by increasing the supply of norepinephrine and/or serotonin at the neuron's receptor sites.
- Antianxiety drugs have a calming effect by facilitating the inhibitory action of the GABA neurotransmitter, thereby reducing nerve impulse transmission.
- Electroconvulsive therapy is an infrequently used physiological treatment for severe depression in which a brief electric shock is administered to an anesthetized patient's brain.
- Psychosurgery is the most radical treatment for psychological disorders and involves destruction of the brain tissue thought to cause the disorder.

14-8 ECONOMIC AND SOCIAL TRENDS IN MENTAL HEALTH TREATMENT

Preview

- *How does managed health care influence the treatment of psychological disorders?*
- *Is psychotherapy effective?*

Private insurance companies have become big economic players in the management and treatment of mental health. This system of insured health care, known as a **managed care system,** has had a significant impact on the treatment of psychological disorders (Alegria et al., 2001; Sharfstein, 2001). Let us briefly examine how the system works and how it is underutilized by certain social groups.

managed care system
A system of insured health care in which the insurance company may determine such issues as which therapists clients may choose, the number of sessions permitted, and which drugs are prescribed.

14-8a Managed Health Care Involves a Trade-Off in Treating Psychological Disorders

The reality of U.S. health care in the twenty-first century is that most people who have an employer-based health-care plan are enrolled in some sort of *managed care system*. Typically run by health maintenance organizations, or HMOs, such managed care has both advantages and disadvantages for members. The advantage is that consumers pay lower prices for their care, but the disadvantage is that they often give up much of their freedom to make health care decisions concerning whom they see and what form of treatment they receive.

Managed care systems have also been guilty at times of limiting or even denying access to medically necessary services in order to keep expenses down so they can turn a profit (Duckworth & Borus, 1999). For example, a national survey tracking children and adolescents' access to mental health care from 1996 to 1998 found that, of those defined as needing mental health services, nearly 80 percent did not receive care (Kataoka et al., 2002). The rate of unmet care was greater among uninsured than insured children.

What sort of impact has managed care had on the treatment of psychological disorders? Largely driven by cost concerns, long-term therapy is rare today, available only to those clients who can afford to continue paying for treatment once their insurance benefits run out. In this new economic reality, treatment goals have shifted from curing mental health problems to helping clients with psychological disorders reestablish a reasonable level of functioning (Zatzick, 1999).

Another impact made by cost-cutting procedures on psychotherapeutic care is that many patients are no longer being treated by highly trained mental health professionals, such as psychiatrists and doctoral-level psychologists. Instead, an increasing number of people suffering from psychological disorders are referred to less well-trained therapists with master's degrees who may not be able to adequately diagnose and treat serious psychological disorders (Pope & Vasquez, 2001).

A further impact made by cost cutting on treatment can be seen in the biomedical therapies. As discussed in section 14-7, pharmaceutical companies are introducing new and improved drugs every year to better treat various psychological disorders. Unfortunately, psychiatrists employed by managed care providers are often required to prescribe the older, less effective drugs because they are considerably cheaper than those newly introduced to the marketplace (Docherty, 1999). In addition, biomedical therapies are most effective when combined with psychotherapy, especially for such disorders as major depression, bipolar disorder, and schizophrenia (Thase, 2000). However, cost management has also led to cutbacks in combining these two therapies, leading to less effective treatment for some individuals (Duckworth & Borus, 1999).

Because of these problems, many therapists and clients dislike managed care programs. Critics claim that the system, rather than trained mental health professionals, is making the important decisions about how therapy should be administered to people suffering from psychological disorders. Unfortunately, there is little evidence that solutions to these problems are on the horizon. Keeping costs down to a manageable level without compromising the delivery of mental health treatment will remain a delicate balancing act for the foreseeable future.

14-8b Efforts to Document Treatment Effectiveness Are Increasing

One possible benefit of managed health care has been a renewed focus on determining which forms of psychotherapy are most effective. The first concerted attempt to determine the effectiveness of psychotherapy occurred in the 1950s, when Hans Eysenck (1952) published an influential study claiming that people with psychological problems who received psychotherapy had a slightly worse outcome than those who did not receive any therapy at all. Based on these results, Eysenck concluded that there was no scientific evidence that psychotherapy is effective.

Although Eysenck's methodology was later found to be flawed, other researchers conducted their own assessments of various forms of psychotherapy, using much larger samples and following more rigorous procedures. The findings from these studies demonstrated that many types of therapy "work," but that they are not always effective for everyone (Orlinsky &

Howard, 1987; Smith & Glass, 1977). Based on these reviews of psychotherapy outcome, the following conclusions can be reached (Lyddon et al., 2001; MacDonald, 2005; Seligman, 1995):

1. Psychotherapy generally has a positive effect.
2. Different types of therapy are often about equally effective for many disorders.
3. Brief therapy helps many clients, with about 50 percent improving by the eighth session.
4. The more treatment clients receive, the more they improve.

The last two findings deserve further comment, given our previous discussion of managed care systems. Short-term psychotherapy—the format employed by most managed care systems—does result in better mental functioning for about half of all clients, but only half of these clients remain well (Westen & Morrison, 2001). Research indicates that the most effective treatments are those psychotherapies lasting more than 2 years (Seligman, 1995). Thus, there appears to be a positive correlation between length of therapy and long-term mental health benefits, but unfortunately, long-term therapy is not currently being offered by most managed care systems.

Another benefit of comparing the outcomes of various forms of psychotherapy is that it can test not only whether new techniques are effective but also whether there is something truly "new" about them that is different from already-established psychotherapeutic procedures. A very popular and relatively new therapy known as *Eye Movement Desensitization and Reprocessing (EMDR)* is currently receiving this type of scrutiny. EMDR was developed in the late 1980s by psychology graduate student Francine Shapiro after she noticed that moving her eyes back and forth while thinking about a disturbing event had the effect of reducing her negative emotions. Based on this personal experience, Shapiro asked 22 individuals suffering from traumatic memories to visually follow her waving finger while thinking about their disturbing events. Like her, these clients reported that their negative emotions and thoughts gradually faded away during and after these eye movement sessions. At first, Shapiro (1989) contended that the eye movements simulated brain activity during REM sleep, which had the effect of "releasing" and "integrating" traumatic memories. Later, she hypothesized that EMDR accelerates a type of "healing" information-processing that helps people overcome anxiety, stress, and trauma (Shapiro & Forrest, 2004). Since 1990, more than 40,000 therapists in more than 50 countries have been trained to use EMDR in treating adults and children with emotional problems. Yet is this use of eye movement really an effective technique in treating emotional trauma?

After assessing EMDR in controlled scientific studies with other therapeutic techniques, a number of psychologists have concluded that there is no credible evidence that the eye movements in EMDR have any therapeutic benefits (Goldstein et al., 2000). In fact, when studies compared treatment effects between the eye movement in EMDR and a "sham" EMDR, in which clients were told to focus their eyes on stationary objects, no significant differences were found (DeBell & Jones, 1997; Goldstein et al., 2000). The psychologists who conducted these studies contend that the reason clients show improvement following EMDR is due to both a hefty placebo effect and systematic desensitization techniques used by the EMDR therapists: Clients are asked to repeatedly think about traumatic events while remaining relaxed, which has the effect of desensitizing them to the feared objects and events (Davidson & Parker, 2001). According to these skeptical psychologists, what is effective in EMDR is not this new eye movement technique but, rather, a behavioral counterconditioning technique that has long been used to treat people with phobias and other intense fears (S. Taylor, 2004). Responding to these critical findings, Shapiro (1996) contended that they were the result of inadequate EMDR training, despite the fact that many of the clinicians conducting these studies were trained by Shapiro's EMDR trainers.

In sorting through this therapeutic controversy, it is important to keep in mind that the critical research did not find that EMDR is an entirely ineffective treatment; some techniques used in the EMDR procedure do help some people suffering from emotional trauma. Advocates of EMDR have also reported these benefits in their own studies (Silver et al., 2005). Yet there is no compelling scientific evidence that these benefits are caused by the eye movement technique. Further complicating this controversy is the fact that Shapiro (1995)

Scientific analysis of psychotherapeutic techniques is essential in identifying those that are effective and those that are either ineffective or simply repackaged versions of already-established techniques. In Eye Movement Desensitization and Reprocessing (EMDR), the client visually follows the therapist's moving finger while thinking about a traumatic memory. The rhythmic eye movements are supposedly accelerating a form of "healing" information-processing. Does scientific research support this claim?

Source: Courtesy of Figzoi.

has modified the EMDR technique to also include the selected use of certain kinds of hand-taps and auditory signals in treating emotional problems. Yet these additional techniques are very similar to the "sham" EMDR comparison procedures that raised such serious doubts about the original EMDR procedure! As you recall from our review of the scientific method in chapter 2, section 2-2f, to qualify as a scientific theory, an explanation must be falsifiable, meaning that it must be possible to find fault with, or disconfirm, the explanation. As of this writing, some psychologists argue that EMDR is based more on "pseudoscience" than science, while other psychologists respond that it is still a promising treatment for certain psychological disorders (Devilly, 2002; Rosen, 1999; Sikes & Sikes, 2003).

The case of EMDR highlights the important role science plays in the development and assessment of effective psychotherapeutic procedures. When therapists use techniques before those techniques have been systematically studied, they run the serious risk of doing a disservice to their clients (Carpenter, 2004; Lilienfeld et al., 2005). Psychologist James Herbert and his colleagues (2000), who were instrumental in exposing some of the problems associated with EMDR, contend that any new therapy should not be widely used by psychotherapists until scientific studies indicate that psychotherapists can answer yes to the following four questions:

- Does the new therapy work better than no therapy?
- Does the new therapy work better than a placebo?
- Does the new therapy work better than established therapies?
- Does the new therapy work in the way hypothesized by its developers?

14-8c Minorities Underutilize Therapeutic Services

A final issue of concern in the treatment of psychological disorders is that a number of studies indicate that ethnic minorities in the United States are less likely to seek mental health treatment and more likely to drop out of therapy than Whites (Vega et al., 1998; Wierzbicki & Pekarik, 1993; Zhang et al., 1998). For example, a recent nationwide survey found that African Americans and Hispanics are only half as likely to seek treatment for psychological problems as are White Americans (Kessler et al., 2005). The causes of these differences in the utilization of psychotherapeutic services are not adequately understood, but a few socio-cultural factors provide some insight into this social problem.

As mentioned in chapter 13, section 13-1b, one factor influencing a person's willing-ness to seek psychotherapy is the belief system in that person's culture. Partly because most modern psychotherapies were developed in Western cultures that have an individualist ori-entation, the primary thrust of contemporary therapies involves focusing on the client's emotions and personal needs. However, in collectivist Asian cultures, talking about personal feelings or even focusing on oneself individually is generally considered socially inappro-priate (Russell & Yik, 1996). Instead, being emotionally nonexpressive and relying on one-self to cope with distress are often interpreted as signs of emotional strength and maturity (Narikiyo & Kameoka, 1992). Thus, one of the possible obstacles Asian Americans face when seeking help for psychological problems is that the conventional Western psychother-apeutic approach may appear to them to be an unwise path for finding mental health.

Another reason ethnic minorities in the United States are less likely than Whites to seek mental health treatment is that a history of institutionalized discrimination based on race and ethnicity has made minorities more mistrustful of the medical and mental health pro-fessions. For example, surveys of African Americans suffering from major depression find that they are more likely than White Americans to cite fears of hospitalization and treatment as reasons for not seeking mental health therapy (Satterfield, 2002; Sussman et al., 1987). Additional surveys find that African Americans, Hispanic Americans, and Native Americans are much more likely than White Americans to believe that their doctors or health providers judge them unfairly or treat them with disrespect because of their race or ethnic background (Brown et al., 2000; LaVeist et al., 2000).

Instead of taking advantage of conventional mental health therapy, many ethnic minorities turn to more culturally comfortable sources of help when they experience pro-longed psychological distress (Peifer et al., 2000; Tan & Dong, 2000). For example, Native Americans and Alaska Natives may rely on traditional healers, while African Americans may seek out their church ministers and rely on spirituality to help them cope with symp-toms of psychological disorders (Trujillo, 2000). Some members of ethnic minorities are also more likely than Whites to delay seeking treatment for mental health concerns until their symptoms are relatively severe. Further, partly due to the stigma surrounding mental illness, when they do seek professional help, ethnic minorities are more likely than Whites to consult primary care physicians and nurses rather than mental health specialists (Chun et al., 1996; Cooper-Patrick et al., 1999). Unfortunately, one of the consequences of this decision is that minority individuals are less likely than Whites to have their psychological problems accurately diagnosed and treated (Borowsky et al., 2000).

What might explain the higher therapy dropout rates among Asian Americans, Hispanic Americans, African Americans, and Native Americans compared to the rates for White Ameri-cans? Some of these differences might be due to the fact that dropout rates are higher among poorer clients, and ethnic minorities are overrepresented in lower-income groups. Another likely factor in explaining these differences is that, although ethnic minorities make up about one-fourth of the population, only about 10 percent of mental health providers are ethnic minorities. Research indicates that clients feel more comfortable when their therapists are sim-ilar to themselves rather than dissimilar, and this may be especially true in regard to race and ethnicity (Snowden & Hu, 1996). Thus, the higher dropout rates among minorities may be at least partly due to problems in establishing rapport with White therapists (Atkinson et al., 1996). A related issue for some Hispanic and Asian clients is a language barrier. Many bilingual minor-ity clients find it easier to discuss their emotions and memories in their native language, some-thing that English-only therapists cannot accommodate (Altarriba, 2003; Biever et al., 2002).

Faced with these cultural divisions that can impede therapeutic effectiveness, an increas-ing number of psychotherapists of all races and ethnicities now receive special training to help them work more effectively with clients from other cultural backgrounds (Basham, 2004; Davis-Russell, 2003; Kersting, 2004b). In such training, therapists might learn, for example, that many Hispanic Americans come from tightly knit families and feel disloyal discussing family problems with outsiders. Psychologist Jeanette Altarriba remarks, "If you come from a society that highly values individualism, you may not think as a therapist to include the family, to ask questions about the family or to interview family members." (Dingfelder, 2005a, p. 69) However, in cultural training sessions, therapists learn to use a family's built-in support system to help Hispanic clients cope with mental health problems (Dingfelder, 2005b, p. 59). Are such training programs effective? Initial studies have found that this cultural training does improve the therapeutic process and reduces the dropout rate of minority clients (Dingfelder, 2005a; Fraga et al., 2004). In fact, in a study of Hispanic students receiving therapy from a university counseling center, researchers found that satisfaction with a therapist was not predicted by the therapist's ethnicity but, instead, depended on the degree to which the Hispanic clients believed their therapists understood their culture (Dingfelder, 2005a).

Although cultural understanding appears to be more important than cultural similarity in establishing client-therapist rapport, the American Psychological Association and other mental health organizations have made concerted efforts to recruit and train more ethnic minority therapists. For example, the APA's Office of Ethnic Minority Affairs runs programs that encourage ethnic minority students to become therapists and researchers in various mental health fields. As the ranks of minority mental health professionals grow in the coming years, this should persuade even more minority students to pursue careers in counseling and clinical psychology (Winerman, 2004).

Section Review

- Managed health care has resulted in more short-term therapies, more reliance on drug therapies, and a shift from curing mental health problems to reestablishing a reasonable level of functioning.
- Early studies of therapy outcome found no scientific evidence that therapy is effective, but more extensive research indicated that psychotherapy generally has a positive effect, that different types of therapy are often about equally effective, and that longer-term therapies are ultimately more beneficial than short-term therapies.
- Ethnic minorities my underutilize therapeutic services due to cultural beliefs about mental illness, previous experiences with institutionalized discrimination, and therapists' lack of understanding of ethnic minority culture.

Psychological Applications

How Do You Select a Psychotherapist?

A recent nationwide survey of Americans found that those suffering from mental illness are more likely to seek treatment now than they were in the early 1990s (Kessler et al., 2005). This is encouraging news, because the rate of mental illness has remained the same during this time period. Yet, given the variety of psychotherapies available, how should you go about selecting a therapist? Working with a therapist on a psychological problem is a sensitive and personal exercise—that is, a therapist who is very successful for one client may not be as helpful for the next client. There are several important questions you can ask when considering seeing a therapist.

First, you should ask whether you actually need a therapist. As noted in chapter 13, on psychological disorders, many people experience mild or "subclinical" levels of a symptom that only in more extreme form may qualify as a psychological disorder. For example,

many people have mild, irrational fears or periods of "the blues" that would not meet diagnostic standards for a psychological disorder. When judging the severity of your symptoms, it is useful to consider the degree to which your daily functioning has been impaired. A person whose symptoms are mildly distressing but do not significantly interfere with daily activities probably does not have a clinical disorder. This individual might benefit from speaking with a psychotherapist, but the therapy would likely be relatively brief. The therapist may provide information about the nature of clinical disorders, provide reassurance that this particular problem is not severe, and make a few suggestions concerning how to better manage the symptoms.

If you determine that your symptoms are producing significant impairment, you must then judge whether you have sufficient resources to cope. When facing a significant stressor, many people muster the resources to

Psychological Applications

—Continued

cope satisfactorily. Just because the symptoms are beginning to interfere with your functioning does not mean that the only way to solve the problem is through the help of a psychotherapist. If a problem is of recent origin, if you have successfully solved comparable problems before, or if you still have many ideas about how to cope with the problem, it may not be necessary to see a therapist. However, if you have exhausted your coping resources and no longer have confidence that you can manage the problem on your own, it may well be appropriate to seek professional help.

When shopping for a therapist, it is also useful to ask several questions. First identify the problem you would like to change: Do you want to reduce your depression? Do you want to stop drinking alcohol? Do you want to be able to go through the school day without having to wash your hands dozens of times? Do you want to get along better with your boyfriend or girlfriend? If you can identify a clear treatment goal, you will be in a better position to select a therapist and an approach to therapy. Clearly, many prospective clients do not have a clear idea of what they would like to change. This may be a part of the problem—they are dissatisfied with their lives but do not know what would help them feel better. In such cases, a psychotherapist can help the client clarify the treatment goal, although this identification process may require some time before actual therapy can begin.

Once you have identified a goal, you can consider the kind of therapy to seek. Some prospective clients have a preference for a specific form of therapy. They may have learned, from previous therapy experiences or from other information about psychotherapy, that they would like cognitive therapy or insight-oriented therapy. In these cases, it makes sense to shop for a therapist who can provide the kind of therapy that fits this preference.

Some psychological disorders have been shown to respond well to particular treatments (Nathan & Gorman, 2002). For example, bipolar disorder is almost always treated with mood-stabilizing medication. Panic disorder has been treated very successfully using cognitive-behavior therapy. Depression has been treated very successfully using cognitive therapy. If you are seeking help for one of these problems, it may be useful to look for a therapist who can provide the treatment that is considered most effective. Several resources are available to help you learn what therapies may be most effective for a particular kind of problem. For example, Martin Seligman (1994) has compiled a consumer guide to psychotherapy *(What You Can Change and What You Can't: The Complete Guide to Successful Self-Improvement)* that summarizes research on which therapies are generally recommended for which disorders. Also, the National Institute of Mental Health, various advocacy groups devoted to specific disorders (such as the Obsessive-Compulsive Foundation), and psychology departments at local universities can provide useful information about the current status of available therapies for a particular disorder.

Again, even if you do not have a clear idea about the kind of problem you have or the kind of therapy that may be helpful, this should not prevent you from seeing a psychotherapist. The therapist can—following an assessment of the problem—suggest one or more possible treatments.

Given that most treatment today is paid for by a third party, such as an insurance company or a social welfare agency, you should check your insurance package to determine whether there are any limits on the mental health coverage. As discussed, many managed care systems list preferred providers, and so your choice of professionals or agencies may be limited. Also as noted, most insurance plans have an upper limit on the number of therapy sessions or the total funds available for mental health services, which may dictate selecting a therapist who provides short-term forms of psychotherapy.

You should also ask some basic questions of prospective therapists: What is the therapist's degree? Is the therapist licensed in the state? Does the therapist have experience in treating problems like the one you have? Does the therapist have a particular theoretical preference? What is the cost of therapy sessions? The receptionist can usually answer these questions before you make an appointment to see the therapist. If the therapist will not allow the receptionist to answer these questions, you might seriously consider calling another therapist.

You can obtain referrals from many sources, including your family doctor, a clergy member, a lawyer, friends, and family members. Many cities have resources to refer mental health patients to psychotherapists, such as a chapter of the Mental Health Association. Local chapters of patient advocacy groups (such as CHADD—Children and Adults with Attention-Deficit/Hyperactivity Disorder) can help steer individuals to experts in the area. Psychology departments at local universities often help people learn about practitioners in the area who may specialize in treating various disorders.

Key Terms

antianxiety drugs (p. 547)

antidepressant drugs (p. 546)

antipsychotic drugs (p. 546)

aversive conditioning (p. 534)

behavior therapies (p. 532)

biomedical therapies (p. 527)

client-centered therapy (p. 539)

cognitive-behavior therapy (CBT) (p. 538)

cognitive therapies (p. 537)

counterconditioning (p. 532)

countertransference (p. 530)

couples therapy (p. 544)

eclectic approach (p. 529)

electroconvulsive therapy (ECT) (p. 548)

empty-chair technique (p. 540)

existential therapy (p. 540)

family systems therapy (p. 543)

family therapies (p. 543)

free association (p. 530)

Gestalt therapy (p. 540)

group therapy (p. 542)

humanistic therapies (p. 538)

managed care system (p. 549)

modeling (p. 536)

open-ended statement (p. 539)

paraphrasing (p. 539)

play therapy (p. 542)

psychodynamic therapies (p. 529)

psychosurgery (p. 548)

psychotherapy (p. 527)

rational-emotive behavior therapy (REBT) (p. 537)

reflection (p. 539)

resistance (p. 530)

response prevention (p. 534)

self-help group (p. 543)

social skills training (p. 536)

systematic desensitization (p. 532)

token economy (p. 537)

transference (p. 530)

Suggested Websites

Psychology Information Online
http://www.psychologyinfo.com
This site provides helpful tips on searching for a psychotherapist.

National Register of Health Service Providers in Psychology
http://www.nationalregister.com
This site can help prospective clients find a registered psychologist in their area.

A Guide to Psychology and Its Practice
http://www.guidetopsychology.com
This site provides information about psychology in general, including various forms of therapy that may be helpful for specific disorders.

Review Questions

Note: You can find the correct answers to these questions by taking the quiz and then submitting your answers in the Online Edition. The program will automatically score your submission. If you miss a question, the program will provide the correct answer, a rationale for the answer, and the section number in the chapter where the topic is discussed.

1. Before Freud developed psychoanalysis, treatment for mental illness emphasized all of the following methods *except*
   a. hypnosis.
   b. altering the brain's functioning with chemical interventions.
   c. terrorizing the patient by threatening to have him or her killed.
   d. emotional support.
   e. draining excess blood from the body.

2. Mental health professionals who deal with psychological disorders and receive extensive training in conducting scientific research are
   a. counseling psychologists with a Psy.D.
   b. psychiatric social workers.
   c. psychiatrists.
   d. clinical psychologists.
   e. psychologists with a Ph.D. or Ed.D.

3. Although there are several varieties of psychodynamic therapies, one thing they all have in common is
   a. a disregard for insight.
   b. an emphasis on sex as the major motivation for human behavior.
   c. the view that psychological disorders stem primarily from unconscious forces.
   d. encouraging resistance as a form of free association.
   e. the view that, to be effective, psychotherapy requires at least 5 years of twice-weekly sessions.

4. Psychodynamic therapists often interpret transference, which involves
   a. feelings that the client experienced toward others early in life.
   b. anything the client does that interferes with therapeutic progress.
   c. only negative feelings clients develop toward their therapist.
   d. the release of pent-up emotion.
   e. free association and Freudian slips.

5. The primary techniques used in behavior therapies are all based on
   a. unconscious learning and insight.
   b. observational learning.
   c. desensitization hierarchies.
   d. principles of learning.
   e. behavior modification.

6. The most effective technique for treating phobias is
   a. sudden and prolonged exposure to the feared object.
   b. response prevention.
   c. reinforcement and punishment.
   d. aversive conditioning.
   e. systematic desensitization.

7. Cognitive therapies may include all of the following *except*
   a. analysis of the meaning underlying dreams.
   b. confronting all-or-none types of thinking.
   c. trying new behaviors that directly challenge irrational beliefs.
   d. highly directive, problem-focused therapeutic techniques.
   e. identifying patients' negative views of themselves, the world, and their future.

8. Cognitive therapy techniques used by Beck and Ellis differ with respect to
   a. their emphasis on faulty thinking.
   b. their use of behavior techniques as well as cognitive techniques.
   c. the therapeutic goal of modifying cognitions.
   d. their response to clients' irrational beliefs.
   e. the overall length of therapy.

9. Carl Rogers is often identified as having the biggest influence on how therapy is practiced, because
   a. he emphasized the facilitation of personal growth.
   b. his client-centered techniques are widely used by therapists of many theoretical orientations.
   c. his principles of conditional positive regard are so effective.
   d. he formulated a highly directive form of therapy used by behavior and cognitive therapists.
   e. his emphasis on closed-ended statements was already used by most therapists.

10. The humanistic technique of paraphrasing
    a. involves analyzing the meaning underlying clients' verbal statements.
    b. acknowledges a client's nonverbal emotions.
    c. is a confrontational challenge of dysfunctional thoughts.
    d. is seen in therapist responses such as "Go on" and "I see."
    e. involves the therapist summarizing the expressed verbal content of clients' statements.

11. Gestalt therapy emphasizes all of the following *except*
    a. focusing on current feelings.
    b. nondirective, client-centered approaches.
    c. the empty-chair technique.
    d. body awareness exercises to stimulate emotional reactions.
    e. the development of self-awareness or insight.

12. Humanistic therapy that deals with finding meaning in life
    a. was developed by Perls.
    b. emphasizes resolving past issues.
    c. is based on Frankl's approach to existential therapy.
    d. has good empirical support.
    e. emphasizes treating the whole person.

13. Children's play therapy involves all of the following *except*
    a. a form of free association.
    b. a nondirective approach.
    c. an educational approach to learning new skills.
    d. directly challenging cognitive distortions.
    e. the use of unconditional positive regard.

14. One of the advantages of group therapy is that
    a. it is less expensive than individual therapy because it doesn't last as long.
    b. it helps clients see that others share similar problems.
    c. therapists are never used, which reduces the cost.
    d. it is based on monthly sessions rather than weekly sessions.
    e. it is more effective than couples therapy in reducing romantic relationship problems.

15. Therapy received on the Internet
    a. is not advised for people who are fearful that others will discover they are seeing a mental health professional.
    b. may make it easier for the therapist to accurately diagnose and treat the person.
    c. should not be used for people in an extreme emotional crisis.
    d. is advised for those suffering from severe depression.
    e. can be effective for complex mental health problems.

16. Antidepressant drugs that affect only serotonin
    a. are called SSRIs, which increase the availability of serotonin by inhibiting its reuptake.
    b. are tricyclic antidepressants, a class of benzodiazepines.
    c. are part of a class of drugs called phenothiazines.
    d. include MAOIs.
    e. are useful only for depression.

17. Most antianxiety drugs
    a. facilitate the action of the neurotransmitter gamma-aminobutyric acid (GABA).
    b. speed up the transmission of nerve impulses.
    c. are safe to use with alcohol.
    d. do not lead to physical dependence.
    e. increase the physiological and psychological changes that occur when a person is under stress.

18. Managed health care has affected the treatment of psychological disorders in all *except* which one of the following ways?
    a. Covered treatment is more often conducted by less well-trained master's level therapists.
    b. Benefits are provided only for short-term therapy, which has been found to be as beneficial as long-term therapy.
    c. Reasonable functioning is emphasized rather than curing problems.
    d. Both diagnoses and treatment may be less adequate.
    e. The use of psychological therapy in conjunction with biomedical therapies has been reduced.

19. Research on the effectiveness of psychotherapy has concluded that
    a. some types of therapy are much more effective than others for most disorders.
    b. about 50 percent of clients improve by the third therapy session.
    c. psychotherapy generally has no effect as often as it has a positive one.
    d. the most effective treatments are those lasting more than 2 years.
    e. there is no correlation between length of therapy and long-term mental health benefits.

20. Which of the following is a possible obstacle to ethnic minorities' use of therapeutic services?
    a. belief systems of one's culture
    b. history of institutionalized discrimination
    c. greater comfort with culturally specific help
    d. stigma surrounding mental health services
    e. all of the above

21. One of the consequences of ethnic minorities underutilizing therapeutic services is that
    a. mental illness among ethnic minorities is underdiagnosed.
    b. higher rates of mental illness are assumed among ethnic minorities.
    c. there is a higher mortality rate among ethnic minorities.
    d. stereotypes are reinforced about mental illness among ethnic minorities.
    e. none of the above

22. Which of the following is *not* true regarding the representation of ethnic minorities in the field of professional psychology and the treatment of these populations?
    a. Only 10 percent of psychologists are from ethnically diverse backgrounds.
    b. Special training is being implemented to increase effectiveness with diverse backgrounds.
    c. The poor, which consists disproportionately of ethnic minorities, have higher therapy dropout rates.
    d. Ethnic minorities receive special benefits to receive therapy but often do not use them.
    e. all of the above

Chapter 15

Stress, Coping, and Health

Source: Courtesy of Figzoi.

Many of you reading this chapter are nearing the end of the semester in your college studies. This is the time in the school year when you have many demands on your time, including the final push to complete term papers and prepare for final exams. For a few of you, the semester has been a breeze, with only minor worries and concerns. For others, events have challenged the limits of your mental and physical endurance. You may now personally understand how sleep deprivation (see chapter 6, section 6-2d) can harm learning and creativity, or how the tip-of-the-tongue phenomenon (see chapter 8, section 8-4b) can mean the difference between a passing and a failing grade on an important exam. So perhaps it is timely that this chapter in our journey of discovery brings us to the psychology of stress and coping—not only stress caused by the demands of college life and other everyday events, but also the stress caused by personal and group hardships and catastrophes. By understanding more about the causes and consequences of stress, you will be better prepared to manage major stressful events in your life as well as the minor hassles that comprise daily living. This exploration of stress will lead us into a broader examination of the psychology of health. Do you know what it means to be healthy? Is being healthy different from being disease-free?

The psychologists and physicians whose work forms the bulk of this chapter are in the interdisciplinary field of **behavioral medicine**, which integrates behavioral and medical knowledge and then applies it to health and illness. Psychologists who study the effects of behavior and mental processes on health and illness are called **health psychologists.** In studying the causes and consequences of health and illness, scientists rely on the **biopsychosocial model,** which assumes that health and overall wellness are influenced by a complex interaction of biological, psychological, and sociocultural factors.

> **behavioral medicine** An interdisciplinary field of science that integrates behavioral and medical knowledge and then applies it to health and illness.

> **health psychologists** Psychologists who study the effects of behavior and mental processes on health and illness.

> **biopsychosocial model** An interdisciplinary model that assumes that health and overall wellness are caused by a complex interaction of biological, psychological, and sociocultural factors.

15-1 WHAT CAUSES STRESS?

Preview

- *What is stress?*
- *What is the general adaptation syndrome?*
- *Are there gender differences in the stress response?*
- *What is the difference between natural immunity and acquired immunity?*

The process by which you perceive and respond to the challenges of college life falls under the general topic that we call stress. I define **stress** as our response to events that disturb, or threaten to disturb, our physical or psychological equilibrium. The events that disrupt our equilibrium are known as **stressors.** Most of us would agree that flunking out of college, experiencing the death of a loved one, or being sexually assaulted would be a very stressful event. Yet most stressors are not of this magnitude, and not all stressors are unpleasant.

> **stress** Our response to events that disturb, or threaten to disturb, our physical or psychological equilibrium.

> **stressors** External or internal events that challenge or threaten us.

15-1a Stressors Can Be Positive or Negative, as Well as Large or Small

Stressors come in various forms. *Major cataclysmic events,* such as the 2004 Southeast Asian tsunami that killed more than 300,000 people, are easily recognized as stressors, as are *personal major events,* such as being a victim of a crime or having a death in the family. Among these events, some may be short-term and acute (for example, surgery to remove a benign tumor), while others may be more chronic in nature (for example, chemotherapy to treat cancer). Historically, these types of major events made up the bulk of early research on stress (Holmes & Rahe, 1967). Such major events can also lead to *post-traumatic stress disorder (PTSD),* which can appear months or even years after experiencing the stressor (see chapter 13, section 13-3a). Symptoms of PTSD include anxiety, social withdrawal, survivor guilt, and flashbacks of the event (Brewin et al., 1996). PTSD is also associated with an increased risk of physical illness (Adams & Adams, 1984).

All the stressors mentioned so far involve negative events. Yet even events that you welcome, such as an outstanding personal achievement, a marriage, or a new job, require major changes in your daily routines and tax your body's resources. For example, although the birth of a child is one of the happiest and most anticipated events in a person's life, studies of married couples have found that the arrival of a child dramatically increases stress and contributes to dissatisfaction with the relationship (Cowan & Cowan, 2000; Levenson et al., 1993). More rarely, among art lovers, exposure to extraordinary art can induce acute stress, sometimes to such an extent that hospitalization is required. This uncommonly intense stress reaction to an overwhelmingly positive experience is known as *Stendhal's syndrome*, named after nineteenth-century French novelist Stendhal, who visited Florence, Italy, and was overwhelmed by the city's rich legacy of art and history. A similar stress reaction sometimes occurs among tourists visiting Jerusalem (the *Jerusalem syndrome*) who are overcome by the mental weight of its history and religious significance. Yet, despite the ability of positive life events to increase stress levels, research indicates that negative events generally induce more stress than do neutral or positive events (Monroe & Simons, 1991).

As disruptive as major events are to your life, they often reflect only a fraction of the stressors that affect your health and well-being. In between each of these major stressful "boulders" occur myriad *hassles* and minor stressful "pebbles," such as losing your keys, arguing with a roommate, or getting a traffic ticket. The more daily hassles you experience, the more your mental and physical health tends to suffer (Nelson et al., 1995; Safdar & Lay, 2003). The negative effects of daily hassles, however, can be alleviated by positive daily experiences (Lazarus & Lazarus, 1994).

Which type of stressor (boulder or pebble) is worse for you? As mentioned, both classes of events can lead to health problems. In part, accumulating pebbles can leave you more vulnerable to major events when they occur. Similarly, major events can leave you unable to deal with the daily hassles of life, causing them to pile up and overwhelm you. Researchers have found that people with high stress levels during the previous year were more than twice as likely to become ill as were people who experienced lower levels of stress (Bieliauskas et al., 1995; Holmes & Rahe, 1967).

This is my father after a 3-day visit with his relatives in northern Italy. Although this was a lifetime dream for my father, he can certainly attest to the fact that wonderful life events can be stressful. The simple fact is that life changes increase stress. Yet do positive events induce less stress than negative events?

Source: Courtesy of Figzoi.

15-1b Hans Selye Viewed Stress as a Specific Set of Responses to Demands

As discussed in chapter 3, section 3-2a, Walter Cannon's (1915) research first described how our bodies respond to threatening situations. If something angers or frightens us, our bodies physiologically prepare for "fight or flight" by slowing digestion, accelerating heart rate, raising blood sugar, and cooling the body with perspiration. If the threatening situation

In rare cases, being in the presence of many artistic masterpieces can induce an intense stress reaction known as Stendhal's syndrome, which is named after the nineteenth-century French novelist who was overcome with emotion upon viewing the artwork in Florence, Italy. Stendhal described his stress reaction in the following way: "I was in a sort of ecstasy, from the idea of being in Florence, close to the great men whose tombs I had seen. . . . I reached the point where one encounters celestial sensations . . . I had palpitations of the heart, what in Berlin they call 'nerves.' Life was drained from me. I walked with the fear of falling."

Source: Courtesy of Figzoi.

does not subside, we remain in this state of heightened arousal. If prolonged, such stress and the accompanying heightened arousal can cause serious health problems.

The General Adaptation Syndrome

One scientist who was instrumental in providing further insight into how our bodies react to stress was Hans Selye (1907–1982). In the 1930s, this European-born physician, while trying to discover new sex hormones, stumbled upon some of the physiological mechanisms of stress. In his experiments with rats, Selye (1936) noticed that exposing the animals to a wide range of physical stressors (cold, heat, swimming, injections) caused their bodies to respond in two ways. The first response was specific to the stressor itself, such as shivering when exposed to cold and sweating when exposed to heat. In contrast, the second response was not specific to any particular stressor but was a general response geared toward energizing and protecting the body from harm. This second response is what Selye (1956) called the *stress response,* and he saw it as occurring in reaction to any significant demand on the body. If the demand continues, particular changes in the body begin to occur. Selye referred to this stress response, and the resulting changes in the body, as the **general adaptation syndrome (GAS),** which consists of three stages: alarm, resistance, and exhaustion. Figure 15-1 depicts these three stages in the body's response to stress.

In stage 1, upon encountering a stressor, the body first reacts with *alarm,* which is essentially the reaction previously referred to as the fight-or-flight response. The alarm reaction produces an initial shock phase, during which the hypothalamus and lower brain structures (such as the amygdala) activate the sympathetic nervous system and the endocrine system to prepare you for action by slowing your digestion, accelerating your heart rate, raising your blood sugar, and cooling your body with perspiration. The adrenal gland's release of the stress hormones *epinephrine* (also called adrenaline) and *norepinephrine* (also called noradrenaline) triggers these rapid and intense physiological changes (Sher, 2003). Your body's resources are now mobilized.

No organism can survive for long in the state of heightened arousal exhibited during the alarm stage. Homeostasis must be achieved, even if the stressor persists. During stage 2, *resistance,* the parasympathetic nervous system returns many physiological functions—such as respiration and heart rate—to normal levels, even while the body focuses its resources against the continuing stressor. Although many stress hormones continue to circulate throughout the body at elevated levels, the outward appearance of the organism generally seems entirely normal. But the body remains on red alert.

If the stressor continues beyond the body's capacity, the organism exhausts its resources and becomes susceptible to disease and death. This is the third stage of the general adaptation syndrome, *exhaustion.* Selye described it as "a kind of premature aging due to wear and tear" (Selye, 1956, p. 31). Organs such as the heart are the first to break down during this stage.

Prolonged Stress and The HPA Axis

Selye's description of the general adaptation syndrome emphasized that the same biological changes that help us deal with stress in the short run can become hazardous to our health in the long run. As described, during the alarm stage of the general adaptation syndrome, the hypothalamus sends messages along a neural pathway, signaling the adrenal glands to release epinephrine and norepinephrine, which sharply heightens physiological arousal. This initial fight-or-flight response is illustrated in pathway 1 of figure 15-2.

general adaptation syndrome (GAS) Selye's model of stress, in which an event that threatens an organism's well-being (a stressor) leads to a three-stage bodily response—alarm, resistance, and exhaustion.

Figure 15-1

The General Adaptation Syndrome

Hans Selye's research suggests that physical reactions to stress include three stages: initial alarm, resistance, and then exhaustion. During the alarm stage, the body's resistance temporarily drops below normal due to the shock of the stressor. The body is at its highest state of resistance to stress during the resistance stage, but resistance declines as the body's resources become depleted in the exhaustion stage.

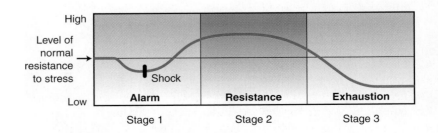

Pathway 1

Hypothalamus

Sympathetic
nervous system

Adrenal glands

Secrete
epinephrine and
norepinephrine

Pathway 2

Hypothalamus

Pituitary gland

Adrenal glands

Kidneys

Secrete cortisol
and other
hormones

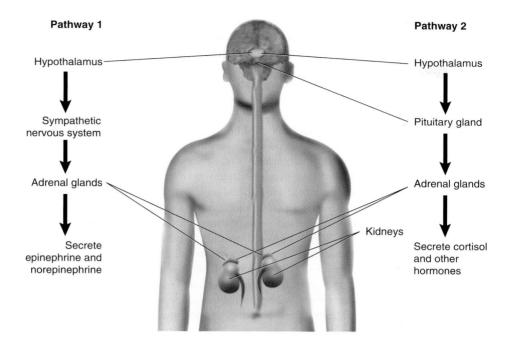

Figure 15-2

Two Stress Pathways from the Hypothalamus to the Adrenal Glands

When a person is under stress, the hypothalamus signals the adrenal glands to secrete hormones using two neural pathways. In pathway 1, the hypothalamus activates the sympathetic division of the autonomic nervous system, which signals the adrenal glands to secrete epinephrine and norepinephrine. The release of these hormones into the bloodstream produces many of the physiological changes associated with the "fight-or-flight" response. If the stress response is prolonged, a second pathway, known as the HPA axis, is used by the hypothalamus. Here, the hypothalamus signals the pituitary gland, which signals the adrenal glands to secrete cortisol and other hormones. This increases the body's energy resources, enhances muscle tone in the heart and blood vessels, and protects the body's tissues from inflammation. What is the danger in these stress hormones remaining at high levels in the body for a prolonged period of time?

Later research revealed that, after this initial stress response, if the threat persists the hypothalamus plays a second important role using a different neural pathway (pathway 2 in figure 15-2). Following prolonged stress, the hypothalamus sends messages along a neural pathway called the *HPA axis,* which stands for hypothalamus (H), pituitary gland (P), and adrenal cortex (A; the outer part of the adrenal glands). Using this second pathway, the hypothalamus signals the pituitary gland, which in turn signals the adrenal cortex to secrete *cortisol* and other hormones. The introduction of these stress hormones into the bloodstream increases the body's energy resources, enhances muscle tone in the heart and blood vessels, and protects body tissues from inflammation.

The increased energy due to HPA axis activation is crucial in helping the body continue resisting or coping with stressors. However, if cortisol and other stress hormones remain high for too long, they can weaken crucial body systems, causing increases in blood pressure, formation of blood clots and clogged arteries, and overall damage to the body's ability to defend itself against disease (see section 15-1e). Elevated cortisol levels also cause increased consumption of fatty foods, which contributes to weight problems. Prolonged stress can also lead to chronic anxiety, depression, and other psychological disorders (see chapter 13).

15-1c The "Fight-or-Flight" Stress Response May Be Gender-Specific

Although Selye's original work assumed that the GAS-type response pattern was the same for men and women, researchers have recently questioned whether women typically respond with fight-or-flight tendencies in the initial alarm stage. Such questioning was prompted by findings indicating that, in response to stress, the pituitary gland releases significantly higher levels of the oxytocin hormone in females than in males (Pedersen, 2004; Windle et al., 1997). As you recall from chapter 3, section 3-2c, the release of oxytocin is associated with increased affiliative and nurturing behaviors. The higher levels of oxytocin released in women compared with men during the stress response have led Shelley Taylor and her coworkers (2000) to propose that, when women are exposed to stressors, instead of experiencing the fight-or-flight response, they are more likely to experience a *tend-and-befriend response.* This response involves women taking action to protect their offspring or befriend members of their social group to reduce their vulnerability.

Evolutionary theorists contend that these stress-response differences are the evolutionary by-products of the different mating strategies of males and females. According to this explanation, males of many species, including our own, are more aggressive and have a stronger social dominance orientation than do females, because aggression and dominance-seeking have been the primary ways males have gained sexual access to females (Buss, 1999a; Buss & Schmitt, 1993). Perhaps, by physically intimidating—and sometimes even killing—less aggressive males, the more aggressive males became socially dominant and, thus, were more likely to sexually reproduce. Unlike that of males, females' reproductive success did not depend on their level of aggression but instead depended on their ability to successfully nurture and protect offspring. Evolutionary psychologists contend that over many generations, the importance of aggression in male reproductive success and the importance of nurturance in female reproductive success led to genetically based differences in male and female responses to stress: Men prepare to fight or flee, while women prepare to tend and befriend (Eisler & Levine, 2002).

An alternative explanation for these gender differences in stress responses proposed by sociocultural theorists is that they are primarily due to gender socialization. Traditionally, the way children are raised in North American culture fosters the construction of an *independent* self-concept among males and a *relational* self-concept among females (Cross & Madson, 1997). As such, girls are more likely than boys to be raised to think, act, and define themselves in ways that emphasize their emotional connectedness to other individuals (Cross et al., 2000). This may lead women to respond to stress with nurturance and affiliation, tending to their offspring and seeking out others for comfort and protection. In contrast, men may tend to exhibit fight-or-flight responses to threat, because they have been raised to be independent and self-sufficient.

At this point, available evidence does not clearly support one view over the other, and both perspectives could explain different aspects of gender differences in stress responses. Consistent with the evolutionary viewpoint, women and men may have evolved different stress responses due to differences in their mating strategies, which account for the greater oxytocin release among women than men. In turn, consistent with the sociocultural perspective, this genetic tendency may be heightened or weakened by existing socialization patterns in contemporary society.

15-1d Headaches Are a Common Reaction to Stress

As you may well be aware from personal experience, the onset of a headache is often preceded by some stressful event (Davenport, 2004; Wittock & Myers, 1998). During a typical year, nearly 95 percent of adults have at least one headache, while 25 percent experiencing long-lasting or recurring head pain (Celentano et al., 1992; Olesen & Lipton, 2004). The Centers for Disease Control and Prevention estimate that the occurrence of disabling headaches has increased over 60 percent during the past 10 years. Stress is by far the most common headache "trigger," and more headaches are caused by everyday hassles than by major life-changing events.

Although the exact causes of tension-type headaches are still unknown, they are frequently associated with the contraction of head and neck muscles, and they are often eased or eliminated by massaging the head and neck or by taking nonprescription analgesics such as aspirin, naproxen sodium, or ibuprofen (Diener & Limmroth, 2004; Jensen et al., 1998). One important built-in protection against headaches appears to be the neurotransmitter serotonin—which helps regulate emotional states and affects sleep and general arousal (see chapter 3, section 3-1d). The beginning of a headache is often associated with a drop in the level of serotonin in the brain.

What may surprise you is that one of the most common causes of chronic headaches is the overuse of nonprescription pain relievers (Warner, 1999; Young, 2004). Initially, sufferers begin taking analgesics to diminish the pain of tension-type headaches. However, by failing to follow label directions—which warn against using the drug for more than a few days—sufferers become physically dependent and experience a "rebound headache" as each dose wears off. Of course, these rebound headaches lead to more pill taking, and the vicious cycle perpetuates itself. Serotonin has now also been implicated in the transformation of tension-type headaches into rebound headaches (Srikiatkhachorn et al., 1998).

Regular consumption of caffeine can also precipitate rebound headaches (Castillo et al., 1999), because caffeine is an addictive drug (see chapter 6, section 6-3g). Once the body becomes physically dependent on caffeine, users experience withdrawal symptoms—principally headaches—when it is not ingested (James, 1998). Caffeine users who experi-

Tension headaches are a common problem in modern-day society. How can the overuse of nonprescription pain relievers cause headaches?

Source: Courtesy of Figzoi.

ence such withdrawal can diminish or eliminate their headaches by drinking something laced with the drug, thus getting their "caffeine fix." Of course, this remedy is as ill advised as the method of those who misuse over-the-counter pain medication. Interestingly, once a headache has begun, caffeine can significantly diminish the pain when used in conjunction with an analgesic, because it enhances the effects of pain medication. That is why caffeine is often added as an ingredient in pain medicines. The remedy for rebound headaches is to stop using the offending drugs—regardless of whether they are analgesics or caffeine—and to tolerate the more severe resulting headaches for a few days or weeks. An alternative strategy is to slowly eliminate the medicine or caffeine from your body.

In rare cases (1 out of 25,000), an acute headache is a symptom of a serious physical disorder. If any of the following symptoms describe your headache pattern, consult a physician:

- The headache is severe, new, and unlike past headaches.
- The headache is the "worst" you have ever experienced.
- The headache becomes much worse over time.
- Headache occurs with exertion, sexual activity, coughing, or sneezing.
- When the headache occurs, you feel drowsy, confused, or feverish.

15-1e Psychophysiological Illnesses Are Stress Related

Medical experts estimate that stress plays a role in 50 to 70 percent of all physical illnesses (Wolkowitz & Rothschild, 2003). These stress-related physical illnesses are referred to as **psychophysiological disorders.** The two body systems that have received the most attention from researchers studying stress-related diseases are the *cardiovascular system* and the *immune system*.

The Cardiovascular System

The cardiovascular system, made up of the heart and all the blood vessels that bring blood to and from the heart, is essential for life. However, this system is also associated with the primary causes of death—namely, heart attacks and stroke. In addition, the cardiovascular system is strongly affected by the emotional responses related to stress (Matthews et al., 2003). People have long believed that strong emotional distress can cause sudden death from cardiac events. Converging evidence from correlational, longitudinal, and animal studies has confirmed such a connection (Kamarck & Jennings, 1991; Krantz et al., 1996). For example, heart attacks and deaths from cardiovascular events were elevated in the weeks that followed air strikes in Tel Aviv during the 1991 Gulf War (Meisel et al., 1991). In particular, stressful events involving anger have been related to heart attacks (Mittleman et al., 1995).

High blood pressure (or *hypertension*) and diseases of the arteries that nourish the heart are primary risk factors behind heart attacks and sudden death. As discussed in section 15-1b, increased sympathetic nervous system activity raises heart rate and blood pressure, placing more strain on the cardiovascular system and damaging the arteries that nourish the heart (Krantz & Manuck, 1984). The majority of instances of *ischemia*, a condition in which the heart does not receive sufficient blood, occur during times of daily mental strain and, in particular, following anger-inducing stressors (Hughes, 2004; Krantz et al., 1996). In addition to this physical strain, when threatening situations persist for extended time periods, stress hormones remain at high levels in the body, which can cause blood clots, artery damage, and heart attacks (Muller et al., 1994).

The Immune System

Another way in which stress responses work with other physical states to place us at greater risk for disease is through their effect on the immune system, our body's primary defense against disease (Anisman & Kusnecov, 2005). The **immune system** is a complex surveillance system of specialized cells, tissues, and organs that react to and destroy microorganisms determined not to be part of the body. Although you might not think of your skin as part of your immune system, it is. Skin tissue prevents many dangerous microorganisms from entering and infecting the body.

The immune system was once thought to act independently of the nervous system, but we now know that the immune system and the brain are in close communication and influence each other's actions (Keller et al., 1994). This communication means that the activity of

psychophysiological disorders Physical conditions, such as high blood pressure and migraine headaches, that are caused or aggravated by psychological factors such as stress.

immune system A complex surveillance system of specialized cells, tissues, and organs that is the body's primary defense against disease.

psychoneuroimmunology
The interdisciplinary field that studies the relationship between psychological factors and physical illness.

one system affects the activity of the other. One pathway is through the stress response. The interdisciplinary field that studies the relationship between psychological factors and illness, especially the effects of stress on the immune system, is known as **psychoneuroimmunology.**

The foreign cells that the immune system seeks to destroy are known as *antigens.* In understanding how the immune system attacks these invading microorganisms, it is useful to distinguish between two immune system responses: natural immunity and specific immunity (Benjamini et al., 2000). *Natural immunity* is created by the body's natural barriers (such as the skin and protective substances in the mouth) and by specialized cells that provide a fast, all-purpose assault on a number of different invading antigens that can cause disease. The largest group of cells involved in natural immunity is the *granulocytes,* which are white blood cells that patrol the body and literally eat antigens and anything else suspicious that they find in the bloodstream, tissues, or lymphatic system. Another cell involved in natural immunity is the *natural killer cell,* which destroys antigens that are causing the early phases of viral infections and tumors, as well as infected body cells (Weiss, 1992).

Natural immunity defense is present at birth, but *specific immunity* (also known as *acquired immunity*) develops from the body being exposed to specific antigens that are "remembered" by the immune system. Later, when these antigens reenter the body, the immune system "remembers" exactly how to respond and produces specific protective white blood cells, called *lymphocytes.* Although the specific immune response creates a population of lymphocyte cells that protects the body against specific antigens, it often takes several days before these cells can effectively fight the infection. The two types of lymphocytes chiefly responsible for the specific immune response to infections are *B lymphocytes* (often simply called *B cells*) and *T lymphocytes* (likewise, called *T cells*). B cells get their name from the fact that they form and mature in the *bone* marrow and produce *antibodies,* which are protein molecules that attach themselves to antigens and mark them for destruction (Weill & Reynaud, 2005). Although T cells also form in the bone marrow, their name comes from the fact that they mature in the thymus. Some T cells directly attack cancer cells, viruses, and other antigens, while other T cells regulate the immune system by directing immune responses (Krogsgaard & Davis, 2005). On occasion, the lymphocytes overreact and attack harmless material, which can trigger allergic reactions to pollen and ragweed, cause the body's rejection of transplanted organs, and lead to *autoimmune diseases,* such as multiple sclerosis and rheumatoid arthritis (Bernard, 2005; Croen et al., 2005; Viau & Zouali, 2005).

A recent meta-analysis of 293 stress studies involving almost 19,000 individuals found that acute, short-term stressors have different effects on the immune system than chronic, long-term stressors (Segerstrom & Miller, 2004). It appears that, when stressors are of the fight-or-flight variety (acute and of short duration), the natural immune system kicks into high gear and adaptively redistributes granulocytes and natural killer cells to fight possible infection and/or injury. This hyperactivation of natural immunity requires only minimal time and energy, but it also causes the body's resources to be directed away from the specific immune response. This suppression of the specific immune system makes evolutionary sense, because during periods of challenge when quick action is necessary, suppressing

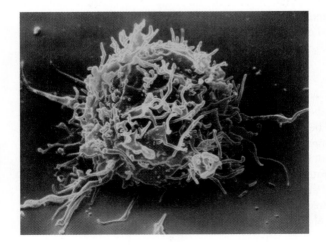

Forming in the bone marrow, lymphocytes are specialized white blood cells that move into certain organs and circulate throughout the bloodstream as an essential part of the body's specific immune response. The type of lymphocyte shown in this photo is a T cell. Some T cells attack and destroy invading microorganisms, while other T cells regulate the immune system by directing immune responses.

Source: Nibsc/Photo Researchers, Inc.

immune responses that require considerable time and energy increases the efficiency of the fight-or-flight response, thus increasing chances of survival (Maier et al., 1994). Following acute stress, the immune system returns to normal. Immune system problems arise, however, when stress is prolonged, because our body's defenses are not designed to efficiently handle long-term challenges. Put simply, chronic stress dramatically reduces the efficiency of the immune system, making the body more susceptible to disease (Moynihan & Stevens, 2001; O'Leary, 1990). The longer the stress lasts, the more likely we are to become ill.

Chronic stress may also hasten the aging process. A study of women who were the primary caregivers for a child suffering from a serious chronic illness found that the women had body cells that looked 10 years older than their chronological age (Epel et al., 2004). Further, the degree of cellular aging was highest in the women who had been caring for a disabled child the longest. One explanation for these findings is that chronic stress disrupts the normal process of cell division in the body, causing damage to cell DNA beyond what normally occurs due to natural aging. Eventually, this DNA damage no longer allows the cell to divide, and it prematurely dies. Researchers are as yet unsure how precisely chronic stress affects cell division and aging, but they believe that chemicals known as *free radicals* are involved in the cell damage.

Another form of chronic stress is bereavement, which is grief following the loss of a loved one. Bereavement is associated with decreased natural killer cell and T-cell activity (Gerra et al., 2003; Segerstrom & Miller, 2004). When grieving spouses were studied over a 2-year period, they were found to be more susceptible to illness and physical ailments and more likely to die than a comparison group of similar adults. These negative health consequences were especially true for the grieving men (Stroebe et al., 2001). Chronic environmental stressors, such as poverty and noisy living conditions, are associated with irritability, fatigue, and high blood pressure, which can lead to a variety of illnesses, including strokes and heart attacks (Adler & Snibbe, 2003; Leather et al., 2003). Even the relatively short-term stressor of final exams can lower the overall effectiveness of the immune system, resulting in greater health risks among college students (Kiecolt-Glaser & Glaser, 2001).

Before complaining to your professors that exams can be hazardous to your health, keep in mind that stress is a subjective experience. As we will discuss more fully in section 15-2a, while one person may perceive a particular situation as highly threatening, another person may perceive the same situation as only mildly stressful. In this regard, it might be useful to recall the discussion in chapter 13, section 13-1c, concerning how a predisposition toward a psychological disorder can lead to its onset following stressful events. This *diathesis-stress model* (Levi, 1974)—which is an excellent example of the biopsychosocial perspective—helps us better understand psychophysiological illnesses. According to the model, several elements are necessary in order for disease to occur. In particular, a *predisposition,* or vulnerability, for a type of disease must exist. In addition, whether or not the disease is allowed to develop will be affected by exposure to something that lowers resistance—notably, stress. This view can help explain not only why different people develop different illnesses following stress, but also why rates of illness change over time (Brannon & Feist, 2000). Let us briefly examine evidence concerning the causal relationship between stress and the following infectious diseases and cancers (Biondi, 2001):

- *Influenza*—Stress diminishes the immune system's response during viral infection and thus reduces the body's ability to fight the virus (Bonneau et al., 2001).
- *West Nile virus*—This mosquito-borne virus can cause encephalitis (inflammation of tissue surrounding the brain) and has been found in a growing number of regions of the United States and Canada. A series of studies demonstrates that the virus is most likely to mutate and become more virulent when the host animal is under stress (Ben-Nathan & Feuerstein, 1990; Ben-Nathan et al., 1996).
- The *"common cold"*—When volunteers were infected with cold virus through nasal drops, they were much more likely to develop cold symptoms if they were experiencing high versus low stress in their daily lives (Cohen & Miller, 2001).
- *Cancer*—A primary defense against cancer is surveillance by the immune system against mutated cells. To date, evidence is mixed as to whether psychosocial stress leads to the development of cancer in the first place. However, the evidence is stronger (though not conclusive) that progression of the disease is greater when people experience high stress. Further, research consistently suggests that people

The stress of living in crowded urban environments can contribute to a variety of illnesses, including strokes and heart attacks. Does everyone react in the same manner to environmental stressors?

Source: Courtesy of Figzoi.

who habitually suppress their emotions are at greater risk for both cancer development and progression, although the degree of risk is as yet unclear (Fox, 1998; Spiegel, 1999; Turner-Cobb et al., 2001).

- *HIV/AIDS*—Logic would suggest that any factor that further suppresses immune functioning, including stress, would affect the progression of HIV/AIDS. Findings from animal and human studies provide preliminary support for the hypothesis that stress negatively affects the efficiency of the body's capacity to fight HIV progression (Cole & Kemeny, 2001).

In summary, substantial evidence from both animal and human studies indicates that changes in immune function in response to stress have negative impacts on health. Clearly, psychosocial stress is one of the important factors affecting vulnerability to various diseases.

Section Review

- Stress is our response to events that disturb, or threaten to disturb, our physical or psychological equilibrium; stressors can be either positive or negative events, with negative events generally inducing more stress.
- According to Selye's general adaptation syndrome, threat first causes the body to react with alarm, then with resistance, and finally with exhaustion as the threat continues.
- There may be gender differences in the initial alarm stage.
- Stress can lead to decreased immune system effectiveness and contribute to a variety of diseases.
- Natural immunity involves the immune system's natural barriers and specialized body cells that make a fast, all-purpose assault on invading microorganisms.
- Specific immunity involves a slower defensive response, in which the immune system creates specific protective cells to attack specific invading microorganisms that the body was exposed to at a previous time.

15-2 WHAT MODERATES STRESS?

Preview

- *How does cognition affect stress?*
- *Can perceived control over a stressor moderate stress?*
- *What personality styles influence stress?*
- *Can friends help you control stress?*
- *Will a spiritual life moderate stress?*

Just because you are exposed to a stressor does not mean that you will become ill. Instead, the way you react to a stressor is shaped by how you perceive it. Your reactions to stress will be moderated by a number of factors, including the *predictability* of the stressor, *perceptions of control,* your *personality,* and the availability of *social support.*

15-2a Cognitive Appraisal Is an Important Part of the Stress Response

Because of Selye's model, stress was catapulted to near the top of the medical community's list of factors contributing to health problems. Yet his theory was developed before most scientists had approached the study of illness from a biopsychosocial perspective. Instead, illness was considered a purely biological phenomenon. Although the GAS easily fit into accepted medical views of the time, by focusing exclusively on the body, this theory all but ignored the role of the mind in the stress response.

Psychological Awareness and Stress

Selye assumed that any severe physiological demand would result in the GAS-type response pattern. However, as more research was conducted, evidence emerged indicating that *psychological awareness of the stressor* is a necessary component in the stress response. In one such study, autopsy reports found evidence of GAS symptoms in people who died while conscious, but not in those who died while comatose (Symington et al., 1955). In other words, the only people who exhibited GAS symptoms were those who were aware that they were dying. Further, starvation studies comparing animals that were fed either nonnutritive pellets or nothing found that only those animals that were aware they were not receiving nutrition showed a GAS response (Mason, 1968). Although the animals given nonnutritive pellets were also being starved, they exhibited no GAS symptoms. None of these findings are consistent with Selye's GAS, suggesting to researchers that a critical weakness in the model is its failure to consider the importance of cognitive processes in the stress response (Frankenhauser, 1975; Mason, 1971, 1975). Realizing that purely biological explanations are inadequate in explaining the stress response was an important step in the development of the biopsychosocial model.

Cognitive Appraisal

Richard Lazarus (1993) was one of the first researchers to examine how we interpret and evaluate stressors in our lives, a process he called *cognitive appraisal.* Cognitive appraisal is essential in defining whether a situation is a threat, how big a threat it is, and what resources you have to deal with the threat (Lazarus & Lazarus, 1994). Some stressors, such as being a crime victim or undergoing surgery, are experienced as threats by almost everyone. However, many other events are defined differently depending on the individuals, their past experiences with similar stressors, and their feelings of competence in dealing with the stressors' demands. For example, starting a new job can fill one person with excitement, while it causes another person to feel apprehensive and overwhelmed. Context is also important. For instance, prior to the anthrax scare of 2001, you probably would not have been alarmed to find powder traces inside a letter you received in the mail. Yet today, with so much concern about biological terrorism, powdered letters are likely to prompt a 911 call.

Lazarus identified two stages in the cognitive appraisal process: primary appraisal and secondary appraisal. *Primary appraisal* involves an initial evaluation of the situation. Here, you assess what is happening, whether it is threatening, and whether you should take some action in response to the threat. If you conclude that some action is necessary, *secondary appraisal* begins. In this second stage of the cognitive appraisal process, you assess whether you have the ability to cope with the stressor. The more competent you perceive yourself to be in dealing with the stressor, the less stress you will experience (Baum & Posluszny, 1999; Croyle, 1992).

Problem-Focused versus Emotion-Focused Coping

In contrast to Selye's model, which viewed the person as a passive recipient of stressors, Lazarus's model conceives of the person as an active participant in evaluating and responding

problem-focused coping
A coping strategy designed to reduce the stress by overcoming the source of the problem.

emotion-focused coping
A coping strategy designed to manage the emotional reactions to stressors rather than to try to change the stressors themselves.

to stressors. Consistent with this activist perspective, Lazarus and Susan Folkman (1984) identified two general coping strategies that people employ during secondary appraisal. **Problem-focused coping** is a strategy aimed at reducing stress by overcoming the source of the problem. For example, if you fail your first exam in an important class, engaging in problem-focused coping might involve such actions as talking to your professor about extra-credit work, changing your study habits, and comparing your class notes with those of someone doing well in the class. A second approach is **emotion-focused coping,** in which you try to manage your emotional reactions to stressors rather than trying to change the stressors themselves (Auerbach & Gramling, 1998). Engaging in this type of coping when faced with class problems might involve trying not to cry when speaking to your professor, seeking sympathy from your friends, or immersing yourself in some other activity to take your mind off your academic troubles. By controlling how you feel, you may be better able to take control of situations, thus limiting the emotional toll of the stressor. Consistent with this idea, research finds that college students experience less daily stress and better physical health if they regularly engage in leisure activities during the school year (Iwasaki, 2003).

We tend to take the active, problem-focused approach to handling stress when we think we have the resources to overcome the problem, but we resort to an emotion-focused strategy when we think the problem is beyond our control (Hagger & Orbell, 2003; Ryden et al., 2003). Of course, at times we employ both types of coping. For example, while devising a plan of action to improve your class performance, you may try to emotionally distance yourself from anxiety by reminding yourself that this is just one exam out of four in the course. Table 15-1 lists some of the specific problem-focused and emotion-focused strategies that people use when coping with stressors (Folkman & Moskowitz, 2000; Kim et al., 2003).

A stressor's actual controllability is one important determinant of what form of coping is appropriate in a given situation. If you can control a stressor, a problem-focused approach is certainly a useful strategy. However, what if you are faced with an uncontrollable stressor? In a fascinating study conducted by the special operations and research staff of the FBI Academy (Auerbach et al., 1994; Strentz & Auerbach, 1988), 57 airline flight attendants voluntarily participated as the victims in a mock terrorist kidnapping. The "terrorists" (actually special agents of the FBI) commandeered a van occupied by the flight attendants, shooting automatic weapons (equipped with blank cartridges) and *flash bangs* (grenades that create noise and light but no shrapnel). The van driver and his assistant soaked their clothes with fake blood and fell to the floor as if shot. The flight attendants were then forcibly pulled from the van, searched, handcuffed, and held in captivity in a building for 4 days with pillowcases placed over their heads. The "terrorists" warned the flight attendants not to communicate with one another or attempt escape, and they were watched so closely that no escape was possible. After 4 days, FBI agents stormed the building and "rescued" the hostages.

Table 15-1 Problem-Focused and Emotion-Focused Coping	
Coping Skills	**Example**
Problem-Focused Coping	
Confronting	Assert yourself and fight for what you want.
Planful problem solving	Develop a plan of action and implement it.
Seeking social support	Seek out others who have information about the stressor.
Emotion-Focused Coping	
Distancing	Redirect your attention to other things or try to downplay the importance of the stressor.
Self-controlling	Keep your feelings to yourself.
Escape/avoidance	Fantasize about the stressor going away (wishful thinking).
Positive reappraisal	Think about positive aspects of yourself not related to the stressor.
Accepting responsibility	Realize that you are responsible for this problem.

Prior to the kidnapping, the flight attendants received one of the following types of preparation: training in escape and intelligence-gathering skills (the problem-focused coping condition); training in relaxation and emotion-control techniques (the emotion-focused coping condition); or information about terrorism and kidnappings (the study's control condition). In this situation of having little control over events, which of the three groups do you think exhibited the highest stress levels?

As expected, the attendants who had been trained to escape and fight back fared the worst during this uncontrollable situation. Put simply, their coping skills were ineffective in dealing with the stressor. In contrast, the attendants who had been trained in emotion-focused coping experienced the least amount of stress, because they were using strategies that best fit this uncontrollable situation. These results are consistent with the reactions of real-life hostages (Auerbach & Gramling, 1998). However, when you are faced with an uncontrollable stressor, it is important to continue monitoring the situation and adjust your coping strategies as the situation changes. Even when a situation is seemingly uncontrollable (for example, being a prisoner of war or suffering from a terminal disease), taking control of what can be controlled (stealing bread when available, controlling pain and comfort levels) helps reduce the negative effects of these intense stressors (Seligman, 1975).

> **Journey of Discovery Question**
>
> It is generally thought that problem-focused coping is maladaptive in situations over which a person has no personal control. Yet a situation that appears on its surface to be uncontrollable may still have controllable aspects. Consider people caring for loved ones with terminal illnesses. During the weeks leading up to death, what sort of problem-focused coping might caregivers engage in to increase their positive moods and lower their stress?

15-2b Predictability and Control Can Moderate the Stress Response

Whether an event will become a harmful stressor is often determined by its *predictability*. If you know that a stressor is coming but are uncertain when it will occur, you tend to experience greater stress (Boss, 1999). In a series of studies assessing stress associated with living in urban environments, David Glass and Jerome Singer (1972) tape-recorded the sounds of office machines and of people speaking a variety of languages. Then, while participants conducted various activities, these loud sounds were played either at predictable or unpredictable intervals. Results indicated that participants who were exposed to the predictable noise adjusted quickly and performed well on almost every task. However, those exposed to the unpredictable noise made more errors and reacted more quickly to frustration. In general, unpredictable stressors have greater impact than those that are predictable, especially when they are intense and occur for relatively brief periods (Parkes & Weiss, 1983).

A host of studies indicate that *perceived control* over a stressor is one of the most important factors moderating the relationship between stress and illness. If people believe that they have some control over a stressor, they usually feel less stressed (Christensen et al., 1998; Theorell, 2003). For example, in one study, elderly nursing home patients who were given greater control over their daily activities experienced fewer health problems and lived longer than those who were not given much control (Rodin, 1986). Similarly, people who work at demanding jobs are least likely to develop coronary heart disease when they believe they have some control over job stressors (Krantz et al., 1988, 1996).

Neurologically, when a stressor is judged to be controllable, a region in the prefrontal cortex involved in thinking and avoidance learning inhibits an acute stress response (Bland et al., 2005). As neuroscientist Steven Maier explains, "It's as if the prefrontal cortex says, 'Cool it brainstem. We have control over this and there is no need to get so excited'" (Kohn, 2005). However, when the stressor is judged to be uncontrollable, the prefrontal cortex activates the brainstem, which triggers a strong fear response.

People differ in their tendency to perceive events as controllable (or uncontrollable). As discussed in chapter 12, section 12-5b, the tendency to assume that outcomes occur because of our own efforts is referred to as an *internal locus of control*, whereas an *external locus of control* reflects a belief that outcomes are outside our control (Rotter, 1966, 1990). A person's

Figure 15-3

Procrastination and Health

When college students who were either procrastinators or nonprocrastinators began the semester in a health psychology class, procrastinators reported slightly fewer symptoms of physical illness than did nonprocrastinators. Later in the semester, as class deadlines loomed, all students showed increased symptoms. However, procrastinators were much more likely to miss those deadlines, and they were much more likely to report an increase in illness symptoms than were nonprocrastinators.

Source: From "Longitudinal study of procrastination, performance, stress, and health: The costs and benefits of dawdling" by D. M. Tice and R. F. Baumeister in *Psychological Science, 8,* 1997, pp. 454–458.

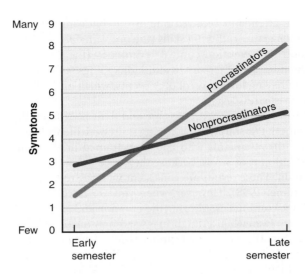

locus of control appears to emerge early in life and is a fairly stable personality trait. Through experience, it is also possible to develop either a sense of mastery or a sense of helplessness toward stressors (see chapter 12, section 12-5b). By experiencing success when attempting to alleviate stressors, you are likely to become more confident that you can gain control over future challenges. Alternatively, repeatedly failing to eliminate stressors can lead to more generalized assumptions of being helpless (Seligman, 1975). This *learned helplessness* can cause you to falsely believe that you have no control over a stressor, thus increasing the likelihood that you will take no action to reduce the threat (Baum et al., 1998).

When people doubt their ability to assert control over a stressor, they are more likely to engage in emotion-focused coping strategies (see section 15-1c). *Procrastination,* which involves delaying the start and completion of *planful problem solving,* is an example of the emotion-focused coping strategy of *escape-avoidance* (refer back to table 15-1). Approximately one out of five adults regularly procrastinates when faced with a stressor, especially when it is severe (Harriot & Ferrari, 1996). These habitually indecisive individuals are easily distracted, have low self-confidence, and have an external locus of control (Ferrari & Dovidio, 2001). Far from reducing stress, however, such delays in tackling problems tend to increase stress and lead to health problems (Ferrari & Tice, 2000). For example, at the beginning of the semester in a health psychology class, researchers identified college students who were either habitually high or low in procrastination (Tice & Baumeister, 1997). As you can see in figure 15-3, although procrastinators reported slightly fewer symptoms of physical illness than did nonprocrastinators early in the semester, procrastinators had significantly greater symptoms later in the semester as term paper deadlines came due. True to form, procrastinators not only turned their assignments in later than nonprocrastinators, but also obtained lower grades on those papers.

15-2c Hostile Persons Are Very Reactive to Stressors

The fact that stressors become less worrisome and more manageable when we perceive them as predictable and controllable highlights how our thinking about events shapes our behavioral responses. Additional research indicates that some people's consistent and distinctive ways of thinking, feeling, and behaving—that is, their personalities—cause them to react negatively to stressors, whereas others respond positively (Masten, 2001). A personality dimension that significantly influences stress responses is *Type A* versus *Type B behavior patterns.*

Type A and Type B Behavior Patterns

During the 1950s, two cardiologists, Ray Rosenman and Meyer Friedman, noted an oddity about their coronary patients: The way these patients sat on the chairs in the cardiologists' waiting room caused the chair upholstery to be worn more in the front than in the back—as if their patients were sitting on the edge of their seats. This observation, coupled with the cardiologists' later findings that many of these same people were also impatient workaholics, led Rosenman and Friedman to identify what they called the **Type A behavior pattern** (Rosenman, 1993; Rosenman et al., 1975). This complex pattern of behaviors and emotions—which is associated with increased risk of heart disease—is characterized by competitiveness, impatience, ambition, hostility, and a hard-driving approach to life (Boyce & Geller, 2002; Le Melledo et al., 2003). The direct opposite of this personality style is the **Type B behavior pattern,** which is characterized by a patient, relaxed, easygoing approach to life, with little hurry or hostility. These individuals are only half as likely to develop coronary heart disease as their Type A counterparts (Lyness, 1993). Spend a few minutes answering the items in Self-Discovery Questionnaire 15-1 to assess yourself for the Type A behavior pattern.

Based on numerous studies, *cynical hostility* appears to be the toxic component of the Type A pattern (Dembroski et al., 1985; Fredrickson et al., 2000). Specifically, people who mistrust and think the worst of others and use anger as a typical response to interpersonal problems appear to be at greatest risk for heart disease (Eysenck, 2000; Vahtera et al., 2000). From a physiological point of view, cynical hostility appears to cause chronic overarousal of the body's stress responses (Everson et al., 1997; Friedman et al., 1994). From a psychosocial point of view, cynical hostility contributes to poor health habits and tense social relationships (Smith, 1992). In general, men are more hostile than women (see section 15-1d), and even at the same level of hostility, men's blood pressure is more adversely affected by their hostility than women's (Räikkönen et al., 1999).

Because of the health problems associated with the Type A behavior pattern, it makes sense to try to convince Type A persons to change their hostile, impatient approach to life.

> **Type A behavior pattern**
> A complex pattern of behaviors and emotions characterized by competitiveness, impatience, ambition, hostility, and a hard-driving approach to life.

> **Type B behavior pattern**
> A pattern of behaviors and emotions characterized by a patient, relaxed, easygoing approach to life, with little hurry or hostility.

Self-Discovery
Questionnaire **15-1**

Do You Have a Type A Personality?

INTERACTIVE BOX

Directions: Indicate how often each of the following applies to you in daily life, using the following three-point scale:

1 = seldom or never   2 = sometimes   3 = always or usually

____ Do you find yourself rushing your speech?

____ Do you hurry other people's speech by interrupting them with "umha, umhm" or by completing their sentences for them?

____ Do you hate to wait in line?

____ Do you seem to be short of time to get everything done?

____ Do you detest wasting time?

____ Do you eat fast?

____ Do you drive over the speed limit?

____ Do you try to do more than one thing at a time?

____ Do you become impatient if others do something too slowly?

____ Does your concentration sometimes wander while you think about what's coming up later?

____ Do you find yourself overcommitted?

____ Do you jiggle your knees or tap your fingers?

____ Do you think about other things during conversations?

____ Do you walk fast?

____ Do you hate dawdling after a meal?

____ Do you become irritable if kept waiting?

____ Do you detest losing in sports and games?

____ Do you find yourself with clenched fists or tight neck and jaw muscles?

____ Do you seem to have little time to relax and enjoy the time of day?

____ Are you a competitive person?

____ *Total Score*

A score of 20–34 may mean low Type A behavior, 35–44 medium Type A behavior, and 45–60 high Type A behavior.

Source: From *Stress Management for Wellness,* 2nd edition, by W. Schafer. Copyright © 1992. Reprinted with permission of Brooks/Cole, an imprint of the Wadsworth Group, a division of Thomson Learning. Fax 800/730-2215.

He who is hurried cannot walk gracefully.

—*Chinese proverb*

God gave us memory so that we can have flowers in December.

—*Percy B. Shelley, English poet, 1792–1822*

> **hardiness** A set of personality traits marked by a sense of commitment, challenge, and control that promotes resistance to stress and illness.

However, one major obstacle to orchestrating such change is that many Type A persons are not unhappy with their behavior. After all, North American culture respects and rewards this hard-driving, hostile lifestyle. (Rush Limbaugh, Donald Trump, and most of the successful contestants on TV reality shows are prototypes of the Type A person.) Yet, for people motivated to reduce their hostility and "smell the roses" in their daily lives, behavior modification and cognitive therapy (see chapter 14, sections 14-3 and 14-4) have been successful in changing Type A behavior (DiGiuseppe & Tafrate, 2003; Zolnierczyk, 2004). Before reading further, check out Explore It Exercise 15-1, on how to alter the Type A behavior pattern.

Hardiness

What sort of person thrives on stress and avoids illness? Suzanne Kobasa and Salvatore Maddi attempted to answer this question by conducting a 5-year longitudinal study of business executives. They found that executives who were illness-resistant tended to possess three personality traits not possessed by those who were illness-prone (Kobasa et al., 1982). These three traits—commitment, control, and challenge—make up what Kobasa and Maddi identify as **hardiness,** or the hardy personality (Maddi, 2004; Maddi & Kobasa, 1984). *Commitment* is a sense of meaning and purpose in life, involving you, others, and work. *Control* is a sense of personal autonomy and believing that you are capable of shaping your life. Finally, *challenge* is a zest for life that leads you to perceive changes as exciting and as opportunities for growth rather than as threats to your security.

Over the years, a number of studies have supported the hypothesis that hardiness is a buffer to life stress. For example, when Norwegian sailors were confined for 7 days within the front section of a submarine as part of a simulated sinking, those with high hardiness experienced the least amount of emotional stress (Eid et al., 2004). Similarly, hardy Latin-American adults who immigrated to Australia reported lower levels of stress while adapting to Australian culture than did similar immigrants with low hardiness (Lopez et al., 2004). Finally, various studies have found that college students, elderly adults, and people living in poverty are significantly more likely to avoid illness when experiencing high levels of stress if they have high hardiness (Smith et al., 2004; Williams & Lawler, 2001).

Although only a few studies have examined the physiological underpinnings of hardiness, there is evidence that hardy individuals have a stronger immune system than nonhardy individuals, making them better prepared to ward off illness and disease (Dolbier et al., 2001). In addition, hardy persons are more likely than nonhardy persons to practice better health habits, such as regularly exercising, not using tobacco products, eating healthy foods, taking vitamins, and seeking early medical attention for minor ailments (S. M. Harris, 2004; Soderstrom et al., 2000; Wiebe & McCallum, 1986). Due to these health benefits, hardiness training programs have been established to teach illness-prone individuals strategies to help them reduce stress and increase their ability to maintain overall health (Maddi & Khoshaba, 2003).

15-2d Pessimism Is Associated with Stress and Illness

> **pessimistic explanatory style** The habitual tendency to explain uncontrollable negative events as caused by one's own stable personal qualities, which affect all aspects of one's life. This pessimistic style is associated with health problems and premature death.

> **optimistic explanatory style** The habitual tendency to explain uncontrollable negative events as caused by temporary factors external to oneself that do not affect other aspects of one's life. This optimistic style is associated with good health and longevity.

Another personality dimension related to health issues is people's *explanatory style*—their degree of habitual pessimism or optimism—regarding negative events in their everyday lives (Haines et al., 1999; Peterson & Steen, 2002). Individuals who have a **pessimistic explanatory style** explain uncontrollable negative events as being caused by internal factors ("It's my fault") that are stable ("It won't ever change") and global ("This affects everything"). Not surprisingly, people who fit this pattern are susceptible to depression (Alloy et al., 1999; Nolen-Hoeksema et al., 1992). In contrast, people with an **optimistic explanatory style** explain uncontrollable negative events as being due to external factors ("It is not my fault") that are unstable or changeable ("It won't happen again") and specific ("This affects only one thing"). Research over the past 20 years indicates that people with an optimistic perspective on life are healthier and more resistant to illness than those with a pessimistic orientation (Peterson & Park, 1998; Scheier & Carver, 2000). In one study, Christopher Peterson and Martin Seligman (1987) measured college students' explanatory styles and asked them to list all the illnesses they had experienced during the previous month, and then again 1 year later (Peterson & Seligman, 1987). Even after controlling for the number of illnesses initially reported, Peterson and Seligman found that students with an optimistic

Based on his research on the Type A behavior pattern, Meyer Friedman (1996) recommends a number of intervention strategies to help Type A persons slow down and reduce their free-floating hostility. Listed next are some of these exercises, plus a few of my own, that you can try during the next week to alter problematic Type A behavior patterns.

Strategies to Modify Time Urgency

Type A persons' habit of always being on the go and thinking of the things they need to accomplish causes them to pay little heed to their current surroundings. Thus, they often fail to notice and appreciate many important people or things in their lives. Here are some exercises you can do to slow down your day and become more present-time oriented:

Exercise 1: *Eat more slowly.* Linger over your meal. Enjoy the various tastes and smells of your food and drink. What do you notice about your meal that you were not aware of before?

Exercise 2: *Take periodic 15-minute breaks from work and notice something beautiful around you.* How does your mood change as you attend to your surroundings?

Exercise 3: *Walk more slowly.* How does this slower pace make you feel? Impatient? Relaxed? Maintain this slower walking pace for at least a week, noticing any changes in your thoughts and feelings over time.

Exercise 4: *Listen to every person who speaks to you without interrupting them, even if you think you have something useful to interject.* How difficult is this for you?

Strategies to Reduce Cynical Hostility

Type A persons' habit of criticizing others is so ingrained that they rarely praise other people. As a result, they rarely receive compliments themselves. Type A persons' free-floating hostility often results in their frowning more than smiling when with others, which often causes people to reciprocate with unfriendly facial expressions and avoidance. Here are some exercises you can do to reverse these negative behavior patterns:

Exercise 1: *Compliment at least two persons during a conversation.* Be sincere and notice their facial expressions as they receive the compliment. How do you feel?

Exercise 2: *Practice smiling as you remember two to three happy events from the past, and then purposely smile while speaking to others.* How do their facial expressions change as you smile?

Exercise 3: *Ask friends or family members about their daily activities, showing genuine interest in what they tell you, asking questions, and avoiding criticisms in your comments.* How do they respond to your expression of interest?

Exercise 4: *Just as you are about to criticize someone, try to avoid doing so; if you must say something critical, first count to 10—or 20, or 30.* Is this a difficult task for you?

One recommendation that helps Type A individuals alter their impatient, hard-driving approach to life is to have them take "time-outs" during their busy daily schedules to appreciate the beauty around them, which they generally fail to notice.

Source: Courtesy of Figzoi.

explanatory style had fewer illnesses 1 year later than those with a pessimistic style. In a second study, using old archived interviews of World War II veterans from 1946, Peterson and Seligman had independent coders classify the men into optimistic or pessimistic categories (Peterson et al., 1988). Although optimism-pessimism did not predict the men's health when they were young adults, by the age of 45, those with a pessimistic explanatory style experienced more health problems than did those with a more optimistic outlook. The researchers found similar results when they studied the deceased members of the Baseball Hall of Fame. Again, using coders to classify players based on how they had explained their sports successes and failures in old newspaper interviews, Peterson and Seligman (1987) found that players with a predominantly pessimistic explanatory style died at a younger age than those with an optimistic style. Other studies that have followed people over a 20- 30-year period have found similar results: Optimists live significantly longer than do pessimists (Levy et al., 2002; Maruta et al., 2000).

Why do optimists live longer, healthier lives? One reason is that pessimists are more vulnerable to accidental or violent death, especially male pessimists (Peterson & Bossio, 2001; Peterson et al., 1998). Apparently, pessimistic thinking is associated with poor problem-solving ability, social difficulties, and risky decision-making, which put pessimists at higher risk of untimely death. A second reason why optimists have greater longevity than pessimists is that they seem to have better immune systems, making them less susceptible to diseases. One study supporting this hypothesis found that optimists had higher numbers of helper T cells (the cells that mediate immune reactions to infection) than did pessimists (Segerstrom et al., 1998). Additional research indicates that optimists have better health habits, more positive social relationships, more positive daily moods, and lower blood pressure than pessimists (Brissette et al., 2002; Mulkana & Hailey, 2001). Combined with the previous findings, it appears that optimists live longer because they are less likely to place themselves in harm's way and are more stress-resistant than pessimists.

Despite these recognized advantages of having an optimistic outlook on life, is there a hidden disadvantage in the optimists' tendency to view the world through rose-colored glasses? Shelley Taylor and her colleagues (2000) examined this question in a longitudinal study of men infected with the HIV virus who were not initially showing any HIV symptoms. Many of these men had seen their close friends and/or partners die from this disease within the past year, and thus, they had plenty of evidence that their own death was a distinct possibility. In this dire situation, the men who maintained the best health and delayed the onset of HIV symptoms were those with the most optimistic beliefs. The researchers concluded that even unrealistic optimistic beliefs about the future may often be beneficial to one's health.

Fortunately, individuals with a pessimistic explanatory style can be taught to change their way of thinking through cognitive therapy (see chapter 14, sections 14-4a and 14-4b). In these *learned optimism training programs,* people are taught to recognize and dispute the inner voices telling them to regularly expect negative events in their daily lives (Seligman & Peterson, 2003). This training typically involves keeping a diary of daily successes and failures, identifying how you contributed to your successes and how external factors caused your failures. Essentially, pessimists are being trained to do what most of us do naturally: take credit for our successes and deny blame for our failures! As discussed in chapter 12, section 12-3d, this beneficial way of explaining your positive and negative outcomes is known as the *self-serving bias.* In a very real sense, research on pessimists and optimists points to the important effects that people's *subjective interpretations* of events have on their health and behavior. Check out Self-Discovery Questionnaire 15-2 to explore your own tendencies toward optimism versus pessimism.

The optimist sees the rose and not its thorns; the pessimist stares at the thorns, oblivious to the rose.

—*Kahlil Gibran, Lebanese poet, 1883–1931*

15-2e Social Support Has Therapeutic Effects

Thus far, we have discussed stress as if it were something you must endure alone. Do you recall what you did when you first learned about the terrorist attacks on New York City and Washington, D.C., on September 11, 2001? If you are like most people, during that time of anxiety, grief, and uncertainty, you sought the companionship of others similarly affected by this tragedy. Our desire to seek out others during times of stress and uncertainty is substantially fueled by the need to compare our emotional state with that of others ("How should I be feeling?") and also to appraise the stressful situation itself ("How much of a threat is this stressor?").

Self-Discovery
Questionnaire **15-2**

Are You Typically an
Optimist or a Pessimist?

The Revised Life Orientation Test developed by Michael Scheier and Charles Carver (1994) measures people's tendencies to believe that they will generally experience good or bad outcomes in their lives. Read the 10 statements below and indicate the degree to which you personally agree with each statement, using the following scale:

0 = strongly disagree
1 = disagree
2 = neutral (neither disagree nor agree)
3 = agree
4 = strongly agree

Try to be as accurate and honest as possible, and try not to let your opinion for one item influence your opinion for other items. There are no correct or incorrect answers.

_____ 1. In uncertain times, I usually expect the best.
_____ 2. It's easy for me to relax.
_____ 3. If something can go wrong for me, it will.
_____ 4. I'm always optimistic about my future.
_____ 5. I enjoy my friends a lot.
_____ 6. It's important for me to keep busy.
_____ 7. I hardly ever expect things to go my way.
_____ 8. I don't get upset too easily.
_____ 9. I rarely count on good things happening to me.
_____ 10. Overall, I expect more good things to happen to me than bad.

Scoring Instructions

_____ **Step 1:** For items 3, 7, and 9, subtract your score from 4.
_____ **Step 2:** Add these corrected scores for items 3, 7, and 9, and record the total here.
_____ **Step 3:** Add your scores for items 1, 4, and 10, and record the total score here.
_____ **Step 4:** Add the totals from steps 2 and 3 to obtain your overall score, which will range from 0 to 40.

Interpretation

Lower scores indicate more pessimism, while higher scores indicate more optimism. In a sample of more than 2,000 college students, the average score was 14.3, with a standard deviation of 4.3. If your score is 10 or lower, this indicates that you tend to be more pessimistic than the average college student. If your score is higher than 10 but lower than 19, this suggests that you tend to have the same level of optimism-pessimism as the average college student. If your score is 19 or higher, this suggests that you tend to be more optimistic than the average college student.

Source: M. F. Scheier, C. S. Carver, & M. W. Bridges, "Distinguishing optimism from neuroticism (and trait anxiety, self-mastery, and self-esteem): A reevaluation of the life orientation test," *Journal of Personality and Social Psychology, 67,* 1073. Copyright 1994 by the American Psychological Association.

The helpful coping resources provided by friends and other people when you are confronting a stressful situation are referred to as **social support.** An overwhelming amount of evidence indicates that having supportive people in our lives provides both psychological and physical benefits (Clark, 2003; S. Cohen et al., 2000; Taylor, 1999). For example, in a longitudinal study of almost 7,000 residents of Alameda County, California, researchers discovered that people lived longest when they had many social and community ties (Berkman & Syme, 1979). This was true of men and women, rich and poor, and people from all racial and ethnic backgrounds. Other studies have found that being socially isolated is, statistically, just as predictive of an early death as high cholesterol or smoking (House et al., 1988; Rogers, 1995). Physiologically, having strong social support networks is associated with a

social support The helpful coping resources provided by friends and other people.

People with more extensive social support networks are happier, have stronger immune systems, and live longer than those who are socially isolated. What are some of the reasons that social connections are so therapeutic?

Source: Courtesy of Figzoi.

stronger immune response to stress (Glaser et al., 1992; Jemmott & Magloire, 1988). For example, a meta-analysis of 81 studies found that having social support during times of stress lowers blood pressure, lessens the secretion of stress hormones, and strengthens immune responses (Uchino et al., 1996).

As mentioned, one common psychological benefit of social support is increased knowledge about the stressor. That is, associating with others often provides us with information about how to understand and emotionally respond to stressful events (Van der Zee et al., 1998). The people who tend to provide us with the most useful information are similar to us in some characteristic related to the stressor (Schachter, 1959). This is the rationale underlying therapeutic support groups for drug abusers, sexual assault victims, and cancer patients (see chapter 14, section 14-6b). In these therapy sessions, people who have experienced the same stressful events can compare themselves with one another while they also provide and receive emotional support.

Although when we are stressed we generally prefer the company of those most similar to us, we sometimes seek out others who are somewhat dissimilar, because they can provide more useful information. For example, a field study (Kulik & Mahler, 1989) found that the vast majority of hospital patients about to undergo coronary bypass surgery preferred to room with someone who had already undergone the procedure rather than with someone like themselves who had not yet had the surgery (78 percent versus 22 percent). A follow-up study found that the information gained from having a postoperative heart patient as a roommate not only did the best job of lowering anxiety but also resulted in faster recovery from surgery (Kulik et al., 1996).

Social support during stressful times can also provide us with opportunities to simply express our feelings, which in turn can lead to physical benefits (Kelly, 1999; Pennebaker et al., 1990). In one relevant experiment, college students spent 15 minutes on each of 4 consecutive nights writing to the experimenter about a traumatic event in their lives. These students subsequently reported fewer illnesses over the next 6 months compared to students who had written to the experimenter about unimportant topics (Pennebaker & Beall, 1986). Similarly, the spouses of suicide or accidental-death victims who confided their feelings to others were less likely to develop physical illnesses during the subsequent year than were spouses who kept their feelings "bottled up" (Pennebaker & O'Heeron, 1984). It appears that such self-disclosing leads to enhanced immune system functioning and, thereby, to better health (Major & Gramzow, 1999; Smyth, 1998). Thus, although "letting out" our feelings about a traumatic event can temporarily upset and arouse us, in the long run, it lowers our stress and improves our health.

As with most things that are good for you, however, too much social support (or support given improperly) can cause negative side effects. For example, receiving overly zealous support can reduce both the recipient's sense of control over a stressor and his or her self-confidence. Receiving social support can also make a person feel beholden to the giver, turning the support into a burden (Greenberg & Frisch, 1972; Gross & Latané, 1974). When providing support to another person, the key is to convey caring for the recipient in a manner that provides real benefits, keeps her or him involved in the solution to the problem (rather than just being "taken care of"), and avoids an inferiority-superiority relationship (Dakof & Taylor, 1990; Dunkel-Schetter et al., 1992).

15-2f Gender Differences Exist in Providing Social Support to Romantic Partners

People involved in long-term romantic relationships often view their partner as their best friend and as the person they would turn to in times of need (Pasch et al., 1997). Receiving such support has four important benefits: The *stress decreases* for those in need, which, in turn, has a positive effect on their *physical health,* while simultaneously increasing their *satisfaction* with and *commitment* to the relationship (Coyne et al., 2001; Sprecher et al., 1995). In heterosexual romance, men rely more on their partners for social support than do women, who also depend on a variety of other sources, including friends, relatives, and neighbors (Cutrona, 1996). However, a woman's psychological well-being is still closely linked to the support she receives from her partner. For example, a longitudinal study of married couples found that lower levels of depression were associated with both women and men receiving a good deal of *emotional support* (tenderness and understanding) and *information support* (advice and guidance) from their partners during the previous 6 months (Cutrona & Suhr, 1994).

Unfortunately for women involved in heterosexual romantic relationships, their skill in providing social support during stressful times—recall the "tend-and-befriend" discussion in section 15-1b—is generally greater than that of their male partners (Fritz et al., 2003; Vinokur & Vinokur-Kaplan, 1990). The most likely explanation for this gender difference is the greater childhood training girls receive in the caregiving role and in emotional attentiveness (Belle, 1982). While female socialization fosters the development of these *relationship-enhancing* behaviors, male socialization is more likely to promote the development of *individual-enhancing* behaviors, such as independence and control. This gender difference may explain why marriage is more beneficial to men than to women: Men marry people who, on average, have been taught to provide care and nurturance, while women marry people who, on average, have spent a lot of time learning how to be independent of others!

How does this gender socialization difference influence social support among lesbian and gay couples? A 5-year longitudinal study suggests that, while the "double dose" of relationship-enhancing skills that lesbians bring to romantic relationships is associated with slightly higher intimacy than that found among heterosexual couples, it doesn't lead to greater relationship satisfaction (Kurdek, 1998). For gay male couples, although their "double dose" of individual-enhancing skills may explain why they tend to have a higher need for autonomy than do heterosexual couples, it doesn't lower their relationship satisfaction.

15-2g Religion and Spirituality Can Positively Influence Health and Longevity

Between 80 and 85 percent of the world's population (more than 6 billion people) is affiliated with some form of religion, with the most popular religions being Christianity, Islam, Hinduism, and Buddhism. Research generally finds that people who regularly attend religious services are somewhat happier and less anxious and depressed, and live about 7 years longer (82 years versus 75 years), than those who do not regularly attend such services (Koenig et al., 2004; McCullough et al., 2000; T. B. Smith et al., 2003). A number of studies point to lifestyle variables as largely accounting for the longevity difference (see chapter 6, section 6-3i). For example, Americans who regularly attend religious services drink less, smoke less, and exercise more than those who do not (Strawbridge et al., 2001). Similarly, Japanese Zen monks, who live significantly longer than the typical Japanese man, smoke less, consume less meat, and live in less crowded parts of the country than the rest of the population (Ogata et al., 1984). Thus, it may well be that the greater longevity of religious persons is substantially due to their healthier lifestyles compared with those of nonreligious persons, and perhaps also due to the social support religious people receive from their fellow worshipers. However, might there be something else contributing to this longevity difference besides health behaviors and social support?

A 60-year longitudinal study of more than 2,500 women and men found that women who identified themselves as highly religious at the age of 30 years regularly reported being in better health and having a slower decline in overall health throughout their lives compared to women who identified themselves as not being very religious (McCullough & Laurenceau, 2005). This was true even after controlling for health behaviors, social support,

People (especially women) who identify themselves as highly religious tend to be healthier and live longer than those who are not very religious. What might explain these health and longevity differences?

Source: Courtesy of Figzoi.

and social activity. In contrast, religiousness had no significant association with any aspect of men's reported health, which is consistent with the findings from other studies indicating that the religiousness-health/longevity link is stronger among women than among men (Clark et al., 1999; McCullough et al., 2000). The reason this link is stronger for women may be due to the fact that women are, on average, more religious than are men in nearly all cultures and throughout most of their lives (Stark, 2002).

What about people who describe themselves as religious but do not participate in formalized religious services? Do they also experience health benefits? A 6-year study of nearly 4,000 people found that those who engaged in some sort of private spiritual practice, such as meditation, prayer, or Bible study, were less likely to die during the course of the study than those who did not engage in such activities, even after controlling for their health behaviors and their levels of social support (Helm et al., 2000).

What about individuals suffering from illnesses and diseases? Is there any evidence that religion or spirituality provides health benefits to the seriously ill? Among women battling breast cancer, one study found that those who had strong religious beliefs had better coping skills than those with weaker religious beliefs (Johnson & Spilka, 1991). Other studies have found that cancer patients who perceived God or Allah as having control over their disease coped better than patients without such beliefs (Ginsburg et al., 1995; Roberts et al., 1997). Finally, among older adults who had coronary bypass surgery, those with strong religious beliefs were less likely to die during the 6-month period following surgery than those with weak beliefs, even after controlling for age, severity of heart problem, and level of social participation (Oxman et al., 1995). One important factor underlying highly religious individuals' greater coping skills in handling the stress of illness and disease appears to be their greater sense of hope and optimism about life and the future (Plante et al., 2000; Salsman et al., 2005).

Of course, religion is certainly not blemish free in promoting health. The biggest negative consequences associated with formal religions are the violence, wars, and intergroup intolerance actively sponsored by some religious leaders and followers (Fontana, 2003). Indeed, formal religions often play a significant—and often negative—role in prejudice and discrimination, which can result in extremely unfortunate physical and mental health consequences for those who are the targets of this intolerance (Levin, 2004; McCann, 1999). It is also true that certain fundamentalist religious groups reject important medical interventions, such as childhood vaccinations and blood transfusions, and that this rejection can have serious health consequences. Finally, although a number of studies indicate that highly religious individuals have better mental health than those who are less religious, this relationship is reversed for certain religious traditions. Several studies indicate that Catholics' religiousness is actually associated with poorer mental health, possibly due to greater feelings of guilt instilled by Roman Catholic Church traditions compared to Protestant traditions (Alferi et al., 1999; C. Park et al., 1990; Tix & Frazier, 2005). Of course, this finding does not mean that the Catholic religious tradition is somehow worse than Protestant traditions, but it does suggest that Catholics who actively "live their faith" might confront somewhat greater mental health challenges than do highly religious Protestants (Pargament, 2002).

Despite these qualifications, scientific studies indicate that religiousness has real health benefits. People with strong religious beliefs appear to have a buffer against stress that is independent of the social support they might receive from fellow worshipers. While many of these health benefits are undoubtedly due to healthier lifestyles, the belief in the ultimate power and control of a Supreme Being may also produce health-inducing thoughts and emotions.

Section Review

- Current views of human stress maintain that it is a continually changing process determined by how a threat is cognitively appraised, what resources (both within and outside the person) are available, and how the person copes with the stressor.
- Events that are predictable and those over which we perceive to have some degree of control are less stressful than unpredictable events that we view as out of our control.
- Hostile and pessimistic individuals are more reactive than others to stressors.
- Strong versus weak social support is associated with a stronger immune response to stress and with better physical and psychological health; women tend to provide better social support than do men.
- Strong religious beliefs are generally beneficial to health, but sometimes religion can be detrimental.

15-3   WHAT BEHAVIORS HURT OR HELP OUR HEALTH?

Preview

- *How do our behaviors affect our health and well-being?*
- *Do young adults generally practice safe sex?*
- *What are the psychological and sociocultural forces behind eating disorders?*
- *Can regular exercise and relaxation training improve health?*

Although stress can take a toll on physical and psychological well-being, as you have learned, both situational and personal factors can buffer many of these negative effects. In this section of the chapter, we will examine how specific behaviors are associated with health and illness.

15-3a   Altering Behaviors Can Often Prevent Premature Death

How you live your life—including the foods you eat, the amount of exercise you get, the precautions you take against accidents, whether you smoke or drink to excess, and your decisions about sexual encounters—will likely affect your life's length and quality. As shown in table 15-2, at all ages, most of the top 10 causes of death have a behavioral component. Risks for heart disease and cancer, the two most common killers, are influenced by eating habits and exercise. Accidents, suicides, and homicides—among the most frequent causes of death for children and young adults—are the direct result of behaviors. Deaths due to HIV infection, many lung diseases, and cirrhosis of the liver are influenced by sexual behaviors, smoking, and alcohol consumption, respectively. Some forms of diabetes—itself a risk factor for heart disease—are the direct result of behaviors, primarily diet.

Table 15-2 The Top 10 Causes of Death in the United States by Age and Gender

Gender and Death Rate per 100,000	All Ages Male (876.4)	All Ages Female (853.5)	Ages 1–4 Male (37.6)	Ages 1–4 Female (31.4)	Ages 5–14 Male (23.4)	Ages 5–14 Female (16.2)	Ages 15–24 Male (119.3)	Ages 15–24 Female (43.5)	Ages 25–44 Male (208.8)	Ages 25–44 Female (107.4)	Ages 45–64 Male (836.9)	Ages 45–64 Female (501.9)	Ages 65 & older Male (5,582.4)	Ages 65 & older Female (4,754.9)
1	Heart diseases	Heart diseases	Accidents	Accidents	Accidents	Accidents	Accidents	Accidents	Accidents	Cancer	Cancer	Cancer	Heart diseases	Heart diseases
2	Cancer	Cancer	Congenital anomalies	Congenital anomalies	Cancer	Cancer	Homicide	Homicide	Heart diseases	Accidents	Heart diseases	Heart diseases	Cancer	Cancer
3	Accidents	Strokes	Homicide	Homicide/ cancer	Homicide	Homicide	Suicide	Cancer	Suicide	Heart diseases	Accidents	Strokes	Strokes	Strokes
4	Strokes	Lung diseases	Cancer		Suicide	Congenital anomalies	Cancer	Suicide	Cancer	Suicide	Strokes	Lung diseases	Lung diseases	Lung diseases
5	Lung diseases	Pneumonia & influenza	Heart diseases	Heart diseases	Congenital anomalies	Heart diseases	Heart diseases	Heart diseases	HIV infection	HIV infection	Cirrhosis & other liver diseases	Diabetes	Pneumonia & influenza	Pneumonia & influenza
6	Pneumonia & influenza	Diabetes	Pneumonia & influenza	Pneumonia & influenza	Heart diseases	Suicide	Congenital anomalies	Congenital anomalies	Homicide	Homicide	Diabetes	Accidents	Diabetes	Diabetes
7	Diabetes	Accidents	Blood poisoning	Birth defects	Lung diseases	Lung diseases/	Lung diseases	Pneumonia & influenza	Cirrhosis & other liver diseases	Strokes	Lung diseases	Cirrhosis & other liver diseases	Accidents	Accidents
8	Suicide	Alzheimer's disease	Birth defects	Blood poisoning	Pneumonia & influenza	pneumonia & influenza	Strokes/ pneumonia & influenza	HIV infection	Strokes	Cirrhosis & other liver diseases	Suicide	Pneumonia & influenza	Kidney diseases	Alzheimer's disease
9	Cirrhosis & other liver diseases	Kidney diseases	Lung diseases	Strokes	Strokes	Other non-cancerous growths		Lung diseases	Diabetes	Diabetes	Pneumonia & influenza	Suicide	Blood poisoning	Kidney diseases
10	Homicide	Blood poisoning	Meningitis	Other non-cancerous growths	Other non-cancerous growths	Strokes	HIV infection	Diabetes	Pneumonia & influenza	Pneumonia & influenza	HIV infection	Blood poisoning	Alzheimer's disease	Blood poisoning

Source: From Murphy, S. (2000). Deaths: Final data for 1998. *National Vital Statistics Reports*, Vol. 48, www.cdc.gov/nchs/data/nvsr48/nvs48_11.pdf

582

As mentioned in chapter 4, section 4-6c, women live an average of 4 years longer than men worldwide, and nearly 7 years longer in the United States and Canada (Coffey et al., 1998). In terms of the 15 leading causes of death, men outrank women in all except one: Alzheimer's disease, which occurs primarily among the elderly. Why might this be so?

Some researchers believe that menstruation and systems related to childbirth better equip women to rid their bodies of toxins. Others suggest that the X chromosome—the sex chromosome that females have two copies of, while males have only one—may contain some protective genes that better enhance women's longevity relative to men's. Still other experts attribute this longevity difference to lifestyle differences between men and women related to gender socialization. Put simply, men are rewarded for taking risks and are often encouraged to ignore danger signals in their lives. Note in table 15-2 the larger number of deaths among males between the ages of 5 and 64. Accidents, suicides, and homicides occur 2 to 7 times more often among boys and men than among girls and women. Additionally, men have 2 to 3 times the rate of death from HIV and cirrhosis of the liver compared with women. They are also twice as likely as women to be hit by lightning or die in a flash flood, often because taking proper precautions to avoid danger in such hazardous weather conditions might be viewed as "unmanly."

Am I suggesting that if you simply behave correctly, you'll never die? No—obviously that isn't true. Death is not preventable, but altering behaviors can prevent premature death and increase the quality of life. Chapter 11 analyzed sex and hunger as motivated behaviors. Now let us examine how unsafe sexual practices and disordered eating behaviors affect health and well-being.

15-3b Knowing about "Safer Sex" Is Not Enough

Do you know how HIV (the virus that causes AIDS) is passed from one person to another? Can you name at least two ways to keep from acquiring a sexually transmitted disease? If you are like most college students, you already know that HIV is spread through body fluids, such as semen and blood, and not through casual contact (including kissing, unless open sores are present) or by mosquitoes (Langer et al., 2001). It also is probably not news to you that HIV and other sexually transmitted diseases can be prevented by abstaining from sex or, if you are sexually active, by practicing safer sex behaviors, such as consistently using a condom (or other barrier), limiting sexual partners, and knowing the sexual histories of your partners (Emmers-Sommer et al., 2005).

The fact that nearly all college students (and the vast majority of other young adults) can correctly answer these questions speaks to the success of educational programs in informing the public about HIV over the past 20 years. However, this knowledge has little relationship to whether or not unmarried adolescents or adults remain abstinent or practice safer-sex behaviors (Bellingham & Gillies, 1993; Rimberg & Lewis, 1994). Instead, college students engage in a number of risky sexual behaviors, including high numbers of sexual partners, "one-night stands" with casual acquaintances, and frequent condomless sex (Bancroft et al., 2004; Reinisch et al., 1995; Simkins, 1995). Even though 1 in 6 sexually active adults reports having had at least one sexually transmitted disease (such as chlamydia, gonorrhea, genital herpes, genital warts, syphilis, or HIV), as many as 9 out of 10 do not use condoms consistently (Michael et al., 1994). Often, the riskier behaviors occur in combination with the use of alcohol or other drugs (Ratliff-Crain et al., 1999). The persistence of these sexually risky behaviors among adults is the primary reason there are 40,000 new HIV cases each year in the United States, with recent indications that this number is slowly increasing (Feig, 2003).

If knowledge about the risks doesn't promote safer behaviors, what does? Additionally, what motivates people to choose unsafe behaviors over those that are safer? Getting people to practice safer-sex behaviors, such as using condoms, takes much more than simply telling them that condoms prevent disease and that they should use them (Bryan et al., 2005; Kalichman, 2005). Here are some of the more common reasons why people don't use condoms:

- *Buying condoms can be embarrassing.* Buying condoms can be an embarrassing event, especially for people who are extremely uncomfortable discussing their sexuality (see chapter 11, section 11-2f). Also, the use of condoms may be inconsistent with an individual's personal or cultural values, diminishing use even further (Huff & Kline,

1999; Locke et al., 2005). Men and women who are comfortable talking about their sexual histories and about safer sex are about 6 times more likely to use condoms than those who are uncomfortable (Catania et al., 1992). Programs that make condoms freely available to everyone often alleviate these barriers to safer sex.

- *Condom use education emphasizes fear and disease prevention.* Sex education programs that use fear of AIDS as the primary focus have been shown to increase awareness but not to change behaviors (Chesney & Coates, 1990). One reason such programs do not lead to safer sexual behavior is that people often associate condoms *with* disease; thus this lowers their motivation to use condoms. Recently, advertisements have begun depicting condoms in a more sexual manner, treating them as a desirable part of the sexual experience rather than as objects associated with disease. If condoms are not part of people's sexual scripts (see chapter 11, section 11-2a), they are less likely to be used in the "heat of the moment."

- *Riskier sexual behaviors are more likely with alcohol consumption.* Alcohol does not necessarily cause people to lose their sexual inhibitions, but it does make them less likely to engage in sound cognitive reasoning (Coates et al., 1988). When people's ability to engage in higher-level reasoning is disrupted, they are much less apt to think about the possible consequences of their behavior (Bryan et al., 2005). When people are intoxicated with alcohol, the more immediate and readily noticeable aspects of a situation will tend to grab their attention and motivate their behavior. In the case of sex, the immediate sexual arousal will be uppermost in people's minds rather than any thought that sexual activity may put them at risk for a disease.

- *Low self-esteem persons are more likely than others to engage in risky sexual behaviors.* Low self-esteem persons have more adverse reactions to negative events in their lives than high self-esteem persons do (Smith & Petty, 1992). When experiencing these negative moods, they also have a heightened need to avoid rejection from others (Heatherton & Vohs, 2000). These reactions to negative events may explain why people with low self-esteem are more likely than high self-esteem persons to have sex without using a condom when they are in a negative mood (MacDonald & Martineau, 2002).

The research findings summarized in the preceding list suggest that effective prevention programs must focus on multiple areas of a person's life in order to increase safer sexual behaviors (Fisher & Fisher, 1992). Such programs need broader interventions, including discussions of nonsexual motivations for seeking intimacy, assertiveness training to help people feel comfortable stating their own preferences with a sexual partner, reducing barriers to obtaining condoms, and providing models and examples of situations in which safer sex is still exciting sex (Coates, 1990).

15-3c Obesity and Eating Disorders Are a Function of Internal and External Forces

As discussed in chapter 11, section 11-3, eating is one of our basic, primary motivated behaviors. You also learned that feelings of hunger and eating behaviors are controlled by much more than what our stomachs tell us. A complex array of physiological, psychological, and social/environmental factors combine to create our motivation to eat.

What Is Obesity?

obesity The excessive accumulation of body fat. Medically, a person with a body mass index (BMI) over 30 is considered obese.

According to the Centers for Disease Control and Prevention (CDC), **obesity,** which is the excessive accumulation of body fat, has become an epidemic in the United States (Mokdad et al., 1999). In diagnosing obesity, physicians calculate a *body mass index (BMI),* which is defined as weight in kilograms divided by height in meters squared (30 kg/m²). To calculate your BMI using pounds and inches, multiply your weight in pounds by 700, divide this number by your height in inches, and then divide by your height again. A ratio over 25 is considered overweight; over 30, obese; over 40, extremely obese. Using the BMI, a 5-foot-4-inch tall woman weighing 174 pounds or more, or a 5-foot-10-inch tall man weighing 207 pounds or more, would be considered obese. Over the past decade, the number of Americans who fall into this excessive body fat category has nearly doubled, increasing from 12

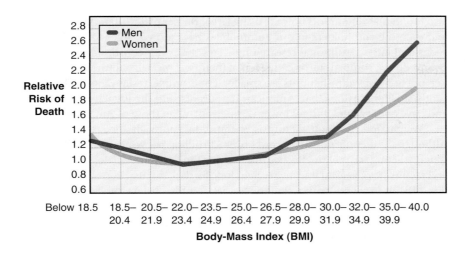

Figure 15-4

Obesity and Mortality

A 14-year study of over 1 million Americans found that men and women with a BMI of 40 were at least two times more likely to have died by the end of the 14-year period than were those with a BMI of 23.

Source: M. J. Thun, J. M. Petrelli, C. Rogriguez, & C. W. Health, Jr. (1999). Body-mass index and mortality in a prospective cohort of U.S. adults. *New England Journal of Medicine,* 1999, 341, 1097–1105.

percent to 21 percent (Yanovski & Yanovski, 1999). Similar increases in heftiness have occurred in Canada, Britain, Australia, and other countries in the developed world (Australian Bureau of Statistics, 2000; Miller, 1999; Statistics Canada, 1999). Healthwise, the ideal BMI differs across racial categories. For example, African Americans' healthiest BMI score, which is around 27, is higher than that for European Americans, which is around 24 to 25 (Brannon & Feist, 2000).

Although being slightly overweight poses no health risks, obesity is closely related to numerous chronic health conditions, including high blood pressure, heart disease, diabetes, arthritis, and sleep disorders (Williams et al., 2005; Wolf & Colditz, 1996). This is especially true for individuals with "apple-shaped" bodies, most of whose weight resides in potbellies, rather than with "pear-shaped" individuals, who have large hips and thighs (Bender et al., 1998; Greenwood, 1989). As depicted in figure 15-4, a recent 14-year longitudinal study of over 1 million Americans found that extreme obesity is a clear risk for premature death (Calle et al., 1999). Further evidence suggests that *changes* in weight due to repeated dieting and weight-gain cycles place people at higher risk for numerous diseases (Brownell & Rodin, 1994; Rexrode et al., 1997).

What Causes Obesity?

Ample evidence shows that people are born with tendencies to be lighter or heavier. Indeed, as much as 70 percent of individual differences in weight are due to genetics (Allison et al., 1994; Bulik et al., 2003). Still, genetics alone cannot explain the rapid increases in obesity in the United States Weight gain occurs when energy intake (through food and drink) exceeds energy expenditure (through body functions and activity). Because Americans' increase in obesity over the past 10 years was not accompanied by a decrease in physical activity, changes in diet and eating habits account for a substantial portion of the national weight gain (Mokdad et al., 1999). Today, Americans' daily diet has increased by 300 calories when compared to 10 years ago, and 31 percent of these total calories come from junk food and alcoholic beverages with little nutritional value. Once digested, these highly refined grains and sugars break down quickly to the sugar glucose in the blood, causing the pancreas to produce extra insulin to process the extra sugar. When sugar levels drop, people feel depleted of energy and experience hunger, and the eating cycle repeats itself. Over time, this cycle leads to excess weight gain (Drewnowski & Levine, 2003).

Fast-food restaurants and food manufacturers contribute to this feeding frenzy by using portion sizes to increase sales and profits. In a national study of restaurants, grocery store products, and cookbook recipes from the 1970s through the late 1990s, nutritionists Lisa Young and Marion Nestle (2002) found that the amount of food allotted for one person dramatically increased. By the late 1990s, portions for restaurant French fries, hamburgers, and sodas were 2 to 5 times as large as they had been 20 years earlier, with similar increases observed in grocery store chocolate bars and bread products. In cookbooks published in the 1990s, authors specified fewer servings—and thereby larger portions for each person—for the same recipes that appeared in earlier editions in the 1970s and 1980s. Young and Nestle also found that restaurants now are using larger dinner plates, pizzerias are using larger pans, and even the cup holders in our automobiles have grown larger to hold our "super-sized" sodas and lattés. Additional research indicates that, after consuming these larger portions, people do not compensate by eating less at their next meal. In cultures where people are thinner, portion sizes at restaurants are smaller. For example, restaurants in France serve significantly smaller portions than American restaurants, and the French are leaner in body mass and have obesity rates 3 times lower (7.4 percent) than those of Americans (21 percent).

Weight loss through dieting is a common approach for trying to control weight. Although the dieting industry receives over $30 billion per year from Americans trying to lose weight, dieting is largely ineffective in achieving long-term weight loss (Stice et al., 2005). Several factors work against effective weight loss. First, as discussed in chapter 11, section 11-3c, it is difficult to change your weight once a set point has been established. Second, many people who diet are already at or below normal weight and therefore shouldn't be dieting. Increased activity in the form of exercise may be the best predictor for long-term weight loss, both before and after dieting (Brownell & Wadden, 1991, 1992; Foreyt et al., 1996). As with other lifestyle changes related to health, effective long-term weight loss for people who are overweight is often achieved only after much work and many failures (Rzewnicki & Forgays, 1987). Yet medical experts remind us that shedding excess weight will significantly lower our risk of premature death, chronic disease, and lower quality of life (Must et al., 1999).

On a national level, one major challenge in fighting the epidemic of obesity will be to improve the activity levels of children and adults. Television viewing and computer use, for example, have been pinpointed as major contributors to sedentary lifestyles and obesity (Dietz & Gortmaker, 1985; Vines, 1995). On average, 10- to 15-year-old girls spend 2-1/2 hours a day watching television or playing video games, and boys spend 3-1/2 hours in these same sedentary activities. If these children also spend 8 hours sleeping, they are spending almost half their day virtually motionless. One recent study suggests that simply reducing the amount of time children spend watching TV or playing video games is sufficient to greatly reduce their weight problems (Robinson, 1999). This reduction in weight occurred even though the children did not decrease their high-fat food intake. As we will discuss in section 15-3d, encouraging increased physical activity may promote better health and well-being, as well as preventing obesity and related health concerns.

Finally, the food industry can play an important role in combating obesity, without necessarily lowering sales and profits. In the summer of 2003, Kraft Foods, the maker of hundreds of different snacks and packaged meals, announced that it would encourage healthier eating by reducing portion sizes for some products. In addition to reducing the amount of food offered to the public, research indicates that food manufacturers can promote healthier eating by selectively lowering the price of healthy foods. For example, in one

Does research suggest that reducing the price of fresh vegetables and fruit increases people's consumption of these healthy foods?

Source: Courtesy of Figzoi.

The Japanese have the longest life expectancy in the world. Not coincidentally, their diet is high in fiber and vitamins and low in fat. For example, shojin cuisine, which was developed by Chinese Zen monks and introduced to Japan more than 700 years ago, consists of vegetables, grains, and seaweed, with no meat of any kind. The tofu contained in many shojin recipes contains substances that may offer protection against cancer and heart disease. How does this diet differ from that consumed by the average American?

Source: Courtesy of Jenny Franzoi.

study of consumer food purchases, epidemiologist Simone French (2003) found that, while highlighting the low-fat content of products had little influence on their popularity, dropping their price by even a nickel increased sales. Further, a 50 percent price reduction on fresh fruit and baby carrots caused a fourfold increase in fresh fruit sales and a twofold increase in baby carrot sales. This study suggests that the food industry can actually be a positive force in reducing obesity and promoting healthier eating among consumers without losing profit margins. In this sense, they can figuratively "have their cake and eat it too."

Cultural Thinness Standards

Being significantly overweight is not just a health problem. In North American culture, obese individuals are often perceived as unattractive, lazy, weak-willed, sloppy, mean, unskilled, and slow (Crandall, 1994; Regan, 1996). In longitudinal studies of obese women and men, researchers find that they are less likely to be hired and they tend to start at lower salaries and receive lower raises than their normal-weight counterparts (Frieze et al., 1991; Gortmaker et al., 1993). Other studies suggest that weight discrimination is more pervasive and widely condoned than race and gender discrimination (Myers & Rothblum, 2005). Obesity is such a strong stigmatizing characteristic in our culture that it even affects how people evaluate individuals seen with obese persons. For example, Michelle Hebl and Laura Mannix (2003) found that male job applicants were rated more negatively when seen with an overweight woman prior to their job interviews than when seen with a woman of normal weight.

Underlying weight discrimination is a social climate that pressures people to reach certain body ideals (Heffernan et al., 2002). Although men are the target of some social pressure in this regard, the female ideal stresses difficult-to-attain thinness standards that actually endanger women's health if women pursue these standards (Posavac & Posavac, 1998; Vohs et al., 2001). One consequence of this cultural obsession with female weight is that women of all age groups are more likely to view their bodies as *objects* of others' attention, and on average women evaluate their bodies more negatively than men (Cash & Henry, 1995; Feingold & Mazzella, 1998; Strelan et al., 2003). By adulthood, women are more likely to habitually experience what researchers identify as *social physique anxiety*, which is anxiety about others observing or evaluating their bodies (Fredrickson et al., 1998). Spend a few minutes completing the Body Esteem Scale in Self-Discovery Questionnaire 15-3.

Although women in North American culture generally experience less positive body esteem than men, evidence shows that minority women and lesbians feel less pressure than White heterosexual women to conform to the unrealistic standards of thinness in the larger culture (Franzoi & Chang, 2002; Lakkis et al., 1999; Rucker & Cash, 1992). As a result, they are less concerned about dieting and weight loss (Mintz & Kashubeck, 1999; M. A. White et al., 2003). This healthier perspective appears to be partly due to a greater valuing of large body sizes in minority and lesbian cultures, but it also may be a by-product of a more general tendency to reject White and heterosexual cultural standards (Kite & Deaux, 1987; Thompson et al., 1996).

Fifty years ago, department store mannequins had body shapes very similar to those of the average American woman. Today, mannequins are extremely thin, with an average hip circumference of 31 inches, compared with the 37-inch average for young adult women. If these mannequins were real, their body fat would be so low that they probably would not menstruate (Brownell, 1991; University of California, 1993). How do you think exposure to such ultrathin representations of female "beauty" affects the body attitudes of American women? Are certain women more susceptible to these cultural beauty standards than other women?

Source: Courtesy of Figzoi.

Self-Discovery
Questionnaire 15-3

What Is Body Esteem?

A person's attitudes toward her or his body are referred to as **body esteem** (Rieves & Cash, 1996). Following is a list of 35 body parts and body functions that make up the *Body Esteem Scale* (Franzoi & Shields, 1984). Please read each item and indicate how you feel about this part or function of your own body, using the following response categories:

> **body esteem** A person's attitudes toward her or his body.

1 = Have strong negative feelings
2 = Have moderate negative feelings
3 = Have no feeling one way or the other
4 = Have moderate positive feelings
5 = Have strong positive feelings

____ **1.** body scent	____ **19.** arms
____ **2.** appetite	____ **20.** chest or breasts
____ **3.** nose	____ **21.** appearance of eyes
____ **4.** physical stamina	____ **22.** cheeks/cheekbones
____ **5.** reflexes	____ **23.** hips
____ **6.** lips	____ **24.** legs
____ **7.** muscular strength	____ **25.** figure or physique
____ **8.** waist	____ **26.** sex drive
____ **9.** energy level	____ **27.** feet
____ **10.** thighs	____ **28.** sex organs
____ **11.** ears	____ **29.** appearance of stomach
____ **12.** biceps	____ **30.** health
____ **13.** chin	____ **31.** sex activities
____ **14.** body build	____ **32.** body hair
____ **15.** physical coordination	____ **33.** physical condition
____ **16.** buttocks	____ **34.** face
____ **17.** agility	____ **35.** weight
____ **18.** width of shoulders	

Dimensions of Female and Male Body Esteem

As you recall from chapter 10, section 10-2a, factor analysis is a statistical technique that allows researchers to identify clusters of variables that are related to—or *correlated* with—one another. In studying body esteem, researchers have asked many people to evaluate different aspects of their own bodies, such as these 35 body items. When these evaluations have been factor analyzed, the findings suggest that body esteem is not one "thing" but at least three different "things" (Franzoi & Shields, 1984). In other words, when people evaluate their bodies, they do so by evaluating different dimensions or aspects. These dimensions differ for women and men, meaning that they think about their bodies differently. For example, whereas women are more likely to think about their appetite, waist, and thighs in terms of *weight concern* (how their body looks), men are more likely to think about how these body items affect their *physical condition* (how their body moves).

The Body Esteem Scale identifies three different body esteem dimensions for both sexes. For women, the Sexual Attractiveness subscale measures attitudes toward aspects and functions of the body associated with facial attractiveness and

---

No woman can be too slim. . . .

> —*Wallis Simpson, the Duchess of Windsor, 1896–1986*

Besides being young, a desirable sex partner—especially a woman—should also be fat.

> —*Observations of the seminomadic Siriono Indians of Bolivia, 1946*

That Black heterosexual women appear to have greater body satisfaction than White heterosexual women does not mean they are unconcerned about weight issues. In general, they are still more dissatisfied with their bodies—particularly their weight—than heterosexual Black men (Harris, 1995). Similar ambivalent feelings appear to describe lesbian body attitudes; interviews with young adult lesbians suggest that they experience a conflict between mainstream and lesbian values about the importance of weight and overall physical appearance (Beren et al., 1997). These findings suggest that Black and lesbian cultural values are not enough to overcome the dominant White heterosexual cultural standard of female thinness.

sexuality (especially those that can be enhanced cosmetically); the Weight Concern subscale includes those body parts that can be altered by controlling functions associated with food intake; and the Physical Condition subscale measures attitudes toward stamina, agility, and strength. For men, the Physical Attractiveness subscale measures attitudes toward facial features and aspects of the physique that influence judgments of attractiveness; the Upper Body Strength subscale measures attitudes toward the upper body (especially those aspects that can be enhanced through anaerobic exercise); and the Physical Condition subscale measures attitudes toward stamina, agility, and general body strength.

Scoring Instructions and Standards

To determine your score for each of the subscales for your sex, simply add up your responses to the items corresponding to each body esteem dimension. For example, for women, to determine self-judgments for the weight concern dimension of body esteem, add up the responses to the 10 items comprising this subscale. For men, the items of "physical coordination" and "figure or physique" are on both the upper-body strength and the physical condition dimensions. The subscale items, plus the means and standard deviations for 964 college men and women (Franzoi & Shields, 1984), are given in the following list:

Women

Sexual attractiveness: Body scent, nose, lips, ears, chin, chest or breasts, appearance of eyes, cheeks/cheekbones, sex drive, sex organs, sex activities, body hair, face. (Mean = 46.9, SD = 6.3)

Weight concern: Appetite, waist, thighs, body build, buttocks, hips, legs, figure or physique, appearance of stomach, weight. (Mean = 29.9, SD = 8.2)

Physical condition: Physical stamina, reflexes, muscular strength, energy level, biceps, physical coordination, agility, health, physical condition. (Mean = 33.3, SD = 5.7)

Men

Physical attractiveness: Nose, lips, ears, chin, buttocks, appearance of eyes, cheeks/cheekbones, hips, feet, sex organs, face. (Mean = 39.1, SD = 5.7)

Upper body strength: Muscular strength, biceps, body build, physical coordination, width of shoulders, arms, chest or breasts, figure or physique, sex drive. (Mean = 34.0, SD = 6.1)

Physical condition: Appetite, physical stamina, reflexes, waist, energy level, thighs, physical coordination, agility, figure or physique, appearance of stomach, health, physical condition, weight. (Mean = 50.2, SD = 7.7)

Source: From "The Body Esteem Scale: Multidimensional structure and sex differences in a college population" by S. L. Franzoi and S. A. Shields in *Journal of Personality Assessment, 48,* 1984, pp. 173–178. Copyright © 1984. Reprinted by permission of Lawrence Erlbaum Associates.

What Are Eating Disorders?

As noted, female body dissatisfaction is fairly common in North American culture, with most of the dissatisfaction focused on weight issues (Cash & Henry, 1995). Sometimes this concern with body weight is taken to such extremes that individuals develop *eating disorders* (Polivy et al., 2005). One eating disorder, **anorexia nervosa,** is diagnosed when a person weighs less than 85 percent of her or his expected weight but still expresses an intense fear of gaining weight or becoming fat (American Psychiatric Association, 1994). Another,

anorexia nervosa An eating disorder in which a person weighs less than 85 percent of her or his expected weight but still expresses an intense fear of gaining weight or becoming fat.

bulimia An eating disorder in which a person engages in recurrent episodes of binge eating followed by drastic measures to purge the body of the consumed calories.

related eating disorder is **bulimia,** which involves recurrent episodes of binge eating—periods of intense, out-of-control eating—followed by drastic measures to compensate for bingeing, such as vomiting, using laxatives, or exercising excessively (American Psychiatric Association, 1994). A person who is anorexic may also be bulimic. Both eating disorders occur 10 times more frequently among women than men, with about 0.5 to 1.0 percent of women in late adolescence and early adulthood being anorexic and 1 to 3 percent being bulimic (American Psychiatric Association, 1994). Because the body is being systematically starved, both disorders pose severe health risks, including death, if left untreated.

Due to the fact that anorexia nervosa and bulimia occur mostly in women and mostly in weight-conscious cultures, psychologists suspect that sociocultural factors significantly shape these disorders. Anorexia always begins as an attempt to lose weight, and the self-induced vomiting typical of bulimia almost always occurs after a person fails to follow the eating restrictions of a weight-loss diet. Further, adolescent girls who suffer from eating disorders tend to be emotionally insecure and have mothers who obsess about both their own weight and their daughters' weight and appearance (Pike & Rodin, 1991; Turner et al., 2005).

The highly critical scrutiny that women with eating disorders direct toward their own and other women's bodies can be described as selective attention to what is perceived as "beautiful" and "ugly." When evaluating themselves, eating-disordered women pay more attention to their "ugly" body parts and less attention to their "beautiful" body parts, which is opposite to the pattern found in healthy women (Jansen et al., 2005). This selective attention is reversed when eating-disordered women evaluate other women's bodies: They are much more likely to notice other women's attractive physical qualities rather than these women's unattractive physical characteristics. Again, healthy women reverse this pattern of selective attention. Thus, women with eating disorders engage in a type of selective attention that reinforces their body dissatisfaction.

What about genetic and motivational influences on eating disorders? A number of studies have found that identical twins are much more likely than fraternal twins to share an eating disorder, and evidence indicates that people with these disorders may have abnormally high levels of certain neurotransmitters that increase their susceptibility to anxiety, depression, and obsessive-compulsive disorder (Kaye et al., 2000; Klump et al., 2001; Strober, 1992). The possible association of obsessive-compulsive disorder with eating disorders suggests to some psychologists that the desire to achieve *psychological control* over one's life may influence disordered eating (Bruch, 1973, 1982). That is, for some individuals suffering from eating disorders, extreme dieting may represent an attempt to control one important factor in life—weight—and this control becomes a source of power and pride. Related to this motivational explanation is the finding that eating disorders are often associated with a history of sexual, physical, or emotional abuse (Ackard & Neumarck-Sztainer, 2001; Silverman et al., 2001). Here again, disordered eating may represent abuse victims' attempts to reassert control over their own bodies and lives.

The most important conclusion in understanding eating disorders may be that they are likely determined by multiple factors (Cash, 1996; Heinberg, 1996). Therefore, successful treatment of these disorders should involve multiple interventions, including appropriate medical attention, family therapy, individual therapy, group therapy, and behavioral training (DeAngelis, 2002a; Geller, 2002; Lock & Grange, 2005; Wanlass et al., 2005).

15-3d Physical Exercise Can Increase Both Physical and Mental Health

Thus far, we have focused on harmful behaviors. What can you do to reduce the likelihood of illness while simultaneously improving your psychological health? Numerous studies have found that people who engage in regular physical exercise are healthier than those who are sedentary. The only way to achieve cardiovascular fitness is through **aerobic exercise,** which is sustained exercise that increases heart and lung fitness. This form of exercise that strengthens the heart and lungs not only has a positive effect on physical health, but also provides benefits to mental health (Thayer, 2001).

aerobic exercise Sustained exercise that increases heart and lung fitness.

When people think about aerobic exercise, the images that often come to mind are rows of sweaty people jazzercising or jogging. But any activity that increases your heart rate into a certain range (defined by your age and maximum possible heart rate) for at least 12 to 20 minutes fits this definition. Vigorous walking, cross-country skiing, bicycling, swimming, dancing, and even strenuous yard work all qualify as aerobic exercise. Accumulating 30 minutes of aerobic exercise three times per week has been recommended for reducing the risk of chronic disease and enhancing the quality of life (Pate et al., 1995). Consistent with this recommendation, physiological studies indicate that such exercise strengthens the heart, lowers blood pressure, and facilitates the metabolism of fats and carbohydrates (Simon, 1991). Additional research finds that adults who exercise regularly live longer than those who are less active (Blair et al., 1989; Paffenbarger et al., 1986).

Does exercise also improve mental health? Based on the results from over 100 studies, mental health experts believe that exercise can be effective in reducing tension and eliminating depressed moods (Thayer et al., 1994; van Doornen et al., 1988). For example, in one representative study, 156 adults with major depression were randomly assigned to one of the following regimens: 4 months of aerobic exercise, treatment with an antidepressant medication, or a combination of both exercise and medication (Babyak et al., 2000). Although a similar number of patients in each group showed mood improvements in the first 4 months, only those in the exercise groups maintained their improvement after 10 months. One possible reason for this beneficial effect is that aerobic exercise heightens the body's supply of mood-enhancing neurotransmitters such as norepinephrine, serotonin, and the endorphins (Jacobs, 1994; Salmon, 2001). It is also possible that these mood benefits are partly a side effect of the muscular relaxation and sounder sleep that often follow aerobic exercise (Brannon & Feist, 2000).

Despite the benefits of regular exercise, it is possible to overdo a good thing. Some athletes overtrain to the point that they begin to experience negative effects such as fatigue and depression (O'Connor, 1997). You can also exceed the body's capacity, resulting in injury, exhaustion, or even death from myocardial infarction or heatstroke. This is exactly what happened to Corey Stringer of the NFL Minnesota Vikings, who died from heatstroke during training camp in the summer of 2001. Other people can become obsessed with exercising, feeling anxious and uncomfortable if they are unable to engage in the activity. Such individuals who feel compelled to exercise often have other unhealthy concerns about weight control and body image (Slay et al., 1998).

15-3e Relaxation Training Is Effective in Reducing Stress and Improving Health

Because stress is associated with physiological arousal, many psychologists recommend relaxation training as an effective stress antidote. Two effective relaxation techniques are hypnosis and meditation, discussed in chapter 6, sections 6-3b and 6-3c. However, the most basic relaxation technique is **progressive relaxation,** which was developed in the 1920s by Edmund Jacobson (1924). Jacobson started with the observation that it is not possible to be physiologically tense and relaxed at the same time. Although his original technique often required months of training, later modifications by Herbert Benson made progressive relaxation far simpler (Benson, 1975; Benson & Stuart, 1992). Once people develop some skill with this technique, they can use it to calm themselves down anywhere and anytime (Barlow & Rapee, 1991; Bernstein et al., 2000).

Progressive relaxation techniques have been used to help heart attack patients manage their stress. For instance, in one study, survivors of a first heart attack were randomly assigned to one of two experimental conditions (Friedman & Ulmer, 1984). In the *medical advice condition,* patients received medical advice about drugs, exercise, work, and diet, whereas in the *relaxation condition,* they were also taught how to relax. Three years after this intervention, the relaxation patients had suffered only half as many repeat heart attacks as those who had only received the standard medical advice. Research suggests that one physiological benefit of relaxation training is that it may improve the effectiveness of the immune response (Hewson-Bower & Drummond, 1996; Lowe et al., 2001). In one such experiment, blood samples were taken from college students 1 month prior to midterm exams and again on the day of the exams (Kiecolt-Glaser et al., 1985). Half the students had been trained in progressive relaxation techniques, while the other half received no training. The students who received the relaxation training exhibited much less of a decrease in activity of natural killer cells—which, as you recall from section 15-1e, fight viruses and tumors—between the first and second measurements. Explore It Exercise 15-2 describes Benson's progressive relaxation procedure.

Aerobic exercise strengthens the heart, lowers blood pressure, and helps the body metabolize fats and carbohydrates. Regular exercise also appears to increase the body's supply of mood-enhancing neurotransmitters, which fosters stress reduction. Thus, if you want to feel happier, sleep better, and live longer, engage in some form of aerobic exercise for 30 minutes three times per week.

progressive relaxation
A stress-reducing technique that involves the successive tensing and relaxing of each of the major muscle groups of the body.

Explore It
Exercise 15-2

How Can You Practice Progressive Relaxation?

Progressive relaxation is an effective technique in managing stress. As originally developed by Edmund Jacobson (1924) and later refined by Herbert Benson (1975), you progressively relax muscle groups in your body, usually starting at the head and slowly moving down to the legs and feet. With practice, you can use this technique to relax quickly and with minimal effort. Practice this technique once or twice daily but not within 2 hours after eating a meal, because digestion can interfere with the relaxation response.

Step 1. Sit or lie comfortably with your eyes shut and your arms and legs bent at a comfortable angle. Take a deep breath, hold it, and exhale slowly. Repeat several times, saying the word *relax* to yourself with each exhale. Step by step, begin tensing different muscle groups one at a time—holding the tension for 5 seconds, concentrating on how that feels, followed by slowly releasing the tension.

Step 2. Start with your arms by clenching your fists while tensing the muscles in your upper arms. Hold. Slowly release. Inhale and exhale slowly. Maintain a passive attitude and permit relaxation to occur at its own pace. When distracting thoughts occur, do not dwell on them but simply return to repeating *relax* to yourself.

Step 3. Next, tense the thigh and calf muscles in your legs by straightening your legs and pointing your toes downward. Hold. Slowly release. Inhale and exhale slowly.

Step 4. Tense your stomach muscles and, at the same time, press your palms together over your chest in order to tighten your chest muscles. Hold. Slowly release. Inhale and exhale slowly.

Step 5. Arch your back and pull your shoulders back (not too far) to tense these muscles. Hold. Slowly release. Inhale and exhale slowly.

Step 6. Tense your jaw and neck muscles by drawing the corners of your mouth back. You may also want to bend your neck first to one side and then the other. Hold. Slowly release. Inhale and exhale slowly.

Step 7. Tense your forehead by pulling your eyebrows together and wrinkling your brow. Hold. Slowly release. Inhale and exhale slowly.

Step 8. Continue to concentrate on your breathing, breathing comfortably into your abdomen (not your chest). Think *relax* with each exhale. Continue this exercise for 10 to 20 minutes. You may open your eyes to check the time, but do not use an alarm. When finished, sit or lie quietly for a few minutes, first with your eyes closed and later with your eyes opened.

Source: Adapted from *The Relaxation Response* by Herbert Benson, M. D., © 1975. Used with permission of the author.

Journey of Discovery Question

Based on your readings, what tactics can you employ to manage your stress and reduce stress-related ailments?

An activity that combines both exercise and relaxation is the ancient Chinese martial arts form of meditation known as *tai chi*. This mind-body relaxation exercise consists of a series of gentle movements and simple postures designed to improve coordination, relieve stress, promote overall well-being, and strengthen the immune system. Typically, these exercise sequences are performed in a slow, relaxed manner over a 30-minute period, with participants focusing their attention on directing life energy ("chi") through the body and mind. In China, many people begin their day by meeting in public places to collectively

Tai chi is a Chinese mind-body relaxation exercise consisting of a series of gentle movements and simple postures. Many elderly adults practice tai chi, which has been shown to be effective in preventing falling injuries due to a loss of balance.

Source: Courtesy of Figzoi.

practice this relaxation exercise. Tai chi is an especially effective exercise activity for elderly adults, and it is becoming increasingly popular in the United States. Various studies have found that older adults who participate in tai chi classes show improvements in their breathing, body balance, and overall physical functioning, which reduces their fear of falling (Kaplan et al., 2003; Li et al., 2005; Tsang & Hui-Chan, 2003).

Section Review

- Altering behaviors can prevent premature death and increase life quality.
- Young adults engage in a variety of risky sexual behaviors that jeopardize their health and well-being.
- Obesity is related to numerous chronic health conditions, including heart disease, diabetes, arthritis, and sleep disorders.
- Body dissatisfaction can lead to eating disorders.
- Reducing meal portions and increasing activity levels can help reduce societal obesity levels.
- Aerobic exercise and progressive relaxation techniques offer many positive influences on health and well-being.

Psychological Applications

Who Is Happy and Why?

In 1776, Thomas Jefferson's penning of the Declaration of Independence was a bold assertion that individuals have the inalienable rights of life, liberty, and "the pursuit of happiness." Well over 200 years after this declaration, researchers who promote the scientific study of positive psychology (see chapter 1, section 1-3b) have been investigating what causes **happiness,** which is often defined as a predominance of positive over negative emotions, and satisfaction with life as a whole (Diener, 1984; Fredrickson, 2001). These studies indicate that happier people have high self-esteem, are optimistic and outgoing, are physically healthy, and have close friendships or satisfying marriages (Diener & Lucas, 1999, 2000b). When researchers compare very

> **happiness** A predominance of positive over negative affect (emotion) and satisfaction with life as a whole.

happy people with average and very unhappy people, they find that the very happy are more extraverted, more agreeable, and less neurotic, and they have stronger romantic and social relationships. Among college students, the most common characteristics shared by the 10 percent of the young adults with the highest happiness and the fewest signs of depression were their strong ties to friends and family and their commitment to spending time with them (Diener & Seligman, 2002). Before reading further, complete Self-Discovery Questionnaire 15-4.

> Though I am grateful for the blessings of wealth, it hasn't changed who I am. My feet are still on the ground. I'm just wearing better shoes.
>
> —*Oprah Winfrey, American talk-show host, b. 1954*

Continued next page—

Psychological Applications
—Continued

Self-Discovery
Questionnaire **15-4**

How Satisfied Are You with Your Life?

Satisfaction with Life Scale

Directions: Below are five statements that you may agree or disagree with. Using the 1–7 scale below, indicate your agreement with each item by placing the appropriate number on the line preceding that item. Please be open and honest in your responses.

1 = Strongly disagree
2 = Disagree
3 = Slightly disagree
4 = Neither agree or disagree
5 = Slightly agree
6 = Agree
7 = Strongly agree

1. In most ways my life is close to my ideal.____
2. The conditions of my life are excellent.____
3. I am satisfied with my life.____
4. So far I have gotten the important things I want in life.____
5. If I could live my life over, I would change almost nothing.____

Scoring and Interpretation of the Scale

Add up your answers to the five items and use the following normative score information to help in the interpretation:

Score	Interpretation
5–9	Extremely dissatisfied with your life.
10–14	Very dissatisfied with your life.
15–19	Slightly dissatisfied with your life.
20	About neutral.
21–25	Somewhat satisfied with your life.
26–30	Very satisfied with your life.
31–35	Extremely satisfied with your life.

Most Americans score in the 21–25 range. A score above 25 indicates that you are more satisfied than most people. A recent 22-year study of American men found that life satisfaction peaks at age 65 and then declines, with extraverts having the most stable high levels of happiness (Mroczek & Spiro, 2005). In general, life satisfaction is fairly stable, although a good deal of fluctuation tends to take place around each person's happiness set point (Fujita & Diener, 2005).

Source: E. Diener, R. Emmons, J. Larson, & S. Griffin, "The satisfaction with life scale," *Journal of Personality Assessment,* 49 (1985): 71–75.

In studying happiness, psychologists have sought to determine what affects both our temporary feelings of happiness and our long-term life satisfaction. Not surprisingly, our moods brighten when we succeed at daily tasks, when others compliment or praise us, and when we feel healthy, while our moods darken when we fall short of goals, are criticized by others, or feel sick (Miley, 1999). We also tend to be happier on days associated with weekend pleasures, such as Fridays and Saturdays, rather than on those associated with work, such as Mondays and Tuesdays (Larsen & Kasimatis, 1990). On average, we experience our most positive moods during the middle of the day (noon to 6:00 P.M.) and our most negative moods in the early morning and late evening (Watson et al., 1999). These mood fluctuations coincide with fluctuations in our circadian rhythms (see chapter 6, section 6-2a): We are happiest when at our highest levels of physiological alertness.

How is happiness affected by dramatic events? Although experiencing the death of a loved one or being the victim of a serious accident, illness, or crime can cause extreme emotional conflict, we usually recover most of our previous levels of day-to-day happiness within a year or two (Gerhart et al., 1994; Gilbert

Psychological Applications

—Continued

et al., 1998; Lucas et al., 2004). This is also the case for dramatically positive events. For example, after the euphoria of winning a state lottery wears off, people usually discover that their overall happiness is unchanged (Brickman et al., 1978).

Research on the happiness of lottery winners raises the following question that many people have asked over the years: Can you buy happiness? As you can see in figure 1, people in richer countries are happier than people in poorer countries (Myers & Diener, 1995). Yet increases in national wealth within developed nations have not, over recent decades, been associated with increases in happiness (Ryan & Deci, 2001). Further, within any given country, the happiness differences between wealthy and middle-income people are modest (Diener et al., 1999). Taken together, this research suggests that, for the most part, money matters in increasing happiness only if people do not have enough of it to cover the basic needs of food, safety, and shelter (Diener et al., 1993; Niemi et al., 1989). Thus, while having adequate resources to be nourished and safe is essential for happiness, once you meet your basic needs, increasing your wealth does not make you appreciably happier.

One interesting research finding regarding wealth and happiness is that people who strongly desire wealth after satisfying their basic needs tend to be less happy than the average person (Kasser & Ryan, 1996; Nickerson et al., 2003). This result has been confirmed in developed countries such as the United States and Germany and in less developed countries such as India and Russia (Ryan et al., 1999; Schmuck et al., 2000). Why might this be the case? One possibility is that plac-

ing too much importance on material possessions—which do not in themselves satisfy basic psychological needs—takes time and energy away from activities that do satisfy those needs. Thus, overall happiness will be lowered when people pursue their love of money rather than romantic, friendship, or familial love. In addition, people with a high desire to accumulate wealth tend to lose their sense of personal autonomy: Their pursuit of wealth makes them feel controlled by external circumstances (Carver & Baird, 1998).

Another possible explanation for why wealth is not a better predictor of happiness—and also why dramatic life events don't permanently alter levels of day-to-day happiness—is that happiness is a fairly stable trait that is substantially determined by our biology. That is, we may each have a biologically determined baseline level of happiness toward which we gravitate (DeNeve, 1999). For example, in a study of more than 2,000 identical and fraternal twins, David Lykken and Auke Tellegen (1996) analyzed the extent to which identical twins and fraternal twins exhibited similar levels of happiness. The twins' happiness levels were measured by self-report questionnaires that asked them to respond to statements such as "Taking the good with the bad, how happy and contented are you on the average now, compared with other people?" When the twins' happiness scores were correlated, levels of happiness were much more strongly correlated (positively) for the identical twins than for the fraternal twins. Overall, twin studies suggest that between 40 and 50 percent of the variability in happiness can be accounted for by genetics.

Continued next page—

Figure 1

Gross National Product and Happiness

Does money make you happy? In a 24-nation study, happiness was strongly correlated with gross national product, which is a measure of national prosperity (Myers & Diener, 1995). Additional research suggests that money has an effect on happiness only if people do not have enough of it to cover their basic needs. After meeting basic needs, those who still strongly desire wealth tend to be relatively unhappy. So, does money make you happy?

Source: From "Who is happy?" by D. Myers and E. Diener in *Psychological Science, 6,* 1995, pp. 10–19. Reprinted by permission of Blackwell Publishing Ltd.

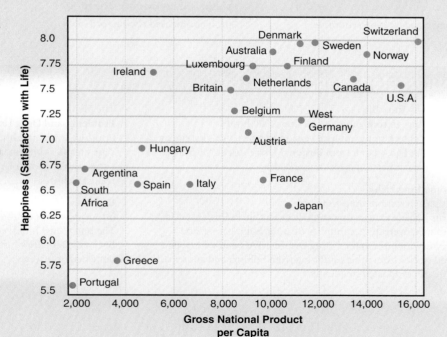

Psychological Applications

—Continued

Finally, some research suggests that people in certain parts of the world are happier than people in other parts. That is, numerous studies indicate that people in individualist cultures report greater levels of happiness than people from cultures with more collectivist orientations (Myers & Diener, 1995). Although some researchers have speculated that these differences are due to quality-of-life factors, others point out that Japan, an economically powerful collectivist country, reports much lower happiness levels than Ireland, an individualist country with a much lower gross national product (Inglehart, 1990). Other researchers speculate that individualists may have been raised to better identify personal, positive feelings that do not rely on the group's well-being (Diener & Diener, 1995). Still others contend that this difference is simply due to the fact that happiness measures have been operationally defined according to individualist standards, such as self-esteem and perceived control over one's life (Lu & Gilmour, 2004). These researchers contend that people in collectivist cultures are more likely than those in individualist cultures to base their happiness on the extent to which they feel valued by others. Thus, happiness in collectivist cultures is related more to collectivist values, such as harmony, social integration, and human heartedness, than in individualist cultures (Lu et al., 2001). So, which type of culture is happier? The answer may well depend on how the questions are asked.

> If only we'd stop trying to be happy we'd have a pretty good time.
>
> —*Edith Wharton, American novelist, 1862–1937*

> There is no duty we so much underrate as the duty of being happy. By being happy, we sow anonymous benefits upon the world.
>
> —*Robert Louis Stevenson, Scottish novelist and poet, 1850–1894*

Key Terms

aerobic exercise (p. 590)

anorexia nervosa (p. 589)

behavioral medicine (p. 560)

biopsychosocial model (p. 560)

body esteem (p. 588)

bulimia (p. 590)

emotion-focused coping (p. 570)

general adaptation syndrome (GAS) (p. 562)

happiness (p. 593)

hardiness (p. 574)

health psychologists (p. 560)

immune system (p. 565)

obesity (p. 584)

optimistic explanatory style (p. 574)

pessimistic explanatory style (p. 574)

problem-focused coping (p. 570)

progressive relaxation (p. 591)

psychoneuroimmunology (p. 566)

psychophysiological disorders (p. 575)

social support (p. 577)

stress (p. 560)

stressors (p. 560)

Type A behavior pattern (p. 573)

Type B behavior pattern (p. 573)

Suggested Websites

Stress by Jim's Big Ego

http://bigego.com/moodyfood/stress2000.html

For an entertaining, musical version of stress, visit this site by Jim's Big Ego, a band from Boston, Massachusetts. (A fast-Internet connection is recommended.)

Something Fishy

http://www.something-fishy.com

This website focuses on eating disorders, including anorexia, bulimia, overeating, compulsive eating, binge eating, and more, with links to the Eating Disorder FAQ and with poems and stories from others suffering from bulimia and anorexia. The site is updated frequently.

The Medical Basis of Stress, Depression, Anxiety, Sleep Problems, and Drug Use

http://www.teachhealth.com

This site offers information on recognizing stress in your life, a stress scale, stress tolerance techniques, and links to other related websites.

Body Mass Index

http://www.halls.md/body-mass-index/bmi.htm

The Body Mass Index website allows you to calculate your BMI and compare yourself to other women and men of the same height and age.

Review Questions

Note: You can find the correct answers to these questions by taking the quiz and then submitting your answers in the Online Edition. The program will automatically score your submission. If you miss a question, the program will provide the correct answer, a rationale for the answer, and the section number in the chapter where the topic is discussed.

1. Stressors are events that have been associated with all of the following *except*
   a. threats to our equilibrium.
   b. positive events such as childbirth.
   c. major cataclysmic events, such as the September 11, 2001, terrorist attacks.
   d. strengthening our ability to maintain equilibrium over time.
   e. daily hassles.

2. Selye's general adaptation syndrome describes
   a. the "fight-or-flight" response.
   b. emotional responses to stress.
   c. a three-stage physical reaction to stress.
   d. the reduction in cortisol that occurs in response to stress.
   e. the body's ability to successfully adapt to stress over time.

3. Concerning gender differences in the response to stress, which one of the following statements is *true*?
   a. Men show higher levels of oxytocin released from the pituitary gland than do women.
   b. According to evolutionary theorists, women needed to respond to stress aggressively to protect their children.
   c. Sociocultural theorists argue that girls are raised to think "flight" instead of "fight."
   d. Women more often use a "tend and befriend" response to stress than do men.
   e. After experiencing a stressor, men are more likely than women to seek out members of their own gender to compare experiences.

4. Research on stress-related disease has indicated all of the following *except* that
   a. stress can reduce the efficiency of the immune system.
   b. strong emotional distress can cause sudden death from heart attacks.
   c. suppression of the immune system during stress makes your response less efficient.
   d. anger-inducing stressors may contribute to ischemia.
   e. both vulnerability and stress are required components of the diathesis-stress model of illness.

5. The biopsychosocial perspective
   a. was favored by medical researchers in the 1940s.
   b. fails to consider the role of cognitive appraisal in stress.
   c. was the foundation of Selye's GAS.
   d. was discounted by research showing that psychological awareness of stressors is a necessary component in the stress response.
   e. assumes that stress-related illness is caused by a complex interaction of factors.

6. Research on stress responses has shown that cognitive appraisal of stressful events
   a. is an unconscious decision-making process.
   b. involves both primary and secondary appraisal processes.
   c. is universal and not affected by individuals' feelings of competence.
   d. occurs after having determined that a threat exists.
   e. results in taking appropriate action in threatening or stressful situations.

7. In general, stress-related research has found all of the following to be true *except* that
   a. the negative effects of stress are cumulative.
   b. men and women generally have different responses to stress.
   c. individuals with low self-esteem are likely to use a problem-focused coping strategy.
   d. focusing on the controllable aspects of uncontrollable situations such as caregiving helps reduce stress.
   e. communication between the immune system and the brain plays a major role in the response to stressful events.

8. The success of a particular coping strategy depends on
   a. the stressor's controllability.
   b. using a problem-focused strategy rather than an emotion-focused strategy.
   c. taking an active approach to removing the source of the threat.
   d. controlling one's emotional response first, followed by controlling one's cognitive response.
   e. its consistency; that is, you should choose one strategy and seek to perfect it.

9. Perceived controllability over a stressor may influence an individual's response
   a. less than predictability, especially with intense, long-lasting stressors.
   b. by leading to procrastination, which is beneficial in the long term.
   c. very little when the individual is an elderly nursing home patient.
   d. through learned helplessness, in which you expect or believe you have no control and thus fail to act to reduce the threat.
   e. by discouraging procrastination, a relatively effective problem-focused coping strategy.

10. Research on stress and personality has found that
    a. optimistic explanatory styles are detrimental because they lead to denial of real threats.
    b. mistrust of others is more harmful to one's health than anger.
    c. there is no difference in functioning between optimists' and pessimists' immune systems.
    d. pessimists explain uncontrollable negative events as due to external factors and positive events as due to internal factors.
    e. Type A behavior patterns are toxic because they often include a component of cynical hostility.

11. Having a strong base of social support has been associated with all of the following *except*
    a. beneficial effects on self-esteem related to being taken care of by others.
    b. a stronger immune response to stress.
    c. gaining information concerning how to understand and emotionally respond to stressors.
    d. reduced control over the stressor due to increased dependence on others.
    e. benefits related to expressing our feelings.

12. Which of the following is *true* regarding religion and health?
    a. Religious beliefs are not related to health.
    b. Cancer fatality rates are actually higher among those who believe in God.
    c. Religious people have greater optimism than others, which helps them handle stress better.
    d. Only people who follow a monotheistic religion experience better health.
    e. all of the above

13. Which of the following is a theory of why women tend to live longer than men?
    a. Women have two X chromosomes, compared to only one for men.
    b. Menstruation and systems related to childbirth help women get rid of toxins.
    c. Men take more risks than do women.
    d. Men are more likely than women to ignore danger signals in their lives.
    e. all of the above

14. Weight gain occurs
    a. when energy intake exceeds energy expenditure.
    b. when energy expenditure exceeds energy intake.
    c. only when there is a genetic predisposition to obesity.
    d. only when there is a lack of will power.
    e. None of the above is true—weight control is arbitrary.

15. Which of the following has contributed to the increase in food intake and ultimately obesity rates in the United States?
    a. Restaurants are using larger plates than in the past.
    b. Cookbooks are specifying fewer portions than in the past for the same recipe.
    c. Cup holders in cars are larger than in the past.
    d. Restaurant servings are 2 to 5 times larger than in the past.
    e. all of the above

16. Eating disorders such as anorexia nervosa and bulimia
    a. occur 3 times more often in women than men.
    b. both involve the body being systematically starved.
    c. are associated more with low self-esteem than with sociocultural factors.
    d. represent learned behaviors; there is no evidence to suggest a genetic component.
    e. are completely separate disorders; they never occur together in the same individual.

17. Physiological methods of decreasing stress
    a. are less effective than relaxation, meditation, or hypnosis.
    b. are effective only if they contain an aerobic exercise component.
    c. include relaxation, associated with a huge decrease in natural killer cell activity.
    d. such as moderate aerobic exercise and progressive relaxation are highly effective.
    e. do not work as well as standard medical advice in reducing heart attacks.

18. Research on positive psychology and happiness has found that
    a. the pursuit of wealth may decrease one's sense of autonomy.
    b. happiness is a highly unstable characteristic, substantially determined by our environment.
    c. dramatic life events permanently alter one's characteristic level of happiness.
    d. people in collectivist cultures report greater levels of happiness than those in individualistic cultures.
    e. happiness is based on biological factors; thus, faith and optimism do not generate greater levels of happiness.

Chapter 16

Understanding Social Behavior

Source: Courtesy of Figzoi.

"Your lecture saved my life!"

It isn't often—make that *it's almost never*—that a college professor hears these words from a student and can take them as literal truth. Yet I had this experience last year during final-exam week. While working in my office, I looked up to see one of my introductory psychology students standing there, visibly shaken, as she made this pronouncement after having had a life-threatening encounter over the weekend. My student, Ferris, had been waiting at a bus stop not far from campus on a Saturday evening when a neatly dressed man walked up to her, put a gun to her stomach, and demanded that she hand over her purse. She was stunned and paralyzed with fear. When she didn't immediately respond, the assailant put the gun to her head and repeated his demand. Ferris noticed that people waiting across the street at another bus stop were watching her plight, but no one was taking action to help. In that moment Ferris recalled the last 5 minutes of my semester-ending lecture the previous morning, when I'd said to the assembled students, "And now I'm going to tell you something that may one day save your life."

Now, in my office, Ferris said that when I'd ended my lecture with this 5-minute recitation of "life-saving" instructions, she dutifully wrote down the information because she thought I might test the class on it during our final exam the following week. However, she hadn't put much stock into the advice. What I'd told students was how bystanders often react—or don't react—when they witness an emergency in which a stranger needs help. My information was based on a series of social psychological experiments conducted in the 1960s by John Darley and Bibb Latané (see chapter 2, section 2-2a). Listening to the lecture, Ferris had scoffed to herself, "People wouldn't just stand around when someone needs help!" Luckily, however, she continued listening as I told the class what these two social psychologists had discovered about the social dynamics of emergency situations and what was necessary to encourage others to intervene when help was needed. It was this knowledge that Ferris drew upon that Saturday night in the moments when the mugger's gun was pointed at her head. And it is this knowledge that Ferris believes probably saved her life.

Now, I am not claiming that this chapter will similarly affect your life, but I am telling you that the reason I love the field of social psychology is that it attempts to understand the social dynamics of everyday living with other people. **Social psychology** is the scientific study of how people's thoughts, feelings, and behavior are influenced by others. Here, perhaps more than in any other leg of this discovery journey in psychology, you can seek answers to a number of questions that you have probably pondered on your own personal journey of discovery. First, you will examine how we judge our social world (social perception and prejudice). Second, you will study how we develop attitudes toward people and events. Third, you will analyze how those around us shape us (social influence). Fourth, you will learn about the factors that either strengthen or weaken our antisocial and prosocial behaviors (aggression and helping). And finally, you will be introduced to some of the scientific insights about interpersonal attraction and romantic love. Along the way, I promise to tell you what I told Ferris and her fellow students on our last day of class. Let's begin.

> **social psychology** The scientific discipline that attempts to understand and explain how the thoughts, feelings, and behaviors of individuals are influenced by others.

16-1   SOCIAL PERCEPTION

Preview

- *How do we form initial impressions of people?*
- *What often happens after we categorize people into social groups?*
- *Are there any benefits to stereotyping?*
- *What is the physical attractiveness stereotype?*
- *What makes women and men look physically attractive?*
- *What is realistic group conflict theory?*
- *Are some people unknowingly prejudiced toward others?*
- *How do we explain other people's behavior?*
- *What is the fundamental attribution error?*

The way we seek to understand other people and events is known as **social perception,** and it can be roughly classified into two areas: impression formation and attribution. This section examines both of these social perception processes.

16-1a The First Step in Impression Formation Is Categorizing People into Groups

Imagine that you are walking down a dark city street at night with no one in sight. Suddenly, you notice the outline of a person walking toward you, three blocks away. At a distance of one block, you can tell that this person is a man. In less than a minute, your paths will cross. Are you in danger?

Every day, you judge people, and often you must react to them based on very little information. How do you "size up" others during initial encounters? As on the hypothetical dark street, the process of gathering information about others can be of vital importance to your health and safety. **Impression formation** is the process by which you combine various sources of information about a person into an overall judgment. It is like developing a theory of a person and then using this theory as a guideline in your actions toward her or him. A theory about a particular person works if it predicts that person's behavior with reasonable accuracy. Social psychologists view this process of forming impressions as dynamic, with judgments continually updated in response to new information.

In our hypothetical nighttime dilemma, the way you respond to the person approaching you will be determined by how you categorize him (Clement & Krueger, 2002; Gawronski et al., 2003). As discussed in chapter 9, section 9-2a, human beings are categorizing creatures. That is, we identify objects—including other people—according to features that distinguish them from other objects (Hampson, 1988; Taylor, 1981). In social categorization, physical features such as race, sex, age, and attractiveness are the most common ways to classify people, especially during first encounters (Park, 1986). Because these categories are used so often, labeling others according to superficial physical features becomes automatic, often occurring without conscious thought or effort (Brewer, 1988; Fiske & Neuberg, 1990).

16-1b Categorizing People into Groups Can Lead to Stereotyping

Not only do we group people into different categories, but also we develop beliefs about them. These social beliefs, which are often learned from others, are called **stereotypes** (McGarty et al., 2002; Van Rooy et al., 2003). Stereotypes are fixed sets of beliefs about people that put them into categories and don't allow for individual variation. In a very real sense, stereotypes are "shortcuts to thinking" that provide us with information about individuals we do not personally know (Dijker & Koomen, 1996; Macrae et al., 1994). Returning to our nighttime example, your stereotypical beliefs about encountering a strange man on a dark, deserted city street would probably result in greater apprehension than if the stranger were a woman or a child.

Although stereotyping people can speed up our social judgments, these cognitive shortcuts can also inhibit our thinking. For example, in one study, Galen Bodenhausen (1988) asked mostly White college students to act as mock jurors in a court case. Some students were told that the defendant's name was Carlos Ramirez, and others were told that his name was Robert Johnson. Half the students in each of these experimental conditions were given information about the case before learning the defendant's name, whereas the other half were given the information afterward. Bodenhausen predicted that hearing the Hispanic-sounding name "Carlos Ramirez" before receiving the evidence would activate students' ethnic stereotypes and that this activation would bias their processing of the information. In other words, instead of "weighing the facts," these students were expected to pay more attention to stereotype-consistent information than to stereotype-inconsistent information. This is exactly what Bodenhausen found. The imaginary Carlos Ramirez was found guilty more often than the imaginary Robert Johnson only when students had learned the name before receiving the evidence. Bodenhausen also found that stereotypes influence information-processing by increasing the amount of attention to and rehearsal of stereotype-consistent information.

social perception The way we seek to know and understand other persons and events; also known as *social cognition.*

impression formation The process of integrating various sources of information about a person into an overall judgment.

Labels are devices for saving talkative persons the trouble of thinking.

—*John Morley, English statesman and author, 1838–1923*

stereotype A fixed set of beliefs about people that puts them into categories and doesn't allow for individual variation.

This study, along with others, suggests that one of the important reasons why stereotyping often results in fast social judgments is that filtering social perceptions through a stereotype causes us to ignore information that is relevant but inconsistent with the stereotype (Kunda & Spencer, 2003; Wigboldus et al., 2003). Additional research finds that, when stereotypes are evoked from memory, they can lead to creation of false memories consistent with the stereotypes (Lenton et al., 2001). Thus, besides inhibiting thinking, stereotypes can also promote thinking that leads to false judgments. Together, these studies inform us that, although stereotyping may often help us when we need to make quick decisions, the cost is that we may sometimes make faulty judgments about whomever we stereotype.

16-1c There Is a Physical Attractiveness Stereotype

As mentioned, when we first meet someone, their physical appearance is generally the first thing we notice, especially if they somehow look different from the average person (McArthur, 1982; Roberts & Herman, 1986). Despite the frequently quoted folk saying "You can't judge a book by its cover," we tend to ignore the wisdom contained within this phrase. Instead, research indicates that we perceive physically attractive people as more sociable, dominant, sexually attractive, mentally healthy, intelligent, and socially skilled than those who are unattractive (Feingold, 1992b; Jackson et al., 1995).

This **physical attractiveness stereotype** is not reserved solely for adults but is found in all age groups (Karraker & Stern, 1990; Vaughn & Langlois, 1983). The physical attractiveness stereotype also occurs in collectivist cultures, but somewhat different cultural values shape its content (Chen et al., 1997). For example, Ladd Wheeler and Youngmee Kim (1997) found that, as in individualist cultures, physically attractive Koreans are perceived to be more sexually warm, mentally healthy, intelligent, and socially skilled than unattractive Koreans. However, consistent with the greater emphasis on harmonious relationships in collectivist cultures, physically attractive Koreans are also assumed to have higher integrity and be more concerned for others than are those who are physically unattractive. Together, these studies from around the world suggest that, as a species, we are drawn to physically attractive people, like bees to honey (Buss, 1987; Davis, 1990). This is especially true for males (Marcus & Miller, 2003).

Within a given culture and during a given time period, people generally agree about what defines physical attractiveness. What is beautiful also often conforms to the current standards of the dominant social group. For example, fine facial features and light skin have been standards for physical attractiveness in North American culture for many generations, and ethnic minority groups have generally mirrored these larger cultural preferences (Hill, 2002; Bond & Cash, 1992).

What shapes beauty standards besides dominant cultural values? Evolutionary theorists believe that the traits valued as desirable and attractive in men and women are those that increase their ability to produce offspring (Buss, 1988; Kenrick & Trost, 1989). Researchers have identified two beauty standards that may be related to reproductive fitness: Weight and its relationship to waist-to-hip ratios influence perceptions of female attractiveness, and facial features influence both sexes but in different ways.

Waist-to-Hip Ratios and Female Attractiveness

Regarding weight and body shape, cross-cultural studies find that men worldwide are generally attracted to women who have a lower waist-to-hip ratio, meaning that the circumference of their waist is smaller than that of their hips (Furnham et al., 2003; Singh, 1993). The most desirable waist-to-hip ratio appears to be 0.7, so a desirable woman with a waist of 25 inches would have a 35-inch hip size, or a desirable woman with a 35-inch waist would have 50-inch hips (Streeter & McBurney, 2003). Evolutionary psychologists contend that this 0.7 waist-to-hip ratio is universally perceived as attractive because it is a biologically accurate indicator that the woman is young and fertile but currently not pregnant—and therefore sexually available (Crandall et al., 2001; Furnham et al., 2002). According to this argument, over the course of human evolution, those men who mated with women with a waist-to-hip ratio of about 0.7 were most likely to successfully conceive an offspring. Con-

physical attractiveness stereotype The belief that physically attractive individuals possess socially desirable personality traits and lead happier, more fulfilling lives than less attractive persons do.

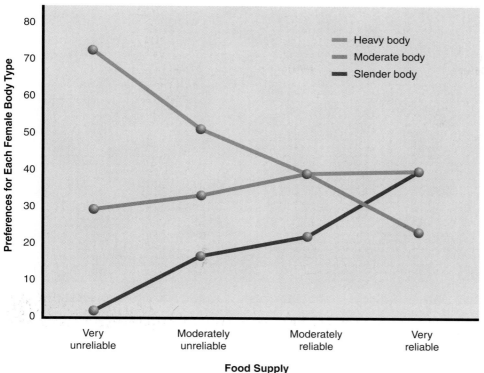

Figure 16-1

Is the Reliability of a Culture's Food Supply Related to Female Body Preferences?

Women with heavy bodies have high waist-to-hip ratios, while women with slender bodies have low waist-to-hip ratios. Cross-cultural research indicates that heavy women are considered more attractive in societies with highly unreliable food supplies. Evolutionary theorists believe that heavier women are perceived as more attractive than slender women in environments with frequent food shortages because heavy women's built-in fat supply helps them remain fertile and produce offspring during food shortages. In environments with more reliable food supplies, why might women with lower waist-to-hip ratios be preferred?

sistent with this reasoning, research indicates that deviations from the 0.7 ratio are associated with decreases in fertility (Van Hooff et al., 2000).

Although the 0.7 waist-to-hip ratio may be the generally preferred female body shape, additional cross-cultural research indicates that this preference is sensitive to the reliability of a culture's food supply (Marlowe & Westman, 2001). For example, as depicted in figure 16-1, Judith Anderson and her colleagues' (1992) analysis of 54 societies found that heavy women were strongly favored in cultures where the availability of food was highly unpredictable (71 percent preference), but they were less popular in those cultures with moderately or very reliable food supplies (40 percent preference). In contrast, slender women were not at all popular in cultures with unreliable food supplies, but their popularity increased to match that of heavy women when the culture's food supply was very reliable. The researchers believe that, in environments with periods of acute food shortages, male preference for heavy women is evolutionarily adaptive because fat represents stored calories. Put simply, heavy women carry a built-in food supply that helps them not only survive food shortages but also be fertile and produce offspring. Thus, in cultures where the food supply is unreliable, the extra fat associated with a higher waist-to-hip ratio overrides the typical evolutionary advantage of choosing women with a lower ratio.

Overall, these findings suggest that men generally prefer women with relatively low waist-to-hip ratios because this body type signifies youth, fertility, and current nonpregnancy. However, in environments where food is often in short supply, male preference shifts to higher female waist-to-hip ratios because this body type signifies greater ability to both produce and nurse offspring during food shortages.

Facial Features and Attractiveness

Cross-cultural research suggests that there may be universal standards of facial attractiveness (Cunningham et al., 2002; Zebrowitz & Rhodes, 2002). Among heterosexuals, possessing youthful or slightly *immature* facial features (large eyes, small nose, full lips, small chin, delicate jaw) enhances female attractiveness, while *mature* facial characteristics related to social dominance (small eyes, broad forehead, thick eyebrows, thin lips, large jaw) increase attractiveness of males. In commenting on these preferences for mature facial features in males and slightly immature features in females, various social scientists have argued that it

In the Old Testament story of King David and Bathsheba, the much older and vastly more powerful king pursues and ultimately possesses the youthful beauty. Throughout history and in cultures around the globe, mate selection has involved a youth-for-status exchange: Women who are sexually mature, yet young, are valued by men as potential mates, while men who are more physically mature and of higher social status are appealing to women. What explanations are offered by evolutionary and sociocultural theorists for this youth-for-status exchange?

Source: Artist unknown, oil on canvas.

suggests a dominant-submissive preference in heterosexual beauty standards. Essentially, heterosexual women and men engage in a *looks-for-status exchange,* in which women exchange their beauty for their mate's social power, and men exchange their social power for their partner's beauty (Fletcher et al., 2004; Gutierres et al., 1999).

In searching for an explanation for this looks-for-status exchange, evolutionary theorists contend that what is valued as desirable and attractive in men and women is that which increases their probability of producing offspring who will carry their genes to the next generation (Kenrick & Luce, 2000; Wade, 2003). Given the biological fact that women have a shorter time span to reproduce than do men, evolution predisposes men to perceive women who *look young* as being most desirable (that is, more physically attractive), because youth implies high reproductive potential. Using this same evolutionary logic, women are much more likely to value maturity over youthfulness in a mate, because a somewhat older man is generally a better provider for his children than is a young man, while still being functionally fertile (Buss, 1989, 1990; Dixson et al., 2003). Male status, ambition, and other signs of *social dominance* trump youthful male looks.

In contrast to this evolutionary explanation, other social scientists maintain that men seek beauty in a woman and women seek power in a man because of the widely different social statuses they have historically held in society. This sociocultural explanation argues that women have been excluded from power and are viewed by men as objects of exchange in the social marketplace (Eagly & Wood, 1999; Howard et al., 1987). Men place a premium on the quality or the beauty of this exchange object, and that is why physical attractiveness is sought in a woman. Because of their historically low status and their restricted ability to socially advance based on their own individual skills, women have been forced to tie their social advancement with the status of their mate. Thus, women seek men who are socially dominant and can be "good providers."

Which of these perspectives provides the best explanation is currently a hotly debated topic. If the sociocultural perspective is correct, recent social advances made by many women in North American and European countries (higher pay and increased social status) may cause shifts in the attractiveness preferences of both women and men. Women may look for more "beauty" in men, and men may look for more "economic status" in women. A handful of recent studies suggests that such changes may be taking place. For example, in Spain, a content analysis of personal ads in newspapers found that while the overall preferences in what men and women seek in a mate are consistent with predictions from evolutionary theory, there was an age difference in women's preferences consistent with sociocultural predictions (Gil-Burmann et al., 2002). Unlike older Spanish women, those younger than age 40 sought mainly physical attractiveness in men, not socioeconomic status. These changes in mate preferences among younger women may be at least partly caused by the financial independence these women are currently enjoying due to Spain's healthy economy. Similarly, in the United States researchers examined male mate preferences by posting four "female seeking male" personal ads on Internet bulletin boards (Strassberg & Holty, 2003). Results indicated that the ad that described a woman as "financially independent . . . successful [and] ambitious" generated over 50 percent more responses than the ad that described a woman as "lovely . . . very attractive and slim." If future research provides additional evidence that mate preferences are indeed changing, this would not necessarily mean that evolutionary forces don't shape perceptions of attractiveness. It may simply mean that, in this instance, inherited tendencies have been overridden by more powerful cultural forces.

16-1d Prejudice Is a Condescending Attitude and Discrimination Is a Negative Action Directed toward Members of Other Groups

The physical attractiveness stereotype illustrates how we treat people differently based on the degree to which their physical appearance matches our standards of beauty. When the stereotypes associated with a particular group of people—such as the physically unattractive—are negative and condescending, they can form the basis for prejudice and discrimination. I'm sure you realize that prejudice and discrimination are socially undesirable behaviors, but what exactly do these terms mean? How is prejudice different from discrimination?

The traditional definition of *prejudice* is a negative attitude toward members of a specific group. However, many forms of prejudice involve complex and contradictory emotions, combining positive attitudes toward group members on some dimensions with negative attitudes on other dimensions. For example, consider the following statement describing the fictional "Snailati" social group:

> I adore the Snailati people. I love their culture, the way they enjoy life. I love their music and the beauty of their women. But if you ever hire a Snailati to do a job, he will only create problems for you.

Using the traditional definition of prejudice, would the first three sentences be classified as prejudicial? No, but the last sentence certainly qualifies. Yet social psychologists who are critical of the traditional definition of prejudice contend that underlying the first three sentences' seemingly positive evaluations is an underlying judgment that the Snailati people are somehow undeserving of an equal social status. For this reason, many social psychologists define **prejudice** as attitudes toward members of specific groups that directly or indirectly suggest they deserve an inferior social status (Glick & Hilt, 2000). This definition can account for seemingly positive attitudes that prejudiced individuals often express toward other social groups that justify placing these groups into a lower social status. It can also account for "upward-directed" prejudices, meaning prejudice expressed by members of lower status groups toward groups with higher status who are seen as undeserving of their higher rank. The prejudice expressed by some women toward men and some working class resentment and envy of the upper social classes are examples of this upward-directed prejudice.

While prejudice is an attitude of condescension, **discrimination** is a negative and/or patronizing action toward members of specific groups. Discrimination can be manifested in many ways (Brewer & Brown, 1998; Hebl et al., 2002). Mild forms may simply involve avoiding people toward whom we hold prejudicial attitudes. As its intensity heightens, however, discrimination may produce actions resulting in violence and death (Hepworth & West, 1988).

How Does Intergroup Competition Cause Prejudice?

Social psychologists have investigated various factors that cause prejudice and discrimination. One social cause is competition between groups. According to **realistic group conflict theory,** when two groups compete for scarce resources such as jobs, housing, consumer sales, or even food, this competition creates a breeding ground for prejudice (Duckitt & Mphuthing, 1998; Levine & Campbell, 1972). Realistic group conflict theory contends that, when groups are in conflict, two important changes occur in each group. The first change involves increased hostility toward the opposing outgroup, and the second change involves

> If we accept and acquiesce in the face of discrimination, we accept the responsibility ourselves and allow those responsible to salve their conscience by believing that they have our acceptance and concurrence. . . . We should, therefore, protest openly everything . . . that smacks of discrimination.
>
> —*Mary McLeod Bethune, U.S. educator and civil rights activist, 1875–1955*

prejudice Attitudes toward members of specific groups that directly or indirectly suggest they deserve an inferior social status.

discrimination A negative and/or patronizing action toward members of a specific social group.

realistic group conflict theory A theory of prejudice contending that when two groups compete for scarce resources this competition creates a breeding ground for prejudice.

ethnocentrism A pattern of increased hostility toward outgroups, accompanied by increased loyalty to one's ingroup.

In the Robbers' Cave study, Sherif and his colleagues (1961) created intergroup hostility between two groups of boys at a summer camp by having them compete against one another. What theory explains how prejudice formed between these two groups due to their competitive relationship? How was prejudice reduced between these two groups?

Source: Figure 3, chapter 5, in Sherif, M., Harvey, O. J., White, B. J., Hood, W. R., & Sherif, C. (1961). *Intergroup conflict and cooperation: The Robbers' Cave experiment.* Norman, OK: Oklahoma Book Exchange.

an intensification of ingroup loyalty. This pattern of behavior is referred to as **ethnocentrism** (Sumner, 1906).

One of the first studies to test the hypotheses derived from realistic group conflict theory was the Robbers' Cave study conducted by Muzafer Sherif and his colleagues in the summer of 1954 at the Robbers' Cave State Park in Oklahoma (Sherif et al., 1961; Sherif & Sherif, 1956). Participants were 20 White, middle-class, well-adjusted 11- and 12-year-old boys who had never met one another. In advance, the researchers divided the boys into two groups, with one group leaving by bus for the camp a day before the other group. Upon arrival, each group was assigned a separate cabin out of sight of the other, and thus, neither knew of the other's existence. The camp counselors were actually the researchers who unobtrusively observed and recorded day-to-day camp events as the study progressed.

The study had three phases. The first phase was devoted to *creating ingroups,* the second was devoted to *instilling intergroup competition,* and the third involved *encouraging intergroup cooperation.* During the first week of ingroup creation, each group separately engaged in cooperative camp activities and developed its own unique identity. One group named itself the "Rattlers" and spent a good deal of time cursing and swearing, while the other group called itself the "Eagles" and instituted a group norm forbidding profanity. As the first week drew to a close, each group became aware of the other's existence, and that's when ingroup-outgroup tensions flared: "*They* better not be in *our* swimming hole!" "*Those* guys are using *our* baseball diamond again!"

During the study's second phase, Sherif tested his hypothesis that intergroup competition would cause prejudice by creating a weeklong tournament between the two groups, consisting of 10 athletic events such as baseball, football, and tug-of-war. True to expectations, the intergroup conflict transformed these normal, well-adjusted boys into what a naive observer would have thought were "wicked, disturbed, and vicious" youngsters (Sherif, 1966, p. 58). The researchers observed a sudden increase in ethnocentrism by both groups: The number of unflattering names used to refer to outgroup members increased (for example, "pig" and "cheater"), while negative attitudes that previously existed between some ingroup members were now redirected toward the outgroup. Soon, intergroup hostility escalated from name calling to acts of physical aggression.

The third phase of the study was designed to reverse the hostility, a task that proved to be much more difficult to accomplish than the others. Simple noncompetitive contact between the groups did not ease tensions. For example, when the two groups were brought together for a meal, food was more likely to be thrown at opposing group members than eaten! Sherif and his colleagues hypothesized that to reduce intergroup conflict they needed to introduce what they called a *superordinate goal,* which is a mutually shared goal that can be achieved only through intergroup cooperation. To test this hypothesis, the researchers arranged for a series of problem situations to develop over the course of the next 6 days, such as the "failure" of the camp's water supply or the "breakdown" of the camp bus. At first, the groups responded to these emergencies by trying to solve the problem on their own, without the other group's assistance. However, when they discovered that intergroup cooperation was necessary, they began to work together, which resulted in a gradual easing of tensions and new friendships forming between the previously competing group members. The Robbers' Cave study is an excellent example of how ethnocentrism can develop when two groups compete for scarce resources. It also demonstrates that having a superordinate goal can lead to peaceful coexistence between previously antagonistic groups. Although this study used children as participants, similar results have been obtained with adult samples (Jackson, 1993; Zárate et al., 2004).

Is There Such a Thing as Unconscious Prejudice?

Intergroup competition often results in open expression of prejudicial feelings, but many instances of prejudice are subtle and difficult to detect. One reason for this is that people who hold prejudicial attitudes often do not openly express them, because they realize that such attitudes are socially unacceptable. So, instead, they consciously conceal their biases from others and publicly express nonprejudiced views. However, on occasion, when their social guard is down and they behave spontaneously, they may unintentionally reveal these prejudices (Crandall & Eshleman, 2003; Dovidio & Gaertner, 1998).

Although some people consciously attempt to deceive others about their prejudice, other people's prejudice may be relatively unconscious, meaning they harbor prejudicial attitudes without being aware of it (Brendl et al., 2001; Dovidio, 2001). *Explicit prejudice* involves consciously holding prejudicial attitudes toward a group, while *implicit prejudice* involves unconsciously holding those attitudes. Individuals with implicit prejudicial attitudes may honestly believe they are not prejudiced, even while they react negatively toward people in the target group. In most instances, individuals who are implicitly prejudiced have explicit attitudes toward the target group that are relatively positive (Wilson et al., 2000).

How is it possible to react in a prejudiced manner toward others without realizing you are doing so? During such interactions, these individuals consciously focus on their positive attitudes toward the target group and actively monitor and regulate their behavior to convey warmth and friendliness. Simultaneously, they try to ignore the feelings of discomfort induced by their implicit prejudice. How do people from the target group react while conversing with individuals who are implicitly prejudiced? Based on past interactions with such individuals, people from the target group may have learned to attend not only to these individuals' consciously constructed self-presentations but also to their nonverbal behavior for evidence of implicit prejudice. Nonverbal behaviors related to negative arousal and tension in face-to-face interactions may include excessive blinking, gaze aversion, and forced smiles. When people from the target group detect these behaviors, they feel more uncomfortable and less satisfied with the interaction than the implicitly prejudiced individuals (Vorauer & Kumhyr, 2001). In other words, the research evidence suggests that, because implicitly prejudiced individuals pay the most attention to their consciously held positive attitudes and overtly friendly self-presentations, whereas their partners from the target group pay the most attention to the others' less consciously controlled—and less friendly—nonverbal behaviors, these two conversational partners often have very different reactions to their exchange (Devine et al., 1996; Dovidio et al., 2002). While implicitly prejudiced individuals often walk away feeling relieved that things "went well" and comforted in the knowledge that they indeed are nonprejudiced, the members from the target group often walk away feeling angry and certain that they have just encountered another prejudiced person.

What Cognitively Perpetuates Prejudiced Thinking?

Why do we sometimes continue to hold negative beliefs about certain groups, even though we know individuals within them who do not fit the negative stereotype? For example, have you ever described people of the other sex as being all alike regarding certain negative characteristics? If so, you voiced this gender stereotype despite the fact that you probably have friends and loved ones of the other sex whom you would not categorize in this manner. Why didn't these friends and lovers automatically serve as a catalyst to alter your stereotype?

One likely explanation for why global negative stereotypes often resist such disconfirming evidence is that they consist of a number of more limited *stereotype subcategories* (Devine & Baker, 1991; Hewstone et al., 1994). These subcategories give us a place to categorize those individuals whose personal characteristics don't fit the global stereotype (Lambert, 1995). For example, Kay Deaux and her colleagues (1985) found that American college students distinguish at least five different subcategories of women: housewives, career women, athletes, feminists, and sex objects. When a man with strong gender stereotypes meets and learns to respect a woman who does not fit any of his stereotypes, he may retain his prior gender beliefs by concluding that this woman is "different" from other women. Instead of revising his global stereotype of women, the man merely creates a new subcategory for this woman. Although subcategories are often more flattering and desirable than many global stereotypes, their very creation allows us to retain more rigid and unflattering views of the social group in question, which can form the basis for discrimination (Kunda & Oleson, 1995).

What Might Explain Some Racial Misunderstandings and Conflicts?

Surveys asking African Americans about their experiences as being targets of racial discrimination find that 60 percent or more report being targeted at some point in their lives, and more than half report having at least 13 racial hassles in the past year (Kessler et al., 1999; Sellers & Shelton, 2003). Most racial hassles involve brief interactions with strangers in which respondents were ignored, overlooked, not given service, treated rudely, or perceived as a threat. Other minorities in the United States report comparable prejudice experiences (Stangor et al., 2003).

Because of their history of being the targets of oppression, people of color are much more likely than others to consider their race and ethnicity an important aspect of their self-concepts (see chapter 4, section 4-5d). When Black and White Americans were questioned about their racial perceptions and attitudes, results suggested that differences in the ways in which these two groups are socialized to think about race increase the likelihood of misunderstandings and conflicts (Judd et al., 1995). Young Whites are generally socialized to avoid thinking about racial differences and stereotypes, because such thinking is considered the source of prejudice and discrimination. In contrast, young Blacks are typically socialized to emphasize their ethnic identity and to recognize the differences between themselves and Whites, because such thinking is considered to help them better deal with ongoing prejudice and discrimination.

Both perspectives have psychological merit: Stereotyping and recognizing group differences can lead to prejudice, and developing an ethnic identity can insulate one from many of the negative effects of prejudice. The former view emphasizes eliminating known causes of prejudice, while the latter perspective emphasizes protecting oneself from existing prejudice. To a certain extent, White Americans' racial views contend that an ideal society should be a "melting pot" or "color-blind," and that in this society everyone should be judged equally regardless of their race or ethnicity. In contrast, Black Americans tend to believe that eliminating their racial identity in a cultural melting pot would strip them of their most important defense against racism. Instead, their perspective on race contends that society is a "patchwork quilt," in which their group's unique strengths and qualities buffer them from ongoing racism.

These two contrasting views on the wisdom of recognizing race in one's life and using it as a basis for making social judgments may partly explain why many Blacks and Whites hold different opinions about social issues such as affirmative action. Whereas Whites may believe that such programs create unhealthy racial divisions and emphasize group differences, Blacks may believe that these programs serve to correct the continuing unfair treatment of minorities in society. Despite the merits in both viewpoints, there is some research indicating that the "patchwork quilt" perspective is more effective in reducing implicit racial bias than the "color-blind" perspective (Richeson et al., 2004). Thus, extolling the virtues of multiculturalism may yield more positive outcomes for intergroup relations than color blindness (Blum, 2002; Bonilla-Silva, 2003).

Can We Control and Eliminate Our Prejudicial Attitudes?

The research discussed thus far suggests that stereotyping and prejudice are social problems that are often difficult to change. Yet change can and does occur for those of us who want to reduce our prejudicial responding. For example, imagine that Virginia, a young White woman, has grown up being taught that Black people are intellectually inferior to Whites and has developed prejudicial views based on this upbringing. However, during the course of her life, Virginia has also been exposed to a number of people who do not fit this racial stereotype. Because of these experiences, she may begin to adopt a more accepting view of Blacks. Although Virginia no longer accepts the negative racial stereotype, she has not eliminated it from her memory. Quite the contrary. During her relearning process, the stereotype may well be more frequently activated from memory than her newly adopted beliefs (Devine, 1989). In a very real sense, for a person like Virginia who wants to be less prejudiced, censoring the negative stereotype and guarding against prejudicial thinking take conscious and deliberate attention—like breaking a bad habit.

Take a look at figure 16-2, which outlines how self-awareness and self-regulation may play a role in reducing prejudiced responses. Whenever Virginia encounters a Black person, the racial stereotype is likely to be involuntarily activated. If she does not consciously monitor her thoughts, she may automatically slip back into acting as though Blacks were intellectually inferior (a discrepant response). Becoming aware of this discrepancy in her actions,

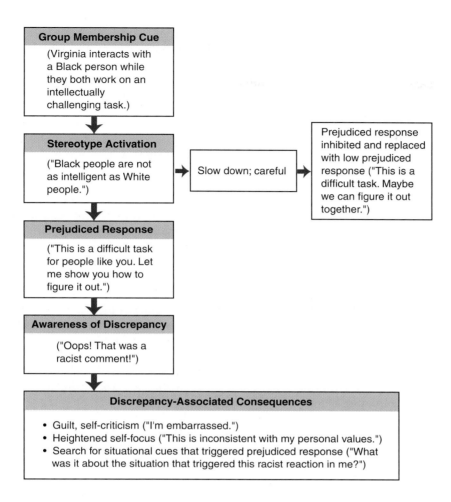

| **Group Membership Cue** |
| (Virginia interacts with a Black person while they both work on an intellectually challenging task.) |

↓

| **Stereotype Activation** |
| ("Black people are not as intelligent as White people.") |

→ | Slow down; careful | → | Prejudiced response inhibited and replaced with low prejudiced response ("This is a difficult task. Maybe we can figure it out together.") |

↓

| **Prejudiced Response** |
| ("This is a difficult task for people like you. Let me show you how to figure it out.") |

↓

| **Awareness of Discrepancy** |
| ("Oops! That was a racist comment!") |

↓

| **Discrepancy-Associated Consequences** |
| • Guilt, self-criticism ("I'm embarrassed.")
• Heightened self-focus ("This is inconsistent with my personal values.")
• Search for situational cues that triggered prejudiced response ("What was it about the situation that triggered this racist reaction in me?") |

Figure 16-2

Reducing Prejudiced Responding through Self-Regulation

When low-prejudiced persons first begin to try to respond in a nonprejudiced manner toward previously denigrated outgroup members, stereotype activation often spontaneously triggers a discrepant (that is, prejudiced) response, which subsequently triggers a series of discrepancy-associated consequences. This cognitive process is depicted by the vertical arrows on the left side of the figure. Over time, through careful self-regulation of one's thoughts and attention to one's nonprejudiced standards, low-prejudiced people break the "prejudice habit" and respond as depicted by the horizontal arrows near the top of the figure. If this model accurately describes how prejudiced behavior can be eliminated, what first step would you need to take to reduce your own prejudiced responding?

Source: From "Self-Regulation of Prejudiced Responses: Implications for Progress in Prejudice-Reduction Efforts" by J. J. Monteith in *Journal of Personality and Social Psychology*, 65, 1993, pp. 469–485. Copyright © 1993 by the American Psychological Association. Adapted with permission.

Virginia will feel guilty. In turn, this guilt will motivate her to heighten her self-awareness and search her memory for the situations that trigger these prejudiced responses (Iyer et al., 2003; Zuwerink et al., 1996). Through such attentiveness, Virginia will slowly be able to monitor and control her prejudicial responding (Monteith, 1993; Monteith et al., 1998).

The lesson here is that you can avoid prejudiced responding if low-prejudiced standards are central to your self-concept and you bring these standards to mind before acting (Macrae et al., 1998; Monteith, 1996). Thus, although the activation of stereotypes from memory makes nonprejudiced responding difficult, you can inhibit such intolerance by consciously and carefully paying attention to what you are thinking. The crucial factor is the strength of your motivation: How committed are you to thinking and acting in a nonprejudiced manner?

One of the biggest obstacles to breaking the prejudice habit involves the tension and distress experienced when interacting with a person from a different social group (Stephan et al., 2000). This **intergroup anxiety** often occurs because the lack of positive previous experiences with people from another group creates negative expectations about what may transpire during the course of the interaction. Due to this intergroup anxiety, people are often "on guard" and seek to limit or entirely avoid such exchanges (Plant & Devine, 2003). But while such avoidance may temporarily reduce anxiety, it does not overcome the reluctance to get to know people from different groups or promote thinking in a nonprejudiced way. Indeed, this pattern of behavior may create a vicious cycle in which the avoidance following intergroup anxiety is likely to sustain and even strengthen the anxiety. What appears effective in such situations is to fight the urge to flee, and instead, actively pursue a positive interaction. If you place yourself in intergroup situations and have positive or even neutral

intergroup anxiety The tension and distress sometimes experienced when interacting with a person from a different social group.

contact with outgroup members, your intergroup anxiety will decrease (Britt et al., 1996; Hyers & Swim, 1998).

16-1e Explaining People's Behavior Hinges on Either Internal or External Attributions

Beyond trying to understand others on the basis of physical appearance and group membership, we also try to understand why they behave the way they do. For example, imagine going shopping and encountering a store clerk who does not smile or talk to you while adding up your purchases. What explains her behavior? The process by which we use information to make inferences about the causes of behavior or events is called **attribution.** Why are we so interested in making attributions about other people's behavior? Put simply, if we think we know why people behave the way they do, we will be much more likely to view the world as coherent and controllable than if we have no clue as to their intentions and dispositions (Heider, 1958).

Primary Dimensions of Causal Experience

In making attributions, the most important judgment concerns whether we attribute a given action to internal qualities of the person or to external factors of the situation. An **internal attribution** consists of any explanation that locates the cause as inside the person, such as personality traits, moods, attitudes, abilities, or effort. An **external attribution** consists of any explanation that locates the cause as outside the person, such as the actions of others, the nature of the situation, or luck. When a clerk at a store doesn't smile at you, you may infer that she is rude and unfriendly (an internal attribution), or you may infer that she is distracted or having a bad day (an external attribution). The attribution you make will guide your future actions toward this person.

The Covariation Model of Making Attributions

Harold Kelley (1967, 1972) developed an influential theory of how people make attributions about the actions of others (whom Kelley called *actors*). According to his **covariation model,** human beings are rational and logical observers, behaving much like naive scientists in the way they test their hypotheses about the behavior of actors. Just as a scientist arrives at a judgment of causality by noticing that a particular variable is associated with a particular effect across a number of different conditions, Kelley asserted that people make causal judgments about everyday events. For example, imagine being grilled by your parents when you tell them that you are going out for the evening with your friend Bart Simpson. Why are they so concerned? What explains their behavior?

In making an attribution for their behavior toward you spending time with Bart, the covariation model predicts that you would rely on the *covariation principle,* which states that for something to be the cause of a particular effect, it must be present when the effect occurs and absent when it does not occur. In other words, the presumed cause (Bart) and the observed effect (parents' grilling) must "covary." Whenever a particular effect (parents' grilling) has several possible causal explanations, you are much less likely to attribute the event to any particular cause (Morris & Larrick, 1995).

How do you narrow down the possible causal explanations? In assessing covariation, Kelley stated that people rely on three basic kinds of information. *Consensus* information deals with the extent to which other people (for example, other parents or your other friends) react in the same way to the stimulus object (Bart) as do the actors (your parents). *Consistency* information concerns the extent to which the actors react to this stimulus object in the same way on other occasions. Finally, *distinctiveness* information refers to the extent to which the actors react in the same way to other, different stimulus objects (for example, your other friends).

In figure 16-3, I've outlined how Kelley's theory might predict specific attributions about your parents' behavior. For consensus, you would look at the behavior of other people: Is everybody suspicious and wary of Bart Simpson (high consensus), or is it only your parents who react this way (low consensus)? For consistency, you would consider your parents' past reactions to your spending time with Bart: Have your parents always been reluctant for you to be around Bart (high consistency), or have they been receptive to him in the past (low consistency)? For

---

attribution The process by which people use information to make inferences about the causes of behaviors or events.

internal attribution An attribution that locates the cause of an event in factors internal to the person, such as personality traits, moods, attitudes, abilities, or effort.

external attribution An attribution that locates the cause of an event in factors external to the person, such as luck, other people, or the situation.

covariation model A theory of attribution asserting that people rely on consensus, consistency, and distinctiveness information when assigning causes for events.

Available Information | What Is the Likely Attribution?

Low Consensus No one else is suspicious of Bart.	**High Consistency** My parents are always suspicious of Bart.	**Low Distinctiveness** My parents are suspicious of all my friends.	**Internal Attribution** My parents' suspicions are caused by something within them: They are distrustful, suspicious people.
High Consensus Everybody is suspicious of Bart.	**High Consistency** My parents are always suspicious of Bart.	**High Distinctiveness** My parents are not suspicious of any of my other friends.	**External Attribution** My parents' suspicions are caused by something outside them: Bart is not a trustworthy person.
Low Consensus No one else is suspicious of Bart.	**Low Consistency** My parents have never been suspicious of Bart before.	**High Distinctiveness** My parents are not suspicious of any of my other friends.	**External Attribution** My parents' suspicions are caused by something outside them: Bart may have done something recently to raise my parents' suspicions.

distinctiveness, you would think about your parents' reactions to your spending time with other friends: Are your parents suspicious and distrustful toward only Bart (high distinctiveness), or do they react this way toward all your friends (low distinctiveness)? According to the covariation model, you are most likely to attribute your parents' behavior to internal causes—such as the personality of your parents—when consensus and distinctiveness are low but consistency is high. On the other hand, external attributions are most likely when consensus and consistency are low and distinctiveness is high, or when all three kinds of information are high.

Research indicates that the covariation model is fairly accurate in explaining the attribution process. However, of the three types of information that we assess, consensus information has the weakest effect on attributions (Chen et al., 1988; Windschild & Wells, 1997). This suggests that, when trying to understand an actor's behavior, we primarily focus on information that can be obtained solely by attending to the actor (Was his or her behavior distinctive or consistent?) and pay less attention to information that requires us to also attend to other people's reactions (consensus information).

Do Individualists and Collectivists Differ in Making Attributions?

When explaining others' actions, people from individualist cultures often make internal attributions rather than external attributions, a bias known as the **fundamental attribution error** (Ross, 1977). In a study that documented these cultural differences, Joan Miller (1984) asked groups of American and Asian-Indian citizens of varying ages to explain the causes of positive and negative behaviors they had seen in their own lives. As figure 16-4 shows, in the youngest children of the two cultures (8- to 11-year-olds), there were no significant attribution differences. However, as the age of the participants increased, the Americans made more internal attributions, and the Asian Indians made more external attributions. This study and others strongly suggest that the fundamental attribution error is more common in individualist cultures than in collectivist cultures and that it is learned through socialization (Lee et al., 1996; Norenzayan & Nisbett, 2000).

Why is the fundamental attribution error more common in individualist cultures than in collectivist cultures? Is it because collectivists are less attentive than individualists to how attitudes and personality traits (internal factors) can shape behavior? Or is it because individualists are less attentive than collectivists to how situational forces (external factors) can influence behavior? Recent studies find that collectivists are just as likely as individualists to take into account people's dispositions when explaining their behavior (Krull et al., 1999). Where they differ is in their awareness of the power of the situation. Collectivists are more attentive to how situational or external factors may influence people's behavior, and that is apparently why they are less susceptible than individualists to the fundamental attribution error (Choi & Nisbett, 1998; Choi et al., 1999). This cultural difference in making attributions

Figure 16-3

Why Did My Parents React So Negatively to My Spending Time with Bart Simpson?

fundamental attribution error The tendency to make internal attributions rather than external attributions in explaining the behavior of others.

Figure 16-4

Is the Fundamental Attribution Error Only an Individualist Bias?

Asian-Indian and American participants of varying ages explained the causes of positive and negative behaviors they had seen in their own lives. Consistent with the fundamental attribution error, the individualist American adults made more internal than external attributions for both positive and negative events. The exact opposite was true for the collectivist Asian-Indian adults. Among the younger children, no attribution differences were found. Why do you think there were differences between the adults but not the children in these two cultures?

Source: From J. G. Miller, "Culture and the Development of Everyday Social Explanation," in *Journal of Personality and Social Psychology, 46* (1984): 961–978.

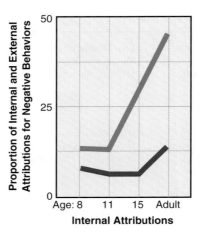

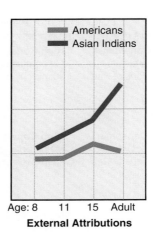

Internal Attributions   **External Attributions**

appears to be rooted in different views of the self. As stated in chapter 4, section 4-2d, individualists view the self as internally driven and relatively uninfluenced by situational forces. In contrast, collectivists view the self as dependent upon the group and strongly influenced by social obligations. The collectivist self-view seems to foster a greater appreciation of how personal and situational factors interact in shaping behavior, which is essentially how social psychology understands social behavior. Based on these findings, some social psychologists suggest that the "rules" that members of collectivist cultures develop in making social judgments about other people often lead to more accurate attributions than those typically developed in individualist cultures (Choi et al., 1999).

The fundamental attribution error can have significant social consequences. Attributing the behavior of others to internal factors often leads us to brush off people's attempts to deny responsibility for negative events with which they are associated (Inman et al., 1993). For example, the tendency to disregard situational forces in explaining the plight of victims within our society (for example, rape victims, street people, disadvantaged minorities) can result in an unsympathetic response, because we hold them responsible for their condition due to "bad" personalities or choices.

Even if we respond with sympathy, where we locate the cause of social problems will shape the type of solutions we seek (Sampson, 1991). That is, if we attribute the difficulties of unfortunate others to personal defects rather than to their circumstances, it is likely that the treatment programs we devise will focus on changing individuals while ignoring social conditions. Yet, if the people in these treatment programs are members of social groups in which failure is often partly due to poverty and discrimination, our attempted interventions will likely be unsuccessful and may even be psychologically damaging.

Section Review

- Impression formation is often based on rapid assessments of easily observable qualities and behaviors in others.
- We group people into different social categories and develop beliefs about them that are known as stereotypes.
- Stereotyping can bring greater speed and efficiency to our social judgments, but it also inhibits thought and can promote prejudice and discrimination.
- Physically attractive people are assumed to possess socially desirable personality traits.
- Women are judged most attractive when they have youthful or immature facial features, while male attractiveness is increased with mature facial characteristics related to social dominance.
- Prejudice involves attitudes toward members of specific groups that directly or indirectly suggest they deserve an inferior social status.
- Realistic group conflict theory contends that when two groups compete for scarce resources this competition creates a breeding ground for prejudice.

- People can hold prejudiced attitudes without being aware of them, but prejudiced thinking can be reduced through self-awareness and self-regulation.
- We attribute others' actions to either internal or external causes.
- The covariation model explains attributions as derived from consensus, consistency, and distinctiveness information.
- People from individualist cultures underestimate the influence of the situation, a judgmental bias known as the fundamental attribution error.

16-2 ATTITUDES

Preview

- *How do we develop attitudes about people, things, and events?*
- *What prompts us to change our attitudes?*
- *Do people have a need to keep their attitudes and behavior consistent?*

Thus far, we have discussed how we form impressions and try to explain others' actions. Through our observations of people and events, we also develop **attitudes,** which are positive or negative evaluations of objects (Schuman, 1995; Zanna & Rempel, 1988). "Objects" include people, things, events, and issues. When we use such words as *like, dislike, love, hate, good,* and *bad,* we are describing our attitudes.

> **attitude** A positive or negative evaluation of an object.

16-2a Two Common Attitude Shapers Are Repeated Exposure and Conditioning

We seem to naturally develop positive attitudes toward objects repeatedly presented to us, be they the unknown students we regularly see in class or the soft drink advertised on television (Zajonc, 1968). This tendency is called the **mere exposure effect,** and it was demonstrated in an interesting experiment conducted by Theodore Mita and his colleagues (1977). They reasoned that people are more commonly exposed to their mirrored facial images than to their true facial images and, thus, should have more positive attitudes toward the former than the latter. To test this hypothesis, they photographed students on campus and later showed them and their close friends their picture along with a mirror image print. When asked to indicate which of the two prints they "liked better," the students preferred the mirror print, while their close friends preferred the actual picture. Overall, the mere exposure effect illustrates how attitudes sometimes develop outside the realm of conscious awareness.

> **mere exposure effect** The tendency to develop more positive feelings toward objects and individuals the more frequently we are exposed to them.

Think about the mere exposure effect the next time you gaze into a mirror. You're probably the only person who knows you well who prefers that image of your face staring back at you!

Attitudes can also be formed through operant and classical conditioning, both of which we considered in chapter 7, sections 7-1 and 7-2. In operant conditioning, if you are praised and encouraged when learning how to dance, for example, you are likely to develop a positive attitude toward this activity. However, if others tease and make fun of your initial awkwardness, you are likely to form a negative attitude. Similarly, in classical conditioning, attitudes may form by pairing a previously neutral stimulus with another stimulus that naturally evokes a positive or negative response in a person. For example, children may develop prejudicial attitudes toward certain groups because the children have heard their parents continuously using negatively evaluated words such as *stupid, lazy, dishonest,* and *dirty* when referring to these people (Cacioppo et al., 1992; Staats & Staats, 1958). By repeatedly pairing the social group's previously neutral name (the conditioned stimulus) with these negative adjectives (the unconditioned stimulus), children can acquire prejudicial attitudes (the conditioned response) toward these people.

16-2b Attitude Change Can Occur with or without Comprehension of the Persuasive Message

Not only do we form attitudes, but also we change attitudes. In fact, every day we are inundated with attempts to change our attitudes. Turn on the television, and commercial spokespersons will try to convince you that their products are better than all others. Go to your doctor's office for your annual physical exam, and your doctor may try to change your attitudes toward salt, fatty foods, and exercise. This process of consciously attempting to change attitudes through the transmission of a particular message is known as **persuasion** (Petty & Wegener, 1996).

One of the most influential persuasion theories is Richard Petty and John Cacioppo's (1986) **elaboration likelihood model.** The term *elaboration likelihood* refers to the probability that a person who receives a persuasive message will elaborate on—that is, carefully analyze and attempt to comprehend—the information contained in the message. According to the model, we tend to engage in either high or low elaboration when processing persuasive messages. When motivated and able to think carefully about the message content (high elaboration), we take the *central route* to persuasion and are influenced by the strength and quality of the arguments. When unable or unwilling to analyze the message, we take the *peripheral route* to persuasion, whereby we pay attention to cues irrelevant to the content or quality of the communication (low elaboration), such as the attractiveness of the communicator or the sheer amount of information presented. By attending to these peripheral cues, we can evaluate a message (for example, "Does the persuader look honest?" "Does she sound knowledgeable?") without engaging in any extensive thinking about the actual issues under consideration. This means that, when you take the peripheral route, it isn't necessary to comprehend the message: Attitude change can occur without comprehension. Figure 16-5 depicts these two persuasion routes.

Although attitude change can occur through either the thoughtful mode of central processing or the lazy mode of peripheral processing, attitudes formed via the lazy route are weaker, less resistant to counterarguments, and less predictive of actual behavior than those formed through the thoughtful route (Haugtvedt & Petty, 1992; Petty et al., 1995). An analogy might be this: If attitudes are like houses, then attitudes changed by the peripheral route are like houses made from straw or sticks—they require little effort to develop and are extremely vulnerable to destruction. In contrast, attitudes changed by the central route are like houses made of bricks—they take a good deal of effort to construct and are strong and durable. This is the reason our psychological journey of discovery has placed so much importance on critical thinking: Such thinking results in a stronger foundation for our knowledge about the world.

16-2c Cognitive Dissonance Theory Explains How the Need for Consistency Can Lead to Attitude Change

Besides changing our attitudes due to others' persuasive messages, sometimes we are motivated by an internal desire to keep our attitudes and behavior consistent. For example, suppose young Jack tells his grade-school friends that he dislikes girls, but later he is seen walking up a hill with Jill. How might Jack respond to this inconsistency between his attitude ("I don't like girls") and his behavior (walking with Jill)? According to Leon Festinger's (1957) cognitive dissonance theory, when aware of an inconsistency between our attitudes and our actions,

---

persuasion The process of consciously attempting to change attitudes through the transmission of some message.

elaboration likelihood model A theory that there are two ways in which persuasive messages can cause attitude change, each differing in the amount of cognitive effort or elaboration they require.

We are not won by arguments that we can analyze but by tone and temper, by the manner which is the man himself.

—Samuel Butler, English author, 1835–1902

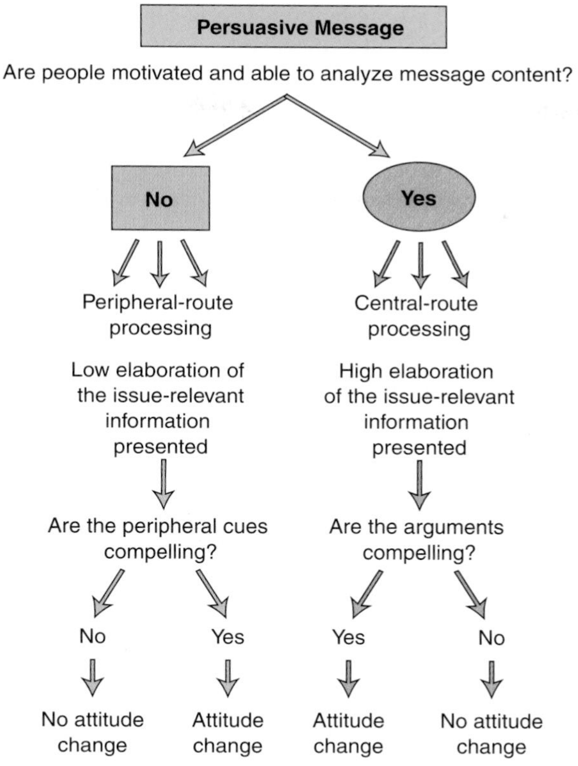

Persuasive Message

Are people motivated and able to analyze message content?

No   **Yes**

Peripheral-route processing

Central-route processing

Low elaboration of the issue-relevant information presented

High elaboration of the issue-relevant information presented

Are the peripheral cues compelling?

Are the arguments compelling?

No   Yes   Yes   No

No attitude change   Attitude change   Attitude change   No attitude change

Figure 16-5

Two Routes to Persuasion

The elaboration likelihood model describes how people evaluate a persuasive message based on their ability and motivation to analyze its contents. As the likelihood of thinking about the attitude-object increases, the processes specified by the central route become more likely determinants of attitudes, and those specified by the peripheral route become less likely determinants. This process is reversed as the likelihood of thinking about the attitude-object decreases. In central-route processing, message contents are carefully scrutinized before they are accepted. However, in peripheral-route processing, evaluation of the message is based on a more shallow analysis of incidental cues, such as the communicator's credibility, status, or likeability. Of the two routes to persuasion, which do you think secures the most enduring attitude change?

cognitive dissonance
A feeling of discomfort caused by performing an action inconsistent with one's attitudes.

we experience an unpleasant psychological state called *cognitive dissonance* (refer back to chapter 2, section 2-3a). **Cognitive dissonance** is a feeling of discomfort caused by performing an action that is inconsistent with our attitudes. To relieve this feeling of discomfort, we often change our attitudes so they are in line with our behavior (Elliot & Devine, 1994). Thus, if no one forced Jack to walk up the hill with Jill, he should experience discomfort due to his dissonant thoughts ("I dislike girls, but I walked with a girl") and could be motivated to change his attitude ("Gee, maybe girls aren't that bad after all"). Since Festinger proposed this attitude theory in the 1950s, hundreds of studies have supported many of its basic principles: When people behave in ways inconsistent with their attitudes and become aware of the discrepancy, they are likely to change their attitudes so their attitudes are consistent with their behavior.

You may have experienced what Festinger called *post-decision dissonance* soon after buying an expensive product, such as a new entertainment system, a computer, or an automobile. If you are like most people, before buying such a pricey item, you read the sales brochures for all the potential choices, weighing each of their advantages and disadvantages. Your final choice probably had more of the qualities you wanted in the product than did the others, but it most likely did not beat its competitors in all areas. Because of this fact, your final choice was to some extent inconsistent with some of your beliefs about what you wanted in this item. That is, as soon as you *committed* yourself and purchased one of the products, the attractive aspects of the unchosen alternatives and the unattractive aspects of your choice were inconsistent with your final decision.

How did you reduce this dissonance? Like most people, you may have lowered your dissonance by not thinking about all the good qualities in the products you did not buy (you tossed out their brochures) and by thinking only about the good qualities in your chosen product (you kept this brochure and read it repeatedly). Such after-the-fact, altered perceptions are regularly found in the behavior of consumers following product choices (Murphy & Miller, 1997), in voters on election day (Regan & Kilduff, 1988), and even in bettors at a racetrack (Knox & Inkster, 1968). Because votes, bets, and many product purchases cannot be changed once a decision has been made, people who commit themselves are motivated to reduce post-decision dissonance. In these circumstances, the only way for people to reduce their dissonance is to convince themselves that they made the right choice.

An initial assumption underlying cognitive dissonance theory was that everyone has an equal desire to think and act consistently. More recent research, however, suggests that this desire for consistency is more common in individualist cultures than in those with a collectivist orientation (Heine & Lehman, 1997; Kashima et al., 1992). That is, because people from collectivist cultures are socialized to think of group needs before their own needs, it is more acceptable for them to behave in a manner inconsistent with their attitudes than it is for individualists. As a result, people from collectivist cultures are less concerned than individualists about maintaining cognitive consistency. Thus, what many North Americans and other individualists consider discrepant and psychologically aversive—namely, believing one thing but saying something else—may not be as troubling to people from cultures with a collectivist orientation.

If you are from an individualist culture, you might be thinking to yourself, "I don't often get upset with acting inconsistently. Why is this so?" Beyond cultural considerations, one possibility is that some of us generally tolerate cognitive inconsistencies better than others do. Spend a few minutes completing Self-Discovery Questionnaire 16-1, which measures individual differences in the preference for consistency. Research employing this measure has found that peo-

> Consistency, madam, is the first of Christian duties.
>
> —*Charlotte Brontë, British author, 1816–1855*

> Consistency is the last refuge of the unimaginative.
>
> —*Oscar Wilde, Irish author, 1854–1900*

Self-Discovery
Questionnaire 16-1

Do You Have a Preference for Consistency?

Instructions: The extent to which people have a preference for consistency is measured by items on the Preference for Consistency Scale (PCS; Cialdini et al., 1995). To take the PCS, read each of the following items and then indicate how well each statement describes you, using the following scale:

1 = strongly disagree
2 = disagree
3 = somewhat disagree
4 = slightly disagree
5 = neither agree nor disagree
6 = slightly agree
7 = somewhat agree
8 = agree
9 = strongly agree

____ 1. It is important to me that those who know me can predict what I will do.
____ 2. I want to be described by others as a stable, predictable person.
____ 3. The appearance of consistency is an important part of the image I present to the world.
____ 4. An important requirement for any friend of mine is personal consistency.
____ 5. I typically prefer to do things the same way.
____ 6. I want my close friends to be predictable.
____ 7. It is important to me that others view me as a stable person.
____ 8. I make an effort to appear consistent to others.
____ 9. It doesn't bother me much if my actions are inconsistent.

Directions for scoring: The last PCS item (number 9) is reverse-scored; that is, for this item a lower rating actually indicates a higher level of consistency preference. Before summing the items, recode item 9 so that 1 = 9, 2 = 8, 3 = 7, 4 = 6, 6 = 4, 7 = 3, 8 = 2, 9 = 1. To calculate your preference for consistency score, add up your responses to the nine items.

When Cialdini and his colleagues developed the PCS in 1995, the mean score for college students was about 48. The higher your score is above this value, the greater your preference for consistency is. The lower your score is below this value, the less of this preference you probably possess.

Source: From "Preference for consistency: The development of a valid measure and the discovery of surprising behavioral implications" by R. Cialdini, M. Trost, and J. Newsom in *Journal of Personality and Social Psychology,* 1995, 69, 318–328 (Appendix, p. 328). Copyright © 1995 by the American Psychological Association. Adapted with permission.

ple with a high preference for consistency are motivated to behave in line with their attitudes, as predicted by cognitive dissonance theory. In contrast, those with a low preference for consistency are not bothered much by inconsistent actions and instead appear open and oriented to flexibility in their behavior (Cialdini et al., 1995). In summarizing cognitive dissonance research, at least two factors can derail expected cognitive dissonance effects: A person's cultural upbringing may make attitude-discrepant behavior an appropriate and acceptable option, or a person's underlying psychological needs may reduce the aversiveness of attitude-discrepant acts.

Section Review

- Attitudes are formed by various means, including mere exposure, operant conditioning, and classical conditioning.
- The elaboration likelihood model describes how attitudes can be changed through either effortful or lazy thinking. Attitudes changed via the lazy route are weaker, less resistant to counterarguments, and less likely to predict later behavior.
- Cognitive dissonance theory explains how attitudes can be changed as a way to maintain cognitive consistency.
- Individualists desire to keep their attitudes and behaviors consistent, while collectivists are more likely to tolerate cognitive inconsistencies.

16-3 SOCIAL INFLUENCE

Preview

- *What is social influence?*
- *What situational factors influence conformity?*
- *Are collectivists more conforming than individualists?*
- *What affects our willingness to grant others' requests?*
- *Are we obedient, and when are we most likely to obey orders?*

Social influence involves the exercise of social power by a person or group to change the attitudes or behavior of others in a certain direction (Cialdini & Goldstein, 2004). *Social power* refers to the force available to the influencer to motivate this change. This power can originate from having access to certain resources (for example, rewards, punishments, information) or from being liked and admired by others (French & Raven, 1959; Tyler, 1997; Zimbardo, 1972). The three main behavioral consequences of social influence are conformity, compliance, and obedience.

> **social influence** The exercise of social power by a person or group to change the attitudes or behavior of others in a certain direction.

16-3a Asch's Research Demonstrates the Power of Conformity Pressure

Can you recall incidents from your past when you behaved a certain way because everyone else was behaving that way? For instance, did you ever join in on Halloween pranks simply because it was "the thing to do"? If not, perhaps you cut classes, took drugs, or volunteered for a local charity drive because others did so. If you engaged in these activities due to perceived group pressure, you were conforming. In **conformity,** our behavior or beliefs become more similar to those of the group. Conformity is not necessarily a bad thing. In fact, if we didn't abide by most of the formal and informal rules of the social groups to which we belong, there would be social chaos.

> **conformity** A yielding to perceived group pressure.

Asch's Line Judgment Studies

In a set of classic conformity studies, Solomon Asch (1951, 1952, 1956) had male college students take part in what was described as a group visual perception experiment. Over a series of trials, six to eight men told Asch which of three comparison lines was equal in length to

Figure 16-6

Asch's Line Judgment Task

In this example of Asch's classic conformity experiments, participants were asked to judge which of the three comparison lines was equal in length to the standard line.

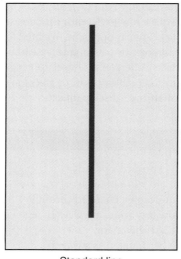

Standard line

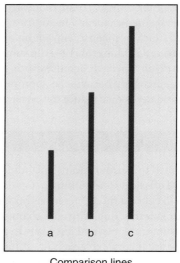

Comparison lines

> Once conform, once do what other people do because they do it, and a lethargy steals over all the finer nerves and faculties of the soul. She becomes all outer show and inward emptiness; dull, callous, and indifferent.
>
> —*Virginia Woolf, British novelist, 1882–1941*

> The fish dies because it opens its mouth.
>
> —*Spanish proverb*

a standard line (see figure 16-6). Although this task may seem easy, there was a catch. Only one person in each group was an actual participant—the rest were confederates of Asch who had been given prior instructions to pick the wrong line. The students made a total of 18 different line judgments and announced them out loud, with the actual participant giving his opinion second to last. What would the participant do when faced with this dilemma? Would he conform to the group's incorrect judgment, or would he stick with what his eyes told him? If you were in his place, what would you do?

Participants conformed on one-third of the critical trials by naming the same incorrect line as that named by the confederates. In contrast, when participants in a control condition made their judgments privately, less than 1 percent conformed (Asch, 1951). What Asch's research and other studies (Tanford & Penrod, 1984) demonstrate is that we often find it easier to conform than to challenge the unanimous opinions of others.

Factors That Influence Conformity

To more fully understand the nature of conformity, we need to identify the types of social settings and personal characteristics that make us more or less susceptible to others' influence. Some of the more important factors that affect conformity are listed here:

- *Group size*—As group size increases, so does conformity, but only up to a point. After the number of people exerting conformity pressure goes beyond three or four, the tendency to yield to the group doesn't increase (Asch, 1955).
- *Group cohesiveness*—In general, groups with a strong sense of togetherness elicit greater conformity than less cohesive groups (Hogg, 1992; Nowak et al., 1990). For example, we are more likely to accept our friends' influence than that of others due to our respect for our friends' opinions, our desire to please them, and our fear of rejection (Crandall, 1988).
- *Social support*—A person who has the support of another is less likely to conform to the influence of the group (Allen & Levine, 1969, 1971). In the line judgment studies, Asch (1956) found that when one of the confederates picked the correct line, conformity dropped dramatically—to one-fourth the level shown by participants faced with a unanimous majority.
- *Desire for personal control*—Sometimes we resist social influence simply in order to feel that we control our own actions (Brehm, 1966; Brehm & Brehm, 1981). Individuals with a high desire for personal control tend to resist conformity more than do those with a low desire for control (Burger, 1987).
- *Culture*—People from collectivist cultures are more concerned than individualists with gaining the approval of their group, and they feel shameful if they fail to get it

(Hui & Triandis, 1986; Triandis, 1989). A person from an individualist culture, on the other hand, has a higher desire for personal control (see the preceding point on this list) and a need to feel unique. As a result of these different orientations, people from collectivist cultures are more conforming to their own group than are individualists (Bond & Smith, 1996). This yielding to the group by collectivists is not considered a sign of weakness as it is in individualist cultures but, rather, is believed to indicate self-control, flexibility, and maturity (Kumagai, 1981; White & LeVine, 1986).

16-3b Compliance Is Influenced by Mood, Reciprocity, and Reason-Giving

In trying to "get our way" with others, the most direct route is to simply ask them to do what we desire. **Compliance** is publicly acting in accord with a direct request. When complying, you may privately agree or disagree with the action the other person is engaging in, or you may have no opinion about the behavior. For example, do you think about what passing the salt to a dinner companion implies about your relationship with this person or your own values? Probably not. You comply out of habit. However, have you ever granted someone's request to copy your answers in an exam, even though you believed it was wrong? This *external compliance*—acting in accord with a direct request despite privately disagreeing with it—occurs because we are concerned about how others might respond if we refuse them. On the other hand, you may often comply with a request because you have a personal allegiance to the values and principles associated with it. Agreeing to donate money to a charity consistent with your own values is an instance of *internal compliance*. Three factors that establish the proper atmosphere in securing compliance are creating positive moods, encouraging reciprocity, and giving reasons for compliance.

> **compliance** Publicly acting in accord with a direct request.

Positive Moods and Compliance

Other people are more likely to comply with our requests when they are in a good mood, especially if the request is prosocial in nature, such as helping someone in need (Forgas, 1998; Isen, 1987). Because of this general awareness that good moods aid compliance, we often try to flatter people before making a request (Liden & Mitchell, 1988). Although those we "butter up" in this manner may be suspicious of our motives after receiving our requests, the preceding flattery is still often effective in securing compliance (Kacmar et al., 1992).

Reciprocity and Compliance

How often has someone come up to you in a public place and offered you a small gift, such as a flower, a pencil, or a flag, and then asked you to donate money to their organization? If so, they were hoping that the small gift would lower your resistance to their request (Burger et al., 1997). The hope rested on a powerful social norm that people in all cultures follow—namely, the **reciprocity norm.** This expectation that one should return a favor or a good deed is based on maintaining fairness in social relationships (Gouldner, 1960; Howard, 1995). Although this norm helps ensure that social exchanges will be roughly equitable between two parties, it can also be used to exert influence over others.

> **reciprocity norm** The expectation that one should return a favor or a good deed.

Giving Reasons for Compliance

Ellen Langer and her colleagues (1978) found evidence for the power of reason-giving in gaining compliance when they had confederates try to cut in line ahead of others at a photocopying machine. In one condition, the confederates gave no reason, merely asking, "May I use the photocopying machine to make five copies?" Sixty percent of those waiting complied with this "no reason" request. Interestingly, when confederates gave a pseudoreason that provided no explanation at all but merely restated their desire to make copies ("May I use the photocopying machine to make five copies because I have to make copies?"), 94 percent of the people waiting complied, identical to the compliance when an actual reason was given ("I'm in a hurry").

Why does giving a reason, any reason, result in greater compliance to requests? Langer (1989) believes that we may often mindlessly grant a request accompanied by a reason

Explore It
Exercise **16-1**

Can You Persuade Others to Comply with a "Reasonable" Request?

People are more likely to grant requests if the requests are accompanied by a reason. Why might this be so?
Source: Courtesy of Figzoi.

Ellen Langer's research found that people will often comply with a request if you give some reason for making the request, even when the given reason is simply a restatement of the request. Apparently, people often mindlessly grant requests accompanied by a reason because they assume the requester would not ask if the request were illegitimate. Test this hypothesis yourself. For example, if you are in line at a grocery store, ask the person in front of you if you can cut ahead of them to pay for your items "because I have to pay for these items." Or, if you are waiting to buy tickets at a movie theater, ask if you can go ahead of others to purchase your ticket "because I have to buy a ticket." Do they comply? Try to gain compliance in similar situations without giving a reason for going ahead of others. Is this strategy less effective, as it was in Langer's research?

because we assume the requester would not ask if the request were illegitimate. When my daughter Lillian was 2 years old, she had already learned the importance of giving reasons when seeking compliance from her parents. In asking to go outside, she would say, "Can I go outside? . . . Because I have to go outside." Based on Langer's findings we see that, when it came to securing compliance, Lillian had already developed sufficient social skills to do quite nicely in the adult world. Before reading further, check out Explore It Exercise 16-1.

16-3c Milgram's Research Demonstrates That People Often Obey Destructive Orders

obedience The performance of an action in response to a direct order.

Unlike the rather subtle social pressures of compliance, **obedience,** which is the performance of an action in response to a direct order, is easily recognized as an exercise of power. Usually the order comes from a person of high status or authority. Because people are often instructed from a very young age to respect and obey those in positions of authority (for example, parents, teachers, and police officers), obedience to those of higher status is common and often perceived as a sign of proper socialization. To understand how situational factors increase or decrease obedience to authority, let's explore the most discussed social-psychological study ever conducted.

Milgram's Obedience Research

Imagine that you volunteer to participate in an experiment investigating the effects of punishment on the learning of word pairs. You will be the teacher, and a 50-year-old man will be the learner. The experimenter explains that you will deliver increasing levels of electrical shock each time the learner makes a mistake. Once the study begins, the learner, who is in an adjacent room, makes many mistakes. Once you have delivered 75 volts of electricity, you hear through the intercom system the learner grunting and moaning in pain whenever you deliver the shocks. At 150 volts, he demands to be released, shouting that his heart is bothering him. Do you stop participating in the study at this point?

Let's imagine that you continue. At 180 volts, the learner shouts that he can no longer stand the pain. Do you now stop delivering the shocks? Why or why not?

Let's imagine that you don't stop. At 300 volts, the learner says that he absolutely refuses to provide any more answers. Now the experimenter turns to you and orders you to treat the absence of a response as equivalent to an error and deliver the appropriate level of shock. Do you do so?

Let's imagine that you obey the experimenter's commands and continue. Now, even though the learner no longer gives answers to your questions, you continue to hear from the adjoining room his screams of agony whenever your finger flips the shock-generator switch. Are these developments now sufficient for you to stop participating in the experiment?

Let's imagine that you continue, despite the learner's pleas to stop. When you surpass the 330-volt switch, the learner falls silent, not to be heard from again. As you continue to increase the shock intensity, you realize that you are getting closer to the last switch, the 450-volt switch. If you hesitate in delivering a shock, the experimenter first tells you, "Please continue," and then says, "The experiment requires that you continue," and then, "It is absolutely essential that you go on," and finally, "You have no other choice; you must go on!" What do you do?

From imagining your responses in this hypothetical situation, when do think you would have disobeyed the experimenter's commands? Would it have been following the learner's first protest? The second? The third? Is it possible that you would have continued, despite the intensity of the learner's pleas?

I am guessing your prediction is that you would have disobeyed the experimenter's orders well before the 450-volt limit was reached. If this is the case, you are in good company, for widespread disobedience is exactly what was predicted by college students, middle-class adults, and psychiatrists who were presented with this hypothetical scenario (Milgram, 1963).

When Stanley Milgram conducted this research in the early 1960s, no one actually received electrical shocks. The learner was a confederate of the experimenter. Even the learner's screams of protest and pain were prerecorded, so all participants heard exactly the same thing. To Milgram's surprise, 65 percent of the participants (26 out of 40) obeyed the experimenter completely, despite the convincing cries of agony from the learner (Milgram, 1965).

Because the findings were so unexpected, Milgram carried out a number of variations of his experiment to better understand the conditions under which obedience and disobedience would be most likely. As illustrated in figure 16-7, these studies found that obedience increased as the distance between the teacher and the learner increased, or as the distance between the teacher and the experimenter decreased. In addition, when college students and women served as participants, the same level of destructive obedience was found (Milgram, 1974). Different researchers also obtained similar results in several other countries, suggesting that these high levels of obedience were not solely an American phenomenon (Kilham & Mann, 1974; Mantell, 1971; Shanab & Yahya, 1977). The participants in these studies were not closet sadists who enjoyed their destructive obedience—in fact, their actions caused them a good deal of stress, although no enduring psychological damage (Elms, 1995; Elms & Milgram, 1966).

Recently, François Rochot and his coworkers (2000) analyzed the audio recordings of one of Milgram's obedience studies to better understand how participants behaved over the course of the experiment. Results indicated that all participants were initially cooperative toward the experimenter, but that this changed as the learner began complaining. What predicted obedience versus disobedience was the timing of the participants' first firm opposition to the shocks they were told to administer. Those who firmly verbally opposed the experimenter by 150 volts all ended up defying his authority by disobeying. In contrast, only about half the participants who began their verbal challenges after 150 volts ever disobeyed. Further, no disobedience ever occurred among those who never took a firm verbal stance against the experimenter. This reanalysis of one of Milgram's classic studies provides additional insight into the social-psychological process of obedience and disobedience. It

---

The person who never submits to anything will soon submit to a burial mat.

—*Nigerian proverb*

Obedience to the law is demanded as a right; not asked as a favor.

—*Theodore Roosevelt, U.S. president, 1858–1919*

. . . far more, and far more hideous, crimes have been committed in the name of obedience than have ever been committed in the name of rebellion.

—*C. P. Snow, English novelist, 1905–1980*

In schools all over the world, little boys learn that their country is the greatest in the world, and the highest honor that could befall them would be to defend it heroically someday. The fact that empathy has traditionally been conditioned out of boys facilitates their obedience to leaders who order them to kill strangers.

—*Myriam Miedzian, U.S. author, 1991*

Figure 16-7

Some Factors That Influence Obedience and Disobedience to Authority

To determine what factors increase or decrease obedience beyond the baseline 5 percent, Milgram varied the location of the experiment, the participant's proximity to the victim and the experimenter, and the presence of obedient or disobedient confederates. As you can see, all these factors influenced obedience levels.

Source: Data from S. Milgram, *Obedience to Authority: An Experimental View,* Harper and Row, Publishers, Inc., 1974; and S. Milgram, *The Individual in a Social World: Essays and Experiments,* Addison-Wesley Publishing Company, 1992.

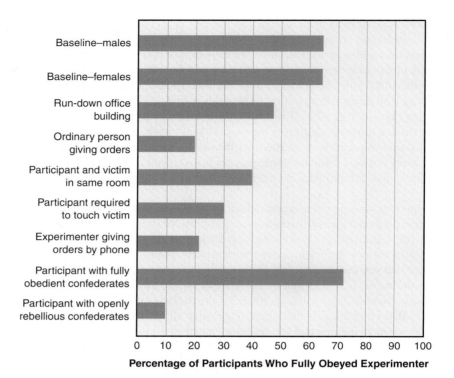

Percentage of Participants Who Fully Obeyed Experimenter

appears that a crucial factor in resisting the destructive commands of authority figures is an early and firm statement of opposition to what is transpiring.

Underestimation of Situational Factors

When describing the situation confronting the participants in the obedience studies, I asked whether you would have fully obeyed the experimenter's commands in the same circumstances. Most people believe they would resist the destructive commands and openly rebel. How do we reconcile these beliefs with the experiments' actual findings?

Before you answer this question, let me remind you about the fundamental attribution error described in section 16-1e. This tendency to assume that others' actions are caused by internal dispositions rather than external forces results in underestimating the power of the situation to shape behavior. Such misrepresentation of how the social world actually operates leaves us vulnerable to manipulation by the very social forces we underestimate. If we were to develop a greater appreciation of how we can be influenced by the wishes, desires, and dictates of others, we might be better able to recognize when we are in danger of falling prey to social manipulation. Before reading further, try Explore It Exercise 16-2 to demonstrate how people are influenced by others' actions.

Section Review

- Social influence is the exercise of social power to change the attitudes or behavior of others in a certain direction.
- Conformity increases as group size and group togetherness increase; it decreases when you have a social supporter.
- Individualists are less conforming to their own groups than are collectivists.
- Compliance is most likely to be secured if you put a person in a good mood, do them a favor, or give them a reason for granting your request.
- Milgram's obedience experiments demonstrated that we will often obey the destructive commands of an authority figure.
- Underestimating situational pressures makes you more susceptible to their power.

People are regularly influenced by the actions of others, conforming to their behavior without even labeling their actions as conformity. If you passed by this person on the left, do you think you would copy her behavior and look up? Do you think you might be more likely to look up if there were five people gazing into the sky rather than just one? Why?

Source: Courtesy of Figzoi.

We often conform to other people's actions, even in subtle and trivial ways. Test this social fact by enlisting a group of your friends to try to get other people to copy their behavior. Have your friends stand together in a public setting, looking up in the air. Tell them to simply tilt their heads up and look skyward. Do not have them point skyward with their arms. Watch passersby from a short distance. Do they look up? How long do they linger? Do they ask your friends any questions? If they do look up, approach them and ask why they looked up in the air. Also ask them if they think their behavior of looking up is an example of conformity. How do they respond?

16-4 HURTING AND HELPING OTHERS

Preview

- *What is the difference between instrumental aggression and hostile aggression?*
- *Do women and men differ in their inclinations to hurt and help others?*
- *What is the culture of honor?*
- *How do we learn to help?*
- *Why does the presence of other bystanders decrease helping in an emergency?*

Although obedience doesn't necessarily result in harm to others, the concept of aggression is directly associated with pain and destruction. **Aggression** is any form of behavior intended to harm another living being (Björkqvist & Niemelä, 1992; Geen, 1996). In contrast, *helping* entails voluntary behavior that is carried out to benefit another person (Batson, 1998). Let us examine these two fundamental aspects of human behavior.

16-4a Aggression Involves the Intention to Harm Another Living Being

Social psychologists have traditionally distinguished two types of aggression. **Instrumental aggression** is the intentional use of harmful behavior in order to achieve some other goal, while **hostile aggression** is the intentional use of harmful behavior simply to cause injury or death to the victim. Instrumental aggression is motivated by the anticipation of rewards or the avoidance of punishment. In that sense, it can be thought of as relatively deliberate and rational. In most robbery attempts, thieves employ aggression as an instrument to achieve

aggression Any form of behavior that is intended to harm or injure a person, oneself, or an object.

instrumental aggression The intentional use of harmful behavior in order to achieve some other goal.

hostile aggression The intentional use of harmful behavior with the goal of causing injury or death to the victim.

their real goal, which is obtaining the victim's money. The aggression that occurs in a military context is also often instrumental. Here, the principal goal may be either to defend one's own territory or to confiscate the enemy's land. By contrast, hostile aggression is not motivated by the anticipation of rewards or the avoidance of punishments, even though these may indeed be ultimate consequences of the aggressive act. Instead, this type of aggression is often impulsive and irrational. We are more apt to engage in hostile aggression when we are very angry.

Although the distinction between instrumental and hostile aggression has been useful in helping researchers understand human aggression, many aggressive actions cannot be neatly placed into only one of the two categories (Bushman & Anderson, 2001). For example, a child may angrily hit another child who has taken his favorite toy, and then he may retrieve the toy while the victim cries. The motives underlying this aggression are both the infliction of pain (hostile aggression) and the recovery of the favored toy (instrumental aggression). In such instances, no clear distinctions can be made between hostile and instrumental aggression. In other instances, aggression might start out instrumentally but then turn hostile. For example, a soldier's "cool" and methodical firing of a weapon at a hidden enemy may turn into impulsive rage when one of her comrades is killed. Because of such multiple motives, in the coming years social psychologists will likely revise this classic distinction between two types of aggression to better represent the complex motivational nature of aggression.

16-4b There Are Gender Differences in Styles of Aggression

A widespread belief in our culture is that men are more aggressive than women. Does research support this cultural belief? Would it surprise you to learn that the answer is both yes and no?

Men and women do differ in one important kind of aggression: physical aggression. That is, men (and boys) are more likely than women (and girls) to engage in aggression that produces pain or physical injury (Bartholow & Anderson, 2002; Eagly & Steffen, 1986). They are also more likely than women and girls to be physically aggressive against others without being provoked (Bettencourt & Miller, 1996). However, in situations where people are provoked, gender differences tend to shrink or even disappear.

Not only do men and women typically differ in their level of physical aggression, but also they appear to experience physical aggression differently (Astin et al., 2003; Campbell & Muncer, 1987). Among North Americans, women tend to view their physical aggression as stress induced, precipitated by a loss of self-control, and a negative experience. Men, in contrast, tend to perceive this type of aggression as an exercise of control over others, provoked by challenges to their self-esteem or integrity, and a positive experience (see the discussion of sexual aggression in chapter 11, section 11-2a). A similar gender difference pattern has been found in Poland (Fraczek, 1992). These results suggest that, when it comes to physical aggression, the more spontaneous and unplanned behaviors typical of hostile aggression tend to describe the antisocial actions of women, while the more planned and calculated actions of instrumental aggression tend to describe male hostility (Campbell et al., 1992).

One form of aggression largely ignored by researchers is indirect aggression—a form of social manipulation in which the aggressor attempts to harm another person without a face-to-face encounter. Gossiping, spreading bad or false stories about someone, telling others not to associate with a person, and revealing someone's secrets are all examples of indirect aggression. Field studies among adolescents in Europe and North America (see figure 16-8) find that girls are more likely than boys to use indirect aggression (Björkqvist et al., 1992; Fry, 1992). One explanation for this gender difference is that girls tend to be discouraged more than boys from engaging in direct acts of aggression. As a result, they may employ indirect aggression simply because it is more socially acceptable. This research further indicates that, whereas male physical aggression decreases significantly during adolescence, teenage girls continue to exhibit higher levels of indirect aggression at all age levels (Campbell, 1999; Theron et al., 2000). Can you think why this might be so? One possibility is that indirect aggression is harder to detect and punish than physical aggression.

Overall, these findings are important because they suggest that we need to reexamine the "peaceful female" stereotype. Although women are generally less physically aggressive than men, they are by no means the "gentle sex." As a species, we all share the capacity to cause harm to one another.

No man can think clearly when his fists are clenched.

—*George Jean Nathan, American critic and writer, 1882–1958*

The wish to hurt, the momentary intoxication with pain, is the loophole through which the pervert climbs into the minds of ordinary men.

—*Jacob Bronowski, British scientist, 1908–1974*

Although males appear to be more physically aggressive than females, research suggests that females may engage in more indirect aggression, such as spreading bad or false stories about others or revealing someone's secrets. What might explain these gender differences?

Source: Courtesy of Figzoi.

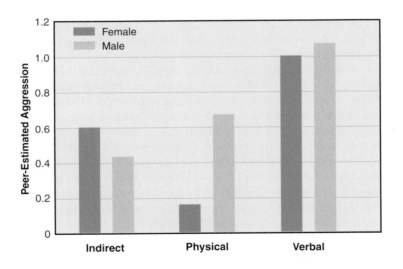

Figure 16-8

Gender Comparisons in Aggressive Strategies

In a study of the aggressive styles used by adolescents in Finland, Björkqvist and his colleagues (1992) found that verbal aggression (for example, yelling, insulting, name-calling) is the type most commonly used by both boys and girls. There are no significant differences in verbal aggression. However, boys display significantly more physical aggression (hitting, kicking, shoving), whereas girls utilize significantly more indirect forms of aggression (gossiping, writing nasty notes about another, telling bad or false stories).

When discussing gender differences in aggression, it is natural to ask what accounts for these differences. In most cases, social psychologists search for social or cultural explanations (see section 16-4c). However, besides these causes, some evidence indicates that biological factors also play a role in the heightened physical aggression among males. For example, men with higher levels of testosterone (an important male sex hormone) in their blood tend to be more physically aggressive than those with lower levels (Berman et al., 1993; Gladue, 1991). This finding is reversed for women: The higher their testosterone levels, the lower their levels of aggression. This evidence suggests that, in addition to social and cultural factors, biological factors may help account for gender differences in aggression.

16-4c The "Culture of Honor" May Explain Certain Types of Male Violence

Cross-cultural research indicates that societies in which the economy is based on the herding of animals have more male violence than farming societies. For example, among the Native American cultures of North America, the herding Navajos were famous for their warring tendencies, while the farming Zunis tended to be nonviolent (Farb, 1978). Within given societies, researchers have also observed this contrast in aggression. In East African cultures, for instance, herders are easily provoked to violence, while farmers go out of their way to get

culture of honor A belief system in which males are socialized to protect their reputation by resorting to violence.

along with their neighbors (Edgerton, 1971). The social psychologists Richard Nisbett and Dov Cohen (1996) believe that the greater violence exhibited by herding people is due to their **culture of honor,** which is a belief system that prepares men to protect their reputation by resorting to violence. In cultures that place a high value on honor, males learn from childhood on that it is important to project a willingness to fight to the death against insults and vigorously protect their property—specifically, their animals—from theft. Nisbett and Cohen hypothesize that this culture of honor is more necessary in herding than farming societies because herders' assets (animals) are more vulnerable to theft—and thus, more in need of aggressive protection—than are the assets of farmers (land).

How does this culture of honor theory relate to contemporary violence in the United States? First, in an analysis of crime statistics in this country, Nisbett and Cohen found that the southern and western states, which were settled by people whose economy was originally based on herding, have higher levels of current violence related to honor than do the northern states, which were originally settled by farmers (Cohen, 1996; Cohen & Nisbett, 1994). Honor-related violence involves arguments, brawls, and lovers' triangles where a person's public prestige and honor have been challenged (Vandello & Cohen, 2003). Second, in a series of experimental studies, Nisbett and Cohen also found that, when insulted, not only did young White men from the South become more stressed and angry than young White men from the North, but also they were more prepared to respond to insults with aggression (Cohen et al., 1996).

These studies suggest that southern White males tend to be more physically aggressive than northern White males in certain situations because they have been socialized to live by a code of honor that requires them to respond quickly and violently to threats to their property or personal integrity (Cohen, 1998). Although the vast majority of these southern men no longer depend on herding for their livelihood, Nisbett and Cohen contend that they still live by their ancestors' culture of honor.

A similar regional difference in violence is not found among young African-American males. That is, Black southern men are not more violent than Black northern men. Thus, the culture of honor in the South is unique to White males. Having stated this, however, Nisbett and Cohen note that the higher incidence of violence among inner-city African-American males compared to African-American males in rural or suburban areas may be partly related to a similar honor code (Nisbett & Cohen, 1996). Thus, just as a culture of honor may exist among southern White men, the inner-city "street" culture may also have a culture of honor that makes violent outbursts more likely here than in other areas. That is, in the inner city, where it is extremely difficult to pull oneself out of poverty by legal means, and where police provide little protection from crime and physical attack, young Black males may strive to gain and maintain respect by responding violently to any perceived insults (Anderson, 1994).

16-4d Aggressive Impulses Can Be Modified by Higher-Order Thinking

A number of biological, personal, and cultural factors can either increase or decrease our individual levels of aggression. Yet what occurs cognitively to trigger or defuse aggressive impulses? Leonard Berkowitz (1984, 1989) developed the **cognitive-neoassociationist model** to explain how aggression is often triggered by circumstances that arouse negative affect, such as frustration, pain, extreme temperatures, and encountering people whom we dislike.

cognitive-neoassociationist model A theory of aggression stating that aversive events produce negative affect, which stimulates the inclination to aggress.

Cognitive-Associative Networks

Berkowitz named his theory the *cognitive-neoassociationist model* because he believes that when we experience negative affect due to some unpleasant event, this affect is encoded into memory and becomes cognitively associated with specific types of negative thoughts, emotions, and reflexive behaviors. Although these cognitive-associative networks are initially weak, the more they are activated, the stronger they become (Berkowitz, 1993; Ratcliff & McKoon, 1994). When these associations are sufficiently strong, activating any one of them will likely activate the others, a process known as *priming* (see chapter 8, section 8-2b). Thus, simply remembering a past occasion when we were angry can prime hostile thoughts, angry feelings, and even reflexive actions, such as clenched fists and gritted teeth. The implication of Berkowitz's notion of priming these negative memories is that, even when our surroundings don't elicit negative affect, simply thinking about aggression can activate it (Miller et al., 2003).

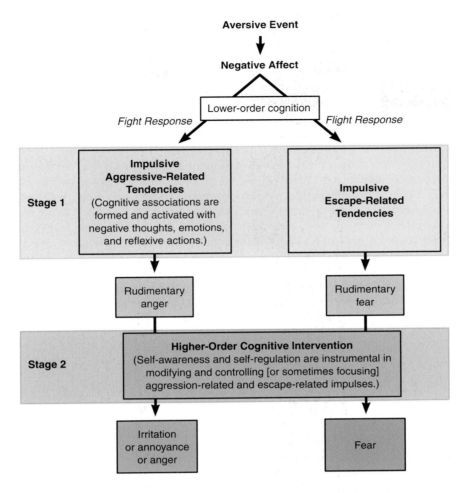

Aversive Event

Negative Affect

Lower-order cognition

Fight Response   *Flight Response*

Stage 1

Impulsive Aggressive-Related Tendencies
(Cognitive associations are formed and activated with negative thoughts, emotions, and reflexive actions.)

Impulsive Escape-Related Tendencies

Rudimentary anger

Rudimentary fear

Stage 2

Higher-Order Cognitive Intervention
(Self-awareness and self-regulation are instrumental in modifying and controlling [or sometimes focusing] aggression-related and escape-related impulses.)

Irritation or annoyance or anger

Fear

Figure 16-9

Cognitive-Neoassociationist Model of Aggression

Leonard Berkowitz's theory of aggression states that aversive events produce negative affect, which stimulates our aggressive inclinations. How does he propose that we can "short-circuit" this aggression?

It should be noted that this conditioning process involves the activation of our sympathetic nervous system in the "fight-or-flight" response, which is also the *alarm* stage in Hans Selye's general adaptation syndrome (see chapter 15, section 15-1b). Whether we react to negative affect with "fight" or with "flight" depends on (1) our biologically inherited aggressive tendencies; (2) our prior conditioning and learning; and (3) our attention to aspects of the situation that facilitate or inhibit aggression (Berkowitz, 1993). Figure 16-9 depicts Berkowitz's model. Because our present objective is to understand how aversive events often lead to aggression, we will concentrate on the fight-response side of the model (the left side of figure 16-9).

"Unthinking" Aggressive Responses

Up to this point in Berkowitz's theory of aggressive responses, the cognitions and feelings we experience due to the aversive event are simply impulsive reactions to negative affect and represent only the potential first stage in aggression. The negative thoughts, emotions, and reflexive actions evoked in the cognitive-associative networks at this stage are primitive and have not yet been shaped and developed by higher-order cognitive thinking. If such aggressive tendencies do not come under the control of more sophisticated thinking, they may cause us to spontaneously lash out with anger or aggression. Berkowitz (1994) states that this impulsive aggression is most likely when we are performing highly routine activities and thus are not consciously monitoring our thoughts, feelings, or actions. Pushing, shoving, or hitting someone after being repeatedly jostled in a crowd at a music concert or sporting event is an example of how negative affect can erupt into an aggressive response.

Journey of Discovery **Question**   "Road rage" has become an all-too-familiar term describing violent outbursts by people driving cars on our nation's highways. Would this type of aggression typically be instrumental or hostile in nature? Why? Beyond harsh penalties, what strategies might public officials employ to reduce road rage?

Higher-Order Cognitive Intervention

If we don't blindly lash out when experiencing negative thoughts, feelings, and impulses during stage 1, Berkowitz contends that higher-order cognitive processes are activated, and this represents stage 2 in the aggressive response. When subjected to higher-level thinking, aggression-related tendencies are often modified and controlled.

What causes the aggression-related tendencies in stage 1 to come under the control of the more complex cognitive processes of stage 2? Research suggests that *self-awareness* and *self-regulation* are crucial in modifying and controlling our aggressive impulses (Mischel et al., 1996). Thus, when angered, we may try to make sense of our negative feelings before acting. If we conclude that no one is to blame for the aversive event, our anger will likely subside. Alternatively, we may assign blame to a particular person but still conclude that retaliation is an inappropriate response. People who regularly consider the future consequences of their behavior tend to be less likely to act aggressively than others when angered (Joireman et al., 2003; Zimbardo & Boyd, 1999). Because of these cognitive control mechanisms in higher-order thinking, negative affect does not always lead to aggression. However, one factor that short-circuits higher-order thinking is alcohol (Bachman & Peralta, 2002; Busch & Rosenberg, 2004). When people drink beverages containing enough alcohol to make them legally intoxicated, they often behave more aggressively than otherwise because the alcohol reduces controlled, effortful thinking while simultaneously leaving more automatic, impulsive responses relatively unaffected (Bartholow et al., 2003).

Of course, even when stone sober, people may strike out at those they blame after carefully considering the consequences. In fact, research indicates that when people believe that aggression will make them feel better, they are more likely to behave aggressively (Bushman et al., 2001). This finding underscores the fact that higher-order thinking does not guarantee a nonaggressive response, but it does make it more likely.

Strategies to Inhibit Aggression in Others

Higher-order thinking often inhibits an aggressive response. Yet what about situations in which people are very angry and probably not engaging in higher-order thinking? As a bystander, what could you do to inhibit their aggressive impulses? Following are two suggestions.

Research indicates that inducing responses or emotions in angry people that are incompatible with their anger may effectively deter them from responding aggressively (Baron, 1976, 1983). Have you ever been in a situation in which people were on the verge of hitting or verbally lashing out at others when suddenly their anger disappeared because someone made them laugh? Inducing laughter or other positive emotions in people who are angry is an effective strategy to short-circuit their aggressive impulses.

Another strategy to inhibit aggression is to employ the most basic and widely used technique to defuse conflict: Offer an apology to those who are angry (Ohbuchi et al., 1989). By admitting blame, offenders demonstrate to those who are offended that the offenders may be worthy of a second chance (Goffman, 1971; Schneider, 2000). When offenders offer apologies, victims of the offense tend to feel greater empathy for the offender, and their desire for revenge diminishes (McCullough et al., 1998). The most effective apologies are those that are offered after, not before, those who are offended have an opportunity to express their feelings about the offense (Frantz & Bennigson, 2005). Why? It appears that the later apologies provide greater reassurance to those who are angry that the offender understands the nature of the offense and will "do the right thing" in the future.

Unfortunately, some people have a hard time apologizing, because they are concerned with "losing face" in a confrontation (Hodgins et al., 1996). This reluctance to apologize is especially true among men: Women are more willing than men to take responsibility for a perceived social transgression (Gonzales et al., 1990). In fact, women tend to become more apologetic when severely reproached for a social transgression, while men respond more defensively to severe reproaches (Hodgins & Liebeskind, 2003). These gender differences may partly explain why men are more likely than women to be involved in physical altercations.

16-4e Helping Others Is Largely a Learned Response

Just as all of us have had personal experiences with aggression, we have also helped and been helped by others. Consider again the chapter-opening story of my student, Ferris, needing help when confronted by a gun-wielding mugger. Would you have gone to her aid if you had been an onlooker? Have you ever wondered how your own degree of helpfulness compares with that of others? Spend a few minutes responding to items in Self-Discovery Questionnaire 16-2 to learn more about the strength of your helping desires.

Learning to Help

Although our inclination to help those in need undoubtedly has a genetic basis (especially if those in need are blood relatives), its strength is substantially strengthened or weakened by our upbringing (McAndrew, 2002). As we mature, parents, teachers, and peers are extremely influential in shaping our personal norms for helping. If helping others becomes an important self-defining value, we will feel proud when responding to others' suffering and ashamed when ignoring them (Schwartz & Howard, 1981, 1982). In this regard, observational learning or modeling (refer back to chapter 7, section 7-3) can have a powerful effect on our willingness to help (Eisenberg & Valiente, 2002). For example, an international study of people who rescued Jews in Nazi-occupied territory during World War II revealed that the rescuers were more likely than nonrescuers to say that they had learned generosity and caring from their parents (Oliner & Oliner, 1988). Similar findings have been obtained in studies of civil rights activists in the United States. Strongly committed activists had parents who had been excellent prosocial models when they were children, whereas less committed activists had parents who tended to be inconsistent models, often preaching prosocial action but not actually practicing it (Rosenhan, 1970). These studies suggest that parents who try to instill prosocial values by preaching helping but not modeling it will likely raise children who are only weakly helpful. Yet parents who not only preach helping but also let their prosocial actions serve as guidelines for their children's behavior are more likely to foster helping responses in the next generation.

Journey of Discovery **Question**   Many of you will be—or currently are—parents. Based on what you have learned about helping, what sort of cultural role models might influence the "helping habits" of boys and girls? How might greater gender-role flexibility influence male and female helping tendencies?

Gender Considerations in Helping

Do you think male bystanders would be more likely than female bystanders to intervene in an emergency like the one confronting my student in the chapter-opening story? The answer appears to be yes. Research indicates that men are more likely than women to help when the situation involves an element of danger and when there is an audience (Eagly & Crowley, 1986). In addition, men more frequently provide help to women than to other men, especially if the women are attractive (West & Brown, 1975). These findings suggest that the help typically offered by men is consistent with the male gender role: It is heroic and chivalrous, and generally directed toward the benefit of female victims.

Women helpers, in contrast, do not show a gender bias in terms of whom they help. Further, although men help more frequently in dangerous situations, women appear to be more helpful than men when assistance is consistent with the female gender role—that is, when the situation involves empathy and devotion. For example, women are more likely than men to provide social and emotional support to others (Shumaker & Hill, 1991), are more likely to volunteer for community service (Trudeau & Devlin, 1996), and are also more likely to take on the caretaking role for children and elderly people (Unger & Crawford, 1992).

16-4f Deciding to Help Often Involves a Series of Decisions

As discussed in chapter 2, section 2-2a, the 1964 murder of Kitty Genovese in New York City prompted social psychologists John Darley and Bibb Latané (1968) to study the

The Helping-Orientation Questionnaire

Directions: While reading these descriptions of hypothetical situations, imagine yourself in each of them and pick the action that best describes what you would do.

1. You have come across a lost wallet with a large sum of money in it, as well as identification of the owner. You
   a. return the wallet without letting the owner know who you are.
   b. return the wallet in hopes of receiving a reward.
   c. keep the wallet and the money.
   d. leave the wallet where you found it.
2. A child riding his or her tricycle past your house appears to be lost. You
   a. ignore the child so as to avoid potential entanglements and misunderstanding.
   b. figure the child can find his or her own way home.
   c. ask the child where he or she lives and take him or her home.
3. When it comes to cooperating when you would rather not, you usually
   a. cooperate if it is helpful to others.
   b. cooperate if it is helpful to yourself.
   c. refuse to get involved.
   d. avoid situations in which you might be asked to cooperate.
4. A neighbor calls you and asks for a ride to a store that is six blocks away. You
   a. refuse, thinking you will never need a favor from him (or her).
   b. explain that you are too busy at the moment.
   c. immediately give the ride and wait while the neighbor shops.
   d. consent if the neighbor is a good friend.
5. Alone in your home, you hear a woman outside calling for help. You
   a. go to her aid.
   b. call the police and join them at the scene.
   c. are afraid to intervene directly, so you take no action.
   d. are sure someone else has heard her, so you wait.
6. You are in a waiting room with another person. If you hear a scream in the adjoining room and the other person fails to respond, you will
   a. help the screaming person whether the other person helps or not.
   b. help the screaming person only if the other person does too.
   c. wait to see if the screaming continues.
   d. leave the room.

conditions that inhibit bystanders from helping in emergencies. Their subsequent bystander intervention model contended that being helpful during an emergency involves not just one decision, but a series of five decisions. As you can see from figure 16-10, at each point in this five-step process of deciding whether or not to help, one decision results in no help being given, while the other decision takes the person one step closer to helping.

According to this model, the first thing you must do as a potential helper is notice that something unusual is happening. Unfortunately, in many social settings, countless sights and sounds distract you, and thus a cry for help may go unnoticed. This is one of the possible reasons why there is a negative correlation between population density and helping (Levine et al., 1994). That is, because of all the distracting sights and sounds, residents of a crowded city are less likely to notice when someone needs help than are those who live in less densely populated urban centers.

As a bystander to an emergency, if you do indeed notice that something unusual is happening, Latané and Darley (1968, 1970) contend that you move to the second step in the decision-making process—namely, deciding whether something is wrong and help is needed. For instance, if you pass an unconscious man lying on the grass in a park, you may ask yourself, "Did he suffer a heart attack, or is he merely sleeping?" This is an extremely

7. A poorly dressed person confronts you on a deserted street and asks for a dime. You
   a. ignore him.
   b. ask him what the money is for.
   c. give him the dime without asking any questions.
   d. refuse him the dime because it's just too much trouble.
8. When asked to volunteer for a needy cause for which you will receive pay, you
   a. volunteer but don't accept the pay.
   b. volunteer and accept the pay.
   c. do not volunteer.
   d. volunteer if you are certain of getting paid and if the work is not demanding.

Scoring: Philosophers and social scientists have identified two different types of helping: egoistic and altruistic. Egoistic helping, in which the person wants something in return, is based on egoism, because the ultimate goal of the helper is to increase his or her own welfare. In contrast, altruistic helping, in which the person expects nothing in return, is based on altruism, because the ultimate goal is to increase another's welfare. The following information shows which answers on the Helping-Orientation Questionnaire indicate altruistic helping, egoistic helping, and unhelpful behavior. It also shows the percent of people who gave each answer in a recent survey. Do your responses indicate that your helping orientation is predominantly altruistic, egoistic, or unhelpful?

Item #	Altruistic Helping	Egoistic Helping	Unhelpful Behavior
1.	a (38%)	b (47%)	c, d (15%)
2.	c (79%)	d (9%)	a, b (13%)
3.	a (61%)	b (20%)	c, d (19%)
4.	c (33%)	d (56%)	a, b (11%)
5.	a (44%)	b (49%)	c, d (7%)
6.	a (50%)	b (10%)	c, d (40%)
7.	c (45%)	b (16%)	a, d (40%)
8.	a (20%)	b (62%)	c, d (19%)

Source: From "A person-situation approach to altruistic behavior" by D. Romer, C. I. Gruder, and T. Lizzardo in *Journal of Personality and Social Psychology,* 1986, 51, 1001–1012 (Appendix, pp. 1011–1012). Copyright © 1986 by the American Psychological Association. Adapted with permission.

important decision, because if you decide he is merely sleeping, you will continue on your way, having defined this as a nonemergency. Yet what if you are mistaken?

When you define the situation as an emergency, the bystander intervention model states that the third decision you must make is to determine the extent to which you have responsibility to help. Failure to assume responsibility results in no helping, while feeling a sense of obligation moves you to the fourth step in Latané and Darley's model.

If you assume responsibility for helping, your next decision is to settle on the appropriate form of assistance to render. Yet, in the heat of the moment, what if you aren't sure what to do? You may become paralyzed with uncertainty. Unable to decide, you may not offer any help at all. If, however, you are able to make a choice in step 4, then in the fifth and final step, you must decide to carry out the helpful behavior.

As you can see, Latané and Darley believe that the decision to intervene in a possible emergency involves a rather complex set of decisions. If we, as bystanders, make an incorrect decision at any point in this process, we will not intervene.

Because many emergency situations are not clearly defined as such, when a group of people witness a possible emergency, each person's reactions will be based partly or exclusively on the reaction of the others. Unfortunately, due to our concern with how others might evaluate us, we often pretend to be calm while witnessing a possible emergency. Acting cool

Figure 16-10

The Model of Bystander Intervention: A Five-Step Decision Process

As outlined by Latané and Darley (1970), the decision to help someone involves a five-step process. At any step, a bystander's decision could lead either to further analysis of the situation or to nonintervention.

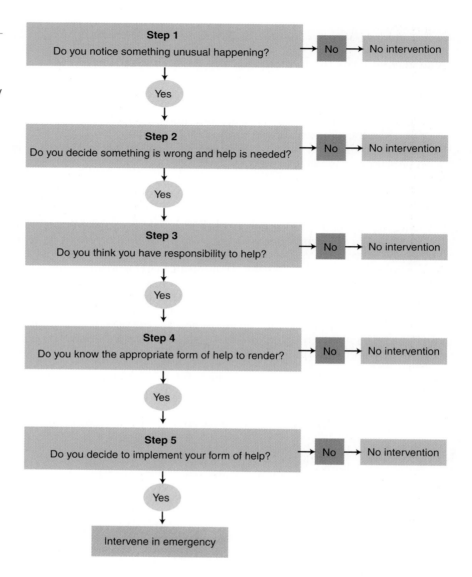

Step 1
Do you notice something unusual happening? → No → No intervention
↓ Yes

Step 2
Do you decide something is wrong and help is needed? → No → No intervention
↓ Yes

Step 3
Do you think you have responsibility to help? → No → No intervention
↓ Yes

Step 4
Do you know the appropriate form of help to render? → No → No intervention
↓ Yes

Step 5
Do you decide to implement your form of help? → No → No intervention
↓ Yes

Intervene in emergency

audience inhibition effect
A situation in which people are inhibited from helping due to a fear of being negatively evaluated by other bystanders if they intervene and it turns out not to be an emergency.

diffusion of responsibility
The belief that the presence of others in a situation makes one less personally responsible for events that occur in that situation.

and calm, we then observe others' behavior for a clue as to how to define what we all are witnessing. Yet, because everyone else is also acting cool and nonchalant, we tend to underestimate the seriousness of the situation and define it as a nonemergency. Thus, in ambiguous emergency situations, the fear of being negatively evaluated, combined with the tendency to look to others for further information, results in the **audience inhibition effect**.

Inhibition in seeking information due to fear of embarrassment is one reason we sometimes don't help in emergencies, but what about those situations in which someone clearly needs help, yet no one intervenes? Darley and Latané believe that the realization that others could also help diffuses bystanders' feelings of individual responsibility (step 3 in the model). They call this response to others' presence the **diffusion of responsibility**—the belief that the presence of other people in a situation makes one less personally responsible for events that occur.

More than 50 laboratory and naturalistic studies have confirmed this effect (Latané & Nida, 1981). On average, in studies where participants believed they were the only bystander to an emergency, 75 percent helped, compared with only 53 percent who helped in the presence of others. Diffusion of responsibility even occurs in Internet chat rooms when people ask for help of some sort (Barron & Yechiam, 2002). In one 30-day study involving over 4,800 chat room participants, diffusion of responsibility increased as the number of people present in a computer-mediated chat group increased. However, this bystander effect was virtually eliminated—and help was received much more quickly—

If bystanders define a situation as an emergency, how might the presence of others inhibit intervention?

Source: Courtesy of Figzoi.

when help was requested by specifying a chat room bystander's name (Markey, 2000). When a specific bystander is singled out of the crowd to help, it is virtually impossible for that individual to diffuse responsibility.

Despite the clear evidence that the presence of others influences our decisions to help, most of us deny that other bystanders have any effect on our actions (or inactions). As discussed, this underestimation of the effect that others have on our own behavior makes it all the more likely that we will fall prey to their influence. After all, how can we guard against being unhelpful when we don't recognize how the simple presence of others not only can inhibit our ability to identify emergencies accurately but also can change our feelings of personal responsibility for helping?

The good news for you, the reader of this textbook, is that knowledge really is power. My student, Ferris, discovered the power of this social psychological knowledge when she implemented the strategies suggested by the bystander intervention model. Indeed, research indicates that people are less likely to fall victim to these bystander effects in emergencies if they have previously learned about them in a psychology course (Beaman et al., 1978). This finding suggests that simply knowing about the social barriers to helping can free one from their antisocial effects. Read Explore It Exercise 16-3 for specific suggestions on what to do if you need help in an emergency.

Section Review

- Instrumental aggression is the intentional use of harmful behavior to achieve some other goal, while hostile aggression is the intentional use of harmful behavior simply to cause injury or death to the victim.
- Men are more likely than women to engage in physical aggression, while women are more likely than men to engage in indirect aggression.
- The culture of honor involves the willingness of men to fight to the death in order to protect their reputation from insults.
- Observational learning has a powerful effect on willingness to help.
- Men are more likely than women to help in dangerous situations, while women are more helpful than men in situations requiring empathy and devotion.
- The bystander intervention model contends that being helpful during an emergency involves a series of five decisions; if bystanders make incorrect decisions at any point in this process, they will not intervene.
- Two factors that make helping less likely when others are present are the audience inhibition effect and diffusion of responsibility.

Explore It
Exercise **16-3**

How Can You Increase Your Chances of Receiving Help in an Emergency?

Social psychological research on bystander effects in helping suggests that people can increase the likelihood of receiving help if they follow a few recommendations. Following these guidelines might save your life someday.

There is a strong likelihood that at some point in your life you will need help in an emergency. Based on what you now know about the bystander intervention model, how can you increase the probability of receiving aid? Here is the gist of the recommendations I told Ferris and my other psychology students, which are based on the insights provided by the experiments conducted by John Darley and Bibb Latané. Learn these guidelines and implement them when you are in need of help.

Guideline 1: A general point to keep in mind is that deciding to intervene in a possible emergency often involves a complex set of decisions. If bystanders make an incorrect decision at any point in this process, they will not intervene. As the victim, you must *attack and neutralize the psychological factors that cause nonintervention.*

Guideline 2: The first psychological hurdle is the audience inhibition effect, in which the fear of being negatively evaluated, combined with the tendency to look to others for further information, leads bystanders to identify emergencies as nonemergencies. You can eliminate this inhibition by *clearly letting everyone know that this is an emergency and you need help.* (Remembering this information while facing her assailant, Ferris began loudly screaming that she was being robbed and needed help. The mugger was so flustered at suddenly becoming the focus of public attention that he fled. However, I told Ferris that if anyone ever again tries to rob her, she should immediately relinquish her belongings. In this instance, she was initially too frightened to comply with the mugger's demand.)

Guideline 3: Even after clearing the audience inhibition hurdle, you must next *attack the diffusion of responsibility,* which is bystanders' tendency to believe they are less personally responsible for helping when others are present. Here, you should implore specific people to help you, because it's hard to deny assistance when singled out. (After the mugger fled, Ferris asked specific people nearby to help her, and they complied. Most other bystanders who were not singled out by Ferris proceeded on their way.)

Guideline 4: Finally, because some people may want to help but are unsure what to do, you can overcome this last hurdle by *specifically giving bystanders instructions.* Using your most authoritative voice will further increase obedience. And obedience is exactly what you are seeking here. (Ferris asked a specific bystander with a cell phone to call the police for assistance, and the police were on the scene within minutes.)

This Explore It Exercise is a bit unconventional, because I am certainly not recommending that you go out and place yourself in dangerous situations to test these guidelines. However, I strongly suggest that you remember these guidelines—they really could help save your life someday.

16-5   INTERPERSONAL ATTRACTION AND LOVE

Preview

- *Why do birds of a feather flock together?*
- *What is the difference between passionate love and companionate love?*
- *How does culture influence the importance placed on love in marriage?*
- *What are common strategies for dealing with romantic problems?*
- *Are positive illusions beneficial in romantic relationships?*

Now that we have examined the psychology of harming and helping others, let's turn our attention to interpersonal attraction and love. We are social creatures by nature, and this is most clearly demonstrated in our desires to seek out others and form lasting close relationships.

16-5a   Proximity and Similarity Often Lead to Attraction

What determines our attraction to others? Social scientists have identified a number of factors that increase the likelihood that close relationships will take root. Two of the most important situational factors that attract us to others are how physically close we are to them (proximity) and the degree to which we share beliefs, attitudes, and other important characteristics (similarity).

Proximity

One of the most powerful factors in determining whether you develop a relationship with another person is his or her proximity to you (Ebbesen et al., 1976; Festinger et al., 1950). For example, spend a minute or two thinking about whom you played with as a child. Chances are, most of your friends were neighbors living nearby. Why does proximity promote liking? As your own childhood experiences suggest, it's easier to develop friendships with those who live close to you simply because they are more accessible. Yet another reason involves the mere exposure effect discussed in section 16-2a: Proximity tends to be associated with repeated exposure, and such familiarity leads to greater liking.

Similarity

Beyond proximity, another ingredient in attraction is similarity. Numerous studies indicate that we choose as friends and lovers those who are similar to us in race, age, social class, education, and attitudes (Kandel, 1978; Whitbeck & Hoyt, 1994). Our belief that similarity attracts is the principal reason why, when trying to match up others as potential friends, we pay close attention to their shared characteristics (Chapdelaine et al., 1994). This tendency to be attracted to similar others is known as the **matching hypothesis** (Berscheid et al., 1971).

The matching hypothesis also operates in the arena of physical attractiveness. Researchers who have observed couples waiting in movie lines, talking in singles bars, and interacting in other social settings have found that they are remarkably well matched in physical attractiveness (Feingold, 1988). One possible reason we are attracted to potential romantic partners who are similar to us in physical attractiveness is that we estimate that we are less likely to be rejected by someone who is roughly our "equal" on the appearance scale. In other words, we learn not to reach too far beyond our own attractiveness value when seeking romance.

Does such matching result in more stable relationships? The answer is "generally, yes." Physically similar couples are more intimate (kissing, holding hands) in public settings and report greater love for one another than mismatched couples do (Murstein, 1972; Silverman, 1971). In addition, studies in North America, Europe, and Asia indicate that matched couples are more likely to get married and stay married than those who are physically mismatched (Peterson & Miller, 1980; White, 1980).

Why Are Similar Others Attractive?

One reason we might seek the company of similar others is because of our desire for social comparison (Festinger, 1954; Goethals, 1986). That is, we are drawn to people with whom we can compare ourselves. The more similar they are to us, the more likely it is that the resulting comparison will provide information we can use in better understanding ourselves

> **matching hypothesis** The proposition that people are attracted to others who are similar to them in certain characteristics, such as attitudes and physical attractiveness.

> To like and dislike the same things, that is indeed true friendship.
>
> —*Gaius Crispus, 86–36 B.C.*

> Live with wolves, howl like a wolf.
>
> —*Russian proverb*

> A balanced relationship: My enemy's enemy is my friend.
>
> —*Old Arab saying*

and our future plans (Goethals & Darley, 1987; Miller, 1984). For example, imagine that you are deciding whether to take a certain college course. You know three people who were previously enrolled in the course: Juan, who always is the top student in every course he takes; Vanessa, who usually receives grades similar to yours; and Sarah, who always seems to be on academic probation. Whom would you seek out for information about the course? Most likely, you would go to Vanessa because of her academic similarity to yours. Her opinions and observations about the course—and her actual final grade—would be more useful in predicting your own performance than information obtained from Juan or Sarah.

Another possible explanation for our attraction to similar others is found in Fritz Heider's (1946, 1958) **balance theory.** Heider proposed that we desire consistency, or "balance," in our thoughts, feelings, and social relationships. Because of this desire for consistency, balanced relationships should be rewarding, while imbalanced relationships—those in which two people hold inconsistent or discrepant thoughts—should be unpleasant (Hummon & Doreian, 2003). Between two people, balance is created when both parties value the same things—that is, when they have similar attitudes.

16-5b Romantic Love Consists of Both Passionate and Companionate Love

Just knowing that proximity and similarity may attract us to one another does not tell us about the psychological nature of romantic love. What can psychologists tell us that poets have not already revealed?

Some psychologists consider that romantic love involves both passionate and companionate love (Hendrick & Hendrick, 2003). **Passionate love** is a state of intense longing for union with another that we typically experience most intensely during the early stages of a romantic relationship (Hatfield, 1988). It is a type of love that we feel with our bodies—a warm-tingling, body-rush, stomach-in-a-knot kind of love. According to Ellen Berscheid and Elaine Hatfield (1974), passionate love is produced, or at least enhanced, during these first romantic encounters due to a rather interesting transference of arousal from one stimulus to another. Drawing on Schachter's (1964) two-factor theory of emotion described in chapter 11, section 11-5f, Berscheid and Hatfield (1974) contend that passionate love is likely to occur when the following three conditions are met:

1. You must learn what love is and come to expect that you will eventually fall in love.
2. You must meet someone who fits your preconceived beliefs of an appropriate lover.
3. While in this person's presence, you must experience a state of physiological arousal.

How does the arousal that develops under these conditions become passionate love? Recall that Schachter's theory of emotion, discussed in chapter 11, section 11-5f, asserts that we use external cues to label our arousal states. According to this two-factor explanation, when arousal occurs in the presence of an appropriate love object, we may well interpret this arousal as romantic and sexual attraction (see figure 16-11).

balance theory A theory that people desire cognitive consistency, or "balance," in their thoughts, feelings, and social relationships.

passionate love A state of intense longing for union with another that we typically experience most intensely during the early stages of a romantic relationship.

Love and eggs are best when they are fresh.

—*Russian proverb*

Figure 16-11

The Two-Factor Theory of Emotion and Passionate Love

According to the two-factor theory of emotion, when we experience physiological arousal in the presence of someone who fits our idea of a suitable romantic partner, we are likely to cognitively interpret this arousal as romantic and sexual attraction. This is the beginning of passionate love.

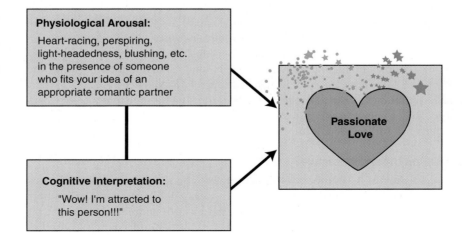

Physiological Arousal:
Heart-racing, perspiring, light-headedness, blushing, etc. in presence of someone who fits your idea of an appropriate romantic partner

Cognitive Interpretation:
"Wow! I'm attracted to this person!!!"

Passionate Love

One reason the emotional roller-coaster ride of early love slows over time to a more smooth and steady experience is that passion generally burns less intensely as a relationship matures (Fletcher, 2002). As we settle into a romantic relationship, the emotional freshness and uncertainty of passionate love are replaced by a more certain and dependable type of love—if love survives at all. Some social scientists explain this lowering of passion as genetically predetermined. According to this perspective, passion is adaptive early in a relationship because it frequently results in children, yet, once children are born, the infants' survival is aided by the parents becoming less obsessed with one another (Kenrick & Trost, 1987).

This less impassioned, more enduring **companionate love** is the affection we feel for those with whom our lives are deeply entwined (Hatfield, 1988). Companionate love exists between close friends as well as between lovers. It develops out of a sense of certainty in one another's love and respect, as well as a feeling of genuine mutual understanding (Hatfield & Rapson, 1996; Singelis et al., 1996; Sprecher, 1999).

Another difference between passionate love and companionate love is in the beliefs we have about our partner. In the early stages of romantic relationships, when passions run high, we tend to see our partners through rose-colored glasses (Brehm, 1988). They are "perfect," the "ideal man" or "ideal woman," our "dream come true." As passion fades and we develop companionate love, this idealization of our beloved gives way to a more realistic view (see section 16-5d).

Companionate love forms the basis for long-term romantic relationships and friendships. It is the affection we feel for those with whom our lives are deeply entwined.

Source: Courtesy of Figzoi.

companionate love The affection we feel for those with whom our lives are deeply entwined.

16-5c The Relationship between Love and Marriage Differs across Cultures

Conceptions of love differ cross-culturally. For example, a study by Robert Levine and his colleagues (1995) examined the importance of love as a basis for marriage in both individualist and collectivist cultures. Results indicate strong cross-cultural differences in the perceived importance of love. Individualist countries, such as the United States, England, and Australia, placed great importance on love in marriage, while collectivist countries, such as India, Pakistan, Thailand, and the Philippines, rated it as much less important. These beliefs appear to have behavioral consequences as well. Those countries placing great importance on love had higher marriage rates, lower fertility rates, and higher divorce rates. Other studies indicate that collectivists tend to select mates who will best "fit into" the extended family, while individualists are more likely to select a mate who is physically attractive or has an "exciting" personality. This doesn't mean, however, that love is not a part of a collectivist marriage. Instead, in collectivist cultures, it is more common for people first to get married and then to fall in love.

People in collectivist cultures place less emphasis than do those in individualist cultures on romantic love as a primary basis for marriage. Instead, they emphasize whether the potential spouse will fit into their extended family. How might this emphasis on family cohesion over personal love lead to more enduring marriages than those found in individualist cultures?

Source: Courtesy of Jenny Franzoi.

One question raised by the researchers was whether there is an inherent conflict between individualist values and the interdependence necessary to maintain romantic love. That is, if you were raised to be autonomous and independent, wouldn't you tend to have difficulty maintaining an intimate relationship defined by partners depending on each other? The curious irony is that, although individualists are more likely to marry due to romantic love, the way they've been socialized may make it less likely that their marriages will survive and that their love will be nurtured.

16-5d Positive Illusions and "Mind Reading" Increase Romantic Satisfaction

There is scientific evidence indicating that if you want happiness in love, you should allow your desire to feel good about your romantic relationship to dominate your desire to critically analyze the imperfections in that relationship (Gagné & Lydon, 2001). In other words, an important component of a satisfying, stable romantic relationship is the ability to mix positive illusion with sober reality when perceiving one's partner. A number of studies indicate that just as there is a *self-serving bias* that leads people with high self-esteem to see themselves in the best possible light (see chapter 12, section 12-3d), people in happy romantic relationships tend to attribute their partner's positive behaviors to dispositional causes (their "wonderful personality") and their negative behaviors to situational factors (a "bad day"). This *partner-enhancing bias* not only makes lovers feel better and increases relationship trust, but also can create a self-fulfilling prophecy (Miller & Rempel, 2004; Murray & Holmes, 1999). In longitudinal studies, married and dating couples who idealized one another more during the initial stages of their romance reported greater increases in satisfaction and decreases in conflicts and doubts over the course of a year than couples who saw each other in a more realistic light (Murray & Holmes, 1997; Murray et al., 1996). Further, during the year, the targets of these positive illusions actually incorporated these idealized images into their own self-concepts. These studies suggest that by taking a "leap of faith" and seeing imperfect relationships in somewhat idealized ways, people not only satisfy their need to feel that their relationships are better than most other relationships, but also create the conditions necessary for their positive illusions to be realized.

Although positive illusions might reinforce the belief that you have found your "perfect match," couldn't there also be benefits to accurately reading your partner's thoughts and feelings? In other words, can accuracy in reading your partner coexist with positive illusions about your partner? New Zealand social psychologists Geoff Thomas and Garth Fletcher (1997) have investigated the ability of relationship partners to read each other's thoughts and feelings, an interpersonal skill they call *mind reading* (also known as *empathic accuracy*). In one of Thomas and Fletcher's typical studies, either married or dating couples are videotaped while they discuss two serious problems in their relationship. Couples are instructed to try to resolve the problems during this 10-minute discussion. After completing this task, couples are separated and partners independently review a videotape of the discussion, stopping the tape at points of time whenever they recall experiencing a thought or emotion and then writing it down. Next, the researchers give each partner the time points the other partner had noted and ask each person to review the tape a second time, but now giving their best guess as to what their partner was thinking and feeling at the indicated time points. Raters later assess the similarity between the pairs of statements from the two partners to determine each one's accuracy in reading the other's thoughts and feelings. For comparison purposes, friends of the couple and strangers also review these tapes and guess what each person was thinking and feeling at the selected time points. The central findings from these studies are that couples are more accurate in assessing what their partners were thinking and feeling than were friends of the dating partners. More importantly, superior mind reading is related to higher relationship satisfaction (Thomas & Fletcher, 2003). Additional research suggests that superior mind readers have higher verbal skills and engage in more complex and effortful thinking when

Things become better when you expect the best instead of the worst.

—Norman Vincent Peale, minister and author, 1899–1993

making attributions of others' behavior than inferior mind readers (Fletcher, 2002). In other words, people who regularly critically analyze social interaction and are also adept at verbal interaction are more accurate in reading their partners' thoughts and feelings, which appears to benefit the relationship. Not surprisingly, women are superior mind readers compared to men (Thomas & Fletcher, 2003).

Is superior mind reading always a good thing for romantic relationships? Maybe not. Individuals in highly committed romantic relationships are sometimes motivated to inaccurately read their partners' minds, such as when they avoid acknowledging that their lover is subtly "checking out" an attractive person while in their presence (Simpson et al., 2003). In such instances, engaging in positive illusions may protect relationship harmony and satisfaction. Overall, it appears that accurate mind reading in romance increases intimacy and satisfaction with the relationship when the partners' thoughts and feelings are not threatening to the relationship (Ickes, 2003). However, when these thoughts and feelings pose a potential danger, positive illusions protect relationship happiness.

16-5e People Use Four Strategies to Handle Relationship Conflict

Rocky periods occur in all romantic relationships. Whether couples remain committed to one another during such times of strife largely depends on how they interact while coping with their problems. Their level of commitment to the relationship greatly influences the strategies they employ, with the more satisfied and invested couples working hardest to solve their problems (Arriaga & Agnew, 2001). The psychologist Caryl Rusbult and her coworkers have identified four strategies people typically use in dealing with a troubled relationship (Rusbult & Martz, 1995; Rusbult et al., 1987). These four strategies differ along the dimensions of *active-passive* and *constructive-destructive*. Figure 16-12 illustrates the primary qualities of these four strategies.

Rusbult states that, in handling conflict, some people adopt a passively constructive approach by exhibiting *loyalty*, which involves simply waiting in the hope that things will improve on their own. Persons who adopt this strategy are often afraid to escalate the conflict by directly acknowledging it, so they say nothing and pray that their loyalty will keep the relationship alive. Others, especially men, adopt the passively destructive strategy of *neglect*. They emotionally ignore their partners and spend less time with them. When partners are together, neglectful persons often treat their partners poorly by constantly criticizing them for things unrelated to the real problem. Those who do not know how to handle their negative emotions, or who are not motivated to improve the relationship but

Figure 16-12

Four Strategies in Dealing with Relationship Problems

In dealing with relationship conflict, people typically use different strategies, which vary along the dimensions of active-passive and constructive-destructive. In dealing with dissatisfactions in your own past and present romantic relationships, which of these four strategies have you used?

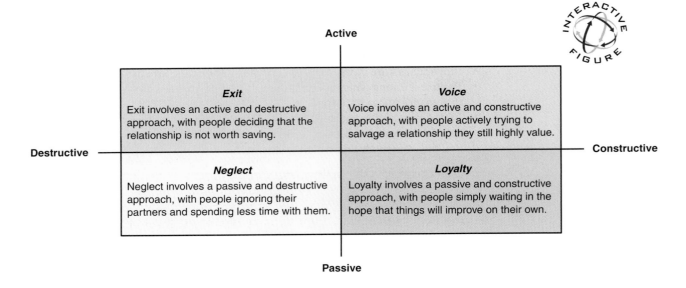

Love doesn't just sit there, like a stone, it has to be made, like bread; re-made all the time, made new.

—*Ursula K. LeGuin, U.S. science fiction writer, b. 1929*

also not ready to end it, often resort to this strategy. When people do conclude that the relationship is not worth saving, they *exit*, which is an active, yet destructive, strategy. A much more constructive and active approach in dealing with conflict is *voice*, in which people discuss their problems, seek compromises, and try to salvage a relationship they still highly value.

One factor that determines which strategies people employ in dealing with their dissatisfaction is their level of psychological masculinity and femininity (Rusbult et al., 1986). In survey studies involving lesbian, gay male, and heterosexual women and men, individuals with many feminine personality traits were much more likely than others to react constructively to relationship problems. They either actively searched for an acceptable resolution or, if a solution did not seem possible, remained quietly loyal. In contrast, those who had many masculine traits and few feminine traits responded destructively, either passively neglecting the problems and allowing the situation to deteriorate further or actively threatening to exit. These patterns were true for both men and women, regardless of sexual orientation. The types of masculine personality characteristics that have this sort of negative impact on solving relationship problems are those related to arrogance and aggressiveness, rather than those involving the more desirable masculine traits related to independence and assertiveness (Bradbury et al., 1995). The reason that feminine personality traits tend to facilitate the resolution of relationship problems is that such traits are characterized by a communal orientation of warmth, intimacy, and concern for interpersonal relations. On the other hand, the negative masculine traits are characterized by a more individualistic orientation of power and dominance. People who have many feminine personality traits appear more interested in resolving conflict through emotional sharing and compromise, whereas those with mostly masculine characteristics, especially the negative ones, prefer to reach decisions on their own and impose their will on others.

In summary, despite the turmoil that love often brings to our lives, most of us yearn for romance even after experiencing romantic failure. While some call this persistence a form of addiction, others describe the desire for romantic intimacy as an expression of one of our most basic needs, the desire to share ourselves as completely as possible with those who have become integral parts of our self-concepts.

Section Review

- Two factors determining interpersonal attraction are proximity and similarity.
- Possible reasons why similarity leads to liking are social comparison, shared genes, and a balanced relationship.
- Passionate love is often experienced during the early stages of romance and is associated with an idealized perception of one's romantic partner, while companionate love is a more enduring kind of love than passionate love; it exists between lovers, as well as between close friends, and is associated with a more realistic view of one's romantic partner.
- Individualists are more likely to marry due to romantic love than are collectivists.
- Positive illusions generally enhance relationship happiness, but accurate mind reading in romance is also important.
- In dealing with relationship dissatisfaction, we typically employ four distinct strategies: loyalty, neglect, exit, and voice, which reflect the active-passive dimension and the constructive-destructive dimension.

Psychological Applications

How Can You Cope with Jealousy?

"O! Beware my lord, of jealousy; It is the green-eyed monster which doth mock."

—*From* Othello, *by William Shakespeare, English dramatist and poet,*
1564–1616

What Is Jealousy?

One emotion that threatens love is jealousy. **Jealousy** is the negative emotional reaction you feel when a real or imagined rival threatens a relationship important to your self-concept (C. R. Harris, 2004). Although some people believe jealousy is a healthy sign in romantic relationships, research indicates that it is actually related to strong feelings of dependence and relationship insecurity (Marelich et al., 2003). It also triggers many negative feelings and behaviors and tends to lower self-esteem (Mathes et al., 1985; Puente & Cohen, 2003).

> **jealousy** The negative emotional reaction experienced when a real or imagined rival threatens a relationship important to one's self-concept.

Ways to Reduce Jealousy

Because jealousy is so destructive to intimate relationships, social scientists and mental health therapists have sought to develop strategies for coping constructively with the "green-eyed monster." What we know is that the people most susceptible to jealousy are those who are highly dependent on the relationship and have few alternative avenues for expressing intimacy (White & Mullen, 1989).

What type of coping strategies—both constructive and destructive varieties—do we employ in contending with jealousy? All jealousy coping strategies boil down to two major goals: (1) trying to maintain the relationship; and (2) trying to maintain self-esteem.

As you can see from table 1, these two goals can be either present or absent in the coping strategy adopted. If you are jealous and desire to maintain both the relationship and your self-esteem, you will probably try to reach a mutually satisfying solution with your partner. However, if you desire to maintain your romantic relationship regardless of any harm to your self-esteem, you may swallow your pride and put up with the part of your partner's behavior that elicits the jealousy. In contrast to these relationship-maintaining strategies, you may use verbal and physical attacks against your partner or your rival when you are more concerned with maintaining self-esteem than with maintaining the relationship. Finally, when you are not principally attempting to either maintain the relationship or bolster your self-esteem, you may engage in self-destructive behavior.

In commenting on these different coping strategies, Sharon Brehm (1992) brings up a good point: When jealous, before acting you should think about both the short-term and the long-term consequences of your coping responses. For example, verbally or physically attacking partners may temporarily intimidate them into not leaving, but this strategy will most likely hasten their exit from the relationship. Similarly, begging and pleading with a partner to end another romance may succeed in the short run, but such emotional clinging not only will threaten self-esteem but probably will also reduce the partner's attraction to the relationship.

The best antidotes to the "green-eyed monster" are to contain emotional outbursts, maintain daily routines, and reevaluate the importance of the relationship (Salovey & Rodin, 1988). Further, to reduce your depression and anger, you should engage in self-bolstering, which involves thinking positively about yourself and doing nice things for yourself. Making new friends and pursuing positive goals in other areas of your life are part of the self-bolstering process, and such activities will increase self-esteem, which in turn will reduce jealousy (Hatfield & Rapson, 1993).

> Let's say I committed this crime [the murder of ex-wife Nicole Brown Simpson]. Even if I did do this, it would have to have been because I loved her very much, right?
>
> —*O. J. Simpson, athlete and infamous celebrity, b. 1947*

Table 1	Different Ways of Coping with Jealousy		
		Relationship-Maintaining Behaviors	
		Yes	No
Self-Esteem– Maintaining Behaviors	Yes	Negotiating a mutually acceptable solution	Verbal/physical attacks against the partner or rival
	No	Clinging to the relationship	Self-destructive behaviors

Source: Adapted from J. B. Bryson, "Situational Determinants of the Expression of Jealousy" in H. Sigall (chair), Sexual Jealousy symposium presented at the annual meeting of the American Psychological Association, San Francisco, 1977.

Key Terms

aggression (p. 623)

attitude (p. 613)

attribution (p. 610)

audience inhibition effect (p. 632)

balance theory (p. 636)

cognitive dissonance (p. 615)

cognitive-neoassociationist model (p. 626)

companionate love (p. 637)

compliance (p. 619)

conformity (p. 617)

covariation model (p. 610)

culture of honor (p. 626)

diffusion of responsibility (p. 632)

discrimination (p. 605)

elaboration likelihood model (p. 614)

ethnocentrism (p. 606)

external attribution (p. 610)

fundamental attribution error (p. 611)

hostile aggression (p. 623)

impression formation (p. 601)

instrumental aggression (p. 623)

intergroup anxiety (p. 609)

internal attribution (p. 610)

jealousy (p. 641)

matching hypothesis (p. 635)

mere exposure effect (p. 613)

obedience (p. 620)

passionate love (p. 636)

persuasion (p. 614)

physical attractiveness stereotype (p. 602)

prejudice (p. 605)

realistic group conflict theory (p. 605)

reciprocity norm (p. 619)

social influence (p. 617)

social perception (p. 601)

social psychology (p. 600)

stereotype (p. 601)

Suggested Websites

Stanford Prison Experiment

http://www.prisonexp.org

This site provides a step-by-step description of a simulation study of the psychology of imprisonment conducted in 1971 at Stanford University.

What Makes Kids Care?

http://www.apa.org/pubinfo/altruism.html

This American Psychological Association website offers suggestions on how to raise children to be more altruistic and supports these suggestions with relevant theories.

Controlling Anger—Before It Controls You

http://www.apa.org/pubinfo/anger.html

This American Psychological Association website provides recommendations for controlling anger before it leads to aggression.

Prejudice and Discrimination

http://www.colorado.edu/conflict/peace/problem/prejdisc.htm

The International Online Training Program on Intractable Conflict at the University of Colorado offers a website on prejudice and discrimination around the world, including possible solutions to these social problems.

Social Psychology Network

http://www.socialpsychology.org

This is the largest social psychology database on the Internet, with more than 5,000 links to psychology-related websites, especially those covering social-psychological topics.

Review Questions

Note: You can find the correct answers to these questions by taking the quiz and then submitting your answers in the Online Edition. The program will automatically score your submission. If you miss a question, the program will provide the correct answer, a rationale for the answer, and the section number in the chapter where the topic is discussed.

1. Stereotyping influences information-processing through all of the following *except*
   a. activation of ethnic stereotypes, which limit critical thinking.
   b. increasing the amount of attention and rehearsal to stereotype-consistent information.
   c. increasing attention to new information rather than old information.
   d. decreasing attention to stereotype-inconsistent information.
   e. decreasing reliance on false information.

2. Which of the following is *not* evaluated in Kelley's covariation model when assessing an event or stimulus?
   a. consensus
   b. consistency
   c. social desirability
   d. distinctiveness
   e. all of the above

3. According to researchers, the fundamental attribution error
   a. is learned at an early age, even before age 5.
   b. is more widespread in collectivist cultures.
   c. is the tendency for people from individualistic cultures to attribute others' behavior to internal causes.
   d. causes Americans to make more external than internal attributions for negative events.
   e. is associated with interactions between internal and external factors.

4. One of your friends has strong political beliefs, and your persuasive arguments do little to change her mind. Your friend's political attitudes have likely been formed through
   a. attending to the credibility of political speakers.
   b. the central route to persuasion.
   c. low elaboration of political arguments.
   d. the peripheral route to persuasion.
   e. the elaboration likelihood model.

5. According to Festinger's theory of cognitive dissonance,
   a. people from collectivist cultures are more prone to feelings of cognitive dissonance than people from individualist cultures.
   b. cognitive dissonance is shaped by conditioning.
   c. people in individualistic cultures are generally motivated to be consistent in their attitudes and behaviors.
   d. someone who exhibits a great deal of flexibility in his or her behavior is bothered by cognitive dissonance.
   e. saying one thing while believing something else is not aversive to individualists.

6. When you arrive at a party, you see that everyone is drinking dark ale, which you dislike. When your host brings you a bottle of ale, you accept graciously, exhibiting
   a. conformity.
   b. obedience.
   c. compliance.
   d. personal consistency.
   e. cognitive dissonance.

7. An individual's willingness to conform may be influenced by all of the following *except*
   a. group size.
   b. the presence of a dissenter.
   c. cultural norms.
   d. desire for personal control.
   e. being given a small gift.

8. If you interpret going along with the group in question 6 as flexibility or maturity, you
   a. have a high need for personal control.
   b. will experience cognitive dissonance.
   c. are complying with the reciprocity norm.
   d. may be from a collectivist culture.
   e. are respecting the authority of your host.

9. The results of Milgram's research were shocking primarily because
   a. only 10 percent of the participants obeyed the experimenter.
   b. proximity to the learner had no effect on participants' conformity.
   c. participants were found to be closet sadists, feeling no negative effects from their actions.
   d. they showed the power of the situation in determining behavior.
   e. they emphasized the power of dispositional factors.

10. Indirect aggression is often associated with
    a. a culture of honor.
    b. being motivated by the anticipation of rewards.
    c. a tendency to be impulsive when angry.
    d. a desire to hurt others.
    e. gossiping about others.

11. Which of the following is associated with a culture of honor?
    a. It is more likely in societies based on farming than in herding societies.
    b. It is related to responding with aggression to perceived insults and threats.
    c. In the United States, it is more common in the North than in the South.
    d. It involves sitting down and honorably addressing issues of personal integrity.
    e. It is rarely observed among African-American men in the inner city.

12. According to the cognitive-neoassociationist model of aggression,
    a. acting aggressively makes us feel better, reinforcing aggression.
    b. pleasant emotions are encoded into memory and help limit aggression.
    c. aggression is most likely when we are thinking about our actions.
    d. remembering a time when we were angry can elicit negative affect and aggression.
    e. activation of the "fight-or-flight" response produces negative affect and aggression.

13. The model of bystander intervention describes a five-step decision-making process involving all of the following *except*
    a. deciding if help is needed.
    b. assuming a sense of personal responsibility.
    c. fear of being hurt.
    d. observing how others respond.
    e. the audience inhibition effect.

14. Which of the following is *false* regarding love and marriage?
    a. Couples around the world universally view love as important for marriage.
    b. Countries placing greater importance on love before marriage have higher divorce rates.
    c. In collectivist cultures, mates are selected who best fit into the extended family.
    d. Lower fertility rates are associated with greater importance attached to love before marriage.
    e. There may be a conflict between individualist values and lifelong dependence on a romantic partner.

15. Which of the following is *not* one of the strategies for handling relationship conflict that Caryl Rusbult identified?
    a. neglect
    b. voice
    c. kindness
    d. loyalty
    e. exit

Appendix A
Statistical Reasoning

As described in chapter 2, section 2-2d, there are two basic kinds of statistics employed by psychologists: descriptive and inferential. *Descriptive statistics* simply summarize and describe the behavior or characteristics of a particular sample of participants in a study, while *inferential statistics* move beyond mere description to make inferences about the larger population from which the sample was drawn. Let us examine in greater detail the purpose, logic, and value of these two different kinds of statistics.

A-1 Descriptive Statistics Are Used to Describe and Summarize Data

Descriptive statistics provide an overview of numerical data. Two important descriptive statistics are *measures of central tendency* and *measures of variability.*

A-1a Measures of Central Tendency

When researchers summarize data, they often describe the typical or average score in their sample, which is referred to as the *central tendency.* There are three measures of central tendency: *mean, median,* and *mode.* The **mean** is the arithmetic average of a distribution. It is the most common measure of central tendency and the one that most people think of when they hear the word *average.* The mean is calculated by adding all the scores in the distribution and then dividing by the number of scores. The second measure of central tendency is the **median,** which is the middle score in a distribution, with half the scores above it and half below it. Finally, the **mode** is the third measure of central tendency, and it is the score that occurs most frequently in a distribution.

> **mean** The arithmetic average of a distribution, obtained by adding all the scores and then dividing by the number of scores.

> **median** The middle score in a distribution; half the scores are above it and half are below it.

> **mode** The score that occurs most frequently in a distribution.

When the scores in your data set are organized in a *normal distribution,* your mean, median, and mode are identical in value. For example, imagine that you ask 38 middle-aged adults in your hometown how many hours they slept the previous night, and their responses yield the normal distribution depicted in figure A-1. As you can see, this distribution peaks at the center and tapers off outwardly while remaining symmetrical with respect to the center. For this reason, a normal distribution is often referred to as a *bell-shaped curve* or a *normal curve.*

When the mean, median, and mode have different values, your data set is described as having a **skewed distribution.** As an example, imagine that you next ask 38 young adults on your col-

> **skewed distribution** A distribution in which the mean, median, and mode have different values; in appearance, the distribution has a long tail before or after the peak.

lege campus how many hours they slept the previous night, and their responses yield the distribution depicted in figure A-2. This distribution is *positively skewed,* meaning that your data contain a small number of very large values, so that when the distribution of scores is drawn, there is a long tail after the peak. The mode is to the left (lowest value), the median is in the middle (middle value), and the mean is to the right (highest value), pulled upward in value by the few very high scores. Reversing this trend gives you a distribution that is *negatively skewed* (figure A-3). Here, imagine that you have asked 38 elderly adults living in a retirement center how many hours they slept the previous night. With a small number of very small values, the tail of your distribution of scores appears before the peak, and the mean is to the left (smallest value), followed by the median (middle value) and the mode (highest value).

A-1b Measures of Variability

Besides knowing the value of the measures of central tendency in your data, it is important to know something about the variation in your data. *Measures of variation* are statistics that tell you how closely distributed your scores are to some measure of central tendency.

The simplest measure of variation is the **range** of scores, meaning the difference between

> **range** The difference between the lowest and highest values in a distribution.

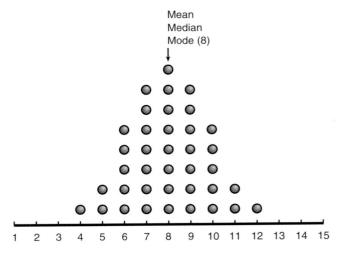

Mean
Median
Mode (8)

Reported Hours of Sleep among Middle-Aged Adults

Figure A-1

Normal Distribution

This graphic representation of the distribution of middle-aged adults' previous night's sleep time illustrates the three measures of central tendency: mean, median, and mode. In a normal distribution, the mean, median, and mode have the same values.

the lowest and highest values in a distribution. To compute the range, you simply subtract the lower value from the higher value. In the middle-aged sample (figure A-1), the range is 8: 12 − 4. In the student sample (figure A-2), the range is 9: 15 − 4. In the elderly sample (figure A-3), the range is 11: 12 − 1.

The range is easy to compute, but it doesn't take into account any of the other scores in the distribution. A more sensitive measure of variation is the **standard deviation,** which takes into account all the scores, as well as indicating the average difference between the scores and their mean. In other words, it is a measure of how much the average score *deviates* from the mean. The value of the standard deviation tells you whether scores are packed close together or spread far apart, with a low score indicating packing and a high score indicating spreading. When the standard deviation value is low, the mean provides a good representation of the entire data set. When the standard deviation is high, the mean is not a good representation of all the data.

> **standard deviation**
> A measure of variation that indicates the average difference between the scores in a distribution and their mean.

Consider again our three different data sets on people's previous night's sleep time. In the middle-aged sample the standard deviation is 1.79, while in the student and elderly adult samples the standard deviation is 3.21. The lower standard deviation value in the middle-aged sample tells you that those scores are closer to the mean, on average, than are the scores in the two other samples. In essence, these standard deviation values numerically represent what your eyes tell you when you look at the distribution of scores in the three figures: The middle-aged adults were more similar to one another in their previous night's sleep time than were the college students and the elderly adults.

A-2 Inferential Statistics Are Used to Interpret Data and Draw Conclusions

After describing and summarizing the data using descriptive statistics, psychologists often use inferential statistics to estimate the likelihood that a difference found in the research sample would also be found if everyone in the population participated in the study. Is the difference found in the sample due to fluctuations of chance, or does it reflect actual differences in the larger population?

For example, imagine that you have a theory that sleep deprivation causes memory problems. Consistent with this theory, you hypothesize that people who are sleep deprived will perform more poorly on a memory task than those who are not sleep deprived. To test this hypothesis, you conduct an experiment in which 50 participants perform a memory task after going without sleep for 24 hours. Your control group in this experiment consists of another 50 participants who perform the same memory task after a normal night's sleep. After scoring the memory task, you discover that the mean score for the sleep-deprived individuals is 15 points lower than the mean score for the control group. You also compute the standard deviation values for the two data sets, and you discover that both are relatively low and roughly equal to one another, indicating that these mean scores provide a good representation of the entire data in the two samples (see section A-1b). However, is this difference in the two sample means simply due to chance variation? Is this difference between the two groups large enough to support your hypothesis? These are the types of questions answered by inferential statistics.

Within each sample, when the deviation from the sample mean indicates low variability, and when the difference between the two sample means is relatively large, it is likely that additional statistical calculations will indicate that these differences are *statistically signifi-*

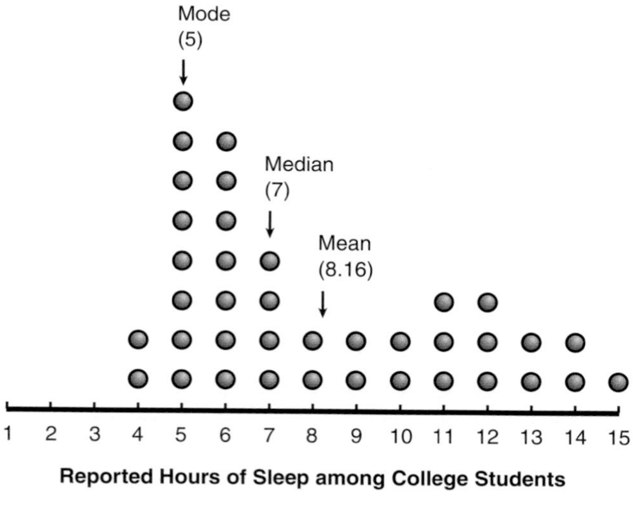

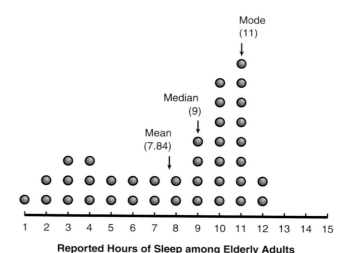

Reported Hours of Sleep among College Students	**Reported Hours of Sleep among Elderly Adults**

Figure A-2

Positively Skewed Distribution

This graphic representation of the distribution of college students' previous night's sleep time illustrates that in a positively skewed distribution the mean, median, and mode have different values. The mode has the lowest value, and the mean has the highest value.

Figure A-3

Negatively Skewed Distribution

This graphic representation of the distribution of elderly adults' previous night's sleep time illustrates that in a negatively skewed distribution the mean, median, and mode have different values. The mean has the lowest value, and the mode has the highest value.

cant. In science, this means that the difference is probably not due to chance variation between the samples. As mentioned in chapter 2, section 2-2d, psychologists generally accept a difference as statistically significant if the likelihood of its having occurred by chance is less than 1 in 20—that is, a probability of less than 5 percent (indicated by the notation $p < .05$).

There are many different types of mathematical formulas for estimating the statistical significance of data sets. Which test is used depends on many factors, including the type of data that has been collected, the number of participants, the number of groups, and the number of variables in the study. In the imaginary sleep-deprivation study, because there is only one independent variable consisting of the experimental group (sleep-deprived participants) and the control group (non-sleep-deprived participants) and one dependent variable (performance on the memory task), you would probably use a very common statistical test, the *t-test*. This test is used when you simply want to know if the difference between the means of two groups is statistically significant. If the t-test indicates that the likelihood that the difference between the group means is due to a 1 in 25 chance (a 4 percent probability level), you would conclude that sleep-deprived participants performed significantly worse on the memory task than non-sleep-deprived participants. More importantly, if your research participants reasonably represent the general population, you would generalize your findings beyond the sample. You now have support for your theory that sleep deprivation causes memory problems in the general population. On the other hand, if the t-test indicates that the likelihood that the difference between the group means is due to a 1 in 5 chance (a 20 percent probability level), you would conclude that sleep-deprived and non-sleep-deprived participants did not significantly differ from one another on the memory task. Your theory, from which your hypothesis was derived, was not supported. These non-significant findings would likely cause you to closely reexamine your study for possible flaws, as well as prompt you to reconsider the ideas underlying your theory. Does the theory need revising? As discussed in chapter 2, section 2-2b, there is a cyclical relationship between a theory and a testable hypothesis. When a research hypothesis is not supported, researchers often reconsider their original theories, revising them and then developing new hypotheses that are tested in another round of empirical studies.

In conclusion, both descriptive and inferential statistics are important tools in the quest to answer scientific questions. However, in science, any conclusion is only a statement of the *probable* relationship between the events being investigated. There are no final truths in science. Every theory is always subject to revision when new data come to light that challenge the hypotheses derived from the original theory.

Key Terms

mean (p. 645)

median (p. 645)

mode (p. 645)

range (p. 645)

skewed distribution (p. 645)

standard deviation (p. 646)

Appendix B

Journey of Discovery Questions and Possible Answers

Chapter 1

Journey of Discovery Question: At the beginning of the twentieth century, Hermann Ebbinghaus (1850–1909), one of psychology's pioneers, stated, "Psychology has a long past, but only a short history." What do you think he meant by this statement?

Possible Answer: Ebbinghaus meant that, well before the science of psychology existed, philosophers wrote extensively about the human condition. Indeed, the study of the mind was once the exclusive domain of philosophers, and many of the issues discussed and analyzed in psychology were originally raised in philosophical circles.

Journey of Discovery Question: Consider the five early perspectives in psychology. What contribution did each make to our understanding of thinking and behavior?

Possible Answer: Perhaps you could say that structuralism contributed to our understanding of thinking and behavior in that this psychological perspective, led by William Wundt, was instrumental in launching the scientific discipline. Wundt is generally credited with establishing the first institute for research in experimental psychology, and he trained many people who went on to make a lasting mark in the field. William James and the functionalists attempted to steer the young science away from the reductionism of Wundt and to instead emphasize how the mind affects what people do and how the mind functions. Of course, Freud and psychoanalysis alerted us to the importance of examining and attending to the unconscious mind. Like Freud, John Watson and behaviorism put psychology "on the map" in people's minds, but for different reasons. Whereas Freud outraged and titillated many people with his emphasis on sex as a primary motive, the behaviorists demonstrated how the findings of psychology could be put to practical use in the real world, such as in conditioning new behavior. Finally, perhaps the Gestaltists' most significant contribution was their proposal that our perceptions are not to be understood as the mind passively responding to a simple combination of individual elements but, rather, as the mind actively organizing stimuli into coherent wholes.

Journey of Discovery Question: Briefly describe the seven contemporary perspectives in psychology. Which of these perspectives appeals to you most, and which least? Why?

Possible Answer: Psychoanalysis is an approach to psychology that studies how the unconscious mind shapes behavior, while behaviorism stresses that psychology should study only observable behavior, rather than hidden mental processes. In contrast to both of these perspectives, the humanistic perspective emphasizes people's innate capacity for personal growth and their ability to consciously make choices. In the 1970s, the cognitive perspective gained prominence, espousing an approach to psychology that attempts to understand behavior by studying how the mind organizes perceptions, processes information, and interprets experiences. At roughly the same time, the neuroscience perspective proposed that psychology should attempt to understand behavior by examining physiological processes, especially those occurring in the brain. Fueled by the growing belief in the social sciences that behavior is at least partly influenced by the effects of evolution, the evolutionary perspective has increasingly been incorporated into psychological theories. Finally, the sociocultural perspective emphasizes social and cultural influences on behavior. Which of these perspectives is most appealing to you? I would suggest that all are important in understanding the full range of psychological processes.

Chapter 2

Journey of Discovery Question: The importance of Kimble's research on implicit personality theories and practicing safe sex is that it not only alerts us to how people often engage in faulty decision making, but also suggests how we might use this knowledge to develop intervention programs aimed at changing young adults' thinking regarding safe sex. If you were developing such a program, how would you explain to participants the role that implicit personality theory plays in their daily social judgments?

Possible Answer: One bit of information you could provide is that the personality judgments we make often defy the rules of cold logic. That is, when we make personality assumptions, we often assume that, if a person is nice and fun to be around, he or she must also have other desirable characteristics, such as being healthy and disease-free. We arrive at this conclusion because the alternative judgment is inconsistent with our assumptions about the relationships between traits and behaviors. To counteract this tendency, you might devise a TV or print advertisement depicting pleasant, clean-cut people who are HIV-positive, with the message that these physical and social qualities should not be the basis for deciding who is and who is not "safe" as a sexual partner.

Journey of Discovery Question: Having digested the research on hindsight bias, why do you think we are less likely to claim hindsight for negative outcomes that personally affect us?

Possible Answer: One possible reason is that it allows us to avoid blaming ourselves: "If I couldn't foresee being laid off, I cannot be blamed for not working harder or changing jobs." In other words, we are unlikely to claim we foresaw a negative event if that claim is likely to lower our esteem in the eyes of others or in our own eyes.

Journey of Discovery Question: Imagine that you are a member of an institutional review board, and a research proposal similar to the Milgram obedience study has been submitted for approval. How would you determine its risk/benefit ratio?

Possible Answer: Using the risk/benefit ratio, you would weigh the potential risks to the participants against the study's potential benefits to society, giving greater weight to the participants' welfare. While assessing a Milgram-type study proposal, you might ask whether there is any other way the researchers could conduct the study to minimize participant stress. In essence, because of the deception being used, full informed consent could not be obtained. As such, you might ask the researchers whether they are going to let the participants know up-front that they cannot reveal all the details of the purpose and procedures to be used in the study. You might also ask the researchers how they would respond to a participant who asked them to stop the study. Would they stop the study after the first request? Because deception and destructive obedience are the topics being studied, you would probably also ask the researchers to specifically detail their debriefing procedures, because these would need to be as sensitive and detailed as possible. You might also require follow-up interviews with participants to determine whether they experienced any delayed stress responses, and you might require that free counseling opportunities with a mental health professional be made available to participants wanting to discuss their research experience.

Would you approve a Milgram-type study? You might decide to do so only if it was seeking to shed light on an aspect of obedience that had not already been investigated. Given the fact that a number of Milgram obedience replications have already been conducted, you might find it difficult to justify approving another replication of the original study, given the possible harm to participants. However, in considering your answer to this question, keep in mind the following thought: The decision not to grant a request to conduct research on a particular topic also has ethical implications. If you do not allow certain research to be conducted because the behavior in question is socially undesirable or destructive when it naturally occurs in the "real world," the social sciences are likely to have crucial gaps in their knowledge base, and these gaps may prevent scientists from developing useful intervention strategies to lessen people's future suffering. What will be potentially lost by not allowing this study to go forward? These are just a few of the tough questions you would grapple with as a member of an institutional review board.

Journey of Discovery Question: For every dog or cat used in a laboratory experiment, 10,000 dogs and cats are abandoned by their owners (Miller, 1985). When these abandoned animals are brought to local humane societies and not adopted, should they be made available as subjects for scientific research? Upon what values would you base your decision?

Possible Answer: For many people, this is a very personal and individual judgment. After arriving at a basis for your judgment, examine Lawrence Kohlberg's theory of moral development in chapter 4, section 4-4a. Can you identify on what level of Kohlberg's theory of moral development your judgment is based?

Journey of Discovery Question: What role should values play in science? Is it possible or desirable to separate values from science?

Possible Answer: For example, the basic research of behavioral psychologists has taught us a great deal about the conditions under which rewards and punishments shape behavior (see chapter 7, section 7-2, for an extended discussion). This knowledge could be utilized by applied psychologists to promote more effective learning in school settings, but it could also be used to encourage gamblers to squander their life savings at casinos. Although most people would have few qualms about using psychological research to facilitate formal education, many would express reservations about using this same research to encourage gambling. Should psychologists use their knowledge only to effect certain changes in the world, or should all areas be open for psychological application? These very concerns have stirred considerable debate about the proper role that psychologists should play in applying their knowledge in the real world (Álvarez, 2001).

One perspective is that the discoveries of any science should be used for whatever purposes interested parties consider important. In such endeavors, scientists should be neutral truth-seekers and should not worry about how their discoveries are used (Kimble, 1989). Followers of this *value-free* perspective believe that psychologists who use their scientific knowledge to influence social policy decisions undermine the scientific basis of the discipline. A second perspective is that psychology and social action should not be separated. Contemporary followers of this *value-laden* perspective assert that studying human behavior without a commitment to changing the quality of life for the better is irresponsible (Álvarez, 2001; Fox, 1985).

A commonly accepted belief within the philosophy of science today is that no science is untouched by values and the politics of the culture in which it is practiced (Harris, 1999). In psychology, the subject matter is very important to people, including the investigators. The personal values of psychologists often determine what sort of research and application they are most interested in undertaking, as well as influencing the theories they develop (Redding, 2001). When psychological theories clash because of different value orientations, science does not grind to a halt. Instead, studies are conducted and published, and new facts are discovered. Thus, the science of psychology will continue to contribute to our understanding of behavior, and many psychologists will also use this knowledge to make changes in their world.

In summary, I think you would agree that there is nothing inherently evil or sinister about a hammer. Indeed, you might be very pleased to have someone use this tool to build a house for you. However, your attitude toward the hammer would be decidedly different if it had been used as a weapon against you in a fight. This example illustrates that the tools of humankind can be used for both beneficial and detrimental purposes, and this is no less true for the tools of the psychologist.

Chapter 3

Journey of Discovery Question: You have probably heard the following statement many times: "We use only 10 percent of our brain." Based on what you have learned about brain functioning, do you think this statement is true? In pondering the merits of this expression, consider another type of human functioning: athletic performance. Do athletes use only 10 percent of their muscles when competing?

Possible Answer: Here is an example of an oft-repeated statement of seeming fact that has absolutely no scientific basis. Just as it would be absurd to suggest that athletes competing in sporting events only use 10 percent of their muscles, it is foolish to suggest such a thing about our everyday thinking. The 10 percent figure was probably pulled out of thin air by someone and gained credence through simple repetition. In reality, there is absolutely no evidence to suggest that only 10 percent of our neurons are active at any given moment. There is also no evidence to suggest that we could remotely behave normally if only 10 percent of any brain area was functioning. Perhaps people who make this statement simply mean to assert that we all have untapped cognitive potential and that there is always something we can do to improve our everyday thinking.

Journey of Discovery Question: After limbs have been amputated, amputees often feel excruciating pain in the area of their lost limb. How might the brain's plasticity play a role in this pain?

Possible Answer: Recent studies suggest that the intense pain that amputees often experience, known as *phantom pain*, is due to the brain's capacity for growth. For example, when the nerve of one finger is severed, brain areas associated with that nerve do not wither away. Instead, neurons activated by nearby fingers take over some of the function of the now-nonexistent neurons in the severed finger, and they fool the brain into thinking that the lost finger is still there.

The more collateral growth that occurs, the more phantom pain the amputee feels (Flor et al., 1995).

Journey of Discovery Question: A common plot device in science fiction movies involves removing a brain from its body and maintaining it alive in a nutrient-rich solution. If this were actually a scientific possibility, do you think this brain would have the same mind as it had when connected to the rest of the body? Underlying this question is the age-old *mind-body debate* concerning where the mind is located in the body.

Possible Answer: In the fourth century B.C., the Greek philosopher Plato made a sharp distinction between the mind and the body, arguing that the mind could exist both before and after it takes up residence in the body. Not only did Plato contend that the mind would remain unaffected if the brain were removed from the rest of the body, but also he argued that destroying the brain itself would not alter the mind. This belief that the body is separate from the mind is known as *dualism*. In contrast, *monism* is the belief that the mind and body are one and the same (Cotterill, 1989; Pert, 2002).

Despite the many discoveries we have made about the brain and mental processes, the mind-body debate remains a matter of speculation. However, the viewpoint that best fits research findings within the biological sciences is a form of monism, proposing that the mind is made up of a mutual interaction between the brain and the body (Prochiantz, 1992). That is, although brain activity generates mental events that significantly influence behavioral responses, our behavioral responses also significantly influence the brain activity that generates mental events. This constant *brain-body interaction* constitutes the mind of a person. Because of this give-and-take influence, most neuroscientists believe that the absence of stimuli from the body would fundamentally change whatever "mind" a disembodied brain might possess.

Chapter 4

Journey of Discovery Question: If you were to tell someone to "just be yourself," what would that mean to a person from an individualist culture? What would it mean to a person from a collectivist culture?

Possible Answer: When Chie Kanagawa and his colleagues (2001) asked U.S. and Japanese college students this question, they received very different responses. For the individualist Americans, this question suggested a group of personal attributes that were not influenced by the situation they happened to be in at the time. Further, these attributes reflected the Americans' unique qualities, and these qualities were mostly positive. In contrast, for the collectivist Japanese, this question called to mind a self that was defined by their social relationships in their group. Here, "being yourself" meant constructing a self-presentation that was fairly self-critical and would help you fit into the group. This research suggests that, for individualists, "being yourself" assumes a relatively fixed and stable self-concept made up of generally positive personal attributes. For collectivists, "being yourself" assumes a self that changes according to the situation in order to better fit in with the group.

Journey of Discovery Question: Why do you think it might be easier to encourage women to expand their gender roles to include "work outside the household" than it is to encourage men to expand their gender roles to include "domestic child-care" responsibilities?

Possible Answer: One possibility is that North American culture places considerably higher value on tasks traditionally defined as masculine than on those defined as feminine. Thus, when women work outside the household, they often reap the rewards that have traditionally been reserved for men (wages and jobs that increase one's social status in the larger culture). In contrast, when men take on the domestic task of child care—a role traditionally assigned to women—few tangible rewards are doled out by the larger culture. Until we value traditionally defined feminine tasks at the same level as traditionally defined masculine tasks, it will be difficult to encourage men to "expand" their gender roles to a level comparable to that exhibited by women.

Chapter 5

Journey of Discovery Question: Based on what you know about your vestibular sense, why do you think it is difficult to walk in a straight line after spinning yourself around on a swing?

Possible Answer: Twirling yourself around on a swing demonstrates the importance of a properly functioning vestibular system in maintaining a sense of balance. When you stop twirling, for a short period of time your brain is still receiving signals from your vestibular sense, indicating that you are still spinning. This perceptual illusion lasts only a few seconds before your vestibular system returns to normal.

Chapter 6

Journey of Discovery Question: Because daydreaming involves thinking about internal thoughts and imaginary situations, what effect might television viewing have on daydreaming? Do you think people who watch a lot of television daydream more or less than those who watch little television? Why?

Possible Answer: Because the content of many television shows offers a great deal of new information and many vivid images to viewers, it's possible that people who watch a lot of television might daydream more than infrequent viewers because they are provided with a lot of raw imaginative material from which to construct daydreams. However, because television viewing often involves rather passive reception of information, it's also possible that people who watch a lot of television daydream less because this passive reception may stifle their ability to actively construct their own compelling internal images and storylines. Of these two possibilities, research suggests that television viewing does lead to increased daydreaming by providing vivid images that form the content of later fantasies (Valkenburg & van der Voort, 1994). However, this same research also suggests that greater television viewing is related to lower creative imagination. Thus, television viewing may encourage people to more often withdraw into their own inner world, but it doesn't appear to encourage much creative thinking during that state of consciousness.

Journey of Discovery Question: Have you ever had a dream that later seemed to come true? Many people who have had this experience, or who hear of it from a close friend or family member, believe that dreams can predict the future. What other potential explanations could there be for a dream that comes true?

Possible Answer: There are many possible reasons that precognitive dreams may appear real. One potential explanation lies in what criteria we use to judge whether the dream is "true." If you are in college now and dream that you will graduate someday, your dream does not necessarily demonstrate psychic ability as much as an awareness of the laws of probability and the logical consequences of completing your requirements. Dreaming about more specific details of the day—what the weather is like, who the speaker is, what you eat for lunch—would be a much more stringent test, a test that most "predictive" dreams are likely to fail.

Another explanation involves the sheer number of dreams you have. Over the course of your life, you will experience thousands upon thousands of dreams. Each dream, in turn, will have many elements. If one element from one dream comes true—for instance, in dreaming about your college graduation, you dream that it rains, and in fact it does rain on your graduation day—that striking occurrence may cause you to believe you have predicted the future. What you have forgotten are the many times you have dreamed of rain when the day has turned out to be sunny, or that in your dream of graduation day, you also predicted that your brother would be late, when in fact he was on time. The tendency to see relationships where there is only coincidence is called *illusory correlation* (Berndsen et al., 1996) and is especially common when people are faced with unusual events—such as seeming to predict the future.

Finally, as you will see in chapter 8, human memory is not a perfect recording device. Our recall of events is influenced by our current circumstances, and dreams are often difficult to recall completely even when they are fresh in our minds. It is difficult to know, looking back across months or years, whether you truly dreamed of rain, or whether the fact that it is now raining is changing your recollection of the dream.

Chapter 7

Journey of Discovery Question: Every year, thousands of drug users die from overdoses. Those who have narrowly survived such overdoses tend to report that the setting in which they took too much of the drug was different from their normal drug-taking environment (Siegel, 1984). How might classical conditioning principles explain why these different settings were more likely to be associated with drug overdoses?

Possible Answer: When drug users repeatedly take drugs in a particular environment, that environment may become a conditioned stimulus. Whenever drug users enter that drug-associated environment, they experience a conditioned response: Their bodies become prepared ahead of time for the drug injection. When the injected drug is an overdose, this prior-occurring conditioned response may partially counteract the effects of the lethal injection. This conditioned response, however, does not occur in an environment where drug users do not normally take drugs, and thus their bodies are less prepared to handle an overdose in unusual settings.

Support for this classical conditioning explanation comes from an actual drug overdose experiment in which rats received injections of either a placebo or heroin on alternating days and in alternating environments (Siegel et al., 1982). Then half of them received a potentially lethal dose of heroin in the setting in which they normally received the heroin, while the other rats received the drug in their normal placebo-associated environment. More rats died of the overdose when they received it in the setting not normally associated with drug injections.

Journey of Discovery Question: Many of the studies that have explored the principles of classical conditioning and operant conditioning were performed on animals, such as rats and pigeons. How can scientists make generalizations about the way people behave based on these studies? Why not just study people?

Possible Answer: Humans clearly differ from other animals in a variety of ways that would seem to challenge these studies. In some cases, it is possible to study people, and psychologists have tested behaviorist principles using human participants. In other cases, ethical concerns make the use of human participants impossible. For example,

can you imagine conducting the electrical-shock learned helplessness study using college students as participants? In such cases, animal participants provide important information in a rigorously controlled experimental setting.

Also, remember that the behaviorist perspective is largely concerned with what organisms do and not with what they think or feel. Once our conscious awareness is removed from the equation, humans appear more similar to nonhuman animals. Thus, animals become a simplified model or analogy of human behavior. This simplification of the model is an asset, not a liability, when scientists are attempting to wrestle with a complex phenomenon; it allows researchers to remove extraneous variables and concentrate on the important theoretical issues. Scientists are also able to argue that, because they are seeking universal principles of behavior, any principle that can be demonstrated in diverse species is a good candidate to be considered universal.

Journey of Discovery Question: Why are the studies on observational learning now mostly based on human populations? And why does observational learning make evolutionary sense for human beings?

Possible Answer: The most obvious difference between observational learning and the other types of learning covered in this chapter is that observational learning requires cognition; the more complex the relationship between the observed behavior and the observed consequences, the greater the sophistication of thought required to learn from it. Because cognition is relevant to this type of learning, it makes sense to study populations with sophisticated cognitive abilities.

Observational learning provides several advantages from an evolutionary standpoint. On a basic level, the ability to learn from your neighbor's errors means that your neighbor, not you, takes the risks. Thus, as your mother used to say, if all your friends jumped off a cliff, you at least would have the opportunity to see what happened to them before deciding to join in. In a primitive and hostile environment, the capacity for that kind of learning could easily enhance reproductive success. In addition, observational learning can result in cumulative cultural evolution, wherein members of societies exhibit behavior that no individual could invent on her or his own (Boyd & Richerson, 1996), leading to increasingly complex adaptive behaviors.

Chapter 8

Journey of Discovery Question: The finding that deep processing leads to more effective encoding and better retention of new information has many practical applications for you as a student. In your own studying, how can you process new information at a deep, rather than shallow, level?

Possible Answer: You can use a number of possible cognitive strategies. The general strategy would be to make connections between new information and information that you already know. One of the most effective ways to retain information is to associate it with something that has a lot of personal meaning—you. Also, actively question new information and try to think of relevant examples of the concepts under study.

Journey of Discovery Question: Could you falsely reconstruct a childhood memory based on your *beliefs* about how memory works? That is, do you think that your beliefs about how memory works could affect your recollection of past events?

Possible Answer: The findings from one recent study raise the possibility that our beliefs about how memory works can indeed affect our recollection of past events. Piotr Winkielman and Norbert Schwarz (2001) asked participants to recall either 4 childhood events or 12 childhood events. Based on past memory studies, Winkielman and Schwarz knew that most people would find that recalling 4 childhood events was rather easy but that recalling 12 events was rather difficult. Following this either easy or difficult memory task, the researchers manipulated participants' beliefs about how memory works by telling them that either pleasant or unpleasant periods of one's life fade from memory. When the recall task was difficult (12 events recalled), participants who had been led to believe that memories from unpleasant periods fade away rated their childhood as less happy than participants who had been led to believe that memories from pleasant periods fade away. The opposite pattern of findings was obtained when the recall task was easy (4 events recalled).

Of what practical importance are these findings that people's memories of past events may be shaped by their beliefs about how memory works? Consider clients in psychotherapy who are asked to recall a large number of childhood events. They are likely to experience recall difficulty. They are also likely to be told by their therapists that unpleasant childhood memories tend to be repressed and difficult to remember (Garry et al., 1997). The findings from Winkielman and Schwarz's study suggest that clients who both experience recall difficulty and share the popular belief that negative events are difficult to remember may incorrectly conclude that their childhoods were unhappy!

Chapter 9

Journey of Discovery Question: Research indicates that infants have an inborn ability to detect phonemes that are not a part of their culture's language repertoire. Given that you cannot ask infants questions, how do you think psychologists tested this ability in newborns? That is, how did they design an experiment to test children's inborn ability to detect phonemes?

Possible Answer: Janet Werker and her colleague (1988) tested infants' inborn capacity to detect phonemes by first using operant conditioning principles to condition infants to turn their heads toward a sound source when they detected a change from one phoneme sound to another. The reward the infants received was seeing a clapping and drumming toy animal. The researchers then measured the infants' ability to differentiate between nonoverlapping English and Hindi phonemes. Using the conditioning technique, they discovered that infants, regardless of which language they were learning, could detect the differences until the age of 8 months. After 8 months, infants could no longer detect phonemes that were not a part of their native language.

Journey of Discovery Question: In Olympic competition, athletes who win an event receive the gold medal, those who come in second receive a silver medal, and third-place finishers get a bronze medal. Fourth-place finishers receive nothing. During the 1992 Olympics, bronze medalists (third-place finishers) exhibited more joy than silver medalists (second-place finishers) after their events (Medvec et al., 1995). How can this finding be explained by the availability heuristic?

Possible Answer: When thinking about where they finished in the competition, the second-place finishers are more likely to think about just missing out on winning their event. For them, the most available memory is just missing out on glory, and thus they don't feel very happy. In contrast, third-place finishers are more likely to think about just beating out the fourth-place finisher for the last medal. Due to this more available memory, they feel joyful.

Chapter 10

Journey of Discovery Question: Women who go to college after their mid-20s receive better grades than would be predicted by their scores on SAT tests taken just before entering college. Why might this be the case?

Possible Answer: A number of reasons are possible. First, these women might score lower on the SATs because their test-taking skills are a bit rusty or they are unduly anxious. Second, being more mature and focused, they may have greater motivation than younger students and thus work harder for their grades in college. Finally, given that these women are older, they may be able to rely more on useful life experiences to manage the stress produced while seeking academic achievement.

Journey of Discovery Question: Imagine that you wanted to develop your own intelligence test. What are some of the pitfalls in early intelligence testing that you would want to avoid?

Possible Answer: Early intelligence tests were developed using one population but then were incorrectly used to test other populations. Thus, in developing an intelligence test, you would need to establish a uniform procedure for administering the test and for interpreting its scores so that such bias did not occur. Because intelligence is assumed to be relatively stable, you would want to make sure that your new test yielded consistent results when taken at different times. Also, to what degree does your test measure what it is designed to measure? Early tests often measured characteristics other than intelligence. Thus, you would need to establish your test's validity. Does your test predict other observable behaviors related to intelligence? If so, you have predictive validity.

Journey of Discovery Question: How are Raymond B. Cattell's concepts of crystallized intelligence and fluid intelligence related to Jean Piaget's concepts of *assimilation* and *accommodation,* discussed in chapter 4, section 4-3a?

Possible Answer: Crystallized intelligence involves using existing knowledge to solve familiar problems. Assimilation is the process of absorbing new information into existing schemas. In essence, a good deal of the knowledge that intelligence researchers consider part of crystallized intelligence is the schemas (the organized clusters of knowledge) that we use to solve problems that are similar to past problems we have successfully solved. Thus, one way to understand these two concepts from two different areas of psychology is that people with high crystallized intelligence are very adept at engaging in assimilation. Similarly, Cattell defines fluid intelligence as the ability to learn or invent new strategies for dealing with new kinds of problems. Piaget defines accommodation as the process of changing existing schemas in order to absorb new information. Thus, consistent with the preceding analysis, people with high fluid intelligence are those who are very adept at engaging in accommodation.

Chapter 11

Journey of Discovery Question: Sometimes, when athletes are paid large sums of money to play their sport, they seem to lose their "love of the game" and become less motivated. How could this change in athletic motivation be explained by intrinsic and extrinsic motivation?

Possible Answer: When playing their sport as amateurs, athletes undoubtedly perceive their actions as intrinsically motivated. However, after receiving large sums of money for playing the sport that they previously played for nothing, some athletes may perceive that they are playing for the money rather than for the "love of the game." This thinking causes a shift from intrinsic to extrinsic motivation. Now believing that their actions are being controlled by external sources (the money), the athletes do not enjoy playing the sport as much as they did previously.

Journey of Discovery Question: What are the similarities and differences between the terms *sexual identity* and *gender identity*?

Possible Answer: Both gender identity and sexual identity involve a type of social identity. Social identities are aspects of a person's self-concept based on her or his group memberships. Gender identity is your knowledge that you are a male or a female and the internalization of this fact into your self-concept. When you develop a gender identity, you cognitively place yourself into the "male" or "female" category. In rare cases, a person who is biologically one sex may identify himself or herself with the other sex. For example, a male adult with a female gender identity may feel that he is a woman "trapped" inside a male body. In contrast to gender identity, sexual identity is your knowledge that you are sexually attracted to either men or women or both, and the internalization of this fact into your self-concept. When you develop a sexual identity, you cognitively place yourself into the "heterosexual," "bisexual," or "homosexual" category.

Journey of Discovery Question: Imagine that you are going out on a date with someone, and you would like this person to fall in love with you. Up to this point in your relationship, this person likes you only "as a friend." Based on your knowledge of the two-factor theory of emotions, what sort of activities might you plan for the date to increase the likelihood that the object of your affections will experience a similar emotion toward you?

Possible Answer: You could take a cue from the Dutton and Aron bridge study and take your date to a place where she or he will become physiologically aroused. The situation could be a scary movie, a fast ride at an amusement park, or an exciting sporting event. While she or he is experiencing this physiological arousal, you should position yourself nearby so the arousal is more likely to be attributed to you. ("Gee, I am romantically attracted to this person!" your date suddenly realizes.) Good luck!!!

Chapter 12

Journey of Discovery Question: An increasing number of contemporary personality theorists pay attention to how culture and evolutionary forces shape personality. Is there any evidence in Freud's theory of personality indicating that he considered the impact of culture and evolution on personality?

Possible Answer: Like many thinkers of his day, Freud was influenced by Charles Darwin's theory of evolution. Freud's emphasis on the sexual and aggressive instincts of the id is compatible with evolutionary explanations of the role these two behaviors play in adaptation and survival. Much less evidence exists indicating that Freud considered the impact of culture on personality development. His explanation that the superego develops as the child internalizes the values of his or her parents perhaps represents some small consideration of cultural factors, but he does not explicitly develop this idea.

Journey of Discovery Question: How do you think Freud would describe the highly conscientious person?

Possible Answer: Highly conscientious people would, from Freud's perspective, be seen as having a highly developed superego. Freud

warned that this has drawbacks as well as advantages. Highly conscientious people may be inflexible, self-righteous, stubborn, stingy, and perfectionistic in addition to being successful at work. People who are low in conscientiousness may be less reliable but much more fun to be with, because they are constantly thinking of new and exciting things to do.

Journey of Discovery Question: Is self-efficacy the same as self-esteem?

Possible Answer: Self-efficacy is not the same as self-esteem. Instead, it is most like what we commonly refer to as self-confidence—but self-confidence related to specific activities. People who have high self-efficacy for many different activities tend to have high self-esteem, but this is not always the case.

Journey of Discovery Question: If people with low self-esteem reject attempts to increase their feelings of self-worth when others lavishly praise them, what strategy might you employ to satisfy their self-enhancement needs without triggering their need for self-verification?

Possible Answer: Self-verification needs are most likely to override self-enhancement needs when low self-esteem people receive positive feedback that, if accepted, would require a major change in their self-concepts. However, research suggests that low self-esteem persons are able to engage in direct forms of self-enhancement when the positive feedback is not related to a highly important aspect of their self-concept (Seta & Donaldson, 1999). Based on this information, you might try to provide them with positive feedback that is not so lavish and not directly associated with a negative belief that you know they hold about themselves. Subtle praise and positive feedback stretched over long periods of time might be effective in slowly nudging low self-esteem people into gradually changing their self-beliefs so they develop more positive attitudes and beliefs about themselves.

Chapter 13

Journey of Discovery Question: How might the *confirmation bias*, a topic of discussion in chapter 9, section 9-2c, explain the decision-making process of the hospital personnel in the Rosenhan study?

Possible Answer: As discussed in chapter 9, the confirmation bias is the tendency to seek only information that verifies our beliefs. Unfortunately, gathering information selectively in this way often prevents us from realizing that our judgments may be incorrect. In forming first impressions of others, research suggests that the questions we ask them tend to be biased in the direction of our initial expectations (Snyder & Swann, 1978). In diagnosing mental illness, these findings suggest that hospital personnel in the Rosenhan study were more likely to ask the pseudopatients questions indicative of mental illness than questions indicative of mental health. In this case, seeking confirmation led to mistakenly diagnosing healthy individuals as psychologically disordered.

Chapter 14

Journey of Discovery Question: Suppose a male college student seeks therapy because he is shy and has been unsuccessful in his attempts to talk to women. He reports that he stammers and has trouble thinking of anything to say. He does not initiate conversations with women classmates, even to make small talk. When he starts to make a phone call to ask someone out, he hesitates and talks himself out of calling. How might a behavior psychotherapist use modeling and social skills training to treat this student's shyness?

Possible Answer: A behavior psychotherapist might begin by modeling different and more effective social behaviors (how to initiate a conversation, how to make small talk). The therapist may also model ways of managing the anxiety that occurs when the client attempts to talk to women. These anxiety management techniques may include both physiological and cognitive exercises. For example, physiological anxiety management may include slow-breathing exercises, while cognitive anxiety management may include telling oneself to "calm down, speak slowly," and "don't anticipate the worst possible outcome." The client would learn these social and coping skills by imitating the therapist and then by practicing them, first in the therapy session under the therapist's guidance and then throughout the week.

Chapter 15

Journey of Discovery Question: It is generally thought that problem-focused coping is maladaptive in situations over which a person has no personal control. Yet a situation that appears on its surface to be uncontrollable may still have controllable aspects. Consider people caring for loved ones with terminal illnesses. During the weeks leading up to death, what sort of problem-focused coping might caregivers engage in to increase their positive moods and lower their stress?

Possible Answer: Research by Judith Moskowitz and Susan Folkman found that when people were caring for loved ones with AIDS-related terminal illnesses, many of them created "to-do" lists made up of seemingly mundane tasks, such as getting a prescription filled, buying groceries, and changing the person's bed linens. These lists served at least two positive functions: (1) They gave caregivers opportunities to feel effective and in control, thereby decreasing their feelings of helplessness, and (2) successfully completing these tasks provided real benefits to the loved one, whose subsequent positive feedback elevated the caregivers' moods. Such problem-focused coping increased the positive moods of caregivers during the weeks leading up to death (Moskowitz et al., 1996).

Journey of Discovery Question: Based on your readings, what tactics can you employ to manage your stress and reduce stress-related ailments?

Possible Answer: A stress management program could include healthy eating habits, combined with aerobic exercise and progressive relaxation. In addition, if you tend to have a Type A behavior pattern, it would be important for you to slow down and relax. We also know that social support helps people cope with stressors, so maintaining family ties, friendships, and romantic relationships will also prove beneficial to your health. Finally, looking on the positive side of life by developing an optimistic explanatory style will help you deal with uncontrollable negative events.

Chapter 16

Journey of Discovery Question: "Road rage" has become an all-too-familiar term describing violent outbursts by people driving cars on our nation's highways. Would this type of aggression typically be instrumental or hostile in nature? Why? Beyond harsh penalties, what strategies might public officials employ to reduce road rage?

Possible Answer: In many reported cases of road rage, the apparent motive underlying the aggression is simply to harm people whom aggressors believe have frustrated their driving goals. The aggression is fueled by anger, and thus most clearly fits the category of hostile aggression. A possible strategy to reduce road rage would be to induce incompatible responses in potentially angry drivers. Brooklyn, New York, has recently employed this strategy by posting signs along the highway containing "knock-knock" jokes. You could also encourage radio stations with "happy" programming formats to advertise their dial numbers on billboards so that drivers would be more likely to tune in to these stations. Billboards could also serve as a means through which to share the insights of social learning theory: Remind adults driving vehicles on the highway that they are role models for children and that how they behave while driving will be observed and learned by younger passengers and drivers. This strategy might prompt drivers to think twice before acting upon their frustration, so their anger doesn't precipitate aggression.

Journey of Discovery Question: Many of you will be—or currently are—parents. Based on what you have learned about helping, what sort of cultural role models might influence the "helping habits" of boys and girls? How might greater gender-role flexibility influence male and female helping tendencies?

Possible Answer: Social modeling studies suggest that children are most likely to imitate the behavior of people with whom they strongly identify, and for most children, this means same-sex adults. Thus, to foster helping habits in children, existing cultural role models for boys and girls could be enlisted to convey prosocial messages in public service announcements.

In Hollywood movies, most leading-male actors play the traditional masculine role of helping people in dangerous situations, while being rather unwilling or ineffective in providing commonplace, long-term help, such as caring for children and the elderly. The underlying message in many of these movies is that this kind of assistance is unmanly.

In contrast, most leading-female actors play characters who have less traditional gender roles, and they are often depicted as being willing to intervene in both dangerous situations and those requiring nurturance and long-term care to needy others. This greater flexibility in helping responses reflects the greater gender flexibility available to women in contemporary culture. For instance, girls are generally allowed to engage in more nontraditional gender behavior than are boys. As a result, you might expect that girls will learn to help in a wider variety of situations than will boys.

Glossary

Absolute threshold The lowest level of intensity of a given stimulus that a person can detect half the time.

Accommodation The process of changing existing schemas in order to absorb new information.

Acetylcholine (ACH) A neurotransmitter involved in muscle contraction and memory formation.

Achievement test A test designed to assess what a person has learned.

Acoustic encoding The encoding of sound, especially the sound of words.

Acquaintance rape Forced sexual intercourse that occurs either on a date or between people who are acquainted or romantically involved; also known as *date rape.*

Acquisition The initial stage of classical conditioning, during which a previously neutral stimulus begins to acquire the ability to elicit a conditioned response.

Action potential The brief shift in a neuron's electrical charge that travels down the axon.

Activation-synthesis theory A theory that dreaming is a by-product of random brain activity, which the forebrain weaves into a somewhat logical story.

Acupuncture An ancient Chinese healing technique in which needles are inserted into the skin at specific points, stimulating the release of pain-reducing endorphins.

Adolescence The transition period between childhood and adulthood.

Adrenal glands Two glands, located near the kidneys, that secrete epinephrine and norepinephrine, which activate the sympathetic nervous system.

Aerobic exercise Sustained exercise that increases heart and lung fitness.

Afterimage A visual image that persists after a stimulus has been removed.

Aggression Any form of behavior that is intended to harm or injure a person, oneself, or an object.

Aging The progressive deterioration of the body that culminates in death.

Agoraphobia A fear of going out to public or open spaces.

Alcoholism Tolerance of and physical dependence on alcohol due to prolonged abuse of that substance.

Algorithm A problem-solving strategy that involves following a specific rule or step-by-step procedure until you inevitably produce the correct solution.

Alpha waves Fast, low-amplitude brain waves associated with a relaxed, wakeful state.

Altered state of consciousness An awareness of oneself and one's environment that is noticeably different from the normal state of consciousness.

Alzheimer's disease A progressive and irreversible brain disorder that strikes older people, causing memory loss and other symptoms.

Anal stage In Freud's theory, the second stage of psychosexual development, during which the child derives pleasure from defecation.

Anorexia nervosa An eating disorder in which a person weighs less than 85 percent of her or his expected weight but still expresses an intense fear of gaining weight or becoming fat.

Anterograde amnesia The inability to form long-term memories due to physical injury to the brain.

Antianxiety drugs Drugs that have an immediate calming effect by facilitating the inhibitory action of the GABA neurotransmitter, thereby reducing nerve impulse transmission.

Antidepressant drugs Drugs that relieve depression by increasing the supply of norepinephrine and/or serotonin at the neuron's receptor sites.

Antipsychotic drugs A group of medications effective in treating the delusions, hallucinations, and loose associations of schizophrenia by blocking dopamine receptors and thereby reducing dopamine activity.

Antisocial personality disorder A personality disorder characterized by a persistent pattern of disregard for and violation of the rights of others.

Anxiety disorders Disorders characterized by distressing, persistent anxiety or maladaptive behavior.

Aphasia The inability to recognize or express language as a result of damage to brain tissue, such as after a stroke.

Applied psychologists Psychologists who use existing psychological knowledge to solve and prevent problems.

Aptitude test A test designed to predict a person's capacity for learning.

Archetypes In Jung's personality theory, inherited images that are passed down from our prehistoric ancestors and that reveal themselves as universal symbols in dreams, religion, and art.

Artificial intelligence (AI) The science of designing and making intelligent machines, especially intelligent computer programs.

Assimilation The process of absorbing new information into existing schemas.

Attachment The strong emotional bond a young child forms with its primary caregiver.

Attitude A positive or negative evaluation of an object.

Attribution The process by which people use information to make inferences about the causes of behaviors or events.

Audience inhibition effect A situation in which people are inhibited from helping due to a fear of being negatively evaluated by other bystanders if they intervene and it turns out not to be an emergency.

Audition The sense of hearing.

Autonomic nervous system A division of the peripheral nervous system that controls the movement of nonskeletal muscles, such as the heart and lung muscles, over which people have little or no voluntary control.

Availability heuristic The tendency to judge the frequency or probability of an event in terms of how easy it is to think of examples of that event.

Aversive conditioning A counterconditioning technique in which a classically conditioned aversive response is conditioned to occur in response to a stimulus previously associated with an undesired behavior.

Axon An extension of the soma that sends information in the form of electrochemical impulses to other neurons.

Balance theory A theory that people desire cognitive consistency, or "balance," in their thoughts, feelings, and social relationships.

Behavioral medicine An interdisciplinary field of science that integrates behavioral and medical knowledge and then applies it to health and illness.

Behavior genetics The study of how the genotype and the environment of an organism influence its behavior.

Behaviorism An approach to psychology that studies observable behavior rather than hidden mental processes; also referred to as the *behavioral perspective.*

Behavior therapies Psychotherapies that apply learning principles to the elimination of unwanted behaviors.

Beta waves Very fast, low-amplitude brain waves associated with an active, alert state of mind.

Binocular cues Depth cues that require information from both eyes.

Biomedical therapies The treatment of psychological disorders by altering brain functioning with physical or chemical interventions.

Biopsychosocial model An interdisciplinary model that assumes that health and overall wellness are caused by a complex interaction of biological, psychological, and sociocultural factors.

Bipolar disorder A mood disorder characterized by swings between the emotional extremes of mania and depression.

Bisexuality The sexual orientation in which a person is sexually attracted to members of both sexes.

Blind spot The area on the retina where the optic nerve leaves the eye; contains no receptor cells.

Blood-brain barrier A semipermeable wall of tiny blood vessels that prevents certain chemicals in the bloodstream from reaching the brain.

Body dysmorphic disorder A somatoform disorder characterized by preoccupation with an imagined physical defect that causes significant distress or interferes with daily functioning.

Body esteem A person's attitudes toward her or his body.

Bulimia An eating disorder in which a person engages in recurrent episodes of binge eating followed by drastic measures to purge the body of the consumed calories.

Cannon-Bard theory A theory that emotion-provoking events simultaneously induce both physiological responses and subjective states that are labeled as emotions.

Case study A descriptive scientific method involving in-depth analysis of a single subject, usually a person.

Categorization The primary means of coding experience through the process of forming concepts.

Central nervous system That portion of the nervous system located in the bony central core of the body and consisting of the brain and spinal cord.

Cerebellum A part of the hindbrain that regulates and coordinates basic motor activities and may also play a role in learning.

Cerebral cortex The largest structure in the forebrain; largely responsible for higher-order mental processes.

Cerebral hemispheres The two main parts of the cerebral cortex; the left and right hemispheres.

Cerebral lateralization The degree to which the right or left hemisphere controls various cognitive and behavioral functions.

Cerebrospinal fluid A clear, cushioning fluid secreted by the brain and circulated inside and around the brain and spinal cord.

Child-directed speech Speech to babies characterized by exaggerated intonations, high pitch, clear enunciation, short sentences, repetition, and slow speech; also called *motherese.*

Chromosomes Threadlike structures carrying genetic information that are found in every cell of the body.

Chunking Organizing items of information into a meaningful unit, or chunk, that can be stored in short-term memory.

Circadian rhythms Internally generated behavioral and physiological changes that occur on a daily basis.

Classical conditioning A type of learning in which a neutral stimulus acquires the capacity to elicit a response after being paired with another stimulus that naturally elicits that response.

Client-centered therapy A humanistic therapy in which the client, rather than the therapist, directs the course of therapy.

Cloning The process of making a genetically identical organism through nonsexual means.

Cochlea The coiled, fluid-filled tube in the inner ear that contains the hairlike auditory receptors.

Cognition The mental activity of knowing and the processes through which knowledge is acquired and problems are solved.

Cognitive-behavior therapy (CBT) The cognitive therapy of Aaron Beck that identifies and then changes negative thinking and behavior by using both cognitive and behavioral principles.

Cognitive dissonance A feeling of discomfort caused by performing an action inconsistent with one's attitudes.

Cognitive-neoassociationist model A theory of aggression stating that aversive events produce negative affect, which stimulates the inclination to aggress.

Cognitive perspective An approach to psychology that attempts to understand behavior by studying how the mind organizes perceptions, processes information, and interprets experiences.

Cognitive therapies Psychotherapies that focus on identifying and then modifying dysfunctional patterns of thought.

Collective unconscious In Jung's personality theory, the part of the unconscious mind containing inherited memories shared by all human beings.

Collectivism A philosophy of life stressing the priority of group needs over individual needs, a preference for tightly knit social relationships, and a willingness to submit to the influence of one's group.

Color blindness A deficiency in the ability to distinguish among colors.

Color constancy Perceiving objects as having consistent color under different conditions of illumination.

Communication The sending and receiving of information.

Companionate love The affection we feel for those with whom our lives are deeply entwined.

Compliance Publicly acting in accord with a direct request.

Computerized axial tomography (CAT) A brain-imaging technique in which thousands of X-ray photographs of the brain are taken and then combined to construct a cross-sectional brain picture.

Concept A mental grouping of objects, ideas, or events that share common properties.

Concrete operational stage The third stage in Piaget's theory of cognitive development (ages 7 to 11), a time when children can perform mental operations on tangible objects or events and gradually engage in logical reasoning.

Conditional positive regard An attitude of acceptance toward another person only when she or he meets your standards.

Conditioned response (CR) In classical conditioning, the learned response to a previously neutral conditioned stimulus.

Conditioned stimulus (CS) In classical conditioning, a previously neutral stimulus that, after repeated pairings with an unconditioned stimulus, comes to elicit a conditioned response.

Cones Receptor neurons in the eye, located near the center of the retina, which mediate color vision.

Confirmation bias The tendency to seek information that supports our beliefs while ignoring disconfirming information.

Conformity A yielding to perceived group pressure.

Conscious mind According to Freud, the relatively small part of our mind that we are aware of at the moment.

Consciousness Awareness of ourselves and our environment.

Conservation The understanding that certain physical properties of an object remain unchanged despite superficial changes in the object's appearance.

Content validity The degree to which the items on a test are related to the characteristic the test supposedly measures.

Continuous reinforcement A schedule of reinforcement in which every correct response is followed by a reinforcer.

Control condition The condition in an experiment in which participants are not exposed to the independent variable.

Conventional morality The second level of moral reasoning in Kohlberg's theory of moral development; characterized by conforming to societal norms and laws.

Convergent thinking Applying logic and conventional knowledge to arrive at (or *converge upon*) a single solution to a problem.

Conversion disorder A somatoform disorder characterized by a specific sensory or motor symptom that has a psychological rather than a physical basis.

Cornea A clear membrane covering the front of the eyeball that aids in visual acuity by bending light that falls on its surface.

Corpus callosum A thick band of nerve fibers connecting the right and left cerebral hemispheres that transmits information between them.

Correlational research Research designed to examine the nature of the relationship between two or more naturally occurring variables.

Correlation coefficient (r) A statistical measure of the direction and strength of the linear relationship between two variables, which can range from −1.00 to +1.00.

Counterconditioning A behavior therapy procedure based on classical conditioning that involves conditioning new responses to stimuli that trigger unwanted behaviors.

Countertransference The process by which the therapist develops feelings for the client that are presumed to reflect feelings the therapist had for others early in life.

Couples therapy Therapy designed to help couples improve the quality of their relationship.

Covariation model A theory of attribution asserting that people rely on consensus, consistency, and distinctiveness information when assigning causes for events.

Creativity The ability to produce novel, high-quality products or ideas.

Critical thinking The process of deciding what to believe and how to act based on careful evaluation of the evidence.

Cryptomnesia A memory illusion in which people believe that some work they have done is a novel creation when, in fact, it is not original.

Crystallized intelligence The ability to acquire knowledge through experience and to use that knowledge to solve familiar problems.

Culture The total lifestyle of people from a particular social grouping, including all the ideas, symbols, preferences, and material objects they share.

Culture-bound syndromes Psychological disorders found only in a few cultural groups.

Culture of honor A belief system in which males are socialized to protect their reputation by resorting to violence.

Daydreaming A relatively passive state of waking consciousness that involves turning attention away from external stimuli to internal thoughts and imaginary situations.

Decay Forgetting due to the passage of time.

Defense mechanisms In Freud's theory, the ego's methods of keeping threatening and unacceptable material out of consciousness and thereby reducing anxiety.

Déjà vu illusion A memory illusion in which people feel a sense of familiarity in a situation that they know they have never encountered before.

Delta waves Slow, high-amplitude brain waves most typical of stage 4 deep sleep.

Dendrites Branchlike extensions of the soma that receive information from other neurons.

Deoxyribonucleic acid (DNA) The complex molecular strands of a chromosome that contain thousands of different genes, located at fixed positions.

Dependent variable The experimental variable that is measured because it is believed to depend on the manipulated changes in the independent variable.

Depressants Psychoactive drugs that slow down—or depress—the nervous system and decrease mental and physical activity.

Depression A mood disorder characterized by extreme and persistent negative moods and the inability to experience pleasure from activities previously enjoyed.

Depth perception The ability to perceive objects three-dimensionally.

Descriptive statistics Numbers that summarize and describe the behavior or characteristics of a particular sample of participants in a study.

Determinism The belief that all events have causes.

Development The systematic physical, cognitive, and social changes in the individual that occur between conception and death.

Diagnosis The process of distinguishing one disorder from another.

Diagnostic and Statistical Manual of Mental Disorders (DSM) The manual of psychological disorders published by the American Psychiatric Association and used for descriptive diagnoses.

Diathesis-stress model A predisposition to a given disorder (diathesis) that combines with environmental stressors to trigger a psychological disorder.

Difference threshold The smallest difference between two stimuli that can be detected half the time; also called *just-noticeable difference*, or *jnd*.

Diffusion of responsibility The belief that the presence of others in a situation makes one less personally responsible for events that occur in that situation.

Discrimination A negative and/or patronizing action toward members of a specific social group.

Displacement A defense mechanism that diverts people's sexual or aggressive urges toward objects that are more acceptable than those that actually stimulate their feelings.

Dissociative amnesia A dissociative disorder characterized by a sudden loss of memory of one's identity and other personal information.

Dissociative disorders Psychological disorders characterized by disruptions in consciousness, memory, sense of identity, or perception.

Dissociative fugue A dissociative disorder characterized by a sudden departure from home or work, combined with the loss of memory of identity and the assumption of a new identity.

Dissociative identity disorder (DID) A dissociative disorder characterized by the presence of two or more distinct identities or personalities that take turns controlling the person's behavior; also known as *multiple personality disorder.*

Divergent thinking Pursuing many different and often unconventional paths to generate many different solutions to a problem.

Divided attention Attention that is split and simultaneously focused on different stimuli.

Dopamine (DA) A neurotransmitter that promotes and facilitates movement as well as influencing thought and emotion.

Down syndrome A form of mental retardation caused by an extra chromosome in an individual's genetic makeup.

Dream A storylike sequence of vivid visual images experienced during sleep.

Drive A physiological state of arousal that moves an organism to meet a need.

Drive-reduction theory The idea that an imbalance in homeostasis creates a physiological need, which in turn produces a drive that motivates the organism to satisfy the need.

Drug abuse Persistence in drug use even when impaired behavior or social functioning results.

Drug tolerance An effect of drug abuse in which greater amounts of the drug are necessary to produce the same effect once produced by a smaller dose.

Dysthymia Chronic low-level depression lasting more than 2 years.

Eardrum A thin, flexible membrane at the end of the auditory canal that vibrates in sequence with sound waves.

Eclectic approach An approach to psychotherapy in which techniques from various theoretical perspectives are used in treating psychological disorders.

Ego The part of our minds that includes our consciousness and that balances the demands of the id, the superego, and reality.

Egocentrism The tendency to view the world from one's own perspective without recognizing that others may have different points of view.

Elaboration likelihood model A theory that there are two ways in which persuasive messages can cause attitude change, each differing in the amount of cognitive effort or elaboration they require.

Elaborative rehearsal Rehearsal that involves thinking about how new information relates to information already stored in long-term memory.

Electroconvulsive therapy (ECT) A physiological treatment for severe depression in which a brief electrical shock is administered to the brain of an anesthetized patient.

Electroencephalograph (EEG) An instrument that records "waves" of electrical activity in the brain using metal electrodes placed on a person's scalp.

Embryonic stage The second stage of prenatal development, lasting from the third week through the eighth week of pregnancy.

Emotion A positive or negative feeling state that typically includes some combination of physiological arousal, cognitive appraisal, and behavioral expression.

Emotional intelligence The ability to recognize and regulate our own and others' emotions.

Emotion-focused coping A coping strategy designed to manage the emotional reactions to stressors rather than to try to change the stressors themselves.

Empty-chair technique A Gestalt technique in which clients engage in emotional expression by imagining that the person to whom they would like to speak is sitting in an empty chair facing them.

Encoding The first memory process, in which information is organized and transformed so it can be entered into memory.

Encoding specificity principle A retrieval rule stating that retrieving information from long-term memory is most likely when the conditions at retrieval closely match the conditions present during the original learning.

Endocrine system A network of glands in various parts of the body that manufacture and secrete hormones directly into the bloodstream.

Endorphins A family of neurotransmitters that are similar to morphine and that play an important role in the experience of pleasure and the control of pain.

Episodic memory Memory for factual information acquired at a specific time and place.

Erotophobia The tendency to respond to sexual cues negatively.

Ethnic identity A person's sense of personal identification with a particular ethnic group.

Ethnocentrism A pattern of increased hostility toward outgroups, accompanied by increased loyalty to one's ingroup.

Etiology The initial cause that led to the development of the disorder.

Eugenics The practice of encouraging supposedly superior people to reproduce, while discouraging or even preventing from doing so those judged to be inferior.

Evolution The genetic changes that occur in a species over generations due to natural selection.

Evolutionary psychology An approach to psychology based on the principle of natural selection.

Existential therapy A philosophical approach to treating clients who are experiencing distress principally related to a lack of meaning in their lives.

Experimental condition The condition in an experiment whereby participants are exposed to different levels of the independent variable.

Experimental research Research designed to test cause-effect relationships between variables.

Explicit memory Memory of previous experiences that one can consciously recollect; also called *declarative memory.*

External attribution An attribution that locates the cause of an event in factors external to the person, such as luck, other people, or the situation.

Extinction In classical conditioning, the gradual weakening and disappearance of the conditioned response when the conditioned stimulus is repeatedly presented without being paired with the unconditioned stimulus.

Extrasensory perception (ESP) The ability to perceive events without using normal sensory receptors.

Extravert A person who is focused on the external world and tends to be confident and socially outgoing.

Extrinsic motivation Motivation to engage in a behavior or an activity because of the external rewards it can provide.

Facial feedback hypothesis A theory of emotion proposing that specific facial expressions trigger the subjective experience of specific emotions.

Factor analysis A statistical technique that allows researchers to identify clusters of variables or test items that correlate with one another.

Family systems therapy A form of family therapy in which the family is treated as a dynamic system, with each member an important interacting element in that system.

Family therapies Therapies designed to constructively modify the dysfunctional relationships among family members.

Fantasy-prone personality A person who has regular, vivid fantasies and who sometimes cannot separate fantasy from reality.

Feature detectors Cells in the visual cortex that respond only to a highly specific feature of a visual stimulus, such as a straight edge, an angle, movement of a spot, or brightness.

Fetal alcohol syndrome Physical and cognitive abnormalities in children that result when pregnant women consume large quantities of alcohol.

Fetal stage The last and longest stage in prenatal development, extending from the ninth week after conception until birth.

Figure-ground relationship The Gestalt principle that, when people focus on an object in their perceptual field, they automatically distinguish it from its surroundings.

Five-factor model A trait theory asserting that personality consists of five traits (neuroticism, extraversion, openness to experience, agreeableness, and conscientiousness).

Fixation A tendency to persist in pleasure-seeking behaviors associated with an earlier psychosexual stage during which conflicts were unresolved.

Fixed-interval schedule A partial reinforcement schedule that reinforces the first response after a fixed time interval has elapsed.

Fixed-ratio schedule A partial reinforcement schedule that reinforces a response after a specified number of nonreinforced responses.

Flashbulb memories Detailed and vivid memories of surprising and emotion-provoking events.

Fluid intelligence The ability to understand the relationships between things in the absence of past experience and the mental capacity to develop strategies for dealing with new kinds of problems.

Flynn effect The tendency for people's performance on IQ tests to improve from one generation to the next.

Forebrain Region of the brain above the midbrain that contains the thalamus, the hypothalamus, and the limbic system.

Formal operational stage The fourth and final stage in Piaget's theory of cognitive development (ages 11 or beyond), during which a person is able to reason abstractly and make predictions about hypothetical situations.

Form perception The process by which sensations are organized into meaningful shapes and patterns.

Fovea The retina's area of central focus.

Framing The way in which choices are structured.

Fraternal twins Twins who develop from the union of two separate sperm and eggs; also known as *dizygotic twins*.

Free association A psychodynamic therapy technique developed by Freud, in which clients say whatever comes to mind, without making any effort to inhibit their speech.

Free will The belief that there are absolutely no limitations on people's power of free choice.

Frequency theory A theory that pitch is determined by the frequency with which the basilar membrane vibrates.

Frontal lobe One of the four major sections of the cerebral cortex, situated in the front of each cerebral hemisphere and behind the forehead; involved in the coordination of movement and higher mental processes.

Functional fixedness The tendency to think of objects as functioning in fixed and unchanging ways and ignoring other less obvious ways in which they might be used.

Functionalism An early approach to psychology that studied how the conscious mind helps humans survive and successfully adapt to their environment.

Functional magnetic resonance imaging (fMRI) A brain-imaging technique that measures over a few seconds the average neural activity in different brain regions by showing fluctuations in blood oxygen levels.

Fundamental attribution error The tendency to make internal attributions rather than external attributions in explaining the behavior of others.

Gate-control theory A theory of pain perception proposing that small and large nerve fibers open and close "gateways" for pain in the spinal cord.

Gender The meanings that societies and individuals attach to being female and male.

Gender identity The knowledge that one is a male or a female and the internalization of this fact into the self-concept.

Gene The basic biochemical unit of inheritance that is located on and transmitted by chromosomes.

General adaptation syndrome (GAS) Selye's model of stress, in which an event that threatens an organism's well-being (a stressor) leads to a three-stage bodily response: alarm, resistance, and exhaustion.

General intelligence factor (g-factor) An intelligence factor that Spearman and other researchers believed underlies all mental abilities.

Generalized anxiety disorder (GAD) An anxiety disorder characterized by a constant state of moderate anxiety.

Generic masculine The use of masculine nouns and pronouns to refer to all people, instead of just males.

Genital stage In Freud's theory, the last stage of psychosexual development during which mature sexual feelings toward others begin to emerge, and the ego learns to manage and direct these feelings.

Genotype The underlying genetic composition of an organism.

Gestalt An organized and coherent whole.

Gestalt psychology An approach to psychology that studies how the mind actively organizes stimuli into coherent wholes.

Gestalt therapy A humanistic psychotherapy that stresses awareness of feelings in the here and now.

Glial cells Non-neuron cells that supply the neurons with support, nutrients, and insulation.

Gonads The two sex glands, called ovaries in females and testes in males.

Grammar The system of rules that determines the proper use and combination of language symbols.

Group therapy The simultaneous treatment of several clients under the guidance of a therapist.

Gustation The sense of taste.

Hallucinogens Psychoactive drugs that distort perception and generate sensory images without any external stimulation.

Happiness A predominance of positive over negative affect (emotion) and satisfaction with life as a whole.

Hardiness A set of personality traits marked by a sense of commitment, challenge, and control that promotes resistance to stress and illness.

Health psychologists Psychologists who study the effects of behavior and mental processes on health and illness.

Heritability coefficient A statistical coefficient, ranging from 0 to 1, that estimates the degree to which heredity determines intelligence within a particular human group.

Heterosexism A system of cultural beliefs, values, and customs that exalts heterosexuality and denies, denigrates, and stigmatizes any nonheterosexual form of behavior or identity.

Heterosexuality The sexual orientation in which a person is sexually attracted primarily to members of the other sex.

Heuristic A problem-solving strategy that involves following a general rule of thumb to reduce the number of possible solutions.

Hierarchy of needs Maslow's progression of human needs, in which those that are the most basic—namely, physiological needs—must be sufficiently satisfied before higher-level safety needs and then psychological needs become activated.

Higher-order conditioning A classical conditioning procedure in which a neutral stimulus becomes a conditioned stimulus after being paired with an existing conditioned stimulus.

Hindbrain Region of the brain above the spinal cord that contains the medulla, the pons, and the cerebellum.

Hindsight bias The tendency, once an event has occurred, to overestimate our ability to have foreseen the outcome.

Homeostasis The tendency for organisms to keep physiological systems internally balanced by adjusting them in response to change.

Homosexuality The sexual orientation in which a person is sexually attracted primarily to members of the same sex.

Hormones Chemical signals manufactured and secreted into the blood in one part of the body that affect other parts of the body.

Hostile aggression The intentional use of harmful behavior with the goal of causing injury or death to the victim.

Humanistic perspective An approach to psychology that emphasizes human beings' innate capacity for personal growth and their ability to consciously make choices.

Humanistic therapies Psychotherapies that help people get in touch with their feelings, with their "true selves," and with their purpose in life.

Hypnogogic state Stage 1 in the sleep cycle; a brief transitional state between wakefulness and sleep, usually lasting only a few minutes.

Hypnosis A psychological state of altered attention and awareness in which a person is unusually receptive to suggestions.

Hypnotizability The degree to which a person can enter a deep hypnotic state.

Hypochondriasis A somatoform disorder characterized by excessive preoccupation with or fear of developing some physical condition.

Hypothalamus A part of the forebrain involved in regulating basic biological processes, such as eating, drinking, sexual activity, emotion, and a stable body temperature.

Hypotheses Specific propositions or expectations about the nature of things derived from a theory.

Id An unconscious part of the mind that contains our sexual and aggressive drives.

Identical twins Twins who develop from the union of the same egg and sperm, and thus share exactly the same genotype; also known as *monozygotic twins*.

Imaginary audience Adolescents' belief that their thoughts, feelings, and behavior are constantly being focused on by other people.

Immune system A complex surveillance system of specialized cells, tissues, and organs that is the body's primary defense against disease.

Implicit memory Memory of previous experiences without conscious recollection; also called *nondeclarative memory*.

Implicit personality theory People's assumptions or naive belief systems about which personality traits go together.

Impression formation The process of integrating various sources of information about a person into an overall judgment.

Incentive A positive or negative environmental stimulus that motivates behavior.

Incentive theory A theory of motivation stating that behavior is directed toward attaining desirable stimuli, called positive incentives, and avoiding undesirable stimuli, called negative incentives.

Independent variable The experimental variable that the researcher manipulates.

Individualism A philosophy of life stressing the priority of personal goals over group goals, a preference for loosely knit social relationships, and a desire to be relatively autonomous of others' influence.

Induced movement The illusory movement of a stationary object caused by the movement of another nearby object.

Infantile amnesia The inability to remember events that occurred during the early part of life (usually before the age of 3).

Inferential statistics Mathematical analyses that move beyond mere description of research data to make inferences about the larger population from which the sample was drawn.

Information-processing model A memory model concerning the sequential processing and use of information, involving encoding, storage, and retrieval.

Insight A problem-solving strategy that involves a sudden realization of how a problem can be solved.

Insomnia A common sleep disorder characterized by the chronic inability to fall or stay asleep.

Instinct An unlearned, relatively fixed pattern of behavior that is essential to a species' survival.

Instinctive drift Species-specific behavior patterns that interfere with operant conditioning.

Instrumental aggression The intentional use of harmful behavior in order to achieve some other goal.

Intelligence The mental abilities necessary to adapt to and shape the environment.

Intelligence quotient (IQ) Originally, the ratio of mental age to chronological age multiplied by 100 (MA/CA $\times$ 100). Today, IQ is calculated by comparing how a person's performance deviates from the average score of her or his same-age peers, which is 100.

Interactionism The study of the combined effects of both the situation and the person on human behavior.

Intergroup anxiety The tension and distress sometimes experienced when interacting with a person from a different social group.

Internal attribution An attribution that locates the cause of an event in factors internal to the person, such as personality traits, moods, attitudes, abilities, or effort.

Internalization A process of cognition in which people absorb knowledge from their social surroundings.

Interneurons Neurons that connect the sensory neurons' input signals with the motor neurons' output signals. One of their most important functions is to link other neurons to one another.

Intrinsic motivation Motivation to engage in a behavior or an activity because one finds it interesting or enjoyable for its own sake.

Introvert A person who is preoccupied with his or her inner world and tends to be hesitant and cautious when interacting with people.

Iris A ring of muscles in the eye that range in color from light blue to dark brown.

James-Lange theory A theory stating that emotion-provoking events induce specific physiological changes in the autonomic nervous system, which our brain automatically interprets as specific emotions.

Jealousy The negative emotional reaction experienced when a real or imagined rival threatens a relationship important to one's self-concept.

Kinesthetic sense A type of proprioceptive sense that provides information about the movement and location of body parts with respect to one another.

Language A systematic way of communicating information using symbols and rules for combining them.

Language acquisition device According to Chomsky's linguistic theory, an innate mechanism that facilitates the learning of language.

Latency stage In Freud's theory, the fourth stage of psychosexual development during which the child is relatively free from sexual desires and conflict.

Latent content The true meaning of the dream that is concealed from the dreamer through the symbols that make up the manifest dream content.

Latent learning Learning that occurs without apparent reinforcement and is not demonstrated until sufficient reinforcement is provided.

Law of effect A basic principle of learning that states that a behavior becomes more or less likely based on its effect in producing desirable or undesirable consequences.

Laws of grouping Simple Gestalt principles describing how people tend to group discrete stimuli together into a meaningful whole.

Learned helplessness The passive resignation produced by repeated exposure to aversive events that cannot be avoided.

Learning A relatively permanent change in behavior that results from experience.

Lens An elastic, disc-shaped structure that focuses light.

Limbic system A part of the forebrain consisting of structures that influence fear and aggression (amygdala) and the acquisition and consolidation of new information in memory (hippocampus).

Linguistic relativity hypothesis The proposal that the structure of language determines the structure of thought, meaning that people who speak different languages also think differently.

Locus of control The degree to which we expect that outcomes in our lives depend on our own actions and personal characteristics versus the actions of uncontrollable environmental forces.

Longitudinal study Research in which the same people are restudied and retested over time.

Long-term memory A durable memory system that has an immense capacity for information storage.

Long-term potentiation The long-lasting strengthening of synaptic transmission along a specific neural circuit, which is believed to be the neural basis for long-term memory.

LSD A synthesized chemical that is the most potent of the hallucinogens; induces hallucinations, distortions, and a blending of sensory experiences.

Lucid dream A dream in which the dreamer is aware of dreaming and is often able to change the plot of the dream.

Magnetic resonance imaging (MRI) A brain-imaging technique that produces three-dimensional images of the brain's soft tissues by detecting magnetic activity from nuclear particles in brain molecules.

Maintenance rehearsal The process of repetitively verbalizing or thinking about information to either extend the usual 18-second duration of short-term memory or transfer the rehearsed information to long-term memory.

Managed care system A system of insured health care in which the insurance company may determine such issues as which therapists clients may choose, the number of sessions permitted, and which drugs are prescribed.

Mania An excessively elated, active emotional state.

Manifest content The dream that is remembered by the dreamer.

Marijuana A mild hallucinogen derived from the leafy material of the hemp, or *Cannabis*, plant; often induces a sense of giddiness or euphoria, as well as heightened sensitivity to various stimuli.

Matching hypothesis The proposition that people are attracted to others who are similar to them in certain characteristics, such as attitudes and physical attractiveness.

Mean The arithmetic average of a distribution, obtained by adding all the scores and then dividing by the number of scores.

Median The middle score in a distribution; half the scores are above it and half are below it.

Medical model The viewpoint from the field of medicine that psychological disorders have a biological basis and can be classified into discrete categories just as physical diseases are.

Meditation A variety of mental exercises that alter the normal flow of consciousness in order to enhance self-knowledge.

Medulla A part of the hindbrain that controls breathing, heart rate, swallowing, and digestion, as well as allowing us to maintain an upright posture.

Memory The mental process by which information is encoded and stored in the brain, and later retrieved.

Menarche The first menstrual period.

Menopause The ending of menstruation.

Mental retardation A diagnostic category used for people who not only have an IQ score below 70 but also have difficulty adapting to the routine demands of independent living.

Mental set The tendency to continue using solutions that have worked in the past, even though a better alternative may exist.

Mere exposure effect The tendency to develop more positive feelings toward objects and individuals the more frequently we are exposed to them.

Meta-analysis The use of statistical techniques to sum up a body of similar studies in order to objectively estimate the reliability and overall size of the effect.

Metacognition An awareness and understanding of one's own cognitive processes.

Midbrain The region of the brain above the hindbrain that contains the reticular formation.

Minnesota Multiphasic Personality Inventory (MMPI) An objective personality test consisting of true-false items that measure various personality dimensions and clinical conditions such as depression.

Misinformation effects Distortions and alterations in witnesses' memories due to receiving misleading information during questioning.

Mnemonics Strategies that make it easier to encode, store, and/or retrieve information.

Mode The score that occurs most frequently in a distribution.

Modeling A behavioral method of psychotherapy in which desirable behaviors are demonstrated as a way of teaching them to clients.

Molecular genetics The subdiscipline in biology that studies the molecular structure and function of genes to determine how they influence behavior.

Monocular cues Depth cues that require information from only one eye.

Mood disorders Psychological disorders characterized by emotional extremes that cause significant disruption in daily functioning.

Moon illusion A perceptual illusion in which the moon appears to be about 1½ times larger when near the horizon than when high in the sky.

Morpheme The smallest unit of language that carries meaning.

Motivated forgetting Forgetting due to a desire to eliminate awareness of some unpleasant or disturbing memory.

Motivation An inner state that energizes behavior toward the fulfillment of a goal.

Motor neurons Neurons that send commands from the brain to glands, muscles, and organs to do, cease, or inhibit something.

Müeller-Lyer illusion A perceptual illusion in which the perceived length of a line is influenced by placing inward- or outward-facing wings on the ends of the line.

Multiple intelligences Gardner's theory contends that there are at least eight distinct and relatively independent intelligences (linguistic, logical-mathematical, spatial, musical, bodily-kinesthetic, naturalist, interpersonal, and intrapersonal), all of which are differently developed in each of us.

Myelin sheath A protective coating of fatty material around an axon that hastens the transmission of the electrochemical charge.

Narcolepsy A sleep disorder characterized by uncontrollable REM sleep attacks during normal waking hours.

Naturalistic observation A descriptive scientific method that investigates behavior in its usual natural environment.

Natural selection The process by which organisms with inherited traits best suited to the environment reproduce more successfully than less well-adapted organisms over a number of generations. Natural selection leads to evolutionary changes.

Nature-nurture debate The question of whether individual differences in behavior are primarily due to inborn biological processes or to environmental factors.

Near-death experience An altered state of consciousness episode in which a person is either briefly clinically dead or in extreme danger of clinical death.

Need for achievement (n-Ach) A desire to overcome obstacles and meet high standards of excellence.

Need for cognition A person's preference for and tendency to engage in effortful cognitive activities.

Negative punishers Stimuli that weaken a response by removing a positive stimulus after a response.

Negative reinforcers Stimuli that strengthen a response by removing an aversive or unpleasant stimulus after a response.

Neodissociation theory A theory that hypnotized persons enter an altered state in which two streams of consciousness operate simultaneously, one actively responding to suggestions and the other passively observing what is going on.

Nerve A bundle of axons from many neurons that are routed together in the peripheral nervous system.

Neurons Specialized cells in the nervous system that send and receive information.

Neuroscience perspective An approach to psychology that attempts to understand behavior and mental processes by examining the nervous system.

Neurotransmitters Chemical messengers released by the synaptic vesicles that travel across the synaptic cleft and either excite or inhibit adjacent neurons.

Night terrors A sleep disorder involving panic attacks that occur during early-night stage 4 NREM sleep.

Nonconscious mimicry The tendency to adopt the behaviors, postures, or mannerisms of interaction partners, without conscious awareness or intention.

Nonverbal communication The sending and receiving of information using gestures, expressions, vocal cues, and body movements rather than words.

Normal distribution The bell-shaped appearance of a distribution that results when the mean, median, and mode are identical in value.

Obedience The performance of an action in response to a direct order.

Obesity The excessive accumulation of body fat. Medically, a person with a body mass index (BMI) over 30 is considered obese.

Objective test A personality test that asks direct, unambiguous questions about a person's thoughts, feelings, and behavior.

Object permanence The realization that an object continues to exist even if you can't see it or touch it.

Observational learning Learning a behavior by observing and imitating the behavior of others (models).

Obsessive-compulsive disorder (OCD) An anxiety disorder characterized by repetitive, unwanted, and distressing actions and/or thoughts.

Occipital lobe One of the four major sections of the cerebral cortex, located at the back of each cerebral hemisphere; primarily responsible for visual processing.

Off-line dream theory A theory that the cognitive process of dreaming consolidates and stores information gathered during the day, thus allowing us to maintain a smaller and more efficient brain.

Olfaction The sense of smell.

Olfactory epithelium A thin layer of tissue at the top of the nasal cavity that contains the olfactory receptor cells.

Open-ended statement A therapy technique in which the therapist encourages the client to speak, without limiting the topic of conversation.

Operant conditioning A type of learning in which behavior is strengthened if followed by reinforcement and weakened if followed by punishment.

Operational definition A scientist's precise description of how a variable has been quantified so that it can be measured.

Opiates A category of depressant drugs, including opium, morphine, and heroin, that depress the nervous system, temporarily relieve pain, and produce a relaxed, dreamlike state.

Opponent-process theory *(1)* A theory of emotion suggesting that every emotion triggers an opposite emotion. *(2)* A theory proposing that color perception depends on receptors that make opposing responses to three pairs of colors.

Optic nerve The bundle of nerve cells that carries information from the retina to the brain.

Optimistic explanatory style The habitual tendency to explain uncontrollable negative events as caused by temporary factors external to oneself that do not affect other aspects of one's life. This optimistic style is associated with good health and longevity.

Oral stage In Freud's theory, the first stage of psychosexual development, during which the child derives pleasure by engaging in oral activities.

Panic disorder An anxiety disorder characterized by episodes of intense fear and dread that usually occur suddenly and unexpectedly.

Parallel distributed processing models Models of memory in which a large network of interconnected neurons, or processing units, distributed throughout the brain simultaneously work on different memory tasks.

Paraphrasing A therapy technique in which the therapist summarizes the expressed verbal content of the client's statements.

Parapsychology The field that studies ESP and other paranormal phenomena.

Parasympathetic nervous system The part of the autonomic nervous system that acts to conserve and maintain the body's energy resources.

Parietal lobe One of the four major sections of the cerebral cortex, situated in front of the occipital lobe in each cerebral hemisphere; involved in touch sensation and in monitoring the body's position in space.

Partial reinforcement A schedule of reinforcement in which correct responses are followed by reinforcers only part of the time.

Participant observation A descriptive scientific method in which a group is studied from within by a researcher who records behavior as it occurs in its usual natural environment.

Passionate love A state of intense longing for union with another that we typically experience most intensely during the early stages of a romantic relationship.

Peak experience A fleeting but intense moment when a person feels happy, absorbed, and extremely capable.

Perception The process that organizes sensations into meaningful objects and events.

Perceptual constancy The tendency to perceive objects as relatively stable despite continually changing sensory information.

Perceptual illusion A misperception of physical reality, often due to the misapplication of perceptual principles.

Perceptual sets Expectations that create a tendency to interpret sensory information in a particular way.

Peripheral nervous system That portion of the nervous system containing all the nerves outside the brain and spinal cord.

Personal fable The tendency for adolescents to believe that their experiences and feelings are unique.

Personality The consistent and distinctive thoughts, feelings, and behaviors an individual engages in.

Personality disorders Psychological disorders characterized by general styles of living that are ineffective and that lead to problems.

Personality style A collection or constellation of traits that describes the functioning of the person across situations and settings.

Persuasion The process of consciously attempting to change attitudes through the transmission of some message.

Pessimistic explanatory style The habitual tendency to explain uncontrollable negative events as caused by one's own stable personal qualities, which affect all aspects of one's life. This pessimistic style is associated with health problems and premature death.

Phallic stage In Freud's theory, the third stage of psychosexual development during which the child derives pleasure from masturbation.

Phenotype The visible and measurable traits of an organism.

Pheromones Airborne chemicals released by animals and detected by other animals using specialized receptors. Pheromones affect the behavior of other animals of the same species.

Phobic disorder An anxiety disorder characterized by strong irrational fears of specific objects or situations.

Phoneme The smallest significant sound unit in speech.

Phonology The rules used in language to combine basic sounds into words.

Physical attractiveness stereotype The belief that physically attractive individuals possess socially desirable personality traits and lead happier, more fulfilling lives than less attractive persons do.

Pituitary gland The body's "master" gland, located in the base of the brain, whose hormones stimulate and regulate the rest of the endocrine system.

Placebo effect A situation in which people experience some change or improvement from an empty, fake, or ineffectual treatment.

Place theory A theory that pitch is determined by which place along the cochlea's basilar membrane is most activated.

Play therapy A therapeutic technique in which the therapist provides children with toys and drawing materials on the assumption that whatever is troubling them will be expressed in their play.

Pleasure principle The process by which the id seeks to immediately satisfy whatever desire is currently active.

Polygraph A machine that measures several of the physiological responses accompanying emotion (such as respiration, heart rate, blood pressure, and palm perspiration).

Pons A part of the hindbrain that is concerned with sleep and arousal.

Ponzo illusion A perceptual illusion in which the perceived lengths of horizontal lines are influenced by their placement between vertical converging lines that serve as distance cues.

Population All the members of an identifiable group from which a sample is drawn.

Positive psychology A relatively new scientific approach to studying optimal human functioning that asserts that the normal functioning of human beings cannot be accounted for within purely negative (or problem-focused) frames of reference.

Positive punishers Stimuli that weaken a response by presenting an aversive stimulus after a response.

Positive reinforcers Stimuli that strengthen a response by presenting a positive stimulus after a response.

Positron emission tomography (PET) A brain-imaging technique that measures over several minutes the average amount of neural activity in different brain regions by showing each region's consumption of the sugar glucose, the brain's chemical fuel.

Postconventional morality The third and final level of moral reasoning in Kohlberg's theory of moral development; characterized by making moral judgments based on abstract universal principles.

Post-traumatic stress disorder (PTSD) An anxiety disorder characterized by flashbacks and recurrent thoughts of life-threatening or other traumatic events.

Preconscious mind According to Freud, those mental processes that are not currently conscious but could become so at any moment.

Preconventional morality The first level of moral reasoning in Kohlberg's theory of moral development; characterized by avoiding punishment and seeking rewards.

Predictive validity The degree to which a test predicts other observable behavior related to the characteristic the test supposedly measures; also known as *criterion validity.*

Prejudice Attitudes toward members of specific groups that directly or indirectly suggest they deserve an inferior social status.

Premack principle The principle stating that more preferred activities act as reinforcers for less preferred activities.

Prenatal development The many changes that transform a fertilized egg into a newborn baby.

Preoperational stage The second stage in Piaget's theory of cognitive development (ages 2 to 7), marked by the full emergence of representational thought.

Primacy effect The increased memory for the first bits of information presented in a string of information.

Primary reinforcers Stimuli that are naturally reinforcing because they satisfy some biological need.

Primary sex characteristics The body organs that make sexual reproduction possible.

Priming A method of activating implicit memories, in which a recently presented bit of information facilitates—or "primes"—responses in a subsequent situation.

Private speech Overt language that is not directed to others but, rather, is self-directed.

Proactive interference Forgetting due to interference from previously learned information.

Problem-focused coping A coping strategy designed to reduce the stress by overcoming the source of the problem.

Problem solving The thought process employed to overcome obstacles.

Problem-solving theory A theory stating that dreams provide people with the opportunity to creatively solve their everyday problems.

Procedural memory Memory of how to perform skilled motor activities, which have become well-learned habits and are carried out automatically (without conscious thought).

Prodigies Individuals who easily master skills in a particular intellectual area.

Prognosis A prediction about the likely course of a disorder.

Progressive relaxation A stress-reducing technique that involves the successive tensing and relaxing of each of the major muscle groups of the body.

Projection A powerful defense mechanism in which people perceive their own aggressive or sexual urges not in themselves, but in others.

Projective test A psychological test that asks people to respond to ambiguous stimuli or situations in ways that will reveal their unconscious motives and desires.

Proprioceptive senses Two additional sources of sensory information that detect body position and movement.

Prototype The most representative member of a concept.

Psychiatry A branch of medicine concerned with the diagnosis and treatment of psychological disorders. The roughly comparable specialty area in psychology is known as clinical psychology.

Psychoactive drugs Chemicals that modify mental processes and behavior.

Psychoanalysis An approach to psychology that studies how the unconscious mind shapes behavior.

Psychodynamic perspective A diverse group of theories descended from the work of Sigmund Freud that assert that behavior is controlled by unconscious forces.

Psychodynamic therapies A diverse group of psychotherapies based on the work of Sigmund Freud that assert that psychological disorders stem primarily from unconscious forces.

Psychological disorder A pattern of atypical behavior that results in personal distress or significant impairment in a person's social or occupational functioning.

Psychology The scientific study of mental processes and behavior.

Psychometrics The measurement of intelligence, personality, and other mental processes.

Psychoneuroimmunology The interdisciplinary field that studies the relationship between psychological factors and physical illness.

Psychophysics The study of how physical stimuli are translated into psychological experience.

Psychophysiological disorders Physical conditions, such as high blood pressure and migraine headaches, that are caused or aggravated by psychological factors such as stress.

Psychosexual stages The fixed sequence of childhood developmental stages during which the id primarily seeks sexual pleasure by focusing its energies on distinct erogenous zones.

Psychosurgery A rarely used surgical procedure to treat psychological disorders in which brain tissue thought to be the cause of the disorder is destroyed.

Psychotherapy The treatment of psychological disorders by employing psychological methods that include a personal relationship between a trained therapist and a client.

Puberty The growth period of sexual maturation, during which a person becomes capable of reproducing.

Punishment The process by which a stimulus decreases the probability of the behavior it follows.

Pupil A hole in the center of the iris that regulates how much light enters the eye.

Random assignment Placement of research participants into experimental conditions in a manner that guarantees that all have an equal chance of being exposed to each level of the independent variable.

Random selection A procedure for selecting a sample of people to study in which everyone in the population has an equal chance of being chosen.

Range The difference between the lowest and highest values in a distribution.

Rape myth The false belief that deep down, women enjoy forcible sex and find it sexually exciting.

Rational-emotive behavior therapy (REBT) The cognitive therapy of Albert Ellis, in which people are confronted with their irrational beliefs and persuaded to develop a more realistic way of thinking.

Rationalization A defense mechanism in which people offer logical self-justifying explanations for their actions in place of the real, more anxiety-producing, unconscious reasons.

Reaction formation A defense mechanism that allows people to express unacceptable feelings or ideas by consciously expressing their exact opposite.

Reaction range The extent to which genetically determined limits on IQ may increase or decrease due to environmental factors.

Realistic group conflict theory A theory of prejudice contending that when two groups compete for scarce resources this competition creates a breeding ground for prejudice.

Reality principle The process by which the ego seeks to delay gratification of id desires until appropriate outlets and situations can be found.

Recall A measure of explicit memory in which a person must retrieve and reproduce information from memory.

Recency effect The increased memory for the last bits of information presented in a string of information.

Reciprocal determinism The social-cognitive belief that personality emerges from an ongoing mutual interaction among people's cognitions, their actions, and their environment.

Reciprocity norm The expectation that one should return a favor or a good deed.

Recognition A measure of explicit memory in which a person need only decide whether or not something has been previously encountered.

Reflection A therapy technique in which the therapist acknowledges an emotion that the client has expressed verbally or nonverbally.

Reflex An automatic, involuntary response to sensory stimuli; many reflexes are facilitated by the spinal nerves.

Regression A defense mechanism in which people faced with intense anxiety psychologically retreat to a more infantile developmental stage at which some psychic energy remains fixated.

Reinforcement The process by which a stimulus increases the probability of the behavior that it follows.

Reinforcer Any stimulus or event that increases the likelihood that the behavior preceding it will be repeated.

Reliability The degree to which a test yields consistent results.

REM (rapid eye movement) sleep A relatively active phase in the sleep cycle, characterized by rapid eye movements, in which dreaming occurs.

Replication Repeating a previous study's scientific procedures using different participants in an attempt to duplicate the findings.

Representativeness heuristic The tendency to make decisions based on how closely an alternative matches (or represents) a particular prototype.

Repression In Freud's theory, a very basic defense mechanism in which people move anxiety-arousing thoughts from the conscious mind into the unconscious mind.

Resistance Anything the client does to interfere with therapeutic progress.

Response prevention A counterconditioning technique commonly used in the treatment of obsessive-compulsive disorder. Clients are exposed to the situation in which they previously exhibited a compulsive behavior but are not permitted to engage in the ritual.

Resting potential The stable, negative charge of an inactive neuron.

Reticular formation A part of the midbrain involved in the regulation and maintenance of consciousness.

Retina A light-sensitive surface at the back of the eye.

Retrieval The third memory process, which involves recovering stored information from memory so it can be used.

Retrieval cue A stimulus that allows us to more easily recall information from long-term memory.

Retroactive interference Forgetting due to interference from newly learned information.

Retrograde amnesia The loss of information previously stored in long-term memory due to physical injury to the brain.

Rods Receptor neurons in the eye located at the edges of the retina that are sensitive to the brightness of light.

Rorschach inkblot test A projective personality test in which people are shown 10 symmetrical inkblots and asked what each might be depicting.

Sample A group of subjects who are selected to participate in a research study.

Satiety Being full to satisfaction—in this case, with food.

Savants Mentally retarded individuals who demonstrate exceptional ability in one specific intellectual area.

Schema An organized cluster of knowledge that people use to understand and interpret information.

Schizophrenia Psychological disorders characterized by severe impairment in thinking, such as hallucinations, delusions, or loose associations.

Scientific method A set of procedures used in science to gather, analyze, and interpret information in a way that reduces error and leads to dependable generalizations.

Seasonal affective disorder (SAD) A subtype of depression characterized by depressive symptoms during the winter months, when daylight hours are reduced.

Secondary reinforcers Stimuli that are learned and become reinforcing by being associated with primary reinforcers.

Secondary sex characteristics The nonreproductive physical features that distinguish the two sexes from one another.

Sedatives Depressants that in mild doses produce relaxation, mild euphoria, and reduced inhibitions.

Selective attention The focused awareness on a single stimulus to the exclusion of all others.

Self-actualization The ultimate goal of growth, being the realization of one's full potential.

Self-awareness A psychological state in which you focus on yourself as an object of attention.

Self-concept The "theory" or "story" that a person constructs about herself or himself through social interaction.

Self-efficacy A person's belief about his or her ability to perform behaviors that should bring about a desired outcome.

Self-esteem A person's overall evaluation of his or her self-concept.

Self-fulfilling prophecy The process by which someone's expectations about a person or group lead to the fulfillment of those expectations.

Self-help group Several people regularly meeting and discussing their problems with one another without the guidance of a therapist.

Self-monitoring A personality trait involving the tendency to use cues from other people's self-presentations in controlling one's own self-presentations.

Self-serving bias The tendency to bolster and defend self-esteem by taking credit for positive events while denying blame for negative events.

Semantic encoding The encoding of meaning, including the meaning of words.

Semantic memory Memory for general knowledge about the world that is not associated with a time and place when the information was learned.

Semantic network model A theory that describes concepts in long-term memory organized in a complex network of associations.

Semantics The rules used in language to communicate the meaning of words, phrases, and sentences.

Sensation The process that detects stimuli from our bodies and our environment.

Sensorimotor stage The first stage in Piaget's theory of cognitive development (birth to age 2), in which infants develop the ability to coordinate their sensory input with their motor actions.

Sensory adaptation The tendency for our sensory receptors to show decreasing responsiveness to stimuli that continue without change.

Sensory memory A memory system that very briefly stores the sensory characteristics of a stimulus.

Sensory neurons Neurons that send information from sensory receptors to the brain, usually by way of the spinal cord.

Separation anxiety The fear and distress that infants display when separated from their primary caregiver.

Serotonin A neurotransmitter that is important in regulating emotional states, sleep cycles, and dreaming, aggression, and appetite.

Set point A level of weight that the body works to maintain.

Sex The biological status of being female or male.

Sex chromosomes One of the 23 pairs of chromosomes, this pair determines whether an individual is male or female.

Sexual identity The identity a person organizes around his or her sexual orientation, typically labeled "heterosexual," "gay," "lesbian," or "bisexual."

Sexual orientation The degree to which a person is sexually attracted to persons of the other sex and/or to persons of the same sex.

Sexual response cycle The four stages of sexual responding—excitement, plateau, orgasm, and resolution; first identified by Masters and Johnson.

Sexual script A learned preconception about how a series of events, perceived as sexual, is likely to occur.

Shape constancy The form of perceptual constancy in which there is a tendency to perceive an object as the same shape no matter from what angle it is viewed.

Shaping In operant conditioning, the process of teaching a new behavior by reinforcing closer and closer approximations to the desired behavior; also known as the *method of successive approximations*.

Short-term memory A limited-capacity memory system through which we actively "work" with information.

Signal-detection theory The theory that explains how detection of a stimulus is influenced by observers' expectations.

Situationism The viewpoint that our behavior is strongly influenced by the situation rather than by personality traits.

Size constancy The form of perceptual constancy in which there is a tendency to perceive objects as stable in size despite changes in the size of their retinal images when they are viewed from different distances.

Skewed distribution A distribution in which the mean, median, and mode have different values; in appearance, the distribution has a long tail before or after the peak.

Sleep A nonwaking state of consciousness characterized by minimal physical movement and minimal responsiveness to one's surroundings.

Sleep apnea A sleep disorder in which a person repeatedly stops breathing during sleep.

Sleep spindles Bursts of rapid, rhythmic electrical activity in the brain characteristic of stage 2 sleep.

Sleepwalking A sleep disorder in which a person arises and wanders about while remaining asleep.

Slips of the tongue Inadvertent speech errors that occur when sounds or words are rearranged.

Social-cognitive perspective A psychological perspective that examines how people interpret, analyze, remember, and use information about themselves, others, social interactions, and relationships.

Social influence The exercise of social power by a person or group to change the attitudes or behavior of others in a certain direction.

Socialization Learning the ways of a given society or group well enough to be able to function according to its rules.

Social learning theory A theory contending that people learn social behaviors mainly through observation and cognitive processing of information.

Social perception The way we seek to know and understand other persons and events; also known as *social cognition.*

Social psychology The scientific discipline that attempts to understand and explain how the thoughts, feelings, and behaviors of individuals are influenced by others.

Social roles Clusters of socially defined expectations that people in given situations are supposed to fulfill, such as the role of son, daughter, student, or employee.

Social skills training A behavioral method of psychotherapy in which clients are taught how to interact with others more comfortably and effectively.

Social support The helpful coping resources provided by friends and other people.

Sociocultural perspective An approach to psychology that emphasizes social and cultural influences on behavior.

Soma The cell body of the neuron; contains the nucleus and other components that preserve and nourish it.

Somatic nervous system A division of the peripheral nervous system that transmits commands to the voluntary skeletal muscles and receives sensory information from the muscles and the skin.

Somatization disorder A somatoform disorder characterized by a series of numerous physical complaints that have a psychological rather than a physical basis.

Somatoform disorders Psychological disorders involving some body symptom, even though there is no actual physical cause of the symptom.

Sound localization The ability to locate objects in space solely on the basis of the sounds they make.

Sound waves Pressure changes in a medium (air, water, solids) caused by the vibrations of molecules.

Speech The oral expression of language.

Spinal cord The slender, tube-shaped part of the central nervous system that extends from the base of the brain down the center of the back; made up of a bundle of nerves.

Spontaneous recovery The reappearance of an extinguished response after a period of nonexposure to the conditioned stimulus.

Standard deviation A measure of variation that indicates the average difference between the scores in a distribution and their mean.

Standardization The process of establishing uniform procedures for administering a test and for interpreting its scores.

Stanford-Binet intelligence test The widely used American revision of the original French Binet-Simon intelligence test.

State-dependent memory The tendency for retrieval from memory to be better when our state of mind during retrieval matches our state during encoding.

Stereotype A fixed set of beliefs about people that puts them into categories and doesn't allow for individual variation.

Stereotype threat The realization that your performance on some task might confirm a negative stereotype associated with your social group.

Stigma An attribute that serves to discredit a person in the eyes of others.

Stimulant-induced psychosis Schizophrenic-like symptoms that can occur following prolonged and excessive use of cocaine and amphetamines.

Stimulants Psychoactive drugs that speed up—or stimulate—the nervous system and increase mental and physical activity.

Stimulus discrimination In classical conditioning, the tendency for a conditioned response not to be elicited by stimuli similar to the conditioned stimulus.

Stimulus generalization In classical conditioning, the tendency for a conditioned response to be elicited by stimuli similar to the conditioned stimulus.

Storage The second memory process, in which information is entered and maintained in memory for a period of time.

Stranger anxiety The fear and distress that infants often display when approached by an unfamiliar person.

Stress Our response to events that disturb, or threaten to disturb, our physical or psychological equilibrium.

Stressors External or internal events that challenge or threaten us.

Stroboscopic movement The illusion of movement produced by a rapid pattern of stimulation on different parts of the retina.

Structuralism An early theory in psychology that sought to identify the components of the conscious mind.

Subliminal perception The processing of information that is just below the absolute threshold of conscious awareness.

Superego The part of our minds that includes our conscience and counterbalances the more primitive demands of the id.

Superstitious behavior A behavior learned simply because it happened to be followed by a reinforcer, even though this behavior was not the cause of the reinforcer.

Suppression Motivated forgetting that occurs consciously.

Survey A structured set of questions or statements given to a group of people to measure their attitudes, beliefs, values, or behavioral tendencies.

Sympathetic nervous system The part of the autonomic nervous system that activates the body's energy resources to deal with threatening situations.

Symptom A sign of a disorder.

Synapse The entire area composed of the terminal button of one neuron, the synaptic cleft, and the dendrite of another neuron.

Synesthesia A rare and extraordinary sensory condition in which people perceive stimuli in other senses, such as by seeing sounds or tasting color.

Syntax The rules used in language to combine words into sentences.

Systematic desensitization A counterconditioning technique commonly used to treat phobias, in which the client is gradually exposed to the feared object while remaining relaxed.

Taste buds Sensory receptor organs located on the tongue and inside the mouth and throat that contain the receptor cells for taste.

Telegraphic speech An early speech phase in which children use short, multiple-word sentences that leave out all but the essential words, as in a telegrammed message.

Temporal lobe One of the four major sections of the cerebral cortex, located below the parietal lobe and near the temple in each cerebral hemisphere; important in audition and language.

Teratogen Any disease, drug, or other noxious agent that causes abnormal prenatal development.

Testosterone A male sex hormone found in both men and women that has a positive influence on sexual desire. The additional testosterone in males stimulates the growth of the male sex organs in the fetus and the development of the male sex characteristics during puberty.

Thalamus A part of the forebrain that is the brain's sensory relay station, sending messages from the senses to higher parts of the brain.

THC The major psychoactive ingredient in marijuana.

Thematic apperception test (TAT) A test in which people "project" their inner feelings and motives through the stories they make up about ambiguous pictures.

Theory An organized system of ideas that seeks to explain why two or more events are related.

Theory of mind The commonsense knowledge about other people's mental states that allows one to understand or predict their behavior in specific situations.

Theta waves Irregular, low-amplitude brain waves associated with stage 1 sleep.

Thyroid gland The gland located just below the larynx in the neck that controls metabolism.

Tip-of-the-tongue phenomenon The temporary inability to remember something you know, accompanied by the feeling that it is just beyond your conscious state.

Token economy A technique often used to modify the behavior of severely disturbed people in institutional settings; involves reinforcing desirable behaviors with tokens that can be exchanged for other forms of reinforcement, such as snacks or television privileges.

Trait A relatively stable tendency to behave in a particular way across a variety of situations.

Trait perspective A descriptive approach to personality that identifies stable characteristics that people display over time and across situations.

Transduction The process by which our sensory organs convert a stimulus's physical properties into neural impulses.

Transference The process by which the client develops feelings for the therapist that are presumed to reflect the client's feelings for significant others early in life.

Trial and error A problem-solving strategy that involves trying one possible solution after another until one works.

Triarchic theory of intelligence Sternberg's theory that three sets of mental abilities make up human intelligence analytic, creative, and practical.

Trichromatic theory A theory of color perception proposing that three types of color receptors in the retina produce the primary color sensations of red, green, and blue.

Two-factor theory A theory of emotion suggesting that our emotional states are sometimes determined by experiencing physiological arousal and then attaching a cognitive label to the arousal.

Type A behavior pattern A complex pattern of behaviors and emotions characterized by competitiveness, impatience, ambition, hostility, and a hard-driving approach to life.

Type B behavior pattern A pattern of behaviors and emotions characterized by a patient, relaxed, easygoing approach to life, with little hurry or hostility.

Unconditional positive regard An attitude of complete acceptance toward another person regardless of what she or he has said or done; based on the belief in that person's essential goodness.

Unconditioned response (UCR) In classical conditioning, the unlearned, automatic response to an unconditioned stimulus.

Unconditioned stimulus (UCS) In classical conditioning, a stimulus that naturally and automatically elicits an unconditioned response.

Unconscious mind According to Freud, the thoughts, desires, feelings, and memories that are not consciously available to us but that nonetheless shape our everyday behavior.

Validity The degree to which a test measures what it is designed to measure.

Variable-interval schedule A partial reinforcement schedule that reinforces the first response after a variable time interval has elapsed.

Variable-ratio schedule A partial reinforcement schedule that reinforces a response after a variable number of nonreinforced responses.

Variables In scientific research, factors that can be measured and that can vary.

Vestibular sense A type of proprioceptive sense that provides information about the position of the body—especially the head—in space; also known as *equilibrium*.

Visual encoding The encoding of picture images, including the sight of words.

Volley theory A theory of pitch stating that neurons work in groups and alternate firing, thus achieving a combined frequency corresponding to the frequency of the sound wave.

Wavelength The distance between two peaks of adjacent waves.

Weber's law The principle that a weak or small stimulus does not require much change before a person notices that the stimulus has changed, but that a strong or large stimulus requires a proportionately greater change before the change is noticed.

Wechsler intelligence scales The most widely used set of intelligence tests, containing both verbal and performance (nonverbal) subscales.

Working memory The term used to describe short-term memory as an active memory system that contains a "central executive" processor and two subsystems for temporarily storing auditory and visual-spatial input.

Yerkes-Dodson law The idea that we perform best when we are at an intermediate level of arousal.

Zone of proximal development (ZPD) The cognitive range between what a child can do on her or his own and what the child can do with the help of adults or more-skilled children.

Zygote stage The first 2 weeks of prenatal development, from conception until the zygote implants itself in the wall of the uterus.

References

Aaker, J. L., Benet-Martinez, V., & Garolera, J. (2001). Consumption symbols as carriers of culture: A study of Japanese and Spanish brand personality constructs. *Journal of Personality and Social Psychology, 81,* 492–508.

Abou-Hatab, F. A.-L. H. (1997). Psychology from Egyptian, Arab, and Islamic perspectives: Unfulfilled hopes and hopeful fulfillment. *European Psychologist, 2,* 356–365.

Abramov, I., & Gordon, J. (1994). Color appearance: On seeing red, or yellow, or green, or blue. *Annual Review of Psychology, 45,* 451–485.

Abramowitz, J. S. (2002). Treatment of obsessive thoughts and cognitive rituals using exposure and response prevention: A case study. *Clinical Case Studies, 1,* 6–24.

Abrams, R. (1993). ECT technique: Electrode placement, stimulus type, and treatment frequency. In C. E. Coffey (Ed.), *The clinical science of electroconvulsive therapy.* Washington, DC: American Psychiatric Press.

Ackard, D., & Neumarck-Sztainer, D. (2001). *Date violence and date rape among adolescents: Associations with disordered eating behaviors and psychological health.* Presented at the 109th Annual Convention of the American Psychological Association, San Francisco, CA.

Ackerman, N. (1966). *Treating the troubled family.* New York: Basic Books.

Acosta, H. M. (2004). Eight factors affecting focal distance and the moon illusion. *Dissertation Abstracts International: Section B: The Physical Sciences & Engineering. Vol. 65*(4-B), 2004, 2130. US: Univ. Microfilms International.

Adams, J. (1995). *Sellout: Aldrich Ames and the corruption of the CIA.* New York: Viking.

Adams, M., & Slayer, S. (2003). *Buffy the Vampire Slayer lexicon.* Oxford, England: Oxford University Press.

Adams, M. J. (1986). *Odyssey: A curriculum for thinking.* Watertown, MA: Mastery Education Corporation.

Adams, P. R., & Adams, G. R. (1984). Mount Saint Helen's ashfall: Evidence for a disaster stress reaction. *American Psychologist, 39,* 252–260.

Adams, R. D., & Victor, M. (1993). *Principles of neurology* (5th ed.). New York: McGraw-Hill.

Adeyemo, S. A. (2002). Can the action of amphetamine on dopamine cause schizophrenia? *Psychology & Education: An Interdisciplinary Journal, 39,* 29–39.

Adler, A. (1929). *The practice and theory of individual psychology.* New York: Harcourt, Brace & World.

Adler, J. (1996, June 17). Building a better dad. *Newsweek,* 58–64.

Adler, N. E., & Snibbe, A. C. (2003). The role of psychosocial processes in explaining the gradient between socioeconomic status and health. *Current Directions in Psychological Science, 12,* 119–123.

Afifi, W. A., & Faulkner, S. L. (2000). On being "just friends": The frequency and impact of sexual activity in cross-sex friendships. *Journal of Social and Personal Relationships, 17,* 205–222.

Ago, Y., Nakamura, S., Baba, A., & Matsuda, T. (2005). Sulpiride in combination with fluvoxamine increases in vivo dopamine release selectivity in rat prefrontal cortex. *Neuropsychopharmacology, 30,* 43–51.

Agrawal, A., Jacobson, K. C., Prescott, C. A., & Kendler, K. S. (2004). A twin study of personality and illicit drug use and abuse/dependence. *Twin Research, 7,* 72–81.

Ahlering, R. F. (1987). Need for cognition, attitudes, and the 1984 presidential election. *Journal of Research in Personality, 21,* 100–102.

Aiken, L. R. (1996). *Assessment of intellectual functioning* (2nd ed.). New York: Plenum.

Ainslie, G. (1975). Specious reward: A behavioral theory of impulsiveness and impulse control. *Psychological Bulletin, 82,* 463–496.

Ainsworth, M. D. S., Blehar, M., Waters, E., & Wall, S. (1978). *Patterns of attachment.* Hillsdale, NJ: Erlbaum.

Akerstedt, T. (1991). Sleepiness at work: Effects of irregular work hours. In T. M. Monk (Ed.), *Sleep, sleepiness, and performance* (pp. 129–152). New York: Wiley.

Akhtar, N., & Tomasello, M. (1996). Two-year-olds learn words for absent objects and actions. *British Journal of Developmental Psychology, 14,* 79–93.

Akil, L. (1982). On the role of endorphins in pain modulation. In A. L. Beckman (Ed.), *The neural bases of behavior* (pp. 311–333). New York: Spectrum.

Akins, C. K., Klein, E. D., & Zentall, T. R. (2002). Imitative learning in Japanese quail *(Coturnix japonica)* using the bidirectional control procedure. *Animal Learning & Behavior, 30,* 275–281.

Akom, A. A. (2000). The house that race built: Some observations on the use of the word nigga, popular culture, and urban adolescent behavior. In L. Weis & M. Fine (Eds.), *Construction sites: Excavating race, class, and gender among urban youth. The teaching for social justice series* (pp. 140–157). New York: Teachers College Press.

Al-Ansari, E. M. (2002). Effects of gender and education on the moral reasoning of Kuwait university students. *Social Behavior & Personality, 30,* 75–82.

Alcock, J. E., Burns, J. E., & Freeman, A. (Eds.). (2003). Psi wars: Getting to grips with the paranormal. Charlottesville, VA: Imprint Academic.

Alegria, M., McGuire, T., Vera, M., Canino, G., Matias, L., & Calderon, J. (2001). Changes in access to mental health care among the poor and nonpoor: Results from health care reform in Puerto Rico. *American Journal of Public Health, 91,* 1431–1434.

Alexander, J., Tharyan, P., Adams, C., John, T., Mol, C., & Philip, J. (2004). Rapid tranquillization of violent or agitated patients in a psychiatric emergency setting: Pragmatic randomised trial of intramuscular lorazepam v. haloperidol plus promethazine. *British Journal of Psychiatry, 185,* 63–69.

Alexander, J. F., & Parsons, B. (1973). Short-term behavioral intervention with delinquent families: Impact on family process and recidivism. *Journal of Abnormal Psychology, 81,* 219–225.

Alexander, J. M., & Schwanenflugel, P. J. (1994). Strategy regulation: The role of intelligence, metacognitive attributions, and knowledge base. *Developmental Psychology, 30,* 709–723.

Alferi, S. M., Culver, J. L., Carver, C. S., Arena, P. L., & Antoni, M. H. (1999). Religiosity, religious coping, and distress: A prospective study of Catholic and evangel-ical Hispanic women in treatment for early-stage breast cancer. *Journal of Health Psychology, 4,* 343–356.

Alicke, M. D., Yurak, T. J., & Vredenburg, D. S. (1996). Using personal attitudes to judge others: The roles of outcomes and consensus. *Journal of Research in Personality, 30,* 103–119.

Alksnis, C., Desmarais, S., & Wood, E. (1996). Gender differences in scripts for types of dates. *Sex Roles, 34,* 321–336.

Allen, L. S., & Gorski, R. A. (1992). Sexual orientation and the size of the anterior commissure in the human brain. *Proceedings of the National Academy of Sciences of the United States of America, 89,* 7199–7202.

Allen, R. E., & Oliver, J. M. (1982). The effects of child maltreatment on language development. *Child Abuse and Neglect, 6,* 299–305.

Allen, V. L., & Levine, J. M. (1969). Consensus and conformity. *Journal of Experimental Social Psychology, 5,* 389–399.

Allen, V. L., & Levine, J. M. (1971). Social support and conformity: The role of independent assessment of reality. *Journal of Experimental Social Psychology, 7,* 48–58.

Allison, D., Heshka, S., Neale, M., Lykken, D., & Heymsfield, S. (1994). A genetic analysis of relative weight among 4,020 twin pairs, with an emphasis on sex effects. *Health Psychology, 13,* 362–365.

Allison, J. A., & Wrightsman, M. R. (1993). *Rape: The misunderstood crime.* Newbury Park, CA: Sage.

Allison, P. D., & Furstenberg, F. F., Jr. (1989). How marital dissolution affects children: Variation by age and sex. *Developmental Psychology, 25,* 540–549.

Alloy, L. B., Abramson, L. Y., & Francis, E. L. (1999). Do negative cognitive styles confer vulnerability to depression? *Current Directions in Psychological Science, 8,* 128–132.

Allport, G. W. (1937). *Personality: A psychological interpretation.* New York: Henry Holt.

Allport, G. W. (1961). *Pattern and Growth in Personality.* New York: Holt Rinehart & Winston.

Allport, G. W. (1967). Gordon W. Allport. In E. G. Boring & G. Lindzey (Eds.), *A history of psychology in autobiography* (Vol. 5). New York: Appleton-Century-Crofts.

Allport, G. W., & Odbert, H. S. (1936). Trait-names: A psycholexical study. *Psychological Monographs, 47* (Whole No. 211).

Allport, G. W., & Postman, L. (1945). The basic psychology of rumor. *Transactions of the New York Academy of Sciences, 11,* 61–81.

Allport, G. W., & Postman, L. (1947). *The psychology of rumor.* New York: Henry Holt.

Almagor, U. (1987). The cycle and stagnation of smells: Pastoralists-fishermen relationships in an East African society. *RES, 14,* 106–121.

Almeida, O. P., Tamai, S., & Garrido, R. (1999). Sleep complaints among the elderly: Results from a survey in a psychogeriatric outpatient clinic in Brazil. *International Psychogeriatrics, 11,* 47–56.

Aloise-Young, P. A., Graham, J. W., & Hansen, W. B. (1994). Peer influence on smoking initiation during early adolescence: A comparison of group members and group outsiders. *Journal of Applied Psychology, 79,* 281–287.

Alston, J. H. (1920). Spatial condition of the fusion of warmth and cold in heat. *American Journal of Psychology, 31,* 303–312.

Altarriba, J. (2003). Does cariño equal "liking"? A theoretical approach to conceptual nonequivalence between languages. *International Journal of Bilingualism, 7,* 305–322.

Álvarez, R. (2001). The social problem as an enterprise: Values as a defining factor. *Social Problems, 48,* 3–10.

Amabile, T. M. (1996). *The context of creativity.* Boulder, CO: Westview.

Amabile, T. M., & Hennessey, B. A. (1992). The motivation for creativity in children. In A. K. Boggiano & T. S. Pittman (Eds.), *Achievement and motivation: A social-developmental perspective.* New York: Cambridge University Press.

Amato, L., Davoli, M., Ferri, M., Gowing, L., & Perucci, C. A. (2004). Effectiveness of interventions on opiate withdrawal treatment: An overview of systematic reviews. *Drug & Alcohol Dependence, 73,* 219–226.

Amato, P. R., & Keith, B. (1991). Parental divorce and the well-being of children: A meta-analysis. *Psychological Bulletin, 110,* 26–46.

Ambady, N., Shih, M., Kim, A., & Pittinsky, T. L. (2001). Stereotype susceptibility in children: Effects of identity activation on quantitative performance. *Psychological Science, 12,* 385–390.

American Psychiatric Association. (1994). *Diagnostic and statistical manual of mental disorders* (4th ed.). Washington, DC: American Psychiatric Press.

American Psychiatric Association. (2000). *Diagnostic and statistical manual of mental disorders* (4th ed., Text Revision). Washington, DC: American Psychiatric Press.

Amsterdam, B. (1972). Mirror self-image reactions before age two. *Developmental Psychobiology, 5,* 297–305.

Anaki, D., Faran, Y., Ben-Shalom, D., & Henik, A. (2005). The false memory and the mirror effects: The role of familiarity and backward association in creating false recollections. *Journal of Memory & Language, 52,* 87–102.

Anch, A. M., Browman, C. P., Mitler, M. M., & Walsh, J. K. (1988). *Sleep: A scientific perspective.* Englewood Cliffs, NJ: Prentice Hall.

Andersen, B. L., Cyranowski, J. M., & Espindle, D. (1999). Men's sexual self-schema. *Journal of Personality and Social Psychology, 76,* 645–661.

Anderson, C., Keltner, D., & John, O. P. (2003). Emotional convergence between people over time. *Journal of Personality and Social Psychology, 84,* 1054–1068.

Anderson, C. A., Berkowitz, L., Donnerstein, E., Huesmann, L. R., Johnson, J. D., Linz, D., Malamuth, N. M., & Wartella, E. (2003a). The influence of media violence on youth. *Psychological Science in the Public Interest, 4*(3), 81–110.

Anderson, C. A., & Bushman, B. J. (2001). Effects of violent video games on aggressive behavior, aggressive cognition, aggressive affect, physiological arousal, and prosocial behavior: A meta-analytic review of the scientific literature. *Psychological Science, 12,* 353–359.

Anderson, C. A., Carnagey, N. L., & Eubanks, J. (2003b). Exposure to violent media: The effects of songs with violent lyrics on aggressive thoughts and feelings. *Journal of Personality and Social Psychology, 84,* 960–971.

Anderson, E. (1994). The code of the streets. *Atlantic Monthly, 5,* 81–94.

Anderson, J. L., Crawford, C. B., Nadeau, J., & Lindberg, T. (1992). Was the Duchess of Windsor right? A cross-cultural review of the socioecology of ideals of female body shape. *Ethology and Sociobiology, 13,* 197–227.

Anderson, J. R. (1983). Retrieval of information from long-term memory. *Science, 220,* 25–30.

Anderson, J. R. (1990). *The adaptive nature of thought.* Hillsdale, NJ: Erlbaum.

Anderson, J. R. (1993a). Problem solving and learning. *American Psychologist, 48,* 35–44.

Anderson, J. R. (1993b). To see ourselves as others see us: A response to Mitchell. *New Ideas in Psychology, 11,* 339–346.

Anderson, M. (2005). Cortex forum on the concept of general intelligence in neuropsychology. *Cortex, 41,* 99–100.

Anderson, N. B., & Nickerson, K. J. (2005). Genes, race, and psychology in the genome era. *American Psychologist, 60,* 5–8.

Anderssen, N. (2002). Does contact with lesbians and gays lead to friendlier attitudes? A two-year longitudinal study. *Journal of Community & Applied Social Psychology, 12,* 124–136.

Andersson, J., & Rönnberg, J. (1997). Cued memory collaboration: Effects of friendship and type of retrieval cue. *European Journal of Cognitive Psychology, 9,* 273–287.

Ando, K., Kripke, D. F., Cole, R. J., & Elliott, J. A. (1999). Light mask 500 lux treatment for delayed sleep phase syndrome. *Progress in Neuro-Psychopharmacology & Biological Psychiatry, 23,* 15–24.

Andre, J., & Owens, D. A. (Eds.). (2003). *Visual perception: The influence of H. W. Leibowitz. Decade of behavior.* Washington, DC: American Psychological Association.

Andrews, G., Clark, M., & Luszcz, M. (2002). Successful aging in the Australian Longitudinal Study of Aging: Applying the MacArthur model cross-nationally. *Journal of Social Issues, 58,* 749–765.

Angermeyer, M. C., & Matschinger, H. (1996). The effect of violent attacks by schizophrenic persons on the attitude of the public towards the mentally ill. *Social Science & Medicine, 43,* 1721–1728.

Anisman, H., & Kusnecov, A. W. (2005). Immune system. In I. Q. Whishaw & B. Kolb (Eds.), *The behavior of the laboratory rat: A handbook with tests* (pp. 245–254). London: Oxford University Press.

Annett, M. (1985). *Left, right, hand and brain: The right shift theory.* Hillsdale, NJ: Erlbaum.

Anstis, S. M. (1978). Apparent movement. In R. Held, H. W. Leibowitz, & H. L. Teuber (Eds.), *Handbook of sensory physiology: Perception* (Vol. 8, pp. 655–673). Berlin: Springer-Verlag.

Antrobus, J. (1987). Cortical hemisphere asymmetry and sleep mentation. *Psychological Review, 94,* 359–368.

Antrobus, J. (1991). Dreaming: Cognitive processes during cortical activation and high afferent thresholds. *Psychological Review, 98,* 96–121.

Appel, J. (1963). Aversive effects of a schedule of positive reinforcement. *Journal of the Experimental Analysis of Behavior, 6,* 423–428.

Arkin, A. M., & Antrobus, J. S. (1991). The effects of external stimuli applied to and during sleep on sleep experience. In S. J. Ellman & J. S. Antrobus (Eds.), *The mind in sleep: Psychology and psychopathology* (2nd ed., pp. 265–307). New York: Wiley.

Arking, R. (1998). *Biology of aging: Observations and principles* (2nd ed.). Sunderland, MA: Sinauer Associates.

Armony, J. L., & LeDoux, J. E. (2000). How danger is encoded: Toward a systems, cellular, and computational understanding of cognitive-emotional interactions in fear. In M. S. Gazzaniga (Ed.), *The new cognitive neurosciences* (2nd ed., pp. 1067–1080). Cambridge, MA: MIT Press.

Armstrong, B. G., & Greenberg, B. S. (1990). Background television as an inhibitor of cognitive processing. *Human Communication Research, 16,* 355–386.

Arnett, J. J. (1999). Adolescent storm and stress reconsidered. *American Psychologist, 54,* 317–326.

Arnett, J. J. (2002). The psychology of globalization. *American Psychologist, 57,* 774–783.

Aron, E. N., & Aron, A. (1982). An introduction to Maharishi's theory of creativity: Its empirical base and description of the creative process. *Journal of Creative Behavior, 16,* 29–49.

Aronoff, S. R., & Spilka, B. (1984–1985). Patterning of facial expressions among terminal cancer patients. *Omega, 15,* 101–108.

Aronow, E., Reznikoff, M., & Moreland, K. L. (1995). The Rorschach: Projective technique or psychometric test? *Journal of Personality Assessment, 64,* 213–228.

Aronson, J., Lustina, M. J., Good, C., Keough, K., Steele, C. M., & Brown, J. (1999). When White men can't do math: Necessary and sufficient factors in stereotype threat. *Journal of Experimental Social Psychology, 35,* 29–46.

Arredondo, P., & Perez, P. (2003). Counseling paradigms and Latina/o Americans. In F. Harper & J. McFadden (Eds.), *Culture and counseling: New approaches* (pp. 115–132). Boston, MA: Allyn & Bacon.

Arriaga, X. B., & Agnew, C. R. (2001). Being committed: Affective, cognitive, and conative components of relationship commitment. *Personality and Social Psychology Bulletin, 27,* 1190–1203.

Asch, S. E. (1946). Forming impressions of personality. *Journal of Abnormal and Social Psychology, 41,* 258–290.

Asch, S. E. (1951). Effects of group pressure upon the modification and distortion of judgments. In H. Guetzkow (Ed.), *Groups, leadership, and men.* Pittsburgh, PA: Carnegie Press.

Asch, S. E. (1952). *Social psychology.* New York: Prentice Hall.

Asch, S. E. (1955, November). Opinions and social pressure. *Scientific American,* 31–35.

Asch, S. E. (1956). Studies of independence and conformity: A minority of one against a unanimous majority. *Psychological Monographs, 70* (Whole No. 416).

Asendorpf, J. B., & Van Aken, M. A. G. (2003). Validity of big five personality judgements in childhood: A 9-year longitudinal study. *European Journal of Personality, 17,* 1–17.

Aserinsky, E. (1996). Memories of famous neuropsychologists: The discovery of REM sleep. *Journal of the History of the Neurosciences, 5,* 213–227.

Aserinsky, E., & Kleitman, N. (1953). Regularly occurring periods of eye mobility and concomitant phenomena during sleep. *Science, 118,* 273–274.

Ash, M. G. (2002). Cultural contexts and scientific change in psychology: Kurt Lewin in Iowa. In W. E. Pickren & D. A. Dewsbury (Eds.), *Evolving perspectives on the history of psychology* (pp. 385–406). Washington, DC: American Psychological Association.

Ashton, G. S. (1982). Handedness: An alternative hypothesis. *Behavior Genetics, 12,* 125–148.

Astin, S., Redston, P., & Campbell, A. (2003). Sex differences in social representations of aggression: Men justify, women excuse? *Aggressive Behavior, 29,* 128–133.

Atkinson, A. (1995). What makes love last. In K. R. Gilbert (Ed.), *Marriage and the family 95/96* (Annual Editions). Guilford, CT: Dushkin/Brown & Benchmark.

Atkinson, D. R., Brown, M. T., Parham, T. A., & Matthews, L. G. (1996). African American client skin tone and clinical judgments of African American and European American psychologists. *Professional Psychology: Research & Practice, 27,* 500–505.

Atkinson, J. (1957). Motivational determinants of risk-taking behavior. *Psychological Review, 64,* 359–372.

Atkinson, J. W. (1977). Motivation for achievement. In T. Blass (Ed.), *Personality variables in social behavior.* Hillsdale, NJ: Erlbaum.

Au, T. K., Knightly, L. M., Jun, S.-A., & Oh, J. S. (2002). Overhearing a language during childhood. *Psychological Science, 13,* 238–243.

Auerbach, S. M., & Gramling, S. (1998). *Stress management: Psychological foundations.* Upper Saddle River, NJ: Prentice Hall.

Auerbach, S. M., Kiesler, D. J., Strentz, T., Schmidt, J. A., & Serio, C. D. (1994). Interpersonal impacts and adjunctment to the stress of simulated captivity: An empirical test of the Stockholm Syndrome. *Journal of Social and Clinical Psychology, 13,* 207–221.

Augusto, J. C. (2005). Temporal reasoning for decision support in medicine. *Artificial Intelligence in Medicine, 33,* 1–24.

Auld, F., Hyman, M., & Rudzinski, D. (2005). Developments in psychoanalytic therapy since Freud. In F. Auld, M. Hyman, & D. Rudzinski (Eds.), *Resolution of inner conflict: An introduction to psychoanalytic therapy* (2nd ed., pp. 237–254). Washington, DC: American Psychological Association.

Australian Bureau of Statistics. (2000). *Apparent consumption of foodstuffs: Australia* (www.abs.gov.au).

Avise, J. C. (2004). *The hope, hype, & reality of genetic engineering: Remarkable stories from agriculture, industry, medicine, and the environment.* New York: Oxford University Press.

Axline, V. M. (1947). *Play therapy.* Boston: Houghton Mifflin.

Ayllon, T., & Azrin, N. H. (1968). *The token economy: A motivational system for therapy and rehabilitation.* New York: Appleton-Century-Crofts.

Baars, B. J. (2003). Reply to comments on "The double life of B. F. Skinner." *Journal of Consciousness Studies, 10,* 79–94.

Babad, E., Hills, M., & O'Driscoll, M. (1992). Factors influencing wishful thinking and predictions of election outcomes. *Basic and Applied Social Psychology, 13,* 461–476.

Babyak, M., Blumenthal, J., Herman, S., Khatri, P., Doraiswamy, M., et al. (2000). Exercise treatment for major depression: Maintenance of therapeutic benefit at 10 months. *Psychosomatic Medicine, 62,* 633–638.

Bachman, R., & Peralta, R. (2002). The relationship between drinking and violence in an adolescent population: Does gender matter? *Deviant Behavior, 23,* 1–19.

Bach-y-Rita, P. (1990). Brain plasticity as a basis for recovery in humans. *Neuropsychologia, 28,* 547–554.

Baddeley, A. (1992). Working memory. *Science, 255,* 556–559.

Baddeley, A. (2002, June). Is working memory still working? *European Psychologist, 7,* 85–97.

Baek, H.-J. (2002). A comparative study of moral development of Korean and British children. *Journal of Moral Education, 31,* 373–391.

Baer, J. (1993). *Creativity and divergent thinking: A task-specific approach.* Hillsdale, NJ: Erlbaum.

Bagby, R. M., Marshall, M. B., Michael, R., Nicholson, R. A., Bacchiochi, J., & Miller, L. S. (2005). Distinguishing bipolar depression, major depression, and schizophrenia with the MMPI-2 clinical and content scales. *Journal of Personality Assessment, 84,* 89–95.

Bahrick, H. P., Bahrick, L. E., Bahrick, A. S., & Bahrick, P. E. (1993). Maintenance of foreign vocabulary and the spacing effect. *Psychological Science, 4*, 316–321.

Bahrick, H. P., Bahrick, P. O., & Wittlinger, R. P. (1975). Fifty years of memory for names and faces: A cross-sectional approach. *Journal of Experimental Psychology: General, 104*, 54–75.

Bailey, J., & Pillard, R. (1991). A genetic study of male homosexual orientation. *Archives of General Psychiatry, 48*, 1089–1097.

Bailey, J., & Pillard, R. (1995). Genetics of human sexual orientation. *Annual Review of Sex Research, 6*, 126–150.

Bailey, J., Pillard, R., Neale, M., & Agyei, Y. (1993). Heritable factors influence sexual orientation in women. *Archives of General Psychiatry, 50*, 217–223.

Bailey, J. M., Bobrow, D., Wolfe, M., & Mikach, S. (1995). Sexual orientation of adult sons of gay fathers. *Developmental Psychology, 31*, 124–129.

Bailey, J. M., & Zucker, K. J. (1995). Childhood sex-typed behavior and sexual orientation: A conceptual analysis and quantitative review. *Developmental Psychology, 31*, 43–55.

Baillargeon, R., & DeVos, J. (1991). Object permanence in young infants: Further evidence. *Child Development, 62*, 1227–1246.

Baker, A., Lee, N. K., Claire, M., Lewin, T., Grant, T., Pohlman, S., Saunders, J. B., Kay-Lambkin, F., Constable, P., Jenner, L., & Carr, V. J. (2004). Drug use patterns and mental health of regular amphetamine users during a reported "heroin drought." *Addiction, 99*, 875–884.

Baker, M. C. (2004). Socially learned antipredator behavior in black-capped chickadees (Poecile atricapillus). *Bird Behavior, 16*, 13–19.

Baker, R. A. (1990). *They call it hypnosis.* Buffalo, NY: Prometheus Books.

Baldwin, E. (1993). The case for animal research in psychology. *Journal of Social Issues, 49*, 121–131.

Balleine, B., & Dickinson, A. (1994). Role of cholecystokinin in the motivational control of instrumental action in rats. *Behavioral Neuroscience, 108*, 590–605.

Balleine, B. W. (2005). Incentive behavior. In I. Q. Whishaw & B. Kolb (Eds.), *The behavior of the laboratory rat: A handbook with tests* (pp. 436–446). London: Oxford University Press.

Balsam, P. D. (1988). Selection, representation, and equivalence of controlling stimuli. In R. C. Atkinson, R. J. Herrnstein, G. Lindzey & R. D. Luce (Eds.), *Stevens' handbook of experimental psychology.* New York: Wiley.

Baltes, P. B., & Kunzmann, U. (2003). Wisdom. *Psychologist, 16*, 131–133.

Baltes, P. B., & Mayer, K. U. (2001). *The Berlin aging study: Aging from 70 to 100.* New York: Cambridge University Press.

Balthasar, N., Coppari, R., McMinn, J., Liu, S. M., Lee, C. E., Tang, V., Kenny, C. D., McGovern, R. A., Chua, S. C., Jr., Elmquist, J. K., & Lowell, B. B. (2004). Leptin receptor signaling in POMC neurons is required for normal body weight homeostasis. *Neuron, 42*, 983–991.

Bancroft, J., Janssen, E., Carnes, L., Goodrich, D., Strong, D., & Long, J.-S. (2004). Sexual activity and risk taking in young heterosexual men: The relevance of sexual arousability, mood, and sensation seeking. *Journal of Sex Research, 41*, 181–192.

Bandura, A. (1965). Influences of models' reinforcement contingencies on the acquisition of initiative responses. *Journal of Personality and Social Psychology, 1*, 589–593.

Bandura, A. (1979). The social learning perspective: Mechanism of aggression. In H. Toch (Ed.), *Psychology of crime and criminal justice.* New York: Holt, Rinehart & Winston.

Bandura, A. (1986). *Social foundations of thought and action: A social-cognitive theory.* Englewood Cliffs, NJ: Prentice Hall.

Bandura, A. (1999). A sociocognitive analysis of substance abuse: An agentic perspective. *Psychological Science, 10*, 214–218.

Bandura, A., Ross, D., & Ross, S. A. (1961). Transmission of aggression through imitation of aggressive models. *Journal of Abnormal and Social Psychology, 63*, 575–582.

Bandura, A., Ross, D., & Ross, S. A. (1963). Vicarious reinforcement and imitative learning. *Journal of Abnormal and Social Psychology, 67*, 601–607.

Banich, M. T. (1998). Integration of information between the cerebral hemispheres. *Current Directions in Psychological Science, 7*, 32–37.

Bankston, C. L., III, & Caldas, S. J. (1997). The American school dilemma: Race and scholastic performance. *The Sociological Quarterly, 38*, 423–429.

Banwell, E. (2004). Balancing individual and organizational values: Walking the tightrope to success. *Journal of Managerial Psychology, 19*, 191–193.

Barbaro, N. M. (1988). Studies of PAG/PVG stimulation for pain relief in humans. *Progress in Brain Research, 77*, 165–173.

Barber, B. L., & Eccles, J. S. (1992). Long-term influence of divorce and single parenting on adolescent family- and work-related values, behaviors, and aspirations. *Psychological Bulletin, 111*, 108–126.

Barber, T. X. (1979). Suggested ("hypnotic") behavior: The trance paradigm versus an alternative paradigm. In E. Fromm & R. E. Shor (Eds.), *Hypnosis: Developments in research and new perspectives.* New York: Aldine.

Barber, T. X. (2000). A deeper understanding of hypnosis: Its secrets, its nature, its essence. *American Journal of Clinical Hypnosis, 42*, 208–272.

Bard, P. (1934). On emotional expression after desortication with some remarks on certain theoretical views. *Psychological Review, 41*, 309–328.

Bargh, J. A., & Churchland, T. L. (1999). The unbearable automaticity of being. *American Psychologist, 54*, 462–479.

Barinaga, M. (1997, June 27). New imaging methods provide a better view into the brain. *Science, 276*, 1974–1976.

Barlow, D., & Rapee, R. (1991). *Mastering stress: A lifestyle approach.* Dallas, TX: American Health.

Barlow, D. H. (1988). *Anxiety and its disorders: The nature and treatment of anxiety and panic.* New York: Guilford.

Barlow, D. H., & Lehman, C. L. (1996). Advances in the psychological treatment of anxiety disorders: Implications for national health care. *Archives of General Psychiatry, 53*, 727–735.

Barnes, S., Gutfreund, M., Satterly, D., & Wells, G. (1983). Characteristics of adult speech which predict children's language development. *Journal of Child Language, 10*, 65–84.

Barnlund, D. C. (1989). *Communicative styles of Japanese and Americans.* Belmont, CA: Wadsworth.

Baron, R. A. (1973). Threatened retaliation from the victim as an inhibitor of physical aggression. *Journal of Research in Personality, 7*, 103–115.

Baron, R. A. (1976). The reduction of human aggression: A field study of the influence of incompatible reactions. *Journal of Applied Social Psychology, 6*, 260–274.

Baron, R. A. (1983). The control of human aggression: A strategy based on incompatible responses. In R. G. Geen & E. I. Donnerstein (Eds.), *Aggression: Theoretical and empirical reviews* (Vol. 2, pp. 173–190). New York: Academic Press.

Baron, R. A., & Kepner, C. R. (1970). Model's behavior and attraction toward the model as determinants of adult aggressive behavior. *Journal of Personality and Social Psychology, 14*, 335–344.

Baron-Cohen, S., Burt, L., Laittan-Smith, F., Harrison, J. E., & Bolton, P. (1996). Synaesthesia: Prevalence and familiarity. *Perception, 25*, 1073–1080.

Barr, C. L. (2001). Genetics of childhood disorders: XXII. ADHD, Part 6: The dopamine D4 receptor gene. *Journal of the American Academy of Child & Adolescent Psychiatry, 40*, 382.

Barr, H. M., Streissguth, A. P., Darby, B. L., & Sampson, P. D. (1990). Prenatal exposure to alcohol, caffeine, tobacco, and aspirin: Effects on fine and gross motor performance in 4-year-old children. *Developmental Psychology, 26*, 339–348.

Barrett, L., Dunbar, R., & Lycett, J. (2002). *Human evolutionary psychology.* Princeton, NJ: Princeton University Press.

Barrett, P. T., & Eysenck, H. J. (1992). Brain evoked potentials and intelligence: The Hendrickson paradigm. *Intelligence, 16*, 361–381.

Barrick, M. R., & Mount, M. K. (1991). The big five personality dimensions and job performance: A meta-analysis. *Personnel Psychology, 44*, 1–26.

Barron, G., & Yechiam, E. (2002). Private e-mail requests and the diffusion of responsibility. *Computers in Human Behavior, 18*, 507–520.

Bartholow, B. D., & Anderson, C. A. (2002). Effects of violent video games on aggressive behavior: Potential sex differences. *Journal of Experimental Social Psychology, 38*, 283–290.

Bartholow, B. D., Pearson, M. A., Gratton, G., & Fabiani, M. (2003). Effects of alcohol on person perception: A social cognitive neuroscience approach. *Journal of Personality and Social Psychology, 85*, 627–638.

Bartlett, F. C. (1932). *Remembering: A study in experimental and social psychology.* London: Cambridge University Press.

Bartoshuk, L. M. (1991). Taste, smell, and pleasure. In R. C. Bolles (Ed.), *The hedonics of taste.* Hillsdale, NJ: Erlbaum.

Bartoshuk, L. M., & Beauchamp, G. K. (1994). Chemical senses. *Annual Review of Psychology, 45*, 419–449.

Bartusiak, M. (1980, November). Beeper man. *Discover,* p. 57.

Baruss, I. (2003). Dreams. In I. Baruss (Ed.), *Alterations of consciousness: An empirical analysis for social scientists* (pp. 79–106). Washington, DC: American Psychological Association.

Basham, K. (2004). Multiculturalism and the therapeutic process. *Smith College Studies in Social Work, 74*, 457–462.

Bass, B. M. (2002). Cognitive, social, and emotional intelligence of transformational leaders. In R. E. Riggio & S. E. Murphy (Eds.), *Multiple intelligences and leadership.* (pp. 105–118). *LEA's organization and management series.* Mahwah, NJ: Erlbaum.

Basson, R. (2002). Women's sexual desire: Disordered or misunderstood? *Journal of Sex and Marital Therapy, 28*, 17–28.

Batejat, D. M., & Lagarde, D. P. (1999). Naps and modafinil as countermeasures for the effects of sleep deprivation on cognitive performance. *Aviation, Space, & Environmental Medicine, 70*, 493–498.

Bates, E., Beeghly-Smith, M., Bretherton, I., & McNew, S. (1983). Social basis of language development: A reassessment. In H. Reese & L. Lipsitt (Eds.), *Advances in child development and behavior* (Vol. 16, pp. 8–75). New York: Academic Press.

Bates, E., & Dick, F. (2002). Language, gesture, and the developing brain. *Developmental Psychobiology, 40*, 293–310.

Bates, E., & MacWhinney, B. (1982). Functionalist approaches to grammar. In E. Wanner & L. Gleitman (Eds.), *Language acquisition: The state of the art* (pp. 173–218). Cambridge: Cambridge University Press.

Bateson, G., Jackson, D. D., Haley, J., & Weakland, J. (1956). Toward a history of schizophrenia. *Behavioral Science, 1*, 252–264.

Batson, C. D. (1998). Prosocial behavior and altruism. In D. T. Gilbert, S. T. Fiske, & G. Lindzey (Eds.), *The handbook of social psychology* (4th ed., pp. 282–316). New York: McGraw-Hill.

Battro, A. M. (2001). *Half a brain is enough: The story of Nico.* New York: Cambridge University Press.

Bauer, P. J. (2002). Long-term recall memory: Behavioral and neuro-developmental changes in the first 2 years of life. *Current Directions in Psychological Science, 11*, 137–141.

Bauer, P. J. (2005). Developments in declarative memory: Decreasing susceptibility to storage failure over the second year of life. *Psychological Science, 16*, 41–47.

Baum, A., Gatchel, R., & Krantz, D. (1998). *An introduction to health psychology* (3rd ed.). New York: McGraw-Hill.

Baum, A., & Posluszny, D. M. (1999). Health psychology: Mapping biobehavioral contributions to health and illness. *Annual Review of Psychology, 50*, 137–163.

Baumeister, A. A., & Francis, J. L. (2002). Historical development of the dopamine hypothesis of schizophrenia. *Journal of the History of the Neurosciences, 11*, 265–277.

Baumeister, R. F. (1998). The self. In D. T. Gilbert, S. T. Fiske, & G. Lindzey (Eds.), *The handbook of social psychology* (4th ed., pp. 680–740). New York: McGraw-Hill.

Baumeister, R. F. (2000). Gender differences in erotic plasticity: The female sex drive as socially flexible and responsive. *Psychological Bulletin, 126*, 347–374.

Baumeister, R. F. (2005). Self-concept, self-esteem, and identity. In V. J. Derlega, B. A. Winstead, & W. H. Jones (Eds.), *Personality: Contemporary theory and research* (3rd ed., pp. 246–280). Belmont, CA: Thomson Wadsworth.

Baumeister, R. F., Catanese, K. R., & Vohs, K. D. (2001). Is there a gender difference in strength of sex drive? Theoretical views, conceptual distinctions, and a review of relevant evidence. *Personality and Social Psychology Review, 5,* 242–273.

Baumeister, R. F., & Heatherton, T. F. (1996). Self-regulation failure: An overview. *Psychological Inquiry, 7,* 1–15.

Baumeister, R. F., & Leary, M. R. (1995). The need to belong: Desire for interpersonal attachments as a fundamental human motivation. *Psychological Bulletin, 117,* 497–529.

Baumrind, D. (1986). Sex differences in moral reasoning: Response to Walker's (1984) conclusion that there are none. *Child Development, 57,* 511–521.

Baumrind, D. (1991). Parenting styles and adolescent development. In J. Brooks-Gunn, R. Lerner, & A. C. Petersen (Eds.), *The encyclopedia of adolescence.* New York: Garland.

Bayley, N. (1949). Consistency and variability in the growth of intelligence from birth to eighteen years. *Journal of Genetic Psychology, 75,* 165–196.

Beach, S. R. H., Whisman, M. A., & O'Leary, K. D. (1994). Marital therapy for depression: Theoretical foundation, current status, and future directions. *Behavior Therapy, 25,* 345–371.

Beaman, A. L., Barnes, P. J., Klentz, B., & McQuirk, B. (1978). Increasing helping rates through information dissemination: Teaching pays. *Personality and Social Psychology Bulletin, 9,* 181–196.

Beasley, D. J., & Amedee, R. G. (2001). Hearing loss. In K. H. Calhoun (Ed.), *Expert guide to otolaryngology* (pp. 53–74). Philadelphia: American College of Physicians.

Beatty, J. (2001). *The human brain: Essentials of behavioral neuroscience.* Thousand Oaks, CA: Sage.

Bebbington, P., & Kuipers, L. (1994). The predictive utility of expressed emotion in schizophrenia: An aggregate analysis. *Psychological Medicine, 24,* 707–718.

Beblo, S., Stark, K. D., Murthy, M., Janisse, J., Rockett, H., Whitty, J. E., Buda-Abela, M., Martier, S. S., Sokol, R. J., Hannigan, J. H., & Salem, N., Jr. (2005). Effects of alcohol intake during pregnancy on docosahexaenoic acid and arachidonic acid in umbilical cord vessels of Black women. *Pediatrics, 115,* 194–203.

Beck, A. T. (1967). *Depression: Clinical, experimental, and theoretical aspects.* New York: Hoeber.

Beck, A. T. (1991). Cognitive therapy: A 30-year retrospective. *American Psychologist, 46,* 368–375.

Beck, A. T. (1997). Cognitive therapy: Reflections. In J. K. Zeig (Ed.), *The evolution of psychotherapy: The third conference.* New York: Brunner/Mazel.

Beck, A. T., & Emery, G. (1985). *Anxiety disorders and phobias: A cognitive perspective.* New York: International Universities Press.

Beck, A. T., Rush, A. J., Shaw, B. F., & Emery, G. (1979). *Cognitive therapy of depression.* New York: Guilford Press.

Beck, C., Silverstone, P., Glor, K., & Dunn, J. (1999). Psychostimulant prescriptions by psychiatrists higher than expected: A self-report survey. *Canadian Journal of Psychiatry, 44,* 680–684.

Beckwith, J., & Alper, J. S. (2002). Genetics of human personality: Social and ethical implications. In J. Benjamin & R. P. Ebstein (Eds.), *Molecular genetics and the human personality* (pp. 315–331). Washington, DC: American Psychiatric Publishing.

Begg, I. M., Anas, A., & Farinacci, S. (1992). Dissociation of processes in belief: Source recollection, statement familiarity, and the illusion of truth. *Journal of Experimental Psychology: General, 121,* 446–458.

Beggs, J. M., Brown, T. H., Byrne, J. H., Crow, T., LeDoux, J. E., LeBar, K., et al. (1999). Learning and memory: Basic mechanisms. In M. J. Zigmond, F. E. Bloom, S. C. Landis, J. L. Roberts, & L. R. Squire (Eds.), *Fundamental neuroscience* (pp. 1411–1454). San Diego, CA: Academic Press.

Beilin, H., & Pufall, P. (Eds.). (1992). *Piaget's theory.* Hillsdale, NJ: Erlbaum.

Békésy, G. von. (1947). The variation of phase along the basilar membrane with sinusoidal vibrations. *Journal of the Acoustical Society of America, 19,* 452–460.

Békésy, G. von. (1957, August). The ear. *Scientific American,* 66–78.

Békésy, G. von. (1960). *Experiments in hearing.* New York: McGraw-Hill.

Bell, A. P., Weinberg, M. S., & Hammersmith, S. K. (1981). *Sexual preference: Its development in men and women.* Bloomington: Indiana University Press.

Bellack, A. S., & Mueser, K. T. (1993). Psychosocial treatment for schizophrenia. *Schizophrenia Bulletin, 19,* 317–336.

Belle, D. (1982). The stress of caring: Women as providers of social support. In L. Goldberger & S. Breznitz (Eds.), *Handbook of stress: Theoretical and clinical aspects* (pp. 496–505). New York: Free Press.

Beller, M., & Gafni, N. (1996). The 1991 international assessment of educational progress in mathematics and sciences: The gender differences perspective. *Journal of Educational Psychology, 88,* 365–377.

Bellingham, K., & Gillies, P. (1993). Evaluation of an AIDS education programme for young adults. *Journal of Epidemiology and Community Health, 47,* 134–138.

Bellus, S. B., Vergo, J. G., Kost, P. P., Stewart, D., & Barkstrom, S. R. (1999). Behavioral rehabilitation and the reduction of aggressive and self-injurious behaviors with cognitively impaired, chronic psychiatric inpatients. *Psychiatric Quarterly, 70,* 27–37.

Bem, S. L. (1983). Gender schema theory and its implications for child development: Raising gender-aschematic children in a gender-schematic society. *Signs, 8,* 598–616.

Ben-Amos, I. K. (1994). *Adolescence and youth in early modern England.* New Haven, CT: Yale University Press.

Benbadis, S. R., Perry, M. C., Sundstad, L. S., & Wolgamuth, B. R. (1999). Prevalence of daytime sleepiness in a population of drivers. *Neurology, 52,* 209–210.

Benbow, C. P., & Stanley, J. C. (1983). Sex differences in mathematical reasoning ability: Fact or artifact? *Science, 222,* 1029–1031.

Bender, R., Trautner, C., Spraul, M., & Berger, M. (1998). Assessment of excess mortality in obesity. *American Journal of Epidemiology, 147,* 42–48.

Benedetti, F., Serretti, A., Colombo, C., Campori, E., Barbini, B., & di Bella, D. (1999). Influence of a functional polymorphism within the promoter of the serotonin transporter gene on the effects of total sleep deprivation in bipolar depression. *American Journal of Psychiatry, 156,* 1450–1452.

Benet-Pagès, A., Orlik, P., Strom, T. M., & Lorenz-Depiereux, B. (2005). An FGF23 missense mutation causes familial tumoral calcinosis with hyperphosphatemia. *Human Molecular Genetics, 14,* 385–390.

Benjamini, E., Coico, R., & Sunshine, G. (2000). *Immunology: A short course* (4th ed.). New York: Wiley-Liss.

Ben-Nathan, D., & Feuerstein, G. (1990). The influence of cold or isolation stress on resistance of mice to West Nile virus encephalitis. *Experientia, 46,* 285–290.

Ben-Nathan, D., Lustig, S., & Kobiler, D. (1996). Cold stress-induced neuroinvasiveness of attenuated arboviruses is not solely mediated by corticosterone. *Archives of Virology, 141,* 1221–1229.

Benson, E. (2003). Intelligence across cultures. *Monitor on Psychology, 34*(2), 56–58.

Benson, H. (1975). *The relaxation response.* New York: Morrow.

Benson, H., & Klipper, M. Z. (1988). *The relaxation response.* New York: Avon.

Benson, H., & Stuart, E. M. (Eds.). (1992). *The wellness book.* New York: Simon & Schuster.

Beren, S. E., Hayden, H. A., Wilfley, D. E., & Striegel-Moore, R. H. (1997). Body dissatisfaction among lesbian college students. *Psychology of Women Quarterly, 21,* 431–445.

Bergin, A. E., & Garfield, S. L. (1994). *Handbook of psychotherapy and behavior change* (4th ed.). New York: Wiley.

Berk, L. E. (1994). Why children talk to themselves. *Scientific American, 271,* 78–83.

Berkman, L., & Syme, S. L. (1979). Social networks, host resistance, and mortality: A nine-year follow-up study of Alameda County residents. *American Journal of Epidemiology, 109,* 186–204.

Berkowitz, L. (1984). Some effects of thoughts on anti- and prosocial influences of media events: A cognitive-neoassociation analysis. *Psychological Bulletin, 95,* 410–427.

Berkowitz, L. (1989). Frustration-aggression hypothesis: Examination and reformulation. *Psychological Bulletin, 106,* 59–73.

Berkowitz, L. (1993). *Aggression: Its causes, consequences, and control.* New York: McGraw-Hill.

Berkowitz, L. (1994). Is something missing? Some observations prompted by the cognitive-neoassociationist view of anger and emotional aggression. In L. R. Huesmann (Ed.), *Aggressive behavior: Current perspectives* (pp. 35–57). New York: Plenum.

Berkowitz, L., & Macaulay, J. (1971). The contagion of criminal violence. *Sociometry, 34,* 238–260.

Berlin, B., & Kay, P. (1969). *Basic color terms: Their universality and evolution.* Berkeley: University of California Press.

Berlyne, D. E. (1974). Studies in the new experimental aesthetics: Steps toward an objective psychology of aesthetic appreciation. Washington, DC: Hemisphere.

Berman, M., Gladue, B., & Taylor, S. (1993). The effects of hormones, Type A behavior pattern and provocation on aggression in men. *Motivation and Emotion, 17,* 182–199.

Bernard, A., Coitot, S., Bremont, A., & Bernard, G. (2005). T and B cell cooperation: A dance of life and death. *Transplantation, 79,* 8–11.

Bernard, H. S. (2005). Countertransference: The evolution of a construct. *International Journal of Group Psychotherapy, 55,* 151–160.

Berndsen, M., Spears, R., & Van Der Pligt, J. (1996). Illusory correlation and attitude-based vested interest. *European Journal of Social Psychology, 26,* 247–264.

Berninger, V. W., Abbott, R. D., Abbott, S. P., Graham, S., & Richards, T. (2002). Writing and reading: Connections between language by hand and language by eye. *Journal of Learning Disabilities, 35,* 39–56.

Bernstein, D. A., Borkovec, T. D., & Hazlette-Stevens, H. (2000). *Progressive relaxation training: A manual for the helping professions* (Rev. ed.). Westport, CT: Greenwood.

Bernstein, I. L. (1978). Learned taste aversions in children receiving chemotherapy. *Science, 200,* 1302–1303.

Bernstein, J. G. (1995). *Handbook of drug therapy in psychiatry* (3rd ed.). St. Louis, MO: Mosby.

Berscheid, E., Dion, K., Hatfield (Walster), E., & Walster, G. W. (1971). Physical attractiveness and dating choice: A test of the matching hypothesis. *Journal of Experimental Social Psychology, 7,* 173–189.

Berscheid, E., & Hatfield (Walster), E. (1974). A little bit about love. In T. Huston (Ed.), *Foundations of interpersonal attraction* (pp. 355–381). New York: Academic Press.

Berube, A. (1990). *Coming out under fire: The history of gay men and women in World War II.* New York: Free Press.

Best, C. T., & Avery, R. A. (1999). Left-hemispheric advantage for click consonants is determined by linguistic significance and experience. *Psychological Science, 10,* 65–70.

Bettencourt, B. N., & Miller, N. (1996). Gender differences in aggression as a function of provocation: A meta-analysis. *Psychological Bulletin, 119,* 422–447.

Beyer, C., Caba, M., Banas, C., & Komisaruk, B. R. (1991). Vasoactive intestinal polypeptide (VIP) potentiates the behavioral effect of substance P intrathecal administration. *Pharmacology, Biochemistry and Behavior, 39,* 695–698.

Beyerstein, B., & Beyerstein, D. (Eds.). (1992). *The write stuff: Evaluations of graphology.* Buffalo, NY: Prometheus Books.

Bidlack, W. R. (1996). Interrelationships of food, nutrition, diet, and health: The National Association of State Universities and Land Grant Colleges White Paper. *Journal of the American College of Nutrition, 15,* 422–433.

Bieliauskas, L. A., Counte, M. A., & Glandon, G. L. (1995). Inventorying stressing life events as related to health change in the elderly. *Stress Medicine, 11,* 93–103.

Biernat, M., & Dovidio, J. F. (2000). Stigma and stereotypes. In T. F. Heatherton, R. E. Kleck, M. R.

Hebl, & J. G. Hull (Eds.), *The social psychology of stigma* (pp. 88–125). New York: Guilford Press.

Bierut, L. J., Dinwiddie, S. H., Begleiter, H., Crowe, R. R., Hesselbrook, V., Nurnberger, J. I., Jr., Porjesz, B., Schuckit, M. A., & Reich, T. (2002). Familial transmission of substance dependence: Alcohol, marijuana, cocaine, and habitual smoking: A report from the collaborative study on the genetics of alcoholism: Erratum. *Archives of General Psychiatry, 59,* 153.

Biever, J. L., Castaño, M. T., de las Fuentes, C., Gonzólez, C., Servín-López, S., & Sprowls, C. (2002). The role of language in training psychologists to work with Hispanic clients. *Professioinal Psychology: Research and Practice, 33,* 330–336.

Billett, E. A., Richter, M. A., & Kennedy, J. L. (1998). Genetics of obsessive-compulsive disorder. In R. P. Swinson & M. M. Antony (Eds.), *Obsessive-compulsive disorder: Theory, research, and treatment* (pp. 181–206). New York: Guilford Press.

Billy, J. O. G., Tanfer, K., Grady, W. R., & Klepinger, D. H. (1993, March/April). The sexual behavior of men in the United States. *Family Planning Perspectives, 25,* 52–60.

Binet, A., & Simon, T. (1905; reprinted 1916). New methods for the diagnosis of the intellectual level of subnormals. In A. Binet & T. Simon (Eds.), *The development of intelligence in children.* Baltimore, MD: Williams & Wilkins.

Biondi, M. (2001). Effects of stress on immune functions: An overview. In R. Ader, D. Felten, & N. Cohen (Eds.), *Psychoneuroimmunology* (Vol. 2, 3rd ed., pp. 189–226). San Diego, CA: Academic Press.

Birbaumer, N., Grodd, W., Diedrich, O., Klose, U., Erb, M., & Lotze, M. (1998). fMRI reveals amygdala activation to human faces in social phobics. *Neuroreport, 9,* 1223–1226.

Birenbaum, M., & Pinku, P. (1997). Effects of test anxiety, information organization, and testing situation on performance on two test formats. *Contemporary Educational Psychology, 22,* 23–38.

Bishop, G. D. (1991). Understanding the understanding of illness: Lay disease representations. In J. A. Skelton & R. T. Croyle (Eds.), *Mental representation in health and illness.* New York: Springer-Verlag.

Björkqvist, K., Lagerspetz, K. M. J., & Kaukiainen, A. (1992). Do girls manipulate and boys fight? Developmental trends regarding direct and indirect aggression. *Aggressive Behavior, 18.*

Björkqvist, K., & Niemelä, P. (1992). New trends in the study of female aggression. In K. Björkqvist & P. Niemelä (Eds.), *Of mice and women: Aspects of female aggression* (pp. 3–16). San Diego, CA: Harcourt Brace Jovanovich.

Black, J. E., Isaacs, K. R., Anderson, B. J., Alcantara, A. A., & Greenough, W. T. (1990). Learning causes synaptogenesis, whereas motor activity causes angiogenesis in cerebellar cortex of adult rats. *Proceedings of the National Academy of Sciences, 87,* 5568–5572.

Blackburn, J. (2005). Rational Emotive Behaviour therapy: Theoretical developments. *Behavioural and Cognitive Psychotherapy, 33,* 122–123.

Blacker, D., & Tsuang, M. T. (1999). Classification and DSM-IV. In A. M. Nichols (Ed.), *The Harvard guide to psychiatry.* Cambridge, MA: Harvard University Press.

Blackmore, S. J. (1997). Probability misjudgment and belief in the paranormal: A newspaper survey. *British Journal of Psychology, 88,* 683–689.

Blackmore, S. J. (2004). *Consciousness.* Oxford, England: Oxford University Press.

Blackwood, N. F., Simmons, A., Bentall, R., Murray, R., & Howard, R. (2004). The cerebellum and decision making under uncertainty. *Cognitive Brain Research, 20,* 46–53.

Blair, S. N., Kohl, H. W., Paffenbarger, R. S., Clark, D. G., Cooper, K. H., & Gibbons, L. W. (1989). Physical fitness and all-cause mortality: A prospective study of healthy men and women. *Journal of the American Medical Association, 262,* 2395–2401.

Bland, S. T., Hargrave, D., Pepin, J. L., Amat, J., Watkins, L. R., & Maier, S. F. (2005). Stressor controllability modulates stress-induced dopamine and serotonin efflux and morphine-induced serotonin efflux in the medial prefrontal cortex. *Neuropsychopharmacology, 28,* 1589–1596.

Blank, H., Fischer, V., & Erdfelder, E. (2003). Hindsight bias in political elections. *Memory, 11,* 491–504.

Blank, S. C., Scott, S. K., Murphy, K., Warburton, E., & Wise, R. J. S. (2002). Speech production: Wernicke, Broca and beyond. *Brain, 125,* 1829–1838.

Blascovich, J. (2002). Social influence within immersive virtual environments. In R. Schroeder (Ed.), *The social life of avatars* (pp. 127–145). Springer-Verlag.

Blascovich, J. (2003). The virtual social animal. Sage Presidential Address to the 4th Annual Meeting of the Society of Personality and Social Psychology. February 6, Los Angeles, CA.

Blass, T. (Ed.). (2000). *Obedience to authority: Current perspectives on the Milgram paradigm.* Mahwah, NJ: Erlbaum.

Blazer, D. G. (1997). Generalized anxiety disorder and panic disorder in the elderly: A review. *Harvard Review of Psychiatry, 5,* 18–27.

Blazer, D. G., Hays, J. C., & Musick, M. A. (2002). Abstinence versus alcohol use among elderly rural Baptists: A test of reference group theory and health outcomes. *Aging & Mental Health, 6,* 47–54.

Blenkiron, P. (2005). Stories and analogies in cognitive behaviour therapy: A clinical review. *Behavioural and Cognitive Psychotherapy, 33,* 45–59.

Bleske-Rechek, A. L., & Buss, D. M. (2001). Opposite-sex friendship: Sex differences and similarities in initiation, selection, and dissolution. *Personality and Social Psychology Bulletin, 27,* 1310–1323.

Bliwise, D. L. (1989). Normal aging. In M. H. Kryger, T. Roth, & W. C. Dement (Eds.), *Principles and practice of sleep medicine.* Philadelphia: Saunders.

Block, N. (2002). How heritability misleads about race. In J. M. Fish (Ed.), *Race and intelligence: Separating science from myth* (pp. 281–296). Mahwah, NJ: Erlbaum.

Bloom, B. S. (1985). *Developing talent in young people.* New York: Ballantine.

Bloom, S., & Polak, J. (Eds.). (1981). *Gut hormones* (2nd ed.). Edinburgh: Churchill-Livingstone.

Blum, L. (2002). *"I'm not a racist, but . . ." The moral quandary of race.* Ithaca, NY: Cornell University Press.

Blumenthal, A. L. A. (2002). A reappraisal of Wilhelm Wundt. In W. E. Pickren & D. A. Dewsbury (Eds.), *Evolving perspectives on the history of psychology* (pp. 65–78). Washington, DC: American Psychological Association.

Boaz, T., Perry, N., Jr., Raney, G., Fischer, I., & Schuman, D. (1991). Detection of guilty knowledge with event-related potentials. *Journal of Applied Psychology, 76,* 788–795.

Bodenhausen, G. V. (1988). Stereotypic biases in social decision making: Testing process models of stereotype use. *Journal of Personality and Social Psychology, 55,* 726–737.

Boehm, S. G., Sommer, W., & Lueschow, A. (2005). Correlates of implicit memory for words and faces in event-related brain potentials. *International Journal of Psychophysiology, 55,* 95–112.

Bogen, J. E. (2000). Split-brain basics: Relevance for the concept of one's other mind. *Journal of the American Academy of Psychoanalysis, 28,* 341–369.

Bogner, H. R., & Gallo, J. J. (2004). Are higher rates of depression in women accounted for by differential symptom reporting? *Social Psychiatry and Psychiatric Epidemiology, 39,* 126–132.

Boiten, F. A. (1998). The effects of emotional behavior on components of the respiratory cycle. *Biological Psychiatry, 49,* 29–51.

Bok, S. (1978). *Lying: Moral choice in public and private life.* New York: Vintage.

Bolles, R. (1980). Some functionalistic thoughts about regulation. In F. Toates & T. Halliday (Eds.), *Analysis of motivational processes* (pp. 63–75). London: Academic Press.

Bolm-Andorff, U., Schwämmle, J., Ehlenz, K., Koop, H., & Kaffarnik, H. (1986). Hormonal and cardiovascular variations during a public lecture. *European Journal of Applied Physiology, 54,* 669–674.

Bonanno, G. A., Keltner, D., Noll, J. G., Putnam, F. W., Trickett, P. K., LeJeune, J., & Anderson, C. (2002). When the face reveals what words do not: Facial expressions of emotion, smiling, and the willingness to disclose childhood sexual abuse. *Journal of Personality & Social Psychology, 83,* 94–110.

Bond, R., & Smith, P. B. (1996). Culture and conformity: A meta-analysis of studies using Asch's (1952b, 1956) line judgment task. *Psychological Bulletin, 119,* 111–137.

Bond, S., & Cash, T. F. (1992). Black beauty: Skin color and body images among African-American college women. *Journal of Applied Social Psychology, 22,* 874–888.

Bonham, V. L., Warshauer-Baker, E., & Collins, F. S. (2005). Race and ethnicity in the genome era: The complexity of the constructs. *American Psychologist, 60,* 9–15.

Bonilla-Silva, E. (2003). *Racism without racists: Color-blind racism and the persistence of racial inequality in the United States.* Lanham, MD: Roman & Littlefield.

Bonneau, R., Padgett, D., & Sheridan, J. (2001). Psychoneuroimmune interactions in infectious disease: Studies in animals. In R. Ader, D. Felten, & N. Cohen (Eds.), *Psychoneuroimmunology* (Vol. 2, 3rd ed., pp. 483–497). San Diego, CA: Academic Press.

Bonson, K. R., Grant, S. J., Contoreggi, C. S., Links, J. M., Metcalfe, J., Weyl, H. L., Kurian, V., Ernst, M., & London, E. D. (2002). Neural systems and cue-induced cocaine craving. *Neuropsychopharmacology, 26,* 376–386.

Boring, E. G. (1923). Intelligence as the tests test it. *New Republic, 35,* 35–37.

Borkenau, P., Riemann, R., Angleitner, A., & Spinath, F. M. (2001). Genetic and environmental influences on observed personality: Evidence from the German observational study of adult twins. *Journal of Personality and Social Psychology, 80,* 655–668.

Borkovec, T., Ray, W., & Stoeber, J. (1998). A cognitive phenomenon intimately linked to affective, physiological, and interpersonal behavioral processes. *Cognitive Therapy & Research, 22,* 561–576.

Bornstein, R. F., Leone, D. R., & Galley, D. J. (1987). The generalizability of subliminal mere exposure effects: Influence of stimuli perceived without awareness on social behavior. *Journal of Personality and Social Psychology, 53,* 1070–1079.

Borowsky, S. J., Rubenstein, L. V., Meredith, L. S., Camp, P., Jackson-Triche, M., & Wells, K. B. (2000). Who is at risk of nondetection of mental health problems in primary care? *Journal of General Internal Medicine, 15,* 381–388.

Boss, P. (1999). *Ambiguous loss: Learning to live with unresolved grief.* Cambridge, MA: Harvard University Press.

Botha, R. P. (1997). Neo-Darwinian accounts of the evolution of language: Questions about their explanatory focus. *Language & Communication, 17,* 249–267.

Bouchard, T. J., Jr. (2004). Genetic influence on human psychological traits. *Current Directions in Psychological Science, 13,* 148–151.

Bouchard, T. J., Jr., Lykken, D. T., McGue, M., Segal, N. L., & Tellegen, A. (1990). Sources of human psychological differences: The Minnesota study of twins reared apart. *Science, 250,* 223–228.

Bouchard, T. J., & McGue, M. (1981). Familial studies of intelligence: A review. *Science, 212,* 1055–1059.

Boudreaux, E., Carmack, C. L., Scarinci, I. C., & Brantley, P. J. (1998). Predicting smoking stage of change among a sample of low socioeconomic status, primary care outpatients: Replication and extension using decisional balance and self-efficacy theories. *International Journal of Behavioral Medicine, 5,* 148–165.

Bougrine, S., Mollard, R., Ignazi, G., & Coblentz, A. (1995). Appropriate use of bright light promotes a durable adaptation to night-shifts and accelerates readjustment during recovery after a period of night-shifts. *Work & Stress, 9,* 314–326.

Bourne, N. K. (2003). Cognitive psychotherapy toward a new millennium: Scientific foundations and clinical practice. *Behaviour Research & Therapy, 41,* 630–631.

Bousfield, W. A. (1953). The occurrence of clustering in the recall of randomly arranged associates. *Journal of General Psychology, 49,* 229–240.

Bovbjerg, D. H., Redd, W. H., Maier, L. A., Holland, J. C., Lesko, L. M., Niedzwiecki, D., Rubin, S. C., & Hakes, T. B. (1990). Anticipatory immune suppression in women receiving cyclic chemotherapy for ovarian cancer. *Journal of Consulting and Clinical Psychology, 58,* 153–157.

Bowen, M. (1960). A family concept of schizophrenia. In D. D. Jackson (Ed.), *The etiology of schizophrenia* (pp. 346–388). New York: Basic Books.

Bowen, M. (1966). The use of family therapy in clinical practice. *Comprehensive Psychiatry, 7,* 345–374.

Bower, B. (1994, October 8). Images of the intellect: Brain scans may colorize intelligence. *Science News, 46,* 236–237.

Bower, B. (1995). Moods and the muse. *Science News, 147,* 378–380.

Bower, G. H., Clark, M. C., Lesgold, A. M., & Winzenz, D. (1969). Hierarchical retrieval schemes in recall of categorized word lists. *Journal of Verbal Learning and Verbal Behavior, 8,* 323–343.

Bower, G. H., & Hilgard, E. R. (1981). *Theories of learning* (5th ed.). Englewood Cliffs, NJ: Prentice Hall.

Bower, G. H., & Mayer, J. D. (1991). In search of mood-dependent retrieval. In D. Kuiken (Ed.), *Mood and memory.* Newbury Park, CA: Sage.

Bowers, K. S., Farvolden, P., & Mermigis, L. (1995). Intuitive antecedents of insight. In S. M. Smith, T. M. Ward, & R. A. Finke (Eds.), *The creative cognition approach* (pp. 27–52). Cambridge, MA: MIT Press.

Bowers, K. S., & Woody, E. Z. (1996). Hypnotic amnesia and the paradox of intentional forgetting. *Journal of Abnormal Psychology,105,* 381–390.

Bowers, T. (1997). Supporting special needs in the mainstream classroom: Children's perceptions of the adult role. *Child: Care, Health and Development, 23,* 217–232.

Bowes, D. E., Tamlyn, D., & Butler, L. J. (2002). Women living with ovarian cancer: Dealing with an early death. *Health Care for Women International, 23,* 135–148.

Bowlby, J. (1969). *Attachment and loss: Vol. I. Attachment.* New York: Wiley.

Bowlby, J. (1988). *A secure base: Parent-child attachment and healthy human development.* New York: Basic Books.

Bowman, C., & Brownell, P. (2000). Prelude to contemporary Gestalt therapy. *Gestalt Journal, 4,* 118–129.

Boyce, T. E., & Geller, E. S. (2002). An instrumented vehicle assessment of problem behavior and driving style: Do younger males really take more risks? *Accident Analysis & Prevention, 34,* 51–64.

Boyd, R., & Richerson, P. J. (1996). Why culture is common, but cultural evolution is rare. In W. G. Runciman, J. M. Smith, et al. (Eds.), *Evolution of social behavior patterns in primates and man. Proceedings of The British Academy* (Vol. 88, pp. 77–93). Oxford, England: Oxford University Press.

Boynton, R. M., & Olson, C. X. (1990). Salience of basic chromatic color terms confirmed by three measures. *Vision Research, 30,* 1311–1317.

Bracken, B. A., Howell, K. K., & Crain, M. R. (1993). Prediction of Caucasian and African-American preschool children's fluid and crystallized intelligence: Contributions of maternal characteristics and home environment. *Journal of Clinical Child Psychology, 22,* 455–463.

Bradburn, N. M., & Sudman, S. (1988). *Polls and surveys: Understanding what they tell us.* San Francisco: Jossey-Bass.

Bradbury, T. N., Campbell, S. M., & Fincham, F. D. (1995). Longitudinal and behavioral analysis of masculinity and femininity in marriage. *Journal of Personality and Social Psychology, 68,* 328–341.

Bradley, R. H., & Caldwell, B. M. (1984). 174 children: A study of the relationship between home environment and cognitive development during the first 5 years. In A. W. Gottfried (Ed.), *Home environment and early cognitive development: Longitudinal research.* Orlando, FL: Academic Press.

Brainerd, C. J., Reyna, V. F., & Brandse, E. (1995). Are children's false memories more persistent than their true memories? *Psychological Science, 6,* 359–364.

Brand, C. (1996). "g," genes and pedagogy: A reply to seven (lamentable) chapters. In D. K. Detterman (Ed.), *Current topics in human intelligence: Vol. 5. The environment* (pp. 113–120). Norwood, NJ: Ablex.

Brandimonte, M. A., Hitch, G. J., & Bishop, D. V. M. (1992). Influence of short-term memory codes on visual image processing: Evidence from image transformation tasks. *Journal of Experimental Psychology: Learning, Memory, and Cognition, 18,* 157–165.

Brannon, L., & Feist, J. (2000). *Health psychology: An introduction to behavior and health* (4th ed.). Belmont, CA: Wadsworth/Thomson Learning.

Branscombe, N. R., Schmidtt, M. T., & Harvey, R. D. (1999). Perceiving pervasive discrimination among African-Americans: Implications for group identification and well-being. *Journal of Personality and Social Psychology, 77,* 135–149.

Bransford, J. D., & Johnson, M. K. (1972). Contextual prerequisites for understanding: Some investigations of comprehension and recall. *Journal of Verbal Learning and Verbal Behavior, 11,* 717–726.

Braun, A. R. (2001). Ecstasy on trial: Seeking insight by prescription. *Cerebrum, 3,* 10–21.

Breedlove, S. M. (1997). Sex on the brain. *Nature, 389,* 801.

Breggin, P. R. (1979). *Electroshock: Its disabling effects.* New York: Springer-Verlag.

Breggin, P. R. (1991). *Toxic psychiatry.* New York: St. Martin's Press.

Brehm, J. (1966). *A theory of psychological reactance.* New York: Academic Press.

Brehm, S. S. (1988). Passionate love. In R. J. Sternberg & M. L. Barnes (Eds.), *The psychology of love* (pp. 232–263). New Haven, CT: Yale University Press.

Brehm, S. S. (1992). *Intimate relationships.* New York: McGraw-Hill.

Brehm, S. S., & Brehm, J. W. (1981). *Psychological reactance: A theory of freedom and control.* New York: Academic Press.

Breitbart, W., Rosenfeld, B., Pessin, H., Kaim, M., Funesti-Esch, J., Galietta, C. J., & Brescia, R. (2000). Depression, hopelessness, and desire for hastened death in terminally ill patients with cancer. *Journal of the American Medical Association, 284,* 2907–2911.

Breland, K., & Breland, M. (1961). The misbehavior of organisms. *American Psychologist, 16,* 681–684.

Brems, C. (1995). Women and depression: A comprehensive analysis. In E. E. Beckham & W. R. Leber (Eds.), *Handbook of depression* (2nd ed., pp. 539–566). New York: Guilford Press.

Brendl, C. M., Markman, A. B., & Messner, C. (2001). How do indirect measures of evaluation work? Evaluating the inference of prejudice in the Implicit Association Test. *Journal of Personality and Social Psychology, 81,* 760–773.

Brennan, P. A., Grekin, E. R., & Mednick, S. A. (1999). Maternal smoking during pregnancy and adult male criminal outcomes. *Archives of General Psychiatry, 56,* 215–219.

Breslau, N., Johnson, E., Hiripi, E., & Kessler, R. (2001). Nicotine dependence in the United States—Prevalence, trends, and smoking persistence. *Archives of General Psychiatry, 58,* 810–816.

Breslau, N., Kessler, R. C., Chilcoat, H. D., Schultz, L. R., Davis, G. C., & Andreski, P. (1998). Trauma and posttraumatic stress disorder in the community: The 1996 Detroit Area Survey of Trauma. *Archives of General Psychiatry, 55,* 626–632.

Bretherton, I. (1985). Attachment theory: Retrospect and prospect. In I. Bretherton & E. Waters (Eds.), Growing points of attachment theory and research. *Monographs of the Society for Research in Child Development, 50*(1-2, Serial No. 209), 3–35.

Breuer, J., & Freud, S. (1893/1955). Studies on hysteria. In J. Strachey (Ed. and Trans.), *The standard edition of the complete psychological works of Sigmund Freud* (Vol. 2, pp. 1–251). London: Hogarth. (Original work published 1893–1895)

Brewer, M. B. (1988). A dual process model of impression formation. In T. K. Srull & R. S. Wyer, Jr. (Eds.), *Advances in social cognition: Vol. 1. A dual process model of impression formation* (pp. 1–36). Hillsdale, NJ: Erlbaum.

Brewer, M. B., & Brown, R. J. (1998). Intergroup relations. In D. T. Gilbert, S. T. Fiske, & G. Lindzey (Eds.), *The handbook of social psychology* (4th ed.). New York: McGraw-Hill.

Brewin, C. R., Dalgleish, T., & Joseph, S. (1996). A dual representation theory of posttraumatic stress disorder. *Psychological Review, 103,* 670–686.

Brickman, P., Coates, D., & Janoff-Bulman, R. J. (1978). Lottery winners and accident victims: Is happiness relative? *Journal of Personality and Social Psychology, 36,* 917–927.

Bridges, J. S., & Etaugh, C. (1994). Black and White college women's perceptions of early maternal employment. *Psychology of Women Quarterly, 18,* 427–431.

Briere, J., & Lanktree, C. (1983). Sex-role related effects of sex bias in language. *Sex Roles, 9,* 625–632.

Briggs, S. R. (2005). Personality measurement. In V. J. Derlega, B. A. Winstead, & W. H. Jones (Eds.), *Personality: Contemporary theory and research* (3rd ed., pp. 27–62). Belmont, CA: Thomson Wadsworth.

Bril, B. (1986). Motor development and cultural attitudes. In H. T. A. Whiting & M. G. Wade (Eds.), *Themes in motor development.* Dordrecht, Netherlands: Martinus Nijhoff.

Brislin, R. (1993). *Understanding culture's influence on behavior.* Fort Worth, TX: Harcourt Brace Jovanovich.

Brissette, I., & Cohen, S. (2002). The contributioin of individual differences in hostility to the associations between daily interpersonal conflict, affect, and sleep. *Personality and Social Psychology Bulletin, 28,* 1265–1274.

Britt, T. W., Boniecki, K. A., Vescio, T. K., Biernat, M., & Brown, L. M. (1996). Intergroup anxiety: A person 3 situation approach. *Personality and Social Psychology Bulletin, 22,* 1177–1188.

Broberg, D. J., & Bernstein, I. L. (1987). Candy as a scapegoat in the prevention of food aversions in children receiving chemotherapy. *Cancer, 60,* 2344–2347.

Brockington, I., Hall, P., Levings, J., & Murphy, C. (1993). The community's tolerance of the mentally ill. *British Journal of Psychiatry, 162,* 93–99.

Brody, C. M. (2002). An existential approach: End-of-life issues for women. In F. K.Trotman & C. M. Brody (Eds.), *Psychotherapy and counseling with older women: Cross-cultural, family, and end-of-life issues* (pp. 239–250). *Springer series, focus on women.* New York: Springer.

Brody, L. R., & Hall, J. A. (1993). Gender and emotion. In M. Lewis & J. M. Haviland (Eds.), *Handbook of emotions* (pp. 447–460). New York: Guilford.

Brody, N. (1992). *Intelligence* (2nd ed.). San Diego, CA: Academic Press.

Brody, N. (2000). History of theories and measurements of intelligence. In R. J. Sternberg (Ed.), *Handbook of intelligence* (pp. 16–33). Cambridge: Cambridge University Press.

Brody, N. (2003). What Sternberg should have concluded. *Intelligence, 31,* 339–342.

Bromet, E. J., & Havenaar, J. M. (2002). Mental health consequences of disasters. In N. Sartorius & W. Gaebel (Eds.), *Psychiatry in society* (pp. 241–261). New York: Wiley.

Brophy, D. R. (2001). Comparing the attributes, activities, and performance of divergent, convergent, and combination thinkers. *Creativity Research Journal, 13,* 439–455.

Broughton, R., De Konick, J., Gagnon, P., Dunham, W., & Stampi, C. (1990). Sleep-wake biorhythms and extended sleep in man. In J. Montplaisir & R. Godbout (Eds.), *Sleep and biological rhythms: Basic mechanisms and applications to psychiatry* (pp. 25–41). New York: Oxford University Press.

Brown, A. D., & Murphy, D. R. (1989). Cryptomnesia: Delineating inadvertent plagiarism. *Journal of Experimental Psychology: Learning, Memory, & Cognition, 15,* 432–442.

Brown, A. S. (1991). A review of the tip-of-the-tongue experience. *Psychological Bulletin, 109,* 204–223.

Brown, A. S. (2002). Consolidation theory and retrograde amnesia in humans. *Psychonomic Bulletin & Review, 9,* 403–425.

Brown, A. S. (2003). A review of the déjà vu experience. *Psychological Bulletin, 129,* 394-413.

Brown, A. S. (2004). *The déjà vu experience: Essays in cognitive psychology.* London: Psychology Press.

Brown, E. R., Ojeda, V. D., Wyn, R., & Levan, R. (2000). *Racial and ethnic disparities in access to health insurance and health care.* Los Angeles: UCLA Center for Health Policy Research and The Henry J. Kaiser Family Foundation.

Brown, G. M. (1994). Light, melatonin, and the sleep-wake cycle. *Journal of Psychiatry and Neuroscience, 19,* 345–353.

Brown, J. (1958). Some tests of the decay theory of immediate memory. *Quarterly Journal of the Behavioral Sciences, 11,* 342–349.

Brown, J. (1979). Motivation. In E. Hearst (Ed.), *The first century of experimental psychology* (pp. 231–274). Hillsdale, NJ: Erlbaum.

Brown, P., & Levinson, S. (1987). *Politeness: Some universals in language usage.* Cambridge, England: Cambridge University Press.

Brown, P. K., & Wald, G. (1964). Visual pigments in single rods and cones of the human retina. *Science, 144,* 45–52.

Brown, R. (1973). *A first language: The early stages.* Cambridge, MA: Harvard University Press.

Brown, R. (1986). Linguistic relativity. In S. H. Hulse & B. F. Green, Jr. (Eds.), *One hundred years of psychological research in America.* Baltimore, MD: Johns Hopkins University Press.

Brown, R., & Kulik, J. (1977). Flashbulb memories. *Cognition, 5,* 73–99.

Brown, S. R. (2000). Tip-of-the-tongue phenomena: An introductory phenomenological analysis. *Consciousness & Cognition: An International Journal, 9,* 516–537.

Brownell, K. D. (1991). Dieting and the search for the perfect body: Where physiology and culture collide. *Behavior Therapy, 22,* 1–12.

Brownell, K. D., & Rodin, J. (1994). Medical, metabolic, and psychological effects of weight cycling. *Archives of Internal Medicine, 154,* 1325–1330.

Brownell, K. D., & Wadden, T. (1991). The heterogeneity of obesity: Fitting treatments to individuals. *Behavior Therapy, 22,* 153–177.

Brownell, K. D., & Wadden, T. (1992). Etiology and treatment of obesity: Understanding a serious, prevalent, and refractory disorder. *Journal of Consulting and Clinical Psychology, 60,* 505–517.

Bruch, H. (1973). *Eating disorders: Obesity, anorexia nervosa, and the person within.* New York: Basic Books.

Bruch, H. (1982). Anorexia nervosa: Therapy and theory. *American Journal of Psychiatry, 139,* 1531–1538.

Brudzynski, S. M. (2001). Pharmacological and behavioral characteristics of 22 kHz alarm calls in rats. *Neuroscience & Biobehavioral Reviews, 25,* 611–617.

Bryan, A., Rocheleau, C. A., Robbins, R. N., & Hutchinson, K. E. (2005). Condom use among high-risk adolescents: Testing the influence of alcohol use on the relationship of cognitive correlates of behavior. *Health Psychology, 24,* 133–142.

Bryant, A. L., & Zimmerman, M. A. (2003). Role models and psychosocial outcomes among African American adolescents. *Journal of Adolescent Research, 18,* 36–67.

Bryant, R. A., Barnier, A. J., Mallard, D., & Tibbits, R. (1999). Posthypnotic amnesia for material learned before hypnosis. *International Journal of Clinical and Experimental Hypnosis, 47,* 46–64.

Bryden, M. P. (1979). Evidence for sex-related differences in cerebral organization. In M. A. Whiting & A. Peterson (Eds.), *Sex-related differences in cognitive functioning* (pp. 121–143). New York: Academic Press.

Bryson, S. E. (1990). Autism and anomalous handedness. In S. Coren (Ed.), *Left-handedness: Behavioral implications and anomalies.* Amsterdam: North-Holland.

Bubar, M. J., McMahon, L. R., De Deurwaerdere, P., Spampinato, U., & Cunningham, K. A. (2003). Selective serotonin reuptake inhibitors enhance cocaine-induced locomotor activity and dopamine release in the nucleus accumbens. *Neuropharmacology, 44,* 342–353.

Buck, R. (1984). *The communication of emotion.* New York: Guilford Press.

Budiansky, S. (1998). *If a lion could talk: Animal intelligence and the evolution of consciousness.* New York: Free Press.

Budney, A. J., Hughes, J. R., Moore, B. A., & Novy, P. L. (2001). Marijuana abstinence effects in marijuana smokers maintained in their home environments. *Archives of General Psychiatry, 58,* 917–924.

Buhusi, C. V., & Schmajuk, N. A. (1999). Timing in simple conditioning and occasion setting: A neural network approach. *Behavioural Processes, 45,* 33–57.

Bulik, C. M., Sullivan, P. F., & Kendler, K. S. (2003). Genetic and environmental contributions to obesity and binge eating. *International Journal of Eating Disorders, 33,* 293–298.

Bullinger, M., Hygge, S., Evans, G. W., Meis, M., & von Mackensen, S. (1999). The psychological cost of aircraft noise for children [Psychologische Beeinträchtigung von Kindern durch Fluglärm]. *Aentralblatt für Hygiene und Umweltmedizin, 202,* 127–138.

Bullough, V. (1980). The Kinsey scale in historical perspective. In D. P. McWhirter, S. A. Sanders, & J. M. Reinisch (Eds.), *Homosexuality/heterosexuality: Concepts of sexual orientation.* New York: Oxford University Press.

Burger, J. M. (1987). Desire for control and conformity to a perceived norm. *Journal of Personality and Social Psychology, 53,* 355–360.

Burger, J. M., Horita, M., Kinoshita, L., Roberts, K., & Vera, C. (1997). Effects of time on the norm of reciprocity. *Basic and Applied Social Psychology, 19,* 91–100.

Burling, R. (1986). The selective advantage of complex language. *Ethology & Sociobiology, 1,* 1–16.

Burnham, M. M., Goodlin-Jones, B. L., Gaylor, E. E., & Anders, T. F. (2003). Use of sleep aids during the first year of life. *Journal of the American Academy of Child & Adolescent Psychiatry, 42,* 92.

Burt, M. (1980). Cultural myths and supports for rape. *Journal of Personality and Social Psychology, 38,* 217–230.

Busch, A. L., & Rosenberg, M. S. (2004). Comparing women and men arrested for domestic violence: A preliminary report. *Journal of Family Violence, 19,* 49–57.

Busch, C. M., Zonderman, A. B., & Costa, P. T. (1994). Menopausal transition and psychological distress in a nationally representative sample: Is menopause associated with psychological distress? *Journal of Aging and Health, 6,* 209–228.

Bushman, B. J., & Anderson, C. A. (2001). Is it time to pull the plug on the hostile versus instrumental aggression dichotomy? *Psychological Review, 108,* 273–279.

Bushman, B. J., Baumeister, R. F., & Phillips, C. M. (2001). Do people aggress to improve their mood? Catharsis beliefs, affect regulation, opportunity, and aggressive responding. *Journal of Personality and Social Psychology, 81,* 17–33.

Buske-Kirschbaum, A., Kirschbaum, C., Stierle, H., Jabaij, L., & Hellhammer, D. (1994). Conditioned manipulation of natural killer (NK) cells in humans using a discriminative learning protocol. *Biological Psychology, 38,* 143–155.

Buss, A. H., & Plomin, R. (1984). *Temperament: Early developing personality traits.* Hillsdale, NJ: Erlbaum.

Buss, D. H. (1999). *Evolutionary psychology.* Boston: Allyn & Bacon.

Buss, D. H., & Kenrick, D. (1998). Evolutionary social psychology. In D. Gilbert, S. Fiske, & G. Lindzey (Eds.), *The handbook of social psychology* (Vol. 2, 4th ed., pp. 982–1026). New York: Oxford University Press.

Buss, D. M. (1987). Sex differences in human mate selection criteria: An evolutionary perspective. In C. Crawford, M. Smith, & D. Krebs (Eds.), *Sociobiology and psychology: Ideas, issues and applications* (pp. 335–351). Hillsdale, NJ: Erlbaum.

Buss, D. M. (1988). The evolution of human intrasexual competition: Tactics of mate attraction. *Journal of Personality and Social Psychology, 54,* 616–628.

Buss, D. M. (1989). Sex differences in human mate preferences: Evolutionary hypotheses tested in 37 cultures. *Behavioral and Brain Sciences, 12,* 1–49.

Buss, D. M. (1990). Evolutionary social psychology: Prospects and pitfalls. *Motivation and Emotion, 14,* 265–286.

Buss, D. M. (1995). Evolutionary psychology: A new paradigm for psychological science. *Psychological Inquiry, 6,* 1–31.

Buss, D. M. (1999a). *Evolutionary psychology: The new science of mind.* Boston, MA: Allyn & Bacon.

Buss, D. M. (1999b). Human nature and individual differences: The evolution of human personality. In L. A. Pervin & O. P. John (Eds.), *Handbook of personality: Theory and research* (pp. 31–56). New York: Guilford Press.

Buss, D. M., Haselton, M. G., Shackelford, T. K., Bleske, A. L., & Wakefield, J. (1998). Adaptations, exaptations, and spandrels. *American Psychologist, 53,* 533–548.

Buss, D. M., & Schmitt, D. P. (1993). Sexual strategies theory: An evolutionary perspective on human mating. *Psychological Review, 100,* 204–232.

Bussey, K., & Bandura, A. (1999). Social cognitive theory of gender development and differentiation. *Psychological Review, 106,* 676–713.

Butcher, J. N. (2005). *A beginner's guide to the MMPI-2* (2nd ed.). Washington, DC: American Psychological Association.

Butcher, J. N., & Rouse, S. V. (1996). Personality: Individual differences and clinical assessment. *Annual Review of Psychology, 47,* 87–111.

Butcher, J. N., & Williams, C. L. (2000). *Essentials of MMPI-2 and MMPI-A interpretation.* Minneapolis, MN: University of Minnesota Press.

Butterworth, G. (1992). Origins of self-perception in infancy. *Psychological Inquiry, 3,* 103–111.

Buunk, B., & Bringle, R. G. (1987). Jealousy in love relationships. In D. Perlman & S. Duck (Eds.), *Intimate relationships: Development, dynamics, and deterioration* (pp. 123–147). Newbury Park, CA: Sage.

Buunk, B. P., & van der Laan, V. (2002). Do women need female role models? Subjective social status and the effects of same-sex and opposite sex comparisons. *Revue Internationale de Psychologie Sociale, 15,* 129–155.

Bybee, J., & Fleischman, S. (Eds.). (1995). *Modality in grammar and discourse.* Philadelphia: Benjamins Publishing.

Byrne, M., Clafferty, B. A., Cosway, R., Grant, E., Hodges, A., Whalley, H. C., Lawrie, S. M., Owens, D. G. C., & Johnstone, E. C. (2003). Neuropsychology, genetic liability, and psychotic symptoms in those at high risk of schizophrenia. *Journal of Abnormal Psychology, 112,* 38–48.

Byrne, R. W. (1995). The ape legacy: The evolution of Machiavellian intelligence and anticipatory interactive planning. In E. N. Goody (Ed.), *Social intelligence and interaction: Expressions and implications of the social bias in human intelligence* (pp. 37–52). Cambridge, England: Cambridge University Press.

Cacioppo, J. T., Lorig, T. S., Nusbaum, H. C., & Bernston, G. G. (2004). Social neuroscience: Bridging social and biological systems. In C. Sansone, C. C. Morf, & A. T. Panter (Eds.), *Handbook of methods in social psychology* (pp. 383–404). Thousand Oaks, CA: Sage.

Cacioppo, J. T., Marshall-Goodell, B. S., Tassinary, L. G., & Petty, R. E. (1992). Rudimentary determinants of attitudes: Classical conditioning is more effective when prior knowledge about the attitude stimulus is low than high. *Journal of Experimental Social Psychology, 28,* 207–233.

Cacioppo, J. T., & Petty, R. E. (1982). The need for cognition. *Journal of Personality and Social Psychology, 42,* 116–131.

Cacioppo, J. T., Petty, R. E., Feinstein, J. A., & Jarvis, W. B. G. (1996). Dispositional differences in cognitive motivation: The life and times of individuals varying in need for cognition. *Psychological Bulletin, 119,* 197–253.

Cacioppo, J. T., Petty, R. E., Kao, C. F., & Rodriguez, R. (1986). Central and peripheral routes to persuasion: An individual differences perspective. *Journal of Personality and Social Psychology, 51,* 1032–1043.

Cain, W. S. (1978). The odoriferous environment and the application of olfactory research. In E. C. Carterette & M. P. Friedman (Eds.), *Handbook of perception* (pp. 277–304). New York: Academic Press.

Cairns-Smith, A. G. (1996). *Evolving the mind: On the nature of matter and the origin of consciousness.* Cambridge: Cambridge University Press.

Caldwell, D. F., & O'Reilly, C. A., III. (1982). Boundary spanning and individual performance: The impact of self-monitoring. *Journal of Applied Psychology, 67,* 124–127.

Caldwell, J. D. (2002). A sexual arousability model involving steroid effects at the plasma membrane. *Neuroscience & Biobehavioral Reviews, 26,* 13–30.

Callahan, C. M. (2000). Intelligence and giftedness. In R. J. Sternberg (Ed.), *Handbook of intelligence* (pp. 159–175). Cambridge: Cambridge University Press.

Calle, E. E., Thun, M. J., Petrelli, J. M., Rogriguez, C., & Health, C. W., Jr. (1999). Body-mass index and mortality in a prospective cohort of U.S. adults. *New England Journal of Medicine, 341,* 1097–1105.

Calvin, W. H. (1996). *How brains think.* New York: Basic Books.

Calvin, W. H., & Ojemann, G. A. (1994). *Conversations with Neil's brain: The neural nature of thought and language.* Reading, MA: Addison-Wesley.

Cameron, A. F., & Webster, J. (2005). Unintended consequences of emerging communication technologies: Instant messaging in the workplace. *Computers in Human Behavior, 21,* 85–103.

Campbell, A. (1999). Staying alive: Evolution, culture, and women's intrasexual aggression. *Behavioral and Brain Sciences, 22,* 203–252.

Campbell, A., & Muncer, S. (1987). Models of anger and aggression in the social talk of women and men. *Journal of the Theory of Social Behaviour, 17,* 489–511.

Campbell, A., Muncer, S., & Coyle, E. (1992). Social representation of aggression as an explanation of gender differences: A preliminary study. *Aggressive Behavior, 18,* 95–108.

Campbell, D. M., Hall, M. H., Barker, D. J. P., Cross, J., Shiell, A. W., & Godfrey, K. M. (1996). Diet in pregnancy and the offspring's blood pressure 40 years later. *British Journal of Obstetrics & Gynecology, 104,* 663–667.

Campbell, F. A., & Ramey, C. T. (1994). Effects of early intervention on intellectual and academic achievement: A follow-up study of children from low-income families. *Child Development, 65,* 684–698.

Campbell, F. A., & Ramey, C. T. (1995). Cognitive and school outcomes for high risk students at middle adolescence: Positive effects of early intervention. *American Educational Research Journal, 32,* 743–772.

Campbell, J. B., & Hawley, C. W. (1982). Study habits and Eysenck's theory of extraversion-introversion. *Journal of Research in Personality, 16,* 139–146.

Campbell, N. A., Mitchell, L. G., & Reece, J. B. (1994). *Biology: Concepts & connections.* Redwood City, CA: Benjamin/Cummings.

Campbell, W. K., & Sedikides, C. (1999). Self-threat magnifies the self-serving bias: A meta-analytic integration. *Review of General Psychology, 3,* 23–43.

Campos, J. L., Langer, A., & Krowitz, A. (1970). Cardiac responses on the visual cliff in prelocomotor human infants. *Science, 170,* 196–197.

Canli, T., & Amin, Z. (2002). Neuroimaging of emotion and personality: Scientific evidence and ethical considerations. *Brain & Cognition, 50,* 414–431.

Canli, T., Zhao, Z., Desmond, J. E., Kang, E., Gross, J., & Gabrieli, J. D. E. (2001). An fMRI study of personality influences on brain reactivity to emotional stimuli. *Behavioral Neuroscience, 115,* 33–42.

Cannon, W. B. (1915). *Bodily changes in pain, hunger, fear, and rage.* Birmingham, AL: Gryphon.

Cannon, W. B. (1927). The James-Lange theory of emotion: A critical examination and an alternative theory. *American Journal of Psychology, 39,* 106–124.

Cannon, W. B., & Washburn, A. (1912). An explanation of hunger. *American Journal of Physiology, 29,* 441–454.

Cantfort, T. V., & Rimpau, J. B. (1982). Sign language studies with children and chimpanzees. *Sign Language Studies, 34,* 14–20.

Capaldi, E. (Ed.). (1996). *Why we eat what we eat: The psychology of eating.* Washington, DC: American Psychological Association.

Capitanio, J. P. (1999). Personality dimensions in adult male rhesus macaques: Prediction of behaviors across time and situation. *American Journal of Primatology, 47,* 299–320.

Capitanio, J. P. (in press). Intra- and interspecific variation in personality. In B. Thierry, M. Singh, & W. Kaumanns (Eds.), *How societies arise: The macaque model.* Cambridge: Cambridge University Press.

Caporael, L. R. (2001). Parts and whole: The evolutionary importance of groups. In C. Sedikides & M. B. Brewer (Eds.), *Individual self, relational self, collective self* (pp. 241–258). Philadelphia: Psychology Press.

Caprara, G. V., Barbaranelli, C., & Zimbardo, P. G. (1996). Understanding the complexity of human aggression: Affective, cognitive, and social dimensions of individual differences in propensity toward aggression. *European Journal of Personality, 10,* 133–155.

Caprara, G. V., Perugini, M., & Barbaranelli, C. (1994). Studies of individual differences in aggression. In M. Potegal & J. F. Knutson (Eds.), *The dynamics of aggression: Biological and social processes in dyads and groups* (pp. 123–153). Hillsdale, NJ: Erlbaum.

Capron, C., & Duyme, M. (1989). Assessment of effects of socioeconomic status on IQ in a full cross-fostering study. *Nature, 340,* 552–553.

Carli, L. L. (1990). Gender, language, and influence. *Journal of Personality and Social Psychology, 59,* 941–951.

Carli, L. L., LaFleur, S. J., & Loeber, C. C. (1995). Nonverbal behavior, gender, and influence. *Journal of Personality and Social Psychology, 68,* 1030–1041.

Carlin, A. S., Hoffman, H. G., & Weghorst, S. (1997). Virtual reality and tactile augmentation in the treatment of spider phobia: A case report. *Behavioral Research and Therapy, 35,* 153–158.

Carmelli, D., Swann, G., Robinette, D., & Fabsitz, R. (1992). Genetic influence on smoking: A study of male twins. *New England Journal of Medicine, 327,* 829–833.

Carnagey, N. L., Bushman, B. J., & Anderson, C. A. (2004). *Video game violence desensitizes players to real world violence.* Manuscript submitted for publication.

Carnap, R. (1966). *An introduction to the philosophy of science.* New York: Basic Books.

Carpenter, J. T. (2004). EMDR as an integrative psychotherapy approach: Experts explore the paradigm prism. *Psychotherapy Research, 14,* 135–136.

Carpenter, P. A., Just, M. A., & Shell, P. (1990). What one intelligence test measures: A theoretical account of the processing in the Raven Progressive Matrices Test. *Psychological Review, 97,* 404–431.

Carpenter, S. (2001). Everyday fantasia: The world of synesthesia. *Monitor on Psychology, 32,* 26–29.

Carroll, J. B. (1993). *Human cognitive abilities: A survey of factor-analytic studies.* Cambridge, England: University of Cambridge Press.

Carroll, K. M. (1997). Listening to smoking researchers: Negative affect and drug abuse treatment. *Psychological Science, 8,* 190–193.

Carter, P. L. (2003). "Black" cultural capital, status positioning, and schooling conflicts for low-income African American youth. *Social Problems, 50,* 136–155.

Cartwright, R. D. (1977). *Night life: Explorations in dreaming.* Englewood Cliffs, NJ: Prentice Hall.

Cartwright, R. D. (1989). Dreams and their meaning. In M. H. Dryger, T. Roth, & W. C. Dement (Eds.), *Principles and practice of sleep medicine.* San Diego, CA: Harcourt Brace Jovanovich.

Cartwright, R. D. (1991). Dreams that work: The relation of dream incorporation to adaptation to stressful events. *Dreaming, 1,* 3–9.

Carver, C. S., & Baird, E. (1998). The American dream revisited: Is it what you want or why you want it that matters? *Psychological Science, 9,* 289–292.

Caryl, P. G. (1994). Early event-related potentials correlate with inspection time and intelligence. *Intelligence, 18,* 15–46.

Case, R. (1985). *Intellectual development: Birth to adulthood.* New York: Academic Press.

Case, R. (1991). *The mind's staircase: Exploring the conceptual underpinnings of children's thought and knowledge.* Hillsdale, NJ: Erlbaum.

Case, R. (1992). Neo-Piagetian theories of child development. In R. J. Sternberg & C. A. Berg (Eds.), *Intellectual development* (pp. 161–196). New York: Cambridge University Press.

Cash, T. (1996). The treatment of body image disturbances. In J. Thompson (Ed.), *Body image, eating disorders, and obesity* (pp. 83–108). Washington, DC: American Psychological Association.

Cash, T., & Henry, P. (1995). Women's body images: The results of a national survey in the U.S.A. *Sex Roles, 33,* 19–28.

Caspi, A., Bem, D. J., & Elder, G. H., Jr. (1989). Continuities consequences of interactional styles across the life course [special issue]. *Journal of Personality, 57,* 375–406.

Cassady, J. D., Kirschke, D. L., Jones, T. F., Craig, A. S., Bermudez, O. B., & Schaffner, W. (2005). Case series: Outbreak of conversion disorder among Amish adolescent girls. *Journal of the American Academy of Child and Adolescent Psychiatry, 44,* 291–297.

Cassel, R. N. (2000). Third force psychology and person-centered theory: From ego-status to ego-ideal. *Psychology: A Quarterly Journal of Human Behavior, 37,* 44–48.

Cassidy, J., & Shaver, P. R. (1999). *Handbook of attachment.* New York: Guilford.

Castillo, J., Munoz, P., Guitera, V., & Pascual, J. (1999). Epidemiology of chronic daily headache in the general population. *Headache, 39,* 190–196.

Catal, L. L., & Fitzgerald, J. M. (2004). Autobiographical memory in two older adults over a twenty-year retention interval. *Memory & Cognition, 32,* 311–323.

Catania, J., Coates, T., Kegeles, S., Thompson-Fullilove, M., Peterson, J., Marin, B., Siegel, D., & Hully, S. (1992). Condom use in multi-ethnic neighborhoods of San Francisco: The population-based AMEN study. *American Journal of Public Health, 82,* 284–287.

Cattell, H. E. P. (2001). The Sixteen Personality Factor (16PF) Questionnaire. In W. I. Dorfman & M. Hersen (Eds.), *Understanding psychological assessment: Perspectives on individual differences* (pp. 187–215). Dordrecht, Netherlands: Kluwer Academic Publishers.

Cattell, R. B. (1963). Theory of fluid and crystallized intelligence: A critical experiment. *Journal of Educational Psychology, 54,* 1–22.

Cattell, R. B. (1965). *The scientific analysis of personality.* Chicago: Aldine.

Cattell, R. B. (1971). *Abilities: Their structure, growth, and action.* Boston: Houghton Mifflin.

Cattell, R. B. (1986). The 16 PF personality structure and Dr. Eysenck. *Journal of Social Behavior and Personality, 1,* 153–160.

Cazden, C. (1972). *Child language and education.* New York: Holt.

Ceci, S. J. (1995). False beliefs: Some developmental and clinical considerations. In D. L. Schacter (Ed.), *Memory distortion: How minds, brains, and societies reconstruct the past* (pp. 91–125). Cambridge, MA: Harvard University Press.

Ceci, S. J., & Bruck, M. (1993). Suggestibility of the child witness: A historical review and synthesis. *Psychological Bulletin, 113,* 403–439.

Ceci, S. J., & Bruck, M. (1995). *Jeopardy in the courtroom: A scientific analysis of children's testimony.* Washington, DC: American Psychological Association.

Ceci, S. J., Crotteau, M. L., Smith, E., & Loftus, E. F. (1995). Repeatedly thinking about a non-event: Source misattributions among preschoolers. *Consciousness and Cognition: An International Journal, 3,* 388–407.

Ceci, S. J., Loftus, E. F., Leichtman, M., & Bruck, M. (1994). The possible role of source misattributions in the creation of false beliefs among preschoolers. *International Journal of Clinical and Experimental Hypnosis, 42,* 304–320.

Celentano, D. D., Stewart, W. F., Lipton, R. B., & Reed, M. I. (1992). Medication use and disability among migraineurs: A national probability sample. *Headache, 32,* 223–225.

Centers for Disease Control and Prevention. (2000). *Obesity epidemic increases dramatically in the United States* (www.cdc.gov/nccdphp/dnpa/obesity-epidemic.htm).

Centers for Disease Control and Prevention. (2002). Web-based injury statistics query and reporting system (WISQARS). National Center for Injury Prevention and Control, Centers for Disease Control and Prevention (Producer). From www.cdc.gov/ncipc/wisqars.

Cervone, D., & Mischel, W. (2002). Personality science. In D. Cervone & W. Mischel (Eds.), *Advances in personality science* (pp. 1–26). New York: Guilford Press.

Cervone, D., & Shoda, Y. (1999). Beyond traits in the study of personality coherence. *Current Directions in Psychological Science, 8,* 27–32.

Chait, L. D., & Pierri, J. (1992). Effects of smoked marijuana on human performance: A critical review. In L. Murphy & A. Bartke (Eds.), *Marijuana/cannabinoids: Neurobiology and neurophysiology* (pp. 387–423). Boca Raton, FL: CRC Press.

Chalmers, I., Hedges, L. V., & Cooper, H. (2002). A brief history of research synthesis. *Evaluation & the Health Professions, 25,* 12–37.

Chambless, D. L. (1990). Spacing of exposure sessions in the treatment of agoraphobia and simple phobia. *Behavior Therapy, 21,* 217–229.

Chang, F. I. F., Isaacs, K. R., & Greenough, W. T. (1991). Synapse formation occurs in association with the induction of long-term potentiation in two-year-old rat hippocampus in vitro. *Neurobiology of Aging, 12,* 517–522.

Chao, J., & Nestler, E. J. (2004). Molecular neurobiology of drug addiction. *Annual Review of Medicine, 55,* 113–132.

Chao, R. K. (1992). Beyond parental control and authoritarian parenting style: Understanding Chinese parenting through the cultural notion of training. *Child Development, 65,* 1111–1119.

Chapdelaine, A., Kenny, D. A., & LaFontana, K. M. (1994). Matchmaker, matchmaker, can you make me a match? Predicting liking between two unacquainted persons. *Journal of Personality and Social Psychology, 67,* 83–91.

Chaplin, W. F., Phillips, J. B., Brown, J. D., Clanton, N. R., & Stein, J. L. (2000). Handshaking, gender, personality, and first impressions. *Journal of Personality and Social Psychology, 79,* 110–117.

Chartrand, T. L., & Bargh, J. A. (1999). The chameleon effect: The perception-behavior link and social interaction. *Journal of Personality and Social Psychology, 76,* 893–910.

Chartrand, T. L., Cheng, C. M., & Jefferis, V. E. (2002). You're just a chameleon: The automatic nature and social significance of mimicry. In M. Jarymowicz & R. K. Ohme (Eds.), *Natura automatyzmow (Nature of automaticity)* (pp. 19–24). Warszawa: IPPAN & SWPS.

Chartrand, T. L., Maddux, W. W., & Lakin, J. L. (in press). Beyond the perception-behavior link: The ubiquitous utility and motivational moderators of nonconscious mimicry. In R. Hassin, J. Uleman, & J. A. Bargh (Eds.), *Unintended thought 2: The new unconscious.* New York: Oxford University Press.

Chase, M. H., & Morales, F. R. (1983). Subthreshold excitatory activity and motorneuron discharge during REM periods of active sleep. *Science, 221,* 1195–1198.

Chase, W. G., & Simon, H. A. (1973). The mind's eye in chess. In W. G. Chase (Ed.), *Visual information processing.* New York: Academic Press.

Chase-Lansdale, P. L., Cherlin, A. J., & Kiernan, K. E. (1995). The long-term effects of parental divorce on the mental health of young adults: A developmental perspective. *Child Development, 66,* 1614–1634.

Chastain, G., & Lundrum, R. E. (1999). *Protecting human subjects: Departmental subject pools and institutional review boards.* Washington, DC: American Psychological Association.

Chaves, J. F. (1999). Applying hypnosis in pain management: Implications of alternative theoretical perspectives. In E. Kirsch & A. Capafons (Eds.), *Clinical hypnosis and self-regulation: Cognitive-behavioral perspectives* (pp. 227–247). *Dissociation, trauma, memory, and hypnosis book series.* Washington, DC: American Psychological Association.

Cheer, S. M., & Goa, K. L. (2001). Fluoxetine: Review of its therapeutic potential in the treatment of depression associated with physical illness. *Drugs, 61,* 81–110.

Chemers, M. M., Hu, L., & Garcia, B. F. (2001). Academic self-efficacy and first year student performance and adjustment. *Journal of Educational Psychology, 93,* 55–64.

Chen, A.-H., Zhou, Y., Gong, H.-Q., & Liang, P.-J. (2004). Firing rates and dynamic correlated activities of ganglion cells both contribute to retinal information processing. *Brain Research, 1017,* 13–20.

Chen, H., Yates, B. T., & McGinnies, E. (1988). Effects of involvement on observers' estimates of consensus, distinctiveness, and consistency. *Personality and Social Psychology Bulletin, 14,* 468–478.

Chen, H.-Y., Yeh, J.-I., Hong, C.-J., & Chen, C.-H. (2005). Mutation analysis of ARVCF gene on chromosome 22q11 as a candidate for a schizophrenia gene. *Schizophrenia Research, 72,* 275–277.

Chen, J.-Y. (2000). Syllable errors from naturalistic slips of the tongue in Mandarin Chinese. *Psychologia: An International Journal of Psychology in the Orient, 43,* 15–26.

Chen, N. Y., Shaffer, D. R., & Wu, C. (1997). On physical attractiveness stereotyping in Taiwan: A revised sociocultural perspective. *Journal of Social Psychology, 137,* 117–124.

Cheney, D. L., & Seyfarth, R. M. (1985). Vervet monkey alarm calls: Manipulation through shared information? *Behavior, 94,* 150–166.

Cherlin, A. J., Furstenberg, F. F., Jr., Chase-Lansdale, P. L., Kiernan, K. E., Robins, P. K., Morrison, D. R., & Teitler, J. O. (1991). Longitudinal studies of effects of divorce on children in Great Britain and the United States. *Science, 252,* 1386–1389.

Cherry, E. C. (1953). Some experiments on the recognition of speech, with one and with two ears. *Journal of the Acoustical Society of America, 25,* 975–979.

Chesney, M., & Coates, T. (1990). Health promotion and disease prevention: AIDS put the models to the test. In S. Petro, P. Franks, & T. Wolfred (Eds.), *Ending the HIV epidemic: Community strategies in disease prevention and health promotion* (pp. 48–62). Santa Cruz, CA: ETR Associates.

Chess, S., & Thomas, A. (1987). *Origins and evolution of behavior disorders: From infancy to early adult life.* Cambridge, MA: Harvard University Press.

Chiroro, P., Bohner, G., Viki, G. T., & Jarvis, C. I. (2004). Rape myth acceptance and rape proclivity: Expected dominance versus expected arousal as mediators in acquaintance-rape situations. *Journal of Interpersonal Violence, 19,* 427–441.

Chochinov, H. M., Hack, T., McClement, S., Harlos, M., & Kristhanson, L. (2002). Dignity in the terminally ill: An empirical model. *Social Science & Medicine, 54,* 433–443.

Choi, I., & Nisbett, R. E. (1998). Situational salience and cultural differences in the correspondence bias and in the actor-observer bias. *Personality and Social Psychology Bulletin, 24,* 949–960.

Choi, I., Nisbett, R. E., & Norenzayan, A. (1999). Causal attribution across cultures: Variation and universality. *Psychological Bulletin, 125,* 47–63.

Chomsky, N. (1957). *Syntactic structures.* The Hague: Mouton.

Chomsky, N. (1965). *Aspects of the theory of syntax.* Cambridge, MA: Harcourt Brace Jovanovich.

Christensen, K. A., Stephens, M. A. P., & Townsend, A. L. (1998). Mastery in women's multiple roles and well-being: Adult daughters providing care to impaired parents. *Health Psychology, 17,* 163–171.

Christensen, L. (1988). Deception in psychological research: When is its use justified? *Personality and Social Psychology Bulletin, 14,* 664–675.

Chui, G. (2004, October. 3). Earth's hum begins deep within its oceans. *Milwaukee Journal Sentinel, 18A.* www.JSONLINE.COM

Chun, C., Enomoto, K., & Sue, S. (1996). Health-care issues among Asian Americans: Implications of somatization. In P. M. Kata & T. Mann (Eds.), *Handbook of diversity issues in health psychology* (pp. 347–366). New York: Plenum.

Church, A. T., & Ortiz, F. A. (2005). Culture and personality. In V. J. Derlega, B. A. Winstead, & W. H. Jones (Eds.), *Personality: Contemporary theory and research* (3rd ed., pp. 420–456). Belmont, CA: Thomson Wadsworth.

Cialdini, R. B., Eisenberg, N., Green, B. L., Rhoads, K., & Bator, R. (1998). Undermining the undermining effect of reward on sustained interest. *Journal of Applied Social Psychology, 28,* 249–263.

Cialdini, R. B., & Goldstein, N. J. (2004). Social influence: Compliance and conformity. *Annual Review of Psychology, 55,* 591–621.

Cialdini, R. B., & Kenrick, D. T. (1976). Altruism as hedonism: A social development perspective on the relationship of negative mood state and helping. *Journal of Personality and Social Psychology, 34,* 907–914.

Cialdini, R., Trost, M., & Newsom, J. (1995). Preference for consistency: The development of a valid measure and the discovery of surprising behavioral implications. *Journal of Personality and Social Psychology, 69,* 318–328.

Cicchetti, D. (2002). How a child builds a brain: Insights from normality and psychopathology. In W. Hartup & R. A. Weinberg (Eds.), *Child psychology in retrospect and prospect: In celebration of the 75th anniversary of the Institute of Child Development. The Minnesota symposia on child psychology* (Vol. 32, pp. 23–71). Mahwah, NJ: Erlbaum.

Civin, C. I., Gewirtz, A. M., Hawley, R. G., & Goodell, M. A. (2005). Advancing the fast-paced field of stem cell research: STEM CELLS increases from 6 to 10 issues in its 23rd year of publication. *Stem Cells, 23,* 1–2.

Clark, D. C. (1995). Epidemiology, assessment, and management of suicide in depressed patients. In E. E. Beckham & W. R. Leber (Eds.), *Handbook of depression* (2nd ed., pp. 526–538). New York: Guilford Press.

Clark, J. D., Beyene, Y., Woldegabriel, G., Hart, W. K., Renne, P. R., Gilbert, H., Defleur, A., Suwa, G., Katoh, S., Ludwig, K. R., Boisserie, J.-R., Asfaw, B., & White, T. D. (2003). *Nature, 423,* 747–752.

Clark, K., Friedman, H., & Martin, L. (1999). A longitudinal study of religiosity and mortality risk. *Journal of Health Psychology, 4,* 381–391.

Clark, K. B. (1950). *The effects of prejudice and discrimination on personality development (Midcentury White House Conference on Children and Youth).* Washington, DC: Federal Security Agency, Children's Bureau.

Clark, K. B., & Clark, M. P. (1939). The development of self and the emergence of racial identification in Negro preschool children. *Journal of Social Psychology, 10,* 591–599.

Clark, K. B., & Clark, M. P. (1947). Racial identification and preference in Negro children. In T. M. Newcomb and E. L. Hartley (Eds.), *Readings in social psychology* (pp. 169–178). New York: Holt.

Clark, K. M., Friedman, H. S., & Martin, L. R. (1999). A longitudinal study of religiosity and mortality risk. *Journal of Health Psychology, 4,* 381–391.

Clark, R. (2003). Self-reported racism and social support predict blood pressure reactivity in Blacks. *Annals of Behavioral Medicine, 25,* 127–136.

Clarke, S., & Thiran, A. B. (2004). Auditory neglect: What and where in auditory space. *Cortex, 40,* 291–300.

Clarkin, J. F., & Carpenter, D. (1995). Family therapy in historical perspective. In B. M. Bongar & L. E. Beutler (Ed.), *Comprehensive textbook of psychotherapy: Theory and practice. Oxford textbooks in clinical psychology* (Vol. 1, pp. 205–227). New York: Oxford University Press.

Classen, C. (1993). *Worlds of sense: Exploring the senses in history and across cultures.* New York: Routledge.

Classen, C., Howes, D., & Synnott, A. (1994). *Aroma: The cultural history of smell.* London: Routledge.

Clausen, J. (1999). *Apples and oranges: My journey through sexual identity.* Boston: Houghton Mifflin.

Clayton, A. H. (2003). Sexual function and dysfunction in women. *Psychiatric Clinics of North America, 26,* 673–682.

Clayton, N. S. (1998). Memory and the hippocampus in food-storing birds: A comparative approach. *Neuropharmacology, 37,* 441–452.

Clayton, N. S., & Dickinson, A. (1998). Episodic-like memory during cache recovery by scrub jays. *Nature, 395,* 272–274.

Clement, R. W., & Krueger, J. (2002). Social categorization moderates social projection. *Journal of Experimental Social Psychology, 38,* 219–231.

Cloninger, G. B., Dinwiddie, S. H., & Reich, T. (1989). Epidemiology and genetics of alcoholism. *Annual Reviews of Psychiatry, 8,* 331–346.

Clopton, N. A., & Sorell, G. T. (1993). Gender differences in moral reasoning: Stable or situational? *Psychology of Women Quarterly, 17,* 85–102.

Cloud, J. (2000, June 5). The lure of ecstacy. *Time,* 62–68.

Coates, J. (1992). *Women, men, and language* (2nd ed.). New York: Longman.

Coates, T. (1990). Strategies for modifying sexual behavior for primary and secondary prevention of HIV disease. *Journal of Consulting and Clinical Psychology, 58,* 57–69.

Coates, T., Stall, R., Catania, J., & Kegeles, S. (1988). Behavioral factors in HIV infection. *AIDS 1988, 2*(Suppl.1), S239–S246.

Cochran, W., & Tesser, A. (1996). The "what the hell" effect: Some effects of goal proximity and goal framing on performance. In L. Martin & A. Tesser (Eds.), *Striving and feeling: Interactions among goals, affect, and self-regulation* (pp. 99–120). Mahwah, NJ: Erlbaum.

Coderre, T. J., Mogil, J. S., & Bushnell, M. C. (2003). The biological psychology of pain. In M. Gallagher & R. J. Nelson, *Handbook of psychology: Biological psychology* (Vol. 3, pp. 237–268). New York: Wiley.

Coffey, C. E. (1993). *Clinical science of electroconvulsive therapy.* Washington, DC: American Psychiatric Press.

Coffey, C. E., Lucke, J. F., Saxton, J. A., Ratliff, G., Unitas, L. J., Billig, B., & Bryan, R. N. (1998). Sex differences in brain aging: A quantitative magnetic resonance imaging study. *Archives of Neurology, 55,* 169–179.

Cogan, J. C., Bhalla, S. K., Sefa-Dedeh, A., & Rothblum, E. D. (1996). A comparison study of United States and

African students on perceptions of obesity and thinness. *Journal of Cross-Cultural Psychology, 27,* 98–113.

Cohen, C. (1994). The case for the use of animals in biomedical research. In E. Erwin, S. Gendin, & L. Kleiman (Eds.), *Ethical issues in scientific research: An anthology* (pp. 253–266). New York: Garland.

Cohen, D. (1996). Law, social policy, and violence: The impact of regional cultures. *Journal of Personality and Social Psychology, 70,* 961–978.

Cohen, D. (1998). Culture, social organization, and patterns of violence. *Journal of Personality and Social Psychology, 75,* 408–419.

Cohen, D., & Nisbett, R. E. (1994). Self-protection and the culture of honor: Explaining southern violence. *Personality and Social Psychology Bulletin, 20,* 551–567.

Cohen, D., & Nisbett, R. E. (1997). Field experiments examining the culture of honor: The role of institutions in perpetuating norms about violence. *Personality and Social Psychology Bulletin, 23,* 1188–1199.

Cohen, D., Nisbett, R. E., Bowdle, B., & Schwarz, N. (1996). Insult, aggression, and the southern culture of honor: An "experimental ethnography." *Journal of Personality and Social Psychology, 70,* 945–960.

Cohen, D., Taieb, O., Flament, M., Benoit, N., Chevret, S., Corcos, M., Fossati, P., Jeammet, P., Allilaire, J. F., & Basquin, M. (2000). Absence of cognitive impairment at long-term follow-up in adolescents treated with ECT for severe mood disorder. *American Journal of Psychiatry, 157,* 460–462.

Cohen, K. M. (2002). Relationships among childhood sex-atypical behavior, spatial ability, handedness, and sexual orientation in men. *Archives of Sexual Behavior, 31,* 129–143.

Cohen, L. B., Diehl, R. L., Oakes, L. M., & Loehlin, J. L. (1992). Infant perception of /aba/versus/apa/: Building a quantitative model of infant categorical discrimination. *Developmental Psychology, 28,* 261–272.

Cohen, M. N. (2002). An anthropological look at "race" and IQ testing. In J. M. Fish (Ed.), *Race and intelligence: Separating science from myth* (pp. 201–223). Mahwah, NJ: Erlbaum.

Cohen, N. J., Eichenbaum, H., Deacedo, B. S., & Corkin, S. (1985). Different memory systems underlying acquisition of procedural and declarative knowledge. *Annals of the New York Academy of Sciences, 444,* 54–71.

Cohen, S., & Miller, G. (2001). Stress, immunity, and susceptibility to upper respiratory infection. In R. Ader, D. Felten, & N. Cohen (Eds.), *Psychoneuroimmunology* (Vol. 2, 3rd ed., pp. 499–509). San Diego, CA: Academic Press.

Cohen, S., Underwood, L. G., & Gottlieb, B. H. (Eds.). (2000). *Social support measurement and intervention: A guide for health and social scientists.* New York: Oxford University Press.

Colcombe, S. J., Erickson, K. I., Raz, N., Webb, A. G., Cohen, N. J., McAuley, E., & Kramer, A. F. (2003). Aerobic fitness reduces brain tissue loss in aging humans. *Journal of Gerontology: Biological and Medical Sciences, 58,* 176–180.

Colcombe, S. J., & Kramer, A. F. (2003). Fitness effects on the cognitive function of older adults: A meta-analytic study. *Psychological Science, 14,* 125–130.

Cole, M. (1992). Culture in development. In M. H. Bornstein & M. E. Lamb (Eds.), *Developmental psychology: An advanced textbook* (3rd ed.). Hillsdale, NJ: Erlbaum.

Cole, M., & Cole, S. R. (1993). *The development of children* (2nd ed.). New York: Freeman.

Cole, S., & Kemeny, M. (2001). Psychosocial influences on the progression of HIV infection. In R. Ader, D. Felten, & N. Cohen (Eds.), *Psychoneuroimmunology* (Vol. 2, 3rd ed., pp. 583–612). San Diego, CA: Academic Press.

Coll, C. G., Bearer, E. L., & Lerner, R. M. (Eds.). (2004). *Nature and nurture: The complex interplay of genetic and environmental influences on human behavior and development.* Mahwah, NJ: Erlbaum.

Collier, G. (1986). The dialogue between the house economist and the resident physiologist. *Nutrition and Behavior, 3,* 9–26.

Colligan, J. (1983). Musical creativity and social rules in four cultures. *Creative Child and Adult Quarterly, 8,* 39–47.

Collins, A. M., & Loftus, E. F. (1975). A spreading-activation theory of semantic processing. *Psychological Review, 82,* 407–428.

Colom, R., Lluis-Font, J. M., & Andres-Pueyo, A. (2005). The generational intelligence gains are caused by decreasing variance in the lower half of the distribution: Supporting evidence for the nutrition hypothesis. *Intelligence, 33,* 83–91.

Colombo, D., & Abend, S. M. (2005). Psychoanalysis: The early years. In E. S. Person & A. M. Cooper (Eds.), *The American Psychiatric Publishing textbook of psychoanalysis* (pp. 375–385). Washington, DC: American Psychiatric Publishing.

Colombo, J. (1995). Cost, utility, and judgments of institutional review boards. *Psychological Science, 6,* 318–319.

Coltheart, M., Hull, E., & Slater, D. (1975). Sex differences in imagery and reading. *Nature, 253,* 438–440.

Comey, G., & Kirsch, I. (1999). Intentional and spontaneous imagery in hypnosis: The phenomenology of hypnotic responding. *International Journal of Clinical and Experimental Hypnosis, 47,* 65–85.

Comrie, B. (2003). On explaining language universals. In M. Tomasello (Ed.), *The new psychology of language: Cognitive and functional approaches to language structure* (Vol. 2, pp. 195–209). Mahwah, NJ: Erlbaum.

Conrad, R. (1964). Acoustic confusions in immediate memory. *British Journal of Psychology, 55,* 75–84.

Conway, M. (1995). *Flashbulb memories.* East Sussex: Erlbaum.

Conway, M. A., Anderson, S. J., Larsen, S. F., Donnelly, C. M., McDaniel, M. A., McClelland, A. G. R., Rawles, R. E., & Logie, R. H. (1994). The formation of flashbulb memories. *Memory and Cognition, 22,* 326–343.

Coombs, R. H., Chopra, S., Schenk, D. R., & Yutan, E. (1993). Medical slang and its functions. *Social Science and Medicine, 36,* 987–998.

Cooney, T. M., Pedersen, F. A., Indelicato, S., & Palkovitz, R. (1993). Timing of fatherhood: Is "on-time" optimal? *Journal of Marriage and the Family, 55,* 205–215.

Cooper, B. Y., Vierck, C. J., Jr., & Yeomans, D. C. (1986). Selective reduction of second pain sensations by systemic morphine in humans. *Pain, 24,* 93–116.

Cooper, D. B. (Ed.). (2000). *Alcohol use.* Oxford, England: Radcliffe Medical Press.

Cooper, J., Kapur, N., Webb, R., Lawlor, M., Guthrie, E., Mackway-Jone, K., & Appleby, L. (2005). Suicide after deliberate self-harm: A 4-year cohort study. *American Journal of Psychiatry, 162,* 297–303.

Cooper, J. R., Bloom, F. E., & Roth, R. H. (1991). *The biochemical basis of neuropharmacology* (6th ed.). New York: Oxford University Press.

Cooper, M. L., Shapiro, C. M., & Powers, A. M. (1998). Motivations for sex and risky sexual behavior among adolescents and young adults. *Journal of Personality and Social Psychology, 75,* 1528–1558.

Cooper, R. S. (2005). Race and IQ: Molecular genetics as deus ex machina. *American Psychologist, 60,* 71–76.

Cooper-Patrick, L., Gallo, J. J., Powe, N. R., Steinwachs, D. M., Eaton, W. W., & Ford, D. E. (1999). Mental health service utilization by African Americans and Whites: The Baltimore Epidemiologic Catchment Area follow-up. *Medical Care, 37,* 1034–1045.

Coppola, K. M., & Trotman, F. K. (2002). Dying and death: Decisions at the end of life. In F. K. Trotman, C. M. Brody, & M. Claire (Eds.), *Psychotherapy and counseling with older women: Cross-cultural, family, and end-of-life issues* (pp. 221–238). *Springer series, focus on women.* New York: Springer.

Corballis, M. C. (1999). Are we in our right minds? In S. D. Sala (Ed.), *Mind myths: Exploring popular assumptions about the mind and brain* (pp. 25–41). London: Wiley.

Corbitt, E. M. (2002). Narcissism from the perspective of the five-factor model. In P. T. Costa, Jr., & T. A. Widiger (Eds.), *Personality disorders and the five-factor model of personality* (2nd ed., pp. 293–298). Washington, DC: American Psychological Association.

Coren, S. (1989). Left-handedness and accident-related injury risk. *American Journal of Public Health, 79,* 1–2.

Coren, S. (1992). *The left-hander syndrome: The causes and consequences of left-handedness.* New York: Free Press.

Coren, S. (1996). *Sleep thieves: The A to ZZZs on sleep.* New York: Free Press.

Coren, S., & Aks, D. J. (1990). Moon illusion in pictures: A multimechanism approach. *Journal of Experimental Psychology: Human Perception & Performance, 16,* 365–380.

Coren, S., & Halpern, D. F. (1991). Left-handedness: A marker for decreased survival fitness. *Psychological Bulletin, 109,* 90–106.

Coren, S., Porac, C., & Theodor, L. H. (1987). Set and subjective contour. In S. Petry & G. E. Meyer (Eds.), *The perception of illusory contours* (pp. 237–245). New York: Springer-Verlag.

Corkin, S. (1984). Lasting consequences of bilateral medial temporal lobectomy: Clinical course and experimental findings in H. M. *Seminars in Neurology, 4,* 249–259.

Cornejo, C. (2001). Piaget, Vigotski and Maturana: Three voices, two constructivisms. *Psykhe: Revista de la Escuela de Psicologia, 10,* 87–96.

Corrigan, P. W., & Penn, D. L. (1998). Lessons from social psychology on discrediting psychiatric stigma. *American Psychologist, 54,* 765–776.

Corsini, R. J., & Wedding, D. (2001). *Current psychotherapies* (6th ed.). Itasca, IL: Peacock.

Cosmides, L., & Tooby, J. (2002). Unraveling the enigma of human intelligence: Evolutionary psychology and the multimodular mind. In R. J. Sternberg & J. C. Kaufman (Eds.), *The evolution of intelligence* (pp. 145–198). Mahwah, NJ: Erlbaum.

Costa, P. T., Jr., & McCrae, R. R. (1992). *Revised NEO Personality Inventory (NEO PI–R) and NEO Five-Factor Inventory (NEO–FFI). Professional Manual.* Odessa, FL: Psychological Assessment Resources.

Costa, P. T., Jr., McCrae, R. R., and Arenberg, D. (1980). Enduring dispositions in adult males. *Journal of Personality and Social Psychology, 38,* 793–800.

Costa, P. T., Jr., McCrae, R. R., and Dembroski, T. M. (1989). Agreeableness versus antagonism: Explication of a potential risk factor for CHD. In A. Siegman & T. M. Dembroski (Eds.), *In search of coronary-prone behavior* (pp. 41–63). New York: Oxford University Press.

Costa, P. T., Jr., McCrae, R. R., Zonderman, A. B., Barbano, H. E., Lebowitz, B., & Larson, D. M. (1986). Cross-sectional studies of personality in a national sample: 2. Stability in neuroticism, extraversion, and openness. *Personality and Aging, 1,* 144–149.

Costa, P. T., Jr., Terracciano, A., & McCrae, R. R. (2001). Gender differences in personality traits across cultures: Robust and surprising findings. *Journal of Personality and Social Psychology, 81,* 322–331.

Cotman, C. W. (1990). Synaptic plasticity, neurotropic factors, and transplantation in the aged brain. In E. L. Schneider & J. W. Rowe (Eds.), *Handbook of the biology of aging* (3rd ed.). San Diego, CA: Academic Press.

Cotterill, R. (1989). *No ghost in the machine: Modern science and the brain, the mind and the soul.* London, England: Heinemann Ltd.

Courage, M. L., & Adams, R. J. (1990). Visual acuity assessment from birth to three years using the acuity card procedures: Cross-sectional and longitudinal samples. *Optometry and Vision Science, 67,* 713–718.

Coutu, D. L. (2001, May). A reading list for Bill Gates—and you: A conversation with literary critic Harold Bloom. *Harvard Business Review,* 63–67.

Covington, M., & Omelich, C. (1987). "I knew it cold before the exam": A test of the anxiety-blockage hypothesis. *Journal of Educational Psychology, 79,* 393–400.

Cowan, C. P., & Cowan, P. (2000). *When partners become parents: The big life change for couples.* Mahwah, NJ: Erlbaum.

Cowan, N. (1995). *Attention and memory: An integrated framework.* New York: Oxford University Press.

Cowan, N. (2001). The magical number 4 in short-term memory: A reconsideration of mental storage capacity. *Behavioral and Brain Sciences, 24,* 87–114.

Cowan, N., Lichty, W., & Grove, T. R. (1990). Properties of memory for unattended spoken syllables. *Journal of Experimental Psychology: Learning, Memory, & Cognition, 16,* 258–269.

Cowart, B. J. (1981). Development of taste perception in humans: Sensitivity and preference through the lifespan. *Psychological Bulletin, 90,* 43–73.

Cowart, B. J. (1989). Relationships between taste and smell across the adult life span. *Annals of the New York Academy of Sciences, 561,* 39–55.

Coyne, J. C., Rohrbaugh, M. J., Shoham, V., Sonnega, J. S., Nicklas, J. M., & Cranford, J. A. (2001). Prognostic importance of marital quality for survival of congestive heart failure. *American Journal of Cardiology, 88,* 526–529.

Crabtree, B. F., & Miller, W. L. (Eds.). (1992). *Doing qualitative research: Multiple strategies.* Thousand Oaks, CA: Sage.

Craig, J. C., & Rollman, G. B. (1999). Somesthesis. *Annual Review of Psychology, 50,* 305–331.

Craik, F. I. M., & Lockhart, R. S. (1972). Levels of processing: A framework for memory research. *Journal of Verbal Learning and Verbal Behavior, 11,* 671–684.

Cramer, P. (1999). Future directions for the Thematic Apperception Test. *Journal of Personality Assessment, 72,* 74–92.

Crandall, C. S. (1988). Social contagion of binge eating. *Journal of Personality and Social Psychology, 55,* 588–598.

Crandall, C. S. (1994). Prejudice against fat people: Ideology and self-interest. *Journal of Personality and Social Psychology, 66,* 882–894.

Crandall, C. S., D'Anello, S., Sakalli, N., Lazarus, E., Wieczorkowska, G., & Feather, N. T. (2001). An attribution-value model of prejudice: Anti-fat attitudes in six nations. *Personality and Social Psychology Bulletin, 27,* 30–37.

Crandall, C. S., & Eshleman, A. (2003). A justification-suppression of the expression and experience of prejudice. *Psychological Bulletin, 129,* 414–446.

Crannell, C. W. (1970). Wolfgang Köhler. *Journal of the History of the Behavioral Sciences, 6,* 267–268.

Crano, W. D., & Brewer, M. B. (2002). *Principles and methods of social research* (2nd ed.). Mahwah, NJ: Erlbaum.

Craske, M. G. (1999). *Anxiety disorders: Psychological approaches to theory and treatment.* Boulder, CO: Westview Press.

Craske, M. G., & Barlow, D. H. (1993). Panic disorder and agoraphobia. In D. H. Barlow (Ed.), *Clinical handbook of psychological disorders: A step-by-step treatment manual* (2nd ed., pp. 1–47). New York: Guilford Press.

Crawford, H. J., & Gruzelier, J. H. (1992). A midstream view of the neuropsychology of hypnosis: Recent research and future directions. In E. Fromm & M. R. Nash (Eds.), *Contemporary hypnosis research* (pp. 227–266). New York: Guilford Press.

Crawford, M., Chaffin, R., & Fitton, L. (1995). Cognition in social context. Special Issue: Psychological and psychobiological perspectives on sex differences in cognition: I. Theory and research. *Learning and Individual Differences, 7,* 341–362.

Crews, F. C. (1998). *Unauthorized Freud: Doubters confront a legend.* New York: Viking Penguin.

Criqui, M. H., & Ringel, B. L. (1994). Does diet or alcohol explain the French paradox? *Lancet, 344,* 1719–1723.

Crocker, J., & Major, B. (1989). Social stigma and self-esteem: The self-protective properties of stigma. *Psychological Review, 96,* 608–630.

Crocker, J., Major, B., & Steele, C. (1998). Social stigma. In D. T. Gilbert, S. T. Fiske, & G. Lindzey (Eds.), *The handbook of social psychology* (4th ed.). New York: McGraw-Hill.

Croen, L. A., Grether, J. K., Yoshida, C. K., Odouli, R., & Van de Water, J. (2005). Maternal autoimmune diseases, asthma and allergies, and childhood autism spectrum disorders: A case-control study. *Archives of Pediatrics and Adolescent Medicine, 159,* 151–157.

Cross, S. E., Bacon, P. L., & Morris, M. L. (2000). The relational-interdependent self-construal and relationships. *Journal of Personality and Social Psychology, 78,* 791–808.

Cross, S. E., & Gore, J. S. (2004).The relational self-construal and the construction of closeness. In A. Aron & D. Mashek (Eds.), *The handbook of closeness and intimacy* (pp. 229–245). Hillsdale, NJ: Earlbaum.

Cross, S. E., & Madson, L. (1997). Models of the self: Self-construals and gender. *Psychological Bulletin, 122,* 5–37.

Cross, W. E. (1991). *Shades of black: Diversity in African-American identity.* Philadelphia: Temple University Press.

Croyle, R. T. (1992). Appraisal of health threats: Cognition, motivation, and social comparison. *Cognitive Therapy and Research, 16,* 165–182.

Crystal, D. S., Chen, C., Fuligni, A.J., Stevenson, H. J., Hsu, C.-C., Ko, H.-J., Kitamura, S., & Kimura, S. (1994). Psychological maladjustment and academic achievement: A cross-cultural study of Japanese, Chinese, and American high school students. *Child Development, 65,* 738–753.

Culp, R. E., Appelbaum, M. I., Osofsky, J. D., & Levy, J. A. (1988). Adolescent and older mothers: Comparison between maternal variables and newborn interaction measures. *Infant Behavior and Development, 11,* 353–362.

Culp, R. E., Watkins, R. V., Lawrence, H., & Letts, D. (1991). Maltreated children's language and speech development: Abused, neglected, and abused and neglected. *First Language, 11,* 377–389.

Cummings, E. M., & Cummings, J. S. (2002). Parenting and attachment. In M. H. Bornstein (Ed.), *Handbook of parenting: Vol. 3. Being and becoming a parent* (2nd ed., pp. 35–58). Mahwah, NJ: Erlbaum.

Cunningham, M. R., Barbee, A. P., & Philhower, C. L. (2002). Dimensions of facial physical attractiveness: The intersection of biology and culture. In G. Rhodes & L. A. Zebrowitz (Eds.), *Facial attractiveness: Evolutionary, cognitive, and social perspectives. Advances in visual cognition* (Vol. 1, pp. 193–238). Westport, CT: Ablex.

Cunningham, S., Scerbo, M. W., & Freeman, F. G. (2000). The electrocortical correlates of daydreaming during vigilance tasks. *Journal of Mental Imagery, 24,* 61–72.

Cursi, A., Luminet, O., Finkenauer, C., & Gislie, L. (2001). Flashbulb memories in social groups: A comparative test-retest study of the memory of French President Mitterrand's death in a French and a Belgian group. *Memory, 9,* 81–101.

Cutler, W. B., Friedmann, E., & McCoy, N. L. (1998). Pheromonal influences on sociosexual behavior in men. *Archives of Sexual Behavior, 27,* 1–13.

Cutrona, C. E. (1996). *Social support in couples.* Thousand Oaks, CA: Sage.

Cutrona, C. E., & Suhr, J. A. (1994). Social support communication in the context of marriage: An analysis of couples' supportive interactions. In B. B. Burleson, T. L. Albrecht, & I. G. Sarason (Eds.), *Communication of social support: Messages, relationships, and community* (pp. 113–135). Thousand Oaks, CA: Sage.

Cytowic, R. E. (2002). *Synesthesia: A union of the senses* (2nd ed.). Cambridge, MA: MIT Press.

Czeisler, C. A., Johnson, M. P., Duffy, J. F., Brown, E. N., Ronda, J. M., & Kronauer, R. E. (1990). Exposure to bright light and darkness to treat physiologic maladaptation to night work. *New England Journal of Medicine, 322,* 1253–1259.

Czeisler, C. A., Moore-Ede, M. C., & Coleman, R. M. (1982). Rotating shift work schedules that disrupt sleep are improved by applying circadian principles. *Science, 217,* 460–463.

Dade, L. A., Zatorre, R. J., & Jones-Gotman, M. (2002). Olfactory learning: Convergent findings from lesion and brain imaging studies in humans. *Brain, 125,* 86–101.

Dakof, G., & Taylor, S. (1990). Victims' perceptions of social support: What is helpful from whom? *Journal of Personality and Social Psychology, 58,* 80–89.

Dallenbach, K. M. (1927). The temperature spots and end organs. *American Journal of Psychology, 54,* 431–433.

Dalzell, T. (1996). *Flappers 2 rappers: American youth slang.* Springfield, MD: Merriam-Webster.

Damasio, A. R. (1994). *Descartes' error: Emotion, reason, and the human brain.* New York: Grosset/Putnam.

Damasio, H., Grabowski, T., Frank, R., Galaburda, A. M., & Damasio, A. R. (1994). The return of Phineas Gage: The skull of a famous patient yields clues about the brain. *Science, 264,* 1102–1105.

Dambrun, M., Duarte, S., & Guimond, S. (2004). Why are men more likely to support group-based dominance than women? The mediating role of gender identification. *British Journal of Social Psychology, 43,* 287–297.

Daniell, H. W. (1971). Smoker's wrinkles: A study in the epidemiology of "Crow's feet." *Annals of Internal Medicine, 75,* 873–880.

D'Argembeau, A., Comblain, C., & Van der Linden, M. (2003). Phenomenal characteristics of autobiographical memories for positive, negative, and neutral events. *Applied Cognitive Psychology, 17,* 281–294.

Darley, J. M., & Latané, B. (1968). Bystander intervention in emergencies: Diffusion of responsibility. *Journal of Personality and Social Psychology, 8,* 377–383.

Daruna, J. H. (2004). The Rorschach Test challenges science with the complexity of imagination. *Journal of Psychopathology & Behavioral Assessment, 26,* 147–149.

Darwin, C. (1859). *On the origin of species.* New York: New York University Press, 1988.

Darwin, C. (1871). *The descent of man.* London: John Murray.

Darwin, C. (1872). *Expression of emotion in man and animals.* London: John Murray.

Dasen, P. R. (1994). Culture and cognitive development from a Piagetian perspective. In W. J. Lonner & R. Malpass (Eds.), *Psychology and culture* (pp. 145–149). Boston: Allyn & Bacon.

Das Gupta, M., & Mari Bhat, P. N. (1997). Fertility decline and increased manifestation of sex bias in India. *Population Studies, 51,* 307–315.

Daum, I., Ackermann, H., Schugens, M. M., Reimold, C., Dichgans, J., & Birbaumer, N. (1993). The cerebellum and cognitive functions in humans. *Behavioral Neuroscience, 104,* 411–419.

Davanloo, H. (1999). Intensive short-term dynamic psychotherapy-central dynamic sequence: Phase of challenge. *International Journal of Short-Term Dynamic Psychotherapy, 13,* 237–262.

Davenport, R. (2004). Diagnosing acute headache. *Clinical Medicine, 4,* 108–112.

Davidson, I., & Noble, W. (1989). The archeology of depiction and language. *Current Anthropology, 30,* 125–156.

Davidson, P., & Parker, K. (2001). Eye movement desensitization and reprocessing (EMDR): A meta-analysis. *Journal of Consulting and Clinical Psychology, 69,* 305–316.

Davidson, P. S. R., & Glisky, E. L. (2002). Is flashbulb memory a special instance of source memory? Evidence from older adults. *Memory, 10,* 99–111.

Davidson, R. (1992). Anterior cerebral asymmetry and the nature of emotion. *Brain and Cognition, 20,* 125–151.

Davidson, R., & Fox, N. (1989). Frontal brain asymmetry predicts infants' response to maternal separation. *Journal of Abnormal Psychology, 98,* 127–131.

Davidson, R. A., & Smith, B. D. (1991). Caffeine and novelty: Effects of electrodermal activity and performance. *Physiology and Behavior, 49,* 1169–1175.

Davidson, R. J. (2005). Affective neuroscience and psychophysiology: Towards synthesis. *Psychophysiology, 40,* 655–665.

Davidson, R. J., Kabat-Zinn, J., Schumacher, J., Rosenkrantz, M., Muller, D., & Santorelli. (2003). Alterations in brain and immune function produced by mindfulness meditation. *Psychosomatic Medicine, 65,* 564–570.

Davidson, R. J., Pizzagalli, D., Nitschke, J. B., & Putnam, K. (2002). Depression: Perspectives from affective neuroscience. *Annual Review of Psychology, 53,* 545–574.

Davies, I. R. L. (1998). A study of colour grouping in three languages: A test of linguistic relativity hypothesis. *British Journal of Psychology, 89,* 433–452.

Davies, M., & McCartney, S. (2003). Effects of gender and sexuality on judgments of victim blame and rape myth acceptance in a depicted male rape. *Journal of Community & Applied Social Psychology, 13,* 391–398.

Davies, M. F. (1997). Positive test strategies and confirmatory retrieval processes in the evaluation of personality feedback. *Journal of Personality and Social Psychology, 73,* 574–583.

Davies, R. J., & Stradling, J. R. (2000). The efficacy of nasal continuous positive airway pressure in the treatment of obstructive sleep apnea syndrome is proven. *American Journal of Respiratory Critical Care Medicine, 161,* 1775–1776.

Davis, J. D., Gallagher, R. J., Ladove, R. F., & Turansky, A. J. (1969). Inhibition of food intake by a humoral factor. *Journal of Comparative and Physiological Psychology, 67,* 407–414.

Davis, M. H. (1996). *Empathy: A social psychological approach.* Boulder, CO: Westview Press.

Davis, S. (1990). Men as success objects and women as sex objects: A study of personal advertisements. *Sex Roles, 23,* 43–50.

Davison, G. C., & Neale, J. M. (2001). *Abnormal psychology* (8th ed.). New York: Wiley.

Davison, K. P., Pennebaker, J. W., & Dickerson, S. S. (2000). Who talks? The social psychology of illness support groups. *American Psychologist, 55,* 205–217.

Davis-Russell, E. (2003). Integrating multicultural issues into graduate clinical psychology training. In P. Bronstein & K. Quina (Eds.), *Teaching gender and multicultural awareness: Resources for the psychology classroom* (pp. 339–346). Washington, DC: American Psychological Association.

Deacon, T. W. (1989). The neural circuitry underlying primate calls and human language. *Human Evolution,* 367–401.

DeAngelis, T. (1996). Women in psychology: Women's contributions large; recognition isn't. *The APA Monitor, 27*(3), 12–13.

DeAngelis, T. (2002a). Binge-eating disorder: What's the best treatment? *Monitor on Psychology, 33*(3), 30.

DeAngelis, T. (2002b). New data on lesbian, gay and bisexual mental health. *Monitor on Psychology, 33,* 46–47.

DeAngelis, T. (2002c). More psychologists needed in end-of-life care. *Monitor on Psychology, 33*(3), 52–55.

Deaux, K., Winton, W., Crowley, M., & Lewis, L. L. (1985). Levels of categorization and content of gender stereotypes. *Social Cognition, 3,* 145–167.

DeBell, C., & Jones, R.D. (1997). As good as it seems? A review of EMDR experimental research. *Professional Psychology: Research and Practice, 28,* 153–163.

de Boysson-Bardies, B., Halle, P., Sagart, L., & Durand, C. (1989). A cross linguistic investigation of vowel formats in babbling. *Journal of Child Language, 16,* 1–17.

DeCasper, A. J., & Fifer, W. P. (1980). Of human bonding: Newborns prefer their mothers' voices. *Science, 208,* 1174–1176.

DeCasper, A. J., & Sigafoos, A. D. (1983). The intrauterine heartbeat: A potent reinforcer for newborns. *Infant Behavior and Development, 6,* 19–25.

DeCasper, A. J., & Spence, M. J. (1986). Prenatal maternal speech influences newborns' perception of speech sounds. *Infant Behavior and Development, 9,* 133–150.

Deci, E., Koestner, R., & Ryan, R. (1999). A meta-analytic review of experiments examining the effects of extrinsic rewards on intrinsic motivation. *Psychological Bulletin, 125,* 627–668.

Deci, E., & Ryan, R. (1985). *Intrinsic motivation and self-determination in human behavior.* New York: Plenum.

Deci, E. L. (2004). Promoting intrinsic motivation and self-determination in people with mental retardation. In H. N. Switzky (Ed.), *Personality and motivational systems in mental retardation* (Vol. 28, pp. 1–29). San Diego, CA: Elsevier Academic Press.

Deci, E. L., Driver, R. E., Hotchkiss, L., Robbins, R. J., & Wilson, I. M. (1993). The relation of mothers' controlling vocalizations to children's intrinsic motivation. *Journal of Experimental Child Psychology, 55,* 151–162.

Deckman, M. (2002). Holy ABCs! The impact of religion on attitudes about education policies. *Social Science Quarterly, 83,* 472–487.

Deepak, K. K., Manchanda, S. K., & Maheshwari, M. C. (1994). Meditation improves clinicoelectro-encephalographic measures in drug-resistant epileptics. *Biofeedback and Self Regulation, 19,* 25–40.

Dehaene, S., Spelke, E., Pinel, P., Stanescu, R., & Tsivkin, S. (1999). Sources of mathematical thinking: Behavioral and brain-imaging evidence. *Science, 284,* 970–974.

Delgado-Gaitan, C. (1994). Socializing young children in Mexican-American families: An intergenerational perspective. In P. M. Greenfield & R. R. Cocking (Eds.), *Cross-cultural roots of minority child development* (pp. 55–86). Hillsdale, NJ: Erlbaum.

Dell, G. S. (1986). A spreading activation theory of retrieval in sentence production. *Psychological Review, 93,* 283–321.

Dell, G. S. (1988). The retrieval of phonological forms in production: Tests of predictions from a connectionist model. *Journal of Memory and Language, 27,* 124–142.

del Olmo, N., Handler, A., Alvarez, L., Bustamante, J., del Rio, R. M., & Solis, J. M. (2003). Taurine-induced synaptic potentiation and the late phase of long-term potentiation are related mechanistically. *Neuropharmacology, 44,* 26–39.

Dembroski, T., MacDougall, J., Williams, R., Haney, T., & Blumenthal, J. (1985). Components of Type A, hostility, and anger in relationship to angiographic findings. *Psychosomatic Medicine, 47,* 219–233.

Dement, W. (1960). The effect of dream deprivation. *Science, 131,* 1705–1707.

Dement, W. C. (1978). *Some must watch while some must sleep.* New York: Norton.

Dement, W. C. (1999). *The promise of sleep.* New York: Delacorte Press.

Dement, W. C., Greenberg, S., & Klein, R. (1966). The effect of partial REM sleep deprivation and delayed recovery. *Journal of Experimental Psychology, 53,* 339–346.

Dement, W. C., & Wolpert, E. (1958). The relation of eye movements, body motility, and external stimuli to dream content. *Journal of Experimental Psychology, 55,* 543–553.

Demetriou, A. (Ed.). (1988). *The neo-Piagetian theories of cognitive development: Toward an integration.* Amsterdam: Elsevier.

DeNeve, K. M. (1999). Happy as an extraverted clam? The role of personality for subjective well-being. *Current Directions in Psychological Science, 124,* 197–229.

Denis, R. G., Bing, C., Brocklehurst, S., Harrold, J. A., Vernon, R. G., & Williams, G. (2004). Diurnal changes in hypothalamic neuropeptide and SOCS-3 expression: Effects of lactation and relationship with serum leptin and food intake. *Journal of Endocrinology, 183,* 173–181.

Dennett, D. C. (1991). *Consciousness explained.* Boston: Little, Brown.

Dennett, D. C. (1994). Real consciousness. In A. Revonsuo & M. Kamppinen (Eds.), *Consciousness in philosophy and cognitive neuroscience* (pp. 55–63). Hillsdale, NJ: Erlbaum.

Dennett, D. C. (1998). *Brainchildren: Essays on designing minds.* Cambridge, MA: MIT Press.

Dennis, W. (1970). Good enough scores, art experience, and modernization. In A. I. Al-Issa & W. Dennis (Eds.), *Cross-cultural studies of behavior* (pp. 134–152). New York: Holt.

De Pascalis, V. (1999). Psychophysiological correlates of hypnosis and hypnotic susceptibility. *International Journal of Clinical and Experimental Hypnosis, 47,* 117–143.

DePaulo, B. M. (1992). Nonverbal behavior and self-presentation. *Psychological Bulletin, 111,* 230–243.

DePaulo, B. M., Charlton, K., Cooper, H. M., Lindsay, J. J., & Muhlenbruck, L. (1997). The accuracy-confidence correlation in the detection of deception. *Personality and Social Psychology Review, 1,* 346–357.

DePaulo, B. M., Kashy, D. A., Kirkendol, S. E., Wyer, M. M., & Epstein, J. A. (1996). Lying in everyday life. *Journal of Personality and Social Psychology, 70,* 979–995.

Deregowski, J. B. (1989). Real space and represented space: Cross-cultural perspectives. *Brain and Behavioral Sciences, 12,* 51–119.

Deslandes, R., & Bertrand, R. (2005). Motivation of parent involvement in secondary-level schooling. *Journal of Educational Research, 98,* 164–175.

Detterman, D. K. (2005). International handbook of intelligence. *Intelligence, 33,* 107–108.

Detterman, D. K., Gabriel, L. T., & Ruthsatz, J. M. (2000). Intelligence and mental retardation. In R. J. Sternberg (Ed.), *Handbook of intelligence* (pp. 141–158). Cambridge: Cambridge University Press.

de Valois, R. L., Abramov, I., & Jacobs, G. H. (1966). Analysis of response patterns of LGN cells. *Journal of the Optical Society of America, 56,* 966–977.

de Valois, R. L., & Jacobs, G. H. (1984). Neural mechanisms of color vision. In I. Darian-Smith (Ed.), *The nervous system* (Vol. 3). Baltimore, MD: Williams & Wilkins.

Devilly, G. (2002). Eye movement desensitization and reprocessing: A chronology of its development and scientific standing. *The Scientific Review of Mental Health Practice, 1,* 113–138.

Devine, P. G. (1989). Stereotypes and prejudice: Their automatic and controlled components. *Journal of Personality and Social Psychology, 56,* 5–18.

Devine, P. G., & Baker, S. M. (1991). Measurement of racial stereotype subtyping. *Personality and Social Psychology Bulletin, 17,* 44–50.

Devine, P. G., Evett, S. R., & Vasquez-Suson, K. A. (1996). Exploring the interpersonal dynamics of intergroup contact. In R. M. Sorrentino & E. T. Higgins (Eds.), *Handbook of motivation and cognition: The interpersonal context* (Vol. 3, pp. 423–464). New York: Guilford.

Devlin, A. M., Cross, J. H., Harkness, W., Chong, W. K., Harding, B., Vargha-Khadem, R., & Neville, B. G. R. (2003). Clinical outcomes of hemispherectomy for epilepsy in childhood and adolescence. *Brain, 126,* 556–566.

DeVoe, M. W. (1977). Cooperation as a function of self-concept, sex, and race. *Educational Research Quarterly, 2,* 3–8.

DeVos, G. A. (1973). Japan's outcasts: The problem of the Burakumin. In B. Whitaker (Ed.), *The fourth world: Victims of group oppression.* New York: Schocken Books.

DeVries, R. (2000). Vygotsky, Piaget, and education: A reciprocal assimilation of theories and educational practices. *New Ideas in Psychology, 18,* 187–213.

de Waal, F. B. M. (2000). Primates—A natural heritage of conflict resolution. *Science, 289,* 586–590.

de Waal, F. B. M. (2002). *The ape and the sushi master: Cultural reflections of a primatologist.* New York: Basic Books.

Dewsbury, D. A. (1992). Triumph and tribulation in the history of American comparative psychology. *Journal of Comparative Psychology, 1067,* 3–19.

Diakidoy, I. A. N., & Spanoudis, G. (2002). Domain specificity in creativity testing: A comparison of performance on a general divergent-thinking test and a parallel, content-specific test. *Journal of Creative Behavior, 36,* 41–61.

Diamond, A. (1985). The development of the ability to use recall to guide action, as indicated by infants' performance on AB. *Child Development, 56,* 868–883.

Diamond, J. (1966). Classification system of primitive people. *Science, 151,* 1102–1104.

Diamond, L. M. (1998). Development of sexual orientation among adolescent and young adult women. *Developmental Psychology, 34,* 1085–1095.

Diamond, L. M. (2000). Sexual identity, attractions, and behavior among young sexual-minority women over a two-year period. *Developmental Psychology, 36,* 241–250.

Diamond, L. M. (2003a). Was it a phase? Young women's relinquishment of lesbian/bisexual identities over a 5-year period. *Journal of Personality and Social Psychology, 84,* 352–364.

Diamond, L. M. (2003b). What does sexual orientation orient? A biobehavioral model distinguishing romantic love and sexual desire. *Psychological Review, 110,* 173–192.

Diamond, L. M., & Savin-Williams, R. C. (2000). Explaining diversity in the development of same-sex sexuality among young women. *Journal of Social Issues, 56,* 297–313.

Diamond, M. C. (1988). *Enriching heredity: The impact of environment on the anatomy of the brain.* New York: Free Press.

Diaz-Guerrero, R., Diaz-Loving, R., & Rodriguez de Diaz, M. L. (2001). In L. L. Adler & U. P. Gielen (Eds.), *Cross-cultural topics in psychology* (2nd ed., pp. 171–184). Westport, CT: Praeger.

Dick, C. L., Bland, R. C., & Newman, S. C. (1994). Panic disorder. *Acta Psychiatrica Scandinavica, 89,* 45–53.

Dick, D. M., & Rose, R. J. (2002). Behavior genetics: What's new? What's next? *Current Directions in Psychological Science, 11,* 70–74.

Dickens, W. T., & Flynn, J. R. (2002). The IQ paradox is still resolved: Reply to Loehlin (2002) and Rowe and Rodgers (2002). *Psychological Review, 109,* 764–771.

Dickinson, A., & Balleine, B. W. (2000). Causal cognition and goal-directed action. In C. Heyes & L. Huber (Eds.), *The evolution of cognition.* Cambridge, MA: MIT Press.

Diehl, W. (1993). *Primal fear.* New York: Villard.

Diener, E. (1984). Subjective well-being. *Psychological Bulletin, 95,* 542–575.

Diener, E., & Diener, M. (1995). Cross-cultural correlates of life-satisfaction and self-esteem. *Journal of Personality and Social Psychology, 68,* 653–663.

Diener E., Emmons, R., Larson, J., & Griffin, S. (1985). The satisfaction with life scale. *Journal of Personality Assessment,* 49, 71–75.

Diener, E., & Lucas, R. E. (1999). Personality and subjective well-being. In D. Kahneman, E. Diener, & N. Schwarz (Eds.). *Well-being: The foundations of hedonic psychology* (pp. 213–229). New York: Russell Sage.

Diener, E., & Lucas, R. E. (2000a). Explaining differences in societal levels of happiness: Relative standards, need fulfillment, culture and evaluation theory. *Journal of Happiness Studies, 1,* 41–78.

Diener, E., & Lucas, R. E. (2000b). Subjective emotional well-being. In M. Lewis & J. M. Haviland (Eds.), *Handbook of emotions* (2nd ed., pp. 325–337). New York: Guilford.

Diener, E., Sandvik, E., Seiditz, L., & Diener, M. (1993). The relationship between income and subjective well-being: Relative or absolute? *Social Indicators Research, 28,* 195–223.

Diener, E., & Seligman, E. P. (2002). Very happy people. *Psychological Science, 13,* 81–84.

Diener, E., Suh, E. M., Lucas, R. E., & Smith, H. L. (1999). Subjective well-being: Three decades of progress. *Psychological Bulletin, 125,* 276–302.

Diener, H., & Limmroth, V. (2004). Medication-overuse headache: A worldwide problem. *The Lancet Neurology, 3,* 475–483.

Dietz, W., Jr., & Gortmaker, S. (1985). Do we fatten our children at the television set? Obesity and television viewing in children and adolescents. *Pediatrics, 75,* 807–812.

DiGiuseppe, R., & Tafrate, R. C. (2003). Anger treatment for adults: A meta-analytic review. *Clinical Psychology: Science and Practice, 10,* 70–84.

Dijker, A. J., & Koomen, W. (1996). Stereotyping and attitudinal effects under time pressure. *European Journal of Social Psychology, 26,* 61–74.

DiLalla, L. F. (Ed.). (2004). *Behavior genetics principles: Perspectives in development, personality, and psychopathology.* Washington, DC: American Psychological Association.

DiLalla, L. F., Kagan, J., & Reznick, J. S. (1994). Genetic etiology of behavioral inhibition among 2-year-old children. *Infant Behavior & Development, 17,* 405–412.

DiLorenzo, P., & Youngentob, S. L. (2003). Olfaction and taste. In M. Gallagher & R. J. Nelson (Eds.), *Handbook of psychology: Biological psychology* (Vol. 3, pp. 269–297). New York: Wiley.

Dilsaver, S. C., Chen, Y. R., Shoaib, A. M., & Swann, A. C. (1999). Phenomenology of mania: Evidence for distinct depressed, dysphoric, and euphoric presentations. *American Journal of Psychiatry, 156,* 426–430.

Dinges, D. F., Pack, F., Williams, K., Gillen, K. A., Powell, J. W., Ott, G. E., Aptowicz, C., & Pack, A. I. (1997). Cumulative sleepiness, mood vigilance performance decrements during a week of sleep restricted to 4–5 hours per night. *Sleep, 20,* 267–273.

Dinges, N. G., & Hull, P. (1992). Personality, culture, and international studies. In D. Lieberman (Ed.), *Revealing the world: An interdisciplinary reader for international studies.* Dubuque, IA: Kendall-Hunt.

Dingfelder, S. F. (2005a). Hispanic psychology: Closing the gap for Latino patients. *Monitor on Psychology, 36*(1), 68–69.

Dingfelder, S. F. (2005b). Hispanic psychology: Lifting as they climb. *Monitor on Psychology, 36*(1), 58–61.

Dittmann, M. (2003). Psychology's first prescribers. *Monitor on Psychology, 34*(2), 36–39.

Dixson, A. F., Halliwell, G., East, R., Wignarajah, P., & Anderson, M. J. (2003). Masculine somatotype and hirsuteness as determinants of sexual attractiveness to women. *Archives of Sexual Behavior, 32,* 29–39.

Docherty, J. P. (1999). Cost of treating mental illness from a managed care perspective. *Journal of Clinical Psychiatry, 60,* 49–53.

Dodson, C., & Reisberg, D. (1991). Indirect testing of eyewitness memory: The (non)effect of misinformation. *Bulletin of the Psychonomic Society, 29,* 333–336.

Dodwell, P. (2000). *Brave new mind: A thoughtful inquiry into the nature and meaning of mental life.* New York: Oxford University Press.

Dohnanyiova, M., Ostatnikova, D., & Laznibatova, J. (2000). Physical development of intellectually gifted children. *Homeostasis in Health & Disease, 40,* 123–125.

Doi, T. (1973). *The anatomy of dependence.* (J. Bester, Trans.). New York: Kodansha International.

Dolbier, C. L., Cocke, R. R., Leiferman, J. A., Steinhardt, M. A., Schapiro, S. J., & Nehete, P. N. (2001). Differences in functional immune responses of high vs. low hardy healthy individuals. *Journal of Behavioral Medicine, 24,* 219–229.

Domhoff, G. W. (2003). *The scientific study of dreams: Neural networks, cognitive development, and content analysis.* Washington, DC: American Psychological Association.

Domino, G., Short, J., Evans, A., & Romano, P. (2002). Creativity and ego defense mechanisms: Some exploratory empirical evidence. *Creativity Research Journal, 14,* 17–25.

Domjan, M. (2005). Pavlovian conditioning: A functional perspective. *Annual Review of Psychology, 56,* 179–206.

Donald, M. (2001). *A mind so rare.* New York: Norton.

Dong, Q., Wang, Y., & Ollendick, T. H. (2002). Consequences of divorce on the adjustment of children in China. *Journal of Community Psychology, 31,* 101–110.

Dorfman, D. D. (1995). Soft science with a neoconservative agenda. *Contemporary Psychology, 40,* 418–421.

Dorfman, J., Shames, V. A., & Kihlstrom, J. F. (1996). Intuition, incubation, and insight: Implicit cognition in problem solving. In G. Underwood (Ed.), *Implicit cognition* (pp. 257–296). Oxford, England: Oxford University Press.

Doty, R. L., Green, P. A., Ram, C., & Tandeil, S. L. (1982). Communication of gender from human breath odors: Relationship to perceived intensity and pleasantness. *Hormones and Behavior, 16,* 13–22.

Douglas, C., & Gardner, W. L. (2004). Transition to self-directed work teams: Implications of transition time and self-monitoring for managers' use of influence tactics. *Journal of Organizational Behavior, 25,* 47–65.

Dovidio, J. F. (2001). On the nature of contemporary prejudice: The third wave. *Journal of Social Issues, 57,* 829–849.

Dovidio, J. F., & Gaertner, S. L. (1998). On the nature of contemporary prejudice: The causes, consequences, and challenges of aversive racism. In J. L. Eberhardt & S. T. Fiske (Eds.), *Confronting racism: The problem and the response* (pp. 3–32). Thousand Oaks, CA: Sage.

Dovidio, J. F., Kawakami, K., & Beach, K. R. (2001). Implicit and explicit attitudes: Examination of the relationship between measures of intergroup bias. In R. Brown & S. L. Gaertner (Eds.), *Blackwell handbook of social psychology:* Vol. 4. *Intergroup relations* (pp. 175–197). Oxford, England: Blackwell.

Dovidio, J. F., Kawakami, K., & Gaertner, S. L. (2002). Implicit and explicit prejudice and interracial interaction. *Journal of Personality and Social Psychology, 82,* 62–68.

Dow, B. M. (2002). Orientation and color columns in monkey visual cortex. *Cerebral Cortex, 12,* 1005–1015.

Drabman, R. S., & Thomas, M. H. (1975). Does TV violence breed indifference? *Journal of Communications, 25*(4), 86–89.

Drachman, D. A. (1997). Aging and the brain: A new frontier. *Annals of Neurology, 42,* 819–828.

Dreher, H. M. (2003). The effect of caffeine reduction on sleep quality and well-being in persons with HIV. *Journal of Psychosomatic Research, 54,* 191–198.

Drewnowski, A., & Levine, A. S. (2003). Sugar and fat: From genes to culture. *Journal of Nutrition, 133,* 829–830.

Dror, I. E., & Thomas, R. D. (2005). The cognitive neuroscience laboratory: A framework for the science of mind. In C. E. Erneling (Ed.), *The mind as a scientific object: Between brain and culture* (pp. 283–292). London: Oxford University Press.

Duckitt, J., & Mphuthing, T. (1998). Group identification and intergroup attitudes: A longitudinal analysis in South Africa. *Journal of Personality and Social Psychology, 74,* 80–85.

Duckworth, K., & Borus, J. F. (1999). Population-based psychiatry in the public sector and managed care. In A. M. Nicholi (Ed.), *The Harvard guide to psychiatry.* Cambridge, MA: Harvard University Press.

Duclos, S. E., Laird, J. D., Schneider, E., Sexter, M., Stern, L., & Van Lighten, O. (1989). Emotion-specific effects of facial expressions and postures on emotional experience. *Journal of Personality and Social Psychology, 57,* 100–108.

Dunbar, R. I. M. (1993). Coevolution of neocortical size, group size and language in humans. *Behavioral and Brain Sciences, 16,* 681–735.

Duncan, J., Seitz, R. J., Kolodny, J., Bor, D., Herzog, H., Ahmed, A., Newell, F. N., & Emslie, H. (2000). A neural basis for general intelligence. *Science, 289,* 457–460.

Duncker, K. (1945). On problem solving. *Psychological Monographs, 58* (5, No. 270).

Dunkel-Schetter, C., Blasband, D., Feinstein, L., & Herbert, T. (1992). Elements of supportive interactions: When are attempts to help effective? In S. Spacapan & S. Oskamp (Eds.), *Helping and being helped: Naturalistic studies* (pp. 83–114). Newbury Park, CA: Sage.

Dunkley, D. M., Zuroff, D. C., & Blankstein, K. R. (2003). Self-critical perfectionism and daily affect: Dispositional and situational influences on stress and coping. *Journal of Personality and Social Psychology, 84,* 234–252.

Dunne, P. E. (2005). Extremal behaviour in multiagent contract negotiation. *Journal of Artificial Intelligence Research, 23,* 41–78.

Dunning, D., Leuenberger, A., & Sherman, D. A. (1995). A new look at motivated inference: Are self-serving theories of success a product of motivational forces? *Journal of Personality and Social Psychology, 69,* 58–68.

Dupre, J. (2003). *Darwin's legacy: What evolution means today.* New York: Oxford University Press.

Durham, R. C., Chambers, J. A., MacDonald, R. R., Power, K. G., & Major, K. (2003). Does cognitive-behavioural therapy influence the long-term outcome of generalized anxiety disorder? An 8–14 year follow-up of two clinical trials. *Psychological Medicine, 33,* 499–509.

Dursan, S. M., & Devarajan, S. (2001). When treating patients with schizophrenia, what clinical points should be considered if lamotrigine is chosen to augment clozapine? *Journal of Psychiatric Neuroscience, 26,* 168.

Durso, F. T., Rea, C. B., & Dayton, T. (1994). Graph-theoretic confirmation of restructuring during insight. *Psychological Science, 5,* 94–98.

Dutton, D. G., & Aron, A. (1974). Some evidence for heightened sexual attraction under conditions of high anxiety. *Journal of Personality and Social Psychology, 30,* 510–517.

Dweck, C. S. (1990). Toward a theory of goals: Their role in motivation and personality. In R. A. Dienstbier (Ed.), *Nebraska Symposium on Motivation* (Vol. 38). Lincoln: University of Nebraska Press.

Dweck, C. S. (1992). The study of goals in psychology [Commentary to feature review]. *Psychological Science, 3,* 165–167.

d'Y'dewalle, G. (2000). Sensation/perception, information processing, attention. In K. Pawlik & M. R. Rosenzweig (Eds.), *International handbook of psychology* (pp. 79–99). London: Sage.

d'Y'dewalle, G., & Rosselle, H. (1978). Text expectations in text learning. In M. M. Gruneberg, P. E. Morris, & R. N. Sykes (Eds.), *Practical aspects of memory.* Orlando, FL: Academic Press.

Dywan, J., & Bowers, K. S. (1983). The use of hypnosis to enhance recall. *Science, 222,* 184–185.

Eagly, A. H., & Crowley, M. (1986). Gender and helping behavior: A meta-analytic review of the social psychological literature. *Psychological Bulletin, 100,* 283–308.

Eagly, A. H., & Steffen, V. J. (1986). Gender and aggressive behavior: A meta-analytic review of the social psychological literature. *Psychological Bulletin, 100,* 309–330.

Eagly, A. H., & Wood, W. (1999). The origins of sex differences in human behavior. *American Psychologist, 54,* 408–423.

Ebbesen, E. B., Kjos, G. L., & Konecni, V. J. (1976). Spatial ecology: Its effects on the choice of friends and enemies. *Journal of Experimental Social Psychology, 12,* 505–518.

Ebbinghaus, H. (1885). *Üzber das gedächtnis: Untersuchugen zur experimentellen psychologie.* Leipzig: Dunker & Humbolt. Translated by H. A. Ruger & C. E. Byssenine as *Memory: A contribution to experimental psychology.* New York: Dover, 1913.

Eble, C. C. (1996). *Slang & sociability: In-group languages among college students.* Chapel Hill: University of North Carolina Press.

Eccles, J., Templeton, J., Barber, B., & Stone, M. (2003). Adolescence and emerging adulthood: The critical passage ways to adulthood. In M. H. Bornstein & L. Davidson (Eds.), *Well-being: Positive development across the life course* (pp. 383–406). *Crosscurrents in contemporary psychology*. Mahwah, NJ: Erlbaum.

Eccles, J. C. (1989). *Evolution of the brain: Creation of the self*. London: Routledge.

Echterling, L. G., & Whalen, J. (1995). Stage hypnosis and public lecture effects on attitudes and beliefs regarding hypnosis. *American Journal of Clinical Hypnosis, 38*, 13–21.

Edelman, S., Lemon, J., & Kidman, A. (2003). The perceived benefits of a group CBT intervention for patients with coronary heart disease. *Journal of Cognitive Psychotherapy, 17*, 59–65.

Edgerton, R. (1971). *The individual in cultural adaptation*. Berkeley: University of California Press.

Edinger, J. D., Wohlgemuth, W. K., Radtke, R. A., Marsh, G. R., & Quillian, R. E. (2001). Cognitive behavioral therapy for treatment of chronic primary insomnia. *Journal of the American Medical Association, 285*, 1865–1874.

Edwards, K., & Smith, E. E. (1996). A disconfirmation bias in the evaluation of arguments. *Journal of Personality and Social Psychology, 71*, 5–24.

Edwards, W. (1977). How to use multiattribute utility measurement for social decision making. *IEEE Transactions in Systems Man and Cybernetics, 17*, 326–340.

Egan, D., & Schwartz, B. (1979). Chunking in recall of symbolic drawings. *Memory & Cognition, 7*, 149–158.

Egas Moñiz, A. (1948). How I came to perform prefrontal leucotomy. *Proceedings of the First International Congress of Psychosurgery* (pp. 7–18). Lisbon: Edicos Atica.

Egeland, J. D., & Sussex, J. N. (1985). Suicide and family loading for affective disorders. *Journal of the American Medical Association, 254*, 915–918.

Ehrlichman, H., & Halpern, J. N. (1988). Affect and memory: Effects of pleasant and unpleasant odors on retrieval of happy and unhappy memories. *Journal of Personality and Social Psychology, 55*, 769–779.

Eible-Eibesfeldt, I., & Sutterlin, C. (1990). Fear, defense and aggression in animals and man: Some ethological perspectives. In P. Brain & S. Parmigiani (Eds.), *Fear and defense*. London: Harwood.

Eich, J. E. (1989). Theoretical issues in state dependent memory. In H. L. Roediger, III & F. I. M. Craik (Eds.), *Varieties of memory and consciousness: Essays in honour of Endel Tulving* (pp. 331–354). Hillsdale, NJ: Erlbaum.

Eichenbaum, H., & Fortin, N. (2003). Episodic memory and the hippocampus: It's about time. *Current Directions in Psychological Science, 12*, 53–57.

Eid, J., Johnsen, B. H., Saus, E.-R., & Risberg, J. (2004). Stress and coping in a week-long disabled submarine exercise. *Aviation, Space, and Environmental Medicine, 75*, 616–621.

Eimer, M., & Schlaghecken, F. (in press). Links between conscious awareness and response inhibition: Evidence from masked priming. *Psychonomic Bulletin & Review*.

Eisenberg, N., Martin, C. L., & Fabes, R. A. (1996). Gender development and gender effects. In D. C. Berliner & R. C. Calfee (Eds.), *Handbook of educational psychology* (pp. 358–396). New York: Prentice Hall.

Eisenberg, N., & Valiente, C. (2002). Parenting and children's prosocial and moral development. In M. H. Bornstein (Ed.), *Handbook of parenting: Vol. 5. Practical issues in parenting* (2nd ed., pp. 111–142). Mahwah, NJ: Erlbaum.

Eisenberger, R., & Cameron, J. (1996). Detrimental effects of reward: Reality or myth? *American Psychologist, 51*, 1153–1166.

Eisler, R., & Levine, D. S. (2002). Nurture, nature, and caring: We are not prisoners of our genes. *Brain & Mind, 3*, 9–52.

Ekman, P. (1970). Universal facial expressions of emotion. *California Mental Health Research Digest, 8*, 151–158.

Ekman, P. (1973). *Darwin and facial expression: A century of research in review*. New York: Academic Press.

Ekman, P. (1993). Facial expression and emotion. *American Psychologist, 48*, 384–392.

Ekman, P. (1994). Strong evidence for universals in facial expressions: A reply to Russell's mistaken critique. *Psychological Bulletin, 115*, 268–287.

Ekman, P., & Davidson, R. J. (1993). Voluntary smiling changes regional brain activity. *Psychological Science, 4*, 342–345.

Ekman, P., Friesen, W. V., & O'Sullivan, M. (1988). Smiling when lying. *Journal of Personality and Social Psychology, 54*, 414–420.

Ekman, P., Friesen, W. V., O'Sullivan, M., Chan, A., Diacoyanni-Tarlatzis, I., Heider, K., Krause, R., LeCompte, W. A., Pitcairn, T., Ricci-Bitti, P. E., Scherer, K., Tomita, M., & Tzavaras, A. (1987). Universals and cultural differences in the judgments of facial expressions of emotion. *Journal of Personality and Social Psychology, 53*, 712–717.

Ekman, P., & O'Sullivan, M. (1991). Who can catch a liar? *American Psychologist, 46*, 913–920.

Elbedour, S., Shulman, S., & Kedem, P. (1997). Adolescent intimacy: A cross-cultural study. *Journal of Cross-Cultural Psychology, 28*, 5–22.

Elkind, D. (1985). Egocentrism redux. *Developmental Review, 5*, 218–226.

Elkind, D., & Bowen, R. (1979). Imaginary audience behavior in children and adolescents. *Developmental Psychology, 15*, 38–44.

Ellenberger, H. (1970). *The discovery of the unconscious*. New York: Basic Books.

Elliot, A. J., & Devine, P. G. (1994). On the motivational nature of cognitive dissonance: Dissonance as psychological discomfort. *Journal of Personality and Social Psychology, 67*, 382–394.

Ellis, A. (1962). *Reason and emotion in psychotherapy*. New York: Lyle Stuart.

Ellis, A. (1999). Why rational emotive therapy to rational emotive behavior therapy? *Psychotherapy, 36*, 154–159.

Ellis, A. (2002). *Overcoming resistance: A rational emotive behavior therapy integrated approach* (2nd ed.). New York: Springer.

Ellis, A., Shaughnessy, M. F., & Mahan, V. (2002). An interview with Albert Ellis about rational emotive behavior therapy. *North American Journal of Psychology, 4*, 355–366.

Ellis, H. C., & Hunt, R. R. (1993). *Fundamentals of cognitive psychology* (5th ed.). Dubuque, IA: Wm. C. Brown.

Elman, J. L. (1999). The emergence of language: A conspiracy theory. In B. MacWhinney (Ed.), *The emergence of language* (pp. 1–27). Mahwah, NJ: Erlbaum.

Elmquist, J. K. (2001). Hypothalamic pathways underlying the endocrine, autonomic, and behavioral effects of leptin. *Physiology & Behavior, 74*, 703–708.

Elms, A. C. (1995). Obedience in retrospect. *Journal of Social Issues, 51*, 21–31.

Elms, A. C., & Milgram, S. (1966). Personality characteristics associated with obedience and defiance toward authoritative command. *Journal of Experimental Research in Personality, 1*, 282–289.

Embretson, S. E., & McCollam, K. M. S. (2000). Psychometric approaches to understanding and measuring intelligence. In R. J. Sternberg (Ed.), *Handbook of intelligence* (pp. 423–444). Cambridge: Cambridge University Press.

Emmelkamp, P. M. G. (1986). Behavior therapy with adults. In S. L. Garfield & A. E. Bergin (Eds.), *Handbook of psychotherapy and behavior change* (3rd ed., pp. 385–442). New York: Wiley.

Emmers-Sommer, T. M., Allen, M., & Duck, S. (Eds.). (2005). *Safer sex in personal relationships: The role of sexual script in HIV infection and prevention*. Mahwah, NJ: Erlbaum.

Enard, W., Przeworski, M., Fisher, S. E., Lai, C. S. L., Wiebe, V., Kitano, T., Monaco, A. P., & Paeaebo, S. (2002). Molecular evolution of FOXP2, a gene involved in speech and language. *Nature, 418*, 869–872.

Endler, N. S., & Speer, R. L. (1998). Personality psychology: Research trends for 1993–1995. *Journal of Personality, 66*, 621–669.

Engels, G. L., Garnefski, N., & Diekstra, R. (1993). Efficacy of rational-emotive therapy: A quantitative analysis. *Journal of Consulting and Clinical Psychology, 61*, 1083–1090.

Epel, E., Blackburn, E. H., Lin, J., Dhabar, F., Adler, N., Morrow, J., & Cawthon, R. (2004). Organismal stress and telomeric aging: An unexpected connection. *Proceedings of the National Academy of Sciences, 101*, 17312–17315.

Epstein, C. J., Erickson, R. P., & Inborn, A. W.-B. (Eds.). (2004). *Errors of development: The molecular basis of clinical disorders of morphogenesis*. New York: Oxford University Press.

Epstein, S. (1979). The stability of behavior: I. On predicting most of the people much of the time. *Journal of Personality and Social Psychology, 37*, 1097–1126.

Epstein, S. (1980). The stability of behavior: II. Implications for psychological research. *American Psychologist, 35*, 790–806.

Epstein, S. (1994). Integration of the cognitive and the psychodynamic unconscious. *American Psychologist, 49*, 709–724.

Epstein, S. (1998). Cognitive-experiential self-theory. In D. F. Barone & M. Hersen (Eds.), *Advanced personality: The Plenum series in social/clinical psychology* (pp. 211–238). New York: Plenum.

Epstein, S. (1999). The interpretation of dreams from the perspective of cognitive-experiential self-theory. In J. A. Singer & P. Salovey (Eds.), *At play in the fields of consciousness: Essays in honor of Jerome L. Singer* (pp. 51–82). Mahwah, NJ: Erlbaum.

Epstein, S., & Morling, B. (1995). Is the self motivated to do more than enhance and verify itself? In M. H. Kernis (Ed.), *Efficacy, agency, and self-esteem* (pp. 9–30). New York: Plenum Press.

Erel, O., Oberman, Y., & Yirmiya, N. (2000). Maternal versus nonmaternal care and seven domains of children's development. *Psychological Bulletin, 126*, 727–747.

Erford, B. T. (1999). A modified time-out procedure for children with noncompliant or defiant behaviors. *Professional School Counseling, 2*, 205–210.

Erickson, B., Lind, E. A., Johnson, B. C., & O'Barr, W. M. (1978). Speech style and impression formation in a court setting: The effects of "powerful" and "powerless" speech. *Journal of Experimental Social Psychology, 14*, 266–279.

Ericsson, K. A., & Kintsch, W. (1995). Long-term working memory. *Psychological Review, 102*, 211–245.

Erikson, E. H. (1950). *Childhood and society*. New York: W. W. Norton.

Erikson, E. H. (1968). *Identity: Youth and crisis*. New York: W. W. Norton.

Erikson, E. H. (1980). *Identity: Youth and crisis*. New York: W. W. Norton.

Eriksson, P. S., Perfilieva, E., Björk-Eriksson, T., Alborn, A.-M., Nordborg, C., Peterson, D. A., & Gage, F. A. (1998). Neurogenesis in the adult hippocampus. *Nature Medicine, 4*, 1313–1317.

Ertekin-Taner, N., Ronald, J., Feuk, L., Prince, J., Tucker, M., Younkin, L., Hella, M., Jain, S., Hackett, A., Scanlin, L., Kelly, J., Kihiko-Ehman, M., Neltner, M., Hersh, L., Kindy, M., Markesbery, W., Hutton, M., de Andrade, M., Petersen, R. C., Graff-Radford, N., Estus, S., Brookes, A. J., & Younkin, S. G. (2005). Elevated amyloid β protein (Aβ42) and late onset Alzheimer's disease are associated with single nucleotide polymorphisms in the urokinase-type plasminogen activator gene. *Human Molecular Genetics, 14*, 447–460.

Erwin, E., Gendin, S., & Kleiman, L. (Eds.). (1994). *Ethical issues in scientific research: An anthology*. New York: Garland.

Erwin, P. G. (1994). Effectiveness of social skills training with children: A meta-analytic study. *Counseling Psychology Quarterly, 7*, 305–310.

Escobar, M., & Miller, R. R. (2004). A review of the empirical laws of basic learning in Pavlovian conditioning. *International Journal of Comparative Psychology, 17*, 279–303.

Esterson, A. (1993). *Seductive mirage: An exploration of the work of Sigmund Freud*. Chicago: Open Court.

Etaugh, C., & Liss, M. B. (1992). Home, school, and playroom: Training grounds for adult gender roles. *Sex Roles, 26*, 129–147.

Evans, E., Hawton, K., & Rodham, K. (2005). Suicidal phenomena and abuse in adolescents: A review of epidemiological studies. *Child Abuse and Neglect, 29*, 45–58.

Evans, M. (2001). Cognitive and contextual factors in the emergence of diverse belief systems: Creation versus evolution. *Cognitive Psychology, 42*, 217–266.

Evans, R. I. (1980). *The making of social psychology: Discussions with creative contributors*. New York: Gardner Press.

Everson, S., Kauhanen, J., Kaplan, G., Goldberg, D., Julkunen, J., Tuomilehto, J., & Salonen, J. (1997). Hostility and increased risk of mortality and acute myocardial infarction: The mediating role of behavioral risk factors. *American Journal of Epidemiology, 146,* 142–152.

Exner, J. E. (1993). *The Rorschach: A comprehensive system.* (Vol. 1, 3rd ed.). New York: Wiley.

Eyeferth, K. (1961). Leistungen vershiedener Gruppen von Besatzungskindern in Hamburg-Wechsler Intelligenztest für Kinder (HAWIK). *Archir für die Gesamte Psychologie, 113,* 224–241.

Eysenck, H. J. (1952). The effects of psychotherapy: An evaluation. *Journal of Consulting Psychology, 16,* 319–324.

Eysenck, H. J. (1967). *The biological basis of personality.* Springfield, IL: Charles C. Thomas.

Eysenck, H. J. (1973). *Eysenck on extraversion.* New York: Wiley.

Eysenck, H. J. (1990). Biological dimensions of personality. In L. A. Pervin (Ed.), *Handbook of personality: Theory and research.* New York: Guilford Press.

Eysenck, H. J. (2000). Personality as a risk factor in cancer and coronary heart disease. In D. T. Kenny & J. G. Carlson (Eds.), *Stress and health: Research and clinical applications* (pp. 291–318). Amsterdam: Harwood Academic.

Eysenck, H. J., & Eysenck, S. B. G. (1983). Recent advances: The cross-cultural study of personality. In J. N. Butcher, and C. D. Spielberger (Eds.), *Advances in personality assessment* (Vol. 2, pp. 41–72). Hillsdale, NJ: Erlbaum.

Eysenck, H. J., & Levey, A. (1972). Conditioning introversion-extraversion and the strength of the nervous system. In V. Nebylitsyn & J. Gray (Eds.), *Biological basis of individual behavior* (pp. 206–220). New York: Academic Press.

Eysenck, S. B. G., & Eysenck, H. J. (1963). The validity of questionnaire and rating assessments of extraversion and neuroticism, and their factorial stability. *British Journal of Psychology, 54,* 51–62.

Fagan, J. F. (1992). Intelligence: A theoretical viewpoint. *Current Directions in Psychological Science, 1,* 82–86.

Fagot, B. I., Leinbach, M. D., & Hagan, R. (1986). Gender labeling and the adoption of sex-typed behaviors. *Developmental Psychology, 17,* 24–35.

Fairburn, C. G., Welch, S. L., Doll, H. A., Davies, B. A., & O'Connor, M. E. (1997). Risk factors for bulimia nervosa. *Archives of General Psychiatry, 54,* 509–511.

Falk, D. (1991). 3.5 million years of hominid brain evolution. *Seminars in the Neurosciences, 3,* 409–416.

Fanselow, M. S., & Poulos, A. M. (2005). The neuroscience of mammalian associative learning. *Annual Review of Psychology, 56,* 207–234.

Farb, P. (1978). *Man's rise to civilization: The cultural ascent of the Indians of North America.* New York: Penguin.

Farrell, P. (1997). The integration of children with severe learning difficulties: A review of the recent literature. *Journal of Applied Research in Intellectual Disabilities, 10,* 1–14.

Farwell, L., & Donchin, E. (1991). The truth will out: Interrogative polygraphy ("lie detection") with event-related potentials. *Psychophysiology, 28,* 531–547.

Fast, K., & Fujiwara, E. (2001). Isolated retrograde amnesia. *Neurocase, 7,* 269–272.

Fauber, J. (2004, September 28). Beauty and the brain: Doctors foresee demand for treatment to enhance abilities. *Milwaukee Journal Sentinel,* 1A. www.JSONLINE.COM

Fauber, J. (2005, March 8). Disorder may precede Alzheimer's. *Milwaukee Journal Sentinel,* 12A. www.JSONLINE.COM

Faust, M. S. (1977). Somatic development of adolescent girls. *Monographs of the Society for Research in Child Development, 42* (Whole No. 169).

Fava, M., & Rosenbaum, J. F. (1995). Pharmacotherapy and somatic therapies. In E. E. Beckham & W. R. Leber (Eds.), *Handbook of depression* (2nd ed., pp. 280–301). New York: Guilford Press.

Faw, B. (2003). Pre-frontal executive committee for perception, working memory, attention, long-term memory, motor control, and thinking: A tutorial review. *Consciousness & Cognition, 12,* 83–139.

Faw, H. W. (1990). Memory for names and faces: A fair comparison. *American Journal of Psychology, 103,* 317–326.

Faymonville, M. E., Laureys, S., Degueldre, C., DelFiore, G., Luxen, A., & Franck, G. (2000). Neural mechanisms of antinociceptive effects of hypnosis. *Anesthesiology, 92,* 1257–1267.

Feather, N. (1994). Values and culture. In W. Lonner & R. Malpass (Eds.), *Psychology and culture.* Boston: Allyn & Bacon.

Fechner, G. T. (1966). *Elements of psychophysics.* (H. E. Alder, Trans.). New York: Holt, Rinehart & Winston. (Original work published 1860)

Federmeier, K. D., & Kutas, M. (2002). Picture the difference: Electrophysiological investigations of picture processing in the two cerebral hemispheres. *Neuropsychologia, 40,* 730–747.

Feig, C. (2003, February 12). Experts fear HIV rates increasing in U.S. From www.cnn.com/2003/ HEALTH/conditins/02/12/hiv.rates/

Feinberg, T. E. (2001). *Altered egos: How the brain creates the self.* Oxford, England: Oxford University Press.

Feingold, A. (1988). Matching for attractiveness in romantic partners and same-sex friends: A meta-analysis and theoretical critique. *Psychological Bulletin, 104,* 226–235.

Feingold, A. (1992a). Cognitive gender differences: A developmental perspective. *Sex Roles, 29,* 91–112.

Feingold, A. (1992b). Good-looking people are not what we think. *Psychological Bulletin, 111,* 304–341.

Feingold, A., & Mazzella, R. (1998). Gender differences in body image are increasing. *Psychological Science, 9,* 190–195.

Feist, G. J., & Barron, F. X. (2003). Predicting creativity from early to late adulthood: Intellect, potential, and personality. *Journal of Research in Personality, 37,* 62–88.

Feldman, D. H. (1999). The development of creativity. In R. Sternberg (Ed.), *Handbook of creativity* (pp. 169–186). Cambridge, England: Cambridge University Press.

Felmlee, D. H. (1999). Social norms in same- and cross-gender friendships. *Social Psychology Quarterly, 62,* 53–67.

Felmlee, D. H., & Sprecher, S. (2000). Close relationships and social psychology: Intersections and future paths. *Social Psychology Quarterly, 63,* 365–376.

Fenigstein, A., Scheier, M. F., & Buss, A. H. (1975). Public and private self-consciousness: Assessment and theory. *Journal of Consulting and Clinical Psychology, 43,* 522–527.

Fenton, W., & McGlashan, T. (1991). Natural history of schizophrenia subtypes: I. Longitudinal study of paranoia, hebephrenic, and undifferentiated schizophrenia. *Archives of General Psychiatry, 48,* 969–977.

Fenwick, P. (1987). Meditation and the EEG. In M. A. West (Ed.), *The psychology of meditation.* Oxford, England: Clarendon Press.

Fergusson, D. M., Horwood, L. J., & Beautrais, A. L. (1999). Is sexual orientation related to mental health problems and suicidality in young people? *Archives of General Psychiatry, 56,* 876–880.

Fernandez, E., & Turk, D. C. (1989). The utility of cognitive coping strategies for altering pain perception: A meta-analysis. *Pain, 38,* 123–135.

Fernberger, S. W. (1933). Wundt's doctorate students. *Psychological Bulletin, 30,* 80–83.

Ferrari, J. R., & Dovidio, J. F. (2001). Behavioral information search by indecisives. *Personality and Individual Differences, 30,* 1–12.

Ferrari, J. R., & Tice, D. M. (2000). Procrastination as a self-handicap for men and women: A task avoidance strategy in a laboratory setting. *Journal of Research in Personality, 34,* 73–83.

Ferster, C. S., & Skinner, B. F. (1957). *Schedules of reinforcement.* New York: Appleton-Century-Crofts.

Festinger, L. (1954). A theory of social comparison processes. *Human Relations, 7,* 117–140.

Festinger, L. (1957). *A theory of cognitive dissonance.* Stanford, CA: Stanford University Press.

Festinger, L., Riecken, H. W., & Schachter, S. (1956). *When prophecy fails.* Minneapolis: University of Minnesota Press.

Festinger, L., Schachter, S., & Back, K. (1950). *Social pressures in informal groups: A study of a housing community.* New York: Harper.

Fetzer, J. H. (Ed.). (2002). *Advances in consciousness research.* Amsterdam: John Benjamins.

Field, T. M. (1982). Individual differences in the expressivity of neonates and young infants. In R. S. Feldman (Ed.), *Development of nonverbal behavior in children.* New York: Springer-Verlag.

Field, T. M., Cohen, D., Garcia, R., & Greenberg, R. (1984). Mother-stranger face discrimination by the newborn. *Infant Behavior and Development, 7,* 19–25.

Fields, J. I. (1997). Measuring giftedness in young children: A comparative study in Malaysia. *Early Development and Care, 131,* 93–106.

Figueredo, A. J., Landau, M. J., & Sefcek, J. A. (2004). Apes and angels: Adaptionism versus panglossianism. *Behavioral and Brain Sciences, 27.*

Findley, M. J., & Cooper, H. M. (1983). Locus of control and academic achievement: A literature review. *Journal of Personality and Social Psychology, 44,* 419–427.

Fine, M. (2004). The power of the *Brown v. Board of Education decision:* Theorizing threats to sustainability. *American Psychologist, 59,* 502–510.

Finger, S., & Wade, N. J. (2002). The neuroscience of Halmholtz and the theories of Johannes Mueller: Part 2: Sensation and perception. *Journal of the History of the Neurosciences, 11,* 234–254.

Fink, J. (1999). *How to use computers and cyberspace in the clinical practice of psychotherapy.* Northvale, NJ: Jason Aronson, Inc.

Fink, M. (1999). *Electroshock: Restoring the mind.* New York: Oxford University Press.

Fink, P., Hansen, M. S., & Oxhoj, M.-L. (2004). The prevalence of somatoform disorders among internal medical inpatients. *Journal of Psychosomatic Research, 56,* 413–418.

Finucane, M. L., Slovic, P., Hibbard, J. H., Peters, E., Mertz, C. K., & MacGregor, D. G. (2002). Aging and decision-making competence: An analysis of comprehension and consistency skills in older versus younger adults considering health-plan options. *Journal of Behavioral Decision Making, 15,* 141–164.

First, M. B., Pincus, H. A., Levine, J. B., Williams, J. B. W., Ustun, B., & Peele, R. (2004). Clinical utility as a criterion for revising psychiatric diagnoses. *American Journal of Psychiatry, 161,* 946–954.

Fish, J. M. (2002). The myth of race. In J. M. Fish (Ed.), *Race and intelligence: Separating science from myth* (pp. 113–141). Mahwah, NJ: Erlbaum.

Fishbach, G. D. (1992, September). Mind and brain. *Scientific American, 267,* 48–57.

Fisher, C. B., Hoagwood, K., Boyce, C., Duster, T., Frank, D. A., Grisso, T., Levine, R. J., Macklin, R., Spencer, M. B., Takanishi, R., Trimble, J. E., & Zayas, L. H. (2002). Research ethics for mental health science involving ethnic minority children and youths. *American Psychologist, 57,* 1024–1040.

Fisher, H. E. (1998). Lust, attraction, and attachment in mammalian reproduction. *Human Nature, 9,* 23–52.

Fisher, J., & Fisher, W. (1992). Changing AIDS-risk behavior. *Psychological Bulletin, 111,* 455–474.

Fisher, W. (1993). Confessions of a sexual scientist. In G. Brannigan and M. Merrens (Eds.), *The undaunted psychologist: Adventures in research* (pp. 13–29). Philadelphia, PA: Temple University Press.

Fisher, W., Byrne, D., Edmunds, M., Miller, C. T., Kelley, K., & White, L. A. (1979). Psychological and situation-specific correlates of contraceptive behavior among university women. *Journal of Sex Research, 15,* 38–55.

Fisher, W., Byrne, D., White, L., & Kelley, K. (1988). Erotophobia-erotophilia as a dimension of personality. *Journal of Sex Research, 25,* 123–151.

Fisher, W., Fisher, J., & Byrne, D. (1977). Consumer reactions to contraceptive purchasing. *Personality & Social Psychology Bulletin, 3,* 293–296.

Fisher, W., Grenier, G., Watters, W., Lamont, J., et al. (1988). Students' sexual knowledge, attitudes toward sex, and willingness to treat sexual concerns. *Journal of Medical Education, 63,* 379–385.

Fiske, S. T., & Neuberg, S. L. (1990). A continuum model of impression formation, from category-based to individuating processes: Influence of information and motivation on attention and interpretation. In M. P. Zanna (Ed.), *Advances in experimental social psychology* (Vol. 23). New York: Academic Press.

Fiske, S. T., & Taylor, S. E. (1991). *Social cognition* (2nd ed.). New York: McGraw-Hill.

Fivush, R., & Nelson, K. (2004). Culture and language in the emergence of autobiographical memory. *Psychological Science, 15,* 573–577.

Flanagan, O. (1996). Deconstructing dreams: The spandrels of sleep. In S. R. Hameroff, A. W. Kaszniak, & A. C. Scott (Eds.), *Toward a science of consciousness: The first Tucson discussions and debates* (pp. 67–88). Cambridge, MA: MIT Press.

Flavell, J. (1982). Structures, stages, and sequences in cognitive development. In W. Collins (Ed.), *The concept of development* (pp. 1–28). Hillsdale, NJ: Erlbaum.

Flavell, J. H. (1992). Cognitive development: Past, present, and future. *Developmental Psychology, 28,* 998–1005.

Flavell, J. H. (1996). Piaget's legacy. *Psychological Science, 7,* 200–203.

Flavell, J. H. (1999). Cognitive development: Children's knowledge about the mind. *Annual Review of Psychology, 50,* 21–45.

Flavell, J. H., Beach, D. R., & Chinsky, J. M. (1966). Spontaneous verbal rehearsal in a memory task as a function of age. *Child Development, 37,* 283–299.

Flavell, J. H., & Flavell, E. R. (2004). Development of children's intuitions about thought-action relations. *Journal of Cognition & Development, 5,* 451–460.

Fletcher, G. (2002). *The new science of intimate relationships.* Malden, MA: Blackwell.

Fletcher, G. J. O., Tither, J. M., O'Loughlin, C., Friesen, M., & Overall, N. (2004). Warm and homely or cold and beautiful? Sex differences in trading off traits in mate selection. *Personality and Social Psychology Bulletin, 30,* 659–672.

Floccia, C., Goslin, J., Schneider, R., & Thommen, E. (2003). Linguistic and conceptual development from one to six years: An introduction. *Developmental Science, 6,* 119–121.

Flor, H., Elbert, T., Knecht, S., & Wienbruch, C. (1995). Phantom-limb pain as a perceptual correlate of cortical reorganization following arm amputation. *Nature, 375,* 482–484.

Flouri, E., & Buchanan, A. (2003). The role of father involvement in children's later mental health. *Journal of Adolescence, 26,* 63–78.

Flynn, J. R. (1987). Massive IQ gains in 14 nations: What IQ tests really measure. *Psychological Bulletin, 101,* 171–191.

Flynn, J. R. (1996). *What environmental factors affect intelligence: The relevance of IQ gains over time.* Norwood, NJ: Ablex Publishing.

Foertsch, J., & Gernsbacher, M. A. (1997). In search of gender neutrality: Is singular *they* a cognitively efficient substitute for generic *he? Behavior Therapy, 16,* 292–302.

Folkman, S., & Moskowitz, J. T. (2000). Positive affect and the other side of coping. *American Psychologist, 55,* 647–654.

Fontana, D. (2003). *Psychology, religion, and spirituality.* Oxford, England: Blackwell.

Ford, C. S., & Beach, F. A. (1951). *Patterns of sexual behavior.* New York: Harper & Brothers.

Ford, D. Y. (1996). *Reversing underachievement among gifted Black students: Promising practices and programs.* New York: Teachers College Press.

Ford, M. (1979). The construct validity of egocentrism. *Psychological Bulletin, 86,* 1169–1188.

Fordham, S., & Ogbu, J. U. (1986). Black students' school success: Coping with the "burden of 'acting white'." *The Urban Review, 18,* 176–206.

Forer, B. R. (1949). The fallacy of personal validation: A classroom demonstration of gullibility. *Journal of Abnormal and Social Psychology, 44,* 118–123.

Foreyt, J., Walker, S., Poston, C., II, & Goodrick, G. (1996). Future directions in obesity and eating disorders. *Addictive Behaviors, 21,* 767–778.

Forgas, J. P. (1998). Asking nicely? The effects of mood on responding to more or less polite requests. *Personality and Social Psychology Bulletin, 24,* 173–185.

Forstmeier, W., & Balsby, T. J. S. (2002). Why mated dusky warblers sing so much: Territory guarding and male quality announcement. *Behaviour, 139,* 89–111.

Fouts, R. (1997). *Next of kin: What chimpanzees have taught me about who we are.* New York: Morrow.

Fowler, C. A. (2003). Speech production and perception. In A. F. Healy & R. W. Proctor (Eds.), *Handbook of psychology: Experimental psychology* (Vol. 4, pp. 237–266). New York: Wiley.

Fowles, D. (1992). Schizophrenia: Diathesis-stress revisited. *Annual Review of Psychology, 43,* 303–336.

Fox, A. T., Fertleman, M., Cahill, P., & Palmer, R. D. (2003). Medical slang in British hospitals. *Ethics & Behavior, 13,* 173–182.

Fox, B. (1998). Psychosocial factors in cancer incidence and progression. In J. Holland (Ed.), *Psycho-oncology.* New York: Oxford University Press.

Fox, B. A. (1988). *Cognitive and interactional aspects of correction in tutoring* (Tech. Rep. No. 88-2). Boulder: University of Colorado, Institute of Cognitive Science.

Fox, D. R. (1985). Psychology, ideology, utopia, and the commons. *American Psychologist, 40,* 48–58.

Fox, N., & Davidson, R. (1991). Hemispheric specialization and attachment behaviors: Developmental processes and individual differences in separation process. In J. Gewirtz & W. Kurtines (Eds.), *Interactions with attachment.* Hillsdale, NJ: Erlbaum.

Fraczek, A. (1992). Patterns of aggressive-hostile behavior orientation among adolescent boys and girls. In K. Björkqvist & P. Niemelä (Eds.), *Of mice and women: Aspects of female aggression* (pp. 107–112). San Diego, CA: Harcourt Brace Jovanovich.

Fraga, E. D., Atkinson, D. R., & Wampold, B. E. (2004). Ethnic group preferences for multicultural counseling competencies. *Cultural Diversity and Ethnic Minority Psychology, 10,* 53–65.

France, P. (1996). *Hermits: The insights of solitude.* New York: St. Martin's.

Frank, L. R. (2002). Electroshock: A crime against the spirit. *Ethical Human Sciences & Services, 4,* 63–71.

Frankenberger, K. D. (2000). Adolescent egocentrism: A comparison among adolescents and adults. *Journal of Adolescence, 23,* 343–354.

Frankenhauser, M. (1975). The experimental psychology research unit. *Man-Environment Systems, 5,* 193–195.

Frankenhauser, M., Myrsten, A., & Post, B. (1970). Psychophysiological reactions to cigarette smoking. *Scandinavian Journal of Psychology, 11,* 237–245.

Frankl, V. (1963). *Man's search for meaning: An introduction to logotherapy.* New York: Vintage Books.

Frankl, V. (1969). *The will to meaning.* New York: World Publishing.

Franks, C. M. (1957). Personality factors and the rate of conditioning. *British Journal of Psychology, 48,* 119–126.

Frantz, C. M., & Bennigson, C. (2005). Better late than early: The influence of timing on apology effectiveness. *Journal of Experimental Social Psychology, 41,* 201–207.

Franzoi, S. L. (1985). Personality characteristics of the cross-country hitchhiker. *Adolescence, 29,* 655–668.

Franzoi, S. L. (1995). The body-as-object versus the body-as-process: Gender differences and gender considerations. *Sex Roles, 33,* 417–437.

Franzoi, S. L., & Chang, Z. (2000). The sociocultural dynamics of the physical self: How does gender shape body esteem? In J. A. Holstein & G. Miller (Eds.), *Perspectives on social problems* (Vol. 12, pp. 179–201). Stamford, CT: JAI Press.

Franzoi, S. L., & Chang, Z. (2002). The body esteem of Hmong and Caucasian young adults. *Psychology of Women Quarterly, 26,* 89–91.

Franzoi S. L., & Davis, M. H. (2005). Self-awareness and self-consciousnesss. In V. J. Derlega, B. A. Winstead, & W. H. Jones (Eds.), *Personality: Contemporary theory and research* (3rd ed., pp. 281–308). Belmont, CA: Thomson Wadsworth.

Franzoi, S. L., Davis, M. H., & Young, R. D. (1985). The effects of private self-consciousness and perspective-taking on satisfaction in close relationships. *Journal of Personality and Social Psychology, 48,* 1584–1594.

Franzoi, S. L., & Shields, S. A. (1984). The Body Esteem Scale: Multidimensional structure and sex differences in a college population. *Journal of Personality Assessment, 48,* 173–178.

Fredrickson, B. L. (2001). The role of positive emotions in positive psychology. *American Psychologist, 56,* 218–226.

Fredrickson, B. L., Maynard, K. E., Helms, M. J., Haney, T. L., Siegler, I. C., & Barefoot, J. C. (2000). Hostility predicts magnitude and duration of blood pressure response to anger. *Journal of Behavioral Medicine, 23,* 229–243.

Fredrickson, B. L., Roberts, T., Noll, S. M., Quinn, D. M., & Twenge, J. M. (1998). That swimsuit becomes you: Sex differences in self-objectification, restrained eating, and math performance. *Journal of Personality and Social Psychology, 75,* 269–284.

Freed, C., & LeVay, S. (2002). *Healing the brain: A doctor's controversial quest for a cure for Parkinson's disease.* Long Beach, NJ: Science News.

Freedman, M. (1971). *Homosexuality and psychological functioning.* Belmont, CA: Brooks/Cole.

French, J. R. P., & Raven, B. H. (1959). The bases of social power. In D. Cartwright (Ed.), *Studies in social power.* Ann Arbor: University of Michigan Press.

French, S. A. (2003). Pricing effects on food choices. *Journal of Nutrition, 133,* 841–843.

Frese, B., Moya, M., & Megias, J. L. (2004). Social perception of rape: How rape myth acceptance modulates the influence of situational factors. *Journal of Interpersonal Violence, 19,* 143–161.

Freud, A. (1936). *The writings of Anna Freud: The ego and the mechanics of defense.* Madison CT: International Universities Press.

Freud, S. (1895/1950/1966). Project for a scientific psychology. In J. Strachey (Ed. and Trans.), *The standard edition of the complete psychological works of Sigmund Freud* (Vol. 1, pp. 282–398). London: Hogarth Press.

Freud, S. (1900/1953). The interpretation of dreams. In J. Strachey (Ed. and Trans.), *The standard edition of the complete psychological works of Sigmund Freud* (Vols. 4 and 5). London: Hogarth.

Freud, S. (1905/1959). Fragments of an analysis of a case of hysteria. *Collected papers* (Vol. 3). New York: Basic Books.

Freud, S. (1909/1957). Mourning and melancholia. In J. Strachey (Ed. and Trans.), *The standard edition of the complete psychological works of Sigmund Freud* (Vol. 14, pp. 243–258). London: Hogarth.

Freud, S. (1909/1963). Analysis of a phobia in a five-year-old boy. In J. Strachey (Ed. and Trans.), *The standard edition of the complete psychological works of Sigmund Freud* (Vol. 10, pp. 3–149). London: Hogarth.

Freud, S. (1917/1959). Introductory lectures on psychoanalysis. Part III: General theory of the neurosis. In J. Strachey (Ed. and Trans.), *The standard edition of the complete psychological works of Sigmund Freud* (Vol. 16, pp. 243–496). London: Hogarth Press.

Freud, S. (1926/1959). Inhibitions, symptoms, and anxiety. In J. Strachey (Ed. & Trans.), *The standard edition of the complete psychological works of Sigmund Freud* (Vol. 20, pp. 89–174). London: Hogarth Press.

Freud, S. (1946). *The ego and the mechanisms of defense.* New York: International Universities Press.

Freud, S. (1949). *A general introduction to psychoanalysis.* New York: Penguin.

Friedman, H., Hawley, P., & Tucker, J. (1994). Personality, health, and longevity. *Current Directions in Psychological Science, 3,* 37–41.

Friedman, H. S., & Schustack, M. W. (1999). *Personality: Classic theories and modern research.* Boston: Allyn & Bacon.

Friedman, J. M. (2000). Obesity in the new millennium. *Nature, 404,* 632–634.

Friedman, L. J. (2001). Erik Erikson on identity, generativity, and pseudospeciation: A biographer's perspective. *Psychoanalysis & History, 3,* 179–192.

Friedman, M. (1996). *Type A behavior: Its diagnosis and treatment.* New York: Plenum.

Friedman, M., & Ulmer, D. (1984). *Treating Type A behavior—and your heart.* New York: Knopf.

Frieze, I. H., Olson, J. E., & Russell, J. (1991). Attractiveness and income for men and women in management. *Journal of Applied Social Psychology, 21,* 1039–1057.

Frisch, K. von. (1950). *Bees: Their vision, chemical senses, and language.* Ithaca, NY: Cornell University Press.

Frisch, K. von. (1962). Dialects in the language of the bees. *Scientific American, 207,* 78–87.

Frisch, K. von. (1967). *The dance language and orientation of bees.* Cambridge, MA: Harvard University Press.

Frith, H., & Kitzinger, C. (2001). Reformulating sexual script theory: Developing a discursive psychology of sexual negotiation. *Theory & Psychology, 11,* 209–232.

Fritz, H. L., Nagurney, A. J., & Helgeson, V. S. (2003). Social interactions and cardiovascular reactivity during problem disclosure among friends. *Personality and Social Psychology Bulletin, 29,* 713–725.

Fromm, E., & Shor, R. E. (Eds.). (1979). *Hypnosis: Developments in research and new perspectives* (2nd ed.). Hawthorne, NY: Aldine.

Fry, D. P. (1992). Female aggression among the Zapotec of Oaxaca, Mexico. In K. Björkqvist & P. Niemelä (Eds.), *Of mice and women: Aspects of female aggression* (pp. 187–199). San Diego, CA: Harcourt Brace Jovanovich.

Fuchs, C. S., Stampfer, M. J., Colditz, G. A., et al. (1995). Alcohol consumption and mortality among women. *New England Journal of Medicine, 332,* 1245–1250.

Fuhriman, A., & Burlingame, G. M. (1994). Group psychotherapy: Research and practice. In A. Fuhriman & G. M. Burlingame (Eds.), *Handbook of group psychotherapy.* New York: Wiley.

Fujita, F., & Diener, E. (2005). Life satisfaction set point: Stability and change. *Journal of Personality and Social Psychology, 88,* 158–164.

Fulero, S. (1997). Personal Internet communication to fellow members of the Society of Personality and Social Psychology.

Fulford, K. W. M. (1999). Nine variations and a coda on the theme of an evolutionary definition of dysfunction. *Journal of Abnormal Psychology, 108,* 412–420.

Fuligni, A. J., & Stevenson, H. W. (1995). Time use and mathematics achievement among American, Chinese, and Japanese high school students. *Child Development, 66,* 830–842.

Funder, D. C. (2001). Personality. *Annual Review of Psychology, 52,* 197–221.

Furio, C., Calatayud, M. L., Barcenas, S. L., & Padilla, O. M. (2000). Functional fixedness and functional reduction as common sense reasonings in chemical equilibrium and in geometry and polarity of molecules. *Science & Education, 84,* 545–565.

Furnham, A. (2001). Internalizing values and virtues. In F. Columbus (Ed), *Advances in psychology research* (Vol. 6, pp. 229–254). Hauppauge, NY: Nova Science Publishers.

Furnham, A., McClelland, A., & Omer, L. (2003). A cross-cultural comparison of ratings of perceived fecundity and sexual attractiveness as a function of body weight and waist-to-hip ratio. *Psychology, Health and Medicine, 8,* 219–230.

Furnham, A., Moutafi, J., & Baguma, P. (2002). A cross-cultural study on the role of weight and waist-to-hip ratio on female attractiveness. *Personality and Individual Differences, 32,* 729–745.

Furomoto, L. (1992). Joining separate spheres—Christine Ladd-Franklin, woman-scientist (1847–1930). *American Psychologist, 47,* 174–182.

Furomoto, L., & Scarborough, E. (2002). Placing women in the history of psychology: The first American women psychologists. In W. E. Pickren & D. A. Dewsbury (Eds.), *Evolving perspectives on the history of psychology* (pp. 527–543). Washington, DC: American Psychological Association.

Fuster, J. M. (1989). *The prefrontal cortex: Anatomy, physiology, and neuropsychology of the frontal lobe* (2nd ed.). New York: Raven Press.

Fuster, J. M. (2005). The cortical substrate of general intelligence. *Cortex, 41,* 228–229.

Gabrieli, J. D. E. (1998). Cognitive neuroscience of human memory. *Annual Review of Psychology, 49,* 87–115.

Gabrieli, J. D. E. (1999). The architecture of human memory. In J. K. Foster & M. Jelicic (Eds.), *Memory: Systems, process, or function?* (pp. 205–231). Oxford, England: Oxford University Press.

Gabrieli, J. D. E., Desmond, J. E., Demb, J. B., Wagner, A. D., Stone, M. V., Vaidya, C. J., et al. (1996). Functional magnetic resonance imaging of semantic memory processes in the frontal lobes. *Psychological Science, 7,* 278–283.

Gafner, G., & Benson, S. (2003). *Hypnotic techniques: For standard psychotherapy and formal hypnosis.* New York: Norton.

Gagliese, L., & Katz, J. (2000). Medically unexplained pain is not caused by psychopathology. *Pain Research & Management, 5,* 251–257.

Gagné, F. M., & Lydon, J. E. (2001). Mindset and relationship illusions: The moderating effects of domain specificity and relationship commitment.

Personality and Social Psychology Bulletin, 27, 1144–1155.

Gagneux, P., Boesch, C., & Woodruff, D. S. (1999). Female reproductive strategies, paternity and community structure in wild West African Chimpanzees. *Animal Behavior, 57,* 9–12.

Gaivoronskaia, G., & Solem, K. E. (2004). Genetic testing: Affected parties and decision making. *Journal of Risk Research, 7,* 481–493.

Galanter, E. (1962). Contemporary psychophysics. In R. Brown (Ed.), *New directions in psychology.* New York: Holt, Rinehart & Winston.

Gallagher, J., Harradine, C. C., & Coleman, M. R. (1997). Challenge or boredom? Gifted students' views on their schooling. *Roeper Review, 19,* 132–141.

Gallagher, T. J., & Lewis, J. M. (2001). Rationalists, fatalists, and the modern superstitious: Test-taking in introductory sociology. *Sociological Inquiry, 71,* 1–12.

Gallup, G. G., Jr. (1977). Self-recognition in primates: A comparative approach to the bidirectional properties of consciousness. *American Psychologist, 32,* 329–338.

Gallup, G. G., Jr., & Povinelli, D. J. (1993). Mirror, mirror on the wall, which is the most heuristic theory of them all? A response to Mitchell. *New Ideas in Psychology, 11,* 327–335.

Galton, F. (1869). *Hereditary genius: An inquiry into its laws and consequences.* New York: Appleton.

Gandevia, S. C., McCloskey, D. I., & Burke, D. (1992). Kinesthetic signals and muscle contraction. *Trends in Neurosciences, 15,* 62–65.

Gangestad, S. W., & Snyder, M. (2000). Self-monitoring: Appraisal and reappraisal. *Psychological Bulletin, 126,* 530–555.

Gantz, B. J., & Turner, C. W. (2003). Combining acoustic and electric hearing. *Laryngoscope, 113,* 1726–1730.

Garcia, C. K., Wilund, K., & Arca, M. (2001). Autosomal recessive hypercholesterolemia caused by mutations in a putative LDL receptor adaptor protein. *Science, 292,* 1394–1398.

Garcia, J., & Koelling, R. A. (1966). Relation of cue to consequence in avoidance learning. *Psychonomic Science, 4,* 123–124.

Garcia, J., Rusniak, K. W., & Brett, L. P. (1977). Conditioning food-illness aversions in wild animals: Caveat Canonici. In H. Davis & H. M. B. Hurwitz (Eds.), *Operant-Pavlovian interactions.* Hillsdale, NJ: Erlbaum.

Gardner, H. (1983). *Frames of mind: The theory of multiple intelligences.* New York: Basic Books.

Gardner, H. (1991). *The unschooled mind: How children think and how schools should teach.* New York: Basic Books.

Gardner, H. (1993a). *Creating minds: An anatomy of creativity seen through the lives of Freud, Einstein, Picasso, Stravinsky, Eliot, Graham, and Gandhi.* New York: Basic Books.

Gardner, H. (1993b). *Multiple intelligences: The theory in practice.* New York: Basic Books.

Gardner, H. (1998). Are there additional intelligences? The case for naturalist, spiritual, and existential intelligence. In J. Kane (Ed.), *Education, information, and transformation* (pp. 111–131). Englewood Cliffs, NJ: Prentice Hall.

Gardner, H. (1999). *Intelligence reframed: Multiple intelligences for the 21st century.* New York: Basic Books.

Gardner, H. (2003). Three meanings of intelligence. In R. J. Sternberg, J. Lautrey, & T. I. Lubart (Eds.), *Models of intelligence: International perspectives* (pp. 43–54). Washington, DC: American Psychological Association.

Gardner, H., Kornhaber, M. L., & Wake, W. K. (1996). *Intelligence: Multiple perspectives.* Ft. Worth, TX: Harcourt Brace.

Gardner, R. A., & Gardner, B. T. (1969). Teaching sign language to a chimpanzee. *Science, 165,* 664–672.

Gardner, R. J. M., & Sutherland, G. R. (1996). *Chromosomal abnormalities and genetic counseling.* New York: Oxford University Press.

Garfinkel, D., Laudon, M., Of, D., & Zisapel, N. (1995). Improvement of sleep quality in elderly people by controlled-release melatonin. *Lancet, 146,* 541–544.

Garlick, D. (2002). Understanding the nature of the general factor of intelligence: The role of individual differences in neural plasticity as an explanatory mechanism. *Psychological Review, 109,* 116–136.

Garrett, K. D., Paul, R. H., Libon, D. J., & Cohen, R. A. (2004). Defining the diagnosis of vascular dementia. *Applied Neuropsychology, 11,* 202–207.

Garry, M., Loftus, E. F., Brown, S. W., & DuBreuil, S. C. (1997). Womb with a view: Memory beliefs and memory-work experiences. In D. G. Payne & F. G. Conrad (Eds.), *Intersections in basic and applied memory research* (pp. 233–255). Mahwah, NJ: Erlbaum.

Gatchel, R. J., & Oordt, M. S. (2003). Acute and chronic pain conditions. In R. J. Gatchel & M. S. Oordt (Eds.), *Clinical health psychology and primary care: Practical advice and clinical guidance for successful collaboration* (pp. 117–134). Washington, DC: American Psychological Association.

Gatchel, R. J., & Turk, D. C. (Eds.). (1999). *Psychosocial factors in pain: Critical perspectives.* New York: Guilford Press.

Gaur, P. D., & Sen, A. K. (1989). A study of deprivation among non-scheduled castes, scheduled castes and mentally retarded children. *Journal of Applied Psychology, 26,* 26–34.

Gawronski, B., Ehrenberg, K., Banse, R., Zukova, J., & Klauer, K. C. (2003). It's in the mind of the beholder: The impact of stereotypic associations on category-based and individuating impression formation. *Journal of Experimental Social Psychology, 39,* 16–30.

Gay, P. (1998). *Freud: A life for our time.* New York: Norton.

Gazzaniga, M. S. (1967). The split brain in man. *Scientific American, 217,* 24–29.

Gazzaniga, M. S. (1970). *The bisected brain.* New York: Appleton-Century-Crofts.

Gazzaniga, M. S. (1988). *Mind matters: How mind and brain interact to create our conscious lives.* Boston: Houghton Mifflin.

Gazzaniga, M. S. (1989). Organization of the human brain. *Science, 245,* 947–952.

Gazzaniga, M. S. (Ed.). (2000). *The new cognitive neuroscience* (2nd ed.). Cambridge, MA: The MIT Press.

Gazzaniga, M. S., & Miller, M. B. (2000). Testing Tulving: The split-brain approach. In E. Tulving (Ed.), *Memory, consciousness, and the brain: The Tallinn Conference* (pp. 307–318). Philadelphia, PA: Psychology Press.

Geary, D. C. (2005a). Evolution of general intelligence. In D. C. Geary (Ed.), *The origin of mind: Evolution of brain, cognition, and general intelligence* (pp. 253–305). Washington, DC: American Psychological Association.

Geary, D. C. (2005b). Heuristics and Controlled Problem Solving. In D. C. Geary (Ed.), *The origin of mind: Evolution of brain, cognition, and general intelligence* (pp. 163–199). Washington, DC: American Psychological Association.

Gedo, J. E. (2001). The enduring scientific contributions of Sigmund Freud. In J. A. Winer & J. W. Anderson (Eds.), *The annual of psychoanalysis: Vol. 29. Sigmund Freud and his impact on the modern world* (pp. 105–115). Hillsdale, NJ: Analytic Press.

Geen, R. G. (1984). Preferred stimulation levels in introverts and extroverts: Effects on arousal and performance. *Journal of Personality & Social Psychology, 46,* 1303–1312.

Geen, R. G. (1996). Aggression and antisocial behavior. In D. T. Gilbert, S. T. Fiske, & G. Lindzey (Eds.), *The handbook of social psychology* (4th ed.). New York: McGraw-Hill.

Gelderloos, P., Walton, K. G., Orme-Johnson, D. W., & Alexander, C. N. (1991). Effectiveness of the Transcendental Meditation program in preventing and treating substance misuse: A review. *The International Journal of Addictions, 26,* 293–325.

Gelfand, S. A. (1981). *Hearing.* New York: Marcel Dekker.

Geller, J. (2002). Estimating readiness for change in anorexia nervosa: Comparing clients, clinicians and research assessors. *International Journal of Eating Disorders, 31,* 251–260.

Genovesio, A., & Ferraina, S. (2004). Integration of retinal disparity and fixation-distance related signals toward an egocentric coding of distance in the posterior parietal cortex of primates. *Journal of Neurophysiology, 91,* 2670–2684.

Georgopoulos, A. P., Whang, K., Georgopoulos, M.-A., Tagaris, G. A., Amirikan, B., Richter, W., Kim, S.-G.,

& Ugurbil, K. (2001). Functional magnetic resonance imaging of visual object construction and shape discrimination: Relations among task, hemispheric lateralization, and gender. *Journal of Cognitive Neuroscience, 13,* 72–89.

Gerbner, G. (1993). Images that hurt: Mental illness in the mass media. *Journal of the California Alliance for the Mentally Ill, 4,* 17–20.

Gerbner, G., & Signorielli, N. (1990). *Violence profile 1967 through 1988–89: Enduring patterns.* Unpublished manuscript, Annenberg School of Communications, University of Pennsylvania.

Gerhart, K. A., Koziol-McLain, J., Lowenstein, S. R., & Whiteneck, G. G. (1994). Quality of life following spinal cord injury: Knowledge and attitudes of emergency care providers. *Annals of Emergency Medicine, 23,* 807–812.

Gerra, G., Monti, D., Panerai, A. E., Sacerdote, P., Anderlini, R., Avanzini, P., Zaimovic, A., Brambilla, F., & Franceschi, C. (2003). Long-term immune-endocrine effects of bereavement: Relationships with anxiety levels and mood. *Psychiatry Research, 121,* 145–158.

Gerra, G., Zaimovic, A., Ferri, M., Zambelli, U., Timpano, M., Neri, E., Marzocchi, G. F., Delsignore, R., & Brambilla, F. (2000). Long-lasting effects of (±)3,4-Methylenedioxymethamphetamine (Ecstacy) on serotonin system function in humans. *Biological Psychiatry, 47,* 127–136.

Gerschwind, N., & Galaburda, A. (1987). *Cerebral lateralization: Biological mechanisms, association and pathology.* Cambridge, MA: Bradford/MIT Press.

Gesheider, G. A. (1985). *Psychophysics: Method and theory.* Hillsdale, NJ: Erlbaum.

Getzmann, S. (2003). A comparison of the contrast effect in sound localization in the horizontal and vertical planes. *Experimental Psychology, 50,* 131–141.

Ghazvini, A., & Mullis, R. L. (2002). Center-based care for young children: Examining predictors of quality. *Journal of Genetic Psychology, 163,* 112–125.

Giambra, L. M. (1989). Task-unrelated-thought frequency as a function of age: A laboratory study. *Psychology and Aging, 4,* 136–143.

Giambra, L. M. (1995). A laboratory method for investigating influences on switching attention to task-unrelated imagery and thought. *Consciousness and Cognition, 4,* 1–21.

Giambra, L. M. (2000). Daydreaming characteristics across the life-span: Age differences and seven to twenty year longitudinal changes. In R.G. Kunzendorf & B. Wallace (Eds.), *Individual differences in conscious experience: Advances in consciousness research* (Vol. 20, pp. 147–206). Amsterdam, Netherlands: John Benjamins.

Gibson, E. J., & Walk, R. D. (1960, April). The "visual cliff." *Scientific American,* 64–71.

Gibson, H. B. (1991). Can hypnosis compel people to commit harmful, immoral, and criminal acts? A review of the literature. *Contemporary Hypnosis, 8,* 129–140.

Gibson, J. J. (1962). Observations on active touch. *Psychological Review, 69,* 477–491.

Gibson, J. J. (1966). *The senses considered as perceptual systems.* Boston: Houghton Mifflin.

Giedd, J. N., Blumenthal, J., Jeffries, N. O., Castellanos, F. X., Liu, H., Zijdenbos, A., Paus, T., Evans, A. C., & Rapoport, J. L. (1999). Brain development during childhood and adolescence: A longitudinal MRI study. *Nature Neuroscience, 2,* 861–863.

Gil, E. (2003). Art and play therapy with sexually abused children. In C. A. Malchiodi (Ed.), *Handbook of art therapy* (pp. 152–166). New York: Guilford Press.

Gilbert, D. T., Pinel, E. C., Wilson, T. D., Blumberg, S. J., & Wheatley, T. P. (1998). Immune neglect: A source of durability bias in affective forecasting. *Journal of Personality and Social Psychology, 75,* 617–638.

Gil-Burmann, C., Pelaez, F., & Sanchez, S. (2002). Mate choice differences according to sex and age: An analysis of personal advertisements in Spanish newspapers. *Human Nature, 13,* 493–508.

Gill, J. H. (1997). *If a chimpanzee could talk: And other reflections on language acquisition.* Tucson: University of Arizona Press.

Gillett, G. R. (2001). Free will and events in the brain. *Journal of Mind & Behavior, 22,* 287–310.

Gilligan, C. (1982). *In a different voice: Psychological theory and women's development.* Cambridge, MA: Harvard University Press.

Gilligan, C. (1990). Teaching Shakespeare's sister. In C. Gilligan, N. Lyons, & T. Hanmer (Eds.), *Making connections: The relational worlds of adolescent girls at Emma Willard School.* Cambridge, MA: Harvard University Press.

Gilligan, C., & Attanucci, J. (1988). Two moral orientations: Gender differences and similarities. *Merrill-Palmer Quarterly, 34,* 223–237.

Gillin, J. C. (1993). Clinical sleep-wake disorders in psychiatric practice: Dyssomnias. In D. L. Dunner (Ed.), *Current psychiatric therapy.* Philadelphia: Saunders.

Gilman, S. L. (2001). Karen Horney, M.D., 1885–1952. *American Journal of Psychiatry, 158,* 1205.

Gilovich, T., & Savitsky, K. (2002). Like goes with like: The role of representativeness in erroneous and pseudo-scientific beliefs. In T. Gilovich, D. Griffin, & D. Kahneman (Eds.), *Heuristic and biases: The psychology of intuitive judgment* (pp. 617–624). New York: Cambridge University Press.

Ginsburg, M. L., Quirt, C., Ginsburg, A. D., & MacKillop, W. J. (1995). Psychiatric illness and psychosocial concerns of patients with newly diagnosed lung cancer. *Canadian Medical Association Journal, 152,* 701–708.

Gladue, B. A. (1991). Aggressive behavioral characteristics, hormones, and sexual orientation in men and women. *Aggressive Behavior, 17,* 313–326.

Glaser, R., Kiecolt-Glaser, J., Bonneau, R., Malarkey, W., Kennedy, S., & Hughes, J. (1992). Stress-induced modulation of the immune response to recombinant hepatitis B vaccine. *Psychosomatic Medicine, 54,* 22–29.

Glass, D., & Singer, J. (1972). *Urban stress: Experiments on noise and social stressors.* New York: Academic Press.

Gleason, J. B. (1997). *The development of language.* Boston: Allyn & Bacon.

Gleaves, D. H. (1996). The sociocognitive model of dissociative identity: A reexamination of evidence. *Psychological Bulletin, 120,* 42–59.

Glick, P., Gottesman, D., & Jolton, J. (1989). The fault is not in the stars: Susceptibility of skeptics and believers in astrology to the Barnum effect. *Personality and Social Psychology Bulletin, 15,* 417–429.

Glick, P., & Hilt, L. (2000). From combative children to ambivalent adults: The development of gender prejudice. In T. Eckes & M. Trautner (Eds.), *Developmental social psychology of gender.* Hillsdale, NJ: Erlbaum.

Gluck, M. A., & Myers, C. E. (2001). *Gateway to memory: An introduction to neural network modeling of the hippocampus and learning.* Cambridge, MA: MIT Press.

Glucksberg, S., & Danks, J. (1968). Effects of discriminative labels and of nonsense labels upon availability of novel function. *Journal of Verbal Learning and Verbal Behavior, 7,* 72–76.

Glucksberg, S., & Weisberg, R. W. (1966). Verbal behavior and problem solving: Some effects of labeling in a functional fixedness problem. *Journal of Experimental Psychology, 71,* 659–664.

Godbout, R., Montplaisir, J., Bédard, M.-A., Doivan, D., & LaPierre, O. (1990). Fundamental and clinical neuropharmacology of sleep disorders: Restless legs syndrome with periodic movements in sleep and narcolepsy. In J. Montplaisir & R. Godbout (Eds.), *Sleep and biological rhythms: Basic mechanisms and applications to psychiatry* (pp. 219–236). New York: Oxford University Press.

Goddard, H. H. (1913). The Binet tests in relation to immigration. *Journal of Psycho-Asthenics, 18,* 105–107.

Goddard, H. H. (1919). *Psychology of the normal and subnormal.* New York: Dodd, Mead.

Goebel, B., & Brown, D. (1981). Age differences in motivation related to Maslow's needs hierarchy. *Developmental Psychology, 17,* 809–817.

Goel, V. (2005). Can there be a cognitive neuroscience of central cognitive systems? In C. E. Erneling (Ed.), *The mind as a scientific object: Between brain and culture* (pp. 265–282). London: Oxford University Press.

Goetestam, K. G. (2002). One session group treatment of spider phobia by direct or modeled exposure. *Cognitive Behaviour Therapy, 31,* 18–24.

Goethals, G. R. (1986). Social comparison theory: Psychology from the lost and found. *Personality and Social Psychology Bulletin, 12,* 261–278.

Goethals, G. R., & Darley, J. M. (1987). Social comparison theory: Self-evaluation and group life. In B. Mullen & G. R. Goethals (Eds.), *Theories of group behavior.* New York: Springer-Verlag.

Goffman, E. (1959). *The presentation of self in everyday life.* Garden City, NY: Doubleday.

Goffman, E. (1963). *Stigma: Notes on the management of spoiled identity.* Englewood Cliffs, NJ: Prentice Hall.

Goffman, E. (1971). *Relations in public.* New York: Basic Books.

Gogtay, N., Sporn, A., Clasen, L. S., Nugent, T. F., III, Greenstein, D., Nicolson, R., Giedd, J. N., Lenane, M., Gochman, P., Evans, A., & Rappoport, J. L. (2004). Comparison of progressive cortical gray matter loss in childhood-onset schizophrenia with that in childhood-onset atypical psychoses. *Archives of General Psychiatry, 61,* 17–22.

Goh, V. H.-H., Tong, Y.-Y., Lim, C.-L., Low, E. C.-T., & Lee, L. K.-H. (2000). Circadian disturbances after night-shift work aboard a naval ship. *Military Medicine, 165,* 101–105.

Gohm, C. L. (2003). Mood regulation and emotional intelligence: Individual differences. *Journal of Personality & Social Psychology, 84,* 594–607.

Goldberg, B. (1995). Slowing down the aging process through the use of altered states of consciousness: A review of the medical literature. *Psychology: A Quarterly Journal of Human Behavior, 32,* 19–21.

Goldberg, C. (2003, May 18). Privacy an issue in brain imaging: Machines can track unconscious preferences, fear. *Boston Globe.*

Goldberg, E. (2001). *The executive brain: Frontal lobes and the civilized mind.* New York: Oxford University Press.

Goldenberg, I., & Goldenberg, H. (1995). Family therapy. In R. J. Corsini & D. Wedding (Eds.), *Current psychotherapies* (5th ed.). Itasca, IL: Peacock.

Goldin-Meadow, S., Nusbaum, H., Kelly, S. D., & Wagner, S. (2001). Explaining math: Gesturing lightens the load. *Psychological Science, 12,* 516–522.

Goldman, J., & Coté, L. (1991). Aging of the brain: Dementia of the Alzheimer's type. In E. R. Kandel, J. H. Schwartz, & T. M. Jessell (Eds.), *Principles of neural science* (3rd ed.). New York: Elsevier.

Goldstein, A.J., de Beurs, E., Chambless, D., & Wilson, K. (2000). EMDR for panic disorder with agoraphobia: Comparison with waiting list and credible attention-placebo control conditions. *Journal of Consulting & Clinical Psychology, 68,* 947–956.

Goldstein, R. B., Wickramaratne, P. J., Horwath, E., & Weissman, M. M. (1997). Familial aggregation and phenomenology of "early"-onset (at or before age 20 years) panic disorder. *Archives of General Psychiatry, 54,* 271–278.

Goldston, D. B. (2003). Assessing risk of suicidal behaviors: Multitiered screening assessments. In D. B. Goldston (Ed.), *Measuring suicidal behavior and risk in children and adolescents* (pp. 205–220). Washington, DC: American Psychological Association.

Golob, E. J., & Starr, A. (2004). Visual encoding differentially affects auditory event-related potentials during working memory retrieval. *Psychophysiology, 41,* 186–192.

Golombok, S., & Tasker, F. (1996). Do parents influence the sexual orientation of their children? Findings from a longitudinal study of lesbian families. *Developmental Psychology, 32,* 3–11.

Gonsiorek, J. C. (1982). Results of psychological testing on homosexual populations. *American Behavioral Scientist, 25*(4), 385–396.

Gonsiorek, J. C. (1991). The empirical basis for the demise of the illness model of homosexuality. In J. Gonsiorek & J. Weinrich (Eds.), *Homosexuality: Research implications for public policy* (pp. 115–136). Thousand Oaks, CA: Sage.

Gonzales, M. H., Pederson, J. H., Manning, D. J., & Wetter, D. W. (1990). Pardon my gaffe: Effects of sex, status, and consequence severity on accounts. *Journal of Personality and Social Psychology, 58,* 610–621.

Goode, E. (1999, February 16). Tales of midlife crisis found greatly exaggerated. *New York Times.*

Goodman, N. (2002). The serotonergic system and mysticism: Could LSD and the nondrug-induced

mystical experience share common neural mechanisms? *Journal of Psychoactive Drugs, 34,* 263–272.
Goodnow, J. J. (1988). Children's household work: Its nature and function. *Psychological Bulletin, 103,* 5–26.
Goosens, K. A., & Maren, S. (2002). Long-term potentiation as a substrate for memory: Evidence from studies of amygdaloid plasticity and Pavlovian fear conditioning. *Hippocampus, 12,* 592–599.
Gootjes, L., Van Strien, J. W., & Bouma, A. (2004). Age effects in identifying and localising dichotic stimuli: A corpus callosum deficit? *Journal of Clinical and Experimental Neuropsychology, 26,* 826–837.
Gopnik, A. (1996). The post-Piaget era. *Psychological Science, 7,* 221–225.
Gopnik, J. J., Meltzoff, A. N., & Kuhl, P. K. (1999). *The scientist in the crib: Minds, brains, and how children learn.* New York: Morrow.
Gorassini, D. R. (1996). Conviction management: Lessons from hypnosis research about how self-images of dubious validity can be willfully sustained. In N. P. Spanos & B. Wallace (Eds.), *Hypnosis and imagination: Imagery and human development series* (pp. 177–198). Amityville, NY: Baywood.
Gordon, P. (1990). Learnability and feedback. *Developmental Psychology, 26,* 217–220.
Gorman, C. (2002, June 10). The science of anxiety. *Time,* 46–54.
Gortmaker, S. L., Must, A., Perrin, J. M., Sobol, A. M., & Dietz, W. H. (1993). Social and economic consequences of overweight in adolescence and young adulthood. *New England Journal of Medicine, 329,* 1008–1012.
Gosling, S. D. (2001). From mice to men: What can we learn about personality from animal research? *Psychological Bulletin, 127,* 45–86.
Gosling, S. D., & John, O. P. (1999). Personality dimensions in nonhuman animals: A cross-species review. *Current Directions in Psychological Science, 8,* 69–75.
Gottesman, I. I. (1991). *Schizophrenic genesis: The epigenetic puzzle.* New York: Cambridge University Press.
Gottfredson, L. S. (2003). Dissecting practical intelligence theory: Its claims and evidence. *Intelligence, 31,* 343–397.
Gottfried, A. W., Gottfried, A. E., Bathurst, K., & Guerin, D. W. (1994). *Gifted IQ: Early developmental aspects: The Fullerton longitudinal study.* New York: Plenum Press.
Gottlieb, G. (2002). Developmental-behavioral initiation of evolutionary change. *Psychological Review, 109,* 211–218.
Gould, E., Reeves, A. J., Graziano, M. S., & Gross, C. G. (1999). Neurogenesis in the neocortex of adult primates. *Science, 286,* 548–552.
Gould, E., Tanapat, P., Rydel, T., & Hastings, N. (2000). Regulation of hippocampal neurogenesis in adulthood. *Biological Psychiatry, 48,* 715–720.
Gould, J. L., & Marler, P. (1987). Learning by instinct. *Scientific American, 256,* 74–75.
Gould, S. J. (1991). *Bully for Brontosaurus: Reflections in natural history.* New York: Norton.
Gould, S. J. (1996). *The mismeasure of man.* New York: Norton.
Gould, S. K. (1993). Mozart and modularity. In S. K. Gould (Ed.), *Eight little piggies: Reflections in natural history* (pp. 249–261). New York: Norton.
Gouldner, A. W. (1960). The norm of reciprocity: A preliminary statement. *American Sociological Review, 25,* 161–178.
Gouras, P. (1991). Color vision. In E. R. Kandel, J. H. Schwartz, & T. M. Jessell (Eds.), *Principles of neural science* (3rd ed., pp. 467–480). New York: Elsevier.
Graffin, N. F., Ray, W. J., & Lundy, R. (1995). EEG concomitants of hypnosis and hypnotic susceptibility. *Journal of Abnormal Psychology, 104,* 123–131.
Grant, B. F., & Dawson, D. A. (1997). Age at onset of alcohol use and its association with DSM-IV alcohol abuse and dependence: Results from the National Longitudinal Alcohol Epidemiologic Survey. *Journal of Substance Abuse, 9,* 103–110.
Graves, F. C., & Hennessy, M. B. (2000). Comparison of the effects of the mother and an unfamiliar adult female on cortisol and behavioral responses of pre- and postweaning guinea pigs. *Developmental Psychobiology, 36,* 91–100.
Grayson, B., & Stein, M. W. (1981). Attracting assault: Victims' nonverbal cues. *Journal of Communication, 31,* 68–75.
Graziano, W. G., & Eisenberg, N. (1997). Agreeableness: A dimension of personality. In R. Hogan, J. Johnson, & S. Briggs (Eds.), *Handbook of personality psychology* (pp. 795–824). San Diego, CA: Academic Press.
Graziano, W. G., Jensen-Campbell, L. A., & Hair, E. C. (1996). Perceiving interpersonal conflict and reacting to it: The case for agreeableness. *Journal of Personality and Social Psychology, 70*(4).
Green, J. (2004). The SSRI debate and the evidence base in child and adolescent psychiatry. *Current Opinion in Psychiatry, 17,* 233–235.
Green, J. T., & Woodruff-Pak, D. S. (2000). Eyeblink classical conditioning: Hippocampal formation is for neutral stimulus associations as cerebellum is for association response. *Psychological Bulletin, 126,* 138–158.
Green, L. (2002). A descriptive study of African American English: Research in linguistics and education. *International Journal of Qualitative Studies in Education, 15,* 673–690.
Green, M. F. (1998). *Schizophrenia from a neurocognitive perspective: Probing the impenetrable darkness.* Boston: Allyn & Bacon.
Green, R. (1987). *The "sissy boy syndrome" and the development of homosexuality.* New Haven, CT: Yale University Press.
Green, R. A., Cross, A. J., & Goodwin, G. M. (1995). Review of the pharmacology and clinical pharmacology of 3,4-methylenedioxymethamphetamine (MDMA or "ecstasy"). *Psychopharmacology, 119,* 247–260.
Greenbank, P. (2003). The role of values in educational research: The case for reflexivity. *British Educational Research Journal, 29,* 791–801.
Greenberg, L. S., & Johnson, S. M. (1988). *Emotionally focused therapy for couples.* New York: Guilford Press.
Greenberg, M., & Frisch, D. (1972). Effects of intentionality on willingness to reciprocate a favor. *Journal of Experimental Social Psychology, 21,* 61–72.
Greenfield, P. M. (1994). Independence and interdependence as developmental scripts: Implications for theory, research, and practice. In P. M. Greenfield & R. R. Cocking (Eds.), *Cross-cultural roots of minority child development* (pp. 1–37). Hillsdale, NJ: Erlbaum.
Greenfield, P. M., Keller, H., Fuligni, A., & Maynard, A. (2003). Cultural pathways through universal development. *Annual Review of Psychology, 54,* 461–490.
Greenfield, P. M., & Lave, J. (1982). Cognitive aspects of informal education. In D. A. Wagner & H. W. Stevenson (Eds.), *Cultural perspectives on child development.* San Francisco: W. H. Freeman.
Greenstein, V. C., Holopigian, K., Seiple, W., Carr, R. E., & Hood, D. C. (2004). Atypical multifocal ERG responses in patients with diseases affecting the photoreceptors. *Vision Research, 44,* 2867–2874.
Greenwald, A. G., McGhee, D. E., & Schwartz, J. L. K. (1998). Measuring individual differences in implicit cognition: The implicit association test. *Journal of Personality and Social Psychology, 74,* 1464–1480.
Greenwald, A. G., Spangenberg, E. R., Pratkanis, A. R., & Eskenazi, J. (1991). Double-blind tests of subliminal self-help audiotapes. *Psychological Science, 2,* 119–122.
Greenwald, D. F., & Harder, D. W. (1997). Fantasies, coping behavior, and psychopathology. *Journal of Clinical Psychology, 53,* 91–97.
Greenwood, M. R. C. (1989). Sexual dimorphism and obesity. In A. J. Stunkard & A. Baum (Eds.), *Perspectives in behavioral medicine: Eating, sleeping, and sex.* Hillsdale, NJ: Erlbaum.
Gregory, R. J. (2004). Psychological testing: History, principles, and applications. Needham Heights, MA: Allyn & Bacon.
Gregory, R. L. (1998). *Eye and brain: The psychology of seeing* (5th ed.). Princeton, NJ: Princeton University Press.
Greif, E. B., & Ulman, K. J. (1982). The psychological impact of menarche on early adolescent females: A review of the literature. *Child Development, 53,* 1413–1430.
Greiffenstein, M. F., Baker, W. J., Axelrod, B., Peck, E., & Gervais, R. (2004). The Fake Bad Scale and MMPI-2 F-Family in detection of implausible psychological trauma claims. *Clinical Neuropsychologist, 18,* 573–590.
Griffiths, R. R., & Mumford, G. K. (1995). Caffeine—A drug of abuse? In F. E. Bloom & D. J. Kupfer (Eds.), *Psychopharmacology: The fourth generation* (pp. 1699–1713). New York: Raven Press.
Grigorenko, E. L. (2000). Heritability and intelligence. In R. J. Sternberg (Ed.), *Handbook of intelligence* (pp. 53–91). Cambridge: Cambridge University Press.
Grillon, C., Smith, K., Haynos, A., & Nieman, L. K. (2004). Deficits in hippocampus-mediated Pavlovian conditioning in endogenous hypercortisolism. *Biological Psychiatry, 56,* 837–843.
Grinker, J. A. (1982). Physiological and behavioral basis for human obesity. In D. W. Pfaff (Ed.), *The physiological mechanisms of motivation.* New York: Springer-Verlag.
Gripps, C. (2002). Sociocultural perspectives on assessment. In G. Wells & G. Claxton (Eds.), *Learning for life in the 21st century: Sociocultural perspectives on the future of education* (pp. 73–83). Malden, MA: Blackwell.
Grohol, J. M. (1998). Future clinical directions: Professional development, pathology, and psychotherapy on-line. In J. Gackenbach (Ed.), *Psychology and the internet: Interpersonal, intrapersonal, and transpersonal implications* (pp. 111–140). San Diego, CA: Academic Press.
Gross, A., & Latané, J. (1974). Receiving help, reciprocating, and interpersonal attraction. *Journal of Applied Social Psychology, 4,* 210–223.
Gross, C. G. (2000). Neurogenesis in the adult brain: Death of a dogma. *Nature Reviews Neuroscience, 1,* 67–73.
Grossman, D. C., Mueller, B. A., Riedy, C., Dowd, M. D., Villaveces, A., Prodzinski, J., Nakagawara, J., Howard, J., Thiersch, N., & Harruff, R. (2005). Gun storage practices and risk of youth suicide and unintentional firearm injuries. *Journal of the American Medical Association, 293,* 707–714.
Grossman, J. B., & Kaufman, J. C. (2002). Evolutionary psychology: Promise and perils. In R. J. Sternberg & J. C. Kaufman (Eds.), *The evolution of intelligence* (pp. 9–25). Mahwah, NJ: Erlbaum.
Groth-Marnat, G. (1997). *Handbook of psychological assessment* (3rd ed.). New York: Wiley.
Grotzer, T. A., & Perkins, D. N. (2000). Teaching intelligence: A performance conception. In R. J. Sternberg (Ed.), *Handbook of intelligence* (pp. 492–515). Cambridge: Cambridge University Press.
Gruzelier, J. (2002). A Janusian perspective on the nature, development and structure of schizophrenia and shizotypy. *Schizophrenia Research, 54,* 95–103.
Guilford, J. P. (1959). Traits of creativity. In H. H. Anderson (Ed.), *Creativity and its cultivation* (pp. 142–161). New York: Harper & Row.
Guilleminault, C. (1976). Cataplexy. In C. Guilleminault, W. C. Dement, & P Passouant (Eds.), *Narcolepsy* (pp. 125–143). New York: Spectrum.
Gulick, W. L., Gesheider, G. A., & Frisina, R. D. (1989). *Hearing: Physiological acoustics, neural coding, and psychoacoustics.* New York: Oxford University Press.
Gumperz, J. J., & Levinson, S. C. (Eds.). (1996). *Rethinking linguistic relativity.* Cambridge: Cambridge University Press.
Guofang, R., & Qinglin, Z. (2004). Three viewpoints on the relationship between praise and intrinsic motivation. *Psychological Science (China), 27,* 1002–1004.
Gur, R. C., Turetsky, B. I., Matsui, M., Yan, M., Bilker, W., Hughett, P., & Gur, R. E. (1999). Sex difference in gray and white matter in healthy young adults: Correlations with cognitive performance. *Journal of Neuroscience, 19,* 4065–4072.
Gustafson, C. R., Garcia, J., Hawkins, W., & Rusniak, K. (1974). Coyote predation control by aversive conditioning. *Science, 184,* 581–583.
Guthrie, J. P., Ash, R. A., & Bendapudi, V. (1995). Additional validity evidence for a measure of morningness. *Journal of Applied Psychology, 80,* 186–190.
Guthrie, R. (1976). *Even the rat was white: A historical view of psychology.* New York: Harper & Row.
Gutierres, S. E., Kenrick, D. T., & Partch, J. J. (1999). Beauty, dominance, and the mating game: Contrast effects in self-assessment reflect gender differences in

mate selection. *Personality and Social Psychology Bulletin, 25,* 1126–1134.

Hackett, T. A., & Kaas, J. H. (2003). Auditory processing in the primate brain. In M. Gallagher & R. J. Nelson (Eds.), *Handbook of psychology: Biological psychology* (Vol. 3, pp. 187–210). New York: Wiley.

Hagger, M. S., & Orbell, S. (2003). A meta-analytic review of the common-sense model of illness representations. *Psychology & Health, 18,* 141–184.

Haggerty, J. J., Stern, R., Mason, G., & Beckwith, J. (1993). Subclinical hypothyroidism: A modifiable risk factor for depression? *American Journal of Psychiatry, 150,* 508–510.

Haier, R. J. (2003). Brain imaging studies of intelligence: Individual differences and neurobiology. In R. J. Sternberg, J. Lautrey, & T. I. Lubart (Eds.), *Models of intelligence: International perspectives* (pp. 185–193). Washington, DC: American Psychological Association.

Haier, R. J., Chueh, D., Touchette, P., Lott, I., Buchsbaum, M. S., MacMillan, D., Sandman, C., LaCasse, L., & Sosa, E. (1995). Intelligence and changes in regional cerebral glucose metabolic rate following learning. *Intelligence, 16,* 415–426.

Haier, R. J., Siegel, B. V., Tang, C., Abel, L., & Buchsbaum, M. S. (1992). Intelligence and changes in regional cerebral glucose metabolic rate following learning. *Intelligence, 16,* 415–426.

Haight, W. L. (2002). *African-American children at church: A sociocultural perspective.* New York: Cambridge University Press.

Haines, B. A., Metalsky, G. I., Cardamone, A. L., & Joiner, T. (1999). Interpersonal and cognitive pathways into the origins of attributional style: A developmental perspective. In T. Joiner & J. C. Coyne (Eds.), *The interactional nature of depression: Advances in interpersonal approaches* (pp. 65–92). Washington, DC: American Psychological Association.

Halaris, A. (2003). Neurochemical aspects of the sexual response cycle. *CNS Spectrums, 8,* 211–216.

Halgren, E., Walter, R. D., Cherlow, A. G., & Crandall, P. H. (1978). Mental phenomena evoked by electrical stimulation of the human hippocampal formation and amygdala. *Brain, 101,* 83–117.

Hall, B. K., Pearson, R. D., & Muller, G. B. (Eds.). (2004). *Environment, development, and evolution: Toward a synthesis.* Cambridge, MA: MIT Press.

Hall, C. D., Smith, A. L., & Keele, S. W. (2001). The impact of aerobic activity on cognitive function in older adults: A new synthesis based on the concept of executive control. *European Journal of Cognitive Psychology, 13,* 279–300.

Hall, D. T., & Nougaim, K. E. (1968). An examination of Maslow's need hierarchy in an organizational setting. *Organizational Behavior and Human Performance, 3,* 12–35.

Hall, E. T. (1969). *The hidden dimension.* New York: Doubleday.

Hall, S., & Brannick, M. T. (2002). Comparison of two random-effects methods of meta-analysis. *Journal of Applied Psychology, 87,* 377–389.

Hall, Z. W. (1992). *Introduction to molecular neurobiology.* Sunderland, MA: Sinauer.

Hallman, R. J. (1970). Toward a Hindu theory of creativity. *Educational Theory, 20,* 368–376.

Hallschmid, M., Benedict, C., Born, J., Fehm, H.-L., & Kern, W. (2004). Manipulating central nervous mechanisms of food intake and body weight regulation by intranasal administration of neuropeptides in man. *Physiology and Behavior, 83,* 55–64.

Halonen, J. (1995). Demystifying critical thinking. *Teaching of Psychology, 22,* 75–81.

Halpern, D. (1995). *Thought and knowledge: An introduction to critical thinking* (3rd ed.). Hillsdale, NJ: Erlbaum.

Halpern, D. F. (1996). *Thinking critically about critical thinking.* Mahwah, NJ: Erlbaum.

Halpern, D. F. (2000). *Sex differences in cognitive abilities* (3rd ed.). Mahwah, NJ: Erlbaum.

Hamann, S. B., Ely, T. D., Hoffman, J. M., & Kilts, C. D. (2002). Ecstasy and agony: Activation of the human amygdala in positive and negative emotion. *Psychological Science, 13,* 135–141.

Hamer, D. H. (2002). Genetics of sexual behavior. In J. Benjamin & R. P. Ebstein (Eds.), *Molecular genetics and the human personality* (pp. 257–272). Washington, DC: American Psychiatric Publishing.

Hamilton, J. T. (1998). *Channeling violence: The economic market for violent television programming.* Princeton, NJ: Princeton University Press.

Hamilton, M. E., Voris, J. C., Sebastian, P. S., Singha, A. K., Krejci, L. P., Elder, I. R., Allen, J. E., Beitz, J. E., Covington, K. R., Newton, A. E., Price, L. T., Tillman, E., & Hernandez, L. L. (1997). Money as a tool to extinguish conditioned responses to cocaine in addicts. *Journal of Clinical Psychology, 54,* 211–218.

Hampson, S. E. (1988). The dynamics of categorization and impression formation. In T. K. Srull & R. S. Wyer, Jr. (Eds.), *Advances in social cognition: Vol. 1. A dual process model of impression formation* (pp. 77–82). Hillsdale, NJ: Erlbaum.

Handen, B. L. (1997). Mental retardation. In E. J. Mash & L. G. Terdal (Eds.), *Assessment of childhood disorders* (3rd ed., pp. 369–407). New York: Guilford Press.

Haney, M., Hart, C. L., Ward, A. S., & Foltin, R. W. (2003). Nefazodone decreases anxiety during marijuana withdrawal in humans. *Psychopharmacology, 165,* 157–165.

Hansen, C. H., & Hansen, R. D. (1988). Finding the face in the crowd: An anger superiority effect. *Journal of Personality and Social Psychology, 54,* 917–924.

Hansen, C. H., & Hansen, R. D. (1990). Rock music videos and antisocial behavior. *Basic and Applied Social Psychology, 11,* 357–369.

Hansen, E. S., Hasselbalch, S., Law, I., & Bolwig, T. G. (2002). The caudate nucleus in obsessive-compulsive disorder. Reduced metabolism following treatment with paroxetine: A PET study. *International Journal of Neuropsychopharmacology, 5,* 1–10.

Hanshaw, J. B., Dudgeon, J. A., & Marshall, W. C. (1985). *Viral diseases of the fetus and newborn.* Philadelphia: Saunders.

Hanson, R. K., Cadsky, O., Harris, A., & Lalonde, C. (1997). Correlates of battering among 997 men: Family, history, adjustment, and attitudinal differences. *Violence and Victims, 12,* 191–208.

Harackiewicz, J. M., Durik, A. M., & Barron, K. E. (2005). Multiple goals, optimal motivation, and the development of interest. In J. P. Forgas, K. P. Williams, & S. M. Lahan (Eds.), *Social motivation: Conscious and unconscious processes.* (pp. 21–39). New York: Cambridge University Press.

Harackiewicz, J. M., & Sansone, C. (2000). Rewarding competence: The importance of goals in the study of motivation. In C. Sansone & J. M. Harackiewicz (Eds.), *Intrinsic and extrinsic motivation: The search for optimal motivation and performance* (pp. 79–103). San Diego, CA: Academic Press.

Harder, D., Maggio, J., & Whitney, G. (1989). Assessing gustatory detection capabilities using preference procedures. *Chemical Senses, 14,* 547–564.

Hardin, C., & Banaji, M. R. (1993). The influence of language on thought. *Social Cognition, 11,* 277–308.

Harkness, S. (2002). Culture and social development: Explanations and evidence. In P. K. Smith & C. H. Hart (Eds.), *Blackwell handbook of childhood social development* (pp. 60–77). Malden, MA: Blackwell Publishers.

Harlow, H. F., & Harlow, M. K. (1962). Social deprivation in monkeys. *Scientific American, 200,* 68–74.

Harlow, H. F., & Zimmermann, R. R. (1959). Affectional responses in the infant monkey. *Science, 130,* 421–432.

Harman, L. D. (1985). Acceptable deviance as social control: The cases of fashion and slang. *Deviant Behavior, 6,* 1–15.

Harnish, R. M. (2002). *Minds, brains, computers: An historical introduction to the foundations of cognitive science.* Malden, MA: Blackwell.

Harpur, T. J., Hart, S. D., & Hare, R. D. (2002). Personality of the psychopath. In P. T. Costa, Jr., & T. A. Widiger (Eds.), *Personality disorders and the five-factor model of personality* (2nd ed., pp. 299–324). Washington, DC: American Psychological Association.

Harrigan, J. A. (1985). Self touching as an indicator of underlying affect and language processing. *Social Science and Medicine, 20,* 1161–1168.

Harrigan, J. A., Lucic, K. S., Kay, D., McLaney, A., & Rosenthal, R. (1991). Effect of expresser role and type of self-touching on observers' perceptions. *Journal of Applied Social Psychology, 21,* 585–609.

Harriot, J., & Ferrari, J. R. (1996). Prevalence of procrastination among samples of adults. *Psychological Bulletin, 78,* 611–616.

Harris, B. (2002). What ever happened to little Albert? In W. E. Pickren & D. A. Dewsbury (Eds.), *Evolving perspectives on the history of psychology* (pp. 237–254). Washington, DC: American Psychological Association.

Harris, C. R. (2004). The evolution of jealousy. *American Scientist, 92,* 62–71.

Harris, M. (1999). *Theories of culture in postmodern times.* Walnut Creek, CA: Alta Mira Press.

Harris, M. J., Milich, R., Corbitt, E. M., Hoover, D. W., & Brady, M. (1992). Self-fulfilling effects of stigmatizing information on children's social interactions. *Journal of Personality and Social Psychology, 63,* 41–50.

Harris, S. (1995). Family, self, and sociocultural contributions to body-image attitudes of African-American women. *Psychology of Women Quarterly, 19,* 129–145.

Harris, S. M. (2004). The effect of health value and ethnicity on the relationship between hardiness and health behaviors. *Journal of Personality, 72,* 379–411.

Harrison, J. (2001). *Synaesthesia: The strangest thing.* Oxford, England: Oxford University Press.

Harrison, P. L., Flanagan, D. P., & Genshaft, J. L. (1997). An integration and synthesis of contemporary theories, tests, and issues in the field of intellectual assessment. In D. P. Flanagan, J. L. Genshaft, & P. L. Harrison (Eds.), *Contemporary intellectual assessment: Theories, tests, and issues* (pp. 533–561). New York: Guilford Press.

Hart, A. J., Whalen, P. J., Shin, L. M., McInerney, S. C., Fischer, H., & Rauch, S. L. (2000). Differential response in the human amygdala to racial outgroup vs. ingroup face stimuli. *Neuroreport, 11,* 2351–2355.

Harte, J. L., Eifert, G. H., & Smith, R. (1995). The effects of running and meditation on beta-endorphin, corticotropin-releasing hormone and cortisol in plasma, and on mood. *Biological Psychology, 40,* 251–265.

Harter, S. (1988). Developmental processes in the construction of the self. In T. D. Yawkey & J. E. Johnson (Eds.), *Integrative processes and socialization: Early to middle childhood.* Hillsdale, NJ: Erlbaum.

Hartley, W. S. (1970). *Manual for the twenty statements problem.* Kansas City, MO: Department of Research, Greater Kansas City Mental Health Foundation.

Hartman, E. (1978). *The sleeping pill.* New Haven, CT: Yale University Press.

Hartshorne, H., & May, M. A. (1928). *Studies in deceit.* New York: Macmillan.

Harvey, E. (1999). Short-term and long-term effects of early parental employment on children of the National Longitudinal Survey of Youth. *Developmental Psychology, 35,* 445–459.

Harvey, J. H., & Martin, R. (1995). Celebrating the story in social perception, communication, and behavior. In R. S. Wyer & T. K. Srull (Eds.), *Knowledge and memory: Advances in social cognition* (Vol. 8). Hillsdale, NJ: Erlbaum.

Harvey, P. H., & Krebs, J. R. (1990). Comparing brains. *Science, 249,* 140–145.

Harwerth, R. S., Fredenburg, P. M., & Smith, E. (2003). Temporal integration for stereoscopic vision. *Vision Research, 43,* 505–517.

Harwood, R. L., Miller, J. G., & Irizarry, N. L. (1995). *Culture and attachment: Perceptions of the child in context.* New York: Guilford Press.

Hasegawa, I., Fukushima, T., Ihara, T., & Miyashita, Y. (1998). Callosal window between prefrontal cortices: Cognitive interaction to retrieve long-term memory. *Science, 281,* 814–818.

Haselton, M. G., & Buss, D. M. (2000). Error management theory: A new perspective on biases in cross-sex mind reading. *Journal of Personality and Social Psychology, 78,* 81–91.

Hasher, L., Chung, C., May, C. P., & Foong, N. (2002). Age, time of testing, and proactive interference. *Canadian Journal of Experimental Psychology, 56,* 200–207.

Haslam, N. (1997). Evidence that male sexual orientation is a matter of degree. *Journal of Personality and Social Psychology, 73,* 862–870.

Hasselmo, M. E., & Bower, J. M. (1993). Acetylcholine and memory. *Trends in Neurosciences, 16,* 218–222.

Hatfield, E. (1988). Passionate and companionate love. In R. J. Sternberg & M. L. Barnes (Eds.), *The psychology of love* (pp. 191–217). New Haven, CT: Yale University Press.

Hatfield, E., & Rapson, R. (1996). *Love and sex: Cross-cultural perspectives.* Boston: Allyn & Bacon.

Hatfield, E., & Rapson, R. L. (1993). *Love, sex, and intimacy: Their psychology, biology, and history.* New York: HarperCollins.

Hatzidimitriou, G., McCann, U. D., & Ricaurte, G. A. (1999). Altered serotonin innervation patterns in the forebrain of monkeys treated with (±)3,4,-methylenedioxymethamphetamine seven years previously: Factors influencing abnormal recovery. *Journal of Neuroscience, 19,* 506–517.

Haugtvedt, C. P., & Petty, R. E. (1992). Personality and persuasion: Need for cognition moderates the persistence and resistance of attitude changes. *Journal of Personality and Social Psychology, 63,* 308–319.

Hauser, R. A., Freeman, T. B., Snow, B. J., Nauert, M., Gauger, L., Kordower, J. H., & Olanow, C. W. (1999). Long-term evaluation of bilateral fetal nigral transplantation in Parkinson's disease. *Archives of Neurology, 56,* 179–187.

Hauser, R. M. (1998). Trends in Black-White test-score differentials: I. Uses and misuses of NAEP/SAT data. In U. Neisser (Ed.), *The rising curve* (pp. 219–249). Washington, DC: American Psychological Association.

Hawkins, D. R. (1986, March). The importance of dreams. *Harvard Medical School Mental Health Letter,* pp. 5–7.

Hawkins, J. D., Catalano, R. F., & Miller, J. Y. (1992). Risk and protective factors for alcohol and other drug problems in adolescence and early adulthood: Implications for substance abuse prevention. *Psychological Bulletin, 112,* 64–105.

Hayes, C. (1951). *The ape in our house.* New York: Harper.

Hayes, M. R., Savastano, D. M., & Covasa, M. (2004). Cholecystokinin-induced satiety is mediated through interdependent cooperation of CCK-A and 5-HT3 receptors. *Physiology and Behavior, 82,* 663–669.

Hayes, N. (2002). *Psychology in perspective* (2nd ed.). Basingstoke, England: Palgrave.

Hayflick, L. (1965). The limited in vitro lifetime of human diploid cell strains. *Experimental Cell Research, 37,* 614–636.

Hazan, C., & Shaver, P. (1987). Romantic love conceptualized as an attachment process. *Journal of Personality and Social Psychology, 52,* 511–524.

Hazelrigg, M. D., Cooper, H. M., & Borduin, C. M. (1987). Evaluating the effectiveness of family therapies: An integrative review and analysis. *Psychological Bulletin, 101,* 428–442.

Healy, A. F. (Ed.). (2005). *Experimental cognitive psychology and its applications.* Washington, DC: American Psychological Association.

Healy, A. F., & Bourne, L. E., Jr. (Eds.). (1995). *Learning and memory of knowledge and skills: Durability and specificity.* Thousand Oaks, CA: Sage.

Heatherton, T. F., & Vohs, K. D. (2000). Interpersonal evaluations following threats to self: Role of self-esteem. *Journal of Personality and Social Psychology, 78,* 725–736.

Hebb, D. (1955). Drives and the C.N.S.—conceptual nervous system. *Psychological Review, 62,* 245–254.

Hebl, M. R., Foster, J. B., Mannix, L. M., & Dovidio, J. F. (2002). Formal and interpersonal discrimination: A field study of bias toward homosexual applicants. *Personality and Social Psychology Bulletin, 28,* 815–825.

Hebl, M. R., & Mannix, L. M. (2003). The weight of obesity in evaluating others: A mere proximity effect. *Personality & Social Psychology Bulletin, 29,* 28–38.

Heffernan, D. D., Harper, S. M., & McWilliam, D. (2002). Women's perceptions of the outcome of weight loss diets: A signal detection approach. *International Journal of Eating Disorders, 31,* 339–343.

Heider, F. (1946). Attitudes and cognitive organization. *Journal of Psychology, 21,* 107–112.

Heider, F. (1958). *The psychology of interpersonal attraction.* New York: Wiley.

Heinberg, L. (1996). Theories of body image disturbance: Perceptual, developmental, and sociocultural factors. In J. Thompson (Ed.), *Body image, eating disorders, and obesity* (pp. 23–26). Washington, DC: American Psychological Association.

Heine, S. J., & Lehman, D. R. (1997). Culture, dissonance, and self-affirmation. *Personality and Social Psychology Bulletin, 23,* 389–400.

Heine, S. J., & Lehman, D. R. (1999). Culture, self-discrepancies, and self-satisfaction. *Personality and Social Psychology Bulletin, 25,* 915–925.

Held, J. D., Alderton, D. E., Foley, P. P., & Segall, D. O. (1993). Arithmetic reasoning gender differences: Explanations found in the Armed Services Vocational Aptitude Battery (ASVAB). *Learning and Individual Differences, 5,* 171–186.

Hellige, J. B. (1990). Hemispheric asymmetry. *Annual Review of Psychology, 41,* 55–80.

Hellige, J. B. (1993). *Hemispheric asymmetry: What's right and what's left?* Cambridge, MA: Harvard University Press.

Hellsten, J., Wennström, M., Bengzon, J., Mohapel, P., & Tingström, A. (2004). Electroconvulsive seizures induce endothelial cell proliferation in adult rat hippocampus. *Biological Psychiatry, 55,* 420–427.

Helm, H., Hays, J. C., Flint, E., Koenig, H. G., & Blazer, D. G. (2000). Does private religious activity prolong survival? A six-year follow-up study of 3,851 older adults. *Journal of Gerontology, 55A,* M400–M405.

Helmholtz, H. von. (1863). *On the sensations of tone as a physiological basis for the theory of music* (A. J. Ellis, Trans.). New York: Dover.

Helms, J. E. (1990). *Black and White racial identity: Theory, research, and practice.* New York: Greenwood Press.

Helms, J. E. (2004). The 2003 Leona Tyler Award Address: Making race a matter of individual differences within groups. *Counseling Psychologist, 32,* 473–483.

Hembree, R. (1988). Correlates, causes, effects, and treatment of test anxiety. *Review of Educational Research, 58,* 47–77.

Henderlong, J., & Lepper, M. R. (2002). The effects of praise on children's intrinsic motivation: A review and synthesis. *Psychological Bulletin, 128,* 774–795.

Hendrick, C., & Hendrick, S. S. (2003). Romantic love: Measuring cupid's arrow. In S. J. Lopez & C. R. Snyder (Eds.), *Positive psychological assessment: A handbook of models and measures* (pp. 235–249). Washington, DC: American Psychological Association.

Heng, M. A. (2000). Scrutinizing common sense: The role of practical intelligence in intellectual giftedness. *Gifted Child Quarterly, 44,* 171–182.

Henningfield, D. R., Schuh, L. M., & Jarvik, M. E. (1995). Pathophysiology of tobacco dependence. In F. E. Bloom & D. J. Kupfer (Eds.), *Psychopharmacology: The fourth generation* (pp. 1715–1729). New York: Raven Press.

Henningfield, J. E., Clayton, R., & Pollin, W. (1990). Involvement of tobacco in alcoholism and illicit drug use. *British Journal of Addiction, 85,* 279–292.

Henriques, J. B. Z., & Davidson, R. J. (1990). Regional brain electrical asymmetries discriminate between previously depressed and healthy control subjects. *Journal of Abnormal Psychology, 99,* 22–31.

Henry, K. R. (1984). Cochlear damage resulting from exposure to four different octave bands of noise at three different ages. *Behavioral Neuroscience, 1,* 107–117.

Hensch, T. K., & Fagiolini, M. (Eds.). (2004). *Excitatory-inhibitory balance: Synapses, circuits, systems.* New York: Kluwer Academic/Plenum Publishers.

Hepper, P. G., Shahidullah, S., & White, R. (1990). Origins of fetal handedness. *Nature, 347,* 431.

Hepworth, J. T., & West, S. G. (1988). Lynchings and the economy: A time-series reanalysis of Hovland and Sears (1940). *Journal of Personality and Social Psychology, 55,* 239–247.

Herbert, J., Lilienfeld, S., Lohr, J., Montgomery, R., O'Donohue, W., Rosen, G., & Tolin, D. (2000). Science and pseudoscience in the development of eye movement desensitization and reprocessing: Implications for clinical psychology. *Clinical Psychological Review, 20,* 945–971.

Herek, G. M. (1991). Myths about sexual orientation: A lawyer's guide to social science research. *Law and Sexuality: A Review of Lesbian and Gay Legal Issues, 1,* 133–172.

Herek, G. M. (2002). Heterosexuals' attitudes toward bisexual men and women in the United States. *The Journal of Sex Research, 39,* 264–274.

Herek, G. M., Cogan, J. C., & Gillis, J. R. (2002). Victim experiences in hate crimes based on sexual orientation. *Journal of Social Issues, 58,* 319–339.

Herman, C. P., & Polivy, J. (1980). Restrained eating. In A. J. Stunkard (Ed.), *Obesity.* Philadelphia: Saunders.

Herman, C. P., & Polivy, J. (2004). The self-regulation of eating: Theoretical and practical problems. In R. F. Baumeister & K. D. Vohs (Eds.), *Handbook of self-regulation: Research, theory, and applications* (pp. 492–508). New York: Guilford Press.

Hermann, C., Ziegler, S., Birbaumer, N., & Flor, H. (2002). Psychophysiological and subjective indicators of aversive Pavlovian conditioning in generalized social phobia. *Biological Psychiatry, 52,* 328–337.

Heron, W. (1957). The pathology of boredom. *Scientific American, 196,* 52–56.

Herrenkohl, E. C., Herrenkohl, R. C., & Toedter, L. J. (1983). Perspectives on the intergenerational transmission of abuse. In D. Finkelhor, R. J. Gelles, G. T. Hotaling, & M. A. Straus (Eds.), *The dark side of families* (pp. 305–316). Beverly Hills, CA: Sage.

Herrera, R. S., & DelCampo, R. L. (1995). Beyond the superwoman syndrome: Work satisfaction and family functioning among working-class Mexican American women. *Hispanic Journal of Behavioral Sciences, 17,* 49–60.

Herring, S. C. (2004). Slouching toward the ordinary: Current trends in computer-mediated communication. *New Media and Society, 6,* 26–36.

Herrnstein, R. J., & Murray, C. (1994). *The bell curve: Intelligence and class structure in American life.* New York: Free Press.

Herrnstein, R. J., Nickerson, R. S., de Sanchez, M., & Swets, J. A. (1986). Teaching thinking skills. *American Psychologist, 41,* 1279–1286.

Hersen, M., & Bellack, A. S. (Eds.). (1999). *Handbook of comparative interventions for adult disorders* (2nd ed.). New York: Wiley.

Hershenson, M. (1982). Moon illusion and spiral aftereffect: Illusions due to the loom-zoom system? *Journal of Experimental Psychology, 111,* 423–440.

Hershenson, M. (2003). A trick of the moonlight: Review of H. Ross & C. Plug, The mystery of the moon illusion. *Nature, 421,* 695.

Hertel, P. T., & Rude, S. S. (1991). Depressive deficits in memory: Focusing attention improves subsequent recall. *Journal of Experimental Psychology: General, 120,* 301–309.

Hess, E. H. (1975, November). The role of pupil size in communication. *Scientific American,* 110–112, 116–119.

Hetherington, A. W., & Ranson, S. W. (1942). The spontaneous activity and food intake of rats with hypothalamic lesions. *American Journal of Physiology, 136,* 609–617.

Hetherington, E. M., & Stanley-Hagen, M. (2002). Parenting in divorced and remarried families. In M. H. Bornstein (Ed.), *Handbook of parenting: Vol. 3. Being and becoming a parent* (2nd ed., pp. 287–315). Mahwah, NJ: Erlbaum.

Hewson-Bower, B., & Drummond, P. D. (1996). Secretory immunoglobulin A increases during relaxation in children with and without recurrent upper respiratory tract infections. *Journal of Developmental and Behavioral Pediatrics, 17,* 311–316.

Hewstone, M., Macrae, C. N., Griffiths, R., Milne, A. B., & Brown, R. (1994). Cognitive models of stereotype change: (5). Measurement, development, and consequences of subtyping. *Journal of Experimental Social Psychology, 30,* 505–526.

Heyman, R. E., Chaudhry, B. R., Treboux, D., Crowell, J., Lord, C., Vivian, D., & Waters, E. B. (2001). How much observational data is enough? An empirical test using marital interaction coding. *Behavior Therapy, 32,* 107–122.

Hicks, D. (1968). Short- and long-term retention of affectively-varied modeled behavior. *Psychonomic Science, 11,* 369–370.

Highstein, S. M., Fay, R. R., & Popper, A. N. (Eds.). (2004). *The vestibular system.* New York: Springer.

Hilgard, E. R. (1965). *Hypnotic susceptibility.* New York: Harcourt Brace Jovanovich.

Hilgard, E. R. (1986). *Divided consciousness: Multiple controls in human thought and action.* New York: Wiley.

Hilgard, E. R. (1992). Dissociation and theories of hypnosis. In E. Fromm & M. R. Nash (Eds.), *Contemporary hypnosis research* (pp. 69–101). New York: Guilford Press.

Hilgard, E. R., Leary, D. E., & McGuire, G. R. (1991). History of psychology: A survey and critical assessment. *Annual Review of Psychology, 42,* 79–107.

Hill, M. E. (2002). Skin color and the perception of attractiveness among African Americans. Does gender make a difference? *Social Pscyhology Quarterly, 65,* 77–91.

Hill, P. (1993). Recent advances in selected areas of adolescent development. *Journal of Child Psychology and Psychiatry, 34,* 69–99.

Hille, B. (1984). *Ionic channels of excitable membranes.* Sunderland, MA: Sinauer.

Hilliard, S. (2003). The Steel Helmet Project: Canine olfactory detection of low concentrations of a surrogate chemical warfare agent. *International Journal of Comparative Psychology, 16,* 193–208.

Hillis, A. E., & Heidler, J. (2002). Mechanisms of early aphasia recovery. *Aphasiology, 16,* 897–902.

Hillix, W. A., & Rumbaugh, D. M. (2004). *Animal bodies, human minds: Ape, dolphin, and parrot language skills.* New York: Kluwer/Plenum.

Hilton, H. (1986). *The executive memory guide.* New York: Simon & Schuster.

Hilts, P. J. (1995). *Memory's ghost: The strange tale of Mr. M. and the nature of memory.* New York: Simon & Schuster.

Hines, M. (1982). Prenatal gonadal hormones and sex differences in human behavior. *Psychological Bulletin, 92,* 56–80.

Hirsch, H. V. B., & Spinelli, D. N. (1970). Visual experience modifies distribution of horizontally and vertically oriented receptive fields in cats. *Science, 168,* 869–871.

Hirsch, J., Fried, S. K., Edens, N. K., & Leibel, R. L. (1989). The fat cell. *Medical Clinics of North America, 73,* 83–96.

Hirsh-Pasek, K., & Golinkoff, R. (1993). Skeletal supports for grammatical learning: What the infant brings to the language learning task. In C. Rovee-Collier & L. Lipsitt (Eds.), *Advances in infancy research* (Vol. 8). Norwood, NJ: Ablex.

Hirt, E. R. (1990). Do I see only what I expect? Evidence for an expectancy-guided retrieval model. *Journal of Personality and Social Psychology, 58,* 937–951.

Ho, D. Y. F., Peng, S. Q., Lai, A. C., & Chan, S. F. (2001). Indigenization and beyond: Methodological relationalism in the study of personality across cultural traditions. *Journal of Personality, 69,* 925–953.

Hoberman, J. (1997). *Darwin's athletes: How sport has damaged Black America and preserved the myth of race.* Boston: Houghton Mifflin.

Hobson, J. A. (1988). *The dreaming brain.* New York: Basic Books.

Hobson, J. A. (1995). *Sleep.* New York: Scientific American Library.

Hobson, J. A. (1999a). *Consciousness.* New York: Scientific American Library.

Hobson, J. A. (1999b). Sleep and dreaming. In M. J. Zigmond, F. E. Bloom, S. C. Landis, J. L. Roberts, & L. R. Squire (Eds.), *Fundamentals of neuroscience* (pp. 1207–1225). San Diego, CA: Academic Press.

Hobson, J. A., & McCarley, R. W. (1977). The brain as a dream state generator: An activation-synthesis hypothesis of the dream process. *The American Journal of Psychiatry, 134,* 1335–1348.

Hobson, J. A., Stickgold, R., & Pace-Schott, E. F. (1998). The neuropsychology of REM sleep dreaming. *NeuroReport, 9*(3), R1–R14.

Hock, R. R. (1992). *Forty studies that changed psychology: Explorations into the history of psychological research.* Englewood Cliffs, NJ: Prentice Hall.

Hockett, C. F. (1960). The origins of speech. *Scientific American, 203,* 89–96.

Hockett, C. F., & Altmann, S. A. (1968). A note on design features. In T. A. Sebeok (Ed.), *Animal communication: Techniques of study and results of research.* Bloomington: Indiana University Press.

Hodapp, V., & Benson, J. (1997). The multidimensionality of test anxiety: A test of different models. *Anxiety, Stress, and Coping, 10,* 219–244.

Hodgins, H. S., & Liebeskind, E. (2003). Apology versus defense: Antecedents and consequences. *Journal of Experimental Social Psychology, 39,* 297–316.

Hodgins, H. S., Liebeskind, E., & Schwartz, W. (1996). Getting out of hot water: Facework in social predicaments. *Journal of Personality and Social Psychology, 71,* 300–314.

Hodos, W., & Butler, A. B. (2001). Sensory system evolution in vertebrates. In G. Roth (Ed.), *Brain evolution and cognition* (pp. 113–133). New York: Wiley.

Hofer, J., & Chasiotis, A. (2004). Methodological considerations of applying a TAT-type picture-story test in cross-cultural research. *Journal of Cross-Cultural Psychology, 35,* 224–241.

Hoff, E. (2003). Language development in childhood. In R. M. Lerner & M. Easterbrooks (Eds.), *Handbook of psychology: Developmental psychology* (Vol. 6, pp. 171–193). New York: Wiley.

Hoffman, C., Lau, I., & Johnson, D. R. (1986). The linguistic relativity of person cognition: An English-Chinese comparison. *Journal of Personality and Social Psychology, 51,* 1097–1105.

Hoffman, L. W. (1989). Effects of maternal employment in the two-parent family. *American Psychologist, 44,* 283–292.

Hogan, J. A. (2005). Motivation. In J. J. Bolhuis (Ed.), *The behavior of animals: Mechanisms, function, and evolution* (pp. 41–70). Malden, MA: Blackwell Publishers.

Hogg, M. A. (1992). *The social psychology of group cohesiveness: From attraction to social identity.* London: Harvester-Wheatsheaf.

Holahan, C. K., & Sears, R. R. (1995). *The gifted group in later maturity.* Palo Alto, CA: Stanford University Press.

Holcomb, W. R., & Anderson, W. P. (1983). Alcohol and drug abuse in accused murderers. *Psychological Reports, 52,* 159–164.

Holden, C. (1993). Wake-up call for sleep research. *Science, 259,* 305.

Holding, P. A., Taylor, H. G., Kazungu, S. D., Mkala, T., Gona, J., Mwamuye, B., Mbonani, L., & Stevenson, J. (2004). Assessing cognitive outcomes in a rural African population: Development of a neuropsychological battery in Kilifi District, Kenya. *Journal of the International Neuropsychological Society, 10,* 246–260.

Holland, R. L., Musch, B. C., & Hindmarch, I. (1999). Specific effects of benzodiazepines and tricyclic antidepressants in panic disorder: Comparisons of clomipramine with alprazolam SR and adinazolam SR. *Human Psychopharmacology: Clinical and Experimental, 14,* 119–124.

Hollander, E., Simon, D., & Gorman, J. M. (1999). Anxiety disorders. In R. E. Hales, S. C. Yudofsky, & J. A. Talbot (Eds.), *American Psychiatric Press textbook of psychiatry.* Washington, DC: American Psychiatric Press.

Hollander, E., Zohar, J., & Marazziti, D. (2002). Introduction: Exploring the foundations of obsessive-compulsive disorder and other anxiety disorders. *Journal of Clinical Psychiatry, 63,* 3–4.

Hollis, K. L. (1997). Contemporary research on Pavlovian conditioning: A "new" functional analysis. *American Psychologist, 52,* 956–965.

Hollon, S. D., & Kendall, P. C. (1980). Cognitive self-statements in depression: Development of an Automatic Thoughts Questionnaire. *Cognitive Therapy and Research, 4,* 383–395.

Holloway, J. D. (2004). Louisiana grants psychologists prescriptive authority. *Monitor on Psychology, 35*(6), 20–21.

Holloway, R. L. (1983). Human brain evolution. *Canadian Journal of Anthropology, 3,* 215–230.

Holm, N. G. (1991). Pentecostalism: Conversion and charismata. *International Journal for the Psychology of Religion, 1,* 135–151.

Holm, N. G. (1995). Role theory and religious experience. In R. W. Hood (Ed.), *Handbook of religious experience* (pp. 397–420). Birmingham, AL: Religious Education Press.

Holman, W. D. (2001). Reaching for integrity: An Eriksonian life-cycle perspective on the experiences of adolescents being raised by grandparents. *Child & Adolescent Social Work Journal, 18,* 21–35.

Holmes, T., & Rahe, R. (1967). The Social Readjustment Rating Scale. *Journal of Psychosomatic Research, 11,* 213–218.

Holowka, S., & Petitto, L.-A. (2002). Left hemisphere cerebral specialization for babies while babbling. *Science, 297,* 1515.

Holtgraves, T. M. (1992). The linguistic realization of face management: Implications for language production and comprehension, person perception, and cross-cultural communication. *Social Psychology Quarterly, 55,* 141–159.

Holtgraves, T. M. (1997). Styles of language use: Individual and cultural variability in conversational indirectness. *Journal of Personality and Social Psychology, 73,* 624–637.

Holtgraves, T. M. (2004). Social desirability and self-reports: Testing models of socially desirable responding. *Personality and Social Psychology Bulletin, 30,* 161–172.

Holtgraves, T. M., & Yang, J. N. (1992). Interpersonal underpinnings of request strategies: General principles and differences due to culture and gender. *Journal of Personality and Social Psychology, 62,* 246–256.

Homeyer, L. E., & DeFrance, E. (2005). Play therapy. In C. A. Malchiodi (Ed.), *Expressive therapies* (pp. 141–161). New York: Guilford Press.

Hong, L. K., & Duff, R. W. (2002). Modulated participant-observation: Managing the dilemma of distance in field research. *Field Methods, 14,* 190–196.

Honts, C., & Perry, M. (1992). Polygraph admissibility: Changes and challenges. *Law and Human Behavior, 16,* 357–379.

Hood, R. W., Jr. (1991). Holm's use of role theory: Empirical and hermeneutical considerations of sacred text as a source of role adoption. *International Journal for the Psychology of Religion, 1,* 153–159.

Hood, R. W., Jr. (1995). The facilitation of religious experience. In R. W. Hood (Ed.), *Handbook of religious experience* (pp. 568–597). Birmingham, AL: Religious Education Press.

Hooker, E. (1957). The adjustment of the male overt homosexual. *Journal of Projective Techniques, 21,* 18–31.

Hopko, D. R., McNeil, D. W., Zvolensky, M. J., & Eifert, G. H. (2001). The relation between anxiety and skill in performance-based anxiety disorders: A behavioral formulation of social phobia. *Behavior Therapy, 32,* 185–207.

Hoppe, R. B. (1988). In search of a phenomenon: Research in parapsychology. [Review of *Foundations of parapsychology*]. *Contemporary Psychology, 33,* 129–130.

Hopper, A., Ciorciari, J., Johnson, G., Spensley, J., Sergejew, A., & Stough, C. (2002). EEG coherence and dissociative identity disorder: Comparing EEG coherence in DID hosts, alters, controls and acted alters. *Journal of Trauma & Dissociation, 3,* 75–88.

Hoptman, M. J., & Davidson, R. J. (1994). How and why do the two cerebral hemispheres interact? *Psychological Bulletin, 116,* 195–219.

Horn, J. L. (1994). Theory of fluid and crystallized intelligence. In R. J. Sternberg (Ed.), *The encyclopedia of human intelligence* (Vol. 1, pp. 443–451). New York: Macmillan.

Horn, J. L. (2002). Selections of evidence, misleading assumptions, and oversimplifications: The political message of *The Bell Curve.* In J. M. Fish (Ed.), *Race and intelligence: Separating science from myth* (pp. 297–325). Mahwah, NJ: Erlbaum.

Horn, J. L., & Cattell, R. B. (1966). Refinement and test of a theory of fluid and crystallized intelligence. *Journal of Educational Psychology, 57,* 253–270.

Horn, J. M. (1983). The Texas adoption project: Adopted children and their intellectual resemblance to biological and adoptive parents. *Child Development, 54,* 268–275.

Horney, K. (1926/1967). *Feminine psychology.* New York: Norton.

Horney, K. (1945). *Our inner conflicts.* New York: Norton.

Hornyak, L. M., & Green, J. P. (Eds.). (2000). *Healing from within: The use of hypnosis in women's health care.* Washington, DC: American Psychological Association.

Horton, R. W., & Santogrossi, D. A. (1978). The effect of adult commentary on reducing the influence of televised violence. *Personality and Social Psychology Bulletin, 4,* 337–340.

Hosman, L. A. (1997). The relationship between locus of control and the evaluative consequences of powerful and powerless speech styles. *Journal of Language and Social Psychology, 16,* 70–78.

Hough, J. V., Matthews, P., Wood, M. W., & Dyer, R. K., Jr. (2002). Middle ear electromagnetic semi-implantable hearing device: Results of the phase II SOUNDTEC direct system clinical trial. *Otolaryngology Neurotology, 23,* 895–903.

House, J., Landis, K., & Umberson, D. (1988). Social relationships and health. *Science, 241,* 540–545.

Howard, D. J. (1995). "Chaining" the use of influence strategies for producing compliance behavior. *Journal of Social Behavior and Personality, 10,* 169–185.

Howard, J. A., Blumstein, P., & Schwartz, P. (1987). Social evolutionary theories? Some observations on preferences in human mate selection. *Journal of Personality and Social Psychology, 53,* 194–200.

Howard, P. J., & Howard, J. M. (2000). *The owner's manual for personality at work.* Austin, TX: Bard Press.

Howe, M. L. (2003). Memories from the cradle. *Current Directions in Psychological Science, 12,* 62–65.

Hsiao, S., Johnson, K., & Yoshioka, T. (2003). Processing of tactile information in the primate brain. In M. Gallagher & R. J. Nelson, *Handbook of psychology: Biological psychology* (Vol. 3, pp. 211–236). New York: Wiley.

Hsieh, D. K., & Kirk, S. A. (2005). The limits of diagnostic criteria: The role of social context in clinicians' judgments of mental disorder. In S. A. Kirk (Ed.), *Mental disorders in the social environment: Critical perspectives* (pp. 45–61). *Foundations of social work knowledge* . New York: Columbia University Press.

Hubel, D. H. (1996). A big step along the visual pathway. *Nature, 380,* 197–198.

Hubel, D. H., & Wiesel, T. N. (1965a). Receptive fields and functional architecture in two non-striate visual areas (18 and 19) of the cat. *Journal of Neurophysiology, 28,* 229–289.

Hubel, D. H., & Wiesel, T. N. (1965b). Binocular interaction in striate cortex of kittens reared with artificial squint. *Journal of Neurophysiology, 28,* 1041–1059.

Huesmann, L. R., & Hasbrouck, J. E. (1996). Television violence: Implications for violence prevention. *School Psychology Review, 25,* 134–151.

Huesmann, L. R., & Miller, L. S. (1994). Long-term effects of repeated exposure to media violence in childhood. In L. R. Huesmann (Ed.), *Aggressive behavior: Current perspectives* (pp. 153–186). New York: Plenum.

Huff, R., & Kline, M. (Eds.). (1999). *Promoting health in multicultural populations: A handbook for practitioners.* Thousand Oaks, CA: Sage.

Huffaker, D. (2004). Spinning yarns around the digital fire: Storytelling and dialogue among youth on the Internet. *Information Technology in Childhood Education Annual, 16,* 63–75.

Huffman, S., Zehner, E., Harvey, P., Martin, P., Piwoz, E., Ndure, K., Combest, C., Mwadime, R., & Quinn, V. (2001, April). *The LINKAGES Project.* www.linkagesproject.org/FAQHtml/EHS/tbrief.htm

Hughes, J., Smith, T. W., Kosterlitz, H. W., Fothergill, L. A., Morgan, B. A., & Morris, H. R. (1975). Identification of two related pentapeptides from the brain with the potent opiate agonist activity. *Nature, 258,* 577–579.

Hughes, T. (2004). Ischemic cerebrovascular disease. *Cognitive Neuropsychology, 21,* 2783.

Hui, C. H., & Triandis, H. C. (1986). Individualism-collectivism, a study of cross-cultural researchers. *Journal of Cross-Cultural Psychology, 17,* 225–248.

Hulit, L. M., & Howard, M. R. (1993). *Born to talk: An introduction to speech and language development,* Needham, MA: Macmillan.

Hull, C. (1952). *A behavior system: An introduction to behavior theory concerning the individual organism.* New Haven, CT: Yale University Press.

Hull, C. L. (1943). *Principles of behavior: An introduction to behavior theory concerning the individual organism.* New Haven, CT: Yale University Press.

Hummon, N. P., & Doreian, P. (2003). Some dynamics of social balance processes: Bringing Heider back into balance theory. *Social Networks, 25,* 17–49.

Humphrey, N. K. (1992). *A history of the mind.* New York: Simon & Schuster.

Humphreys, L. G. (1939). Acquisition and extinction of verbal expectations in a situation analogous to conditioning. *Journal of Experimental Psychology, 25,* 294–301.

Hunn, E. (1982). The utilitarian factor in folk biological classification. *American Anthropologist, 84,* 830–847.

Hunn, E. (1990). *Nch'i-Wana "The Big River": Mid-Columbia Indians and their land.* Seattle: University of Washington Press.

Hunsley, J., & Bailey, J. M. (1999). The clinical utility of the Rorschach: Unfulfilled promises and an uncertain future. *Psychological Assessment, 11,* 266–277.

Hunt, E. (1995). The role of intelligence in modern society. *American Scientist, 83,* 356–368.

Hunt, M. (1982). *The universe within.* New York: Simon & Schuster.

Hunt, R. W. G. (1998). *Measuring colour* (3rd ed). London: Fountain Press.

Hunter, R. S., & Kilstrom, N. (1979). Breaking the cycle in abusive families. *American Journal of Orthopsychiatry, 56,* 142–146.

Hurst, R. D., Harrington, S., & Tan, K. H. (2002). Peroxynitrite elicits the damaging effect of nitric oxide on the blood-brain barrier. *The Journal of Physiology, 539,* 88.

Hutchings, B., & Mednick, S. A. (1977). Criminality in adoptees and their adoptive and biological parents: A pilot study. In S. A. Mednick & K. O. Christiansen (Eds.), *Biosocial bases of criminal behavior* (pp. 127–141). New York: Plenum Press.

Huth-Bocks, A. C., Levendosky, A. A., Bogat, G. A., & von Eye, A. (2004). The impact of maternal characteristics and contextual variables on infant-mother attachment. *Child Development, 75,* 480–496.

Hutnik, N. (1991). *Ethnic minority identity: A social psychological perspective.* New York: Oxford University Press.

Hyde, J. S., Fennema, E., & Lamon, S. J. (1990). Gender differences in mathematics performance: A meta-analysis. *Psychological Bulletin, 107,* 139–155.

Hyers, L., & Swim, J. (1998). A comparison of the experiences of dominant and minority group members during an inter-group encounter. *Group Process and Intergroup Relations, 1,* 143–163.

Hygge, S., Evans, G. W., & Bullinger, M. (2002). A prospective study of some effects of aircraft noise on cognitive performance in school children. *Psychological Science, 13,* 469–474.

Hyman, R. (1994). Anomaly or artifact? Comments on Bem and Honorton. *Psychological Bulletin, 115,* 19–24.

Hyman, R. (1996, March/April). Evaluation of the military's twenty-year program on psychic spying. *The Skeptical Inquirer, 27,* 21–23.

Iaccino, J. F. (1993). *Left brain-right brain differences: Inquiries, evidence, and new approaches.* Hillsdale, NJ: Erlbaum.

Iacono, W., & Lykken, D. (1997). The validity of the lie detector: Two surveys of scientific opinion. *Journal of Applied Psychology, 82,* 426–433.

Ickes, W. (2003). *Everyday mind reading: Understanding what other people think and feel.* Amherst, NY: Prometheus Books.

Ikeda, H. (2001). Buraku students and cultural identity: The case of a Japanese minority. In N. K. Shimahara, I. Z. Holowinsky, et al. (Eds.), *Ethnicity, race, and nationality in education: A global perspective* (pp. 81–100). *The Rutgers invitational symposium on education series.* Piscataway, NJ: Rutgers University Press.

Ikonomovic, M. D., Mufson, E. J., Wuu, J., Bennett, D. A., & DeKosky, S. T. (2005). Reduction of choline acetyltransferase activity in primary visual cortex in mild to moderate Alzheimer's disease. *Archives of Neurology, 62,* 425–430.

Illes, J., & Raffin, T. A. (2002). Neuroethics: An emerging new discipline in the study of brain and cognition. *Brain & Cognition, 50,* 341–344.

Impett, E., & Peplau, L. A. (2003). Sexual compliance: Gender, motivational, and relationship perspectives. *Journal of Sex Research, 40,* 87–100.

Ingbar, D. H., & Gee, J. B. L. (1985). Pathophysiology and treatment of sleep apnea. *Annual Review of Medicine, 36,* 369–395.

Inglehart, R. (1990). *Culture shift in advanced industrial society.* Princeton, NJ: Princeton University Press.

Inglehart, R., & Oyserman, D. (in press). Individualism, autonomy and self-expression: The human development syndrome. In H. Vinken, J. Soeters, & P. Ester (Eds.), *Comparing cultures: Dimensions of culture in a comparative perspective.* Leiden, The Netherlands: Brill.

Ingram, D. M. (2001). The Hofgeismar lectures: A contemporary overview of Horneyan psychoanalysis. *American Journal of Psychoanalysis, 60,* 113–141.

Inhelder, B., & Piaget, J. (1958). *The growth of logical thinking from childhood to adolescence.* New York: Basic Books.

Inman, M. L., Reichl, A. J., & Baron, R. S. (1993). Do we tell less than we know or hear less than we are told? Exploring the teller-listener extremity effect. *Journal of Experimental Social Psychology, 29,* 528–550.

Innis, N. K. (1992). Animal psychology in America as revealed in APA presidential addresses. *Journal of Experimental Psychology: Animal Behavior Processes, 18,* 3–11.

Intons-Peterson, M. J., & Newsome, G. L. (1992). External memory aids: Effects and effectiveness. In D. J. Herrmann, H. Weingartner, A. Searleman, & C. L. McEvoy (Eds.), *Memory improvement: Implications for memory theory* (pp. 101–121). New York: Springer-Verlag.

Ioannides, A. A., Kostopoulos, G. K., Laskaris, N. A., Liu, L., Shibata, T., Schellens, M., Poghosyan, V., & Khurshudyan, A. (2002). Timing and connectivity in the human somatosensory cortex from single trial mass electrical activity. *Human Brain Mapping, 15,* 231–246.

Irle, E., Lange, C., & Sachsse, U. (2005). Reduced size and abnormal asymmetry of parietal cortex in women with borderline personality disorder. *Biological Psychiatry, 57,* 173–182.

Isaac, G. L. (1983). Aspects of human evolution. In D. S. Bendall (Ed.), *Evolution from molecules to men.* Cambridge: Cambridge University Press.

Isada, N. B., & Grossman, J. H., III. (1991). Perinatal infections. In S. G. Gabbie, J. R. Niebyl, & J. L. Simpson (Eds.), *Obstetrics: Normal and problem pregnancies.* New York: Churchill Livingstone.

Isen, A. M. (1987). Positive affect, cognitive processes, and social behavior. In L. Berkowitz (Ed.), *Advances in experimental social psychology* (Vol. 20, pp. 203–253). New York: Academic Press.

Ito, H. (1967). Japan's outcasts in the United States. In G. A. DeVos & H. Wagatsuma (Eds.), *Japan's invisible race.* Berkeley: University of California Press.

Ito, T. A., Miller, N., & Pollock, V. E. (1996). Alcohol and aggression: A meta-analysis on the moderating effects of inhibitory cues, triggering effects, and self-focused attention. *Psychological Bulletin, 120,* 60–82.

Iversen, I. (1992). Skinner's early research: From reflexology to operant conditioning. *American Psychologist, 47,* 1318–1328.

Iwasaki, Y. (2003). Roles of leisure in coping with stress among university students: A repeated-assessment field study. *Anxiety, Stress, & Coping, 16,* 31–57.

Iyengar, S. S., & Lepper, M. R. (1999). Rethinking the value of choice: A cultural perspective on intrinsic motivation. *Journal of Personality and Social Psychology, 76,* 349–366.

Iyer, A., Leach, C. W., & Crosby, F. (2003). White guilt and racial compensation: The benefits and limits of self-focus. *Personality and Social Psychology Bulletin, 29,* 117–129.

Izard, C. (1989). The structure and functions of emotions: Implications for cognition, motivation, and personality. In I. S. Cohen (Ed.), *The G. Stanley Hall Lecture Series* (Vol. 9, pp. 39–73). Washington, DC: American Psychological Association.

Izard, C. E. (1994). Innate and universal facial expressions: Evidence from developmental and cross-cultural research. *Psychological Bulletin, 115,* 288–299.

Izard, C. E., Fantauzzo, C. A., Castle, J. M., Haynes, O. M., Rayias, M. F., & Putnam, P. H. (1995). The ontogeny and significance of infants' facial expressions in the first 9 months of life. *Developmental Psychology, 31,* 997–1013.

Jablonski, N. G. (1998). Ultraviolet light-induced neural tube defects in amphibian larvae and their implications for the evolution of melanized pigmentation and declines in amphibian populations. *Journal of Herpetology, 32,* 455–457.

Jablonski, N. G., & Chaplin, G. (in press). Natural selection and the evolution of hominid patterns of growth and development. In N. Minugh-Purvis & K. McNamara (Eds.), *Human Evolution through Developmental Change.*

Jackson, J. W. (1993). Realistic group conflict theory: A review and evaluation of the theoretical and empirical literature. *Psychological Record, 43,* 395–413.

Jackson, L. A., Hunter, J. E., & Hodge, C. N. (1995). Physical attractiveness and intellectual competence: A meta-analytic review. *Social Psychology Quarterly, 58,* 108–122.

Jacob, S., Kinnunen, L. H., Metz, J., Cooper, M., & McClintock, M. K. (2001). Sustained human chemosignal unconsciously alters brain function. *NeuroReport, 12,* 2391–2394.

Jacob, S., & McClintock, M. K. (2000). Psychological state and mood effects of steroidal chemosignals in women and men. *Hormones & Behavior, 37,* 57–78.

Jacobs, B., Schall, M., & Scheibel, A. B. (1993). A quantitative dendritic analysis of Wernicke's area in humans: II. Gender, hemispheric, and environmental factors. *Journal of Comparative Neurology, 327,* 97–106.

Jacobs, B. L. (1994). Serotonin, motor activity, and depression-related disorders. *American Scientist, 82,* 456–463.

Jacobs, R. A. (2002). Visual cue integration for depth perception. In R. P. N. Rao & B. A. Bruno (Eds.), *Probabilistic models of the brain: Perception and neural function* (pp. 61–76). *Neural information processing series.* Cambridge, MA: The MIT Press.

Jacobson, E. (1924). The technique of progressive relaxation. *Journal of Nervous and Mental Disease, 60,* 568–578.

Jacobson, N. S., & Margolin, G. (1979). *Marital therapy: Strategies based on social learning and behavior exchange principles.* New York: Brunner/Mazel.

Jacobson, S. W., & Jacobson, J. L. (2001). Alcohol and drug-related effects on development: A new emphasis on contextual factors. *Infant Mental Health Journal, 22,* 416–430.

Jaffee, S., & Hyde, J. S. (2000). Gender differences in moral orientation: A meta-analysis. *Psychological Bulletin, 126,* 703–726.

James, J. E. (1997). *Understanding caffeine: A biobehavioral analysis.* Newbury Park, CA: Sage.

James, J. E. (1998). Acute and chronic effects of caffeine on performance, mood, headache, and sleep. *Neuropsychobiology, 38,* 32–41.

James, L. E., & Burke, D. M. (2000). Phonological priming effects on word retrieval and tip-of-the-tongue experiences in young and older adults. *Journal of Experimental Psychology: Learning, Memory, & Cognition, 26,* 1378–1391.

James, O. (2003). Seeking the middle ground in the "memory wars." *British Journal of Psychology, 94,* 125–139.

James, S. (1990). *Normal language acquisition.* Austin, TX: Pro-Ed.

James, W. (1884). What is an emotion? *Mind, 9,* 188–205.

James, W. (1890). *The principles of psychology* (2 vols.). New York: Henry Holt.

James, W. (1899). *Talks to teachers on psychology and to students on some of life's ideals.* New York: Henry Holt.

James, W. (1902/1985). *The varieties of religious experience.* Cambridge, MA: Harvard University Press.

James, W. (1909/1986). The confidences of a "psychical researcher." In F. Burkhardt & F. Bowers (Eds.), *The Works of William James: Essays in Psychical Research.* Cambridge, MA: Harvard University Press. (Reprinted from *American Magazine,* October 1909, 68: 580–589)

Jameson, D. (1985). Opponent-colors theory in light of physiological findings. In D. Ottoson & S. Zeki (Eds.), *Central and peripheral mechanisms of color vision* (pp. 8–102). New York: Macmillan.

Jamieson, D. W., Lydon, J. E., & Zanna, M. P. (1987). Attitude and activity preference similarity: Differential

bases of interpersonal attraction for low and high self-monitors. *Journal of Personality and Social Psychology, 53,* 1052–1060.

Jamison, K. R. (1995). Manic-depressive illness and creativity. *Scientific American,* 62–67.

Janos, P. M., & Robinson, N. M. (1985). Psychosocial development in intellectually gifted children. In F. D. Horowitz & M. O'Brien (Eds.), *The gifted and talented: Developmental perspectives* (pp. 149–195). Washington, DC: American Psychological Association.

Jansen, A., Nederkoorn, C., & Mulkens, S. (2005). Selective visual attention for ugly and beautiful body parts in eating disorders. *Behaviour Research and Therapy, 43,* 183–196.

Jansen, A., Theunissen, N., Slechten, K., Nederkoorn, C., Boon, B., Mulkens, S., & Roefs, A. (2003). Overweight children overeat after exposure to food cues. *Eating Behaviors, 4,* 197–209.

Jarvis, E. D., Ribeiro, S., da Silva, M. L., Ventura, D., Vielliard, J., & Mello, C. V. (2000). Behaviourally driven gene expression reveals song nuclei in hummingbird brain. *Nature, 406,* 628–632.

Jaschinski, U., & Wentura, D. (2002). Misleading postevent information and working memory capacity: An individual differences approach to eyewitness memory. *Applied Cognitive Psychology, 16,* 223–231.

Jausovek, N., & Jausovek, K. (2003). Spatiotemporal brain activity related to intelligence: A low resolution brain electromagnetic tomography study. *Cognitive Brain Research, 16,* 267–272.

Jayakar, K. (1994). Women of the Indian Subcontinent. In L. Comas-Diaz & B. Greene (Eds.), *Women of color.* New York: Guilford Press.

Jaycox, L. H., Stein, B. D., Kataoka, S. H., Wong, M., Fink, A., Escudero, P., & Zaragoza, C. (2002). *Journal of the American Academy of Child Adolescent Psychiatry, 41,* 1104–1110.

Jefferis, V. E., van Baaren, R., & Chartrand, T. L. (2003). *The functional purpose of mimicry for creating interpersonal closeness.* Manuscript under review, The Ohio State University.

Jemmott, J., III, & Magloire, K. (1988). Academic stress, social support, and secretory immunoglobulin A. *Journal of Personality and Social Psychology, 55,* 803–810.

Jenkins, J. G., & Dallenbach, K. M. (1924). Oblivescence during sleep and waking. *American Journal of Psychology, 35,* 605–612.

Jensen, A. R. (1969). How much can we boost IQ and scholastic achievement? *Harvard Educational Review, 39,* 1–123.

Jensen, A. R. (1973). *Educability and group differences.* New York: Harper & Row.

Jensen, A. R., & Johnson, F. W. (1994). Race and sex differences in head size and IQ. *Intelligence, 18.*

Jensen, J. K., & Neff, D. L. (1993). Development of basic auditory discrimination in preschool children. *Psychological Science, 4,* 104–107.

Jensen, R., Bendtsen, L., & Olesen, J. (1998). Muscular factors are of importance in tension-type headache. *Headache, 38,* 10–17.

Jensvold, M. L. A., & Gardner, R. A. (2000). Interactive use of sign language by cross-fostered chimpanzees *(Pan troglodytes). Journal of Comparative Psychology, 114,* 335–346.

Jerison, H. J. (1975). Fossil evidence of the evolution of the human brain. *Annual Review of Anthropology, 16,* 403–426.

Jerison, H. J. (1991). Brain size and the evolution of mind. *Fifty-ninth James Arthur Lecture.* American Museum of Natural History.

Jiang, Y., Luo, Y. J., & Parasuraman, R. (2002). Neural correlates of perceptual priming of visual motion. *Brain Research Bulletin, 57,* 211–219.

Johanson, D., & Edgar, B. (1996). *From Lucy to language.* New York: Simon & Schuster.

John, O. P., Cheek, J. M., & Klohnen, E. C. (1996). On the nature of self-monitoring: Construct explication with Q-sort ratings. *Journal of Personality and Social Psychology, 71,* 763–776.

John, O. P., & Srivastava, S. (1999). The big five trait taxonomy: History, measurement, and theoretical perspectives. In L. A. Pervin & O. P. John (Eds.), *Handbook of personality* (2nd ed., pp. 102–138). New York: Guilford.

Johnson, A. M., Vernon, P. A., Harris, J., Aitken, J., & Kerry, L. (2004). A behavior genetic investigation of the relationship between leadership and personality. *Twin Research, 7,* 27–32.

Johnson, D. L., Wiebe, J. S., Gold, S. M., Andreasen, N. C., Hichwa, R. D., Watkins, G. L., et al. (1999). Cerebral blood flow and personality: A positron emission tomography study. *American Journal of Psychiatry, 156,* 252–257.

Johnson, F., & Wardle, J. (2005). Dietary restraint, body dissatisfaction, and psychological distress: A prospective analysis. *Journal of Abnormal Psychology, 114,* 119–125.

Johnson, J. D., Jackson, L. A., & Gatto, L. (1995). Violent attitudes and deferred academic aspirations: Deleterious effects of exposure to rap music. *Basic and Applied Social Psychology, 16,* 27–41.

Johnson, J. D., Noel, N. E., & Sutter-Hernandez, J. (2000). Alcohol and male acceptance of sexual aggression: The role of perceptual ambiguity. *Journal of Applied Social Psychology, 30,* 1186–1200.

Johnson, J. G., Cohen, P., Smailes, E. M., Kasen, S., & Brook, J. S. (2002). Television violence and aggressive behavior during adolescence and adulthood. *Science, 295,* 2468–2471.

Johnson, M. E., & Brems, C. (1991). Comparing theoretical orientations of counseling and clinical psychologists: An objective approach. *Professional Psychology: Research and Practice, 22,* 133–137.

Johnson, M. H., & Karmiloff-Smith, A. (2004). Neuroscience perspectives on infant development. In G. Bremner & A. Slater (Eds.), *Theories of infant development.* (pp. 121–141). Malden, MA: Blackwell Publishers.

Johnson, M. K., & Raye, C. L. (2000). Cognitive and brain mechanisms of false memories and beliefs. In D. L. Schacter & E. Scarry (Eds.), *Memory, brain, and belief* (pp. 35–86). Cambridge, MA: Harvard University Press.

Johnson, S. C., & Spilka, B. (1991). Outcome research and religious psychotherapies: Where are we and where are we going? *Journal of Psychology and Theology, 21,* 297–308.

Johnson, W., Bouchard, T. J., Jr., Krueger, R. F., McGue, M., & Gottesman, I. I. (2004). Just one g: Consistent results from three test batteries. *Intelligence, 32,* 95–107.

Johnson, W., & Krueger, R. F. (2005). Higher perceived life control decreases genetic variance in physical health: Evidence from a national twin study. *Journal of Personality and Social Psychology, 88,* 165–173.

Johnston, J. H., Driskell, J. E., & Salas, E. (1997). Vigilant and hypervigilant decision making. *Journal of Applied Psychology, 82,* 614–622.

Johnston, K. L., & White, K. M. (2003). Binge-drinking: A test of the role of group norms in the theory of planned behaviour. *Psychology & Health, 18,* 63–77.

Johnston, T. D., & Edwards, L. (2002). Genes, interactions, and the development of behavior. *Psychological Review, 109,* 26–34.

Joiner, T. (1999). The clustering and containing of suicide. *Current Directions in Psychological Science, 8,* 89–92.

Joireman, J., Anderson, J., & Strathman, A. (2003). The aggression paradox: Understanding links among aggression, sensation seeking, and the consideration of future consequences. *Journal of Personality and Social Psychology, 84,* 1287–1302.

Jollant, F., Bellivier, F., Leboyer, M., Astruc, B., Torres, S., Verdier, R., Castelnau, D., Malafosse, A., & Courtet, P. (2005). Impaired decision making in suicide attempters. *American Journal of Psychiatry, 162,* 304–310.

Jones, E. (1957). *Sigmund Freud: Life and work* (Vol. 3). London: Hogarth.

Jones, M. C. (1924). A laboratory study of fear: The case of Peter. *Pedagogical Seminary and Journal of Genetic Psychology, 31,* 308–315.

Jonides, J., Lacey, S. C., & Nee, D. E. (2005). Processes of working memory in mind and brain. *Current Directions in Psychological Science, 14,* 2–5.

Joseph, R. (2000). The evolution of sex differences in language, sexuality, and visual-spatial skills. *Archives of Sexual Behavior, 29,* 35–66.

Josephs, R. A., Larrick, R. P., Steele, C. M., & Nisbett, R. E. (1992). Protecting the self from the negative consequences of risky decisions. *Journal of Personality and Social Psychology, 62,* 26–37.

Judd, C. M., Park, B., Ryan, C., Brauer, M., & Kraus, S. (1995). Stereotypes and ethnocentrism: Diverging interethnic perceptions of African American and White American youth. *Journal of Personality and Social Psychology, 69,* 460–481.

Julien, R. M. (1998). *A primer of drug action: A concise nontechnical guide to the actions, uses, and side effects of psychoactive drugs* (8th ed.). New York: Freeman.

Julien, R. M. (2001). *A primer of drug action: Nontechnical guide to the actions, uses, and side effects of psychoactive drugs* (9th ed.). New York: Freeman.

Jung, C. G. (1916). *Analytical psychology.* New York: Moffat.

Jung, C. G. (1921). *Psychological types.* New York: Harcourt Brace.

Jung, C. G. (1963). *Memories, dreams, reflections.* New York: Random House.

Jung, C. G. (1964). *Man and his symbols.* New York: Dell.

Jussim, L. (1989). Teacher expectations: Self-fulfilling prophecies, perpetual biases, and accuracy. *Journal of Personality and Social Psychology, 57,* 469–480.

Jussim, L., Yen, H., & Aiello, J. R. (1995). Self-consistency, self-enhancement, and accuracy in reactions to feedback. *Journal of Experimental Social Psychology, 31,* 322–356.

Just, M. A., & Carpenter, P. A. (1987). *The psychology of reading and language comprehension.* Newton, MA: Allyn & Bacon.

Just, M. A., Carpenter, P. A., Keller, T. A., Emery, L., Zajac, H., & Thulborn, K. R. (2001). Interdependence of nonoverlapping cortical systems in dual cognitive tasks. *Neuroimage, 14,* 417–426.

Kacmar, K. M., Delery, J. E., & Ferris, G. R. (1992). Differential effectiveness of applicant impression management tactics on employment interview decisions. *Journal of Applied Social Psychology, 22,* 1250–1272.

Kaelber, C. T., Moul, D. E., & Farmer, M. E. (1995). Epidemiology of depression. In E. E. Beckham & W. R. Leber (Eds.), *Handbook of depression* (2nd ed., pp. 3–35). New York: Guilford Press.

Kaeppler, C., & Hohagen, F. (2003). Psychosocial aspects of insomnia: Results of a study in general practice. *European Archives of Psychiatry & Clinical Neuroscience, 253,* 49–52.

Kafka, J. S. (2002). History of psychoanalysis: Freud and dream contributing to and celebrating the centenary of "The Interpretation of Dreams" as the origin of the psychoanalytic method. *International Journal of Psychoanalysis, 83,* 483–486.

Kagan, J., Snidman, N., & Arcus, D. (1998). Childhood derivatives of high and low reactivity in infancy. *Child Development, 69,* 1483–1493.

Kagan, J., Snidman, N., & Arcus, D. M. (1992). Initial reactions to unfamiliarity. *Current Directions in Psychological Science, 1,* 171–174.

Kagan, J., Snidman, N., McManis, M., & Woodward, S. (2001). Temperamental contributions to the affect family of anxiety. *Psychiatric Clinics of North America, 24,* 677–688.

Kagan, S., & Knight, G. P. (1979). Cooperation-competition and self-esteem: A case of cultural relativism. *Journal of Cross-Cultural Psychology, 10,* 457–467.

Kagee, A. (2004). Present concerns of survivors of human rights violations in South Africa. *Social Science and Medicine, 59,* 625–635.

Kâgitçibasi, C. (1994). A critical appraisal of individualism and collectivism: Toward a new formulation. In U. Kim, H. C. Triandis, C. Kâgitçibasi, S. Choi, & G. Yoon (Eds.), *Individualism and collectivism: Theory, method, and applications* (pp. 52–65). Thousand Oaks, CA: Sage.

Kahn, D., & Hobson, J. A. (1993). Self-organization theory of dreaming. *Dreaming: Journal of the Association for the Study of Dreams, 3,* 151–178.

Kahn, E., Fisher, C., & Edwards, A. (1991). Night terrors and anxiety dreams. In S. J. Ellman & J. S. Antrobus (Eds.), *The mind in sleep: Psychology and psychopathology* (2nd ed., pp. 437–447). New York: Wiley.

Kail, R. (1991). Processing time declines exponentially during childhood and adolescence. *Developmental Psychology, 27,* 259–266.

Kail, R. (2002). Developmental change in proactive interference. *Child Development, 73,* 1703–1714.

Kalat, J. (1998). *Biological psychology* (6th ed.). Pacific Grove, CA: Brooks/Cole.

Kalichman, S. C. (2000). HIV transmission risk behaviors of men and women living with HIV-AIDS: Prevalence, predictors, and emerging clinical interventions. *Clinical Psychology: Science and Practice, 7,* 32–47.

Kalichman, S. C. (2005). The other side of the healthy relationships intervention: Mental health outcomes and correlates of sexual risk behavior change. *AIDS Education and Prevention, 17,* 66–75.

Kalish, R. (1981). *Death, grief, and caring relationships.* Monterey, CA: Brooks-Cole.

Kalish, R. (1985). The social context of death and dying. In R. H. Binstock & E. Shanas (Eds.), *Handbook of aging and the social sciences* (2nd ed.). New York: Van Nostrand Reinhold.

Kamarck, T., & Jennings, R. (1991). Biobehavioral factors in sudden cardiac death. *Psychological Bulletin, 109,* 42–75.

Kanagawa, C., Cross, S. E., & Markus, H. R. (2001). "Who am I?" The cultural psychology of the conceptual self. *Personality and Social Psychology Bulletin, 27,* 90–103.

Kandel, D. B. (1978). Similarity in real-life adolescent friendship pairs. *Journal of Personality and Social Psychology, 36,* 306–312.

Kandel, E. R. (1995). Cellular mechanisms of learning and memory. In E. R. Kandel, J. H. Schwartz, & T. M. Jessell (Eds.), *Essentials of neural science and behavior.* Norwalk, CT: Appleton & Lange.

Kandel, E. R., & Schwartz, J. H. (1982). Molecular biology of learning: Modulation of transmitter release. *Science, 218,* 433–443.

Kaplan, H., Brooks, R., Cassone, P., Estepan, H., Hore, P., Knott, V., McAlvanah, T., Messbauer, L., Ndongo, M., Khafra, P. L., & Revell, S. (2003). The effects of tai-chi on seniors with developmental disabilities. *Physical and Occupational Therapy in Geriatrics, 21,* 41–51.

Kapur, N. (1999). Syndromes of retrograde amnesia: A conceptual and empirical synthesis. *Psychological Bulletin, 125,* 800–825.

Karni, A., Tanne, D., Rubenstein, B. S., Askenazy, J. J. M., & Sagi, D. (1994). Dependence on REM sleep of overnight improvement of a perceptual skill. *Science, 265,* 679–682.

Karno, M., Golding, J. M., Sorenson, S. B., & Burnam, M. A. (1988). The epidemiology of obsessive-compulsive disorder in five U.S. communities. *Archives of General Psychiatry, 45,* 1094–1099.

Karraker, K. H., & Stern, M. (1990). Infant physical attractiveness and facial expression: Effects on adult perceptions. *Basic and Applied Social Psychology, 11,* 371–385.

Karraker, K. H., Vogel, D. A., & Lake, M. A. (1995). Parents' gender-stereotyped perceptions of newborns: The eye of the beholder revisited. *Sex Roles, 33,* 687–701.

Kasamatsu, M., & Hirai, T. (1969). An electroencephalographic study of the Zen meditation (*zazen*). In C. Tart (Ed.), *Altered states of consciousness* (pp. 489–501). New York: Wiley.

Kashima, Y., Kokubo, T., Kashima, E. S., Boxall, D., Yamaguchi, S., & Macrae, K. (2004). Culture and self: Are there within-culture differences in self between metropolitan areas and regional cities? *Personality and Social Psychology Bulletin, 30,* 816–823.

Kashima, Y., Siegel, M., Tanaka, K., & Kashima, E. S. (1992). Do people believe behaviours are consistent with attitudes? Towards a cultural psychology of attribution processes. *British Journal of Social Psychology, 31,* 111–124.

Kashy, D. A., & DePaulo, B. M. (1996). Who lies? *Journal of Personality and Social Psychology, 70,* 1037–1051.

Kasser, T., & Ryan, R. M. (1996). Further examining the American dream: Differential correlates of intrinsic and extrinsic goals. *Personality and Social Psychology Bulletin, 22,* 20–287.

Kassin, S. M., Tubb, V. A., Hosch, H. M., & Memon, A. (2001). On the "general acceptance" of eyewitness testimony research: A new survey of the experts. *American Psychologist, 56,* 405–416.

Kataoka, S. H., Zhang, L., & Wells, K. B. (2002). Unmet need for mental health care among U.S. children: Variation by ethnicity and insurance status. *American Journal of Psychiatry, 159,* 1548–1555.

Katigbak, M. S., Church, A. T., Guanzon-Lapena, M. A., Carlota, A. J., & del Pilar, G. H. (2002). Are indigenous personality dimensions culture specific? Philippine inventories and the five-factor model. *Journal of Personality and Social Psychology, 82,* 89–101.

Katkin, E. S., Wiens, S., & Ohman, A. (2001). Nonconscious fear conditioning, visceral perception, and the development of gut feeling. *Psychological Science, 12,* 366–370.

Katz, P. (1986). Gender identity: Development and consequences. In R. Ashmore & F. Del Boca (Eds.), *The social psychology of female-male relations* (pp. 21–67). Orlando, FL: Academic Press.

Katz, R., & McGuffin, P. (1993). The genetics of affective disorders. In D. Fowles (Ed.), *Progress in experimental personality and psychopathology research.* New York: Springer.

Katzenberg, D., Young, T., Finn, L., Lin, L., King, D. P., Takahashi, J. S., & Mignot, E. (1998). A CLOCK polymorphism associated with human diurnal preference. *Sleep, 21,* 569–576.

Kaufman, A. S. (1990). *Assessing adolescent and adult intelligence.* Boston: Allyn & Bacon.

Kaufman, A. S. (2000). Tests of intelligence. In R. J. Sternberg (Ed.), *Handbook of intelligence* (pp. 445–476). Cambridge: Cambridge University Press.

Kaufman, A. S., Kaufman, J. C., Chen, T. H., & Kaufman, N. L. (1996). Differences on six horn abilities for 14 age groups between 15–16 and 75–94 years. *Psychological Assessment, 8,* 161–171.

Kaufman, L., & Rock, I. (1962). The moon illusion (Vol. 1). *Science, 136,* 953–961.

Kaufman, M. H. (1997). The teratogenic effects of alcohol following exposure during pregnancy, and its influence on the chromosome constitution of the pre-ovulatory egg. *Alcohol & Alcoholism, 32,* 113–128.

Kaut, K. P. (2002). Religion, spirituality, and existentialism near the end of life. *American Behavioral Scientist, 46,* 220–234.

Kawamoto, K., Ishimoto, S., Minoda, R., Brough, D. E., & Raphael, Y. (2003). Math1 gene transfer generates new cochlear hair cells in mature guinea pigs in vivo. *Journal of Neuroscience, 23,* 4395–4400.

Kaye, W., Klump, K., Frank, G., & Strober, M. (2000). Anorexia and bulimia nervosa. *Annual Review of Medicine, 51,* 299–313.

Kayumov, L., Rotenberg, V., Buttoo, K., Auch, C., Pandi-Perumal, S. R., & Shapiro, C. M. (2000). Interrelationships between nocturnal sleep, daytime alertness, and sleepiness: Two types of alertness proposed. *Journal of Neuropsychiatry & Clinical Neurosciences, 12,* 86–90.

Kazak, A. E., Alderfer, M., Rourke, M. T., Simms, S., Streisand, R., & Grossman, J. R. (2004). Posttraumatic stress disorder (PTSD) and posttraumatic stress symptoms (PTSS) in families of adolescent childhood cancer survivors. *Journal of Pediatric Psychology, 29,* 211–219.

Kazdin, A. E. (1982). The token economy: A decade later. *Journal of Applied Behavior Analysis, 15,* 431–445.

Keefauver, S. P., & Guilleminault, C. (1994). Sleep terrors and sleepwalking. In M. Kryger, T. Roth, & W. C. Dement (Eds.), *Principles and practices of sleep medicine* (2nd ed., pp. 567–573). Philadelphia: Saunders.

Keen, C., & Howard, A. (2002). Experiential learning in Antioch College's work-based learning program as a vehicle for social and emotional development for gifted college students. *Journal of Secondary Gifted Education, 13,* 130–140.

Keenan, J. P., Nelson, A., O'Connor, M., & Pascual-Leone, A. (2001). Self-recognition and the right hemisphere. *Nature, 409,* 305.

Keesey, R. E. (1995). A set-point model of weight regulation. In K. D. Brownell & C. G. Fairburn (Eds.), *Eating disorders and obesity* (pp. 46–50). New York: Guilford Press.

Keith, J. R., & McVety, K. M. (1988). Latent place learning in a novel environment and the influences of prior training in rats. *Psychobiology, 16,* 146–151.

Keller, A., Castellanos, F., Vaituzis, A. C., Jeffries, N. O., Giedd, J. N., & Rapoport, J. L. (2003). Progressive loss of cerebellar volume in childhood-onset schizophrenia. *American Journal of Psychiatry, 160,* 128–133.

Keller, S., Shiflett, S., Schleifer, S., & Bartlett, J. (1994). Stress, immunity, and death. In R. Glaser & J. Kiecolt-Glaser (Eds.), *Handbook of human stress and immunity* (pp. 217–244). San Diego, CA: Academic Press.

Kellett, K. (2005). Nature and nurture: The complex interplay of genetic and environmental influences on human behavior and development. *Educational Gerontology, 31,* 84–85.

Kelley, H. H. (1967). Attribution theory in social psychology. In D. L. Vine (Ed.), *Nebraska symposium on motivation.* Lincoln: University of Nebraska Press.

Kelley, H. H. (1972). Causal schemata and the attribution process. In E. Jones, D. Kanouse, H. Kelley, R. Nisbett, S. Valms, & B. Weiner (Eds.), *Attribution: Perceiving the causes of behavior.* Morristown, NJ: General Learning Press.

Kellogg, W. N., & Kellogg, L. A. (1933). *The ape and the child.* New York: McGraw-Hill.

Kelly, A. E. (1999). Revealing personal secrets. *Current Directions in Psychological Science, 8,* 105–109.

Kelly, G. (2001). *Sexuality today: The human perspective* (7th ed.). Boston: McGraw-Hill.

Kelly, I. W. (1997). Modern astrology: A critique. *Psychological Reports, 81,* 1035–1066.

Kelly, K., Jones, W. H., & Adams, J. M. (2002). Using the Imaginary Audience Scale as a measure of social anxiety in young adults. *Educational & Psychological Measurement, 62,* 896–914.

Kelly, L. (1997). Skills training as a treatment for communication problems. In J. A. Daly, J. C. McCroskey, J. Ayres, T. Hopf, & D. M. Ayres (Eds.), *Avoiding communication: Shyness, reticence, and communication apprehension* (2nd ed., pp. 331–365). Creskill, NJ: Hampton Press.

Kelman, H. C. (1998). The place of ethnic identity in the development of personal identity: A challenge for the Jewish family. *Studies in contemporary Jewry: An annual* (pp. 3–26). New York: Oxford University Press.

Keltner, D., & Haidt, J. (1999). Social functions of emotions at four levels of analysis. *Cognition & Emotion, 13,* 505–521.

Keltner, D., & Haidt, J. (2003). Approaching awe, a moral, spiritual, and aesthetic emotion. *Cognition & Emotion, 17,* 297–314.

Kempermann, G., & Gage, F. H. (1999a). Experienced-dependent regulation of adult hippocampal neurogenesis: Effects of long-term stimulation and stimulus withdrawal. *Hippocampus, 9,* 321–332.

Kempermann, G., & Gage, F. H. (1999b, May). New nerve cells for the adult brain. *Scientific American,* 48–53.

Kempler, W. (1974). *Principles of Gestalt family therapy.* Salt Lake City, UT: Deseret.

Kendler, H. H. (2004). Politics and science: A combustible mixture. *American Psychologist, 59,* 122–123.

Kendler, K. S., Gardner, C. O., & Prescott, C. A. (1999a). Clinical characteristics of major depression that predict risk of depression in relatives. *Archives of General Psychiatry, 56,* 322–327.

Kendler, K. S., Karkowski, L. M., & Prescott, C. A. (1999b). Fears and phobias: Reliability and heritability. *Psychological Medicine, 29,* 539–553.

Kendler, K. S., Myers, J., & Prescott, C. A. (2002a). The etiology of phobias: An evaluation of the stress-diathesis model. *Archives of General Psychiatry, 59,* 242–248.

Kendler, K. S., Neale, M. C., Thornton, L. M., Aggen, S. H., Gilman, S. E., & Kessler, R. C. (2002b). Cannabis use in the last year in a U.S. national sample of twin and sibling pairs. *Psychological Medicine, 32,* 551–554.

Kendler, K. S., Thornton, L. M., Gilman, S. E., & Kessler, R. C. (2000). Sexual orientation in U.S. national sample of twin and nontwin sibling pairs. *American Journal of Psychiatry, 157,* 1843–1846.

Kenrick, D. T., & Luce, C. L. (2000). An evolutionary life-history model of gender differences and similarities. In T. Eckes & H. M. Trautner (Eds.), *The developmental social psychology of gender* (pp. 35–63). Mahwah, NJ: Erlbaum.

Kenrick, D. T., & Maner, J. K. (2004). One path to balance and order in social psychology: An evolutionary perspective. *Behavioral and Brain Sciences, 27,* 346–347.

Kenrick, D. T., & Trost, M. R. (1987). A biosocial theory of heterosexual relationships. In K. Kelly (Ed.), *Females, males, and sexuality.* Albany: State University of New York Press.

Kenrick, D. T., & Trost, M. R. (1989). Reproductive exchange model of heterosexual relationships: Putting proximate relationships in ultimate perspective. In C. Henrick (Ed.), *Review of personality and social psychology* (Vol. 10). Newbury Park, CA: Sage.

Keppel-Benson, J. M., Ollendick, T. H., & Benson, M. J. (2002). Post-traumatic stress in children following motor vehicle accidents. *Journal of Child Psychology & Psychiatry & Allied Disciplines, 43,* 203–212.

Kerr, S., & Jowett, S. (1994). Sleep problems in pre-school children: A review of the literature. *Child Care, Health, and Development, 20,* 379–391.

Kersting, K. (2004a). Brown contributor Clark reflects back. *Monitor on Psychology, 35*(8), 58–59.

Kersting, K. (2004b). Cross-cultural training: 30 years and going strong. *Monitor on Psychology, 35*(8), 48–49.

Kessler, R. C., Demler, O., Frank, R. G., Olfson, M., Pincus, H. A., Walters, E. E., Wang, P., Wells, K. B., & Zaslavsky, A. M. (2005). Prevalence and treatment of mental disorders, 1990 to 2003. *New England Journal of Medicine, 24,* 2515–2523.

Kessler, R. C., McGonagle, K. A., Zhao, S., Nelson, C. B., Hughes, M., Eshleman, S., Wittchen, H. U., & Kendler, K. S. (1994). Lifetime and 12-month prevalence of *DSM-III-R* psychiatric disorders in the United States. *Archives of General Psychiatry, 51,* 8–19.

Kessler, R. C., Mickelson, K. D., & Williams, D. R. (1999). The prevalence, distribution, and mental health correlates of perceived discrimination in the United States. *Journal of Health and Social Behavior, 40,* 208–230.

Kessler, R. C., Sonnega, A., Bromet, E., Hughes, M., & Nelson, C. B. (1995). Post traumatic stress disorder in the National Comorbidity Study. *Archives of General Psychiatry, 52,* 1048–1060.

Kessner, D. M. (1973). *Infant death: An analysis by maternal risk and health care.* Washington, DC: National Academy of Sciences.

Ketter, T. A., & Wang, P. W. (2002). Predictors of treatment response in bipolar disorders: Evidence from clinical and brain imaging studies. *Journal of Clinical Psychiatry, 63,* 21–25.

Kettlewell, H. B. D. (1973). *The evolution of melanism.* Oxford, England: Oxford University Press.

Key, W. B. (1973). *Subliminal seduction.* Englewood Cliffs, NJ: Signet.

Key, W. B. (1989). *The age of manipulation.* New York: Holt.

Keys, A., Brozek, J., Henschel, A., Mickelsen, O., & Taylor, H. (1950). *The biology of human starvation* (Vols. I and II). Minneapolis: University of Minnesota Press.

Khaleque, A. (1999). Sleep deficiency and quality of life of shift workers. *Social Indicators Research, 46,* 181–189.

Khalid, R. (1991). Personality and academic achievement: A thematic apperception perspective. *British Journal of Projective Psychology, 36,* 25–34.

Kiecolt-Glaser, J. K., Glaser, R. (2001). Psychological stress and wound healing. *Advances in Mind-Body Medicine, 17,* 15–17.

Kiecolt-Glaser, J. K., Glaser, R., Williger, D., Stout, J., Messick, G., Sheppard, S., Ricker, D., Romisher, S. C., Briner, W., Bonnell, G., & Donnerberg, R. (1985). Psychosocial enhancement of immunocompetence in a geriatric population. *Health Psychology, 4,* 25–41.

Kihlstrom, J. F. (1985). Hypnosis. *Annual Review of Psychology, 36,* 385–418.

Kihlstrom, J. F. (1989). On what does mood-dependent memory depend? *Journal of Social Behavior and Personality, 4,* 23–32.

Kilham, W., & Mann, L. (1974). Level of destructive obedience as a function of transmitter and executant roles in the Milgram obedience paradigm. *Journal of Personality and Social Psychology, 29,* 696–702.

Kilpatrick, D. G., & Resnick, H. S. (1993). Posttraumatic stress disorder associated with exposure to criminal victimization in clinical and community populations. In J. R. T. Davidson & E. B. Foa (Eds.), *Posttraumatic stress disorder: DSM-IV and beyond* (pp. 113–143). Washington, DC: American Psychiatric Press.

Kim, H.-W., Greenberg, J. S., Seltzer, M. M., & Krauss, M. W. (2003). The role of coping in maintaining the psychological well-being of mothers of adults with intellectual disability and mental illness. *Journal of Intellectual Disability Research, 47,* 313–327.

Kimble, D. L., Covell, N. H., Weiss, L. H., Newton, K. J., & Fisher, J. D. (1992). College students use implicit personality theory instead of safer sex. *Journal of Applied Social Psychology, 22,* 921–933.

Kimble, G. A. (1989). Psychology from the standpoint of a generalist. *American Psychologist, 44,* 491–499.

Kimmel, E. B. (1992). Women's contributions to psychology. *Contemporary Psychology, 37,* 201–202.

Kimura, D. (1987). Are men's and women's brains really different? *Canadian Journal of Psychology, 28,* 133–147.

Kimura, D. (1992). Sex differences in the brain. *Scientific American, 267,* 81–87.

Kimura, D., & Hampson, E. (1994). Cognitive pattern in men and women is influenced by fluctuations in sex hormones. *Current Directions in Psychological Science, 3,* 57–61.

King, S. A., & Moreggi, D. (1998). Internet therapy and self-help groups—The pros and cons. In J. Gackenbach (Ed.), *Psychology and the Internet: Interpersonal, intrapersonal, and transpersonal implications* (pp. 77–109). San Diego, CA: Academic Press.

Kingery, P. M., Alford, A. A., & Coggeshall, M. B. (1999). Marijuana use among youth: Epidemiologic evidence from the US and other nations. *School Psychology International, 20,* 9–21.

Kingsbury, S. J. (1987). Cognitive differences between clinical psychologists and psychiatrists. *American Psychologist, 42,* 152–156.

Kinsey, A., Pomeroy, W., & Martin, C. (1948). *Sexual behavior in the human male.* Philadelphia: Saunders.

Kinsey, A., Pomeroy, W., Martin, C., & Gebhard, P. (1953). *Sexual behavior in the human female.* Philadelphia: Saunders.

Kiple, K. F., & Ornelas, K. C. (2001). Experimental animals in medical research: A history. In E. F. Paul & J. Paul (Eds.), *Why animal experimentation matters: The use of animals in medical research. New studies in social policy* (pp. 23–48). New Brunswick, NJ: Transaction Publishers.

Kirchner, M. (2000). Gestalt therapy theory: An overview. *Gestalt Journal, 4,* 200–210.

Kirsch, I., & Braffman, W. (2001). Imaginative suggestibility and hypnotizability. *Current Directions in Psychological Science, 10,* 57–61.

Kirsch, I. L., Steven, J., Vigorito, M., & Miller, R. R. (2004). The role of cognition in classical and operant conditioning. *Journal of Clinical Psychology, 60,* 369–392.

Kirschenbaum, H. (2004). Carl Rogers's life and work: An assessment on the 100th anniversary of his birth. *Journal of Counseling and Development, 82,* 116–124.

Kish, S. J. (2002). How strong is the evidence that brain serotonin neurons are damaged in human users of ecstasy? *Pharmacology, Biochemistry, & Behavior, 71,* 845–855.

Kite, M. E., & Deaux, K. (1987). Gender belief systems: Homosexuality and the implicit inversion theory. *Psychology of Women Quarterly, 11,* 83–96.

Kite, M. E., Russo, N. F., Brehm, S. S., Hall, C. C. I., Hyde, J. S., & Keita, G. P. (2001). Women psychologists in academe: Mixed progress, unwarranted complacency. *American Psychologist, 56,* 1080–1098.

Kittler, P., Krinsky-McHale, S. J., & Devenny, D. A. (2004). Sex differences in performance over 7 years on the Wechsler Intelligence Scale for Children—Revised among adults with intellectual disability. *Journal of Intellectual Disability Research, 48,* 114–122.

Kjaer, T. W., Bertelsen, C., Piccini, P., Brooks, D., Alving, J., & Lou, H. C. (2002). Increased dopamine tone during meditation-induced change of consciousness. *Cognitive Brain Research, 13,* 255–259.

Klayman, J., & Ha, Y.-W. (1987). Confirmation, disconfirmation, and information in hypothesis testing. *Psychological Review, 94,* 211–228.

Klein, M. (1932). *The psycho-analysis of children.* London: Hogarth.

Klein, O., Snyder, M., & Livingston, R. W. (2004). Prejudice on the stage: Self-monitoring and the public expression of group attitudes. *British Journal of Social Psychology, 43,* 299–314.

Kleinknecht, R. A. (1991). *Mastering anxiety: The nature and treatment of anxious conditions.* New York: Plenum.

Kleinknecht, R. A. (2000). Social phobia. In M. Hersen & M. K. Biaggio (Eds.), *Effective brief therapies: A clinician's guide.* New York: Academic Press.

Kleinmuntz, B., & Szucko, J. (1984). Lie detection in ancient and modern times: A call for contemporary scientific study. *American Psychologist, 39*, 766–776.

Klerman, G. (1987). Clinical epidemiology of suicide. *Journal of Clinical Psychiatry, 48*, 33–38.

Kline, S., & Groninger, L. D. (1991). The imagery bizarreness effect as a function of sentence complexity and presentation time. *Bulletin of the Psychonomic Society, 29*, 25–27.

Klinger, E. (1990). *Daydreaming: Using waking fantasy and imagery for self-knowledge and creativity.* Los Angeles: Tarcher.

Klinger, E. (1999). Thought flow: Properties and mechanisms underlying shifts in content. In J. A. Singer & P. Salovey (Eds.), *At play in the fields of consciousness: Essays in honor of Jerome L. Singer* (pp. 29–50). Mahwah, NJ: Erlbaum.

Kloos, H., & Amazeen, E. L. (2002). Perceiving heaviness by dynamic touch: An investigation of the size-weight illusion in preschoolers. *British Journal of Developmental Psychology, 20*, 171–184.

Kluger, R. (1976). *Simple justice: The history of Brown v. Board of Education and Black Americans' struggle for equality.* New York: Alfred A. Knopf.

Klump, K., Kaye, W., & Strober, M. (2001). The evolving genetic foundations of eating disorders. *Psychiatric Clinics of North America. Special Issue: Eating Disorders, 24*(2), 215–225.

Knight, A., Underhill, P. A., Mortensen, H. M., Zhivotovsky, L. A., Lin, A. A., Henn, B. M., Louis, D., Ruhlen, M., & Mountain, J. L. (2003). African Y chromosome and mtDNA divergence provides insight into the history of click languages. *Current Biology, 13*, 464–473.

Knox, R. E., & Inkster, J. A. (1968). Postdecision dissonance at post-time. *Journal of Personality and Social Psychology, 8*, 319–323.

Kobasa, S. C., Maddi, S. R., & Kahn, S. (1982). Hardiness and health: A prospective study. *Journal of Personality and Social Psychology, 42*, 168–177.

Koenig, H. G., George, L. K., & Titus, P. (2004). Religion, spirituality, and health in medically ill hospitalized older patients. *Journal of the American Geriatrics Society, 52*, 554–562.

Koester, J. (1995). Membrane potential. In E. R. Kandel, J. H. Schwartz, & T. M. Jessell (Eds.), *Essentials of neural science and behavior.* Norwalk, CT: Appleton & Lange.

Kohlberg, L. (1981). *Essays on moral development.* New York: Harper & Row.

Kohlberg, L. (1984). The psychology of moral development: The nature and validity of moral stages. In *Essays on moral development* (Vol. 2). New York: Harper & Row.

Kohn, A. (1993). *Punished by rewards: The trouble with gold stars, incentive plans, A's, praise, and other bribes.* New York: Houghton Mifflin.

Kohn, C. K. (2005, March 7). Rat brain's executive hub quells alarm center if stress is controllable. *Mental Health Weekly Digest,* p. 7.

Kolb, B. (1989). Brain development, plasticity, and behavior. *American Psychologist, 44*, 1203–1212.

Kolb, B., Gibb, R., & Robinson, T. E. (2003). Brain plasticity and behavior. *Current Directions in Psychological Science, 12*, 1–5.

Kolb, B., & Whishaw, I. Q. (1990). *Fundamentals of human neuropsychology* (3rd ed.). New York: Freeman.

Kolb, B., & Whishaw, I. Q. (1998). Brain plasticity and behavior. *Annual Review of Psychology, 49*, 43–64.

Kopelowicz, A., Liberman, R. P., & Zarate, R. (2002). Psychosocial treatments for schizophrenia. In P. E. Nathan & J. M. Gorman (Eds.), *A guide to treatments that work* (2nd ed., pp. 201–228). London: Oxford University Press.

Koren, D., Norman, D., Cohen, A., Berman, J., & Klein, E. M. (2005). Increased PTSD risk with combat-related injury: A matched comparison study of injured and uninjured soldiers experiencing the same combat events. *American Journal of Psychiatry, 162*, 276–282.

Korn, J. H., Davis, R., & Davis, S. F. (1991). Historians' and chairpersons' judgments of eminence among psychologists. *American Psychologist, 46*, 789–792.

Kornreich, J., Hearn, K. D., Rodriguez, G., & O'Sullivan, L. F. (2003). Sibling influence, gender roles, and the sexual socialization of urban early adolescent girls. *Journal of Sex Research, 40*, 101–110.

Koss, M. (1993). Rape: Scope, impact, interventions, and public policy responses. *American Psychologist, 48*, 1062–1069.

Kotzer, A. M. (2000). Factors predicting postoperative pain in children and adolescents following spine fusion. *Issues in Comprehensive Pediatric Nursing, 23*, 83–102.

Koutsaal, W., Schacter, D. L., Johnson, M. K., & Gallucio, L. (1999). Facilitation and impairment of event memory produced by photographic review. *Memory & Cognition, 27*, 478–493.

Kozulin, A. (1990). *Vygotsky's psychology: A biography of ideas.* Cambridge, MA: Harvard University Press.

Kramer, A. F., Larish, J. F., & Strayer, D. L. (1995). Training for attentional control in dual task settings: A comparison of young and old adults. *Journal of Experimental Psychology: Applied, 1*, 50–76.

Kramlinger, K. (Ed.). (2001). *Mayo Clinic on depression.* Rochester, MN: Mayo Clinic Health Information.

Kramrisch, S., Otto, J., Ruck, C., & Wasson, R. (1986). *Persephone's quest: Etheogens and the origins of religion.* New Haven, CT: Yale University Press.

Krantz, D., & Manuck, S. (1984). Acute psychophysiologic reactivity and risk of cardiovascular disease: A review and methodologic critique. *Psychological Bulletin, 96*, 435–464.

Krantz, D. S., Contrada, R. J., Hill, D. R., & Fiedler, E. (1988). Environmental stress and biobehavioral antecedents of coronary heart disease. *Journal of Consulting and Clinical Psychology, 56*, 333–341.

Krantz, D. S., Kop, W., Santiago, H., & Gottdiener, J. (1996). Mental stress as a trigger of myocardial ischemia and infarction. *Cardiology Clinics of North America, 14*, 271–287.

Kraus, R., Zack, J., & Stricker, G. (Eds.). (2004). *Online counseling: A handbook for mental health professionals.* San Diego, CA: Elsevier Academic Press.

Kravitz, E. A. (1988). Hormonal control of behavior: Amines and the biasing of behavioral output in lobsters. *Science, 241*, 1775–1782.

Kreitler, S. (1999). Consciousness and meaning. In J. A. Singer & P. Salovey (Eds.), *At play in the fields of consciousness: Essays in honor of Jerome L. Singer* (pp. 207–224). Mahwah, NJ: Erlbaum.

Kribbs, N. B. (1993). Siesta. In M. A. Carskadon (Ed.), *Encyclopedia of sleep and dreaming.* New York: Macmillan.

Kristeller, P. O. (1983). "Creativity" and "tradition." *Journal of the History of Ideas, 44*, 105–114.

Kristensen, K. B., Slife, B. D., & Yanchar, S. C. (2000). On what basis are evaluations possible in a fragmented psychology? An alternative to objectivism and relativism. *Journal of Mind & Behavior, 21*, 273–288.

Kroger, J. (1996). *Identity in adolescence: The balance between self and other.* London: Routledge.

Krogsgaard, M., & Davis, M. M. (2005). How T cells "see" antigen. *Nature Immunology, 6*, 239–245.

Kroll, N. E. A., Yonelinas, A. P., Dobbins, I. G., & Frederick, C. M. (2002). Separating sensitivity from response bias: Implications of comparisons of yes-no and forced-choice tests for models and measures of recognition memory. *Journal of Experimental Psychology: General, 131*, 241–254.

Kruglanski, A. W., & Freund, T. (1983). The freezing and unfreezing of lay inferences: Effects on impressional primacy, ethnic stereotyping, and numerical anchoring. *Journal of Experimental Social Psychology, 19*, 448–468.

Kruglanski, A. W., & Webster, D. M. (1996). Motivated closing of the mind: "Seizing" and "freezing." *Psychological Review, 103*, 263–283.

Krull, D. S., Loy, M. H.-M., Lin, J., Wang, C.-F., Chen, S., & Zhao, X. (1999). The fundamental attribution error: Correspondence bias in individualist and collectivist cultures. *Personality and Social Psychology Bulletin, 25*, 1208–1219.

Kryger, M. H., Roth, T., & Dement, W. C. (Eds.). (2000). *Principles and practice of sleep medicine* (4th ed.). Philadelphia: Saunders.

Kübler-Ross, E. (1969). *On death and dying.* New York: Macmillan.

Kübler-Ross, E. (1981). *Living and dying.* New York: Macmillan.

Kuczmarski, R. J., Flegal, K. M., Campbell, S. M., & Johnson, C. L. (1994). Increasing prevalence of overweight among U.S. adults. The National Health and Nutrition Examination Surveys, 1960 to 1991.

Journal of the American Medical Association, 272, 205–211.

Kuhn, T. (1977). *The essential tension.* Chicago: University of Chicago Press.

Kulik, J. A., Bangert-Downs, R. L., & Kulik, C. (1984). Effectiveness of coaching for aptitude tests. *Psychological Bulletin, 95*, 179–188.

Kulik, J. A., & Mahler, H. I. M. (1989). Stress and affiliation in a hospital setting: Preoperative roommate preferences. *Personality and Social Psychology Bulletin, 15*, 183–193.

Kulik, J. A., Mahler, H. I. M., & Moore, P. J. (1996). Social comparison and affiliation under threat: Effects on recovery from major surgery. *Journal of Personality and Social Psychology, 71*, 967–979.

Kulynych, J. (2002). Legal and ethical issues in neuroimaging research: Human subjects protection, medical privacy and the public communication of research results. *Brain & Cognition, 50*, 345–357.

Kumagai, H. A. (1981). A dissection of intimacy: A study of "bipolar posturing" in Japanese social interaction—amaeru and amayakasu, indulgence and deference. *Culture, Medicine, and Psychiatry, 5*, 249–272.

Kumar, V. K., Pekala, R. J., & Cummings, J. (1996). Trait factors, state effects, and hypnotizability. *International Journal of Clinical and Experimental Hypnosis, 44*, 232–249.

Kunda, Z., & Oleson, K. C. (1995). Maintaining stereotypes in the face of disconfirmation: Constructing grounds for subtyping deviants. *Journal of Personality and Social Psychology, 68*, 565–579.

Kunda, Z., & Spencer, S. J. (2003). When do stereotypes come to mind and when do they color judgment? A goal-based theoretical framework for stereotype activation and application. *Psychological Bulletin, 129*, 522–544.

Kuo, T. B. J., Shaw, F.-Z., Lai, C., Lai, C.-W., & Yang, C. C. H. (2004). Changes in sleep patterns in spontaneously hyperactive rats. *Sleep: Journal of Sleep & Sleep Disorders Research, 27*, 406–412.

Kuo, Y.-Y. (1996). Taoistic psychology of creativity. *Journal of Creative Behavior, 30*, 197–212.

Kurdek, L. A. (1994a). Conflict resolution styles in gay, lesbian, heterosexual non-parent, and heterosexual parent couples. *Journal of Marriage and the Family, 56*, 705–722.

Kurdek, L. A. (1994b). Areas of conflict for gay, lesbian, and heterosexual couples: What couples argue about influences relationship satisfaction. *Journal of Marriage and the Family, 56*, 923–934.

Kurdek, L. A. (1995). Lesbian and gay couples. In A. R. D'Augelli & C. J. Patterson (Eds.), *Lesbian, gay, and bisexual identities over the lifespan: Psychological perspectives* (pp. 243–261). New York: Oxford University Press.

Kurdek, L. A. (1998). Relationship outcomes and their predictors: Longitudinal evidence from heterosexual married, gay cohabiting, and lesbian cohabiting couples. *Journal of Marriage and the Family, 60*, 553–568.

Kurtzberg, T. R., & Amabile, T. M. (2001). From Guilford to creative synergy: Opening the black box of team-level creativity. *Creativity Research Journal, 13*, 285–294.

Kutash, I. L., & Wolf, A. (1990). Object relational groups. In I. L. Kutash & A. Wolf (Eds.), *The group psychotherapist's handbook: Contemporary theory and technique* (pp. 99–115). New York: Columbia University Press.

Kutchins, H., & Kirk, S. A. (1997). *Making us crazy: DSM—The psychiatric Bible and the creation of mental disorders.* New York: Free Press.

Kwate, N. O. (2001). Intelligence or misorientation? *Journal of Black Psychology, 27*, 221–238.

LaBerge, S. P. (1992). *Physiological studies of lucid dreaming.* Hillsdale, NJ: Erlbaum.

LaBerge, S. P., & DeGracia, D. J. (2000). Varieties of lucid dreaming experience. In R. G. Kunzendorf & B. Wallace (Eds.), *Individual differences in conscious experience: Advances in consciousness research* (Vol. 20, pp. 269–307). Amsterdam, Netherlands: John Benjamins.

Labov, W. (1973). The boundaries of words and their meanings. In C. J. N. Bailey & R. W. Shiny (Eds.), *New ways of analyzing variation in English* (Vol. 1). Washington, DC: Georgetown University Press.

Lachman, M. E., & Weaver, S. L. (1998). The sense of control as a moderator of social class differences in health and well-being. *Journal of Personality and Social Psychology, 74,* 763–773.

Ladd-Franklin, C. (1929). *Colour and colour theories.* New York: Harcourt, Brace & Company.

LaGrenade, L., Graham, D., & Trontell, A. (2001). Myocarditis and cardiomyopathy associated with clozapine use in the United States. *New England Journal of Medicine, 345,* 224–225.

Laing, D. G., Prescott, J., Bell, G. A., & Gillmore, R. (1993). A cross-cultural study of taste discrimination with Australians and Japanese. *Chemical Senses, 18,* 161–168.

Laing, R. D. (1967). *The politics of experience.* New York: Pantheon.

Laird, J. D. (1974). Self-attribution of emotion: The effects of expressive behavior on the quality of emotional experience. *Journal of Personality and Social Psychology, 29,* 475–486.

Laitmann, J. T. (1983, August). The anatomy of human speech. *Natural History,* 20–27.

Lakkis, J., Ricciardelli, L. A., & Williams, R. J. (1999). Role of sexual orientation and gender-related traits in disordered eating. *Sex Roles, 31,* 1–16.

Lakoff, R. T. (1975). *Language and woman's place.* New York: Harper & Row.

Lakoff, R. T. (1990). *Talking power: The politics of language in our lives.* New York: Basic Books.

Lamar, J. (2000). Suicides in Japan reach a record high. *British Medical Journal, 321,* 528.

Lamb, M., Sternberg, K. J., & Prodromidis, M. (1992). Nonmaternal care and the security of the infant-mother attachment: A reanalysis of the data. *Infant Behavior and Development, 15,* 71–83.

Lamb, M. E. (Ed.). (1987). *The father's role: Cross-cultural perspectives.* Hillsdale, NJ: Erlbaum.

Lamb, M. E., Pleck, J. H., Charnov, E. L., & Levine, J. A. (1987). A biosocial perspective on paternal behavior and involvement. In J. B. Lancaster, A. Rossi, J. Altmann, & L. R. Sherrod (Eds.), *Parenting across the lifespan: Biosocial perspectives.* Hawthorne, NY: Aldine de Gruyter.

Lambert, A. J. (1995). Stereotypes and social judgment: The consequences of group variability. *Journal of Personality and Social Psychology, 68,* 388–403.

Laming, D. (1985). Some principles of sensory analysis. *Psychological Review, 92,* 462–485.

Lamprecht, F., & Sack, M. (2002). Posttraumatic stress disorder revisited. *Psychosomatic Medicine, 64,* 222–237.

Land, E. H. (1986). Recent advances in retinex theory. *Vision Research, 26,* 7–21.

Landolt, H.-P., Werth, E., Borbely, A. A., & Dijk, D.-J. (1995). Caffeine intake (200 mg) in the morning affects human sleep and EEG power spectra at night. *Brain Research, 675,* 67–74.

Landrine, H. (1988). Revising the framework of abnormal psychology. In P. Bronstein & K. Quina (Eds.), *Teaching a psychology of people.* Washington, DC: American Psychological Association.

Lang, P. (1995). The emotion probe: Studies of motivation and attention. *American Psychologist, 50,* 372–385.

Langens, T. A. (2003). Daydreaming mediates between goal commitment and goal attainment in individuals high in achievement motivation. *Imagination, Cognition and Personality, 22,* 103–115.

Langens, T. A., & Schmalt, H.-D. (2002). Emotional consequences of positive daydreaming: The moderating role of fear of failure. *Personality and Social Psychology Bulletin, 28,* 1725–1735.

Langer, E. J. (1989). Minding matters: The consequences of mindlessness-mindfulness. In L. Berkowitz (Ed.), *Advances in experimental social psychology* (Vol. 22, pp. 137–173). San Diego, CA: Academic Press.

Langer, E. J., Blank, A., & Chanowitz, B. (1978). The mindlessness of ostensibly thoughtful action. *Journal of Personality and Social Psychology, 36,* 635–642.

Langer, L. M., Warheit, G. J., & McDonald, L. P. (2001). Correlates and predictors of risky sexual practices among a multi-racial/ethnic sample of university students. *Social Behavior and Personality, 29,* 133–144.

Larsen, R. J., & Kasimatis, M. (1990). Individual differences in entrainment of mood to the weekly calendar. *Journal of Personality and Social Psychology, 58,* 164–171.

Lashley, K. S. (1950). In search of the engram. *Symposium of the Society for Experimental Biology, 4,* 454–482.

Latané, B., & Darley, J. M. (1968). Group inhibition of bystander intervention in emergencies. *Journal of Personality and Social Psychology, 10,* 216–221.

Latané, B., & Darley, J. M. (1970). *The unresponsive bystander: Why doesn't he help?* Englewood Cliffs, NJ: Prentice Hall.

Latané, B., Liu, J. H., Nowak, A., & Bonevento, M. (1995). Distance matters: Physical space and social impact. *Personality & Social Psychology Bulletin, 21,* 795–805.

Latané, B., & Nida, S. (1981). Ten years of research on group size and helping. *Psychological Bulletin, 89,* 308–324.

Latta, F., & Van Cauter, E. (2003). Sleep and biological clocks. In M. Gallagher & R. J. Nelson (Eds.), *Handbook of psychology: Biological psychology* (Vol. 3, pp. 355–377). New York: Wiley.

Laumann, E., Gagnon, J., Michael, R., & Michaels, S. (1994). *The social organization of sexuality: Sexual practices in the United States.* Chicago: University of Chicago Press.

LaVeist, T. A., Diala, C., & Jarrett, N. C. (2000). Social status and perceived discrimination: Who experiences discrimination in the health care system, how, and why? In C. Hogue, M. Hargraves, & K. Scott-Collins (Eds.), *Minority health in America* (pp. 194–208). Baltimore, MD: Johns Hopkins University Press.

Lavie, P. (2003). *Restless nights: Understanding snoring and sleep apnea.* New Haven, CT: Yale University Press.

Lavond, D. G., & Steinmetz, J. E. (2003). *Handbook of classical conditioning.* Dordrecht, Netherlands: Kluwer Academic Publishers.

Lavrakas, P. J. (1993). *Telephone survey methods: Sampling, selection, and supervision* (2nd ed.). Newbury Park, CA: Sage.

Law, D. J., Pellegrino, J. W., & Hunt, E. B. (1993). Comparing the tortoise and the hare: Gender differences and experience in dynamic spatial reasoning tasks. *Psychological Science, 4,* 35–40.

Lazar, S. W., Bush, G., Gollub, R. L., Fricchione, G. L., Khalsa, G., & Benson, H. (2000). Functional brain mapping of the relaxation response and meditation. *Neuroreport: For Rapid Communication of Neuroscience Research, 11,* 1581–1585.

Lazarus, R., & Folkman, S. (1984). *Stress, appraisal, and coping.* New York: Springer.

Lazarus, R. S. (1993). From psychological stress to the emotions: A history of changing outlooks. *Annual Review of Psychology, 44,* 1–21.

Lazarus, R. S., & Lazarus, B. N. (1994). *Passion and reason: Making sense of our emotions.* New York: Oxford University Press.

Leahey, T. H. (1991). *A history of modern psychology.* Englewood Cliffs, NJ: Prentice Hall.

Leary, D. E. (2002). William James and the art of human understanding. In W. E. Pickren & D. A. Dewsbury (Eds.), *Evolving perspectives on the history of psychology* (pp. 101–120). Washington, DC: American Psychological Association.

Leary, M. R. (2005). The scientific study of personality. In V. J. Derlega, B. A Winstead, & W. H. Jones (Eds.), *Personality: Contemporary theory and research* (3rd ed., pp. 2–26). Belmont, CA: Thomson Wadsworth.

Leary, M. R., Nezlek, J. B., Downs, D., Radford-Davenport, J., Martin, J., & McMullen, A. (1994). Self-presentation in everyday interactions: Effects of target familiarity and gender composition. *Journal of Personality and Social Psychology, 67,* 664–673.

Leather, P., Beale, D., & Sullivan, L. (2003). Noise, psychosocial stress and their interaction in the workplace. *Journal of Environmental Psychology, 23,* 213–222.

Leck, K., & Simpson, J. (1999). Feigning romantic interest: The role of self-monitoring. *Journal of Research in Personality, 33,* 69–91.

Leckman, J. F., & Herman, A. E. (2002). Maternal behavior and developmental psychopathology. *Biological Psychiatry, 51,* 27–43.

LeDoux, J. (1995). Emotion: Clues from the brain. *Annual Review of Psychology, 46,* 209–235.

LeDoux, J. (1998). *The emotional brain.* New York: Simon & Schuster.

Lee, F., Hallahan, M., & Herzog, T. (1996). Explaining real-life events: How culture and domain shape attributions. *Personality and Social Psychology Bulletin, 22,* 732–741.

Lee, G. P., Meador, K. J., Loring, D. W., Allison, J. D., Brown, W. S., Paul, L. K., Pillai, J. J., & Lavin, T. B. (2004). Neural substrates of emotion as revealed by functional magnetic resonance imaging. *Cognitive and Behavioral Neurology, 17,* 9–17.

Lee, T. M. C., Liu, H.-L., Tan, L.-H., Chan, C. C. H., Mahankali, S., Feng, C.-M., Hou, J., Fox, P. T., & Gao, J.-H. (2002). Lie detection by functional magnetic resonance imaging. *Human Brain Mapping, 15,* 157–164.

Leff, J., & Vaughn, C. (1985). *Expressed emotion in families: Its significance for mental illness.* New York: Guilford.

Lefkowitz, J. (2003). *Ethics and values in industrial-organizational psychology.* Mahwah, NJ: Erlbaum.

Lehman, A. F., Steinwachs, D. M., Dixon, L. B., Goldman, H. H., Osher, F., Postrado, L., Scott, J. E., Thompson, J. W., Fahey, M., Fischer, P., Kasper, J. A., Lyles, A., Skinner, E. A., Buchanan, R., Carpenter, W. T., Jr., Levine, J., McGlynn, E. A., Rosenheck, R., & Zito, J. (1998). Translating research into practice: The schizophrenia patient outcomes research team (PORT) treatment recommendations. *Schizophrenia Bulletin, 24,* 1–10.

Lehman, D. R., Lempert, R. O., & Nisbett, R. E. (1988). The effects of graduate training on reasoning. *American Psychologist, 43,* 431–442.

Lei, T., Askeroth, C., Lee, C.-T., Burshteyn, D., & Einhorn, A. (2004). Indigenous Chinese healing: A criteria-based meta-analysis of outcomes research. In U. P. Gielen, J. M. Fish, & J. G. Draguns (Eds.), *Handbook of culture, therapy, and healing* (pp. 213–251). Mahwah, NJ: Erlbaum.

Leippe, M. R., & Elkin, R. A. (1987). When motives clash: Issue involvement and response involvement as determinants of persuasion. *Journal of Personality and Social Psychology, 52,* 269–278.

Leitenberg, H., & Henning, K. (1995). Sexual fantasy. *Psychological Bulletin, 117,* 469–496.

Le Melledo, J.-M., Arthur, H., Dalton, J., Woo, C., Lipton, N., Bellavance, F., Koszycki, D., Boulenger, J.-P., & Bradwejn, J. (2003). The influence of Type A behavior pattern on the response to the panicogenic agent CCK-4. *Journal of Psychosomatic Research, 51,* 513–520.

Lemonick, M., & Dorfman, A. (2002, July 22). Father of us all? *Time,* 40–47.

Lenton, A. P., Blair, I. V., & Hastie, R. (2001). Illusions of gender: Stereotypes evoke false memories. *Journal of Experimental Social Psychology, 37,* 3–14.

Leonard, C. M., Lombardino, L. J., Mercado, L. R., Browd, S. R., Brier, J. I., & Agee, O. F. (1996). Cerebral asymmetry and cognitive development in children: A magnetic resonance imaging study. *Psychological Science, 7,* 89–95.

Lepper, M., Greene, D., & Nisbett, R. (1973). Undermining children's intrinsic interest with extrinsic rewards: A test of the overjustification hypothesis. *Journal of Personality and Social Psychology, 23,* 129–137.

Lerner, A. G., Gelkopf, M., Skladman, I., Rudinski, D., Nachshon, H., & Bleich, A. (2003). Clonazepam treatment of lysergic acid diethylamide-induced hallucinogen persisting perception disorder with anxiety features. *International Clinical Psychopharmacology, 18,* 101–105.

Lerner, R., & Steinberg, L. (Eds.). (2004). *Handbook of adolescent psychology* (2nd ed.). New York: Wiley.

Leslie, A. M., German, T. P., & Polizzi, P. (2005). Belief-desire reasoning as a process of selection. *Cognitive Psychology, 50,* 45–85.

Levant, R. F. (1984). *Family therapy: A comprehensive overview.* Englewood Cliffs, NJ: Prentice Hall.

LeVay, S. (1991). A difference in hypothalamic structure between heterosexual and homosexual men. *Science, 253,* 1034–1037.

Levenson, R. W. (1992). Autonomic nervous system differences among emotions. *Psychological Science, 3,* 23–27.

Levenson, R. W. (2005). Presidential column: Desperately seeking Phil. *Observer, 18,* 4.

Levenson, R. W., Carstensen, L. L., & Gottman, J. M. (1993). Long-term marriage: Age, gender, and satisfaction. *Psychology and Aging, 8,* 301–313.

Levenson, R. W., Ekman, P., Heider, K., & Friesen, W. V. (1992). Emotion and autonomic nervous system activity in the Minangkabau of West Sumatra. *Journal of Personality and Social Psychology, 62,* 972–988.

Levi, L. (1974). Psychological stress and disease: A conceptual model. In E. Gunderson & R. Rahe (Eds.), *Life stress and illness.* Springfield, IL: Charles C. Thomas.

Levin, H. S., Papanicolaou, A., & Eisenberg, H. (1984). Observations on amnesia after nonmissie head injury. In L. R. Squire & N. Butters (Eds.), *Neuropsychology of memory.* New York: Guilford Press.

Levin, I. P., & Gaeth, J. (1988). How consumers are affected by the framing of attribute information before and after consuming the product. *Journal of Consumer Research, 15,* 374–378.

Levin, S. (2004). Perceived group status differences and the effects of gender, ethnicity, and religion on social dominance orientation. *Political Psychology, 25,* 31–48.

Levine, H. G. (1992). Temperance cultures: Alcohol as a problem in Nordic and English-speaking cultures. In M. Lader, G. Edwards, & D. Drummond (Eds.), *The nature of alcohol and drug-related problems* (pp. 16–36). New York: Oxford University Press.

Levine, R., & Norenzayan, A. (1999). The pace of life in 31 countries. *Journal of Cross-Cultural Psychology, 26,* 554–571.

Levine, R. A., & Campbell, D. T. (1972). *Ethnocentrism.* New York: Wiley.

Levine, R. V., Martinez, T. S., Brase, G., & Sorenson, K. (1994). Helping in 36 U.S. cities. *Journal of Personality and Social Psychology, 67,* 69–82.

Levine, R. V., Sata, S., Hashimoto, T., & Verma, J. (1995). Love and marriage in eleven cultures. *Journal of Cross-Cultural Psychology, 26,* 554–571.

Levitan, I. B., & Kaczmarek, L. K. (1991). *The neuron: Cell and molecular biology.* New York: Oxford University Press.

Levy, B. R., Slade, M. D., Kunkel, S. R., & Kasl, S. V. (2002). Longevity increased by positive self-perceptions of aging. *Journal of Personality and Social Psychology, 83,* 261–270.

Levy, J. (1969). Possible basis for the evolution of lateral specialization of the human brain. *Nature, 224,* 614–615.

Levy, J. (1972). Lateral specialization of the human brain: Behavioral manifestations and possible evolutionary basis. In J. A. Kiger (Ed.), *The biology of behavior.* Corvallis: Oregon State University.

Levy, J., Heller, W., Banich, M., & Burton, L. A. (1983). Asymmetry of perception in free viewing of chimeric faces. *Brain and Cognition, 2,* 404–419.

Lewandowsky, S., & Murdock, B. B., Jr. (1989). Memory for serial order. *Psychological Review, 96,* 25–57.

Lewin, R. (1993a). *Human evolution: An illustrated introduction.* Boston: Blackwell Scientific Publications.

Lewin, R. (1993b). *The origin of modern humans.* New York: Scientific American Library.

Lewin, T. J., Slade, T., Andrews, G., Carr, V. J., & Hornabrook, C. W. (2005). Assessing personality disorders in a national mental health survey. *Social Psychiatry and Psychiatric Epidemiology, 40,* 87–98.

Lewinsohn, P. M., & Gotlib, I. H. (1995). Behavioral theory and treatment of depression. In E. E. Beckham & W. R. Leber (Eds.), *Handbook of depression* (2nd ed., pp. 352–375). New York: Guilford Press.

Lewinsohn, P. M., & Rosenbaum, M. (1987). Recall of parental behavior by acute depressives, remitted depressives, and nondepressives. *Journal of Personality and Social Psychology, 52,* 611–619.

Lewis, M., & Brooks, J. (1978). Self-knowledge in emotional development. In M. Lewis & L. Rosenblum (Eds.), *The development of affect* (pp. 205–226). New York: Plenum.

Lewis, M., & Weintraub, M. (1979). Origins of early sex-role development. *Sex Roles, 5,* 135–153.

Lewontin, R. (1995). *Human diversity.* New York: Scientific American Library.

Leyens, J.-P. (Ed.). (1991). Prolegomena for the concept of implicit theories of personality. *European Bulletin of Cognitive Psychology, 11,* 131–136.

Leyens, J.-P., Camino, L., Parke, R. D., & Berkowitz, L. (1975). Effects of movie violence on aggression in a field setting as a function of group dynamics and cohesiveness. *Journal of Personality and Social Psychology, 32,* 346–360.

Li, F., Fisher, K.-J., Harmer, P., & McAuley, E. (2005). Falls self-efficacy as a mediator of fear of falling in an exercise intervention for older adults. *Journals of Gerontology, 60,* 34–40.

Li, J. (2004). High abilities and excellence: A cultural perspective. In L. V. Shavinina & M. Ferrari (Eds.), *Beyond knowledge: Extracognitive aspects of developing high ability* (pp. 187–208). *The educational psychology series.* Mahwah, NJ: Erlbaum.

Lichtenberg, J. D. (1989). *Psychoanalysis and motivation.* Hillsdale, NJ: The Analytic Press.

Lichtenstein, E., & Brown, R. A. (1980). Smoking cessation methods: Review and recommendations. In W. R. Miller (Ed.), *The addictive behaviors: Treatment of alcoholism, drug abuse, smoking, and obesity* (pp. 169–206). New York: Pergamon.

Liden, R. C., & Mitchell, T. R. (1988). Ingratiatory behaviors in organizational settings. *Academy of Management Review, 13,* 572–587.

Lieberman, M. A. (1990). A group therapist perspective on self-help groups. *International Journal of Group Psychotherapy, 40,* 251–278.

Lieberman, P. (1984). *The biology and evolution of language.* Cambridge: Harvard University Press.

Liebert, R., & Morris, L. (1967). Cognitive and emotional components of test anxiety: A distinction and some initial data. *Psychological Reports, 20,* 975–978.

Lilienfeld, S. (1999, November/December). Research review: New analyses raise doubts about replicability of ESP findings. *The Skeptical Inquirer.* Full text available at http://www.csicop.org/si/9911/lilienfeld.html

Lilienfeld, S. O., Fowler, K. A., Lohr, J. M., & Lynn, S. J. (2005). Pseudoscience, nonscience, and nonsense in clinical psychology: Dangers and remedies. In R. H. Wright, N. Cummings, & A. Nicholas (Eds.), *Destructive trends in mental health: The well-intentioned path to harm* (pp. 187–218). New York: Routledge.

Lilienfeld, S. O., Kirsch, I., Sarvin, T. R., Lynn, S. J., Chaves, J. F., Ganaway, G. K., & Powell, R. A. (1999). Dissociative identity disorder and the sociocognitive model: Recalling the lessons of the past. *Psychological Bulletin, 125,* 507–523.

Lilienfeld, S. O., & Lynn, S. J. (2003). Dissociative identity disorder: Multiple personalities, multiple controversies. In S. O. Lilienfeld & S. J. Lynn (Eds.), *Science and pseudoscience in clinical psychology* (pp. 109–142). New York: Guilford Press.

Lilienfeld, S. O., Wood, J. M., & Garb, H. N. (2000). The scientific status of projective techniques. *Psychological Science in the Public Interest, 1,* 27–66.

Lin, C. (1998). Comparison of the effects of perceived self-efficacy on coping with chronic cancer pain and coping with chronic low back pain. *Clinical Journal of Pain, 14,* 303–310.

Lin, K. M., & Cheung, F. (1999). Mental health issues for Asian Americans. *Psychiatric Services 50,* 774–780.

Linden, D. R., Savage, L. M., & Overmier, J. B. (1997). General learned irrelevance: A Pavlovian analog to learned helplessness. *Learning and Motivation, 28,* 230–247.

Linehan, M. M. (1993). *Cognitive-behavioral treatment of borderline personality disorder.* New York: Guilford Press.

Link, B. G., Andrews, H., & Cullen, F. T. (1992). The violent and illegal behavior of mental patients reconsidered. *American Sociological Review, 57,* 275–292.

Lipman, J. J., Miller, B. E., Mays, K. S., & Miller, M. N. (1990). Peak B endorphin concentration in cerebrospinal fluid: Reduced in chronic pain patients and increased during the placebo response. *Psychopharmacology, 102,* 112–116.

Lipp, O. V., Siddle, D. A., & Dall, P. J. (2003). The effects of unconditional stimulus valence and conditioning paradigm on verbal, skeleto-motor and autonomic indices of human Pavlovian conditioning. *Learning & Motivation, 34,* 32–51.

Lippa, R. A. (2002). Gender-related traits of heterosexual and homosexual men and women. *Archives of Sexual Behavior, 21,* 83–98.

Lippa, R. A. (2005). Sex and gender. In V. J. Derlega, B. A. Winstead, & W. H. Jones (Eds.), *Personality: Contemporary theory and research* (3rd ed., pp. 332–365). Belmont, CA: Thomson Wadsworth.

Littleton, H. L., & Axsom, D. (2003). Rape and seduction scripts of university students: Implications for rape attributions and unacknowledged rape. *Sex Roles, 49,* 465–475.

Littleton, J. M., & Little, H. J. (1989). Adaptation in neuronal calcium channels as a common basis for physical dependence on central depressant drugs. In A. J. Goudie & M. W. Emmett-Oglesby (Eds.), *Psychoactive drugs: Tolerance and sensitization* (pp. 461–518). Clifton, NJ: Human Press.

Lock, J., & Grange, D. L. (2005). *Help your teenager beat an eating disorder.* New York: Guilford Press.

Locke, E., & Latham, G. (1990). *A theory of goal setting and task performance.* Englewood Cliffs, NJ: Prentice Hall.

Locke, T. F., Newcomb, M. D., & Goodyear, R. K. (2005). Childhood experiences and psychosocial influences on risky sexual behavior, condom use, and HIV attitudes-behaviors among Latino males. *Psychology of Men and Masculinity, 6,* 25–38.

Lockhart, R. S., & Craik, F. I. (1990). Levels of processing: A retrospective commentary on a framework for memory research. *Canadian Journal of Psychology, 44,* 87–112.

Loehlin, J. C., Horn, J. M., & Willerman, L. (1989). Modeling IQ change: Evidence from the Texas Adoption Project. *Child Development, 60,* 993–1004.

Loehlin, J. C., Horn, J. M., & Willerman, L. (1997). Heredity, environment, and IQ in the Texas Adoption Project. In R. J. Sternberg & E. L. Grigorenko (Eds.), *Intelligence, heredity, and environment* (pp. 105–125). Cambridge, England: Cambridge University Press.

Loehlin, J. C., Vandenberg, S., & Osborne, R. (1973). Blood group genes and negro-White ability differences. *Behavior Genetics, 3,* 263–270.

Loftus, E. F. (1992). When a lie becomes memory's truth: Memory distortion after exposure to misinformation. *Current Directions in Psychological Science, 1,* 121–123.

Loftus, E. F. (1993). The reality of repressed memories. *American Psychologist, 48,* 518–537.

Loftus, E. F., & Coan, D. (1995). The construction of childhood memories. In D. Peters (Ed.), *The child witness in context: Cognitive, social and legal perspectives.* New York: Kluwer.

Loftus, E. F., Feldman, J., & Dashiell, R. (1995). The reality of illusory memories. In D. L. Schacter (Ed.), *Memory distortion: How minds, brains, and societies reconstruct the past* (pp. 47–68). Cambridge, MA: Harvard University Press.

Loftus, E. F., & Palmer, J. C. (1974). Reconstruction of automobile destruction: An example of the interaction between language and memory. *Journal of Verbal Learning and Verbal Behavior, 13,* 585–589.

LoLordo, V. M., & Droungas, A. (1989). Selective associations and adaptive specializations: Taste aversions and adaptive specializations: Taste aversions and phobias. In S. B. Klein & R. R. Mower (Eds.), *Contemporary learning theories: Instrumental conditioning and the impact of biological constraints on learning.* Hillsdale, NJ: Erlbaum.

Long, C. R., Seburn, M., Averill, J. R., & More, T. A. (2003). Solitude experiences: Varieties, settings, and individual differences. *Personality and Social Psychology Bulletin, 29,* 678–583.

Long, G. M., & Beaton, R. J. (1982). The case for peripheral persistence: Effects of target and background luminance on a partial-report task. *Journal of Experimental Psychology: Human Perception and Performance, 8,* 383–391.

Lonsway, K. A., Klaw, E. L., Berg, D. R., Waldo, C. R., Kothari, C., Mazurek, C. J., & Hegeman, K. E. (1998). Beyond "no means no": Outcomes of an intensive program to train peer facilitators for campus acquaintance rape education. *Journal of Interpersonal Violence, 13,* 73–92.

Lopez, A., & Carrillo, E. (Eds.). (2001). *The Latino psychiatric patient: Assessment and treatment.* Washington, DC: American Psychiatric Press.

Lopez, O., Haigh, C., & Burney, S. (2004). Relationship between hardiness and perceived stress in two generations of Latin American migrants. *Australian Psychologist, 39,* 238–243.

Lopez, S. R., & Guarnaccia, P. J. (2000). Cultural psychopathology: Uncovering the social world of mental illness. *Annual Review of Psychology, 51,* 571–598.

Loring, D. W., Meador, K., Lee, G., Murro, A., Smith, J., Flanigin, H., Gallagher, B., & King, D. (1990). Cerebral language lateralization: Evidence from intracarotid amobarbital testing. *Neuropsychologia, 28,* 831–838.

Lott, B. (2002). Cognitive and behavioral distancing from the poor. *American Psychologist, 57,* 100–110.

Lotto, R. B., & Purves, D. (2002). The empirical basis of color perception. *Consciousness & Cognition, 11,* 609–629.

Lounsbury, J. W., Hutchens, T., & Loveland, J. M. (2005). An investigation of Big Five personality traits and career decidedness among early and middle adolescents. *Journal of Career Assessment, 13,* 25–39.

Lourenço, O., & Machado, A. (1996). In defense of Piaget's theory: A reply to 10 common criticisms. *Psychological Review, 103,* 143–164.

Lovibond, P. F. (2004). Cognitive processes in extinction. *Learning and Memory, 11,* 495–500.

Lowe, G., Bland, R., Greenman, J., Kirkpatrick, N., & Lowe, G. (2001). Progressive muscle relaxation and secretory immunoglobulin A. *Psychological Reports, 88,* 912–914.

Lowery, C. R., & Settle, S. A. (1985). Effects of divorce on children: Differential impact of custody and visitation patterns. *Family Relations: Journal of Applied Family and Child Studies, 34,* 455–463.

Lu, L., & Gilmour, R. (2004). Culture and conceptions of happiness: Individual oriented and social oriented swb. *Journal of Happiness Studies, 5,* 269–291.

Lu, L., Gilmour, R., Kao, S., Weng, T., Hu, C., Chern, J., Huang, S., & Shih, J. (2001). Two ways to achieve happiness: When the East meets the West. *Personality and Individual Differences, 30,* 1161–1174.

Lubart, T. I. (1999). Creativity across cultures. In R. J. Sternberg (Ed.), *Handbook of creativity* (pp. 339–350). Cambridge, England: Cambridge University Press.

Lubart, T. I., & Sternberg, R. J. (1994). An investment approach to creativity. In R. J. Sternberg (Ed.), *Thinking and problem solving* (pp. 289–332). San Diego, CA: Academic Press.

Lubinski, D., Webb, R. M., Morelock, M. J., & Benbow, C. P. (2001). Top 1 in 10,000: A 10-year follow-up of the profoundly gifted. *Journal of Applied Psychology, 86,* 718–729.

Lucas, R. E., Clark, A. E., Georgellis, Y., & Diener, E. (2004). Unemployment alters the set point for life satisfaction. *Psychological Science, 15,* 8–13.

Lucas, R. E., Diener, E., Grob, A., Suh, E., & Shao, L. (2000). Cross-cultural evidence for the fundamental features of extraversion. *Journal of Personality and Social Psychology, 79,* 452–468.

Lucas, W. (1985). Police use of psychics: A waste of resources and tax money. *Campus Law Enforcement Journal, 15,* 15–21.

Luchins, A. S. (1942). Mechanization in problem solving. *Psychological Monographs, 54* (6, No. 248).

Lucy, J. A. (1992). *Language diversity and thought: A reformulation of the linguistic relativity hypothesis.* New York: Cambridge University Press.

Lucy, J. A. (1997). Linguistic relativity. *Annual Review of Anthropology, 26,* 291–312.

Ludy, B. T., Jr., & Crouse, E. M. (2002). The American Psychological Association's response to *Brown v. Board of Education:* The case of Kenneth B. Clark. *American Psychologist, 57,* 38–50.

Luo, M., Fee, M. S., & Katz, L. C. (2003). Encoding pheromonal signals in the accessory olfactory bulb of behaving mice. *Science, 299,* 1196–1201.

Luria, A. R. (1968). *The mind of a mnemonist: A little book about a vast memory* (L. Solotaroff, Trans.). New York: Basic Books.

Lyddon, W. J., & Chatkoff, D. K. (2001). Empirically supported treatments: Recent trends, current limitations, and future promise. In W. J. Lyddon & J. V. Jones, Jr. (Eds.), *Empirically supported cognitive therapies: Current and future application* (pp. 235–246). New York: Springer.

Lykken, D. T. (1984). Polygraph interrogation. *Nature, 307,* 681–684.

Lykken, D. T. (1995). *The antisocial personalities.* Hillsdale, NJ: Erlbaum.

Lykken, D. T. (1998). *A tremor in the blood: Uses and abuses of the lie detector.* New York: Plenum.

Lykken, D. T., & Tellegen, A. (1996). Happiness is a stochastic phenomenon. *Psychological Science, 65,* 56–68.

Lynch, M. (1994). Developmental psychology. In D. Matsumoto (Ed.), *People: Psychology from a cultural perspective* (pp. 65–81). Pacific Grove, CA: Brooks/Cole.

Lyness, S. A. (1993). Predictors of differences between Type A and Type B individuals in heart rate and blood pressure reactivity. *Psychological Bulletin, 114,* 266–295.

Lynn, R. (1994). Sex differences in intelligence and brain size: A paradox resolved. *Personality and Individual Differences, 17,* 257–271.

Lynn, R. (1996). Racial and ethnic differences in intelligence in the U.S. on the Differential Ability Scale. *Personality and Individual Differences, 20,* 271–273.

Lynn, S. J., Lock, T., Loftus, E. F., Krackow, E., & Lilienfeld, S. O. (2003). The remembrance of things past: Problematic memory recovery techniques in psychotherapy. In S. O. Lilienfeld & S. J. Lynn (Eds.), *Science and pseudoscience in clinical psychology* (pp. 205–239). New York: Guilford.

Lynn, S. J., & Neufeld, V. A. (1996). Fantasy styles, hypnotic dreaming, and fantasy proneness. *Contemporary Hypnosis, 12,* 4–12.

Lynn, S. J., Neufeld, V. A., Green, J. P., Sandberg, D., et al. (1996). Daydreaming, fantasy, and psychopathology. In R. G. Kunzendorf, N. P. Spanos, & B. Wallace (Eds.), *Hypnosis and imagination. Imagery and human development series.* Amityville, NY: Baywood.

Lynn, S. J., & Ruhe, J. W. (1986). The fantasy-prone person: Hypnosis, imagination, and creativity. *Journal of Personality and Social Psychology, 51,* 404–408.

Lyons, M. J., True, W. R., Eisen, S. A., Goldberg, J., Meyer, J. M., Faraone, S. V., Eaves, L. J., & Tsuang, M. T. (1995). Differential heritability of adult and juvenile antisocial traits. *Archives of General Psychiatry, 52,* 906–915.

Lytton, H., & Gallagher, L. (2002). Parenting twins and the genetics of parenting. In M. H. Bornstein (Ed.), *Handbook of parenting: Vol. 1. Children and parenting* (2nd ed., pp. 227–253). Mahwah, NJ: Erlbaum.

Lyvers, M., Brooks, J., & Matica, D. (2004). Effects of caffeine on cognitive and autonomic measures in heavy and light caffeine consumers. *Australian Journal of Psychology, 56,* 33–41.

Ma, H. K. (1988). The Chinese perspective on moral judgment and development. *International Journal of Psychology, 23,* 201–227.

Ma, V., & Schoeneman, T. J. (1997). Individualism versus collectivism: A comparison of Kenyan and American self-concepts. *Basic and Applied Social Psychology, 19,* 261–273.

Maas, J. B. (1998). *The sleep advantage: Preparing your mind for peak performance.* New York: Villard.

Maccoby, E. E. (1990). Gender and relationships: A developmental account. *American Psychologist, 45,* 513–520.

Maccoby, E. E., & Martin, J. A. (1983). Socialization in the context of the family: Parent-child interaction. In E. M. Hetherington (Ed.), *Handbook of child psychology: Vol. 4. Socialization, personality, and social development* (4th ed.). New York: Wiley.

MacDonald, A. J. (2005). Brief therapy in adult psychiatry: Results from fifteen years of practice. *Journal of Family Therapy, 27,* 65–75.

MacDonald, K. (1998). Evolution, culture, and the five-factor model. *Journal of Cross-Cultural Psychology, 29,* 119–149.

MacDonald, T. K., & Martineau, A. M. (2002). Self-esteem, mood, and intentions to use condoms: When does low self-esteem lead to risky health behaviors? *Journal of Experimental Social Psychology, 38,* 299–306.

Macfarlane, A. (1975). Olfaction in the development of social preferences in the human neonate. *CIBA Foundation Symposium 33: Parent-infant interaction.* Amsterdam, The Netherlands: Elsevier.

MacFarlane, J. G., Cleghorn, J. M., Brown, G. M., & Streiner, D. L. (1991). The effects of exogenous melatonin on the total sleep time and daytime alertness of chronic insomniacs: A preliminary study. *Biological Psychiatry, 30,* 371–376.

MacKay, D. G., & Ahmetzanov, M. V. (2005). Emotion, memory, and attention in the Taboo Stroop Paradigm. *Psychological Science, 16,* 25–32.

MacLeod, C. M. (1988). Forgotten but not gone: Savings for pictures and words in long-term memory. *Journal of Experimental Psychology: Learning, Memory, and Cognition, 14,* 195–212.

MacPherson, S. E., Sala, S. D., & Logie, R. H. (2004). Dual-task interference on encoding and retrieval processes in healthy and impaired working memory. *Cortex, 40,* 183–184.

Macrae, C. N., Bodenhausen, G. V., & Milne, A. B. (1998). Saying no to unwanted thoughts: Self-focus and the regulation of mental life. *Journal of Personality and Social Psychology, 74,* 578–589.

Macrae, C. N., Milne, A. B., & Bodenhausen, G. V. (1994). Stereotypes as energy-saving devices: A peek inside the cognitive toolbox. *Journal of Personality and Social Psychology, 66,* 37–47.

Madden, D. J. (1992). Adult age differences in attentional selectivity and capacity. *European Journal of Cognitive Psychology, 2,* 229–252.

Madden-Derdich, D. A., & Leonard, S. A. (2002). Shared experiences, unique realities: Formerly married mothers' and fathers' perceptions of parenting and custody after divorce. *Family Relations: Interdisciplinary Journal of Applied Family Studies, 51,* 37–45.

Maddi, S. R. (2004). Hardiness: An operationalization of existential courage. *Journal of Humanistic Psychology, 44,* 279–298.

Maddi, S. R., & Khoshaba, D. M. (2003). Hardiness training for resiliency and leadership. In D. Paton & J. M. Violanti (Eds.), *Promoting capabilities to manage posttraumatic stress: Perspectives on resilience* (pp. 43–58). Springfield, IL: Charles C. Thomas.

Maddi, S. R., & Kobasa, S. C. (1984). *The hardy executive: Health under stress.* Homewood, IL: Dow Jones-Irwin.

Madigan, S., & O'Hara, R. (1992). Short-term memory at the turn of the century. *American Psychologist, 47,* 170–174.

Madsen, T. M., Yeh, D. D., Valentine, G. W., & Duman, R. S. (2005). Electroconvulsive seizure treatment increases cell proliferation in rat frontal cortex. *Neuropsychopharmacology, 30,* 27–34.

Maestripieri, D. (1997). The evolution of communication. *Language & Communication, 17,* 269–277.

Magnavita, J. J. (2002). *Theories of personality: Contemporary approaches to the science of personality.* New York: Wiley.

Magnusson, D., & Endler, N. S. (1977). Interaction psychology: Present status and future prospects. In D. Magnusson & N. S. Endler (Eds.), *Personality at the crossroads* (pp. 3–31). New York: Wiley.

Maher, W. B., & Maher, B. A. (1985). Psychopathology: II. From the eighteenth century to modern times. In G. A. Kimble & K. Schlesinger (Eds.), *Topics in the history of psychology* (pp. 295–329). Hillsdale, NJ: Erlbaum.

Maheu, M. M., & Gordon, B. L. (2000). Counseling and therapy on the Internet. *Professional Psychology: Research & Practice, 31,* 484–489.

Mahoney, D. J., & Restak, R. M. (1998). *The longevity strategy: How to live to 100 using the brain-body connection.* New York: Wiley.

Maier, S. F., Seligman, M. E. P., & Solomon, R. L. (1969). Pavlovian fear conditioning and learned helplessness: Effects on escape and avoidance behavior of (a) the CS-US contingency, and (b) the independence of the US and voluntary responding. In B. A. Campbell & R. M. Church (Eds.), *Punishment and aversive behavior.* New York: Appleton-Century-Crofts.

Maier, S. F., Watkins, L. R., & Fleshner, M. (1994). Psychoneuroimmunology: The interface between behavior, brain, and immunity. *American Psychologist, 49,* 1004–1017.

Major, B., & Gramzow, R. H. (1999). Abortion as stigma: Cognitive and emotional implications of concealment. *Journal of Personality and Social Psychology, 77,* 735–745.

Major, B., Spencer, S., Schmader, T., Wolfe, C., & Crocker, J. (1998). Coping with negative stereotypes about intellectual performance: The role of psychological disengagement. *Personality and Social Psychology Bulletin, 24,* 34–50.

Mak, M. H. J. (2002). Accepting the timing of one's death: An experience of Chinese hospice patients. *Omega-Journal of Death & Dying, 45,* 245–260.

Makin, J. W., & Porter, R. H. (1989). Attractiveness of lactating females' breast odors to neonates. *Child Development, 60,* 803–810.

Makin, P. J., & Hoyle, D. J. (1993). The Premack principle: Professional engineers. *Leadership and Organization Development Journal, 14,* 16–21.

Makoul, G. (1998). Perpetuating passivity: Reliance and reciprocal determinism in physician-patient interaction. *Journal of Health Communication, 3,* 233–259.

Malik, M. L., & Beutler, L. E. (2002). The emergence of dissatisfaction with the DSM. In L. E. Beutler & M. L. Malik (Eds.), *Rethinking the DSM: A psychological perspective* (pp. 3–15). *Decade of behavior.* Washington, DC: American Psychological Association.

Malka, A., & Chatman, J. A. (2003). Intrinsic and extrinsic work orientations as moderators of the effect of annual income on subjective well-being: A longitudinal study. *Personality and Social Psychology Bulletin, 29,* 737–746.

Malnic, B., Hirono, J., Sato, T., & Buck, L. B. (1999). Combinatorial receptor codes for odors. *Cell, 96,* 713–723.

Malone, J. C., & Cruchon, N. M. (2001). Radical behaviorism and the rest of psychology: A review/précis of Skinner's "About Behaviorism." *Behavior & Philosophy, 29,* 31–57.

Malone, S. M., Taylor, J., Marmorstein, N. R., McGue, M., & Iacono, W. G. (2004). Genetic and environmental influences on antisocial behavior and alcohol dependence from adolescence to early adulthood. *Development and Psychopathology, 16,* 943–966.

Malt, B. C. (1995). Category coherence in cross-cultural perspective. *Cognitive Psychology, 29,* 85–148.

Manabe, T., Noda, Y., Mamiya, T., Katagirl, H., Houtani, T., Nishi, M., Noda, T., Takahashi, T., Sugimoto, T., Nabeshima, T., & Takeshima, H. (1998). Facilitation of long-term potentiation and memory in mice lacking nociceptin receptors. *Nature, 394,* 677–581.

Mancia, M. (1981). On the beginning of mental life in the foetus. *International Journal of Psycho-Analysis, 62,* 351–357.

Mandler, G., & Pearlstone, Z. (1966). Free and constrained concept learning and subsequent recall. *Journal of Verbal Learning and Verbal Behavior, 5,* 126–131.

Mann, C. C. (1994). Behavioral genetics in transition. *Science, 264,* 1686–1689.

Mantell, D. M. (1971). The potential for violence in Germany. *Journal of Social Issues, 27,* 101–112.

Mantyla, T. (1986). Optimizing cue effectiveness: Recall of 500 and 600 incidentally learned words. *Journal of Experimental Psychology: Learning, Memory, and Cognition, 12,* 66–71.

Manuck, S. B., Flory, J. D., Muldoon, M. F., & Ferrell, R. E. (2002). Central nervous system serotonergic responsivity and aggressive disposition in men. *Physiology & Behavior, 77,* 705–709.

Marcincuk, M. C., & Roland, P. S. (2002). Geriatric hearing loss: Understanding the causes and providing appropriate treatment. *Geriatrics Advisor, 57,* 44–59.

Marcus, B. H., Lewis, B. A., King, T. K., Albrecht, A. E., Hogan, J., Bock, B., Parisi, A. F., & Abrams, D. B. (2003). Rationale, design, and baseline data for Commit to Quit II: An evaluation of the efficacy of moderate-intensity physical activity as an aid to smoking cessation in women. *Preventive Medicine, 36,* 479–492.

Marcus, D. K., & Miller, R. S. (2003). Sex differences in judgments of physical attractiveness: A social relations analysis. *Personality and Social Psychology Bulletin, 29,* 325–335.

Marcus, G. F. (1996). Why do children say "breaked"? *Current Directions in Psychological Science, 5,* 81–85.

Marczinski, C. A., Davidson, W., & Kertesz, A. (2004). A longitudinal study of behavior in frontotemporal dementia and primary progressive aphasia. *Cognitive & Behavioral Neurology, 17,* 185–190.

Marechal, J., & Thorold, A. I. (2004). *The psychology of the mystics.* Mineola, NY: Dover.

Marelich, W. D., Gaines, S. O., Jr., & Branzet, M. R. (2003). Commitment, insecurity and arousability: Testing a transactional model of jealousy. *Representative Research in Social Psychology, 27,* 23–31.

Margalit, M. (1995). Effects of social skills training for students with an intellectual disability. *International Journal of Disability, Development and Education, 42,* 75–85.

Margolskee, R. (1995). Receptor mechanisms in gustation. In R. L. Doty (Ed.), *Handbook of olfaction and gustation.* New York: Marcel Dekker.

Marín, G. (1994). The experience of being a Hispanic in the United States. In W. J. Lonner & R. Malpass (Eds.), *Psychology and culture.* Boston: Allyn & Bacon.

Mark, M. M., & Mellor, S. (1991). Effect of self-relevance of an event on hindsight bias: The foreseeability of a layoff. *Journal of Applied Psychology, 76,* 569–577.

Markey, P. M. (2000). Bystander intervention in computer-mediated communication. *Computers in Human Behavior, 16,* 183–188.

Markman, A. B. (1999). *Knowledge representation.* Mahwah, NJ: Erlbaum.

Markman, A. B., & Gentner, D. (2001). Thinking. *Annual Review of Psychology, 52,* 223–247.

Marks, I. M. (2004). The Nobel prize award in physiology to Ivan Petrovich Pavlov - 1904. *Australian & New Zealand Journal of Psychiatry, 38,* 674–677.

Marks, S. B. (1997). Reducing prejudice against children with disabilities in inclusive settings. *International Journal of Disability, Development and Education, 44,* 117–131.

Markus, H., & Kitayama, S. (1991). The cultural psychology of personality. *The Journal of Cross-Cultural Psychology, 29,* 63–87.

Marlowe, F., & Westman. Preferred waist-to-hip ratio and ecology. *Personality and Individual Differences, 30,* 481–489.

Marsh, H. W., Craven, R. G., & Debus, R. (1991). Self-concepts of young children 5 to 8 years of age: Measurement and multidimensional structure. *Journal of Educational Psychology, 83,* 377–392.

Marshall, N. L. (2004). The quality of early child care and children's development. *Current Directions in Psychological Science, 13,* 165–168.

Marshall, S. P. (1995). *Schemas in problem solving.* Cambridge: Cambridge University Press.

Martens, R. (1969). Effects of an audience on learning and performance of a complex motor skill. *Journal of Personality and Social Psychology, 12,* 252–260.

Marthol, H., & Hilz, M. J. (2004). Female sexual dysfunction: A systematic overview of classification, pathophysiology, diagnosis and treatment. *Fortschritte der Neurologie, Psychiatrie, 72,* 121–135.

Martin, B. R. (1995). Marijuana. In F. E. Bloom & D. J. Kupfer (Eds.), *Psychopharmacology: The fourth generation* (pp. 1757–1765). New York: Raven Press.

Martin, C. L., & Ruble, D. (2004). Children's search for gender cues: Cognitive perspectives on gender development. *Current Directions in Psychological Science, 13,* 67–70.

Martin, E. (Ed.). (2000). *Dictionary of medicines.* New York: Market House Books.

Martin, P., & Bateson, P. (1993). *Measuring behaviour: An introductory guide* (2nd ed.). Cambridge, England: Cambridge University Press.

Martindale, C. (1991). *Cognitive psychology: A neural-network approach.* Pacific Grove, CA: Brooks/Cole.

Martino, G., & Marks, L. E. (2001). Synesthesia: Strong and weak. *Current Directions in Psychological Science, 10,* 61–65.

Maruta, T., Colligan, R. C., Malinchoc, M., & Offord, K. P. (2000). Optimism versus pessimism: Survival rate among medical patients over a 30-year period. *Mayo Clinic Proceedings, 75,* 140–143.

Marx, E. (1999). Gender processing in speech production: Evidence from German speech errors. *Journal of Psycholinguistic Research, 28,* 601–621.

Masaki, T., Chiba, S., Noguchi, H., Yasuda, T., Tobe, K., Suzuki, R., Kadowaki, T., & Yoshimatsu, H. (2004). Obesity in insulin receptor substrate-2-deficient mice: Disrupted control of arcuate nucleus neuropeptides. *Obesity Research, 12,* 878–885.

Masataka, N. (1996). Perception of motherese in a signed language by 6-month-old deaf infants. *Developmental Psychology, 32,* 874–879.

Maslow, A. (1970). *Motivation and personality* (2nd ed.). New York: Harper & Row.

Maslow, A. (1971). *The farther reaches of human nature.* New York: Viking Press.

Mason, D. J., Humphreys, G. W., & Kent, L. (2004). Visual search, singleton capture, and the control of attentional set in ADHD. *Cognitive Neuropsychology, 21,* 661–687.

Mason, J. (1968). A review of the psychoendocrine research on the pituitary adrenal cortisol system. *Psychosomatic Medicine, 30,* 576–607.

Mason, J. (1975). A historical review of the stress field. *Journal of Human Stress, 1,* 22–36.

Mason, J. W. (1971). A re-evaluation of the concept of non-specificity in stress theory. *Journal of Psychiatric Research, 8,* 323–333.

Mason, W. A. (1997). Discovering behavior. *American Psychologist, 52,* 713–720.

Masson, J. M. (1999). *The emperor's embrace: Reflections on animal families and fatherhood.* New York: Pocket Books.

Masten, A. S. (2001). Ordinary magic: Resilience, processes in development. *American Psychologist, 56,* 227–238.

Masters, M. S., & Sanders, B. (1993). Is the gender difference in mental rotation disappearing? *Behavior Genetics, 23,* 337–341.

Masters, R. E. L., & Houston, J. (1966). *The varieties of psychedelic experience.* New York: Delta.

Masters, W., & Johnson, V. (1966). *Human sexual response.* Boston: Little, Brown.

Mathes, E. W., Adams, H. E., & Davies, R. M. (1985). Jealousy: Loss of relationship rewards, loss of self-esteem, depression, anxiety, and anger. *Journal of Personality and Social Psychology, 48,* 1552–1561.

Matsumoto, D. (1994). *People: Psychology from a cultural perspective.* Pacific Grove, CA: Brooks/Cole.

Matsumoto, D., Kudoh, J., Scherer, K., & Wallbott, H. (1988). Antecedents and reactions to emotions in the United States and Japan. *Journal of Cross-Cultural Psychology, 19,* 267–286.

Matthews, K. A. (1992). Myths and realities of the menopause. *Psychosomatic Medicine, 54,* 1–9.

Matthews, K. A., Salomon, K., Brady, S. S., & Michael, T. (2003). Cardiovascular reactivity to stress predicts future blood pressure in adolescence. *Psychosomatic Medicine, 65,* 410–415.

Mattingly, J. B., Rich, A. N., Yelland, G., & Bradshaw, J. L. (2001). Unconscious priming eliminates automatic binding of colour and alphanumeric form in synaesthesia. *Nature, 410,* 580–582.

Mattlar, C.-E. (2004). The Rorschach comprehensive system is reliable, valid, and cost-effective. In A. Andronikof (Ed.), *Rorschachiana XXVI: Yearbook of the International Rorschach Society* (pp. 158–186). Ashland, OH: Hogrefe & Huber Publishers.

Matusov, E., & Hayes, R. (2000). Sociocultural critique of Piaget and Vygotsky. *New Ideas in Psychology, 18,* 215–239.

Matute, H. (1995). Human reactions to uncontrollable outcomes: Further evidence for superstitions rather than helplessness. *Quarterly Journal of Experimental Psychology: Comparative and Physiological Psychology, 48,* 142–157.

Mavromatis, A. (1991). *Hypnagogia: The unique state of consciousness between wakefulness and sleep.* London: Routledge.

Mawhinney, V. T., Boston, D. E., Loaws, O. R., Blumenfeld, G. T., & Hopkins, B. L. (1971). A comparison of students' studying behavior produced by daily, weekly, and three-week testing schedules. *Journal of Applied Behavior Analysis, 4,* 257–264.

May, J., & Kline, P. (1987). Measuring the effects upon cognitive abilities of sleep loss during continuous operations. *The British Psychological Society, 78,* 443–455.

May, R. (1959). *The discovery of being: Writings in existential psychology.* New York: Norton.

May, R. (1990). Will, decision, and responsibility. *Review of Existential Psychiatry, 20,* 269–278.

Mayer, J. D., & Salovey, P. (1997). What is emotional intelligence? In P. Salovey & D. Sluyter (Eds.), *Emotional development, emotional literacy, and emotional intelligence.* New York: Basic Books.

Mayer, J. D., Salovey, P., & Caruso, D. (2000). In R. J. Sternberg (Ed.), *Handbook of intelligence* (pp. 396–420). Cambridge: Cambridge University Press.

Maynard, A. E. (2002). Cultural teaching: The development of teaching skills in Maya sibling interactions. *Child Development, 73,* 969–982.

Mayrhauser, R. T. V. (2002). The mental testing community and validity: A prehistory. In W. E. Pickren & D. A. Dewsbury (Eds.), *Evolving perspectives on the history of psychology* (pp. 303–324). Washington, DC: American Psychological Association.

McAdams, D. P. (1988). Personal needs and personal relationships. In S. Duck (Ed.), *Handbook of personal relationships: Theory, research and interventions* (pp. 7–22). New York: Wiley.

McAdoo, H. P. (2002). The village talks: Racial socialization of our children. In H. P. McAdoo (Ed.), *Black children: Social, educational, and parental environments* (2nd ed., pp. 47–55). Thousand Oaks, CA: Sage.

McAndrew, F. T. (2002). New evolutionary perspectives on altruism: Multilevel-selection and costly-signaling theories. *Current Directions in Psychological Science, 11,* 79–82.

McArthur, L. Z. (1982). Judging a book by its cover: A cognitive analysis of the relationship between physical appearance and stereotyping. In A. H. Hastorf & A. M. Isen (Eds.), *Cognitive social psychology* (pp. 149–211). New York: Elsevier/North Holland.

McAuliffe, S. P., & Knowlton, B. J. (2001). Hemispheric differences in object identification. *Brain & Cognition, 45,* 119–128.

McBride, R. E., Xiang, P., & Wittenburg, D. (2002). Dispositions toward critical thinking: The preservice teacher's perspective. *Teachers & Teaching: Theory & Practice, 8,* 29–40.

McBride, W. (2004). Health of thalidomide victims and their progeny. *Lancet, 363,* 169.

McCabe, R., & Quayle, E. (2002). Knowing your own mind. *Psychologist, 15,* 14–16.

McCall, R. B., & Carriger, M. S. (1993). A meta-analysis of infant habituation and recognition memory performance as predictors of later IQ. *Child Development, 64,* 57–79.

McCann, S. J. H. (1999). Threatening times and fluctuations in American church memberships. *Personality and Social Psychology Bulletin, 25,* 325–336.

McCarthy, G. (1995). Functional neuroimaging of memory. *The Neuroscientist, 1,* 155–163.

McCarthy, R. E. (1992). *Secrets of Hollywood: Special effects.* Stoneham, MA: Focal Press.

McCaul, K. D., & Malott, J. (1984). Distraction and coping with pain. *Psychological Bulletin, 95,* 516–533.

McClain, C. S., Rosenfeld, B., & Breitbart, W. (2003). The influence of spirituality on end-of-life despair among terminally ill cancer patients. *Lancet, 361,* 1603–1607.

McClearn, G. E. (1993). Behavioral genetics: The last century and the next. In R. Plomin & G. E. McClearn (Eds.), *Nature, nurture, and psychology.* Washington, DC: American Psychological Association.

McClelland, D. C. (1985). *Human motivation.* Glenview, IL: Scott, Foresman.

McClelland, D. C. (1995). Achievement motivation in relation to achievement-related recall, performance, and urine flow, a marker associated with release of vasopressin. *Motivation and Emotion, 19,* 59–76.

McClelland, D. C., Atkinson, J., Clark, R., & Lowell, E. (1953). *The achievement motive.* New York: Appleton-Century-Crofts.

McClelland, J. L. (1994). The organization of memory: A parallel distributed processing perspective. *Revue Neurologique, 150,* 570–579.

McClelland, J. L., & Rumelhart, D. E. (1981). An interactive activation model of context effects in letter perception: Part I. An account of basic findings. *Psychological Review, 102,* 375–407.

McClintock, M. K. (1971). Menstrual synchrony and suppression. *Nature, 229,* 244–245.

McConkey, K. M. (1992). The effects of hypnotic procedures on remembering: The experimental findings and their implications for forensic hypnosis. In E. Fromm & M. R. Nash (Eds.), *Contemporary hypnosis research* (pp. 405–426). New York: Guilford Press.

McConnell, A. R., & Fazio, R. H. (1996). Women as men and people: Effects of gender-marked language. *Personality and Social Psychology Bulletin, 22,* 1004–1013.

McCoy, S. K., & Major, B. (2003). Group identification moderates emotional responses to perceived prejudice. *Personality and Social Psychology Bulletin, 29,* 1005–1017.

McCrae, R. R. (1994). Openness to experience: Expanding the boundaries of Factor V. *European Journal of Personality, 13,* 39–55.

McCrae, R. R. (1996). Social consequences of experiential openness. *Psychological Bulletin, 52,* 509–516.

McCrae, R. R., and Costa, P. T., Jr. (1987). Validation of a five-factor model of personality across instruments and observers. *Journal of Personality and Social Psychology, 52,* 81–90.

McCrae, R. R., & Costa, P. T., Jr. (1990). Personality trait structure as a human universal. *American Psychologist, 52,* 509–516.

McCrae, R. R., & Costa, P. T., Jr. (1997a). Conceptions and correlates of openness to experience. In R. Hogan, J. Johnson, & S. Briggs (Eds.), *Handbook of personality psychology* (pp. 825–847). San Diego, CA: Academic Press.

McCrae, R. R., & Costa, P. T., Jr. (1997b). Personality structure as a human universal. *American Psychologist, 52,* 509–516.

McCrae, R. R., Costa, P. T., Jr., de Lirna, M. P., Simoes, A., Ostendorf, F., Angleitner, A., Marusic, I., Bratko, D., Caprara, G. V., Barbaranelli, G., Chae, J.-H., & Piedmont, R. L. (1999). Age differences in personality across the adult life span: Parallels in five cultures. *Developmental Psychology, 35,* 466–477.

McCrae, R. R., Costa, P. T., Jr., del Pilar, G. H., Rolland, J. P., & Parker, W. D. (1998). Cross-cultural assessment of the five-factor model: The revised NEO personality inventory. *Journal of Cross-Cultural Psychology, 29,* 171–188.

McCrae, R. R., & John, O. P. (1992). An introduction to the five-factor model and its applications. *Journal of Personality, 60,* 175–215.

McCready, D. (1999). *The moon illusion explained.* Mailed to illusion researchers and placed on http://facstaff.uww.edu/mccreadd/. Revised December 2002.

McCullough, M., Rachal, K., Steven, J., Worthington, E., Brown, S., & Hight, T. (1998). Interpersonal forgiving in close relationships II: Theoretical elaboration and measurement. *Journal of Personality and Social Psychology, 75,* 1586–1603.

McCullough, M. E., Hoyt, W. T., Larson, D. B., Koenig, H. G., & Thoresen, C. E. (2000). Religious involvement and mortality: A meta-analytic review. *Health Psychology, 19,* 211–222.

McCullough, M. E., & Laurenceau, J.-P. (2005). Religiousness and the trajectory of self-rated health across adulthood. *Personality and Social Psychology Bulletin, 31,* 560–573.

McDougall, I., Brown, F. H., & Fleagle, J. G. (2005). Stratigraphic placement and age of modern humans from Kibish, Ethiopia. *Nature, 433,* 733–736.

McDougall, W. (1908). *Introduction to social psychology.* London: Methuen & Co.

McEwen, B. S. (2000). The effects of stress on structural and functional plasticity in the hippocampus. In D. S. Charney, E. J. Nestler, & B. S. Bunney (Eds.), *Neurobiology of mental illness* (pp. 475–493). New York: Oxford University Press.

McGarry-Roberts, P. A., Stelmack, R. M., & Campbell, K. B. (1992). Intelligence, reaction time, and event-related potentials. *Intelligence, 16,* 289–313.

McGarty, C., Yzerbyt, V. Y., & Spears, R. (Eds.). (2002). *Stereotypes as explanations: The formation of meaningful beliefs about social groups.* New York: Cambridge University Press.

McGaugh, J. L. (2004). The amygdala modulates the consolidation of memories of emotionally arousing experiences. *Annual Review of Neuroscience, 27,* 1–28.

McGee, M. T. (1989). *Beyond ballyhoo: Motion picture promotion and gimmicks.* Jefferson, NC: McFarland.

McGeoch, J. A., & McDonald, W. T. (1931). Meaningful relation and retroactive inhibition. *American Journal of Psychology, 43,* 579–588.

McGlone, J. (1978). Sex differences in functional brain asymmetry. *Cortex, 14,* 122–128.

McGlynn, F. D., Moore, P. M., Lawyer, S., & Karg, R. (1999). Relaxation training inhibits fear and arousal during in vivo exposure to phobia-cue stimuli. *Journal of Behavior Therapy and Experimental Psychiatry, 30,* 155–168.

McGue, M., Bouchard, T. J., Jr., Iacono, W. G., & Lykken, D. T. (1993). Behavioral genetics of cognitive ability: A life-span perspective. In R. Plomin & G. E. McClearn (Eds.), *Nature, nurture and psychology.* Washington, DC: American Psychological Association.

McGue, M., Pickens, R. W., & Svikis, D. S. (1992). Sex and age effects on the inheritance of alcohol problems: A twin study. *Journal of Abnormal Psychology, 202,* 3–17.

McHugh, P. R. (1995). Witches, multiple personalities, and other psychiatric artifacts. *Nature Medicine, 1,* 110–114.

McHugh, P. R., Lief, H. I., Freyd, P. P., & Fetkewicz, J. M. (2004). From refusal to reconciliation: Family relationships after an accusation based on recovered memories. *Journal of Nervous & Mental Disease, 192,* 525–531.

McKinnon, J. W. (1976). The college student and formal operations. In J. W. Renner, D. G. Stafford, A. E. Lawson, J. W. McKinnon, F. E. Friot, & D. H. Kellog (Eds.), *Research training and learning with the Piaget model* (pp. 110–129). Norman: University of Oklahoma Press.

McKinnon, J. W., & Renner, J. W. (1971). Are colleges concerned with intellectual development? *American Journal of Psychology, 39,* 1047–1052.

McLean, J. H., & Shipley, M. T. (1992). Neuroanatomical substrates of olfaction. In M. J. Serby & K. L. Chobor (Eds.), *Science of olfaction* (pp. 126–171). New York: Springer-Verlag.

McManis, M. H., Kagan, J., Snidman, N. C., & Woodward, S. A. (2002). EEG asymmetry, power, and temperament in children. *Developmental Psychobiology, 41,* 169–177.

McMillan, B., Sherlock, K., & Conner, M. (2003). Expanding the traditional user versus non-user dichotomy amongst ecstasy users. *Journal of Community & Applied Social Psychology, 13,* 15–28.

McMullin, E. (1983). Values in science. In P. D. Asquith & T. Nickles (Eds.), *Proceedings of the 1982 Philosophy of Science Association* (Vol. 2, pp. 3–23). East Lansing, MI: Philosophy of Science Association.

McNally, R. J. (2003). *Remembering trauma.* Cambridge, MA: Harvard University Press.

McNamera, P., McLaren, D., Smith, D., Brown, A., & Stickgold, R. (2005). A "Jekyll and Hyde" within: Aggressive versus friendly interactions in REM and non-REM dreams. *Psychological Science, 16,* 130–136.

McNaughton, B. L., Barnes, C. A., Battaglia, F. P., Bower, M. R., Cowen, S. L., Ekstrom, A. D., Gerrard, J. L., Hoffman, K. L., Houston, F. P., Karten, Y., Lipa, P., Pennartz, C. M. A., & Sutherland, G. R. (2003). Off-line reprocessing of recent memory and its role in memory consolidation: A progress report. In P. Maquet, C. Smith, & R. Stickgold (Eds.), *Sleep and brain plasticity* (pp. 225–246). Oxford, England: Oxford University Press.

McNeil, B. J., Pauker, S. G., Sox, H. C., Jr., & Tversky, A. (1982). On the elicitation of preferences for alternative therapies. *New England Journal of Medicine, 306,* 1259–1262.

McNeill, M. C., & Wang, C. K. J. (2005). Psychological profiles of elite school sports players in Singapore. *Psychology of Sport and Exercise, 6,* 117–128.

McShane, D. A., & Plas, J. M. (1984). The cognitive functioning of American Indian children: Moving from the WISC to the WISC-R. *School Psychology Review, 13,* 61–73.

Mebert, C., & Michel, G. (1980). Handedness in artists. In J. Herron (Ed.), *Neuropsychology of left handedness.* New York: Academic Press.

Medin, D. L. (1989). Concepts and conceptual structure. *American Psychologist, 44,* 1469–1481.

Mednick, S. A. (1958). A learning theory approach to research in schizophrenia. *Psychological Bulletin, 55,* 316–327.

Mednick, S. A., Gabrielli, W. F., & Hutchings, B. (1987). Genetic factors in the etiology of criminal behavior. In S. A. Stacks (Ed.), *The causes of crime: New biological approaches* (pp. 267–291). Cambridge, MA: Cambridge University Press.

Medvec, V. H., Madley, S. F., & Gilovich, T. (1995). When less is more: Counterfactual thinking and satisfaction among Olympic medallists. *Journal of Personality and Social Psychology, 69,* 603–610.

Mehrabian, A. (1972). *Nonverbal communication.* Chicago: Aldine-Atherton.

Meichenbaum, D., & Turk, D. (1976). The cognitive-behavioral management of anxiety, anger, and pain. In P. O. Davidson (Ed.), *The behavioral management of anxiety, depression and pain* (pp. 1–34). New York: Brunner/Mazel.

Meichenbaum, D. H., Bowers, K. S., & Ross, R. R. (1969). A behavioral analysis of teacher expectancy effects. *Journal of Personality and Social Psychology, 13*, 306–316.

Meikle, L., McMullen, J. R., Sherwood, M. C., Lader, A. S., Walker, V., Chan, J. A., & Kwiatkowski, D. J. (2005). A mouse model of cardiac rhabdomyoma generated by loss of *Tsc1* in ventricular myocytes. *Human Molecular Genetics, 14*, 429–435.

Meins, E. (1999). Sensitivity, security, and internal working models: Bridging the transmission gap. *Attachment and Human Development, 1*, 325–342.

Meisel, S., Kutz, I., Dayan, K., et al. (1991). Effect of Iraqi missile war on incidence of acute myocardial infarction and sudden death in Israeli civilians. *Lancet, 338*, 660–661.

Melis, M. R., & Argiolas, A. (1993). Nitric oxide synthase inhibitors prevent apomorphine- and oxytocin-induced penile erection and yawning in male rats. *Brain Research Bulletin, 32*, 71–74.

Mellinger, G. D., Balter, M. B., & Uhlenhuth, E. H. (1985). Insomnia and its treatment: Prevalence and its correlates. *Archives of General Psychiatry, 42*, 225–232.

Melton, A. W. (1963). Implications of short-term memory for a general theory of memory. *Journal of Verbal Learning and Verbal Behavior, 2*, 1–21.

Meltzer, H. Y. (1979). Biochemical studies in schizophrenia. In L. Bellak (Ed.), *Disorders of the schizophrenic syndrome* (pp. 45–135). New York: Basic Books.

Meltzer, H. Y. (2000). Genetics and etiology of schizophrenia and bipolar disorder. *Biological Psychiatry, 47*, 171–173.

Meltzoff, A. N., & Moore, M. K. (1977). Imitation of facial and manual gestures by human neonates. *Science, 198*, 75–78.

Meltzoff, A. N., & Moore, M. K. (1989). Imitation in newborn infants: Exploring the range of gestures imitated and the underlying mechanisms. *Developmental Psychology, 25*, 954–962.

Melzack, R. (1973). *The puzzle of pain.* New York: Basic Books.

Melzack, R. (1986). Neurophysiological foundations of pain. In R. A. Sternbach (Ed.), *The psychology of pain* (pp. 1–24). New York: Raven Press.

Melzack, R. (1992, April). Phantom limbs. *Scientific American, 266*, 120–126.

Melzack, R., & Wall, P. D. (1982a). *The challenge of pain.* Harmondsworth, England: Penguin.

Melzack, R., & Wall, P. D. (1982b). Pain mechanisms: A new theory. *Science, 13*, 971–979.

Menson, V., Boyett-Anderson, J. M., Schatzberg, S. F., & Reiss, A. L. (2002). Relating semantic and episodic memory systems. *Cognitive Brain Research, 13*, 261–265.

Menyuk, P., Liebergott, J. W., & Schultz, M. C. (1995). *Early language development in full-term and premature infants.* Hillsdale, NJ: Erlbaum.

Menzel, R., & Backhaus, W. (1989). Color vision in honey bees: Phenomena and physiological mechanisms. In D. G. Stavenga & R. C. Hardie (Eds.), *Facets of vision* (pp. 281–297). Berlin: Springer-Verlag.

Merikle, P. M., & Skanes, H. E. (1992). Subliminal self-help audiotapes: A search for placebo effects. *Journal of Applied Psychology, 77*, 772–776.

Merton, R. (1948). The self-fulfilling prophecy. *Antioch Review, 8*, 193–210.

Mesquita, B., & Frijda, N. (1992). Cultural variations in emotions: A review. *Psychological Bulletin, 112*, 179–204.

Messman, S. J., Canary, D. J., & Hause, K. S. (2000). Motives to remain platonic, equity, and the use of maintenance strategies in opposite-sex friendships. *Journal of Social and Personal Relationships, 17*, 67–94.

Michael, R., Gagnon, J., Laumann, E., & Kolata, G. (1994). *Sex in America.* New York: Little, Brown.

Middlebrooks, J. C., & Green, D. M. (1991). Sound localization by human listeners. *Annual Review of Psychology, 42*, 135–159.

Mihaylov, I. R., Batchelor, P., & Abbott, N. J. (2002). Quantitative evidence for production and convective flow of brain interstitial fluid. *The Journal of Physiology, 539*, 90.

Mikulincer, M., & Erev, I. (1991). Attachment style and the structure of romantic love. *British Journal of Social Psychology, 30*, 273–291.

Miley, W. M. (1999). *The psychology of well being.* Westport, CT: Praeger.

Milgram, S. (1963). Behavioral study of obedience. *Journal of Abnormal and Social Psychology, 67*, 371–378.

Milgram, S. (1965). Some conditions of obedience and disobedience to authority. *Human Relations, 18*, 57–76.

Milgram, S. (1974). *Obedience to authority: An experimental view.* New York: Harper & Row.

Miller, C., & Swift, K. (1991). *Words and women.* New York: HarperCollins.

Miller, E. M. (1994). Intelligence and brain myelination: A hypothesis. *Personality and Individual Differences, 17*, 803–832.

Miller, G. A. (1956). The magical number seven, plus or minus two: Some limits on our capacity to process information. *Psychological Review, 63*, 81–97.

Miller, G. A., & Gildea, P. M. (1987). How children learn words. *Scientific American, 257*, 94–99.

Miller, I. J., Jr. (1995). Anatomy of the peripheral taste system. In R. L. Doty (Ed.), *Handbook of olfaction and gustation.* New York: Marcel Dekker.

Miller, J. G. (1984). Culture and the development of everyday social explanation. *Journal of Personality and Social Psychology, 46*, 961–978.

Miller, J. G. (1994). Cultural diversity in the morality of caring: Individually-oriented versus duty-oriented interpersonal codes. *Cross-Cultural Research, 28*, 3–39.

Miller, J. J., Fletcher, K., & Kabat-Zinn, J. (1995). Three-year follow-up and clinical implications of a mindfulness meditation-based stress reduction intervention in the treatment of anxiety disorders. *General Hospital Psychiatry, 17*, 192–200.

Miller, L. C., Berg, J. H., & Archer, R. L. (1983). Openers: Individuals who elicit intimate self-disclosure. *Journal of Personality and Social Psychology, 44*, 1234–1244.

Miller, N., Pedersen, W. C., Earleywine, M., & Pollock, V. E. (2003). A theoretical model of triggered displaced aggression. *Personality and Social Psychology Review, 7*, 75–97.

Miller, N. E. (1985). The value of behavior research on animals. *American Psychologist, 40*, 423–440.

Miller, P. J. E., & Rempel, J. K. (2004). Trust and partner-enhancing attributions in close relationships. *Personality and Social Psychology Bulletin, 30*, 695–705.

Miller, R. R., & Grace, R. C. (2003). Conditioning and learning. In A. F. Healy, R. W. Proctor, & W. Robert (Eds.), *Handbook of psychology: Experimental psychology* (Vol. 4, pp. 357–397). New York: Wiley.

Miller, R. S. (1997). We always hurt the ones we love: Aversive interactions in close relationships. In R. M. Kowalski (Ed.), *Aversive interpersonal behaviors* (pp. 11–29). New York: Plenum Press.

Miller, W. C. (1999). Fitness and fatness in relation to health: Implications for a paradigm shift. *Journal of Social Issues, 55*, 207–220.

Miller, W. I. (1997). *The anatomy of disgust.* Cambridge, MA: Harvard University Press.

Miller, W. R., & Hester, R. K. (1980). Treating the problem drinker. In W. R. Miller (Ed.), *The addictive behaviors: Treatment of alcoholism, drug abuse, smoking, and obesity* (pp. 11–141). New York: Pergamon.

Mills, C. B., Viguers, M. L., Edelson, S. K., Thomas, A. T., Simon-Dack, S. L., & Innis, J. A. (2002). The color of two alphabets for a multilingual synesthete. *Perception, 31*, 1371–1394.

Mills, D. L., Coffey-Corina, S., & Neville, H. J. (1997). Language comprehension and cerebral specialization from 13 to 20 months. *Developmental Neuropsychology, 13*, 397–445.

Mills, M., & Stunkard, A. (1976). Behavioral changes following surgery for obesity. *American Journal of Psychiatry, 133*, 527–531.

Mills, S. L., & Catania, K. C. (2004). Identification of retinal neurons in a regressive rodent eye (the naked mole-rat). *Visual Neuroscience, 21*, 107–117.

Milner, B., Corkin, S., & Teuber, H. L. (1968). Further analysis of the hippocampal amnesic syndrome: 14-year follow-up study of H. M. *Neuropsychologia, 6*, 317–338.

Miltenberger, R. G. (2001). *Behavior modification: Principles and procedures.* Pacific Grove, CA: Wadsworth.

Mindell, J. A. (1999). Sleep disorders. In A. J. Goreczny & M. Hersen (Eds.), *Handbook of pediatric and adolescent*

health psychology (pp. 371–386). Boston: Allyn & Bacon.

Mineka, S., & Öhman, A. (2002). Phobias and preparedness: The selective, automatic, and encapsulated nature of fear. *Biological Psychiatry, 52*, 927–937.

Mineka, S., & Zinbarg, R. (1995). Conditioning and ethological models of anxiety disorders: Stress-in-Dynamic-Context models. In D. A. Hope (Ed.), *Nebraska symposium on motivation, 1995: Perspectives of anxiety, panic, and fear. Current theory and research in motivation* (Vol. 43, pp. 135–210). Lincoln: University of Nebraska Press.

Minton, H. (2000). Psychology and gender at the turn of the century. *American Psychologist, 55*, 613–615.

Minturn, L., Grosse, M., & Haider, S. (1969). Cultural patterning of sexual beliefs and behavior. *Ethnology, 8*, 301–313.

Mintz, L. B., & Kashubeck, S. (1999). Body image and disordered eating among Asian American and Caucasian college students: An examination of race and gender differences. *Psychology of Women Quarterly, 23*, 781–796.

Mintzer, M. Z., & Griffiths, R. R. (2003). Triazolam-amphetamine interaction: Dissociation of effects on memory versus arousal. *Journal of Psychopharmacology, 17*, 17–29.

Mirmiran, M., & Ariagno, R. L. (2003). Role of REM sleep in brain development and plasticity. In P. Maquet, C. Smith, & R. Stickgold (Eds.), *Sleep and brain plasticity* (pp. 181–187). Oxford, England: Oxford University Press.

Mischel, W. (1968). *Personality and assessment.* New York: Wiley.

Mischel, W. (1984). Convergences and challenges in the search for consistency. *American Psychologist, 39*, 351–364.

Mischel, W., Cantor, N., & Feldman, S. (1996). Principles of self-regulation: The nature of willpower and self-control. In E. T. Higgins & A. W. Kruglanski (Eds.), *Social psychology: Handbook of basic principles* (pp. 329–360). New York: Guilford Press.

Mischel, W., & Shoda, Y. (1999). Integrating dispositions and processing dynamics within a unified theory of personality: The cognitive-affective personality system. In L. A. Pervin & O. P. John (Eds.), *Handbook of personality: Theory and research* (2nd ed., pp. 197–218). New York: Guilford Press.

Miserandino, M. (1991). Memory and the seven dwarfs. *Teaching of Psychology, 18*, 169–171.

Mistry, J., & Rogoff, B. (1994). Remembering in a cultural context. In W. J. Lonner & R. S. Malpass (Eds.), *Psychology and culture.* Boston: Allyn & Bacon.

Mita, T. H., Dermer, M., & Knight, J. (1977). Reversed facial images and the mere-exposure hypothesis. *Journal of Personality and Social Psychology, 35*, 597–601.

Mitchell, C. M., Novins, D. K., & Holmes, T. (1999). Marijuana use among American Indian adolescents: A growth curve analysis from ages 14 through 20 years. *Journal of the American Academy of Child & Adolescent Psychiatry, 38*, 72–78.

Mitchell, D. E. (1980). The influence of early visual experience on visual perception. In C. S. Harris (Ed.), *Visual coding and adaptability.* Hillsdale, NJ: Erlbaum.

Mittleman, M., Maclure, M., Sherwood, J., et al. (1995). Triggering of acute myocardial infarction onset by episodes of anger: Determinants of myocardial infarction onset study investigators. *Circulation, 92*, 1720–1725.

Moeller, A. T., & Steel, H. R. (2002). Clinically significant change after cognitive restructuring for adult survivors of childhood sexual abuse. *Journal of Rational-Emotive & Cognitive Behavior Therapy, 20*, 49–64.

Moely, B. E., Olson, F. A., Halwes, T. G., & Flavell, J. H. (1969). Production deficiency in young children's clustered recall. *Developmental Psychology, 1*, 26–34.

Mogg, K., & Bradley, B. P. (1999). Orienting of attention to threatening facial expressions presented under conditions of restricted awareness. *Cognition and Emotion, 12*, 713–740.

Mokdad, A., Serdula, M., Dietz, W., Bowman, B., Marks, J., & Koplan, J. (1999). The spread of the obesity epidemic in the United States, 1991–1998. *Journal of the American Medical Association, 282*, 1519–1522.

Mollon, J. D. (1990). The club-sandwich mystery. *Nature, 343,* 16–17.

Monane, M. (1992). Insomnia in the elderly. *Journal of Clinical Psychiatry, 53*(6, Suppl.), 23–28.

Mondloch, C. J., Lewis, T. L., Budreau, D. R., Maurer, D., Dannemiller, J. L., Stephens, B. R., & Kleiner-Gathercoal, K. A. (1999). Face perception during early infancy. *Psychological Science, 10,* 419–422.

Monk, T. H. (2000). What can the chronobiologist do to help the shift worker? *Journal of Biological Rhythms, 15,* 86–94.

Monk, T. M., & Folkard, S. (1992). *Making shift work tolerable.* London: Taylor & Francis.

Monroe, S. M., & Simons, A. D. (1991). Diathesis-stress theories in the context of life stress research: Implications for the depressive disorders. *Psychological Bulletin, 110,* 406–425.

Monsour, M. (1997). Communication and cross-sex friendship across the lifecycle: A review of the literature. *Communication Yearbook, 20,* 375–414.

Monteith, M. J. (1993). Self-regulation of prejudiced responses: Implications for progress in prejudice-reduction efforts. *Journal of Personality and Social Psychology, 65,* 469–485.

Monteith, M. J. (1996). Affective reactions to prejudice-related discrepant responses: The impact of standard salience. *Personality and Social Psychology Bulletin, 22,* 48–59.

Monteith, M. J., Sherman, J. W., & Devine, P. G. (1998). Suppression as a stereotype control strategy. *Personality and Social Psychology Review, 2,* 63–82.

Montepare, J. M., & Zebrowitz-McArthur, L. (1988). Impressions of people created by age-related qualities of their gaits. *Journal of Personality and Social Psychology, 55,* 547–556.

Moore, B. E., & Fine, B. D. (Eds). (1990). *Psychoanalytic terms and concepts.* New Haven, CT: The American Psychoanalytic Association and Yale University Press.

Moore, K. L., & Persaud, T. V. N. (1993). *Before we are born* (4th ed.). Philadelphia: Saunders.

Moore, R. Y. (1990). The circadian system and sleep-wake behavior. In J. Montplaisir & R. Godbout (Eds.). *Sleep and biological rhythms: Basic mechanisms and applications to psychiatry* (pp. 3–10). New York: Oxford University Press.

Moore, T. E. (1995). Subliminal self-help auditory tapes: An empirical test of perceptual consequences. *Canadian Journal of Behavioural Science, 27,* 9–20.

Moran, M. G., & Stoudemire, A. (1992). Sleep disorders in the medically ill patient. *Journal of Clinical Psychiatry, 53*(6, Suppl.), 29–36.

Morgan, D. L., & Morgan, R. K. (2001). Single-participant research design. *American Psychologist, 56,* 119–127.

Morgan, J. (1986). *From simple input to complex grammar.* Cambridge, MA: MIT Press.

Morgan, J., & Travis, L. (1989). Limits on negative information in language input. *Journal of Child Language, 16,* 531–532.

Morganstern, J., Labouvie, E., McGrady, B. S., Kahler, C. W., & Frey, R. M. (1997). Affiliation with Alcoholics Anonymous after treatment: A study of its therapeutic effects and mechanism of action. *Journal of Consulting and Clinical Psychology, 65,* 768–777.

Mori, R. C., Telles, M. M., Guimaraes, R. B., Novo, N. F., Juliano, Y., Nascimento, C. M., & Ribeiro, E. B. (2004). Feeding induced by increasing doses of neuropeptide Y: Dual effect on hypothalamic serotonin release in normal rats. *Nutritional Neuroscience, 7,* 235–239.

Morikawa, K. (2003). An application of the Mueller-Lyer illusion. *Perception, 32,* 121–123.

Morin, A. (2001). The split-brain debate revisited: On the importance of language and self-recognition for right hemispheric consciousness. *Journal of Mind and Behavior, 22,* 107–118.

Morin, C. M., Mimeault, V., & Gagne, A. (1999). Nonpharmacological treatment of late-life insomnia. *Journal of Psychosomatic Research, 46,* 103–116.

Morin, C. M., Rodrigue, S., & Ivers, H. (2003). Role of stress, arousal, and coping skills in primary insomnia. *Psychosomatic Medicine, 65,* 259–267.

Morley, J. (1998). The private theater: A phenomenological investigation of daydreaming. *Journal of Phenomenological Psychology, 29,* 116–134.

Morley, J., Levine, A., Bartness, T., Nizielski, S., Shaw, M., & Hughes, J. (1985). Species differences in the response to cholecystokinin. *Annals of the New York Academy of Sciences, 448,* 413–416.

Morling, B., & Epstein, S. (1997). Compromises produced by the dialectic between self-verification and self-enhancement. *Journal of Personality and Social Psychology, 73,* 1268–1283.

Morris, C. D., Bransford, J. D., & Franks, J. J. (1977). Levels of processing versus transfer appropriate processing. *Journal of Verbal Learning and Verbal Behavior, 16,* 519–533.

Morris, M. W., & Larrick, R. P. (1995). When one cause casts doubt on another: A normative analysis of discounting in causal attribution. *Psychological Review, 102,* 331–355.

Morton, J., & Johnson, M. H. (1991, April). CONSPEC and CONLEARN: A two-process theory of infant face recognition. *Psychological Review, 98,* 164–181.

Moses, L. J., & Chandler, M. J. (1992). Traveler's guide to children's theories of mind. *Psychological Inquiry, 3,* 286–301.

Moses, P., & Stiles, J. (2002). The lesion methodology: Contrasting views from adult and child studies. *Developmental Psychobiology, 40*(3), 266–277.

Moskowitz, J. T., Folkman, S., Collette, L., & Vittinghoff, E. (1996). Coping and mood during AIDS-related caregiving and bereavement. *Annals of Behavioral Medicine, 18,* 49–57.

Moss, D. (1999). Abraham Maslow and the emergence of humanistic psychology. In D. Moss (Ed.), *Humanistic and transpersonal psychology: A historical and biographical sourcebook* (pp. 24–37). Westport, CT: Greenwood Press.

Moss, E., Bureau, J.-F., Cyr, C., Mongeau, C., & St. Laurent, D. (2004). Correlates of attachment at age 3: Construct validity of the preschool attachment classification system. *Developmental Psychology, 40,* 323–334.

Motley, M. T. (1985). Slips of the tongue. *Scientific American, 253,* 116–127.

Motley, M. T., & Baars, B. J. (1979). Effects of cognitive set upon laboratory-induced verbal (Freudian) slips. *Journal of Speech and Hearing Research, 22,* 421–432.

Mouritsen, H., & Frost, B. J. (2002). Virtual migration in tethered flying monarch butterflies reveals their orientation mechanisms. *Proceedings of the National Academy of Sciences, 99,* 10162–10166.

Mowrer, O. H. (1947). On the dual nature of learning—A reinterpretation of "conditioning" and "problem-solving." *Harvard Education Review, 17,* 102–148.

Moynihan, J., & Stevens, S. (2001). Mechanisms of stress-induced modulation of immunity in animals. In R. Ader, D. Felten, & N. Cohen (Eds.), *Psychoneuroimmunology* (Vol. 2, 3rd ed., pp. 227–250). San Diego, CA: Academic Press.

Mozell, M. M., Smith, B. P., Smith, P. E., Sullivan, R. L., & Swender, P. (1969). Nasal chemoreception in flavor identification. *Archives of Otolaryngology, 90,* 131–137.

Mroczek, D. K., & Spiro, A. (2005). Change in life satisfaction during adulthood: Findings from the Veterans Affairs Normative Aging Study. *Journal of Personality and Social Psychology, 88,* 189–202.

Mulac, A., & Lundell, T. L. (1986). Linguistic contributors to the gender-linked language effect. *Journal of Language and Social Psychology, 5,* 81–101.

Mulkana, S. S., & Hailey, B.-J. (2001). The role of optimism in health-enhancing behavior. *American Journal of Health Behavior, 25,* 388–395.

Muller, J., Abela, G., Nestro, R., & Tofler, G. (1994). Triggers, acute risk factors, and vulnerable plaques: The lexicon of a new frontier. *Journal of the American College of Cardiology, 23,* 809–813.

Mulvany, F., O'Callaghan, E., Takei, N., Byrne, M., Fearson, P., & Larkin, C. (2001). Effect of social class at birth on risk and presentation of schizophrenia: Case control study. *British Medical Journal, 323,* 1398–1401.

Murphy, P. L., & Miller, C. T. (1997). Postdecisional dissonance and the commodified self-concept: A cross-cultural examination. *Personality and Social Psychology Bulletin, 23,* 50–62.

Murphy, S. (2000). Deaths: Final data for 1998. *National Vital Statistics Reports* (Vol. 48.) From www.cdc.gov/nchs/data/nvsr/nvsr48/nvs4811.pdf

Murray, C. J., & Lopez, A. D. (Eds.). (1996). *The global burden of disease: A comprehensive assessment of mortality and disability from diseases, injuries, and risk factors in 1990 and projected to 2020.* Cambridge, MA: Harvard University Press.

Murray, H. A. (1938). *Explorations in personality: A clinical and experimental study of fifty men of college age, by the workers at the Harvard Psychological Clinic.* New York: Oxford University Press.

Murray, H. A. (1948). *Assessment of men.* New York: Science Editions.

Murray, J. B. (1980). *Television and youth: 25 years of research and controversy.* Boys Town, NE: Boys Town Center for the Study of Youth Development.

Murray, S. L., & Holmes, J. G. (1997). A leap of faith? Positive illusions in romantic relationships. *Personality and Social Psychology Bulletin, 23,* 586–604.

Murray, S. L., & Holmes, J. G. (1999). The (mental) ties that bind: Cognitive structures that predict relationship resilience. *Journal of Personality and Social Psychology, 77,* 1228–1244.

Murray, S. L., Holmes, J. G., Bellavia, G., Griffin, D. W., & Dolderman, D. (2002). Kindred spirits? The benefits of egocentrism in close relationships. *Journal of Personality and Social Psychology, 82,* 563–581.

Murray, S. L., Holmes, J. G., & Griffin, D. W. (1996). The benefits of positive illusions: Idealization and the construction of satisfaction in close relationships. *Journal of Personality and Social Psychology, 70,* 79–98.

Murstein, B. I. (1972). Physical attractiveness and marital choice. *Journal of Personality and Social Psychology, 22,* 8–12.

Mussone, L., Ferrari, A., & Oneta, M. (1999). An analysis of urban collisions using an artificial intelligence model. *Accident Analysis and Prevention, 31,* 705–718.

Must, A., Spadano, J., Coakley, E., Field, A., Colditz, G., & Dietz, W. (1999). The disease burden associated with overweight and obesity. *Journal of the American Medical Association, 282,* 1523–1529.

Myers, A. M., & Rothblum, E. D. (2005). Coping with prejudice and discrimination based on weight. In J. L. Chin (Ed.), *The psychology of prejudice and discrimination: Disability, religion, physique, and other traits: Vol. 4. Race and ethnicity in psychology* (pp. 112–134). Westport, CT: Praeger/Greenwood.

Myers, D., & Diener, E. (1995). Who is happy? *Psychological Science, 6,* 10–19.

Nabuzoka, D., & Ronning, J. A. (1997). Social acceptance of children with intellectual disabilities in an integrated school setting in Zambia: A pilot study. *International Journal of Disability, Development and Education, 44,* 105–115.

Nadeau, S. N. (2001). Phonology: A review and proposals from a connectionist perspective. *Brain & Language, 79,* 511–579.

Nadel, L., & Zola-Morgan, S. (1984). Infantile amnesia: A neurobiological perspective. In M. Moscovitch (Ed.), *Infant memory.* New York: Plenum Press.

Nair, K. U., & Ramnarayan, S. (2000). Individual differences in need for cognition and complex problem solving. *Journal of Research in Personality, 34,* 305–328.

Nairne, J. S. (2003). Sensory and working memory. In A. F. Healy & R. W. Proctor (Eds.), *Handbook of psychology: Experimental psychology* (Vol. 4, pp. 423–444). New York: Wiley.

Nakajima, M., Nakajima, S., & Imada, H. (2000). General learned irrelevance and its prevention. *Learning and Motivation, 30,* 265–280.

Nakiyingi, J. S., Bracher, M., Whitworth, J. A. G., Ruberantwari, A., Busingye, J., Mbulaiteye, S. M., & Zaba, B. (2003). Child survival in relation to mother's HIV infection and survival: Evidence from a Ugandan cohort study. *AIDS, 17,* 1827–1834.

Nardi, P. M., & Sherrod, D. (1994). Friendship in the lives of gay men and lesbians. *Journal of Social and Personal Relationships, 11,* 185–199.

Narikiyo, T. A., & Kameoka, V. A. (1992). Attributions of mental illness and judgments about help seeking among Japanese-American and white American students. *Journal of Counseling Psychology, 39,* 363–369.

Narrow, W. E., Rae, D. S., Robins, L. N., & Regier, D. A. (2002). Revised prevalence based estimates of mental disorders in the United States: Using a clinical signficance criterion to reconcile 2 surveys' estimates. *Archives of General Psychiatry, 59,* 115–123.

Nash, J. M. (1997, May 5). Addicted: Why do people get hooked? Mounting evidence points to a powerful brain chemical dopamine. *Time,* 68–76.

Nash, M. (1987). What, if anything, is regressed about hypnotic age regression? A review of the empirical literature. *Psychological Bulletin, 102,* 42–52.

Nathan, P. (1982). *The nervous system* (2nd ed.). Oxford, England: Oxford University Press.

Nathan, P. E., & Gorman, J. M. (Eds.). (2002). *A guide to treatments that work* (2nd ed.). London: Oxford University Press.

National Academy of Sciences. (1999). Marijuana and medicine: Assessing the science base (by J. A. Benson, Jr., and S. J. Watson, Jr.). Washington, DC: National Academy Press.

National Opinion Research Center. (2003). General Social Survey. www.norc.org/

National Research Council and Institute of Medicine, Division of Behavioral and Social Sciences and Education, Board on Children, Youth, and Families, Committee on Family and Work Policies. (2003). *Working families and growing kids: Caring for children and adolescents* (E. Smolensky & J. A. Gootman, Eds.). Washington, DC: National Academies Press. http://www.nap.edu/openbook/0309087031/html/R1.html

National Sleep Foundation. (2002). *2001 Sleep in America Poll.* Retrieved July 30, 2002, from www.sleepfoundation.org/img/2002sleepInAmericaPoll.pdf

Naveh-Benjamin, M. (1990). The acquisition and retention of knowledge: Exploring mutual benefits to memory research and the educational setting. *Applied Cognitive Psychology, 4,* 295–320.

Neher, A. (1996). Jung's theory of archetypes: A critique. *Journal of Humanistic Psychology, 36,* 61–91.

Neisser, U. (1982). Snapshots or benchmarks? In U. Neisser (Ed.), *Memory observed* (pp. 43–48). San Francisco: Freeman.

Neisser, U., Boodoo, G., Bouchard, T. J., Jr., Boykin, A. W., Brody, N., Ceci, S. J., Halpern, D. F., Loehlin, J. C., Perloff, R., Sternberg, R. J., & Urbina, S. (1996). Intelligence: Knowns and unknowns. *American Psychologist, 51,* 77–101.

Neisser, U., & Harsch, N. (1992). Phantom flashbulbs: False recollections of hearing the news about *Challenger.* In E. Winograd & U. Neisser (Eds.), *Affect and accuracy in recall: Studies of "flashbulb" memories* (pp. 9–31). New York: Cambridge University Press.

Nelson, C. A. (1999). Neural plasticity and human development. *Current Directions in Psychological Science, 8,* 42–45.

Nelson, D. L., Schreiber, T. A., & McEvoy, C. L. (1992). Processing implicit and explicit representations. *Psychological Review, 99,* 322–348.

Nelson, E. S., Karr, K. M., & Coleman, P. K. (1995). Relationships among daily hassles, optimism and reported physical symptoms. *Journal of College Student Psychotherapy, 10,* 11–26.

Nelson, K., Skwerer, D. P., Goldman, G. S., Henseler, S., Presler, N., & Walkenfeld, F. F. (2003). Entering a community of minds: An experiential approach to "theory of mind." *Human Development, 46,* 24–46.

Nelson, L., Badger, S., & Wu, B. (2004). The influence of culture in emerging adulthood: Perspectives of Chinese college students. *International Journal of Behavioral Development, 28,* 26–36.

Nelson, R. (2000). *An introduction to behavioral endocrinology* (2nd ed.). Sunderland, MA: Sinauer Associates.

Nelson, T. F., & Wechsler, H. (2003). School spirits: Alcohol and collegiate sports fans. *Addictive Behaviors, 28,* 1–11.

Nemeroff, C. B. (1998, June). The neurobiology of depression. *Scientific American,* 42–49.

Nettelbeck, T., & Wilson, C. (2004). The Flynn effect: Smarter not faster. *Intelligence, 32,* 85–93.

Neugarten, B. L., Wood, V., Kraines, R. J., & Loomis, B. (1963). Women's attitudes toward the menopause. *Vita Humana, 6,* 140–151.

Neumeister, A., Praschak-Rieder, N., Hebelmann, B., Rao, M.-L., Glück, J., & Kasper, S. (1997). Effects of tryptophan depletion on drug-free patients with seasonal affective disorder during a stable response to bright light therapy. *Archives of General Psychiatry, 54,* 133–138.

Neville, B., & Parke, R. D. (1997). Waiting for paternity: Interpersonal and contextual implications of the timing of fatherhood. *Sex Roles, 37,* 45–59.

Newberg, A. B., d'Aquili, E. G., & Rause, V. (2001). *Why God won't go away: Brain science and the biology of belief.* New York: Ballantine Books.

Newcombe, N. S., Drummey, A. B., Fox, N. A., Lie, E., & Ottinger-Alberts, W. (2000). Remembering early childhood: How much, how, and why (or why not). *Current Directions in Psychological Science, 9,* 55–58.

Newman, A. W., & Thompson, J. W., Jr. (1999). Constitutional rights and hypnotically elicited testimony. *Journal of the American Academy of Psychiatry & the Law, 27,* 149–154.

Newman, S. D., Just, M. A., Keller, T. A., Roth, J., & Carpenter, P. A. (2003). Differential effects of syntactic and semantic processing on the subregions of Broca's area. *Cognitive Brain Research, 16,* 297–307.

Newport, F., & Strausberg, M. (2001, June 8). Americans' belief in psychic and paranormal phenomena is up over last decade. Princeton, NJ: The Gallup Organization (www.gallup.com/poll/releases/pr010608.asp).

Ng, C. H. (1997). The stigma of mental illness in Asian cultures. *Australian and New Zealand Journal of Psychiatry, 31,* 382–390.

NICHD Early Child Care Research Network. (2002). Parenting and family influences when children are in child care: Results from the NICHD study of early child care. In J. G. Borkowski & S. L. Ramey (Eds.), *Parenting and the child's world: Influences on academic, intellectual, and social-emotional development* (pp. 99–123). *Monographs in parenting.* Mahwah, NJ: Erlbaum.

Nicholson, A. N., Pascoe, P. A., Spencer, M. B., Stone, B. M., Roehis, T., & Roth, T. (1986). Sleep after transmeridian flights. *Lancet, 2,* 1205–1208.

Nicholson, I. A. M. (2002). Gordon Allport, character, and the "Culture of Personality." In W. E. Pickren & D. A. Dewsbury (Eds.), *Evolving perspectives on the history of psychology* (pp. 325–345). Washington, DC: American Psychological Association.

Nickerson, C., Schwarz, N., Diener, E., & Kahneman, D. (2003). Zeroing on the dark side of the American dream: A closer look at the negative consequences of the goal for financial success. *Psychological Science, 14,* 531–536.

Nickerson, R. S. (2000). Null hypothesis significance testing: A review of an old continuing controversy. *Psychological Methods, 5,* 241–301.

Nickerson, R. S., & Adams, M. J. (1979). Long-term memory for a common object. *Cognitive Psychology, 11,* 287–307.

Nicolaus, L. K., & Nellis, D. W. (1987). The first evaluation of the use of conditioned taste aversion to control predation by mongooses upon eggs. *Applied Animal Behaviour Science, 17,* 329–346.

Nielsen, C. (1995). *Animal evolution: Interrelationships of the living phyla.* Oxford, England: Oxford University Press.

Nielsen, L. L., & Sarason, I. G. (1981). Emotion, personality, and selective attention. *Journal of Personality and Social Psychology, 41,* 945–960.

Niemi, R., Mueller, J., & Smith, T. (1989). *Trends in public opinion: A compendium of survey data.* New York: Greenwood Press.

Nietzel, M. T., Speltz, M. L., McCauley, E. A., & Bernstein, D. A. (1998). *Abnormal psychology.* Boston: Allyn & Bacon.

Nijhawan, R. (1991). Three-dimensional Müeller-Lyer illusion. *Perception & Psychophysics, 49,* 333–341.

Niles, S. (1998). Achievement goals and means: A cultural comparison. *Journal of Cross-Cultural Psychology, 29,* 656–667.

Nisbet, M. (1998, May/June). Psychic telephone networks profit on yearning, gullibility. *The Skeptical Inquirer,* 5–6.

Nisbett, R. (1995). Race, IQ, and scientism. In S. Fraser (Ed.), *The Bell Curve wars: Race, intelligence and the future of America* (pp. 36–57). New York: Basic Books.

Nisbett, R. E., & Cohen, D. (1996). *Culture of honor: The psychology of violence in the South.* Boulder, CO: Westview Press.

Nisbett, R. E., & Wilson, T. D. (1977). Telling more than we can know: Verbal reports on mental processes. *Psychological Review, 84,* 231–259.

Noben-Trauth, K., Zheng, Q. Y., & Johnson, K. R. (2003). Association of Cadherin 23 with polygenic inheritance and genetic modification of sensorineural hearing loss. *Nature Genetics, 35,* 21–23.

Nogrady, H., McConkey, K., & Perry, C. (1985). Enhancing visual memory: Trying hypnosis, trying imagination, and trying again. *Journal of Abnormal Psychology, 94,* 195–204.

Noice, T., & Noice, H. (2002). Very long-term recall and recognition of well-learned material. *Applied Cognitive Psychology, 16,* 259–272.

Nolen-Hoeksema, S., Girgus, J. S., & Seligman, M. E. P. (1992). Predictors and consequences of childhood depressive symptoms: Five-year longitudinal study. *Journal of Abnormal Psychology, 101,* 405–422.

Nolen-Hoeksema, S., & Larson, J. (1999). *Coping with loss.* Mahwah, NJ: Erlbaum.

Norden, K. A., Klein, D. N., Donaldson, S. K., Popper, C. M., & Klein, L. M. (1995). Reports of the early home environment in *DSM-III-R* personality disorders. *Journal of Personality Disorders, 9,* 213–223.

Norenzayan, A., Choi, I., & Nisbett, R. E. (2002). Cultural similarities and differences in social inference: Evidence from behavioral predictions and lay theories of behavior. *Personality and Social Psychology Bulletin, 28,* 109–120.

Norenzayan, A., & Nisbett, R. E. (2000). Culture and causal cognition. *Current Directions in Psychological Science, 9,* 132–135.

Norris, J. E., & Tinsdale, J. A. (1994). *Among generations: The cycle of adult friendships.* New York: Freeman.

North, M. M., North, S. M., & Coble, J. R. (2002). Virtual reality therapy: An effective treatment for phobias. In K. M. Stanney (Ed.), *Handbook of virtual environments: Design, implementation, and applications* (pp. 1065–1078). *Human factors and ergonomics.* Mahwah, NJ: Erlbaum.

Norwich, K. H. (1987). On the theory of Weber fractions. *Perception & Psychophysics, 42,* 286–298.

Nowak, A., Szamrej, J., & Latané, B. (1990). From private attitude to public opinion: A dynamic theory of social impact. *Psychological Review, 97,* 362–376.

Nyberg, L., Forkstam, C., Petersson, K. M., Cabeza, R., & Ingvar, M. (2002). Brain imaging of human memory systems: Between-systems similarities and within-system differences. *Cognitive Brain Research, 13,* 281–292.

Nyberg, L., Marklund, P., Persson, J., Cabeza, R., Forkstam, C., Petersson, K. M., & Ingvar, M. (2003). Common prefrontal activations during working memory, episodic memory, and semantic memory. *Neuropsychologia, 41,* 371–377.

Nygard, L. (2004). Responses of persons with dementia to challenges in daily activities: A synthesis of findings from empirical studies. *American Journal of Occupational Therapy, 58,* 435–445.

Oatley, K., & Jenkins, J. (1996). *Understanding emotions.* Cambridge, MA: Blackwell.

O'Brien, C. P., Eckardt, M. J., & Linnoila, M. I. (1995). Pharmacotherapy of alcoholism. In F. E. Bloom & D. J. Kupfer (Eds.), *Psychopharmacology: The fourth generation* (pp. 1745–1755). New York: Raven Press.

Ochse, R. (1990). *Before the gates of excellence: The determinants of creative genius.* Cambridge, England: Cambridge University Press.

O'Conner, E. (2001). Psychology's diversity leaps "beyond 2000." *Monitor on Psychology, 32,* 36–38.

O'Connor, K. J., Cunningham, W. A., Funayama, E. S., Gatenby, J. C., Gore, J. C., & Banaji, M. R. (2000). Performance on indirect measures of race evaluation predicts amygdala activation. *Journal of Cognitive Neuroscience, 12,* 729–738.

O'Connor, N., Cowan, R., & Samella, K. (2000). Calendrical calculation and intelligence. *Intelligence, 28,* 31–48.

O'Connor, P. (1997). Overtraining and staleness. In W. Morgan (Ed.), *Physical activity and mental health* (pp. 145–160). Washington, DC: Taylor & Francis.

Oda, Ryo. (2001). Lemur vocal communication and the origin of human language. In T. Matsuzawa (Ed.), *Primate origins of human cognition and behavior* (pp. 115–134). New York: Springer-Verlag.

Oetting, E. R., & Beauvais, F. (1990). Adolescent drug use: Findings of national and local surveys. *Journal of Consulting and Clinical Psychology, 58,* 385–394.

Oettingen, G. (1997). *Psychologie des Zukunftsdenkens* [On the psychology of future thought]. Goettingen, Germany: Hogrefe.

Oettingen, G., Pak, H., & Schnetter, K. (2001). Self-regulation and goal-setting: Turning free fantasy about the future into binding goals. *Journal of Personality and Social Psychology, 80,* 736–753.

O'Farrell, T., & Murphy, C. M. (1995). Marital violence before and after alcoholism treatment. *Journal of Consulting and Clinical Psychology, 63,* 256–262.

Offit, K., Groeger, E., Turner, S., Wadsworth, E. A., & Weiser, M. A. (2004). The "duty to warn" a patient's family members about hereditary disease risks. *Journal of the American Medical Association, 292,* 1469–1473.

Ogata, M., Ikeda, M., & Kuratsune, M. (1984). Mortality among Japanese Zen priests. *Journal of Epidemiology and Community Health, 38,* 161–166.

Ogbu, J. U. (1978). *Minority education and caste: The American system in cross-cultural perspective.* New York: Academic Press.

Ogbu, J. U. (1986). Class stratification, racial stratification and schooling. In L. Weis (Ed.), *Race, class and schooling: Special studies in comparative education* (Vol. 17, pp. 6–35). New York: Comparative Education Center, State University of New York at Buffalo.

Ogbu, J. U. (1993). Differences in cultural frame of reference. *International Journal of Behavioral Development, 16,* 483–506.

Ogbu, J. U. (2002). Cultural amplifiers of intelligence: IQ and minority status in cross-cultural perspective. In J. M. Fish (Ed.), *Race and intelligence: Separating science from myth* (pp. 241–278). Mahwah, NJ: Erlbaum.

Ogbu, J. U., & Simons, H. D. (1998). Voluntary and involuntary minorities: A cultural-ecological theory of school performance with some implications for education. *Anthropology and Education Quarterly, 29,* 155–188.

Oghalai, J. S. (2005). Cochlear hearing loss. In R. Jackler & D. Brackmann (Eds.), *Neurotology,* 2nd ed. Philadelphia: Mosby.

Ohayon, M. M., Guilleminault, C., & Priest, R. G. (1999). Night terrors, sleepwalking, and confusional arousals in the general population: Their frequency and relationship to other sleep and mental disorders. *Journal of Clinical Psychiatry, 60,* 268–276.

Ohbuchi, K., Kamdea, M., & Agarie, N. (1989). Apology as aggression control: Its role in mediating appraisal of and response to harm. *Journal of Personality and Social Psychology, 56,* 219–227.

Öhman, A., Flykt, A., & Esteves, F. (2001). Emotion drives attention: Detecting the snake in the grass. *Journal of Experimental Psychology: General, 130,* 466–478.

Öhman, A., Lundqvist, D., & Esteves, F. (2001). The face in the crowd revisited: A threat advantage with schematic stimuli. *Journal of Personality and Social Psychology, 80,* 381–396.

Öhman, A., & Mineka, S. (2003). The malicious serpent: Snakes as a prototypical stimulus for an evolved module of fear. *Current Directions in Psychological Science, 12,* 5–9.

Öhman, A., & Soares, J. J. F. (1994). "Unconscious anxiety": Phobic responses to masked stimuli. *Journal of Abnormal Psychology, 103,* 231–240.

Ohnishi, T., Moriguch, Y., Matsuda, H., Mori, T., Hirakata, M., Imabayashi, E., Hirao, K., Nemoto, K., Kaga, M., Inagaki, M., Yamada, M., & Uno, A. (2004). The neural network for the mirror system and mentalizing in normally developed children: An fMRI study. *Neuroreport: For Rapid Communication of Neuroscience Research, 15,* 1483–1487.

Oishi, S., Diener, E. F., Lucas, R. E., & Suh, E. M. (1999). Cross-cultural variations in predictors of life satisfaction: Perspectives from needs and values. *Personality and Social Psychology Bulletin, 25,* 980–990.

Olausson, H., Lamarre, Y., Backlund, H., Morin, C., Wallin, B. G., Starck, G., Ekholm, S., Strigo, I., Worsley, K., Vallbo, Å. B., & Bushnell, M. C. (2002). Unmyelinated tactile afferents signal touch and project to insular cortex. *Nature Neuroscience, 5,* 900–904.

Oldfield, R. C. (1971). The assessment and analysis of handedness: The Edinburgh Inventory. *Neuropsychologia, 9,* 97–114.

O'Leary, A. (1990). Stress, emotion, and human immune function. *Psychological Bulletin, 108,* 363–382.

O'Leary, K. D., Vivian, D., & Malone, J. (1992). Assessment of physical aggression in marriage: The need for multimodal assessment. *Behavioral Research and Therapy, 14,* 1–10.

Olesen, J., & Lipton, R. B. (2004). Headache classification update 2004. *Current Opinion in Neurology, 17,* 275–282.

Oliner, S. P., & Oliner, P. M. (1988). *The altruistic personality: Rescuers of Jews in Nazi Europe.* London: Free Press.

Oliver, M. B., & Hyde, J. S. (1993). Gender differences in sexuality: A meta-analysis. *Psychological Bulletin, 114,* 29–51.

Oller, D. K., & Eilers, R. E. (1988). The role of audition in infant babbling. *Child Development, 59,* 441–449.

Olson, K. R., Lambert, A. J., & Zacks, J. M. (2004). Graded structure and the speed of category verification: On the moderating effects of anticipatory control for social vs. non-social categories. *Journal of Experimental Social Psychology, 40,* 239–246.

Olweus, D. (1980). Familial and temperamental determinants of aggressive behavior in adolescent boys: A causal analysis. *Developmental Psychology, 16,* 644–666.

O'Mahony, J. F. (1986). Development of person description over adolescence. *Journal of Youth and Adolescence, 15,* 389–403.

Orlinsky, D. E., & Howard, K. I. (1987). The relation of process to outcome in psychotherapy. In S. L. Garfield & A. E. Bergin (Eds.), *Handbook of psychotherapy and behavior change* (3rd ed., pp. 311–381). New York: Wiley.

Ortmann, A., & Hertwig, R. (1997). Is deception acceptable? *American Psychologist, 52,* 746–747.

Osaka, N. (2003). Working memory-based consciousness: An individual difference approach. In N. Osaka (Ed.), *Neural basis of consciousness. Advances in consciousness research* (Vol. 49, pp. 27–44). Amsterdam, Netherlands: John Benjamins.

Ossorio, P., & Duster, T. (2005). Race and genetics: Controversies in biomedical, behavioral, and forensic sciences. *American Psychologist, 60,* 115–128.

Ostatnikova, D., Laznibatova, J., Putz, Z., Mataseje, A., Dohnanyiova, M., & Pastor, K. (2000). Salivary testosterone, handedness, allergy and cognition in children. *Homeostasis in Health and Disease, 40,* 121–123.

Ostatnikova, D., Laznibatova, J., Putz, Z., Mataseje, A., Dohnanyiova, M., & Pastor, K. (2001). Biological aspects of intellectual giftedness. *Studia Psychologica, 44,* 3–13.

O'Sullivan, C., & Yeager, C. P. (1989). Communicative context and linguistic competence: The effects of a social setting on a chimpanzee's conversational skill. In R. A. Gardner, B. T. Gardner, & T. E. Van Cantfort (Eds.), *Teaching sign language to chimpanzees.* New York: State University of New York Press.

O'Sullivan, M. (2005). Emotional intelligence and deception detection: Why most people can't "read" others, but a few can. In R. E. Riggio, E. Ronald, R. S. Feldman, & S. Robert (Eds.), *Applications of nonverbal communication* (pp. 215–253). Mahwah, NJ: Erlbaum.

Otani, H., Kusumi, T., Kato, K., Matsuda, K., Kern, R. P., Widner, R., Jr., & Ohta, N. (2005). Remembering a nuclear accident in Japan: Did it trigger flashbulb memories? *Memory, 13,* 6–20.

Ouellet, C., Le Norman, M.-T., & Cohen, H. (2001). Language evolution in children with cochlear implants. *Brain & Cognition, 46,* 231–235.

Ouimette, P. C., Finney, J. W., & Moos, R. H. (1997). Twelve-step and cognitive behavioral treatment for substance abuse: A comparison of treatment effectiveness. *Journal of Consulting and Clinical Psychology, 65,* 230–240.

Overmier, J. B., & Leaf, R. C. (1965). Effects of discriminative Pavlovian fear conditioning upon previously or subsequently acquired avoidance responding. *Journal of Comparative and Physiological Psychology, 60,* 213–218.

Oxman, T. E., Freeman, D. H., & Manheimer, E. D. (1995). Lack of social participation or religious strength and comfort as risk factors for death after cardiac surgery in the elderly. *Psychosocial Medicine, 57,* 5–15.

Oyserman, D., Coon, H. M., & Kemmelmeier, M. (2002). Rethinking individualism and collectivism: Evaluation of theoretical assumptions and meta-analyses. *Psychological Bulletin, 128,* 3–72.

Paffenbarger, R. S., Jr., Hyde, R. T., Wing, A. L., & Hsieh, C. (1986). Physical activity, all-cause mortality, and longevity of college alumni. *New England Journal of Medicine, 314,* 605–613.

Pagel, J. F. (1994). Treatment of insomnia. *American Family Physician, 49,* 1417–1421.

Pahnke, W. N. (1970). Drugs and mysticism. In B. Aarson & H. Osmond (Eds.), *Psychedelics.* New York: Anchor.

Paignon, A., Desrichard, O., & Bollon, T. (2003). A connectionist model of social learning: The case of learning a simple task by observation. *Canadian Journal of Experimental Psychology, 58,* 46–60.

Paivio, S. C., & Greenberg, L. S. (1995). Resolving "unfinished business": Efficacy of experiential therapy using empty-chair dialogue. *Journal of Consulting and Clinical Psychology, 63,* 419–425.

Pakkenberg, B., & Gunderson, H. J. G. (1997). Neocortical neuron number in humans: Effect of sex and age. *The Journal of Comparative Neurology, 384,* 312–320.

Palazzo-Craig, J. (1986). *The upside-down boy.* Mahwah, NJ: Troll Associates.

Palmer, G., & Broud, W. (2002). Exceptional human experiences, disclosure, and a more inclusive view of physical, psychological, and spiritual well-being. *Journal of Transpersonal Psychology, 34,* 29–61.

Parasuraman, R., Greenwood, P. M., Kumar, R., & Fosella, J. (2005). Beyond heritability: Neurotransmitter genes differentially modulate visuospatial attention and working memory. *Psychological Science, 16,* 200–207.

Pargament, K. I. (2002). The bitter and the sweet: An evaluation of the costs and benefits of religiousness. *Psychological Inquiry, 13,* 168–181.

Parham, T. A., & Helms, J. E. (1985). Attitudes of racial identity and self-esteem in Black students: An exploratory investigation. *Journal of College Student Personnel, 26,* 143–147.

Paris, J. (1997). Childhood trauma as an etiological factor in the personality disorders. *Journal of Personality Disorders, 11,* 34–49.

Park, B. (1986). A method for studying the development of impressions of real people. *Journal of Personality and Social Psychology, 51,* 907–917.

Park, C., Cohen, L. H., & Herb, L. (1990). Intrinsic religiousness and religious coping as life stress moderators for Catholics versus Protestants. *Journal of Personality and Social Psychology, 59,* 562–574.

Parke, R. D., & Buriel, R. (1998). Socialization in the family: Ethnic and ecological perspectives. In W. Damon & N. Eisenberg (Eds.), *Handbook of child psychology: Vol. 3. Social, emotional, and personality development* (5th ed., pp. 463–552). New York: Wiley.

Parker, G. (2004). Concise guide to mood disorders. *American Journal of Psychiatry, 161,* 2147–2148.

Parker, S. T. (2000). *Homo erectus* infancy and childhood: The turning point in the evolution of behavioral development in hominids. In S. T. Parker, J. Langer, & M. L. McKinney (Eds.), *Biology, brains, and behavior: The evolution of human development* (pp. 279–318). *School of American Research Advanced Seminar Series.*

Parker, S. T., Langer, J., & McKinney, M. L. (Eds.). (2000). *Biology, brains, and behavior: The evolution of human development. School of American Research Advanced Seminar Series.*

Parkes, C. M. P., & Weiss, R. S. (1983). *Recovery from bereavement.* New York: Basic Books.

Parkinson Study Group. (2002). Dopamine transporter brain imaging to assess the effects of pramipexole vs. levodopa on Parkinson's disease progression. *JAMA: Journal of the American Medical Association, 287,* 1653–1661.

Parry, J. K., & Ryan, A. (1995). *A cross-cultural look at death, dying and religion.* New York: Nelson Hall.

Pasch, L. A., Bradbury, T. N., & Sullivan, K. T. (1997). Social support in marriage: An analysis of intraindividual and interpersonal components. In G. R. Pierce, B. Lakey, I. G. Sarason, & B. R. Sarason (Eds.), *Sourcebook of social support and personality* (pp. 229–256). New York: Plenum.

Pashler, H. (1992). Attentional limitations in doing two tasks at the same time. *Current Directions in Psychological Science, 1,* 44–48.

Pashler, H., Johnston, J. C., & Ruthruff, E. (2000). Attention and performance. *Annual Review of Psychology, 52,* 629–651.

Passman, R. H., & Weisberg, P. (1975). Mothers and blankets as agents for promoting play and exploration by young children in a novel environment: The effects of social and nonsocial attachment objects. *Developmental Psychology, 11,* 170–177.

Pate, R., Pratt, M., Blair, S., Haskell, W., Macera, C., et al. (1995). Physical activity and public health: A recommendation from the Centers for Disease Control and Prevention and the American College of Sports Medicine. *Journal of the American Medical Association, 273,* 402–407.

Patenaude, A. F. (2005). Children and genetic testing. In A. F. Patenaude (Ed.), *Genetic testing for cancer: Psychological approaches for helping patients and families* (pp. 229–250). Washington, DC: American Psychological Association.

Pato, M. T., Pato, C. N., & Pauls, D. L. (2002). Recent findings in the genetics of OCD. *Journal of Clinical Psychiatry, 63,* 30–33.

Patrick, A., & Durndell, A. (2004). Lucid dreaming and personality: A replication. *Dreaming, 14,* 234–239.

Patterson, F. (1978, October). Conversations with a gorilla. *National Geographic,* 438–465.

Pauls, D. L., Alsobrook, J. P., Goodman, W., Rasmussen, S., & Leckman, J. F. (1995). A family study of obsessive-compulsive disorder. *American Journal of Psychiatry, 152,* 76–84.

Paunonen, S. V. (2003). Big five factors of personality and replicated predictions of behavior. *Journal of Personality and Social Psychology, 84,* 411–424.

Paunonen, S. V., & Ashton, M. C. (2001). Big five factors and facets and the prediction of behavior. *Journal of Personality and Social Psychology, 81,* 524–539.

Pavlides, C., & Ribeiro, S. (2003). Recent evidence of memory processing in sleep. In P. Maquet, C. Smith, & R. Stickgold (Eds.), *Sleep and brain plasticity* (pp. 227–362). Oxford, England: Oxford University Press.

Pavlides, C., & Winson, J. (1989). Influences of hippocampal place cell firing in the awake state on the activity of these cells during subsequent sleep episodes. *Journal of Neuroscience, 9,* 2907–2918.

Pavlov, I. P. (1927). *Conditioned reflexes* (G.V. Anrep, Trans.). London: Oxford University Press.

Pavlov, I. P. (1997). Excerpts from *The work of the digestive glands. American Psychologist, 52,* 936–940. (Original work published 1897)

Pearson, J., Brandeis, L., & Cuello, A. C. (1982). Depletion of substance P-containing axons in substantia gelatinosa of patients with diminished pain sensitivity. *Nature, 295,* 61–63.

Pedersen, C. A. (2004). Biological aspects of social bonding and the roots of human violence. *Annals of the New York Academy of Sciences, 1036,* 106–127.

Pedersen, C. A., & Boccia, M. L. (2002). Oxytocin maintains as well as initiates female sexual behavior: Effects of a highly selective oxytocin antagonist. *Hormones & Behavior, 4,* 170–177.

Pedersen, W. C., Miller, L. C., Putcha-Bhagavatula, A. D., & Yang, Y. (2002). Evolved sex differences in the number of partners desired? The long and the short of it. *Psychological Science, 13,* 157–161.

Pederson, D. R., Moran, G., Sitko, C., Campbell, K., Ghesquire, K., & Acton, H. (1990). Maternal sensitivity and the security of infant-mother attachment: A q-sort study. *Child Development, 61,* 1974–1983.

Peele, S. (1993). The conflict between public health goals and the temperance mentality. *American Journal of Public Health, 83,* 805–810.

Peele, S. (1997). Utilizing culture and behaviour in epidemiological models of alcohol consumption and consequences for Western nations. *Alcohol & Alcoholism, 32,* 51–64.

Peifer, K. L., Hu, T. W., & Vega, W. (2000). Help seeking by persons of Mexican origin with functional impairments. *Psychiatric Services, 51,* 1293–1298.

Peigneux, P., Melchior, G., Schmidt, C., Dang-Vu, T., Boly, M., Laureys, S., & Maquet, P. (2004). Memory processing during sleep mechanisms and evidence from neuroimaging studies. *Psychologica Belgica, 44,* 121–142.

Pekkanen, J. (1982, June). Why do we sleep? *Science, 82,* 86.

Penfield, W. W. (1958). *The excitable cortex in conscious man.* Springfield, IL: Charles Thomas.

Penfield, W. W., & Perot, P. (1963). The brain's record of auditory and visual experience: A final summary and discussion. *Brain, 86,* 595–696.

Penn, D. L., & Martin, J. (1998). The stigma of severe mental illness: Some potential solutions for a recalcitrant problem. *Psychiatric Quarterly, 69,* 235–247.

Pennebaker, J. W., & Beall, S. (1986). Confronting a traumatic event: Toward an understanding of inhibition and disease. *Journal of Abnormal Psychology, 95,* 274–281.

Pennebaker, J. W., Colder, M., & Sharp, L. K. (1990). Accelerating the coping process. *Journal of Personality and Social Psychology, 58,* 528–537.

Pennebaker, J. W., & O'Heeron, R. C. (1984). Confiding in others and illness rate among spouses of suicide and accidental death victims. *Journal of Abnormal Psychology, 93,* 473–476.

Penny, L. (1996). *The Whorf theory complex: A critical reconstruction.* Philadelphia: John Benjamins Publishing.

Peplau, L. A. (2003). Human sexuality: How do men and women differ? *Current Directions in Psychological Science, 12,* 37–40.

Peplau, L. A., Fingerhut, A., & Beals, K. (2004). Sexuality in the relationships of lesbians and gay men. In J. Harvey, A. Wenzel, & S. Sprecher (Eds.), *Handbook of sexuality in close relationships.* Mahwah, NJ: Erlbaum.

Peplau, L. A., & Garnets, L. D. (2000). A new paradigm for understanding women's sexuality and sexual orientation. *Journal of Social Issues, 56,* 329–350.

Peplau, L. A., & Taylor, S. E. (Eds.). (1997). *Sociocultural perspectives in social psychology: Current readings.* Upper Saddle River, NJ: Prentice Hall.

Pepperberg, I. M. (2002). Cognitive and communicative abilities of grey parrots. *Current Directions in Psychological Science, 11,* 83–87.

Perakh, M. (2004). *Unintelligent design.* Amherst, NY: Prometheus Books.

Perkins, D. (1995). *Outsmarting IQ: The emerging science of learnable intelligence.* New York: The Free Press.

Perls, F. S. (1969). *Gestalt therapy verbatim.* Lafayette, CA: Real People Press.

Perls, F. S., Heffertine, R. F., & Goodman, P. (1951). *Gestalt therapy.* New York: Julian Press.

Pernot-Marino, E., Danion, J.-M., & Hedelin, G. (2004). Relations between emotion and conscious recollection of true and false autobiographical memories: An investigation using lorazepam as a pharmacological tool. *Psychopharmacology, 175,* 60–67.

Persky, H. (1983). Psychosexual effects of hormones. *Medical Aspects of Human Sexuality, 17,* 74–101.

Pert, C. B. (1999). *Molecules of emotion.* New York: Simon & Schuster.

Pert, C. B. (2002). The wisdom of the receptors: Neuropeptides, the emotions, and bodymind. *Advances in Mind-Body Medicine, 18,* 30–35.

Pert, C. B., & Snyder, S. H. (1973). Opiate receptor: Demonstration in nervous tissue. *Science, 179,* 1011–1014.

Pervin, L. A. (1996). *The science of personality.* New York: Wiley.

Pescosolido, B. A., Monahan, J., Link, B. G., Stueve, A., & Kikuzawa, S. (1999). The public's view of the competence, dangerousness, and need for legal coercion of persons with mental health problems. *American Journal of Public Health, 89,* 1339–1345.

Peters, M. F. (2002). Racial socialization of young Black children. In H. P. McAdoo (Ed.), *Black children: Social, educational, and parental environments* (2nd ed., pp. 57–72). Thousand Oaks, CA: Sage.

Peters, V. B., Thomas, P., Liu, K. L., Gill, B., Dominguez, K. L., Frederick, T., Melville, S., Hsu, H., & Orengo, J. C. (2002, July 7–12). Missed opportunities of perinatal HIV prevention among HIV-exposed infants born 1996–2000, Pediatric spectrum of HIV disease cohort. *International Conference on AIDS.* Abstract No. ThOrD1429.

Peterson, B. D., West, J., Pincus, H. A., & Kohout, J. (1996). An update on human resources in mental health. In R. W. Manderscheid & M. A. Sonnenschein (Eds.), *Mental Health, United States 1996* (DHHS Publication No. SMA 96-3098). Washington, DC: U.S. Department of Health and Human Services.

Peterson, C., & Bossio, L. M. (2001). Optimism and physical well-being. In E. C. Chang (Ed.), *Optimism and pessimism: Implications for theory, research, and practice* (pp. 127–145). Washington, DC: American Psychological Association.

Peterson, C., Maier, S. F., & Seligman, M. E. P. (1993). *Learned helplessness: A theory for the age of personal control.* New York: Oxford University Press.

Peterson, C., & Park, C. (1998). Learned helplessness and explanatory style. In D. F. Barone, M. Hersen, & V. B. Van Hasselt (Eds.), *Advanced personality.* New York: Plenum.

Peterson, C., & Seligman, M. E. (1984). Causal explanations as a risk factor for depression: Theory and evidence. *Psychological Review, 91,* 347–374.

Peterson, C., & Seligman, M. E. P. (1987). Explanatory style and illness. *Journal of Personality, 55,* 237–265.

Peterson, C., Seligman, M. E. P., & Vaillant, G. E. (1988). Pessimistic explanatory style is a risk factor for physical illness: A thirty-five-year longitudinal study. *Journal of Personality and Social Psychology, 55,* 23–27.

Peterson, C., Seligman, M. E. P., Yurko, K. H., Martin, L. R., & Friedman, H. S. (1998). Catastrophizing and untimely death. *Psychological Science, 9,* 49–52.

Peterson, C., & Steen, T. A. (2002). Optimistic explanatory style. In C. R. Snyder & S. J. Shane (Eds.), *Handbook of positive psychology* (pp. 244–256). London: Oxford University Press.

Peterson, J. L., & Miller, C. (1980). Physical attractiveness and marriage adjustment in older American couples. *Journal of Psychology, 105,* 247–252.

Peterson, L., Brown, D., & Aronson, H. (1998). Faculty gender, status, roles, and privileges in applied doctoral programs. *The Clinical Psychologist, 51,* 11–16.

Peterson, L. R., & Peterson, M. J. (1959). Short-term retention of individual verbal items. *Journal of Experimental Psychology, 58,* 193–198.

Peterson, Z. D., & Muehlenhard, C. L. (2004). Was it rape? The function of women's rape myth acceptance and definitions of sex in labeling their own experiences. *Sex Roles, 51,* 129–144.

Petitto, A. (2000). On the biological foundations of human language. In H. Lane & K. Emmorey (Eds.), *The signs of language revisited* (pp. 447–471). Mahwah, NJ: Erlbaum.

Peto, R., Lopez, A. D., Boreham, J., & Thun, M. (1992). Mortality from tobacco in developed countries: Indirect estimation from national vital statistics. *Lancet, 339,* 1268–1278.

Petrides, K. V., & Furnham, A. (2003). Trait emotional intelligence: Behavioural validation in two studies of emotion recognition and reactivity to mood induction. *European Journal of Personality, 17,* 39–57.

Petrill, S. A., Luo, D., Thompson, L. A., & Detterman, D. K. (1996). The independent prediction of general intelligence by elementary cognitive tasks: Genetic and environmental influences. *Behavior Genetics, 26,* 135–147.

Petty, R. E., & Cacioppo, J. T. (1986). *Communication and persuasion: Central and peripheral routes to attitude change.* New York: Springer-Verlag.

Petty, R. E., Haugtvedt, C. P., & Smith, S. M. (1995). Elaboration as a determinant of attitude strength: Creating attitudes that are persistent, resistant, and predictive of behavior. In R. E. Petty & J. A. Krosnick (Eds.), *Attitude strength: Antecedents and consequences.* Hillsdale, NJ: Erlbaum.

Petty, R. E., & Wegener, D. T. (1996). Attitude change: Multiple roles for persuasion variables. In D. Gilbert, S. Fiske, & G. Lindzey (Eds.), *The handbook of social psychology* (4th ed.). New York: McGraw-Hill.

Pezze, M. A., Feldon, J., & Murphy, C. A. (2002). Increased conditioned fear response and altered balance of dopamine in the shell and core of the nucleus accumbens during amphetamine withdrawal. *Neuropharmacology, 42,* 633–643.

Pezzo, M. V. (2003). Surprise, defense, or making sense: What removes the highsight bias? *Memory, 11,* 421–441.

Pfaffmann, C. (1978). The vertebrate phylogeny, neural code, and integrative process of taste. In C. Carteerette & M. P. Friedman (Eds.), *Handbook of perception* (Vol. 6A). New York: Academic Press.

Phelps, J. A., Davis, J. O., & Schartz, K. M. (1997). Nature, nurture, and twin research strategies. *Current Directions in Psychological Science, 6,* 117–121.

Phillips, D. P. (1983). The impact of mass media violence on U.S. homicides. *American Sociological Review, 48,* 560–568.

Phillips, D. P. (1986). Natural experiments on the effects of mass media violence on fatal aggression: Strengths and weaknesses of a new approach. In L. Berkowitz (Ed.), *Advances in experimental social psychology* (Vol. 19, pp. 207–250). Orlando, FL: Academic Press.

Phillips, D. P., & Brugge, J. F. (1985). Progress in neurophysiology of sound localization. *Annual Review of Psychology, 36,* 245–274.

Phillips, M. R., Li, S., & Zhang, Y. (2002). Suicide rates in China: 1995–99. *Lancet, 359,* 835–840.

Phillips, R. D., Wagner, S. H., Fells, C. A., & Lynch, M. (1990). Do infants recognize emotion in facial expressions? Categorical and "metaphorical" evidence. *Infant Behavior and Development, 13,* 71–84.

Phinney, J., & Kohatsu, E. (1997). Ethnic and racial identity and mental health. In J. Schulenberg, J. Maggs, & K. Hurrelmann (Eds.), *Health risks and developmental transitions during adolescence* (pp. 420–443). New York: Cambridge University Press.

Phinney, J. S., Cantu, C. L., & Kurtz, D. A. (1997). Ethnic and American identity and self-esteem. *Journal of Youth and Adolescence, 26,* 165–185.

Phinney, V. G., Jensen, L. C., Olsen, J. A., & Cundick, B. (1990). The relationship between early development and psychosexual behaviors in adolescent females. *Adolescence, 25,* 321–332.

Piaget, J. (1972a). Development and learning. In C. S. Lavatelli & F. Stendler (Eds.), *Readings in child behavior and development* (3rd ed.). New York: Harcourt Brace Jovanovich.

Piaget, J. (1972b). Intellectual evolutions from adolescence to adulthood. *Human Development, 15,* 1–12.

Piaget, J., & Inhelder, B. (1956). *The child's conception of space* (F. J. Langdon & J. L. Lunzer, Trans.). London: Routledge & T. K. Paul.

Piaget, J., & Inhelder, B. (1969). *The psychology of the child.* New York: Basic Books.

Piasecki, T. M., Kenford, S. L., Smith, S. S., Fiore, M. C., & Baker, T. B. (1997). Listening to nicotine: Negative affect and the smoking withdrawal conundrum. *Psychological Science, 8,* 184–189.

Piccione, C., Hilgard, E. R., & Zimbardo, P. G. (1989). On the degree of stability of measured hypnotizability over a 25-year period. *Journal of Personality and Social Psychology, 56,* 289–295.

Pickens, R. W., Svikis, D. S., McGue, M., Lykken, D. T., Heston, L. L., & Clayton, P. J. (1993). Heterogeneity in the inheritance of alcoholism: A study of male and female twins. *Archives of General Psychiatry, 48,* 19–28.

Pike, K. M., & Rodin, J. (1991). Mothers, daughters, and disordered eating. *Journal of Abnormal Psychology, 100,* 198–204.

Pillemer, D. B. (1984). Flashbulb memories on the assassination attempt on President Reagan. *Cognition, 14,* 709–715.

Pine, F. (1990). *Drive, ego, object, and self: A synthesis for clinical work.* New York: Basic Books.

Pinel, J. (1997). *Biopsychology.* Boston: Allyn & Bacon.

Pinel, J., Assanand, S., & Lehman, D. (2000). Hunger, eating, and ill health. *American Psychologist, 55,* 1105–1116.

Pinel, J. P. J., Lehman, D. R., & Assanand, S. (2002). Eating for optimal health: How much should we eat?: Comment. *American Psychologist, 57,* 372–373.

Pines, A. M. (1993). Burnout. In L. Goldberger & S. Breznitz (Eds.), *Handbook of stress: Theoretical and clinical aspects.* New York: Free Press.

Pinker, S. (1994). *The language instinct: How the mind creates language.* New York: Morrow.

Pinker, S. (1999). *Words and rules: The ingredients of language.* New York: Basic Books.

Piotrowski, C., Belter, R. W., & Keller, J. W. (1998). The impact of "managed care" on the practice of psychological testing: Preliminary findings. *Journal of Personality Assessment, 70,* 441–447.

Pittman, T. (1998). Motivation. In D. Gilbert, S. Fiske, & G. Lindzey (Eds.), *The handbook of social psychology* (Vol. 1, 4th ed., pp. 549–590). New York: Oxford University Press.

Plant, E. A., & Devine, P. G. (2003). The antecedents and implications of interracial anxiety. *Personality and Social Psychology Bulletin, 29,* 790–801.

Plante, T. G. (2005). *Contemporary clinical psychology* (2nd ed.). New York: Wiley.

Plante, T. G., Yancey, S., Sherman, A., & Guertin, M. (2000). The association between strength of religious faith and psychological functioning. *Pastoral Psychology, 38,* 405–412.

Plaut, D. C., & Kello, C. T. (1999). The emergence of phonology from the interplay of speech comprehension and production: A distributed connectionist approach. In B. MacWhinney (Ed.), *The emergence of language* (pp. 381–415). Mahwah, NJ: Erlbaum.

Pliner, P., & Pelchat, M. L. (1991). Neophobia in humans and the special status of foods of animal origin. *Appetite, 16,* 205–218.

Plomin, R. (1984). Childhood temperament. In B. Lahey & A. Kazdin (Eds.), *Advances in clinical child psychology* (Vol. 6). New York: Plenum.

Plomin, R. (2004). Genetics and developmental psychology. *Merrill-Palmer Quarterly, 50,* 341–352.

Plomin, R., & Crabbe, J. (2000). DNA. *Psychological Bulletin, 128.*

Plomin, R., DeFries, J. C., McClearn, G. E., & Rutter, M. (1997). *Behavioral genetics* (3rd ed.). New York: Freeman.

Plomin, R., & McClearn, G. E. (Eds.). (1993). *Nature-nurture and psychology.* Washington, DC: American Psychological Association.

Plous, S. (1996a). Attitudes toward the use of animals in psychological research and education: Results from a national survey of psychologists. *American Psychologist, 51,* 1167–1180.

Plous, S. (1996b). Attitudes toward the use of animals in psychological research and education: Results from a national survey of psychology majors. *Psychological Science, 7,* 352–358.

Plous, S. (1998). Signs of change within the animal rights movement: Results from a follow-up survey of activists. *Journal of Comparative Psychology, 112,* 48–54.

Plutchik, R. (1994). *The psychology and biology of emotion.* New York: HarperCollins.

Pohl, R. F., Bender, M., & Lachman, G. (2002). Hindsight bias around the world. *Experimental Psychology, 49,* 270–282.

Pokorny, J., Shevell, S. K., & Smith, V. C. (1991). Colour appearance and colour constancy. In P. Gouras (Ed.), *The perception of colour: Vol. 6. Vision and visual dysfunction* (pp. 43–61). Boca Raton, FL: CRC.

Polivy, J., Herman, C., & McFarlane, T. (1994). Effects of anxiety on eating: Does palatability moderate distress-induced overeating of dieters? *Journal of Abnormal Psychology, 103,* 505–510.

Polivy, J., Herman, C.-P., & Boivin, M. (2005). Eating disorders. In J. E. Maddux & B. A. Winstead (Eds.), *Psychopathology: Foundations for a contemporary understanding* (pp. 229–254). Mahwah, NJ: Erlbaum.

Pomerantz, E. M., Wang, Q. N., & Florrie, F.-Y. (2005). Mothers' affect in the homework context: The importance of staying positive. *Developmental Psychology, 41,* 414–427.

Pomerantz, J. M. (2002). Is social phobia a serious medical disorder? *Drug Benefit Trends, 14,* 5.

Pope, H., Gruber, A., Hudson, J., Huestis, M., & Yurgelun-Todd, D. (2001). Neuropsychological performance in long-term cannabis users. *Archives in General Psychiatry, 58,* 909–915.

Pope, K. S., & Vasquez, M. J. T. (2001). *Ethics in psychotherapy and counseling: A practical guide* (2nd ed.). San Francisco: Jossey-Bass.

Porac, C., & Coren, S. (1981). *Lateral preferences and human behavior.* New York: Springer-Verlag.

Porter, F. L., Porges, S. W., & Marshall, R. E. (1988). Newborn pain cries and vagal tone: Parallel changes in response to circumcision. *Child Development, 59,* 495–505.

Porter, R. H. (1991). Human reproduction and the mother-infant relationship. In T. V. Getchell et al. (Eds.), *Taste and smell in health and disease.* New York: Raven Press.

Porter, R. H., & Moore, J. D. (1981). Human kin recognition by olfactory cues. *Physiology and Behavior, 27,* 493–495.

Posavac, H. D., & Posavac, S. S. (1998). Exposure to media images of female attractiveness and concern with body weight among young women. *Sex Roles, 38,* 187–201.

Posner, M. I. (2002). Convergence of psychological and biological development. *Developmental Psychobiology, 40,* 339–343.

Povinelli, D. J., & Bering, J. M. (2002). The mentality of apes revisited. *Current Directions in Psychological Science, 11,* 115–119.

Powers, D. E. (1993). Coaching for the SAT: A summary of the summaries and an update. *Educational Measurement Issues and Practice, 12,* 24–30.

Pratkanis, A. R. (1989). The cognitive representation of attitudes. In A. R. Pratkanis, S. J. Breckler, & A. G. Greenwald (Eds.), *Attitude structure and function* (pp. 71–98). Hillsdale, NJ: Erlbaum.

Pratt, D. D. (1991). Conceptions of self within China and the United States: Contrasting foundations for adult education. *International Journal of Intercultural Relations, 15,* 285–310.

Premack, D. (1959). Toward empirical behavior laws: I. Positive reinforcement. *Psychological Review, 66,* 219–233.

Premack, D. (1962). Reversibility of the reinforcement relation. *Science, 136,* 235–237.

Premack, D., & Premack, A. (1983). *The mind of an ape.* New York: Norton.

Prepeliczay, S. (2003). Sociocultural and psychological aspects of contemporary LSD use in Germany. *Journal of Drug Issues, 32,* 431–458.

Presson, P. K., & Benassi, V. A. (1996). Locus of control and depressive symptomatology: A meta-analysis. *Journal of Social Behavior and Personality, 11,* 201–212.

Preston, S. D., & de Waal, F. B. M. (2002). Empathy: Its ultimate and proximal bases. *Brain and Behavioral Sciences, 25,* 1–72.

Priester, J. R., Godek, J., Nayakankuppum, D. J., & Park, K. (2004). Brand congruity and comparative advertising: When and why comparative advertisements lead to greater elaboration. *Journal of Consumer Psychology, 14,* 115–123.

Priluck, R., & Till, B. D. (2004). The role of contingency awareness, involvement, and need for cognition in attitude formation. *Journal of the Academy of Marketing Science, 32,* 329–344.

Pritchard, C., & Hansen, L. (2005). Comparison of suicide in people aged 65–74 and 75+ by gender in England and Wales and the major Western countries 1979–1999. *International Journal of Geriatric Psychiatry, 20,* 17–25.

Pritchard, R. (1991). The effects of cultural schemata on reading processing strategies. *Reading Research Quarterly, 24,* 273–293.

Pritchard, R. M. (1961, June). Stabilized images on the retina. *Scientific American,* 72–78.

Prochiantz, A. (1992). *How the brain evolved.* New York: McGraw-Hill.

Provins, K. A. (1997). Handedness and speech: A critical reappraisal of the role of genetic and environmental factors in the cerebral lateralization of function. *Psychological Review, 104,* 544–571.

Puente, S., & Cohen, D. (2003). Jealousy and the meaning (or nonmeaning) of violence. *Personality and Social Psychology Bulletin, 29,* 449–460.

Pugh, E. N., Jr. (1988). Vision: Physics and retinal physiology. In R. C. Atkinson, R. J. Herrnstein, G. Lindzey, & R. D. Luce (Eds.), *Stevens' handbook of experimental psychology* (Vol. 1). New York: Wiley.

Putnam, S. P., Sanson, A. V., & Rothbart, M. K. (2002). Child temperament and parenting. In M. H. Bornstein (Ed.), *Handbook of parenting: Vol. 1. Children and parenting* (2nd ed., pp. 255–277). Mahwah, NJ: Erlbaum.

Pyryt, M. C. (1993). The fulfillment of promise revisited: A discriminant analysis of factors predicting success in the Terman study. *Roeper Review, 15,* 178–179.

Pytlik Zillig, L. M., Hemenover, S. H., & Dienstbier, R. A. (2002). What do we assess when we assess a Big 5 trait? A content analysis of the affective, behavioral and cognitive processes represented in the Big 5 personality inventories. *Personality and Social Psychology Bulletin, 28,* 847–858.

Qin, Y., Carter, C. S., Silk, E. M., Stenger, V. A., Fissell, K., Goode, A., & Anderson, J. R. (2004). The change of the brain activation patterns as children learn algebra equation solving. *Proceedings of the National Academy of Sciences,* 101, 5686–5691.

Querido, J. G., Warner, T. D., & Eyberg, S. M. (2002). Parenting styles and child behavior in African American families of preschool children. *Journal of Clinical Child Psychology, 31,* 272–277.

Rabbitt, P., Chetwynd, A., & McInnes, L. (2003). Do clever brains age more slowly? Further exploration of a nun result. *British Journal of Psychology, 94,* 63–71.
Rabin, M. D., & Cain, W. S. (1986). Determinants of measured olfactory sensitivity. *Perception & Psychophysics, 39,* 281–286.
Raffaelli, M., & Ontai, L. L. (2004). Gender socialization in Latino/a families: Results from two retrospective studies. *Sex Roles, 50,* 287–299.
Raffone, A., & Leeuwen, C. V. (2001). Activation and coherence in memory processes: Revisiting the parallel distributed processing approach to retrieval. *Connection Science: Journal of Neural Computing, Artificial Intelligence & Cognitive Research, 13,* 349–382.
Räikkönen, K., Matthews, K. A., Flory, J. D., & Owens, J. F. (1999). Effects of hostility on ambulatory blood pressure and mood during daily living in healthy adults. *Health Psychology, 18,* 44–53.
Rainville, P. D., Duncan, G. H., Price, D. D., Carrier, B., & Bushnell, M. C. (1997). Pain affect encoded in human anterior cingulated but not somatosensory cortex. *Science, 277,* 968–971.
Raithatha, N., & Smith, R. (2004). Disclosure of genetic tests for health insurance: Is it ethical not to? *Lancet, 363,* 395–396.
Rajimehr, R., Vaziri-Pashkam, M., Afraz, S.-R., & Esteky, H. (2004). Adaptation to apparent motion in crowding condition. *Vision Research, 44,* 925–931.
Rakison, D. H., & Oakes, L. M. (Eds.). (2003). *Early category and concept development: Making sense of the blooming, buzzing confusion.* London: Oxford University Press.
Ramachandran, V. S. (1992, May). Blind spots. *Scientific American,* 102–109.
Ramanathan, L., Gulyani, S., Nienhuis, R., & Siegel, J. M. (2002). Sleep deprivation decreases superoxide dismutase activity in rat hippocampus and brainstem. *Neuroreport: For Rapid Communication of Neuroscience Research, 13,* 1387–1390.
Ramirez-Amaya, V., & Bermudez-Rattoni, F. (1999). Conditioned enhancement of antibody production is disrupted by insular cortex and amygdala but not hippocampal lesions. *Brain, Behavior, and Immunity, 13,* 46–60.
Rammsayer, T. H. (2003). NMDA receptor activity and the transmission of sensory input into motor output in introverts and extraverts. *Quarterly Journal of Experimental Psychology: Comparative and Physiological Psychology, 56,* 207–221.
Rampon, C., Jiang, C. H., Dong, H., Tang, Y. P., Lockhart, D. J., Schultz, P. G., Tsien, J. Z., & Hu, Y. (2000). Effects of environmental enrichment on gene expression in the brain. *Proceedings of the National Academy of Sciences,* 97, 12880–12884.
Ramus, F., Hauser, M. D., Miller, C., Morris, D., & Mehler, J. (2001). Language discrimination by human newborns and by cotton-top tamarin monkeys. In M. Tomasello (Ed.), *Language development: The essential readings* (pp. 34–41). *Essential readings in developmental psychology.* Malden, MA: Blackwell.
Randi, J. (1980). *Flim-flam!* New York: Lippincott.
Ranganath, C., Johnson, M. K., D'Esposito, M. (2003). Prefrontal activity associated with working memory and episodic long-term memory. *Neuropsychologia, 41,* 378–389.
Rao, S. M., Huber, S. J., & Bornstein, R. A. (1992). Emotional changes with multiple sclerosis and Parkinson's disease. *Journal of Consulting and Clinical Psychology, 60,* 369–378.
Rapee, R. M. (1995). Psychological factors influencing the affective response to biological challenge procedures in panic disorder. *Journal of Anxiety Disorders, 9,* 59–74.
Ratcliff, R., & McKoon, G. (1994). Retrieving information from memory: Spreading-activation theories versus compound-cue theories. *Psychological Review, 101,* 177–184.
Rathunde, K. (2001). Toward a psychology of optimal human functioning: What positive psychology can learn from the "experiential turns" of James, Dewey, and Maslow. *Journal of Humanistic Psychology, 41,* 135–153.
Ratliff-Crain, J., Donald, K., & Ness, J. (1999). The relative impact of knowledge, beliefs, peer norms, and past behaviors on current risky sexual behaviors among college students. *Psychology and Health, 14,* 625–641.
Ravasia, S. (2001). Risperidone-induced edema. *Canadian Journal of Psychiatry, 46,* 453–454.
Raven, P. H., & Johnson, G. B. (1999). *Biology* (5th ed.). New York: McGraw-Hill.
Raynor, H. A., & Epstein, L. H. (2003). The relative-reinforcing value of food under differing levels of food deprivation and restriction. *Appetite, 40,* 15–24.
Raz, A., & Shapiro, T. (2002). Hypnosis and neuroscience: A cross talk between clinical and cognitive research. *Archives of General Psychiatry, 59,* 85–90.
Raz, S., & Raz, N. (1990). Structural brain abnormalities in the major psychoses: A quantitative review of the evidence from computerized imaging. *Psychological Bulletin, 108,* 93–108.
Redding, R. E. (2001). Sociopolitical diversity in psychology. *American Psychologist, 56,* 205–215.
Reed, G. (1979). Everyday anomalies of recall and recognition. In J. F. Kihlstrom & F. J. Evans (Eds.), *Functional disorders of memory* (pp. 1–28). Hillsdale, NJ: Erlbaum.
Reed, I. C. (2005). Creativity: Self-perceptions over time. *International Journal of Aging and Human Development, 60,* 1–18.
Reed, S. K. (1996). *Cognition: Theory and applications* (4th ed.). Pacific Grove, CA: Brooks/Cole.
Reeder, H. M. (2000). "I like you . . . as a friend": The role of attraction in cross-sex friendship. *Journal of Social and Personal Relationships, 17,* 329–348.
Reese, H. W., Lee, L.-J., Cohen, S. H., & Puckett, J. M., Jr. (2001). Effects of intellectual variables, age, and gender on divergent thinking in adulthood. *International Journal of Behavioral Development, 25,* 491–500.
Reeve, J. (1992). *Understanding motivation and emotion.* Fort Worth, TX: Harcourt Brace.
Regan, D., & Beverley, K. I. (1984). Figure-ground segregation by motion contrast and by luminance contrast. *Journal of the Optical Society of America A, 1,* 433–442.
Regan, D. T., & Kilduff, M. (1988). Optimism about elections: Dissonance reduction at the ballot box. *Political Psychology, 9,* 101–107.
Regan, P. C. (1996). Sexual outcasts: The perceived impact of body weight and gender on sexuality. *Journal of Applied Social Psychology, 26,* 1803–1815.
Regan, P. C., Levin, L., Sprecher, S., Christopher, F. S., & Cate, R. (2000). Partner preferences: What characteristics do men and women desire in their short-term sexual and long-term romantic partners? *Journal of Psychology & Human Sexuality, 12,* 1–21.
Reichman, J. (1998). *I'm not in the mood: What every woman should know about improving her libido.* New York: Morrow.
Reinisch, J., Hill, C., Sanders, S., & Ziemba-Davis, M. (1995). High-risk sexual behavior at a midwestern university: A confirmatory survey. *Family Planning Perspectives, 27,* 79–82.
Reiser, M. (1982). *Police psychology: Collected papers.* Los Angeles: Lehi Publishing Company.
Reiss, S., & Havercamp, S. M. (2005). Motivation in developmental context: A new method for studying self-actualization. *Journal of Humanistic Psychology, 45,* 41–53.
Reissland, N. (1988). Neonatal imitation in the first hour of life: Observations in rural Nepal. *Developmental Psychology, 24,* 464–469.
Reitman, D., Hupp, S. D. A., O'Callaghan, P. M., Gulley, V., & Northup, J. (2001). The influence of a token economy and methylphenidate on attentive and disruptive behavior during sports with ADHD-diagnosed children. *Behavior Modification, 25,* 305–323.
Remington, G., Shammi, C. M., Sethna, R., & Lawrence, R. (2001). Antipsychotic patterns for schizophrenia in three treatment settings. *Psychiatric Services, 52,* 96–98.
Reneman, L., Booij, J., Schmand, B., van den Brink, W., & Gunning, B. (2000). Memory disturbances in "Ecstasy" users are correlated with an altered brain serotonin neurotransmission. *Psychopharmacology, 148,* 322–324.
Renner, J. W., Abraham, M. R., Grzybowski, E. B., & Marek, E. A. (1990). Understandings and misunderstandings of eighth graders of four physics concepts found in textbooks. *Journal of Research in Science in Teaching, 27,* 35–54.
Rescorla, R. A. (1968). Probability of shock in the presence and absence of CS in fear conditioning. *Journal of Comparative and Physiological Psychology, 66,* 1–5.
Rescorla, R. A. (1992). Hierarchical associative relations in Pavlovian conditioning and instrumental training. *Current Directions in Psychological Science, 1,* 66–70.
Rescorla, R. A., & Wagner, A. R. (1972). A theory of Pavlovian conditioning: Variations in the effectiveness of reinforcement and nonreinforcement. In A. H. Black & W. F. Perokasy (Eds.), *Classical conditioning II: Current theory.* New York: Appleton-Century-Crofts.
Ressler, K. J., Sullivan, S. L., & Buck, L. B. (1994). A molecular dissection of spatial patterning in the olfactory system. *Current Opinion in Neurobiology, 4,* 588–596.
Reuter-Lorenz, P. A., & Miller, A. C. (1998). The cognitive neuroscience of human laterality: Lessons from the bisected brain. *Current Directions in Psychological Science, 7,* 15–20.
Rexrode, K., Carey, V., Hennekens, C., Walters, E., Colditz, G., Stampher, M., Willett, W., & Manson, J. (1997). A prospective study of body mass index, weight change, and risk of stroke in women. *Journal of the American Medical Association, 277,* 1539–1545.
Rhine, J. B. (1934). Extra-sensory perception of the clairvoyant type. *Journal of Abnormal and Social Psychology, 29,* 151–171.
Riccio, D. C., Millin, P. M., & Gisquet-Verrier, P. (2003). Retrograde amnesia: Forgetting back. *Current Directions in Psychological Science, 12,* 41–44.
Riccio, D. C., Rabinowitz, V. C., & Axelrod, S. (1994). Memory: When less is more. *American Psychologist, 49,* 917–926.
Rice, G., Anderson, C., Risch, N., & Ebers, G. (1999). Male homosexuality: Absence of linkage to microsatellite markers at Xq28. *Science, 284,* 665–667.
Rice, M. E. (1997). Violent offender research and implications for the criminal justice system. *American Psychologist, 52,* 414–423.
Richardson, J. (1993). The curious case of coins: Remembering the appearance of familiar objects. *The Psychologist: Bulletin of the British Psychological Society, 6,* 360–366.
Richardson, J. T. E. (2003). Howard Andrew Knox and the origins of performance testing on Ellis Island, 1912–1916. *History of Psychology, 6,* 143–170.
Richardson, J. T. E., Engle, R. W., Hasher, L., Logie, R. H., Stoltzfus, E. R., & Zacks, R. T. (Eds.). (1996). *Working memory and human cognition.* New York: Oxford University Press.
Richardson, J. T. E., & Zucco, G. M. (1989). Cognition and olfaction: A review. *Psychological Bulletin, 105,* 352–360.
Richeson, J. A., & Nussbaum, R. J. (2004). The impact of multiculturalism versus color-blindness on racial bias. *Journal of Experimental Social Psychology, 40,* 417–423.
Ridley, J., Yu, D. W., & Sutherland, W. J. (2005). Why long-lived species are more likely to be social: The role of local dominance. *Behavioral Ecology, 16,* 358–363.
Riedel, B. W., Robinson, L. A., Klesges, R. C., & McLain-Allen, B. (2003). Ethnic differences in smoking withdrawal effects among adolescents. *Addictive Behaviors, 28,* 129–140.
Rieves, L., & Cash, T. (1996). Social developmental factors and women's body-image attitudes. *Journal of Social Behavior and Personality, 11,* 63–78.
Riger, S. (1992). Epistomological debates, feminist voices: Science, social values, and the study of women. *American Psychologist, 47,* 730–740.
Riley, L. R. (1987). *Psychology of language development: A primer.* Toronto: C. J. Hogrefe.
Rimberg, H., & Lewis, R. (1994). Older adolescents and AIDS: Correlates of self-reported safer sex practices. *Journal of Research on Adolescence, 4,* 453–464.
Rimmele, C. T., Howard, M. O., & Hilfrink, M. L. (1995). Aversion therapies. In R. K. Hester & W. R. Miller (Eds.), *Handbook of alcoholism treatment approaches: Effective alternatives* (2nd ed., pp. 134–147). Boston: Allyn & Bacon.
Riso, L. P., du Toit, P. L., Blandino, J. A., Penna, S., Dacey, S., Duin, J. S., Pacoe, E. M., Grant, M. M., Merida, M., & Ulmer, C. S. (2003). Cognitive aspects of chronic depression. *Journal of Abnormal Psychology, 112,* 72–80.

Roberts, B., Wood, D., & Smith, J. L. (2005). Evaluating Five Factor Theory and social investment perspectives on personality trait development. *Journal of Research in Personality, 39,* 166–184.

Roberts, B. W., Caspi, A., & Moffitt, T. E. (2001). The kids are alright: Growth and stability in personality development from adolescence to adulthood. *Journal of Personality and Social Psychology, 81,* 670–683.

Roberts, B. W., & DelVecchio, W. F. (2000). The rank-order consistency of personality traits from childhood to old age: A quantitative review of longitudinal studies. *Psychological Bulletin, 126,* 3–25.

Roberts, J. A., Brown, D., Elkins, T., & Larson, D. B. (1997). Factors influencing views of patients with gynecologic cancer about end-of-life decisions. *American Journal of Obstetrics and Gynecology, 176,* 166–172.

Roberts, J. V., & Herman, C. P. (1986). The psychology of height: An empirical review. In C. P. Herman, M. P. Zanna, & E. T. Higgins (Eds.), *Physical appearance, stigma, and social behavior: The Ontario symposium* (Vol. 3, pp. 113–140). Hillsdale, NJ: Erlbaum.

Roberts, R. E., Phinney, J. S., Masse, L. C., Chen, Y., Roberts, C. R., & Romero, A. (1999). The structure of ethnic identity of young adolescents from diverse ethno-cultural groups. *Journal of Early Adolescence, 19,* 301–322.

Robinson, E. L., & Nagel, R. J. (1992). The comparability of the test of cognitive skills with the Wechsler Intelligence Scale for Children-Revised and the Stanford-Binet: Fourth edition with gifted children. *Psychology in School, 29,* 107–112.

Robinson, P. (1989). *The modernization of sex.* Ithaca, NY: Cornell University Press.

Robinson, T. (1999). Reducing children's television viewing to prevent obesity: A randomized controlled trial. *Journal of the American Medical Association, 282,* 1561–1567.

Robinson, T. N., Wilde, M. L., Navracruz, L. C., Haydel, K. F., & Varady, A. (2001). Effects of reducing children's television and video game use on aggressive behavior: A randomized controlled trial. *Archives of Pediatrics and Adolescent Medicine, 155,* 17–23.

Rochot, F., Maggioni, O., & Modigliani, A. (2000). The dynamics of obeying and opposing authority: A mathematical model. In T. Blass (Ed.), *Obedience to authority: Current perspectives on the Milgram paradigm* (pp. 161–192). Mahwah, NJ: Erlbaum.

Rodin, J. (1986). Aging and health: Effects of the sense of control. *Science, 233,* 1271–1276.

Rodin, J., & Wing, R. R. (1988). Behavioral factors in obesity. *Diabetes/Metabolism Reviews, 4,* 701–725.

Roediger, H. L., III. (1990). Implicit memory: Retention without remembering. *American Psychologist, 45,* 1043–1056.

Roediger, H. L., III, & Marsh, E. J. (2003). Episodic and autobiographical memory. In A. F. Healy & R. W. Proctor (Eds.), *Handbook of psychology: Experimental psychology* (Vol. 4, pp. 475–497). New York: Wiley.

Roehrs, T., Papineau, K., Rosenthal, L., & Roth, T. (1999). Sleepiness and the reinforcing and subjective effects of methylphenidate. *Experimental and Clinical Psychopharmacology, 7,* 145–150.

Rogers, C. R. (1951). *Client-centered therapy: Its current practice, implications, and theory.* Boston: Houghton Mifflin.

Rogers, C. R. (1959). A theory of therapy, personality, and interpersonal relationships as developed in the client-centered framework. In S. Koch (Ed.), *Psychology: A study of a science* (Vol. 3, pp. 184–256). New York: McGraw-Hill.

Rogers, C. R. (1961). *On becoming a person.* Boston: Houghton Mifflin.

Rogers, L. (2001). *Sexing the brain.* London: Weidenfeld & Nicolson.

Rogers, R. G. (1995). Marriage, sex, and mortality. *Journal of Marriage and the Family, 57,* 515–526.

Rogers, T. B., Kuiper, N. A., & Kirker, W. S. (1977). Self-reference and the encoding of personal information. *Journal of Personality and Social Psychology, 35,* 677–688.

Rogoff, B. (1984). *Children's learning in the "zone of proximal development."* San Francisco: Jossey-Bass.

Rogoff, B. (1990). *Apprenticeship in thinking: Cognitive development in a social context.* New York: Oxford University Press.

Rogoff, B., Paradise, R., Arauz, R. M., Correa-Chavez, M., & Angelillo, C. (2003). Firsthand learning through intent participation. *Annual Review of Psychology, 54,* 175–203.

Rolls, A., & Deco, G. (2002). *Computational neuroscience of vision.* London: Oxford University Press.

Rolls, B. (1986). Sensory-specific satiety. *Nutrition Reviews, 44,* 93–101.

Rolls, B., Rolls, E., Rowe, E., & Sweeney, K. (1981). Sensory specific satiety in man. *Physiology and Behavior, 27,* 137–142.

Romer, D., Gruder, C. I., & Lizzadro, T. (1986). A person-situation approach to altruistic behavior. *Journal of Personality and Social Psychology, 51,* 1001–1012.

Rorschach, H. (1921). *Psychodiagnostics.* Bern: Bircher (Transl. Hans Huber Verlag, 1942).

Rosch, E. H. (1973). Natural categories. *Cognitive Psychology, 4,* 328–350.

Rosch, E. H. (1978). Principles of categorization. In E. Rosch & B. L. Lloyd (Eds.), *Cognition and categorization.* Hillsdale, NJ: Erlbaum.

Rose, R. J., & Ditto, W. B. (1983). A developmental-genetic analysis of common fears from early adolescence to early adulthood. *Child Development, 54,* 361–368.

Rose, S., & Zand, D. (2000). Lesbian dating and courtship from young adulthood to midlife. *Journal of Gay and Lesbian Social Services, 11,* 77–104.

Rosen, G., Lohr, J., McNally, R., & Herbert, J. (1999). Power therapies: Evidence vs. miraculous claims. *Behavioural & Cognitive Psychotherapy, 27,* 9–12.

Rosen, H. J., Narvaez, J. M., Hallam, B., Kramer, J. H., Wyss-Coray, C., Gearhart, R., Johnson, J. K., & Miller, B. L. (2004). Neuropsychological and functional measures of severity in Alzheimer disease, frontotemporal dementia, and semantic dementia. *Alzheimer Disease & Associated Disorders, 18,* 202–207.

Rosen, K. S., & Rothbaum, F. (1993). Quality of parental caregiving and security of attachment. *Developmental Psychology, 29,* 358–367.

Rosenberg, M. (1965). *Society and the adolescent self-image.* Princeton, NJ: Princeton University Press.

Rosenberg, M. (1979). *Conceiving the self.* New York: Basic Books.

Rosenberg, M. L., & Mercy, J. A. (1991). Assaultive violence. In M. L. Rosenberg & M. A. Fenley (Eds.), *Violence in America: A public health approach* (pp. 14–50). New York: Oxford University Press.

Rosenberg, M. L., Mercy, J. A., & Potter, L. B. (1999). Firearms and suicide. *New England Journal of Medicine, 341,* 1609–1611.

Rosenhan, D. L. (1970). The natural socialization of altruistic autonomy. In J. Macaulay & L. Berkowitz (Eds.), *Altruism and helping behavior.* New York: Academic Press.

Rosenhan, D. L. (1971). On being sane in insane places. *Science, 179,* 250–258.

Rosenman, R. H. (1993). Relationships of the Type A behavior pattern with coronary heart disease. In L. Goldberger & S. Breznitz (Eds.), *Handbook of stress: Theoretical and clinical aspects* (2nd ed.). New York: Free Press.

Rosenman, R. H., Brand, R. J., Jenkins, C. D., Freidman, M., Straus, R., & Wurm, M. (1975). Coronary heart disease on the Western collaborative group study: Final follow-up experience of 8 1/2 years. *Journal of the American Medical Association, 233,* 872–877.

Rosenthal, N. E., Sack, D. A., Gillin, C., Lewy, A. J., Goodwin, F. K., Davenport, Y., Mueller, P. S., Newsome, D. A., & Wehr, T. A. (1984). Depression and length of daylight in seasonal affective disorder. *Archives of General Psychiatry, 41,* 72–80.

Rosenthal, R. (1994). Science and ethics in conducting, analyzing, and reporting psychological research. *Psychological Science, 5,* 127–134.

Rosenthal, R. (1995). Ethical issues in psychological science: Risk, consent, and scientific quality. *Psychological Science, 6,* 322–323.

Rosenthal, R., & Jacobson, L. (1968). *Pygmalion in the classroom: Teacher expectation and pupils' intellectual development.* New York: Holt.

Rosenzweig, M. R. (1984). Experience, memory, and the brain. *American Psychologist, 47,* 718–722.

Rosenzweig, M. R., Breedlove, S. M., & Leiman, A. L. (2002). *Biological psychology: An introduction to behavioral, cognitive, and clinical neuroscience* (3rd ed.). Sunderland, MA: Sinauer Associates.

Ross, C. A. (1991). Epidemiology of multiple personality disorder and dissociation. *Psychiatric Clinics of North America, 14,* 503–516.

Ross, C. A., Norton, G. R., & Wozney, K. (1989). Multiple personality disorder: An analysis of 236 cases. *Canadian Journal of Psychiatry, 34,* 413–418.

Ross, H., & Plug, C. (2002). *The mystery of the moon illusion.* Oxford: Oxford University Press.

Ross, H. E. (2000). Sensation and perception. In D. S. Gupta & R. M. Gupta (Eds.), *Psychology for psychiatrists* (pp. 20–40). London: Whurr Publishers.

Ross, L. (1977). The intuitive psychologist and his shortcomings: Distortions in the attribution process. In L. Berkowitz (Ed.), *Advances in experimental social psychology* (Vol. 10, pp. 174–221). New York: Academic Press.

Ross, M., & Wilson, A. E. (2002). It feels like yesterday: Self-esteem, valence of personal past experiences, and judgments of subjective distance. *Journal of Personality and Social Psychology, 82,* 792–803.

Ross, M., & Wilson, A. E. (2003). Autobiographical memory and conceptions of self: Getting better all the time. *Current Directions in Psychological Science, 12,* 66–69.

Rossini, P. M., & Pauri, F. (2000). Neuromagnetic integrated methods tracking human brain mechanisms of sensorimotor areas' "plastic" reorganization. *Brain Research Reviews, 33,* 131–154.

Rosso, I. M., Cintron, C. M., Steingard, R. J., Renshaw, P. F., Young, A. D., & Yurgelum-Todd, D. A. (2005). Amygdala and hippocampus volumes in pediatric major depression. *Biological Psychiatry, 57,* 21–26.

Rossow, I., Groholt, B., & Wichstrom, L. (2005). Intoxicants and suicidal behaviour among adolescents: Changes in levels and associations from 1992 to 2002. *Addiction, 100,* 79–88.

Roszak, T. (1975). *The unfinished animal.* New York: Harper & Row.

Roth, G. (2001). The evolution of consciousness. In G. Roth (Ed.), *Brain evolution and cognition* (pp. 555–582). New York: Wiley.

Rothbart, M. K. (1989). Biological process in temperament. In G. A. Kornstramm, J. Bates, & M. K. Rothbart (Eds.), *Handbook of temperament in childhood* (pp. 77–110). Sussex, England: Wiley.

Rothbaum, B. O., Hodges, L. F., Kooper, R., Opdyke, D., Williford, J., & North, M. M. (1995). Effectiveness of computer-generated (virtual reality) graded exposure in the treatment of acrophobia. *American Journal of Psychiatry, 152,* 626–628.

Rothbaum, F., Weisz, J., Pott, M., Miyake, K., & Morelli, G. (2000). Attachment and culture: Security in the United States and Japan. *American Psychologist, 55,* 1093–1104.

Rothkopf, J. S., & Blaney, P. H. (1991). Mood congruent memory: The role of affective focus and gender. *Cognition and Emotion, 5,* 53–64.

Rothstein, H. R., McDaniel, M. A., & Borenstein, M. (2002). Meta-analysis: A review of quantitative cumulation methods. In F. Drasgow & N. Schmitt (Eds.), *Measuring and analyzing behavior in organizations: Advances in measurement and data analysis. The Jossey-Bass business & management series.* San Francisco: Jossey-Bass.

Rotter, J. (1966). Generalized expectancies for internal versus external control of reinforcement. *Psychological Monographs, 80* (Whole No. 609).

Rotter, J. (1990). Internal versus external control of reinforcement: A case history of a variable. *American Psychologist, 45,* 489–493.

Rovee-Collier, C., Hayne, H., & Colombo, M. (2001). *The development of implicit and explicit memory.* Philadelphia: John Benjamins.

Rowatt, W. C., Cunningham, M. R., & Druen, P. B. (1998). Deception to get a date. *Personality and Social Psychology Bulletin, 24,* 1228–1242.

Rowe, C. C., & Van den Oord, E. J. C. G. (2005). Genetic and environmental influences. In V. J. Derlega, B. A Winstead, & W. H. Jones (Eds.), *Personality: Contemporary theory and research* (3rd ed., pp. 63–97). Belmont, CA: Thomson Wadsworth.

Rowe, D. C. (1997). Genetics, temperament, and personality. In R. Hogan, J. Johnson, & S. Briggs (Eds.), *Handbook of personality psychology* (pp. 267–286). San Diego, CA: Academic Press.

Rowland, D. L., & Burnett, A. L. (2000). Pharmacotherapy in the treatment of male sexual dysfunction. *Journal of Sex Research, 37,* 226–243.

Roy, N., Gordon, G., & Thrun, S. (2005). Finding approximate POMDP solutions through belief compression. *Journal of Artificial Intelligence Research, 23,* 1–40.

Roy-Byrne, P. P., & Cowley, D. S. (2002). Pharmacological treatments for panic disorder, generalized anxiety disorder, specific phobia, and social anxiety disorder. In P. E. Nathan & J. M. Gorman (Eds.), *A guide to treatments that work* (2nd ed., pp. 337–365). London: Oxford University Press.

Rozin, P. (1996). Sociocultural influences on human food selection. In E. Capaldi (Ed.), *Why we eat what we eat: The psychology of eating* (pp. 233–263). Washington, DC: American Psychological Association.

Rozin, P., Dow, S., Moscovitch, M., Rajaram, S. (1998). What causes humans to begin and end a meal? A role for memory for what has been eaten, as evidenced by a study of multiple meal eating in amnesic patients. *Psychological Science, 9,* 392–396.

Rubin, D. C., & Wallace, W. T. (1989). Rhyme and reason: Analyses of dual retrieval cues. *Journal of Experimental Psychology: Learning, Memory, and Cognition, 15,* 698–709.

Rubin, E. (1915/1958). Synoplevede Figurer (Figure and ground). In D. C. Beardslee & M. Wertheimer (Eds.), *Readings in perception* (pp. 194–203). Princeton, NJ: Von Nostrand.

Rubin, K. H., Burgess, K. B., & Coplan, R. J. (2002). Social withdrawal and shyness. In P. K. Smith & C. H. Hart (Eds.), *Blackwell handbook of childhood social development* (pp. 330–352). Malden, MA: Blackwell.

Rucker, C., III, & Cash, T. (1992). Body images, body-size perceptions, and eating behaviors among African-American and White college women. *International Journal of Eating Disorders, 12,* 291–299.

Ruggerio, V. R. (1988). *Teaching thinking across the curriculum.* New York: Harper & Row.

Rumbaugh, D. M. (1990). Comparative psychology and the great apes: Their competency in learning, language, and numbers. *Psychological Record, 40,* 15–39.

Rumbaugh, D. M., & Savage-Rumbaugh, S. (1986). Reasoning and language in chimpanzees. In R. J. Hoage & L. Goldman (Eds.), *Animal intelligence.* Washington, DC: Smithsonian Institution Press.

Rumbaugh, D. M., & Washburn, D. A. (2003). *Intelligence of apes and other rational beings.* New Haven, CT: Yale University Press.

Rusbult, C. E., & Martz, J. M. (1995). Remaining in an abusive relationship: An investment model analysis of nonvoluntary dependence. *Personality and Social Psychology Bulletin, 21,* 558–571.

Rusbult, C. E., Morrow, G. D., & Johnson, D. J. (1987). Self-esteem and problem-solving behaviour in close relationships. *British Journal of Social Psychology, 26,* 293–303.

Rusbult, C. E., Zembrodt, I., & Iwaniszek, J. (1986). The impact of gender and sex-role orientation on responses to dissatisfaction in close relationships. *Sex Roles, 15,* 1–20.

Ruscio, J. (2001). Administering quizzes at random to increase students' reading. *Teaching of Psychology, 28,* 204–206.

Rushton, J. P. (1995). *Race, evolution, and behavior,* New Brunswick, NJ: Transaction.

Rushton, J. P., & Ankney, C. D. (1996). Brain size and cognitive ability: Correlations with age, sex, social class, and race. *Psychonomic Bulletin and Review, 3,* 21–36.

Rushton, J. P., & Rushton, E. W. (2003). Brain size, IQ, and racial-group differences: Evidence from musculoskeletal traits. *Intelligence, 31,* 139–155.

Rushton, J. P., Skuy, M., & Bons, T. A. (2004). Construct validity of Raven's Advanced Progressive Matrices for African and Non-African engineering students in South Africa. *International Journal of Selection and Assessment, 12,* 220–229.

Russell, J. A., & Yik, S. M. (1996). Emotion among the Chinese. In M. H. Bond (Ed.), *The handbook of Chinese psychology.* Hong Kong, China: Oxford University Press.

Russell, J. D., & Roxanas, M. (1990). Psychiatry and the frontal lobes. *Australian & New Zealand Journal of Psychiatry, 24,* 113–132.

Russell, S., & Norvig, P. (2003). *Artificial intelligence: A modern approach* (2nd ed.). Englewood Cliffs, NJ: Prentice Hall.

Russo, J. E., & Schoemaker, P. J. H. (2002). *Winning decisions: Getting it right the first time.* New York: Doubleday.

Russo, P., Persegani, C. M., Papeschi, L. L., & Trimarchi, M. (2001). Sex differences in EEG correlates of a self-reported measure of hemisphere preference. *International Journal of Neuroscience, 106,* 109–121.

Rutherford, E. (1886). A new theory of hearing. *Journal of Anatomy and Physiology, 21,* 166–168.

Rutter, M. (2002). Nature, nurture, and development: From evangelism through science toward policy and practice. *Child Development, 73,* 1–21.

Ryan, R. M., Chirkov, V. I., Little, T. D., Sheldon, K. M., Timoshina, E., & Deci, E. L. (1999). The American dream in Russia: Extrinsic aspirations in two cultures. *Personality and Social Psychology Bulletin, 25,* 1509–1524.

Ryan, R. M., & Deci, E. L. (2000). When rewards compete with nature: The undermining of intrinsic motivation and self-regulation. In C. Sansone & J. M. Harackiewicz (Eds.), *Intrinsic and extrinsic motivation: The search for optimal motivation and performance* (pp. 13–78). San Diego, CA: Academic Press.

Ryan, R. M., & Deci, E. L. (2001). On happiness and human potentials: A review of research on hedonic and eudaimonic well-being. *Annual Review of Psychology, 52,* 141–166.

Ryden, A., Karlsson, J., Sullivan, M., Torgerson, J. S., & Taft, C. (2003). Coping and distress: What happens after intervention? A 2-year follow-up from the Swedish obese subjects (SOS) study. *Psychosomatic Medicine, 65,* 435–442.

Rymer, R. (1993). *Genie: An abused child's flight from silence.* New York: HarperCollins.

Rzewnicki, R., & Forgays, D. (1987). Recidivism and self-cure of smoking and obesity: An attempt to replicate. *American Psychologist, 42,* 97–100.

Saakvitne, K. W. (2005). Holding hope and humanity in the face of trauma's legacy: The daunting challenge for group therapists. *International Journal of Group Psychotherapy, 55,* 137–149.

Saarni, C. (1999). *The development of emotional competence.* New York: Guilford.

Sachs, J. (1989). Communication development in infancy. In J. Berko-Gleason (Ed.), *The development of language.* Columbus, OH: Merrill/Macmillan.

Sachs, J., Bard, B., & Johnson, M. L. (1981). Language learning with restricted input: Case studies of two hearing children of deaf parents. *Applied Psycholinguistics, 2,* 33–54.

Sackheim, H. A., Prudic, J., Devanand, D. P., Nobler, M. S., Lisanby, S. H., Peyser, S., Fitzsimons, L., Moody, B. J., & Clark, J. (2000). A prospective, randomized, double-blind comparison of bilateral and right unilateral electroconvulsive therapy at different stimulus intensities. *Archive of General Psychiatry, 57,* 425–434.

Sadler, P., & Woody, E. (2003). Is who you are who you're talking to? Interpersonal style and complementarity in mixed-sex interactions. *Journal of Personality & Social Psychology, 84,* 80–95.

Safdar, S., & Lay, C. H. (2003). The relations of immigrant-specific and immigrant-nonspecific daily hassles to distress controlling for psychological adjustment and cultural competence. *Journal of Applied Social Psychology, 33,* 299–320.

Sage, C., Huang, M., Karimi, K., Gutierrez, G., Vollrath, M. A., Zhang, D.-S., García-Añoveros, J., Hinds, P. W., Corwin, J. T., Corey, D. P., & Chen, Z.-Y. (2005). Proliferation of functional hair cells in vivo in the absence of the retinoblastoma protein. *Science Express Reports,* published online January 14, 2005, www.sciencemag.org

Sagi, A., Koren-Karie, N., Gini, M., Ziv, Y., & Joels, T. (2002). Shedding further light on the effects of various types and quality of early child care on infant-mother attachment relationship: The Haifa Study of Early Child Care. *Child Development, 73,* 1166–1186.

Sagi, A., Lamb, M. E., Lewkowicz, K. S., Shoman, R., Dvir, R., & Estes, D. (1985). Security of infant-mother, -father, and metapelet attachment among kibbutz-reared Israeli children. *Monographs of the Society for Research in Child Development, 50* (1-2, Serial No. 209).

Sagie, A., Elizur, S., & Hirotsugu, Y. (1996). The structure and strength of achievement motivation: A cross-cultural comparison. *Journal of Organization Behavior, 17,* 431–444.

Sahi, T. (1994). Hypolactasia and lactase persistence: Historical review and the terminology. *Scandinavian Journal of Gastroenterology, 202* (Suppl.), 1–6.

Saks, E. R., Jeste, D. V., Granholm, E., Palmer, B. W., & Schneiderman, L. (2002). Ethical issues in psychosocial interventions research involving controls. *Ethics & Behavior, 12,* 87–101.

Sales, B., & Folkman, S. (2000). *Ethics in research with human participants.* Washington, DC: American Psychological Association.

Salmon, P. (2001). Effects of physical exercise on anxiety, depression, and sensitivity to stress: A unifying theory. *Clinical Psychology Review, 21,* 33–61.

Salovey, P., & Mayer, J. (1994). Some final thoughts about personality and intelligence. In R. J. Sternberg & P. Ruzgis (Eds.), *Personality and intelligence* (pp. 303–318). New York: Cambridge University Press.

Salovey, P., Mayer, J. D., Caruso, D., & Lopes, P. N. (2003). Measuring emotional intelligence as a set of abilities with the Mayer-Salovey-Caruso Emotional Intelligence Test. In S. J. Lopez & C. R. Snyder (Eds.), *Positive psychological assessment: A handbook of models and measures* (pp. 251–265). Washington, DC: American Psychological Association.

Salovey, P., & Pizarro, D. A. (2003). The value of emotional intelligence. In R. J. Sternberg, J. Lautrey, & T. I. Lubart (Eds.), *Models of intelligence: International perspectives* (pp. 263–278). Washington, DC: American Psychological Association.

Salovey, P., & Rodin, J. (1988). Coping with envy and jealousy. *Journal of Social and Clinical Psychology, 7,* 15–33.

Salsman, J. M., Brown, T. L., Brechting, E. H., & Carlson, C. R. (2005). The link between religion and spirituality and psychological adjustment: The mediating role of optimism and social support. *Personality and Social Psychology Bulletin, 31,* 522–535.

Sameroff, A., Seifer, R., Baldwin, A., & Baldwin, C. (1993). Stability of intelligence from preschool to adolescence: The influence of social and family risk factors. *Child Development, 64,* 80–97.

Sampson, E. E. (1991). *Social worlds, personal lives: An introduction to social psychology.* San Diego, CA: Harcourt Brace Jovanovich.

Sandage, S. J., & Hill, P. C. (2001). The positive virtues of positive psychology: The rapprochement and challenges of an affirmative postmodern perspective. *Journal for the Theory of Social Behaviour, 31,* 241–260.

Sanders, G., Sjodin, M., & de Chastelaine, M. (2002). On the elusive nature of sex differences in cognition: Hormonal influences contributing to within-sex variation. *Archives of Sexual Behavior, 31,* 145–152.

Sandfort, T. G. M., de Graaf, R., Bijl, R. V., & Schnabel, P. (2001). Same-sex sexual behavior and psychiatric disorders. *Archives of General Psychiatry, 58,* 85–91.

Sandler, W. (2003). On the complementarity of signed and spoken languages. In Y. Levy & J. Schaeffer (Eds.), *Language competence across populations: Toward a definition of specific language impairment* (pp. 383–409). Mahwah, NJ: Erlbaum.

Sappington, A. A. (1990). Recent psychological approaches to the free will versus determinism issue. *Psychological Bulletin, 108,* 19–29.

Sarason, I. (1984). Stress, anxiety, and cognitive interference: Reactions to tests. *Journal of Personality and Social Psychology, 46,* 929–938.

Sarason, I., Sarason, B., & Pierce, G. (1990). Anxiety, cognitive interference, and performance. *Journal of Social Behavior and Personality, 5,* 1–18.

Satterfield, J. M. (2002). Culturally sensitive cognitive-behavioral therapy for depression with low-income and minority clients. *Comprehensive handbook of psychotherapy: Cognitive-behavioral approaches, Vol. 2* (pp. 519–545). New York: Wiley.

Saudino, K. J., Plomin, R., Pedersen, N. L., & McClearn, G. E. (1994). The etiology of high and low cognitive ability during the second half of the life span. *Intelligence, 19,* 359–371.

Saufley, W. H., Otaka, S. R., & Bavaresco, J. L. (1985). Context effects: Classroom tests and context independence. *Memory & Cognition, 13,* 522–528.

Savage-Rumbaugh, S., Shanker, S. G., & Taylor, T. J. (1998). *Apes, language, and the human mind.* New York: Oxford University Press.

Savic, I., Berglund, H., & Lindstro, P. (2005). Brain response to putative pheromones in homosexual men. *Proceedings of the National Academies of Science, 102,* 7356–7361.

Savin, H. B. (1973). Professors and psychological researchers: Conflicting values in conflicting roles. *Cognition, 2,* 147–149.

Saxena, S., & Rauch, S. L. (2000). Functional neuroimaging and the neuroanatomy of obsessive-compulsive disorder. *Psychiatric Clinics of North America, 23,* 563–586.

Scarr, S., Pakstis, A. J., Katz, S. H., & Barker, W. B. (1977). The absence of a relationship between degree of white ancestry and intellectual skills within a black population. *Human Genetics, 39,* 69–86.

Scarr, S., & Weinberg, R. A. (1976). IQ test performance of Black children adopted by White families. *American Psychologist, 31,* 726–739.

Scarr, S., & Weinberg, R. A. (1983). The Minnesota adoption studies: Genetic differences and malleability. *Child Development, 54,* 260–267.

Scaturo, D. J. (2005). Transference, countertransference, and resistance: Unconscious determinants of dilemmas. In D. J. Scaturo & J. Douglas (Eds.), *Clinical dilemmas in psychotherapy: A transtheoretical approach to psychotherapy integration* (pp. 127–142). Washington, DC: American Psychological Association.

Scepkowski, L. A., Wiegel, M., Bach, A. K., Weisberg, R. B., Brown, T. A., & Barlow, D. H. (2004). Attributions for sexual situations in men with and without erectile disorder: Evidence from a sex-specific Attributional Style Measure. *Archives of Sexual Behavior, 33,* 559–569.

Schachter, S. (1959). *The psychology of affiliation: Experimental studies of the sources of gregariousness.* Stanford, CA: Stanford University Press.

Schachter, S. (1964). The interaction of cognitive and physiological determinants of emotional state. In L. Berkowitz (Ed.), *Advances in experimental social psychology* (Vol. 1, pp. 49–80). New York: Academic Press.

Schachter, S. (1966). The interaction of cognitive and physiological determinants of emotional state. In C. Spielberger (Ed.), *Anxiety and behavior.* New York: Academic Press.

Schachter, S., & Singer, J. (1962). Cognitive, social, and physiological determinants of emotional state. *Psychological Review, 69,* 379–399.

Schachtman, T. (2004). Pavlovian conditioning: Basic associative processes. *International Journal of Comparative Psychology, 17,* 14–15.

Schacter, D. L. (1992). Understanding implicit memory: A cognitive neuroscience approach. *American Psychologist, 47,* 559–569.

Schacter, D. L. (1996). *Searching for memory.* New York: Basic Books.

Schacter, D. L., & Badgaiyan, R. D. (2001). Neuroimaging of priming: New perspectives on implicit and explicit memory. *Current Directions in Psychological Science, 10,* 1–4.

Schacter, D. L., Chiu, C.-Y. P., & Ochsner, K. N. (1993). Implicit memory: A selective review. *Annual Review of Neuroscience, 16,* 159–182.

Schacter, D. L., & Scarry, E. (2003). Memory, brain and belief. *Quarterly Journal of Experimental Psychology, 56,* 185–187.

Schafer, D. W. (1996). *Relieving pain: A basic hypnotherapeutic approach.* Northvale, NJ: Jason Aronson.

Schafer, W. (Ed.). (1992). *Stress management for wellness* (2nd ed.). New York: Holt, Rinehart.

Schaie, K. W. (1996). Intellectual development in adulthood. In J. E. Birren, K. Schaie, R. P. Abeles, M. Gatz, & T. A. Salthouse (Eds.), *Handbook of the psychology of aging* (4th ed., pp. 266–286). San Diego, CA: Academic Press.

Schaie, K. W. (2005). *Developmental influences on adult intelligence: The Seattle longitudinal study.* London: Oxford University Press.

Schaller, M. (1997). Beyond "competing," beyond "compatible." *American Psychologist, 52,* 1379–1380.

Scharf, B. (1983). Loudness. In J. V. Tobias & E. D. Schubert (Eds.), *Hearing research and theory* (pp. 1–56). New York: Academic Press.

Scharff, C. (2000). Chasing fate and function of new neurons in adult brains. *Current Opinion in Neurobiology, 10,* 774–783.

Scharfstein, B.-A. (1973). *Mystical experience.* Indianapolis, IN: Bobbs-Merrill.

Schatzberg, A. F., & Nemeroff, C. B. (Eds.). (1995). *The American Psychiatric Press textbook of psychopharmacology.* Washington, DC: American Psychiatric Press.

Scheier, M., & Carver, C. (2000). Optimism, coping, and health: Assessment and implications of generalized outcome expectancies. *Health Psychology, 4,* 219–247.

Schiavi, R. C., & Schreiner-Engel, P. (1988). Nocturnal penile tumescence in healthy aging men. *Journal of Gerontology: Medical Sciences, 43,* 146–150.

Schifano, F., Oyefeso, A., Webb, L., Pollard, M., Corkery, J., & Ghodse, A. H. (2003). Review of deaths related to taking ecstasy, England and Wales, 1997–2000. *British Medical Journal, 326,* 80–81.

Schiff, M., Duyme, M., Dumaret, A., Steward, J., Tomkiewicz, S., & Feingold, J. (1978). Intellectual status of working class children adopted early into upper middle-class families. *Science, 200,* 1503–1504.

Schiffman, S. S. (1997). Taste and smell losses in normal aging and problem disease. *Journal of the American Medical Association, 278,* 1357–1363.

Schiffman, S. S., Graham, B. G., Sattely-Miller, E. A., & Warwick, Z. S. (1998). *Current Directions in Psychological Science, 7,* 137–143.

Schluter, N. D., Krams, M., Rushworth, M. F. S., & Passingham, R. E. (2001). Cerebral dominance for action in the human brain: The selection of actions. *Neuropsychologia, 39,* 105–113.

Schmidt, L. A., & Fox, N. A. (2002). Molecular genetics of temperamental differences in children. In J. Benjamin & R. P. Ebstein (Eds.), *Molecular genetics and the human personality* (pp. 245–255). Washington, DC: American Psychiatric Publishing.

Schmidt, S. J. (2004). Developmental needs meeting strategy: A new treatment approach applied to dissociative identity disorder. *Journal of Trauma and Dissociation, 5,* 55–78.

Schmitt, D. P. (2003). Universal sex differences in the desire for sexual variety: Tests from 52 nations, 6 continents, and 13 islands. *Journal of Personality and Social Psychology, 85,* 85–104.

Schmitt, D. P., Shackelford, T. K., & Buss, D. M. (2001a). Are men really more "oriented" toward short-term mating than women? A critical review of research and theory. *Psychology, Evolution, and Gender, 3,* 211–239.

Schmitt, D. P., Shackelford, T. K., Duntley, J., Tooke, W., & Buss, D. M. (2001b). The desire for sexual variety as a key to understanding basic human mating strategies. *Personal Relationships, 8,* 425–455.

Schmitter-Edgecombe, M., & Nissley, H. M. (2002). Effects of aging on implicit covariation learning. *Aging Neuropsychology & Cognition, 9,* 61–75.

Schmolck, H., Buffalo, E. A., & Squire, L. R. (2000). Memory distortions develop over time: Recollections from the O. J. Simpson trial verdict after 15 and 32 months. *Psychological Science, 11,* 39–45.

Schmuck, P., Kasser, T., & Ryan, R. M. (2000). The relationship of well-being to intrinsic and extrinsic goals in Germany and the U.S. *Social Indicators Research, 50,* 225–241.

Schmuck, P., & Sheldon, K. M. (Eds.). (2001). *Life goals and well-being: Towards a positive psychology of human striving.* Kirkland, WA: Hogrefe & Huber.

Schnaitter, R. (1987). American practicality and America's psychology [Review of *The origins of behaviorism: American psychology, 1870–1920*]. *Contemporary Psychology, 32,* 736–737.

Schneider, B. (1985). Organizational behavior. *Annual Review of Psychology, 36,* 573–611.

Schneider, C. D. (2000). What it means to be sorry: The power of apology in mediation. *Mediation Quarterly, 17,* 265–280.

Schneider, F., Weiss, U., Kessler, C., Mueller-Gaertner, H.-W., Posse, S., Salloum, J. B., Grodd, W., Himmelmann, F., Gaebel, W., & Birbaumer, N. (1999). Subcortical correlates of differential classical conditioning of aversive emotional reactions in social phobia. *Biological Psychiatry, 45,* 863–871.

Schneider, M. L., Moore, C. F., Kraemer, G. W., Roberts, A. D., & DeJesus, O. T. (2002). The impact of prenatal stress, fetal alcohol exposure, or both on development: Perspectives from a primate model. *Psychoneuroendocrinology, 27,* 285–298.

Schneider, R. H., Castillo-Richmond, A., Alexander, C. N., Myers, H., Kaushik, V., Aranguri, C., Norris, K., Haney, D., Rainforth, M., Calderon, R., & Nidich, S. (2001). Behavioral treatment of hypertensive heart disease in African Americans: Rationale and design of a randomized controlled trial. *Behavioral Medicine, 27,* 83–95.

Schneidman, E. S. (1987). A psychological approach to suicide. In G. VandenBos & B. K. Bryant (Eds.), *Cataclysms, crises, and catastrophes: Psychology in action. The master lectures* (Vol. 6, pp. 147–183). Washington, DC: American Psychological Association.

Schooler, J. W., Gerhard, D., & Loftus, E. F. (1986). Qualities of the unreal. *Journal of Experimental Psychology: Learning, Memory, and Cognition, 12,* 171–181.

Schultz, D. P., & Schultz, S. F. (2000). *A history of modern psychology* (7th ed.). Fort Worth, TX: Harcourt Brace.

Schulz, R., & Alderman, D. (1974). Clinical research and the stages of dying. *Omega, 5,* 137–143.

Schulze, C., Karie, T., & Dickens, W. (1996). *Does the bell curve ring true?* Washington, DC: Brookings Institution.

Schulze, D., Beauducel, A., & Brocke, B. (2005). Semantically meaningful and abstract figural reasoning in the context of fluid and crystallized intelligence. *Intelligence, 33,* 143–159.

Schuman, H. (1995). Attitudes, beliefs, and behavior. In K. S. Cook, G. A. Fine, & J. S. House (Eds.), *Sociological perspectives on social psychology* (pp. 68–89). Boston: Allyn & Bacon.

Schunk, D. H. (1996). *Learning theories* (2nd ed.). Englewood Cliffs, NJ: Merrill.

Schwartz, B., & Robbins, S. J. (1995). *Psychology of learning and behavior.* New York: W. W. Norton.

Schwartz, B. L. (2001). The relation of tip-of-the-tongue states and retrieval time. *Memory and Cognition, 29,* 117–126.

Schwartz, B. L. (2002). *Tip-of-the-tongue states: Phenomenology, mechanism, and lexical retrieval.* Mahwah, NJ: Erlbaum.

Schwartz, G. E., Davidson, R. J., & Maer, F. (1975). Right hemisphere lateralization for emotion in the human brain: Interactions with cognition. *Science, 190,* 286–288.

Schwartz, J. H. (1995). The neuron. In E. R. Kandel, J. H. Schwartz, & T. M. Jessell (Eds.), *Essentials of neural science and behavior.* Norwalk, CT: Appleton & Lange.

Schwartz, M. W., & Porte, D., Jr. (2005). Diabetes, obesity, and the brain. *Science, 307,* 375–379.

Schwartz, R. H. (1993). Chronic marijuana smoking and short-term memory impairment. In G. G. Nahas & C. Latour (Eds.), *Cannabis: Physiopathology, epidemiology, detection* (pp. 61–71). Boca Raton, FL: CRC Press.

Schwartz, S., & Maquet, P. (2002). Sleep imaging and the neuro-psychological assessment of dreams. *Trends in Cognitive Sciences, 6,* 23–30.

Schwartz, S. H. (2003). Mapping and interpreting cultural differences around the world. In H. Vinken, J. Soeters, & P. Ester (Eds.), *Comparing cultures: Dimensions of culture in a comparative perspective.* Leiden, The Netherlands: Brill.

Schwartz, S. H., & Howard, J. A. (1981). A normative decision-making model of altruism. In J. P. Rushton & R. M. Sorrentino (Eds.), *Altruism and helping behavior: Social, personality, and developmental perspectives* (pp. 189–211). Hillsdale, NJ: Erlbaum.

Schwartz, S. H., & Howard, J. A. (1982). Helping and cooperation: A self-based motivational model. In V. J. Derlega & J. Grzelak (Eds.), *Cooperation and helping behavior: Theories and research* (pp. 327–353). New York: Academic Press.

Schwarz, B. E. (1960). Ordeal by serpents, fire and strychnine: A study of some provocative psychosomatic phenomena. *Psychiatry Quarterly, 34,* 405–429.

Schwarz, N., & Vaughn, L. A. (2002). The availability heuristic revisited: Ease of recall and content of recall as distinct sources of information. In T. Gilovich, D. Griffin, & D. Kahneman (Eds.), *Heuristics and biases: The psychology of intuitive judgment* (pp. 103–119). New York: Cambridge University Press.

Schwarz, S., & Stahlberg, D. (2003). Strength of hindsight bias as a consequence of meta-cognitions. *Memory, 11,* 395–410.

Sclafani, A. (1995). How food preferences are learned: Laboratory animal models. *Proceedings of the Nutrition Society, 54,* 419–427.

Scott, A. J. (1994). Chronobiological considerations in shiftworker sleep and performance and shiftwork scheduling. *Human Performance, 7,* 207–233.

Scott, W. A., Scott, R., & McCabe, M. (1991). Family relationships and children's personality: A cross-cultural, cross-source comparison. *British Journal of Social Psychology, 30,* 1–20.

Sealey, A. (2000). *Childly language: Children, language and the social world.* Harlow, England: Pearson.

Searle, J. R. (1995). Ontology is the question. In P. Baumgartner & S. Payr (Eds.), *Speaking minds: Interviews with twenty eminent cognitive scientists* (pp. 202–213). Princeton, NJ: Princeton University Press.

Searleman, A., & Herrmann, D. (1994). *Memory from a broader perspective.* New York: McGraw-Hill.

Sears, L. L., Finn, P. R., & Steinmetz, J. E. (1994). Abnormal classical eye-blink conditioning in autism. *Journal of Autism and Developmental Disorders, 24,* 737–751.

Sedgwick, J. (1995). Inside the Pioneer Fund. In R. Jacoby & N. Glauberman (Eds.), *The bell curve debate: History, documents, opinions* (pp. 144–161). New York: Random House.

Sedikides, C., & Strube, M. J. (1997). Self-evaluation: To thine own self be good, to thine own self be sure, to thine own self be true, and to thine own self be better. In M. P. Zanna (Ed.), *Advances in experimental social psychology* (Vol. 29, pp. 209–269). San Diego, CA: Academic Press.

Seeman, P., Guan, H., & Hubert, H. (1993). Dopamine D4 receptors elevated in schizophrenia. *Nature, 365,* 441–445.

Segall, M. H., Campbell, D. T., & Herskovits, M. J. (1966). *The influence of culture on visual perception.* Indianapolis, IN: Bobbs-Merrill.

Segall, M. H., Dasen, P. R., Berry, J. W., & Poortinga, Y. H. (1990). *Human behavior in global perspective: An introduction to cross-cultural psychology.* New York: Pergamon.

Segerstrom, S., Taylor, S., Kemeny, M., & Fahey, J. (1998). Optimism is associated with mood, coping, and immune change in response to stress. *Journal of Personality and Social Psychology, 74,* 1646–1655.

Segerstrom, S. C., & Miller, G. E. (2004). Psychological stress and the human immune system: A meta-analytic study of 30 years of inquiry. *Psychological Bulletin, 130,* 601–630.

Seifer, R., Schiller, M., Sameroff, A. J., Resnick, S., & Riordin, A. J. (1996). Attachment, maternal sensitivity, and infant temperament during the first year of life. *Developmental Psychology, 32,* 12–25.

Seipp, B. (1991). Anxiety and academic performance: A meta-analysis of findings. *Anxiety Research, 4,* 27–41.

Sekuler, R., & Blake, R. (1994). *Perception* (3rd ed.). New York: McGraw-Hill.

Seldon, H. L. (2005). Does brain white matter growth expand the cortex like a balloon? Hypothesis and consequences. *Laterality: Asymmetries of Body, Brain and Cognition, 10,* 81–95.

Selemon, L. D., Wang, L., Nebel, M. B., Csernansky, J. G., Goldman-Rakic, P. S., & Rakic, P. (2005). Direct and indirect effects of fetal irradiation on cortical gray and white matter volume in the Macaque. *Biological Psychiatry, 57,* 83–90.

Seligman, M. E. P. (1970). On the generality of laws of learning. *Psychological Review, 77,* 406–418.

Seligman, M. E. P. (1971). Phobias and preparedness. *Behavior Therapy, 2,* 307–321.

Seligman, M. E. P. (1975). *Helplessness: On depression, development, and death.* San Francisco: Freeman.

Seligman, M. E. P. (1994). *What you can change and what you can't: The complete guide to successful self-improvement.* New York: Knopf.

Seligman, M. E. P. (1995). The effectiveness of psychotherapy: The Consumer Reports study. *American Psychologist, 50,* 965–974.

Seligman, M. E. P. (2003). Positive psychology: Fundamental assumptions. *Psychologist, 16,* 126–127.

Seligman, M. E. P., & Maier, S. F. (1967). Failure to escape traumatic shock. *Journal of Experimental Psychology, 74,* 1–9.

Seligman, M. E. P., & Peterson, C. (2003). Positive clinical psychology. In L. G. Aspinwall & U. M. Staudinger (Eds.), *A psychology of human strengths: Fundamental questions and future directions for a positive psychology* (pp. 305–317). Washington, DC: American Psychological Association.

Selkoe, D. J. (1992). Aging brain, aging mind. *Scientific American, 267,* 135–142.

Sellers, R. M., & Shelton, J. N. (2003). The role of racial identity in perceived racial discrimination. *Journal of Personality and Social Psychology, 84,* 1079–1092.

Selye, H. (1936). A syndrome produced by nocuous agents. *Nature, 138,* 32.

Selye, H. (1956). *The stress of life.* New York: McGraw-Hill.

Sémon, M., Mouchiroud, D., & Duret, L. (2005). Relationship between gene expression and GC-content in mammals: Statistical significance and biological relevance. *Human Molecular Genetics, 14,* 421–427.

Senior, C., Ward, J., & David, A. S. (2002). Representational momentum and the brain: An investigation into the functional necessity of V5/MT. *Visual Cognition, 9,* 81–92.

Seppa, N. (1996, May). A multicultural guide to less spanking and yelling. *APA Monitor,* p. 37.

Serbin, L. A., & Sprafkin, C. (1986). The salience of gender and the process of sex typing in three- to seven-year-old children. *Child Development, 57,* 1188–1199.

Serpell, R. (2000). Intelligence and culture. In R. J. Sternberg (Ed.), *Handbook of intelligence* (pp. 549–577). Cambridge: Cambridge University Press.

Serpell, R., & Haynes, B. P. (2004). The cultural practice of intelligence testing: Problems of international export. In R. J. Sternberg & E. L. Grigorenko (Eds.), *Culture and competence: Contexts of life success* (pp. 163–185). Washington, DC: American Psychological Association.

Servan-Schreiber, E., & Anderson, J. R. (1990). Learning artificial grammars with competitive chunking. *Journal of Experimental Psychology: Learning, Memory, & Cognition, 16,* 592–608.

Seta, J. J., & Donaldson, S. (1999). Self-relevance as a moderator of self-enhancement and self-verification. *Journal of Research in Personality, 33,* 442–462.

Sevy, S., Mendlewicz, J., & Mendelbaum, K. (1995). Genetic research in bipolar illness. In E. E. Beckham & W. R. Leber (Eds.), *Handbook of depression* (2nd ed., pp. 203–212). New York: Guilford Press.

Sewell, K. W. (2005). The experience cycle and the sexual response cycle: Conceptualization and application to sexual dysfunctions. *Journal of Constructivist Psychology, 18,* 3–13.

Seyfarth, R. M., & Cheney, D. L. (1992). Meaning and mind in monkeys (vocalizations and intent). *Scientific American, 267,* 122–128.

Shadish, W. R., Montgomery, L. M., Wilson, P., Wilson, M. R., Bright, I., & Okwumabua, T. (1993). Effects of family and marital psychotherapies: A meta-analysis. *Journal of Consulting and Clinical Psychology, 61,* 992–1002.

Shaffer, D., & Greenberg, T. (2002). Suicide and suicidal behavior in children and adolescents. In D. Shaffer & B. D. Waslick (Eds.), *The many faces of depression in children and adolescents. Review of psychiatry* (Vol. 21, No. 2, pp. 129–178). Washington, DC: American Psychiatric Association.

Shakow, D. (2002). Clinical psychology seen some 50 years later. In W. E. Pickren & D. A. Dewsbury (Eds.), *Evolving perspectives on the history of psychology* (pp. 433–451). Washington, DC: American Psychological Association.

Shalev, A., & Munitz, H. (1986). Conversion without hysteria: A case report and review of the literature. *British Journal of Psychiatry, 148,* 198–203.

Shanab, M. E., & Yahya, K. A. (1977). A behavioral study of obedience in children. *Journal of Personality and Social Psychology, 35,* 530–536.

Shanahan, T. L., Kronauer, R. E., Duffy, J. F., Williams, G. H., & Czeisler, C. A. (1999). Melatonin rhythm observed throughout a three-cycle bright-light stimulus designed to reset the human circadian pacemaker. *Journal of Biological Rhythms, 14,* 237–253.

Shapiro, D. H., Jr. (1987). Implications of psychotherapy research for the study of meditation. In M. A. West (Ed.), *The psychology of meditation.* Oxford, England: Clarendon Press.

Shapiro, F. (1989). Efficacy of the eye movement desensitization procedure in the treatment of traumatic memories. *Journal of Traumatic Stress, 2,* 199–223.

Shapiro, F., (1995). *Eye movement desensitization and reprocessing: Basic principles, protocols and procedures.* New York: Guilford Press.

Shapiro, F. (1996). Eye movement desensitization and reprocessing (EMDR): Evaluation of controlled PTSD research. *Journal of Behavior Therapy and Experimental Psychiatry, 27,* 209–218.

Shapiro, F., & Forrest, M. S. (2004). *EMDR: The breakthrough therapy for overcoming anxiety, stress, and trauma.* New York: Basic Books.

Shapiro, S. L., Schwartz, G. E., & Bonner, G. (1998). Effects of mindfulness-based stress reduction on medical and premedical students. *Journal of Behavioral Medicine, 21,* 581–599.

Sharfstein, S. S. (2001). The President's Advisory Commission on Consumer Protection and Quality in the Health Care Industry. In B. Dickey & L. I. Sederer (Eds.), *Improving mental health care: Commitment to quality* (pp. 5–20). Washington, DC: American Psychiatric Publishing.

Sharp, S. E. (1898). Individual psychology: A study of psychological method. *American Journal of Psychology, 10,* 329–391.

Shaywitz, B. A., Shaywitz, S. E., Pugh, K. R., Constable, R. T., Skudlarski, P., Fulbright, R. K., Bronen, R. A., Fletcher, J. M., Shankweller, D. P., Katz, L., & Gore, J. C. (1995). Sex differences in the functional organization of the brain for language. *Nature, 373,* 607–609.

Shaywitz, J., & Liebowitz, M. R. (2003). Antiepileptic treatment of anxiety disorders. *Primary Psychiatry, 10,* 51–56.

Shedler, J., & Westen, D. (2004). Refining personality disorder diagnosis: Integrating science and practice. *American Journal of Psychiatry, 161,* 1350–1365.

Shekim, W. O., Bylund, D. B., Frankel, F., Alexson, J., Jones, S. B., Blue, L. D., Kirby, J., & Corchoran, C. (1989). Platelet MAO activity and personality variations in normals. *Psychiatry Research, 27,* 81–88.

Sheldon, K. M., & King, L. (2001). Why positive psychology is necessary. *American Psychologist, 56,* 216–217.

Shepperd, J. A., Ouellette, J. A., & Fernandez, J. K. (1996). Abandoning unrealistic optimism: Performance estimates and the temporal proximity of self-relevant feedback. *Journal of Personality and Social Psychology, 70,* 844–855.

Sher, L. (2002a). Genetics of seasonal affective disorder. *Lancet, 359,* 803–804.

Sher, L. (2002b). Suicidal behaviour and seasonality. *Nordic Journal of Psychiatry, 56,* 67.

Sher, L. (2003). Daily hassles, cortisol, and depression. *Australian & New Zealand Journal of Psychiatry, 37,* 383–384.

Sherif, M. (1966). *In common predicament: Social psychology of intergroup conflict and cooperation.* Boston: Houghton Mifflin.

Sherif, M., Harvey, O. J., White, B. J., Hood, W. R., & Sherif, C. (1961). *Intergroup conflict and cooperation: The Robbers' Cave experiment.* Norman, OK: Oklahoma Book Exchange.

Sherif, M., & Sherif, C. W. (1956). *An outline of social psychology.* New York: Harper & Brothers.

Shestowsky, D., Wegener, D. T., & Fabrigar, L. R. (1998). Need for cognition and interpersonal influence: Individual differences in impact on dyadic decisions. *Journal of Personality and Social Psychology, 74,* 1317–1328.

Shields, J., Konold, T. R., & Glutting, J. J. (2004). Validity of the Wide Range Intelligence Test: Differential effects across race/ethnicity, gender, and educational level. *Journal of Psychoeducational Assessment, 22,* 287–303.

Shields, S. A. (1987). Women, men, and the dilemma of emotion. In P. R. Shaver & C. Hendrick (Eds.), *Sex and gender* (*Review of Personality and Social Psychology*, Vol. 7, pp. 229–250). Beverly Hills, CA: Sage.

Shields, S. A. (1995). The role of emotion beliefs and values in gender development. In N. Eisenberg (Ed.), *Review of Personality and Social Psychology* (Vol. 15, pp. 212–232). Thousand Oaks, CA: Sage.

Shields, S. A. (2002). *Speaking from the heart: Gender and the social meaning of emotion.* Cambridge: Cambridge University Press.

Shields, S. A. (2005). The politics of emotion in everyday life: "Appropriate" emotion and claims on identity. *Review of General Psychology, 9,* 3–15.

Shiho, Y., Tohru, T., Shinji, S., Manabu, T., Yuka, T., Eriko, T., Ikuko, S., & Naoki, W. (2005). Suicide in Japan: Present condition and prevention measures. *Crisis, 26,* 12–19.

Shimahara, K. N. (1991). Social mobility and education: Burakumin in Japan. In M. A. Gibson & J. U. Ogbu (Eds.), *Minority status and schooling: A comparative study of immigrant and involuntary minorities* (pp. 342–353). New York: Garland.

Shimahara, K. N., Holowinsky, I. Z., et al. (Eds.). (2001). *Ethnicity, race, and nationality in education: A global perspective* (pp. 81–100). *The Rutgers invitational symposium on education series.* Piscataway, NJ: Rutgers University Press.

Shin, L. M., Kosslyn, S. M., McNally, R. J., Alpert, N. M., Thompson, W. L., Raush, S. L., Macklin, M. L., & Pitman, R. K. (1997). Visual imagery and perception in posttraumatic stress disorder: A positron emission tomographic investigation. *Archives of General Psychiatry, 54,* 233–241.

Shneidman, E. (1992). *Death: Current perspectives* (3rd ed.). Mountain View, CA: Mayfield.

Shumaker, S. A., & Hill, D. R. (1991). Gender differences in social support and physical health. *Health Psychology, 10,* 102–111.

Shumaker, S. A., Legault, C., Rapp, S. R., Thal, L., Wallace, R. B., Ockene, J. K., Hendrix, S. L., Jones, B. N., III, Assaf, A. R., Jackson, R. D., Kotchen, J. M., Wassertheil-Smoller, S., & Wactawski-Wende, J. (2003). Estrogen plus progestin and the incidence of dementia and mild cognitive impairment in postmenopausal women: The Women's Health Initiative Memory Study: A randomized controlled trial. *Journal of the American Medical Association, 289,* 2651–1662.

Shweder, R. A., Mahapatra, M., & Miller, J. G. (1990). Culture and moral development. In J. W. Stigler, R. A. Shweder, & G. Herdt (Eds.), *Cultural psychology* (pp. 130–204). New York: Cambridge University Press.

Sicotte, N. L., Woods, R. P., & Mazziotta, J. C. (1999). Handedness in twins: A meta-analysis. *Laterality, 4,* 265–286.

Sidanius, J., Levin, S., Liu, J., & Pratto, F. (2000). Social dominance orientation, antiegalitarianism and the political psychology of gender: An extension and cross-cultural replication. *European Journal of Social Psychology, 30,* 41–67.

Siegel, J. M. (2003, November). Why we sleep. *Scientific American,* 92–97.

Siegel, S. (1984). Pavlovian conditioning and heroin overdose: Reports by overdose victims. *Bulletin of the Psychonomic Society, 22,* 428–430.

Siegel, S., Hinson, R. E., Krank, M. D., & McCully, J. (1982). Heroin "overdose" death: The contribution of drug-associated environmental cues. *Science, 216,* 436–437.

Siegler, R. S. (1996). *Emerging minds: The process of change in children's thinking.* New York: Oxford University Press.

Siegler, R. S. (1998). *Children's thinking* (3rd ed.). Upper Saddle River, NJ: Prentice Hall.

Siegler, R. S., & Ellis, S. (1996). Piaget on childhood. *Psychological Science, 7,* 211–215.

Sigelman, L., & Tuch, S. A. (1997). Metastereotypes: Blacks' perceptions of whites' stereotypes of blacks. *Public Opinion Quarterly, 61,* 87–101.

Sigurdson, J. (1993). Frequency-modulated whistles as a medium for communication with the bottlenose dolphin (*Tursiops truncatus*). In H. L. Roitblat, L. M. Herman, & P. E. Nachtigall (Eds.), *Language and communication: Comparative perspectives* (pp. 153–173). Hillsdale, NJ: Erlbaum.

Sigvardsson, S., von Knorring, A. L., Bohman, M., & Cloninger, C. R. (1984). An adoption study of somatoform disorders: I. The relationship of somaticization to psychiatric disability. *Archives of General Psychiatry, 41,* 853–859.

Sikes, C., & Sikes, V. (2003). EMDR: Why the controversy? *Traumatology, 9,* 169–181.

Silber, M. H. (2001). Sleep disorders. *Neurology Clinics, 19,* 173–186.

Silva, C. E., & Kirsch, I. (1992). Interpretive sets, expectancy, fantasy proneness, and dissociation as predictors of hypnotic response. *Journal of Personality and Social Psychology, 63,* 847–856.

Silver, S. M., Rogers, S., Knipe, J., & Colelli, G. (2005). EMDR therapy following the 9/11 terrorist attacks: A community-based intervention project in New York City. *International Journal of Stress Management, 12,* 29–42.

Silverman, I. (1971, September). Physical attractiveness. *Sexual Behavior,* 22–35.

Silverman, J., Raj, A., Mucci, L., & Hathaway, J. (2001). Dating violence against adolescent girls and associated substance use, unhealthy weight control, sexual risk behavior, pregnancy, and suicide. *Journal of the American Medical Association, 286,* 572–579.

Silverstein, L. B. (1996). Fathering is a feminist issue. *Psychology of Women Quarterly, 20,* 3–37.

Simcock, G., & Hayne, H. (2002). Breaking the barrier? Children fail to translate their preverbal memories into language. *Psychological Science, 13,* 225–231.

Simkins, L. (1995). Risk of HIV transmission in sexual behaviors of college students. *Psychological Reports, 76,* 787–799.

Simmons, R. G., Blyth, D. A., Van Cleave, E. F., & Bush, D. M. (1979). Entry into adolescence: The impact of school structure, puberty, and early dating on self-esteem. *American Sociological Review, 44,* 948–967.

Simon, H. A. (1957). *Models of man.* New York: Wiley.

Simon, H. B. (1991). Exercise and human immune function. In R. Ader, D. E. Felton, & N. Cohen (Eds.), *Psychoneuroimmunology* (2nd ed., pp. 869–895). New York: Academic Press.

Simons, D. J., & Levin, D. T. (1998). Failure to detect changes to people during a real-world interaction. *Psychonomic Bulletin and Review, 5,* 644–649.

Simons, R. C., & Hughes, C. C. (1993). Culture-bound syndromes. In A. C. Gaw (Ed.), *Culture, ethnicity, and mental illness* (pp. 75–99). Washington, DC: American Psychological Association.

Simonton, D. K. (1992). The social context of career success and course for 2,026 scientists and inventors. *Personality and Social Psychology Bulletin, 18,* 452–463.

Simonton, D. K. (2000a). Creativity: Cognitive, personal, developmental, and social aspects. *American Psychologist, 55,* 151–158.

Simonton, D. K. (2000b). Creative development as acquired expertise: Theoretical issues and an empirical test. *Developmental Review, 20,* 283–318.

Simoons, F. (1970). Primary adult lactose intolerance and the milking habit: A problem in biologic and cultural interrelations: II. A cultural-historical hypothesis. *American Journal of Digestive Diseases, 15,* 695–710.

Simoons, F. (1982). Geography and genetics as factors in the psychobiology of human food selection. In L. Baker (Ed.), *The psychobiology of human food selection* (pp. 204–225). Westport, CT: AVI.

Simpson, J. A., Rholes, W. S., Campbell, L., & Wilson, C. L. (2003). Changes in attachment orientations across the transition to parenthood. *Journal of Experimental Social Psychology, 39,* 317–331.

Sims, E. (1974). Studies in human hyperphagia. In G. Bray & J. Bethune (Eds.), *Treatment and management of obesity.* New York: Harper & Row.

Sims, E., & Horton, E. (1968). Endocrine and metabolic adaptation to obesity and starvation. *American Journal of Clinical Nutrition, 21,* 1455–1470.

Singelis, T., Choo, P., & Hatfield, E. (1996). Love schemas and romantic love. *Journal of Social Behavior and Personality, 10,* 15–36.

Singelis, T. M., Triandis, H. C., Bhawuk, D. S., & Gelfand, M. (1995). Horizontal and vertical dimensions of individualism and collectivism: A theoretical and measurement refinement. *Cross-Cultural Research, 29,* 240–275.

Singer, J. A., & Salovey, P. (1988). Mood and memory: Evaluating the network theory of affect. *Clinical Psychology Review, 8,* 211–251.

Singer, J. A., Singer, J. L., & Zittel, C. (2000). Personality variations in autobiographical memories, self-representations, and daydreaming. In R. G. Kunzendorf & B. Wallace (Eds.), *Individual differences in conscious experience: Advances in consciousness research* (Vol. 20, pp. 269–307). Amsterdam, Netherlands: John Benjamins.

Singer, J. L. (1975). *The inner world of daydreaming.* New York: Harper & Row.

Singh, A., & Selesnick, S. H. (2005). Meningiomas. In R. K. Jackler & D. E. Brackmann (Eds.), *Neurotology,* 2nd ed. Philadelphia: Lippincott, Williams & Wilkins.

Singh, D. (1993). Adaptive significance of female physical attractiveness: Role of waist-to-hip ratio. *Journal of Personality and Social Psychology, 65,* 293–307.

Singhal, R., & Misra, G. (1994). Achievement goals: A situational-contextual analysis. *International Journal of Intercultural Relations, 18,* 239–258.

Siskind, D. (2005). Psychotherapy with children and parents during divorce. In L. Gunsberg & P. Hymowitz (Eds.), *A handbook of divorce and custody: Forensic, developmental, and clinical perspectives* (pp. 331–341). Hillsdale, NJ: Analytic Press.

Skinner, B. F. (1938). *The behavior of organisms.* New York: Appleton-Century-Crofts.

Skinner, B. F. (1948a). *Walden two.* New York: Macmillan.

Skinner, B. F. (1948b). "Superstition" in the pigeon. *Journal of Experimental Psychology, 38,* 168–172.

Skinner, B. F. (1957). *Verbal behavior.* New York: Appleton-Century-Crofts.

Skinner, B. F. (1979). *The shaping of a behaviorist.* New York: Knopf.

Skinner, B. F. (1990). Can psychology be a science of the mind? *American Psychologist, 45,* 1206–1210.

Skodol, A. E. (2005). The borderline diagnosis: Concepts, criteria, and controversies. In J. G. Gunderson (Ed.), *Understanding and treating borderline personality disorder: A guide for professionals and families* (pp. 3–19). Washington, DC: American Psychiatric Publishing.

Skokal, M. M. (2002). Origins and early years of the American Psychological Association. In W. E. Pickren & D. A. Dewsbury (Eds.), *Evolving perspectives on the history of psychology* (pp. 141–167). Washington, DC: American Psychological Association.

Skoyles, J. R., & Sagan, D. (2002). *Up from dragons: The evolution of human intelligence.* New York: McGraw-Hill.

Slade, L. A., & Rush, M. C. (1991). Achievement motivation and the dynamics of task difficulty choices. *Journal of Personality and Social Psychology, 60,* 165–172.

Slaughter, M. (1990). The vertebrate retina. In K. N. Leibovic (Ed.), *Science of vision.* New York: Springer-Verlag.

Slavney, P. R. (1990). *Perspectives on hysteria.* Baltimore, MD: Johns Hopkins University Press.

Slay, H., Hayaki, J., Napolitano, M., & Brownell, K. (1998). Motivations for running and eating attitudes in obligatory versus nonobligatory runners. *International Journal of Eating Disorders, 23,* 267–275.

Slife, B. D., & Fisher, A. M. (2000). Modern and postmodern approaches to the free will/determinism dilemma in psychotherapy. *Journal of Humanistic Psychology, 40,* 80–107.

Slutske, W., Eisen, S., Xian, H., True, W., Lyons, M. J., Goldberg, J., & Tsuang, M. (2001). A twin study of the association between pathological gambling and antisocial personality disorder. *Journal of Abnormal Psychology, 110,* 297–308.

Smedley, A., & Smedley, B. D. (2005). Race as biology is fiction, racism as a social problem is real: Anthropological and historical perspectives on the social construction of race. *American Psychologist, 60,* 16–26.

Smilek, D., Dixon, M. J., Cudahy, C., & Merikle, P. M. (2002). Concept driven color experiences in digit-color synesthesia. *Brain & Cognition, 48,* 570–573.

Smith, A. E., Jussim, L., & Eccles, J. (1999). Do self-fulfilling prophecies accumulate, dissipate, or remain stable over time? *Journal of Personality and Social Psychology, 77,* 548–565.

Smith, C. (2003). The REM sleep window and memory processing. In P. Maquet, C. Smith, & R. Stickgold (Eds.), *Sleep and brain plasticity* (pp. 117–133). Oxford, England: Oxford University Press.

Smith, C. T. (1995). Sleep states and memory processes. *Behavioural Brain Research, 69,* 137–145.

Smith, D. (1982). Trends in counseling and psychotherapy. *American Psychologist, 37,* 802–809.

Smith, D. V. (1985). Brainstem processing of gustatory information. In D. W. Pfaff (Ed.), *Taste, olfaction, and the central nervous system* (pp. 151–177). New York: Rockefeller University Press.

Smith, E. J., Partridge, J. C., Parsons, K. N., White, E. M., Cuthill, I. C., Bennett, A. T. D., & Church, S. C. (2002). Ulraviolet vision and mate choice in the guppy (Poecilia reticulata). *Behavioral Ecology, 13,* 1–19.

Smith, J., & Baltes, P. B. (1990). Wisdom-related knowledge: Age/cohort differences in response to life-planning problems. *Developmental Psychology, 26,* 494–505.

Smith, J. M., & Szathmáry, E. (1995). *The major transitions in evolution.* Oxford, England: W. H. Freeman.

Smith, L. D. (2002). On prediction and control: B. F. Skinner and the technological ideal of science. In W. E. Pickren & D. A. Dewsbury (Eds.), *Evolving perspectives on the history of psychology* (pp. 255–272). Washington, DC: American Psychological Association.

Smith, M. L., Cottrell, G. W., Gosselin, F., & Schyns, P. G. (2005). Transmitting and decoding facial expressions. *Psychological Science, 16,* 184–189.

Smith, M. L., & Glass, G. V. (1977). Meta-analysis of psychotherapy outcome studies. *American Psychologist, 32,* 752–760.

Smith, N., Young, A., & Lee, C. (2004). Optimism, health-related hardiness and well-being among older Australian women. *Journal of Health Psychology, 9,* 741–752.

Smith, P., & Bond, M. (1994). *Social psychology across cultures.* Boston: Allyn & Bacon.

Smith, R. A. (2002). *Challenging your preconceptions: Thinking critically about psychology* (2nd ed.). Belmont, CA: Wadsworth/Thomson Learning.

Smith, S. M., Gleaves, D. H., Pierce, B. H., Williams, T. L., Gilliland, T. R., & Gerkens, D. R. (2003). Eliciting and comparing false and recovered memories: An experimental approach. *Applied Cognitive Psychology, 17,* 251–279.

Smith, S. M., Glenberg, A. M., & Bjork, R. A. (1978). Environmental context and human memory. *Memory & Cognition, 6,* 342–355.

Smith, S. M., & Petty, R. E. (1992). Personality moderators of mood congruency effects on cognitions: The role of self-esteem and negative mood regulation. *Journal of Personality and Social Psychology, 68,* 1092–1107.

Smith, S. S., & Richardson, D. (1983). Amelioration of deception and harm in psychological research: The important role of debriefing. *Journal of Personality and Social Psychology, 44,* 1075–1082.

Smith, T. (1992). Hostility and health: Current status of a psychosomatic hypothesis. *Health Psychology, 11,* 139–150.

Smith, T. B., McCullough, M. E., & Poll, J. (2003). Religiousness and depression: Evidence for a main effect and the moderating influence of stressful life events. *Psychological Bulletin, 129,* 614–636.

Smith, T. L. (1994). *Behavior and its causes: Philosophical foundations of operant psychology.* Dordrecht, The Netherlands: Kluwer Academic Publishers.

Smith-Rohrberg, D., Bruce, R., & Altice, F. L. (2004). Research note—Review of corrections-based therapy for opiate-dependent patients: Implications for buprenorphine treatment among correctional populations. *Journal of Drug Issues, 34,* 451–480.

Smolensky, P. (1995). On the proper treatment of connectionism: In C. Macdonald & G. Macdonald (Eds.), *Connectionism: Debates on psychological explanation.* Cambridge, MA: Blackwell.

Smyth, J. M. (1998). Written emotional expression: Effect sizes, outcome types, and moderating variables. *Journal of Consulting and Clinical Psychology, 66,* 174–184.

Snarey, J. R. (1985). Cross-cultural universality of social-moral development: A critical review of Kohlbergian research. *Psychological Bulletin, 97,* 202–233.

Sneed, C. D., McCrae, R. R., & Funder, D. C. (1998). Lay conceptions of the Five-Factor Model and its indicators. *Personality and Social Psychology Bulletin, 24,* 115–126.

Snidman, N., Kagan, J., Riordan, L., & Shannon, D. C. (1995). Cardiac function and behavioral reactivity during infancy. *Psychophysiology, 32,* 199–207.

Sno, H. N. (2000). Deja vu and jamais vu. In G. E. Berrios & J. R. Hodges (Eds.), *Memory disorders in psychiatric practice* (pp. 338–347). New York: Cambridge University Press.

Snow, C. E. (1999). Social perspectives on the emergence of language. In B. MacWhinney (Ed.), *The emergence of language* (pp. 257–276). Mahwah, NJ: Erlbaum.

Snowden, L. R., & Hu, T. W. (1996). Outpatient service use in minority-serving mental health programs. *Administration and Policy in Mental Health, 24,* 149–159.

Snyder, C. R. (2000). The past and possible futures of hope. *Journal of Social and Clinical Psychology, 19,* 11–28.

Snyder, C. R., & Lopez, S. J. (Eds.). (2002). *Handbook of positive psychology.* London: Oxford University Press.

Snyder, M. (1974). The self-monitoring of expressive behavior. *Journal of Personality and Social Psychology, 30,* 526–537.

Snyder, M. (1987). *Public appearances/private realities: The psychology of self-monitoring.* New York: Freeman.

Snyder, M., & Copeland, J. (1989). Self-monitoring processes in organizational settings. In R. A. Giacalone & P. Rosenfeld (Eds.), *Impression management in the organization* (pp. 7–19). Hillsdale, NJ: Erlbaum.

Snyder, M., & Gangestad, S. (1982). Choosing social situations: Two investigations of self-monitoring processes. *Journal of Personality and Social Psychology, 43,* 123–135.

Snyder, M., & Simpson, J. A. (1984). Self-monitoring and dating relationships. *Journal of Personality and Social Psychology, 47,* 1281–1291.

Snyder, M., & Swann, W. B. (1978). Hypothesis-testing processes in social interaction. *Journal of Personality and Social Psychology, 36,* 1202–1212.

Soares, J. F. J., & Öhman, A. (1993). Preattentive processing, preparedness and phobias: Effects of instruction on conditioned electrodermal responses to masked and non-masked fear-relevant stimuli. *Behavior Research and Therapy, 31,* 87–95.

Soderstrom, M., Dolbier, C., Leiferman, J., & Steinhardt, M. (2000). The relationship of hardiness, coping strategies, and perceived stress to symptoms of illness. *Journal of Behavioral Medicine, 23,* 311–328.

Solanto, M. V. (2002). Dopamine dysfunction in AD/HD: Integrating clinical and basic neuroscience research. *Behavioural Brain Research, 130,* 65–71.

Solomon, D. A., Leon, A. C., Endicott, J., Mueller, T. I., Coryell, W., Shea, M. T., & Keller, M. B. (2004). Psychosocial impairment and recurrence of major depression. *Comprehensive Psychiatry, 45,* 423–430.

Solomon, R. L. (1980). The opponent-process theory of acquired motivation: The costs of pleasure and the benefits of pain. *American Psychologist, 35,* 691–712.

Solomon, R. L., & Corbit, J. D. (1974). An opponent-process theory of motivation: I. Temporal dynamics of affect. *Psychological Review, 81,* 119–145.

Sommers, S. R., & Kassin, S. M. (2001). On the many impacts of inadmissible testimony: Selective compliance, need for cognition, and the overcorrection bias. *Personality and Social Psychology Bulletin, 27,* 1368–1377.

Sonnert, G., & Holton, G. (1995). *Gender differences in science careers: The Project Access Study.* New Brunswick, NJ: Rutgers University Press.

Sorokin, A. A., Maksimov, A. L., & Jermain, J. (2000). Human circadian rhythm synchronization by social timers: The role of motivation: IV. Individual features of the free-running 24-hour sleep-wake cycle under simulated conditions of vital activity. *Human Physiology, 26,* 41–47.

Sorrentino, R., & Hewitt, E. (1984). The uncertainty-reducing properties of achievement tasks revisited. *Journal of Personality and Social Psychology, 47,* 884–899.

Sowell, E. R., Thompson, P. M., Leonard, C. M., Welcome, S. E., Kan, E., & Toga, A. W. (2004). Longitudinal mapping of cortical thickness and brain growth in normal children. *Journal of Neuroscience, 24,* 8223–8231.

Sowell, E. R., Thompson, P. M., & Toga, A. W. (2004). Mapping changes in the human cortex throughout the span of life. *Neuroscientist, 10,* 372–392.

Spangler, W. D. (1992). Validity of questionnaire and TAT measures of need for achievement: Two meta-analyses. *Psychological Bulletin, 112,* 140–154.

Spanos, N. P. (1986). Hypnosis and the modification of hypnotic susceptibility: A social psychological perspective. In P. L. N. Naish (Ed.), *What is hypnosis? Current theories and research* (pp. 85–120). Philadelphia: Open University Press.

Spanos, N. P., & Chaves, J. F. (1989). The cognitive-behavioral alternative to hypnosis research. In N. P. Spanos & J. F. Chaves (Eds.), *Hypnosis: The cognitive-behavioral perspective* (pp. 9–16). Buffalo, NY: Prometheus Books.

Spanos, N. P., & Coe, W. C. (1992). A social-psychological approach to hypnosis. In E. Fromm & M. R. Nash (Eds.), *Contemporary hypnosis research* (pp. 102–130). New York: Guilford Press.

Spanos, N. P., Flynn, D. M., & Niles, J. (1989–1990). Rapport and cognitive skill training in the enhancement of hypnotizability. *Imagination, Cognition, and Personality, 9,* 245–262.

Spear, L. P. (2003). Neurodevelopment during adolescence. In D. Cicchetti & E. Walker (Eds.), *Neurodevelopmental mechanisms in psychopathology* (pp. 62–83). New York: Cambridge University Press.

Spearman, C. E. (1927). *The abilities of man.* London: Macmillan.

Speier, P. L., Sherak, D. L., Hirsch, S., & Cantwell, D. P. (1995). Depression in children and adolescents. In E. E. Beckham & W. R. Leber (Eds.), *Handbook of depression* (2nd ed., pp. 467–493). New York: Guilford Press.

Spelke, E. S., Breinlinger, K., Macomber, J., & Jacobson, K. (1992). Origins of knowledge. *Psychological Review, 99,* 605–632.

Spence, C., Shore, D. I., Gazzaniga, M. S., Soto-Faraco, S., & Kingstone, A. (2001). Failure to remap visuotactile space across the midline in the split-brain. *Canadian Journal of Experimental Psychology, 55,* 133–140.

Spencer, S. J., Steele, C. M., & Quinn, D. M. (1999). Stereotype threat and women's math performance. *Journal of Experimental Social Psychology, 35,* 4–28.

Spencer, S. M., & Norem, J. K. (1996). Reflection and distraction: Defensive pessimism, strategic optimism, and performance. *Personality and Social Psychology Bulletin, 22,* 354–365.

Sperling, G. (1960). The information available in brief visual presentation. *Psychological Monographs: General and Applied, 74,* 1–29.

Sperry, R. W. (1964). The great cerebral commissure. *Scientific American, 210,* 42–52.

Sperry, R. W. (1968). Hemisphere deconnection and unity in conscious experience. *American Psychologist, 23,* 723–733.

Spiegel, D. (1999). Healing words. Emotional expression and disease outcome. *Journal of the American Medical Association, 281,* 1328–1329.

Spielman, A., & Herrera, C. (1991). Sleep disorders. In S. J. Ellman & J. S. Antrobus (Eds.), *The mind in sleep: Psychology and psychopathology* (2nd ed., pp. 437–447). New York: Wiley.

Spitzer, R. L., Forman, J. B. W., & Nee, J. (1979). *DSM-III* field trials: II. Initial experience with the multiaxial system. *American Journal of Psychiatry, 136,* 815–817.

Spoormaker, V. I., van den Bout, J., & Meijer, E. J. G. (2003). Lucid dreaming treatment for nightmares: A series of cases. *Dreaming, 13,* 181–186.

Sporn, A. L., Greenstein, D. K., Gogtay, N., Jeffries, N. O., Lenane, M., Gochman, P., Clasen, L. S., Blumenthal, J., Giedd, J. N., & Rappoport, J. L. (2003). Progressive brain volume loss during adolescence in childhood-onset schizophrenia. *American Journal of Psychiatry, 160,* 2181–2189.

Sprecher, S. (1999). "I love you more today than yesterday": Romantic partners' perceptions of changes in love and related affect over time. *Journal of Personality and Social Psychology, 76,* 46–53.

Sprecher, S., Metts, S., Burleson, B., Hatfield, E., & Thompson, A. (1995). Domains of expressive interaction in intimate relationships: Associations with satisfaction and commitment. *Family Relations, 44,* 1–8.

Springer, S. P., & Deutsch, G. (1998). *Left brain, right brain: Perspectives from cognitive neuroscience* (5th ed.). New York: W. H. Freeman.

Squire, L. R. (1992). Memory and the hippocampus: A synthesis from findings with rats, monkeys, and humans. *Psychological Review, 99,* 195–231.

Squire, L. R., & Kandel, E. R. (1999). *Memory: From mind to molecules.* New York: Scientific American Library.

Srikiatkhachorn, A. (2002). Chronic daily headaches: A scientist's perspective. *Headache, 42,* 532–537.

Srikiatkhachorn, A., Maneesri, S., Govitrapong, P., & Kasantikul, V. (1998). Derangement of serotonin system in migrainous patients with analgesic abuse headache: Clues from platelets. *Headache, 38,* 43–49.

Srivastava, S., John, O. P., Gosling, S. D., & Potter, J. (2003). Development of personality in early and middle adulthood: Set like plaster or persistent change? *Journal of Personality & Social Psychology, 84,* 1041–1053.

Staats, A. W., & Staats, C. K. (1958). Attitudes established by classical conditioning. *Journal of Abnormal and Social Psychology, 57,* 37–40.

Staddon, J. E. R., & Simmelhag, V. L. (1971). The "superstition" experiment: A reexamination of its implications for the principles of adaptive behavior. *Psychological Review, 78,* 3–43.

Stallard, P., Salter, E., & Velleman, R. (2004). Posttraumatic stress disorder following road traffic accidents: A second prospective study. *European Child and Adolescent Psychiatry, 13,* 172–178.

Stamps, A. E., III. (2002). Meta-analysis. In R. B. Bechtel & A. Churchman (Eds.), *Handbook of environmental psychology* (pp. 222–232). New York: Wiley.

Stangor, C., Swim, J. K., Sechrist, G. B., DeCoster, J., & Van Allen, K. L. (2003). Ask, answer, and announce: Three stages in perceiving and responding to discrimination. *European Review of Social Psychology, 14.*

Stanley, B., Kyrkouli, S., Lampert, S., & Leibowitz, S. (1986). Neuropeptide Y chronically injected in the hypothalamus: A powerful neurochemical inducer of hyperphagia and obesity. *Peptides, 7,* 1189–1192.

Stanley, J. (1993). Boys and girls who reason well mathematically. In G. R. Bock & K. Ackrill (Eds.), *The origins and development of high ability.* Chichester, England: Wiley.

Stark, R. (1965). A taxonomy of religious experience. *Journal for the Scientific Study of Religion, 3,* 3–21.

Stark, R. (2002). Physiology and faith: Addressing the "universal" gender difference in religious commitment. *Journal for the Scientific Study of Religion, 41,* 495–507.

Statistics Canada. (1999). *Statistical report.*

Steadman, H. J., Mulvey, E. P., Monahan, J., Robbins, P. C., Appelbaum, P. S., Grisso, T., Roth, L. H., & Silver, E. (1998). Violence by people discharged from acute psychiatric inpatient facilities and by others in the same neighborhoods. *Archives of General Psychiatry, 55,* 393–401.

Stebbins, W. C. (1980). The evolution of hearing in the mammals. In A. N. Popper & R. R. Fay (Eds.), *Comparative studies of hearing in vertebrates* (pp. 421–436). New York: Springer-Verlag.

Steele, C. M. (1992, April). Race and the schooling of Black Americans. *The Atlantic Monthly,* 68–78.

Steele, C. M. (1997). A threat in the air: How stereotypes shape intellectual identity and performance. *American Psychologist, 52,* 613–629.

Steele, C. M., & Aronson, J. (1995). Stereotype threat and the intellectual test performance of African Americans. *Journal of Personality and Social Psychology, 69,* 797–811.

Steele, C. M., & Josephs, R. A. (1988). Drinking your troubles away: I. The psychology of drunken excess. *Journal of Personality and Social Psychology, 48,* 18–34.

Steil, J. M. (1994). Equality and entitlement in marriage. In M. J. Lerner & G. Mikula (Eds.), *Entitlement and the affectional bond: Justice in close relationships* (pp. 229–258). New York: Plenum Press.

Stein, D. G., Brailowsky, S., & Will, B. (1995). *Brain repair.* New York: Oxford University Press.

Stein, E. A., Pankiewicz, J., Harsch, H. H., Cho, J.-K., Fuller, S. A., & Hoffmann, R. G. (1998). Nicotine-induced limbic cortical activation in the human brain: A functional MRI study. *American Journal of Psychiatry, 155,* 1009–1015.

Steinberg, J. (1995). The graying of the senses. *Journal of NIMH Research, 7,* 32–33.

Steinberg, L. (2004). *The 10 basic principles of good parenting.* New York: Simon & Schuster.

Steinberg, L. (in press). Cognitive and affective development in adolescence. *Trends in Cognitive Sciences.*

Steinberg, L., Dornbusch, S. M., & Brown, B. B. (1992). Ethnic differences in adolescent achievement: An ecological perspective. *American Psychologist, 47,* 723–729.

Steiner, J. E. (1979). Human facial expressions in response to taste and smell stimulation. In H. E. Reese & L. Lipsitt (Eds.), *Advances in child development and behavior* (Vol. 13). New York: Academic Press.

Steinmetz, J. E. (1999). A renewed interest in human classical eyeblink conditioning. *Psychological Science, 10,* 24–25.

Steketee, G. S. (1993). *Treatment of obsessive-compulsive disorder.* New York: Guilford.

Stellar, E. (1954). The physiology of motivation. *Psychological Review, 61,* 5–22.

Stemberger, R. T., Turner, S. M., Beidel, D. C., & Calhoun, K. S. (1995). Social phobia: An analysis of possible developmental factors. *Journal of Abnormal Psychology, 104,* 526–531.

Stener-Victorin, E., Kruse-Smidje, C., & Jung, K. (2004). Comparison between electroacupuncture and hydrotherapy, both in combination with patient education and patient education alone, on the symptomatic treatment of osteoarthritis of the hip. *Clinical Journal of Pain, 20,* 179–185.

Stephan, G. W., Diaz-Loving, R., & Duran, A. (2000). Integrated threat theory and intercultural attitudes: Mexico and the United States. *Journal of Cross-Cultural Psychology, 31,* 240–249.

Stephan, W., Stephan, C., & de Vargas, M. (1996). Emotional expression in Costa Rica and the United States. *Journal of Cross-Cultural Psychology, 27,* 147–160.

Steriade, M., Ropert, N., Kitsikis, A., & Oakson, G. (1980). Ascending activating neuronal networks in midbrain reticular core and related rostral systems. In S. A. Hobson & A. M. Brazier (Eds.), *The reticular formation revisited: Specifying function for a nonspecific system.* New York: Raven.

Stern, D. (1985). *The interpersonal world of the infant: A view from psychoanalysis and developmental psychology.* New York: Basic Books.

Stern, W. (1914). *The psychological methods of testing intelligence.* Baltimore, MD: Warwick & York.

Sternbach, H. (1998). Age-associated testosterone decline in men: Clinical issues for psychiatry. *American Journal of Psychiatry, 155,* 1310–1318.

Sternbach, R. A. (1963). Congenital insensitivity to pain: A review. *Psychological Bulletin, 60,* 252–264.

Sternberg, R. J. (1985). *Beyond IQ: A triarchic theory of human intelligence.* New York: Cambridge University Press.

Sternberg, R. J. (1996). *Successful intelligence: How practical and creative intelligence determine success in life.* New York: Penguin Books.

Sternberg, R. J. (1997). The concept of intelligence and its role in lifelong learning and success. *American Psychologist, 52,* 1030–1037.

Sternberg, R. J. (2003). Construct validity of the theory of successful intelligence. In R. J. Sternberg, J. Lautrey, & T. I. Lubart (Eds.), *Models of intelligence: International perspectives* (pp. 55–77). Washington, DC: American Psychological Association.

Sternberg, R. J. (2005). The importance of converging operations in the study of human intelligence. *Cortex, 41,* 243–244.

Sternberg, R. J., & Davidson, J. E. (1999). Insight. In M. A. Runco & S. R. Pritzker (Eds.), *Encyclopedia of creativity* (Vol. 2). San Diego, CA: Academic Press.

Sternberg, R. J., & Jarvin, L. (2003). Alfred Binet's contributions as a paradigm for impact in psychology. In R. J. Sternberg (Ed.), *The anatomy of impact: What makes the great works of psychology great?* (pp. 89–107). Washington, DC: American Psychological Association.

Sternberg, R. J., & Kaufman, J. C. (Eds.). (2002). *The evolution of intelligence.* Mahwah, NJ: Erlbaum.

Sternberg, R. J., & Lubart, T. I. (1995). *Defying the crowd: Cultivating creativity in a culture of conformity.* New York: The Free Press.

Sternberg, R. J., & Lubart, T. I. (1996). Investing in creativity. *American Psychologist, 51,* 677–688.

Sternberg, R. J., & O'Hara, L. A. (2000). Intelligence and creativity. In R. J. Sternberg (Ed.), *Handbook of intelligence* (pp. 611–630). Cambridge: Cambridge University Press.

Sternberg, R. J., Wagner, R. K., Williams, W. M., & Horvath, J. A. (1995). Testing common sense. *American Psychologist, 50,* 913–927.

Stevens, A., & Price, J. (1996). *Evolutionary psychiatry: A new beginning.* New York: Routledge.

Stevens, J. C. (1989). Food quality reports from noninstitutionalized aged. *Annals of the New York Academy of Sciences, 561,* 87–93.

Stevens, S. S. (1955). The measurement of loudness. *Journal of the Acoustical Society of America, 27,* 815–819.

Stevenson, H. W., Chen, C., & Lee, S. (1993). Mathematics achievement of Chinese, Japanese, and American children: Ten years later. *Science, 259,* 53–58.

Stevenson, H. W., Lee, S., & Stigler, J. W. (1986). Mathematics achievement of Chinese, Japanese, and American children. *Science, 231,* 693–699.

Stevenson, H. W., & Zusho, A. (2002). Adolescence in China and Japan: Adapting to a changing environment. In B. B. Brown, R. Larson, & T. S. Saraswathi (Eds.), *The world's youth: Adolescence in eight regions of the globe* (pp. 141–170). New York: Cambridge University Press.

Stewart, K. T., Hayes, B. C., & Eastman, C. I. (1995). Light treatment for NASA shift workers. *Chronobiology International, 12,* 141–151.

Stice, E., Presnell, K., Shaw, H., & Rohde, P. (2005). Psychological and behavioral risk factors for obesity onset in adolescent girls: A prospective study. *Journal of Consulting and Clinical Psychology, 73,* 195–202.

Stickgold, R. (2003). Human studies of sleep and off-line memory reprocessing. In P. Maquet, C. Smith, & R. Stickgold (Eds.), *Sleep and brain plasticity* (pp. 41–63). Oxford, England: Oxford University Press.

Stirling, L. J., & Yeomans, M. R. (2004). Effect of exposure to a forbidden food on eating in restrained and unrestrained women. *International Journal of Eating Disorders, 35,* 59–68.

Stone, M. H. (2002). Treatment of personality disorders from the perspective of the five-factor model. In P. T. Costa, Jr., & T. A. Widiger (Eds.), *Personality disorders and the five-factor model of personality* (2nd ed., pp. 405–430). Washington, DC: American Psychological Association.

Stonovich, K. (1996). *How to think straight about psychology* (4th ed.). New York: HarperCollins.

Stores, G. (2001). *A clinical guide to sleep disorders in children and adolescents.* Cambridge: Cambridge University Press.

Storms, M. D. (1983). *Development of sexual orientation.* Washington, DC: Office of Social and Ethical Responsibility, American Psychological Association.

Strack, F., Martin, L. L., & Stepper, S. (1988). Inhibiting and facilitating conditions of facial expressions: A nonobtrusive test of the facial feedback hypothesis. *Journal of Personality and Social Psychology, 54,* 768–777.

Strakowski, S. M., Adler, C. M., & DelBello, M. P. (2002). Volumetric MRI studies of mood disorders: Do they distinguish unipolar and bipolar disorder? *Bipolar Disorders, 4,* 80–88.

Strassberg, D. S., & Holty, S. (2003). An experimental study of women's internet personal ads. *Archives of Sexual Behavior, 32,* 253–260.

Strausfeld, N. J. (2001). Insect brain. In G. Roth & M. F. Wullimann (Eds.), *Brain evolution and cognition* (pp. 367–400). New York: Wiley.

Strawbridge, W. J., Sjema, S. J., Cohen, R. D., & Kaplan, G. A. (2001). Religious attendance increases survival by improving and maintaining good health behaviors, mental health, and social relationships. *Annals of Behavioral Medicine, 23,* 68–74.

Strayer, D. L., & Johnston, W. A. (2001). Driven to distraction: Dual-task studies of simulated driving and conversing on a cellular phone. *American Psychological Society, 12,* 462–466.

Street, L. L., & Luoma, J. B. (2002). Control groups in psychosocial intervention research: Ethical and methodological issues. *Ethics & Behavior, 12,* 1–30.
Streeter, S. A., & McBurney, D. H. (2003). Waist-to-hip ratio and attractiveness: New evidence and a critique of a "critical test." *Evolutioin and Human Behavior, 24,* 88–98.
Streissguth, A. P., Bookstein, F. L., Sampson, P. D., & Barr, H. M. (1993). *The enduring effects of prenatal alcohol exposure on child development: Birth through seven years, a partial least squares solution.* Ann Arbor: University of Michigan.
Strelan, P., Mehaffey, S. J., & Tiggemann, M. (2003). Self-objectification and esteem in young women: The mediating role of reasons for exercise. *Sex Roles, 48,* 89–95.
Strentz, H. (1986, January 1). Become a psychic and amaze your friends! *Atlanta Journal,* p. 15A.
Strentz, T., & Auerbach, S. (1988). Adjustment to the stress of simulated captivity: Effects of emotion-focused versus problem-focused preparation on hostages differing in locus of control. *Journal of Personality & Social Psychology, 55,* 652–660.
Stricker, G. (1996). Empirically validated treatment, psychotherapy manuals, and psychotherapy integration. *Journal of Psychotherapy Integration, 6,* 217–226.
Strickland, B. R. (1995). Research on sexual orientation and human development: A commentary. *Developmental Psychology, 31,* 137–140.
Strigini, P., Sansone, R., Carobbi, S., & Pierluigi, M. (1990). Radiation and Down's syndrome. *Nature, 347,* 717.
Stringer, C. (2003). Human evolution: Out of Ethiopia. *Nature, 423,* 692–695.
Strober, M. (1992). Family-genetic studies. In K. Halmi (Ed.), *Psychobiology and treatment of anorexia nervosa and bulimia nervosa* (pp. 61–76). Washington, DC: American Psychiatric Press.
Stroebe, M., Stroebe, W., & Schut, H. (2001). Gender differences in adjustment to bereavement: An empirical and theoretical review. *Review of General Psychology, 5,* 62–83.
Stromswold, K., Caplan, D., Alpert, N., & Rauch, S. (1996). Localization of syntactic comprehension by positron emission tomography. *Brain and Language, 52,* 452–473.
Stumpf, H., & Stanley, J. C. (1998). Stability and change in gender-related differences on the College Board Advanced Placement and Achievement Tests. *Current Directions in Psychological Science, 7,* 192–196.
Stunkard, A. J., Harris, J. R., Pedersen, N. L., & McClearn, G. E. (1990). The body-mass index of twins who have been reared apart. *New England Journal of Medicine, 322,* 1483–1487.
Suarez, S. D., & Gallup, G. G., Jr. (1981). Self-recognition in chimpanzees and orangutans, but not gorillas. *Journal of Human Evolution, 10,* 175–188.
Subotnik, R. F., Karp, D. E., & Morgan, E. R. (1989). High IQ children at midlife: An investigation into the generalizability of Terman's genetic studies of genius. *Roeper Review, 11,* 139–144.
Suddath, R. L., Christison, G. W., Torrey, E. F., Casanova, M. F., & Weinberger, D. R. (1990). Anatomical abnormalities in the brains of monozygotic twins discordant for schizophrenia. *The New England Journal of Medicine, 322,* 789–794.
Sue, S., & Chu, J. Y. (2003). The mental health of ethnic minority groups: Challenges posed by the supplement to the Surgeon General's report on mental health. *Culture, Medicine and Psychiatry, 27,* 447–465.
Suler, J. (2001, August 1). The future of online psychotherapy and clinical work. In *The psychology of cyberspace.* www.rider.edu/users.suler/psycyber/psycyber.html
Sumner, W. (1906). *Folkways.* New York: Ginn.
Sun, W.-L., & Rebec, G. V. (2005). The role of prefrontal cortex D1-like and D2-like receptors in cocaine-seeking behavior in rats. *Psychopharmacology, 177,* 315–323.
Super, C. W. (1980). Cross-cultural research on infancy. In H. C. Triandis & A. Heron (Eds.), *Handbook of cross-cultural psychology: Vol. 4. Developmental psychology.* Boston: Allyn & Bacon.
Super, C. W. (1981). Behavioral development in infancy. In R. H. Munroe, R. L. Munroe, & B. B. Whiting (Eds.), *Handbook of cross-cultural human development* (pp. 181–269). Chicago: Garland.
Surgeon General. (1999). *Mental health: A report of the Surgeon General.* Rockville, MD: U.S. Department of Health and Human Services.
Susan, T. A. (1990). How to handle the process litigation effectively under the Education for All Handicapped Children Act of 1975. *Journal of Reading, Writing, and Learning Disabilities International, 6,* 63–70.
Sussman, L. K., Robins, L. N., & Earls, F. (1987). Treatment-seeking for depression by Black and White Americans. *Social Science and Medicine, 24,* 187–196.
Sutton, S. K., & Davidson, R. J. (1997). Prefrontal brain symmetry: A biological substrate of the behavioral approach and inhibition systems. *Psychological Science, 8,* 204–210.
Suzuki, L. A., & Gutkin, T. B. (1994a). Hispanic. In R. J. Sternberg (Ed.), *Encyclopedia of intelligence* (pp. 539–545). New York: Macmillan.
Suzuki, L. A., & Gutkin, T. B. (1994b). Asian Americans. In R. J. Sternberg (Ed.), *Encyclopedia of intelligence* (pp. 140–144). New York: Macmillan.
Swann, G. E., & Carmelli, D. (1996). Curiosity and mortality in aging adults: A 5-year follow-up of the Western Collaborative Group Study. *Psychology and Aging, 11,* 449–453.
Swann, W. B., Jr. (1997). The trouble with change: Self-verification and allegiance to the self. *Psychological Science, 8,* 177–183.
Swanson, L. W. (2004). *Brain maps: Structure of the rat brain* (3rd ed.). San Diego, CA: Elsevier/Academic Press.
Swayze, V. W. (1995). Frontal leucotomy and related psychosurgical procedures in the era before antipsychotics (1935–1954): A historical overview. *American Journal of Psychiatry, 152,* 505–515.
Sweat, J. A., & Durm, M. W. (1993). Psychics: Do police departments really use them? *The Skeptical Inquirer, 17,* 148–158.
Swerdlow, J. L. (1995). Quiet miracles of the brain. *National Geographic, 187*(6), 2–41.
Swets, J. A. (1992). The science of choosing the right decision threshold in high-stakes diagnostics. *American Psychologist, 47,* 522–532.
Symington, T., Currie, A., Curran, R., & Davidson, J. (1955). The reactions of stress. In *Ciba Foundation's colloquia on endocrinology* (Vol. 8). Boston: Little, Brown.
Symons, C. S., & Johnson, B. T. (1997). The self-reference effect in memory: A meta-analysis. *Psychological Bulletin, 121,* 371–394.
Szasz, T. (1961). *The myth of mental illness: Foundations of a theory of personal conduct.* New York: Harper.
Szasz, T. (1990). *Insanity: The idea and its consequences.* New York: Wiley.
Szeto, H. H., Wu, D. L., Decena, J. A., & Cheng, Y. (1991). Effects of single and repeated marijuana smoke exposure on fetal EEG. *Pharmacology, Biochemistry, and Behavior, 40,* 97–101.

Tabaee, A., Roach, M., & Selesnick, S. H. (2004). Middle ear congenital disorders. In A. Lalwani (Ed.), *Current diagnosis and treatment in otolaryngology-head and neck surgery.* New York: McGraw Hill.
Tacey, D. (2001). *Jung and the new age.* Philadelphia: Brunner-Routledge.
Takeshige, C. (1985). Differentiation between acupuncture and non-acupuncture points by association with analgesia inhibitory system. *Acupuncture and Electro-Therapeutics Research, 10,* 195–202.
Tamminga, C. A. (2005). The hippocampus. *American Journal of Psychiatry, 162,* 25.
Tan, S.-Y., & Dong, N. J. (2000). Psychotherapy with members of Asian American churches and spiritual traditions. In P. S. Richards & A. E. Bergin (Eds.), *Handbook of psychotherapy and religious diversity* (pp. 421–444). Washington, DC: American Psychological Association.
Tanaka, K. (2002). Effect of the cognitive load of being a photo-model and dieting on eating behavior. *Japanese Journal of Health Psychology, 15,* 41–48.
Tanford, S., & Penrod, S. (1984). Social influence model: A formal integration of research on majority and minority influence. *Psychological Bulletin, 95,* 189–225.
Tang, T.-P., Shimizu, E., Dube, G. R., Rampon, C., Kerchner, G. A., Zhuo, M., Liu, G., & Tsien, J. Z. (1999). Genetic enhancement of learning and memory in mice. *Memory, 401,* 63–69.
Tango, R. A., & Kolodinsky, P. (2004). Investigation of placement outcomes 3 years after a job skills training program for chronically unemployed adults. *Journal of Employment Counseling, 41,* 80–92.
Tanner, J. M. (1990). *Foetus into man: Physical growth from conception to maturity* (Rev. & enl. ed.). Cambridge, MA: Harvard University Press.
Tansley, K. (1965). *Vision in vertebrates.* London: Chapman & Hall.
Tashkin, D. P. (1999). Effects of marijuana on the lung and its defenses against infection and cancer. *School Psychology International, 20,* 23–37.
Taylor, F. K. (1965). Crypomnesia and plagiarism. *British Journal of Psychiatry, 111,* 1111–1118.
Taylor, F. R. (2004). Diagnosis and classification of headache. *Primary Care, 31,* 243–259.
Taylor, S. (2004). Efficacy and outcome predictors for three PTSD treatments: Exposure therapy, EMDR, and relaxation training. In S. Taylor (Ed.), *Advances in the treatment of posttraumatic stress disorder: Cognitive-behavioral perspectives* (pp. 13–37). New York: Springer Publishing.
Taylor, S. E. (1981). A categorization approach to stereotyping. In D. L. Hamilton (Ed.), *Cognitive processes in stereotyping and intergroup behavior.* Hillsdale, NJ: Erlbaum.
Taylor, S. E. (1999). *Health psychology* (4th ed.). New York: McGraw-Hill.
Taylor, S. E., Klein, L. C., Lewis, B. P., Gruenewald, T. L., Gurung, R. A. R., & Updegraff, J. A. (2000). Biobehavioral responses to stress in females: Tend-and-befriend, not fight-or-flight. *Psychological Review, 107,* 411–429.
Teasdale, T. W., & Owen, D. R. (1984). Heredity and familial environment in intelligence and educational level: A sibling study. *Nature, 309,* 620–622.
Tedlock, B. (2004). The poetics and spirituality of dreaming: A Native American enactive theory. *Dreaming, 14,* 183–189.
Teigen, K. H. (1994). Yerkes-Dodson: A law for all seasons. *Theory and Psychology, 4,* 525–547.
Tekcan, A. I., & Peynircioglu, Z. F. (2002). Effects of age on flashbulb memories. *Psychology & Aging, 17,* 416–422.
Tellegen, A., Lykken, D. T., Bouchard, T. J., Jr., Wilcox, K. J., Segal, N. L., & Rich, S. (1988). Personality similarity in twins reared apart and together. *Journal of Personality and Social Psychology, 54,* 1020–1030.
te Nijenhuis, J., Tolboom, E., Resing, W., & Bleichrodt, N. (2004). Does cultural background influence the intellectual performance of children from immigrant groups? The RAKIT Intelligence Test for immigrant children. *European Journal of Psychological Assessment, 20,* 10–26.
Tercyak, K. P. (2003). Genetic disorders and genetic testing. In M. C. Roberts (Ed.), *Handbook of pediatric psychology* (3rd ed., pp. 719–734). New York: Guilford Press.
Teri, L., & Lewinsohn, P. M. (1985). Group intervention for unipolar depression. *Behavior Therapist, 8,* 109–111.
Terman, L. M. (1916). *The measurement of intelligence.* Boston: Houghton Mifflin.
Terman, L. M. (1925). *Genetic studies of genius: Vol. 1. Mental and physical traits of a thousand gifted children.* Stanford, CA: Stanford University Press.
Terman, L. M., & Childs, H. G. (1912). Tentative revision and extension of the Binet-Simon Measuring Scale of Intelligence. *Journal of Educational Psychology, 3,* 61–74, 133–143, 198–208, 277–289.
Terman, L. M., & Oden, M. H. (1947). *Genetic studies of genius: Vol. 4. The gifted child grows up: Twenty-five years' follow-up of a superior group.* Stanford, CA: Stanford University Press.
Terr, L. C. (1988). What happens to early memories of trauma? A study of 20 children under age five at the time of documented traumatic events. *Journal of the American Academy of Child and Adolescent Psychiatry, 27,* 96–104.
Terrace, H. S. (1979). *Nim: A chimpanzee who learned sign language.* New York: Washington Square Press.
Terrace, H. S., Petitto, L. A., Saunders, R. J., & Bever, T. G. (1979). Can an ape create a sentence? *Science, 206,* 891–902.
Teti, D. M., Nakagawa, M., Das, R., & Wirth, O. (1991). Security of attachment between pre-schoolers and their mothers: Relations among social interaction,

parenting stress, and mothers' sorts of the Attachment Q-Set. *Developmental Psychology, 27,* 440–447.
Thalassis, N. (2004). Measuring minds: Henry Herbert Goddard and the origins of American intelligence testing. *British Journal of Psychology, 95,* 119–123.
Thase, M. E. (2000). Relapse and recurrence of depression: An updated practical approach for prevention. In K. J. Palmer (Ed.), *Drug treatment issues in depression* (pp. 35–52). Kwai Chung, Hong Kong: Adis International Publications.
Thase, M. E., & Howland, R. H. (1995). Biological processes in depression: An updated review and integration. In E. E. Beckham & W. R. Leber (Eds.), *Handbook of depression* (2nd ed., pp. 213–279). New York: Guilford Press.
Thayer, R. (2001). *Calm energy: How people regulate mood with food and exercise.* Oxford, England: Oxford University Press.
Thayer, R., Newman, J., & McClain, T. (1994). Self-regulation of mood: Strategies for changing a bad mood, raising energy, and reducing tension. *Journal of Personality and Social Psychology, 67,* 910–925.
Theorell, T. (2003). To be able to exert control over one's own situation: A necessary condition for coping with stressors. In J. C. Quick & L. E. Tetrick (Eds.), *Handbook of occupational health psychology* (pp. 201–219). Washington, DC: American Psychological Association.
Theron, W. H., Matthee, D. D., Steel, H. R., & Ramirez, J. M. (2000). Direct and indirect aggression in women: A comparison between South African and Spanish university students. In J. M. Ramirez & D. S. Richardson (Eds.), *Cross-cultural approaches to research on aggression and reconciliation* (pp. 99–109). Huntington, NY: Nova.
Thigpen, C. H., & Cleckley, H. M. (1957). *The three faces of Eve.* New York: McGraw-Hill.
Thoman, E. B. (1999). Morningness and eveningness: Issues for study of the early ontogeny of these circadian rhythms. *Human Development, 42,* 206–212.
Thomas, D. R. (1992). Discrimination and generalization. In L. R. Squire (Ed.), *Encyclopedia of learning and memory.* New York: Macmillan.
Thomas, G., & Fletcher, G. J. O. (1997). Empathic accuracy in close relationships. In W. Ickes (Ed.), *Empathic accuracy* (pp. 194–218). New York: Guilford Press.
Thomas, G., & Fletcher, G. J. O. (2003). Mind-reading accuracy in intimate relationships: Assessing the roles of the relationship, the target, and the judge. *Journal of Personality and Social Psychology, 85,* 1079–1094.
Thomas, M. H., Horton, R. W., Lippincott, E. C., & Drabman, R. S. (1977). Desensitization to portrayals of real-life aggression as a function of exposure to television violence. *Journal of Personality and Social Psychology, 35,* 450–458.
Thomas, P. (2004). The many forms of bipolar disorder: A modern look at an old illness. *Journal of Affective Disorders, 79,* S3–S8.
Thomas, R. M. (2001). *Recent theories of human development.* Thousand Oaks, CA: Sage.
Thompson, C., Thompson, S., & Smith, R. (2004). Prevalence of seasonal affective disorder in primary care: A comparison of the seasonal health questionnaire and the seasonal pattern assessment questionnaire. *Journal of Affective Disorders, 78,* 219–226.
Thompson, P. M., Vidal, C., Giedd, J. N., Gochman, P., Blumenthal, J., Nicolson, R., Toga, A. W., & Rapoport, J. L. (2001). Mapping adolescent brain change reveals dynamic wave of accelerated gray matter loss in very early-onset schizophrenia. *Proceedings of the National Academy of Sciences, 98,* 11650–11655.
Thompson, R. F. (2000). *The brain: A neuroscience primer* (3rd ed.). New York: Freeman.
Thompson, R. F. (2005). In search of memory traces. *Annual Review of Psychology, 56,* 1–23.
Thompson, S. H., Sargent, R. G., & Kemper, K. A. (1996). Black and White adolescent males' perceptions of ideal body size. *Sex Roles, 34,* 391–406.
Thorndike, E. L. (1898). Animal intelligence: An experimental study of the associative processes in animals. *Psychological Review Monograph Supplement, 2* (No. 8).
Thorndike, E. L. (1911). *Animal intelligence: Experimental studies.* New York: Macmillan.
Thorndike, E. L. (1914). *The psychology of learning.* New York: Teachers College.
Thurstone, L. L. (1938). Primary mental abilities. *Psychometric Monographs, Vol. 1.* Chicago: Chicago University Press.
Tice, D., & Baumeister, R. F. (1993). Anger control. In D. Wegner & J. Pennebaker (Eds.), *Handbook of mental control.* Englewood Cliffs, NJ: Prentice Hall.
Tice, D. M. (1993). The social motivations of people with low self-esteem. In R. F. Baumeister (Ed.), *Self-esteem: The puzzle of low self-regard* (pp. 37–53). New York: Plenum Press.
Tice, D. M., & Baumeister, R. F. (1997). Longitudinal study of procrastination, performance, stress, and health: The costs and benefits of dawdling. *Psychological Science, 8,* 454–458.
Tice, D. M., Butler, J. L., Muraven, M. B., & Stillwell, A. M. (1995). When modesty prevails: Differential favorability of self-presentation to friends and strangers. *Journal of Personality and Social Psychology, 69,* 1120–1138.
Tilley, A. J., & Empson, J. A. (1978). REM sleep and memory consolidation. *Biological Psychology, 6,* 293–300.
Timberlake, W. (2004). Trends in the study of Pavlovian conditioning. *International Journal of Comparative Psychology, 17,* 119–130.
Timmermann, L., Ploner, M., Freund, H. J., & Schnitzler, A. (2000). Separate representations of static and dynamic touch in human somatosensory thalamus. *Neurology, 54,* 2024–2026.
Timmers, M., Fischer, A. H., & Manstead, A. S. R. (1998). Gender differences in motives for regulating emotions. *Personality and Social Psychology Bulletin, 24,* 974–985.
Tinbergen, N. (1969). *The study of instinct.* Oxford, England: Clarendon Press.
Ting-Toomey, S., Gao, G., Trubisky, P., Yang, Z., Kim, H. S., Lin, S., & Nishida, T. (1991). Culture, face maintenance, and styles of handling interpersonal conflict: A study in five cultures. *International Journal of Conflict Management, 2,* 275–296.
Tinker, M. A. (1932). Wundt's doctorate students and their theses, 1875–1920. *American Journal of Psychology, 44,* 630–637.
Titone, D. A. (2002). Memories abound: The neuroscience of dreams. *Trends in Cognitive Sciences, 6,* 4–5.
Tix, A. P., & Frazier, P. A. (2005). Mediation and moderation of the relationship between intrinsic religiousness and mental health. *Personality and Social Psychology Bulletin, 31,* 295–306.
Todd, J. T., & Norman, J. F. (2003). The visual perception of 3-D shape from multiple cues: Are observers capable of perceiving metric structure? *Perception & Psychophysics, 65,* 31–47.
Todes, D. P. (1997). From the machine to the ghost within: Pavlov's transition from digestive physiology to conditional reflexes. *American Psychologist, 52,* 947–955.
Toga, A. W., & Mazziota, J. C. (Eds.). (1999). *Brain mapping.* New York: Morgan Kaufman.
Tolman, E. C. (1922). A new formula for behaviorism. *Psychological Review, 29,* 44–53.
Tolman, E. C. (1932). *Purposive behavior in animals and men.* New York: Appleton-Century-Crofts.
Tolman, E. C., & Honzik, C. H. (1930). Insight in rats. *University of California Publications in Psychology, 4,* 215–232.
Tomarken, A. J., Davidson, R. J., & Henriques, J. B. (1990). Resting frontal brain asymmetry predicts affective responses to films. *Journal of Personality and Social Psychology, 59,* 791–801.
Tonigan, J. S., Miller, W. R., & Connors, G. J. (2000). Project MATCH client impressions about Alcoholics Anonymous: Measurement issues and relationship to treatment outcome. *Alcoholism Treatment Quarterly, 18,* 25–41.
Torgersen, S. (1983). Genetic factors in anxiety disorders. *Archives of General Psychiatry, 40,* 1085–1089.
Torres, A., Rodrigues, D., Andre M., Crepaldi, A. L., & Miguel, E. C. (2004). Obsessive-compulsive symptoms in patients with panic disorder. *Comprehensive Psychiatry, 45,* 219–224.
Torrey, E. F. (1997). *Out of the shadows: Confronting America's mental illness crisis.* New York: Wiley.
Torvik, A., Lindhoe, C., & Rogde, S. (1982). Brain lesions in alcoholics—A neuropathological study with clinical correlations. *Journal of Neurological Science, 75,* 43–51.
Tower, R. K., Kelly, C., & Richards, A. (1997). Individualism, collectivism and reward allocation: A cross-cultural study in Russia and Britain. *British Journal of Social Psychology, 36,* 331–345.
Tramer, M. R., Carroll, D., Campbell, F. A., Reynolds, D. J., Moore, R. A., & McQuay, H. J. (2001). Cannabinoids for control of chemotherapy-induced nausea and vomiting: Quantitative systematic review. *British Medical Journal, 323,* 16–21.
Trappey, C. (1996). A meta-analysis of consumer choice and subliminal advertising. *Psychology and Marketing, 13,* 517–530.
Travis, J. (1994). Glia: The brain's other cells. *Science, 266,* 970–972.
Treffert, D. A. (1989). *Extraordinary people: Understanding savant syndrome.* New York: Ballantine Books.
Treffert, D. A. (1992). Savant syndrome. In L. R. Squire (Ed.), *Encyclopedia of learning and memory* (pp. 573–574). New York: Macmillan.
Trepper, T. S. (1990). In celebration of the case study. *Journal of Family Psychotherapy, 1,* 5–13.
Triandis, H. C. (1989). The self and social behavior in differing cultural contexts. *Psychological Review, 96,* 506–520.
Triandis, H. C. (1995). *Individualism & collectivism.* Boulder, CO: Westview Press.
Trigg, A. B. (2004). Deriving the Engel Curve: Pierre Bourdieu and the social critique of Maslow's hierarchy of needs. *Review of Social Economy, 62,* 393–406.
Trimpop, R., & Kirkcaldy, B. (1997). Personality predictors of driving accidents. *Personality & Individual Differences, 23,* 147–152.
Trivers, R. (1972). Parental investment and sexual selection. In B. Campbell (Ed.), *Sexual selection and the descent of man: 1871–1971* (pp. 136–179). Chicago: Aldine-Atherton.
Truax, C. B., & Carkhuff, R. R. (1967). *Toward effective counseling and psychotherapy: Training and practice.* Chicago: Aldine.
Trudeau, K. J., & Devlin, A. S. (1996). College students and community service: Who, with whom, and why? *Journal of Applied Social Psychology, 26,* 1867–1888.
Trujillo, A. (2000). Psychotherapy with Native Americans: A view into the role of religion and spirituality. In P. S. Richards & A. E. Bergin (Eds.), *Handbook of psychotherapy and religious diversity* (pp. 445–466). Washington, DC: American Psychological Association.
Tryon, G. (1980). The measurement and treatment of test anxiety. *Review of Educational Research, 50,* 343–372.
Trzesniewski, K. H., Donnellan, M. B., & Robins, R. W. (2003). Stability of self-esteem across the life span. *Journal of Personality and Social Psychology, 84,* 205–220.
Tsang, W. W.-N., & Hui-Chan, C. W.-Y. (2003). Effects of tai chi on joint proprioception and stability limits in elderly subjects. *Medicine and Science in Sports and Exercise, 35,* 1962–1971.
Tsuang, M. (2000). Schizophrenia: Genes and environment. *Biological Psychiatry, 47,* 210–220.
Tucker, J. S., & Riggio, R. E. (1988). The role of social skills in encoding of posed and spontaneous facial expressions. *Journal of Nonverbal Behavior, 12,* 87–97.
Tuerlinckx, F., De Boeck, P., & Lens, W. (2002, March). Measuring needs with the Thematic Apperception Test: A psychometric study. *Journal of Personality & Social Psychology, 82*(3), 448–461.
Tulving, E. (1962). Subjective organization in free-recall of "unrelated" words. *Psychological Review, 69,* 344–354.
Tulving, E. (1997). Human memory. In M. S. Gazzaniga (Ed.), *Conversations in the cognitive neurosciences.* Cambridge, MA: MIT Press.
Tulving, E. (1999). Study of memory: Processes and systems. In J. K. Foster & M. Jelicic (Eds.), *Memory: Systems, process, or function?* (pp. 11–30). Oxford, England: Oxford University Press.
Tulving, E. (2002). Episodic memory: From mind to brain. *Annual Review of Psychology, 53,* 1–25.
Tulving, E., & Lepage, M. (2000). Where in the brain is the awareness of one's past? In D. L. Schacter & E. Scarry (Eds.), *Memory, brain, and belief* (pp. 208–228). Cambridge, MA: Harvard University Press.
Tulving, E., & Schacter, D. L. (1990). Priming and human memory systems. *Science, 247,* 301–306.

Tulving, E., & Thomson, D. M. (1973). Encoding specificity and retrieval processes in episodic memory. *Psychological Review, 80,* 352–373.

Turkheimer, E. (1991). Individual and group differences in adoption studies of IQ. *Psychological Bulletin, 110,* 392–405.

Turksen, K. (Ed.). (2004). *Adult stem cells.* Totowa, NJ: Humana Press.

Turnbull, C. (1989). *The mountain people.* London: Paladin.

Turner, C. W., Gantz, B. J., Vidal, C., & Behrens, A. (in press). Speech recognition in noise for cochlear implants. *Listeners: Benefits of Residual Acoustic Hearing.*

Turner, H. M., Rose, K. S., & Cooper, M. J. (2005). Parental bonding and eating disorder symptoms in adolescents: The mediating role of core beliefs. *Eating Behaviors, 6,* 113–118.

Turner, H. S., & Watson, T. S. (1999). Consultant's guide for the use of time-out in the preschool and elementary classroom. *Psychology in the Schools, 36,* 135–148.

Turner, J., Meyer, D., Cox, K., Logan, C., DiCintio, M., & Thomas, C. (1998). Creating contexts for involvement in math. *Journal of Educational Psychology, 90,* 730–745.

Turner-Cobb, J., Sephton, S., & Spiegel, D. (2001). Psychosocial effects on immune function and disease progression in cancer: Human studies. In R. Ader, D. Felten, & N. Cohen (Eds.), *Psychoneuroimmunology* (Vol. 2, 3rd ed., pp. 565–582). San Diego, CA: Academic Press.

Turvey, M. T. (1996). Dynamic touch. *American Psychologist, 51,* 1134–1152.

Tutty, S., Gephart, H., & Wurzbacher, K. (2003). Enhancing behavioral and social skill functioning in children newly diagnosed with attention-deficit hyperactivity disorder in a pediatric setting. *Journal of Developmental & Behavioral Pediatrics, 24,* 51–57.

Tversky, A., & Kahneman, D. (1973). Availability: A heuristic for judging frequency and probability. *Cognitive Psychology, 5,* 207–232.

Tversky, A., & Kahneman, D. (1974). Judgment under uncertainty: Heuristics and biases. *Science, 185,* 1124–1131.

Tversky, A., & Kahneman, D. (1981). The framing of decisions and the psychology of choice. *Science, 211,* 453–458.

Tygart, C. E. (2000). Genetic causation attribution and public support of gay rights. *International Journal of Public Opinion Research, 12,* 259–275.

Tyler, T. R. (1997). The psychology of legitimacy: A relational perspective on voluntary deference to authorities. *Personality and Social Psychology Review, 1,* 323–345.

Tyrrell, R. A., & Leibowitz, H. W. (1990). The relation of vergence effort to reports of visual fatigue following prolonged near work. *Human Factors, 32,* 341–357.

Uchino, B. N., Cacioppo, J. T., & Kiecolt-Glaser, J. K. (1996). The relationship between social support and physiological processes: A review with emphasis on underlying mechanisms and implications for health. *Psychological Bulletin, 119,* 488–531.

Uhl, G. R., Elmer, G. I., LaBuda, M. C., & Pickens, R. W. (1995). Genetic influences in drug abuse. In F. E. Bloom & D. J. Kupfer (Eds.), *Psychopharmacology: The fourth generation* (pp. 1793–1806). New York: Raven Press.

Ukrainetz, T. A., & Blomquist, C. (2002). The criterion validity of four vocabulary tests compared to a language sample. *Child Language Teaching & Therapy, 18,* 59–78.

Ulfberg, J., Carter, N., & Edling, C. (2000). Sleep-disorder breathing and occupational accidents. *Scandinavian Journal of Work, Environment, & Health, 26,* 237–242.

Underwood, G., & Bright, J. E. H. (1996). Cognition with and without awareness. In G. Underwood (Ed.), *Implicit cognition* (pp. 1–40). Oxford, England: Oxford University Press.

Unger, R. K., & Crawford, M. (1992). *Women and gender: A feminist psychology.* New York: McGraw-Hill.

University of California. (1993, December). The new American body. *University of California at Berkeley Wellness Letter,* pp. 1–2.

Urbach, T. P., Windmann, S. S., Payne, D. G., & Kutas, M. (2005). Mismaking memories: Neural precursors of memory illusions in electrical brain activity. *Psychological Science, 16,* 19–24.

Urdan, T., & Maehr, M. (1995). Beyond a two-goal theory of motivation and achievement: A case for social goals. *Review of Educational Research, 65,* 213–243.

Uribe, F. M. T., LeVine, R. A., & LeVine, S. E. (1994). Maternal behavior in a Mexican community: The changing environments of children. In P. M. Greenfield & R. R. Cocking (Eds.), *Cross-cultural roots of minority child development* (pp. 41–54). Hillsdale, NJ: Erlbaum.

U.S. Bureau of the Census. (2001a). *Poverty in the United States: 2000.* Washington, DC: U.S. Government Printing Office.

U.S. Bureau of the Census. (2001b). *Statistical abstract of the United States, 2001.* Washington, DC: U.S. Government Printing Office.

Vahali, H. O. (2002). From affirming silence to finding voice: Psychology and the circle of human protest. *Psychological Studies, 47,* 5–10.

Vahtera, J., Kivimaeki, M., Uutela, A., & Pentti, J. (2000). Hostility and ill health: Role of psychosocial resources in two contexts of working life. *Journal of Psychosomatic Research, 48,* 89–98.

Valbak, K. (2003). Specialized psychotherapeutic group analysis: How do we make group analysis suitable for "non-suitable" patients? *Group Analysis, 36,* 73–86.

Valentine, T., Brennen, T., & Brédart, S. (1996). *The cognitive psychology of proper names: On the importance of being Ernest.* London: Routledge.

Valeriani, M., Ranghi, F., & Giaquinto, S. (2003). Corrigendum to "The effects of aging on selective attention to touch: A reduced inhibitory control in elderly subjects?" *International Journal of Psychophysiology, 49,* 75–87.

Valkenburg, P. M., & van der Voort, T. H. A. (1994). Influence of TV on daydreaming and creative imagination: A review of research. *Psychological Bulletin, 116,* 316–339.

Vallerand, R. J., Fortier, M. S., & Guay, F. (1997). Self-determination and persistence in a real-life setting: Toward a motivational model of high school dropout. *Journal of Personality and Social Psychology, 72,* 1161–1176.

Valleroy, L. A., Harris, J. R., & Way, P. O. (1990). The impact of HIV infection on child survival in the developing world. *AIDS, 4,* 667–672.

van Baaren, R. B., Holland, R. W., Kawakami, K., & van Knippenberg, A. (2004). Mimicry and prosocial behavior. *Psychological Science, 15,* 71–74.

Van Bakel, H. J. A., & Riksen-Walraven, J. M. (2002). Quality of infant-parent attachment as reflected in infant interactive behaviour during instructional tasks. *Journal of Child Psychology & Psychiatry & Allied Disciplines, 43,* 387–394.

Vandello, J. A., & Cohen, D. (2003). Male honor and female infidelity: Implicit cultural scripts that perpetuate domestic violence. *Journal of Personality and Social Psychology, 84,* 997–1010.

van den Heuvel, H., Tellegen, G., & Koomen, W. (1992). Cultural differences in the use of psychological and social characteristics in children's self-understanding. *European Journal of Social Psychology, 22,* 353–362.

Van der Heijden, A. H. C. (1981). *Short-term visual information forgetting.* London: Routledge & Kegan Paul.

Van der Zee, K., Oldersma, F., Buunk, B. P., & Bos, D. (1998). Social comparison preferences among cancer patients as related to neuroticism and social comparison orientation. *Journal of Personality and Social Psychology, 75,* 801–810.

van Doornen, L., de Geus, E., & Orlebeke, J. (1988). Aerobic fitness and physiological stress response: A critical evaluation. *Social Science and Medicine, 26,* 303–307.

Van Hooff, M. H., Voorhorst, F. J., Kaptein, M. B., Hirasing, R. A., Koppenaal, C., & Schoemaker, J. (2000). Insulin, androgen, and gonadotropin concentration, body mass index, and waist-to-hip ratio in the first years after menarche in girls with regular menstrual cycles, irregular menstrual cycles, or oligomenorrhea. *Journal of Clinical Endocrinology and Metabolism, 85,* 1394–1400.

Van Lommel, P., van Wees, R., & Meyers, V. (2001). Near-death experiences in survivors of cardiac arrest: A prospective study in the Netherlands. *The Lancet, 358,* 2039–2045.

Van Overwalle, R., & Labiouse, C. (2004). A recurrent connectionist model of person impression formation. *Personality and Social Psychology Review, 8,* 28–61.

Van Rooy, D., Van Overwalle, F., Vanhoomissen, T., Labiouse, C., & French, R. (2003). A recurrent connectionist model of group biases. *Psychological Review, 110,* 536–563.

Vansteenkiste, M., Simons, J., Lens, W., Sheldon, K. M., & Deci, E. L. (2004). Motivating learning, performance, and persistence: The synergistic effects of intrinsic goal contents and autonomy-supportive contexts. *Journal of Personality and Social Psychology, 87,* 246–260.

Varela, F. J., Palacios, A. G., & Goldsmith, T. H. (1993). Color vision of birds. In H. P. Ziegler & H.-J. Bishof (Eds.), *Vision, brain and behavior in birds* (pp. 77–98). Cambridge: MIT Press.

Vargas, J. S. (2003). A commentary on "The double life of B. F. Skinner" by B. J. Baars. *Journal of Consciousness Studies, 10,* 68–73.

Vartanian, L. R. (2000). Revisiting the imaginary audience and personal fable constructs of adolescent egocentrism: A conceptual review. *Adolescence, 35,* 639–661.

Vasta, R., Knott, J. A., & Gaze, C. E. (1996). Can spatial training erase the gender differences on the water-level task? *Psychology of Women Quarterly, 20,* 549–568.

Vaughn, B. E., & Langlois, J. H. (1983). Physical attractiveness as a correlate of peer status and social competence in preschool children. *Developmental Psychology, 19,* 561–567.

Vaughn, L. A., & Weary, G. (2002). Roles of the availability of explanations, feelings of ease, and dysphoria in judgments about the future. *Journal of Social and Clinical Psychology, 21,* 686–704.

Vega, W. A., Kolody, B., Aguilar-Gaxiola, S., Alderate, E., Catalano, R., & Carveo-Anduaga, J. (1998). Lifetime prevalence of DSM–III–R psychiatric disorders among urban and rural Mexican Americans in California. *Archives of General Psychiatry, 55,* 771–778.

Vein, A. M., Sidorov, A. A., Martazaev, M. S., & Karlov, A. V. (1991). Physical exercise and nocturnal sleep in healthy humans. *Human Physiology, 17,* 391–397.

Veniegas, R. C., & Peplau, L. A. (1997). Power and the quality of same-sex friendships. *Psychology of Women Quarterly, 21,* 279–297.

Verma, G. K. (1988). Educational adaptation and achievement of ethnic minority adolescents in Britain. In S. H. Irvine & J. W. Berry (Eds.), *Human abilities in cultural context* (pp. 509–533). Cambridge, England: Cambridge University Press.

Vernon, P. A., & Mori, M. (1992). Intelligence, reaction times, and peripheral nerve conduction velocity. *Intelligence, 16,* 273–288.

Vernon, P. A., Wickett, J. C., Bazana, P. G., & Stelmack, R. M. (2000). The neuropsychology and psychophysiology of human intelligence. In R. J. Sternberg (Ed.), *Handbook of intelligence* (pp. 245–264). Cambridge: Cambridge University Press.

Vgontzas, A. N., & Kales, A. (1999). Sleep and its disorders. *Annual Review of Medicine, 50,* 387–400.

Viau, M., & Zouali, M. (2005). B-lymphocytes, innate immunity, and autoimmunity. *Clinical Immunology, 114,* 17–26.

Vierikko, E., Pulkkinen, L., Kaprio, J., & Rose, R. J. (2004). Genetic and environmental influences on the relationship between aggression and hyperactivity-impulsivity as rated by teachers and parents. *Twin Research, 7,* 261–274.

Vigliocco, G. V., Vinson, D. P., Martin, R. C., & Garrett, M. F. (1999). Is "count" and "mass" information available when the noun is not? An investigation of tip of the tongue states and anomia. *Journal of Memory & Language, 40,* 534–558.

Villejoubert, G. (2005). Could they have known better? *Applied Cognitive Psychology, 19,* 140–143.

Vines, G. (1995, July 22). Fight fat with feeling. *New Scientist,* 14–15.

Vingerhoets, A. (1985). The role of the parasympathetic division of the autonomic nervous system in stress and the emotions. *International Journal of Psychosomatics, 32*(3), 28–34.

Vining, E. P. G., Freeman, J. M., Pillas, D. J., Uematsu, S., Carson, B. S., Brandt, J., Boatman, D., Pulsifer, M. B., & Zukerberg, A. (1997). Why would you remove half a brain? The outcome of 58 children after hemispherectomy—The Johns Hopkins Experience: 1968 to 1996. *Pediatrics, 100,* 163–171.

Vinokur, A. D., & Vinokur-Kaplan, D. (1990). In sickness and in health: Patterns of social support and undermining in older married couples. *Journal of Aging and Health, 2,* 215–241.

Vitaterna, M. H., King, D. P., Chang, A. M., Kornhauser, J. M., Lowrey, P. L., McDonald, J. D., Dove, W. F., Pinto, L. H., Twek, F. W., & Takahashi, J. S. (1994). Mutagenesis and mapping of a mouse gene, *Clock,* essential for circadian behavior. *Science, 264,* 719–725.

Vitterso, J. (2004). Subjective well-being versus self-actualization: Using the flow-simplex to promote a conceptual clarification of subjective quality of life. *Social Indicators Research, 65,* 299–331.

Vives, F., & Oltras, C. M. (1992). Plasma levels of beta-endorphin, ACTH, glucose, free fatty acids and lactate in athletes after running races of different distances. *Medical Science Research, 20,* 67–69.

Voegtlin, W. L. (1940). The treatment of alcoholism by establishing a conditioned reflex. *American Journal of the Medical Sciences, 199,* 802–810.

Vogel, G. (1996). School achievement: Asia and Europe top in the world, but reasons are hard to find. *Science, 274,* 1296.

Vohs, K. D., Heatherton, T. F., & Herrin, M. (2001). Disordered eating and the transition to college: A prospective study. *International Journal of Eating Disorders, 29,* 280–288.

Volkow, N. D., Chang, L., Wang, G. J., Fowler, J. S., Franceschi, D., & Sedler, M. J. (2001). Higher cortical and lower subcortical metabolism in detoxified methamphetamine abusers. *American Journal of Psychiatry, 158,* 383–389.

Vorauer, J. D., & Kumhyr, S. M. (2001). Is this about you or me? Self- versus other-directed judgments and feelings in response to intergroup interaction. *Personality and Social Psychology Bulletin, 27,* 706–719.

Vrij, A., & Semin, G. R. (1996). Lie experts' beliefs about nonverbal indicators of deception. *Journal of Nonverbal Behavior, 20,* 65–80.

Vygotsky, L. S. (1986). *Thought and language* (A. Kozulin, Trans.). Cambridge, MA: MIT Press. (Original work published 1934)

Wade, N. (1999, September 23). Number of human genes is put at 140,000, a significant gain. *New York Times,* p. 86.

Wade, T. J. (2003). Evolutionary theory and African American self-perception: Sex differences in body-esteem predictors of self-perceived physical and sexual attractiveness, and self-esteem. *Journal of Black Psychology, 29,* 123–141.

Wagar, B. M., Dixon, M. J., Smilek, D., & Cudahy, C. (2002). Colored photisms prevent object-substitution masking in digit-color synesthesia. *Brain & Cognition, 48,* 606–611.

Wagenaar, W. A., & Groeneweg, J. (1990). The memory of concentration camp survivors. *Applied Cognitive Psychology, 4,* 77–87.

Wagner, H. (2001). Hunting in barn owls: Peripheral and neurobiological specializations and their general relevance in neural computation. In G. Roth (Ed.), *Brain evolution and cognition* (pp. 205–235). New York: Wiley.

Wagner, R. K. (2000). Practical intelligence. In R. J. Sternberg (Ed.), *Handbook of intelligence* (pp. 380–395). Cambridge: Cambridge University Press.

Wahl, O. F. (1999). Mental health consumers' experience of stigma. *Schizophrenia Bulletin, 25,* 467–478.

Wahlbeck, K., Cheine, M., Essali, A., & Adams, C. (1999). Evidence of clozapine's effectiveness in schizophrenia: A systematic review and meta-analysis of randomized trials. *American Journal of Psychiatry, 156,* 990–999.

Wakefield, J. C. (1999). Evolutionary versus prototype analyses of the concept of disorder. *Journal of Abnormal Psychology, 108,* 374–399.

Wald, G. (1964). The receptors of human color vision. *Science, 145,* 1007–1017.

Waldman, I. D., Weinberg, R. A., & Scarr, S. (1994). Racial-group differences in IQ in the Minnesota

transracial adoption study: A reply to Levin and Lynn. *Intelligence, 19,* 29–44.

Waldsmith, J. (1991). *Stereoviews: An illustrated history and price guide.* Iola, WI: Krause Publications.

Walk, R. D. (1981). *Perceptual development.* Monterey, CA: Brooks/Cole.

Walk, R. D., & Gibson, E. J. (1961). A comparative and analytical study of visual depth perception. *Psychological Monographs,* No. 75.

Walker, E., & Bollini, A. M. (2002). Pubertal neurodevelopment and the emergence of psychotic symptoms. *Schizophrenia Research, 54,* 17–23.

Walker, E. F., & Diforio, D. (1998). Schizophrenia: A neural diathesis-stress model. *Psychological Review, 104,* 667–685.

Walker, L. J. (1989). A longitudinal study of moral reasoning. *Child Development, 60,* 157–166.

Wall, P. (2000). *Pain: The science of suffering.* New York: Columbia University Press.

Wallace, B. (1993). Day persons, night persons, and variability in hypnotic susceptibility. *Journal of Personality and Social Psychology, 64,* 827–833.

Wallace, P. (1977). Individual discrimination of humans by odor. *Physiology and Behavior, 19,* 577–579.

Waller, D., Loomis, J. M., Gollege, R. G., & Beall, A. C. (2002). Place learning in humans: The role of distance and direction information. *Spatial Cognition and Computation, 2,* 333–354.

Walsh, R. (1996). Meditation research: The state of the art. In B. W. Scotton, A. B. Chinen, & J. R. Battista (Eds.), *Textbook of transpersonal psychiatry and psychology* (pp. 167–175). New York: Basic Books.

Walsh, S. (1993). Cited in Toufexis, A. (1993, February 15). *Time,* 49–51.

Walsh, V. (2000). Hemispheric asymmetries: A brain in two minds. *Current Biology, 10,* 460–462.

Walters, J. M., & Gardner, H. (1986). The theory of multiple intelligences: Some issues and answers. In R. Sternberg & R. Wagner (Eds.), *Practical intelligences* (pp. 163–183). New York: Cambridge University Press.

Wanberg, C. R., Kenfer, R., & Rotundo, M. (1999). Unemployed individuals: Motives, job-search constraints as predictors of job seeking and reemployment. *Journal of Applied Psychology, 54,* 897–910.

Wang, G.-J., Volkow, N. D., Thanos, P. K., & Fowler, J. S. (2003). Positron emission tomographic evidence of similarity between obesity and drug addiction. *Psychiatric Annals, 33,* 104–111.

Wang, Q. (2001). Culture effects on adults' earliest childhood recollection and self-description: Implications for the relation between memory and the self. *Journal of Personality and Social Psychology, 81,* 220–233.

Wanlass, J., Moreno, J.-K., & Thomson, H. M. (2005). Group therapy for eating disorders: A retrospective case study. *Journal for Specialists in Group Work, 30,* 47–66.

Ward, C. (1994). Culture and altered states of consciousness. In W. J. Lonner & R. S. Malpass (Eds.), *Psychology and Culture.* Boston: Allyn & Bacon.

Wardhaugh, R. (1993). *Investigating language: Central problems in linguistics.* Oxford, England: Blackwell Publishers.

Warner, J. S. (1999). What's in a name? *Headache, 39,* 136–137.

Warren, R. M. (1970). Perceptual restoration of missing speech sounds. *Science, 167,* 392–393.

Waschbusch, D. A., Sellers, D. P., LeBlanc, M., & Kelley, M. L. (2003). Helpless attributions and depression in adolescents: The roles of anxiety, event valence and demographics. *Journal of Adolescence, 26,* 169–183.

Wason, P. C. (1960). On the failure to eliminate hypotheses in a conceptual task. *Quarterly Journal of Experimental Psychology, 12,* 129–140.

Wass, H., Christian, M., Myers, J., & Murphey, M. (1978–1979). Similarities and dissimilarities in attitudes toward death in a population of older persons. *Omega, 9,* 337–354.

Wasserman, D., Lempert, R. O., & Hastie, R. (1991). Hindsight and causality. *Personality and Social Psychology Bulletin, 17,* 30–35.

Wasserman, E. A., & Miller, R. R. (1997). What's elementary about associative learning? *Annual Review of Psychology, 48,* 573–607.

Wasserman, J. D. (2003). Assessment of intellectual functioning. In J. R. Graham & J. A. Naglieri (Eds.), *Handbook of psychology: Assessment psychology* (Vol. 10, pp. 417–442). New York: Wiley.

Watkins, M. J., & Tulving, E. (1975). Episodic memory: When recognition fails. *Journal of Experimental Psychology: General, 104,* 5–29.

Watson, D., & Clark, L. A. (1997). Extraversion and its positive emotional core. In R. Hogan, J. Johnson, & S. Briggs, (Eds.), *Handbook of personality psychology.* San Diego, CA: Academic Press.

Watson, D., Wiese, D., Vaidya, J., & Tellegen, A. (1999). The two general activation systems of affect: Structural findings, evolutionary considerations, and psychobiological evidence. *Journal of Personality and Social Psychology, 76,* 820–838.

Watson, J. B. (1913). Psychology as the behaviorist views it. *Psychological Review, 20,* 158–177.

Watson, J. B. (1924). *Behaviorism.* New York: Norton.

Watson, J. B., & Rayner, R. (1920). Conditioned emotional responses. *Journal of Experimental Psychology, 3,* 1–14.

Waxman, S. G. (Ed.). (2001). *Form and function in the brain and spinal cord: Perspectives of a neurologist.* Cambridge, MA: MIT Press.

Waxman, S. R. (2003). Links between object categorization and naming: Origins and emergence in human infants. In D. H. Rakison & L. M. Oakes (Eds.), *Early category and concept development: Making sense of the blooming, buzzing confusion* (pp. 213–241). London: Oxford University Press.

Way, N., Cowal, K., Gingold, R., Pahl, K., & Bissessar, N. (2001). Friendship patterns among African American, Asian American, and Latino adolescents from low-income families. *Journal of Social and Personal Relationships, 18,* 29–53.

Wearden, A. J., Tarrier, N., Barrowclough, C., Zastowny, T. R., & Rahill, A. A. (2000). A review of expressed emotion research in health care. *Clinical Psychology Review, 20,* 633–666.

Webb, W. B. (1992). *Sleep: The gentle giant.* Bolton, MA: Anker Publishing.

Weber, E. H. (1834). *De pulen, resorptione, auditu et tactu: Annotationes anatomicae et physiologicae.* Leipzig: Koehler.

Wechsler, H., Lee, J. E., Kuo, M., Seibring, M., Nelson, T. F., & Lee, H. (2002). Trends in college binge drinking during a period of increased prevention efforts: Findings for 4 Harvard School of Public Health College Study Surveys: 1993–2001. *Journal of American College Health, 50,* 203–217.

Wegener, D. T., & Petty, R. E. (1995). Flexible correction processes in social judgment: The role of naive theories in corrections for perceived bias. *Journal of Personality and Social Psychology, 68,* 36–51.

Wegner, D. M., Erber, R., & Raymond, P. (1991). Transactive memory in close relationships. *Journal of Personality and Social Psychology, 61,* 923–929.

Weick, K. E. (1985). Systematic observational methods. In G. Lindzey & E. Aronson (Eds.), *Handbook of social psychology* (Vol. 1, pp. 567–634). New York: Random House.

Weill, J. C., & Reynaud, C. A. (2005). Do developing B cells need antigen? *Journal of Experimental Medicine, 201,* 7–9.

Weinberg, R. A., Scarr, S., & Waldman, I. D. (1992). The Minnesota Transracial Adoption Study: A follow-up of IQ test performance at adolescence. *Intelligence, 16,* 117–135.

Weiner, T., Johnston, D., & Lewis, N. (1995). *Betrayal: The story of Aldrich Ames, an American spy.* New York: Random House.

Weingardt, K. R., Loftus, E. F., & Lindsay, D. S. (1995). Misinformation revisited: New evidence on the suggestibility of memory. *Memory and Cognition, 23,* 72–82.

Weinstock, H., Berman, S., & Cates, W. (2000). Sexually transmitted diseases among American youth: Incidence and prevalence estimates, 2000. *Perspectives on Sexual and Reproductive Health, 36,* 6–10.

Weir, W. (1984, October 15). Another look at subliminal "facts." *Advertising Age,* 46.

Weisbuch, M., Mackie, D. M., & Garcia-Marques, T. (2003). Prior source exposure and persuasion: Further evidence for misattributional processes. *Personality and Social Psychology Bulletin, 29,* 691–700.

Weisenberg, M. (1977). Pain and pain control. *Psychological Bulletin, 84,* 1008–1044.

Weiss, C. S. (1992). Depression and immuno-competence: A review of the literature. *Psychological Bulletin, 111,* 475–489.

Weiss, L. G., Saklofske, D. H., & Prifitera, A. (2005). Interpreting the WISC-IV index scores. In A. Prifitera, D. H. Saklofske, & L. G. Weiss (Eds.), *WISC-IV clinical use and interpretation: Scientist-practitioner perspectives* (pp. 71–100). San Diego, CA: Elsevier Academic Press.

Weissman, M. M., Bland, R. C., Canino, G. J., Faravelli, C., Greenwald, S., & Hwu, H.-G. (1997). The cross-national epidemiology of panic disorder. *Archives of General Psychiatry, 54,* 305–309.

Weissman, M. M., Bland, R. C., Canino, G. J., Faravelli, C., Greenwald, S., Hwu, H.-G., Joyce, P. R., Karam, E. G., Lee, C.-K., Lellouch, J., Lepine, J.-P., Newman, S. C., Rubio-Stepic, M., Wells, J. E., Wickramaratne, P. J., Wittchen, H.-U., & Yeh, E.-K. (1996). Cross-national epidemiology of major depression and bipolar disorder. *Journal of the American Medical Association, 276,* 293–299.

Weissman, M. M., Bruce, M., Leaf, P., Florio, L., & Holzer, C. (1991). Affective disorders. In L. N. Robins & D. A. Regier (Eds.), *Psychiatric disorders in America* (pp. 53–80). New York: Free Press.

Weitzman, E. R., Nelson, T. F., & Wechsler, H. (2003). Taking up binge drinking in college: The influences of person, social group, and environment. *Journal of Adolescent Health, 32,* 26–35.

Weldon, M. S. (1999). The memory chop shop: Issues in the search for memory systems. In J. K. Foster & M. Jelicic (Eds.), *Memory: Systems, process, or function?* (pp. 162–205). Oxford, England: Oxford University Press.

Wellman, H. M., Cross, D., & Watson, J. (2001). Meta-analysis of theory-of-mind development: The truth about false belief. *Child Development, 72,* 655–684.

Welsh, D. K. (1993). Timing of sleep and wakefulness. In M. A. Carskadon (Ed.), *Encyclopedia of sleep and dreaming.* New York: Macmillan.

Weng, J., McClelland, J., Pentland, A., Sporns, O., Stockman, I., Sur, M., & Thelan, E. (2001). Autonomous mental development by robots and animals. *Science, 291,* 599–600.

Werker, J. F., & Lalond, F. M. (1988). Cross-language speech perception: Initial capabilities and developmental change. *Developmental Psychology, 24,* 672–683.

Werking, K. (1997). *We're just good friends.* New York: Guilford Press.

Wert, B. Y., & Neisworth, J. T. (2003). Effects of video self-modeling on spontaneous requesting in children with autism. *Journal of Positive Behavior Interventions, 5,* 30–34.

Wertsch, J. V., & Tulviste, P. (1992). L. S. Vygotsky and contemporary developmental psychology. *Developmental Psychology, 28,* 548–557.

West, S. G., & Brown, T. J. (1975). Physical attractiveness, the severity of the emergency and helping: A field experiment and interpersonal simulation. *Journal of Experimental Social Psychology, 11,* 531–538.

Westen, D. (1998). The scientific legacy of Sigmund Freud: Toward a psychodynamically informed psychological science. *Psychological Bulletin, 124,* 333–371.

Westen, D., & Gabbard, G. O. (1999). Psychoanalytic approaches to personality. In L. A. Pervin & O. P. John (Eds.), *Handbook of personality: Theory and research* (pp. 57–101). New York: Guilford Press.

Westen, D., & Morrison, K. (2001). *A meta-analytic investigation of empirically supported treatments for depression, anxiety, and generalized anxiety disorder.* Unpublished manuscript, Boston University.

Wever, E. G. (1949). *Theory of hearing.* New York: Wiley.

Wever, E. G., & Bray, C. W. (1937). The perception of low tones and the resonance-volley theory. *Journal of Psychology, 3,* 101–114.

Wever, R. A. (1979). *The circadian system in man.* Berlin: Springer-Verlag.

Whaley, A. L. (2004). A two-stage method for the study of cultural bias in the diagnosis of schizophrenia in African Americans. *Journal of Black Psychology, 30,* 167–186.

Wheeler, L., & Kim, Y. (1997). What is beautiful is culturally good: The physical attractiveness stereotype

has different content in collectivist cultures. *Personality and Social Psychology Bulletin, 23,* 795–800.

Whitbeck, L. B., & Hoyt, D. R. (1994). Social prestige and assortive mating: A comparison of students from 1956 and 1988. *Journal of Social and Personal Relationships, 11,* 137–145.

Whitbourne, S. K. (1985). *The aging body: Physiological changes and psychological consequences.* New York: Springer-Verlag.

White, C. E. (2002, February 2). A conversation with Jasper Fforde. *Writers Write: The Internet Writing Journal,* http://www.writerswrite.com/journal/feb02/fforde.htm

White, G. L. (1980). Physical attractiveness and courtship progress. *Journal of Personality and Social Psychology, 39,* 660–668.

White, G. L., & Mullen, P. E. (1989). *Jealousy: Theory, research, and clinical strategies.* New York: Guilford Press.

White, J. R., Froeb, H. F., & Kulik, J. A. (1991). Respiratory illness in nonsmokers chronically exposed to tobacco smoke in the workplace. *Chest, 100,* 39–43.

White, L., Katzman, R., & Losonczy, K. (1994). Association of education with incidence of cognitive impairment in three established populations for epidemiologic studies of the elderly. *Journal of Clinical Epidemiology, 47,* 363–371.

White, M., & LeVine, R. A. (1986). What is an Ii ko (good child)? In H. Stevenson, H. Azuma, & K. Hakuta (Eds.), *Child development and education in Japan* (pp. 55–62). New York: Freeman.

White, M. A., Kohlmaier, J. R., Varnado-Sullivan, P., & Williamson, D. A. (2003). Racial/ethnic differences in weight concerns: Protective and risk factors for the development of eating disorders and obesity among adolescent females. *Eating & Weight Disorders, 8,* 20–25.

White, T. D., Berhane, A., Degusta, D., Gilbert, H., Richards, G. D., Suwa, G., & Howell, F. C. (2003). Pleistocene *Homo sapiens* from Middle Awash, Ethiopia. *Nature, 423,* 742–747.

Whitehead, W., III, & Kuhn, W. F. (1990). Chronic pain: An overview. In T. W. Miller (Ed.), *Chronic pain* (Vol. 1, pp. 5–48). Madison, CT: International Universities Press.

Whitehurst, G. J., Arnold, D. S., Epstein, J. N., Angell, A. L., Smith, M., & Gischel, J. E. (1994). A picture book reading intervention in day care and home for children from low-income families. *Developmental Psychology, 30,* 679–689.

Whorf, B. L. (1956). Science and linguistics. In J. B. Carroll (Ed.), *Language, thought, and reality: Selected writings of Benjamin Lee Whorf.* Cambridge, MA: MIT Press.

Wich, S. A., Assink, P. R., Becher, F., & Sterck, E. H. M. (2002). Playbacks of loud calls to wild Thomas langurs (primates; *Presbytis thomasi*): The effect of familiarity. *Behaviour, 139,* 79–87.

Wickelgren, W. A. (1965). Acoustic similarity and intrusion errors in short-term memory. *Journal of Experimental Psychology, 70,* 102–108.

Wickens, C. D. (1992a). Virtual reality and education. In *Proceedings of the IEEE International Conference on Systems, Man and Cybernetics.* New York: IEEE.

Wickens, C. D. (1992b). *Engineering psychology and human performance* (2nd ed.). New York: HarperCollins.

Widner, B., Laich, A., Sperner-Unterweger, B., Ledochowski, M., & Fuchs, D. (2002). Neopterin production, tryptophan degradation, and mental depression: What is the link? *Brain, Behavior, & Immunity, 16,* 590–595.

Wiebe, D. J., & McCallum, D. M. (1986). Health practices and hardiness as mediators in the stress-illness relationship. *Health Psychology, 5,* 425–438.

Wiederhold, B. K., Gevirtz, R. N., & Spira, J. L. (2001). Virtual reality exposure therapy vs. imagery desensitization therapy in the treatment of flying phobia. In R. Giuseppe & C. Galimberti (Eds.), *Towards cyberpsychology: Mind, cognition and society in the Internet age* (pp. 253–272). Amsterdam: IOS Press.

Wierzbicki, M. (1993). *Issues in clinical psychology: Subjective versus objective approaches.* Boston: Allyn & Bacon.

Wierzbicki, M. (1997). *Introduction to clinical psychology: Scientific foundations to clinical practice.* Boston: Allyn & Bacon.

Wierzbicki, M., & Pekarik, G. (1993). A meta-analysis of psychotherapy dropout. *Professional Psychology: Research and Practice, 24,* 190–195.

Wierzbicki, M., & Rexford, L. (1989). Cognitive and behavioral correlates of depression in clinical and nonclinical populations. *Journal of Clinical Psychology, 45,* 872–877.

Wiesel, T. N. (1982). Postnatal development of the visual cortex and the influence of environment. *Nature, 299,* 583–591.

Wigboldus, D. H. J., Dijksterhuis, A., & Van Knippenberg, A. (2003). When stereotypes get in the way: Stereotypes obstruct stereotype-inconsistent trait inferences. *Journal of Personality & Social Psychology, 84,* 470–484.

Wiggins, J. S. (Ed.). (1996). *The five factor model of personality: Theoretical perspectives.* New York: Guilford Press.

Willerman, L., & Cohen, D. B. (1990). *Psychopathology.* New York: McGraw-Hill.

Williams, C. L., Haines, J., & Sale, I. M. (2003). Psychophysiological and psychological correlates of dissociation in a case of dissociative identity disorder. *Journal of Trauma & Dissociation, 4,* 101–118.

Williams, D., & Lawler, K. A. (2001). Stress and illness in low-income women: The roles of hardiness, John Henryism, and race. *Women and Health, 32,* 61–76.

Williams, J., Wake, M., Hesketh, K., Maher, E., & Waters, E. (2005). Health-related quality of life of overweight and obese children. *Journal of the American Medical Association, 293,* 1–5.

Williams, R. W., & Herrup, K. (1988). The control of neuron number. *Annual Review of Neuroscience, 11,* 423–453.

Williams, S. D. (2002). Self-esteem and the self-censorship of creative ideas. *Personnel Review, 31,* 495–503.

Williams, W. L. (1992). The relationship between male-male friendship and male-female marriage. In P. M. Nardi (Ed.), *Men's friendships* (pp. 186–200). Newbury Park, CA: Sage.

Williams, W. M., & Ceci, S. J. (1997). Are Americans becoming more or less alike? Trends in race, class, and ability differences in intelligence. *American Psychologist, 52,* 1126–1235.

Willis, C. M., Church, S. M., Guest, C. M, Cook, W., McCarthy, N., Bransbury, A. J., Church, M. R. T., & Church, J. C. T. (2004). Olfactory detection of human bladder cancer by dogs: Proof of principle study. *British Medical Journal, 329,* 7468.

Willis, W. D. (1985). *The pain system: The neural basis of nociceptive transmission in the mammalian nervous system.* Basel: Karger.

Wills, T. A., Yaeger, A. M., & Sandy, J. M. (2003). Buffering effect of religiosity for adolescent substance use. *Psychology of Addictive Behaviors, 17,* 24–31.

Willson, A. E. (2003). Race and women's income trajectories: Employment, marriage, and income security over the life course. *Social Problems, 50,* 87–110.

Wilson, A. E., & Ross, M. (2001). From chump to champ: People's appraisals of their earlier and current selves. *Journal of Personality and Social Psychology, 80,* 572–584.

Wilson, B. (1970). *Religious sects.* London: Weidenfeld & Nicolson.

Wilson, B. J., Donnerstein, E., Linz, D., Kunkel, D., Potter, J., Smith, S. L., Blumenthal, E., & Gray, T. (1998). Content analysis of entertainment television: The importance of context. In J. T. Hamilton (Ed.), *Television violence and public policy* (pp. 13–53). Ann Arbor, MI: University of Michigan Press.

Wilson, E. O. (1997). *In search of nature.* Washington, DC: Island Press.

Wilson, S. C., & Barber, T. X. (1983). The fantasy-prone personality: Implications for understanding imagery, hypnosis, and parapsychological phenomena. In A. A. Sheikh (Ed.), *Imagery: Current theory, research, and applications.* New York: Wiley.

Wilson, T. D., Lindsey, S., & Schooler, T. Y. (2000). A model of dual attitudes. *Psychological Review, 107,* 101–126.

Windle, R. J., Shanks, N., Lightman, S. L., & Ingram, C. D. (1997). Central oxytocin administration reduces stress-induced corticosterone release and anxiety behavior in rats. *Endocrinology, 138,* 2829–2834.

Windschitl, P. D. (1996). Memory for faces: Evidence of retrieval-based impairment. *Journal of Experimental Psychology: Learning, Memory, and Cognition, 22,* 1101–1122.

Windschitl, P. D., & Wells, G. L. (1997). Behavioral consensus information affects people's inferences about population traits. *Personality and Social Psychology Bulletin, 23,* 148–156.

Winerman, L. (2004). Back to her roots. *Monitor on Psychology, 35*(8), 46–47.

Wingood, G. M., DiClemente, R. J., Bernhardt, J. M., Harrington, K., Davies, S. L., Robillard, A., & Hook, E. W., III. (2003). A prospective study of exposure to rap music videos and African American female adolescents' health. *American Journal of Public Health, 93,* 437–439.

Winkielman, P., & Schwarz, N. (2001). How pleasant was your childhood? Beliefs about memory shape inferences from experienced difficulty of recall. *Psychological Science, 12,* 176–179.

Winn, P. (1995). The lateral hypothalamus and motivated behavior: An old syndrome reassessed and a new perspective gained. *Current Directions in Psychological Science, 4,* 182–187.

Winner, E. (1997). Exceptionally high intelligence and schooling. *American Psychologist, 52,* 1070–1081.

Winograd, E., & Killinger, W. A. (1983). Relating age at encoding in early childhood to adult recall: Development of flashbulb memories. *Journal of Experimental Psychology: General, 112,* 413–422.

Winson, J. (1990, November). The meaning of dreams. *Scientific American,* 86–96.

Wise, R. A. (2004). Drive, incentive, and reinforcement: The antecedents and consequences of motivation. In R. A. Bevins & M. T. Bardo (Eds.), *Motivational factors in the etiology of drug abuse. Nebraska Symposium on Motivation* (Vol. 50, pp. 159–195). Lincoln, NE: University of Nebraska Press.

Wise, S. M. (2000). *Rattling the cage: Toward legal rights for animals.* Cambridge, MA: Perseus Books.

Wiseman, R., & Greening, E. (2002). The mind machine: A mass participation experiment into the possible existence of extra-sensory perception. *British Journal of Psychology, 93,* 487–499.

Wissler, C. (1901). The correlation of mental and physical tests. *Psychological Review Monograph Supplement 3,* No. 6.

Witelson, S. F., Kigar, D. L., & Harvey, T. (1999). The exceptional brain of Albert Einstein. *Lancet, 353,* 2149–2153.

Wittock, D. A., & Myers, T. C. (1998). The comparison of individuals with recurrent tension-type headache and headache-free controls in physiological response, appraisal, and coping with stressors: A review of the literature. *Annals of Behavioral Medicine, 20,* 118–134.

Wixted, J. T., & Ebbesen, E. B. (1991). On the form of forgetting. *Psychological Science, 2,* 409–415.

Wolf, A., & Colditz, G. (1996). Social and economic effects of weight in the United States. *American Journal of Nutrition, 63* (Suppl. 3), 466S–469S.

Wolkowitz, O. M., & Rothschild, A. J. (Eds.). (2003). Psychoneuroendocrinology: The scientific basis of clinical practice. Arlington, VA: American Psychiatric Publishing.

Woll, S. (2002). *Everyday thinking: Memory, reasoning, and judgment in the real world.* Mahwah, NJ: Erlbaum.

Wolpe, J. (1958). *Psychotherapy by reciprocal inhibition.* Stanford, CA: Stanford University Press.

Wolpe, J., & Plaud, J. J. (1997). Pavlov's contributions to behavior therapy: The obvious and the not-so-obvious. *American Psychologist, 52,* 966–972.

Wood, B. (2002). Palaeoanthropology: Hominid revelations from Chad. *Nature, 418,* 133–135.

Wood, D. J., Bruner, J. S., & Ross, G. (1976). The role of tutoring in problem solving. *Journal of Child Psychology and Psychiatry, 17,* 89–100.

Wood, D. J., & Middleton, D. (1975). A study of assisted problem-solving. *British Journal of Psychology, 66,* 181–191.

Wood, E., Agster, K., & Eichenbaum, H. (2004). One trial odour-reward association: A form of event memory not dependent on hippocampal function. *Behavioral Neuroscience, 118,* 526–539.

Wood, J. M., Lilienfeld, S. O., Garb, H. N., & Nezworski, M. T. (2000). The Rorschach Test in clinical diagnosis: A critical review, with a backward look at Garfield (1947). *Journal of Clinical Psychology, 56,* 395–430.

Wood, J. V., Giordano-Beech, M., Taylor, K. L., Michela, J. L., & Gaus, V. (1994). Strategies of social comparison among people with low self-esteem: Self protection and self-enhancement. *Journal of Personality of Social Psychology, 67,* 713–731.

Wood, N., & Cowan, N. (1995). The cocktail party phenomenon revisited: How frequent are attention shifts to one's name in an irrelevant auditory channel? *Journal of Experimental Psychology: Learning, Memory, and Cognition, 21,* 255–260.

Wood, W., Wong, F. Y., & Chachere, J. G. (1991). Effects of media violence on viewers' aggression in unconstrained social interaction. *Psychological Bulletin, 109,* 371–383.

Woodruff, M. L. (1993). Report: Electroencephalograph taken from Pastor Liston Pack, 4:00 P.M., 7 Nov. 1985. In T. Burton, *Serpent-handling believer* (pp. 142–144). Knoxville: University of Tennessee Press.

Woodruff-Pak, D. S. (1999). New directions for a classical paradigm: Human eyeblink conditioning. *Psychological Science, 10,* 1–3.

Woods, S. (1991). The eating paradox: How we tolerate food. *Psychological Review, 98,* 488–505.

Woods, S., Schwartz, M., Baskin, D., & Seeley, R. (2000). Food intake and the regulation of body weight. *Annual Review of Psychology, 51,* 255–277.

Woodward, S. A., McManis, M. H., Kagan, J., Deldin, P., Snidman, N., Lewis, M., & Kahn, V. (2001). Infant temperament and the brainstem auditory evoked response in later childhood. *Developmental Psychology, 37,* 533–538.

World Health Organization. (2002). *Mental Health: Responding to the call for action.* From www.who.int/gb/EBWHA/PDF/WHA55/ ea5518.pdf

Worth, B. L., & Yates, J. L. (Ed.). (1996). *The near death experience: A reader.* London: Routledge.

Wright, I. C., Rabe, H. S., Woodruff, P. W. R., David, A. S., Murray, R. M., & Bullmore, E. T. (2000). Meta-analysis of regional brain volumes in schizophrenia. *American Journal of Psychiatry, 157,* 16–25.

Wright, P. H., & Scanlon, M. B. (1991). Gender role orientations and friendship: Some attenuation, but gender differences abound. *Sex Roles, 24,* 551–566.

Wu, T.-C., Tashkin, D. P., Djahed, B., & Rose, J. E. (1988). Pulmonary hazards of smoking marijuana as compared with tobacco. *New England Journal of Medicine, 318,* 347–351.

Wyatt, F., & Teuber, H. L. (1944). German psychology under the Nazi system, 1933–1940. *Psychological Review, 51,* 229–247.

Wyche, K. F. (1993). Psychology and African American women: Findings from applied research. *Applied & Preventive Psychology, 2,* 115–121.

Yacoubian, G. S. (2003). Correlates of ecstasy use among high school seniors surveyed through Monitoring the Future. *Drugs: Education, Prevention & Policy, 10,* 65–72.

Yaffe, K., Barnes, D., Nevitt, M., Lui, L.-Y., & Covinsky, K. (2001). A prospective study of physical activity and cognitive decline in elderly women. *Archives of Internal Medicine, 161,* 1703–1708.

Yager, J. (2005). Masters of the mind: Exploring the story of mental illness from ancient times to the new millennium. *American Journal of Psychiatry, 162,* 407–408.

Yalom, I. D. (1995). *The theory and practice of group psychotherapy* (4th ed.). New York: Basic Books.

Yamaguchi, S., Hale, L. A., D'Esposito, M., & Knight, R. T. (2004). Rapid prefrontal-hippocampal habituation to novel events. *Journal of Neuroscience, 24,* 5356–5363.

Yamane, D., & Polzer, M. (1994). Ways of seeing ecstasy in modern society: Experimental-expressive and cultural-linguistic views. *Sociology of Religion, 55,* 1–25.

Yancey, A. K., Siegel, J. M., & McDaniel, K. L. (2002). Role models, ethnic identity, and health-risk behaviors in urban adolescents. *Archives of Pediatric Adolescent Medicine, 156,* 55–61.

Yanovski, J., & Yanovski, S. (1999). Recent advances in basic obesity research. *Journal of the American Medical Association, 282,* 1504–1506.

Yeargin-Allsopp, M., Murphy, C. C., Cordero, J. F., & Decoufle, P. (1997). Reported biomedical causes and associated medical conditions for mental retardation among 10-year-old children. *Developmental Medicine & Child Neurology, 39,* 142–149.

Yehuda, R. (2000). The biology of post traumatic stress disorder. *Journal of Clinical Psychiatry, 61* (Suppl. 7), 14–21.

Yelena, P., Leo, M. A., Kroll, W., & Lieber, C. S. (2002). Effects of alcohol consumption on eight circulating markers of liver fibrosis. *Alcohol & Alcoholism, 37,* 256–260.

Yoder, J. D. (1999). *Women and gender: Transforming psychology.* Upper Saddle River, NJ: Prentice Hall.

Yoder, J. D., & Schleicher, T. L. (1996). Undergraduates regard deviation from occupational gender stereotypes as costly for women. *Sex Roles, 34,* 171–188.

Young, L. J. (2002). The neurobiology of social recognition: Approach and avoidance. *Biological Psychiatry, 51,* 18–26.

Young, L. R., & Nestle, M. (2002). The contribution of expanding portion sizes to the U.S. obesity epidemic. *American Journal of Public Health, 92,* 246–249.

Young, W. B. (2004). Drug-induce headache. *Neurological Clinic, 22,* 173–184.

Yousem, D. M., Maldjian, J. A., Siddiqi, F., Hummel, T., Alsop, D. C., Geckle, R. J., Bilker, W. B., & Doty, R. L. (1999). Gender effects on odor-stimulated functional magnetic resonance imaging. *Brain Research, 818,* 480–487.

Yousem, D. M., Oguz, K. K., & Li, C. (2001). Imaging of the olfactory system. *Seminars in Ultrasound, CT & MR, 22,* 456–472.

Yu, B., Zhang, W., Jing, Q., Peng, R., Zhang, G., & Simon, H. A. (1985). STM capacity for Chinese and English language materials. *Memory and Cognition, 13,* 202–207.

Yule, G. (1996). *The study of language.* Cambridge: Cambridge University Press.

Yzerbyt, V. Y., Rocher, S., & Schadron, G. (1996). Stereotypes as explanations: A subjective essentialistic view of group perception. In R. Spears, P. J. Oakes, N. Ellemers, & S. A. Haslam (Eds.), *The social psychology of stereotyping and group life.* Cambridge, England: Blackwell.

Zajonc, R. B. (1968). Attitudinal effects of mere exposure. *Journal of Personality and Social Psychology Monograph Supplement, 9* (2, Part 2), 1–27.

Zamansky, H. S., & Bartis, S. P. (1985). The dissociation of an experience: The hidden observer observed. *Journal of Abnormal Psychology, 94,* 243–248.

Zanna, M. P., & Rempel, J. K. (1988). Attitudes: A new look at an old concept. In D. Bar-Tal & A. W. Kruglanski (Eds.), *The social psychology of knowledge* (pp. 315–334). New York: Cambridge University Press.

Zanot, E. J., Pincus, J. D., & Lamp, E. J. (1983). Public perceptions of subliminal advertising. *Journal of Advertising, 12,* 37–45.

Zaragoza, M. S., & Mitchell, K. J. (1996). Repeated exposure to suggestion and the creation of false memories. *Psychological Science, 7,* 294–300.

Zárate, M. A., Garcia, B., Garza, A. A., & Hitlan, R. T. (2004). Cultural threat and perceived realistic group conflict as dual predictors of prejudice. *Journal of Experimental Social Psychology, 40,* 99–105.

Zatzick, D. F. (1999). Managed care and psychiatry. In R. E. Hales, S. C. Yudofsky, & J. A. Talbott (Eds.), *American Psychiatric Press textbook of psychiatry.* Washington, DC: American Psychiatric Press.

Zebrowitz, L. A., & Montepare, J. M. (1992). Impressions of babyfaced individuals across the life span. *Developmental Psychology, 28,* 1143–1152.

Zebrowitz, L. A., & Rhodes, G. (2002). Nature let a hundred flowers bloom: The multiple ways and wherefores of attractiveness. In G. Rhodes & L. A. Zebrowitz (Eds.), *Facial attractiveness: Evolutionary, cognitive, and social perspectives. Advances in visual cognition* (Vol. 1, pp. 261–293). Westport, CT: Ablex.

Zebrowitz, L. A., Voinescu, L., & Collins, M. A. (1996). "Wide-eyed" and "crooked-faced": Determinants of perceived and real honesty across the life span. *Personality and Social Psychology Bulletin, 22,* 1258–1269.

Zeman, A. (2005). Tales from the temporal lobes. *New England Journal of Medicine, 352,* 119–121.

Zhang, A. Y., Snowden, L. R., & Sue, S. (1998). Differences between Asian- and White-Americans' help-seeking and utilization patterns in the Los Angeles area. *Journal of Community Psychology, 26,* 317–326.

Zhang, D. R., Li, Z. H., Chen, X. C., Wang, Z. X., Zhang, X. C., Meng, X. M., He, S., & Hu, X. P. (2003). Functional comparison of primacy, middle and recency retrieval in human auditory short-term memory: An event-related fMRI study. *Cognitive Brain Research, 16,* 91–98.

Zhang, W., & Zhang, N. L. (2005). Restricted value iteration: Theory and algorithms. *Journal of Artificial Intelligence Research, 23,* 123–165.

Zhiyan, T., & Singer, J. L. (1997). Daydreaming styles, emotionality and the Big Five personality dimensions. *Imagination, Cognition & Personality, 16,* 399–414.

Zhou, L., Yang, W., Liao, S., & Zou, H. (1999). Experimental study of lie detection with P300 in simulated crime. *Chinese Journal of Clinical Psychology, 7,* 31–33.

Zhou, P., Shah, B., Prasad, K., & David, R. (2005). Letrozole significantly improves growth potential in a pubertal boy with growth hormone deficiency. *Pediatrics, 115,* 245–248.

Zimbardo, P. G. (Producer). (1972). *The Stanford prison experiment* . [Slide/tape presentation].

Zimbardo, P. G., & Boyd, J. N. (1999). Putting time in perspective: A valid, reliable individual differences metric. *Journal of Personality and Social Psychology, 77,* 1271–1288.

Zinn, M. B., Hondagneu-Sotelo, P., & Messner, M. A. (2000). *Gender through the prism of difference* (2nd ed.). Needham Heights, MA: Allyn & Bacon.

Zipursky, R. B., & Schulz, S. C. (Eds.). (2002). *The early stages of schizophrenia.* Washington, DC: American Psychiatric Publishing, Inc.

Zola-Morgan, S., & Squire, L. R. (1993). Neuroanatomy of memory. *Annual Review of Neuroscience, 16,* 547–563.

Zolnierczyk, D. (2004). Perceived job stressors and mindfulness-based cognitive stress management intervention: The role of Type A and reactivity. *Polish Psychological Bulletin, 35,* 25–33.

Zorick, F. (1989). Overview of insomnia. In M. H. Dryger, T. Roth, & W. C. Dement (Eds.), *Principles and practice of sleep medicine.* San Diego, CA: Harcourt Brace Jovanovich.

Zrenner, E., Abramov, I., Akita, M., Cowey, A., Livingstone, M., & Valberg, A. (1990). Color perception: Retina to cortex. In L. Spillman & J. S. Werner (Eds.), *Visual perception: The neurophysiological foundations.* San Diego, CA: Academic Press.

Zucker, K. J., Wilson-Smith, D. N., Kurita, J. A., & Stern, A. (1995). Children's appraisal of sex-typed behavior in their peers. *Sex Roles, 33,* 703–725.

Zuckerman, M. (1984). Sensation seeking: A comparative approach to a human approach. *The Behavioral and Brain Sciences, 7,* 413–471.

Zuckerman, M. (1999). *Vulnerability to psychopathology: A biosocial model.* Washington, DC: American Psychological Association.

Zurbriggen, E. L., & Yost, M. R. (2004). Power, desire, and pleasure in sexual fantasies. *Journal of Sex Research, 41,* 288–300.

Zuwerink, J. R., Devine, P. G., Monteith, M. J., & Cook, D. A. (1996). Prejudice toward Blacks: With and without compunction? *Basic and Applied Social Psychology, 18,* 131–150.

Zwislocki, J. J. (1981). Sound analysis in the ear: A history of discoveries. *American Scientist, 69,* 184–192.

Name Index

Law, I., 504, 505
Lawler, K. A., 574
Lawlor, M., 520
Lawrence, H., 326
Lawrence, R., 546
Lawrie, S. M., 515
Lawyer, S., 533
Lazar, S. W., 222
Lazarus, B. N., 561, 569
Lazarus, R., 222
Lazarus, R. S., 569
Laznibatova, J., 92, 380
Le Melledo, J.-M., 573
Le Norman, M.-T., 326
Leach, C. W., 609
Leaf, P., 505, 506
Leaf, R. C., 265
Leahey, T. H., 359
Leary, D. E., 5, 12
Leary, M. R., 406, 449, 483
Leather, P., 567
LeBar, K., 307
LeBlanc, M., 265
Lebowitz, B., 467
Leboyer, M., 520
Leck, K., Simpson, J., 483
Leckman, J. F., 65, 503
Ledochowski, M., 59
LeDoux, J., 436
LeDoux, J. E., 307, 436
Lee, C., 574
Lee, C. E., 411
Lee, C.-K., 506
Lee, C.-T., 176
Lee, F., 611
Lee, G., 92
Lee, G. P., 437
Lee, H., 227, 233
Lee, J. E., 227, 233
Lee, K. K.-H., 209
Lee, L.-J., 393
Lee, N. K., 228
Lee, S., 391
Lee, T. M. C., 67, 434
Leeuwen, C. V., 295
Leff, J., 544
Legault, C., 140
Lehman, A. F., 48, 546
Lehman, C. L., 534
Lehman, D., 408, 409, 412
Lehman, D. R., 407, 474, 616
Lei, T., 176
Leibel, R. L., 412
Leibowitz, H. W., 181
Leibowitz, S., 408
Leichtman, M., 306
Leiferman, J., 574
Leiferman, J. A., 574
Leiman, A. L., 12, 53, 58, 80
Leinbach, M. D., 116
Leippe, M. R., 345
Leitenberg, H., 205, 419
LeJeune, J., 430
Lellouch, J., 506
Lemon, J., 542
Lemonick, M., 71
Lempert, R. O., 26
Lenane, M., 515
Lens, W., 405, 426
Lenton, A. P., 602
Leo, M. A., 226
Leonard, C. M., 79, 126
Leonard, S. A., 111
Leone, D. R., 196
Lepage, M., 288
Lepine, J.-P., 506
Lepper, M., 405
Lepper, M. R., 405
Lerner, A. G., 231
Lerner, R., 131
Lerner, R. M., 12
Lesgold, A. M., 310
Lesko, L. M., 251
Leslie, A. M., 125

Letts, D., 326
Leuenberger, A., 474
Levan, R., 553
Levant, R. F., 543
LeVay, S., 59, 423
Levendosky, A. A., 108
Levenson, R. W., 434, 435, 527, 561
Levey, A., 481, 482
Levi, L., 567
Levin, D. T., 303
Levin, H. S., 309
Levin, I. P., 344
Levin, L., 417
Levin, S., 129, 580
Levine, A., 408
Levine, A. S., 585
Levine, D. S., 564
Levine, H. G., 233
Levine, J., 48, 546
Levine, J. A., 139
Levine, J. B., 500
Levine, J. M., 618
Levine, R., 38
LeVine, R. A., 115, 619
Levine, R. A., 605
Levine, R. J., 33
Levine, R. V., 630, 637
LeVine, S. E., 115
Levings, D., 498
Levinson, S., 332
Levinson, S. C., 331
Levitan, I. B., 54
Levy, B. R., 575
Levy, J., 77, 78, 92
Levy, J. A., 99
Lewandowsky, S., 277
Lewin, R., 71, 318
Lewin, T., 228
Lewin, T. J., 518
Lewis, B. A., 228
Lewis, B., 428
Lewis, B. P., 129, 563, 575
Lewis, J. M., 262
Lewis, L. L., 607
Lewis, M., 78, 111, 482
Lewis, N., 434
Lewis, R., 583
Lewis, T. L., 105
Lewkowicz, K. S., 109
Lewontin, R., 90, 38
Lewy, A. J., 509, 510
Leyens, J.-P., 25
Leyens, J.-P., 45
Li, C., 172
Li, F., 593
Li, J., 391
Li, S., 491
Li, Z. H., 279
Liang, P.-J., 157
Liao, S., 434
Liberman, R. P., 535
Libon, D. J., 141
Lichtenberg, J. D., 460
Lichtenstein, E., 534
Lichty, W., 281
Liden, R. C., 619
Lie, E., 309
Lieber, C. S., 226
Liebergott, J. W., 327
Lieberman, M. A., 543
Lieberman, P., 321
Liebert, R., 442
Liebeskind, E., 628
Liebowitz, M. R., 227
Lief, H. I., 307
Lightman, S. L., 563
Lilienfeld, S. O., 306, 477, 478, 511, 552
Lilienfeld, S., 193, 512
Lim, C.-L., 209
Limmroth, V., 564
Lin, A. A., 319
Lin, C., 471
Lin, J., 567, 611

Lin, K. M., 493
Lin, L., 208
Lin, S., 332
Lind, E. A., 351
Lindberg, T., 603
Linden, D. R., 246
Lindhoe, C., 80
Lindsay, D. S., 301
Lindsay, J. J., 335
Lindsey, S., 607
Lindstro, P., 172
Linehan, M. M., 538
Link, B. G., 498
Links, J. M., 229, 246
Linnoila, M. I., 226
Linz, D., 268, 269
Lipa, P., 216
Lipman, J. J., 177
Lipp, O. V., 242
Lippa, R. A., 88, 424
Lippincott, E. C., 269
Lipton, N., 573
Lipton, R. B., 564
Lisanby, S. H., 548
Liss, M. B., 116
Little, H. J., 225
Little, T. D., 595
Littleton, H. L, 415
Littleton, J. M., 225
Liu, G., 307
Liu, H., 101
Liu, H.-L., 67, 434
Liu, J., 129
Liu, J. H., 334
Liu, L., 295
Liu, S. M., 411
Livingston, R. W., 483
Livingstone, M., 163
Lizzadro, T., 631
Loaws, O. R., 261
Lock, J., 590
Lock, T., 306
Locke, E., 428
Locke, T. F., 584
Lockhart, D. J., 377
Lockhart, R. S., 278, 285
Loeber, C. C., 352
Loehlin, J. C., 357, 365, 383, 385
Loehlin, J. L., 327
Loftus, E. F., 291, 301, 306
Logan, C., 405
Logie, R. H., 277, 282, 301
Lohr, J., 552
Lohr, J. M., 552
LoLordo, V. M., 252
Lombardino, L. J., 79
London, E. D., 229, 246
Long, C. R., 222
Long, G. M., 281
Long, J.-S., 583
Loomis, B., 140
Loomis, J. M., 46
Lopes, P. N., 373
Lopez, A., 544
Lopez, A. D., 228, 491
Lopez, O., 574
Lopez, S. R., 544
Lord, C., 38
Lorenz-Depiereux, B., 86
Lorig, T. S., 12
Loring, D. W., 92, 437
Losonczy, K., 81
Lott, B., 495
Lott, I., 376
Lotto, R. B., 163
Lotze, M., 482
Lou, H. C., 222
Louis, D., 319
Lounsbury, J. W., 467
Lourenço, O., 125
Loveland, J. M., 467
Lovibond, P. F., 246
Low, E. C.-T., 209
Lowe, G., 591
Lowell, B. B., 411

Lowell, E., 427
Lowenstein, S. R., 594
Lowery, C. R., 591
Lowrey, P. L., 208
Loy, M. H.-M., 611
Lu, J., 595
Lubart, T. I., 394, 395
Lubinski, D., 380
Lucas, R. E., 112, 474, 481, 593, 594, 595
Lucas, W., 194
Luce, C. L., 604
Luchins, A. S., 341
Lucic, K. S., 335
Lucke, J. F., 140, 583
Lucy, J. A., 331
Ludy, B. T., Jr., 20
Lueschow, A., 296
Lui, L.-Y., 141
Luminet, O., 301
Lundell, T. L., 351
Lundqvist, D., 252, 334
Lundrum, R. E., 32
Lundy, R., 220
Luo, D., 381
Luo, M., 172
Luo, Y. J., 159
Luoma, J. B., 33
Luria, A. R., 276
Lustig, S., 567
Lustina, M. J., 390
Luszcz, M., 141
Luxen, A., 221
Lycett, J., 13, 402
Lyddon, W. J., 551
Lydon, J. E., 484, 638
Lykken, D., 434, 585
Lykken, D. T., 86, 233, 382, 433, 467, 519, 595
Lyles, A., 48, 546
Lynch, M., 105, 113
Lyness, S. A., 573
Lynn, R., 384, 385
Lynn, S. J., 206, 219, 306, 511, 552
Lyons, M. J., 519
Lytton, H., 85, 382

Ma, H. K., 129
Ma, V., 16
Maas, J. B., 214
Macaulay, J., 267
Maccoby, E. E., 116
MacDonald, A. J., 551
MacDonald, K., 450, 466
MacDonald, R. R., 538
MacDonald, T. K., 584
MacDougall, J., 573
Macera, C., 591
Macfarlane, A., 105
Macfarlane, J. G., 208
MacGregor, D. G., 141
Machado, A., 125
MacKay, D. G., 302
Mackie, D. M., 196
MacKillop, W. J., 580
Mackinosh, N. J., 385
Macklin, M. L., 504
Macklin, R., 33
Mackway-Jone, K., 520
MacLeod, C. M., 303
Maclure, M., 565
MacMillan, D., 376
Macomber, J., 125
MacPherson, S. E., 277
Macrae, C. N., 601, 607, 609
Macrae, K., 16
MacWhinney, B., 326
Madden, D. J., 204
Madden-Derdich, D. A., 111
Maddi, S. R., 574
Maddux, W. W., 336
Madigan, S., 9

Madley, S. F., 347
Madsen, T. M., 548
Madson, L., 564
Maehr, M., 428
Maer, F., 439
Maestripieri, D., 318
Maggio, J., 152
Maggioni, O., 621
Magloire, K., 578
Magnavita, J. J., 450
Magnusson, D., 470
Mahan, V., 537
Mahankali, S., 67, 434
Mahapatra, M., 129
Maher, B. A., 526
Maher, E., 585
Maher, W. B., 526
Maheshwari, M. C., 222
Maheu, M. M., 544
Mahler, H. I. M., 578
Mahoney, D. J., 80
Maier, A., 251
Maier, S. F., 265, 567, 571
Major, B., 388, 389, 578
Major, K., 538
Mak, M. H. J., 142
Makin, J. W., 105
Makin, P. J., 256
Makoul, G., 471
Maksimov, A. L., 208
Malafosse, A., 520
Malamuth, N. M., 268
Malarkey, W., 578
Maldjian, J. A., 172
Malik, M. L., 500
Malka, A., 404
Mallard, D., 219
Malnic, B., 170
Malone, J., 544
Malone, J. C., 11
Malone, S. M., 233
Malott, J., 176
Malt, B. C., 294
Mamiya, T., 307
Manabe, T., 307
Manabu, T., 506
Manchanda, S. K., 222
Mancia, M., 211
Mandler, G., 291
Maneesri, S., 564
Maner, J. K., 13
Manheimer, E. D., 580
Mann, C. C., 383
Mann, L., 621
Manning, D. J., 628
Mannix, L. M., 587, 605
Manson, J., 585
Manstead, A. S. R., 136
Mantell, D. M., 621
Mantyla, T., 298
Manuck, S., 565
Manuck, S. B., 59
Maquet, P., 214, 216
Marazziti, D., 500
Marcincuk, M. C., 168
Marcus, B. H., 228
Marcus, D. K., 602
Marcus, G. F., 328
Marczinski, C. A., 141
Marechal, J., 224
Marek, E. A., 124
Marelich, W. D., 641
Margalit, M., 536
Margolin, G., 543
Margolskee, R., 172
Mari Bhat, P. N., 87
Marin, B., 584
Marín, G., 450
Mark, M. M., 26
Markesbery, W., 86
Markey, P. M., 633
Marklund, P., 288
Markman, A. B., 337, 339, 607
Marks, I. M., 241

Marks, J., 584, 585
Marks, L. E., 177
Marks, S. B., 379
Markus, H., 428
Markus, H. R., 114
Marler, P., 263
Marmorstein, N. R., 233
Marsh, E. J., 288
Marsh, G. R., 235
Marsh, H. W., 112
Marshall, M. B., 479
Marshall, N. L., 110
Marshall, R. E., 105
Marshall, S. P., 293
Marshall, W. C., 101
Marshall-Goodell, B. S., 614
Martazaev, M. S., 211
Martens, R., 312
Marthol, H., 418
Martier, S. S., 100
Martin, B. R., 231, 231
Martin, C., 400, 419
Martin, C. L., 89, 116
Martin, E., 547, 547
Martin, J., 483, 498
Martin, L., 580
Martin, L. L., 435
Martin, L. R., 576
Martin, P., 38, 99
Martin, R., 26
Martin, R. C., 298
Martindale, C., 281
Martineau, A. M., 584
Martinez, T. S., 630
Martino, S., 177
Martz, J. M., 639
Marusic, I., 466
Maruta, T., 575
Marx, E., 330
Masaki, T., 407
Masataka, N., 328
Maslow, A., 406, 461
Mason, D. J., 204
Mason, G., 65
Mason, J. W., 569
Mason, W. A., 106
Masse, L. C., 135
Masson, J. M., 138
Masten, A. S., 572
Masters, M. S., 384
Masters, R. E. L., 224
Masters, W., 418
Mataseje, A., 92, 380
Mathes, E. W., 641
Matias, R., 549
Matschinger, H., 498
Matsuda, H., 102
Matsuda, K., 302
Matsuda, T., 58, 547
Matsui, M., 384
Matsumoto, D., 331, 430
Matthee, D. M., 624
Matthews, K. A., 140, 565, 573
Matthews, L. G., 553
Matthews, P., 169
Mattingly, J. B., 178
Mattlar, C.-E., 477
Matusov, E., 126
Matute, H., 262
Maurer, D., 105
Mavromatis, A., 210
Mawhinney, V. T., 261
May, C. P., 137
May, J., 215
May, M. A., 469
May, R., 540
Mayer, J., 373
Mayer, J. D., 298, 373
Mayer, K. U., 142
Maynard, A., 365
Maynard, A. E., 365
Maynard, K. E., 573
Mayrhauser, R. T. V., 358
Mays, K. S., 177

Subject Index